D1562294

Routledge Handbook of International Environmental Law

The *Routledge Handbook of International Environmental Law* is an advanced level reference guide which provides a comprehensive and contemporary overview of the corpus of international environmental law (IEL). The Handbook features specially commissioned papers by leading experts in the field of international environmental law, drawn from a range of both developed and developing countries in order to put forward a truly global approach to the subject. Furthermore, it addresses emerging and cross-cutting issues of critical importance for the years ahead.

The book is split into six parts for ease of reference:

- **The Legal Framework, Theories and Principles of International Environmental Law** – focuses on the origins, theory, principles and development of the discipline.
- **Implementing International Environmental Law** – addresses the implementation of IEL and the role of various actors and institutions, including corporations, intergovernmental organisations and NGOs.
- **Key Issues and Legal Frameworks** – brings fresh perspectives of the common general issues of international environmental law, such as biological diversity and marine environmental law.
- **Regional Environmental Law** – explores the specific regimes developed to address regional environmental issues, considering the evolution, prospects and relationship of regional law and mechanisms to IEL.
- **Cross-Cutting Issues** – considers the engagement of international environmental law with other key fields and legal regimes, including international trade, human rights and armed conflict.
- **Contemporary and Future Challenges** – analyses pressing current and emerging issues in the field including environmental refugees and climate change, REDD and deforestation, and 'treaty congestion' in IEL.

This up-to-date and authoritative book makes it an essential reference work for students, scholars and practitioners working in the field.

Shawkat Alam is a Senior Lecturer and Director of the Centre for International and Environmental Law at Macquarie University in Sydney, Australia, where he teaches and researches in the areas of international and environmental law. His recent publications include *Sustainable Development and Free Trade* (Routledge, 2008).

Md Jahid Hossain Bhuiyan teaches law in the Department of Law, ASA University Bangladesh. He was a visiting scholar of Emory Law School, USA. During his studies in Belgium he gained experience in legal practice. He is co-editor of *Globalization, International Law, and Human Rights* (Oxford University Press, 2012).

Tareq M.R. Chowdhury is Professor and Dean at the Faculty of Law, ASA University Bangladesh. He was a faculty member of Stockholm University, Sweden. He has contributed many research articles. He is the author of *Legal Framework of International Supervision* (Stockholm University, 1986).

Erika J. Techera is a Professor at The University of Western Australia where she teaches and researches in international and comparative environmental law. She is the author of *Marine Environmental Governance: from International Law to Local Practice* (Routledge, 2012) and previously practised as a barrister.

Routledge Handbook of International Environmental Law

Edited by Shawkat Alam, Md Jahid Hossain Bhuiyan,
Tareq M.R. Chowdhury and Erika J. Techera

LONDON AND NEW YORK

First published 2013
by Routledge
2 Park Square, Milton Park, Abingdon, Oxon OX14 4RN

Simultaneously published in the USA and Canada
by Routledge
711 Third Avenue, New York, NY 10017

Routledge is an imprint of the Taylor & Francis Group, an informa business

British Library Cataloguing in Publication Data
A catalogue record for this book is available from the British Library

Library of Congress Cataloging in Publication Data
Routledge handbook of international environmental law /
ed. by: Shawkat Alam ... [et al.].
   p. cm.
   ISBN 978-0-415-68717-1 (hardback) — ISBN 978-0-203-09347-4 (e-book)
   1. Environmental law, International.   I. Alam, Shawkat.   II. Title: Handbook
   of international environmental law.
   K3585.R68 2012
   344.04′6—dc23
                                                                    2012013451

ISBN: 978-0-415-68717-1 (hbk)
ISBN: 978-0-203-09347-4 (ebk)

Typeset in Bembo
by RefineCatch Limited, Bungay, Suffolk

Contents

Contents

Contents

Preface

The global environment is indivisible and the degradation of any part of it affects – in the course of time – the global environment itself. The realities of climate change are a rude reminder of the above fact. Increasingly, concern for protection of the environment has become an important agenda item for the governments of every nation. International environmental law has evolved and expanded to become a significant area of international law and a vital subject to be studied, researched and talked about in the important circles of academics, lawyers, policy-makers, practitioners and administrators.

The *Routledge Handbook of International Environmental Law* provides a comprehensive and contemporary overview of the corpus of international environmental law from a range of perspectives. It recognises that international environmental law is not a self-contained discipline, but is interconnected with other issues and branches of law, through an examination of key areas where international environmental law intersects with other fields. It includes contributions from scholars in different parts of the world and at different stages of their careers. In doing so it attempts to capture the diversity of international environmental law scholarship in a dynamic and developing field.

This book explores the existing international environmental law – governance frameworks, regimes and institutions – and examines their strengths and weaknesses and the techniques, barriers and challenges to successful implementation. In doing so it offers a comprehensive and contemporary overview of international environmental law, as well as addressing emerging and cross-cutting issues of critical importance for the years ahead. The up-to-date and authoritative articles in this book make it an essential reference work for students, scholars and practitioners working in the field.

Acknowledgements

This publication represents a considerable amount of work by a significant number of contributors. We wish to thank all those who have come together to make this such a stimulating publication on international environmental law.

Sadly, during the preparation of this book the international environmental law community suffered a significant loss with the passing of Svitlana Kravchenko. We would like to pay tribute to her considerable work in the areas of international law, human rights and the environment.

We are most grateful to Katie Carpenter and Stephen Gutierrez from Routledge for their support and assistance with this challenging project. We would also like to thank Shannon Kelly for his superior research assistance in the final editing of this volume.

Finally, we would all like to thank our families. This work would not have been possible without their continuing patience and ongoing support.

SA
JB
TC
ET

Contributors

Shawkat Alam is a Senior Lecturer at Macquarie Law School, Macquarie University, Australia where he teaches and researches in areas of international law, international environmental law, international trade and sustainable development. He is the author of the book, *Sustainable Development and Free Trade* (Routledge, 2008). He has published extensively in his areas of expertise. Shawkat holds an LLB (Honours) from Rajshahi University, an LLM from Dhaka University and a PhD from Macquarie University. He is Director of the Centre for International and Environmental Law at Macquarie University and editor of the *Macquarie Journal of International and Comparative Environmental Law.*

Abdullah Al Faruque is a Professor of Law and former Head of the Department of Law at the University of Chittagong, Bangladesh. He holds an LLM from the University of Dhaka and a PhD from Dundee University. He was awarded a Commonwealth Scholarship in 2002 to pursue his PhD programme in Petroleum Law in the UK. He was a post-doctoral fellow at Dundee University during 2009 and 2010 under a Commonwealth Staff Fellowship. He has published two books: *Petroleum Contracts: Stability and Risk Management in Developing Countries* (BILIA, 2011) and *Essentials of Legal Research* (Palal Prokashoni, 2009). He has also published many articles in national and international refereed law journals.

Donald K. Anton is an Associate Professor of Law at the Australian National University. He teaches, researches and advises in core areas of international law and organisation and has an active international law practice. In 2010 he appeared as Counsel on behalf of the International Union for the Conservation of Nature in the Seabed Disputes Chamber of the International Tribunal for the Law of the Sea in *Responsibilities and Obligations of States Sponsoring Persons and Entities with Respect to Activities in the Area.*

Md Jahid Hossain Bhuiyan teaches law in the Department of Law, ASA University Bangladesh. During his studies in Belgium he gained experience in legal practice with lawyers from European countries. Bhuiyan was a visiting scholar of Emory Law School, Emory University, USA. He has articles in journals published in Australia, Bangladesh, India and Malta. He is co-editor of *International Humanitarian Law: An Anthology* (LexisNexis Butterworths, 2009), *Issues in Human Rights* (Atlantic Publishers, 2010), *An Introduction to International Human Rights Law* (Martinus Nijhoff, 2010) and *Globalization, International Law, and Human Rights* (Oxford University Press, 2012).

Ulrike M. Bohlmann earned her doctoral degree at the University of Cologne, Germany, after the completion of her bar exam. She joined the legal department of the European Space Agency

(ESA) in 2002 and has since covered a multitude of legal issues embracing both public international law and private law aspects, and represented ESA at the international level. She has published a book on commercial space activities and intellectual property, a number of book chapters, conference papers and articles in law and policy journals. She contributes to academic research projects and lectures regularly on space law and policy at the university level.

Klaus Bosselmann, PhD, is a Professor and Director of the New Zealand Centre for Environmental Law at the University of Auckland Faculty of Law. He is chair of various international professional bodies including the IUCN Commission on Environmental Law Ethics Specialist Group and the Global Ecological Integrity Group. Professor Bosselmann has been an advisor to UNEP, IUCN, the EU and the New Zealand and German governments on legal issues related to hazardous substances, biodiversity, climate change and sustainable development. He has authored or edited 25 books in the area of international environmental law, domestic environmental law and sustainability approaches to law-making and global governance.

Rebecca M. Bratspies is a Professor of Law at the CUNY School of Law, New York. She directs the CUNY Center for Urban Environmental Reform. Her scholarly research focuses on the international dimensions of environmental regulation and on environmental democracy. Professor Bratspies has published widely on the topics of environmental liability, international fisheries management and genetically modified food crops. She co-edited *Transboundary Harm in International Law: Lessons from the Trail Smelter Arbitration* (Cambridge University Press, 2006) and *Progress in International Law* (Martinus Nijhoff, 2008). Professor Bratspies holds a BA in Biology from Wesleyan University and graduated with honours from the University of Pennsylvania Law School.

Susan Breau is Professor of International Law at Flinders University in Adelaide, Australia. She has published widely on the law of armed conflict. Her main focus of research is civilian casualties in armed conflict as her PhD research focused on humanitarian intervention. Recently she was co-author with Kerim Yilidiz of a book entitled *The Kurdish Conflict, International Humanitarian Law and Post-Conflict Mechanisms* (Routledge, 2010). She is currently a consultant with the Oxford Research Group on their Recording of Civilian Casualties of Armed Conflict project.

Maxine Burkett is an Associate Professor of Law at the William S. Richardson School of Law, University of Hawaii and serves as the Director of the Center for Island Climate Adaptation and Policy (ICAP). Professor Burkett attended Williams College and Exeter College, Oxford University, and received her law degree from Boalt Hall School of Law at the University of California, Berkeley. Professor Burkett's current research focuses on 'Climate Justice', writing on the disparate impact of climate change on vulnerable communities, in the United States and globally. As the Director of ICAP, she leads projects to address climate change law, policy and planning for island communities in Hawaii, the Pacific region and beyond.

Elizabeth Burleson is a Professor at Pace Law School, has an LLM in International Law from the London School of Economics (LSE), a JD from the University of Connecticut, and is a Fulbright Senior Specialist whose research addresses emerging International Environmental and Human Rights Law. She began participating in the treaty negotiation process at the United Nations in 1991 during proceedings for the United Nations Conference on Environment and Development and helped draft the United Nations Framework Convention on Climate Change (UNFCCC), Agenda 21 and the Rio Declaration. She has written reports for the United Nations and delivered presentations at United Nations conferences.

Indira Carr (MA, BPhil, LLM, PhD) is a Professor of Law at the University of Surrey, UK. Her research interests include various aspects of international trade law and information technology law. Of late, she has been working on corruption in international business. This research has been funded by the UK Arts & Humanities Research Council (AHRC) and the British Academy. Professor Carr is also the founder editor of the journal *Information & Communications Technology* and Joint Founder Editor (with Brian Carr) of the journal *Asian Philosophy*, both published by Taylor & Francis.

Tareq M.R. Chowdhury BA (Hons), MA, LLB (Dhaka) PGDSS, PGDLS, DBC, LLD (Stockholm University, Sweden) is Professor and Dean at the Faculty of Law, ASA University Bangladesh. He was a faculty member of Stockholm University, Sweden. He has participated in several national and international conferences, and made substantial contributions through his papers. He has contributed many research articles. He is the author of *Legal Framework of International Supervision* (Stockholm University, 1986) and co-editor of *Globalization, International Law, and Human Rights* (Oxford University Press, 2012).

Marie-Claire Cordonier Segger (MEM (Yale) BCL and LLB (McGill) BA Hons) is Head of Economic Growth and Trade at the International Development Law Organization (IDLO); Senior Director, Centre for International Sustainable Development Law (CISDL); Affiliated Fellow, Lauterpacht Centre for International Law (LCIL), Cambridge University; and International Professor, Faculty of Law, University of Chile. She is a Councillor of the World Future Council, an expert on the International Law Association's Committee on International Law on Sustainable Development, and author/editor of 14 books and over 80 papers on law and policy for sustainable development.

Damien Cremean (MA (Phil), LLB (Hons 1st Class), PhD, Barrister-at- Law) is an Adjunct Professor at the Law School, University of Queensland, Australia, attached to the Maritime and Shipping Law Unit. Dr Cremean is a practising barrister and a specialist admiralty and maritime lawyer. He has published widely in those areas and has taught maritime law subjects.

Erin Daly is a Professor of Law and the H. Albert Young Fellow in Constitutional Law at Widener Law School in Delaware, United States. She is the author, with Jeremy Sarkin, of *Reconciliation in Divided Societies: Finding Common Ground* (University of Pennsylvania Press, 2006), and of the forthcoming *Dignity Rights: Courts, Constitutions and the Worth of the Human Person* (University of Pennsylvania, 2012), and, with James R. May, of *Environmental Rights and Constitutional Protections: Implications for Present and Future Generations* (Cambridge University Press, 2013).

Michael Eburn is a Senior Fellow at the ANU College of Law and the Fenner School of Environment and Society, the Australian National University. Dr Eburn has written extensively on Australian and international disaster law. His PhD benchmarked Australia's legal arrangements against Red Cross international disaster response law guidelines and he has contributed, as a member of a panel of experts, to the development of the *Model Act on International Disaster Assistance*. Dr Eburn is a member of the advisory panel for the *Australian Journal of Emergency Management* and is a visiting presenter at the Australian Emergency Management Institute.

Douglas E. Fisher holds the degrees of MA, LLB and PhD of the University of Edinburgh. He has practised law in Scotland and in Queensland in Australia. He has held positions at Edinburgh University and Dundee University in Scotland, at Queensland University and the Australian National University in Australia and at Victoria University in Wellington in New Zealand. He is currently a Professor of law at Queensland University of Technology in Australia. The focus of his academic and professional activities over the last 40 years has been environmental and natural resources law.

Steven Freeland is Professor of International Law at the University of Western Sydney, Visiting Professor in International Law at the University of Copenhagen, and Faculty Member at the London Institute of Space Policy and Law. He has been a Visiting Professional at the International Criminal Court and a member of the Australian delegation to the United Nations Committee on the Peaceful Uses of Outer Space. Among other appointments, he is a Director of the International Institute of Space Law, and a member of the Space Law Committee of the International Law Association. He lectures and publishes widely on various aspects of International Law and Space Law.

Paolo Galizzi is Clinical Professor of Law and Director of the Sustainable Development Legal Initiative (SDLI) of the Leitner Center for International Law and Justice at Fordham Law School in New York City. He previously taught at Imperial College London, the University of Nottingham and the University of Verona. His research interests lie in international environmental law and law of sustainable development and he has published extensively in these areas. His recent publications include *The Future of African Customary Law* with Tracy Higgins and Jeanmarie Fenrich (Cambridge University Press, 2011) and *The Role of the Environment in Poverty Alleviation* (Fordham University Press, 2008).

Markus W. Gehring is Deputy Director of the Centre for European Legal Studies (CELS) at the University of Cambridge, Faculty of Law and Fellow in Law at Robinson College in the UK. He holds an *ad personam* Jean Monnet Chair in Sustainable Development Law at the University of Ottawa in Canada and serves as Lead Counsel for Sustainable International Trade, Investment and Competition Law with the Centre of International Sustainable Development Law (CISDL), based at McGill University. He holds an LLM from Yale and a Dr Jur from Hamburg. His most recent book is titled *Sustainable Development in World Investment Law* (Kluwer Law International, 2010).

Renée Gift (LLB (University of the West Indies), with Honours, member of the Trinidad and Tobago Bar, LLM (Lewis and Clark Law School) Natural Resources and Environmental Law) is an environmental lawyer practising in Trinidad and Tobago and Legal Researcher at the Centre for International Sustainable Development Law (CISDL). Renée has worked on legal matters advocating for the expansion of the rights of private individuals to bring citizen suits against the local environmental regulator, increased public consultation in permitting applications, and increased enforcement of environmental standards by local regulators, and also provides pro bono assistance to local non-profit environmental groups.

Carmen G. Gonzalez is a Professor of Law at Seattle University School of Law, who writes in the areas of international environmental law, environmental justice, trade and the environment, and food security. After graduating from Yale University and Harvard Law School, Professor Gonzalez clerked for Judge Thelton E. Henderson, US District Court for the

Northern District of California, and practised environmental law in the private sector and with the US Environmental Protection Agency. Professor Gonzalez was a Fulbright scholar in Argentina, a Fellow at the US Supreme Court and a Visiting Scholar at the University of Cambridge, UK. From 2011 to 2012, she served as Chair of the Environmental Law Section of the Association of American Law Schools.

Paul Govind is a lecturer at Macquarie University Law School and a member of The Centre for International and Environmental Law at Macquarie University, Sydney, Australia. His research interests include international climate change law with a particular emphasis on adaptation and climate finance.

Anita M. Halvorssen received her law degree from the University of Oslo, Norway and an LLM and doctorate in the science of law (JSD) from Columbia University, New York. She is the Director of Global Legal Solutions, an international think tank and consultancy, focusing on developing countries and sustainable development. She also teaches Sustainable Development and Trade and Global Climate Change Law and Policy at the University of Denver, Sturm College of Law. Dr Halvorssen has also taught international law and international environmental law at the University of Colorado. She is a member of the Committee on Legal Principles Relating to Climate Change of the International Law Association (ILA).

Cameron Holley is a Senior Lecturer at the University of New South Wales Law School in Australia and Research Affiliate at the National Centre for Groundwater Research and Training. Prior to joining UNSW, Cameron worked as a researcher and lecturer at the Centre for Legal Governance and the Centre for International and Environmental Law at Macquarie University and as a postdoctoral research associate at the Regulatory Institutions Network at the Australian National University. Cameron's research interests are in the areas of environmental law, natural resources law and water law, with a focus on regulation and governance.

Kamrul Hossain is a Senior Researcher at the Northern Institute for Environmental and Minority Law in the Arctic Centre of the University of Lapland. He holds a degree of Doctor of Laws in international law from the University of Lapland. His research interests lie in the field of international environmental law as applied in the Arctic with special focus on energy and mineral development, marine pollution, indigenous people's human rights, continental shelf development and law of the sea. He has recently served as the Special Editor of the third volume of the *Yearbook of Polar Law* (Martinus Nijhoff, 2011).

Md Saiful Karim is an Associate Lecturer at the School of Law and Justice, Southern Cross University, Lismore, Australia. Before joining Southern Cross University, he was a Sessional Lecturer at Macquarie University. He has also worked as a consultant for the University of South Pacific, Vanuatu. After completing his LLB (Honours) and LLM at Chittagong University in 2004, Saiful worked for the Bangladesh Environmental Lawyers Association (BELA). In 2008 he completed his LLM by research programme at the Faculty of Law, National University of Singapore and then practised at a Singapore law firm.

J. Patrick Kelly is the Vice-Dean and Professor of Law at Widener University School of Law, Pennsylvania. Professor Kelly received his JD degree from Harvard Law School and a BA from the University of Delaware. He has served as Counsel to the House Banking Committee of the US House of Representatives and the Federal Trade Commission. Professor Kelly is a specialist in the areas of international law, international trade and international environmental law. He is admitted to practise in the District of Columbia and the United States Supreme Court as well as being an associate member of the Delaware Bar Association. His articles have appeared in many international journals including those of Yale, Virginia, Duke, Cornell, Northwestern and Michigan law schools.

Avidan Kent (LLM (McGill University)) is a PhD candidate at Cambridge University (POLIS), a Visiting Fellow at Bristol University School of Law, and a Legal Research Fellow with the Centre for International Sustainable Development Law (CISDL). Avidan's research interests include the field of international trade and investment law and its intersection with other legal disciplines such as competition law and climate change law. Avidan has supervised in European Union environmental law at undergraduate level at Cambridge University. He is a member of the Israeli Bar.

Michael Kidd has a BCom LLB LLM PhD (all from the University of Natal) and is Professor of Law at the University of KwaZulu-Natal in Pietermaritzburg, South Africa. He teaches environmental law and administrative law and is the author of *Environmental Law*, a leading South African textbook. He is the principal editor of the *South African Journal of Environmental Law and Policy* and is on the governing board of the IUCN Academy of Environmental Law. His principal research interests within environmental law are water, environmental impact assessment, enforcement and climate change.

Svitlana Kravchenko was Professor and Director of the LLM Programme in Environmental and Natural Resources Law, the University of Oregon Law School, USA. She was the author of 12 books, numerous book chapters and scholarly articles. Kravchenko was an advisor to the Ministry of Environment and the Parliament of Ukraine. She was the founder and served as president of Environment-People-Law, the first public interest environmental law firm in Ukraine. She was co-founder and co-director of the Association of Environmental Law of Central and Eastern Europe. She also served as Vice Chair of the IUCN Commission of Environmental Law.

Koh Kheng-Lian is an Emeritus Professor, founder member and Director of the Asia-Pacific Centre for Environmental Law (established in 1996 by the Faculty of Law, National University of Singapore, in partnership with the IUCN Commission on Environmental Law (IUCN-CEL) in collaboration with the United Nations Environment Programme (UNEP)). She has published extensively on environment and other areas of law. She was the IUCN-CEL Regional Vice-Chair for South and East Asia, and a member of its Steering Committee from 1996 to 2004. She was formerly legal officer in the Secretariat of the United Nations Commission on International Trade Law in Vienna.

Zada Lipman is an Emeritus Professor in the School of Law, Macquarie University, Sydney. Over the past 26 years, she has been involved in teaching and researching in the area of environmental law. Zada is the Australian editor of the *Environmental Liability Journal*, and the New South Wales and Pollution Special Editor of the *Environmental and Planning Law Journal*. Zada is a member of the IUCN – the World Conservation Union Commission on Environmental Law. She is a member of the Commission's Special Working Groups on Enforcement and Compliance and the Special Working Group on Oceans, Coasts and Coral Reefs.

Rowena Maguire is a Lecturer in the Faculty of Law at Queensland University of Technology, Australia. Dr Maguire completed her doctoral thesis in 2010 on the topic of 'The International Regulation of Sustainable Forest Management'. This work is currently in preparation for publication as a manuscript with Edward Elgar Publishers for release in mid-2012. In 2011, Rowena was awarded a Queensland–China Climate Change Fellowship to further explore issues of land tenure and forest carbon markets. Rowena has published articles on forest carbon markets in the *Carbon and Climate Law Review* and the *Environmental and Planning Law Journal*.

James R. May is a Professor of Law, co-director of the Environmental Law Center, Professor of Graduate Engineering (Adjunct), and founder and co-director of the Masters of Marine Policy (MMP) program at Widener University, Pennsylvania. He serves as a Fellow of the American College of Environmental Lawyers, and is a former H. Albert Young Constitutional Law Fellow. He is widely published. His most recent book is *Principles of Constitutional Environmental Law* (American Bar Assn, Envtl L Inst, 2011). May has served as a pro bono litigator on public interest environmental cases throughout the country, working on cases at every level from state boards to the United States Supreme Court.

Elisa Morgera is a Lecturer in European Environmental Law and Director of the LLM Programme in Global Environment and Climate Change Law at the University of Edinburgh School of Law, UK. Dr Morgera specialises in international, EU and comparative environmental law, with a focus on biodiversity and corporate accountability. She authored *Corporate Accountability in International Environmental Law* (Oxford University Press, 2009), and co-authored *Environmental Integration in the EU's External Relations: Beyond Multilateral Dimensions* (Hart, 2012) and *A Commentary to the 2010 Nagoya Protocol on Access and Benefit-Sharing* (Martinus Nijhoff, forthcoming).

Chidi Oguamanam (LLM, PhD) is an Associate Professor in the Faculty of Law, University of Ottawa, Canada. He writes, teaches and consults in the areas of law and technology (including biotechnologies), biodiversity, agricultural knowledge systems, indigenous knowledge, intellectual property, human rights, globalisation and global knowledge governance. He is a Senior Research Fellow in the Centre for International Sustainable Development Law at McGill University, Montreal and a member of Nova Scotia Barristers' Society and the Nigerian Bar Association. He is the author of *International Law and Indigenous Knowledge* (University of Toronto Press, 2006) and *Intellectual Property in Global Governance* (Routledge, 2011).

Robert V. Percival is the Robert F. Stanton Professor of Law and the Director of the Environmental Law Program at the University of Maryland, Francis King Carey School of Law. He has been a visiting professor at Harvard Law School and Georgetown University Law Center and a Fulbright Scholar at the China University of Political Science and Law in Beijing and Comenius University Law School in Bratislava. The principal author of the leading environmental law casebook in the US, Percival has lectured in 25 countries on six continents. He maintains a website and blog on global environmental law at www.globalenvironmentallaw.com.

Tony George Puthucherril is a JSD candidate at the Schulich School of Law, Dalhousie University, Canada, researching climate change, sea level rise and integrated coastal zone management. In 2010, Puthucherril was awarded the Vanier Canada Graduate Scholarship and the Dalhousie University Presidents' award for his academic achievements. His Master's thesis on ship recycling has been published as *From Ship Breaking to Sustainable Ship Recycling: Evolution of a Legal Regime* (Martinus Nijhoff, 2010). Puthucherril's research interests include the rights of marginalised populations, and environmental, coastal and climate change law.

Jona Razzaque is an Associate Professor in Environmental Law at the University of the West of England (UWE) in Bristol, UK. Jona is a barrister and holds a PhD in law from the University of London. Prior to joining UWE, she worked as a staff lawyer with the Foundation for International Environmental Law and Development (FIELD). She has researched widely on access to justice and participatory rights in environmental matters and her publications include *Public Interest Environmental Litigation in India, Pakistan and Bangladesh* (Kluwer, 2004) and *Globalisation and Natural Resources Law* (Edward Elgar, 2011).

Alistair Rieu-Clarke (LLB (Hons), LLM (Distinction), PhD) is a Senior Lecturer at the IHP-HELP Centre for Water Law, Policy and Science (under the auspices of UNESCO), University of Dundee, Scotland, UK. Dr Rieu-Clarke's research interests centre on examining the effectiveness of transboundary watercourse treaty regimes, where he has a particular interest in the interface between international law and science (including hydrology, ecology and the political economy). He has taught, published and led numerous international research projects.

Tim Stephens is an Associate Professor in the Faculty of Law, University of Sydney, Australia. He has published widely on public international law, national and international environmental law and the law of the sea. His most recent book is *The International Law of the Sea* (Hart, 2010), co-authored with Professor Donald R Rothwell. Dr Stephens is Co-Director of the Sydney Centre for International Law and Co-Editor in Chief of the *Asia Pacific Journal of Environmental Law*. Tim holds a PhD in law from the University of Sydney, and an MPhil in geography from the University of Cambridge. In 2010 Tim was awarded the IUCN Academy of Environmental Law Junior Scholarship Prize for his contribution to environmental law.

Vernon I. Tava holds an LLM (First Class Honours) from the University of Auckland in New Zealand. He was the 2010 winner of the university's Fowld's Memorial Prize for Most Distinguished Postgraduate Student in Law. He works as a Research Fellow at the New Zealand Centre for Environmental Law, Faculty of Law, University of Auckland.

Erika J. Techera (LLB (Hons), M Env Law, LLM, PhD) is a Professor in the Faculty of Law, University of Western Australia. Dr Techera teaches and researches in environmental law including international and comparative marine environmental governance and cultural heritage law. She is the author of *Marine Environmental Governance: From International Law to Local Practice* (Routledge, 2011). She has been a Visiting Scholar at the University of Hawaii, was formerly Director of the Centre for International and Environmental Law at Macquarie University and has practised as a barrister. She is a member of the IUCN Commission on Environmental Law and World Commission on Protected Areas.

Anastasia Telesetsky is an Associate Professor of Law at the University of Idaho, College of Law where she teaches and writes in the area of international environmental law. Her scholarship focuses on the general international legal principle of restoration and the protection of living marine resources.

Justin Wolst holds LLM degrees in international environmental law and EU law. International environmental law has been the cornerstone of his education and professional career. After his initial studies he interned at UNEP and at an environmental non-governmental organisation. Following his graduation he was accepted in the Netherlands' government traineeship and subsequently worked for the international affairs department of the Netherlands' Ministry of Infrastructure and the Environment in international climate change and environmental affairs. Currently he works as an analyst in a private sector consultancy firm as a specialist in European affairs and international energy and environmental law.

Alexander Zahar is a Senior Lecturer in law at Macquarie Law School, Sydney, Australia. Dr Zahar is the editor of the journal *Climate Law* and an expert reviewer (energy sector) of national communications and state greenhouse gas inventories under the auspices of the UN Framework Convention on Climate Change. His book *Australian Climate Law in a Global Context* (co-authored with Jacqueline Peel and Lee Godden) is to be published by Cambridge University Press in September 2012.

List of abbreviations and acronyms

AAU	assigned amount unit
ABS	access and benefit-sharing
ACB	ASEAN Centre for Biodiversity
ACCC	Adaptation to Climate Change in the Caribbean Project
ACP	African Caribbean and Pacific
ACT	Amazon Cooperation Treaty
ACTO	Amazon Cooperation Treaty Organization
AEA	Andean Environmental Agenda
AEC	ASEAN Economic Community
AHPs	ASEAN Heritage Parks
ALIDES	Central American Alliance for Sustainable Development
AMCEN	African Ministerial Conference on the Environment
ANCSA	Alaska Native Claims Settlement Act
AOSIS	Alliance of Small Island States
APSC	ASEAN Political Security Community
ARCBC	ASEAN Regional Centre for Biodiversity Conservation
ASCC	ASEAN Socio-Cultural Community
ASEAN	Association of South East Asian Nations
ASEAN-WEN	ASEAN Wildlife Law Enforcement Network
ASEPs	ASEAN Environmental Programmes
ASPAE	ASEAN Strategic Plan of Action on the Environment
ATCA	Alien Tort Claims Act
ATME	Antarctic Treaty Meeting of Experts
ATS	Antarctic Treaty System
AWGNCB	ASEAN Working Group on Nature Conservation and Biodiversity
BAP	Bali Action Plan
BCRCs	Regional and Coordinating Centres for Capacity Building and Technology Transfer
BIT	bilateral investment treaty
BPOA	Barbados Programme of Action
BRL	Biodiversity Resources Law
CAAAM	Andean Community of Environmental Authorities
CAFOs	confined animal feeding operations
CAFTA-DR	US–Dominican Republic–Central American Free Trade Agreement
CAN	Andean Community
CAP	Caribbean Action Plan

CARICOM	Caribbean Community
CBD	Convention on Biological Diversity
CBDR/CDR	common but differentiated responsibility
CBMU	capacity-building management unit
CCAD	Central American Commission for Environment and Development
CCAMLR	Convention on the Conservation of Antarctic Marine Living Resources
CCAP	Climate Change Action Plan
CCCCC	Caribbean Community Climate Change Centre
CCD	Convention to Combat Desertification
CCSC	Climate Change Steering Committee
CDEMA	Caribbean Disaster Emergency Management Agency
CDM	Clean Development Mechanism
CDR	see CBDR
CEC	Commission for Environmental Cooperation
CELDF	Community Environmental Legal Defense Fund
CEP	Caribbean Environmental Programme
CER	Certified Emission Reduction
CETA	Comprehensive Economic and Trade Agreement
CFCs	chlorofluorocarbons
CHM	clearinghouse mechanism
CICOS	Commission for the Congo-Oubangui-Sangha Basin
CIL	customary international law
CIS	Commonwealth of Independent States
CITES	Convention on International Trade in Endangered Species of Wild Fauna and Flora
CJEU	Court of Justice of the European Union
CLC	International Convention on Civil Liability for Oil Pollution Damage
CLRTAP	Convention on Long-Range Transboundary Air Pollution
CMP	Conference of the Parties (to the Kyoto Protocol)
CMS	Convention on the Conservation of Migratory Species of Wild Animals
COM	Conference of Parties Committee (ASEAN)
COMESA	Common Market for Eastern and Southern Africa
CONDESAN	Consortium for the Sustainable Development of the Andean Eco-region
COP	Conference of the Parties
COSPAR	Committee on Space Research
CPACC	Caribbean Planning for Adaptation to Climate Change Project
CPRS	Carbon Pollution Reduction Scheme
CRAMRA	Convention on the Regulation of Antarctic Mineral Resources
CSD	Commission for Sustainable Development
CSR	corporate social responsibility
CWC	Convention on Certain Conventional Weapons
DDT	dichlorodiphenyltrichloroethane
DOE	Designated Operational Entity
DRC	Division of Regional Cooperation (UNEP)
DSD	Department of Sustainable Development (OAS)
DSU	Dispute Settlement Understanding
EBRD	European Bank for Reconstruction and Development
EA	environmental assessment

EC	European Community
ECA	Environment Conservation Act (Bangladesh)
ECA	Environmental Cooperation Agreement
ECACC	Enhancing Capacity for Adaptation to Climate Change
ECC	Environmental Cooperation Commission
ECHR	European Convention on Human Rights
ECJ	European Court of Justice
ECOSOC	Economic and Social Council (UN)
ECP	Eastern Canadian Premiers
ECP	Environmental Cooperation Program
ECT	Energy Charter Treaty
ECtHR	European Court of Human Rights
EEC	European Economic Community
EEZ	Exclusive Economic Zone
EIA	environmental impact assessment
EMEP	European Monitoring and Evaluation Programme
EMG	Environment Management Group
ENMOD	Convention on the Prohibition of Military and any other Hostile Use of Environmental Modification Techniques
ENSO	El Niño Southern Oscillation
EPBC	Environment Protection and Biodiversity Conservation
EPG	Group of Eminent Persons
ER	environmental review
ERB	Regional Strategy for the Conservation and Sustainable Use of Biodiversity in Mesoamerica
ERTs	Expert Review Teams
ESD	ecologically sustainable development
ESM	environmentally sound management
ETS	Emissions Trading Schemes
EU	European Union
EUETS	European Union Emissions Trading Scheme
FAO	Food and Agriculture Organization
FCPF	Forest Carbon Partnership Facility
FDI	foreign direct investment
FER	fundamental environmental right
FIDA	Inter-American Forum on Environmental Law
FIPA	Foreign Investment Protection Agreement
FOC	flags of convenience
FTAs	free trade agreements
G-77	Group of Developing Countries and China
GATS	General Agreement on Trade in Services
GATT	General Agreement on Tariffs and Trade
GEF	Global Environmental Facility
GFCM	General Fishery Commission for the Mediterranean
GHG	greenhouse gas
GHS	Globally Harmonised System
GNI	Gross National Income
GNP	Gross National Product

GNSS	global navigation satellite system
GRAIN	Genetic Resources Action International
HCFC	hydrochlorofluorocarbon
HDI	Human Development Index
HFC	hydrofluorocarbon
HPA	ASEAN Hanoi Plan of Action
IABIN	Inter-American Biodiversity Information Network
IADC	Inter-Agency Space Debris Coordination Committee
IAEA	International Atomic Energy Agency
IBCD	Index of Biocultural Diversity
ICCAT	International Convention for the Conservation of Atlantic Tunas
ICCPR	International Covenant on Civil and Political Rights
ICCROM	International Centre for the Study of the Preservation and Restoration of Cultural Property
ICESCR	International Covenant on Economic, Social and Cultural Rights
ICIMOD	International Centre for Integrated Mountain Development
ICJ	International Court of Justice
ICOMOS	International Council on Monuments and Sites
ICP	United Nations Informal Consultation Process
ICRC	International Committee of the Red Cross
ICRW	International Convention for the Regulation of Whaling
ICSID	International Centre for Settlement of Investment Disputes
ICSU	International Council of Scientific Unions
ICTSD	International Centre for Trade and Sustainable Development
ICTY	International Criminal Tribunal for Yugoslavia
ICUN	International Union for the Conservation of Nature
IDP	internally displaced person
IDRL Guidelines	Guidelines for the Domestic Facilitation and Regulation of International Disaster Relief and Initial Recovery Assistance (ICRC)
IEA	International Energy Agency
IEA Database	International Environmental Agreements Database
IEL	International Environmental Law
IFC	International Finance Corporate
IFF	Intergovernmental Forum on Forests
IFRC	International Federation of Red Cross and Red Crescent Societies
IFSD	Institutional Framework for Sustainable Development
IGC	intergovernmental committee
IGO	intergovernmental organisation
IGY	International Geophysical Year
IIA	international investment agreement
IIL	Institute of International Law
IISD	International Institute for Sustainable Development
IJC	International Joint Commission
ILA	International Law Association
ILC	International Law Commission
ILM	International Legal Materials
ILO	International Labour Organization
IMDG Code	International Maritime Dangerous Goods Code

IMF	International Monetary Fund
IMO	International Maritime Organization
IPCC	Intergovernmental Panel on Climate Change
IOTC	Indian Ocean Tuna Commission
IPF	Intergovernmental Panel on Forests
IPOA-IUU	International Plan of Action to Prevent, Deter and Eliminate Illegal, Unreported and Unregulated Fishing
IR	international relations
IRPTC	International Register of Potentially Toxic Chemicals
ISBA	International Seabed Authority
ISI	import substitution industrialisation
ISS	International Space Station
ITLOS	International Tribunal for the Law of the Sea
ITPGRFA	International Treaty on Plant Genetic Resources for Food and Agriculture
IUCN	International Union for Conservation of Nature
IUU	illegal, unreported and unregulated fishing
JI	Joint Implementation
LAC	Latin America and the Caribbean
LCA	long-term cooperative action
LGA	Local Government Act
LMO	living modified organism
LRTAP	long-range transboundary air pollution
LULUCFG	Land-use, Land-use Change and Forestry guidelines
MACC	Mainstreaming and Adaptation to Climate Change
MARPOL	International Convention for the Prevention of Pollution from Ships
MBRS	Mesoamerican Barrier Reef System
MDB	multilateral and regional development banks
MDGs	Millennium Development Goals
MEA	Multilateral environmental agreement
MERCOSUR	Southern American Common Market
MGR	marine genetic resources
MIKE	Monitoring the Illegal Killing of Elephants
MIT	Massachusetts Institute of Technology
MMPA	Marine Mammal Protection Act
MNC	multinational corporation
MNE	multinational enterprise
MNES	matters of national environmental significance
MOP	Meeting of the Parties
MPA	marine protected area
MPMF	Montreal Protocol Multilateral Fund
MRC	Mekong River Commission
MRV	measurement, reporting, and verification
MSFD	Marine Strategy Framework Directive
MSY	maximum sustainable yield
MTR	multilateral treaty regimes
NAAEC	North American Agreement on Environmental Cooperation
NAFO	Northwest Atlantic Fisheries Organization
NAFTA	North American Free Trade Agreement

NAMAs	Nationally appropriate mitigation actions
NAP	National Action Programme
NAPPO	North American Plant Protection Organization
NATO	North Atlantic Treaty Organisation
NAWM	North American Waterfowl Management Plan
NCP	National contact point
NEAFC	North East Atlantic Fisheries Commission
NEG	New England Governors
NEPAD	New Partnership for Africa's Development
NGO	non-governmental organisation
NIEO	New International Economic Order
NIMBY	not in my backyard
NPM	non-precluded measures
NPS	nuclear power source
NPT	Non-Proliferation Treaty
NTS	non-traditional security
NZ	New Zealand
NZETS	New Zealand Emissions Trading Scheme
OAS	Organization of American States
OAU	Organisation of African Unity
ODA	official development aid/ overseas development assistance
ODS	ozone-depleting substances
OECD	Organisation for Economic Co-operation and Development
OECS	Organisation of Eastern Caribbean States
OPRC	International Convention on Oil Pollution Preparedness, Response, and Co-operation
OSPAR	Convention for the Protection of the Marine Environment of the North-East Atlantic
PARCA	Central American Environmental Plan
PCA	Permanent Court of Arbitration
PCBs	polychlorinated biphenyls
PCIJ	Permanent Court of International Justice
PCT	Patent Cooperation Treaty
PDD	Project Design Document
PES	Payment for Ecosystem Services
PFM	Participatory Forestry Management
PIC	prior informed consent
PIL	public interest litigation
PLT	Patent Law Treaty
POPs	persistent organic pollutants
PPP	public private partnerships
PROARCA	Regional Environmental Program for Central America
PRTR	Regional Pollutant Release and Transfer Register
R&D	research and development
REAs	sub-regional or bi-lateral environmental agreements
REDD	Reduced emissions from deforestation and degradation
RFMOs	regional fishery management organisations
RICO	racketeer influenced and corrupt organisations

RMA	Resource Management Act
RMU	removal unit
ROLAC	Regional Office for Latin America and the Caribbean (UNEP)
RONA	Regional Office for North America (UNEP)
RRACC	Reducing risk to human and natural assets resulting from climate change
SADC	South African Development Community
SBSTA	Subsidiary Body for Scientific and Technological Advice
SBSTTA	Subsidiary Body for Scientific, Technical and Technological Advice
SEA	Single European Act
SEA	Strategic Environmental Assessment of Plans and Policies (Canada)
SEA	strategic environmental assessment
SEAFO	Southeast Atlantic Fishery Organization
SFM	sustainable forest management
SIA	Sustainability Impact Assessment
SICA	Central American Integration System
SIDS	Small Island Developing States
SIDSnet	Small Island Developing States Network
SPACC	Special Program on Adaptation to Climate Change
SPLT	Substantive Patent Law Treaty
SPRFMO	South Pacific Regional Fishery Management Organisation
SPS Agreement	Agreement on Sanitary and Phytosanitary Measures
STAP	Scientific and Technical Advisory Panel
STSC	Scientific and Technical Subcommittee
TAC	total allowable catch
TBT	technical barriers to trade
TEU	Treaty of the European Union
TFEU	Treaty on the Functioning of the European Union
TIAS	Treaties and other International Acts Series
TNC	Transnational Corporations
TOMA	tropospheric ozone management area
TRIPS	Trade-Related Aspects of Intellectual Property Rights
UDRME	Universal Declaration on the Rights of Mother Earth
UK	United Kingdom
UN	United Nations
UNCCD	United Nations Convention to Combat Desertification
UNCED	United Nations Conference on Environment and Development
UNCHR	United Nations Commission on Human Rights
UNCITRAL	United Nations Commission on International Trade Law
UNCLOS	United Nations Convention on the Law of the Sea
UNCOPUOS	United Nations Committee on the Peaceful Uses of Outer Space
UNCSD	United Nations Commission on Sustainable Development
UNCTC	United Nations Commission on Transnational Corporations
UNDP	United Nations Development Programme
UNDRIP	United Nations Declaration on the Rights of Indigenous Peoples
UNECE	United Nations Economic Commission for Europe
UNEP	United Nations Environment Programme
UNESCAP	United Nations Economic and Social Commission for Asia and the Pacific

UNESCO	United Nations Educational, Scientific and Cultural Organization
UNFCCC	United Nations Framework Convention on Climate Change
UNFF	United Nations Forum on Forests
UNGA	United Nations General Assembly
UNGASS	Special Session of the United Nations General Assembly
UNICITRAL	United Nations Commission on International Trade Law
UNIDROIT	International Institute for the Unification of Private Law
UNTS	United Nations Treaty System
US	United States
USD	US Dollars
VCLT	Vienna Convention on the Law of Treaties
VISC	Voluntary Indicative Scale of Contributions
VOC	volatile organic compound
WCED	World Commission on Environment and Development
WCS	World Conservation Strategy
WEEE	waste electrical and electronic equipment
WHO	World Health Organization
WIPO	World Intellectual Property Organization
WMO	World Meteorological Organization
WSSD	World Summit on Sustainable Development
WTO	World Trade Organization
WWF	World Wide Fund for Nature (formerly World Wildlife Fund)
YRITWC	Yukon River Inter-Tribal Watershed Council
ZAMCOM	Agreement on the Establishment of the Zambezi Watercourse Commission

Introduction

Shawkat Alam, Md Jahid Hossain Bhuiyan,
Tareq M.R. Chowdhury and Erika J. Techera

Overview

The *Handbook of International Environmental Law* aims to provide comprehensive coverage of this growing and evolving field from a range of perspectives. The global environment is indivisible and the degradation of any part of it affects – in the course of time – the global environment itself. The realities of climate change are a rude reminder of the above fact. Over the last four decades a worldwide concern for protection of the environment has become an increasingly important agenda item for the international community and the governments of every nation. During this time there have been significant developments in international environmental law, extending from global conferences to aspirational documents and binding instruments. In 1972 at the time of the *United Nations Conference on the Human Environment* in Stockholm there were only a handful on international laws focusing on environmental protection. Today there are over 1,000 environmental law instruments covering areas such as water, marine, climate, biodiversity, habitats, heritage, pollution and waste, each of which is addressed in this book. In addition, it engages with the broader governance issues such as environmental principles and institutions, public participation and access to information and justice, funding and finance as well as the dominating paradigm of sustainable development. Thus the book covers general principles of international environmental law as well as including empirical chapters and case studies. This inclusion of both theory and practice is intended to improve both the accessibility and the utility of the volume.

Increasingly, international environmental law intersects with other issues such as energy production, conflicts and disasters, trade and investment, and human and indigenous collective rights. The *Handbook* thus includes important contemporary and novel issues such as the regulation of nuclear energy, deforestation and REDD, constitutionally embedded environmental rights, climate refugees and space law. This *Handbook* explores these areas and in doing so seeks to pave the way for those interested in analysing specific aspects or the entire range of international environmental laws. By examining the cross-cutting nature of these issues, the *Handbook* integrates international environmental law norms and practices into the broader context of law, politics, economics and society. The *Handbook* is also truly global in scope. This is particularly reflected by the conscious effort to include contributions addressing

1

all regions of the world – Europe, the Americas, Asia, the Pacific, Africa and the Polar regions.

The rapid expansion of international environmental law has led to a number of challenges, not least of which is its breadth and complexity. Much of this law was reactive, responding to specific environmental issues, and what has emerged is often criticised as piecemeal and fragmented rather than seen as a coherent regime for environmental protection. A further issue is what some commentators refer to as 'treaty congestion' given the large number of operative instruments. The realisation of positive environmental outcomes remains a challenge and for many countries the implementation of these laws presents a significant hurdle. However, all countries are not in the same position and the consideration of different regional approaches is critical. Thus international environmental law has become an important subject to be studied, researched and discussed in many circles, including academics, lawyers, policy-makers, administrators and practitioners. This *Handbook* provides a comprehensive and contemporary overview of international environmental law, as well as addressing emerging and cross-cutting issues of critical importance for the next decade.

This *Handbook* explores the existing international legal framework for the protection of the environment and seeks to demonstrate the dimensions of the problems that the world is facing today. But the mere identification of the problems and the presence of rules are not enough to combat rapidly accelerating global environmental degradation. The need of the hour is to examine the status, strengths and weaknesses of existing procedures and processes for the implementation of those laws. The book analyses the operationalisation of international environmental law and assesses the contribution of non-state actors, from courts to communities, for the protection and improvement of the environment. Economic elements remain influential on the implementation of international environmental law and the book also explores this issue and offers suggestions as to how to tackle the problems of raising funds at the international level. The negative impacts of globalisation are now well recognised and this is also explored within the context of the sustainable development paradigm.

Scope

The *Handbook* includes contributions from a diverse range of authors in the field from around the world, ensuring that the text is inclusive, truly global and representative. It is also important because current approaches to international environmental law have not resulted in positive global outcomes. This situation can only be improved by engaging with regional and developing country issues. A particular strength of this publication is that it draws upon expertise from both developing and developed countries including Australia, Bangladesh, Canada, Germany, India, the Netherlands, New Zealand, Singapore, South Africa, the United Kingdom, the United States and the West Indies. The authors range from senior professors to post-doctoral researchers and more junior scholars and include government and private sector practitioners. Thus the volume incorporates a diverse range of expertise, perspectives and methodologies.

The *Handbook* will be an important reference book for teachers and researchers in the field of international environmental law. For teachers and students the volume will have particular relevance to courses on international environmental law, including those involved with advanced undergraduate, postgraduate and higher degree research students. Such courses are offered at most universities around the world. It will also be a necessary volume for practitioners and law- and policy-makers, as well as non-lawyers working in government, business and the public interest sector. Thus it will be both an essential publication for those researching in the field, and will also set the research agenda for the future. The volume is strengthened by its consideration of cutting-edge issues, making it a comprehensive, innovative addition to the discipline, and a vital work of reference for students, scholars and practitioners. Protection of environment is an issue that is intrinsic to international law. Therefore, the book will also be a key reference source for scholars, practitioners, teachers and students researching and practising in international law more broadly and in specialist areas such as international human rights law, international humanitarian law and international trade law.

The *Handbook of International Environmental Law* provides a comprehensive and contemporary global examination of international environmental law. The intention has been to capture the dynamic and evolving nature of international environmental law. The vast and complex nature of international environmental law today means that it is of course impossible to cover the entire field in depth. The contents of the *Handbook* have thus been selected on the basis of their contemporary relevance, importance and diversity of perspective. The result is a wide-ranging account of international environmental law and the problems and prospects it currently faces. The inclusion of up-to-date and new information, as well as the latest initiatives in the field including existing and emerging legal frameworks, guarantees that this will be a text that inspires both present and future scholarship on international environmental law.

Structure

The book is divided into six parts involving 40 chapters. The first part, entitled 'The legal framework, theories and principles of international environmental law', covers the origin, theory, principles and development of the discipline. The second part, 'Implementing international environmental law', addresses the implementation of international environmental law and the role of various actors and institutions, including corporations, intergovernmental organisations and non-governmental organisations. The third part, entitled 'Key issues and legal frameworks', brings fresh perspectives on the commonly encountered aspects of international environmental law, such as air, water, biodiversity, habitats, pollution and marine environmental governance, as well as some lesser explored areas including space, nuclear energy and heritage law. The fourth part, 'Regional environmental law', explores regional approaches to the implementation of international environmental law as well as the specific regimes developed to address regional environmental issues. It therefore engages with the evolution, implementation, future prospects and relationship of international environmental law in various regions of the world more broadly. The fifth part, entitled 'Cross-cutting issues', explores the engagement of international environmental law with other key fields and legal regimes, such as international trade, human rights and armed conflict. The final part, 'Contemporary and future challenges', addresses pressing current and emerging issues including governance challenges posed by the rapid growth in international environmental law, sustainable development, environmental refugees and climate change.

In the first chapter, entitled 'The environment and international society: issues, concepts, and context', James R. May and J. Patrick Kelly consider the definitional subtext of what is properly 'international environmental law'. In fact, this issue is extremely complicated, invoking old unsettled scores, politics, population, diplomacy, war, disaster relief and the human condition. The authors are of the opinion that 'one of the great challenges of the twenty-first century will be to develop authoritative processes for making new international law and solving common environmental problems binding on all that are viewed by nations and their peoples as legitimate'.

Anita M. Halvorssen, in her chapter entitled 'The origin and development of international environmental law', vividly traces the history of international environmental law and states that the environment, as the whole biosphere, consisting of independent ecosystems, was first introduced as a matter of importance on the international scene with the UN Conference on the Human Environment, held in Stockholm in 1972. The author is concerned about climate change and expresses the view that '[h]ow effective the international community is in solving' the problem of climate change 'will determine the fate of future generations, yet the pace of the climate negotiations needs to reach a whole new level of cooperation and progress for there to be much hope'.

Svitlana Kravchenko, Tareq M.R. Chowdhury and Md Jahid Hossain Bhuiyan, in their chapter 'Principles of international environmental law', state that principles play an important role in the arena of international law as they help to improve the environment. The authors examine the legal status of sustainable development, the precautionary principle, common but differentiated responsibilities, intergenerational equity, access to information and public participation (good governance). They are in favour of achieving global consensus on the principles having the force of law.

Kamrul Hossain, in his chapter entitled 'The international environmental law-making process', mentions that in addition to states, international organisations, non-governmental organisations and various non-state actors, including financial institutions, companies and stakeholders, local companies and individuals participate in the international environmental law-making process. He opines that the inclusion of thousands of organisations and millions of individuals in the structure of environmental law-making makes this process special.

Carmen G. Gonzalez's chapter on 'Environmental justice and international environmental law' examines the roots of environmental justice and notes that environmental justice norms and politics must be integrated into the broader corpus of international law in order to protect the environment and advance social and economic development. She states that '[t]he achievement of environmental justice also requires cooperation and collective action among nations to regulate the extraterritorial conduct of transnational corporations'.

Paul Govind in 'International environmental institutions' discusses the role of international environmental institutions in maintaining effective environmental governance. This includes an array of actors such as governments, intergovernmental and non-governmental organisations. He expresses the view that the challenges for modern environmental governance are the proliferation of multilateral environmental agreements since 1972 and the lack of coordination between them.

Vernon I. Tava, in his chapter entitled 'The role of non-governmental organisations, peoples and courts in implementing international environmental laws', states that a fundamental tenet of neoliberal globalisation has been the devolution of state power. The approach of international law has been shifted from government to governance 'to explore more coordinated, effective and integrated ways in which to manage environmental issues'. The result has been a substantial democratisation of the area. Non-governmental organisations, indigenous peoples and grass-roots environmental movements have become major sources of developments in international environmental law. He argues that '[a]lthough courts have been reluctant to make definitive judgments on matters of international environmental law, they are becoming more accessible and receptive to non-state parties'.

Jona Razzaque, in her chapter entitled 'Information, public participation and access to justice in international environmental matters', states that 20 years after the 1992 Rio Declaration a significant development took place in the area of participatory rights. This development deals with the process through which an administrative or judicial decision is taken and typically encompasses public consultation, access to information and access to justice. The author expresses the view that global, regional and national collaboration can promote sustainable resource governance.

Justin Wolst in his chapter entitled 'The funding of international environmental law' provides an overview of the history, structure and different types of funding for international environmental law. He takes the position that financial and technical assistance for environmental purposes has been playing a significant role in the development of international environmental law.

Tim Stephens in 'The settlement of disputes in international environmental law' notes that environmental disputes are now litigated in international courts, including the International Court of Justice. The author highlights the limitations of international courts to settle environmental disputes and expresses the view that environmental compliance procedures should be welcomed to reduce the relentless march of global environmental degradation.

Increasingly the power and range of multinational corporations (MNCs) is being felt. Elisa Morgera in her chapter entitled 'Multinational corporations and international environmental law' traces the evolution of these corporations, highlighting environmentally sound and responsible conduct of MNCs. The author is of the opinion that '[e]ven if international law does not impose legally binding obligations directly on MNCs, minimum international standards', such as environmental impact self-assessment and ongoing/continuous assessment, 'are emerging that may be legitimately expected to be respected by private companies even in the absence of national laws to that effect'.

Chidi Oguamanam in his chapter on 'Biological diversity' states that the concept of biological diversity (or 'biodiversity') is central to any serious discussion on the environment. Underscoring the imperative for biodiversity conservation, the author writes about generalised ecological analysis of biological diversity. He is of the opinion that striking the right balance between biological conservation and development imperatives remains an ongoing challenge for credible international environmental law and policy.

Douglas Fisher in his chapter demonstrates the interconnection of freshwater, habitats and ecosystems. He states that they 'should be managed on a coherent, integrated and sustainable basis'. He is of the opinion that though there is no single mechanism for the conservation of freshwater resources, habitats and ecosystems, they are capable of protection and conservation within the existing set of arrangements.

The governance of transboundary freshwater involves issues of ownership, control and use of water as a resource. Alistair Rieu-Clarke in his chapter entitled 'International freshwater law' considers the role and relevance of international law in addressing global water-related issues. He explores the reasons why the United Nations (UN) Watercourse Convention adopted by the UN General Assembly in 1997 has not entered into force, and opines that 'more work is needed to increased awareness, training and understanding of law's role in this increasingly important field of international relations'.

Rebecca M. Bratspies and Anastasia Telesetsky in their chapter entitled 'Marine environmental law: UNCLOS and fisheries' argue that the future success of fisheries law to protect and manage marine living resources depends on creating a more robust governance regime. They continue that 'it must be forward-thinking in creating proactive policies and laws that will protect fisheries and marine ecosystems for multiple generations'.

Damien Cremean and Erika J Techera in their chapter on 'Marine pollution law' explore the development and evaluate the contribution of relevant international conventions to the protection of the marine environment. The authors are of the opinion that though those conventions are designed to protect and preserve the marine environment, nevertheless some implementation challenges do remain.

Tony George Puthucherril in his chapter 'Two decades of the Basel Convention' states that the treaty has been hailed as the most comprehensive global multilateral environmental agreement to regulate the adverse effects ensuing from the generation, management, transboundary movements and disposal of hazardous and other wastes. Right from the time of its inception, the Basel Convention established a regulatory framework to control the transboundary movements of wastes based on several innovative legal principles such as environmentally sound management and prior informed consent. Nevertheless, the amount of illegal traffic in hazardous waste continues to be a matter of serious concern.

The topic of pollution is continued in Zada Lipman's chapter on 'Pollution control and the regulation of chemicals and e-waste'. She states that although internationally binding legal instruments, such as the Rotterdam, Stockholm and Basel Conventions, are designed to protect human health and the environment from the dangers of hazardous chemicals and pesticides, their implementation has been difficult. She argues that governmental regulation in developed and developing countries should reinforce international measures and '[d]eveloped countries should assume responsibility for waste they have generated instead of exporting it to developing countries'.

International environmental law has engaged with several air pollution issues. Atmospheric pollution is a global concern which causes serious environmental degradation. Paolo Galizzi in his chapter entitled 'Air, atmosphere and climate change' states that international rules in relation to the atmosphere are effective to 'address atmospheric pollution with the proven financial and regulatory approaches innovated in the arenas of transboundary air pollution and ozone depletion'.

Alexander Zahar in his chapter on 'The climate change regime' examines the provisions of the United Nations Framework Convention on Climate Change (UNFCCC) and the Kyoto Protocol that deal with pressing environmental issues. He discusses key mechanisms and institutions of the climate change regime that have been created under these two instruments, and more recent developments in this contemporary field of international environmental law.

Ulrike M. Bohlmann and Steven Freeland in their chapter entitled 'The regulation of space activities and the space environment' discuss international legal regulations in relation to exploration and use of the outer space environment. The authors take the position that 'the existing body of international space law does not provide a comprehensive legal framework for the protection of the environment of outer space'.

In 'Nuclear energy and the environment' Abdullah Al Faruque explores the relationship between energy and environment. The author argues that among renewable energy sources, nuclear energy will be considered one of the most viable options. The reason behind this view is that it produces significantly little environmental pollution and greenhouse gas emissions compared with other options. In that context he notes that the nuclear safety regime should be developed 'so that any nuclear power plant can withstand any natural calamity of catastrophic scale'.

Erika J. Techera explores 'International cultural heritage law' in her chapter. She states that good environmental governance is necessary for the protection and preservation of both the natural and cultural environments and that recent developments have expanded the coverage of international law in this field. She argues that international heritage law offers many valuable lessons 'not only in terms of substantive law but also of the tools and processes embedded within the different treaty regimes'.

6

Moving on to the regional chapters, Elisa Morgera in 'European environmental law' states that though the European Union (EU), which is a party to more than 40 multilateral environmental agreements, is a prominent international actor in the effective enforcement of international environmental law, EU environmental law faces significant challenges. Complex strategies such as the EU's use of 'its domestic and external legislative action to support the implementation of international environmental law' do not always provide positive results.

Marie-Claire Cordonier Seggar and Renée Gift continue the regional examination in their chapter on 'The Americas' environmental and sustainable development law'. The Americas consist of 35 countries and the authors analyse the approach that has been taken to protect the region's ecology and promote sustainable development. The authors are of the opinion that collaboration for environmental protection and sustainable development among the countries of the Americas 'is a massive task, and for effective stewardship of significant ecological and hydrological systems, a great deal remains to be done to address the many environmental and sustainable development challenges'.

Koh Kheng-Lian and Md Saiful Karim in their chapter on 'South East Asian environmental legal governance' analyse and evaluate the laws and policies in the Association of South East Asian Nations (ASEAN) which consists of ten member states. The authors take the position that it 'has not fully achieved effective environmental governance for sustainable development' but it is now time for ASEAN to play an effective role in bringing environmental governance forward.

Cameron Holley in his chapter entitled 'International environmental law and Australia and New Zealand' states that although these countries have been leaders in effective implementation of international law, 'there are weaknesses, as well as key issues on which more work could be done to ensure consistency with and more effective implementation of international environmental law obligations'. For instance, there is ineffective legal cooperation and coordination between levels of government in Australia and New Zealand.

In exploring 'Environmental law in Africa' Michael Kidd notes that although the African continent, consisting of 54 states, is blessed with enormous biodiversity, it is 'also facing environmental problems that resonate on the world stage'. He further states that although most African countries have developed domestic environmental laws in light of international environmental law, weak implementation is still evident in some countries because of political instability, corruption, lack of political will, capacity constraints or financial constraints.

Elizabeth Burleson in 'Polar law and good governance' explores the governance regimes that exist in the Antarctic and Arctic and in particular assesses the Antarctic Treaty System. Stating that the Antarctic and Arctic regions are vulnerable to pollution, she expresses the view that '[g]lobal cooperation in the face of unprecedented environmental and security challenges remains a sensible path forward.'

The first chapter in the cross-cutting issues section is presented by Indira Carr. In 'International trade rules and environmental effects' she states that the World Trade Organization (WTO), in particular the General Agreement on Tariffs and Trade (GATT), promotes free trade to encourage economic growth and raise standards of living, guided by a liberalist ideology. The issue of whether there is a conflict between GATT and environmental measures has been extensively debated since 1991 as a result of the Tuna–Dolphin dispute. The author examines the trade and environmental debate and analyses some other case law and environmentally focused provisions in other WTO agreements. She is of the opinion that 'the trade–environment interface is a complex one, but it is possible to reconcile the two fields by adopting a sensitive and pragmatic approach that does not at the same time forget the need to achieve a balance'.

Markus W. Gehring and Avidan Kent in their chapter entitled 'International investment agreements and sustainable development: future pathways' state that international investment agreements (IIAs), which 'are designed to provide security and certainty for foreign investors, in order to promote FDI (foreign direct investment), with the object of achieving the ultimate goal of development', mainly regulate the promotion of FDI. The authors put forward some tools available for states to incorporate sustainable development objectives into their IIAs.

In the first of two chapters on rights-based approaches to environmental governance, Shawkat Alam explores 'Collective indigenous rights and the environment'. He states that since indigenous peoples are closely linked with their land, they are significantly affected by environmental degradation and the adverse effect of climate change. This relationship to their environment also shows the interconnected nature of their rights to self-determination, lands and cultural integrity. The author is of the opinion that if that environment is endangered then these collective rights are themselves endangered as well. So a searching reappraisal of existing models of approaching climate change and indigenous peoples is needed to ensure and uphold indigenous peoples' heritage and future.

James R. May and Erin Daly in their assessment of 'Global constitutional environmental rights' examine the extent to which these rights have met the promise of ensuring a right to a healthy, adequate or quality environment. The authors, in stating that courts have had to 'make sense of and take seriously constitutional environmental rights', take the position that no judicial order can resolve environmental or climate change problems; 'in many cases, the most that a court can do is galvanise the political process to take environmental protection seriously. But this, in and of itself, is worth the effort to vindicate constitutional environmental rights.'

Susan Breau in her chapter entitled 'Protection of environment during armed conflict' opines that international custom and treaty law applicable to the protection of the environment in armed conflict is not effective in protecting the environment during armed conflict or in dealing with the environmental degradation following armed conflict. She notes, however, that the International Committee of the Red Cross's (ICRC) 'customary humanitarian law study is a tremendous boost to the customary status of environmental protection obligations in armed conflict'.

Michael Eburn explores the emerging area of 'International disaster law'. He states that natural hazard events such as flood, storm or wildfire, rising sea levels and coastal erosion may qualify as a disaster if they impact upon a vulnerable population. He is of the opinion that the basic problem in relation to international responses to disaster is the concept of state sovereignty which 'allows affected states to determine if and when they will call for aid, and from whom they will accept assistance, and leaves donor states free to offer help if and when, and on what terms that they choose'.

The rapid development of international environmental law in the last 30 years of the twentieth century has posed a number of problems including so-called 'treaty congestion'. Arguably the sheer number of international instruments is now hampering implementation. In particular many developing countries are confronted with the challenge of operationalising the numerous laws, policies, programmes and plans. Donald K. Anton in his chapter entitled ' "Treaty congestion" in contemporary international environmental law' opines that '[a]s greater international cooperation is required to address global problems, the need for more law to implement cooperation accompanies'.

Increasingly sustainable development is being seen as the dominant paradigm in environmental governance. Klaus Bosselmann in his chapter entitled 'Sustainable development and international environmental law' states that the current environmental problems are global. The demands on natural resources across the globe have been increasing. Thus adjustments are necessary if this world is to 'live sustainably within the limits of ecological systems, whether local or global'.

Early attention was drawn to the issue of liability with the Trail Smelter Arbitration setting standards which are now part of the corpus of customary international law. Robert V. Percival in his chapter entitled 'International responsibility and liability for environmental harm' explores the evolution of this area. The author is of the opinion that though the nations of the world and international tribunals hearing environmental cases have accepted the norm of state responsibility for transboundary environmental harm, 'international law has failed to develop efficient liability and compensation regimes for most forms of global environmental harm despite pledges to do so in Stockholm in 1972 and Rio in 1992.'

One of the most pressing contemporary issues is that of climate change. Within that topic, reduced emissions from deforestation and degradation (REDD) has become perhaps the most topical issue. Rowena Maguire in her chapter on 'Deforestation, REDD and international law' discusses the impact of existing law on the protection of forests. She states that, since the United Nations Forum on Forests has been unable to deal effectively with forest regulation, a number of international forestry institutions have evolved. Finally, she highlights the REDD policy and expresses the view that it 'will play a dominant role in international forest regulation for the foreseeable future'.

The final chapter addresses another critical issue. Climate change is likely to result in significant displacement. Maxine Burkett in her chapter entitled 'Climate refugees' states that although environmental disturbances push people to migrate, some countries, such as India, are not willing to accept climate-induced migrants. She notes that 'the question of statelessness still requires significant attention and clarification' and urges the international community to bring emissions under control.

Emerging themes and final words

This book incorporates multiple perspectives on a range of international environmental law issues in different contexts. Despite this diversity there are several themes which emerge. First, the rapid expansion of international environmental law has led to fragmentation and congestion. Fragmentation is not necessarily a problem but treaty congestion reduces the effectiveness of international environmental law. Furthermore, this expansion also challenges those tasked with implementing international environmental law – in the South as well as the North.

Second, international environmental law has within it the flexibility to address contemporary and emerging challenges. Throughout many chapters of this book novel and effective mechanisms are highlighted. But in order for these to be harnessed, international environmental law must become more coordinated in terms of both the different governance regimes themselves and its engagement with other disciplines; including embedding science in law and policy, addressing trade and investment-related issues and securing human rights, for example.

Finally, it must be noted that 2012 is a key year for this volume to be produced as it is another milestone along the international environmental law timeline – 20 years since the seminal Rio Conference, the Earth Summit, held in Rio de Janeiro in 1992. If international environmental law is to continue to evolve and develop to address persistent, emerging and future challenges then it will require global cooperation and commitment. It is hoped that Rio+20 will provide an opportunity for both renewed commitments and the exploration of innovative solutions. Only with renewed effort will improved legal governance and environmental security be assured for present and future generations.

Part I
The legal framework, theories and principles of international environmental law

The environment and international society

Issues, concepts and context

James R. May and J. Patrick Kelly*

International environmental law is the study of the norms, means and processes to address global and regional environmental challenges. The world's domestic and transboundary ecosystems are under enormous strain. International environmental law includes the study of how treaties, principles, custom and other sources of international law can be used to address these strains. Accordingly, this section provides a brief survey of threshold principles in international law, including common issues, concepts and definitions, and associated international law constructs. In addition, it views how these concepts are shaped by external and emerging notions of global trade, economics, sustainability and environmental rights.

Introduction

The world's resources are under enormous strain. The population of the planet has eclipsed seven billion people, many if not most of whom desire a better quality of life. Population stress naturally contributes to the rising demand for food, energy, metals and materials. These demands create enormous pressure on domestic and transboundary ecosystems.

International environmental law is the study of how treaties, principles, custom and other sources of international law can be used to address these strains. This book examines what international environmental law is, and how it is or can be used to address the planet's wide array of complex and seemingly intractable challenges, including human-induced climate change, resources-based conflict, rising sea levels, loss of timber, biological and cultural diversity loss, diminution of liveable land and fresh water, pollution of the oceans, seas and coastal areas, persistent organic pollutants, by-products of technology and nanotechnology, overharvesting of forests and oceans, global disposal of chemical and hazardous wastes, trade in endangered plants and animals, minerals harvesting in the polar regions and a human right to a quality environment.

Part I of this volume introduces the legal framework, theories and principles of international environmental law, and how it is implemented and enforced, including ethical considerations. This section provides a brief survey of threshold principles in international

* The proofreading assistance of Corey Bolander, Widener L. '11, is noted with gratitude.

law, including common issues, concepts and definitions, and associated international law constructs. In addition, it views how these concepts are shaped by external and emerging notions of global trade, economics, sustainability and environmental rights.

What is international environmental law? Common issues, concepts and definitions

As discussed elsewhere in Part I, international environmental law provides and describes the global institutional means for engaging the global ecological challenges. It is conceptually commodious, a reflection of interconnected ends that can be global, parochial and everything in between. It consists of a loose affiliation of treaties, principles and customs that define and describe norms, relationships and responses among and between states to meet these many global ecological challenges.[1] It can be poetic and inscrutable, as shown by the definition of 'sustainable development': 'development . . . that . . . meets the needs of the present without compromising the ability of future generations to meet their own needs.'[2] Regardless of whether it appears as positive hard law, normative soft law, or a hybrid of these, international environmental law is essential to the global order of environmental law.[3]

International environmental law is also evolutionary. It reflects the confluence of 500 years of *opinio juris, lex suprema* and customary law coupled with more modern conventions and general principles of international environmental law, with added ingredients of environmental ethics, ecology and economics and human rights.

Moreover, as Part II of this book suggests, most treaty negotiations – from climate change to fish stocks – reflect endogenous political, cultural, religious and ethnic consilience and division, and exogenous influences respecting who should pay for what and when, who participates, and who decides. It reflects the inescapable binomialism of the global age: north and south, east and west, developed and developing, financially rich and poor, biologically endowed and barren, givers and takers around the globe. Part II considers concepts of implementation, including international environmental institutions, stakeholders, funding, dispute settlement and the role of multinational corporations. Confounding, cross–cutting factors also serve as a kind of proxy for global *realpolitik*, including trade, economics, property rights, constitutional constraints and conflict, as addressed in Part V.

Sceptics argue that international environmental law is unnecessary at best and unwise at worst. This view invites a political and societal backlash by trivializing huge moral and ethical challenges, engendering unnecessary counter-colonial effects, facilitating scapegoating, diluting sovereignty and autonomy, creating 'spill over' effects that curtail private property, and undermining more sensible cooperative efforts. International environmental law is also shaped by principles of geography, population distribution, engineering, land use planning and the applied sciences.

As suggested in Part II, international environmental law also has a dizzying array of stake-holders. It is shaped by nation-states, international institutions such as the United Nations

---

1 See generally, P. Sands, *Principles of International Environmental Law*, 2nd edition, Cambridge: Cambridge University Press, 2003.
2 World Commission on Environment and Development, *Our Common Future*, Oxford: Oxford University Press, 1987, p. 8.
3 See generally, T. Yang and R. Percival, 'The Emergence of Global Environmental Law', *Ecology Law Quarterly* 36, 2009.

Environment Programme (UNEP), non-governmental organizations (NGOs) such as the International Union for Conservation of Nature (IUCN), corporate associations, individuals, academics and the concern for future generations.[4]

To complicate matters, as Part IV on regional environmental law suggests, no two countries implement international law in the same way. The constitutions of some countries allow the head of state to negotiate and implement binding agreements unilaterally. Other countries require parliamentarian ratification and legislation to implement an international accord. Many countries fall somewhere in between. Domestic implementation is also complicated by domestic policies concerning the use and disposition of natural resources, energy policies and national security. Many countries lack the resources and statutory and regulatory architectures to implement, or the wherewithal and resources to enforce, international laws. Correspondingly, Part V addresses cross-cutting issues, including trade, financial investment, intellectual property, human rights, global constitutional environmental rights and environmental protection during conflict.

The international legal constructs

International law constructs include principles, rules and norms that are binding on nations and sub-national actors. Environmental legal principles and policy prescriptions emerge from the use of international sources and processes to make law and to cooperate to solve problems. While international law and legal processes may be mechanisms to address transboundary environmental problems, it is a relatively undeveloped and cumbersome system, not an integrated, hierarchical system of universal rules and principles.

International law is complex, to say the least. The international legal system is a decentralized system of independent nation-states with different histories, values and interests. The international system lacks a legislature with the authority to make law, an authoritative court with mandatory jurisdiction to articulate norms, an executive with delegated authority to make law or execute legal norms, or an international police force to enforce norms.

Accordingly, international society has been conceived as made up of independent states that must consent to restraints on their authority. These limitations make solving problems on the basis of consent or consensus difficult and slow.

Hence, the international legal system has been criticized for its anarchic character. Critics particularly within the international legal community have called for a new sense of common humanity to transcend the limited vision of states asserting sovereignty rather than solving common problems.

The primary means of creating international environmental norms are treaty, customary law, general principles of law and soft law processes. Under conventional theory, substantive international law is largely consensual. International law is formed by express consent in the case of treaty law and implied consent in the case of customary international law (CIL).[5]

Treaties negotiated, signed and ratified by nations have several distinct advantages as a form of law-making. The norms created and nations bound are clearly identified. Nations have agreed in advance to accept such norms as law and to comply. In several cases the treaties

---

4 See generally, E.B. Weiss, *In Fairness to Future Generations: International Law, Common Patrimony, and Intergenerational Equity*, New York: Transnational Publishers, 1988.
5 See generally, I. Brownlie, *Principles of Public International Law*, 6th edition, Oxford: Oxford University Press, 2003, pp. 3–4. For a brief summary of the history of the triumph of positivism over natural law, see S.C. McCaffrey, *Understanding International Law*, 2006, pp. 36–7.

contain the means of resolving disputes and the sanctions or procedures for encouraging or policing compliance. In some cases specific legal norms in treaties may become CIL if the requirements for customary law are met. On the other hand, treaty norms do not generally bind non-parties states that may be useful or necessary to achieve the ends of a treaty.

One of the most significant developments of the last 50 years has been the birth of Multilateral Treaty Regimes (MTR). Such MTRs are not just treaties with defined norms. The treaty instruments, by their terms, create ongoing legislative and administrative bodies that expand the limited contractual nature of treaties themselves. For example, the Ozone Layer Treaty Regime discussed elsewhere in this book began with a framework convention that created an ongoing institution, a conference of parties that meets regularly and a means for resolving disputes and/or managing compliance.[6]

The conference of parties or another mechanism with the authority to make decisions such as the Ministerial Conference of the World Trade Organization (WTO) will typically monitor new information, technology and needs. The Conference of Parties will then assess the need for amendments or protocols that may define the standards with greater particularity or expand the subject matter of the treaty to new areas such as the expansion of the trade regime into intellectual property. As discussed in chapters by Stephens and Carr, some MTRs such as the WTO have formal dispute settlement bodies that adjudicate disputes and render formal opinions that become a form of precedent that creates law or at least ongoing rules of decision.

Such treaty regimes must be interpreted to clarify norms and settle disputes. There are two general approaches: (1) interpreting a treaty using the ordinary meaning and context of the treaty in light of the object and purpose[7] at the time of the conclusion of the treaty; or (2) interpreting the treaty as an evolutionary instrument in light of the contemporary principles of international law and the contemporary concerns of the international community.[8]

This latter process of interpretation may lead and has led to the expansion of norms beyond what appeared to be prior agreed principles. For example, in the *Shrimp-Turtle* case discussed by Carr in Part V, the Appellate Body (AB) of the WTO re-examined the meaning of 'conservation of exhaustible natural resources' in Article XX (g) of the general exceptions section of the GATT agreement under an 'evolutionary methodology' that included the contemporary concerns of the international community and the meaning of 'natural resources' in several recent environmental treaties to conclude that 'natural resources' now included living as well as inanimate resources.

The norms of CIL are created by state practice generally accepted as law by the international community of states.[9] States impliedly consent to norms by their participation in state practice and their demonstrated attitude of acceptance. Custom, then, consists of two elements: (1) the practice of states as the material element that provides evidence of customary norms; and (2) the general acceptance of a norm as a legal obligation by the world community

---

6 See Chapter 19 by P. Galizzi in this volume.
7 *Vienna Convention on the Law of the Treaties*, 23 May 1969, 1155 UNTS 331 (entered into force 27 January 1980) ('VCLT') Art 31(1). Text online. Available HTTP: <http://untreaty.un.org/ilc/texts/instruments/english/conventions/1_1_1969.pdf> (accessed 27 November 2011).
8 See e.g. *Legal Consequences for States of the Continued Presence of South Africa in Namibia (Southwest Africa) Notwithstanding Security Council Resolution 276 (1970), Advisory Opinion of 21 June 1971*, ICJ Rep 16, 31.
9 Brownlie, op. cit., pp. 3, 6.

as the attitudinal requirement.[10] Note that this is not actual consent, but rather acceptance by the community as a whole. Consent is implied from community acceptance. The great advantage of CIL is that it binds all states. Even new members of the international community of states are said to be bound by existing customary law. However, an existing state is generally said to not be bound by emerging customary law if it persistently objects during the formation of custom.[11]

Several CIL norms, particularly in the field of international environmental law, are controversial because few states participate in the practice that may form a norm and there is no objective way to determine if the generality of states has accepted a given norm. The arbitrator in the *Trail Smelter Arbitration*, for example, invoked a general principle of international law, the *sic utere tuo* principle that states must not use their territory in a manner that injures another state, to decide a transboundary air pollution matter without reference to state practice or proof that the principle in question had been generally accepted. Since then the *sic utere tuo* principle has been affirmed in the Stockholm and Rio Declarations and recognized by the International Court of Justice (ICJ) in the *Nuclear Weapons Advisory Opinion* of 1996.[12]

The disadvantages of CIL as a form of law-making include that the precise contours of CIL norms are often not clear, and require further definition in treaties or non-binding instruments. Nor is it clear when there is sufficient general acceptance to create a legally binding norm. Many states may, for example, object to a norm because they did not specifically consent or participate in the process that created the norm and were unaware of its formation. Moreover, CIL processes do not create institutions to adjudicate disputes or provide for sanctions or other mechanisms to enforce such norms, as do several MTR.

General principles of law are an exception to the consent or consensus bases of international law. The Statute of the International Court of Justice in Article 38 lists 'general principles of law recognized by civilized nations' as a source of law to be applied by the Court.[13] Putting aside the anachronism or perhaps misnomer of which countries are 'civilized nations,' the general principles referred to appear to be the rules generally accepted in the domestic laws of the major legal systems of the world. Since the international legal system is inherently incomplete, resort may be had to rules and procedures that are common to the major legal cultures as gap-fillers to this incomplete system.

There are several different theories or approaches as to which principles of law are appropriate as binding rules of international law. At a minimum international tribunals have looked to common domestic doctrine when necessary to make the law of nations a viable system that can be applied in a judicial process.[14] International tribunals have looked to domestic systems for procedural and equitable principles such as *res judicata*, laches, good faith and estoppel. This implies a limiting methodology of a systemic search through the domestic law of all the major legal systems of the world for evidence of a particular principle.

---

10 A. D'Amato, *The Concept of Custom in International Law*, New York: Cornell University Press, 1971, pp. 47–72.
11 The major treaties, as well as the US Restatement, agree on the formal elements of this paradigm. See e.g. Brownlie, op. cit., pp. 6–12; R. Jennings and A. Watts (eds.) *Oppenheim's International Law*, 9th edition, Boston: Addison Wesley Publishing, 1996, pp. 25–31.
12 *Advisory Opinion on the Legality of the Threat and Use of Nuclear Weapons (UNGA)*, opinion of 8 July 1996, 1996, ICJ Rep 95, para 29
13 *Statute of the International Court of Justice*, Art. 38.
14 Brownlie, op. cit.

Some theorists, and at times the ICJ, have used the concept of general principles as a form of natural law to discern principles of justice.[15] For example, the ICJ in its *Advisory Opinion on the Legality of the Threat or Use of Nuclear Weapons* indicated that there existed prior principles of law to protect nations and peoples based on usages, the laws of humanity and the dictates of public conscience.[16]

The general principles of international environmental law have often been referred to as a similar non-consensual source of substantive principles limiting state actions. One such principle, the *sic utere tuo* principle that a nation should not use its territory in a manner that harms the interests of another nation in its territory, was used by the ICJ to help resolve the Corfu Channel case involving the mine that destroyed a British ship.[17]

Numerous non-binding international instruments, such as the Stockholm Declaration on Human Environment, contain norms, principles or standards that are termed 'soft law'. Soft law norms are non-binding social norms that may lead to binding legal norms and, as an empirical matter, may create expectations of compliance that limit or influence state behaviour. While states consider such instruments as political commitments and not legal norms, they nevertheless may treat political commitments as defining standards of behaviour that if violated may significantly diminish a nation's reputation as a trustworthy partner and as a responsible member of the international community. In that respect, soft law can and does have real-world effects.

Economics, trade and the international policy process

As addressed by Part V on cross-cutting issues, on one level economic ideas and tools are a means to achieve environmental goals in an efficient manner; on the other hand, there is considerable tension between environmental goals and rapid economic development, particularly in less developed countries. Many environmental problems such as air and water pollution, ozone layer protection, the protection of endangered species, the transboundary movement of toxic substances and climate change may be seen as the overuse of public goods. Public goods, such as the atmosphere and the oceans, are treated as the property of no one without a price to reduce their exploitation. Such resources are overused and degraded. This is the tragedy of the commons. Public resources degrade with increases in population unless there is a mechanism to regulate their use or put a price on its consumption as, for example, a carbon tax or cap and trade system would do. Economic theory suggests that the external costs of production, including the effect on human and animal health, should be placed on the producer as a cost of production. National and international legal institutions may place the cost back on the manufacturer or manage the externalities (emissions) by regulations to reduce the external effects of the various activities of modern life from manufacturing to residential construction to energy production.

The principles of economics help shape and provide alternative approaches to achieving international policy goals. Treaty negotiators have a number of means or alternative policy tools to mandate or encourage actions to safeguard the environment. These include a tax on the damaging activity (air or water pollution) to discourage such pollution and encourage

---

15 S. Rosenne, *Practice and Method of International Law*, New York: Oceania, 1984, p. 69.
16 *Advisory Opinion on the Threat or Use of Nuclear Weapons* (1996), 35 ILM 809.
17 *Corfu Channel (United Kingdom v Albania) (Merits)*, 1949 ICJ 4.

alternative less polluting processes, thereby channelling the spending of resources. Command and control regulations, including the prohibition in the Montreal Protocols on producing or consuming listed ozone-depleting chemicals, limit permissible activity and force producers to discover or invent new chemicals as substitutes for the damaging ones.

Tradable permits and permit exchanges, such as the cap and trade system, currently used under the Kyoto Protocol in Europe and the sulphur dioxide regulations within the domestic law of the USA, provide an economic incentive to emit fewer greenhouse gases in both the production process and the consumption of energy. Under the tradable permit approach a government places a cap on permissible greenhouse gas (GHG) emissions and then grants property rights to those who emit levels below the cap. The more GHG-efficient producers may then sell the right to emit up to their cap to other producers via commodity exchanges. This effectively places a price on pollution and encourages all producers to create new, less polluting processes to reduce their costs.

Subsidies may be used to encourage the development of new energy sources to reduce GHGs. Similarly, the reduction of subsidies to industries that are more carbon-based may reduce the overuse of environmental resources, returning the industry to the full cost of production. Several international treaties establish multilateral environmental funds to help defer or reduce the costs of technology transfer or encourage the adaptation of new less polluting production methods. The Montreal Protocol as amended in London, for example, created a Multilateral Fund to provide financial and technical assistance to developing countries in adopting ozone-friendly technologies instead of ozone-depleting ones. Finally, sanctions or prohibitions on trade may be a very effective means of enforcement of international agreements and norms. The Convention on Trade in Endangered Species (CITES) prohibits trade in listed species, thereby limiting the markets for such goods and reducing the incentive to kill such species.

Indeed, as discussed in Part V, the rapid growth in international trade and increased economic interdependence among nations are transforming the organization of economic life, placing pressure on the ecosystems of the world. As explored by Part VI on contemporary and future challenges, globalization, a more open international trading system and the spread of new technologies have increased productivity, incomes and wealth.

In general, nations with higher levels of economic development have cleaner environments, a larger middle class that puts demands on government for reduced pollution, and possess more democratic political systems.[18] Unfortunately, not all nations and people share equally in this growth. There is evidence of increased income inequality in and among some countries even as average income rises. There is another fundamental cost: the cost of the internationalization of production. As production, goods, services and people move from

---

18 Economists suggest that growth in income will lead to greater resources to attack pollution and more demands for a cleaner environment: J. Bhagwati, 'Trade and the Environment: The False Conflict?', in D. Zaelke, R. Housman and P. Orbach (eds) *Trade and the Environment: Law, Economics and Policy*, Washington DC: Island Press, 1995, pp. 162–3; G. Grossman and A. Krueger, 'Environmental Impacts of a North American Free Trade Agreement', Washington DC: NBER Working Paper No. 3914, 1991 (study of levels of sulphur dioxide and smoke in 42 countries indicated that pollution levels rose until per capita income reached $4,000–$5,000 measured in 1985 US dollars. At higher levels of income pollution declined). While increased trade and income provide more resources for pollution abatement, political institutions often fail to develop proper environmental policies to reduce the pollution created: H. Nordström and S. Vaughan, *Trade and Environment*, Special Studies 4, World Trade Organization, 1999, pp. 2–5.

one country to another, environmental and other costs are transferred to those nations with fewer economic and political resources to internalize those costs. Rather, many developing countries suffer from the increased pollution from rapid economic development with little regulation or enforcement of what environmental laws may exist, as discussed in Parts IV and VI.

A question often arises as to the extent that trade sanctions used as a means to enforce multilateral treaties and domestic unilateral environmental laws may violate the WTO agreements. The GATT and its successor, the WTO, by reducing tariffs and opening markets to trade have stimulated this globalization phenomenon. The Dispute Settlement Understanding, one of the package of WTO agreements, creates a mandatory dispute settlement system to resolve disputes about rule violations. Yet dispute settlement or treaty solutions to regional problems, for example, raise issues of festering unsettled scores, politics, population pressure, diplomacy, ongoing or potential war over resources, disaster relief and the human condition. The solutions to environmental problems are intertwined with the old debates of north and south, east and west, rich and poor, developing and developed. The relationship between trade and the environment and other cross-cutting issues are addressed in Part V.

Emerging issues

Some of the most important emerging issues in international environmental law revolve around concepts of sustainability and environmental human rights, as Part VI explores in depth.

The principle of 'sustainability' is approaching its 40th anniversary. It is a concept that has experienced both evolution and stasis. It has shaken the legal foundation, and is often engaged, recited and even revered by policy-makers, law-makers and academics worldwide. Sustainability entered the general public conscience in 1972 with the Stockholm Declaration on the Human Environment.[19] In 1987 it secured centre stage when the World Commission on Environment and Development released its pioneering study, *Our Common Future*,[20] which defines 'sustainable development' as 'development . . . that . . . meets the needs of the present without compromising the ability of future generations to meet their own needs'.[21] In 1992 the Earth Summit's Rio Declaration declared that sustainable development must 'respect the interests of all and protect the integrity of the global environmental and developmental system'.[22] The Rio Declaration's blueprint document, *Agenda 21*, provides that sustainable development must coincidently raise living standards while preserving the environment: 'integration of environment and development concerns . . . will lead to the fulfilment of basic needs, improved living standards for all, better protected and managed ecosystems and a safer, more prosperous future.'[23]

While disparate, the unmistakable thread that runs through threshold definitions of sustainability is the interconnectedness of living things, opportunity and hope. Recognition

---

19 Stockholm Declaration on the Human Environment (1972), 11 ILM 1416 ('Stockholm Declaration').
20 World Commission on Environment and Development, *Our Common Future*, New York: Oxford University Press, 1987.
21 Ibid., p. 8.
22 *Rio Declaration on Environment and Development* (1992), 31 ILM 874 ('Rio Declaration').
23 *Agenda 21: A Programme for Action for Sustainable Development*, Report of the UN Conference on Environment and Development, Annex II, 12 August 1992, UN Doc A./Conf. 151/26 ('Agenda 21').

of the importance of sustainability has grown exponentially since the Earth Summit.[24] Since then, the concept of sustainability has been regularly recognized in international accords,[25] by nations in constitutional, legislative and regulatory reform,[26] by states, municipalities and localities in everything from policy statements to building codes,[27] and in corporate mission statements and practices worldwide.[28] Sustainability principles are shape-shifters, adaptive to most environmental decision-making, including water and air quality, species conservation and national environmental policy in the USA and around the globe.[29] Furthermore, it has entered the bloodstream of courts around the globe as a guiding principle of judicial discretion in environmental cases.[30]

Next, as discussed in Part V, human rights have emerged as an important area in international environmental law.[31] Fundamental human rights to life and liberty, for example, cannot be achieved without adequate environmental conditions of clean water, air and land.[32] Forty years ago the Universal Declaration of Human Rights first recognized the link between the human condition and the environment.[33] Next were efforts to have foundational international environmental measures expressly recognize a human right to a quality environment. For the most part, domestic courts have declined to find that these normative developments

24 J. Dernbach (ed.) *Agenda for a Sustainable America*, Washington DC: Environmental Law Institute, 2009, pp. 2–3.
25 See e.g. R.K.L. Panjabi, *The Earth Summit at Rio: Politics, Economics, and the Environment*, New England: Northeastern University Press, 1997, p. 17 (describing how the Earth Summit in Rio led to a new global consciousness of sustainability in treaty-making).
26 See e.g. M. Berry and A. Nelson, 'Steering Sustainability: What, When, and Why', in A. Nelson (ed.) *Steering Sustainability in an Urbanizing World: Policy Practice and Performance*, 2007, pp. 1, 2–3 (explaining the national policy and reform considerations behind urban sustainability); J. May, 'The North American Symposium on the Judiciary and Environmental Law: Constituting Fundamental Environmental Rights Worldwide', *Pace Environmental Law Review* 23, 2005/2006, p. 113, Appendix B (listing countries that have constitutionally entrenched environmental policies as governing principles, some including sustainability).
27 See e.g. V. MacLaren, A. Morris and S. Labatt, 'Engaging Local Communities in Environmental Protection with Competitiveness: Community Advisory Panels in Canada and the United States', in J.J. Kirton and P. Hajnal (eds) *Sustainability, Civil Society and International Governance*, Aldershot: Ashgate Publishing, 2006, pp. 31, 36 (examining examples of Community Advisory Panels in the United States and Canada and how they affect sustainability in the communities).
28 See e.g. I. Biagiotti, 'Emerging Corporate Actors in Environment and Trade Governance: New Vision and Challenge for Norm-setting Processes', in S. Thoyer and B. Martimort-Asso (eds) *Participation for Sustainability in Trade*, Aldershot: Ashgate Publishing, 2007, pp. 121, 122 (describing how global corporations are focusing more on environmental sustainability).
29 J. May, 'Of Development, daVinci and Domestic Legislation: The Prospects for Sustainable Development in Asia and its Untapped Potential in the United States', *Widener Law Symposium Journal* 3, 1998, p. 197.
30 R. Higgins, 'Natural Resources in the Case Law of the International Court', in A. Boyle and D. Freestone, *International Law and Sustainable Development: Past Achievements and Future Challenges*, Oxford: Oxford University Press, 1999, at pp. 87, 111 (using the International Court of Justice to highlight environmental sustainability in international courts and other arenas).
31 R.R. Churchill, 'Environmental Rights in Existing Human Rights Treaties', in A. Boyle and M. Anderson (eds) *Human Rights Approaches to Environmental Protection*, Oxford: Oxford University Press, 1996, p. 89.
32 See generally S. Kravchenko and J. Bonine, *Human Rights and the Environment: Cases, Law and Policy*, North Carolina: Carolina Academic Press, 2008,
33 *Universal Declaration of Human Rights* (1948), GA Res 217A, UN GAOR, 3rd Sess, 1st Plen Mtg, UN Doc A/810.

in international law amount to domestically enforceable environmental human rights.[34] Meanwhile, many countries still lack the laws, agencies, resources or political will to protect environmental rights.[35]

While some people question whether applying existing human rights to environmental challenges is effective,[36] most conclude that the point is academic because international human rights do not encompass environmental rights. To be sure, of the two human rights treaties that equate human and environmental rights, one is not in force and the other 'suffers from weak institutional and compliance mechanisms'.[37] International law generally does not provide for protection of substantive environmental rights.[38] First, there is no international 'environmental rights' treaty. International accords that bespeak environmental rights, such as the 1972 Stockholm Declaration[39] and the Rio Declaration,[40] are not enforceable. Second, international legal customs and norms do not provide an enforceable right. The protection of fundamental human rights is the closest international law comes to protecting fundamental rights to the environment. Indeed, the extent to which human rights embody environmental rights has engendered ample commentary.[41] Some contend that existing international human rights treaties include fundamental environmental rights (FERs).[42] Third, general principles of international environmental law fall short of protecting fundamental environmental rights, including those involving environmental procedural rights[43] and notions of intergenerational equity.[44]

Embedding environmental human rights domestically can be preferable to international, multilateral or bilateral treaties, if for no other reason than that treaties must usually

---

34 See e.g. *Flores v S. Peru Copper Corp*, 343 F.3d 140, 160 (2d Cir. 2003) (finding customary international law does not include a 'right to life' or 'right to health').

35 For a discussion of the variety of ways to reconcile environmental and human rights in concept, see J.G. Merrills, 'Environmental Protection and Human Rights: Conceptual Aspects', in Boyle and Anderson (eds) op. cit., pp. 25–42.

36 D. Shelton, 'Human Rights, Environmental Rights, and the Right to the Environment,' 28 *Stanford Journal of International Law* 28, 1991, 103, pp. 112–13, 116 (noting that 'the scope of protection for the environment based on existing human rights norms remains narrow because environmental degradation is not itself a cause for complaint, but rather must be linked to an existing right').

37 N. Dorsen, S. Baer, A. Sajo and M. Rosenfeld, *Comparative Constitutionalism, Cases and Materials*, St Paul, MN: West, 2003, p. 1319.

38 I. Hodkova, 'Is There a Right to a Healthy Environment in the International Legal Order?', 7 *Connecticut Journal of International Law* 7, 1991, pp. 65, 66; M. Thorme, 'Establishing Environment as a Human Right', *Denver Journal of International Law and Policy* 19, 1991, pp. 301, 317.

39 The Stockholm Declaration provides: 'Both aspects of a man's environment, the natural and the man-made, are essential to his well-being and to the enjoyment of basic human rights and the right to life itself.'

40 The Rio Declaration reads, in the pertinent part: 'States shall enact effective environmental legislation. Environmental standards, management objectives and priorities should reflect the environmental and developmental context to which they apply.'

41 M. Anderson, 'Human Rights Approaches to Environmental Protection: An Overview', in Boyle and Anderson (eds), op. cit., pp. 1–24; A. Boyle, 'The Role of International Human Rights Law in the Protection of the Environment', in ibid., pp. 43–70.

42 For a discussion of such rights, see R. Churchill, 'Environmental Rights in Existing Human Rights Treaties', in Boyle and Anderson (eds), op. cit., pp. 89–108.

43 See e.g. M. Dejeant-Pons, 'Human Rights to Environmental Procedural Rights', in Boyle and Anderson (eds) op. cit., pp. 23–46.

44 For an argument that all nations can accept environmental human rights, at least for intergenerational equity, see R. Hiskes, 'The Right to a Green Future: Human Rights, Environmentalism, and Intergenerational Justice', *Human Rights Quarterly* 27, 2005, pp. 1346–64.

be ratified by the country's legislature, and then must often be implemented by domestic legislation.[45] Courts worldwide are with growing frequency recognizing that human rights and the environment are inextricably intertwined.[46] Some countries have opted to adopt constitutional protections to a quality environment.[47] As Part V describes, constitutional provisions in dozens of countries embed individualized rights to some form of healthy, adequate or quality environment.[48] Domestic courts and international tribunals are enforcing constitutionally enshrined environmental rights with growing frequency,[49] recognizing basic human rights to clean water, air, land and environmental opportunity.[50] These provisions are inherently complex for five reasons, revolving around form, scope, parties, remedies and justiciability.[51]

While many judicial opinions mention constitutionally embedded rights, including procedural rights, surprisingly few have reached the merits and implemented constitutionally enshrined environmental rights provisions.[52] Regardless of the legal apparatus – international, national, or sub-national – environmental rights run into some basic inertial truisms: economic concerns usually trump environmental concerns, and property rights usually prevail over environmental rights.[53]

45 For example, the European Court of Human Rights (ECtHR) has interpreted the European Convention on Human Rights (ECHR) as providing a right to a healthy environment. See B. Pontin, 'Environmental Rights under the UK's "Intermediate Constitution" ', *Natural Resources & Environment* 17, 2002, p. 21 (discussing *Lopez Ostra v Spain*, 20 ECHR 277 (1995), in which the Court held that the ECHR's protection of human rights includes a right to a healthy environment). The UK has incorporated this interpretation to a certain extent through domestic legislation. Ibid., pp. 22–3 (discussing the UK Human Rights Act's incorporation of the ECHR).

46 See generally, S. Turner, *A Substantive Environmental Right: An Examination of the Legal Obligations of Decision-makers Towards the Environment*, The Hague: Kluwer Law International, 2008; C. Bruch, *Constitutional Environmental Law: Giving Force to Fundamental Principles in Africa*, Washington DC: Environmental Law Institute, 2nd edition; T. Hayward, *Constitutional Environmental Rights*, Oxford: Oxford University Press, 2005, pp. 12–13; M. Pallemaerts, 'The Human Right to a Healthy Environment as a Substantive Right', in M. Déjeant-Pons and M. Pallemaerts (eds) *Human Rights and the Environment*, Brussels: Council of Europe Publishing, 2002, pp. 11–21 (discussing the extent to which international law recognizes the existence of a substantive individual right to a healthy environment).

47 See e.g. E. Brandl and H. Bungert, 'Constitutional Entrenchment of Environmental Protection: A Comparative Analysis of Experiences Abroad', *Harvard Environmental Law Review* 16, 1992, p. 1; D. Shelton, 'Human Rights, Environmental Rights, and the Right to Environment', *Stanford Journal of International Law* 28, 1991, p. 103; Symposium, 'Earth Rights and Responsibilities: Human Rights and Environmental Protection', *Yale Journal of International Law* 18, 1993, p. 215; J. Sax, 'The Search for Environmental Rights', *Journal of Land Use and Environmental Law* 6, 1990, p. 93; Compare this to J. Fernandez, 'State Constitutions, Environmental Rights Provisions, and the Doctrine of Self-Execution: A Political Question?', *Harvard Environmental Law Review* 17, 1993, p. 333 (objecting to enforcement of constitutional environmental rights).

48 See, generally J. May, 'Constituting Fundamental Environmental Rights Worldwide', *Pace Environmental Law Review* 23, 2006, p. 113; D. Boyd, *The Environmental Rights Revolution*, Vancouver: UBC Press, 2012, p. 59.

49 See generally, J.R. May and E. Daly, 'Vindicating Constitutionally Entrenched Environmental Rights Worldwide', *Oregon Review of International Law* 11, 2010, p. 365.

50 See, generally, Kravchenko and Bonine, op. cit.

51 For further discussion see Chapter 33 by J.R. May and E. Daly in this volume.

52 May, 'Constituting Fundamental Environmental Rights Worldwide', op. cit., pp. 133–6.

53 For a multi-dimensional discussion about the relationship between property and land use of commons on an international scale, see S. Hanna, C. Folke and K-G. Mäler (eds) *Rights to Nature*, Washington DC, Island Press, 1996.

Conclusion

We are amidst a period of unprecedented species and habitat loss due to accelerated climate change, continued population growth, half-lives of persistent pollution, biodiversity loss, oceanic and atmospheric acidification, habitat destruction, persistent organic pollutants and water, air and soil pollution, to name but a few. Accelerated and decidedly non-Darwinian adaptation, then, is an inevitable condition. Humans must adapt, mitigate or face the inevitable consequences.

International environmental law contributes some of the means to address intractable global challenges. International treaty regimes such as the WTO, the Ozone Layer Treaty Regime and the Climate Change Treaty Regime are essentially specialized legislative bodies created by treaties with the ongoing capacity to react to events and create new norms generally under the principle of consent by member nations. These institutions conduct negotiations that may lead to new treaties or protocols with specific binding norms. In the case of the WTO's dispute settlement system, the Appellate Body, as a judicial-like body that decides specific cases, may create new norms or expand existing understandings through the process of interpretation much like domestic courts do.[54] These structures must be used to create legal norms binding on all.

One of the great challenges of the twenty-first century will be to develop authoritative processes for making new international law and solving common environmental problems, binding on all, that are viewed by nations and their peoples as legitimate. The chapters that follow examine how treaties, CIL, principles and soft law have helped to shape international environmental law for us and future generations.

---

54 J.P. Kelly, 'The Seduction of the Appellate Body: Shrimp/Sea Turtle I and II and the Proper Role of States in WTO Governance', *Cornell International Law Journal* 38, 2005.

2

The origin and development of international environmental law

*Anita M. Halvorssen**

The interdependence of elements of the natural environment is a global phenomenon, yet most of our past actions to protect the environment have focused on 'local' problems. The 1972 Stockholm Conference on the Human Environment gave legitimacy to environmental policy as a universal concern among nations. This chapter will cover the history of international environmental law and how it became a new branch of international law, in an attempt to protect a steadily degraded environment. Essentially, international environmental law is the application of public international law to environmental issues. It is a product of awareness that the environment does not respect political boundaries.

Introduction

The interdependence of the elements of the natural environment is a global phenomenon, yet most of our past actions to protect the environment have focused on 'local' problems.[1] Current environmental problems, such as air pollution, hazardous waste, depletion of the ozone layer and climate change, have global ramifications. For instance, Chinese coal-fired plants are contributing to a large extent to particulate pollution over Los Angeles.[2]

The United Nations (UN) Conference on the Human Environment, held in Stockholm in 1972, gave legitimacy to environmental policy as a universal concern among nations.[3] International efforts before the Stockholm Conference were mostly focused on resource conservation, for strategic and economic reasons. National movements for environmental

* The author wishes to thank her research assistant, Brittany Bilderback, for all her assistance.

1 A.J. Barnes, 'The Growing International Dimension to Environmental Issues', *Columbia Journal of Environmental Law* 13, 1988, p. 389.
2 J. Kahn and J. Yardley, 'As China Roars, Pollution Reaches Deadly Extremes', *New York Times*, 26 August, 2007. Online. Available HTTP: <http://www.nytimes.com/2007/08/26/world/asia/26china.html> (accessed 4 June 2010).
3 L.K. Caldwell, *International Environmental Policy: Emergence and Dimensions*, Durham, NC: Duke University Press, 1984, p. 19. *Stockholm Declaration on the Human Environment* (1972), 11 ILM 1416 ('Stockholm Declaration').

protection and conservation, resulting in national environmental laws in a few states by the end of the 1960s and early 1970s, were followed by regional conservation efforts made by several industrialised nations and ultimately preceded cooperation on a global scale. It became clear that transboundary environmental problems had to be addressed by the world community in order to find effective solutions.[4]

This chapter will cover the history of international environmental law and how it became a new branch of international law, in an attempt to protect a steadily degraded environment. Essentially, international environmental law is the application of public international law to environmental issues.[5] It is a product of awareness that the environment does not respect political boundaries, hence activities which are carried out within nations often cross borders and cause environmental damage in other nations or global commons, thus requiring international regulation. In reflecting on the development of this new field, this chapter will also examine how effective international environmental law has been in protecting the environment.

Pre-Stockholm

Since international environmental law is the application of international law to environmental issues, it is useful to explain how states operating on the international plane base their actions on the concept of sovereignty. Modern international law dates back to the 1648 Treaty of Westphalia, when the principle of state sovereignty was adopted in Europe at the end of the Thirty Years War.[6] The principle centres on the relationship between states. The main consequences of sovereignty and equality of states are:

(1) exclusive jurisdiction of a territory and the population living there;
(2) a duty of non-intervention in other states' area of exclusive jurisdiction; and
(3) the dependence of obligations arising from customary international law and treaties on the consent of the obligor.[7]

This principle was originally referred to as 'absolute sovereignty', meaning states had unrestrained control over their citizens and the use of natural resources on their territory, both of which were considered a domestic concern. Beyond territorial borders, such as in the high seas, natural resources were available to all states on a first-come, first-served basis.[8] This concept of sovereignty is one of the reasons international management of the environment was largely ineffectual before Stockholm.[9]

---

4 V. Nanda, 'Trends in International Environmental Law', *Californian Western International Law Journal*, 1990, p. 187.
5 P. Birnie and A. Boyle, *International Law and the Environment*, Oxford: Oxford University Press, 2002, p. 2.
6 *Treaty of Westphalia*, 24 October 1648. Online. Available HTTP: <http://avalon.law.yale.edu/17th_century/westphal.asp>. See also L. Gross, 'The Peace of Westphalia, 1648–1948', *American Journal of International Law* 42(1), 1948, pp. 20, 26.
7 I. Brownlie, *Principles of Public International Law*, Oxford: Oxford University Press, 2003, p. 287.
8 E.B. Weiss, 'Environmental Equity: The Imperative for the Twenty-First Century', in W. Lang (ed.) *Sustainable Development and International Law*, 1995, p. 17.
9 V. Nanda and G. Ping, *International Environmental Law & Policy for the 21st Century*, Leiden: Brill Academic Publishers, 2003, p. 65.

At the time, it was commonly thought that the oceans contained inexhaustible amounts of natural resources and that the actions or resource exploitations by one state would have no impact on other states' access to those resources. However, technological innovations arising from the Industrial Revolution made clear that actions within one state's borders and on the high seas could have grave economic, social and environmental implications, not only for its neighbours but for the entire global commons.[10] In addition, states eventually realised that the uncontrolled exploitation of wildlife beyond national jurisdiction led to a depletion of these resources, which, without close monitoring and protection, would soon become extinct.[11] For instance, overfishing enabled by huge factory ships has led to the depletion and extinction of many fish species.

Protecting endangered species and other conservation efforts

Early realisation of the destructive effects of human activities on nature came in 1864 when George Perkins Marsh published *Man and Nature*. In this text, he argued that '[t]he action of man upon the organic world tends to subvert the original balance of its species' and '[i]t is evidently a matter of the utmost importance that the public . . . be roused to a sense of the dangers to which the indiscriminate clearing of the woods may expose . . . to future generations'.[12] On a global scale, it was becoming clear that, with the increase of trade, absolute sovereignty would no longer be viable in the international setting. The drive by some states to protect what in effect were finite natural resources resulted in cooperation between countries and the creation of legal instruments to protect and conserve endangered species, which in turn led to the voluntary limitation of the sovereignty of the states involved.

The 1893 *Behring Fur Seal Arbitration* between the United States (US) and Great Britain is an early example of how a natural resource, the fur seal, had been exploited to the point of near extinction, thus forcing a transition from international coexistence to cooperation.[13] After an unsuccessful attempt to agree on international rules to protect the fur seal fisheries, the US seized British Columbian and British fur sealing vessels.[14] The US alleged that Great Britain was over-exploiting fur seals, which were of great value for their pelts, by pelagic sealing in the North Pacific Ocean.[15] The issue was whether the US could legally adopt regulations to protect fur seals in this area, outside its national jurisdiction.[16] The parties to the dispute agreed to establish a tribunal to decide the case.[17] The arbitrators granted an award in favour of Great Britain and then adopted specific regulations to protect fur seals outside of any nation's national jurisdiction, in the global commons.[18] The tribunal essentially upheld

10 Ibid., p. 12
11 P. Sands, *Principles of International Environmental Law I: Frameworks, Standards and Implementation*, Cambridge: Cambridge University Press, 2003, p. 26.
12 G.P. Marsh, *Man and Nature, or, Physical Geography as Modified by Human Action*, New York: Charles Scribner and Co, 1867, pp. iv, 234.
13 Sands, op. cit., p. 881.
14 Ibid., p. 416.
15 New York Times, *Bering Sea Arbitration*, March 2, 1982. Online. Available HTTP: <http://query.nytimes.com/mem/archive-free/pdf?_r=1&res=9500E3D81631E033A25751C0A9659C94639ED7CF> (accessed 10 June 2010). (Pelagic sealing is the killing of seals in the sea where the animals' gender cannot be determined, resulting in the killing of females and their pups.)
16 Sands, op. cit., p. 416.
17 Ibid.
18 Ibid.

Grotius' absolute freedom to exploit natural resources on the high seas, unless states agreed to limitations.[19]

In 1911 the *Convention between the US, Great Britain, Russia and Japan for the Preservation and Protection of Fur Seals* was adopted by these four states to stop the hunting of seals on the high seas because the animals were on the brink of extinction.[20] This treaty included a provision on policing adherence to treaty provisions and represented one of the earliest examples of the voluntary limitation of sovereignty for the protection of a natural resource.[21]

Other efforts at environmental agreements at the international level at the end of the nineteenth century were made when riparian states from the Rhine basin adopted a treaty to protect North Atlantic salmon spawning grounds.[22] France and Britain agreed to a treaty for the protection of oysters by outlawing fishing outside certain dates.[23] At the time, however, conservation still served an economic purpose rather than indicating an awareness of degradation of the environment. Only natural resources used for the pursuit of economic interests were taken into account; protecting biodiversity was not yet an issue.

Conservation of wildlife in a particular region was first addressed in a treaty in 1900, in which European colonies in Africa limited the trade and export of animal skins and furs. This treaty was superseded by a new convention in 1933.[24] The 1933 *Convention on the Preservation of Fauna and Flora in their Natural State* was, in turn, superseded by a new treaty in 1968 entered into by the newly independent African nations.[25] The 1900 and 1933 Conventions did not have any stipulations on monitoring or compliance. The trade restrictions they contained, however, were combined with economic incentives.[26]

The first treaty to address a particular species, the 1902 *Convention to Protect Birds Useful to Agriculture*, was formulated by the International Ornithological Committee, which was established in 1884.[27] This treaty focused on birds of a commercial interest, not birds in general, and was adopted upon the realisation that the birds were being overexploited and populations were rapidly dwindling. The whaling industry's concern for the overexploitation of whales resulted in the first Whaling Convention in 1931.[28] This treaty was superseded by the

19 M. Tolba, *Global Environmental Diplomacy*, Cambridge, MA: MIT Press, 1998, p. 11. (The Dutch jurist Hugo Grotius, in his book *Mare Liberum*, the first major work on international law, wrote that the oceans are beyond the reach of any nation's shore, therefore beyond national jurisdiction, and hence the high seas should be free for all to use.)
20 *Convention between the United States, Great Britain, Russia and Japan for the Preservation and Protection of Fur Seals*, signature 7 July 1911. Online. Available HTTP: <http://docs.lib.noaa.gov/noaa_documents/NOS/ORR/TM_NOS_ORR/TM_NOS-ORR_17/HTML/Pribilof_html/Documents/THE_FUR_SEAL_TREATY_OF_1911.pdf> (accessed 9 May 2012).
21 Ibid.
22 Tolba, op. cit., p. 12.
23 *Convention between France and Great Britain relative to Fisheries*, signature 11 November 1867, XXI *IPE* 1, Art. XI. See also Sands, op. cit., p. 26.
24 Sands, op. cit., p. 27.
25 *African Convention on the Conservation of Nature and Natural Resources*, opened for signature 15 September 1968, CAB/LEG/24. Online. Available HTTP: <http://www.paxafrica.org/documents/resources/african-union-documents/african-convention-on-the-conservation-of-nature-and-natural-resources-algiers-convention–1968/view> (accessed 8 July 2010).
26 Sands, op. cit., p. 28.
27 *Convention to Protect Birds Useful to Agriculture*, signature 19 March 1902. Online. Available HTTP: <http://eelink.net/~asilwildlife/bird_1902.html> (accessed 8 July 2010).
28 *Convention for the Regulation of Whaling*, signature 24 September 1931, 155 LNTS 351. Also see L.L. Leonard, 'Recent Negotiations Toward the International Regulation of Whaling', *American Journal of International Law* 35, 1941, p. 90.

1937 Agreement which, in turn, was replaced by the 1946 *International Convention for the Regulation of Whaling* that established the Whaling Commission.[29] The goal of the convention was to 'provide for the proper conservation of whale stocks and thus make possible the orderly development of the whaling industry'.[30] However, by the early 1980s, the majority of the Convention's membership consisted of anti-whaling nations which, in 1982, used their three-fourths majority to institute a moratorium prohibiting all commercial whaling after the 1986 season.[31]

In the 1960s and 1970s, the environment in general became a hot topic nationally, especially in the US. Rachel Carson's book *Silent Spring*[32] and similar European books promoted the awareness of environmental issues within nations.[33] *Silent Spring* played a decisive role in the development of pesticide legislation in the US.[34] Also, concerned citizen groups, communicating with one another across national borders, pressured their governments for administrative action to protect and restore the quality of the environment.[35] At the same time, enlightened public environmental awareness quickly expanded from local to national and from national to international levels.[36]

Pollution

Pollution was not the focus of treaties at the turn of the twentieth century. Instead, most treaties focused on the conservation of living natural resources and shared waterways. The exception was the 1909 *Water Boundary Treaty* between Canada and the United States, which stipulated that neither country should pollute the water because it was a shared natural resource.[37]

The landmark arbitral award addressing air pollution is the *Trail Smelter* case of 1938, which established clear limitations on state sovereignty with regard to activities with transboundary effects.[38] An arbitral tribunal resolved the dispute between Canada and the United States which arose when sulphur dioxide fumes emitted by a Canadian smelter plant located in Trail, British Columbia, caused damage to farms in the State of Washington.[39] The tribunal concluded that 'no State has a right to use or permit the use of its territory in such a manner as to cause injury by fumes in the territory of another . . . when the case is of serious consequence and the injury is established by clear and convincing evidence',[40] affirming the

---

29 *1 International Convention for the Regulation of Whaling*, opened for signature 2 December 1946, 161 UNTS 77 (entered into force 10 November 1948). Online. Available HTTP: <http://www.iwc office.org/_documents/commission/convention.pdf> (accessed 16 June 2010).

30 Ibid., Preamble.

31 Sands, op. cit., p. 594.

32 R. Carson, *Silent Spring*, Boston: Houghton Mifflin Company, 2002 (concerning new chemical pesticide technology).

33 See E.B. Weiss, 'International Environmental Law: Contemporary Issues and the Emergence of a New World Order', 81 *Georgetown Law Journal*, 1993, p. 677.

34 *Federal Insecticide, Fungicide, and Rodenticide Act*, 1947, 7 USCA §136a-y (revised in 1972).

35 Caldwell, op. cit., p. 29.

36 Ibid.

37 *Treaty between the United States and Great Britain Relating to Boundary Waters, and Questions Arising Between the United States and Canada*, signature 11 January 1909, US-Great Britain, 11 IPE 5704, 36 Stat. 2448. Online. Available HTTP: <http://bwt.ijc.org/index.php?page=Treaty-Text&hl=eng> (accessed 16 June 2010).

38 *Trail Smelter*, 3 UN Reports of International Arbitration Awards, 1905 (1938 and 1941).

39 Ibid.

40 Ibid.; L.F. Damrosch, L. Henkin, H. Smit and S.D. Murphy, *International Law, Cases, and Materials*, St Paul: Thomson/West, 2009, p. 1493.

principle of good neighbourliness.[41] This is one of the guiding principles of international environmental law today and is the origin of norms of state responsibility regarding trans-boundary pollution.[42] Canada was found responsible, and the tribunal directed injunctive relief and payment of an indemnity.[43]

Long-range transboundary pollution was first addressed in a multilateral agreement in the 1970s. First, the framework agreement, the *Convention on Long-Range Transboundary Air Pollution* (LRTAP)[44] was adopted in 1979, under the aegis of the UN Economic Commission for Europe (UNECE).[45] The LRTAP Convention was followed by eight protocols setting specific limits for industrial pollutants, such as sulphur dioxide. Yet this only addressed pollution on both sides of the Atlantic Ocean, broadly speaking, including the European Union (EU), non–EU Western and Eastern Europe, South-East Europe, the Commonwealth of Independent States (CIS), the United States and Canada, amounting to a regional approach. Other air pollution issues, such as substances depleting the stratospheric ozone layer and greenhouse gases causing climate change have been addressed on a global level, as described below.

At the beginning of the twentieth century, the international community became aware of the problems of oil pollution at sea as the transportation of oil moved from ships carrying barrels to bulk, in addition to ships running on diesel.[46] The League of Nations tried unsuc-cessfully through agreements in the 1920s and 1930s to address territorial seas and control marine pollution caused by ships.[47] Further international efforts to address marine oil pollu-tion were made at the 1926 Washington Conference on Oil Pollution of Navigable Waters, which produced a draft text dealing with oil pollution.[48] This draft formed the basis of the 1954 *International Convention for the Prevention of Pollution of the Sea by Oil*, the first treaty tack-ling marine pollution by oil.[49] Provisions to address pollution and conservation of natural resources related to oceans then followed in the 1958 Geneva Conventions on the law of the sea.[50] This treaty, in turn, was superseded by the UN *Convention on the Law of the Sea*.[51]

International efforts to deal with pollution have been largely reactive, often triggered by disasters. On 18 March 1967, a supertanker called the *Torrey Canyon* ran aground off the shore

---

41 Nanda and Ping, op. cit., p. 73 (good neighbourliness refers to a State using its property without injuring that of another, historically referring to harms involving property rights).
42 Ibid.
43 Ibid., p. 42.
44 *Convention on Long-Range Transboundary Air Pollution*, opened for signature 13 November 1979, 18 ILM 1440 (entered into force 16 March 1983).
45 Sands, op. cit., p. 319.
46 L. Juda, *International Law and Ocean Use Management: The Evolution of Ocean Governance*, London: Routledge, 1996, p. 54.
47 Ibid.
48 Sands, op. cit., p. 393.
49 *International Convention for the Prevention of Pollution of the Sea by Oil*, opened for signature 12 May 1954, 327 UNTS 3 (entered into force 2 October 1983). Online. Available HTTP: <http://sedac. ciesin.org/entri/texts/pollution.of.sea.by.oil.1954.html> (accessed 16 July 2010).
50 *Convention on Fishing and Conservation of the Living Resources of the High Seas*, opened for signature 29 April 1958, 559 UNTS 285 (entered into force 20 March 1966); *Convention on the Continental Shelf*, opened for signature 29 April 1958, 499 UNTS 311 (entered into force 10 June 1964); *Convention on the High Seas*, opened for signature 29 April 1958, 450 UNTS 82 (entered into force 30 September 1962); Sands, op. cit., p. 393.
51 *United Nations Convention on the Law of the Sea*, opened for signature 10 December 1982, 1834 UNTS 397 (entered into force 16 November 1994) ('UNCLOS'). Online. Available HTTP: <http://www. un.org/depts/los/convention_agreements/texts/unclos/unclos_e.pdf> (accessed 9 May 2012).

of England and spilled its entire cargo of 118,000 tons of crude oil.[52] This spill killed an estimated 25,000 birds.[53] This accident drew universal attention to the potential that human activities have to cause large-scale, irreversible destruction to ecosystems.[54] In response, maritime states adopted the *International Convention Relating to Intervention on the High Seas in Cases of Oil Pollution Casualties*, focusing on the right of coastal states to intervene,[55] and the *International Convention on Civil Liability for Oil Pollution Damage*, establishing a liability regime.[56] Two years later, in January 1969, there was another massive spill off the coast of Santa Barbara, California.[57] A drilling platform erupted while parts were being changed, and although the well was capped, nearby faults continued to leak oil until December of that year.[58] The total amount of leaked oil reached 100,000 barrels.[59] This spill brought to the fore the fact that even those spills not causing massive environmental damage may still have serious economic implications, especially in those regions that rely heavily on tourist revenue.[60]

Moving from the protection of local wildlife used for economic development to addressing pollution problems on a regional level, the need for a global perspective on environmental protection was the focus when the international community met in Stockholm in 1972.

From Stockholm to Johannesburg

Stockholm Conference

Initiated by the Nordic countries suffering from acid rain resulting from industrial activities in Germany and Great Britain, the Stockholm Conference on the Human Environment was convened in 1972.[61] Bringing together 6,000 people from 114 countries, it was the largest gathering of its kind and spurred the interest of politicians in developed and developing countries alike.[62] It was the first international meeting to address development and environment as interrelated issues in industrialised and developing countries.

Stockholm represents a turning point in the context of international environmental law because, unlike earlier efforts that focused on the environmental problems of the

---

52 NOAA/Hazardous Materials Response and Assessment Division, *Oil Spill Case Histories*, Seattle, 1992. Online. Available HTTP: <http://response.restoration.noaa.gov/sites/default/files/Oil_Spill_Case_Histories.pdf> (accessed 9 May 2012).

53 Ibid.

54 Ibid.

55 *International Convention Relating to Intervention on the High Seas in Cases of Oil Pollution Casualties*, opened for signature 29 November 1969, ILM 25–44 (entered into force 6 May 1975). Online. Available HTTP: <http://sedac.ciesin.org/entri/texts/intervention.high.seas.casualties.1969. html> (accessed 18 July 2010).

56 *International Convention on Civil Liability for Oil Pollution Damage*, opened for signature 29 November 1969, 973 UNTS 3 (entered into force 19 June 1975). Online. Available HTTP: <http://www.imo. org/About/Conventions/ListOfConventions/Pages/International-Convention-on-Civil-Liability-for-Oil-Pollution-Damage-(CLC).aspx> (accessed 9 May 2012).

57 Ibid., p. 57.

58 Ibid.

59 Ibid.

60 M. Baldwin, 'The Santa Barbara Oil Spill', *University of Colorado Law Review* 42, 1970–1971, p. 38.

61 Stockholm Declaration, op. cit., 4. D. Bodansky, *The Art and Craft of International Environmental Law*, Cambridge, MA: Harvard University Press, 2009, p. 28.

62 Ibid., pp. 28–9.

industrialised countries, developing countries actively participated at Stockholm, insisting that the environment had to be examined in the context of development issues.[63] The following remark by the Sri Lankan ambassador to the UN in 1970 illustrates the outlook of most developing countries at the time:

> Developing countries have of late been warned of the price that has to be paid in the form of environmental pollution for industrial development. All developing countries are aware of the risks, but they would be quite prepared to accept from the developed countries even 100 percent of their gross national pollution if thereby they could diversify their economies through industrialization.[64]

However, the attitude among developing countries began to change as the international community realised it faced a common threat: the degradation of the global environment. On the international plane, '[n]ations cooperate when convinced that their interests will be served by cooperation.'[65] This cooperation is evidenced by the hundreds of environmental treaties that have been adopted since Stockholm. Most countries eventually established environmental ministries and adopted environmental regulations, yet the bigger issue now is whether these laws are actually being enforced.

At the Stockholm Conference, the states did not adopt any treaties, yet they did agree on two important documents: the *Declaration of Principles for the Preservation and Enhancement of the Human Environment* (Stockholm Declaration) and an Action Plan making suggestions for environmental management.[66] Furthermore, states agreed to one of the most important outcomes of the Stockholm Conference: the establishment of the United Nations Environment Programme (UNEP), the first UN body to focus specifically on environmental issues.[67] It was also the first UN body to be located in a developing country, specifically Kenya.

The Stockholm Declaration, unlike a convention, is a non-binding 'soft law' document consisting of 26 principles, which form the precursor to the Rio Declaration of 1992.[68] While the Stockholm Declaration was the first of its kind and, for the most part, was merely reiterated in the Rio Declaration, it is the latter document that is most often referred to. However, the Stockholm Declaration is credited as introducing the most ambitious and forward-looking set of environmental principles by the international community at the time.[69]

The rights included in Principle 1 are 'freedom, equality and adequate conditions of life, in an environment of a quality that permits a life of dignity and well-being'.[70] Linked to the rights is the responsibility for the 'protect[ion] and improve[ment] of the environment

---

63 Bodansky, op. cit., p. 30.
64 H.J. Leonard and D. Morrell, 'Emergence of Environmental Concern in Developing Countries: A Political Perspective', *Stanford Journal of International Law* 17, 1981, p. 281.
65 Caldwell, op. cit., p. 3.
66 Stockholm Declaration, op. cit.
67 UNEP was established through the General Assembly Resolution 2997 (XXVII) *Institutional and Financial Arrangements for International Cooperation* (1972), GA Res 2997, 27 UN GAOR Supp. No 30, UN Doc A/8730.
68 *Rio Declaration on Environment and Development* (1992), 31 ILM 874 ('Rio Declaration'). Online. Available HTTP: <http://www.unep.org/Documents.Multilingual/Default.asp?documentid=78 &articleid=1163> (accessed 18 July 2010).
69 Nanda and Ping, op. cit., p. 83.
70 Ibid.

for present and future generations'.[71] This principle connects environmental protections to individual rights or human rights norms.[72] The rights of human beings in the Rio Declaration focus more narrowly on environmental issues, stipulating the right to a 'healthy and productive life in harmony with nature'.[73] It is important to remember, however, that these principles are not legally binding, just aspirational. However, several states have since incorporated such rights into their domestic legislation and some also into their constitutions, operationalising the principle as, for instance, the Philippines did in 1987 and Norway in 1992.[74]

Addressing natural resources, Principles 2 through 7 focus on rational planning, management and pollution control in order to safeguard natural resources for the benefit of future generations.[75] Before the term 'sustainable development' was invented, the relationship between environment and development was already being addressed.

Six of the principles included in the Stockholm Declaration specifically addressed the special circumstances of developing countries. Principle 9 emphasised how the transfer of technical and financial assistance to developing countries is necessary to solve the environmental problems caused by underdevelopment.[76] Principle 10 focused on the importance of the stability of prices and adequate earnings for primary commodities and raw material for environmental management.[77]

Principles 11, 12 and 23 addressed the importance of implementing environmental policies in all states and the impact that such implementation will have on development in developing countries.[78] These standards sought to avoid any adverse impact on the development potential of developing countries and were to take into consideration the unique systems and values of each country.[79] In addition, technical and financial assistance was to be made available to developing countries for incorporating such measures into their own development planning.[80]

---

71 Ibid.
72 Sands, op. cit., pp. 38–9.
73 Rio Declaration, Principle 1.
74 *Constitution of the Republic of the Philippines* (1987), Art. 2 on Declaration of Principles and State Policies, Section 16: 'the State shall protect and advance the right of the people to a balanced and healthful ecology in accord with the rhythm and harmony of nature.' Online. Available HTTP: <http://www.unescap.org/DRPAD/VC/orientation/legal/constit_phl.htm> (accessed 20 July 2010). For a further consideration of constitutional environmental rights see Chapter 33 by May and Daly in this volume. *Kongeriket Norges Grunnlov* 1814 (The Constitution of the Kingdom of Norway), Article 110b:

> Every person has a right to an environment that is conducive to health and to a natural environment whose productivity and diversity are maintained. Natural resources should be managed on the basis of comprehensive long-term considerations whereby this right will be safeguarded for future generations as well.
>
> In order to safeguard their right in accordance with the foregoing paragraph, citizens are entitled to information on the state of the natural environment and on the effects of any encroachment on nature that is planned or carried out.

Online. Available HTTP: <http://www.stortinget.no/In-English/About-the-Storting/The-Constitution/The-Constitution> (accessed 20 July 2010).

75 Stockholm Declaration, Principle 2.
76 Ibid., Principle 9.
77 Ibid.
78 Ibid., Principles 11, 12, 23.
79 Ibid., Principle 23.
80 Ibid., Principles 12, 20.

Principle 21 of the Stockholm Declaration, practically identical to Principle 2 of the Rio Declaration, reflects customary international law and is, therefore, considered binding international law. This principle reaffirms the award in the Trail Smelter case, recognising both states' sovereignty over their natural resources and the responsibility of all states to ensure that activities within their jurisdiction or control do not harm other states.[81] The recognition of such a duty represents a landmark in international environmental law.

To give effect to Principle 21, governments recognised the need to develop a specific body of international environmental law.[82] Principle 22 states: 'States shall cooperate to develop further the international law regarding liability and compensation for victims of pollution and other environmental damage caused by activities within the jurisdiction or control of such States to areas beyond their jurisdiction.'[83]

On the whole, the Stockholm principles have not significantly improved the state of the environment, and environmental degradation on a global scale is steadily becoming worse.[84] This is, in part, due to a lack of political will and public awareness of the problems, and a lack of funding. However, the Stockholm Conference did emphasise how human actions can irreversibly harm the environment and therefore staked out the course: that the human environment needs to be protected and enhanced through common efforts at the local, national and international levels.[85]

After Stockholm, several treaties were adopted on environmental issues, some under the auspices of UNEP and others under different arms of the UN. The UN *Convention on the Law of the Sea*, a comprehensive treaty addressing the rights of states with regard to the world's oceans, including environmental protection, was adopted in 1982.[86] The *Convention on the International Trade in Endangered Species* (CITES) adopted in 1973 is regarded as one of the most significant treaties addressing living natural resources.[87] Due to economic incentives several animal and plant species were being driven to extinction. The realisation that there was a value in preserving these species for the sake of biodiversity moved states to take action. Under CITES, a system was set up where trade in certain listed species was either prohibited or needed consent from the state of origin, thus reducing and controlling the trade in endangered species.

During the 1980s ozone depletion, nuclear hazards and global warming began to be viewed as truly global problems that required concerted international action.[88] International efforts were considered imperative if the severe consequences of stratospheric ozone depletion and climate change were to be avoided.[89] The global ramifications of human actions were no longer hypothetical, but imminently real. The question was no longer *if* climate change would occur, but *when*, and actors at the international level were instilled with the sense of

---

81 Rio Declaration, Principle 2; Tolba, op. cit., p. 15.
82 O. Schachter, *International Law in Theory and Practice*, Dordrecht: Martinus Nijhoff Publishers, 1991, p. 363.
83 Stockholm Declaration, Principle 22.
84 Millennium Ecosystem Assessment Board (MEAB), *Living Beyond Our Means: Natural Assets and Human Well-Being. Statement from the Board* (MEAB 2005), 5. Online. Available HTTP: <http://pdf.wri.org/ma_board_final_statement.pdf> (accessed 9 May 2012).
85 Caldwell, op. cit., p. 30.
86 UNCLOS, op. cit., p. 56.
87 *Convention on International Trade in Endangered Species of Wild Fauna and Flora*, opened for signature 3 March 1973, 12 ILM 1088 (entered into force 1 July 1975) ('CITES').
88 Bodansky, op. cit., p. 30.
89 Ibid.

urgency needed to provide the impetus for action. Work on the *UN Framework Convention on Climate Change* began in 1988 and it was adopted in 1992 at the Rio Conference, to be addressed below.

Negotiations to address depletion of the stratospheric ozone layer had a successful outcome when the international community agreed to the *Vienna Convention for the Protection of the Ozone Layer* in 1985, which set up the framework, and then the *Montreal Protocol on Substances that Deplete the Ozone Layer* was adopted in 1987, mandating cuts in the production and consumption of ozone-depleting substances such as chlorofluorocarbons (CFCs).[90] The Montreal Protocol applied several of the principles that were later agreed to in the Rio Declaration, among them the principle of common but differentiated responsibilities. Hence, the developing countries were given a ten-year delayed compliance schedule.[91]

The World Commission on Environment and Development (Brundtland Commission)

In 1983 Gro Harlem Brundtland, former prime minister of Norway, was appointed chair of the World Commission on Environment and Development by the UN Secretary General.[92] The Brundtland Commission's mandate was to examine the divergence between continued economic growth and an environment that was steadily deteriorating. Synthesising earlier aims enunciated in instruments such as the *World Charter for Nature*, the Brundtland Commission introduced the concept of sustainable development to the broader international community and defined it as 'development that meets the needs of the present without compromising the needs of future generations'.[93]

The Brundtland Commission intended to demonstrate how human survival might depend on the international community's ability to elevate sustainable development to a global ethic.[94] In its report, *Our Common Future*, it set forth the main challenges to the world community: achieving sustainable development by the year 2000 and beyond by agreeing on multilateral solutions and a restructured economic system.[95] The Commission called for greater cooperation to eradicate international poverty, manage the global commons and to maintain peace and security worldwide.[96] In order to broaden the spectrum of issues addressed, it defined the 'environment' as 'where we all live', not a sphere separate from human actions and needs, and it defined 'development' as 'what we do in attempting to improve our lot within that abode', not the limited focus of development assistance for poor nations.[97] Hence, the Commission stated that the environment and development are inseparable, recognising the

---

90 *Montreal Protocol on Substances that Deplete the Ozone Layer*, opened for signature 16 September 1987, 1522 UNTS 3 (entered into force 1 January 1989) ('Montreal Protocol').

91 Ibid., Article 5.

92 *World Commission on Environment and Development* (WCED), 11 Dec. 111987, A/RES/42/187.

93 World Commission on Environment and Development (WCED), *Our Common Future*, New York: Oxford University Press, 1987, pg. 8 and chapter 8. Online. Available HTTP: <http://www.un-documents.net/wced-ocf.htm>. See Birnie and Boyle, op. cit., p. 4. *World Charter for Nature*, 28 Oct. 1982, A/RES/37/7. Online. Available HTTP: <http://www.un.org/documents/ga/res/37/a37r007.htm> (accessed 23 July 2010) (a set of ecological principles adopted by the UN General Assembly in 1982).

94 Ibid., WCED, *Our Common Future*, p. 308.

95 Ibid., p. ix.

96 Ibid.

97 Ibid., p. xi.

growing interdependence among nations in dealing with economic and environmental problems.[98]

Rio Conference

In 1992, on the twentieth anniversary of the Stockholm Conference, the international community gathered for the UN Conference on Environment and Development (UNCED or Earth Summit) in Rio de Janeiro, Brazil. No fewer than 176 states sent representatives to the conference, in addition to over 50 intergovernmental organisations and thousands of non-governmental organisations.[99] Essentially, the findings of the Brundtland Commission were confirmed when the nations gathered at Rio formally adopted the concept of 'sustainable development' as the new paradigm for international environmental law: to achieve progress or economic development while simultaneously protecting the environment.

Five legal instruments were adopted at Rio: the *UN Framework Convention on Climate Change* (UNFCCC),[100] the *Convention on Biodiversity* (CBD),[101] the Rio Declaration on Environment and Development, Agenda 21,[102] and the Non-Legally Binding Principles on Forests.[103] The first two documents are binding; the last three are considered soft law. Furthermore, as a means of ensuring the effective follow-up to the conference and to monitor the implementation of these agreements, the UN Commission on Sustainable Development (UNCSD) was established in December 1992.[104]

The adoption of the UNFCCC in 1992 was the beginning of a long and ongoing process dealing with climate change issues. The UNFCCC entered into force in 1994 and the *Kyoto Protocol* to the UNFCCC was adopted in 1997 and entered into force in 2005.[105] The latest development on this front occurred on 10 December 2010 when the 16th UN Conference of the Parties to the UNFCCC (COP–16) adopted the Cancun Agreements,[106] a non-legally binding, political agreement.[107] This decision by COP–16 incorporated the Copenhagen

---

98 Ibid.
99 Sands, op. cit., p. 52.
100 *United Nations Framework Convention on Climate Change*, opened for signature 4 June 1992, 1771 UNTS 107 (entered into force 21 March 1994) ('UNFCCC').
101 *Convention on Biological Diversity*, opened for signature 5 June 1992, 31 ILM 818 (entered into force 29 December 1993) ('CBD').
102 *Agenda 21: A Programme for Action for Sustainable Development*, Report of the UN Conference on Environment and Development, Annex II, 12 August 1992, UN Doc A./Conf. 151/26 (Vol. 2) ('Agenda 21'). Online. Available HTTP: <http://www.un.org/esa/dsd/agenda21/res_agenda21_00.shtml> (accessed 24 July 2010).
103 *Non-Legally Binding Authoritative Statement of Principles for a Global Consensus on the Management, Conservation, and Sustainable Development of All Types of Forests*, opened for signature 13 June 1992, 31 ILM 881 ('Forest Principles').
104 *Institutional arrangements to follow up the United Nations Conference on Environment and Development*, A/RES/47/191. Online. Available HTTP: <http://www.un.org/documents/ga/res/47/ares47–191.htm> (accessed 11 May 2012); Agenda 21, para. 38.11.
105 *Kyoto Protocol to the United Nations Framework Convention on Climate Change*, opened for signature 11 December 1997, 2303 UNTS 148 (entered into force 16 February 2005) ('Kyoto Protocol').
106 *UNFCCC Conference of the Parties Fifteenth session* (2009), Copenhagen, 7–18 December 2009, FCCC/CP/2009/L.7, ('Copenhagen Accord').
107 D. Bodansky, 'The Copenhagen Climate Change Conference: A Post-Mortem', *American Journal of International Law* 104, 2010. 231. Online. Available HTTP: <http://papers.ssrn.com/sol3/papers.cfm?abstract_id=1553167> (accessed 26 July 2010).

Accord which was the first time all states agreed to emission reduction cuts or mitigation action.[108] However, the whole climate change process can now be considered stalled, due mainly to disagreements on burden-sharing as described below.

The *Convention on Biodiversity* also entered into force in 1994. It is the first global treaty dealing with the comprehensive protection of biological diversity.[109] Its Protocol, the *Cartagena Protocol on Biosafety* dealing with genetically modified organisms, was adopted in 2000 and entered into force in 2003.[110] The Cartagena Protocol addresses the movements of living modified organisms (LMOs) resulting from modern biotechnology from one country to another. States are to be provided with the information necessary to make informed decisions before agreeing to the import of such organisms into their territory.[111] A second Protocol was adopted in 2010 – the *Nagoya Protocol on Access to Genetic Resources and the Fair and Equitable Sharing of Benefits Arising from their Utilization*. This instrument provides a legal framework for access to and sharing of the benefits of genetic resources covered by the CBD.

The Rio Declaration is, in part, a renewed version of most of the Stockholm Principles. Principle 2 is the mirror image of Stockholm Principle 21, except Principle 2 has the added words 'and development'. It also includes new principles, such as the right to development.[112] The Rio Declaration represents a careful balance of the principles prioritised by both developed and developing countries.[113] An important principle that has been operationalised in later agreements is the common but differential treatment for developing countries, stipulated in Principle 7 of the Rio Declaration. Focusing on a cooperative approach, it stipulates how the developed countries recognise their responsibility for historic environmental degradation, hence leading to common, but differentiated, responsibilities.[114] It appears in the UNFCCC both in the preamble and under Principle 3, and in general, in the notion that the industrialised countries should take the lead in reducing their greenhouse gas (GHG) emissions.[115]

Agenda 21 is a comprehensive but non-binding action program for governments, development agencies, UN organisations and independent sectors in all major areas affecting the relationship between the environment and the economy. It is designed to merge the goals of continued economic development and environmental protection. Agenda 21 represents a plan of action which needs to be implemented in order for states to achieve sustainable development. Consisting of nearly 500 pages, it is divided into four parts: (I) social and economic dimensions; (II) conservation and management of resources for development; (III) strengthening of major groups; and IV) means of implementation.[116]

After the Rio Conference, conferences have been held on many different issues relating to international environmental law, including high-seas fisheries, sustainable development of small island states, population and development, women and social issues. In addition, the *UN*

---

108 Copenhagen Accord, op. cit., paras 4, 5.
109 Sands, op. cit., p. 516.
110 *Cartagena Protocol on Biosafety*, opened for signature 29 January 2000, 39 ILM 1027 (entered into force 11 September 2003).
111 Convention on Biodiversity, Cartagena Protocol, *About the Protocol*, 1760 UNTS 79, 143; 31 ILM 818 (1992). Online. Available HTTP: <http://bch.cbd.int/protocol/background/> (accessed 28 July 2010).
112 Rio Declaration, Principle 3.
113 S. Johnson, *The Earth Summit: The United Nations Conference on Environment and Development (UNCED)*, London: Kluwer Law International, 1993, p. 117.
114 Rio Declaration, Principle 7.
115 UNFCCC, Art. 3.
116 Agenda 21, p. 115.

Convention to Combat Desertification, called for at the Rio Conference, was adopted in 1994 and entered into force in 1996.[117] In 1997, a Special Session of the UN General Assembly (UNGASS) was held to review progress made since the Rio Conference, as called for in Agenda 21.[118] In its report, *Programme for Further Implementation of Agenda 21*, UNGASS acknowledged that some positive results had been achieved, including the adoption of new treaties, but stated that 'the overall trends for sustainable development are worse today than they were in 1992'.[119]

In 2000, at the end of Millennium Summit in New York, 192 world leaders unanimously adopted the *UN Millennium Declaration*, which is a statement of values, principles and common objectives in areas such as peace and security, poverty eradication, environmental protection and good governance for the international community for the twenty-first century.[120] The Millennium Development Goals (MDGs) emerged from this Declaration, focusing on poverty eradication, disease control, a global partnership for development and environmental sustainability.[121]

Johannesburg Summit

The international community gathered again in 2002 on the tenth anniversary of the Rio Conference, this time in Johannesburg, South Africa, for the World Summit on Sustainable Development (WSSD). Since Rio, poverty had been deepening, environmental degradation worsening and unsustainable patterns of development continued. The goal of Johannesburg was for the world leaders to 'adopt concrete steps and identify quantifiable targets for better implementing Agenda 21'.[122] Kofi Annan, the UN Secretary General, stated that it was an 'opportunity to rejuvenate the quest to build a more sustainable future'.[123]

Johannesburg was to go beyond debate and move to action and results, unlike Agenda 21, by instituting targets and timetables. The Summit reaffirmed the Rio Declaration and Agenda 21 and produced two new documents: the *Johannesburg Declaration on Sustainable Development* and the *Johannesburg Plan of Implementation*, but these are both non-legally-binding soft-law instruments.[124] Many of the goals reiterated the MDGs from 2000, but governments also

---

117 *United Nations Convention to Combat Desertification in Those Countries Experiencing Serious Drought and/or Desertification, Particularly in Africa*, opened for signature 17 June 1994, 33 ILM 1016 (entered into force 26 December 1996). Online. Available HTTP: <http://www.unccd.int>.

118 *Special Session of the UN General Assembly to Review and Appraise the Implementation of Agenda 21*, 23–27 June 1997 (UNGASS). Online. Available HTTP: <http://www.un.org/esa/earthsummit> (accessed 28 July 2010).

119 Ibid.

120 *United Nations Millennium Declaration*, Millennium Summit of the United Nations, 6–8 September 2000. Online. Available HTTP: <http://www.un.org/millennium/declaration/ares552e.htm> (accessed 9 May 2012).

121 United Nations, *Millennium Development Goals*. Online. Available HTTP: <http://www.un.org/millenniumgoals/poverty.shtml> (accessed 23 July 2010).

122 *World Summit on Sustainable Development*, 10 December 2002, A/C.2/57/L.83. Online. Available HTTP: <http://www.johannesburgsummit.org/html/documents/documents.html> (accessed 9 May 2012). See also United Nations, *Johannesburg Summit 2002, Basic Information*. Online. Available HTTP: <http://un.org/jsummit/html/basic_info/basicinfo.html> (accessed 26 July 2010).

123 *Johannesburg Summit 2002: World Summit on Sustainable Development*. Online. Available HTTP: <http://un.org/jsummit/html/brochure/brochure12.pdf> (accessed 26 July 2010).

124 *Report of the World Summit on Sustainable Development*, 26 August–4 September 2002, A/CONF.199/20. Online. Available HTTP: <http://daccess-dds-ny.un.org/doc/UNDOC/GEN/N02/636/93/PDF/N0263693.pdf?OpenElement> (accessed 26 July 2010).

committed to expand access to safe water and proper sanitation (by 2015) and modern, clean energy services, as well as to reverse the decline of ecosystems by restoring fisheries (by 2015), curtailing illegal logging and limiting the harm caused by toxic chemicals.[125] Furthermore, over 200 voluntary partnerships were agreed upon in Johannesburg by governments, NGOs and businesses to contribute to the implementation of Agenda 21 and the Johannesburg Plan of Implementation through specific projects.[126]

There is an upside and a downside of agreeing to targets and timetables. The upside is that they are easily measureable. The downside is that when such targets have not been met or when progress towards them is not moving as quickly as anticipated you lose momentum and the will to make progress. With less than five years remaining until most of the deadlines of the MDGs and the Johannesburg Plan of Implementation expire, progress toward achieving the targets has not occurred at the rate expected or hoped for. It is true that poverty has been reduced tremendously in China,[127] for instance, but unfortunately economic development has come at the cost of a degraded environment. After surpassing the US, China has now become the largest emitter of GHGs.[128]

As a whole, the WSSD created a new emphasis on sustainable development consisting of three elements: economic development, social development and environmental protection. Many environmentalists were disappointed that new and stronger commitments were not agreed upon in the environmental field. The focus was more on the issues central to developing countries, such as poverty eradication and clean drinking water. This seems only natural, since developing countries are reaching the stage of development where these matters are important, but it was the first time that safe drinking water and sanitation were dealt with on the international level.

Looking to the future – a maturing international environmental law

The vision of shared prosperity within the carrying capacity of the Earth's ecosystems is the ultimate goal of sustainable development.[129] Having discerned this in Stockholm and then confirmed and reconfirmed it at Rio and Johannesburg, respectively, the international community is now mobilising to celebrate the twentieth anniversary of the Rio Conference, returning to Rio in 2012.[130] Progress with regard to the environmental pillar has been the slowest, compared to the economic and social pillars.[131] International environmental law has

---

125 Ibid.
126 UN Division for Sustainable Development, *Partnerships for Sustainable Development.* Online. Available HTTP: <http://www.un.org/esa/dsd/dsd_aofw_par/par_index.shtml> (accessed 28 July 2010).
127 United Nations Development Programme: China, *Poverty Reduction.* Online. Available HTTP: <http://www.undp.org.cn/modules.php?op=modload&name=News&file=article&catid=10&sid=10> (accessed 28 July 2010).
128 J. Vidal and D. Adam, 'China overtakes US as world's biggest CO2 emitter', *The Guardian,* 19 June 2007. Online. Available HTTP: <http://www.guardian.co.uk/environment/2007/jun/19/china.usnews> (accessed 28 July 2010).
129 Preparatory Committee for the United Nations Conference on Sustainable Development, First session, 17–19 May 2010, A/CONF.216/PC/2. Online. Available HTTP: <http://daccess-dds-ny.un.org/doc/UNDOC/GEN/N10/302/56/PDF/N1030256.pdf?OpenElement> (accessed 30 July 2010).
130 Ibid., p. 13.
131 Ibid., p. 8.

led to a lot of improvements, yet the challenges are ever-growing, with climate change being the most high-stakes issue to date. International cooperation, as the Brundtland Commission called for, is needed more than ever.

The necessity to coordinate long-term international interests versus states' national interests is paramount in the international environmental law field, since there is no escaping the fact that we all share the same planet.[132] Nations recognise that no state can guarantee the welfare of its own people in the future simply by focusing on its own interests. However, there are deep differences among states, especially between the developing and industrialised states, regarding the equitable allocation of burdens and benefits in coordinating their interests.[133] This is the most important issue with which international environmental law scholars must currently contend, especially in the context of climate change.[134] Common but differential responsibility is the guiding principle to deal with this problem, meaning that there should be less stringent commitments and more financial transfers to developing countries based on which states historically caused the problem and their capacity to deal with it.[135]

With regard to international environmental negotiations, the dynamics have changed. Industrialised countries realise that they cannot solve the climate change problem without the cooperation of developing countries; hence, developing countries are having a much greater influence on the talks than previously. A negotiating system that uses consensus, as the UN climate change negotiations do, also affects the dynamics, as do the sheer numbers – there are four times as many developing countries as industrialised countries in the world. The new dynamics are also due to economic globalisation, which has created a group of fast-growing developing countries, such as India and China, and global environmental challenges, such as climate change. All nations need to be in agreement to reach a consensus, or at least not object, and that is not possible if they feel their interests are not being served.

At the climate discussions in Copenhagen in December 2009,[136] China vetoed any talk of pledging emission reduction commitments for 2050 even by industrialised countries unilaterally, because of the effect it would have on how much China could emit in 2050.[137] Until recently, smaller states did not dare speak against the powerful nations, and certainly not outside of their 'block' of nations (such as G–77). Now, however, smaller states are finding their voices and stalling negotiations, as in the case of Sudan, Venezuela and Bolivia in Copenhagen.[138] Because these three countries objected to the Copenhagen Accord, preventing COP–15 from reaching a consensus, instead of adopting it, COP–15 just took 'note of' the Copenhagen Accord, thus making its status uncertain until the Cancun Agreements, elaborating on the Copenhagen Accord, were adopted a year later.[139] Major compromises will have to be reached to solve these problems, yet they cannot come at the cost of our ecosystems

132 Weiss, op. cit., p. 701.
133 Ibid.
134 See e.g. A. Halvorssen, *Equality Among Unequals in International Environmental Law – Differential Treatment for Developing Countries*, Boulder: Westview Press, 1999. See also L. Rajamani, *Differential Treatment in International Environmental Law*, Oxford: Oxford University Press, 2006.
135 Rio Declaration, Principle 7.
136 UNFCCC, op. cit.
137 Z. Zhang, 'Copenhagen and Beyond: Reflections on China's Stances and Responses', *East-West Center Working Papers, Economic Series* 111, June 2010. Online. Available HTTP: <http://papers.ssrn.com/sol3/papers.cfm?abstract_id=1586058> (accessed 30 July 2010).
138 Bodansky, op. cit., p. 118.
139 Ibid.; COP–15 Report, op. cit., p. 117.

(including the atmosphere) and the services they provide, which we all depend on for economic development.

International environmental law has evolved through several phases: first, a recognition of the different environmental problems, followed by efforts to tackle them through various types of agreements. Now that most areas of the environment have been addressed with international regulations, the next step is to focus on compliance with the treaties. There has been greater attention given to this, starting in the 1990s. The effectiveness of these treaties is being questioned because the environment is still being degraded. Some good news is surfacing, however. The stratospheric ozone layer is on the mend, due to the efforts made through the Montreal Protocol.[140] In addition, in Brazil, 'large-scale deforestation fell dramatically last year [2009]', meaning that the rainforest is no longer being diminished at the normal rate of an area the size of Belgium per year.[141] Brazil has put greater effort into enforcing its environmental laws, thus complying with its international commitments, and this is having a positive effect on the rainforests which will, in turn, have a positive effect on biodiversity and the climate change issue, since rainforests, are one of the most biologically diverse ecosystems and are a sink for carbon dioxide.

Conclusion

International environmental law has evolved from the protection of individual species for economic reasons to whole ecosystem protection, such as the CBD. Rather than being swallowed up by the new field, the law of sustainable development, international environmental law has come into its own as a vibrant branch of international law. Environmental degradation, sadly, continues to be a problem. Human activity will inevitably interfere with ecosystems, to a greater or smaller extent. The goal is to focus on sustainable development, where the environment must be taken into account in the process of economic development. This is often referred to as internalising the externalities; if the costs of development include the impact it has on the environment, then better ways will be sought to develop, using energy efficiency and renewable energy. Industrialised countries have made progress in this area, with their environmental policies and laws, though developing countries often struggle with the implementation of their environmental laws. However, as the recent spill in the Gulf of Mexico proves, reactive rather than preventative law-making is still the norm and this newest disaster will likely prompt new international regulation to address offshore drilling.[142]

Economic development without consideration of the environment or social issues is coming more and more into focus regarding the challenge of climate change, due to the effect that GHGs have on the planet as a whole. How effective the international community is in solving this problem will determine the fate of future generations, yet the pace of the climate negotiations needs to reach a whole new level of cooperation and progress for there to be much hope.

140 United Nations Development Programme, *Protecting the Ozone Layer and Safeguarding the Global Climate*. Online. Available HTTP: <http://web.undp.org/ozone/> (accessed 9 May 2012). See also Montreal Protocol, op. cit., p. 95.

141 PRI's The World, *Cautious Optimism in the Amazon*, 28 July 2010. Online. Available HTTP: <http://www.theworld.org/2010/07/28/cautious-optimism-in-the-amazon/> (accessed 30 July 2010).

142 T. Johnson, 'Law of Sea Implications for Gulf Spill', interview with Caitlyn Antrim, Executive Director, Rule of Law Committee for the Oceans, Council on Foreign Relations, 2 July 2010. Online. Available HTTP: <http://www.cfr.org/publication/22585/law_of_sea_implications_for_gulf_spill.html> (accessed 30 July 2010).

3

Principles of international environmental law

*Svitlana Kravchenko, Tareq M.R. Chowdhury
and Md Jahid Hossain Bhuiyan*

This chapter will explore and evaluate the general principles and sources of international environmental law and discuss their status and role in the global context. International environmental law is a highly fragmented area and determining the meaning and status of general principles is thus a complex task. Many revolve around the core issue of sustainable development, which is a difficult and contested concept itself. Principles that will be discussed include the notion of sustainable development, the precautionary principle, common but differentiated responsibility, inter- and intra-generational equity and the polluter pays principle.

Introduction

Principles of international environmental law are 'reflected in treaties, binding acts of international organizations, state practice, and soft law commitments . . . they are potentially applicable to all members of the international community'.[1] Some of them are universally accepted and frequently endorsed in state practice.

Article 38 of the Statute of International Court of Justice recognises 'general principles of law recognized by civilized nations' as a source of law. General principles fill the gaps in international law which have not already been covered by treaty or custom. Therefore, courts rely on general principles in the absence of treaty or customary law.

After World War II, the geographical, industrial and scientific scenario of the world dramatically changed. The emergence of modern industrial society and consequent urbanisation has had a tremendously negative effect on the global environment.[2] The international community became concerned and to contain the damage, and also improve the environment, it recognised certain legal principles: for example, sustainable development, intergenerational equity, intra-generational equity, prevention of harm, common but differentiated responsibility, precaution, polluter pays, the right to a healthy environment and access to

---

1 P. Sands, *Principles of International Environmental Law*, 2nd edition, Cambridge: Cambridge University Press, 2003, p. 231.
2 A.S. Rao, 'Enforcement of Environmental Laws', *AIR Journal* 88, 2001, 222–4, p. 222.

information and public participation in environmental decision-making (good governance). These principles, though recognised by the international community, and in the absence of judicial decisions, opened a floodgate of conflicting interpretations making it difficult to determine their actual legal status. Each of these principles has to be interpreted in turn and their legal status should be considered taking into account the textual content, the transparency of the language and the circumstances of their creation. In the overall context of environmental governance many of these general principles are of less importance, but some play a significant role in protecting the environment and many states have already declared their allegiance to them.[3]

The aim of this chapter is to examine some of these principles in detail, including sustainable development, the precautionary principle, the polluter pays principle, the common but differentiated responsibility principle and relatively new and evolving principles such as access to information and public participation in environmental decision-making.

Sustainable development

In the Brundtland Report, prepared by the World Commission on Environment and Development, the expression 'sustainable development' was formally introduced.[4] It was defined as 'development that meets the needs of the present without compromising the ability of future generations to meet their own needs'. It essentially drew attention to two things: (1) the basic needs of the world's poor, and (2) the technological and social limitations on the ability of the environment to meet present and future needs. 'Needs' were given overriding priority.[5]

The International Union for the Conservation of Nature (IUCN) maintains that by ensuring ecological sustainability, economic viability and social desirability, quality of life or standards of living can be maintained for many generations. According to the IUCN this is the main meaning of sustainable development.[6] According to Jena, the conservation of nature and maintenance of ecological order, which preserves biodiversity and thereby makes life on Earth possible now and in the future, is the real meaning of sustainable development.[7]

Subsequently, 'sustainable development' was included in the 1992 Rio Declaration which recognised the entitlement of human beings to a healthy and productive life in harmony with

3 P. Sands, *Principles of International Environmental Law I: Frameworks, Standards and Implementation*, Manchester: Manchester University Press, 1995, p. 183.
4 However, according to many, the concept of sustainability was reflected in state practice much earlier. Philippe Sands, for example, mentions that in 1983 the United States asserted the right to ensure legitimate and proper use of seals to protect them for the benefit of mankind and save them from wanton destruction. Subsequently, many treaties and other Acts have supported, directly or indirectly, the sustainable use of natural resources and advanced the idea that states have a legal obligation and responsibility to conserve natural resources and support the concept of sustainable development. Ibid., p. 199.
5 World Commission on Environment and Development, *Our Common Future*, Oxford: Oxford University Press, 1987, p. 43.
6 IUCN – World Conservation Union, *Guide to Preparing and Implementing National Sustainable Development Strategies and Other Multi-sectoral Environmental and Development Strategies*, prepared by the IUCN's Commission on Environment Strategies Working Group on Strategies for Sustainability, the IUCN Secretariat and the Environment Planning Group of the IIED, pre-publication review Draft 1993, p. 6.
7 K.C. Jena, 'Ecology and Environmental Protection Movements: A Brief Conspectus', *AIR Journal* 92, 2005, 288–94, p. 289.

nature, and thus put humankind at the centre of concerns for sustainable development.[8] It also recognised the fact that in order to achieve sustainable development environmental protection should constitute an integral part of the development process and must not be considered in isolation from it.[9] Furthermore, treaties such as the 1992 UN Framework Convention on Climate Change (UNFCCC) recognise that all countries – especially developing countries – need access to resources required to achieve sustainable, social and economic development and thus acknowledged sustainable development as an instrument of interaction between states.[10]

Sustainable development has not been defined in such a precise way that its legal status can clearly be determined. Its paradigm-changing nature raises many questions and at present the lack of adequate articulation inhibits confident generalisations from being made. Indeed, whether it is a 'principle' or a 'concept' remains an issue. The argument that sustainable development has achieved the status of customary international law or a general principle has some support from the International Court of Justice (ICJ) and particularly the separate opinion of Judge Weeramantry.[11] Judge Weeramantry asserted that sustainable development was 'more than a mere concept' and was a 'principle with normative value'.[12] He went on to state that 'the right to development and the right to environmental protection . . . are important principles of current international law'[13] and 'the principle of sustainable development . . . is an integral part of modern international law'.[14] This was, however, a minority decision.

Birnie and Boyle question the obligations of states with respect to conservation and sustainable development of natural resources and protection of the natural environment and conclude that it is still an open question.[15] They do, however, agree with the proposition that the *Icelandic Fisheries* case and various treaties do support the existence of customary obligations to cooperate in the conservation and sustainable development of common property resources of the high seas. Handl in 1991 expressed the view that the notion of sustainable development has not yet become a norm of international law, but that it might in time even become a peremptory norm of international law.[16]

The understanding of sustainable development that has emerged from various international instruments does not really solve the problem of ascertaining its essential elements that apply in any particular context. However, they do underlie the fact that sustainable development is emerging as a principle of international law.[17]

Though a universally accepted definition of sustainable development is absent, global and regional treaties relating to international watercourses, wildlife conservation, habitat protection, endangered species and cultural and natural heritage also suggest that a wider legal

8 *Rio Declaration on Environment and Development* (1992), 31 ILM 874 ('Rio Declaration'), Principle 1; S.P. Johnson, *The Earth Summit: The United Nations Conference on Environment and Development (UNCED)* Dordrecht: Martinus Nijhoff, 1992, p. 118.
9 Rio Declaration, Principle 4.
10 Ibid., Preamble.
11 *Gabčíkovo-Nagymaros Project (Hungary v Slovakia)* (separate opinion of Judge Weeramantry) [1997] ICJ Reports 7.
12 Ibid., para. 88.
13 Ibid., para. 89. See also his summary of the right to development and the right to environmental protection, paras 91–2.
14 Ibid.
15 P.W. Birnie and A.E. Boyle, *International Law and the Environment*, reprint 1994, Oxford: Clarendon Press, 1992, pp 122–4.
16 Referred to by Birnie and Boyle, ibid., p. 5.
17 Ibid., pp. 122–4.

significance has been achieved regarding conservation and sustainable development.[18] It is clear that a meaning of sustainable development, requiring activities to be carried out without causing harm to the environment, is broadly respected by the world community.[19]

Precautionary principle

The precautionary principle provides guidance on the development and application of international environmental law in the absence of scientific certainty.[20] Where there is no firm scientific evidence on the measures to be taken in a development activity that may have an environmental effect, the principle advocates protective anticipatory action.[21] The precautionary principle provides that lack of scientific certainty should not be used as a reason to postpone measures to be taken for the protection of human life, health and environment.[22] The precautionary principle was first advocated in the 1970s under the name of *Vorsorgeprinzip* during discussions relating to West German environmental law.[23] While it is difficult to find the existence of such a concept in early legal writings in the United States (US),[24] there are some laws which have a precautionary nature, and the principle underlies much of the early environmental legislation in this country: for example, the *National Environmental Policy Act*, the *Clean Water Act* and the *Pollution Prevention Act*.

In the international context the precautionary principle compels a state to act in the face of scientific uncertainty to take measures to protect the natural environment.[25] Where a *prima facie* case is established that a measure or development programme may cause environmental damage, and there is a lack of full scientific certainty about the nature and dimension of the environmental damage that may happen if the activity is realised, this should not prevent action.[26] Thus the principle obligates authorities to take precautionary measures where there is a lack of scientific certainty about the consequence of its action and induces authorities

---

18 Ibid.
19 For a further discussion of sustainable development, see Chapter 37 by K. Bosselmann in this volume.
20 Sands, op. cit., p. 208.
21 See J.A. Herrera Izaguirre, 'International Law and GMOS: Can the Precautionary Principle Protect Biological Diversity', *Boletin Mexicano de Derecho Comparado* 11, 2007, 97–136, p. 99. Online. Available HTTP: <http://www.estig.ipbeja.pt/~ac_direito/HerreraIz.pdf > (accessed 26 April 2012).
22 J. Ellis and A. FitzGerald, 'The Precautionary Principle in International Law: Lessons from Fuller's Internal Morality', *McGill Law Journal* 49, 2004, 780–800, p. 782. Online. Available HTTP: <http://lawjournal.mcgill.ca/documents/Ellis_and_FitzGerald.pdf> (accessed 23 November 2011).
23 P. Sandin, *The Precautionary Principle: From Theory to Practice*, Stockholm, 2002, p. 3. Online. Available HTTP: <http://kth.diva-portal.org/smash/get/diva2:7408/FULLTEXT01> (accessed 23 November 2011).
24 C.R. Sunstein, 'Beyond the Precautionary Principle', *University of Pennsylvania Law Review* 1(151), 2003, 1003–51, p. 1005. Online. Available HTTP: <http://sciencepolicy.colorado.edu/students/envs_5000/sunstein_2003.pdf> (accessed 23 November 2011).
25 D. Anton, J. Kohout and N. Pain, 'Nationalizing Environmental Protection in Australia: The International Dimensions', *Environmental Law* 23, 1993, 763–83. Online. Available HTTP: <http://www.ciesin.org/docs/010–567/010–567.html> (accessed 23 November 2011).
26 D. Freestone and E. Hey, 'Origins and Development of the Precautionary Principle', in D. Freestone and E. Hey (eds) *The Precautionary Principle and International Law: The Challenge of Implementation*, The Hague: Kluwer Law International, 1996, p. 13.

undertaking development activities based on exploitation of nature to take precautionary measures to minimise the possible degradation of nature.[27] It also encourages such bodies to consider less intrusive alternative approaches.[28]

Usually the burden of proof lies with the individual, who refuses or opposes the carrying out of an activity, to prove that such activity is likely to cause environmental harm. However, in the case of the precautionary principle the burden of proof lies with the individual who wants to carry out an activity that may affect the environment to prove that such activity will not have any negative impact on the environment. This shifting of the burden of proof is explained by Birnie and Boyle in the following words:

> A stronger version of the precautionary principle goes further by reversing the burden of proof altogether. In this form, it becomes impermissible to carry out an activity unless it can be shown that it will not cause unacceptable harm to the environment. Examples of its use in this sense include the resolution suspending disposal of low-level radioactive waste at sea without the approval of the London Dumping Convention Consultative Parties, the suspension of industrial dumping in the Oslo Commission area without prior justification . . . and the moratorium on whaling. The main effect of the principle in these situations is to require states to submit proposed activities affecting the global commons to international scrutiny.[29]

It was in the Second International Conference on the Protection of the North Sea, in 1987, that the first explicit formulation of the precautionary concept was discussed at the international level. It was stated that a precautionary approach was necessary to protect the North Sea from possibly damaging effects of the most dangerous substances and it may require that action be taken even before a causal link has been established by absolutely clear scientific evidence.[30] During the Third Conference on the Protection of the North Sea, ministers agreed to abide by the rules of this principle under the 1990 Bergen Ministerial Declaration on Sustainable Development.[31] The Declaration stated that the precautionary principle must serve as the foundation on which policies should be created in order to achieve sustainable development. Environmental degradation must be prevented with measures that predict and diminish threats to the environment. In cases where damage to the environment is inevitable, lack of scientific evidence should not be used to delay execution of measures to prevent environmental degradation.[32] The amendment of the Montreal Protocol on Substances that Deplete the Ozone Layer in London in 1990 added a precautionary measure as a further safeguard to protect the

---

27 D.M. Dharmadhikari, 'Environment – Problems and Solutions', *AIR Journal* 90, 2003, 161–70, p. 163.
28 J.M. Van Dyke, *The Evolution and International Acceptance of the Precautionary Principle*, p. 359. Online. Available HTTP: <http://mmc.gov/sound/internationalwrkshp/pdf/vandyke.pdf> (accessed 23 November 2011).
29 Birnie and Boyle, op. cit., p. 98.
30 Para. VII, London, 24–25 November 1987. Online. Available HTTP: <www.vliz.be/imisdocs/publications/140155.pdf> (accessed 23 November 2011).
31 *Bergen Ministerial Declaration on Sustainable Development* (1990), The Hague, UN Doc A/CONF.151/PC/10. Online. Available HTTP: <http://www.seas-at-risk.org/1mages/1990%20Hague%20Declaration.pdf> (accessed 23 November 2011).
32 Ibid., para. 7.

ozone layer.[33] At the 1991 Bamako Convention on the Ban of the Import into Africa and the Control of Transboundary Movement and Management of Hazardous Wastes within Africa, it was set forth that parties should put some effort into implementing the precautionary approach to pollution, which would in turn prevent the release of substances which may be toxic to humans or the environment, without waiting for scientific proof to affirm the presence of such harm. The parties would have to work together to implement the precautionary principle and would have to adopt hygienic production methods to inhibit pollution.[34] The Protocol on Water and Health to the 1992 Convention on the Protection and Use of Transboundary Watercourses and International Lakes incorporates the precautionary principle by providing that action to prevent, control or minimise water-related disease shall not be delayed on the basis that the scientific research has not fully proved a causal link between the factor at which such action is aimed, on the one hand, and the potential contribution of that factor to the prevalence of water-related disease and/or transboundary impacts, on the other hand.[35] In the 1992 OSPAR (Convention for the Protection of the Marine Environment of the North-East Atlantic) it was agreed upon that the precautionary principle has to be executed by contracting parties.[36] A further example of the principle is seen in the Protocol to the regional 1979 Convention on Long-Range Transboundary Air Pollution on Further Reduction of Sulphur Emissions, which called on states to take precautionary measures to predict, prevent and reduce hazardous air emissions and diminish their potentially detrimental effects. Similar to later protocols, it provides that where there are threats of serious or irreversible damage, lack of scientific certainty should not be used to defer precautionary measures, taking into consideration that such measures would be worthwhile to invest financially.[37]

The use of the precautionary principle by parties as a medium to predict, prevent or reduce the causes of climate change and alleviate its harmful effects was included in the 1992 United Nations Framework Convention on Climate Change (UNFCCC). The Convention calls for parties to 'take precautionary measures' but 'taking into account that policies and measures to deal with climate change should be cost-effective so as to ensure global benefits at the lowest

33 *Montreal Protocol on Substances that Deplete the Ozone Layer*, opened for signature 16 September 1987, 1522 UNTS 3 (entered into force 1 January 1989) ('Montreal Protocol') Preamble. Online. Available HTTP: <http://ozone.unep.org/pdfs/Montreal-Protocol2000.pdf> (accessed 23 November 2011).

34 *Bamako Convention on the Ban of the Import to Africa and the Control of Transboundary Movement and Management of Hazardous Wastes within Africa*, opened for signature 30 January 1991, 30 ILM 773 (entry into force 22 April 1998), Art. 4(3)(f). Online. Available HTTP: <http://www.africa-union.org/Official_documents/Treaties_%20Conventions_%20Protocols/hazardouswastes.pdf> (accessed 23 November 2011).

35 *Protocol on Water and Health to the 1992 Convention on the Protection and Use of Transboundary Watercourses and International Lakes*, opened for signature 17 June 1999 (entered into force 4 August 2005) Article 5(a). Online. Available HTTP: <http://www.unece.org/fileadmin/DAM/env/documents/2000/wat/mp.wat.2000.1.e.pdf> (accessed 23 November 2011).

36 *Convention for the Protection on the Marine Environment of the North-East Atlantic*, opened for signature 22 September 1992, 32 ILM 1069 (entered into force 25 March 1998) ('OSPAR Convention') Article 2(2)(a). Online. Available HTTP: <http://www.ospar.org/html/documents/ospar/html/OSPAR_Convention_e_updated_text_2007.pdf> (accessed 2 October 2007).

37 *Protocol to the Regional 1979 Convention on Long-Range Transboundary Air Pollution on Further Reduction of Sulphur Emissions*, opened for signature 14 June 1994, UN Doc EB.AIR/R.84 (entered into force 5 August 1998) Preamble. Online. Available HTTP: <http://www.unece.org/fileadmin/DAM/env/lrtap/full%20text/1994.Sulphur.e.pdf> (accessed 23 November 2011).

possible cost'.[38] Although the 1992 Convention on Biological Diversity (CBD) does not put much emphasis on the precautionary principle it does state that in cases where there is a major risk of reduction or loss of biological diversity in significant magnitude, inadequate scientific knowledge should not be used as an excuse for delaying necessary measures to avoid or diminish such a threat.[39] Furthermore, the precautionary approach contained in Principle 15 of the 1992 Rio Declaration was reiterated in the 2000 Cartagena Protocol on Biosafety.[40] An outline of a plan for the application of the precautionary principle was presented as part of the 2000 Communication from the Commission on the Precautionary Principle.[41] The precautionary principle also received recognition in the 2001 Stockholm Convention on Implementing International Action on Certain Persistent Organic Pollutants.[42]

In terms of soft law the 1992 Rio Declaration stated that the states shall widely apply the precautionary principle in accordance with their capabilities for shielding the environment against harm. For situations in which the threats of damage to the environment cannot be avoided, inadequacy of scientific results shall not be used for postponing cost-effective procedures to prevent deterioration of the environment.[43]

According to Agenda 21 an approach that would anticipate and take action against environmental threats is crucial; in other words a precautionary approach rather than a reactive one.[44]

Academics do not agree as to the legal status of the precautionary principle. Cameron and Abouchar argue that there is sufficient evidence of state practice to make a good argument that the principle has become a norm of international law.[45] According to Birnie and Boyle, in spite of its importance and the novel and far-reaching effects of some applications, the late reception of the precautionary principle in international instruments suggests that it is not yet a principle of international law. Difficult questions, concerning the point at which it becomes applicable, remain unanswered and seriously undermine its normative character and realistic utility, although support for it does show greater prudence on the part of those states that intend to accept it.[46] Sands remarks that the legal status of the principle is still evolving.[47]

---

38 *United Nations Framework Convention on Climate Change*, opened for signature 4 June 1992, 1771 UNTS 107 (entered into force 21 March 1994) (UNFCCC) Article 3(3).
39 *Convention on Biological Diversity*, opened for signature 5 June 1992, 31 ILM 818 (entered into force 29 December 1993) ('CBD') Preamble.
40 *Cartagena Protocol on Biosafety*, opened for signature 29 January 2000, 39 ILM 1027 (entered into force 11 September 2003) Preamble. Online. Available HTTP: <http://bch.cbd.int/protocol/text/> (accessed 23 November 2011).
41 *Communication from the Commission on the Precautionary Principle*, Commission of the European Communities, Brussels, 2000. Online. Available HTTP: <http://ec.europa.eu/dgs/health_consumer/library/pub/pub07_en.pdf> (accessed 23 November 2011).
42 *Stockholm Convention on Implementing International Action on Certain Persistent Organic Pollutants*, opened for signature 22 May 2001, 40 ILM 532 (entered into force 17 May 2004) Preamble, Arts. 1, 8(9). Online. Available HTTP: <http://www.pops.int/documents/convtext/convtext_en.pdf> (accessed 23 November 2011).
43 Rio Declaration, Principle 15; Johnson, op. cit., p. 120.
44 *Agenda 21: A Programme for Action for Sustainable Development*, Report of the UN Conference on Environment and Development, Annex II, 12 August 1992, UN Doc A./Conf. 151/26 (Vol II-IV) Chapter 17, para. 17.21; Ibid., p. 311.
45 J. Cameron and J. Abouchar, 'The Status of the Precautionary Principle in International Law', in Freestone and Hey, op. cit., p. 30.
46 Birnie and Boyle, op. cit., p. 98.
47 Sands, op. cit, pp. 212–13.

Udemgba, noticing the progress that has been made at the international level relating to the application of the principle, agrees with Sands and remarks that the precautionary principle seems to be emerging as a customary norm. He considers that the uncertainties in the meaning, application and implications of the principle make it difficult to reach a conclusion that the precautionary principle is a rule of customary law.[48]

There is little doubt that the precautionary principle is now widely recognised and is taken into consideration by states and international organisations whenever they initiate large-scale environmental change. Moreover, it is incorporated into different international instruments and many states have adopted the principle at the national level. Despite the difference among academics about the legal status of the precautionary principle, the broad support and evidence of state practice in instruments such as the Rio Declaration, the UNFCCC and the CBD justify a strong argument that it reflects a principle of customary international law.[49]

Polluter pays principle

The polluter pays principle is essentially based on a commonsense approach for the mitigation of environmental degradation. It simply means that s/he who damages the environment should bear the cost of rectifying that damage. In a broader sense producers of goods and other items should be responsible for any pollution which the process of production causes and therefore must also pay for prevention or rectification of the damage caused to the environment by such pollution.[50] Underlying the meaning of the polluter pays principle is the belief that when public authorities take measures to prevent potential and actual environmental damage, the expenses incurred should be borne by the person responsible for the pollution.[51] In the event of environmental pollution the principle can be applied to require the producer and/or resource user to meet the costs of implementing an environmental standard. Where it is required, the resource user should also meet the necessary expenses for implementation of technical regulations. It is also suggested that introduction of liability regimes be introduced to make resource users liable for causing environmental harm and thus pay for the pollution caused by their authorities.[52] It appears in Principle 16 of the Rio Declaration where it is noted that 'the polluter should, in principle, bear the cost of pollution'.

The polluter pays principle was first referred to at the international level explicitly in 1972 in a Council Recommendation on Guiding Principles Concerning the International Economic Aspects of Environmental Policies of the Organisation for Economic Co-operation and Development (OECD). In the Recommendation of the Council it was stated that:

> the polluter should bear the expenses of carrying out the . . . measures decided by public authorities to ensure that the environment is in an acceptable state. In other words, the

48 S. Udemgba, 'The Precautionary and Differentiated Responsibility Principles in the Climate Change Context', Master of Law Thesis, 2005, University of Saskatchewan, Canada, pp. 23–4. Online. Available HTTP: <http://library.usask.ca/theses/available/etd–09132005–171902/unrestricted/LLMTHESIS.pdf> (accessed 27 April 2012).

49 Sands, op.cit, pp. 212–13.

50 S. Ball and S. Bell, *Environmental Law*, 2nd edition, Delhi: Universal Law Publishing, 1994, p. 97.

51 H. Smets, 'The Polluter Pays Principle in the Early 1990s', in L. Campiglio, L. Pineschi, D. Siniscalco and T. Treves (eds.) *The Environment After Rio: International Law and Economics*, London: Martinus Nijhoff, 1994, pp. 136–7.

52 C. Coffey and J. Newcombe, *The Polluter Pays Principle and Fisheries: The Role of Taxes and Charges*, London: Institute for European Environmental Policy, p. 1. Online. Available HTTP: <http://www.ieep.eu/assets/238/thepolluterpaysprincipleandfisheries.pdf > (accessed 27 April 2012).

cost of these measures should be reflected in the cost of goods and services which cause pollution in production and/or consumption. Such measures should not be accompanied by subsidies that would create significant distortions in international trade and investment.[53]

The 1972 OECD Council Recommendation added the polluter pays principle to allocate costs of pollution prevention and control measures to promote frugal use of environmental resources and to prevent likely falsehood in figures on international trade and investment.[54] The polluter pays principle was reaffirmed as a fundamental principle for Member States during the 1974 OECD Council Recommendation on the Implementation of the Polluter-Pays Principle.[55] The 1989 OECD Council Recommendation concerning the Application of the Polluter-Pays Principle to Accidental Pollution provides that the principle implies that the operator of a hazardous installation is under an obligation to bear the cost of reasonable measures to prevent and control accidental pollution from that installation in conformity with domestic law before the occurrence of an accident in order to protect human health or the environment.[56] One particular application of the polluter pays principle in the Recommendation consists of adjusting fees or taxes, in concurrence with domestic law, to pay more fully for the cost of certain exceptional measures to prevent and control unexpected pollution in specific hazardous installations. Such measures are taken by public authorities to protect human health and the environment, and must be rational and directly related to accident prevention or the control of accidental pollution released by the hazardous installation.[57] Another application of the principle in the Recommendation consists of charging the cost of basic pollution control measures to the operator of the hazardous installation following an accident. Such a measure would allow the operator or the authorities to take prompt action, to completely avoid or at least minimise dissemination of environmental damage and to put a lid on the release of toxic substances, thus preventing any adverse effects on the environment.[58] However, the application of the principle does not extend to the point that would require the person at the origin of the accident or the operator to pay other costs connected with the public authorities' response to an accident or with the occurrence of the accident. But public authorities may demand compensation from the person responsible for the accident.[59]

53 OECD, *Council Recommendation on Guiding Principles Concerning the International Economic Aspects of Environmental Policies of the Organisation for Economic Co-operation and Development* (1972), C(72) 128, para A.4. Online. Available HTTP: <http://acts.oecd.org/Instruments/ShowInstrumentView.aspx?InstrumentID=4&Lang=en&Book=False> (accessed 27 April 2012).

54 Ibid.

55 OECD, *Council Recommendation on the Implementation of the Polluter-Pays Principle* (1974), C(74) 223, para I(1). Online. Available HTTP: <http://acts.oecd.org/Instruments/ShowInstrumentView.aspx?InstrumentID=11&InstrumentPID=9&Lang=en&Book=False> (accessed 17 February 2012).

56 OECD, *Council Recommendation concerning the Application of the Polluter-Pays Principle to Accidental Pollution* (1989), C(89)88/Final, para. 4. Online. Available HTTP: <http://acts.oecd.org/Instruments/ShowInstrumentView.aspx?InstrumentID=38&InstrumentPID=35&Lang=en&Book=False> (accessed 17 February 2012).

57 Ibid., para. 10.

58 Ibid., para. 11.

59 Ibid., para. 16.

The OECD initiative was the result of demands on governments and other institutions to introduce policies and mechanisms for the protection of the environment and the public from the threats posed by pollution in a modern industrialised society.[60] The principle was subsequently endorsed in 1973 when the European Community (EC) adopted a programme of action on the environment. Subsequently, an EC Council Recommendation (1975) provided that Member States should apply the polluter pays principle. It further provided that natural or legal persons must pay the price of such measures that are necessary to reduce or remove the pollution to meet the standards or equivalent measures laid down by public authorities.[61] Although the EC Recommendation is not legally binding (unlike the OECD Recommendation), it encompasses many more issues with regards to the costs of environmental damage. The EC took another step in 1986 when it adopted the Single European Act regarding the environment, in which it stated that preventive action should be taken as a priority to rectify environmental damage at the source and the polluter shall be liable to bear the cost.[62] This Act is legally enforceable. The polluter pays principle was also adopted in the ASEAN Agreement on Conservation on Nature and Natural Resources adopted in 1985. It provides that the originator of the activity that causes environmental degradation is to be held responsible for its prevention, reduction and control, and also for rehabilitation and remedial measures.[63]

The polluter pays principle was recognised as a general principle of international environmental law in the 1990 International Convention on Oil Pollution, Preparedness, Response and Cooperation.[64] The Protocol on Water and Health to the 1992 Convention on the Protection and Use of Transboundary Watercourses and International Lakes gives recognition to the polluter pays principle to place the costs of pollution prevention, control and reduction on the polluter.[65] A similar provision was adopted by the 1992 OSPAR Convention for the Protection of the Marine Environment of the North–East Atlantic.[66] The 1992 Convention on the Protection of the Marine Environment of the Baltic Sea Area also includes

60 *Indian Council for Enviro-Legal Action* v *Union of India*, (1996) 3 SCC 212.
61 Council Recommendation 75/436/EURATOM, para. 2. Online. Available HTTP: <http://eur-lex.europa.eu/LexUriServ/LexUriServ.do?uri=CELEX:31975H0436:EN:HTML> (accessed 17 February 2012).
62 *Single European Act regarding the environment*, Art. 25. Online. Available HTTP: <http://ec.europa.eu/economy_finance/emu_history/documents/treaties/singleuropeanact.pdf> (accessed 17 February 2012).
63 ASEAN, *Agreement on Conservation on Nature and Natural Resources* (1985), Art. 10(d). Online. Available HTTP: <http://sedac.ciesin.org/entri/texts/asean.natural.resources.1985.html> (accessed 17 February 2012).
64 *International Convention on Oil Pollution, Preparedness, Response and Cooperation*, opened for signature 30 November 1990, 30 ILM 733 (entered into force 13 May 1995) ('OPRC Convention') Preamble. Online. Available HTTP: <http://www.admiraltylawguide.com/conven/oilpolresponse1990.html> (accessed 17 February 2012).
65 *Protocol on Water and Health to the 1992 Convention on the Protection and Use of Transboundary Watercourses and International Lakes*, op. cit., Art. 5(b). Online. Available HTTP: <http://www.unece.org/env/documents/2000/wat/mp.wat.2000.1.e.pdf> (accessed 17 February 2012).
66 *OSPAR Convention for the Protection of the Marine Environment of the North East Atlantic*, opened for signature 22 September 1992, 32 ILM 1069 (entered into force 25 March 1998) ('OSPAR Convention') Art. 2(2)(b). Online. Available HTTP: <http://www.ospar.org/html_documents/ospar/html/OSPAR_Convention_e_updated_text_2007.pdf> (accessed 17 February 2012).

the polluter pays principle and directs the contracting parties to be guided by the principle.[67] It was recognised as a general principle of international environmental law by the 1992 Convention on the Transboundary Effects of Industrial Accidents.[68]

The initiative to promote the polluter pays principle, taken by the OECD during the 1970s, has subsequently been widely endorsed in relation to the protection of the global environment. In essence, it could be said to be based on three elements: the need for preventive action; the need for environmental damage to be rectified at the source; and that the polluter should pay. However, the precise scope of the principle, and its implications for those involved in potentially polluting activities, has never been satisfactorily agreed. Furthermore, it is not yet unquestionably accepted as a principle of international law. For example, according to Sands, the polluter pays principle is yet to receive broad geographic and subject-matter support over the long term. He has serious doubts whether the principle has achieved the status of a generally applicable rule of customary international law.[69] On the other hand, there is strong support among academics, who have expressed the view that the polluter pays principle has obtained significant endorsement from a large number of states and international organisations. For example, Birnie and Boyle are of the view that as a policy the polluter pays principle represents an important strategy for controlling environmentally harmful activities by emphasising responsibility for their true economic costs and complementing the more obvious regulatory measures adopted under global and regional treaties.[70] Grossman has stated that the polluter pays principle has developed legal status and is now considered as a general principle of international environmental law.[71]

To conclude the above discussion, it can be safely stated that the international community has accepted the polluter pays principle as a strategic tool to protect the environment from pollution and degradation, and it has perhaps emerged as a customary rule of international law.

Common but differentiated responsibilities

The principle of common but differentiated responsibility has developed from the application of equity in international law and the recognition that the special needs of developing countries have to be taken into account.[72] This principle is widely accepted in treaties and soft-law instruments. The Stockholm Declaration in Principle 23 emphasised the importance of assessing the 'applicability of standards which are valid for the most advanced countries but which may be

---

67 *Convention on the Protection of the Marine Environment of the Baltic Sea Area*, opened for signature 9 April 1992, 13 ILM 546 (entered into force 17 January 2000) ('Helsinki Convention') Art. 3(4). Online. Available HTTP: <http://www.helcom.fi/stc/files/Convention/Conv0704.pdf> (accessed 17 February 2012).

68 *Convention on the Transboundary Effects of Industrial Accidents*, opened for signature 18 March 1992, 32 ILM 1330 (entered into force 19 April 2000) Preamble. Online. Available HTTP: <http://sedac.ciesin.org/entri/texts/industrial.accidents.1992.html> (accessed 17 February 2012).

69 Sands, op.cit., p. 213.

70 Birnie and Boyle, op. cit., p. 111.

71 M. Rosso Grossman, 'Agriculture and Polluter Pays Principle', *Netherlands Comparative Law Association*, p. 2. Online. Available HTTP: <http.//www.ejcl.org/113/article113–15.pdf> (accessed 17 March 2012).

72 Sands, op. cit., p. 285.

inappropriate and of unwarranted social cost for the developing countries'.[73] Building on this statement, 20 years later, Principle 7 of the Rio Declaration formulated it as follows:

> States shall cooperate in a spirit of global partnership to conserve, protect and restore the health and integrity of the Earth's ecosystem. In view of the different contributions to global environmental degradation, States have common but differentiated responsibilities. The developed countries acknowledge the responsibility that they bear in the international pursuit to sustainable development in view of the pressures their societies place on the global environment and of the technologies and financial resources they command.[74]

The principle of common but differentiated responsibilities consists of two prongs. First, all states have a common responsibility for the protection of the environment. Second, this common responsibility needs to take into account different circumstances, resources and capabilities to carry it out and different contributions to the particular environmental problem. It requires all states to participate in the international response to the problem and take measures to address it. However, obligations imposed on different states have to be varied depending on the level of their economic development, circumstances and capabilities.

The most successful Multilateral Environmental Agreement (MEA) – the Montreal Protocol on Substances that Deplete the Ozone Layer – took into account the special situation and needs of developing countries, giving them a grace period of ten years allowing them to delay compliance with control measures.[75] However, after that period, commencing in 1999, developing countries started to participate in control schedules and phase-outs for the consumption of the controlled substances that deplete the ozone layer. Fulfilment of developing country obligations, to comply with the control measures, will depend upon the effective implementation of financial cooperation and the transfer of technology.[76]

Support for the principle of common but differentiated responsibility can also be found in the preamble of the CBD, where it is acknowledged that 'special provision is required to meet the needs of developing countries, including the provision of new and additional financial resources and appropriate access to relevant technologies'.[77] The CBD includes in Article 20:

1. Each Contracting Party undertakes to provide, in accordance with its capabilities, financial support and incentives in respect of those national activities which are intended to achieve the objectives of this Convention, in accordance with its national plans, priorities and programmes.
2. The developed country Parties shall provide new and additional financial resources to enable developing country Parties to meet the agreed full incremental costs to them of implementing measures which fulfil the obligations of this Convention.

[. . .]

---

73 *Stockholm Declaration on the Human Environment* (1972), 11 ILM 1416 ('Stockholm Declaration').
74 Rio Declaration, op. cit.
75 Montreal Protocol, op. cit., Art. 5.
76 Ibid.
77 CBD, op. cit.

4. The extent to which developing country Parties will effectively implement their commitments under this Convention will depend on the effective implementation by developed country Parties of their commitments under this Convention related to financial resources and transfer of technology and will take fully into account the fact that economic and social development and eradication of poverty are the first and overriding priorities of the developing country Parties.[78]

Common but differentiated responsibilities is a key principle in the climate change regime. Article 3 of the UNFCCC defines this principle as follows:

The Parties should protect the climate system for the benefit of present and future generations of humankind, on the basis of equity and in accordance with their common but differentiated responsibilities and respective capabilities. Accordingly, the developed country Parties should take the lead in combating climate change and the adverse effects thereof.[79]

Differences between obligations and commitments under the UNFCCC and the Kyoto Protocol for developed (Annex I) and developing (non-Annex I) countries are intended to fairly represent the historical contributions of developed countries to the climate change problem. The differences also take into account the right of developing countries to develop and to compensate climate change victims for harm caused to them and their territories as a result of climate change. Developing countries tend to be more vulnerable to climate change impacts, especially small island states. They have fewer resources and capabilities to combat the effects. Therefore, in the first commitment period of the Kyoto Protocol (2008 to 2012) developing countries do not have any mandatory commitments.

Reporting requirements are also different for developed and developing countries. Annex I parties are required to report greenhouse gas (GHG) emissions and transactions of emissions units under the Kyoto Protocol flexibility mechanisms in order to assess their compliance with emissions targets.[80] Non-Annex 1 Parties report nationally appropriate mitigation actions (NAMAs).[81] Further developments include the Bali Action Plan, which anticipated that a new climate agreement would provide for the measurement, reporting and verification (MRV) of three different categories of action: developed country mitigation commitments or actions, developing country mitigation actions and the provision of support for developing country mitigation actions.[82]

The principle of common but differentiated responsibilities can be controversial. It requires developed countries to provide financial assistance to developing countries, to transfer technology and build capacity to allow them to comply with international agreements. It also allows developing countries to have less rigorous compliance with MEAs. This issue was

78 Ibid., Art. 20.
79 UNFCCC.
80 UNFCCC, National Reports. Online. Available HTTP: <http://unfccc.int/national_reports/items/1408.php> (accessed 19 June 2010).
81 Ibid.
82 UNFCCC, *Thirteenth Conference of the Parties* (2008), Bali, Indonesia, 3–15 Dec. 2007, *Report of the Conference of the Parties*, UN Doc FCCC/CP/2007/6/Add.1 ('Bali Action Plan') paras 1(b)(i)–(iii). Online. Available HTTP: <http://unfccc.int/resource/docs/2007/cop13/eng/06a01.pdf> (accessed 5 July 2011).

difficult during the negotiation of the Kyoto Protocol. The lack of binding commitments for developing countries was a major reason for the US failure to ratify the Kyoto Protocol in 2001.[83] This controversy prevented consensus being reached between the 192 countries during negotiations at the Fifteenth Session of the UNFCCC Conference of the Parties (COP 15) in Copenhagen. Instead of a legally binding agreement, COP 15 resulted in only the Copenhagen Accord, which is a non-binding political document. Thus COP 15 only took note of the Accord and it appears unlikely that consensus will be achieved for a legally binding agreement in the near future. This is because developed countries want some level of *common* responsibility for all countries including developing ones, especially rapidly developing economies such as China (currently the main contributor to climate change), India and Brazil. And of course the world expects the US, not currently a party to the Kyoto Protocol, to be part of a new agreement and offer a serious commitment to reduce GHG emissions.

The Copenhagen Accord recognises that meeting the objective of deep GHG emission reductions will take 'longer in developing countries . . . bearing in mind that social and economic development and poverty eradication are the first and overriding priorities of developing countries . . . .'[84] The Accord states that 'developed countries shall provide adequate, predictable and sustainable financial resources, technology and capacity building to support the implementation of adaptation action in developing countries'.[85] The Copenhagen Accord addressed common responsibility, stating that non-Annex I Parties to the Convention will implement mitigation actions in the context of sustainable development and least developed countries (including small island developing states) may undertake actions voluntarily and on the basis of support.[86] The Copenhagen Accord also established the Copenhagen Green Climate Fund to support projects, programmes, policies and other activities in developing countries related to mitigation, adaptation, capacity building, technology development and transfer.[87] This is consistent with the principle of common but differentiated responsibility and takes a step in the right direction towards a new legally binding treaty beyond (or as a successor to) the Kyoto Protocol.[88]

Intergenerational equity

The principle of intergenerational equity is well known in international law. The interests of future generations were recognised as early as 1946 in the International Convention on the Regulation of Whaling, which states in its preamble the 'interest of the nations of the world in safeguarding for future generations the great natural resources represented by the whale stocks'. Another example is found in Article 4 of the World Heritage Convention (1972), where parties agreed to 'protect, conserve, present and transmit cultural and natural heritage to future generations'.[89]

---

83 D. Hunter, J. Salzman and D. Zaelke, *International Environmental Law and Policy*, 3rd edition, NSW Australia: Foundation Press, 2007, p. 495.
84 *UNFCCC Conference of the Parties Fifteenth Session* (2009), Copenhagen, 7–18 December 2009, FCCC/CP/2009/L.7, ('Copenhagen Accord') para. 2. Online. Available HTTP: <http://unfccc.int/resource/docs/2009/cop15/eng/l07.pdf> (accessed 6 July 2011).
85 Ibid., Art. 3.
86 Ibid., Art. 5.
87 Ibid., Art. 10.
88 For further discussion of the international climate regime see Chapter 20 by A. Zahar in this volume.

In the Brundtland Commission Report *Our Common Future* the definition of sustainable development includes meeting the needs of the present generation without sacrificing the needs of future generations. This focus on future generations as beneficiaries of environmental protection has led to the principle of intergenerational equity.[90] The essence of this principle is that present generations cannot leave the environment in a worse condition than it had for itself. The principle of intergenerational equity requires taking into consideration impacts of current activities on future generations, giving them a 'seat at the table' where decisions are made, to avoid irreversible environmental damage.

Several MEAs include this principle in their preamble or substantive provisions. In the preamble of the Convention on International Trade in Endangered Species of Wild Fauna and Flora (CITES) the contracting parties recognised that 'wild fauna and flora in their many beautiful and varied forms are an irreplaceable part of the natural systems of the earth which must be protected for this and the generations to come'.[91] Article 2(5)(c) of the UNECE (UN Economic Commission for Europe) Water Convention states that '[w]ater resources shall be managed so that the needs of the present generation are met without compromising the ability of future generations to meet their own needs'.[92] The preamble of the CBD notes the parties' determination 'to conserve and sustainably use biological diversity for the benefit of present and future generations'.[93] Article 3(1) of the UNFCCC acknowledges among its principles that '[p]arties should protect the climate system for the benefit of present and future generations of humankind'.[94]

This principle is well established in soft law as well. The preamble of the Stockholm Declaration states that 'to defend and improve the human environment for present and future generations has become an imperative goal of humankind'.[95] Principle 1 of the Declaration states that man 'bears a solemn responsibility to protect and improve the environment for present and future generations'.[96] Principle 2 requires safeguarding of natural resources and ecosystems 'for the benefit of present and future generations'.[97] The Rio Declaration's Principle 3 recognises that '[t]he right to development must be fulfilled so as to equitably meet developmental and environmental needs of present and future generations'.[98]

Professor Edith Brown Weiss, a leading scholar on this principle, proposed three basic conservation elements of intergenerational equity. First, each generation should be required to conserve the diversity of the natural and cultural resource base, so it does not unduly restrict the options available to future generations – 'conservation of options'. Second, each generation should be required to maintain the quality of the planet so that it is passed on in no worse condition than that in which it was received – 'conservation of quality'. Third, each

89 *Convention Concerning the Protection of the World Natural and Cultural Heritage*, opened for signature 16 November 1972, 1037 UNTS 151 (entered into force 17 December 1975) ('World Heritage Convention'). Online. Available HTTP: <http://whc.unesco.org/archive/convention-en.pdf> (accessed 6 July 2011).
90 Hunter et al., op. cit., p. 491.
91 *Convention on International Trade in Endangered Species of Wild Fauna and Flora*, opened for signature 3 March 1973, 12 ILM 1088 (entered into force 1 July 1975) ('CITES').
92 *Convention on the Protection and Use of Transboundary Watercourses and International Lakes*, op. cit.
93 CBD, op. cit.
94 UNFCC, op. cit.
95 Stockholm Declaration, op. cit.
96 Ibid.
97 Ibid.
98 Rio Declaration, op. cit.

generation should provide its members with equitable rights of access to the legacy of past generations and should conserve this access for future generations – 'conservation of access'.[99]

The principle of intergenerational equity has been recognised by the ICJ in its Advisory Opinion on the Threat of Use of Nuclear Weapons: 'the environment is not an abstraction but represents the living space, the quality of life, and the very health of human beings, including generations unborn.'[100]

Access to information and public participation (good governance)

The principle of access to information and public participation (good governance) is relatively new and less well recognised in international environmental law. However, in the last decade it has been included in declarations, in about one hundred conventions and in jurisprudence in domestic courts. It consists of three pillars: access to information, public participation and access to justice in environmental decision-making (the third pillar is not covered here). It was formulated for the first time in Principle 10 of the Rio Declaration:

> Environmental issues are best handled with participation of all concerned citizens, at the relevant level. At the national level, each individual shall have appropriate access to information concerning the environment that is held by public authorities, including information on hazardous materials and activities in their communities, and the opportunity to participate in decision-making processes. States shall facilitate and encourage public awareness and participation by making information widely available. Effective access to judicial and administrative proceedings, including redress and remedy, shall be provided.[101]

Public participation as a principle in international environmental law was first articulated in Agenda 21:

> One of the fundamental prerequisites for the achievement of sustainable development is broad public participation in decision making. Furthermore, in the more specific context of environment and development, the need for new forms of participation has emerged. This includes the need of individuals, groups and organizations to participate in environmental impact assessment procedures and to know about and participate in decisions, particularly those which potentially affect the communities in which they live and work.[102]

Subsequently this principle was included in many global and regional MEAs.[103] For instance, Article 4(1)(i) of the UNFCCC obliges parties to 'encourage the widest participation in this

---

99 E.B. Weiss, *In Fairness to Future Generations: International Law, Common Patrimony, and Intergenerational Equity*, New York: Transnational Publishers, 1996, pp. 37–8.
100 *Nuclear Tests Cases (New Zealand v France)* 1974 ICJ Rep. 253.
101 Rio Declaration, Principle 10.
102 *Agenda 21: A Programme for Action for Sustainable Development*, Report of the UN Conference on Environment and Development, Annex II, 12 August 1992, UN Doc A/Conf. 151/26, para. 23.2.
103 Joint UNEP-OHCHR Expert Seminar on Human Rights and the Environment, Geneva, Switzerland, 14–16 January 2002, *Background Paper No. 1: Human Rights and Environment Issues in Multilateral Treaties Adopted Between 1991 and 2001* (prepared by D. Shelton). Online. Available HTTP: <http://www2.ohchr.org/english/issues/environment/environ/bp1.htm> (accessed 7 July 2011).

process, including that of non–governmental organizations'.[104] Article 6 further provides that parties shall promote and facilitate the public's access to information and public participation.[105]

The Espoo Convention on Environmental Impact Assessment in a Transboundary Context guarantees non–discriminatory public participation in environmental impact procedures.[106] Article 2(6) states that:

> The Party of origin shall provide . . . an opportunity to the public in the areas likely to be affected to participate in relevant environmental impact assessment procedures regarding proposed activities and shall ensure that the opportunity provided to the public of the affected Party is equivalent to that provided to the public of the Party of origin.[107]

A comprehensive approach to public participation is established by the Aarhus Convention on Access to Information, Public Participation in Decision-Making and Access to Justice in Environmental Matters, which was adopted in 1998 and has now been ratified by 44 parties.[108] According to the former United Nations Secretary-General Kofi Annan, the Aarhus Convention is the most impressive elaboration of Principle 10 of the Rio Declaration. As such it is the most ambitious venture in the area of 'environmental democracy' so far undertaken under the auspices of the United Nations. According to Article 6, public participation is guaranteed and required in regards to all decisions on whether to permit activities which may have a significant impact on the environment. The public shall be informed about the proposed activity 'early in the decision-making procedure and in an adequate, timely and effective manner'.[109] The public participation procedures shall include reasonable time, allowing the public 'to prepare and participate effectively during the environmental decision-making'.[110] The public must have access to all relevant information on the proposed activities including, *inter alia*, a description of environmental impacts, measures to prevent or mitigate the effects, a non-technical summary of documents and main alternatives.[111] Public participation can be in the form of written or oral comments[112] and the outcomes shall be taken into account.[113] All decisions shall be made public, along with the reasons and considerations on which the decision is based. In addition to providing for public participation regarding decisions on specific projects, the Aarhus Convention promotes public participation in the preparation of environmental plans, programmes, policies[114] and regulations.[115]

---

104 UNFCCC, Arts 6(a), 6(a)(ii).
105 Ibid, Arts 6(a), 6(a)(ii)–(iii).
106 *Convention on Environmental Impact Assessment in a Transboundary Context*, opened for signature 25 February 1991, 1989 UNTS 309 (entered into force 10 September 1997) ('Espoo Convention').
107 Ibid., Art. 2(6).
108 *Convention on Access to Information, Public Participation in Decision-Making and Access to Justice in Environmental Matters*, opened for signature 25 June 1998, 2161 UNTS 447 (entered into force 30 October 2001) ('Aarhus Convention'). Online. Available HTTP: <http://www.unece.org/env/pp/documents/cep43e.pdf> (accessed 7 July 2011).
109 Ibid., Art. 6(2).
110 Ibid., Art. 6(3).
111 Ibid., Art. 6(6).
112 Ibid., Art. 6(7).
113 Ibid., Art. 6(8).
114 Ibid., Art. 7.
115 Ibid., Art. 8.

Public participation is particularly important in environmental impact assessment (EIA) procedures. Environmental impact assessment in a transboundary context[116] can evaluate and take into account environmental degradation or impacts of an activity of a country of origin and provide procedural rights of access to information and public participation in the decision-making process to those affected, including residents of the country of origin and the affected country. Public participation in EIA procedures (including in the transboundary context) has become a recognised norm and practice of civilised nations of the world. Indeed this is supported by the recent *Pulp Mills on the River Uruguay* ICJ decision, in which it was held that the requirement to prepare environmental impact assessments has become part of general international law.[117]

Furthermore, the UN High Commissioner for Human Rights has stressed the role that public participation should play:

> [Public] participation in decision-making is of key importance in efforts to tackle climate change . . . . The right to participation in decision-making is implied in Article 25 of the International Covenant on Civil and Political Rights which guarantees the right to 'take part in the conduct of public affairs'.[118]

Conclusion

So far scientific progress, while contributing to the well-being and comfort of humankind, has also had a significant, negative effect on the global environment. The consequences of this have recently drawn the attention of developed and developing nations and the world has united in its effort to face the challenge of global environmental degradation including climate change.

In checking the progress of environmental degradation, a significant contribution has been made through the development of a framework of cooperation based on legal principles, such as sustainable development, intergenerational equity, prevention of harm, common but differentiated responsibility, the precautionary principle, the polluter pays principle and access to information and public participation in environmental decision-making (good governance). The above-cited principles developed by jurists, environmentalists and policy-makers, if followed by all nations, are a great step forward in mitigating the environmental crisis. Many states and international organisations have already accepted these principles in broad outline; what is now needed is consensus that the principles have the force of law.

116 Joint UNEP-OHCHR Expert Seminar on Human Rights and the Environment, op. cit.
117 *Case Concerning Pulp Mills on the River Uruguay (Argentina v Uruguay)* ICJ Reports 2010, para. 204.
118 Report of the Office of the United Nations High Commissioner for Human Rights on the relationship between climate change and human rights (2009), UN Doc A/HRC/10/61, para. 79. Online. Available HTTP: <http://www.ohchr.org/Documents/Press/AnalyticalStudy.pdf> (accessed 7 July 2011).

4

The international environmental law-making process

Kamrul Hossain

Although apparently identical to that of the traditional international law-making process, international environmental law is heavily influenced by diverse actors, formal and informal sources of law and a unique negotiation process. This chapter presents a concise overview of these fundamental aspects. In particular it addresses the involvement of multiple actors in the process of negotiation, including states, international organisations, non-governmental organisations, the scientific community and individuals as well as indigenous peoples. The framework type treaty – commonly used in international environmental law – is another progressive development which this chapter also explores along with the broader range of international environmental law sources.

Introduction

International environmental law (IEL), as part of general international law, inherits the traditional law-making process including a set of formal sources embodied in the Statute of the International Court of Justice.[1] Article 38(1) of the Statute suggests that the Court, while performing its function, shall apply international conventions, international customs, general principles of law and, as a subsidiary means, judicial decisions and the teachings of the most highly qualified publicists of various nations. While scholars mostly consider treaties to be the pre-eminent method of law-making, in practice, the international environmental law-making process accepts other broader schemes, such as normative principles, programmes of action, recommendations and policy guidelines etc. Indeed, through the negotiation of treaties, states develop detailed substantive rules and international supervisory machinery to address particular environmental problems.[2] International environmental law nevertheless involves both formal and informal sources, which offer a dynamic approach to the legislative

---

1 *Statute of the International Court of Justice*, adopted in 1920, which later was attached to the Charter of the United Nations, adopted in 1945. The text of the Statute is online. Available HTTP: <http://www.icj-cij.org/documents/index.php?p1=4&p2=2&p3=0> (accessed 10 October 2011).
2 D. Bodansky, 'Customary (And Not So Customary) International Environmental Law', *Indiana Journal of Global Legal Studies* 3(1), 1995, p. 106.

process. Therefore, while the process is identical to that of general international law, there are specific characteristics applied to law-making in IEL.

In addition to states, a large number of international organisations, national and international non-governmental organisations (NGOs), and various non–state actors, including financial institutions, companies and stakeholders, local communities and individuals take part in the process. However, in the end, it is the state that consents to be bound by the rules of international law. In this sense, the classical understanding of international law-making, as developed in case law jurisprudence, and embodied in the famous *Lotus* case in 1927, is still valid. The Permanent Court of International Justice (PCIJ) stated that international law governs relations between independent states. The rules of law impose binding obligations upon states. They, therefore, emanate from states' free will, as expressed in conventions or in their usage, which is generally accepted as expressing principles of law.[3] While IEL is based on the same foundation, the inclusion of diverse actors, the uniqueness of the negotiation process and the adoption of both formal and informal sources make the law-making process special.

This chapter focuses on the process of law-making in IEL, a process that includes a diverse range of both actors and sources. While both formal and informal sources are crucial in law-making, it is important to note how the general negotiation process in IEL takes place. To the extent that law-making is an action contingent on the actors behind the action, it is important to widen an understanding of the players and their conduct in the negotiating process. Subsequently, the nature of the sources of IEL requires some attention, in particular hard and soft law. Therefore, the sources of IEL include binding conventions, on the one hand, and other more liberal guiding principles on the other. Both eventually contribute to the process of law-making, as well as to an understanding of the content of specific rules. Together, they ultimately provide an effective law-making process in IEL.

IEL negotiation process

The negotiation of a particular issue through bilateral or multilateral mechanisms requires firstly sufficient interest by the states concerned. Thereafter, other immediate issues include the choice of a negotiating forum and the adoption of a negotiation mandate.[4] Despite the absence of a defined procedure on how to negotiate a Multilateral Environmental Agreement (MEA), the negotiation process for IEL adopts a relatively novel and effective process by including numerous non-traditional actors and diverse procedures. The law-making process involves not only states, but also various other actors, as well as structures, strategies and outcomes.[5] The whole procedure has been developed through state practice over the last few decades.

The negotiation process begins with a common agenda requiring multilateral legislative action. However, prior to initiating such legislative action, states are usually required to follow an internal governmental process as national interests are often contested and

---

3 *Lotus Case*, PCIJ (1927) Ser. A. No. 10.
4 D. Bodansky, *The Art and Craft of International Environmental Law*, Cambridge, MA: Harvard University Press, 2011, p. 167.
5 B.I. Spector, 'International Environmental Negotiation: Insights for Practice', *The Processes of International Negotiation Project*, Executive Report (ER–21), 1992. Online. Available HTTP: <http://www.iiasa.ac.at/Admin/PUB/Documents/ER–92–021.pdf> (accessed 6 December 2011).

contingent on complex interactions between sub-state actors.[6] This process involves various governmental agencies, including departments and ministries, as well as local communities, who may have an interest in the issue at stake. At times, this process also includes legislatures by a means of parliamentary hearings. Such a hearing facilitates the accommodation of scientific theories and explores conflicting economic and social interests. The process, in its entirety, essentially provides a coordinated approach toward a uniform national policy. Absence of such a uniform position complicates the negotiation process at the intergovernmental level. An example of such a non-coordinated national position has been seen during the post-Kyoto climate change negotiations, where Russia's position varied due to conflicting views held by multiple agencies simultaneously acting as Russia's delegations.[7]

The negotiation of IEL generally takes place at a forum established by the interested parties. In most cases, the United Nations General Assembly (UNGA), its subsidiary bodies, as well as other bodies associated with it, such as the United Nations Environment Programme (UNEP) and the United Nations Economic Commission for Europe (UNECE), are chosen as negotiating platforms. Often, an international organisation convenes a conference to initiate negotiations. However, there might be other fora as well. States may establish an informal ad hoc group of experts associated with a formal structure. The UN Framework Convention on Climate Change (UNFCCC), for example, was negotiated in a specially established body called the 'Intergovernmental Negotiating Committee'. In some cases, a particular government may develop a draft text for negotiation. In other cases, the International Law Commission (ILC) may first draft certain treaties. Nevertheless, in all cases the subsequent negotiation process is performed at an intergovernmental level. In some cases a regional intergovernmental organisation (IGO) facilitates negotiations culminating in the adoption of a treaty. The Arctic Council initiative, for example, has recently facilitated the adoption of the Arctic Search and Rescue Agreement in 2011 by acting as a negotiating forum.[8] In order to negotiate a subsequent instrument, a body under the existing treaty regime may also serve as a forum for negotiation. For example, pursuant to Article 19(3) of the Convention on Biological Diversity (CBD), the Conference of the Parties (COP), by decision II/5, established an Open-ended Ad Hoc Working Group on Biosafety to develop a draft protocol, which later resulted in an agreement on the text and subsequent adoption of the Cartagena Protocol on Biosafety.[9] In the negotiation process another important issue is the mandate, which needs to be established before the start of real negotiations. Typically a negotiation mandate includes the scope of the negotiation, the legal status of the intended outcome, the types of provisions to be included, the target date for completion and rules regarding decision-making and participation.[10]

6 Bodansky, *Art and Craft*, op. cit., p. 112.

7 Ibid., pp. 115–16.

8 At the Seventh Ministerial Meeting of the Arctic Council held in Nuuk, Greenland in May 2011, the first legally binding agreement – the Search and Rescue Agreement (SRA) – was adopted. Online. Available HTTP: <http://www.arctic-council.org/index.php/en/about/documents/category/5-declarations> (accessed 25 April 2012).

9 The text of the Cartagena Protocol (2000) is online. Available HTTP: <http://www.cbd.int/doc/legal/cartagena-protocol-en.pdf> (accessed 4 December 2011).

10 Bodansky, *Art and Craft*, op. cit., p. 168. In the drafting for the Kyoto Protocol, for example, developing countries succeeded in including a provision that expressly excluded them from any new commitments while on the other hand the developed countries proved more successful in negotiating the mandate for the post-Kyoto climate change negotiations.

While states continue to have the greatest power, both hard and soft, of any international actors,[11] non-state actors increasingly contribute to treaty regimes. The scientific community, for example, plays a significant role in IEL. Scientists establish a bridge between government agencies and policy-makers at both the national and international level. International scientific assessments are essential in order to draw basic parameters and narrow the range of uncertainty. Scientists play a significant role in the negotiation process by transcending the narrow political and commercial interests of sovereign states. The Vienna Convention on the Protection of the Ozone Layer and the Protocol attached to it are examples where scientists collaborated with government officials in the negotiation process, thus assuming responsibility for the implication of their findings for policy options.[12] Other global, regional and scientific institutions also contribute to the process of negotiation. In the ozone treaty negotiations, for example, UNEP, the World Meteorological Organization (WMO) and the International Council of Scientific Unions (ICSU) were engaged.[13]

International institutions and their secretariats provide objective information needed to clarify issues, summarise proceedings and undertake the systematic comparison of key elements in national position papers. These activities may help negotiating parties find common ground. Often, the secretariat performs the role of a mediator.[14] The environment is the only area where NGOs make significant contributions.[15] Today, some national delegations at intergovernmental negotiations contain NGO representatives. Considering the notable influence on outcomes, some smaller states even rely on NGOs to represent them.[16] NGOs can facilitate support for negotiations and contribute to structuring the agenda by helping authorities set priorities. On the ground, they create public awareness and push the community to move forward with an environmental agenda, they lobby state decision-makers to affect domestic and foreign policies related to the environment, they coordinate boycotts in efforts to alter corporate practices harmful to nature and they help monitor and implement international agreements.[17] At times, however, it has been argued that NGOs create substantial uncertainty in upsetting the negotiation process by criticising states for taking the wrong position. Yet, the inclusion of NGOs in the negotiation process is seen as representing a wider trend towards viewing international society in broader terms than a community of states alone.[18]

In general, public opinion also increasingly influences the IEL negotiation process. It is ultimately individuals whose concerns are the subject of legislation. However, individuals themselves are ill-equipped with essential scientific knowledge unless it is properly communicated to them. In this respect, public lecture events, academic discourse, press conferences, NGO-initiated workshops and media dissemination play a major role in raising individual consciousness. Individuals' voices can contribute to a community's influence on the negotiation process via both direct and indirect participation.[19] The Aarhus

---

11 Ibid., p. 110.
12 Spector, op. cit.
13 Negotiating Multilateral Environmental Agreement, op. cit.
14 Ibid.
15 Spector, op. cit.
16 Negotiating Multilateral Environmental Agreement, op. cit.
17 M.M. Betsill and E. Corell, 'NGO Influence in International Environmental Negotiations: A Framework for Analysis', *Global Environmental Politics* 1, 2001, 4, p. 67. See also Bodansky, *Art and Craft*, op. cit., p. 125.
18 Negotiating Multilateral Environmental Agreement, op. cit.
19 Ibid.

Convention,[20] for example, ensures public participation by providing citizens with access to environmental information, the possibility of participating in decision-making, as well as access to justice. It offers transparency in environmental regulation and creates trustworthy relations amongst civil society, government and the general public at large. Indigenous peoples' participation as a community, for example, is an important element of the IEL negotiation process. While in most cases negotiations rely heavily on complex, yet uncertain, scientific and technical information, clear interdependence and joint collaboration between actors are crucial in all aspects of the IEL-making process. Broad participation facilitates the integration of science, technology, strategy and diplomacy, which assists in making international environmental instruments an effective form of regulation.

The relationship between developed and developing countries is also important in the law-making process. Developed countries are thought to be in an advantageous position due to their easy access to a wide range of information and resources. On the other hand, developing countries are often dependent on these developed countries. In the negotiation process of the Basel Convention, for example, African countries were particularly concerned with their capacity, in terms of resources, to implement the potential treaty. This has, arguably, led to the situation where none of the African countries has signed the 'Final Act' of the Convention. It is important to note that such non-capacity on the part of the weaker states may often upset the negotiation process as developing states may be unwilling to participate in the negotiation due to their lack of resources to implement the potential treaty at the end. This issue has been recognised in IEL.[21] Consequently, in many negotiation processes, a compromise is reached in terms of differentiated responsibilities for actions to achieve a common goal. The promotion of this idea was initially embodied in the Rio Declaration.[22]

Indigenous peoples in the negotiation process

The role of indigenous peoples in the development of international environmental law has been significant in recent decades. This is primarily due to their profound and strong connection to nature and their knowledge in regard to nature conservation and biodiversity management. Such knowledge has been recognised in the CBD.[23] Today, indigenous peoples are actively involved in international bodies, such as the United Nations,[24] the Organization of

---

20 *Convention on Access to Information, Public Participation in Decision Making and Access to Justice in Environmental Matters*, opened for signature 25 June 1998, 38 ILM 517 (entered into force on 30 October 2001). Online. Available HTTP: <http://www.unece.org/fileadmin/DAM/env/pp/documents/cep43e.pdf> (accessed 30 November 2011).

21 Negotiating Multilateral Environmental Agreement, op. cit.

22 *Rio Declaration on Environment and Development* (1992), 31 ILM 874, Principle 7 states that:

> States shall cooperate in a spirit of global partnership to conserve, protect and restore the health and integrity of the Earth's ecosystem. In view of the different contributions to global environmental degradation, States have common but differentiated responsibilities.

Text online. Available HTTP: <http://www.unep.org/Documents.Multilingual/Default.asp?documentid=78&articleid=1163> (accessed 8 December 2011).

23 *Convention on Biological Diversity*, opened for signature 5 June 1992, 31 ILM 818 (entered into force 29 December 1993) ('CBD') Article 8(j). Text online. Available HTTP: <http://www.cbd.int/traditional/> (accessed 22 November 2011).

24 UN Permanent Forum on Indigenous Issues. Online. Available HTTP: <http://www.un.org/esa/socdev/unpfii/> (accessed 22 November 2011). An advisory body established within the framework of the UN System that reports to the UN Economic and Social Council.

American States (OAS)[25] and the Arctic Council.[26] In addition to institutional engagements, indigenous peoples have gained important recognition in numerous international instruments.[27] Their participatory role in decision-making, especially in the making of IEL, has increasingly been realised in those instruments.[28] As a result, they have gradually achieved a large measure of legal personality as distinct societies with collective rights, as well as a separate role in national and international decision-making.[29] While this development does not suggest any concrete legal status for indigenous peoples as legal persons in international law, their gradual and increasingly participatory role, at least in matters that concern them, arguably provides them with a limited legal personality. As their participation highlights a multi-layered approach to international law-making via both informal avenues of knowledge production and norm-generation, as well as formal top-down structures engaged in decision-making,[30] indigenous peoples profoundly affect the law-making process in regards to nature, nature conservation, and in matters concerning them.

Nature of regulations

Today, international law is elaborated through a variety of instruments to an impressive degree.[31] These instruments include formal sources of law of legally binding character, as well as other informal sources that are not strictly enforceable, but ethically, morally or politically binding in character. In the legal literature these forms are respectively termed 'hard law' and 'soft law'. While IEL acknowledges both forms of regulation, it is noteworthy that there are an emerging number of soft-law instruments used in the law-making process.

Hard law

Hard law refers to regulations that establish legally binding obligations and delegate authority for their interpretation and implementation.[32] Hard law is conceived as the classical form of international law where treaties, conventions and other instruments expressive of consent are freely given by states with the intention of being legally binding upon them. Consequently,

---

25 Organization of American States. Online. Available HTTP: <http://www.oas.org/dil/indigenous_peoples.htm> (accessed 22 November 2011).
26 Arctic Council. Online. Available HTTP: <http://www.arctic-council.org/index.php/en/> (accessed 22 November 2011). In the Arctic Council, for example, the indigenous peoples are given a 'permanent participant' status by means of which they participate both in dialogues and in discussions on matters that affect them.
27 In addition to the CBD, the UN Declaration on the Rights of the Indigenous Peoples, adopted in 2007, is of significant importance.
28 ILO Convention No. 169 of 1989, Art. 6; the Human Rights Committee (treaty monitoring body within the framework of the ICCPR); and the instruments endorsed in the Rio Summit etc. suggest the greater participatory role of the indigenous peoples. Many of these instruments also highlighted the free and prior informed consent of the indigenous peoples in matters that affect them.
29 L.R. Barsh, 'Indigenous Peoples in the 1990s: From Object to Subject of International Law', *Harvard Human Rights Journal* 33, 1994, reprinted in L. Watters (ed.) *Indigenous Peoples, the Environment and Law*, Durham, NC: Carolina Academic Press, 2004, 15–42, p. 23.
30 L.A. Miranda, 'Indigenous Peoples as International Lawmakers', *University of Pennsylvania Journal of International Law* 32(1), 2010, p. 217.
31 K.W. Abbott and D. Snidal, 'Hard and Soft Law in International Governance', *International Organization* 54(3), 2000, p. 421.
32 Ibid., p. 421.

hard law refers to legally binding laws. In international law, hard law includes both international agreements and customary law. Hard law strengthens the credibility of the commitments of states and expands their available political strategies accordingly. Hard law restricts states' behaviour and limits their sovereignty.[33]

Soft law

Soft laws are regulations that have emerged from policy dialogues, including resolutions adopted in international conferences and in other relevant fora. In other words, anything 'lawlike', but not binding in the formal sense, is described as soft law. It may, for instance, be in the form of a written document signed by states, but which has, for some reason, not satisfied the requirements of a treaty. In addition, the informal exchange of promises through diplomatic correspondence, votes in international organisations and the decisions of some international tribunals are also considered to be soft-law instruments. Despite the debate on whether soft law qualifies as law, in the case of environmental regulation it plays a significant role. Legal scholars who argue that 'soft law [is] not a law at all' find it difficult to acknowledge that it may also not simply be regarded as politics.[34] According to Higgins, the adoption of binding decisions is not the only way in which law develops. Legal consequences may also result from acts which are not formally binding.[35] Soft law is best understood as a continuum, or spectrum, running between fully binding treaties and political positions that can be changed at will.[36] It has, however, a legal effect as it shapes states' understanding of what constitutes compliant behaviour with the underlying binding rule.[37] The recommendatory nature of soft law includes language as well as instruments: for example, 'should' instead of 'shall'. Since states apply soft law, it has an important influence on international life. This is particularly the case as it expresses a consensus of norms, which should guide a state's behaviour. Such an acceptance and regular compliance with non-obligatory rules can lead to the creation of customary law, which may then become obligatory.

A consideration of the precautionary principle, for example, raises the question whether it has become an 'emerging customary' norm.[38] This discussion has matured in the event of the 1998 World Trade Organization (WTO) *Hormones in Beef* dispute.[39] While the European Union (EU) (the then European Commission) held that the precautionary principle had

---

33 Ibid., p. 422.

34 See e.g. P. Weil, 'Toward Relative Normativity in International Law', *American Journal of International Law* 77, 1983, pp. 413, 414–17.

35 R. Higgins, *Problems and Process: International Law and How We Use It*, New York: Oxford University Press, 1995, p. 25.

36 A.T. Guzman and T.L. Meyer, *Explaining Soft Law*, American Society of International Law. Online. Available HTTP: <http://www.asil.org/files/guzman.pdf> (accessed 20 November 2011).

37 Ibid.

38 For detailed discussion on this matter see O. McIntyre and T. Mosedale, 'The Precautionary Principle as a Norm of Customary International Law', *Journal of Environmental Law*, 1997, p. 221; D. Freestone, 'The Precautionary Principle', in R. Churchill and D. Freestone (eds) *International Law and Global Climate Change*, London: Graham and Trotman, 1991; D. Freestone and E. Hey, 'Origins and Development of the Precautionary Principle', in D. Freestone and E. Hey (eds) *The Precautionary Principle and International Law: The Challenge of Implementation*, The Hague: Kluwer Law International, 1996, p. 3.

39 *EC Measures Concerning Meat and Meat Products* (the *Hormones Case*), WTO Doc. WT/DS48/AB/R (6 January 1998).

become a fully fledged principle of international law, both the US and Canada denied that it was a principle of international law due to its lack of consistent formulation. Instead, they regarded precaution as an approach.[40] While customary rules ultimately emerge out of a combination of behaviour and belief, the precautionary principle arguably carries ambiguity in terms of both its content and consistency.[41] The discussion, however, suggests that a concrete soft-law norm may, over time, become a consistent state practice and may thereby be characterised as a customary norm in international law.

The structure of IEL

As discussed, law-making in IEL involves various sources, including hard- and soft-law instruments, from strictly legally binding agreements to more loosely adopted documents and resolutions by international organisations. Although it is essentially a treaty that provides a hard source for international environmental law as with any other branch of international law, it increasingly acknowledges other informal sources, which are discussed below.

Treaties

Treaties refer to agreements concluded primarily between states. Such agreements may also occur between states and international organisations, as well as between various international organisations. In international law, the two Vienna Conventions regulate treaties.[42] Treaties are concluded in written form and governed by international law. A treaty can be composed of one single instrument or several related instruments. As there is no precise designation required for a treaty, it may be called one of many names including treaty, convention, covenant, agreement, protocol or exchange of letters.[43] Its only decisive factor is the intent of the parties in regards to the document's binding nature. An agreement may be regarded as a treaty when it clearly intends to establish international legal rights and obligations between the parties. Such an objective is often clear in its characteristics and the circumstances under which it was adopted.[44] Generally, a typical treaty consists of a preamble, an operative part and annexes. The preamble is declaratory, and provides normative principles, whereas the operative part refers to obligatory actions on the part of the parties to the treaty. A treaty typically includes the following in its operative part: specific objectives, precise obligations, implementation rules, regular conference of the parties, functioning of the bodies within the treaty framework, creation of an international secretariat, reservation provisions, provisions

40 See, for more detailed discussion on the Precautionary Principle, M. Fitzmaurice, *Contemporary Issues in International Environmental Law*, Cheltenham: Edward Elgar, 2009, pp. 22–6.

41 J. Ellis and A. FitzGerald, 'The Precautionary Principle in International Law: Lessons from Fuller's Internal Morality', *McGill Law Journal* 49, 2004, pp. 787–8.

42 *Vienna Convention on the Law of Treaties*, 23 May 1969, 1155 UNTS 331 (entered into force 27 January 1980) (VCLT). Text online. Available HTTP: <http://untreaty.un.org/ilc/texts/instruments/english/conventions/1_1_1969.pdf> (accessed 27 November 2011); *Vienna Convention on the Law of Treaties between States and International Organizations or between International Organizations*, 21 March 1986, 25 ILM 543 (not yet entered into force). Text online. Available HTTP: <http://untreaty.un.org/ilc/texts/instruments/english/conventions/1_2_1986.pdf> (accessed 27 November 2011).

43 VCLT, op. cit., Art. 2.

44 P. Sands, *Principles of International Environmental Law*, 2nd edition, Cambridge: Cambridge University Press, 2003, p. 126.

related to entry into force, adhesion to the treaty, how to make amendments, and so on. Technical details are normally annexed to the treaty. They generally include lists of issue areas or activities in which the treaty applies. The Convention on International Trade in Endangered Species of Wild Fauna and Flora (CITES),[45] for example, provides a number of appendices listing endangered species, as well as those that are not yet endangered, but will be so if parties to the Convention do not take any proactive measures.

While the treaty does not legally bind non-contracting countries, it may, however, affect them.[46] At the same time, treaties that have not yet come into force may also have certain legal consequences. Under the 1969 Vienna Convention on the Law of Treaties (VCLT), signatory states must refrain from acts that would defeat the objectives and purposes of the treaty that they have signed (unless they have indicated their intent not to become party to the agreement) even though the treaty has not entered into force.[47] The US, for example, has noted that it intends not to become a party to the Kyoto Protocol after it signed the UNFCCC. A treaty which has not yet entered into force may contribute to the development of customary international law or reflect, in clearer terms, pre-existing customary international law.[48]

Today it is estimated that there are more than 700 MEAs.[49] Most MEAs were concluded over the past three decades. After the 1992 Rio Conference, almost all treaties began to include more or less developed principles concerning environmental protection. Some of these treaties promote global norms regulating the entire international community. Important international conventions, with a worldwide scope, include, for example, the United Nations Convention on the Law of the Sea (UNCLOS) adopted in 1982 and the CBD adopted in 1992. The UNCLOS provides a holistic approach to oceans governance and dedicates a chapter to the protection of the marine environment. There are also some other chapters that refer to environmental concerns. In addition, IEL includes both sectoral and regional regulations. The Ramsar Convention on Wetlands, for example, pursues the goal of conservation and wise use of all wetlands. An important regional convention adopted by the UNECE is, for example, the 1991 Espoo Convention on Environmental Impact Assessment in a Transboundary Context.[50]

45 *Convention on International Trade in Endangered Species of Wild Fauna and Flora*, opened for signature 3 March 1973, 12 ILM 1088 (entered into force 1 July 1975) (CITES). Text online. Available HTTP: <http://www.fws.gov/le/pdffiles/CITES_Treaty.pdf> (accessed 27 November 2011).
46 See, e.g., *Bamako Convention on the Ban of the Import to Africa and the Control of Transboundary Movement and Management of Hazardous Wastes within Africa*, opened for signature 30 January 1991, 30 ILM 773 (entry into force 22 April 1998), Art. 14. Text online. Available HTTP: <http://www.cetim.ch/en/documents/conv-bamako-ang.pdf> (accessed 27 November 2011). The Article states that:

> all Parties shall take appropriate legal, administrative and other measures within the area under their jurisdiction to prohibit the import of all hazardous wastes, for any reason, into Africa from non-Contracting Parties,

which produces direct effects for the non-contracting states.
47 VCLT, op. cit., Art. 18.
48 Sands, op. cit., p. 134.
49 UNEP, *Manual on Compliance with and Enforcement of Multilateral Environmental Agreements*, 2006, p. 29.
50 *Convention on Environmental Impact Assessment in a Transboundary Context*, opened for signature 25 February 1991, 1989 UNTS 309 (entered into force 10 September 1997) ('Espoo Convention').

The framework treaty

The framework type treaty is a relatively recent development. While it is mostly used in IEL, it is not, however, limited to this area.[51] The general understanding is that it is a legally binding agreement establishing general guidelines and principles for international governance on a particular issue. Such a treaty generally carries basic objectives and obligations for contracting parties. In addition, a framework treaty also establishes institutions and procedures for decision-making and dispute settlements. Within the umbrella of such a treaty, more specific and detailed regulations are invoked in separate instruments, which are then attached to the agreement. These instruments are typically called protocols. Hence, protocols are built upon the parent agreement and provide specific commitments and institutional arrangements while the parent agreement merely provides general obligations. Whereas the parent agreement is broad and general, a protocol is specific and detailed. Together, they attempt to address an issue of international law in an effective manner.[52] At times, protocols are envisaged from the beginning and are even negotiated parallel to the framework convention. In other cases, the framework merely provides the procedure for the adoption of specific rules via protocols.[53] There are a number of examples of framework agreements available in IEL.[54] The one that is most repeatedly used is the UNFCCC and its Kyoto Protocol. Although both the parent agreement and attached protocols are binding upon the contracting parties they are, by nature, separate agreements. A party to the parent agreement may not necessarily be a party to the attached protocols. The US, for example, is a party to the UNFCCC, but has not ratified the Kyoto Protocol. On the other hand, a non-contracting party to the framework treaty cannot be a party to the protocols. This precondition guarantees that states are bound by the guiding principles of the framework when interpreting and implementing the rights and obligations under the protocol.[55]

As environmental regimes are not static, they require a remarkable dynamism.[56] The framework convention normally addresses more complex problems,[57] for which general

---

51 B. Janusz, 'The Framework Convention for the Protection of the Marine Environment of the Caspian Sea', *Chinese Journal of International Law* 4(1), 2005, pp. 257–70; *Framework Convention Concept*, Economic Commission for Europe, the Committee on Housing and Land Management, seventy-second session, Geneva 3–4 October 2011. Online. Available HTTP: <http://www.unece. org/fileadmin/DAM/hlm/sessions/docs2011/informal.notice.5.pdf> (accessed 20 November 2011); see also N. Matz-Lück, 'Framework Conventions as a Regulatory Tool', *Goettingen Journal of International Law* 1(3), 2009, pp. 440, 448. The author states that regulation of international issues by framework conventions is a relatively recent regulatory technique in international law and has mainly been employed in the field of international environmental law.
52 Ibid., Matz-Lück, p. 446.
53 Ibid., p. 452.
54 Among others, the 1985 *Vienna Convention for the Protection of Ozone Layer* and the attached *Montreal Protocol on Substances That Deplete the Ozone Layer* adopted two years later, the 1992 *Convention on Biological Diversity* and the attached *Cartagena Protocol on Bio-safety* adopted in 2000, the 2010 *Nagoya Protocol*, the 2003 the *World Health Organization Framework Convention on Tobacco Control* (FCTC) etc. are mentionable.
55 Matz-Lück, op. cit., p. 451; see also the *Vienna Convention for the Protection of Ozone Layer*, Art. 16 (1); CBD, op. cit., Art. 32; *World Health Organisation Framework Convention on Tobacco Control*, Art. 33(4). The Vienna Convention, for example, states that state or a regional economic integration organisation may not become a party to a protocol unless it is, or becomes at the same time, a party to the Convention.
56 Bodansky, *Art and Craft*, op. cit., p. 183.
57 Janusz, op. cit., p. 257.

guiding principles firstly need to be established before penetrating into details regarding specific obligations. Once a coherent overarching agreement has been concluded with the general broader obligation, a consensus may more easily be achieved in the adoption of details and specific obligations.[58] The aim is to begin with relatively modest commitments in order to encourage participation and then, over time, to broaden the scope of the commitments via subsequent regulations. The features of the framework convention are linked to the standard rules and norms of current international law, applicable to the agreements concluded both at the international as well as at the regional level.[59] The negotiation, adoption, modification, interpretation and termination processes are identical to that of other treaties. Both the framework convention and protocol instruments are legally binding and they are ratified by national parliaments, which then follow the same domestic procedure of adopting and implementing legislation.[60] A framework treaty allows for the possibility of further regulations in response to the demand for global environmental protection, as a whole, on certain priority areas, in a more flexible and timely manner.[61] The process of such regulation makes a treaty a 'living instrument'. Furthermore, such a treaty is built upon a permanent structure that allows, for example, for the establishment and support of working groups for the preparation of protocols, and the supervision of the effectiveness of the regime.[62] In order to give a treaty a life adaptable to new situations, the framework treaty establishes organs, such as a plenary body for decision-making, which is called the Conference of the Parties (COP) or the Meeting of the Parties (MOP), a secretariat for handling administrative matters and a body for scientific advice.[63]

The COP sets priorities and reviews the implementation of the convention based on reports submitted by governments, considers new information given by governments, NGOs and individuals to make recommendations to the parties on implementation, makes decisions necessary to promote effective implementation, revises the treaty if necessary and acts as a forum for discussion on matters of importance.[64] Some MEAs contain provisions authorising the COPs to consider additional action within the framework of the treaty and to exercise such other functions required for the fulfilment of the objective of the treaty.[65] Through such specific powers, the COPs are generally provided with authority, at the internal level,

---

58 UNECE, *Framework Convention Concept*, op. cit.
59 Janusz, op. cit., p. 258.
60 UNECE, *Framework Convention Concept*, op. cit.
61 P. Birnie, A. Boyle and C. Redgwell, *International Law and the Environment*, Oxford: Oxford University Press, 2009, p. 14.
62 Matz-Lück, op. cit., p. 444.
63 Ibid.
64 UNEP, GEO–2000, 'Chapter Three: Policy Responses – Global and Regional Synthesis – MEAs and Non-binding Instruments'. Online. Available HTTP: <http://www.grida.no/geo2000/english/0136.htm> (accessed 21 October 2011).
65 See e.g. *Convention on the Preservation of Marine Pollution by Dumping of Wastes and Other Matter*, opened for signature 29 December 1972, 26 UST 2403, 1046 UNTS 120 (entered into force 15 July 1977) ('London Convention') Art. XIV (4)(f); *United Nations Framework Convention on Climate Change*, opened for signature 4 June 1992, 1771 UNTS 107 (entered into force 21 March 1994) ('UNFCCC') Art. 7(2)(m). Online. Available HTTP: <www.unfccc.de> (accessed 12 November 2011). See also Bodansky, *Art and Craft*, op. cit., p. 119, where the COP's authority is discussed. According to the author, decision-making authority and procedures of COPs vary from agreement to agreement. Some COPs have limited authority to adopt new environmental rules that bind all the treaty parties unless there are any specific objections.

corresponding to that found in the constitutions of IGOs.[66] The management of COPs is normally linked to the treaty secretariat, which is responsible for the day-to-day operation of the treaty. Together, they contribute to the development of substantive norm-making in IEL with which state parties are required to comply. They help ensure that the treaty is not static, but a robust and ongoing process of law-making, normative discussion and flexibility.[67]

Customs

Custom consists of two elements: general state practice as a material component and state acceptance with the conviction that such practice is applied believing that it constitutes existing law. This latter element is referred to as the psychological component, which means that states apply such general practice with a sense of legal obligation. In international law, it is termed *opinio juris*. Customary law is, therefore, a combination of state practice and *opinio juris*. Even though state practice is 'notoriously difficult to prove',[68] it is commonly understood that it must be general, consistent, uniform and repeated. While the practice must be extensive, it is not required to be long-standing. Nor is there any requirement for the participation of all states across the globe or in a particular region. However, practice must include states particularly affected by the purported custom.[69]

In IEL, customary law includes those norms that are of a substantive nature as well as principles that inform and guide decision-making. Such substantive rules are reflected in many treaties. Principle 21 of the Stockholm Declaration[70] and Principle 2 of the Rio Declaration,[71] for example, reiterate the 'no harm' doctrine, which has been developed as a classic and fundamental customary norm in IEL. The doctrine restricts absolute territorial sovereignty, which is replaced by a responsibility not to cause harm to another state by an action taken within one's own territory. The doctrine is now widely recognised as an international legal rule, whereby a state has the responsibility to prevent, reduce and control the risk of environmental harm to other states. The emergence of the norm was first found in early nineteenth-century international law jurisprudence, which was a major step back from the so-called 'Harmon Doctrine' – the absolute territorial sovereignty

66 L.K. Camenzuli, 'The Development of International Environmental Law at the Multilateral Environmental Agreements' Conference of the Parties and its Validity'. Online. Available HTTP: <http://cmsdata.iucn.org/downloads/cel10_camenzuli.pdf> (accessed 23 November 2011).
67 M. Drumbl, 'Actors and Law-making in International Environmental Law', *Research Handbook of International Environmental Law*, Cheltenham: Edward Elgar, 2011.
68 Sands, op. cit., p. 144.
69 Drumbl, op. cit.
70 *Stockholm Declaration on the Human Environment* (1972), 11 ILM 1416 ('Stockholm Declaration'), Principle 21: States have, in accordance with the Charter of the United Nations and the principles of international law, the sovereign right to exploit their own resources pursuant to their own environmental policies, and the responsibility to ensure that activities within their jurisdiction or control do not cause damage to the environment of other States or of areas beyond the limits of national jurisdiction. Text online. Available HTTP: <http://www.unep.org/Documents.Multilingual/Default.asp?documentid=97&articleid=1503> (accessed 23 November 2011).
71 Rio Declaration, Principle 2, op. cit.

doctrine.[72] The *Trail Smelter* dispute first contributed to the development of this substantive norm in international environmental law.[73] The arbitration tribunal concluded that 'no State has the right to use or permit the use of its territory in such a manner as to cause injury by fumes in or to the territory of another or the properties or persons therein'.[74] The International Court of Justice in the *Corfu Channel* case later assumed a similar approach. Although the case was not concerned with environmental issues, its relevance for IEL is significant as it confirms the initial assertion of the norm invoked in the *Trail Smelter* case. The norm is, thus, linked to general international law. The Court confirmed 'every State's obligation not to allow knowingly its territory to be used for acts contrary to the rights of other states'.[75] Consequently, the doctrine of 'no harm' is established as a generally binding norm for all states.

Today, more and more customary norms are included in treaties. The more customary norms are incorporated in treaties, the more general obligations are placed upon actors in international law. While treaty laws are only binding on contracting states, customary laws are generally binding on all states, unless they persistently object to the development of such norms. Whereas a treaty may be terminated by states, customary norms may only be amended by state practice that is accepted as law. On the other hand, a customary norm may also be amended or abrogated by treaties.[76] Nevertheless, customary law develops the understanding of substantive norms in the making of treaties, while customary rules also emerge from identical provisions of treaty law, which exist simultaneously with treaty obligations.[77] Today, such customary law includes an obligation to cooperate on environmental problems especially with respect to shared natural resources, the obligation to adopt general measures to protect the marine environment, as well as the responsibility to take measures that ensure the conservation of, and prevent the harming of, endangered species of fauna and flora.[78]

72 The Doctrine was developed in the context of shared water resources of the Rio Grande River between Mexico and the United States in 1895. While the US was the upstream country utilising most of the waters of the river for irrigation and causing low water flow down the river, Mexico suffered from loss of natural water flow in its territory. The then US Attorney General Judson Harmon came up with the doctrine of 'absolute sovereignty', which he illustrated by stating that a state is free to dispose, within its territory, of the waters of an international river in any manner it deems fit, without concern for the harm or adverse impact that such use may cause to other riparian states. However, the doctrine has largely been criticised. See M.A. Salman, 'The Helsinki Rules, the UN Watercourses Convention and the Berlin Rules: Perspectives on International Water Law', *Water Resources Development* 23(4), 2007, p. 627.

73 The dispute was about transboundary air pollution and it lasted for 13 years from 1928 to 1941 between the US and Canada, where fumes caused by the Trail Smelter located close to the US border on the Canadian side resulted in damage to the State of Washington in the US through air pollution. See, out of a huge amount of literature, e.g. M. van de Kerkhof, 'The Trail Smelter Case Re-examined: Examining the Development of National Procedural Mechanisms to Resolve a Trail Smelter Type Dispute', *Merkourios – International and European Environmental Law* 27(73), 2011, p. 69.

74 See *Trail Smelter Case (United States v Canada)*, Report of the International Arbitral Awards, the United Nations (2006), Volume III pp. 1905–1982 at 1965. Online. Available HTTP: <http://untreaty.un.org/cod/riaa/cases/vol_III/1905–1982.pdf> (accessed 22 November 2011).

75 *Corfu Channel Case*, ICJ Reports 1949, p. 22.

76 G. Tunkin, 'Is General International Law Customary Law Only?', *European Journal of International Law* 4, 1993, p. 539.

77 Sands, op. cit., p. 147.

78 Ibid., p. 148.

Other sources of law

The ICJ (International Court of Justice) also recognises general principles of international law accepted by civilised nations as sources of international law and, in addition, the judicial decisions, works and teaching of the most highly qualified publicists of various nations as subsidiary sources,[79] which the Court applies in cases brought before it. However, as mentioned above, IEL generally includes a diverse range of other sources in addition to these formal ones. The most important of these are soft-law documents on which states often rely to justify their legal rights and duties.[80] These additional sources contribute to law-making in the IEL and are briefly discussed below.

General principles of law include principles of municipal laws, which are common to a large number of national legal systems. Although the scope of these principles is unclear, a general understanding is that such principles are 'recognized by civilized nations'. While in practice these principles are occasionally relied upon, they are looked upon as directives to fill gaps in the decision-making. Often, such principles assist the Court in order to reach a conclusion in the absence of any clear legal provisions, either in treaties or in customary law. The principle of good faith, for example, is a general principle of law, which has been widely considered both in the ICJ and in other arbitral tribunals. On many occasions, the principle has touched upon international environmental issues.[81] The ICJ regarded the principle as '[o]ne of the basic principles governing the creation and performance of legal obligations'.[82] Today, many of the general principles of law frequently referred to in judicial decisions have become part of international law. Such principles include principles of equity, estoppel and due diligence, among others.

Judicial decisions and the teaching of the most highly qualified publicists do not consist of sources of international environmental law in a strict sense. However, as a means of recognising norms in the other sources they are helpful. As a matter of fact, in addition to the ICJ, various national and regional courts and other judicial bodies issue opinions of relevance to the content of international law, including IEL, which interprets legal sources.[83] In this way, judicial decisions and the work of the publicists play a role in the development of the rules of IEL.

Resolutions of international organisations[84] also create IEL. Whether they are binding or not depends on the constituent document of the organisation itself and the nature of the resolution. In most cases, however, international organisations issue non-binding resolutions, largely composed of three categories: normative recommendations, declarations of principles and programmes of action. Compared to treaties, they have several advantages: they may be adopted and changed more quickly and flexibly than treaties as they do not

79 Statute of the International Court of Justice, op. cit., Art. 38(1).
80 See e.g. P.M. Dupuy, 'Soft Law and the International Law of the Environment', *Michigan Journal of International Law* 12, 1991, pp. 420–35.
81 See e.g. *Fur Seal Arbitration* of 1893, the *Trail Smelter Case* of 1928–1941 and the *Nuclear Test Cases* of 1974.
82 See *Nuclear Tests Cases (Australia v France; New Zealand v France)*, [1974] ICJ Reports 253 at 268.
83 The WTO Dispute Settlement Panels and the Appellate Body have issued important reports, for example, in the Shrimp/Turtle, Asbestos and Hormones disputes. The Federal courts in the United States have assessed the content of international environmental law, in particular in customary international law, within the framework of civil claims brought under the Alien Tort Claims Act for violations of the 'laws of nations'. See Drumbl, op. cit., pp. 18–19.
84 See for a detailed discussion, A. Kiss, *Introduction to International Environmental Law*, 2nd edition, Geneva: United Nations Institute for Training and Research, 2005, p. 52.

require ratification, they are easier to negotiate as they represent a weaker commitment level, and they give states a way to test an approach without fully committing, which is attractive.[85] Although these instruments generate non-binding commitments, they embody normative considerations that motivate states.[86]

Normative recommendations[87] consist of rules of behaviour and standards, which member states should observe. By participating in an international organisation, a state freely accepts certain obligations that are often general, and drafted in abstract terms. Although such obligations are not legally binding by nature, states are inclined to follow them in most cases. The Organisation for Economic Co-operation and Development (OECD) has adopted a series of recommendations which have led to important developments in different fields related to the environment, such as the management of natural resources, coastal zones, waste and the control of chemicals, as well as others.

Declarations of principles[88] consist of norms that are fundamental. Unlike normative recommendations they do not require any action to be undertaken, but provide a significant influence on the development of IEL in the formation of both treaty law and customary law. They provide policy-oriented guidelines, which are often reflected in both international and national legislations. The declarations are normally adopted at international conferences, such as the Rio Declaration adopted at the UN Conference on Environment and Development in 1992.

Programmes of action[89] involve the transformation of principles into practices. Both the Stockholm and Rio Conferences adopted vast programmes of action designated respectively as the 'Action Plan' and 'Agenda 21'. While the immediate legal significance of these actions is limited, they provide long-term implications for the achievement of environmental agenda.

Conclusion

As discussed in this chapter, the law-making process in IEL is both diverse and dynamic. While it is substantially identical to that of the traditional method of international law-making, multiple actors, including various non-state and sub-state-level actors, with both direct and indirect influences make IEL law-making significant and effective. Ultimately, only states develop legal commitments and they are assumed to comply with the obligations to which they commit. Only a few rules of IEL create rights or duties for companies, individuals or other non-state actors.[90] Due to the rapid changes that the international system is undergoing, the structure of international environmental law-making today includes thousands of organisations and millions of individuals as relevant actors[91] with differentiated responsibilities. Such a broad inclusion makes the law-making process of IEL special. It, unlike traditional international law-making, is dynamic as it adopts a process of providing a treaty with life and the possibility of subsequent and continuous adaptation in the event of new challenges that may emerge over time.

85 Bodansky, *Art and Craft*, op. cit., p. 156.
86 Ibid., p. 112.
87 See for a detailed discussion, Kiss, op. cit., p. 52.
88 Ibid.
89 Ibid.
90 Bodansky, *Art and Craft*, op. cit., p. 109.
91 E.B. Weiss, Chapter 5, 'The Emerging Structure of International Environmental Law', in N.J. Vig and R.S. Axelrod (eds) *The Global Environment Institutions, Law and Policy*, London: Earthscan, 1999, p. 99.

5

Environmental justice and international environmental law

*Carmen G. Gonzalez**

Environmental justice lies at the heart of most environmental disputes between the global North and South as well as grass-roots environmental struggles within nations. However, the discourse of international environmental law is often ahistorical and technocratic. It neither educates the North about its inordinate contribution to global environmental problems nor responds to the grievances of nations and communities disproportionately burdened by poverty and environmental degradation. This chapter examines the root causes of environmental injustice among and within nations from the colonial period to the present, and discusses strategies to integrate environmental justice into international law so as to promote social and economic justice while protecting natural resources for present and future generations.

Introduction

The global economy is currently exceeding ecological limits, and producing a variety of destructive impacts, including climate change, desertification, deforestation, degradation of arable land, freshwater shortages, depletion of fish stocks, unprecedented species extinction, and widespread chemical contamination of air, land, and water.[1] The United Nations Millennium Ecosystem Assessment concluded that human economic activity during the last half-century has produced more rapid and severe ecosystem degradation than in any comparable era of human history. The loss of ecosystem services intensifies poverty, exacerbates inequality, and poses significant obstacles to the achievement of the Millennium Development Goals (MDGs). Ecosystem degradation will also diminish the benefits that future generations derive from the planet's natural capital.[2]

* The author would like to thank Shawkat Alam, Richard Delgado, Sheila Foster, Eileen Gauna, Angela Harris, David Skover, and Faith Stevelman for helpful comments on an earlier draft of this chapter.
1 J.G. Speth, *The Bridge at the Edge of the World: Capitalism, the Environment, and Crossing from Crisis to Sustainability*, New Haven: Yale University Press, 2008, pp. 1–9; W. Sachs and T. Santorius (eds) *Fair Future: Resource Conflicts, Security and Global Justice*, London/New York: Zed Books, 2007, pp. 22–4.
2 See United Nations Millennium Ecosystem Assessment (2005), *Synthesis Report: Ecosystems and Human Well-Being*. Online. Available HTTP: <http://www.maweb.org/documents/document.356.aspx.pdf> (accessed 28 December 2011), pp. 1–24.

The primary cause of global environmental degradation is the unsustainable consumption of environmental resources by the most economically privileged, most of whom reside in the global North or in the industrial centres of the global South.[3] Twenty per cent of the world's population consumes approximately 85 per cent of the planet's timber, 70 per cent of its energy, and 60 per cent of its food.[4] This population is also responsible for more than 90 per cent of the world's annual production of hazardous waste, some of which is exported to Southern countries and contributes to illness and widespread environmental harm.[5]

While the affluent reap the benefits of unsustainable economic activity, the burdens are borne disproportionately by the global South and by the world's most vulnerable communities, including indigenous peoples, racial and ethnic minorities, and the poor. Some scholars have described the ecological segregation of the world's population along economic and racial lines as 'eco-apartheid'.[6]

This chapter uses the framework of environmental justice to analyse the responses of international environmental law to disparities between the North and South and between privileged and vulnerable communities within each nation. Efforts to understand the role of environmental justice in international environmental law are complicated by the inherent ambiguity of the term and by the failure of many environmental treaties to explicitly reference ethics and justice. The chapter begins by defining environmental justice and discussing its application to North–South environmental conflicts and grass-roots environmental struggles. It then examines the colonial and post-colonial roots of environmental injustice among and within nations, and highlights several legal strategies to promote a more equitable and sustainable social order. The chapter concludes by calling for an approach to international environmental law that recognises historic injustices, and seeks holistic solutions that integrate international human rights law, international environmental law, and international economic law.

Environmental justice: North and South

This chapter adopts a four-part definition of environmental justice consisting of distributive justice, procedural justice, corrective justice, and social justice.[7] Distributive justice calls for the fair allocation of the benefits and burdens of natural resource exploitation among and within nations.[8] Procedural justice requires open, informed, and inclusive decision-making

---

3 Sachs and Santorius, op. cit., pp. 77–80; W.E. Rees and L. Westra, 'When Consumption Does Violence: Can There be Sustainability and Environmental Justice in a Resource-Limited World?', in J. Agyeman, R.D. Bullard and B. Evans (eds) *Just Sustainabilities: Development in an Unequal World*, Cambridge, MA: MIT Press, 2003, p. 116; C. Gonzalez, 'Beyond Eco-Imperialism: An Environmental Justice Critique of Free Trade', *Denver University Law Review* 78, 2001, pp. 1001–2.

4 W. Sachs, *Planet Dialectics: Explorations in Environment and Development*, London/New York: Zed Books, 1999, p. 171; T. Athanasiou, *Divided Planet: The Ecology of Rich and Poor*, Athens, GA: University of Georgia Press, 1998, p. 53.

5 D.N. Pellow, *Resisting Global Toxics: Transnational Movements for Environmental Justice*, Cambridge, MA: MIT Press, 2007, p. 8; Gonzalez, 'Beyond Eco-Imperialism', op. cit., pp. 991–2.

6 Rees and Westra, op. cit., pp. 100–3.

7 R.R. Kuehn, 'A Taxonomy of Environmental Justice', *Environmental Law Reporter* 30, 2000, p. 10681.

8 D. French, 'Sustainable Development and the Instinctive Imperative of Justice in the Global Order', in D. French (ed.) *Global Justice and Sustainable Development*, Leiden: Martinius Nijhoff Publishers, 2010, p. 8.

processes.[9] Corrective justice imposes an obligation to provide compensation for historic inequities and to refrain from repeating the conduct that caused the harm.[10] Social justice, the fourth and most nebulous aspect of environmental justice, recognises that environmental struggles are inextricably intertwined with struggles for social and economic justice.[11] Environmental injustice cannot be separated from economic inequality, race and gender subordination, and the colonial and post-colonial domination of the global South.[12] As a practical matter, environmental disputes frequently involve several aspects of environmental justice, and do not fit neatly into one of the four categories.

Environmental justice has an important North–South dimension. Through overconsumption of natural resources, wealthy countries have contributed disproportionately to a variety of environmental problems. Despite their far smaller contribution to global environmental degradation, poor countries bear most of the harm due to their vulnerable geographic locations, lack of resources and limited administrative infrastructure.[13] In addition to this *distributive injustice*, North–South relations are also plagued by *procedural inequities*. The North dominates decision-making in the International Monetary Fund (IMF), the World Bank, the World Trade Organization (WTO), and multilateral environmental treaty fora as a consequence of its greater economic and political clout. While the South can present alternative points of view, the preferences of the powerful generally dictate the substantive outcomes.[14] *Corrective injustice* is evident in the plight of small island states whose very existence is threatened by climate change, but who possess no legal mechanism to obtain compensation or cessation of the harmful conduct.[15] In addition, North–South environmental conflicts reflect broader *social injustice* because they are inextricably intertwined with colonial and post-colonial economic policies that impoverished the global South and facilitated the North's appropriation of its natural resources.[16]

The concept of environmental justice draws its moral force from grass-roots social struggles in both the North and the South. Beginning in the 1980s, the environmental justice movement emerged in the United States (US) in response to the concentration of polluting industry

---

9 Kuehn, op. cit., p. 10688.

10 K. Mickelson, 'Competing narratives of justice in North-South environmental relations: the case of ozone layer depletion', in J. Ebbesson and P. Okowa (eds) *Environmental Law and Justice in Context*, Cambridge: Cambridge University Press, 2009, pp. 299–300.

11 C.G. Gonzalez, 'An Environmental Justice Critique of Comparative Advantage: Indigenous Peoples, Trade Policy, and the Mexican Neoliberal Economic Reforms', *University of Pennsylvania Journal of International Law* 32, 2011, p. 728; R. Guha, *Environmentalism: A Global History*, New York: Longman, 2000, p. 105.

12 Gonzalez, 'Beyond Eco-Imperialism', op. cit., pp. 1014; T. Yang, 'International Environmental Protection: Human Rights and the North–South Divide', in K.H. Mutz, G. Bryner and D. Kenney (eds) *Justice and Natural Resources: Concepts, Strategies and Applications*, Washington DC: Island Press, 2002 pp. 94–8.

13 R. Anand, *International Environmental Justice: A North–South Dimension*, Burlington: Ashgate, 2004, pp. 128–30; Gonzalez, 'Beyond Eco-Imperialism', op. cit., pp. 987–1000.

14 Anand, op. cit., pp. 132–3; P. Hossay, *Unsustainable: A Primer for Global Environmental and Social Justice*, London/New York: Zed Books, 2006, pp. 191–8; R. Peet, *Unholy Trinity: The IMF, World Bank and WTO.* London/New York: Zed Books, 2003, pp. 200–4.

15 M. Burkett, 'Climate Reparations', *Melbourne Journal of International Law* 10, 2009, pp. 513–20.

16 C.G. Gonzalez, 'Genetically Modified Organisms and Justice: The International Environmental Justice Implications of Biotechnology', *Georgetown International Environmental Law Review* 19, 2007, pp. 595–602.

and hazardous waste disposal facilities in low-income and minority communities.[17] The movement soon expanded to encompass additional environmental issues.[18] Environmental justice advocates alleged distributive injustice in the form of disproportionate exposure to environmental hazards; procedural unfairness in environmental decision-making; corrective injustice due to inadequate environmental enforcement; and social injustice because environmental degradation cannot be separated from other problems plaguing low-income communities and communities of colour (such as unemployment and underfunded schools).[19]

Environmental justice struggles are taking place on every continent. Many environmental justice struggles in the global South have been spearheaded by local and indigenous communities in opposition to development projects that threaten their lands, livelihoods, and natural resources.[20] Scholars have dubbed these grass-roots social movements 'the environmentalism of the poor'.[21]

The root causes of environmental injustice

In order to remedy environmental injustice, it is important to understand its historic roots. When European nations conquered America, they laid the groundwork for contemporary disparities in wealth and well-being.[22] The riches of the New World triggered a scramble among European countries for colonies in Asia, Africa, and the Americas. By 1800, Europe controlled 55 per cent of the global land mass. By 1914, 84.4 per cent of the planet's territory was under the effective control of Europe and the US.[23]

Colonialism transformed subsistence economies into economic satellites of Europe, and wreaked havoc on the peoples and environments of the colonised territories. Asia, Africa, and Latin America were incorporated into the global economy as exporters of raw materials and importers of manufactured products. Mining, logging, and plantation agriculture destroyed forests, displaced indigenous communities, and disrupted local ecosystems. The diversion of prime agricultural lands to export production created poverty and inequality by concentrating landholding in the hands of local elites, converting farmers into landless

17 L. Cole and S. Foster, *From the Ground Up: Environmental Racism and the Rise of the Environmental Justice Movement*, New York: New York University Press, 2001, pp. 19–33; R.D. Bullard, 'Environmental Justice in the Twenty-First Century' in R.D. Bullard (ed.) *The Quest for Environmental Justice: Human Rights and the Politics of Pollution*. San Francisco: Sierra Club Books, 2005, pp. 18–25.

18 Gonzalez, 'Genetically Modified Organisms and Justice', op, cit., pp. 727–8; A.H. Alkon and J. Agyeman, 'Introduction: The Food Movement as Polyculture', in A.H. Alkon and J. Agyeman (eds) *Cultivating Food Justice: Race, Class, and Sustainability*, Cambridge, MA: MIT Press, 2011, pp. 4–10; D.N. Suagee, 'Tribal Self-Determination and Environmental Federalism: Cultural Values as a Force for Sustainability', *Widener Law Symposium* 3, 1998, pp. 236–9.

19 Kuehn, op. cit., pp. 10685, 10689, 10694–5, 10700–2.

20 Guha, op. cit., pp. 99–100, 115–19.

21 Ibid., pp. 98–108; R. Guha and J. Martinez-Alier, *Varieties of Environmentalism: Essays North and South*, London: Earthscan, 1997, pp. 3–21.

22 J.H. Elliott, *Empires of the Atlantic World: Britain and Spain in America 1492–1830*, New Haven: Yale University Press, 2006, pp. 85–108.

23 J.M. Cypher and J.L. Dietz, *The Process of Economic Development*, London/New York: Routledge, 1997, pp. 69, 89.

peasants, promoting the use of slave labour, and degrading the natural resource base necessary for food production. Resistance to colonial domination was brutally repressed.[24]

Colonialism also introduced racial hierarchies that linger to the present day. The colonial enterprise was justified by the ideology of European racial and cultural superiority. Europeans asserted a moral obligation to subjugate non-white 'savages' in order to 'civilise' them and convert them to Christianity.[25] Post-colonial elites would later internalise European cultural norms and subordinate indigenous communities in the name of modernisation and development.[26]

When political independence failed to eliminate the former colonies' crippling economic dependence on the export of primary commodities, many nations in the global South embarked on a state-led development strategy known as import substitution industrialisation (ISI). These countries sought to industrialise their economies by substituting imported manufactured goods with domestically produced equivalents.[27] Beginning in the 1960s, these nations came together as the Group of 77 (G–77) to demand the establishment of a New International Economic Order (NIEO), under the auspices of the United Nations (UN), that would restructure the international economic system to achieve a more equitable distribution of global wealth.[28] Recognising that Southern poverty was due to Northern dominance of the international economic system, the G–77 nations demanded full and effective participation in global governance, debt forgiveness, technology transfer, special trade preferences, and stabilisation of export prices for the commodities produced by the global South.[29] They asserted permanent sovereignty over their natural resources and the right to nationalise foreign companies exploiting these resources. In other words, the G–77 nations attempted to leverage their control over the raw materials needed by the global North in order to create a more just economic order.[30] The G–77 nations (whose current membership far exceeds the original 77 members) remain a significant force in negotiations, and their demands for justice have profoundly influenced international environmental law. Given the lack of a precise definition of developing countries in most environmental treaties, the G–77 nations are generally regarded as 'developing countries' in conventions that impose differential obligations on Northern and Southern countries.[31]

24 Hossay, op. cit., pp. 52–5; C.G. Gonzalez, 'Trade Liberalization, Food Security, and the Environment: The Neoliberal Threat to Sustainable Rural Development', *Transnational Law & Contemporary Problems* 14, 2004, pp. 433–37.
25 R. Gordon, 'Saving Failed States: Sometimes a Neocolonialist Notion', *American University Journal of International Law and Policy* 19, 1997, pp. 929–40; Elliott, op. cit., p. 85.
26 J. Ngugi, 'The Decolonization–Modernization Interface and the Plight of Indigenous Peoples in Post-Colonial Development Discourse in Africa', *Wisconsin International Law Journal* 20, 2002, p. 324–6; R. Stavenhagen, 'Indigenous Peoples and the State in Latin America: An Ongoing Debate', in R. Sieder (ed.) *Multiculturalism in Latin America: Indigenous Rights, Diversity and Democracy*, New York: Palgrave Macmillan, 2002, pp. 24–6.
27 C.G. Gonzalez, 'China in Latin America: Law, Economics, and Sustainable Development', *Environmental Law Reporter* 40, 2010, p. 10173.
28 L. Rajamani, *Differential Treatment in International Environmental Law*, Oxford: Oxford University Press, 2006, pp. 17–18.
29 Ibid., p. 18; R. Gordon and J.H. Sylvester, 'Deconstructing Development', *Wisconsin International Law Journal* 22, 2004, pp. 56–8.
30 R. Gordon, 'The Dawn of a New, New International Economic Order?' *Law and Contemporary Problems* 72, 2009, pp. 142–9.
31 Rajamani, op. cit., pp. 92, 115.

The debt crisis of the 1980s marked the demise of both the NIEO and ISI and ushered in the free market economic reforms known as the Washington Consensus. Lured into borrowing money from commercial banks to finance expensive development projects, many Southern nations struggled to repay these loans. In order to secure IMF and World Bank assistance, these debtor nations were required to adopt free market reforms that included privatisation of industry and public services; trade liberalisation; curtailment of government expenditures on health, education, and social programmes; the implementation of laws and policies favourable to foreign investors; and the maximisation of primary product exports in order to service the foreign debt. These policies were designed to put an end to state-led development strategies and to open up the global South to foreign exporters and investors.[32]

By promoting specialisation in primary commodities, the Washington Consensus reinforced the South's dependence on the export of raw materials rather than fostering investment in more dynamic economic sectors.[33] The lifting of tariff and non-tariff barriers in the agricultural sector rendered small farmers in the global South destitute by placing them in direct competition with highly subsidised US and European Union agribusiness.[34] The opening of domestic markets to cheap, imported manufactured goods jeopardised nascent industries. Finally, the mass privatisations of the 1990s enabled transnational corporations to dominate key economic sectors in the global South.[35]

The Washington Consensus's emphasis on export-led growth facilitated the global North's overconsumption of natural resources by increasing the supply and lowering the price of primary commodities.[36] The intense competition among debt-ridden Southern countries to maximise exports in order to obtain badly needed foreign exchange drove down prices and encouraged overproduction and overconsumption. Much of the environmental degradation in the global South has been caused not by local consumption of natural resources but by export-oriented production designed to satisfy Northern demand.[37] For example, chemical-intensive agro-export production in the global South accelerated deforestation, eroded agro-biodiversity, depleted aquifers, and contaminated water supplies with toxic agrochemicals. It also drove subsistence farmers from the land, fractured the integrity of rural communities, and accelerated rural-to-urban migration.[38]

Scholars, activists, and Southern governments have argued that the global North owes an ecological debt to the global South.[39] Having prospered on the basis of resources extracted from its colonial possessions, the global North continues to exploit the global South at prices that do not reflect social and environmental externalities. In addition, the global North

32 Gordon, 'The Dawn of a New, New International Economic Order?', op. cit., pp. 145–50; Gonzalez, 'China in Latin America', op. cit., pp. 10173–4.
33 Gordon, 'The Dawn of a New, New International Economic Order?', op. cit., pp. 149–50.
34 Gonzalez, 'Trade Liberalization, Food Security, and the Environment', op. cit., p. 466.
35 Gonzalez, 'China in Latin America', op. cit., pp. 10174, 10177.
36 Ibid., p. 10174; J. Martinez-Alier, *The Environmentalism of the Poor: A Study of Ecological Conflicts and Valuation*, Cheltenham: Edward Elgar, 2002, p. 220.
37 Rees and Westra, op. cit., pp. 105, 110.
38 Gonzalez, 'Trade Liberalization, Food Security, and the Environment', op. cit., pp. 467–71.
39 K. Mickelson, 'Competing narratives of justice in North-South environmental relations: the case of ozone layer depletion', in Ebbesson and Okowa (eds) op. cit., pp. 153–7.

industrialised rapidly and cheaply by using more than its fair share of the global commons, and its per capita ecological footprint continues to dwarf that of the global South.[40] Based on empirical evidence regarding material and energy flows from extraction of natural resources through production of finished goods, economists have confirmed that Northern economies 'are draining ecological capacity from extractive regions by importing resource-intensive products and have shifted their environmental burdens to the South through the export of waste'.[41]

The ecological debt concept is particularly compelling in the context of climate change, and it has achieved at least partial recognition in binding legal instruments. Between 1880 and 1990, the global North was responsible for 84 per cent of all fossil fuel-related carbon dioxide emissions and 75 per cent of all deforestation-related carbon dioxide emissions.[42] The United Nations Framework Convention on Climate Change (UNFCCC) acknowledges the North's disproportionate contribution to climate change by noting 'that the largest share of historical and current global emissions has originated in developed countries, that per capita emissions in developing countries are still relatively low and that the share of global emissions originating in developing countries will grow to meet their social and developmental needs'.[43] In order to mitigate this North–South distributive inequity, Article 3(1) of the UNFCCC requires the global North to take the lead in combating climate change.[44]

By promoting trade and investment while restricting the ability of the state to intervene in the economy, the Washington Consensus increased corporate power. Corporations comprise 53 of the hundred largest economies in the world. They produce half of the world's greenhouse gas (GHG) emissions and control half of the global extraction of oil, gas, and coal. Due to their economic power and political influence, corporations are adept at evading regulatory oversight and democratic control.[45]

The burdens of the Washington Consensus are borne disproportionately by the planet's poorest and most marginalised communities. Economic inequality and environmental degradation have increased in most countries and regions in recent decades. Poor and indigenous rural communities that depend on natural resources for physical and economic survival are harmed by declining fish stocks, soil erosion, water scarcity, desertification, and deforestation. Women are particularly affected because they are often responsible for subsistence farming, gathering of fuel wood, water collection, and cooking. In urban areas, slum dwellers face the greatest risks from climate change-related sea level rises and increases in extreme weather events due to precarious living conditions, inadequate disaster preparation and response, and

40 A. Simms, *Ecological Debt: The Health of the Planet & the Wealth of Nations*, London: Pluto Press, 2005, pp. 86–109; D. McLaren, 'Environmental Space, Equity and the Ecological Debt', in Alkon and Agyeman (eds) op. cit., pp. 30–2; Martinez-Alier, op. cit., pp. 213–29; Rees and Westra, op. cit., pp. 109–12.

41 J.T. Roberts and B.C. Parks, *A Climate of Injustice: Global Inequality, North–South Politics, and Climate Policy*, Cambridge, MA: MIT Press, 2007, p. 168.

42 K. Mickelson, 'Leading Towards a Level Playing Field, Repaying Ecological Debt, or Making Environmental Space: Three Stories about International Environmental Cooperation', *Osgoode Hall Law Journal* 43, 2005, pp. 154–5.

43 *United Nations Framework Convention on Climate Change*, opened for signature 4 June 1992, 1771 UNTS 107 (entered into force 21 March 1994) (UNFCCC), preamble, para. 3.

44 Ibid., Art. 3(1).

45 Speth, op. cit., pp. 166–73.

lack of social safety nets.[46] In general, 'the most disadvantaged people carry a double burden of deprivation: more vulnerable to the wider effects of environmental degradation, they must also cope with threats to their immediate environment posed by indoor air pollution, dirty water and unimproved sanitation.'[47]

Finally, even nations that reject the Washington Consensus have adopted economic development strategies that mimic the development paths of the global North and impose disparate environmental burdens on vulnerable populations. China, for example, pursued an unorthodox development strategy based on proactive state intervention in the economy. However, its 'grow first, clean up later' economic policies have produced environmental degradation of staggering proportions within China, and have contributed to global environmental problems, such as climate change, transboundary air pollution, and the illegal timber trade.[48] Invoking the need for local sacrifices to promote national well-being, even populist Southern governments, such as the left-of-centre regimes in Ecuador, Bolivia, Venezuela, and Brazil, have embraced growth-at-any-cost development strategies based on mining and petroleum extraction despite these industries' devastating impacts on the livelihoods and natural resources of impoverished rural and indigenous communities.[49]

Environmental justice and international law

In order to foster equitable and effective solutions to global environmental problems, international environmental law must be informed by a morally compelling narrative that recognises the historic roots of environmental injustice and seeks to provide redress to the nations and communities disproportionately burdened by environmental degradation. Regrettably, the discourse of international environmental law is often technocratic and ahistorical. It does not educate the world's wealthy about their inordinate contribution to global environmental problems, and it frequently alienates the world's poor, who demand fairness and equity in the distribution of finite resources. As one observer points out in connection with climate change:

> Public outrage in the United States at the collapse in the livelihood of hundreds of millions is virtually non-existent. A discussion distinct from 'caps' and 'trades', and 'costs to the average consumer' will help to illuminate [the] suffering of the climate vulnerable, and the developed world's understanding of its own responsibility.[50]

Reframing international environmental law with justice at its core may facilitate the development of international environmental regimes that are more effective and more responsive to the inequities in global resource allocation.

Environmental justice requires the mitigation of structural inequities that impose a disproportionate share of the environmental costs of global economic activity on the global South

---

46 United Nations Development Programme (UNDP), *Human Development Report 2011: Sustainability and Equity: A Better Future for All*, New York: Palgrave Macmillan, 2011, pp. 4–5, 28–30, 51, 59.
47 UNDP, op. cit., p. 5.
48 Gonzalez, 'China in Latin America', op. cit., pp. 10175–76.
49 E. Gudynas, 'Más allá del nuevo extractivismo: transiciones sostenibles y alternativas al desarrollo', in F. Wanderley (ed.) *El desarrollo en cuestión. Reflexiones desde América Latina*, La Paz, Bolivia: Oxfam, 2011, pp. 385–90.
50 Burkett, op. cit., pp. 510–11.

and on vulnerable populations in both affluent and poor countries. Environmental justice necessitates the implementation of measures to scale back the North's overconsumption of the world's resources, to reduce North–South inequality, to curb the power of transnational corporations, and to guarantee full and effective participation in international, national, regional, and local governance by Southern nations and vulnerable communities. Lastly, environmental justice calls for a bold rethinking of the dominant economic paradigm so as to promote economic and social development while respecting the planet's biophysical limits.

The remainder of this chapter describes several strategies for bringing justice to the forefront of environmental protection and mitigating the stark disparities in social and economic development within and among nations.

Environmental human rights

Environmental justice is grounded in international human rights, including the rights to life, health, and cultural integrity, the right to be free from race and sex discrimination, the rights to information, participation, and redress for environmental harm, and the right to a healthy environment.[51] The enjoyment of internationally protected human rights depends upon a healthy environment, and serious environmental degradation is often accompanied by human rights abuses. Similarly, environmental protection is strengthened by the exercise of human rights, such as the right to information and the right to participate in governmental decision-making.[52] Invoking human rights law and institutions when human rights are threatened by environmental degradation ensures that 'the environment does not deteriorate to the point where the human right to life, the right to health, the right to a family and private life, the right to culture, the right to safe drinking water, or other human rights are seriously impaired'.[53]

Recognising entitlements as human rights protects them from the tyranny of the majority, the dictatorship of the minority, and the reciprocal exchange of obligations that takes place in the negotiation of international trade and investment agreements.[54] Although most human rights treaties do not contain explicit environmental provisions, global and regional human rights tribunals have interpreted these agreements to permit claims against states based on human rights violations caused by inadequate environmental protection.[55] These tribunals have recognised that environmental degradation may interfere with the rights to life, health, property, privacy, food, water, and an adequate standard of living and with the collective rights of indigenous peoples to their ancestral lands and resources.[56] Human rights

---

51 Gonzalez, 'Genetically Modified Organisms and Justice', op. cit., p. 626.
52 D. Shelton, 'Environmental Rights', in Philip Alston (ed.) *Peoples' Rights*, New York: Oxford University Press, 2001, pp. 187–94; Gonzalez, 'Beyond Eco-Imperialism', op. cit., pp. 1014–15.
53 Shelton, 'Environmental Rights', op. cit., p. 187.
54 Ibid., pp. 187–94; Gonzalez, 'Genetically Modified Organisms and Justice', op. cit., pp. 777–8.
55 J. Knox, 'Climate Change and Human Rights Law', *Virginia Journal of International Law* 50, 2009, pp. 168–70; D. Shelton, 'The Environmental Jurisprudence of International Human Rights Tribunals', in R. Picolotti and J.D. Taillant (eds) *Linking Human Rights and the Environment*, Tucson: University of Arizona Press, 2003, pp. 11–12.
56 D. Shelton, 'Environmental Rights and Brazil's Obligations in the Inter-American Human Rights System', *George Washington International Law Review* 40, 2009, pp. 750–67; A. Boyle, 'Human Rights or Environmental Rights? A Reassessment', *Fordham Environmental Law Review* 18, 2007, p. 487; Knox, 'Climate Change and Human Rights Law', op. cit., pp. 170–8.

tribunals have held that states have a duty to refrain from directly violating these rights and an obligation to protect these rights by regulating the conduct of private parties.[57]

Human rights violations linked to environmental degradation have been recognised under the International Covenant on Civil and Political Rights (ICCPR), the International Covenant on Economic, Social and Cultural Rights (ICESCR), the European Convention for the Protection of Human Rights and Fundamental Freedoms, and the American Convention on Human Rights despite the lack of explicit environmental human rights provisions in these treaties. The African Charter on Human and People's Rights and the Additional Protocol to the American Convention on Human Rights in the Areas of Economic, Social and Cultural Rights (San Salvador Protocol) do recognise substantive environmental human rights.[58] International human rights law is therefore an essential tool for victims of environmental injustice.

A human rights approach to environmental protection reveals some of the deficiencies of the current state-centric model of international environmental law. Most environmental treaties seek to constrain environmentally deleterious behaviour, but do not address human impacts. The environmental treaty regime tends to focus on transboundary consequences or impacts on the global commons, but lacks mechanisms to address harm that is purely domestic.[59] Environmental treaties generally lack citizen complaint mechanisms, and human rights tribunals are often the only international forum in which victims of environmental injustice can challenge governmental action or inaction related to the environment.[60]

International environmental law can better address environmental injustice by incorporating complaint procedures into environmental treaties so as to permit members of civil society to bring claims against states for non-compliance – whether or not such non-compliance results in transboundary harm. This approach is not unprecedented. The Aarhus Convention, for example, creates a Compliance Committee of independent experts and authorises any member of the public and any non-governmental organisation (NGO) to file a communication with the Committee alleging a party's non-compliance. The Compliance Committee can issue declarations of non-compliance, make recommendations to the party concerned, suspend the party's rights under the treaty, or make recommendations to the Meeting of the Parties regarding the imposition of punitive measures.[61] In addition, the North American Agreement on Environmental Cooperation (NAAEC), popularly known as the NAFTA (North American Free Trade Agreement) environmental side agreement, permits members of the public to file complaints against the parties (the US, Canada, and Mexico) for failure to effectively enforce their environmental laws. However, this mechanism is less effective than that of the Aarhus Convention because it is controlled by the very governments whose conduct is challenged and because the public is largely excluded from the

---

57 Knox, 'Climate Change and Human Rights Law', op. cit., pp. 170–1, 178–9.
58 S. Kravchenko and J.E. Bonine, *Human Rights and the Environment: Cases, Law, and Policy*, Durham, NC: Carolina Academic Press, 2008, pp. 3–4.
59 H.M. Osofsky, 'Learning from Environmental Justice: A New Model for International Environmental Rights', *Stanford Environmental Law Journal* 24, 2005, 71–131, pp. 78–87.
60 Shelton, 'Environmental Jurisprudence of International Human Rights Tribunals', op. cit., pp. 1–2.
61 S. Kravchenko, 'The Aarhus Convention and Innovations in Compliance with Multilateral Environmental Agreements', *University of Colorado Journal of International Environmental Law and Policy* 18, 2007, pp. 10–18, 30.

decision-making process. Moreover, the process results in a non-binding 'factual record' rather than a legal determination on the merits of the complaint.[62]

The Aarhus Convention is a ground-breaking contribution to procedural human rights that promotes environmental justice by empowering citizens to challenge governmental non-compliance with environmental commitments. Individuals and NGOs can bring claims of non-compliance against their own country or against any other party to the treaty in order to secure the rights guaranteed therein, including access to information, public participation, and access to justice. The Convention's complaint process promotes transparency, democracy, and accountability, and serves as a potential model for citizen participation in future environmental treaties.[63]

An environmental justice approach to environmental protection must be particularly attentive to public participation by vulnerable communities. Poverty, illiteracy, lack of information, and government indifference or hostility have excluded vulnerable communities from effective participation in decision-making regarding climate change, biodiversity protection, and environmental impact assessments for local, regional, or national development projects.[64] Once again, the Aarhus Convention's minimum requirements for access to information, public participation, and access to justice are instructive, requiring governments to provide support to facilitate participation in environmental decision-making. Among the types of support provided are financial grants, technical assistance, capacity-building, and free legal representation offered by the government or financed by domestic or foreign donors.[65]

Reducing North–South inequality through differential treatment

Environmental justice requires recognition and redress of the enduring inequalities between states arising from the colonial encounter and the post-colonial development practices described in this chapter. One important tool to mitigate North–South inequality is differential treatment in international law. Norms of differential treatment in favour of Southern countries are designed to redress historic inequities, and have been utilised in both international economic law and international environmental law. While differential treatment has been on the wane in international economic law since the early 1990s, it has been on the rise in international environmental law.[66] The following subsections explore the principles that have arisen to promote differential treatment: (1) special and differential treatment in international trade law; and (2) common but differentiated responsibility in international environmental law.

62 J.H. Knox, 'The Neglected Lessons of the NAFTA Environmental Regime', *Wake Forest Law Review* 45, 2010, p. 397; T. Yang, 'The Effectiveness of the NAFTA Environmental Side Agreement's Citizen Submission Process: A Case Study of Metales y Derivados', *University of Colorado Law Review*, 2005, pp. 463–74.
63 M. Fitzmaurice, 'Environmental Justice through International Complaint Procedures? Comparing the Aarhus Convention and the North American Agreement on Environmental Cooperation', in Ebbesson and Okowa (eds) op. cit., pp. 222–3; Kravchenko, 'Aarhus Convention and Innovations in Compliance', op. cit., pp. 1–2.
64 S. Kravchenko, 'The Myth of Public Participation in a World of Poverty', *Tulane Environmental Law Journal* 23, 2009, pp. 35–46.
65 Ibid., pp. 48 55.
66 Rajamani, op. cit., pp. 47–8.

International economic law: special and differential treatment

Differential treatment in international law may appear to violate the doctrine of sovereign equality of states, but it is entirely consistent with international law and is justified by the need to promote social and economic development. Given the economic disparities among states, formal equality would exacerbate poverty and inequality. Differential treatment seeks to narrow the gap between the colonisers and the formerly colonised by providing more advantageous treatment to the latter. Since states have the sovereign right to elect to be bound by treaties that confer special treatment on other states, differential treatment in international legal instruments does not run afoul of international law.[67]

Differential treatment has its origins in the demands of the G–77 nations for a more equitable distribution of the planet's resources. Differential norms were adopted initially in international economic law and were subsequently incorporated into international environmental law.[68]

The 1947 General Agreement on Tariffs and Trade (GATT) was negotiated when most of the South was under colonial rule. The GATT benefited the global North by reducing tariffs on manufactured goods, but it did not address the global South's needs for economic diversification and industrialisation or compel the global North to open its highly protected agricultural markets to Southern imports.[69] By the mid–1950s, Southern nations had mobilised to demand a variety of measures to promote economic development, including removal of the global North's trade-distorting agricultural subsidies and import barriers; preferential market access and non-reciprocal tariff reductions for Southern country products; and the right to protect infant industries through tariffs, subsidies, and quotas.[70]

The concerted efforts of the global South introduced the principle of special and differential treatment into the GATT through a series of amendments that permitted (but did not require) the global North to provide differential and more favourable treatment to its Southern trading partners.[71] Pursuant to this principle, Southern countries were granted preferential market access and non-reciprocal tariff concessions, and were not required to become parties to all of the side agreements resulting from the 1973 to 1979 Tokyo Round of trade negotiations.[72]

However, the advantages of special and differential treatment generally proved illusory. The benefits of preferential market access to Northern markets declined as Northern tariff levels were reduced. The most significant products of the global South (clothing, textiles, agriculture) were either excluded or received less preference. Because the norms imposing differential treatment were often drafted in aspirational rather than mandatory language, the compliance of the global North was strictly voluntary, and non-compliance did not result in sanctions.[73] For example, GATT Article XXXVII requires Northern countries to 'accord

---

67 Ibid., pp. 2, 48–9.
68 Ibid., pp. 17–19, 48–9.
69 Gonzalez, 'China in Latin America', op. cit., pp. 10178–9; Gonzalez, 'Trade Liberalization, Food Security, and the Environment', op. cit., pp. 456–7.
70 Gonzalez, 'China in Latin America', op. cit., p. 10179; F. Ismail, 'Rediscovering the Role of Developing Countries in GATT Before the Doha Round', *Law and Development Review* 1, 2008, pp. 59–67.
71 Ismail, op. cit., pp. 65–7.
72 Gonzalez, 'Genetically Modified Organisms and Justice', op. cit., pp. 633–4.
73 Ibid., pp. 634–5.

high priority' to the export products of interest to the global South and to refrain from introducing or increasing import barriers to such products.[74] However, this provision excuses Northern countries from complying with these obligations if they invoke 'compelling reasons', including contrary legal obligations.[75] In other words, 'developed countries may escape from those so-called commitments by legislating against them'.[76]

The WTO, which succeeded the 1947 GATT, eroded differential treatment by imposing the same obligations on all countries but merely giving the global South more time to comply. The WTO failed to phase out the Northern import barriers on clothing, textiles, and agricultural products, but managed to constrain the development options of Southern nations. Reinforcing the free market reforms imposed by the IMF in the wake of the debt crisis, the WTO required the global South to eliminate the import barriers that had formerly protected domestic industries from more technologically advanced foreign competitors; restricted the ability of the state to use tariffs and subsidies to promote dynamic new industries; and imposed new and expensive obligations on the global South in the areas of intellectual property, services, and investment.[77]

The free market reforms imposed by international trade and financial institutions deprive the global South of the protectionist tools used by the global North and by the rising powers of the global South to achieve economic prosperity. The US, Germany, France, Japan, the United Kingdom, China, South Korea, and Taiwan deployed a broad array of state interventionist measures (industrial policy) in order to diversify and industrialise their economies. These measures included subsidies, tariffs, state financing of major industries, local content requirements, technology transfer requirements, and even state-sponsored theft of intellectual property through industrial espionage.[78] Regrettably, nations that arrive at the pinnacle of economic success through protectionism often advocate free trade so as to 'kick away the ladder' and prevent others from climbing up.[79]

As a matter of fairness and justice, the regulatory framework for international trade must be modified to permit Southern countries to make use of tariffs, subsidies, and other protectionist measures to end their dangerous and debilitating dependence on the export of primary commodities. Only a regime of asymmetrical obligations that facilitates economic diversification in the global South while restricting protectionism in the global North will overcome the colonial legacy. Indeed, in response to the dissatisfaction of the global South with the current WTO framework, the ministerial declaration that launched the Doha Round of WTO negotiations reaffirmed the commitment of WTO members to special and differential treatment and pledged that 'all special and differential treatment provisions shall be

74 General Agreement on Tariffs and Trade, opened for signature 30 October 1947, 55 UNTS 187 (entered into force 1 January 1948) (GATT), Art. XXXVII(1).
75 Ibid., Art. XXXVII(1).
76 Y.S. Lee, *Reclaiming Development in the World Trading System.* Cambridge: Cambridge University Press, 2006, p. 35.
77 Ibid., pp. 41–3; F.J. Garcia, 'Beyond Special and Differential Treatment', *Boston College International and Comparative Law Review* 27, 2004, pp. 297–9.
78 H. Chang, 'The East Asian Development Experience', in H. Chang (ed.) *Rethinking Development Economics*, London/New York: Anthem Press, 2003, pp. 111–17; H. Chang, *Kicking Away the Ladder: Development Strategy in Historical Perspective*, London/New York: Anthem Press, 2002, pp. 19–51, 59–66; Gonzalez, 'China in Latin America', op. cit., pp. 10174–5.
79 Chang, *Kicking Away the Ladder*, op. cit., pp. 4–5.

reviewed with a view to strengthening them and making them more precise, effective and operational'.[80]

International environmental law: common but differentiated responsibility

States differ in terms of their contribution to global environmental degradation, their vulnerability to environmental harm, and their capacity to address environmental problems. Northern proposals to protect the global environment without taking these differences into account have sparked scepticism in the global South.[81] Indeed, Northern environmentalism was initially regarded as yet another effort to 'kick away the ladder' and perpetuate Southern poverty by depriving the global South of the polluting technologies that the North had used to industrialise.[82]

Nevertheless, the global South has been an active partner in the development of international environmental law. However, Southern nations have generally articulated a different concept of environmentalism. While the North has typically focused on global environmental problems (such as ozone depletion, climate change, and biodiversity loss), the South has often pressed for action on environmental problems with more immediate impacts on vulnerable local populations, including desertification, food security, the hazardous waste trade, access to safe drinking water and sanitation, and indoor air pollution caused by lack of access to sustainable energy.[83] As awareness of the potentially devastating local and global consequences of climate change grew, the South demanded an aggressive response based on the North's disproportionate contribution to the problem.[84]

During the major diplomatic conferences on the environment convened by the United Nations, the South has emphasised responsibility for historic environmental harm and the need to address poverty and inequality.[85] From the 1972 Stockholm Conference through the 2002 World Summit on Sustainable Development, the South played an instrumental role in the development of soft-law principles and treaty mechanisms that introduced differential treatment into international environmental law so as to foster social and economic development. The relevant soft-law principles include Principles 3, 5, 6, and 9 of the Rio Declaration, which endorse the right to development, require states to cooperate to decrease disparities in living standards, express concern for the special needs and circumstances of developing countries, and recognise the need for technology transfer to achieve sustainable development.[86] The relevant treaty mechanisms include provisions exempting the South from substantive obligations (such as the Kyoto Protocol, which does not impose binding emission reduction

80 World Trade Organization, Ministerial Declaration of 14 November 2001, WT/MIN(01)/DEC/1, 41 ILM 746 (2002), ¶44.
81 Gonzalez, 'Beyond Eco-Imperialism', op. cit., pp. 1008–9.
82 R. Falk, 'The Second Cycle of Ecological Urgency: An Environmental Justice Perspective' in Ebbesson and Okowa (eds) op. cit., p. 45.
83 Gonzalez, 'Beyond Eco-Imperialism', op. cit., pp. 1008–9; L. Guruswamy, 'Energy Justice and Sustainable Development', *Colorado Journal of International Environmental Law and Policy* 12, 2010, pp. 235–8.
84 Roberts and Parks, op. cit., pp. 132–50.
85 K. Mickelson, 'South, North, International Environmental Law, and International Environmental Lawyers', *Yearbook of International Environmental Law*, 2000, pp. 70–1.
86 *Rio Declaration on Environment and Development* (1992), Report of the UN Conference on Environment and Development, UN Doc A/CONF.151/26 (vol. I), reprinted in 31 ILM 874 ('Rio Declaration') Principles 3, 5, 6 and 9; Rajamani, op. cit., p. 60.

obligations on Southern countries); giving Southern countries more time to comply (such as the Montreal Protocol's differential phase-out schedules for ozone-depleting chemicals); and conditioning the South's duty to comply with treaty provisions on the North's transfer of financial resources and technology (such as the Convention on Biological Diversity (CBD) and the UNFCCC).[87]

The principle of common but differentiated responsibility is perhaps the most significant expression of differential treatment in international environmental law. Principle 7 of the Rio Declaration articulates the principle as follows:

> In view of the different contributions to global environmental degradation, States have common but differentiated responsibilities. The developed countries acknowledge the responsibility that they bear in the international pursuit of sustainable development in view of the pressures their societies place on the global environment and of the technologies and financial resources they command.[88]

The principle of common but differentiated responsibility finds use in international environmental law to impose asymmetrical obligations on the North and the South in light of: (1) the North's disproportionate contribution to global environmental degradation; (2) the North's superior financial and technical resources; and (3) the South's economic and ecological vulnerability.[89] The principle of common but differentiated responsibility appears in a variety of environmental treaties, including the Vienna Convention for the Protection of the Ozone Layer, the Montreal Protocol on Substances that Deplete the Ozone Layer, the UNFCCC, the Kyoto Protocol, the CBD, and the United Nations Convention on the Law of the Sea (UNCLOS).[90]

Notwithstanding the incorporation of common but differentiated responsibility into so many treaties, its meaning remains contested – particularly in climate change negotiations. From the perspective of the global South, the principle acknowledges 'the historic, moral, and legal responsibility of the North to shoulder the burdens of environmental protection, just as it has enjoyed the benefits of economic and industrial development largely unconstrained by environmental concerns'.[91] However, there is disagreement as to whether the principle operates in terms of corrective or distributive injustice. One prominent scholar argues that the principle 'provides a corrective justice basis for obliging the developed world to pay for past harms as well as present and future harms' through the transfer of financial resources and technology.[92] Others are not persuaded that the principle unequivocally mandates Northern financing of Southern adaptation and mitigation measures.[93] To the extent that the principle merely requires the North to scale back its own emissions in order

87 D. Shelton, 'Describing the Elephant: International Justice and Environmental Law', in Ebbesson and Okowa (eds) op. cit., p. 62.
88 Rio Declaration, op. cit., Principle 7.
89 C.D. Stone, 'Common But Differentiated Responsibilities in International Law', *American Journal of International Law* 98, 2004, pp. 279–80.
90 Gonzalez, 'Genetically Modified Organisms and Justice', op. cit., p. 632.
91 Mickelson, 'South, North, International Environmental Law', op. cit., p. 70.
92 Shelton, 'Describing the Elephant', op. cit., pp. 67–8.
93 J. Brunnée, 'Climate change, global environmental justice and international environmental law', in Ebbesson and Okowa (eds) op. cit., pp. 325–6.

to permit the South to increase its emissions to the degree necessary to improve living standards, then the principle would appear to be more consistent with distributive justice.

Northern countries, however, have refused to accept responsibility for historical acts of environmental degradation, and have instead attributed their leadership role in the climate regime to their greater wealth, technical expertise, and capacity to take response measures.[94] In addition to refusing to ratify the Kyoto Protocol, the US went so far as to submit an interpretive statement on Principle 7 of the Rio Declaration rejecting legal responsibility for past actions.[95]

The global North's ahistorical understanding of global environmental problems is one of the fundamental obstacles to North–South environmental collaboration. This approach 'seeks to wipe the colonial past from our collective memories and start afresh, as if past patterns of exploitation have little bearing on current inequities, and the efforts of developing countries to raise them time and again are no more than special pleading'.[96] Instead of acknowledging responsibility for past wrongs, the global North ascribes its differential commitments under the climate regime and other environmental treaties to *noblesse oblige* – benevolence, morality, and good will. This justification ensures that the North's obligations are drafted in discretionary rather than binding language, and are included in soft law rather than hard law instruments. The North's ahistorical approach is inconsistent with the polluter pays principle, which requires the polluter to bear the cost of environmental degradation. It is also at odds with the climate regime's use of 1990 as the baseline for mitigation – a baseline that grandfathers the historical emissions of the global North.[97]

The principle of common but differentiated responsibility, no matter how contested or how imperfectly implemented, serves as a reminder of the historic and contemporary unequal contributions to global environmental degradation and as an important vehicle for securing North–South environmental justice. Southern countries do bear responsibility for their own polluting behaviour, and must contribute their fair share to collective solutions. International environmental law must continue to right historic wrongs by apportioning responsibility on the basis of past and current contribution to environmental degradation – as well as vulnerability and capacity to address environmental problems.

Mitigating the power of transnational corporations

Corporations are frequently implicated in serious human rights and environmental abuses. While corporations have begun to adopt voluntary codes of conduct, the magnitude of corporate influence in the global economy requires a stronger response.[98]

An environmental justice approach to international environmental law requires creative use of international and domestic law to regulate the extraterritorial conduct of transnational corporations. When these corporations engage in environmentally irresponsible conduct in

---

94 Rajamani, op. cit., pp. 76, 81.
95 J.D. Kovar, 'A Short Guide to the Rio Declaration', *University of Colorado Journal of International Environmental Law and Policy* 4, 1993, pp. 129–30.
96 Rajamani, op. cit., p. 87.
97 Ibid., pp. 86–7.
98 A. Sinden, 'Power and Responsibility: Why Human Rights Should Address Corporate Environmental Wrongs', in D. McBarnet, A. Voiculescu and T. Campbell (eds) *The New Corporate Accountability: Corporate Social Responsibility and the Law*, Cambridge: Cambridge University Press, 2009, pp. 501–3.

the global South, they are externalising the costs on local populations while internalising the economic benefits. The geographic separation between the home state and the host state obscures the injury and may prevent shareholders and the public in the home state from experiencing moral culpability.[99] Furthermore, if these activities proceed via a subsidiary, the legal separation between the parent company in the home state and the subsidiary in the host state may make it difficult for the legal system to hold the parent company and its shareholders liable despite the profits that they derive from this activity.[100] Under well-settled legal principles, the corporate subsidiary is deemed a separate legal person, and the parent company is not generally liable for the actions of its subsidiary.[101] Because Southern governments are often implicated in human rights and environmental abuses or are vulnerable to exploitation by transnational corporations due to their staggering foreign debts, the host country may not be able to adequately regulate the corporation's activities. Transnational regulation may therefore be the best solution.[102] The remainder of this section considers several regulatory strategies that may promote socially responsible corporate behaviour.

Some scholars have argued that corporations should be treated like states under international human rights law.[103] Transnational corporations, like states, could elect to be bound by human rights treaties, and would be subject to *jus cogens* norms and to norms that have achieved the status of customary international law. Transnational corporations, like states, would also be liable for complicity in the human rights violations of another state, including knowingly aiding and assisting; directing and controlling; and coercing another state in the commission of human rights violations.[104] The problem with this approach is that corporations would likely refuse to be bound by human rights treaties and refuse to consent to the jurisdiction of international or regional human rights tribunals. In the absence of consent, there may be no mechanism to enforce applicable customary international law norms against recalcitrant corporations.

A second strategy calls for legislation subjecting the corporation to liability in the home state for violations of legal norms abroad. This strategy may be appealing to victims of human rights and environmental abuses if significant barriers frustrate justice in the host state. An example of this approach is the US Alien Tort Claims Act (ATCA), which gives federal courts jurisdiction over civil suits by aliens for torts 'committed in violation of the law of nations or a treaty of the United States'.[105] The statute has been invoked against transnational corporations for complicity in human rights violations.[106] Despite high-profile settlements in cases brought against Unocal and Shell, few ATCA cases have been successful due, in part, to the significant procedural hurdles that these cases encounter, including the doctrines of *forum non conveniens*, act of state, political question, sovereign immunity, and

---

99 Yang, 'International Environmental Protection', op. cit., p. 105.

100 J. Overland, 'A Multi-Faceted Journey: Globalisation, Transnational Corporations, and Corporate Social Responsibility', in S. Alam, N. Klein and J. Overland (eds) *Globalisation and the Quest for Social and Environmental Justice: the Relevance of International Law in an Evolving World Order*, New York: Routledge, 2011, pp. 136–7.

101 A. De Jonge, *Transnational Corporations and International Law: Accountability in the Global Business Environment*, Cheltenham: Edward Elgar, 2011, pp. 83–4.

102 Yang, 'International Environmental Protection', op. cit., pp. 97, 105–6.

103 Sinden, op. cit., p. 519.

104 De Jonge, op. cit., pp. 150–1.

105 *Alien Torts Claims Act*, 28 USC §1350.

106 De Jonge, op. cit., pp. 100–1.

comity.[107] In addition, the plaintiffs will need to establish the liability of the parent for breaches that are most commonly committed by its subsidiaries.[108] Thus, the threat of a successful lawsuit in the home state may not be sufficient to deter misconduct in the host state. In addition, on 17 September 2010, the US Court of Appeals for the Second Circuit ruled in the case of *Kiobel v Royal Dutch Petroleum* that corporations cannot be sued under the ATCA because no international tribunal has ever held a corporation liable for human rights violations.[109] In October 2011, the US Supreme Court granted *certiorari* to hear this case.[110] The decision will determine the fate of corporate liability in the US under the ATCA.

A third strategy is extraterritorial legislation in the home state regulating the conduct of its corporations abroad or state responsibility for failure to regulate. Many states already impose liability on corporations for money-laundering and bribery in their operations abroad, and could expand existing legislation to encompass human rights and environmental standards.[111] States that fail to regulate could be held responsible for the extraterritorial conduct of their corporate nationals. Under customary international law, states have a duty to refrain from causing transboundary harm, including a due diligence obligation to regulate the conduct of private parties within their territories. States that have ratified the ICESCR have an additional obligation to ensure that corporations under their jurisdiction and control respect economic, social, and cultural rights in other countries.[112] Where a state has actual or constructive knowledge that extraterritorial corporate activity (such as oil drilling) may violate human rights (including environmental human rights) and fails to exercise due diligence to prevent such violations, the state may incur liability on that basis.[113] Furthermore, capital exporting countries that enter into bilateral investment treaties (BITs) with capital importing countries may be liable for the human rights violations of their corporate nationals to the extent that the BITs restrict the ability of the host state to regulate the foreign investor in a manner that protects human rights.[114]

A fourth strategy is to incorporate sustainable development into BITs and free trade agreement investment chapters. These agreements have historically protected foreign investors while limiting the regulatory authority of the host state.[115] For example, arbitration tribunals have interpreted the key operative clauses of BITs to require host state governments to compensate foreign investors when health, safety, and environmental regulations diminish the profitability of the investment – with little or no deference to the state's exercise of regulatory authority and with no opportunity for the state to complain of the foreign investor's conduct.[116] Drawing upon the model investment agreement developed by the International

107 Ibid., pp. 99–100; 108–17.
108 Overland, op. cit., p. 138.
109 De Jonge, op. cit., pp. 105–6.
110 M. Sacks, 'Supreme Court to Rule on Corporate Personhood for Crimes Against Humanity', Huffington Post, 17 October 2011. Online. Available HTTP: <http://www.huffingtonpost.com/2011/10/17/supreme-court_n_1015953.html> (accessed 26 November 2011).
111 De Jonge, op. cit., pp. 91–3.
112 R. McCorquodale and P. Simons, 'Responsibility Beyond Borders: State Responsibility for Extraterritorial Violations by Corporations of International Human Rights Law', *Modern Law Review* 70, 2007, pp. 617–19.
113 Ibid., pp. 619–21.
114 Ibid., pp. 621–3.
115 X. Fuentes, 'The Impact of Foreign Investment Rules on Domestic Law', in D. French (ed.) op. cit., pp. 192–203.
116 Ibid., pp. 199–206.

Institute for Sustainable Development (IISD), states might enter into BITs that: (1) make sustainable development the objective of the agreement and affirm the right of the host state to regulate in the public interest; (2) revise the substantive obligations of the host state to explicitly preserve regulatory flexibility; (3) require the host state to adopt high levels of environmental and human rights protection in its national legislation; (4) require foreign investors to comply with domestic and international human rights and environmental norms; (5) establish civil liability in the investor's home state for breach of these domestic and international norms; and (6) permit the host state to make counterclaims against the foreign investor for failure to comply with the obligations set forth in the BIT.[117] This approach imposes standards of conduct on transnational corporations, requires the home country of the foreign investor to more closely monitor and regulate the extraterritorial activities of its companies, and expands the rights of victims of human rights and environmental abuses. Indeed, these BITs should also include a hierarchy of norms clause that recognises the primacy of human rights and environmental norms in the event of a conflict with other BIT obligations.

The foregoing list of regulatory strategies is illustrative rather than exhaustive. It highlights the need for creative interventions to ensure corporate accountability for extraterritorial misconduct.

Re-conceptualising development

Climate change jeopardises the health and well-being of present and future generations, and represents the single greatest threat to sustainable development. It is also one of the most devastating manifestations of a deeper problem: a failed development model premised on the fallacy of unlimited economic growth. Since the Second World War, Northern trade, aid and financial institutions have trumpeted the growth-at-any-cost economic model as the solution to global poverty and inequality.[118] This 'has brought us to the point where sustained material growth destroys ecosystems, impoverishes the planet, diminishes the human spirit, and visits violence upon whole poor communities'.[119] The world's wealthiest countries (the US, the European Union, and Japan) and its rising powers (China, India, Russia, and Brazil) are currently responsible for almost 70 per cent of global GHG emissions, and these emissions are growing.[120] This practice is sustainable only if poor countries freeze their development and consume only a fraction of the planet's resources. If all countries of the world simultaneously pursue the growth-at-any-cost economic model, the result would be global environmental catastrophe.[121] It is

117 H. Mann, K. von Moltke, L.E. Peterson and A. Cosbey (2005), *International Institute for Sustainable Development Model International Agreement for Sustainable Development.* Online. Available HTTP: <http://www.iisd.org/pdf/2005/investment_model_int_agreement.pdf> (accessed 28 December 2011).
118 Sachs and Sartorius, op. cit., pp. 30–1.
119 Rees and Westra, op. cit., p. 107.
120 Climate Analysis Indicators Tool (CAIT), Version 9.0, Washington, DC: World Resources Institute, 2011. Online. Available HTTP:<http://cait.wri.org> (accessed 28 December 2011). This figure is based on emissions data for 2005, and does not include anthropogenic greenhouse gas emissions associated with deforestation.
121 C. Flavin and G. Gardner, 'China, India, and the New World Order', in Worldwatch Institute, *State of the World 2006: Special Focus: India and China*, New York: W. W. Norton and Company, 2006, pp. 16–18; Gonzalez, 'Beyond Eco-Imperialism', op. cit., pp. 1002–3.

therefore necessary to develop alternative models of economic development that require reductions in per capita energy and resource consumption by the affluent so as to create the ecological space necessary to improve the living standards of the poor.

One solution to the impasse in the climate change negotiations is a reinvigorated conception of common but differentiated responsibility that imposes differential mitigation obligations on *all* nations based on historic responsibility, vulnerability, and capacity to reduce GHG emissions. Popularly known as contraction and convergence, this approach would cap and reduce greenhouse gas emissions by allocating emissions entitlements to each nation based on the above criteria with the ultimate goal of having Northern and Southern per capita emissions converge. Excluding the global South from mandatory emissions caps is fundamentally unjust because it equates countries such as India and China (with their significant and growing emissions) with Sudan and Tuvalu (with their minimal emissions, limited capacity, and significant vulnerability) and guarantees gridlock in the climate nego-tiations as the planet teeters on the brink of catastrophe.[122] The contraction and convergence approach to climate change will promote environmental justice by scaling back the North's overconsumption of the planet's resources so that the South will be able to improve living standards – instead of simply grandfathering the global North's emissions based on the climate regime's 1990 baseline.[123]

Foregrounding justice in the climate change negotiations can also produce a new model of economic development that reduces GHG emissions, improves the well-being of the world's poor, and facilitates the transition to renewable energy. A large percentage of humanity relies on animal dung, crop residues, rotted wood, and other forms of biomass for energy. Biomass can be used for cooking and heating, but it exacts a terrible toll on the health of women and children exposed to indoor pollution, and produces black carbon, a powerful contributor to global warming. In addition, biomass cannot provide the energy necessary to power water pumps and agricultural machinery or to provide water filtration and lighting for homes and schools – all of which contribute to the fulfilment of the MDGs of reducing hunger, increasing access to safe water and sanitation, and providing primary education.[124] Instead of ignoring the plight of the most vulnerable, climate negotiators should deploy the Kyoto Protocol's Clean Development Mechanism (CDM) and develop new mechanisms in the Kyoto Protocol's successor to finance renewable energy projects (such as small-scale hydroelectric, wind, or solar power) in the poorest countries of the global South in order to simultaneously reduce black carbon emissions, decrease indoor air pollution, contribute to the achievement of the MDGs, and enable countries in the global South to leapfrog the fossil fuel-based development path taken by the global North.[125]

An environmental justice approach to climate policy would prioritise the needs of the most vulnerable by placing greater emphasis on climate adaptation. Consistent with the principle of common but differentiated responsibility, the nations that contributed the most to climate change would have an obligation to increase the adaptive capacity of the poorest,

122 J. Ngugi, 'The "Curse" of Ecological Interdependence: Africa, Climate Change and Social Justice', in W.H. Rodgers, Jr and M. Robinson-Dorn (eds) *Climate Change: A Reader*, Durham, NC: Carolina Academic Press, 2011, pp. 982–3.
123 Simms, op. cit., pp. 171–7.
124 Guruswamy, op. cit., pp. 233–8.
125 R. Gordon, 'Climate Change and the Poorest Nations: Further Reflections on Global Inequality', *University of Colorado Law Review* 78, 2007, p. 1615.

least culpable, and most vulnerable.[126] Adaptation funds should focus on the poorest countries and target the neediest segments of society.[127] Adaptation funding would build resilience to climate change, combat poverty and inequality, contribute to the fulfilment of the MDGs, and promote North–South cooperation. Climate change adaptation will require coordination of environmental policy with trade, investment, finance, immigration, public health, land use, energy, and national security law and policy. As one observer puts it, 'climate change adaptation policy is going to transcend environmental law quickly and decisively.'[128]

Conclusion

Environmental injustice is rooted in colonial and post-colonial economic policies that subordinated the global South and enabled the global North to secure a disproportionate share of the planet's finite resources. One of the obstacles to the achievement of environmental justice is the fragmentation of international law into three distinct fields: international economic law, international human rights law, and international environmental law. If international law is to advance environmental protection and social and economic development, then environmental justice norms and policies must be integrated into the broader corpus of international law. The achievement of environmental justice also requires cooperation and collective action among nations to regulate the extraterritorial conduct of transnational corporations. Economic and environmental cooperation between the global North and the global South must rest on a shared understanding of historic injustices and a shared commitment to right these injustices for the benefit of present and future generations.

126 Ngugi, 'The "Curse" of Ecological Interdependence', op. cit. p. 985.
127 Verchik, 'Adaptive Justice' in Rodgers, op. cit., pp. 891–93.
128 J.B. Ruhl, 'Climate Change Adaptation and the Structural Transformation of Environmental Law', *Environmental Law* 40, 2010, p. 415.

Part II

Implementing international environmental law

6

International environmental institutions

Paul Govind

International environmental institutions fulfil a significant role in maintaining effective environmental governance. Governance suggests an evolving process that is representative of diverse interests and changing circumstances. The composition of international environmental institutions has developed and includes a vast array of disparate actors. A key challenge of effective governance relates to facilitating and coordinating cooperation to help provide solutions to environmental problems. Principal among the challenges is the growth of global environmental problems, the proliferation of multilateral environmental agreements and the limited means to coordinate solutions.

Introduction

Any discussion of international environmental institutions is more effectively explored under the heading of 'governance'. Governance includes all bodies responsible for 'formulating and implementing international environmental policy and law'.[1] Governance involves:

> a continuing process through which conflicting or diverse interests may be accommodated and cooperative action may be taken. It includes formal institutions and regimes empowered to enforce compliance, as well as informal arrangements... There is no single model or form of global governance, nor is there a single structure or set of structures. It is a broad, dynamic, complex, process of interactive decision-making.[2]

Therefore, central to understanding international environmental governance are the linkages and interactions between different institutional actors. This is particularly important in the context of international environmental law and policy given the absence of a central organisation – such as an equivalent to the World Trade Organization (WTO) or World

1 P. Birnie, A. Boyle and C Redgwell, *International Law and The Environment*, Oxford: Oxford University Press, 2009, p. 41.
2 A. Roberts and B. Kingsbury (eds) *United Nations, Divided World. The UN's Role in International Relations*, Oxford: Oxford University Press, 1993, pp. 14–17.

Health Organization (WHO). The lack of such a central international organisation means that a number of different actors fill the void, including governments, intergovernmental and non-governmental organisations (NGOs). Analysing international environmental law and policy in terms of governance recognises the diversity of relevant and pertinent international institutions – not necessarily restricted to those actors that possess law-making power.[3] This diversity of actors, all of whom contribute to the advancement of law- and policy-making, is a feature of modern international environmental law.

The definition of 'international environmental institutions' is itself subject to debate. Ellen Hey has described them as a 'heterogeneous set of actors' that emerged in the context of international cooperative efforts.[4] Schermers and Blokker define them as 'forms of cooperation founded on an international agreement creating at least one organ with a will of its own under international law'.[5] A common theme is cooperation.

In the context of international environmental law, actors fall into one of two preeminent groups: the United Nations (UN) and related 'governance' organisations and 'the extensive network of supervisory bodies, conference of the parties and commissions established by environmental treaties'.[6] The latter group are described as 'autonomous treaty bodies' and are entrusted with guiding the development of individual treaty regimes.[7] There is little doubt that autonomous treaty bodies and the UN-related organisations share a complementary relationship.

This chapter first outlines prospects and challenges of environmental governance. Andresen and Hey underline that modern international environmental governance reflects the synthesis between environmental, development and social concerns.[8] Of particular significance is the presence of fragmentation and the need for coherence. It will subsequently discuss the role of the UN as a primary actor within international environmental governance. Analysis shows that a number of factors influence the effectives of institutions such as the United Nations Environment Programme (UNEP) such as limited finance and an increasingly broad mandate. This chapter maintains that the current status of international environmental governance has been complicated by the growth of multilateral environmental agreements (MEAs) and attendant administrative regimes. These highly specific treaty-based institutions predictably lack coherence and coordination. Coordination is a primary task of the UN, specifically the UNEP, and this chapter concludes by arguing that the extent to which the UNEP, and related UN organs, complement the operation of MEA regimes is a fundamental challenge for contemporary environmental governance.

3   Birnie et al., op. cit., pp. 46–7.
4   E. Hey, 'International Institutions', in D. Bodansky, J. Brunnée and E. Hey (eds) *The Oxford Handbook of International Environmental Law*, Oxford: Oxford University Press, 2007, p. 750.
5   H.G Schermers and N.M Blokker, *International Institutional Law. Unity Within Diversity*, Leiden: Martinus Nijhoff Publishers, 2004.
6   Birnie et al., op. cit., p 44.
7   R. Churchill and G. Ulfstein, 'Autonomous Institutional Arrangements in Multilateral Environmental Agreements: A Little-Noticed Phenomenon in International Law', *American Journal of International Law* 94, 2000, 623–59.
8   S. Andresen and E. Hey, 'The Effectiveness and Legitimacy of International Environmental Institutions', *International Environmental Agreements* 5, 2006, 211–26, pp. 212–13.

Challenges of effective international environmental governance

Effective environmental governance is 'critical' in responding to urgent environmental issues but the current system exhibits 'fragmentation'.[9] At the conclusion of 2010 the international environmental governance system included over 500 MEAs, each with an attendant administrative and decision-making regime that adds to the potential for a rich complexity of environmental governance. Between 1992 and 2007 Member States of 18 MEAs were called for a total of 540 meetings that resulted in 5,084 decisions.[10] Whilst these decisions varied in nature and scope they reflect the sheer volume of information that underlies international environmental governance.[11]

The Nusa Dua Declaration, released in 2010, explicitly recognised that the increasing level of complexity and fragmentation was undermining the effectiveness of international environmental governance:

> We note the fact that the current international environmental governance architecture has many institutions and instruments and has become complex and fragmented. It is therefore sometimes not as effective and efficient as it should be. We commit to further efforts to make it more effective.[12]

The Declaration adopted a progressive outlook and established a Consultative Group of Ministers to develop options for reform of the current architecture and increased synergy among MEAs in the lead-up to the 2012 Conference on Sustainable Development (Rio+20). The Consultative Group has developed nine options for strengthening governance, including reinforcing the relationship between environmental science and policy, improving channels for financial and technical assistance and providing legal advice to nations on the implementation of MEAs.[13]

Global environmental problems largely affect the community of nations as a whole. Whilst the extent of such problems will vary among different states, effective solutions must be based on cooperation and the use of common rules, standards and mechanisms that facilitate regular decision-making among the relevant nations.[14] A feature of modern international environmental governance is the increasing diversity found among the actors that contribute to the formulation, implementation and enforcement of international law. Traditional definitions of international institutions focused principally upon law-making capabilities. However, a broader view recognises that international environmental governance requires the participation of different types of institutions. Equally important is acknowledging the linkages between the different actors. Hey reviews the contribution of these bodies in the context of both normative development of international rules and decision-making and adopts a broader perspective that recognises the multitude of different actors and characterises them according to the roles fulfilled.[15] Analysis of 'normative development' encompasses a broad process that

---

9 United Nations Environment Programme, *United Nations Environment Programme Yearbook 2011. Emerging Issues in our Global Environment*, Nairobi: UNEP, 2011, p. 70.
10 Ibid.
11 For further discussion of 'treaty congestion' see Chapter 36 by D. Anton in this volume.
12 *Nusa Dua Declaration* (2010), UNEP/GCSS.XI/L.6, para. 8.
13 United Nations Environment Programme, *United Nations Environment Programme Annual Report 2010*, Nairobi: UNEP, 2010.
14 Hey, op. cit., p. 750.
15 Ibid.

includes the fomenting conditions that promote and facilitate the creation of international law. It also highlights the different avenues by which normative standards can be created – a trend that is of particular significance with regard to treaty regimes and the operation of Conferences of the Parties (COPs).

An indispensable part of exercising a facilitative role is providing a forum that allows states to engage in dialogue and negotiations. This affords states the opportunity to reach agreements in a conciliatory environment that helps alleviate many of the economic, social and cultural differences that exist between nations.[16] This has led commentators to conclude that 'international organizations have become an important part of the law making process, even if they are not in themselves *the* process'.[17] This underlines the importance of the facilitative role they play but also hints at the inherent limitations within which such bodies operate in trying to progress law and policy. Decisions that represent the outcome of negotiations and meetings facilitated by international organisations ultimately reflect the interests and concerns of the Member States as influenced by the particular voting structure that the specific treaty regime or organisation employs.[18]

The United Nations

The primary international organisation remains the United Nations (UN). The Economic and Social Council (ECOSOC) along with the UN General Assembly and Security Council constitute the principal organs of the UN. Two subsidiary bodies responsible for implementing sustainable development/environment policy are the UNEP and the Commission for Sustainable Development (CSD). Whilst the two bodies adopt slightly different perspectives and emphasis, the issue of cooperation with other intergovernmental bodies remains a high priority for each. However, achieving cooperation and coherence remains challenging as there are 44 agencies within the UN system that are engaged in environmental activity in some way. This can be viewed as positive in the sense that it indicates mainstreaming of environmental issues, yet coherence remains problematic in many instances.[19]

Throughout the history of the UN the promotion of environmental issues has developed slowly. The UN Charter does not contain any overt references to environmental protection nor to sustainable development. Birnie, Boyle and Redgwell indicate that the lack of explicit references to protecting the environment mean that the 'subsequent evolution of UN power to adopt policies or take measures directed at environmental objectives has to be derived from a broad interpretation of the Charter and of the implied powers of the organization'.[20] An example of such 'broad interpretation' recognises the links between the natural environment and economic and social development, health and human rights mentioned in provisions such as Articles 1 and 55 of the UN Charter.[21]

16 Ibid., p. 45.
17 A. Boyle and C.M. Chimkin, *The Making of International Law*, Oxford: Oxford University Press, 2007, p. 12.
18 Birnie et al., op. cit., p. 46.
19 *Environment in the United Nations system*, UNEP/GC.26/INF/23 (21–24 February, 2011).
20 Birnie et al., op. cit., p. 58.
21 The decision in the *Reparations for Injuries Case* underlined the legitimacy of this method of interpreting the UN Charter by holding that 'the rights and duties of an entity such as the Organization must depend upon its purpose and functions as specified or implied in its constituent documents and developed in practice'.

The environmental duties and responsibilities performed by specialised agencies such as the International Maritime Organization (IMO), the Food and Agriculture Organization (FAO) and the UN Educational, Scientific and Cultural Organization (UNESCO) provide further evidence of the fragmented nature of international environmental governance. The majority of such agencies have only incidental relevance to environmental protection to the extent that environmental concerns impact on their core mandate – be it related to maritime concerns or agriculture etc. Their power to regulate environmental matters has necessarily had to be developed through interpretation and practice.[22] Any such powers must be very closely related to the specific objects and purpose of the organisation – a position affirmed in the International Court of Justice (ICJ) *Advisory Opinions on the Legality of the Threat or Use of Nuclear Weapons*.[23] The ICJ discerned the general, broad power of the UN General Assembly from the exclusively health-related powers of the WHO. Consequently it decided that the WHO lacked competence to seek an advisory opinion on the legality of nuclear weapons despite the obvious dangers to human health and the environment more broadly. The environmental scope of the IMO is restricted to marine pollution from vessels whilst the FAO is concerned with sustainable use of resources in the context of agriculture.

A recent comment by the UNEP Governing Council reflected the importance of coordination:

> Central to coherence in the environment–development nexus at intergovernmental level is UNGA, ECOSOC, functional commissions under ECOSOC, including CSD, the governing boards of UN agencies … and the COPs of MEAs.[24]

UN General Assembly

The General Assembly (UNGA) can deal with any matter that is within the mandate of the UN Charter. In terms of environmental issues the General Assembly has passed resolutions that whilst not binding do act as recommendations, for example the 1982 World Charter for Nature.[25] Even though environmental and sustainable development matters are delegated among various organs including the UNEP, the United Nations Development Programme (UNDP) and the CSD, the UNGA has historically fulfilled a crucial coordinating role in terms of 'initiating processes, establishing the institutional machinery and adopting benchmarks for environmental cooperation'.[26] The UNGA does not possess an explicit law-making power – rather it fulfils the role of commencing and facilitating the law-making process among Member States. It performs this role through such activities as adopting resolutions and convening conferences that can place a particular environmental issue on the international agenda. For example, landmark international conferences initially spearheaded by the UNGA include the 1972 Stockholm Conference on the Human Environment, the

---

22 Birnie et al., op. cit., p. 59.
23 *Advisory Opinions on the Legality of the Threat or Use of Nuclear Weapons*.
24 *Environment in the United Nations System* UNEP/GC.26/INF/23, p. 11, para. 18.
25 *World Charter for Nature* (1982), GA Res 37/7, UN GAOR, 37th Sess, 51st Supp, UN Doc A/37/7.
26 G. Ulfstein, 'International Framework for Environmental Decision-making', in M. Fitzmaurice, D.M. Ong and P. Merkouris (eds) *Research Handbook on International Environmental Law*, Cheltenham: Edward Elgar, 2010, p. 28.

1973 Law of the Sea Conference and the 1992 Rio Conference on Environment and Development.[27] Promotion of international dialogue on environmental issues is crucial given the fractured state of international environmental governance.

ECOSOC and the Commission on Sustainable Development

The UNEP and the CSD are two areas of the UN dedicated to environmental protection and sustainable development. Both are programmes rather than bodies and operate under the auspices of the ECOSOC.

The UN Charter states that the ECOSOC is the principal UN organ responsible for the promotion of international cooperation on economic and social matters. It has a strong influence upon regulating environmental issues, as the UNEP is included as one of the various specialised agencies, commissions and programmes that report to the ECOSOC. Each agency will bring a different perspective to a common environmental issue and represent different constituencies. As Birnie, Boyle and Redgwell have pointed out, the ability to coordinate across a number of diverse interests is critical as 'no single forum is self-evidently the right one to undertake the development of new law'.[28]

Criticisms aimed at the UN and its constituent organs focus on inefficiency and duplication of tasks largely caused by the unsystematic structure of subsidiary bodies. The ECOSOC is often implicated in this criticism and has been described as 'unable to rise to the task'.[29] It was decided at the Rio Conference not to institute reforms concerning the operation of the ECOSOC with regard to its environmental interests and duties.[30] Ultimately it was agreed that the most appropriate course of action was to implement the sustainable development objectives through the establishment of another subsidiary body dedicated to this purpose – leading to the creation of the CSD. It was recognised that the implementation of sustainable development is 'dynamic' and capable of evolving as conditions demand. The UN General Assembly underlined its coordinating role by giving the CSD a rather broad mandate:

- Promote the incorporation of the Rio Declaration and the Forest Principles in the implementation of Agenda 21;
- Monitor the progress of Agenda 21, the Rio Declaration and Forest Principles made by governments and the UN system;
- Review the adequacy of the financial and technology transfer provisions;
- Enhance the dialogue between the UN, NGOs and other outside bodies;
- Consider information on the implementation of environmental conventions;
- Make recommendations to ECOSOC and the General Assembly on the above matters.

Whilst the responsibilities are broad the CSD is given little power and few resources with which to meet its objectives. The CSD provides a forum for continued discussion at the

---

27 Note that the UNGA employs a voting system that affords each Member State one vote – consequently giving developing states a majority.
28 Birnie et al., op. cit., p. 60.
29 W.B. Chambers and J.F. Green, *Reforming International Environmental Governance. From Institutional Limits to Innovative Reform*, Tokyo: United Nations University Press, 2005, p. 35.
30 Proposals included 're-instituting the UNEP's coordinating role, or establishing an Intergovernmental Standing Committee in a supervisory role, or adapting the role of the Security Council or Trusteeship Council to take on environmental responsibilities'; see Birnie et al., op. cit., p. 66.

international level related to how to broadly meet sustainable development objectives and little else. For example, in order to monitor the progress of Agenda 21 the CSD requires reports from nation states and other UN institutions; yet despite its obvious importance these reports remain voluntary and it is within the discretion of national governments to decide the timing, content and format. Consequently reviewing and comparing reports is difficult as there is no formal baseline for measuring performance.

UNEP

Background

The UNEP fulfils a dual role of catalyst and coordinator – helping to establish new MEAs and coordinating such treaties as part of international environmental governance. More specifically the roles of the UNEP include:

- Setting the environmental agenda;
- Promoting the coherent implementation of the environmental dimension of sustainable development within the UN system;
- Catalysing the development and implementation of environmental policies and instruments;
- Supporting efforts to implement agreed environmental goals and objectives.

The UNEP has been recognised as having made a 'significant contribution to the development of new global and regional conventions, to further development and strengthening of existing legal agreements and to the promotion of wide participation in existing agreements'.[31] The UNEP has provided legal advice and other logistical and political support that has led to the following MEAs:

- Cartagena Protocol on Biosafety;
- Rotterdam Convention on the Prior Informed Consent Procedure for Certain Hazardous Chemicals and Pesticides in International Trade;
- Stockholm Convention on Persistent Organic Pollutants;
- Revised Protocol on Shared Watercourses;
- Convention for Cooperation in the Protection and Sustainable Development of the Marine and Coastal Environment of the North East Pacific;
- African Convention on the Conservation of Nature and Natural Resources;
- ASEAN Agreement on Transboundary Haze Pollution.

It has its headquarters in Nairobi, Kenya; however, it also has an office in New York in the UN headquarters. The New York Office is vital in ensuring that the UNEP is represented in the context of UNGA and ECOSOC deliberations that concern environmental and sustainable development. It further consolidates the UNEP's coordination role within the

---

31 Fourth Programme for the Development and Periodic Review of Environmental Law, Governing Council/Global Ministerial Forum at Nairobi, 16–20 February, UNEP/GC.25/INF/15/Add.1, para. 32.

UN system by participating in inter-UN meetings such as the UN Development Group and Environmental Management Group.[32]

The UNEP is also one of three implementing agencies of the Global Environmental Facility (GEF), along with the UNDP and the World Bank, that acts at the funding mechanism for the following MEAs:

- Convention on Biological Diversity (CBD);
- Convention on Climate Change (UNFCCC);
- Convention to Combat Desertification (CCD);
- Stockholm Convention on Persistent Organic Pollutants.[33]

As a 'programme' the UNEP does not hold a highly influential or independent role in terms of the UN structure as it is not a separate organisation and is integrated into the UN hierarchy. Programmes in the UN system are small and their membership is not universal. The UNEP was not established by treaty but through decisions of the UNGA. As such it cannot make binding decisions and is an example of a soft-law institution that reports to the UNGA via ECOSOC. Given that the UNGA oversees the UNEP all members have an indirect voice in the governance of the body. However, it remains prolific in its contribution to the coordination and development of international environmental law and governance. The programme is piloted by the Governing Council, which consists of 58 members elected by the UN General Assembly for three-year terms. The election of members represents the principle of equitable regional representation.[34] The Governing Council also constitutes the forum of the Global Ministerial Environment Forum that is convened annually to review environmental policy issues. Described as a 'catalyst, advocate, educator and facilitator to promote the wise use and sustainable development of the global environment' the UNEP performs this role by working in conjunction with a variety of actors including other UN bodies, international organisations, NGOs, national governments and private interests.

The UNEP was created in 1972. In the course of the Stockholm Conference Member States recognised the need for a 'permanent institutional arrangement within the United Nations for the protection and improvement of the environment'.[35] The UNEP is not bestowed with the responsibility for initiating the development of international environmental law and policy. Rather it is associated with coordinating action in the international environmental arena through the adoption of a cooperative approach. The UNGA imposed a set of responsibilities upon the Governing Council including, *inter alia*:

---

32 The UNEP has regional offices in Africa, Asia and the Pacific, Europe, Latin America and the Caribbean and West Asia. The role of the UNEP is to enhance the capacity of domestic governments to implement programmes in the various regions.

33 For further discussion of international environmental funding see Chapter 9 by J. Wolst in this volume.

34 The breakdown of representation on the Governing Council is as follows:

- 16 seats for African States;
- 13 seats for Asian States;
- 6 seats for Eastern European States;
- 10 seats for Latin American States;
- 13 seats for Western European and other States.

35 See *Report of the United Nations Conference on the Human Environment, Stockholm, 5–16 June 1972.*

- To promote international cooperation in the field of the environment and to recommend, as appropriate, policies to this end;
- To provide general policy guidance for the direction and coordination of environmental programmes within the UN system;
- To keep under review the world environmental situation in order to ensure that emerging environmental problems of wide international significance receive appropriate and adequate consideration by governments;
- To review and approve the programme of utilisation of resources of the Environment Fund.

Further to the realisation of these objectives the UNGA decided that the UNEP Executive Director would have the responsibility, *inter alia*, to 'coordinate, under the guidance of the Governing Council, environmental programmes within the United Nations system, to keep their implementation under review and to assess their effectiveness'.[36] This might have motivated the first Executive Director to describe the role of the UNEP as 'to remind others of, and help them to take into account all the systems, interactions and ramifications implied in their work'.[37]

The decisions of the Stockholm Declaration indicated that the UNEP was never to be given operational powers. The mandate underlined functions including coordination and providing expertise to solve environmental crises but also expressed that it was to be flexible and grow into its mandate as new issues emerged. It is clear that the role and mandate of the UNEP has evolved since its inception in 1972.

Arguably the most notable change to the UNEP's role was contained in Agenda 21 established in 1992. The document mandates the UNEP to specifically give priority, *inter alia*, to development of international environmental law, promoting its implementation through coordinating (or clustering) the operation of different MEAs and their respective regimes.[38] Explicit references to 'development of international environmental law' represented the culmination of a number of previous initiatives aimed at enhancing the role of UNEP in promoting both binding and non-binding instruments. In 1982, ten years after the inception of the UNEP, the Programme for the Development and Periodic Review of Environmental Law ('the Montevideo Programme') was adopted.[39] The Montevideo Programme plotted future progress in international environmental law and policy and identified treaties on issues such as ozone protection as representing markers of such progress. Implementation of the Programme was to be performed by the UNEP in conjunction with other UN bodies, regional organisations and NGOs. It was subject to revisions in 1993 following the Rio Conference and once again in 2001. Since the release of the Montevideo Programme and the World Summit on Sustainable Development in 2002, international environmental governance has focused upon achieving existing goals and objectives contained in UN frameworks such as Agenda 21 and the UN Millennium Development Goals in addition to various treaties.

36 UNEP Governing Council, *Introductory Statement by the Executive Director* (11 February 1975) UNEP/GC/31, UNEP/GC/31/Add 1, UNEP/GC/31/Add 2, UNEP/GC/31/Add 3.
37 Ibid.
38 *Agenda 21*, Ch. 38, para. H (1)(h); UNGA Res S/19–2; UNGA Res 53/242 (1999).
39 *Montevideo Programme for the Development and Periodic Review of Environmental Law*, Ad Hoc Meeting of Senior Government Officials Expert in Environmental Law, Montevideo, 6 November 1981, Decision 10/21 of Governing Council of UNEP of 31 May 1981.

Facilitating coordination and coherence

The coordination role for the UNEP outlined in Agenda 21 was intended to 'achieve coherence and compatibility, and to avoid overlapping or conflicting regulation' between different environmental regimes.[40] However, the effectiveness of the UNEP in fulfilling its list of objectives and responsibilities has been undermined by problems relating to the structure of the UN. Its failure to coordinate the environmental work of the UN has been a constant source of criticism. The Governing Council of the UNEP recently reported that current demands have hindered fulfilment of the UNEP's original mandate: 'The expanding environmental agenda and its emerging integration into the development agenda … has made the performance of UNEP's originally envisaged system-wide role more demanding, while UNEP's own system-wide role has been eroding.'[41]

An innovation that has been spearheaded by the UNEP, and that is particularly prevalent in modern international environmental law, is the development of framework treaties. Under this approach the UNEP initiates a process of gathering scientific information and building consensus towards a broad framework that identifies an environmental problem and provides loosely developed legal strategies, often containing limited commitments and obligations, to solve the identified problem.

The UNEP has also helped facilitate subsequent negotiations – with the notable exception of the climate change regime.[42] The relationship between the UNEP and various MEA regimes can affect the capacity for coordination.[43] Conferences of the Parties (COPs) are the supreme authority under each individual MEA and decide upon any joint efforts within any treaty regime. As Andresen comments, COPs do not appear to hold much faith in the UNEP process.[44] In support of this proposition Andresen cites events that took place during a meeting of the COP to the CBD in 2004. The meeting witnessed the establishment of the Biodiversity Liaison Group, which excluded the UNEP even though it had played a major role in creating all the conventions included as part of the Group. A potential reason for this omission is that the UNEP is not regarded as performing its coordination role particularly well. Andresen has commented that:

> [the] UNEP … has traditionally been well equipped as a 'founding father' for new institutions but has not really been able to 'keep the children in the nest when they are ready to fly'.[45]

40 *Agenda 21*, op. cit.
41 *Environment in the United Nations System*, UNEP/GC.26/INF/23 (21–24 February 2011).
42 At its first session in 1995 the COP decided that 'the Convention secretariat will be institutionally linked to the United Nations, while not being fully integrated in the work programme and management structure of any particular department or programme'. FCCC/CP/1995/7/Add.1 Decision 14.
43 In 1998 the UN General Assembly formed a Task Force to undertake a review of the UNEP. Of particular relevance the Task Force Report called for stronger linkage among MEAs through such measures as periodic meetings between the UNEP Governing Council and the COPs of the different MEAs.
44 S. Andresen, 'The Effectiveness of UN Environmental Institutions', *International Environmental Agreements* 7, 2007, 317–36, pp. 331, 333.
45 Ibid., p. 333.

Funding

The UNEP is widely criticised for having an excessively broad mandate yet insufficient funding to match. The UNEP is funded through the regular budget of the UN, the Environment Fund, trust funds and earmarked contributions related to the Environment Fund and Trust Fund Support account. Funding for the UNEP is vastly inferior to that of the UNDP – a problem that is exacerbated by the 'turf wars' that exist among UN bodies competing for territory and status.

The UNEP is heavily dependent on voluntary contributions, with the bulk being channelled through the Environment Fund. Theoretically all UN Member States, taking into account their individual economic and social circumstances, should contribute financially to the UNEP. In order to facilitate this, a Voluntary Indicative Scale of Contributions (VISC) was developed to provide a guide to the amount of contributions that should be made. This has proved an 'efficient approach in stimulating voluntary contributions to the Environment Fund'.[46] Currently contributions are sourced from over 110 donor countries (on average), representing a significant increase from the 76 donor countries in 2003. The 2008–2009 biennium witnessed unprecedented contributions totalling US $174 million.[47] It was reported that the 2010–2011 biennium had a less positive outlook as the global economic crisis and exchange rate fluctuations had a negative impact on the level of contributions made in currencies outside US dollars.[48]

The Environment Fund was also established in 1972. The overall effect of the fund is to finance environmental programmes. Through the history of the UNEP payments to the Environmental Fund have fluctuated, leaving the organisation on the verge of a funding crisis on numerous occasions. After the establishment of the UNEP in 1972 there was strong initial financial support that peaked in 1977. However, by the time of the Brundtland Report in 1987 the level of financial support had shrunk by 60 per cent compared to 1977. Despite a resurgence in 1992, no doubt coinciding with the Rio Conference, the figures fell to new lows in 2000. Over the period from 1973 to 2011 a total of 181 countries have made at least one contribution. However, only 12 countries have continued to give regular annual contributions over this period. Thus contributions are still concentrated among a small number of countries. In 2008, 92.7 per cent of total contributions came from 15 donor countries – in comparison to 2007 the number of country pledges decreased in 2008 from 104 to 92 yet the amount of paid contributions increased from US$66.83 million to US$88.25 million.[49]

The number of trust funds currently active stood at 84 in 2010. Of these 52 directly supported the UNEP Programme of Work whilst the remaining 32 financed MEAs and Regional Seas Programmes.[50] Most trust funds are designed to provide finance for specific projects. The most prolific trust fund is the Multilateral Fund under the Montreal Protocol

---

46 United Nations Environment Programme, *Financing of the UNEP*: Online. Available HTTP: <http://www.unep.org/rms/en/Financing_of_UNEP/Environment_Fund/index.asp> (accessed 12 December 2011).

47 Ibid.

48 Ibid.

49 Status of the Environment Fund and Other Sources of Funding of the UNDP, 25th Session of the Governing Council/Global Ministerial Forum, 16–20 February 2009, Nairobi, UNEP/GC.25. INF/5, 13 January 2009

50 United Nations Environment Programme, *Financing of the UNEP*: Online Available HTTP: <www.unep.org/rms/en/Financing_of_UNEP/Trustfunds/index.asp> (accessed 12 December 2011).

on substances that Deplete the Ozone Layer. In terms of general trust funds the key function is the provision of financial resources for activities related to the programme of work of the UNEP, MEAs (including activities of secretariats) and Regional Seas Programmes.[51]

The Financial Rules of the UNEP Fund allow the Director of the UNEP to accept earmarked contributions. These contributions take the form of agreements between the UNEP and governments and other bodies and are made in cash to support specific activities outlined in project documents.[52] Funding from earmarked contributions during the 2008–2009 period amounted to $67.6 million.[53] Significant contributions are channelled through the Partnership Agreements between the UNEP and major donors. Funding under this arrangement is much more targeted and focuses on UNEP programme priorities. It helps provide predictable and additional funding for projects. The current biennium of 2010–2011 had US$228 million in earmarked support.[54]

The UN regular budget was originally envisaged as providing funds for costs of servicing the Governing Council under UNGA Resolution 2997 (XXVII). In the 2008–2009 period US$13.8 million was designated from the UN regular budget with US$10.3 million allocated to and directly administered by the UNEP in its Nairobi headquarters.[55] Examples of specific activities funded through the use of the regular budget contribution include policy-making, executive direction and management, development of programmes of work and programme support. In 2008–2009 US$12.93 million was allocated from the UN regular budget for the UNEP whilst in 2010–2011 the contribution increased to US$13.4 million.[56] The contribution from the UN regular budget represents less than 4 per cent of the UNEP's total budget. Further funds are allocated to the UNEP from the UN Development Account – part of the UN regular budget. During the 2010–2011 biennium funding under this category exceeded US$2.7 million.[57]

Environment Management Group

The Environment Management Group (EMG) was established in 2001 in accordance with UNGA Resolution 53/242 passed in 1999.[58] It is principally designed to effect system-wide coordination within the UN. The group specialises in identifying environmental issues that require cooperation and seeks to find coherent solutions that utilise the various actors. An important aspect of this role is coordinating UN-wide support in the implementation of MEAs. In particular the EMG will investigate the operation of particular MEAs that require cooperation with other regimes – examples include the UN climate neutral initiative, the 2010 biodiversity targets and the EMG land initiative. Fulfilment of this task complements other initiatives undertaken by the UNEP to coordinate implementation of MEAs through

51 Ibid.
52 Ibid.
53 Ibid.
54 Ibid.
55 United Nations Environment Programme, *Financing of the UNEP:* Online. Available HTTP: <www.unep.org/rms/en/Financing_of_UNEP/Regular_Budget/index.asp> (accessed 12 December 2011).
56 Ibid.
57 Ibid.
58 *Report of the Secretary General on the Environment and Human Settlements* UNGA Res 53/242, 53rd session, Agenda item 30, A/RES/53/242, 10 August 1999.

measures such as harmonisation of national reporting based on either 'clustering' relevant MEAs or common themes that intersect different regimes.

The EMG has a broad membership including UN specialised agencies, programmes, the secretariats of various MEAs, Bretton Woods Institutions and the WTO. The different members engage in information sharing, consultation regarding new initiatives and an agreed set of priorities. In terms of administration the EMG is highly dependent upon the UNEP, which provides a secretariat whilst the UNEP Executive Director also chairs the group. The EMG also contributes to the work of the Consultative Group of Ministers that was established to consider broad reform of the international environmental governance system.

Criticism and possible future direction

The UN environmental operations have been heavily criticised. Whilst a thorough analysis is beyond the scope of this chapter, commentary on how to improve the situation focuses strongly on efficiency and effectiveness. Effective environmental governance must be cognisant of the role played by economic development goals and priorities. A measure of effectiveness is the extent to which environmental goals are integrated into development strategies and pathways. A report by the Secretary-General's High-Level Panel in 2006, entitled *Delivering as One*, commissioned to highlight ways in which the UN can improve overall coherency, commented upon environmental policy in the context of fulfilling the Millennium Development Goals.[59] A major focus of the report is systematic fragmentation and the need for better focus on performance.[60] These concerns appear to stem from a failure within the UN to measure and evaluate outcomes.

The current structure of the UN is also criticised for not facilitating effective environmental governance. Environmental issues are pervasive and increasing relevance to a number of UN organs places competitive pressure upon resources. The *Delivering as One* report recommended that UN agencies, programmes and funds with responsibilities in the area of the environment should cooperate more effectively on a thematic basis, for example atmosphere, water and endangered species.[61] The report commented, 'This would be based on a combined effort towards agreed common activities and policy objectives to eliminate duplication and focus on results.'[62] In terms of environmental policy the overall view of the Report was that:

> [t]o improve effectiveness and targeted action of environmental activities, the system of international environmental governance should be strengthened and more coherent, featuring an upgraded UN Environment Programme with real authority as the UN's 'environment policy' pillar.[63]

59 Secretary-General's High-Level Panel on UN System-Wide Coherence in the Areas of Development, Humanitarian Assistance, and the Environment, *Delivering as One. Report of the Secretary-General's High-Level Panel*, New York: United Nations, 2006.
60 Ibid., p. 18.
61 Ibid., p. 21.
62 Ibid.
63 Ibid., pp. 18–19.

A number of these issues are encapsulated in the preparatory negotiations and documents guiding the 'Rio+20' UN Conference on Sustainable Development in 2012.[64] Strengthening and reforming the institutional framework of environmental governance constitute a key theme of Rio+20 and the overall goal of enhancing sustainable development. The so-called zero-draft of the outcome document has outlined a number of improvements to be made across ECOSOC, the CSD and the UNEP. With regard to the former two bodies improvements to be sought focus in particular upon mainstreaming sustainable development and enhancing implementation of agreements and decisions.[65] In relation to the CSD, options that allow it to focus on a more limited set of issues will be considered and as an alternative the transformation of the CSD into a Sustainable Development Council will be submitted.[66]

Regarding the UNEP the zero-draft states that the parties (the heads of state and government) agree to strengthen the capacity of the UNEP through establishing universal membership in its Governing Council together with a substantial budgetary increase; or alternatively resolve to form a UN specialised agency based on the UNEP but existing on an equal footing with other such bodies.[67]

Financial institutions[68]

Provision of finance and funding channels are essential to the implementation of international environmental law and policy. The two most prominent financial institutions are the World Bank and the Global Environmental Facility (GEF).

The World Bank's overall purpose is to provide funds, usually in the form of long-term loans, that will foster reforms leading to economic development or supporting reconstruction projects. In the past this has led to inevitable conflict with environmental groups concerned about the implications of such development projects. Despite the economic focus of its mandate the World Bank, like other UN agencies, is expected to promote sustainable development. This commitment is reflected in current World Bank policy that requires proposed development projects to fulfil certain environmental criteria before funding is provided. This is aimed at ensuring that the development project is environmentally sound through the use of Environmental Action Plans that outline the borrowing countries' environmental problems and strategies for addressing them.

The International Finance Corporation, the private financial wing of the World Bank, has instituted a policy that forbids funding of any activity that does not meet the social and environmental standards it sets. In this case the criteria reflect the provisions of several different MEAs.[69] A unique aspect of the World Bank's operations relates to monitoring of the environmentally conscious aspects of its funding strategies. The Inspection Panel was created to

64 United Nations, *The Future We Want – zero-draft of the outcome document, January 10, 2012*: Online. Available HTTP: <www.uncsd2012.org/rio20/content/documents/370The%20Future%20 We%20Want%2010Jan%20clean.pdf> (accessed 11 January 2012).
65 Ibid., p. 9.
66 Ibid., p. 10.
67 Ibid., p. 11.
68 The issue of funding international environmental law is considered in detail by J. Wolst in Chapter 9 of this volume.
69 See The World Bank, *Introduction to the WBG's Environment Strategy*: Online. Available HTTP: <http://web.worldbank.org/WBSITE/EXTERNAL/TOPICS/ENVIRONMENT/0,,contentM DK:20268515~menuPK:242145~pagePK:148956~piPK:216618~theSitePK:244381,00.html> (accessed 12 December 2011).

provide affected groups with an avenue to challenge any perceived failure of the World Bank to adhere to its own environmental policies. Birnie, Boyle and Redgwell have remarked that the Inspection Panel is an 'innovative and … unique method for introducing a measure of public accountability to the operations of an international organization'.[70]

Further criticism relates to the voting structure and consequent lack of developing country representation of both the World Bank and the GEF. The control of the World Bank is determined by those nations that contribute the most capital – predictably rich, developed and industrialised economies. As a consequence developing countries are marginalised.

The World Bank, in conjunction with the UNEP and the UNDP, created the GEF in 1991. During the Rio Conference in 1992 decisions were taken to restructure the GEF and integrate the principles of 'universality, transparency and democracy' into its operations through a new instrument which was ultimately revised in 2002. The role of the GEF is to provide funding to developing countries to meet 'agreed incremental costs' of measures taken in accordance with Agenda 21 and is aimed at achieving 'agreed global environmental benefits' in relation to the following:

- climate change;
- biological diversity;
- international waters;
- ozone layer depletion;
- deforestation;
- desertification;
- persistent organic pollutants.

The GEF is also the designated financial mechanism for a number of MEA regimes including the UNFCCC, the CBD and the Convention on Persistent Organic Pollutants.

The GEF remains a separate and distinct entity despite being an inter-agency body with the World Bank acting as trustee. The GEF has its own Governing Council, with decision-making power, constituted by 32 members representing an equal balance between developed and developing countries.[71] The voting system was purposely redesigned in 1992 in order to prevent the lack of developing country representation witnessed in the World Bank's structure.[72] The World Bank, the UNDP and the UNEP are all accountable to the Council for activities funded by the GEF.[73] The GEF also utilises an independent secretariat that receives administrative support from the World Bank. Decisions are made via consensus, and in the event that no consensus is attainable a formal vote is taken. In such a situation decisions must receive approval through a double majority (that is of developed and developing countries) of 60 per cent of all members and a majority of 60 per cent (in terms of contribution) of donors before they are passed.[74] The second condition has attracted some criticism suggesting

---

70 Birnie et al., op. cit., p. 81.
71 Global Environmental Facility, *What is the GEF?* Online. Available HTTP: <www.thegef.org/gef/whatisgef> (accessed 12 December 2011).
72 L. Boisson de Chazournes, 'The Global Environment Facility (GEF): A Unique and Crucial Institution', *Review of European Community and International Environmental Law*, 14(3), 2005, pp. 193 201.
73 Ibid.
74 Ibid.

that the power of decision-making still rests heavily with rich, developed nations. It should be noted that the GEF has never been forced to resort to a vote.[75]

The GEF remains an important institution for the promotion of developing country interests particularly by acting as a conduit for the delivery of funds originating in the developed world. The GEF's operations reflect the principles of Common but Differentiated Responsibility (CBDR) and additionality that are critical from the developing countries' perspective. The two principles are enshrined in the Rio Declaration and other MEAs and operate to ensure equitable treatment of developing countries in terms of environmental commitments and the maintenance of a predictable, steady flow of funding that is designated for specific environmental purposes and not diverted from pre-existing funding streams.

The GEF Trust Fund is financed through 'replenishments' that take the form of pledged contributions. The GEF Replenishment operates in the context of broader negotiations where replenishment participants negotiate and ultimately agree to a set of policy reforms together with the level of resources that the GEF will attempt to provide during the replenishment period.[76] Further, replenishment participants will review independent 'Overall Performance Studies' of the operations of the GEF. The current replenishment period, the fifth replenishment period in the history of the GEF, operates from 1 July 2010 to 30 June 2014 – whilst negotiations for the sixth replenishment are to start in 2013.[77] The negotiations for the fifth replenishment period broke with tradition by allowing non-donor recipient countries to participate as well as NGO representatives.[78] This acknowledged the increasing role of developing countries in international environmental governance and a commitment to increasing values such as transparency, accountability and inclusion. Overall 34 countries made pledges, resulting in a 53.4 per cent increase in funding from the fourth replenishment period and a total GEF Trust Fund figure of US$4.34 billion for the fifth replenishment period.[79]

International autonomous regulatory regimes

Background

International regulatory regimes are based upon MEAs and accompanying administrative institutions. These regimes include a number of bodies, all of which are created through the constitutive documents of the respective MEA; for example, Conferences/Meetings of the Parties and Scientific and Technical Bodies. Such regimes are a hallmark of contemporary international environmental governance as they provide a flexible system of regulation with the capacity for 'dynamic evolution'.[80] This is of great importance when attempting to regulate environmental issues such as climate change that have clear global consequences and require consistent re-evaluation of commitments in accordance with the increasing severity of environmental damage as reflected in scientific findings. The parties to the MEA meet regularly through Conferences/Meetings of the Parties (COP/MOP). Generally provision

---

75 Ibid., p. 197.
76 Global Environment Facility, *GEF Replenishments*: Online. Available HTTP: <www.thegef.org/gef/replenishment> (accessed 12 December 2011).
77 Ibid.
78 Ibid.
79 Ibid.
80 T. Gehring, 'International Dynamic Regimes: Dynamic Sectoral Legal Systems', *Yearbook of International Environmental Law*, 1, 1990, 35–49, pp. 35–6.

for the existence and operation of the COP/MOP is made in the constitutive documents of the treaty; however, meetings can be convened by order of the UNGA or a specialised agency or a commission specifically set up for the purpose of managing the treaty. The COP is bestowed with authority to establish subsidiary bodies and the secretariat and is instrumental in developing cooperation through instruments such as subsequent protocols. For example, under the climate change regime the COP is the supreme body in the 'institutional machinery' pursuant to Article 7(2) of the UNFCCC. Churchill and Ulfstein list functions such as managing internal matters, contributing to the development of new substantive obligations of the parties, amending an MEA and supervising compliance; and they may act at the external level by adopting arrangements with international organisations.[81] Despite being bodies created through MEAs, COPs are 'freestanding and distinct from ... state parties to a particular agreement and feature their own law making powers and compliance mechanisms'.[82] A secretariat can act as a link between the treaty regime and existing international institutions. A number of MEAs have secretariats such as the UNEP that means the treaty regime is integrated into the UN structure. The functions, though, are detailed in the provisions of the relevant MEA and include, *inter alia*, conducting studies, preparing draft decisions for the COPs and receiving and circulating reports on the implementation of commitments.

Operation of autonomous regulatory regimes

MEAs that feature 'framework' agreements, such as the UNFCCC, are designed to provide an initial broad-based legal solution to an environmental problem, thereby allowing further legal developments through subsequent protocols, annexes, amendments and recommendations that 'flesh out' commitments. As such there is a necessary overlap between the Protocol, for example, and the Convention – but the former does enjoy its own unique institutional structure. In some cases the body that convenes for annual meetings is constituted differently. This reflects differences in terms of which nations are parties to the Convention as opposed to the Protocol. For example, under the ozone layer regime the Vienna Convention features a different COP as compared to the MOP that operates under the Montreal Protocol. In the case of the climate change regime the Kyoto Protocol outlines that the COP (under the UNFCCC) and MOP under the Protocol are the same – but only parties to the Kyoto Protocol can participate in the MOP.

Another core element relates to reviewing the treaty. The COP/MOP cannot create substantive legal commitments in the absence of ratification by parties to the MEA. However, the COP/MOP does have a prominent role to play in developing substantive commitments through direct and indirect law-making powers. Indirect powers, for instance, allow negotiations of amendments whilst an example of direct powers relates to developing rules for emissions trading within the climate change regime. Emissions trading, as originally outlined in the UNFCCC, lacked detail regarding the operation of the scheme and is an example of where the substance of the rules was to be provided through COP decisions – see Article 17 of the Convention.[83] It can in certain contexts, however, help develop the

---

81 Churchill and Ulfstein, op. cit., p. 623.
82 Ibid.
83 *United Nations Framework Convention on Climate Change*, opened for signature 4 June 1992, 1771 UNTS 107 (entered into force 21 March 1994) (UNFCCC) Art. 17.

operation of legal commitments through interpreting provisions of the relevant MEA or Protocol. Article 31(3)(a) describes COP-related decisions as a 'subsequent agreement between the Parties regarding the interpretation of the treaty or the application of its provisions'. The implications of this role should not be underestimated. Whilst the COP meets annually it presents the most regular contact point between parties and the Convention and is therefore well equipped to examine and reassess the parties' commitments with particular regard to emerging environmental challenges. It is an important vehicle that helps drive the evolution of the regime. Reviewing the treaty is essentially concerned with ensuring that the overall objects and purpose are being met. In completing this task Member States can consider the adoption of new measures and commitments. In dispensing this responsibility the COP can overlap with the treaty secretariat that is responsible for the daily operations of the regime. In some instances, such as the Vienna Convention on Ozone Depletion, the UNEP serves as the secretariat for a treaty regime.

This is complemented by the work performed by expert bodies. This includes subsidiary bodies that provide scientific and technical expertise to evaluate whether commitments are helping to achieve the environmental objects of the MEA. In addition expert bodies can provide advice on legal issues such as implementation and even compliance measures. Each expert body can recommend changes to ensure that the purpose and objects of the treaty are fulfilled.

The elements of treaty regimes operate to ensure that the MEA continues to develop in the context of changing environmental conditions. Drumbl adds that the treaty regime approach represents a 'robust and ongoing process of law making ... and agility'. He therefore concludes that 'treaty bodies effectively serve as actors involved in making international environmental law'.[84]

'Law-making' powers of autonomous regulatory regimes

The primary concern with law-making through treaty regimes relates to consent and legitimacy. Bodansky has argued that the consensual basis of international environmental law has helped preserve it against allegations of a lack of legitimacy and the 'democracy deficit'.[85] Adoption of COP decisions occurs on a majority, rather than unanimous basis. The ability to redefine obligations and commitments in the context of a protocol or even an amendment to a protocol allows a regime a measure of flexibility and progression. Some commentators have characterised COP decisions as 'endeavours to soften the edges of consent' and representative of 'creative legal engineering'.[86] The treatment of consent appears to be the most significant difference between international law-making operating through COP decisions as opposed to the more traditional system. Opinions on the status of COPs range from descriptions of 'issue specific global legislatures'[87] with the capacity to adopt binding standards, through to 'autonomous institutional arrangements' and arguments that a COP best resembles a

---

84 M. Drumbl, 'Actors and Law-making in International Environmental Law', in M. Fitzmaurice, D.M. Ong and P. Merkouris (eds) *Research Handbook on International Environmental Law*, Cheltenham: Edward Elgar, 2010, p. 10.

85 D. Bodansky, 'The Legitimacy of International Governance: A Coming Challenge for International Law?', *American Journal of International Law* 93(3), 1999, 596–627, p. 609.

86 R. Lefeber, 'Creative Legal Engineering', *Leiden Journal of International Law* 13, 2000, 1–9, p. 1.

87 D. Anderson, 'Law-Making Processes in the UN System – Some Impressions', *Max Planck UN Law* 2, 1998, 23–81, p. 49.

diplomatic conference and little else. Two key issues are independence and autonomy, and the range of views on the status of COPs reflects different opinions of the extent to which these themes are represented through the actions of the COP.

An example where the consent requirements have been relaxed relates to the adoption or addition of annexes to protocols or framework agreements. This often serves the purpose of providing technical detail that substantiates existing treaty terms rather than creating new obligations or commitments – examples being Articles 16 and 21.1 of the UNFCCC.[88] These types of additions or annexes are managed by the COP and are usually adopted by consensus yet no formal, explicit expression of consent is necessarily required to give binding legal force to the amendment or annex. It will enter into force and bind all parties except those that object and signify their non-acceptance. Brunnée has argued that the role is evolving to a level 'whereby significant regulatory detail is developed in the COP or its subsidiary bodies, and then adopted by a simple COP decision – without the treaty envisaging a separate consent step to trigger the commitment of individual parties'.[89]

In terms of explicit authority provided within the MEA, the highpoint is found in Article 2.9 of the Montreal Protocol on Substances that Deplete the Ozone Layer.[90] The provision deals with the ozone-depleting substances that are included under annexes to the treaty, and it specifically allows for changes to the ozone-depleting potential of substances or its phase-out schedule. Article 2.9 allows for adoption of these adjustments following a two-thirds majority decision that is then binding on all parties irrespective of whether a sovereign nation voted against the proposed adjustment. The requirement of a two-thirds majority vote ensures that a large measure of consent is still necessary before it can become a binding commitment, but as Brunnée points out, 'Article 2.9 is remarkable in that it allows for formally binding law making by the Meeting of the Parties in relation to alterations of the treaty's substance, indeed, of its central commitments.'[91] Given that control and ultimate phasing out of ozone-depleting substances is central to the very purpose of the Montreal Protocol the MOP can exert influence over the creation of legal norms upon which the architecture of the regime is built. Under the climate change regime the COP/MOP is assigned the role of developing and adopting a decision but with little clarification regarding the legal contours and parameters of the role. Unlike the example of Article 2.9 under the Montreal Protocol there is no legal status for a COP decision.[92]

Relationship to financial institutions

There are practical links between the operation of MEAs and financial institutions. This occurs through the presence of the GEF as the designated financial mechanism in a number of MEAs that provides links to its three operating entities – the World Bank, the UNEP and the UNDP. In the context of MEAs all Member States formally participate equally in

---

88 UNFCCC, op. cit., Arts 16 and 21.1.
89 J. Brunnée, 'Reweaving the Fabric of International Law? Patterns of Consent in Environmental Framework Agreements', in R. Wolfrum and V. Roben (eds) *Developments of International Law in Treaty Making*, Berlin: Springer, 2005, p. 109.
90 *Protocol on Substances that Deplete the Ozone Layer (Montreal)*, opened for signature 16 September 1987, UKTS 19 (1990) Cm.977; 26 *ILM* (1987) 1550 (entered into force 1 January 1989). Current amended text in UNEP, *Handbook of the Montreal Protocol*. (Montreal Protocol).
91 Brunnée, op. cit., p. 109.
92 Montreal Protocol, Art. 2.9.

decision-making. Andresen and Hey maintain that this result is a compromise between developed and developing country interests and is an 'effort to balance legitimacy and effectiveness'.[93] A number of MEAs, such as the climate change and ozone regimes, incorporate principles such as CBDR that places financial obligations on developed countries that are owed to developing countries. The responsibility for funding these obligations is often transferred to the GEF that brings the World Bank into the equation. Given the central role of funding to achieving environmental objectives financial institutions such as the World Bank play a key role in environmental governance.[94]

Criticism and possible future direction

The proliferation of bodies responsible for environmental governance has become self-defeating because the increasing number and complexity of environmental issues is not matched by changes to the structure of relevant international organs or attempts to better coordinate disparate MEAs. Developing countries in particular feel overburdened and cannot meet the necessary administrative costs. The *Delivering as One* Report revealed that the three Rio MEAs (dealing with climate change, biodiversity and desertification) have up to 230 meetings annually.[95]

The high number of MEAs helps to identify different environmental problems but it exacerbates the fragmentation that besets environmental governance. The public attention that environmental issues attract is positive but in order to provide effective governance the current system must be reformed to increase coherency and cooperation among different actors. The Report recommended that:

> National reporting requirements for related multilateral environment agreements should be consolidated into one comprehensive annual report, to ease the burden on countries and improve coherence … Governing bodies of MEAs should promote administrative efficiencies, reducing the frequency and duration of meetings.[96]

Conclusion

The UN system has not generated a system that facilitates the synthesis of environmental and developmental goals. Marrying these two objectives is at the centre of sustainable development but coordination, particularly within UN institutions, has proven difficult.

Whilst the UN bodies are to be compatible and complementary there are advantages in differences which encourage interactions that cut across multiple sectors and recognise competing perspectives. However, the UN bodies have not been effective in monitoring and reviewing the outcomes of its programmes. Whilst treaty regimes might possess the necessary administrative machinery to rectify compliance issues with respect to their own specific provisions there is little they can contribute to overall coordination failures.

93 Andresen and Hey, op. cit., p. 216.
94 Ibid., p. 217.
95 Secretary-General's High-Level Panel on UN System-Wide Coherence in the Areas of Development, Humanitarian Assistance, and the Environment, op. cit., p. 20.
96 Ibid., pp. 21–2.

There is debate as to whether a world environmental organisation akin to the WTO or WHO could alleviate many of the coordination problems discussed above. The proliferation of MEA regimes since 1972 has added another dimension to the debate. These regimes have surged to the forefront of international environmental governance and the lack of coordination between them has resulted in inefficiency and in some cases tension.[97] Whilst the problems concerning coordination are broadly acknowledged, opinion varies as to whether the creation of a world environmental organisation would be of assistance. The primary attraction is centralising the operation of core MEAs and attendant regimes and providing a 'gravity centre' as described by Oberthur and Gehring.[98] Such a move appears desirable but could have negative consequences and will no doubt encounter political resistance. It must also be pointed out that the creation of a world environmental organisation will not in and of itself result in better governance. Charnovitz has commented that:

> Analysts sometimes make the mistake that reorganization (or organizational changes) can drive policy. That almost never happens. Reorganization can only be useful when they implement policy changes.[99]

Charnovtiz reminds observers that the key is the provision of effective governance.[100] This might seem an overly simplistic point but it remains the overall purpose of any proposed reform. Organisations and regimes are very similar in terms of administrative structure – both feature bureaucracies including secretariats.[101] There is a misconception that organisational structures, such as the WTO, necessarily have a broader mandate and area of concern than regimes and are therefore better equipped to deal with environmental regulation. This overlooks the wide-ranging, cross-sector issues that are dealt with under such MEAs as the climate change regime.

Ultimately it is difficult to assess the utility of a world environmental agency until it is clear what model of organisational structure will be employed. One proposal, released by the UN, would simply group all MEA regimes under the one umbrella with no change in the scope of issue areas and decision-making procedures. Such an organisation would essentially be symbolic and make no discernible change to governance. However, a model based on the WTO would present a fundamental change to the decision-making process by adopting 'world environmental rounds' to debate issues. It should be noted, though, that the track record of successfully negotiating rounds in the WTO is not great. There remains little doubt that any structure that is adopted should employ majority decision-making rather than relying upon consensus.

97 S. Oberthur and T. Gehring, 'Reforming International Environmental Governance. An Institutionalist Critique of the Proposal for a World Environmental Organisation', *International Environmental Agreements. Politics, Law and Economics* 4, 2004, 359–381. Oberthur and Gehring cite the example of carbon sequestration activities under the Kyoto Protocol undermining the objectives of the CBD.
98 Ibid.
99 S. Charnovitz, 'A World Environment Organization', *Columbia Journal of Environmental Law* 27, 2002, 323–62, p. 337.
100 Ibid.
101 For a broader discussion of the structure of 'organisations' in international environmental law see F. Biermann, 'Strengthening Green Global Governance in a Disparate World Society. Would a World Environment Organisation Benefit the South?', *International Environmental Agreements: Politics, Law and Economics*, 2002, 297–315.

7

The role of non-governmental organisations, peoples and courts in implementing international environmental laws

Vernon I. Tava

A consequence of neoliberal globalisation has been the devolution of state power to non-state actors. The traditional model of international law has shifted from 'government' to 'governance', challenging states as the sole agents in the establishment and implementation of international environmental agreements. Self-organised NGOs have become major sources of international environmental policy and legislation. Indigenous peoples have forged global solidarity movements and advanced an alternative 'ethno-ecological identity' which is inherently ecocentric and is finding its way into domestic bodies of law. This chapter explores these issues and also examines how international specialist courts deal with the unique considerations of environmental law.

Introduction

In the second half of the twentieth century and into the twenty-first, the practice of international law has dramatically changed and international environmental law has emerged as a distinct discipline. The approach of global governance has supplanted government regulation within national borders to explore more coordinated, effective and integrated ways in which to manage environmental issues. Global civil society in the form of non-governmental organisations (NGOs), indigenous peoples and grass-roots environmental movements working together more closely seeks to change the nature of international environmental law to one that is less state-centric and has begun to challenge the legal treatment of the environment as the property of individuals or states. We are also seeing increasing recognition of indigenous claims for self-determination and, concomitantly, the world view of indigenous peoples informs the principles of sustainable development. Although international courts and arbitration bodies have generally been open only to state actors, there is a developing trend toward the acceptance of submissions from non-state parties. This chapter will examine the role of courts, peoples and NGOs in implementing international law by looking at their interconnected roles within the framework of global environmental governance.

Globalisation has fundamentally altered the nature of relations between and within nation-states. Globalisation's three major characteristics of instantaneous information exchange, a weakening of the nation-state and strengthening of decentralisation processes[1] have also profoundly changed the formation and operation of international environmental law. The nation-state is no longer the sole type of actor on the world stage and can no longer claim a monopoly on policy-making or even areas such as provision of social services or public infrastructure.[2] The easing of restrictions on capital flows across national borders has allowed for the flourishing of a transnational capitalist class who are supra-national in their operation and world view. This has facilitated a 'neo-colonial' global economic order continuing a centuries-old unequal exchange in which the role of developing countries was generally centred around extraction of natural resources and the provision of cheap labour.[3] To compete, governments engaged in a 'race to the bottom' in terms of environmental and social standards. Simultaneously, neoliberal reforms instigated by international financial institutions in the 1990s and 2000s 'rolled back' the state from involvement in the social and ecological spheres through measures such as reforms devolving governance to local centres, minimisation of social welfare schemes and shedding regulation of markets and the environment.[4]

Conventional accounts of international environmental law conceive of a world legal order consisting solely in relations between nation-states. But law lacking an enforcement mechanism requires some other means for its effective implementation. This is the unique quality of the governance discourse and its de-emphasis on the state as the sole agent of legitimacy and implementation. Along with this is a shift in emphasis from the national and international scale of action to the regional, local and community level: in accordance with the principle of subsidiarity, that decision-making and implementation should be carried out at the level closest to that at which the effects will be felt. This chapter will explore the alternative paths to implementation of international environmental law by examining the role of courts, indigenous peoples, civil society groups and NGOs in this process.

The role of these non-governmental entities in implementing international environmental laws will be seen to be interrelated and overlapping, particularly the roles and competencies of international NGOs, civil society and 'grass-roots' groups, and indigenous peoples. The 'laws' relating to international environmental matters are less enactments to be carried out and more a complex network of ongoing formulations of the principle of sustainability reached by consultation and cooperation between state and non-state actors.

NGOs

From governability to governance

As part of the disengagement of the state from the realm of environmental protection and a general trend of decentralisation of the state and devolution of state power, non-governmental groups became increasingly significant from the 1990s onwards as they emerged to deal with

---

1 D. Harvey, *A Brief History of Neoliberalism*, Oxford: Oxford University Press, 2005.
2 The divestment of public utilities into private hands is usually one of the first stages of a privatisation regime.
3 W. Rodney, *How Europe Underdeveloped Africa*, London: Bogle-L'Ouverture Press, 1972; E. Galeano, *Open Veins of Latin America: Five Centuries of the Pillage of a Continent*, Cedric Belfrage (trans.), New York: Monthly Review Press, 1973.
4 For a critical treatment of one of the most thorough cases of neoliberal reform in the 1980s see J. Kelsey, *Rolling Back the State: Privatisation of Power in Aotearoa/New Zealand*, Wellington: Bridget Williams Books, 1993.

the failure of states to address continuing and accelerating environmental degradation. Traditional models of 'government' were no longer adequate to describe the increasingly diffuse reality of international law and decision-making. The new discourse of global 'governance' entered mainstream discourse with the UN Commission on Global Governance's 1995 report, *Our Global Neighbourhood*.[5] The Commission defined global governance as:

> [T]he sum of the many ways individuals and institutions, public and private, manage their common affairs. It is a continuing process through which conflicting or diverse interests may be accommodated and co-operative actions may be taken. It includes formal as well as informal arrangements that people and institutions either have agreed to or perceive to be in their interest . . . At the global level, governance has been viewed primarily as intergovernmental relationships, but it must now be understood as also involving non-governmental organizations (NGOs), citizens' movements, multinational corporations, and the global capital market. Interacting with these are the global mass media of dramatically enlarged influence.[6]

As such, NGOs have become an avenue for international democratic participation by groups and interests that would traditionally have been excluded from dealings between states and their delegated representatives. This has been characterised as a 'participatory revolution'[7] in international environmental law.

What is an NGO?

The definition of what is an NGO is by no means settled but the starting point in international law is Article 71 of the UN Charter, which provides for the Economic and Social Council (ECOSOC) to grant 'consultative status' to international NGOs satisfying certain criteria. This consultative status allows the NGO to designate representatives to be present at meetings of the Commission. They may also make written submissions to the Commission and may, with consent, address the meetings but have no formal negotiating role.[8]

The definition given by ECOSOC for 'international NGO' is:

> [A] non-profit entity whose members are citizens or associations of citizens of one or more countries and whose activities are determined by the collective will of its members in response to the needs of the members or of one or more communities with which the NGO cooperates.[9]

---

5 UN Commission on Global Governance, *Our Global Neighbourhood*, Oxford: Oxford University Press, 1995. Although the term can be traced back at least as far as the Trilateral Commission's report of 1975: M. Crozier, S. Huntington and J. Watanuki, *The Crisis of Democracy: Report on the Governability of Democracies to the Trilateral Commission*, New York: New York University Press, 1975.
6 UN Commission on Global Governance, op. cit., pp. 2–3.
7 K. Rustiala, 'The Participatory Revolution in International Environmental Law', *Harvard Environmental Law Review* 21, 1997, 537.
8 A. Kiss and D. Shelton, *International Environmental Law*, 2nd edition, Ardsley: Transnational Publishers, 2000, p. 136.
9 United Nations Economic and Social Council, *Open-Ended Working Group on the Review of Arrangements for Consultations with Non-Governmental Organizations* (1994), Report of the Secretary-General, UN Doc E/AC.70/1994/5.

For the purposes of international environmental law, it must be noted that only 'international' NGOs are included within the definition above and it is their role which will be examined in this section. National NGOs, civil society and 'grass-roots' movements will be treated as part of a broader movement (frequently in alliance with indigenous movements) in the later section of this chapter dealing with 'peoples'.

The role of NGOs

There are a number of important roles played by NGOs in the implementation of international environmental law. They have a direct role in Multilateral Environmental Agreement (MEA) bodies but with no legal personality they may not bring actions in international fora themselves.[10] Essentially, their role is one of 'contributing without negotiating',[11] a standard that began with the 1992 United Nations Conference on Environment and Development (UNCED).[12] However, many conventions have afforded a role to international NGOs in the negotiation process, allowing observers to attend the Conferences of the Parties as observers and in some cases assisting the treaty secretariat.[13] Where many NGOs come into their own is as 'watchdogs' in instances when states lack the resources (or, indeed, the inclination) to effectively monitor compliance with treaties. International and local NGOs will engage in labour- and capital-intensive tasks such as monitoring and information-gathering to keep track of adherence to agreed-upon norms. Many NGOs are uniquely well placed to provide such information given their level of funding, degree of specialisation and scientific, technical or policy expertise. When matters come up for adjudication or arbitration, NGOs may provide *amicus* briefs.[14] Even the Dispute Settlement Body of the World Trade Organization, which grants standing only to states parties, has been receptive to these. However, although they are empowered to do so, no international adjudicative body is bound to accept or consider *amicus* briefs. They are not always accepted and their impact is, in many cases, negligible.[15]

---

10 I. Brownlie, *Principles of Public International Law*. 6th edition, Oxford: Oxford University Press, 2003, p. 57.

11 UNCED PrepCom Declaration 1/1, 14 August 1990.

12 Known informally as the 'Earth Summit' or 'Rio Summit', held in Rio de Janeiro, Brazil from 13 to 14 June 1992.

13 See e.g. *Convention on International Trade in Endangered Species* ('CITES'), Arts 11, 12; *International Convention for the Regulation of Whaling*, Art. 4; *Montreal Protocol*, Art. 11.5; *Convention on Biological Diversity*, Art. 23(5).

14 Provided by an *amicus curiae*, literally 'friend of the court' (Latin). The role of the *amicus curiae* is to assist the court in deciding a matter before it as an impartial source of information or interpretation. The court accepts this input at its discretion.

15 See e.g. *United States – Import Prohibition of Certain Shrimp and Shrimp Products*, WTO Doc WT/DS58/AB/R (report of the Appellate Body) (1998). Although in a later proceeding (*United States – Import Prohibition on Certain Shrimp and Shrimp Products; recourse to article 21.5*, WTO Doc WT/DS58/AB/RW (report of the Appellate Body)(2001)) the Appellate Body refused to accept the sole *amicus* brief it received without giving reasons for its refusal; *Methanex v United States of America*, Decision of the Tribunal on Petitions from Third Persons to Intervene as 'Amici Curiae', 15 January 2001 (ruling that Art. 15(1) of the United Nations Convention on International Trade Law ('UNCITRAL') rules empower the Tribunal to accept written *amicus* submissions). For further comment, see B.S. Chimni, 'WTO and Environment: Shrimp-Turtle and EC-Hormones Cases', *Economic and Political Weekly*, 2000, 1752.

The ability of NGOs to bring public interest litigation is limited. Although this role is heavily circumscribed by the rules of standing, a number of national jurisdictions have been prepared to grant access to the courts, as will be seen in the following section on the role of courts in implementing international environmental law.

International NGOs wield very significant political and public influence. This is particularly important with regard to international environmental commitments given the general lack of direct enforcement mechanisms available. With the dissemination of information that would not otherwise reach the eyes and ears of the world's population, NGOs – particularly well-resourced and globally connected international ones – have proven themselves capable of raising public awareness and effectively mobilising public opinion against environmentally harmful activities. A famous example of a positive employment of the phenomenon of globalisation is the Greenpeace-organised consumer boycott of Royal Dutch Shell gasoline in 1995. This was in response to the company's proposal to scuttle the Brent Spar oil rig in the North Atlantic. Within weeks, Shell reversed its decision when sales in Germany had dropped by 30 per cent.[16]

But this is not to say that all environmental NGOs are focused on conservation or protection of global commons. There are also very well-resourced and staffed organisations lobbying on behalf of the automotive, oil and fishing industries, for example, and they are perceived to benefit the interests of corporations and the developed countries to the detriment of developing nations, indigenous peoples and nature.[17] Their involvement in negotiations has also left its mark on international environmental agreements.[18] The involvement of NGOs in international decision-making is not synonymous with the participation of social movements; or at least, not all social movements. Rajagopal observes that NGOs are institutionalised forms of a small number of social movements, often specialised and limited in their scope and operation.[19] Indeed, developing nations have often opposed the acceptance of *amicus* briefs on the basis that NGOs from developed countries and with better access to the work and documents of international bodies will be unduly advantaged and further that they are often funded by, or serve the purposes of, corporations from their own country.[20] However, altruistic or not, on balance NGOs provide a voice for civil society in international environmental legal bodies that would not otherwise be heard.

IUCN

A uniquely effective NGO worthy of special mention is the International Union for the Conservation of Nature (IUCN). The IUCN is something of an anomaly among NGOs by being a hybrid organisation, non-governmental but also allied with conservation groups, states and public law entities such as universities and research institutes. This status gives it a

---

16 Kiss and Shelton, op. cit., p. 136.
17 G. Marceau and M. Stilwell, 'Practical Suggestions for *Amicus Curiae* Briefs before WTO Adjudicating Bodies', *Journal of International Economic Law* 4, 2001, 161.
18 P.W. Birnie, A.E. Boyle and C. Redgwell, *International Law and the Environment*, 3rd edition, Oxford: Oxford University Press, 2009, p. 101.
19 B. Rajagopal, 'International Law and Social Movements: Challenges of Theorizing Resistance', *Columbia Journal of Transnational Law* 41, 2003, 409
20 B. S. Chimni, 'International Institutions Today: An Imperial Global State in the Making', *European Journal of International Law* 15, 2004, 26.

unique capacity to 'play a catalytic role in initiating or supporting new legal developments'.[21] It was one of the first entities to perceive the connection between environment and development – and one of the very earliest users of the term 'sustainable development' in the IUCN/ World Wildlife Fund/United Nations Environment Programme World Conservation Strategy published in 1980.[22] The IUCN was key in the drafting and passage of the World Charter for Nature (adopted by the UN General Assembly in 1982) and also initiated work on the Convention on Biological Diversity and the mooted Earth Charter for the UNCED. The IUCN has contributed to the negotiation of the World Heritage Convention (1972), the Convention on Trade in Endangered Species (CITES) (1973), the Convention on Conservation of Migratory Species of Wild Animals (1979), and the Ramsar Convention on Wetlands of International Importance (1971), also serving as the treaty secretariat on this last agreement.[23] The IUCN Environmental Law Centre and the IUCN Commission on Environmental Law have prepared draft treaties that have formed the basis of negotiations. Further, they aim to provide expert advice and guidance to developing countries in drafting domestic law and regional agreements as well as working together with other NGOs in order to assist with the discussion and integration of novel and emerging scientific and legal principles. The IUCN has a significant role in fostering legal academic work in international environmental law by producing publications such as policy and law working papers, coordinating international scholarship initiatives, maintaining an IUCN Academy of universities and giving awards for exceptional scholarship in the area.

However, international NGOs are rather abstract or sectional entities without the input and involvement of grass-roots groups grounded in local and specific concerns and struggles. Any analysis of NGO functioning in the frame of global environmental governance would be incomplete without considering the role of peoples as comprised of indigenous peoples and civil society groups.

Peoples

Civil society

In the consultation and drafting processes, as well as in implementation of international environmental law, civil society groups and indigenous peoples are closely connected in their extra-legal status and often work together in an alliance on a global scale. The ECOSOC definition of NGOs most relevant to international law includes only NGOs that are 'international' in their outlook or operation. This excludes national NGOs and 'grass-roots' groups, hence their inclusion here as movements of 'peoples'.

As communities become more connected to national and global processes, they become 'vulnerable to pressures and incentives that originate at other levels of social, political, and economic organization'.[24] As such, self-organisation of communities at all levels becomes a highly important factor in the creation of social movements that are equipped to forge links

---

21 Birnie et al., op. cit., p. 102.
22 IUCN, UNEP and WWF, *World Conservation Strategy: Living Resource Conservation for Sustainable Development*, Gland: International Union for the Conservation of Nature and Natural Resources, 1980.
23 Birnie et al., op. cit., p. 102.
24 F. Berkes, 'Commons in a Multilevel World', *International Journal of the Commons* 2, 2008, 1.

horizontally or vertically between other groups engaged in parallel struggles around the world. One of the defining characteristics of globalisation is an unprecedented compression of space and time scales,[25] so the success of groups in forming these links is instrumental in their ability to cross these scales and work together toward common goals. What is more, there is a 'growing relationship between human rights and environmental discourse at the international level'.[26] In practical terms this has meant that rights to a healthy environment and in some jurisdictions rights of nature have been given practical effect.[27]

Indigenous peoples

Indigenous peoples have been the populations most harmed by neoliberal globalisation and are traditionally the most excluded group. Scholars have noted that the rise of indigenous movements is directly correlated to the ascendancy of neoliberal globalisation in their countries.[28] There is a growing trend in international environmental law to recognise the traditional wisdom of indigenous peoples as guardians of the environment and draw upon their unique knowledge of the carrying capacity of ecosystems and world views for living in harmony with the land. As stated in the IUCN's Inter-Commission Task Force on Indigenous Peoples:

> They are the sole guardian of vast habitats critical to modern societies . . . [and] in the case of many indigenous peoples, their ecological knowledge is an asset of incalculable value.[29]

The 'inherent link'[30] between the rights of indigenous peoples to self-determination and the contribution that they can make to sustainable development is central to understanding the role of indigenous peoples in implementing international environmental law; not so much as the implementation of specific norms of international law as approaches to effecting a sustainable relationship between humans and nature through traditional practices. Understood this way, self-determination is inseparable from indigenous visions of sustainable development and the ability of international law to protect the environment.[31]

25 D. Harvey, *The Conditions of Postmodernity*, London: Basil Blackwell, 1989, cited in O.R. Young, F. Berkhout, G.C. Gallopin, M.A. Janssen, E. Ostrom and S. van der Leeuw, 'The Globalisation of Socio-Ecological Systems: An Agenda for Scientific Research', *Global Environmental Change* 16, 2006, 308.

26 P. Sands, *Principles of International Environmental Law*, 2nd edition, Cambridge: Cambridge University Press, 2003, p. 117.

27 For further consideration of constitutional environmental rights see Chapter 33 by J.R. May and E. Daly in this volume.

28 C.A. Rodríguez-Garavito and L.C. Arenas, 'Indigenous Rights, Transnational Activism, and Legal Mobilisation', in B. de Sousa-Santos and C.A. Rodríguez-Garavito (eds.) *Law and Globalisation from Below*, Cambridge: Cambridge University Press, 2005, p. 242.

29 IUCN Inter-Commission Task Force on Indigenous Peoples, *Indigenous Peoples and Sustainability: Cases and Actions*, Utrecht: International Books, 1997, p. 35. See also, World Commission on Environment and Development, *Our Common Future*, Oxford: Oxford University Press, 1987, p. 115.

30 B. Richardson, 'Indigenous Peoples, International Law and Sustainability', *Review of European Community and International Environmental Law and Policy* 10, 2001, 1, p. 12.

31 K. Bosselmann, 'The Right to Self-Determination and International Environmental Law: An Integrative Approach', *New Zealand Journal of Environmental Law* 1, 1997, 1.

At the level of localities and within nation–states, the vindication of claims to territory and autonomy to live by local laws, customs and traditional wisdom are ends in themselves. Furthermore, these successes have something of a 'demonstration effect' in providing a positive example and templates for resistance to other indigenous peoples in other localities. Solidarity amongst these groups leads to coordination and communication between other national and regional indigenous groups. Increasingly, these movements join forces with transnational ethnic and indigenous groups and at this level often have sufficient commonality with environmental and global social justice movements that they coordinate efforts on a global scale.

The rights of indigenous peoples to self-determination are recognised specifically in the ILO (International Labour Organization) Convention No. 169[32] and the 2007 UN Declaration on the Rights of Indigenous Peoples (UNDRIP).[33] Article 7(4) of the ILO Convention obliges the state to take measures, in cooperation with the peoples concerned, to protect and preserve the environment of the territories they inhabit. Article 13(1) invokes respect for the special importance of these peoples' relationship with their lands or territories for their cultures and spiritual values and for the collective aspects of this relationship. Recognition of the rights of ownership and possession of the peoples concerned of the lands which they traditionally occupy is advanced in Article 14(1). Under Article 15(1), the state must safeguard their rights, including their rights of use, management and conservation, to the natural resources in their lands and territories. The UNDRIP reiterates many of the same rights in more detail.[34] Indigenous peoples and NGOs may also work together across national boundaries. A recent example of this is the pioneering importation of the constitutional provision for rights of nature[35] in Articles 71 to 74[36] of the 2008 Constitution of Ecuador. As part of a broad local, national and international consultation process employed in drafting the Constitution, the Ecuadorian Constituent Assembly worked with the Pennsylvania, US-based Community Environmental Legal Defense Fund (CELDF) in concert with the Pachamama Alliance.[37] Although the incorporation of legal recognition for non-human organisms is unprecedented in national constitutions, the CELDF had in fact drafted similar provisions for municipal bodies in the US.[38]

---

32 International Labour Organization No. 169, 28 ILM 1382 (1989).

33 *Declaration on the Rights of Indigenous Peoples* (2007), GA Res 295, UN GAOR, 61st Sess, 107th Plen Mtg, UN Doc A/Res/295 ('UNDRIP').

34 See particularly, ibid., Arts 3, 4, 9, 11, 25, 26, 29 and 31.

35 C.D. Stone, 'Should Trees Have Standing? – Toward Legal Rights for Natural Objects', *Southern California Law Review* 45, 1972, 450.

36 See particularly, UNDRIP, Art. 71: 'Nature or Pachamama, where life is reproduced and exists, has the right to exist, persist, maintain and regenerate its vital cycles, structure, functions and its processes in evolution ...' and Art. 74: 'Nature has the right to an integral restoration. This integral restoration is independent of the obligation on natural and juridical persons or the State to indemnify the people and the collectives that depend on the natural systems ...'

37 The Pachamama Alliance is an NGO based in San Francisco, USA and Ecuador. A delegation from the CELDF visited Montecristi, Ecuador on two occasions in November 2007 and February 2008 to consult with the Constitutional Assembly as a whole and also with several *mesa* or committees.

38 See *Tamaqua Borough Corporate Waste and Local Control Ordinance* of 1 May 2007 (Schuylkill County, Pennsylvania, USA). Online. Available HTTP: <http://www.celdf.org/article.php?id=439> (accessed 15 May 2012). This ordinance prohibits the use of corporate personality to avoid liability for the dumping of toxic wastes. Similar provisions have now been passed in over 100 municipalities in Pennsylvania and Maine.

The Global People's Conference on Climate Change and the Rights of Mother Earth

Recently, a new phenomenon has emerged in the process of creation of international environmental law. Disillusioned with the failure of the UN Fifteenth Conference of the Parties to the Kyoto Protocol (COP15)[39] to reach an agreement acceptable to all[40] and the active exclusion of non-state actors from deliberations, the President of Bolivia, Evo Morales, initiated an alternative conference on climate change to be held in Cochabamba, Bolivia. This conference was conceived as being primarily animated by the input of global civil society. Known as the Global People's Conference on Climate Change and the Rights of Mother Earth,[41] from the outset this gathering had a particular emphasis on engaging with civil society and indigenous peoples. Maria Souviron, the Bolivian ambassador in London, stressed the multilevel participation on which the conference was focused: 'The invitation is to heads of state but chiefly to civil society. We think that social movements and non-government groups, people not at decision level, have an important role in climate talks.'[42] The Conference had an ambitious agenda, proposing the establishment of an international climate change tribunal and a global referendum on climate and environment. Most significant was the negotiation and approval of a Universal Declaration on the Rights of Mother Earth (UDRME).[43] This Declaration includes such concepts as legal personality for non-human organisms[44] and the recognition of the planet as a single living organism.[45] The intention of developing the UDRME is that it will be presented to the UN General Assembly for adoption and, where necessary, further developed through appropriate UN organs.

But the claims of individuals, peoples, NGOs and nature itself, however exalted in international declarations, must be enforceable in domestic or international courts to have practical effect.

Courts

Domestic courts

Upon agreeing to an international treaty or declaration, a state should bring its law into compliance with the principles and rules of that international agreement. Unless this has been done,

---

39 Held in Copenhagen, Denmark, 7–18 December 2009.

40 Fifteenth Conference of the Parties to the United Nations Framework Convention on Climate Change, *Copenhagen Accord*, Decision 2/CP.15 in *Report of the Conference of the Parties in its Fifteenth Session*, addendum one, part two, UN Doc FCCC/CP/2009/11/Add.1, at 4–7 ('Copenhagen Accord').

41 *Conferencia Mundial de los Pueblossobre Cambio Climático (CMPCC) y Derechos de la Madre Tierra*: The Global Peoples Conference on Climate Change and the Rights of Mother Earth. Held in Cochabamba, Bolivia, 20–22 April 2010.

42 J. Vidal, 'China, India, Brazil and South Africa Prepare for Post-Copenhagen Meeting', *Guardian*, 13 January 2010. Online. Available HTTP: <http://www.guardian.co.uk/environment/2010/jan/13/developing-countries-basic-climate-change> (accessed 8 March 2012).

43 *Universal Declaration on the Rights of Mother Earth* (1997), UN Doc FCCC/AWGLCA/2009/17, first proposed in the *Kyoto Protocol to the United Nations Framework Convention on Climate Change*, opened for signature 11 December 1997, 2303 UNTS 148 (entered into force 16 February 2005) ('Kyoto Protocol').

44 As pioneered in the 2008 Constitution of Ecuador, Arts. 71–4. For the origin of this idea, see Stone, op. cit., p. 450.

45 The *Universal Declaration on the Rights of Mother Earth* can be viewed online. Available HTTP: <http://motherearthrights.org/2010/04/27/world-peoples-conference-on-climate-change-and-the-rights-of-mother-earth/>.

international obligations cannot trump domestic legislation. Where the state has not fully brought domestic law into line with international standards, enforcement can be attempted in one of two ways. The judiciary may incorporate international legal precedent into case law as non-binding but persuasive authority or the courts may use international instruments to interpret domestic legislation consistently with international obligations. An exception to this general principle is the European Community (EC) member countries, in which failure to implement EC law has been successfully challenged in the European Court of Justice (ECJ).[46]

The great obstacle to public interest litigation both domestically and internationally is the doctrine of *locus standi* (standing). To be granted standing by a court, a prospective party to legal proceedings must be able to demonstrate that they have some legal right or interest in the matter beyond simply that of concern for the environment. Many common law countries, such as England,[47] the United States[48] and New Zealand,[49] have allowed standing for administrative review but many more impose restrictive rules of standing.[50] A legal instrument that circumvents this impasse is the 1998 Aarhus Convention on Access to Information, Public Participation in Decision-making and Access to Justice in Environmental Matters.[51] This is a regional convention to which countries of the European Union and many of the former Soviet Union are signatories. The focus is on participatory rights, granting access to the elements listed in its title; these are specifically guaranteed under Article 6. This is a practical implementation of Principle 10 of the Rio Declaration.[52] Article 4 of the Convention entitles 'the public', including NGOs 'promoting environmental protection', to request information according to international law. There is no requirement of standing. Article 9 guarantees enforcement of these rights under the Convention in national courts of participating countries.[53]

46 R. Wagenbaur, 'The European Community's Policy on Implementation of Environmental Directives', *Fordham International Law Journal* 14, 1990, 455; L. Krämer, 'The Implementation of Community Environmental Directives Within Member States: Some Implications of Direct Effect Doctrine', *Journal of Environmental Law* 3, 1991, 39.

47 *R v Secretary of State for Foreign and Commonwealth Affairs, ex parte World Development Movement* [1995] 1 All ER 611. Requirement of 'sufficient interest' in Supreme Court Act 1981 s 31(3), and in RSC Ord 53, r 3(7). Holding that the World Development Movement had sufficient interest to initiate administrative review of a decision to finance a dam in Malaysia.

48 *Sierra Club v Morton* 405 US 727 (1972); *Lujan v Defenders of Wildlife* 504 US 555 (1992); *Friends of the Earth v Laidlaw* 120 SCt 693 (2000).

49 *Environmental Defence Society v South Pacific Aluminium* (No 3) (1981) 1 NZLR 216.

50 For a more detailed review of *locus standi* in international jurisdictions see Birnie et al., op. cit., pp. 288–98.

51 United Nations Economic Commission for Europe, *Aarhus Convention on Access to Information, Public Participation in Decision-Making and Access to Justice in Environmental Matters*, UN Doc ECE/CEP/43, 21 April 1998.

52 Principle 10, United Nations Conference on Environment and Development (UNCED), *United Nations Declaration on Environment and Development*, 31 ILM (1992) ('Rio Declaration'):

> Environmental issues are best handled with participation of all concerned citizens, at the relevant level. At the national level, each individual shall have appropriate access to information concerning the environment that is held by public authorities, including information on hazardous materials and activities in their communities, and the opportunity to participate in decision-making processes. States shall facilitate and encourage public awareness and participation by making information widely available. Effective access to judicial and administrative proceedings, including redress and remedy, shall be provided.

53 For further consideration of this convention see Chapter 8 by J. Razzaque in this volume.

A number of treaties establish international rules of civil liability hence allowing an enforcement role for individuals. Some allow victims of transboundary pollution to choose between bringing suit in the country where the harm was suffered or in the jurisdiction in which the pollution originated. Others, such as the nuclear liability conventions, require the victims of nuclear harms to make their claims in the country responsible for incurring that damage. These would almost inevitably be great distances from the area harmed, imposing a significant burden upon the claimants.[54] The oil pollution conventions, however, provide for individuals to enforce their terms in the courts of any party state in which pollution has been caused.[55] Another class of conventions allow for non-state actors to bring actions under private international law regulating civil and commercial transactions. Actions in tort may also be possible under these conventions with the possibility of victims choosing a *forum conveniens* in which to have the matter adjudicated. Although it has application only to EC countries, the 1968 Brussels Convention[56] extends jurisdiction for an action to be brought for 'tort, delict or quasi-delict' in the court of the state 'where the harmful event occurred'.[57]

International courts

International environmental law is primarily legislative in its origin. It is formed by MEAs and bilateral treaties between sovereign states, declarations, resolutions and other soft-law instruments. These treaties generally include their own mechanisms for dispute resolution which obviate the necessity to resort to international courts. Commercial and trade law (especially the WTO rules) often take primacy over other laws and tend to be rigorously enforced and obeyed by states and transnational corporations. These rules and the impacts of associated activities, for instance heavy industry and large-scale development projects, largely escape the ambit of the courts and disputes that are raised are often arbitrated under conditions that lack many of the hallmarks of natural justice, instead favouring secrecy of proceedings and with no avenue for appeal or review. That said, adjudication has its own shortcomings[58] and has 'invoked the criticism that courts are essentially bilateral institutions

---

54 *Convention on Third Party Liability in the Field of Nuclear Energy*, opened for signature 29 July 1960, 956 UNTS 264 (entered into force 1 April 1968) ('Paris Convention'), Art. 13; *Vienna Convention on Civil Liability for Nuclear Damage*, opened for signature 21 May 1963, 1063 UNTS 266 (entered into force 12 November 1977) ('1963 Vienna Convention'), Art. XI(1). It should also be noted that these conventions do not specifically allow claims for environmental damage.

55 *International Convention on Civil Liability for Oil Pollution Damage*, opened for signature 29 November 1969 (entered into force 19 June 1975) (replaced by the *1992 Protocol*, opened for signature 27 November 1992, entered into force 30 May 1996; amended by the *2000 Amendments*, opened for signature 18 October 2000, entered into force 1 November 2003), Art. IX(1); International Convention on the Establishment of an International Fund for Compensation for Oil Pollution Damage 1971, opened for signature 18 December 1971 (entered into force 16 October 1978) (as superseded by the *1992 Protocol*; amended by the *2000 Amendments*; supplemented by the *2003 Protocol*, opened for signature 16 May 2003, entered into force 3 March 2005), Art. 7(1).

56 *Convention on Jurisdiction and Enforcement of Judgments in Civil and Commercial Matters*, opened for signature 27 September 1968 8 ILM 229 (entered into force 1 February 1973) ('Brussels Convention').

57 Ibid., Art. 5(3); *Council Regulation 44/2001 (EC) on jurisdiction and enforcement of judgements in civil and commercial matters* (2001), OJ L12, 1. See *Handelskwekerij GJ Bier v Mines de Potasses D'Alsace* [1976] ECR 1735 (holding that Art. 5(3) is to be interpreted 'in such a way as to acknowledge that the plaintiff has an option to commence proceedings either at the place where the damage occurred or the place of the event giving rise to it').

58 L. Fuller, 'The Form and Limits of Adjudication', *Harvard Law Review* 92, 1978, 353.

that cannot embrace the multilateral character of international environmental disputation'.[59] This is particularly problematic in dealing with exploitation of and damage to the global commons that involve many, if not all, states. Overall, a managerial approach favouring mediation and the avoidance of conflict is preferred to an adjudicative one and even international courts are reluctant to definitively rule on an issue when they can encourage state parties to resolve it themselves. Another of the difficulties that has kept many environmental matters from adjudication in international courts is the improbability of matters being determined as 'wholly or predominantly environmental' in nature.[60]

International Court of Justice (ICJ)

A body of international jurisprudence has developed that advances the concept of sustainable development. The watershed judgment was the 1997 *Case Concerning the Gabčíkovo-Nagymaros Project*.[61] The Court considered the principle of sustainable development to be central to the reconciliation of a conflict between Hungary and Slovakia over the construction of a massive damming project of the River Danube. In his separate opinion, Vice-President Weeramantry identified sustainable development as 'one of the most ancient ideas of the human heritage'.[62] While this judgment is celebrated as a definitive moment in the development of the principle of sustainable development, the Court also avoided determining whether there was in fact a breach of international environmental law, failed to make any clear findings regarding the environmental damage likely to be caused by the project, and instead encouraged the parties to seek their own mutually agreed resolution.

The ICJ has not dealt extensively with environmental issues.[63] A significant part of the reason for this is that the environmental concerns are generally secondary to or subsumed within international trade law as 'trade barriers', leaving the courts to deal with those issues rather than specifically with the environmental impacts. Another reason is that there remains no functional international environmental court, although there is a substantial body of literature arguing for the establishment of such a body.[64] In 1993, the ICJ instituted a seven-member Permanent Chamber for Environmental Matters.[65] The judges were to be specialist to some degree, with Article 16(2) of the Statute directing the Court in selecting appointees to 'have regard to any special knowledge, expertise or previous experience which any members of the Court may have in relation to the category of case the Chamber is being formed to deal with'. However, no cases have ever been submitted to the Chamber; even a

59 T. Stephens, *International Courts and Environmental Protection*, Cambridge: Cambridge University Press, 2009, p. 93.
60 Ibid., p. 39–40.
61 *Gabčíkovo-Nagymaros Project Case (Hungary/Slovakia)* [1997] ICJ Rep 7.
62 Ibid., 110.
63 D. Tarlock, 'The Role of Non-Governmental Organizations in the Development of International Environmental Law', contribution to the Chicago-Kent Dedication symposium 'Environmental Law', *Chi-Kent L Rev* 68, 1992–1993, 61, p. 73.
64 See e.g. G. Palmer, 'New Ways to Make International Environmental Law', *American Journal of International Law* 86, 1992, 259; J. Pauwelyn, 'Judicial Mechanisms: Is There a Need for a World Environment Court?', in W.B. Chambers and J.F. Green (eds) *Reforming International Environmental Governance: From Institutional Limits to Innovative Reforms*, Tokyo: United Nations University Press, 2005.
65 Under Art. 26(1) of the Statute of the International Court of Justice.

seemingly obviously suited matter, the *Pulp Mills on the River Uruguay* case,[66] dealing with industrial pollution of the river between Uruguay and Argentina, was dealt with in the main Court and on other grounds. The Chamber is now essentially defunct with the Court ceasing annual elections for its membership in 2006.

International Tribunal for the Law of the Sea (ITLOS)

The International Tribunal for the Law of the Sea (ITLOS) is charged with resolution of disputes under the UN Convention on the Law of the Sea (UNCLOS).[67] Like the ICJ, it has been reluctant to pronounce judgment on breaches of law and prefers to encourage states to resolve their differences. A representative view is the following observation of Judge ad hoc Shearer in the *Southern Bluefin Tuna* provisional measures order of 1999:

> [T]he tribunal, in its prescription of provisional measures in this case, has behaved less as a court of law and more as an agency of diplomacy. While diplomacy, and a disposition to assist the parties in resolving their dispute amicably have their proper place in the judicial settlement of international disputes, the Tribunal should not shrink from the consequences of proven facts.[68]

Permanent Court of Arbitration (PCA)

Some of the seminal decisions in international environmental law have been arbitrations.[69] The Permanent Court of Arbitration (PCA), based in The Hague, was established by the Hague Convention in 1889 (later revised in 1907). It is commonly observed that it is neither permanent nor a court.[70] The PCA overcomes one of the major limitations of both arbitration and adjudication by allowing for multi-party proceedings in its *Optional Rules for the Arbitration of Disputes Concerning the Environment and/or Natural Resources* (2001) (Natural Resources Rules).[71] The Introduction and Article 1(1) of the Natural Resources Rules allow for involvement of international organisations, NGOs and corporations. 'Given the nature of PCA arbitration (involving party control over the course of the procedure), it may seem unlikely that a tribunal would accept third party *amicus curiae* briefs unless the parties to a case so agree.'[72] But while the Hague Conventions and the Natural Resources Rules make no specific provision for *amicus* briefs, Article 15(1) of the Natural Resources Rules is similarly worded

---

66 *The Case Concerning Pulp Mills on the River Uruguay (Argentina v Uruguay)*. Filed in the ICJ in 2006, the Court delivered its latest judgment on 20 April 2010.

67 *United Nations Convention on the Law of the Sea*, opened for signature 10 December 1982, 1834 UNTS 397, 21 ILM 1245 (entered into force 16 November 1994) (UNCLOS).

68 *Southern Bluefin Tuna order* (1999) 38 ILM 1624, [14].

69 *Pacific Fur Seals Arbitration* (Great Britain v United States) [1893] Moore's International Arbitration 755; *Trail Smelter Case* (United States v Canada) (1935/1941) 3 RIAA 1905; *Lac Lanoux Arbitration* (France v Spain) (1957) 12 RIAA 281; 24 ILR 101.

70 R. Mackenzie, C. Romano, Y. Shany and P. Sands, *The Manual on International Courts and Tribunals*, 2nd edition, Oxford: Oxford University Press, 2010, p. 102.

71 *Permanent Court of Arbitration, Optional Rules for Arbitration of Disputes Relating to Natural Resources and the Environment* (19 June 2001) 41 ILM 202. Online Available HTTP: <http://www.pca-cpa.org/upload/files/ENVIRONMENTAL(3).pdf> (accessed 15 May 2012).

72 Ibid., 117.

to Article 15 of the UNCITRAL rules which have been interpreted to allow *amicus* briefs.[73] To date, although many environmental cases have come before the PCA, these rules have not been used. Nonetheless, they are a fine normative model for future arrangements as they were expressly designed to take into account the polycentric nature of public international law and the Natural Resources Rules allow for interim measures to be sought to prevent serious harm to the environment.[74]

Conclusion

Globalisation has defined the nature of international environmental governance for better and for worse. Means have been devised to overcome the limitations of standing and the discourse of governance has explored more coordinated, effective and integrated ways in which to manage environmental issues. As global civil society in the form of NGOs, indigenous peoples and grass-roots environmental movements works together more closely, visions of international environmental law are emerging which are less state-centric and, in more recent developments, less anthropocentric. Furthermore, as indigenous claims for self-determination are recognised, the unique ecocentric perspectives of these peoples inform the corpus of sustainable development law. Although courts have been reluctant to make definitive judgments on matters of international environmental law, they are becoming more accessible and receptive to non-state parties. What may be lacking in finality is somewhat ameliorated by inclusiveness and flexibility. With sufficient international legal recognition, peoples and NGOs can provide the much-needed link between global obligations and domestic implementation. The evolving matrix of governance in the creation and implementation of international environmental law can be seen as possessed of the complexity and nuance necessary to deal with the multifocal, multi-party realities of an interconnected world in which now, more than ever, the global commons must be protected rather than carved up between competing nation-states.

73 See *Methanex*, op. cit., and accompanying text.
74 *Natural Resources Rules*, Art. 26(1).

8

Information, public participation and access to justice in environmental matters

Jona Razzaque

In the twenty years since the Rio Declaration, there have been a number of developments in the field of participatory rights where environmental agreements emphasise the need to include communities in the environmental decision-making. Lack of community engagement, along with weak information and consultation procedures that disregard the voice of the affected communities, have resulted in unsustainable resource management. Examples from developed and developing countries show the need for increased participation of non-state actors, joint management of shared natural resources and stronger government obligations to involve communities in decisions. Along with an effective global framework dealing with participatory rights, regional collaboration can help to promote sustainable resource governance.

Introduction

Even twenty years after the 1992 Rio Summit,[1] increasing depletion of resources (such as land, water, energy, forests, ecosystems) as well as restricted access to these resources remain issues of global concern. The conventional model of economic growth has caused potentially irreversible social, environmental and economic cost and is no longer sufficient to secure growth, development and poverty alleviation. What is needed is an economy that improves human well-being, sustainably manages natural resources, preserves natural capital and reduces inequalities in decision-making. Along with investing in the sustainable management of key resources and establishing the right market and regulatory conditions, there is a need to improve governance and community involvement in resource decisions. Sustainable management of resources and ecosystems should be shaped by those who are most at risk. Community participation in decisions and projects concerning natural resources is crucial to the creation and maintenance of a healthy and stable society that can balance states' exclusive right to explore, exploit and develop the natural resource sector.

---

1 *United Nations Declaration on Environment and Development* (1992), UN Doc A/CONF.151/5/Rev. 1 ('Rio Declaration').

Participatory rights deal with the process through which a decision (administrative or judicial) is taken and typically encompass public consultation, information provision and access to courts.[2] The core issues involved are procedural fairness – allowing people to be part of the process – and community empowerment – enabling people to take an active role in decisions affecting their lives. Access to information, public participation and justice improve the credibility, effectiveness and accountability of government decision-making processes.[3] The importance of participatory rights along with its current interpretation and approaches in international and national laws has been reviewed in a number of academic papers.[4] This chapter aims to examine the development of participatory rights (including rights to information, public participation and access to effective remedies) 20 years after the 1992 Rio Declaration with a brief discussion on the development of participatory rights that has been influenced by human rights,[5] the involvement of non-state actors and the proactive interpretation of these rights by the judiciary.

This chapter examines some of these developments and approaches in the context of ecosystem services, resource management and state sovereignty. These three topics are chosen because of their present importance to participatory rights. First, the economic valuation of natural resources without community engagement leads to an unsustainable pattern of resource development. As confirmed by the Millennium Ecosystem Assessment,[6] involving communities in the management and payment of ecosystem services scheme is essential for its success and sustainability. Second, the lack of access to information and consultation with affected and indigenous communities results in more resource conflicts. Allowing communities to participate in the decision-making processes, implementation and monitoring of resource-related projects creates greater trust in the process itself. Third, states' sovereign rights to natural resources are now restricted with the influence of a number of international and regional agreements. This recalibration of sovereign rights over natural resources has given the public more access to courts in order to protect the natural resource sector. Undoubtedly, sustainable natural resource management requires strong substantive rights supported by inclusive participatory rights. However, the issue is not only about having a liberal judiciary, strong environmental legislation dealing with information and consultation, and explicit constitutional provisions. There should also be public access to affordable and cost-effective remedies and the emphasis is now more on meaningful participation with

2 J. Ebbesson, 'The Notion of Public Participation in International Environmental Law', *Yearbook of International Environmental Law* 8, 1997, 70–5.

3 E. Petkova, C. Maurer, N. Henninger and F. Irwin, *Closing the Gap: Information, Participation, and Justice in Decision-making for the Environment*, Washington DC: World Resources Institute, 2002, pp. 121–32.

4 M. Fitzmaurice, 'Some Reflections on Public Participation in Environmental Matters as a Human Right in International Law', *Non-State Actors & International Law* 2, 2002, 1–22; G. Pring and S.Y. Noe, 'The Emerging International Law of Public Participation Affecting Global Mining, Energy and Resource Development', in D.N. Zillman, A. Lucas and G. Pring (eds) *Human Rights in Natural Resource Development: Public Participation in the Sustainable Development of Mining and Energy Resources*, Oxford: Oxford University Press, 2002, pp. 11–76; J. Ebbesson, op. cit; B. Richardson and J. Razzaque, 'Public Participation in Environmental Decision-making', in B.J. Richardson and S. Wood (eds) *Environmental Law for Sustainability*, London: Hart Publishing, 2006, pp. 165–94.

5 UN Department of Economic and Social Affairs, *Participatory Governance and the Millennium Development Goals*, New York, 2008, chapter 3.

6 Millennium Ecosystem Assessment, *Ecosystems and Human Well-being: General Synthesis*, Washington DC: Island Press, 2005, p. v.

timely information. The chapter concludes that, in order to achieve more effective routes to participation and a transparent, inclusive and accountable system of governance, there is a need for increased participation of non-state actors, joint management of shared resources and stronger obligations of government agencies to include communities in resource decisions. Along with a global framework, strong regional collaboration can help to promote sustainable resource governance.

At the international level, the absence of a global treaty on participatory rights and the lack of any international compliance mechanism means that the effectiveness of participatory rights depends heavily on the national legal system, courts and other government agencies. At the national level, some countries have advanced procedural tools, while some national legal frameworks fail to provide adequate mechanisms for access to information, participation and justice. While it is not possible to provide all the recent legal developments or an exhaustive list of approaches followed in various domestic and regional laws in this short span, this chapter attempts to highlight some of the recent trends in participatory rights. Along with developing countries, examples are brought from Europe, where participatory rights have gone through some exciting developments due to the 1998 Aarhus Convention[7] and several legal instruments in the European Union (EU) that promote participatory rights to protect the environment.

Development of participatory rights: pre and post 1992

The period between the 1972 Stockholm and 1992 Rio Declarations has seen a growing recognition of participatory tools to protect the environment. The 1972 Stockholm Declaration indirectly refers to public participation and talks about equitable sharing of common efforts of citizens, communities, governments and private sectors in order to 'defend and improve the human environment'.[8] Apart from the 1972 Stockholm Declaration, there were some other non-binding[9] and binding[10] instruments until 1992 where governments recognised the crucial role of participatory mechanisms in environmental protection.

Prior to 1972, it was mostly human rights treaties that included provisions of participatory rights. As early as 1948, the Universal Declaration of Human Rights provided generalised rights of access to information and justice and recognised political participation and freedom of assembly, opinion and expression.[11] The 1966 International Covenant on Civil and Political Rights also addressed these obligations.[12] Similar provisions on information and justice can be

---

7 UNECE Convention on Access to Information, Public Participation and Access to Justice in Environmental Matters, opened for signature on 25 June 1998, 38 ILM 517 (entered into force 30 October 2001) ('Aarhus Convention').

8 Declaration of the United Nations Conference on the Human Environment (1972), UN Doc A/CONF.48/14/Rev.1, para. 7 ('Stockholm Declaration') Preamble.

9 *Draft Principles of Conduct in the Field of Environment for Guidance of States in the Conservation and Harmonious Utilization of Natural Resources Shared by Two or More States* (1978); *World Charter for Nature* (1982); *WCED Experts Group on Environmental Law for Environmental Protection and Sustainable Development* (1986); *UNEP Goals and Principles of Environmental Impact Assessment* (1987); *IUCN Draft Covenant on Environmental Conservation and Sustainable Use of Natural Resources* (1991).

10 *World Heritage Convention* (1972); *Basel Convention on the Control of Transboundary Movement of Hazardous Wastes and their Disposal* (1989); *Protocol on Environmental Protection to the Antarctic Treaty* (1991).

11 *Universal Declaration of Human Rights* (1948), GA Res 217 (AIII), UN GAOR, 3rd Sess, pt 1, at 71, UN Doc A/810, Arts. 8, 10, 19, 20.

12 *International Covenant on Civil and Political Rights* (1966), 999 UNTS 171, Arts 19, 25.

found in the 1950 European Convention on Human Rights[13] and the 1981 African Charter on Human and Peoples' Rights.[14]

The 1980s movement to make a connection between human rights and the environment underscored the need for more concrete commitments[15] and culminated in the 1994 Draft Declaration of Principles on Human Rights and the Environment.[16] In addition to the substantive rights (e.g. the right to a clean environment), the draft document recognised that participatory rights – such as access to information, public participation in decision-making and access to justice – are essential for the realisation of the substantive rights to the environment. The 1992 Rio Declaration elaborates on the three pillars of public participation in its Principle 10, *participation of all concerned citizens* at the relevant level of decision-making; *access to information* concerning the environment; and *access to judicial and administrative proceedings* including redress and remedy.[17] At the same time, Agenda 21 emphasises the need to strengthen the role of major groups as critical to the effective implementation of sustainable development and outlines different forms of participatory mechanisms.[18]

While the 1972 Stockholm and 1992 Rio Declarations offer a general language, they have played a crucial role in the development of public participation at the national level. After these declarations, further non-binding[19] and binding[20] environmental instruments incorporated specific provisions on information, participation and access to justice. These obligations fell short of creating an enforceable right that can be asserted by individuals; however, Principle 10 of the 1992 Rio Declaration continues to influence legal instruments promoting participatory environmental rights. Along with a number of actors and instruments, other branches of international law (e.g. human rights law, economic law) have also played a crucial role.[21]

Largely influenced by the Stockholm Declaration, many developing countries went through a phase of legal reform for better environmental management during the 1970s and 1980s.[22] After 1992, reforms in access to justice and information began slowly, if at all, in some developing countries.[23] In some Asian countries, for example, non-state actors such as

---

13 *European Convention for the Protection of Human Rights and Fundamental Freedoms* (1950), 213 UNTS 222, Arts 6, 10.

14 *African Charter on Human and Peoples' Rights* (1981), 1520 UNTS 217, (1981) 21 ILM 59, Arts 3, 7, 9(1), 13, 24.

15 *Final Report on the Human Rights and the Environment for the Sub-Commission on Prevention of Discrimination and Protection of Minorities* (1994), E/CN.4/Sub.2/1994/9.

16 *Draft Principles On Human Rights And The Environment* (1994), E/CN.4/Sub.2/1994/9, Annex I.

17 *Rio Declaration on Environment and Development* (1992), UN Doc A/CONF.151/26/Rev.1.

18 *Agenda 21*, Report of the UNCED, I (1992) UN Doc A/CONF.151/26/Rev.1, (1992) 31 ILM 874, chapters 12, 19, 27, 36, 37, 40.

19 *The Millennium Declaration* (2000); the *Johannesburg Plan of Implementation of the World Summit on Sustainable Development* (2002); *United Nations Environment Programme, Guidelines for the Development of National Legislation on Access to Information, Public Participation and Access to Justice in Environmental Matters* (2010), Decision SS.XI/5, part A.

20 *Montreal Protocol on Substances that deplete the Ozone Layer* (1987), *Climate Change Convention* (1992), *Convention on Biological Diversity* (1992).

21 Pring and Noe, op. cit., pp. 11–76.

22 D. Craig, N. Robinson and K. Kheng-Lian (eds) *Capacity Building for Environmental Law in the Asian and Pacific Region: Approaches and Resources*, Manila: Asian Development Bank, 2003, Volume I and II.

23 Ibid. For examples from Latin America, Africa and Asia, see J Foti, L. de Silva, H. McGray, L. Shaffer, J. Talbot and J. Werksman, *Voice and Choice: Opening the Door to Environmental Democracy*, Washington DC: World Resources Institute, 2008.

international financial institutions, NGOs, donor agencies and UN agencies have played an important role in developing the concept of participation in these countries, implementing participatory environmental reforms and also integrating it into policies and regulations.[24] Moreover, the development of participation provisions in environmental decision-making was also influenced by participation provisions in multilateral environmental agreements – a large number of Asian countries are parties to these agreements.[25]

In Europe, the 1998 Aarhus Convention contributed to putting Principle 10 of the Rio Declaration into practice and brought about one of the unique developments in participatory rights to protect the environment. The Convention adopts a rights-based approach to information, participation and justice, makes reference to a substantive right to a healthy environment and allows people to enforce their procedural and substantive environmental rights in court. It provides for the right to receive *environmental information* held by public authorities,[26] the right of active involvement and *participation* from an early stage in environmental decision-making,[27] and access to *justice* in environmental matters.[28] The Convention and its Protocol[29] demonstrate that participatory rights are linked to the legal, political and administrative arrangements at the national level. Although the Aarhus Convention has a European basis, it is open to all states and provides standards that might usefully be drawn upon at the international level to protect the environment.[30] However, developing countries may not be willing to ratify this Convention as it contains a detailed environmental impact assessment (EIA) procedure for development projects (e.g. power plants, pipelines and infrastructure projects) which may be expensive and time-consuming.

Participatory rights and ecosystem services

The degradation of ecosystem services[31] has been identified as a significant barrier to achieving the Millennium Development Goals.[32] The depletion of ecosystems has a more direct impact and a greater effect upon the world's poorest people and is often the main factor contributing to poverty. With regard to access to ecosystem services, the Millennium Ecosystem Assessment has found that there is a growing inequity and disparity among groups of people.[33] The poor, women and indigenous communities are the most affected by externalities, such as adverse climatic conditions and the destruction or unavailability of ecosystem services.

---

24 R. Mushkat, 'The Principle of Public Participation: A Selective Asia-Pacific Perspective', in N. Schrijver and F. Weiss (eds) *International Law and Sustainable Development: Principles and Practice*, Boston/Leiden: Martinus Nijhoff Publishers, 2004, pp. 607–30.

25 J. Razzaque, 'Participatory Rights in Natural Resource Management: Role of the Communities in South Asia', in J. Ebbesson and P. Okowa (eds) *Environmental Law and Justice in Context*, Cambridge: Cambridge University Press, 2009, pp. 117–38.

26 Ibid., Arts 4, 5, 2 (3).

27 Ibid., Arts 6–8 and 2 (2), Annex I.

28 Ibid., Art. 9.

29 *Pollution Release and Transfer Registers Protocol*, opened for signature 21 May 2003 at an extraordinary meeting of the MOP, Kiev (entered into force 8 October 2008).

30 Aarhus Convention, op. cit., Art. 19(3).

31 Ecosystem services are the benefits people obtain from ecosystems, including services from food, water and timber. Millennium Ecosystem Assessment, op. cit., v.

32 United Nations, Millennium Development Goals (2000). Online. Available HTTP: <http://www.un.org/millenniumgoals/> (accessed 26 April 2012).

33 Millennium Ecosystem Assessment, op. cit., p. 12.

At the same time, these marginalised communities are traditionally excluded from participation in decision-making and from policies of empowerment with respect to ownership of natural resources and access to ecosystem services.[34] As a consequence, they have little or no control over the processes, resulting in destruction of ecosystem services or changes in use.

Substantive as well as participatory rights are equally essential to manage ecosystem services at the national and regional levels and are often connected. For example, a substantive right to ecosystem services usually requires procedural rights to be heard in decisions that might affect the substantive right.[35] The fact that 60 per cent of all ecosystem services are being degraded or used unsustainably underscores that conflicting economic, social and environmental interests are affecting these services.[36] In most cases, this degradation and unsustainable use takes place in order to increase the supply of other ecosystem services, e.g. turning forest into agricultural land disrupts water flows and creates climate externalities. It is crucial to establish a system that takes into account these competing interests, equity considerations and the inclusiveness of stakeholders. This is more important in the context of food, water and forests as public goods.[37]

Tropical forests are an example of an ecosystem that attracts internal claims as well as external actors with respect to its management, highlighting the competing parties that need them for survival. Concepts such as sustainable forest management (SFM)[38] try to integrate these competing claims and concerns. For example, the joint forest management scheme in Madhya Pradesh (India) actively involves local people in the management and ownership of the forest products.[39] The problems with SFM and the introduction of market instruments (e.g. incentives, certification, regulation) are that they tend to ignore social costs associated with market development and fail to provide for those who are most vulnerable and directly dependent on the resources.[40] The lack of rights (e.g. tenure, resource and environment) for the forest-dependent poor, limited information and weak institutional support are the main obstacles to improving SFM.[41] No market-based instrument can reshape ecosystem

---

34 J. Razzaque, 'Implementing International Procedural Rights and Obligations: Serving the Environment and Poor Communities', in T. Bigg and D. Satterthwaite (eds) *How to Make Poverty History – The Central Role of Local Organisations in Meeting the MDGs*, London: International Institute for Economic Development, 2005, p. 175.

35 E. Blanco and J. Razzaque, 'Ecosystem Services and Human Well-being in a Globalized World: Assessing the Role of Law', *Human Rights Quarterly* 31, 2009, 692–720.

36 Millennium Ecosystem Assessment, *Health Synthesis*, World Health Organisation, 2005, iii.

37 Public goods are non-rivalrous (available for all to consume) and non-excludable (no one can be effectively excluded from using the good): F. Wijen, K. Zoetman and J. Pieters (eds) *A Handbook of Globalisation and Environmental Policy: National Government Intervention in A Global Arena*, Cheltenham: Edward Elgar, 2005, pp. 89–91.

38 SFM is 'a dynamic and evolving concept which aims to maintain and enhance the economic, social and environmental value of all types of forests, for the benefit of present and future generations'. *Non-legally binding instrument on all types of forests* (2008), GA Res, UN GAOR, A/RES/62/98.

39 P.B. Durst, C. Brown, H.D. Tacio and M. Ishikawa (eds) *In Search of Excellence: Exemplary Forest Management in Asia and the Pacific*, Bangkok: Food and Agriculture Organisation, 2005.

40 A. Wells, C. Luttrell, D. Brown and N. Bird, 'Public Goods and Private Rights: The Illegal Logging Debate and the Rights of the Poor', London: Overseas Development Institute Forestry Briefings, 2006, pp. 2–3.

41 A. Wilson and S. Guéneau, 'Enhancing the compatibility of market-based policy instruments for sustainable forest management', Paris: Institute of Sustainable Development and International Relations, 2004, pp. 16–18.

management if the basic problems of rights allocation, access and participation are not addressed by national governments.[42]

Individuals or groups will only willingly participate in a system that they perceive as fair. Equity encourages the cooperative behaviour necessary to reach decisions on the management and enjoyment of public goods and which is essential at the organisational level to encourage participation.[43] Participation in environmental decision-making is a complex area: it includes determination of interested and affected parties and their inclusion in a deliberative process.[44] Without equal participation in decision-making and access to the management of ecosystem services, rural communities will remain desperately poor. In Brazil, for example, unequal land distribution is proving incredibly difficult to redress despite measures taken by the government since 1995.[45] In this case, restricted participatory rights did not provide the affected people with a say.[46] This example highlights that the realisation of the substantive right to food and water largely depends on the rights of participation by stakeholders in decisions affecting their ecosystems.[47] The FAO Guidelines also confirm the link between substantive and procedural rights while acknowledging that any rights-based approach to food security needs to take into account socio-economic circumstances (e.g. good governance, rule of law, property rights, land tenure systems, strong governmental organisations) that surround those individuals and groups whose entitlement to food is endangered.[48]

Information, public participation and resource management

Sustainable resource management is closely connected to the principles of good governance to strengthen public participation.[49] Participatory rights create a sense of 'ownership' in the decision itself. Involving people at the early stage of decision-making processes creates greater trust in the process and decreases the possibility of later conflicts.[50] Accountability of public

---

42 For examples of engaging communities in environmental markets and payments for ecosystem services, see R. Vonada, T. Herbert and S. Waage, *Introduction to Payments for Ecosystem Services: A Reference Book for Uganda*, Uganda: National Environment Management Authority, 2011, pp. 15–23.

43 M. Rao, 'Equity in a Global Public Goods Framework', in I. Kaul, I. Grunberg and M.A. Stern (eds) *Global Public Goods: International Cooperation in the 21st Century*, New York: Oxford University Press, 1999, pp. 68–70.

44 J. Steele, 'Participation and Deliberation in Environmental Law: Exploring and Problem-Solving Approach', *Oxford Journal of Legal Studies* 21, 2001, 437–8.

45 Rome Declaration on World Food Security (1996), FAO, Report of the World Food Summit, WFS96/Rep, Part One, Appendix. Also see, FAO, *Contemporary Thinking on Land Reforms* (1998). Online. Available HTTP: <http://www.fao.org/sd/ltdirect/ltan0037.htm> (accessed 26 April 2012).

46 Ibid. Also see, *Right to Food Case Study: Brazil* (2004), Study conducted for FAO in support of the Intergovernmental Working Group on the Elaboration of a set of Voluntary Guidelines for the Realization of the Right to Adequate Food in the context of National Food Security, IGWG RTFG /INF 4/APP.1.

47 The FAO Voluntary Guidelines highlight the importance not only of including all stakeholders in access to food production and consumption but of creating an enabling environment through widening participation. Annex I, Section II(6), (8). FAO, *Voluntary Guidelines to Support the Progressive Realisation of the Right to Adequate Food in the Context of National Food Security* (2004), Report of the 30th Session of the Committee on World Food Security, Rome.

48 Ibid., Annex I, § II (7) and (8).

49 Economic Commission for Europe, *Rio plus Aarhus – 20 Years On: Bearing Fruit and Looking Forward* (2011), ECE/MP.PP/2011/CRP.4/rev 1

50 P. Birnie, A. Boyle and C. Redgwell, *International Law and the Environment*, 3rd edition, Oxford: Oxford University Press, 2009, p. 288.

bodies and participation of all stakeholders remain a crucial but underdeveloped component of resource rights, for example the right to food and water. A new breed of laws, policies and regulatory techniques provide some opportunities to individuals and communities to participate actively and lead to transparent and accountable decisions. At the national level, the constitutions of many countries include rights to information, participation and justice – in some instances, with specific reference to the environment or natural resource protection.[51] National regulations also elaborate these rights and some countries have specific laws to give effect to participatory rights to resource management.[52] Moreover, these laws may include specific procedures providing guidelines on consultation and post-project monitoring and ensuring information and participation (e.g. plans for large infrastructure projects). Under national laws, as discussed below, citizens may have access to administrative or judicial review of private or governmental actions that violate a resource protection law. Additionally, some countries have guaranteed citizens the right to seek judicial review when access to information or public participation is wrongfully denied.

In many developing countries, laws and policies are influenced by Principle 10 of the 1992 Rio Declaration. In some countries (e.g. South Africa, Thailand), environmental protection laws provide specific provisions for environmental information,[53] complementing access to information laws. Some constitutions accommodate provisions on rights to information (e.g. Thailand, Indonesia, Philippines) and public participation.[54] Without specific constitutional provision or information laws, it is difficult for the community groups and individuals to challenge a development project or participate effectively during the consultation. Effective participation also depends on the quality of information available to the community. For example, in cases relating to dam projects (e.g. Nam Choan dam in Thailand and Chico dam in the Philippines) information relating to loss of forests, wetlands or livelihoods was not available to the local communities.[55] In Europe, on the other hand, information regulations are influenced by regional agreements such as the Aarhus Convention. In order to comply with this agreement, some countries have reformed their constitution to include a right to information, formulated new laws regulating access to information and developed general environmental codes with provisions on access to courts.[56]

National EIA legislation may also include participatory provisions allowing public consultation and participation at every stage (e.g. screening, scoping) in the process.[57] Although it is argued that public participation slows down the EIA process, the real goal of EIA is to ensure

51 J. Razzaque,' Linking Human Rights, Environment and Development: Experience from Litigation in South Asia', *Fordham Journal of Environmental Law* 18(3), 2007, 587–608. World Resources Institute, Partnership for Principle 10. Online. Available HTTP: <www.pp10.org> (accessed 8 March 2012).

52 E. Blanco and J. Razzaque, *Globalisation and Natural Resources Law*, Cheltenham: Edward Elgar, 2011, pp. 131–70.

53 World Resources Institute, *World Resources 2002–2004 – Decisions for the Earth: Balance, Voice and Power*, Washington DC: World Resources Institute, 2004, Chapter 3.

54 Petkova et al., op. cit.

55 A.S. Tolentino, 'Legislative Reform for Good Governance through Popular Participation in the Sustainable Development of Wetlands', *Bulletin on APEC Marine Resources Conservation* 4(4), 2002.

56 Economic Commission for Europe, *Synthesis Report on the Status of Implementation of the Convention* (2008), ECE/MP.PP/2008/4. Online. Available HTTP: <http://www.unece.org/env/docu­ments/2008/pp/mop3/ece_mp_pp_2008_4_e.pdf>.

57 J. Holder, *Environmental Assessment: the Regulation of Decision Making*, Oxford: Oxford University Press, 2005, pp. 32–42.

sound environmental results and sustainable management of resources.[58] One example is China where, with the growing importance of environmental protection, participatory procedures such as access to information and public participation are being integrated into regulatory frameworks.[59] In South Asia (e.g. India, Pakistan), national legislation also provides some opportunities, albeit restricted, for public consultation with potentially affected communities in the decision-making process.[60] There are also examples of foreign assistance funding in some Asian countries (e.g. Bangladesh, Pakistan) which require public participation during the preparation of EIA reports.[61] In addition, EIA could be seen as a route to involve people at the project level and can be used as a form of social bargaining. For example, the Malampaya Deepwater Gas-to-Power Project in the Philippines integrated communities' views in business decision-making with resulting benefits on costs and sustainability.[62] However, because of its project-based nature, an EIA may come too late to result in major changes in proposed activities. In those cases, strategic environmental assessment (SEA) may be more beneficial as it allows people to participate at the policy-making (or plans and programmes) level.[63]

A more consistent route is followed in Europe, where some countries have adopted a participatory approach in managing shared natural resources (e.g. watercourses, forests). Within the EU, both EIA and SEA Directives ask Member States to consult with individuals of other Member States if the proposed development activity (project, plan or programme) is likely to have a 'significant effect' on these people.[64] One example of such an inclusive approach is the Water Framework Directive, where public participation plays a key role in managing shared water resources.[65] Another example is the EIA Convention, where members of the public in one state (the area likely to be affected) have the right to receive information and participate in decision-making about activities proposed to be conducted in another state (the state of origin).[66]

While examples from the EU highlight a more homogeneous approach to protect shared resources, there are sporadic instances of the inclusive management of shared resources in the developing world.[67] One such example is inclusive basin management in the Mekong River

58 W.A. Tilleman, 'Public Participation in the Environmental Impact Assessment Process: A Comparative Study of Impact Assessment in Canada, the United States and the European Community', *Columbia Journal of Transnational Law* 33(2), 1995, 337–439.

59 Economic Commission for Europe, *Global and Regional Developments on Issues Related to Principle 10 of the Rio Declaration on Environment and Development* (2008), ECE/MP.PP/2008/8.

60 Razzaque, 'Participatory Rights in Natural Resource Management', op. cit., pp. 117–38.

61 Examples of such EIAs can be found in gas pipeline, thermal power plants, hydropower project, water management, biodiversity conservation sectors. Ibid., pp. 123–6.

62 J. Sohn (ed.) *Development Without Conflict: The Business Case for Community Consent*, Washington DC: World Resources Institute, 2007.

63 B. Dalal-Clayton and B. Sadler, *Strategic Environmental Assessment: A Sourcebook and Reference Guide to International Experience*, London: Earthscan, 2005.

64 EIA Directive 85/337/EEC as amended by 97/11/EC and 2003/35/EC, Art. 7. SEA Directive 2001/42/EC, Arts 7–9.

65 *Directive 2000/60/EC of the European Parliament and of the Council of 23 October 2000 establishing a framework for Community action in the field of water policy* (2000), OJL 327, Preamble, Art. 14.

66 The 1991 UNECE Convention on Environmental Impact Assessment in a Transboundary Context provides provisions on participation (Arts 2, 3) and information (Arts 3,4,6). 30 ILM (1991) 802.

67 For examples of community participation in shared water management in developed and developing countries, see J. Razzaque, 'Public Participation in Water Governance', in J. Dellapenna and J. Gupta (eds) *The Evolution of Law and Politics of Water*, Dordrecht: Springer, 2008, pp. 353–72.

Agreement.[68] It establishes a framework for cooperation between the riparian states in all fields of the river basin's sustainable development under the auspices of the Mekong River Commission (MRC).[69] The MRC has developed policies on information exchange and public participation to promote bottom-up processes in decision-making.[70] Individuals or groups have a right to participate in the Lower Mekong Basin development planning process by contributing their knowledge, voicing their opinions, and learning along with other participants during the planning process.

The above discussion highlights how regional agreements can guide participatory rights with information regulations, consultation procedures to assess impacts and guidelines to manage shared resources such as water. There are, however, some instances of non-compliance with the Aarhus Convention in Europe due to financial and administrative constraints.[71] In developing countries, there are inadequate applications of a rights-based approach, restricted access to public hearings and a lack of regional guidelines on shared resources.[72] Moreover, participatory challenges in many Asian countries relate primarily to the lack of regulated public participation procedures.[73] Excessive technical and bureaucratic procedures for public involvement along with financial costs make it difficult for poor communities to participate effectively in resource decisions.[74] Without a true opportunity to take part in decision-making and impact assessment processes, communities are unable to influence the outcome.

Sovereignty, access to justice and the environment

The non-absolute form of sovereign rights over natural resources allows individuals to access remedies in the international and national legal fora. Sovereignty[75] over natural resources includes a bundle of rights – for example the right to possess, the right to use and the right to manage[76] – along with the ability to legitimately use these rights, duties and competences.[77]

---

68 *Cooperation for the Sustainable Development of the Mekong River Basin*, opened for signature 5 April 1995, 2069 UNTS 3 (entered into force 5 April 1995). The 4,800 km-long Mekong River originates in China, and flows through Myanmar, Lao PDR, Thailand and Cambodia before ending in the Mekong Delta of Vietnam.

69 Ibid. Signed between Cambodia, Lao PDR, Thailand and Vietnam. China and Myanmar are not signatories to the Agreement.

70 *Public participation in the context of MRC* (MRC, 1999). Online. Available HTTP: <http://www. mekonginfo.org/assets/midocs/0002009-society-public-participation-in-the-context-of-the-mrc. pdf> (accessed 9 May 2012). Also see: MRC Public Participation Strategy, MRC, 2002.

71 Economic Commission for Europe, *Synthesis Report on the Status of Implementation of the Convention* (2008), ECE/MP.PP/2008/4.

72 Razzaque, 'Participatory Rights in Natural Resource Management', op. cit., pp. 117–38; Razzaque, 'Public Participation in Water Governance' op. cit., pp. 353–72.

73 Mushkat, 'The Principle of Public Participation', op. cit., pp. 607–30.

74 Foti et al., op. cit.

75 Sovereignty of a state is an integral part of its existence along with three other elements – a permanent population, a defined territory and government. M. Shaw, *International Law*, Cambridge: Cambridge University Press, 2008, pp. 197–204.

76 N. Schrijver, *Sovereignty over Natural Resources: Balancing Rights and Duties*, Cambridge: Cambridge University Press, 1997, chapters 2 and 3; R. Barnes, *Property Rights and Natural Resources*, Oxford: Hart Publishing, 2009, pp. 228–30.

77 W.G. Werner and J.H. De Wilde, 'The Endurance of Sovereignty', *European Journal of International Relations* 7(3), 2001, 283–313, p. 297.

With the exclusive control and use of the natural resources within the territory, states have the right to profits gained from the resources, and to conserve, explore and exploit these resources.[78] However, '[p]ermanent sovereignty over natural resources has to be exercised for national development and the well-being of the people.'[79] With the wide discretion to interpret, the way states exercise this duty may not always be beneficial to the people or natural resource management. States also have the duty to enter into foreign investment agreements in good faith and respect the 'sovereignty of peoples and nations over their natural wealth and resources'.[80] Moreover, the state has a duty to protect the interests of indigenous peoples.[81] This shows that the rule of law reshapes the internal sovereignty of the state, puts the constitutions above the state and gives resource rights to people. The rule of law imposes significant constraints upon how law is made and how it is adjudicated and implies that the court should be impartial and accessible to all.[82]

Several state actions have reshaped the conventional definition of sovereignty. First, states by accepting the authority of international law, ratifying international agreements (e.g. UN Charter, human rights and environmental treaties) and agreeing to abide by the rules of international institutions (e.g. the World Trade Organization) have imposed restrictions on their resource sovereignty. The rules of some international courts and tribunals include provisions allowing people to participate in court proceedings. Direct participation by private citizens and NGOs is allowed, for example in the World Bank Inspection Panel.[83] In addition, indirect participation, for example through *amicus* briefs from NGOs, industry and academics, is allowed in the International Tribunal for the Law of the Sea,[84] the WTO Dispute Settlement Body[85] and the International Centre for the Settlement of Investment Disputes.[86]

The EU provides a unique example because the membership of this regional body limits the power of the Member States to adopt decisions in certain areas. This surrender of absolute sovereignty means the supremacy of EU law.[87] The EU jurisprudence and legislation apply between the supranational level and the Member States, and at the level of

78 Barnes, op. cit., pp. 228–30.
79 *Permanent Sovereignty over Natural Resources* (1962), GA Res 1803 (XVII), 17 UN GAOR Supp (no. 17) 15, UN Doc A/5217, para. 1; International Covenant on Civil and Political Rights, Art. 1(2); Schrijver, op. cit., p. 168.
80 *Permanent Sovereignty over Natural Resources*, op. cit., paras 4 and 8.
81 *United Nations Declaration on the Rights of Indigenous Peoples* (2007), GA Res 61/295, UN GAOR, 61st Sess, 68th Plen Mtg, UN Doc A/RES/61/295.
82 Werner and Wilde, op. cit., p. 297.
83 D. Hunter, 'Using the World Bank Inspection Panel to Defend the Interests of Project-Affected People', *Chicago Journal of International Law* 4, 2003, 201.
84 *Rules of the Tribunal*, Arts 77, 82, 84.
85 *Import Prohibition of Certain Shrimp and Shrimp Products*, report of the Appellate Body, 12 October 1998, *DSR* 1998: VII, 2755 (paras 104–6, 110). *Imposition of Countervailing Duties on Certain Hot-rolled Lead and Bismuth Carbon Steel Products Originating in the United Kingdom*, report of the Appellate Body, 7 June 2000, *DSR* 2000: V, 2601 (paras 39–42). *Measures Affecting Asbestos and Asbestos-containing Products*, report of the Appellate Body, 5 April 2001, *DSR* 2001: VII, 3243 (paras 51–5).
86 *Aguas Argentinas, SA, Suez, Sociedad General de Aguas de Barcelona, SA and Vivendi Universal, SA and the Argentine Republic*, ICSID Case No. ARB/03/19, Order in response to a petition for transparency and participation as *amicus curiae*, 19 May 2005 (paras 17–29). *Aguas Provinciales de Santa Fe SA and Others v Argentina* (17 March 2006), Order in Response to a Petition for Participation as *Amicus Curiae*, ICSID Case No. ARB/03/17.
87 *Costa v ENEL* (case 6/64), 1964, ECR 585.

Union citizens.[88] However, the EU should only act where 'the objectives of the proposed action cannot be achieved sufficiently by the Member States' and 'by reason of the scale or effects of the proposed action', the EU could achieve better results.[89] Applying the principle of subsidiarity, the EU has the power to adopt measures in order to achieve its environmental objectives protecting habitats, migratory species or water.[90] Thus, the Aarhus Convention has considerably influenced law-making at the European level.[91] Apart from taking necessary measures to apply the provisions of the Aarhus Convention to the EU's own institutions,[92] the EU has adopted and amended several directives concerning public access to environmental information and public participation reflecting the provisions of the Convention.[93]

Second, the transformation of sovereignty (thus prioritising the rule of law) is apparent when a state allows human rights bodies to determine the quality of life of citizens and to ascertain the property and ownership rights of indigenous people. The limited nature of resource sovereignty allows individuals, NGOs or groups of individuals to come to the European Court of Human Rights,[94] Inter-American Commission on Human Rights[95] and African Commission on Human Rights[96] if they are victims of any violation. In addition, these regional courts allow NGOs to submit *amicus curiae* briefs during the written procedure and, in some cases, take part in oral hearings.[97] Unfortunately, access for individuals and communities to the Court of Justice of the EU (CJEU) is still quite restricted.[98] Noting these practices in other regional courts along with the access to justice provision of the Aarhus Convention, it is time to rethink the standing of individuals at the CJEU.

Third, the recognition of the rights of indigenous peoples over their resources affirms their cultural rights and rights to lands, waters, territories and natural resources, genetic resources and traditional knowledge. The UN Declaration acknowledges the collective rights of indigenous peoples to genetic resources and associated traditional knowledge as well as a right to

---

88 L. Kramer, 'The EU: a Regional Model?', in G. Winter (ed.) *Multilevel Governance of Global Environmental Change*, Cambridge: Cambridge University Press, 2006, p. 333.

89 *Treaty of the European Union*, Art. 5(3). Official Journal of EU, C83/13, 30 March 2010.

90 *Treaty on the Functioning of the European Union*, Official Journal of the European Union, C115/49, Arts 191, 192; W.P.J. Wils, 'Subsidiarity and EC Environmental Policy: Taking People's Concerns Seriously', *Journal of Environmental Law* 6, 1994, 85–91, pp. 88–9.

91 The EU signed the Aarhus Convention in 1998 and approved it in early 2005.

92 Regulation (EC) No 1367/2006 on the application of the provisions of the Aarhus Convention on Access to Information, Public Participation in Decision-making and Access to Justice in Environmental Matters to Community institutions and bodies.

93 Council Directive 2003/4/EC, Council Directive 2011/92/EU (EIA Directive), Directive 2008/1/EC (IPPC Directive).

94 However, the application of margin of appreciation gives the Court the flexibility needed to avoid damaging confrontations between the Court and the member states and enables it to balance the sovereignty of Member States with their obligations under the Convention. For example, *Hatton v The UK*, judgment of 8 July 2003, § 122. See also *Guerra and Others v Italy*, 1998-I ECHR, Judgment of 19 February 1998. *Lopez-Ostra v Spain*, ECHR (1994), Series A, No. 303C.

95 *American Convention on Human Rights*, OAS Treaty Series No. 36, 1144 UNTS 123, Art. 44.

96 Decision regarding Communication 155/96 (Social and Economic Rights Action Center/Center for Economic and Social Rights v Nigeria), Case No. ACHPR/COMM/A044/1, 27 May 2002.

97 *European Convention on Human Rights*, as amended by Protocol 11, Art. 36; *Rule of the European Court of Human Rights* (2009), Art. 44(2); *Rules of Procedure* (2009), Arts 2(3), 44.

98 *Treaty of the EU*, op. cit., Art. 19; *Treaty on the Functioning of the EU*, op. cit., Art. 263.

participate in the development of national laws on access and benefit-sharing and traditional knowledge.[99] They have the right to redress or compensation if there is no free, prior informed consent.[100] Although the Declaration is by nature aspirational and is not legally binding, the significance of its full and unqualified recognition of the sovereign rights of indigenous peoples to natural resources has far-reaching implications.[101]

Communities (including indigenous people) and NGOs at the national level can access courts if there is a violation of constitutional or other rights. The nature, scope and strength of these rights depend on the legal systems, democratic traditions and legal cultures of states. In Europe, rights to access courts, for example, can be protected by the Constitution.[102] Judicial review is one procedural technique by which decisions of public bodies exercising environmental responsibilities can be challenged in court and a means by which the courts supervise public bodies in the exercise of their powers or the carrying out of their duties.[103] Another option lies in civil suits. A class action may be used in tort-based claims that have an impact on a large number of people (e.g. climate litigation in the US).[104] However, examples from Europe show that litigation costs, lawyers' fees, lack of legal aid for environmental cases as well as strict interpretation of standing rules remain major obstacles in bringing an environmental matter to the court.[105]

In both European and non-European countries, environmental or general administrative laws provide possibilities for private persons to challenge acts or omissions by public authorities which contravene provisions of national environmental law.[106] In some countries, individuals and environmental NGOs may seek the intervention of competent authorities under environmental legislation as well as directly sue the operators of activities that pose a threat to the environment.[107] In determining whether public interest groups or NGOs have standing, the court may consider a number of factors including the merits of the challenge, the importance of vindicating the rule of law, the importance of the issues raised and the nature of the breach.[108] The national law may give standing to community groups or individuals to challenge a government decision on resource development.[109] An example of the challenges of standing is the case of the coastal native

---

99 UN Declaration (2007), op. cit., Art. 27.

100 Ibid., Art. 2.

101 Economic and Social Council, *Prevention of Discrimination and Protection of Indigenous Peoples and Minorities* (2001), E/CN.4/Sub.2/2001/21. *Report on Indigenous Peoples' Permanent Sovereignty over Natural Resources, Special Rapporteur of the Commission on Human Rights* (2004), E/CN.4/Sub.2/2004/30 and Add. 1.

102 Economic Commission for Europe (2008), op. cit., note 56.

103 H. Woolf, J. Jowell and A.P. Le Sueur, *De Smith, Woolf and Jowell's Principles of Judicial Review*, London: Sweet and Maxwell, 1999, part I.

104 *Connecticut v American Electric Power Company, Inc.; Comer v Murphy Oil Co.; California v General Motors Corp.* D. Grossman, 'Tort Based Climate Litigation', in W.C.G. Burns and H. Osofsky (eds) *Adjudicating Climate Change: State, National and International Approaches*, Cambridge: Cambridge University Press, 2009, pp. 193–229.

105 Economic Commission for Europe, *Synthesis Report on the Status of Implementation of the Convention* (2008), ECE/MP.PP/2008/4.

106 Economic Commission for Europe (2008), op. cit., note 56 and 59. Foti (2008), op.cit.

107 Ibid.

108 Economic Commission for Europe, *Implementation Report Submitted by the United Kingdom* (2008), ECE/MP.PP/IR/2008/GBR.

109 Ibid.

Alaskan village of Kivalina,[110] which deals with internally displaced persons. Kivalina residents filed a federal lawsuit in the US alleging that 20 energy companies were responsible for thinning sea ice and increasing storm surges that are forcing the villagers to relocate and therefore hold those greenhouse gas producers responsible for the alleged climate change.[111] One of the grounds used to dismiss the action by the District Court for the Northern District of California was that the plaintiffs lacked standing to pursue their claim as there was no causal link between the alleged injuries and the alleged harm committed by the defendants.[112] In similar circumstances, it may be possible to bring an action in the regional human rights courts. However, as the Inuit case (2005) in the Inter-American Commission on Human Rights[113] shows, it may not be easy to prove standing in that forum either.

Public interest litigation (PIL) is another legal mechanism that allows individuals and NGOs to vindicate a 'public interest', and it has been widely used to uphold environmental law.[114] It is a form of legal proceeding in which redress is sought in respect of injury to the public in general. Individuals or NGOs can bring PIL against government bodies, companies or private individuals.[115] Examples of PIL challenging government decisions can be found in Africa (Uganda, Tanzania, South Africa), Asia (India, Pakistan, Philippines, Nepal, Bangladesh, Sri Lanka) and South America (Argentina, Chile, Peru), enabling poorer sections of the community to access the courts.[116] The historical development of PIL in India shows that the judiciary has been very active in relaxing the standing rules, giving access to marginalised communities to courts and interpreting the constitutional rights in a liberal manner in order to enhance the rule of law.[117] A large number of these cases allow indigenous communities to bring action in the court.[118] In Europe, PIL is not as well developed as in some developing countries. Individuals and communities have a number of alternative routes to challenge a decision by government agencies or activities of a polluting company. The public can, for example, report potential breaches of environmental legislation to the appropriate regulator (e.g. in England and Wales, to the Environment Agency).[119] With regard to access to

---

110 US District Court for the Northern District of California Oakland Division, *Native Village of Kivalina and City of Kivalina v Exxon Mobil Corp., et al.*, Case No: C08–1138 SBA. The case is pending at the Ninth Circuit Court of Appeals. *Native Village of Kivalina v Exxon Mobil*, No. 09–17490 (9th Cir. filed 5 Nov 2009).

111 *Native Village of Kivalina v Exxon Mobil Corp.*, 663 F. Supp. 2d 863 (N.D. Cal. 2009).

112 Ibid.

113 While the Commission declined to review the merits of the petition, it initiated a 'Hearing of a General Nature' on human rights and global warming in 2007. Press Release, Inter-American Commission on Human Rights, 'IACHR Announces Webcast of Public Hearings of the 127th Regular Period of Sessions', No 8/07 (26 Feb 2007). Online. Available HTTP: <http://www. cidh.org/Comunicados/English/2007/8.07eng.htm> (accessed 21 January 2012).

114 J. Cassels 'Judicial Activism and Public Interest Litigation in India: Attempting the Impossible?', *American Journal of Comparative Law* 37, 1989, 495–519, p. 498.

115 J. Razzaque, *Public Interest Environmental Litigation in India, Pakistan and Bangladesh*, The Hague: Kluwer, 2004, chapters 1–2; Mushkat, 'The Principle of Public Participation', op. cit., pp. 607–30.

116 Partnership for Principle 10, op. cit.

117 R. Dhavan 'Whose Law? Whose interest?', in J. Cooper and R. Dhavan (eds) *Public Interest Law*, Oxford: Blackwell, 1986, p. 21.

118 *Banawasi Seva Ashram v State of Uttar Pradesh* AIR 1987 SC 374, *Olga Tellis v Bombay Municipal Corporation* AIR 1986 SC 180, *Karajan Jalasay Y.A.S.A.S. Samity v State of Gujarat*, AIR 1987 SC 532 and *Gramin Sewa Sanstha v State of Uttar Pradesh*, 1986(Supp) SCC 578.

119 Economic Commission for Europe, *Implementation Report Submitted by the UK*, op. cit.

environmental information, the relevant Information Commissioner may offer a review procedure which involves no expense.[120]

It is clear from the history of the development of PIL that lack of cooperation from the government and weak regulations to protect natural resources forced people to take effective action in the court. One criticism of PIL is that it does not change the policy of the government and public authorities are free to make the same decision again in a similar situation. Therefore, access to the courts may not ensure procedural justice or a just substantive outcome. Criticisms regarding costs and lengthy procedures aside,[121] PIL in the developing world has become a forum for people to voice their concerns on environmental matters and reflects a communitarian approach.

Conclusion

The above discussion shows that, along with the regulation of ecosystem services, rights to access natural resources and participate in resource-related decision-making can strongly influence the sustainability of ecosystem management. However, government agencies in many developing countries do not always follow a coordinated approach due to time, financial and manpower constraints. Second, some countries have advanced procedural tools while some national legal frameworks do not provide adequate mechanisms for access to information, participation and justice. While states require regulation to protect the resource sector, strong substantive rights are not enough – these rights need to be complemented by participatory rights (i.e. information, participation and access to legal remedies). Third, even if there is an effective judicial system, in many instances it is not cost-effective, standing rules are often restricted and legal assistance is rarely available for environmental cases.

Most examples of public participation considered in this chapter emphasise public access to environmental information, participation in decision-making (e.g. environmental assessments) and access to justice (e.g. standing in courts). While these participatory reforms have improved the quality of many environmental decisions, they have hardly engendered a major paradigm shift to ecologically sustainable development. Most participatory techniques so far hardly threaten existing political institutions, since they operate within those institutions, and leave power and authority mostly unfettered. Many deficiencies with public participation can be traced to flaws in the enabling legal and institutional frameworks. For example, the terms of reference of an EIA may be drafted narrowly by authorities to exclude certain contentious issues or may be conducted when the development decision has already been approved.[122] Along with the financial costs and procedural technicalities of participation procedures, there are difficulties in gaining access to clear information that would allow the public to provide a meaningful voice in resource decisions. Access to the courts can also be prohibitively expensive for most individuals, and therefore PIL is unlikely in the absence of generous state legal aid or other similar funding schemes. Apart from strengthening government agencies' obligations to initiate effective consultation, provisions for public participation watchdogs to

---

120 Ibid.
121 Razzaque, *Public Interest Environmental Litigation*, op. cit., Chapter 5; M.I. Jeffrey, 'Intervenor Funding as Key to Effective Citizen Participation in Environmental Decision-Making', *Arizona Journal of International and Comparative Law* 19, 2002, p. 660.
122 Richardson and Razzaque, 'Public Participation in the Environmental Decision-making', op. cit., pp. 165–94.

monitor environmental decision-making processes can also lead to transparent, participatory and accountable decisions.[123]

The experience over the last two decades shows that the development of the participatory rights, to a large extent, depends on knowledge sharing among the public bodies, judiciary, private sectors and NGOs. It also shows that improved participatory governance will require greater transparency and accountability in local decision-making and a redefinition of the role of states.[124] It is evident that achieving good environmental decision-making at the national level is closely related to environmental governance at the global level. Following the global participation agenda,[125] recent environmental and development policies in many developing countries aim to strengthen the institutional capacity of local government and non-state actors to create a more participatory ambience. However, people in many developing and developed countries lack information on their participatory rights and fail to actively participate in decision-making processes. In many developed countries (e.g. in Europe), the participation agenda is generally integrated in the public consultation and review mechanisms and has tended to take a more legal form than into many developing countries where it has, to some extent, been confined to policy mechanisms.[126]

Experience also demonstrates that, in order to achieve a transparent, inclusive and accountable system of governance at the national level, resource development decisions need to have support from most affected communities including resource right holders. To proactively include the poor and marginalised groups in resource decisions will require both the project proponent and the government adapting their strategies of information dissemination and adopting methods of citizen participation that take into account the social, economic, cultural and geographic characteristics of the population in question. Greening of the economy needs to promote transparency and accountability through access to information and stakeholder involvement in decision-making, open processes that engage citizens and ensure social inclusion supported by institutions and interest groups.

With the inadequate legal regime to manage natural resources and the increased pressure from private actors to influence a decision on development activities, regional initiatives can offer some guidance to developing countries to push for transparent and accountable decisions. It is time for regional bodies to support and encourage countries to jointly manage transboundary shared resources (e.g. rivers, wetlands, biological resources) with rules on EIA, SEA, access to information and courts for affected communities. These regional platforms could be instrumental in sharing experiences among countries with similar legal system and economic development – to develop, explore and manage natural resources sustainably. Such inclusive management can improve the relationship among neighbouring countries as well. For example, the Indus–Ganges–Brahmaputra–Meghna Basin is surrounded by Afghanistan, China, Pakistan, Nepal, Bhutan, India and Bangladesh. The terrain is varied and so are the

123 For further examples, see W.M. Lafferty and J. Meadowcroft (eds) *Democracy and the Environment: Problems and Prospects*, Cheltenham: Edward Elgar, 1996.

124 Asian Development Bank, *What is Governance? Governance in Asia: From Crisis to Opportunity*, Bangkok, 1999.

125 For example, international (e.g. Climate Change Convention, Biodiversity Convention, Desertification Convention) and regional conventions (e.g. Espoo Convention, Aarhus Convention)

126 O. Renn, T. Webler and P. Wiedemann (eds) *Fairness and Competence in Citizen Participation: Evaluating Models for Environmental Discourse*, Dordrecht: Kluwer, 1995, pp. 17–33.

political situations in this basin. All these are developing countries and, noting the adverse effect of climate change in this region, their collaboration in basin-based management is urgently needed.[127]

The recent economic crisis does offer a 'second chance' to many countries in following a sustainable path to development and making correct choices – but, unfortunately, nature does not allow bailouts. Participatory rights are crucial to the greening of the economy; it is time to reflect the economic as well as social values of the environment in all resource decisions, which in effect can lead to the sustainability and well-being of society.

---

127 *Kathmandu to Copenhagen: A Regional Climate Change Conference*, Nepal, 2009, Final Statement.

9

The funding of international environmental law

Justin Wolst

This chapter will provide an overview of how international environmental law is funded. It will explore the structure, different types of funding and current and emerging trends. Central to this chapter will be the role and effectiveness of the funding mechanisms, such as trust funds, market mechanisms and the Global Environment Facility. This chapter will consider the international environmental treaty regimes for which funding mechanisms provide financial resources, and the way that they have evolved.

Introduction

'Money makes the world go round'. This famous phrase from the musical play, *Cabaret* in the 1960s referred to the important role that money played in the world then as it still does today. Environmental protection is no exception to this. Awareness of the need to protect the environment rose in the 1970s. It became quickly evident that one of the main difficulties in creating a fair and sound legal system for environmental protection is money – or rather the lack of it. Industrialised countries' development increased their social and economic position but often at the cost of the environment. Developing countries lack financial resources but still hold a substantial portion of the earth's biological resources. Additionally, in addressing global environmental issues developing countries often demand financial and technical assistance for environmental conservation and the use of environmentally friendly technologies. Thus financial and technical assistance for environmental purposes has been a key element in the development of international environmental law.

This chapter will first provide a brief overview of the history and the main principles of funding will be described. The second part will address the structure of international environmental law funding. This refers to the financial arrangements that support the operation of multilateral environmental agreements (MEAs) and institutions. The third part will explore the funding used to pursue the objectives of international environmental law and in particular MEAs. The different types of funding considered are treaty-specific mechanisms, overseas development assistance and funding by multilateral development banks. The final part will critically examine a number of trends in the funding of international environmental law.

History and principles of funding of international environmental law

Principles and responsibilities

Funding has been the subject of debate since international environmental law first emerged. Initial references date back to the *Declaration of the United Nations Conference on the Human Environment* in 1972 (Stockholm Declaration)[1] which stated that 'environmental deficiencies . . . can best be remedied by accelerated development through the transfer of substantial quantities of financial and technological assistance . . . to . . . developing countries'.[2] The need for funding of international environmental law by industrialised countries was later addressed in the *World Commission on Environment and Development,* in their 1987 report (*Brundtland Report*).[3]

Neither the Stockholm Declaration nor the Brundtland Report directly addressed or led to concrete funding commitments by industrialised countries. They did, however, create awareness that led to the recognition by developed countries of the responsibility they must take for global environmental degradation. Although some early initiatives were undertaken, such as treaty-specific trust funds, it took almost two decades for the international community to create more comprehensive financial mechanisms for environmental objectives.[4] Significantly, the establishment of the financial mechanism of the *Montreal Protocol on Substances that Deplete the Ozone Layer* (Montreal Protocol) in 1990 was a turning point.[5] In 1992 a next step was taken at the *United Nations Conference on Environment and Development* (UNCED), where allocation of financial resources for environmental purposes became a central issue. The *Rio Declaration on Environment and Development* (Rio Declaration) and *Agenda 21: Programme of Action for Sustainable Development* (Agenda 21) addressed the differentiation between industrialised and developing countries as donors and receivers of funding.[6] The way in which this was achieved was through the principle of 'common but differentiated responsibilities' (CBDR).[7] This principle can be described as acceptance of the different responsibilities states have and is the basis for the transfer of financial resources from industrialised countries to developing countries for remediation of existing environmental degradation and to prevent repetition of mistakes industrialised countries made during their own development.[8] Although non-binding, the Rio Declaration and Agenda 21 are political agreements

---

1 *Declaration of the United Nations Conference on the Human Environment* (1973), UN Doc A/CONF.48/14/Rev. 1 ('Stockholm Declaration').
2 Stockholm Declaration, Principle 9.
3 See e.g. United Nations World Commission on Environment and Development, *Our Common Future*, 1987, Oxford: Oxford University Press ('Brundtland Report') Ch. 3.1.
4 See e.g. *Convention Concerning the Protection of the World Cultural and Natural Heritage*, opened for signature 16 November 1972, 11 ILM 1358 (entered into force 17 December 1975) ('World Heritage Convention'), Art. 17, which established the World Heritage Trust Fund in 1972; *Montreal Protocol on Substances that Deplete the Ozone Layer*, opened for signature 16 September 1987, 26 ILM 1550 (1987) (entered into force 1 January 1989) ('Montreal Protocol'), Art. 10, which established the *Montreal Protocol Multilateral Fund*.
5 Montreal Protocol, Art. 10.
6 See, e.g., Rio Declaration, Principle 7; *Agenda 21: Programme of Action for Sustainable Development*, UN Doc A/Conf.151/26 (1992) ('Agenda 21'), Ch. 33.3, which states that 'the provision to developing countries of effective means, *inter alia*, financial resources and technology . . . will serve the common interests of developed and developing countries . . .'.
7 Rio Declaration, Principle 7.
8 See also Sands, op. cit., pp. 285–6; N. Matz, 'Environmental Financing and Coherence of Financial Mechanisms in International Environmental Agreements', *Max Planck Yearbook of United Nations Law* 6, 2002, 473–534 ('Matz 2002'), p. 477.

in which industrialised countries showed their commitment to provide funding for the prevention of further, and remediation of existing, environmental degradation.[9] The acceptance of the principle of common but differentiated responsibilities formed a basis for funding of international environmental law and led to a number of financial mechanisms in MEAs that will be discussed in this chapter.

Simultaneously, another important principle emerged that is related specifically to funding of international environmental law. The Stockholm Declaration called for 'additional international technical and financial assistance' to be made available for environmental purposes in developing countries.[10] A similar reference was made to 'new and additional financial resources, particularly to developing countries' in Agenda 21.[11] This meant that funding for environmental protection purposes should be additional to existing financial resources for developmental purposes.[12] This concept of 'new and additional' resources has found its way into the text of many MEAs.[13] However, not all the funding that has been promised by developed countries has been delivered to developing countries.[14] This has subsequently led to tensions between developing and developed countries and unfortunately a lack of trust.[15]

The structure of funding commitments

Funding of international environmental law can be roughly divided into two categories: first, financial support for treaty regimes and frameworks; and second the funding of objectives and substantive obligations. The former refers to the establishment of and costs involved in MEA regimes and other environmental initiatives. The latter means the financial resources that are used to pursue the goals set out in the different MEAs including *inter alia* compliance, monitoring and capacity-building.

---

9 Agenda 21, Ch. 33.
10 Stockholm Declaration, Principle 12.
11 Agenda 21, Ch. 33.1.
12 Ibid. One of the reasons to use the term 'new and additional resources' was to differentiate the funding for environmental purposes from economic development aid or poverty alleviation; see Agenda 21, Ch. 33.13.
13 See, e.g., *Stockholm Convention on Persistent Organic Pollutants*, opened for signature 22 May 2001, 40 ILM 532 (entered into force 17 May 2004) (Stockholm Convention) Art. 13; *Convention on Biological Diversity*, opened for signature 5 June 1992, 31 ILM 818 ('Convention on Biological Diversity') Preamble; *Kyoto Protocol to United Nations Framework Convention on Climate Change*, opened for signature 11 December 1997, 37 ILM 22 (entered into force 16 February 2005) ('Kyoto Protocol') Art. 11 sub 2 (a).
14 The 0.7 per cent ODA pledge made by developed countries in Agenda 21, for example, has not been met, except by a couple of countries; see more below. See also R.L. Hicks, B.C. Parks, J.T. Roberts and M.J. Tierney, *Greening Aid? Understanding the Environmental Impacts of Developing Assistance*, Oxford: Oxford University Press, 2008.
15 See e.g. J. Drexhage and D. Murphy, 'From Brundtland to Rio 2012', *International Institute for Sustainable Development Background Paper prepared for consideration by the High Level Panel on Global Sustainability at its first meeting*, 2010, p 7. Online. Available HTTP: <http://www.un.org/wcm/webdav/site/climatechange/shared/gsp/docs/GSP1-6_Background%20on%20Sustainable%20Devt.pdf> (accessed 19 February 2012).

Effectiveness of international environmental law

Effectiveness is gauged by the achievement of international environmental law goals. In national legal systems effectiveness is often measured by changes in human behaviour.[16] Although in both national and international law the standards set are directed to change human behaviour, the effectiveness of international environmental law is more focused upon tangible goals. The foremost reason for this distinction is the lack of means of enforcing international law, and especially international environmental law. A clear example is the *Convention on Biological Diversity* (CBD), where in the two decades since its adoption a decline in species is still clearly evident.[17] Although the number of MEAs has grown significantly, with the exception of the Montreal Protocol very few have been deemed successful. This limited effectiveness could affect contributions made by donors.[18]

Players within international environmental law

Generally, MEAs are agreements between states that set certain environmental standards for signatory parties. In addition, other players, such as international institutions, supranational bodies and non-governmental organisations (NGOs), can have observer status or play a facilitative role in implementing treaties or in the executive agency. Although the private sector is often not included in negotiation or implementation processes, it is becoming increasingly important, especially within the context of *funding* of international environmental law. This is due to the (potential) amount of private sector funding flowing to developing countries.[19]

Supporting the structure of international environmental law

Literature on funding of international environmental law often focuses on financial resources that flow from developed to developing countries to facilitate compliance with MEAs and pursue global environmental benefits. In addition to this there are also financial resources used to support the governance structure of treaty regimes themselves. Among the requirements of MEAs are regular meetings, secretariats for administrative purposes and the

16 N. Matz, 'Financial Institutions between Effectiveness and Legitimacy – A Legal Analysis of the World Bank, Global Environment Facility and Prototype Carbon Fund', *International Environmental Agreements* 5, 2005, 265–302 ('Matz 2005'), p. 267.
17 See e.g. COP 10 Decision X/2 Convention on Biological Diversity, which states: '*Noting with concern* the conclusions of the third edition of the Global Biodiversity Outlook, which confirm that the 2010 biodiversity target has not been met in full . . .'.
18 For example, although not conclusive of this matter, contributions to the UNEP Environment Fund have been declining since 2009. From 1973 until 2008 contributions increased every year, but in the last two years available they have declined from US$89 million in 2008 to US$81 million in 2010. *Contributions to UNEP's Environment Fund 1973–2010*, UNEP. Online. Available HTTP: <http://www.unep.org/rms/en/Financing_of_UNEP/Environment_Fund/pdf/Contributions%20by%20year%201973-2010.18.2.2011.Web.pdf> (accessed 14 February 2012).
19 See e.g. B.S. Gentry and D.C. Esty, 'Private Capital Flows: New and Additional Resources for Sustainable Development', in J.A. Miller and J. Coppock (eds) *Bridges to Sustainability: Business and Government Working Together for a Better Environment*, Yale School of Forestry & Environmental Studies Bulletin 101, 1997, pp. 18–19, where the authors show that the private capital flows to developing countries are substantial. See also Organisation for Economic Co-operation and Development (OECD) report on 2010 development aid results. Online. Available HTTP: <http://www.oecd.org/document/10/0,3746,en_2649_33721_44774218_1_1_1_1,00.html> (accessed 18 February 2012).

participation of as many countries as possible. Financial resources supporting the governance structure of MEAs are, in general, financed through contributions by parties. Contributions are often agreed upon by the Conference of Parties (COP) of a MEA and can be voluntary, required by legal agreement, or mandatory as an obligation assumed on membership.[20] In addition to mandatory contributions, parties or other entities can choose to donate voluntarily. Parties contribute in accordance with their capabilities, with developed countries paying more than developing countries. An example of a commonly used contribution scale is the UN scale of assessments:

> Contributions made each year by Parties . . . based on such a scale of assessments of the United Nations as may be adopted from time to time by the General Assembly, adjusted so as to ensure that no party contributes less than 0.01 per cent of the total, that no one contribution exceeds 22 per cent of the total and that no contribution from a least developed country exceeds 0.01 per cent of the total.[21]

An important organisational part of the structure of international environmental law is the MEA secretariat. Secretariats prepare meetings, disseminate information, report to the COPs and often have an advisory role to assist parties in compliance-related issues.[22] Secretariats are responsible for the financial sustainability of the MEA and its mechanisms.[23] Secretariats are financed by the contributions of the parties to the MEA.[24] Some countries provide a location and headquarters for a secretariat and other secretariats are placed under the auspices of an international (environmental) organisation, such as the United Nations Environment Programme (UNEP).[25] For some MEAs a special secretariat is founded with the sole purpose of supporting that MEA, such as the Secretariat for the CBD or the United Nations Framework Convention on Climate Change (UNFCCC).[26]

In general MEAs target environmental protection and preservation in a global context. Their aim is to include as many parties as possible to address international environmental problems. However, developing nations often do not have the resources or capability to participate in all negotiations. Therefore, developed parties are requested to assist developing

20 See also, J. Klabbers, *An Introduction to International Institutional Law*, Cambridge: Cambridge University Press, 2004, p. 128.
21 *Decision SC-1/3*, adopted at the Conference of the Parties at its first meeting, Stockholm Convention, Rule 5.1(a). See also 'Committee on Contributions', *UN Regular Budget*, online. Available HTTP: <http://www.un.org/Depts/dhl/resguide/specrb.html#contrib> (accessed 14 February 2012).
22 See e.g. *United Nations Framework Convention on Climate Change*, opened for signature 4 June 1992, 31 ILM 849 (entered into force 21 March 1994) ('UNFCCC') Art. 8.
23 UNFCCC, Art. 8; see also, Decision SC-1/3 Stockholm Convention, Rule 3.
24 See e.g. Decision SC-1/3 Stockholm Convention, Rule 4.
25 See e.g. Stockholm Convention, Art. 20.3. The Stockholm Convention has UNEP as its Secretariat. In total UNEP hosts 11 secretariats for MEAs. *About UNEP*. Online. Available HTTP: <http://www.unep.org/Documents.multilingual/Default.asp?DocumentID=43&ArticleID=234> (accessed 14 February 2012).
26 See e.g. *Convention on Biological Diversity*, opened for signature 5 June 1992, 1760 UNTS 143 (entered into force 29 December 1993) ('CBD') Art. 24 (the CBD Secretariat is established in Montreal, Canada); UNFCCC, Arts 8, 21.1 (the UNFCCC Secretariat is established in Bonn, Germany).

countries to participate. Some MEAs allocate specific funds for participation of developing countries.[27]

Funding for environmental objectives and compliance

The greater part of funding of international environmental law is for the achievement of the substantive objectives and ensuring compliance. The standards and obligations agreed on in MEAs need to be implemented, monitored and verified. Developing countries often lack resources and/or capacity to do so. As embedded in the principle of common but differentiated responsibilities, industrialised countries have acknowledged their obligation to assist developing countries financially in pursuing environmentally sound and sustainable development.[28]

Funding for international environmental law is not limited to the mere provision of money. Different but very valuable types of funding are for the transfer of technology and technical assistance which developing countries often lack.[29] Clean technologies are often protected under intellectual property rights law and are difficult to apply.[30] A mechanism that focuses on the transfer of technologies and technical assistance is the 'clearinghouse mechanism' (CHM).[31] A CHM is a network, often digital, facilitating technical and scientific cooperation, transparency and capacity-building through information exchange.[32] However, the success of a CHM depends on the participation of different parties. The *Biosafety Clearing House Mechanism*, for example, has tried to counter this challenge by linking the usage of the CHM to compliance with the *Cartagena Protocol on Biosafety to the Convention on Biological Diversity*.[33]

Incremental costs

Financial mechanisms in international environmental law generally finance the incremental costs of projects – defined as the additional costs that contribute to implementation of and compliance with MEAs. Implementation refers to the translation of standards and rules in MEAs into national legislation. Compliance involves meeting the standards set out in MEAs.[34] In this context funding that supports national reporting and capacity-building can also fall within this definition and thus the wide-ranging scope of incremental costs.

---

27 See e.g. Financial rules as Annex to Decision RC-1/4 adopted by the Conference of Parties at its first meeting, *Convention on the Prior Informed Consent Procedure for Certain Hazardous Chemicals and Pesticides in International Trade*, opened for signature 10 September 1998, 38 ILM 1 (entered into force 24 February 2004) ('Rotterdam Convention') Art. 9 (c).
28 See Rio Declaration, Principle 7; Agenda 21, Ch. 33.
29 See e.g. Stockholm Declaration, Principles 12, 20; Rio Declaration, Principle 7.
30 See e.g. Sands, op. cit., p. 1044; Stockholm Declaration, Principles 12, 20. See also M. Blakeney, *Legal Aspects of the Transfer of Technology to Developing Countries*, Oxford: ESC, 1989.
31 See e.g. CBD, Art. 18.3; *Cartagena Protocol on Biosafety*, opened for signature 29 January 2000, 39 ILM 1027 (entered into force 11 September 2003) ('Biosafety Protocol') Art. 20.
32 See e.g. CBD, Art. 18.3.
33 See e.g. Biosafety Protocol, Art. 11.1.
34 R. Mitchell 'Compliance Theory: An Overview', in J. Cameron, J. Werksman and P. Roderick, *Improving Compliance with International Environmental Law*, London: Earthscan, 1996, p. 24; UNEP, *Compliance Mechanisms Under Selected Multilateral Environmental Agreements*, p. 19. Online. Available HTTP: <http://www.unep.org/DEC/docs/Compliance%20mechanisms%20under%20selected %20MEAs.pdf> (accessed 14 February 2012).

The *Global Environment Facility* (GEF) defines incremental costs as 'additional costs associated with transforming a project with national benefits into one with global environmental benefits'.[35] The GEF only finances the additional part of funding that is needed to achieve global environmental benefits. This ensures that funding by the GEF is 'new and additional' and not a substitute for official development aid (ODA).[36] Interpretation of the principle of incremental costs by the GEF has often been subject to criticism. The COPs of the CBD and the UNFCCC, which provide guidance on the eligibility of projects, prefer a very wide interpretation.[37] This has led to tension, with COPs (and in particular the national focal points') preferring that every project preventing biodiversity loss or reducing greenhouse gas (GHG) emissions be considered to have global environmental benefits. The GEF argued that such an interpretation would create too many eligible projects.[38] This would mean that, for example, all energy efficiency projects would be eligible for funding. The problem has been addressed by the GEF in its governing meetings and it has redefined its policy over the years.[39] In addition, the GEF has established guidelines for the determination of incremental costs for project funding.

Treaty-specific funding

In terms of the achievement of substantive international environmental law goals, two types of funding can be distinguished:

1. Treaty-specific funding established under an MEA for specific or global environmental objectives.[40]
2. Other funding including bilateral or multilateral donations or (private) investments that are subject to compliance with international environmental standards.[41]

---

35 Based on Agenda 21 GEF adopted the definition of incremental costs accordingly; see e.g. Agenda 21, Preamble para. 4; Agenda 21, Ch. 33, Art. 14 iii. See also Global Environment Facility, 'Operational Guidelines for the Application of the Incremental Cost Principle', 14 May 2007, GEF 31.1/12. Online. Available HTTP: <http://www.thegef.org/gef/policy/incremental_costs> (accessed 13 February 2012).

36 See, e.g., Global Environment Facility, 'Evaluation of Incremental Costs Assessment', GEF/ME/C.30/2, 2 November 2006. Online. Available HTTP: <http://www.thegef.org/gef/sites/thegef.org/files/documents/GEFME-C30-2-IncrementalCostEvaluation110206.pdf> (accessed 13 February 2012).

37 See e.g. Decision V/13 of COP 5 Convention on Biological Diversity, Doc UNEP/CBD/COP/5/23, 130 onwards; see also Matz 2002, op. cit., p. 506.

38 See e.g. R. Lake, 'Finance for the Global Environment: the Effectiveness of the GEF as the Financial Mechanism to the Convention on Biological Diversity', *Review of European Community & International Environmental Law* 7, 1998, 68–75, p. 68; see also Matz 2002, op. cit., p. 508.

39 See e.g. GEF, 'Evaluation of Incremental Costs Assessment', op. cit.; Global Environment Facility, 'Operational Guidelines for the Application of the Incremental Cost Principle', op. cit.; Global Environment Facility, 'Report on the Incremental Costs', GEF/C.14/5, 5 November 1999. Online. Available HTTP: <http://www.thegef.org/gef/sites/thegef.org/files/documents/gef_c14_5.pdf> (accessed 13 February 2012). Currently the GEF uses a five-step approach to determine project eligibility: (1) determine the environmental problem, threat, or barrier, and the 'business-as-usual' scenario; (2) identify the global environmental benefits . . . and priorities linked to the GEF focal area; (3) develop the results framework of the intervention; (4) provide the incremental reasoning and GEF's role; and (5) negotiate the role of co-financing. Online. Available HTTP: <http://www.thegef.org/gef/policy/incremental_costs> (accessed 13 February 2012)

40 Sands, op. cit., p. 1021.

41 Ibid.

An early example of a treaty-specific fund is the *World Heritage Fund* in 1972.[42] Governed by the *World Heritage Committee* this fund is a grant-orientated trust fund.[43] Most of its funding has been spent on technical cooperation and capacity-building.[44] In the same year the voluntary *UNEP Environment Fund* was established, which accepts earmarked and general contributions for UN environmental policy and initiatives.[45] Up until 1990 a number of trust funds were established, but most of them focused on capacity-building efforts and site conservation.[46] A real shift in financial mechanisms for MEAs came with the establishment of the *Montreal Protocol Multilateral Fund* (MPMF) in 1990.[47] Its purpose was to provide 'financial and technical co-operation, including the transfer of technologies . . . to enable . . . compliance with . . . control measures'.[48] The MPMF provides for the incremental costs of compliance, including capacity-building, the search for substitutes and alteration of installations.[49] The MPMF finances its secretariat and has an Executive Committee that works in cooperation with UNEP, UNDP (United Nations Development Programme), the United Nations Industrial Development Organization and the World Bank.[50] With the creation of the MPMF and the political commitment displayed by donor states at the UNCED in 1992 the way was open for more treaty-specific funding mechanisms that addressed global environmental issues such as the GEF.

Global Environment Facility (GEF)

The GEF is probably the most comprehensive financial mechanism for environmental objectives. It was established in 1990 as a three-year pilot to provide grants for investment projects, technical assistance and research to developing countries to protect the global environment, transfer environmentally benign technologies and to promote environmentally sound and sustainable economic development.[51] After the initial successful pilot phase, the GEF was

---

42 World Heritage Convention, Art. 15.
43 World Heritage Convention, Art. 15; Financial Regulations for the World Heritage Fund, Art. IV. Online. Available HTTP: <http://whc.unesco.org/en/financialregulations/> (accessed 16 February 2012).
44 Sands, op. cit., p. 1030.
45 *United Nations General Assembly Resolution 2997* (1972), GA Res 2997 (XXVII).
46 See e.g. the establishment of the Wetland Conservation Fund, Conf. Res. C.4.3 *Convention on Wetlands of International Importance especially as Waterfowl Habitat*, opened for signature 2 February 1971, 11 ILM 963 (entered into force 21 December 1975); *Convention on the Control of Transboundary Movement of Hazardous Wastes and Their Disposal*, opened for signature 22 March 1989, 28 ILM 657 (entered into force 5 May 1992) (Basel Convention), Art. 14.1.
47 Montreal Protocol, Art. 10. Online. Available HTTP: <http://www.multilateralfund.org/default. aspx>; see also, E. DeSombre and J. Kauffman, 'The Montreal Protocol Multilateral Fund: Partial Success Story', in R.O. Keohane and M.A. Levy (eds) *Institutions for Environmental Aid: Pitfalls and Promise*, Cambridge, MA: MIT Press, 1996, 89–126, p. 89; Matz 2002, op. cit., pp. 495–6.
48 Montreal Protocol, Art. 10.
49 See the Indicative List of Incremental Costs in Annex VIII of the report of the Fourth Meeting of the Parties. Online. Available HTTP: <http://ozone.unep.org/Publications/MP_Handbook/ Section_3.6_Annexes_The_Multilateral_Fund/Indicative_list.shtml> (accessed 16 February 2012).
50 Montreal Protocol, Art. 10(5).
51 Res. No. 91-5 of the Executive Directors of the World Bank, 14 March 1991. See also Sands op. cit., pp. 727 and 1032; J. Werksman, 'Consolidating Governance of the Global Commons: Insights from the GEF', *Yearbook of International Environmental Law* 47(6), 1995, 27–63, p. 27; Matz 2002, op. cit., p. 503.

restructured in 1994 via the *Instrument for the Establishment of the Restructured Global Environmental Facility*.[52] Every four years the GEF is replenished by new pledges from donor countries.[53] The main reason for its restructuring was criticism from developing countries directed at the role of the World Bank as the only implementing agency. The World Bank, according to the criticism, was under the control of donor countries and therefore influenced by them, because voting rights were related to the amount a country donated.[54] The amendments in 1994 increased the number of implementing agencies to three, that is UNEP, UNDP and the World Bank,[55] assuring developing countries that environmental considerations were prioritised and that they would have influence over the operational policy of GEF. For environmental purposes UNEP was included and provides *inter alia* environmental expertise and ensures project consistency with existing environmental treaties.[56] Other issues include equal voting rights and accountability of the GEF to MEA COPs, where GEF is the treaty-specific financial mechanism. Despite the amendments the role of the World Bank remains significant, for it is the trustee of the GEF Trust Fund and often co-finances projects.[57]

The GEF provides environmental subsidies aimed at internalising the external benefits of projects and additionally leverages a significant amount in co-financing.[58] It provides treaty-specific funding for projects in developing countries and those with an economy in transition, and is the designated funding instrument or mechanism for four MEAs: the CBD, the UNFCCC, the *Stockholm Convention on Persistent Organic Pollutants* and the *United Nations Convention to Combat Desertification in Countries Experiencing Serious Drought and/or Desertification, Particularly in Africa* (CCD). The GEF also finances projects that support other MEAs, including the Montreal Protocol, and projects addressing international waters. The most important criterion for GEF funding is that the project should have global environmental benefits.

A unique characteristic of the GEF is the combination of its main objective, to target global environmental benefits, and its designation as the treaty-specific financial mechanism for five MEAs. This allows project funding to mainstream a range of environmental objectives and avoids duplication.[59] The role of the implementing agencies is important in this

52 Another name commonly used in literature is the 'Restructured GEF' or the 'Instrument'. See also United Nations Environment Programme, Division of Environmental Policy Development and Law, *Training Manual on International Environmental* Law, 2006, Nairobi: Publishing Section of UNON ('UNEP Training Manual') p. 65.

53 The GEF has been replenished every four years: in 1994, 1998, 2002 and 2006 with the last negotiations on the fifth replenishment concluding in May 2010 with a total amount of pledged funds of US$4.25 billion.

54 IBRD Articles of Agreement, Art. V, section 3.

55 *Instrument for the Establishment of the Restructured Global Environment Facility*, October 2011, Arts 22, 23. Online. Available HTTP: <http://www.thegef.org/gef/sites/thegef.org/files/publication/ GEF_Instrument_Oct2011_final_0.pdf> (accessed 22 February 2012).

56 Matz 2002, op. cit., p. 505. See also, UNEP Training Manual, p. 71.

57 *Instrument for the Establishment of the Restructured Global Environment Facility 2011*, Art. 8. Annex B of the Instrument further elaborates on the role and fiduciary responsibilities of the trustee.

58 See e.g. Matz 2002, op. cit., p. 503; Global Environment Facility, Annual Report 2010. Online. Available HTTP: <http://www.thegef.org/gef/sites/thegef.org/files/publication/WBAnnualReport Text.revised.pdf> (accessed 16 February 2012).

59 Matz 2002, op. cit., p. 505.

process with project funding often flowing through UNEP and UNDP as they provide necessary knowledge.[60]

The internal structure of the GEF is divided into four organs.[61] The Council and the Assembly provide governance. The Council consists of 32 members, 16 from developing countries, 2 from economies in transition and 14 from developed countries, and meets biannually to provide guidance on operational policies.[62] The Assembly meets every four years and includes all participating countries. It reviews the GEF policies and amendments to the instrument.[63] Representation, daily business and administrative support is provided for by the independent Secretariat and its Chief Executive Officer.[64] It also monitors implementation and prepares the meetings. It is independent but administratively supported by the World Bank.[65] The Scientific and Technical Advisory Panel (STAP) provides guidance to the Council and its secretariat is organised by UNEP.[66] Finally, the GEF Office of Monitoring and Evaluation is responsible for monitoring the effectiveness of projects.

The GEF provides direct funding and co-financing of incremental costs. Direct funding is through its established mechanisms, such as trust funds. Co-financing means that the GEF invests part of the sum needed if the participants invest the rest that is required for the project. From 1991 until 2009 the GEF invested US$8.6 billion directly and leveraged US$36.1 billion in co-financing.[67] There are generally five different types of projects sponsored by the GEF: full-size and medium-sized projects, enabling activities, pragmatic approach projects, climate change adaptation projects and the small grants programme. The difference between full-size and medium-sized projects is the amount of funds the projects require (medium-sized projects are limited to US$1 million). Enabling activities are often grants that will assist countries in basic data collection and reporting to MEAs.[68] Programmatic approach projects are partnerships between governments and other entities such as private actors or NGOs. Climate change adaptation projects are trust fund projects for climate change adaptation purposes. The small grants programme is a corporate programme for small community projects that is implemented by UNDP.[69]

---

60 *Instrument for the Establishment of the Restructured Global Environment Facility 2011*, Arts. 22, 23. See also, *Instrument with the principles of cooperation between implementing agencies*, Annex D. Next to the implementing agencies that are responsible for the operation of GEF, there are seven executive agencies that contribute supportively to project development and implementation in their respective areas of expertise: the Food and Agriculture Organization, the International Fund for Agricultural Development, the UN Industrial Development Organization, the Inter-American Development Bank, the European Bank for Reconstruction and Development, the Asian Development Bank and the African Development Bank. See also UNEP Training Manual, p. 65.
61 Ibid., Art. 11.
62 Ibid., Arts 13, 14. See also, *Instrument for the designation of the seats per region*, Annex E.
63 Ibid., Arts 15–20.
64 Ibid., Art. 21.
65 Ibid.
66 Ibid., Art. 24.
67 Global Environment Facility information report, 'About the Global Environment Facility 2009'. Online. Available HTTP: <http://www.thegef.org/gef/> (accessed 10 September 2011).
68 Global Environment Facility, 'Project Cycle: An Update', GEF/C.22/Inf.9 5 November 2003, para. 10. Online. Available HTTP: <http://www.thegef.org/gef/sites/thegef.org/files/documents/Loc... Update__FINAL__Nov_5_2003.pdf> (accessed 13 February 2012). See also UNEP Training Manual, pp. 65–71.
69 Global Environment Facility, 'Project types and Programmatic Approach'. Online. Available HTTP: <http://www.thegef.org/gef/project_types> (accessed 12 February 2012).

Given the amount that has been invested by the GEF in environmental projects, it can be deemed successful. However, it has also been criticised. As mentioned above, the influence of the World Bank (and donor countries) has been substantial. As a result of criticism the GEF was changed and developing countries' influence is provided for in the GEF Council and Assembly, and by the guidance that COPs provide for the treaty-specific funding. The amount of allocated funds and the new pledges confirm the trust that countries still have in the GEF as a comprehensive financial mechanism.[70]

Market mechanisms

In addition to 'classic' type of treaty-specific funding mechanisms, alternative instruments have been established. Trust funds and subsequently the project funding via the GEF were a start but still more monies were needed, leading to the establishment of market-based mechanisms. The *Kyoto Protocol to the United Nations Framework Convention on Climate Change* ('Kyoto Protocol') was one of the first to establish market-based financial instruments: the *Clean Development Mechanism, Joint Implementation* and *Emission Trading Scheme*.[71]

The Clean Development Mechanism (CDM) allows Annex B Parties (those states that have an emission reduction target under the Kyoto Protocol) to invest in emission reduction projects in developing countries.[72] The reduced emissions generate *Certified Emission Reduction* (CER) credits that developed countries can use for their own emission reduction target.[73] Joint Implementation (JI) is similar to the CDM but allows Annex B Parties to earn *Emission Reduction Units* (ERUs) from projects that acquire offsets in other Annex B Parties.[74] It has often been used for investment in projects in countries with an economy in transition because the incremental costs for abatement of GHG are relatively lower in those countries.[75] In Emissions Trading Schemes (ETS) – also known as the cap-and-trade system – a ceiling is set for emitting entities, while the same entities are allocated with a maximum emission level that gradually declines over time.[76] The entities can emit less than their allocated maximum emission level and sell their surplus of emission allowances or buy additional emission allowances where they have emitted more than allowed.[77] This produces an incentive to emit less while also creating a market. An advantage of market mechanisms is that they also involve the private sector. An ETS is therefore a tool for governments to involve private industry in reducing GHG emissions. The above-mentioned market mechanisms can be linked together, increasing their attractiveness. For example, in the European Union (EU)

---

70 See above; for the fifth replenishment in May 2010 donors pledged a total amount of US$4.25 billion to the GEF.
71 Kyoto Protocol, Arts 6, 12, 17.
72 Ibid., Art. 12 and Annex B; Annex B contains a list of quantified emission reduction commitments for each Party.
73 Ibid., Art. 12.
74 Ibid., Art. 6.
75 See e.g. report of the Organisation for Economic Co-Operation and Development and the International Energy Agency, K. Karousakis, 'Joint Implementation: Current Issues and Emerging Challenges', 2006. Online. Available HTTP: <http://www.oecd.org/dataoecd/45/32/37672335.pdf> (accessed 19 February 2012).
76 Kyoto Protocol, Art. 17.
77 Ibid.

ETS CERs from CDM projects can be used by private entities to fulfil their targets under the ETS.[78]

In theory, market mechanisms should be win–win situations for all parties. However, their practical application has not been easy and they have been criticised.[79] For example, large hydroelectric/dam projects were already planned or being constructed and received additional funding through CDM; and monocultures to produce biofuels have often led to vulnerable crops, while these types of projects also have had negative effects on communities.[80] More recent criticism has targeted CDM industrial gas projects, and in particular the hydrofluorocarbon (HFC) gas capture projects.[81] Here refrigerant-producing factories in developing countries, which produce hydrochlorofluorocarbon 22 (HCFC-22), capture the unwanted by-product hydrofluorocarbon 23 (HFC-23) – a potent GHG. The return for the capture of HFC-23 is so high that it could create an incentive for factories to increase production of HCFC-22 to capture more HFC-23 and thus increase profits.[82] This negative incentive forced the CDM Executive Board, the overall guidance and executing agency, to review the criteria for these types of industrial gas projects and suspend them until new criteria are drafted that remedy this problem.[83] Additionally, the UNFCCC market mechanisms have led, inherently, to transfer of funding to areas where the biggest return is possible. The focus of CDM projects has been on China and India, while least developed

---

78 *Directive 2004/101/EC of the European Parliament and the of the Council of 27 October 2004 amending Directive 2003/87/EC establishing a scheme for greenhouse gas emission allowance trading within the Community, in respect of the Kyoto Protocol's project mechanisms,* OJ L 338/18, 13 November 2004; *Directive 2009/29/EC of the European Parliament and the of the Council of 23 April 2009 amending Directive 2003/87/EC so as to improve and extend the greenhouse gas emission allowance trading scheme of the Community,* OJ L 140/63, 5 June 2009.

79 The practical application of market mechanisms has been difficult, mostly because of the minimal participation of countries (and players) in them. E.g., the Kyoto Protocol has not been ratified by all parties to the UNFCCC. Of the parties that have ratified the Kyoto Protocol, 37 countries have an emission reduction target and not all of them participate actively in market mechanisms. The United States, although a major emitter, did not ratify the Protocol and developing countries (including China and India) did not have emission reduction targets and do not participate in the market mechanisms. The limited number of countries that have implemented market mechanisms creates an unbalanced market for the Kyoto mechanisms because their aim is global. Furthermore, the current emission levels have changed in the last 20 years (following the signing of the UNFCCC and Kyoto Protocol) so that the Parties to the Kyoto Protocol, that have emission reduction targets, do not represent a similar level of global greenhouse emissions as at the time the parties negotiated the Kyoto Protocol. The subsequent participants in the market mechanisms do not reflect the current emissions in the world, resulting in an unbalanced market for the mechanisms.

80 B. Haya, P. McCully and B. Pearson, 'Damming the CDM: Why Big Hydro Is Ruining the Clean Development Mechanism', (2002) *International Rivers Network/CDM Watch.* Online. Available HTTP: <http://unfccc.int/cop8/se/kiosk/cm2.pdf> (accessed 19 February 2012). See also J. Conant, 'Massive UN-Supported African Palm Plantations Leading to Oppression Kidnapping and Murder', (2011) *Rainforest Rescue.* Online. Available HTTP: <http://www.rainforest-rescue.org/news/3319/massive-un-supported-african-palm-plantations-leading-to-oppression-kidnapping-and-murder> (accessed 19 February 2012).

81 See e.g. M. Sharpiro, Report on the Amount of Funding that Flows to China under CDM. Online. Available HTTP: <http://e360.yale.edu/feature/perverse_co2_payments_send_flood_of_money_to_china/2350/> (accessed 19 February 2012).

82 Ibid.

83 58th Executive Board Meeting report, Ref: CDM-EB-58, 26 November 2010, para. 28.

countries are often left out.[84] It is up to the parties, the COP and in this case the CDM Executive Board to establish a solid and reliable framework that would encourage market participants to invest in projects in other regions of the world.

As a mechanism, ETS has not yet reached its full potential. The best results would be gained if all developed countries would participate to create a level playing field for the private entities involved. So far, only a few countries have established an ETS. For example New Zealand[85] and the EU[86] have enacted cap-and-trade systems for GHG reductions and in the US a similar system has been enacted for its Acid Rain Program.[87]

The linking of market mechanisms had also been criticised. For example in the EU, CERs (from CDM projects) could be used in the EU ETS.[88] This increased the attractiveness of CERs and investments in industrial gas projects under the CDM, such that the EU is planning to ban the usage of CERs from some HFC-23 gas projects after 2012. There are other factors that impinge upon the effectiveness of the system, for example carbon leakage, fraud and volatility of prices. These and the above-mentioned challenges need to be addressed before ETS and the other market mechanisms can contribute to their full potential.

Other funding of IEL

There are three substantial other types of funding discussed in this chapter: multilateral development banks, overseas development aid and private sector funding.

Multilateral development banks

Multilateral and regional development banks (MDBs) originally focused on funding projects that supported economic and social development. The need to prevent further environmental degradation and previous criticism resulted in important policy adjustments in MDBs' project funding to increase contributions to global environmental outcomes and sustainable development.[89] In 1980 the World Bank, five development banks, the European Commission, the

---

84 'CDM Registered Projects by Region', (2012). Online. Available HTTP: <http://cdm.unfccc.int/ Statistics/Registration/RegisteredProjByRegionPieChart.html> (accessed 19 February 2012).

85 *Climate Change Response (Emissions Trading) Amendment Act 2008* (NZ), 2008 No. 85, 25 September 2008.

86 *Directive 2003/87/EC the European Parliament and the of the Council of 13 October 2003 establishing a scheme for greenhouse gas emission allowance trading within the Community and amending Council Directive 96/61/EC*, OJ L 275, 25 October 2003; and, *Directive 2009/29/EC*, OJ L 140/63, 23 April 2009. In the EU ETS, other European countries that are not in the EU also participate in the scheme, such as Norway and Switzerland.

87 *Clean Air Act (1990)* (US) 42 USC paras 7401–671g, P.L. 88–206, 77 Stat. 392, as amended by *Clean Air Act Amendments of 1990* (104 Stat. 2468, PL 101–549). Other countries, such as Australia and Japan, have been trying to establish an ETS, but up until now have not succeeded.

88 *Directive 2003/87/EC*, OJ L 275, 25 October 2003 and *Directive 2009/29/EC*, OJ L 140/63, 23 April 2009. See also A.D. Ellerman and B.K. Buchner, 'The European Union Emissions Trading Scheme: Origins, Allocations, and Early Results', *Environmental Economics and Policy* 1(1), 2007, 66–87, p. 84.

89 The international criticism focused on negative environmental effects of funding and the influence that donor states have in the allocation of funds. See e.g. S.D. Krasner, 'Power Structures and Regional Development Banks', *International Organization* 35, 1981, 303–28; Matz 2005, op. cit., p. 275; E. Johnston in *The Japan Times* on the effectiveness of the Asian Development bank after the Tsunami, 'Large-scale ADB projects draw criticism', May 2007 Online. Available HTTP: <http://www.japantimes.co.jp/text/nn20070508a5.html> (accessed 20 February 2012). See also the reference in Agenda 21 to multilateral development banks, Ch. 33.15 (a).

Organization of American States, UNEP and UNDP adopted the *Declaration of Environmental Policies and Procedures Relating to Economic Development* supporting the principles and actions laid down in the Stockholm Declaration[90] and agreed to include environmental impact standards in financial allocation policies.[91]

Another motivation for MDBs to green their policies was their degree of international personality. In this context, they could become responsible where environmental harm was caused by economic aid, and might even be legally liable for damages.[92] Therefore, banks incorporated environmental policies, such as the EBRD (European Bank for Reconstruction and Development), which was the first bank to have environmental objectives included in its rules of procedure.[93]

The MDBs' original goal of limiting negative environmental effects has gradually shifted to a more proactive approach towards the environment and, in particular, natural resources. Most of the MDBs use environmental impact assessments as a common tool.[94] Some work on a regional basis; a great advantage of regional MDBs is the local knowledge they bring, making them efficient partners in projects funded under MEAs and the GEF.[95] Furthermore, new funding initiatives are often set up in partnerships with NGOs to increase environmental considerations.[96]

Overseas development assistance

Overseas development assistance (or official development assistance – ODA) is the transfer of financial resources from an industrialised country to a developing country, or an economy in transition, for developmental purposes. It can be bilateral, direct, or through multilateral, supernatural or other international institutions or funds.[97] Originally, ODA was based on economic development and poverty alleviation. In the Rio Declaration countries

90 *Declaration of Environmental Policies and Procedures Relating to Economic Development*, opened for signature 1 February 1980, 19 ILM 524. The five development banks were the Asian Development Bank, the African Development Bank, the Inter-American Development Bank, the Arab Bank for Economic Development in Africa and the Caribbean Development Bank. See also Sands, op. cit., p. 1024.
91 *Declaration of Environmental Policies and Procedures Relating to Economic Development*, op. cit., paras 3, 4.
92 Sands, op. cit., p. 1024; Advisory opinion of the International Court of Justice in *Reparation for Injuries Suffered in the Service of the United Nations*, Advisory Opinion (1949) ICJ Reports 174.
93 *Agreement Establishing the European Bank for Reconstruction and Development*, signed on 29 May 1990 (entered into force 29 March 1991) Art. 2 sub vii. See also the Asian Development Bank's *Safeguard Policy Statement* (2009). Online. Available HTTP: <http://beta.adb.org/documents/safeguard-policy-statement> (accessed 18 February 2012).
94 See e.g. European Bank for Reconstruction and Development, *Environmental and Social Policy Guidelines*, para. 7. Online. Available HTTP: <http://www.ebrd.com/downloads/about/sustainability/2008policy.pdf> (accessed 18 February 2012).
95 Cooperation of the GEF with regional development banks; co-financing policy of the GEF, GEF/C.20/6 September 16, 2005. See also figures of co-financing between GEF and MDBs such as Inter-American Development Bank, Asian Development Bank. *Co-financing data related to GEF operations*. Online. Available HTTP: <http://www.thegef.org/gef/sites/thegef.org/files/Docs/GEF_R5_Inf9%2520Co-financing%2520Data%2520Related%2520to%2520GEF%2520Operations.pdf> (accessed 18 February 2012).
96 See e.g. the cooperation between the Asian Development Bank and the World Wide Fund for Nature. Online. Available HTTP: <http://beta.adb.org/features/wwf-and-adb-two-heads-are-better-one> (accessed 20 February 2012).
97 See e.g. the Congo Basin Forest Fund. Online. Available HTTP: <http://www.cbf-fund.org/> (accessed 22 February 2012).

acknowledged that environmental protection should be an integral part of sustainable development and therefore of development assistance.[98] In time it became clear that development aid should target more than just economic development, and should also include social and environmental development.[99]

Environmentally related ODA can include allocation of financial resources for compliance efforts, sustainable environmental projects and environmentally sound projects with non-environmental purposes; ODA includes development aid for economic, social and/or environmental objectives and is often only partly for environmental purposes. A substantial part of ODA funding is meant for *ad hoc* remedial purposes following natural disasters – for example the earthquake in Haiti in 2009.[100] The ODA funding often flows through MDBs and it can also include debt relief provided by developed countries.[101]

The transition to more environmental development aid is also referred to as the 'greening' of ODA. Two types of green development aid can be distinguished. The first is meant for economic, social or poverty alleviation goals that also take into account environmental impacts and therefore directly or partly has environmental goals, for example using environmental impact assessments on development aid projects. The second is development aid solely (or mostly) aimed at environmental improvement, for example environmental protection and compliance with MEAs. One reason for greening ODA was the need to include environmental considerations to reduce the negative environmental effects of purely economic development. Another reason for greening ODA was that by consolidating objectives in ODA funding, more could be achieved at the same time. However, there have also been other more questionable motives for industrialised countries to green their development aid, including ensuring participation of developing countries in MEAs.[102] Another reason was to create the perception of addressing global environmental degradation whereas achieving this through ODA could be considered low-hanging fruit.[103]

At the 1992 UNCED developed countries agreed on a political commitment to allocate 0.7 per cent of their Gross National Product (GNP) for ODA.[104] Unfortunately, few countries

---

98 Rio Declaration, Principle 4.

99 Organisation for Economic Co-Operation and Development, *Recommendation of the Council on Measures Required to Facilitate the Environmental Assessment of Development Assistance Projects and Programmes*, 23 October 1986 – C(86)26/FINAL.

100 'Haiti Quake Aid Pledges Country Donations', *Guardian*. Online. Available HTTP: <http://www.guardian.co.uk/news/datablog/2010/jan/14/haiti-quake-aid-pledges-country-donations> (accessed 18 February 2012) with an overview of all pledged aid to Haiti after the earthquake in 2009.

101 Part of the ODA funding can consist of debt relief, meaning that developed countries cancel the debt developing countries have with them. In 2005 and 2006 in the US a relatively high percentage of the ODA consisted of debt relief; see 'Debt Relief is Down: Other ODA Rises Slightly', OECD. Online. Available HTTP: <http://www.oecd.org/document/8/0,3343,en_2649_201185 _40381960_1_1_1_1,00.html> (accessed 18 February 2012).

102 Hicks et al. op. cit.; Å. Persson, 'Environmental Policy Integration and Bilateral Development Assistance: Challenges and Opportunities with an Evolving Governance Framework', *International Environmental Agreements* 9, 2009, 409–29.

103 Ibid.

104 Agenda 21, Ch. 33.15, See also the *Proceedings of the United Nations Conference on Trade and Development* (UNCTAD), Second Session, Annex 1, Decision 27(II), para. 7; 'History of the 0.7 ODA Target', *DAC Journal 2002* 3(4), III-9 (Revised June 2010).

in the world have actually reached the 0.7 per cent target.[105] The biggest net contributors, the US, the United Kingdom (UK) and France, have not done so.[106] Although the target has not been met by most developed countries, in 2011 the OECD (Organisation for Economic Co-operation and Development) reported that 2010 had been the year with the highest rate of ODA funding ever.[107] Developing countries still refer to the 0.7 per cent target and use it in current negotiations.[108]

Despite the high amount of ODA in 2010, there are factors that might influence the amount of environmentally related ODA funding. First, the financial crisis that still affects the world economy.[109] Unemployment in developed countries is rising, governments are becoming bankrupt and recovery is very slow. Some effects of the financial crises have been environmentally beneficial, for without it the EU would probably not be as on track to achieve their emission reduction target under the Kyoto Protocol.[110] However, one negative consequence is that governments review their expenditure, which might place pressure on financial resources allocated for environmental purposes.[111] Another factor that might influence ODA is effectiveness and interest return-rate. Most institutions and financial mechanisms established for environmental purposes were created 20 years ago or earlier.[112] Although some of the institutions have adapted to changing needs and challenges, others might have become obsolete or less apparent in their contribution to the field. As mentioned earlier, international environmental law is often measured by its effectiveness in achieving its goals. Not achieving the intended goal has led to re-evaluation of the funding by, for example, the effective return-rate of the money spent for different development purposes, instead of providing more financial resources.[113] The UK has recently conducted a comprehensive research programme to evaluate the effectiveness of ODA funding used for different international development and environmental institutions.[114] The result will be used in the allocation of future funding. Research such as this can result in less

105 Sweden, Norway, Denmark, Luxembourg and the Netherlands are countries that fulfilled their pledge. See also, the OECD information note. Online. Available HTTP: <http://www.oecd.org/dataoecd/16/38/45539274.pdf> (accessed 18 February 2012).

106 Despite these countries not reaching the 0.7 per cent target, these countries finance a substantial amount of the total ODA recorded in 2011. See *Statistics from A to Z*, OECD. Online. Available HTTP: <http://www.oecd.org/document/0,3746,en_2649_201185_46462759_1_1_1_1,00.html> (accessed 21 February 2012).

107 See OECD ODA report on 2010 results. Online. Available HTTP: <http://www.oecd.org/document/10/0,3746,en_2649_33721_44774218_1_1_1_1,00.html> (accessed 18 February 2012).

108 See e.g. the Submission by Bangladesh to the Ad-Hoc Working Group on Long-term Cooperative Action of the UNFCCC of 23 April 2009, FCCC/AWGLCA/2009/MISC.4, p. 26.

109 See e.g. *United Nations General Assembly Resolution on the Financial Crises* (2011), GA Res 63/303, UN GAOR, UN Doc A/RES/63/303.

110 *Communication by the Commission: Analysis of options to move beyond 20% greenhouse gas emission reductions and assessing the risk of carbon leakage*, Brussels, (2010) p. 3.

111 Although ODA funding has been recorded as the highest ever in 2010, a number of governments have announced their intention to re-evaluate their development aid expenditure. See also OECD Secretariat estimates on expected ODA. Online. Available HTTP: <http://www.oecd.org/dataoecd/17/12/44981982.pdf> (accessed 18 February 2012).

112 The Restructured GEF was established in 1994, whilst institutions like UNEP were established far earlier than that (1972).

113 Department for International Development (UKAID), *Multilateral Aid Review: Ensuring maximum value for money for UK aid through multilateral organisations* (2011). Online. Available HTTP: <http://www.dfid.gov.uk/Documents/publications1/mar/multilateral_aid_review.pdf> (accessed 22 February 2012).

114 Ibid.

funding for established instruments but also creates a healthy incentive for international institutions to develop and adjust policy in line with current problems and available resources.

Private sector funding

The last type of funding is that of the private sector. As mentioned above, developed governments have tried to include the private sector. The past 30 years has shown that solely transferring funding via established mechanisms has some effect, but has not yet achieved intended goals. Additionally, private sector funding that flows from developed to developing countries has surpassed ODA.[115] Private sector funding generally seeks an interest return-rate and therefore often participates at the local level to encourage commitment at a local level. Commitment at a local level is increasingly seen as an important factor for success of development projects.[116]

Although private sector investments are intended to create profits, market mechanisms under the Kyoto Protocol, for example, have been a first step in facilitating private investment for environmental projects. Other examples of private sector finance are public private partnerships (PPP) in which governments and the private sector work together.

Conclusion

From the above discussion several trends in the funding of international environmental law can be distinguished: the tensions between developing and developed countries; a shift in the types of mechanisms that are used for the funding of international environmental law; and changes in the players in international environmental law.

Tension between developed and developing countries

The tension between developing and developed countries is still evident. The tension was created and defined by the acknowledgement of environmental principles some 50 years ago and later by the commitment of developed countries to provide new and additional resources. Although the world changes, some countries develop quickly and others more slowly, while environmental problems have increased and funding is still an issue at the negotiating table. New developments, such as the financial crisis, have not increased trust and more developed countries want to ensure the maximum value for their donations.[117] In the meantime there have been few developed countries that have met their ODA pledge. These factors, and more, can negatively affect the relationship between developed and developing countries and increase tension. To mend fences and increase trust, it is important that the international

---

115 OECD reported that net official development assistance in 2010 was a total of US$128,492 million while private flows of development aid were US$330,104 million. *Statistics from A to Z*. Online. Available HTTP: <http://www.oecd.org/document/0,3746,en_2649_201185_46462759_1_1_1_1,00.html> (accessed 21 February 2012).

116 See e.g. *Accra Agenda for Action*, as part of *the Paris Declaration on Aid Effectiveness Ownership, Harmonisation, Alignment, Results and Mutual Accountability*, opened for signature 4 September 2008, paras 13, 14, 18. Online. Available HTTP: <http://www.oecd.org/document/18/0,374 6,en_2649 3236398_35401554_1_1_1_1,00.html> (accessed 21 February 2012).

117 Department for International Development (UKAID), 'Multilateral Aid Review: Ensuring Maximum Value for Money for UK Aid Through Multilateral Organisations'.

community shows each other how large sums of funding are used for environmental development. Central to achieving this is transparency. An example of this is a Dutch initiative for fast-start finance of climate change funding.[118] In this initiative developed countries publish the amount of fast-start finance they provide as committed to in the Cancun Agreements.[119] Although a first step, transparency is of great value and a start to increasing trust.

From trust funds to market mechanisms

A visible trend in treaty-specific funding started with the establishment of particular trust funds followed by global funds, such as the GEF, and later by market mechanisms. A consolidated trust fund has more potential to address interlinked global environmental issues in one package. This not only allows projects to take into account other environmental considerations, it is also a more acceptable one-stop-shop for developed countries. Other instruments, such as the technology transfer CHM, are under continuous development and still have difficulty reaching their full potential. A visible shift came with the UNFCCC market mechanisms. Market mechanisms are, for obvious reasons, more difficult to manage than a mere trust fund but they increase attractiveness for project participants. The experience so far has not been very hopeful, with alleged abuse in CDM projects and lack of participation in ETSs indicating that the differences between states are still a considerable hurdle, even between developed countries.[120] In addition, limitations of market mechanisms, including the geographical spread of funding, are still evident. Most investments go to projects that generate the highest return-rate in the easiest countries, thus leaving out the least developed countries.[121] However, previous mistakes in market mechanisms will lead to improvements and new criteria so that they become less vulnerable to fraud in the future and more open to all countries. More important is the potential of market mechanisms to include the private sector and unlock a vast amount of resources. This will no doubt take time, for the current trust in environmental market mechanisms is not very high; but a giant step forward can be made in creating a framework to facilitate private sector investments. In the ongoing climate change negotiations the search for new market mechanisms has been difficult but continues. In 2010 in Cancun the parties to the UNFCCC agreed on the construction of a Green Climate Fund that is to help developing countries in mitigation and adaptation to climate change.[122] It is supposed to include public, private and bilateral funding and is currently under construction.[123] Another example

---

118 *Fast Start Finance.* Online. Available HTTP: <http://www.faststartfinance.org> (accessed 15 September 2011).
119 Draft Decision -/CP.15, FCCC/CP/2009/L.7 that US$30 billion was pledged from 2010–2012 as fast-start finance of new and additional resources.
120 See 85, 86 above: only a few countries have established an ETS. Other countries, like Australia and Japan, have been trying to.
121 See 84 above: the market focuses on the cheapest options with the highest return-rate. Such type of effects should be countered by governments, for example, to increase their attractiveness and gain the participation of more countries.
122 Although originally included in the *Copenhagen Agreement* in 2009, the COP/MOP formally adopted the creation of the Green Climate Fund in the *Cancun Agreements*, para. 100 of Decision 1/CP.16, FCCC/CP/2010/7/Add.1.
123 A transitional committee is established and started drafting the framework and guidelines for the Green Climate Fund. *Transitional Committee for the design of the Green Climate Fund*, UNFCCC. Online. Available HTTP: <http://unfccc.int/cooperation_and_support/financial_mechanism/green_climate_fund/items/5869.php> (accessed 19 February 2012).

is the inclusion of the private sector in UNFCCC initiatives via, for example, the *Adaptation Private Sector Initiative* that aims to increase participation of the private sector in climate adaptation.[124]

From state funding to private funding

The original players in the funding of international environmental law have been states. The original trust funds were simple: the developed countries donated and the developing countries used the funding for environmental projects. The increased importance of international environmental law, the lack of results and the need for more funding have increased the number of stakeholders. As a result MDBs, and in particular regional MDBs, have countered the need for more local involvement in projects. The private sector has been and will become more involved in the funding of international environmental law, as it unlocks potentially unlimited financial resources and has more prospect of increasing local participation. The role of the private sector (and PPPs) is also one of the central topics scheduled for the Rio+20 conference in 2012.[125]

The original definitions of the funding of international environmental law have changed according to their need; where initially only governments negotiated, now NGOs have a regular seat at the table and more funding is required from private parties. Trust is still an issue in international environmental law funding, and common ground between actors needs to be found. Transparency is essential, as is inclusion of all parties, and perhaps, while we aim for the best and continue to finance the environment globally, money will make the world go round a little bit greener.

---

124 See *Adaptation Private Sector Initiative*, UNFCCC. Online. Available HTTP: <http://unfccc. int/adaptation/nairobi_work_programme/private_sector_initiative/items/4623.php> (accessed 23 February 2012).

125 See e.g, *The Future We Want – Zero draft of the outcome document of the Rio+20 conference that is planned from 20–21 June 2012*, UNCSD. Online. Available HTTP: <http://www.uncsd2012.org/rio20/ index.php?menu=140> (accessed 19 February 2012).

10

The settlement of disputes in international environmental law

Tim Stephens

The view that many environmental questions are effectively non-justiciable in international courts has been challenged by real-world practice that shows that states are increasingly referring environmental disputes to international judicial and quasi-judicial forums. However, while traditional dispute settlement mechanisms are increasingly being used to litigate environmental questions, a distinctive approach has been taken within some international environmental regimes. International environmental law has been a laboratory for experimentation with a new form of dispute management: the 'compliance procedure'. This chapter provides an overview of contemporary international environmental dispute settlement, a discussion of compliance procedures in multilateral environmental regimes and an assessment of the limits to the 'judicialisation' of international environmental dispute settlement.

Introduction

Until recently it was received wisdom that international environmental law raised 'polycentric' disputes involving fundamental competing values and interests that are not amenable to effective adjudication through the traditional machinery of inter-state dispute settlement.[1] The view that many environmental questions are effectively non-justiciable in international courts has been challenged by real-world practice that shows that states are increasingly referring environmental disputes to international judicial and quasi-judicial forums. Environmental disputes now appear as likely as controversies over other issues of international law, such as territorial sovereignty or the limits of state jurisdiction, to be litigated in international courts, including the International Court of Justice (ICJ). The ICJ currently has three environmental cases before it (*Proceedings with regard to 'violations of Nicaraguan sovereignty and major environmental damages to its territory' (Nicaragua v Costa Rica), Aerial Herbicide Spraying (Ecuador v Colombia)* and *Whaling in the Antarctic (Australia v Japan)*) and recently decided a riverine dispute involving environmental issues in *Pulp Mills on the River Uruguay (Argentina v Uruguay)*.[2]

---

1 See e.g. E.B. Weiss, 'Understanding Compliance with International Environmental Agreements: The Baker's Dozen Myths', *University of Richmond Law Review* 32, 1999, 1555.
2 *Pulp Mills on the River Uruguay (Argentina v Uruguay)*, Judgment of 20 April 2010. Online. Available HTTP: <www.icj-cij.org> (accessed 30 April 2012).

However, while traditional dispute settlement mechanisms are increasingly being used to litigate environmental questions it is also the case that a distinctive approach has been taken within some international environmental regimes to address disputes arising from them. International environmental law has been a laboratory for experimentation with a new form of dispute management: the 'compliance procedure'. Compliance procedures have been established under a host of multilateral environmental regimes, the earliest and best-known being the 1987 *Montreal Protocol on Substances that Deplete the Ozone Layer*.[3] Whereas traditional dispute settlement relies on states to instigate a complaint, compliance procedures have been driven by the governance institutions of the relevant regime themselves, thus circumventing the main hurdle to international environmental litigation, namely the reluctance of states to bring proceedings against other states.[4] However, compliance procedures are in addition to rather than a replacement for existing mechanisms of dispute settlement, with the consequence that in contemporary international environmental law there are a constellation of dispute settlement options that are open to litigants including both state and, in some limited contexts, also non-state actors.[5]

This chapter provides an overview of contemporary international environmental dispute settlement. Following a discussion of the nature of international environmental disputes in the twenty-first century, it sets out the main mechanisms of dispute settlement and discusses how they have been utilised in the environmental context. The chapter then turns to the ways in which environmental disputes have been addressed in specialised forums that do not have an avowed environmental focus such as the World Trade Organization's (WTO) Dispute Settlement Understanding (DSU),[6] raising the spectre that international environmental law may be the victim of 'fragmentation'. There is then discussion of compliance procedures in multilateral environmental regimes and in conclusion an assessment of the limits to the 'judicialisation' of international environmental dispute settlement.

Contemporary international environmental disputation

The character of international environmental disputes

The arbitration in the *Trail Smelter* case[7] over transboundary environmental damage is often cited as the classic inter-state environmental dispute. That case concerned a history of significant air pollution from a metals smelter in Canada that caused damage to farming land in the United States. Decided in the 1930s by an arbitral tribunal convened by both states, the *Trail Smelter* case itself makes little mention of the environment.[8] Instead the case was decided

---

3 *Montreal Protocol on Substances that Deplete the Ozone Layer*, opened for signature 16 September 1987, 1522 UNTS 29 (entered into force 1 January 1989).

4 D.A. Wirth, 'Re-examining Decision-Making Processes in International Environmental Law', *Iowa Law Review* 79, 1994, 769, p. 779.

5 An example is the range of disputes that may arise out of the operation of the Kyoto Protocol: C. Brown, 'The Settlement of Disputes Arising in Flexibility Mechanism Transactions under the Kyoto Protocol', *Arbitration International* 21, 2005, 361.

6 *Marrakesh Agreement Establishing the World Trade Organization*, opened for signature 15 April 1994, 1869 UNTS 190 (entered into force 1 January 1995), Annex 2.

7 (Canada/United States of America) *Reports of International Arbitral Awards* 3, 1938 and 1941, 1911.

8 For a comprehensive analysis see R.M. Bratspies and R.A. Miller (eds) *Transboundary Harm in International Law: Lessons from the Trail Smelter Arbitration*, Cambridge: Cambridge University Press, 2006.

primarily on the basis that states have an obligation not to interfere unreasonably within the territory of other states by failing to prevent damaging substances from passing across international boundaries. Preventing transboundary environmental damage is now a central concern of international environmental law, as seen in Principle 2 of the 1992 Rio Declaration[9] and the efforts of the International Law Commission (ILC) to develop general rules applicable to such situations through the *2001 Draft Articles on the Prevention of Transboundary Harm from Hazardous Activities*,[10] and the *2004 Draft Principles on the Allocation of Loss in the Case of Transboundary Harm Arising out of Hazardous Activities*.[11] Transboundary harm issues have been raised in the *Aerial Herbicide Spraying* case currently before the ICJ, in which Ecuador claims that by spraying toxic herbicides to control illicit coca and poppy plantations in border regions with Ecuador, Colombia has 'failed to meet its obligations of prevention and precaution' and caused damage to human health, property and the environment within Ecuador.[12]

It is increasingly difficult to identify international disputes that are solely environmental in character. The expansion in the content and complexity, and the connections between areas of international law inevitably means that a dispute having some environmental aspects will also involve a host of other legal questions. The challenge of climate change shows that it is seldom, if ever, the case that an international environmental dispute will be purely environmental in character. In reality disputes involving environmental issues are almost always intertwined with other issues, and with other fields of international law. Witness for instance the potential international trade law implications of measures taken by individual states or groups of states to impose taxes on products or services with a substantial carbon footprint. Just such measures are being implemented by the European Union in its emissions trading scheme which from 1 January 2012 requires all airlines (including foreign carriers) to purchase permits under the EU's emissions trading system. In December 2011 the European Court of Justice (ECJ) upheld the legality of the EU directive in terms of EU and international law.[13] However, there is a very strong likelihood that such measures, adopted in conformity with the objective of UNFCCC (United Nations Framework Convention on Climate Change) and the Kyoto Protocol to prevent dangerous climate change, will be challenged in the WTO. That environmental disputes cannot be divorced from international law disputes generally is one reason among several why a specialised global court for the environment is unlikely ever to be established.[14]

---

9 *United Nations Declaration on Environment and Development* (1992), UN Doc A/CONF.151/5/Rev. 1 ('Rio Declaration'):

> States have, in accordance with the Charter of the United Nations and the principles of international law, the sovereign right to exploit their own resources pursuant to their own environmental and developmental policies, and the responsibility to ensure that activities within their jurisdiction or control do not cause damage to the environment of other States or of areas beyond the limits of national jurisdiction.

10 Report of the International Law Commission, 53rd Session, UN Doc A/56/10 (2001).
11 Report of the International Law Commission, 56th Session, UN Doc A/59/10 (2004).
12 *Aerial Herbicide Spraying (Ecuador v Colombia)*, Application of Ecuador, 31 March 2008, [37].
13 *Air Transport Association of America and Others v Secretary of State for Energy and Climate Change*, Case C 366/10, 21 December 2011.
14 See further T. Stephens, *International Courts and Environmental Protection*, Cambridge: Cambridge University Press, 2009, ch. 2.

The 'hardening' of international environmental law

While the boundaries of the class of disputes classified as international environmental controversies are inevitably fluid and permeable, with the rise of multilateral environmental regimes it is now the case that there is an extensive body of 'hard' international environmental law supplying a core of rules over which states may litigate.

This is a relatively recent development. The origins of international environmental law lie in general principles of customary international law (such as the obligation to prevent transboundary harm addressed in the *Trail Smelter* case) and also principles and concepts set out in 'soft-law' instruments such as the 1972 Stockholm[15] and 1992 Rio Declaration.[16] International environmental law continues to feel the influence of its soft-law origins, with principles such as sustainable development and precaution prominent in international environmental discourse.[17] The soft-law character of some aspects of international environmental law has led some commentators to question whether it is really suitable as a basis for litigation before an international court as general principles provide very uncertain guidance to courts seeking to resolve concrete disputes.[18]

While that objection once had some force, many elements of international environmental law today are as detailed and enforceable as any other area of public international law. Evidence of this development includes the exceptionally finely textured body of law relating to marine pollution and maritime safety as set out in a collection of widely subscribed treaties adopted under the auspices of the International Maritime Organization.[19] Environmental principles nonetheless continue to perform an important function in bringing conceptual order and direction to a host of prescriptive rules, and international courts are increasingly being given the task of overseeing this. An example of this process in action is the development of environmental rules to prevent marine environmental damage when states engage in mining activities on the deep seabed, the area beyond national jurisdiction that is the common heritage of humankind. The rules for the deep seabed 'Area' are found in the 1982 *United Nations Convention on the Law of the Sea* (UNCLOS),[20] the 1994 Implementation Agreement for Part XI of the UNCLOS,[21] and the 'Mining Code' promulgated by the International Seabed Authority (ISBA),[22] and they were recently considered by the Seabed Disputes Chamber of the International Tribunal for the Law of the Sea (ITLOS). The Seabed Disputes Chamber was asked by ISBA to consider the nature and extent of state liability for mining activities in the Area. In *Responsibilities and Obligations of States Sponsoring Persons and Entities*

---

15 Declaration of the United Nations Conference on the Human Environment, UN Doc. A/CONF.48/14/Rev. 1 (1973).

16 Rio Declaration.

17 On the discursive character of international environmental law see B. Jessup and K. Rubenstein (eds) *Environmental Discourses in International and Public Law*, Cambridge: Cambridge University Press, 2011.

18 See e.g. M. Koskenniemi, 'Peaceful Settlement of Environmental Disputes', *Nordic Journal of International Law* 60, 1991, 73.

19 See D.R. Rothwell and T. Stephens, *The International Law of the Sea*, Oxford: Hart Publishing, 2010, 347ff.

20 *United Nations Convention on the Law of the Sea*, opened for signature 10 December 1982, 1833 UNTS 397 (entered into force 16 November 1994) ('UNCLOS').

21 *Implementation Agreement for Part XI of the UNCLOS*, opened for signature 28 July 1994, 1836 UNTS 42 (entered into force 28 July 1996).

22 The *Mining Code* is available on the ISBA website. Online. Available HTTP: <http://www.isa.org.jm/en/documents/mcode> (accessed 30 April 2012).

with Respect to Activities in the Area[23] the Chamber rendered a unanimous opinion which drew heavily upon the precautionary principle in concluding that states are under a due diligence obligation to ensure that activities carried out on the deep seabed do not damage the marine environment.

The *Seabed Advisory Opinion* also shows a particular dimension of international environmental law that has acquired increasing sophistication, and that is in regulating the process by which governments make decisions that may have transboundary environmental effects. Environmental governance by individual governments or groups of states involves making difficult decisions about how to balance various objectives, as seen most obviously in the contest between the objectives of economic development and environmental protection, a contest that the principle of sustainable development seeks to resolve.[24] In many situations it is difficult or impossible to determine in the abstract and in advance whether a certain activity should or should not be permitted. In such circumstances a significant contribution that international environmental law can make is to ensure that the procedure for making a decision on whether to approve a particular project or allow a certain activity places before decision-makers appropriate information, and allows those states and non-state actors affected by a decision some participation in the process.

This is where what is termed 'procedural' international environmental law can have an important role to play. It is also where international environmental law may be said to be at the forefront of developments in 'global administrative law', that is the body of rules and principles designed to improve participation, accountability and transparency in decision-making and potentially even the international judicial review of such decisions. Obligations of a procedural character are an important component of many environmental regimes, and include requirements such as that states should notify other states of activities that may have a transboundary environmental impact and that states should carry out an environmental impact assessment (EIA).[25]

The distinction between substantive and procedural obligations was recently addressed in the *Pulp Mills* case between Argentina and Uruguay, in which Argentina argued that Uruguay had breached the 1975 Statute of the River Uruguay[26] (1975 Statute) in authorising the construction of pulp mills that Argentina said would damage the River Uruguay by discharging pollutants. The ICJ examined the procedural and substantive obligations under the 1975 Statute and found that they were closely linked, in that satisfaction of the former assists in ensuring that the parties comply with the latter. The Court held that Uruguay had violated several procedural obligations including the requirement to notify Argentina of the EIAs that had been carried out before going ahead and authorising the mills.[27] However, in

---

23 Advisory Opinion of the Seabed Disputes Chamber of the International Tribunal for the Law of the Sea (1 February 2011) ('*Seabed Mining Advisory Opinion*'). Online. Available HTTP: <http://www.itlos.org/fileadmin/itlos/documents/cases/case_no_17/adv_op_010211.pdf> (accessed 30 April 2012). For commentary see D. Anton, 'Seabed Mining: Advisory Opinion on Responsibility and Liability', *Environmental Policy and Law* 41, 2011, 60.

24 D. French, *International Law and Policy on Sustainable Development*, Manchester: Manchester University Press, 2004; D. French (ed.) *Global Justice and Sustainable Development*, Leiden: Martinus Nijhoff, 2010.

25 N. Craik, *The International Law of Environmental Impact Assessment: Process, Substance and Integration*, Cambridge: Cambridge University Press, 2008.

26 *Statute of the River Uruguay*, opened for signature 26 February 1975, 1295 UNTS 340 (entered into force 18 September 1976) ('1975 Statute').

27 *Pulp Mills on the River Uruguay (Argentina v Uruguay)*, op. cit., [121].

dealing with the substantive obligations, such as the obligation to prevent pollution and preserve the aquatic environment in Article 41 of the 1975 Statute, the Court found that Uruguay was not in breach. The Court concluded that the duty to notify of the EIA was a procedural obligation, but that the EIA itself was part of the substantive obligation to act with due diligence in seeking to prevent pollution. This can be interpreted as the Court imbuing what is in essence a fairly narrow procedural obligation with a broader and more meaningful content, and in so doing ensuring that an EIA is not simply a 'rubber-stamping' exercise. However, on the evidence before it, the Court was not satisfied that Uruguay's EIA was insufficient, and it found that Uruguay had complied with all of its substantive obligations under the 1975 Statute. As a consequence the Court concluded that the only remedy for Argentina was the declaration in the judgment that the procedural obligations had been violated.

Traditional mechanisms for resolving international environmental disputes

Before examining the various mechanisms for dispute settlement in international environmental law it is necessary to say something about its purpose. As the very term suggests, the primary purpose of dispute settlement has been to resolve disagreements between states in service to the overriding aim, expressed in the United Nations Charter's foremost goal, 'to save succeeding generations from the scourge of war'. With the development of an increasingly detailed body of international law the objective of maintaining peaceful relations has been coupled with additional aims, the most important being to provide authoritative interpretations of international regimes, and to ensure that states comply with their international legal obligations. Compliance is a particularly important objective for international environmental law because environmental disputes are best seen as involving not only a competing set of 'private' interests between two (or more) states, but also the 'public' interest of the international community in safeguarding the natural environment. Hence a dispute settlement system that is geared towards resolving disagreements between states is not necessarily suited to protecting the environment per se.

Romano has suggested that dispute settlement mechanisms engaged in addressing international environmental disputes may be divided into two main categories.[28] First there are endogenous mechanisms, that is to say those established by, or referred to, within environmental regimes. An example is ITLOS, established by the UNCLOS, a treaty that has a major environmental focus. The second category of dispute settlement systems are exogenous mechanisms, external to environmental regimes, that can be used to deal with environmental (or other) types of dispute. An example is the ICJ which has general subject-matter jurisdiction. In contemporary practice both endogenous and exogenous dispute settlement mechanisms are being utilised to resolve environmental disputes. Both draw upon but differ in some important respects from the long tradition of dispute settlement in public international law.

The traditional dispute settlement methods are listed in Article 33 of the United Nations Charter, and these are negotiation, enquiry, mediation, conciliation, arbitration and resort to regional agencies or arrangements. Most of these have been utilised to greater or lesser extent in international environmental dispute resolution. In this regard there is quite a degree of

---

28 C.P.R. Romano, 'International Dispute Settlement', in D. Bodansky, J. Brunnee and E. Hey (eds) *The Oxford Handbook of International Environmental Law*, Oxford: Oxford University Press, 2007, 1036.

diversity among environmental regimes. A number of environmental treaties make no provision for dispute settlement at all,[29] many simply repeat the formulation in Article 33 and state that the parties are free to choose a procedure of their liking,[30] while relatively few provide for compulsory settlement via conciliation,[31] arbitration or judicial settlement.[32]

Diplomatic forms of environmental dispute settlement

As with international dispute settlement generally, negotiation has proven to be the most commonly used method for resolving disputes. It is less common for states to turn from negotiation, which involves only the parties themselves, to other forms of dispute settlement involving a third party such as mediation, conciliation, arbitration and judicial settlement.

Negotiation (which is used interchangeably with the term consultation) can take place at any stage in the emergence or resolution of a dispute, and both general international law and specific environmental and other regimes place states under an obligation to consult with other states before approving activities in their jurisdiction or control that may have transboundary impacts. This was seen in the *Lake Lanoux* case in which an arbitral tribunal held that France was under an obligation to consult with Spain in relation to a hydroelectricity project that affected the flow of water from French to Spanish territory.[33]

Mediation, which is a process of dispute settlement in which a third party becomes involved in order to assist in structuring a settlement between the disputing states, is widely referred to in environmental treaties as a dispute settlement option, but does not appear to have been used in practice. Conciliation differs from mediation in that it not only involves a third party, but one which takes a more active role and which delivers a non-binding report. Several environmental treaties make reference to conciliation as an option for resolving disputes, an example being the 1992 *Convention on Biological Diversity*[34] which the New Zealand government reportedly considered invoking against France in response to the latter's resumption of nuclear testing in the South Pacific in the 1990s.[35] Ultimately New Zealand decided instead to pursue the complaint in the ICJ.[36]

Related to conciliation is the commission of an inquiry or fact-finding process whereby an individual or panel is engaged to investigate the factual basis of a given dispute. An example is the 1997 *UN Convention on the Non-Navigational Uses of International Watercourses*,[37] which establishes a compulsory fact-finding process, unless the parties have agreed to an alternative

---

29 See e.g. *International Convention for the Regulation of Whaling*, opened for signature 2 December 1946, 161 UNTS 72 (entered into force 10 November 1938).

30 See e.g. *Convention for the Conservation of Southern Bluefin Tuna*, opened for signature 10 May 1993, 1819 UNTS 359 (entered into force 20 May 1994).

31 See e.g. *Convention on Biological Diversity*, opened for signature 5 June 1992, 1760 UNTS 143 (entered into force 29 December 1993) ('CBD').

32 See e.g. UNCLOS, op. cit., Pt. XV.

33 *Lake Lanoux case (France/Spain)* (1957) 12 RIAA 285.

34 CBD, Art. 27(2).

35 P. Sands and R. MacKenzie, 'Guidelines for Negotiating and Drafting Dispute Settlement Clauses for International Environmental Agreements', in International Bureau of the Permanent Court of Arbitration, *International Investments and Protection of the Environment*, Leiden: Kluwer, 2001, 305, p. 314.

36 *Nuclear Tests, request for an examination of the situation in accordance with paragraph 63 of the Court's judgment of 20 December 1974 in the Nuclear Tests (New Zealand v France) case* [1995] ICJ Rep 288.

37 *UN Convention on the Non-Navigational Uses of International Watercourses*, opened for signature 21 May 1997, 36 ILM 700 (has not entered into force).

procedure or have declared their acceptance of judicial settlement by the ICJ or arbitration by an arbitral tribunal.[38] The goal of any fact-finding process is to narrow the range of issues in dispute between the parties, allowing legal issues to be resolved.

Legal forms of dispute settlement

Negotiation, mediation, conciliation and inquiry can all be characterised as diplomatic or political forms of dispute settlement, although legal considerations can and do play some role when they are used. Arbitration and judicial settlement are by contrast truly legal forms of dispute settlement in which rules of international law are ostensibly the determining criteria for resolving the matters in contention. Further emphasising their legal importance, arbitration and judicial settlement normally produce decisions that are binding on the parties to the dispute. Moreover, arbitral awards and judicial decisions may contribute to the development of international law as recognised in Article 38(1)(d) of the *Statute of the International Court of Justice*.

Arbitration and judicial settlement are usually both described as being legal forms of dispute settlement, but this was not always the case. Historically arbitration was mostly political in character. However, with the establishment of the Permanent Court of Arbitration at the beginning of the twentieth century arbitration became more legal in nature. Today it is largely indistinguishable from judicial settlement, that is by a standing court or tribunal. Nonetheless, some important differences remain, chief among them being that arbitration is more closely controlled by the parties than judicial settlement. In an arbitration, the parties will be responsible not only for selecting the arbitrators, but also for the adoption of the rules of procedure. Arbitral panels are therefore more dependent on party control and it can be argued that they are not as suitable as permanent international courts for dealing with questions of a truly public order character such as many environmental issues.

As with other areas of international law, international environmental law has experienced the twin processes of 'legalisation' and 'judicialisation' under which there has been a turn to more formal, legal processes of dispute settlement, in particular international courts and tribunals. This is an incident of the phenomenon of 'proliferation' in international courts and tribunals. There is now a patchwork of courts and tribunals that have some jurisdictional capacity to address environmental issues[39] that range from the classic international courts such as the ICJ through to more recently established bodies such as the WTO dispute settlement system, regional institutions such as the European Court of Justice, and human rights courts and complaints procedures.

What is striking about this 'patchwork' is that there is no dedicated court for environmental matters. This illustrates a related point, which is that very few multilateral environmental treaties rely upon arbitration or judicial settlement as the primary means of resolving disputes arising from them. Put another way, few environmental regimes establish a system involving compulsory adjudication of disputes. Several conventions such as the 1985 *Vienna Convention for the Protection of the Ozone Layer*[40] allow for compulsory and binding adjudication where the parties have opted in to the procedure, while several others such as the 1980

---

38 Ibid., Art. 33(3).
39 Stephens, op. cit., ch 2.
40 *Vienna Convention for the Protection of the Ozone Layer*, opened for signature 22 March 1985, 1513 UNTS 324 (entered into force 22 September 1988).

Convention for the Physical Protection of Nuclear Material[41] provide for compulsory and binding adjudication unless the parties have opted out. However, it is only UNCLOS that establishes a mechanism for compulsory and binding adjudication that is automatically applicable.

The absence of a dedicated international environmental court has prompted proposals for such a body to be established;[42] however, there are no indications of any significant support by states for an international court for the environment. It is highly questionable whether such a court would attract any business, and it would instead be preferable for there to be improvements to the capacity of existing courts to address environmental disputes.[43] Such capacity could be enhanced in several respects, including by making provision for courts to draw upon expert assistance when addressing technical or scientific matters relating to the environment. This would help ensure that environmental matters are dealt with appropriately in whatever forum they are litigated. Mindful of this, some courts and tribunals have sought to improve their environmental credentials, as seen in the establishment by the ICJ of a Permanent Chamber for Environmental Matters in 1993. Perhaps underscoring the reluctance of states to utilise an environmental court, that Chamber has never decided a dispute, and the ICJ no longer holds annual elections for the Chamber.

The 'fragmentation' of international environmental law disputation

Because international environmental law disputes may be brought before any number of diverse processes the concern has been expressed that this may lead to 'fragmentation'. This is because it may result in environmental disputes being resolved in forums which do not have an avowed environmental focus of specialisation, leading potentially to decisions that are skewed in favour of the particular regime which the dispute settlement procedure serves. There is also a related apprehension that the multiplicity of dispute settlement options will produce practical problems of forum shopping and in some cases even proceedings on the same issue in multiple forums.

Nowhere has this anxiety been more strongly expressed than in the context of the relationship between international trade law and international environmental law.[44] This is because of the strength of the WTO dispute settlement system that is readily invoked to respond to trade measures taken by states, including where those measures have an environmental purpose. There are certainly legitimate questions to be asked as to whether international trade law and international environmental law can operate harmoniously. The trade liberalisation agenda places fetters on the capacity of states to limit trade in products or services where they are associated with environmental damage.

There is certainly the prospect that the WTO will be a roadblock to progressive environmental measures. However, WTO jurisprudence to date suggests that the Appellate Body is alive to the possibility of fragmentation and is seeking to avoid open conflict between trade and environmental norms, to the extent that this is possible. The dispute most frequently

---

41 *Convention for the Physical Protection of Nuclear Material*, opened for signature 3 March 1980, 1456 UNTS 124 (entered into force 8 February 1987).

42 See in particular A. Postiglione, *The Global Environmental Crisis: The Need for an International Court of the Environment*, Rome: Giunti, 1996.

43 Stephens, op. cit., p. 61.

44 R. Eckersley, 'The Big Chill: The WTO and Multilateral Environmental Agreements', (2004) *Global Environmental Politics* 4, 24.

cited in this respect is the *Shrimp-Turtle* cases,[45] in which the Appellate Body referred to multi-lateral environmental agreements in reaching the decision that a trade measure adopted by the United States to protect sea turtles was one relating to the conservation of an exhaustible natural resource under Article XX(g) of the 1994 General Agreement on Tariffs and Trade (GATT).[46] In more recent decisions panels have not been quite so willing to look beyond the strictures of the WTO agreements themselves. This was seen in the *Biotech Products* case,[47] where a WTO Panel took a restrictive view of Article 31(3)(c) of the 1969 *Vienna Convention on the Law of Treaties*[48] (VCLT) in concluding that only environmental treaties binding on all parties to the WTO could possibly be relevant when interpreting WTO rules. As noted at the outset of this chapter, the WTO is likely to be at the centre of disputes between states over climate change policies that have trade effects, and as there are ultimate limits to which Article XX(g) of the GATT can be stretched.

The concerns that international environmental law may be destabilised by the proliferation of courts and tribunals applies not only in the context of the WTO but also in other areas such as human rights where there is a fairly well-developed system of dispute settlement. The reality is that litigants will tend to use whatever forums are available, even if they are not ideally suited to the dispute at hand, as seen in the use of the United Nations Human Rights Committee and similar regional bodies by complainants bringing what are really environmental claims. This is not necessarily a process that will bring dissonance to international environmental law, as there are well-established principles in international law for reconciling norms that appear inconsistent. In its study of the general phenomenon of fragmentation in international law, a study group of the ILC chaired by Martti Koskenniemi noted that the VCLT supplies rules of interpretation which perform this function.[49] These include the principle set out in Article 31(3)(c) of the VCLT that provides that in interpreting a treaty '[t] here shall be taken into account . . . any relevant rules of international law applicable in the relations between the parties'.

Compliance procedures

One of the most significant developments in international environmental dispute settlement was the advent of the compliance procedure established by the 1987 Montreal Protocol to supervise compliance with the ozone regime.[50] Compliance procedures are best seen as one institution among various bodies established under multilateral environmental agreements that have responsibilities for monitoring state adherence to environmental regimes. Such bodies include treaty secretariats and subsidiary bodies such as scientific committees.

---

45 *United States – Import Prohibition of Certain Shrimp and Shrimp Products*, WTO Doc WT/DS58/R (1998) (report of the Panel), WTO Doc WT/DS58/AB/R (1998) (report of the Appellate Body).

46 *Marrakesh Agreement Establishing the World Trade Organization*, opened for signature 15 April 1994, 1869 UNTS 190 (entered into force 1 January 1995), Annex 1A.

47 *European Communities – Measures Affecting the Approval and Marketing of Biotech Products*, WTO Docs WT/DS291/R, WT/DS292/R, WT/DS293/R (2006) (report of the Panel).

48 *Vienna Convention on the Law of Treaties*, opened for signature 23 May 1969, 1155 UNTS 332 (entered into force 27 January 1980).

49 *Fragmentation of International Law: Difficulties Arising from the Diversification and Expansion of International Law: Report of the Study Group of the International Law Commission*, Finalised by Chairman M. Koskenniemi ILC, UN Doc. A/CN.4/L.682.

50 Decision IV/5, Report of the Fourth Meeting of the Parties to the Montreal Protocol, UN Doc UNEP/Oz.L.Pro.4/15 (1992).

Compliance procedures operate in a more structured manner, and are designed as a halfway approach between legal and political dispute settlement in that they are generally non-confrontational and aim to assist states comply rather than imposing sanctions.

Given the failure of states to agree upon a second commitment period for the Kyoto Protocol at COP17/CMP7 in Durban in December 2011, and Canada's withdrawal from the Protocol in the same month, the future of the Kyoto Protocol is highly uncertain. Nonetheless, the Kyoto Protocol compliance procedure[51] illustrates well the way in which compliance systems can function. The Kyoto Protocol compliance system operates through a plenary session, a bureau and two branches – the facilitative branch and the enforcement branch – both of which are composed of independent rather than government representatives. The facilitative and enforcement branches have somewhat different functions, with the former more concerned to provide advice and assistance than the latter, which determines what consequences should flow from breach. Those consequences can be serious, including the suspension of a Kyoto Protocol party from participation in the emissions trading and other flexibility mechanisms, and the imposition of a 30 per cent penalty for failing to meet an emissions reduction or limitation target. In line with the tenor of the compliance system as a whole, which is concerned with compliance rather than violations of legal obligations, the language of breach is avoided altogether in favour of the more oblique terminology of 'questions of implementation'.

One of the most important features of the Kyoto Protocol compliance procedure, and one shared with other similar procedures, is that 'questions of implementation' can be raised not only by other states but also by expert review teams and even non-compliant parties themselves. This enables compliance issues to be raised far more readily. And the practice in the Kyoto system shows that they have been. Seven parties to the Kyoto Protocol have had compliance issues raised against them by expert review teams: Greece, Canada, Croatia, Bulgaria, Romania, Ukraine and Lithuania. Most of these 'cases' have related to the failure by parties to have in place appropriate inventories for measuring greenhouse gases or registries for the trade in Kyoto carbon units such as those from Clean Development Mechanism projects in developing states.

Compliance procedures are rightly described as being quasi-judicial not only because they involve assessment by independent experts but also because the process is highly developed in order to provide due process protections for parties involved. Yet by contrast with courts compliance procedures are more proactive, and preventative in their focus, and to that end involve a range of options to assist parties meet their obligations by providing technical and other assistance. This has been particularly important in the context of the Kyoto Protocol, which imposes demanding obligations of a technical character upon parties and where the compliance system has been used to assist states, particularly those with economies in transition, improve their internal governance arrangements.

Conclusion

International environmental law has reached a depth and breadth that would have seemed inconceivable at the time of the 1972 Stockholm Conference or even the 1992 Rio Conference. Now on the eve of Rio+20 it must be asked whether the machinery of dispute settlement

---

51 Decision 24/CP.7, Report of the Conference of the Parties on its Seventh Session, UN Doc FCCC/CP/2001/13/Add.3 (2002).

established alongside the substantive rules of international environmental law is suited to the task of enhancing international environmental governance. The answer to this question depends in large part on determining what precisely the function of dispute settlement in international environmental law should be. Is the primary aim to promote more harmonious relations among states and avoid major controversies? Or alternatively should it serve a higher objective to ensure that the fundamental objective of international environmental law, to preserve the planet's natural systems for future generations, is achieved?

Despite the major advances that have been made, dispute settlement remains largely a quasi-diplomatic or facilitative process in international environmental law. This is illustrated starkly by a comparison of two cases in the ICJ, one in the 1970s, the *Nuclear Tests* case,[52] and one four decades later, the *Pulp Mills* case. In the *Nuclear Tests* case the ICJ was able to avoid entering into the merits of the dispute by reframing the case as one relating to the legal effect of a unilateral statement by France of its intention to cease atmospheric nuclear testing. In so doing the Court sought to promote a diplomatic and mutually agreeable settlement without making a hard-and-fast decision about the legal rights of the parties in relation to the environment. In the *Pulp Mills* case the Court showed a greater willingness to engage with substantive rules and principles of international environmental law, yet once again the ICJ sought to avoid confrontation as far as possible, reaching a decision that found Uruguay in technical breach of certain procedural obligations, while imposing no real penalty for the infractions. Notwithstanding the strength of Australia's arguments in the *Scientific Whaling* case or Ecuador's submissions in the *Aerial Herbicide Spraying* case, it seems likely that the Court will seek yet again to invoke a Solomonic approach in both of these disputes. While such an approach has been commended by some commentators as one in which the Court is being alive to the realities of complex and contested international environmental dispute settlement,[53] it risks the *private* ordering of what are ultimately *public* values in that the Court is essentially achieving a settlement of the dispute that diffuses the controversy rather than addressing the underlying environmental problem.

Despite the limitations of turning to international courts to address environmental threats the continued use of litigation appears inevitable as states pursue proceedings in the court as one strategy among several for achieving their environmental policy objectives. One domain where this is most likely is in relation to climate change. Given the slow and uncertain pace of negotiations on an effective international climate change regime, states are considering their options. Several Pacific Island states declared on signing and ratifying the 1992 UNFCCC[54] and the 1997 Kyoto Protocol[55] that joining the climate regime in no way constituted a renunciation of any rights under international law concerning

52 *Nuclear Tests (Australia v France) (New Zealand v France)* (merits) [1974] ICJ Rep 253 and 457.
53 See e.g. D.M. Johnston, 'Fishery Diplomacy and Science and the Judicial Function', *Yearbook of International Environmental Law* 10, 1999, 33, p. 38; N. Klein, 'Settlement of International Environmental Disputes', in M. Fitzmaurice, D.M. Ong and P. Merkouris (eds) *Research Handbook on International Environmental Law*, Cheltenham: Edward Elgar, 2010, 379, p. 395.
54 *United Nations Framework Convention on Climate Change*, opened for signature 4 June 1992, 1771 UNTS 165 (entered into force 21 March 1994).
55 *Kyoto Protocol*, opened for signature 11 December 1997, 37 ILM 22 (entered into force 16 February 2005).

state responsibility for the adverse effects of climate change.[56] And in September 2011 the Pacific island nation of Palau called on the United Nations General Assembly to request an advisory opinion of the ICJ on the legal responsibility of states to prevent damage to other states caused by climate change.[57] Contentious or advisory proceedings in relation to climate change are unlikely to bear a great deal of fruit in terms of outcome, because despite the seriousness of the climate change problem, which is no less than an existential threat to humanity, it is not a regulatory challenge that is readily soluble through inter-state dispute settlement. Climate change is a global commons problem given that the sources of pollution are dispersed and the effects are widely felt and not ascribable to emissions from particular states.[58]

Given the limitations of traditional forms of dispute settlement invoking international courts and tribunals, the continued development and strengthening of a tailored system of compliance control through environmental compliance procedures is to be welcomed, as the litigation of international environmental disputes is not a strategy for international environmental governance that can produce the kinds of stark outcomes that are needed to reverse the relentless march of global environmental decline.

---

56 See UNFCCC Declarations by Parties. Online. Available HTTP: <http://unfccc.int/essential_background/convention/items/5410.php>; Kyoto Protocol Declarations and Reservations by Parties. Online. Available HTTP: <http://unfccc.int/kyoto_protocol/status_of_ratification/items/5424.php> (both accessed 30 April 2012).

57 'Palau seeks UN World Court opinion on damage caused by greenhouse gases', *UN News Centre*, 22 September 2011. Online. Available HTTP: <http://www.un.org/apps/news/story.asp?NewsID=39710&Cr=pacific+island&Cr1> (accessed 30 April 2012).

58 See generally T. Stephens, 'International Courts and Climate Change: Progression, Regression and Administration', in R. Lyster (ed.) *In the Wilds of Climate Change Law*, Brisbane: Australian Academic Press, 2010, p. 53; E.A. Posner, 'Climate Change and International Human Rights Litigation: A Critical Appraisal', *University of Pennsylvania Law Review* 155, 2007, p. 1938.

11

Multinational corporations and international environmental law

Elisa Morgera

This contribution analyses the evolution of international law and practice concerning the environmentally responsible conduct of multinational corporations, highlighting continuing challenges. To this end, the chapter distinguishes three approaches: international regulation, partnerships and human rights-based approaches. In each case, the role of multilateral environmental agreements and principles of international environmental law is identified.

Introduction

The economic power and worldwide scale of activities of multinational corporations (MNCs)[1] makes these entities highly significant in the development and implementation of international environmental law. Both their day-to-day activities and major accidents due to their sub-standard practices have been documented as contributing to environmental degradation. At the same time, MNCs' financial, technological and managerial resources make them influential and creative contributors to the protection of the environment and the sustainable use of natural resources. In addition, MNCs that depend on natural capital for their long-term operations ultimately have a vested interest in environmental protection. Against this complex background comprising very concrete threats and opportunities for international environmental law, MNCs are also associated with complex legal challenges. On the one hand, they defy national law due to the inefficacy of the legal control exercised by host states over a subsidiary and by home states over a parent company. On the other hand, MNCs benefit from the formidable protection afforded to them by international investment law.[2] They are not, however, subject to corresponding international obligations, and can profit from the gaps of international criminal and civil liability regimes with respect to environmentally damaging conduct.[3]

---

1 P. Muchlinski, *Multinational Enterprises and the Law*, New York: Oxford University Press, 2007.
2 M. Sornarajah, *The International Law on Foreign Investment*, Cambridge: Cambridge University Press, 2004.
3 E. Morgera, *Corporate Accountability in International Law*, Oxford: Oxford University Press, 2009, ch. 3.

These difficulties are reflected in the ongoing debate on the status of MNCs – as business entities with activities in more than one country, and more than one owner in more than one home state – in international law. Multinationals have been seen as 'significant actors',[4] indispensable interlocutors to states;[5] 'participants' rather than subjects in a system of international law;[6] members of the international community;[7] 'entities *sui generis*', whose treatment in international law needs to be approached on a pragmatic, case-by-case basis to reflect the functions they perform;[8] or as holders of 'limited and functional legal personality'.[9] It may therefore be cautioned from the outset that 'much of the debate on international legal personality of transnational corporations . . . is rather abstract and may be of little help in an actual understanding of the form and scope of corporate accountability'.[10] Increasingly international practice avoids defining MNCs or distinguishing them from other business enterprises.[11]

This contribution will discuss the evolution of international law vis-à-vis MNCs, highlighting the variety of approaches adopted at the international level to ensure the environmentally sound and responsible conduct of MNCs, and continuing challenges. To this end, it will distinguish and analyse three approaches: international regulation, partnerships and human rights-based approaches. All of these, with one exception, have been developed on the basis of international environmental law in as far as corporate environmental accountability standards were concerned. Attention will be drawn in particular to the standard-setting functions performed by international organizations, only touching upon their equally significant monitoring functions,[12] with a view to pointing to relevant linkages with multilateral environmental agreements.

---

4 Indeed, the UN Group of Eminent Persons in 1974 concluded that 'multinational corporations are important actors on the world stage', in 'Report of the Group of Eminent Persons, The Impact of Multinational Corporations on the Development Process and on International Relations' (1974), UN Doc E/5500/Add.1.

5 H. Hosein, 'Unsettling: Bhopal and the Resolution of International Disputes Involving an Environmental Disaster', *Boston College International and Comparative Law Review* 16, 1993, 285–319, p. 308.

6 R. Higgins, *Problems and Processes. International Law and How We Use It*, Oxford: Clarendon Press, 1994, pp. 48–55.

7 D. Thurer, 'The Emergence of Non-governmental Organizations and Transnational Enterprises in International Law and the Changing Role of the State', in R. Hofmann and N. Geissler (eds) *Non-State Actors as New Subjects of International Law*, Berlin: Duncker & Humblot, 1999, p. 54. Although according to some doctrines, the international community is itself not yet a subject of international law: C. Tomuschat, 'International Liability for Injurious Consequences Arising out of Acts Not Prohibited by International Law: The Work of the International Law Commission', in F. Francioni and T. Scovazzi (eds) *International Responsibility for Environmental Harm*, London: Graham & Trotman, 1991, p. 78.

8 V. Lowe, 'Corporations as International Actors and International Law Makers', *Italian Yearbook of International Law* 13, 2004, 23–38, p. 25.

9 P.M. Dupuy, *L'unité de l'ordre juridique international*, Leiden: Martinus Nijhoff Publishers, 2003, pp. 102–18.

10 A. Nollkaemper, 'Responsibility of Transnational Corporations in International Environmental Law: Three Perspectives', in G. Winter (ed.) *Multilevel Governance of Global Environmental Change: Perspectives from Science, Sociology and the Law*, Cambridge: Cambridge University Press, 2006, p. 186.

11 Morgera, op. cit., p. 60; see also D. Weissbrodt and M. Kruger, 'Norms on the Responsibilities of Transnational Corporations and Other Business Enterprises with regard to Human Rights', *American Journal of International Law* 97, 2003, 901–23, p. 910.

12 For a discussion of international monitoring of corporate environmental accountability, see E. Morgera, 'From Corporate Social Responsibility to Accountability Mechanisms', in P.M. Dupuy and J. Vinales (eds), *Protecting the Environment in the XXIst Century: The Role of the Private Sector*, Cambridge: Cambridge University Press, 2012.

An old problem in need of new solutions?

The international community has debated the need for international regulation and oversight of MNCs for almost forty years.[13] As early as 1972, during the United Nations Conference on the Human Environment, discussions took place with regard to the role of business in the global protection of the environment and on the necessity of integrating environmental concerns into corporate decision-making.[14] Indeed, the preamble of the resulting Stockholm Declaration made a broad reference to the environmental responsibility of business in sharing efforts with other stakeholders towards global environmental goals.[15]

A 1991 resolution of the UN Economic and Social Council (ECOSOC) refers to the observance by MNCs of international environmental principles, particularly polluter pays, prevention and precaution.[16] In a 1991 report of the UN Secretary-General it was suggested that MNCs were expected to conduct their activities in accordance with intergovernmental environmental policies and standards representing internationally agreed-upon minimum standards.[17]

More debate on the role of private companies, and particularly MNCs, and environmental protection occurred at the United Nations Conference on Environment and Development (UNCED) in 1992. The resulting Rio Declaration emphasized the necessity of internalizing environmental costs through economic instruments, which has some direct relevance for corporations,[18] but did not provide more specific guidance. Agenda 21, in turn, dedicated a whole chapter (Chapter 30) to 'Strengthening the Role of Business and Industry', explicitly and implicitly[19] making reference to the role of MNCs.

At the World Summit on Sustainable Development (WSSD) in Johannesburg in 2002, discussions on the role of the private sector were more detailed than in previous international conferences. The WSSD Political Declaration includes two references to the role of business for sustainable development: the *'duty'* of the private sector 'to contribute to the evolution of equitable and sustainable communities and societies' and 'the need for corporations to

13 Early attempts were undertaken in the context of the UN Economic and Social Council, who adopted a resolution in 1972 acknowledging the lack of an international regulatory framework for multinational corporations and the need to institutionalize international debate on that issue: ECOSOC Res 1721 (LIII), 28 July 1972.

14 'Business and the UNCED Process', in UNCTC, 'Activities of Transnational Corporations and Management Division and its Joint Units: Follow-up to the UN Conference on Environment and Development as related to Transnational Corporations' (1993), UN Doc E/C.10/1993/7, which indicated that more than 900 firms were involved in the preparatory process. H. Gleckman, 'Transnational Corporations' Strategic Responses to 'Sustainable Development', in H.O. Bergenses, G. Parmann and Ø.B. Thommessen (eds) *Green Globe Yearbook of International Cooperation on Environment and Development*, Oxford: Oxford University Press, 1995, p. 95.

15 *Declaration of the United Nations Conference on the Human Environment* (1972), UN Doc A/ CONF.48/14/Rev.1, para. 7 ('Stockholm Declaration').

16 ECOSOC Res 1991/55 (26 July 1991), paras 28(c) and (i).

17 ECOSOC, 'Report of the UN Secretary-General: Transnational Corporations and Issues Relating to the Environment' (1991), UN Doc E/C.10/1991/3.

18 Rio Declaration on Environment and Development (1992), UN Doc A/CONF.151/6/Rev.1 ('Rio Declaration') Principle 16.

19 ECOSOC, 'Follow-up to the United Nations Conference on Environment and Development as Related to Transnational Corporations: Report of the Secretary General' (1993), UN Doc E/C.10/1993/7, note 44, 35, indicates that MNCs were referred to with the following terms: 'foreign direct investment, multinationals, commerce and industry including MNCs', etc.

enforce corporate accountability within a transparent and stable regulatory environment'.[20] The WSSD Plan of Implementation further refers to the issue of corporate accountability, in three separate instances: it encourages voluntary initiatives; it calls upon the international community to promote corporate responsibility and accountability; and it urges them to:

> actively promote corporate responsibility and accountability, based on the Rio principles including through the full development and effective implementation of intergovern- mental agreements and measures, international initiatives and public–private partner- ships and appropriate national regulations, and support continuous improvement in corporate practices in all countries.[21]

The term 'corporate accountability' was thus endorsed by the international community at the WSSD. It can be understood as the legitimate expectation that reasonable efforts will be put in place, according to international standards, by private companies and MNCs for the attain- ment of a certain internationally agreed environmental objective.[22] This concept is often paired or used interchangeably with corporate responsibility. Ultimately, however, corporate responsibility and accountability seem to refer to two different legal approaches in addressing the role of business, and MNCs in particular, in the global protection of the environment.[23] On the one hand, corporate responsibility makes reference to the need for substantive, result-oriented standards for the conduct of MNCs and other companies that go beyond what is required at the national level of the host state. Corporate responsibility seeks to ensure direct contributions to environmental protection and more generally to sustainable development from the private sector. Corporate accountability, on the other hand, makes reference to the need for procedural standards, in terms of transparency, reporting and disclosure of information to the public. It focuses on the indirect means for ensuring the environmentally sound conduct of MNCs on the basis of public expectations.

Against this background of increasing international debate on MNCs and international environmental law, three approaches have emerged internationally with regard to the need to ensure or at least support the environmentally sound conduct of MNCs. These approaches will be analysed in turn in the following sections.

International regulation?

The first major initiative within the UN on the question of the international regulation of MNCs arose in the context of the General Assembly's debates on permanent sovereignty over natural resources.[24] These were initiated in the early 1970s by the Group of Developing

---

20 WSSD, 'Political Declaration' (2002), UN Doc A/CONF.199/20, 2002, Resolution 1 (WSSD Declaration), paras 27 and 29.
21 WSSD, 'Johannesburg Plan of Implementation' (2002), UN Doc A/CONF.199/20, Resolution 2 (WSSD Plan of Implementation), paras 18, 140(f) and 49.
22 Morgera, *Corporate Accountability*, op. cit., ch. 2.
23 The UN General Assembly has implicitly recognized such duality in 2005, when framing the mandate of the UN Special Representative on issues of Human Rights and Transnational Corporations (discussed below) in terms of 'identify[ing] and clarify[ing] standards of corporate responsibility and accountability': Commission on Human Rights Res 2005/69 (20 April 2005).
24 Permanent Sovereignty over Natural Resources (1962), GA Res 1803 (XVII).

Countries and China (G-77/China),[25] leading to the negotiations of a UN code of conduct for transnational corporations. Thus, ECOSOC created a permanent body, the UN Commission on Transnational Corporations (UNCTC),[26] with the mandate to: monitor the activities of MNCs and report on developments in international investment activities; provide developing countries with expertise and advice in their dealings with MNCs; and draft proposals for normative frameworks governing the activities of transnational corporations. The last task was consistently given the highest priority.[27] A Working Group charged with the drafting of a UN Code of Conduct for Transnational Corporations initiated work in 1977. The first draft was presented in 1982 but negotiations collapsed in 1992. The latest text of the Draft Code dates back to 1990.[28]

The Draft Code represented the first attempt at a universal and complete instrument on MNCs, because of both its global scope and its comprehensive subject matter.[29] It was initially agreed that it would reflect, to some degree, existing regulatory agreements or relevant instruments under development in other international fora.[30] The question of the legal nature of the Draft Code was from the start a contentious issue, so much so that the Working Group decided to postpone it to a subsequent phase of the negotiations. According to the developing country proponents, the Draft Code was to deal only with the regulation of MNC activities.[31] However, in 1980 a compromise was reached to have two sections in the draft. The first focused on the activities of transnational corporations (and their regulation), providing rules of conduct directly applying to MNCs. The second section focused on MNCs' treatment (i.e. their protection), providing rules of conduct applying to capital-importing countries.[32] This decision aimed to strike a balance between the rights and the responsibilities of MNCs and of governments in a single document.[33] Thus, the objective of the Draft Code was twofold: to contribute to ensuring a stable, predictable and transparent framework for the strengthening of international investments; and to help minimize the negative effects of

---

25 P. Muchlinski, 'Attempts to Extend the Accountability of Transnational Corporations: The Role of UNCTAD', in M.T. Kamminga and S. Zia-Zarifi (eds) *Liability of Multinational Corporations under International Law*, The Hague: Kluwer Law International, 2000, p. 99; J.M. Kline, 'Business Codes of Conduct in a Global Political Economy', in O.F. Williams (ed.) *Global Codes of Conduct: An Idea Whose Time Has Come*, Indiana: University of Notre Dame Press, 2000, p. 43.

26 ECOSOC Res 1913(LVII) (5 December 1974).

27 M. Hansen, 'Environmental Regulation of Transnational Corporations', in P. Utting (ed.) *The Greening of Business in Developing Countries*, London: Zed Books in association with UNRISD, 2002, p. 161; S.J. Rubin, 'Transnational Corporations and International Codes of Conduct: a Study of the Relationship between International Legal Cooperation and Economic Development', *American University Journal of International Law and Policy* 10, 1994–1995, 1275–89; S. Coonrod, 'The United Nations Code of Conduct for Transnational Corporations', *Harvard International Law Journal* 18, 1977, 273–307.

28 UN Commission on Transnational Corporations (UNCTC), 'Proposed Text of the Draft Code of Conduct on Transnational Corporations' (1990) UN Doc E/1990/94 ('UN Draft Code of Conduct').

29 K.P. Sauvant and V. Aranda, 'The International Legal Framework for Transnational Corporations', in A.A. Fatouros (ed.) *Transnational Corporations: The International Legal Framework*, London: Routledge, 1994, p. 86; and Coonrod, op. cit., p. 274.

30 Rubin, op. cit., p. 1284.

31 F. Francioni, 'International Codes of Conduct for Multinational Enterprises: An Alternative Approach', *The Italian Yearbook of International Law* 3, 1977, 143–71.

32 ECOSOC Res 60 (24 July 1980); P. Muchlinski, 'Attempts to Extend the Accountability of Transnational Corporations, op. cit., p. 100.

33 Sauvant and Aranda, op. cit., p. 105.

MNCs, while promoting their contribution to development efforts of host countries.[34] The first section, on the activities of MNCs, covered, *inter alia*, respect for national sovereignty, adherence to the economic and development goals of host countries, respect for human rights, non-interference with the host countries' internal affairs, abstention from corrupt practices, employment conditions, and consumer and environmental protection. Its aim was not to oppose the establishment of MNCs in developing countries, but rather to require their regulation in order to ensure their contribution to development.[35] The second section, on the treatment of MNCs, focused on compensation for nationalization, jurisdiction and dispute settlement.

The UN Draft Code of Conduct devoted three paragraphs to the protection of the environment.[36] It prescribed that MNCs carry out their activities in accordance with national laws, regulations, administrative practices and policies, but also with 'due regard to relevant *international* standards'.[37] In addition, corporations were expected to take steps to protect the environment and, where it was damaged, to restore it.[38] The Code also called upon MNCs to supply relevant information to competent authorities regarding their products, processes and services whose characteristics could be harmful to the environment,[39] as well as to be responsive to requests from their host country governments and to cooperate with international organizations in their efforts to promote national and international environmental standards.[40]

Although the language of the Draft Code was vague and exhortatory,[41] its most significant contribution lay in the unprecedented attribution to the international community of the task of developing a set of international general standards on the proper role of MNCs.[42] It is of great importance to note that, whereas fundamental disagreement persisted on the second part of the Draft Code (regarding the protection of FDI (foreign direct investment)),[43] substantial agreement had already been reached on the first part (containing the environmental protection section) by 1981.[44] The remaining disagreement led to the collapse of the negotiations in 1992, since the Draft Code was discussed as a package deal.[45]

Certainly, the Draft Code's failure showed the lack of political will of negotiating states to have an international instrument regulating MNCs' responsibility, partly due to the changed political and economic background to the negotiations. Its failure had 'substantial psychological and political implications'[46] that have been reflected in the new strategies adopted

---

34 W. Sprote, 'Negotiations on a United Nations Code of Conduct on Transnational Corporations', *German Yearbook of International Law* 33, 1990, 331–48.

35 Muchlinski, 'Attempts to Extend the Accountability of Transnational Corporations', op. cit., p. 100.

36 UN Code of Conduct, paras 41–3.

37 Ibid., para. 41 (emphasis added).

38 Ibid.

39 Ibid., para. 42.

40 Ibid., para. 43.

41 R.J. Waldmann, *Regulating International Business through Codes of Conduct*, Washington DC: American Enterprise Institute for Public Policy Research, 1980, p. 84.

42 Coonrod, op. cit., p. 296.

43 P. Hansen and V. Aranda, 'An Emerging International Framework for Transnational Corporations', *Fordham International Law Journal* 14, 1990, 881–91; Sprote, op. cit., p. 341.

44 A.A. Fatouros, 'Looking for an International Legal Framework for Transnational Corporations', in Fatouros (ed.) op. cit., p. 9; Sauvant and Aranda, op. cit., p. 102.

45 Sprote, op. cit., p. 339.

46 Rubin, op. cit., p. 1289.

within the UN to tackle the issue of corporate accountability, such as the partnership approach and the human rights-based approach discussed below. The adoption of these new strategies showed the increasing initiative of the UN in the face of continued resistance by states.

At the height of the discussion on a Draft Code of Conduct on Transnational Corporations within the United Nations, the Organisation for Economic Cooperation and Development (OECD) approved its voluntary *Guidelines for Multinational Enterprises*[47] in 1976. They were part of the *Declaration on International Investment and Multinational Enterprises*,[48] which was designed to improve the international investment climate and to strengthen the basis for mutual confidence between enterprises and the society in which they operate.[49] As opposed to the UN Draft Code, which focused both on the regulation of the activities of MNCs and their protection from the unlawful conduct of capital-importing countries, the OECD Guidelines were drafted solely as governmental recommendations formulated to directly address MNCs operating in adhering countries.

The OECD Guidelines contain a specific and quite detailed provision on the environment, referring both to general standards of environmental protection and to a list of specific tools for corporate environmental accountability. Accordingly, MNCs should generally conduct their activities:

> within the framework of laws, regulations and administrative practices in the countries in which they operate, and in consideration of relevant international agreements, principles, objectives, and standards, take due account of the need to protect the environment, public health and safety, and generally . . . conduct their activities in a manner contributing to the wider goal of sustainable development.[50]

With a pragmatic approach, the following, more detailed provisions list a series of tools for corporate environmental accountability: environmental managements systems, communication and stakeholder involvement, life-cycle assessment and environmental impact assessment, risk prevention and mitigation, continuous improvement of corporate environmental performance, education and training of employees, and contribution to public policies.[51] Probably the most interesting feature of the environmental provisions of the OECD Guidelines is the implicit reference to the precautionary approach:

> Consistent with the scientific and technical understanding of risks, where there are threats of serious damage to the environment, taking also into account human health and safety, [enterprises should] not use the lack of full scientific certainty as a reason for postponing cost-effective measures to prevent or minimise such damage.[52]

The 2011 review of the OECD Guidelines stressed stakeholder engagement as an interactive and two-way process based on good faith for planning and decision-making concerning projects or

---

47 OECD, *The OECD Guidelines for Multinational Enterprises* (OECD, 2011) ('OECD Guidelines').
48 OECD, *The OECD Declaration and Decisions on International Investment and Multinational Enterprises: Basic Texts* (2000), OECD Doc DAFFE/IME (2000) 20.
49 J. Huner, 'The Multilateral Agreement on Investment and the Review of the OECD Guidelines for Multinational Enterprises', in Kamminga and Zia-Zafiri, op. cit., p. 198.
50 OECD Guidelines, ch. VI.
51 Ibid., paras 1–8.
52 Ibid, para. 4.

activities 'that may significantly impact local communities', such as those involving the intensive use of land and water. It also pointed to the need for MNCs to disclose climate change and biodiversity-specific information.[53] In addition, the 2011 review included references to due diligence, thanks to the influence of the UN Framework on Business and Human Rights (discussed below). It further addressed a more specific recommendation on exploring and assessing ways to improve environmental performance with reference to emission reduction, efficient resource use, the management of toxic substances and the conservation of biodiversity.[54]

Although the OECD Guidelines themselves are a voluntary initiative, they have their 'implementation procedure'.[55] This procedure is based on one formal obligation for adhering countries, which is setting up national contact points (NCPs).[56] These NCPs handle inquiries ('specific instances') at the national level.[57] Specific instances are basically a means for any 'interested party' to draw the NCP's attention to a company's alleged non-observance of the Guidelines.[58] The NCPs make an initial assessment of the issue and then offer their services as mediators.

Although the performance of the OECD Guidelines implementation procedure has been mixed, there have been notable cases in which NCPs significantly contributed to clarifying how international environmental standards are expected to be complied with by MNCs. For instance, an NCP affirmed that a UK multinational involved in mining operations in Indian forest land did not respect the Convention on Biological Diversity[59] and its Akwé: Kon Guidelines on environmental and socio-cultural impact assessment[60] when consulting an indigenous group affected by its operations.[61]

Partnerships

In the late 1990s, a new trend of promoting UN–business partnerships developed to become an 'integral part' of the work of the UN[62] with a view to addressing the whole private sector,

53 OECD Council, *OECD Guidelines for Multinational Enterprises: Update 2011 – Note by the Secretary-General* (2011), OECD doc. C (2011) 59, Appendix II, para. II. A.14; OECD Council, *OECD Guidelines for Multinational Enterprises: Update 2011 – Commentaries* (2011), OECD Doc C (2011) 59/ADD1, paras 25, 33.
54 OECD Guidelines, section VI.6.d.
55 The Implementation Procedure of the OECD Guidelines for Multinational Enterprises is included in Part II of the OECD Guidelines, section I.
56 Huner, op. cit., p. 200.
57 Ibid.
58 P. van der Gaag, 'OECD Guidelines for Multinational Enterprises: Corporate Accountability in a Liberalised Economy?', p. 3. Online. Available HTTP: <http://www.oecdwatch.org/docs/paper%20NC%20IUCN.pdf> (accessed 10 April 2008).
59 Convention on Biological Diversity, opened for signature 5 June 1992, 1760 UNTS 79 (entered into force 29 December 1993).
60 Akwé: Kon Voluntary Guidelines for the Conduct of Cultural, Environmental and Social Impact Assessment regarding Developments Proposed to Take Place on, or which are Likely to Impact on, Sacred Sites and on Lands and Waters Traditionally Occupied or Used by Indigenous and Local Communities, in Article 8(j) and related provisions (CBD Decision VII/16F, 13 April 2004).
61 UK NCP, Final Statement on the Complaint from Survival International against Vedanta Resources plc, 25 September 2009.
62 GA, Report of the Secretary-General: Enhanced Cooperation between the United Nations and all Relevant Partners, in particular the Private Sector (2003), UN Doc.A/58/227. For a detailed analysis of UN-private sector partnerships, see A. Zammit, *Development at Risk. Rethinking UN-Business Partnerships*, Geneva: UNRISD, 2003.

and no longer MNCs alone. This trend became increasingly relevant for the environmental sector,[63] and has been coupled with the adoption of a multi-stakeholder participation approach in the definition and implementation of international environmental standards for corporate accountability.[64]

The highest profile example of this approach is the Global Compact,[65] launched by former UN Secretary-General Kofi Annan to assist companies in the development and promotion of global value-based management.[66] In time, the Global Compact received an intergovernmental endorsement through General Assembly resolutions,[67] but the question of its intergovernmentally agreed mandate remains open.[68]

The Compact has been widely publicized and criticized,[69] due to its innovative approach according to which 'confrontation' with the business community has been replaced with 'cooperation'.[70] Its main aim is to build collaborative relations with the private sector with a view to the establishment of partnerships, on the basis of internationally agreed principles of good corporate citizenship (human rights, labour standards, environmental sustainability and anti-corruption.) Specifically, it builds on ten principles, all drawn from existing UN documents, including the Rio Declaration, that are framed in general terms.[71]

The scope of the Compact is thus to encourage the private sector to commit to ten international principles, integrate them into their core business operations and pursue activities that advance implementation of the principles and other UN-related objectives. Adhering companies are further expected to post on the Global Compact website, at least once a year, a report of the concrete steps taken and lessons learnt on any of the principles. Under these

---

63 The most notable, although controversial, outcome of WSSD was 'Type II Partnerships', namely opportunities for the private sector to engage actively in the process through multi-stakeholder involvement, as an alternative to Type I (formal) commitments. See C. Streck, 'The World Summit on Sustainable Development: Partnerships as the New Tool in Environmental Governance', *Yearbook of International Environmental Law* 13, 2003, 63–95.

64 Morgera, *Corporate Accountability*, op. cit., pp. 85–7.

65 UN Global Compact, *The Ten Principles*: Online. Available HTTP: <http://www.unglobal compact.org/AboutTheGC/TheTenPrinciples/index.html> (accessed 7 January 2012). K. Bruno and J. Karliner, 'The UN's Global Compact, Corporate Accountability and the Johannesburg Earth Summit', *Development* 45, 2002, 33–8.

66 UN Global Compact Office, *United Nations Guide to the Global Compact: A Practical Understanding of the Vision and the Nine Principles*, p. 4 ('United Nations Guide to the Global Compact'). Online. Available HTTP: <http://www.cosco.com/en/pic/research/7573381391844063.pdf> (accessed 9 May 2012).

67 Towards Global Partnership (2009) GA Res 64/223, para. 13; Towards Global Partnership (2007) GA Res 62/211, para. 9.

68 Joint Inspection Unit, 'United Nations Corporate Partnerships: The Role and Functioning of the Global Compact' (2010), UN Doc. JIU/REP/2010/9, paras 13–18 and recommendation 1; and UN Global Compact Office, 'A response from the Global Compact Office', 2. Online. Available HTTP: <http://www.unglobalcompact.org/docs/news_events/9.1_news_archives/2011_03_24/gco_jiu_response.pdf> (accessed 7 January 2012).

69 For an overview of opinions on the Global Compact, see M. Shaughnessy, 'The United Nations Global Compact and the Continuing Debate about the Effectiveness of Corporate Voluntary Codes of Conduct', *Colorado Journal of International Environmental Law and Policy Yearbook*, 2000, 159–62; W.H. Meyer and S. Boyka, 'Human Rights, the UN Global Compact, and Global Governance', *Cornell International Law Journal* 34, 2001, 501–21.

70 Bruno and Karliner, op. cit.

71 F. Calder and M. Culverwell, *Following up the WSSD Commitments on Corporate Responsibility & Accountability*, London: Royal Institute of International Affairs, 2004, p. 37.

conditions, business enterprises are free to publicize their participation in the Global Compact.[72]

The UN qualifies it as a 'voluntary corporate citizenship initiative based on a learning approach',[73] thus highlighting its non-regulatory character: the initiative is therefore a platform designed to promote institutional learning, through transparency, dialogue with stakeholders and dissemination of best practices. The Global Compact makes it clear that it is not a substitute for effective action by governments, nor does it supplant other voluntary initiatives. It is further specified that it does not endorse the companies participating in the initiative.[74] Nonetheless, it has developed a procedure to handle 'credible allegations of systematic or egregious abuse of the Global Compact's overall aims and principles', with a view to safeguarding the reputation, integrity and good efforts of the initiative, as well as to promoting continuous quality improvement and assisting participants in aligning their actions with their commitments. Abuse in that connection includes 'severe environmental damage'.[75] Regrettably, information on the complaints dealt to date by the Global Compact is very limited[76] and does not allow for a more detailed discussion of its impact on corporate environmental abuse.

The most prominent feature of the Global Compact is the application of the precautionary approach to adhering companies,[77] which entails that businesses should take the most cost-effective, early action to prevent the occurrence of irreversible environmental damage.[78] To this end, companies are expected to carry out assessments of their environmental impacts and environmental risks, invest in sustainable production methods and research and develop environmentally friendly products.[79]

In addition, the Compact encourages businesses to undertake initiatives to promote greater environmental responsibility[80] through resource productivity, cleaner production, corporate governance and multi-stakeholder dialogue.[81] Finally, the Compact expects adhering companies to encourage the development and diffusion of environmentally friendly

72 D. Shelton, 'The Utility and Limits of Codes of Conduct for the Protection of the Environment', in A. Kiss, D. Shelton and K. Ishibashi (eds) *Economic Globalization and Compliance with International Environmental Agreements*, The Hague: Kluwer Law International, 2003, p. 216.

73 United Nations Guide to the Global Compact, op. cit., p. 4.

74 Ibid., 4.

75 UN Global Compact Office, *Frequently Asked Questions on the Integrity Measures*. Online. Available HTTP: <http://www.unglobalcompact.org/docs/news_events/9.1_news_archives/2009_08_21/Integrity_Measures.FAQ.pdf> (accessed 7 January 2012).

76 The lack of transparency concerning the complaint procedure was highlighted by the Joint Inspection Unit, op. cit., paras 70–3 and recommendation 6(d). See also 'A response from the Global Compact Office', op. cit., p. 5, where it is stressed that information on integrity cases is included in the Global Compact Annual Review (UN Global Compact Office, 2011, at 42) starting from the 2009 edition. The 2010 edition of the Annual Report, though, limits itself to report that '21 separate matters alleging abuses of the Ten Principles by business entities were raised with the Global Compact Office in 2010 [of which] 3 matters were handled under the Integrity Measures dialogue facilitation mechanism'. No additional information is provided, not even with reference to the specific principles that were alleged to be seriously violated by the company. (Similar information is provided in the 2009 review, p. 20.)

77 The Global Compact Principle, 7.

78 United Nations Guide to the Global Compact, op. cit., p. 52.

79 Ibid., p. 54.

80 Global Compact, Principle 8.

81 United Nations Guide to the Global Compact, op. cit., p. 58.

technologies.[82] These are defined in the *Guide* to the Compact by express reference to Agenda 21, including technologies that allow for limited pollution, protection of the environment, sustainable use of natural resources, and reduction or reuse of waste.[83]

Ultimately, the relevance of the UN Global Compact may be its underlying implication as to the direct applicability of principles of international environmental law to private enterprises.[84] Regrettably it is still unclear to what extent such an understanding finds concrete application through the Compact implementation and its 'allegations' procedure.

Human rights-based approach

In parallel with the launch of the Global Compact, the UN Sub-Commission on the Promotion and Protection of Human Rights, which was the 'think tank' of the former UN Commission on Human Rights (UNCHR), started work on corporate accountability with specific reference to transnational corporations.[85] These activities resulted in the preparation by the Sub-Commission of Norms on the Responsibility of Transnational Corporations and Other Business Enterprises with regards to Human Rights.[86]

The Norms[87] were drafted as a comprehensive 'restatement of international legal principles applicable to business',[88] covering human rights, labour law, humanitarian law, environmental and consumer protection and anti-corruption law. They purported to reflect, interpret and elaborate primarily upon legally binding treaties and non-binding guidelines adopted by the vast majority of states and international organizations. A commentator highlighted the 'hybrid nature' of the Norms – recommendations and clarification of states' obligations, and at the same time identification of the need to further develop direct corporate obligations.[89] The Norms asserted from the outset that the primary responsibility for human rights protection is that of national governments, and that companies are not requested to replace governments in such a task.[90] Whereas the Norms do not intend to create new obligations

---

82 Global Compact, Principle 9.

83 United Nations Guide to the Global Compact, op. cit., p. 64.

84 P. Utting, 'The Global Compact: Why All the Fuss?', *UN Chronicle* 40, 2003, 1.

85 On the relationship between Sub-Commission and the Commission in relation to the Norms, S. Walker's contribution in UNRISD, 'Corporate Social Responsibility and Development: Towards a New Agenda: Summaries of Presentations', Geneva, Switzerland, 17–18 November 2003, p. 83. The mandate of the Sub-Commission is detailed in 'The Work of the Sub-Commission on the Promotion and Protection of Human Rights' (2003), UNCHR Res 2003/59 and 'The work of the Sub-Commission on the Promotion and Protection of Human Rights' (2004), UNCHR Res 2004/60.

86 'UNCHR Sub-Commission on the Promotion and Protection of Human Rights, Norms on the Responsibilities of Transnational Corporations and Other Business Enterprises with regard to Human Rights' (2003), UN Doc E/CN.4/Sub.2/2003/12/Rev.2 (UN Norms). For a full account of the drafting of the Norms, see Weissbrodt and Kruger, op. cit., p. 904. Prof. Weissbrodt was one of the drafters of the Norms.

87 T. Rathgeber, 'UN Norms on the Responsibilities of Transnational Corporations', Friedrich-Ebert-Stiftung Occasional Geneva Papers n. 22, 2006, who claims that the Norms have a 'systemizing function' and are 'a benchmark for negotiations on a future standard.'

88 Weissbrodt and Kruger, op. cit., p. 327.

89 N. Rosemann, 'The UN Norms on Corporate Human Rights Responsibilities: An Innovating Instrument to Strengthen Business' Human Rights Performance', Friedrich-Ebert-Stiftung Occasional Geneva Papers n. 20, 2005.

90 UN Norms, para. A 'General Obligations'; Weissbrodt and Kruger, op. cit., p. 911.

Elisa Morgera

for governments in relation to human rights,[91] they intend to provide for an allocation of responsibility between governments and business.[92] In this light, the Norms require, at a minimum, that businesses refrain from activities that directly or indirectly violate human rights or benefit from human rights violations, and use due diligence in avoiding harm.[93]

Unlike the UN draft Code of Conduct, the Norms not only addressed MNCs, but also 'other' business enterprises. Generally, they were expected to be applied by all businesses. Unlike the Global Compact, however, which applies to all business companies regardless of their size, the Norms pay special attention to MNCs. They also refer to other business enterprises that, although not transnational in character, have relationships with MNCs, and have activities that produce delocalized impacts, or that involve violations of the right to security.[94] The Norms expressly acknowledge, however, that MNCs raise the greatest international concerns and are the least susceptible to national regulations, thus leading to a system of 'relative application'.[95]

The Sub-Commission's Norms provide the most detailed provisions on corporate environmental accountability with the imprimatur of the UN. The preamble highlights the obligation for MNCs and other business enterprises to respect 'generally recognised responsibility and norms contained in UN treaties and other international instruments'. Among these, reference was made, even in the earlier drafts, to the Convention on Civil Liability for Oil Pollution Damage and the Convention on Civil Liability for Damage Resulting from Activities Dangerous to the Environment,[96] which are two examples in international environmental law of civil liability of private business entities.[97] The 2003 version of the document[98] also includes reference to the Convention on Biological Diversity, the Rio Declaration, the WSSD Plan of Implementation and the Millennium Declaration.[99] The operational section on environmental protection of the Norms[100] is framed in obligatory terms and requires 'accordance with national laws, regulations, administrative practices and policies of the countries in which MNCs operate'. Most importantly, the same section also requires 'accordance with relevant international agreements, principles, objectives, responsibilities and standards' on the environment, human rights, public health, safety, bioethics and the precautionary principle. In addition, the activities of MNCs are

91 Weissbrodt and Kruger, op. cit., p. 912.
92 Ibid., 915; and Amnesty International, *The UN Human Rights Norms for Business: Towards Legal Accountability*, London: Amnesty International Publications, 2004, p. 7.
93 Amnesty International, op. cit., p. 8.
94 UN Norms, Section I 'Definitions', para. 21; C.F. Hillemanns, 'UN Norms on the Responsibility of Transnational Corporations and Other Business Enterprises with Regard to Human Rights', *German Law Journal* 4, 2003, 1065–80.
95 Weissbrodt and Kruger, op. cit., p. 910.
96 UNCHR Sub-Commission, 'Draft Universal Human Rights Guidelines for Companies' (2001), UN Doc E/CN.4/Sub.2/2001/WG.2/WP.1/Add.1; UNCHR Sub-Commission, 'Human Rights, Principles and Responsibilities for Transnational Corporations and Other Business Enterprises with Commentary on the Principles' (2002), UN Doc E/CN.4/Sub.2/2002/XX/Add.2.
97 Convention on Civil Liability for Nuclear Damage, opened for signature 29 May 1963, 1063 UNTS 265 (entered into force 12 November 1977), Arts I(1)(k) and II(1); International Convention on Civil Liability for Oil Pollution Damage, opened for signature 29 November 1969, 973 UNTS 3 (entered into force 19 June 1975), Arts II and III(1).
98 UN Norms, Preamble.
99 Millennium Declaration (2000), GA Res 55/2.
100 UN Norms, Section G, para. 14.

200

expected to be conducted 'in a manner contributing to the wider goal of sustainable development'.[101]

The Commentary to the Norms greatly expands on these standards, first of all by calling for the respect of the right to a clean and healthy environment, respect of the concerns for intergenerational equity, and respect of 'internationally recognized *standards*' on air and water pollution, land use, biodiversity and hazardous waste.[102] Secondly, the Commentary underscores the expectation that companies assume responsibility for the environmental and human health impacts of all their activities. Thirdly, business enterprises are expected to assess the environmental impacts of their activities on a periodic basis, in order to ensure that the burden of the negative environmental consequences does not fall on vulnerable racial, ethnic and socio-economic groups. The reports of such assessments are to be circulated in a timely and accessible manner to the UN Environment Programme and other international bodies, to the national governments of the host and home countries, and to other affected groups. In addition, the reports should be accessible to the general public.[103] Fourthly, companies are to respect the prevention and precautionary principles, and to take appropriate steps to reduce the risk of accidents and damage to the environment, by adopting best management practices and technologies.[104] Finally, the Commentary points to the obligation to ensure effective means of collecting the remains of products or services for recycling, reuse or other environmentally responsible disposal.[105]

The Norms became very controversial: they enjoyed a level of expert legitimacy based on the adoption by the Sub-Commission, but lacked political legitimization, which could have derived from their adoption by the Commission.[106] Instead, the Commission only 'took note' of the Norms[107] and underlined that they had 'not been requested by the Commission and, as a draft proposal, had no legal standing, and that the Sub-Commission should not perform any monitoring function in this regard'.[108] Therefore, the Norms remain a document representing the opinion of experts but lacking the political endorsement of states.

With a view to continuing the debate on a human rights-based approach to MNCs following the rejection of the UN Norms, the UNCHR in April 2005 requested the UN Secretary-General to appoint a Special Representative with the mandate to identify and clarify standards of corporate responsibility and accountability for MNCs and other business; elaborate on the role of states in effectively regulating and adjudicating on the role of MNCs, including through international cooperation; develop methodologies for human rights impact assessment of activities of MNCs and other business; and compile a compendium of best practices of states, MNCs and other businesses.[109]

---

101 Ibid., para. 14.
102 Ibid., Section G, Commentary, para. (a) (emphasis added).
103 Ibid., paras (b) and (c).
104 Ibid., paras (e) and (g).
105 Ibid., para. (f).
106 Walker's contribution in UNRISD, op. cit., p. 85.
107 Responsibilities of Transnational Corporations and Related Business Enterprises with Regard to Human Rights (2004), UNCHR Decision 2004/116.
108 Ibid., para. C. This is particularly significant as the Sub-Commission has instead proposed the creation of an initial implementation procedure for the Norms through the Sub-Commission's consideration of information from NGOs, business and individuals: Weissbrodt and Kruger, op. cit.
109 Human Rights and Transnational Corporations and Other Business Enterprises (2005), UNCHR Res 2005/69.

John Ruggie, appointed by the UN Secretary-General as the UN Special Representative on Business and Human Rights, produced the *UN Framework on Business and Human Rights*,[110] which received intergovernmental support.[111] The Framework emerged from the rejection of the idea that there are direct legal obligations under international law for companies, and the support for international standards that are in 'the process of being socially constructed'[112] in the face of the 'fluidity' in the applicability of international legal principles to companies' acts.[113] The Special Representative thus pointed to 'standards' governing corporate 'responsibility' – understood as the legal, social or moral obligations imposed on companies – and on corporate 'accountability' – understood as the mechanisms to hold companies to their obligations.[114] Ruggie emphasized that corporations are under growing scrutiny by international human rights mechanisms and have been the object of the standard-setting, and accountability mechanisms created by international organizations, in light of 'social expectations by States and other actors'.[115] Such practice was seen as 'blurring the lines between strictly voluntary, and mandatory' and recognizing the need to 'exercise shared responsibility'.[116] As a result, the Representative put forward a framework built on three pillars ('Protect, Respect and Remedy'), namely: the state duty to protect against human rights abuses by business; the corporate responsibility to respect human rights; and the need for greater access to effective remedies. The second pillar consists of the prevailing societal expectation that companies 'do no harm' and exercise 'due diligence', as the 'process whereby companies not only ensure compliance with national laws but also manage the risk of human rights harm with a view to avoiding it', based on reasonable expectations.[117]

While the Special Representative stressed the importance for the Framework of international policy coherence,[118] particularly with specific regard to 'prevailing social norms . . . that have acquired near-universal recognition by all stakeholders',[119] there was, however, no clear attempt to seek or acknowledge synergies between the UN Framework and relevant widely ratified international environmental agreements. This is particularly troubling in the

---

110 'Report of the Special Representative of the Secretary-General on the issue of Human Rights and Transnational Corporations and Other Business Enterprises, Protect, Respect and Remedy: A Framework for Business and Human Rights' (2008), UN Doc A/HRC/8/35 ('UN Framework').
111 'Mandate of the Special Representative of the Secretary- General on the Issue of human rights and transnational corporations and other business enterprises' (2008), HRC Res 8/7.
112 'Interim Report of the Special Representative of the Secretary-General on the Issue of Human Rights and Transnational Corporations and other Business Enterprises' (2006), UN Doc E/CN.4/2006/97, para. 55.
113 Ibid., para. 64.
114 'Report of the Special Representative of the Secretary-General on the Issue of Human Rights and Transnational Corporations and Other Business Enterprises: Mapping International Standards of Responsibility and Accountability for Corporate Acts' (2007), UN Doc A/HRC/4/35, para. 6.
115 Ibid., paras 44–6.
116 Ibid., paras 61–2.
117 HRC, 'Report of the Special Representative of the Secretary-General on the Issue of Human Rights and Transnational Corporations and Other Business Enterprises: Protect, Respect and Remedy: A Framework for Business and Human Rights' (2008), UN Doc A/HRC/8/35, paras 25 and 58.
118 UN Framework, para. 52.
119 Ibid., p. 13.

specific case of natural resource exploitation,[120] which is an area in which serious corporate abuses of human rights have been documented, and departs from all other international initiatives examined above. Nonetheless, the Special Representative developed the procedural aspect of his proposed human rights due diligence process on concepts and approaches[121] that have been developed and experimented with in the environmental sphere, notably environmental impact assessment, stakeholder involvement in environmental decision-making and life-cycle environmental management.[122]

In 2011, the Special Representative adopted Guiding Principles to implement the UN Framework, which received intergovernmental endorsement, in order to clarify that there is a 'global standard of expected conduct for all business enterprises wherever they operate', independent of states' ability and willingness to fulfil their human rights obligations. Such a global standard is seen to operate 'over and above compliance with national laws and regulations protecting human rights', basically requiring business entities to take adequate measures to prevent, mitigate and remedy adverse human rights impacts.[123] The Guidelines further clarify that the human rights due diligence process entails periodically assessing actual and potential impacts with 'meaningful consultations' with potentially affected groups and other stakeholders; integrating the assessment findings in internal decision-making budget allocation and oversight processes; acting upon those findings; tracking responses (including by drawing on feedback from affected stakeholders); and communicating how impacts are addressed to right-holders in a manner that is sufficient for stakeholders to evaluate the adequacy of the company's response.[124] Companies are expected to prioritize the prevention and mitigation of most severe impacts or those that a delayed response would make irremediable.[125] Finally, enterprises 'should establish or participate in' legitimate, transparent, predictable, equitable and right-compatible grievance mechanisms that are directly accessible to individuals and communities that may be directly impacted by their business operations. These grievance mechanisms are expected both to support the identification of adverse impacts and systematic problems, and remedy adverse impacts.[126] The Guiding Principles, therefore, continue the self-referential trend of the UN Framework, with no

---

120 The UN Representative indicated that the scope of corporate responsibility to respect human rights is defined by the actual and potential human rights impacts generated by business, which can be identified on the basis of an authoritative list of international recognized rights including the 'International Bill of Rights', relevant conventions of the International Labour Organization and also depending on circumstances human rights instruments concerning specifically indigenous peoples and other vulnerable groups: 'Report of the Special Representative of the Secretary-General on the Issue of Human Rights and Transnational Corporations and Other Business Enterprises, Business and Human Rights: Towards Operationalizing the "Protect, Respect and Remedy" Framework' (2009), UN Doc. A/HRC/11/13, p. 15.

121 Ibid., p. 14.

122 E. Morgera, (2010) 'Expert Report Corporate Responsibility to Respect Human Rights in the Environmental Sphere', European Commission-funded project, p. 12, University of Edinburgh. Online. Available HTTP: <http://www.law.ed.ac.uk/euenterpriseslf/documents/files/CSREnvironment.pdf> (accessed 28 December 2011).

123 UN Special Representative on Human Rights and Business Enterprises, 'Guiding Principles on Business and Human Rights to Implement the UN Protect, Respect and Remedy Framework' (2011), UN Doc A/HRC/17/31, para. 11; 'Human rights and transnational corporations and other business enterprises' (2011), HRC Res 17/4.

124 'Guiding Principles on Business and Human Rights', paras 17–21.

125 Ibid., para. 24.

126 Ibid., paras 29, 31.

specific reference to the relevance of multilateral environmental agreements or principles of international environmental law.

Conclusion

Even if international environmental law does not impose legally binding obligations directly on MNCs, minimum international standards are emerging that may be legitimately expected to be respected by private companies even in the absence of national laws to that effect. These standards have already reached a significant level of detail and international acceptance, regardless of the approach taken (regulation, partnership, human rights-based approach).

These standards include the environmental impact self-assessment as the ongoing assessment, beyond legal requirements at the national level, of the possible environmental impacts of private companies' activities before and during their operations, on the basis of scientific evidence and communication with likely-to-be-affected communities. As a result of such continuous assessment, private companies are further to elaborate environmental management systems to assist in controlling direct and indirect impacts on the environment and possibly to continually improve their environmental performance. In accordance with their environmental impact assessments and management systems, private companies are further reasonably expected to take active steps, including the suspension of certain activities, to prevent or minimize environmental damage, particularly in cases of likely transboundary environmental harm or environmental harm with serious human rights consequences. In addition, in the face of scientific uncertainty, private companies are further expected to undertake precautionary action by taking the most cost-effective early action to prevent the occurrence of environmental harm, or avoiding delays in preventing or minimizing such harm. Disclosure of public information, direct consultations with the public and the creation of a review or appeal process for communities to express their complaints are further complementary and mutually reinforcing procedural standards. Although less convergence has been seen in the identification of substantive standards, the 2011 review of the OECD Guidelines reveals increased focus on climate change, biodiversity and efficient resource use.[127] These concepts are also incorporated and expanded upon in the Performance Standards of the World Bank's International Finance Corporate (IFC),[128] which identify the responsibility of the private sector on the basis of international environmental agreements,[129] and have been widely followed by regional development banks as well as major commercial banks.[130]

In conclusion, these international instruments and initiatives have provided an initial 'translation' of inter-state obligations contained in international environmental law into practical guidelines for the conduct of MNCs and of the private sector more generally. As

---

127 Morgera, 'From Corporate Social Responsibility', op. cit.
128 IFC, 'Performance Standards on Social and Environmental Sustainability', adopted by the IFC Board in 2011, with implementation starting on 1 January 2012. Online. Available HTTP: <http://www.ifc.org/ifcext/policyreview.nsf/Content/2012-Edition#PerformanceStandards> (accessed 30 April 2012).
129 For a more in-depth discussion, see Morgera, *Corporate Accountability*, op. cit., ch. 7.
130 C. Wright, 'Setting Standards for Responsible Banking: Examining the Role of the International Finance Corporation in the Emergence of the Equator Principles', in F. Biermann, B. Siebenhüner and A. Schreyrögg (eds) *International Organizations in Global Environmental Governance*, Abingdon: Routledge, 2009.

such, they can be used as benchmarks to assess the conduct of MNCs. Existing international efforts to monitor corporate environmental accountability have on this basis called upon MNCs to respect multilateral environmental agreements and even voluntary guidelines adopted by the governing bodies of these agreements, although relevant international practice is still evolving.[131]

---

131 Morgera, 'From Corporate Social Responsibility', op. cit.

Part III

Key issues and legal frameworks

12
Biological diversity

Chidi Oguamanam

This chapter situates the concept of biological diversity within the corpus of international environmental law. It briefly explores the evolution of global environmental consciousness toward the protection of biological diversity which crystallised in the '1992 Rio Package' of international environmental instruments, most notably the Convention on Biological Diversity (CBD). It identifies key international, regional and other relevant levels of regulatory instruments and initiatives at the core and periphery of the CBD framework that shape the subject of conservation of biological diversity. It concludes by reflecting on the mutually re-enforcing nature of the environment, especially biodiversity conservation, with developmental imperatives.

Introduction

The accuracy and meaning of 'international environmental law' (IEL), its actual legal status and basic undergirding principles remain contentious.[1] Indeed, on a broad conceptual plane, both the 'environment' and 'international law' are hardly candidates for legal or definitional precision. The same can be said of the concept of biological diversity (biodiversity), which is pivotal to any serious discourse on the environment. The conceptual affinity between 'bio-diversity' and 'the environment' makes the former a critical touchstone for an integrated discourse of contemporary environmental issues at both policy and philosophical levels. In this chapter, the notion of biodiversity is located within the corpus of IEL, and a brief ecological and economic analysis of biodiversity is provided while highlighting relevant key biodiversity conservation instruments as pivotal components of IEL.

To understand the concept of biodiversity, a few considerations that have shaped its integration and elaboration within the corpus of IEL warrant highlighting upfront. First, even though biodiversity assumes an important and seemingly independent space, it is an integral part of IEL's engagement with natural resources. Second, the emphasis on biodiversity relates to living organisms or the 'biosphere'. Practically, however, it is impossible to separate those

---

1 See P. Birnie, A. Boyle and C. Redgwell, *International Law and the Environment*, 3rd edition, Oxford: Oxford University Press, 2009, p. 2.

from non-living structural, geographic and geologic features of the environment that often constitute the natural habitats for complex biotic networks and interactions that support biodiversity. Third, the isolation of biodiversity from the broader environment framework serves a convenient purpose only and is not sustainable for the most part. Fourth, there are a number of factors that have led to the prominence which biodiversity currently enjoys,[2] as well as the tensions associated with it, including:

(a) the unprecedented decline of global biological diversity;
(b) the historic demand for biological resources in the wake of modern biotechnology;
(c) the natural concentration of biodiversity and biological resources in the tropical regions of the globe, which are the home of many of the world's indigenous and local communities, and developing countries of the South;
(d) the pre-eminence and concentration in the North or industrialised countries of the Research and Development (R&D), technology, capital and legal schemes for the exploitation of biological resources;
(e) disparate epistemological approaches between Western nations, and the inchoate categories of non-Western or indigenous or local communities, in regard to differing perspectives on environmental ethics.

Finally, the subject of biodiversity conservation is a site for practical translation and exploration of the basic principles which scholars and policy-makers associate with IEL. It is hardly surprising, therefore, that even though biodiversity is conceptually a subset of the complex mass of issue areas within the ambit of IEL, it provides an important context for an appraisal or general overview of the latter's complex and indeterminate scope.

What is biodiversity?

Biological diversity is a novel phrase credited to American scientists, perhaps as recently as 1987.[3] Specifically, Harvard biologist Edward O. Wilson credits Walter G. Rosen for introducing the term,[4] which has since been co-opted by scientists, conservationists, lawyers and environmental policy bureaucrats. Despite finding favour with policy-makers and stakeholders, the meaning and definition of biodiversity is not quite settled. First, biodiversity is not a synonym for natural or biological resources, even if it is inseparable from them. Second, unlike biological resources which are tangible, biodiversity is essentially an intangible phenomenon which is better appreciated as a conceptual abstraction. Along these lines Birnie, Boyle and Redgwell counsel that biodiversity 'is not, as often wrongly assumed, the sum of all ecosystems, species and genetic materials'.[5] They endorse the International Union for Conservation of Nature and Natural Resources (IUCN) observation that, in a way, biodiversity is 'an attribute of life, in contrast to "biological resources" which are tangible biotic

---

2 In 2007, the United Nations declared 2010 the International Year of Biodiversity. See UNGA Res A/Res/61/203, 19 January 2007; see also CBD website: Online. Available HTTP: <www.cbd. int/2010> (accessed 8 March 2012).
3 C. Oguamanam, *International Law and Indigenous Knowledge: Intellectual Property, Plant Biodiversity, and Traditional Medicine*, Toronto: University of Toronto Press, 2006, p. 36.
4 Ibid., note 2.
5 Birnie et al., op. cit., p. 588.

components of ecosystems'.[6] Similarly, Paul Wood makes a case for distinguishing the concept of biodiversity from biological resources, and notes that one is the source of the other.[7] Because biodiversity is a conceptual abstraction, it is not amenable to ownership or necessarily limited to national or political boundaries in the sense applicable to specific biological resources.

For the foregoing reasons, it can be argued that biodiversity is a concept more in need of explanation than definition. Most definitions of biodiversity neither underscore the conceptual morass inherent in the concept nor highlight its abstracted nature. For example, the symbiotic relationship between biodiversity and biological resources is not an issue that is readily captured by even the most conventional definitions of biodiversity. For instance, Birnie, Boyle and Redgwell define biodiversity as 'the variability of life in all its forms, levels and combinations'.[8] Other authoritative definitions of biodiversity do not reflect any radical departure from this framework.

According to Jeffrey McNeeley, biodiversity:

> encompasses all species of plants, animals, and microorganisms and the ecosystems and ecological processes of which they are parts. It is an umbrella term for the degree of nature's variety . . . usually considered at three different levels: genetic diversity, species diversity and ecosystem diversity.[9]

Elsewhere, it has been noted that, as an umbrella term, 'biodiversity includes every interaction that obtains within and between life forms [and that] those interactions can be abstracted and/or empirical'.[10] Lastly, the Convention on Biological Diversity (CBD) defines its subject matter as 'the variability among living organisms from *all* sources including, *inter alia*, terrestrial, marine and other aquatic ecosystems and the ecological complexes of which they are part; this includes diversity within species, between species and of ecosystems'.[11]

From these definitions, we can surmise that biodiversity is a conceptual way of depicting diversity as a core attribute of life on Earth in its complex ecological domains, including their natural regenerative processes. However, biodiversity cannot be treated in isolation both in terms of its complex nature but also in relation to its impact and practical translation to broader environmental considerations. In this sense the line between biodiversity and bioresources is blurred.

Ensuring ecosystem diversity and species diversity (to mention but two aspects) is the primary preoccupation of biodiversity conservation and critical to sustaining life forms which in turn represent biological resources. According to the CBD, the latter include 'genetic resources, organisms or parts thereof, populations, or any other biotic component of ecosystems with actual or potential use or value for humanity'.[12]

---

6 Ibid.
7 P.M. Wood, *Biodiversity and Democracy: Re-Thinking Society and Nature*, Vancouver: UBC Press, 2000, p. 37.
8 Birnie et al., op. cit., p. 588.
9 J.A. McNeely, *Conserving the World's Biological Diversity*, Washington DC: IUCN, 1990, p. 17.
10 Oguamanam, op. cit., p. 37.
11 *United Nations Convention on Biological Diversity*, opened for signature 5 June 1992, 30619 UNTS (entered into force 29 December 1993) Art. 2 [emphasis added].
12 Ibid.

Humanity has a vested interest in the state of the world's biological diversity, due to our dependence on nature. Paul Wood puts it more aptly when he observes that 'biodiversity is the *source* of bioresources, and therein lies its value to humanity'.[13] So, the imperative for the conservation of biodiversity issues from both intrinsic and anthropocentric considerations. In regard to the latter, humanity's dependence on biological resources easily provides the warrant for conservation of biological diversity.

Conservation of biodiversity

The use of the word 'conservation' is commonplace in international environmental instruments. However, for the most part, there is no deliberate attempt to associate references to conservation with specific technical or scientific meanings. In this ambiguous state, the meaning to be ascribed to a treaty's use of conservation can be glimpsed or 'implied from the nature of the measures presented to achieve the aims of conservation expressed in the preamble or substantive articles'.[14]

The issue of conservation arises mostly against the backdrop of concerns regarding species endangerment and sustainability for human-driven utilitarian objectives. Consequently, key aspects of the use of the term in many international environmental instruments include its association with or moderation by anthropocentric objectives: sustainability, economic, social and development considerations. For example, the 1980 World Conservation Strategy (WCS) defines conservation as 'the management of human use of the biosphere so that it may yield the greatest sustainable benefit to current generations while maintaining its ability to meet the needs and aspirations of the future generations'. It further claims that 'conservation, like development is for people'.[15] Similarly, the 1980 Convention on the Conservation of Antarctic Marine Living Resources (CCAMLR) depicts conservation principles in the form of 'prevention of decrease in the size of any harvested population to levels below those which ensure its stable recruitment' or, alternatively as 'aggregate of the measure rendering possible the optimum sustainable yield . . .'.[16]

Despite an expanded scientific outlook on conservation, a fixation on anthropocentric, social, economic and developmental objectives remains the driving motivation for conservation. The ensuing understanding and application of conservation strategies has largely failed to recognise that even in the context of an ordinary meaning of conservation, 'a higher standard of care is necessary to fulfil conservation objectives than is actually required by existing conventions',[17] including, of course, the CBD.

The CBD was concluded well after the IUCN's 1980 landmark WCS,[18] as well as other antecedent instruments (discussed below) that elaborated on a more expansive vision of conservation. The IUCN document earned significant recognition among credible members

---

13 Wood, op. cit., p. 37 (emphasis in the original).
14 Birnie et al., op. cit., pp. 588–9.
15 IUCN, UNEP and WWF, *World Conservation Strategy: Living Resource Conservation for Sustainable Development*, Gland: International Union for Conservation of Nature and Natural Resources, 1980, chapter 1, paras 4, 5 and 7.
16 *Convention on the Conservation of Antarctic Marine Living Resources*, Art. 3(a). Online. Available HTTP: <www.ccamlr.org/pu/e/e_pubs/bd/pt1.pdf> (accessed 8 March 2012); see also Birnie et al., op. cit., p. 589.
17 Ibid.
18 IUCN, UNEP and WWF, *World Conservation Strategy*.

of the global environment advocacy community. It has since 'evolved to take account of the developmental implications of environmental measures within the context of sustainable development advocated in the Rio Declaration, Agenda 21 and related instruments'.[19] In the words of one analyst, the WCS is hailed as incorporating the ' "classic" elements of protection and preservation, including restoration and the safeguarding of ecological processes and genetic diversity besides management of natural resources in order to sustain their maintenance by sustainable utilization'.[20] However, the CBD completely eschews reference to preservation as a component of its conservation strategy while embracing oblique references to 'conservation' and 'sustainable use'[21] and emphasising 'fair and equitable sharing of the benefits arising out of the utilization of genetic resources'.[22]

It may be argued that the CBD is a framework regime negotiated under very contentious circumstances that required high profile compromises. As such, the CBD's approach to conservation may be better gleaned not necessarily from its preambles or text but perhaps from the measures adopted under its programmes of work, resulting protocol(s) and decisions of its Conference of the Parties (COP) on specific subject areas pursuant to the Convention's overall objectives. However, on this consideration, the CBD's focus on the use of a market economic approach to advance or incentivise conservation does not buttress the foregoing alibi. Another downside is the obvious and unmistakeable language of the CBD text which makes reference to economic, sustainable human use and overall development objectives as the primary *raison d'être* for biodiversity conservation.[23]

In sum, the CBD adopts a narrow instrumentalist approach to conservation which falls short of a higher standard in which conservation measures transcend human- and economic-driven objectives. Therefore, as in the majority of international environmental instruments, the CBD does not provide a clear outlook on conservation. Rather, its conservation strategy is primarily a management concept that it may be inclined to adopt under its implementation programmes. For example, pursuant to the 1995 Jakarta Mandate on the Conservation and Sustainable Use of Marine and Coastal Biodiversity, the CBD established a programme of work on marine and coastal biodiversity. One of the programme's five elements includes the encouragement of a coordinated national, regional and global approach to marine and coastal protected areas. This is an indication that the Convention has the capacity, albeit peripherally, to accommodate a higher standard of preservation measures within its 'conservation' strategy. Generally, however, the CBD's approach to conservation is inchoate and falls short of higher standards. Its principal focus is on economic and human-centred objectives for biodiversity conservation. The next section highlights the ecological and economic significance of biodiversity.

Ecological and economic significance of biodiversity

Biodiversity is a touchstone for appraising the complex, interrelated and, perhaps more appropriately, the holistic nature of environmental issues. For example, industrial and other

---

19 Birnie et al., op. cit., p. 590.
20 V. Heijnsbergen, *International Legal Protection of Wild Fauna and Flora*, Amsterdam: IOS Press, 1997 (cited in Birnie et al., op. cit.).
21 Ibid.
22 *United Nations Convention on Biological Diversity*, Art. 1.
23 See e.g. *United Nations Convention on Biological Diversity*, Arts 2 (definition), 8(j), 11, 12, 15 19, 20.

forms of pollution, climate change or global warming, ozone layer depletion, forest fires, oil spills, industrial agriculture, deforestation, habitat destruction, mass migration, overconsumption and a host of other specific environmental threats that occupy current environmental law and policy have direct ramifications for biodiversity.

This raises a number of points. First, biodiversity has a symbiotic relationship with the ecosystem. The CBD identifies principal ecosystems or ecological sites that are the sources of biodiversity to include 'terrestrial, marine, and other aquatic ecosystems'.[24] Within these broad systems we can identify other more specific or endemic ecological categories such as island, desert, forest, polar and other climatic-driven or geographical characteristics that demarcate ecological profiles. Further, within the broad range of terrestrial and marine ecosystems, for example, we can also distinguish species – animals, plants and micro-organisms – some of which inhabit either land or water and others both.

Second, human economic activities, especially in regard to the direct exploitation of biological resources, and other miscellaneous development endeavours, are critical to the distortion of ecological balance with its consequential impact on biodiversity. Biological resources, and the biodiversity that sustains them within a given ecological setting, drive a significant aspect of human economic activities. Ironically, however, those economic activities constitute a threat to biodiversity. Thus, perhaps no single environmental concept other than biodiversity provides a more convenient and logical understanding of the tension between environment and development and the imperative for sustainability. Whereas bioresources and, by extension, biodiversity are important to human economic and developmental endeavours, the sustainability of such endeavours is largely dependent on adopting a sustainable approach to biodiversity. In a way, in the realm of biodiversity, the often conflicted nature of the relationship between environment and development takes a mutually supportive or symbiotic turn.

Third, the focus of biodiversity is on living biotic components of ecosystems. The latter support the diversity of life on Earth as complex vital resources with great economic ramifications. Nonetheless, such a depiction of biodiversity does not reflect ecological accuracy. Rather, biodiversity and, by extension, biological resources, transcends the discrete mass of exploitable resources of the biosphere, but perhaps more importantly, it incorporates integrated but yet overlapping ecosystems, which include non-living elements of the environment such as lands, oceans and mountains, and diverse categories of natural resources on which they depend. Understood in this fashion, biodiversity, bioresources and their components do not exist in isolation. Hence, they are explored more appropriately as subject matters at the overlapping intersection of nature conservation, natural resources law and environmental law.

The ideological bases for biodiversity conservation and, more broadly, environmental protection draw from economic/instrumentalist and intrinsic rationales. By some accounts, intrinsic or value-oriented considerations are peripheral and of more recent origin. While that may be partly true, an intrinsic value-based approach to environmental protection is not necessarily of novel origin. In many indigenous, non-Western or traditional communities, the idea of intrinsic value in regard to the environment enjoys pre-eminence. In such societies, there are higher considerations for biodiversity conservation or environmental

---

24 *United Nations Convention on Biological Diversity*, Art. 2.

protection that transcend anthropocentric or economic logic.[25] Despite this recognition, economic/instrumentalist considerations and their inherent anthropocentricism remain the predominantly shared ethical system for biodiversity conservation.

Global biodiversity crisis in historical context

From an exclusively scientific narrative, within the Earth's four-billion-year history, the evolution of biodiversity is owed essentially to oxidisation of the atmosphere. An oxygen-rich atmosphere and various complex geological processes combined to shape the character and nature of life forms. From the early onset of life on Earth, speciation and diversity have remained progressive and dynamic evolutionary features of the planet. The occasional interruption of ecological processes by natural occurrences and consequential changes in the pattern of speciation and biodiversity is a normal feature of the evolutionary process of life forms. This phenomenon demonstrates the Earth's natural ability to maintain its carrying capacity and overall ecological balance.

In the current epoch, the Earth has witnessed perhaps the greatest threat to global biodiversity in the form of human-driven interventions. Although not solely culpable, 'humanity's contribution to upsetting global ecological balance remains the most far-reaching'.[26] Since the late twentieth century, the alarming decline of global biodiversity has arisen from a combination of factors, including rapid human population growth; aggressive construction/developmental initiatives and industrial agriculture; unsustainable settlement programmes; changes in migration demographics; environmental pollution; unprecedented generation of industrial waste; increased volume of trade and consumption patterns; and demand for endangered or exotic species. These phenomena have attracted the attention of policy-makers, warranting the proactive inclusion of concerns about biodiversity loss, and other environmental issues of our time such as global warming and climate change, into the corpus of IEL.

Several scientific studies and diverse surveys of global biodiversity paint a very bleak picture.[27] In contrast to the impact of natural occurrences on the state of global biodiversity, anthropogenic impacts do not come with the assurance of Earth's natural capacity for self-regeneration. Put differently, 'the current global biodiversity crisis appears to undermine nature's regenerative capacity'.[28] Summing up the state of global biodiversity, Jeffrey McNeely and Peter Raven note that 'we are confronting an episode of species extinction [greater] than anything that the world has experienced in the past 65 million years'.[29]

Geo-political dynamic of biodiversity

Collective consciousness over the state of global biodiversity coincides with the period of unprecedented scientific and industrial advancements in biotechnology. The latter loosely

---

25 See, generally, M. Battiste and J. Henderson, *Protecting Indigenous Knowledge and Heritage: A Global Challenge*, Saskatoon: Purich, 2000.
26 Oguamanam, op. cit., p .41.
27 See e.g. *Global Biodiversity Outlook 3*: Online. Available HTTP: <http://www.cbd.int/gbo3/> (accessed 8 March 2012).
28 Oguamanam, op. cit., p. 41.
29 P.H. Raven and J.A. McNeely, 'Biological Extinction: Its Scope and Meaning for Us', in L.D. Guruswamy and J.A. McNeely, *Protection of Global Biodiversity: Converging Strategies*, Durham: Duke University Press, 1988, p. 13.

refers to diverse techniques for manipulating the genetic materials of living organisms and for exploring the complex chemistry of biological systems for food and agriculture, medicine and therapeutics and for other complex indeterminate ends.[30] Biological resources, and, by extension, biodiversity is the mainstay of biotechnology. By some accounts, over 70 per cent of global biological resources are found in mega-biodiverse hotspots of the world which happen to be the home of many indigenous and local communities.[31] However, in the global power equation, the technological and legal infrastructure for harnessing the benefits of biotechnology resides in the developed countries of the global north and the centres of global finance capital.

A number of reasons, particularly ecological factors, account for the uneven concentration of global biodiversity in tropical areas in the south in contrast to the more temperate north.[32] Centres of biodiversity are also often centres of cultural, linguistic and epistemic diversity. Because of their natural dependence on genetic and biological resources endemic to their traditional homelands, indigenous and local communities are naturally rich in traditional or local knowledge systems. Dealings with biological resources through biotechnology and various industrial applications implicate the issue of access to and insight into the knowledge of indigenous and local communities.[33] Thus, biotechnology implicates a complex issue linkage in regard to ownership, control, appropriation (or misappropriation), access to and benefit-sharing of biological resources and associated local knowledge.[34]

Also, biotechnology and indigenous bio-cultural knowledge represent dual sites for the interplay of competing environmental philosophical outlooks. Essentially, biotechnology is an industrial process for dealing with genetic resources within the broad capitalist market economic framework. On the other hand, traditional bio-cultural knowledge of indigenous and local communities is first and foremost a socio-cultural process of knowledge production and dissemination which, for the most part, happens within a communal framework. It is also an integral part of a people's philosophical engagement with and understanding of their environment and ecological worldviews.[35] The diverging orientation between global industrial

---

30 M.J. Fecenko, *Biotechnology Law: Corporate-Commercial Practice*, Toronto: Butterworths, 2002, pp. 6–7; C. Oguamanam, 'Agro-Biodiversity and Food Security: Biotechnology and Traditional Agricultural Practices at the Periphery of International Intellectual Property Regime Complex', *Michigan State Law Review* 215, 2007, 222; C. Oguamanam, 'Canada: Time to Take Access and Benefit Sharing Over Genetic Resources Seriously', *University of New Brunswick Law Journal* 60, 2010, 139.

31 Oguamanam, *International Law and Indigenous Knowledge*, op. cit.

32 See McNeely, op. cit., p. 4.

33 E. Arezzo, 'Struggling Around the Natural Divide: The Protection of Tangible and Intangible Indigenous Property', *Cardozo Arts & Entertainment Law Journal* 25, 2007, 371; W. Weeraworawit, 'Formulating an International Legal Protection for Genetic Resources, Traditional Knowledge and Folklore: Challenges of the Intellectual Property System', *Cardozo Journal of International and Comparative Law* 11, 2003, 769; Oguamanam, 'Regime Complex'; G. Martin and S. Vermeylen, 'Intellectual Property, Indigenous Knowledge and Biodiversity', *Capitalism, Nature, Socialism* 26, 2005, 27.

34 N. Zerbe, 'Biodiversity, Ownership, and Indigenous Knowledge: Exploring Legal Frameworks for Community, Farmers, and Intellectual Property Rights in Africa', *Ecological Economics* 53, 2005, 493; I. Mgbeoji, 'Patents and Traditional Knowledge of Uses of Plants: Is a Communal Patent Regime Part of the Solution to the Scourge of Biopiracy?' *Indiana Journal of Global Legal Studies* 9, 2001, 163; P. Drahos, 'Indigenous Knowledge, Intellectual Property and Biopiracy: Is a Global Bio-collecting Society the Answer', *European Intellectual Property Law Review* 22, 2000, 245.

35 D.A. Posey, *Cultural and Spiritual Values of Biodiversity*, Nairobi: United Nations Environment Programme, 1999.

proprietors of biotechnology and custodians of traditional bio-cultural knowledge has implications for fashioning an overall approach to biodiversity conservation. This is part of the reason access and benefit-sharing (ABS) is now an important aspect of the biodiversity conservation law and policy lexicon.

Because of the converging nature of knowledge systems in the global knowledge economy, biodiversity and related conservation strategies are a site for engagement between modern biotechnologies with traditional bio-cultural knowledge.[36] The notion that earlier and present-day traditional societies are purely resource-based is fast losing credibility. As Graham Dutfield has rightly noted, 'there is a growing recognition that traditional knowledge technologies are not just old, obsolete and maladaptive; they can be highly evolutionary, adaptive, creative and even novel.'[37] In the realm of biotechnology, the traffic or exchange of information between formal science and traditional knowledge or insight regarding genetic resources has brought novel phenomena such as biopiracy to the fore.[38] Also, this form of knowledge convergence has tasked intellectual property jurisprudence with demands for equity in the allocation of benefits.

In sum, the extreme and troubling crisis of global biodiversity loss, the rise in biotechnology, and the latter's status as an integral part of the convergence in knowledge systems dealing with biological or genetic resources constitute major factors that have shaped the recent international legal and policy response toward the conservation of biodiversity. Consequently, that response provides the premise for the full incorporation of biodiversity conservation into the framework of IEL. The principal instrument for a holistic approach to biodiversity conservation is the 1992 CBD.

Emergence of biodiversity conservation in IEL

Before the CBD, there was no unified ecosystem or holistic approach to biodiversity conservation. Instead, national and international conservation initiatives followed a pattern of ad hoc species-specific approaches to what may be called in today's diction, biodiversity conservation. For the most part, in early initiatives '[l]iving species were not treated very differently from other sources such as minerals . . . [until lately they have been] included within the general description of natural resources'.[39] Consequently, as in the contemporary approach, early legal instruments covered an open-ended scope of diversity in terms of species and ecosystems including animal, plant, terrestrial, marine and other aquatic ecosystems and their 'biotic components'.

In addition to the lack of a holistic ecosystem approach to biodiversity conservation, early instruments tended to be driven by trade-based priorities. They linked the prevention of cruelty against animals in transit, sustainable harvest or hunting and general welfare of

---

36 For perspectives on knowledge convergence, see M.F. Brown, 'Can Culture be Copyrighted', *Current Anthropology* 39, 1998, 193; C. Oguamanam, 'Local Knowledge as a Trapped Knowledge: Intellectual Property, Culture, Power and Politics', *Journal of World Intellectual Property* 11, 2008, 29.

37 G. Dutfield, *Protecting Traditional Knowledge: Pathways to the Future*, ICTSD Issue Paper No. 6 (2006), p. 1.

38 See I. Mgbeoji, *Global Biopiracy: Patents, Plants and Indigenous Knowledge*, Vancouver: UBC Press, 2005; contrast with P.J. Heald, 'The Rhetoric of Biopiracy' *Cardozo Journal of International and Comparative Law* 11, 2003, 519

39 Ibid., p. 594; even the CBD defines biodiversity to include 'other biotic components of the ecosystem': see *United Nations Convention on Biological Diversity*, Art. 2.

animals to the efficiency and sustainability of international trade in those animals. That explains the ambiguity over the role of animal welfare in the evolution of national and international law on the protection of biodiversity.[40] The following examples of pre-CBD agreements reflect the narrow context of some of the instruments as well as the open-ended range of subject matters implicated in the biodiversity protection policy arena. They include: the 1882 North Sea Overfishing Convention, the 1882 Convention for the Uniform Regulation of the Rhine, the 1946 International Convention for the Regulation of Whaling (ICRW), the 1959 Antarctic Treaty, the 1966 International Convention for the Conservation of Atlantic Tunas (ICCAT), the 1971 Convention on Wetlands of International Importance, especially as Waterfowl Habitat, the 1972 Convention Concerning the Protection of the World Cultural and Natural Heritage (World Heritage Convention), the 1973 Convention on the International Trade in Endangered Species of Wild Fauna and Flora (CITES), the 1979 Convention on the Conservation of Migratory Species of Wild Animals (CMS), the 1980 Convention for the Conservation of Antarctic Marine Living Resources (CCAMLR) and the 1983 FAO International Undertaking on Plant Genetic Resources.[41]

Some of these instruments have a regional focus while others have global appeal. They could be the subject of different classificatory regimen from marine and terrestrial to general nature or natural resource conservation. Beyond these instruments, it is logical to draw in various other international environmental agreements,[42] including those dealing with pollution and hazardous substances as complements to international biodiversity protection regimes. The 1972 London Convention on the Prevention of Marine Pollution by Dumping of Waste and Other Matter, the 1985 FAO International Code of Conduct on the Distribution and Use of Pesticides and the 1989 Basel Convention on the Control of Transboundary Movement of Hazardous Wastes and their Disposal are examples of such regimes that have direct and indirect relevance to the protection of biodiversity.

An obvious paradigm shift in environmental philosophy and management strategy in the twentieth century was the realisation of the inadequacy of previous approaches to biodiversity protection and conservation. The alarming havoc stemming from the transboundary effects of hazardous environmental activities, the over-exploitation of certain migratory species, increasing interest in marine biology as well as the awareness of the transboundary migratory nature of marine creatures, to mention a few, underscored the imperative for a more concerted and cooperative approach to biodiversity protection. Progressive inclination to explore species management and biodiversity issues via transnational exchange of scientific and research data in the twentieth century coincided with a change in philosophical outlook on environmental matters. Such matters were identified as being of 'common interest' and 'common concern' of humankind, thus requiring a cooperative approach. In a way, science, law and policy forged an unconscious alliance of convenience to replace species-specific and ad hoc approaches with a more holistic ecosystem model.

40 According to Birnie et al., op. cit., p. 600: 'Animal welfare issues are thus not wholly irrelevant to the development of international and national law protecting biodiversity, but they are not yet a dominant concern.'
41 This metamorphosed into the 2004 International Treaty of Plant Genetic Resources for Food and Agriculture. See *International Treaty on Plant Genetic Resources for Food and Agriculture*, opened for Signature 3 November 2001, FAO Res. 3/2003. Online: Available FTP:<http://www.fao.org/legal/treaties/033t-e.htm> (accessed 18 May 2012) (ITPGRFA).
42 Even the World Heritage Convention's dedication to protection of significant sites of natural heritage is an integral piece of overall global biodiversity conservation.

This transformation happened gradually through developments in at least eight institutional and policy sites.[43] The first is the 1972 Declaration of the United Nations Conference on the Human Environment in Stockholm (Stockholm Declaration). That Declaration provided the earliest pointer to a holistic and cooperative approach to environmental management, including biodiversity and wildlife conservation. The second is the 1978 United Nations Environment Programme (UNEP) principles and guidelines to support conservation and harmonious exploitation of natural resources shared by more than one state. This document is credited with influencing major wildlife conventions, and is consistent with the general framework of the Stockholm Declaration. The third instrument is the UN General Assembly's World Charter for Nature, adopted in 1983, which enunciated key principles for biodiversity, nature and wildlife conservation.

The fourth instrument is the 1987 Report of the World Commission on Environment and Development (WCED), the Brundtland Report, titled *Our Common Future*.[44] This high-profile report was recommended and actively promoted by the United Nations General Assembly (UNGA) as an environmental policy instrument for national policy formulation. As such, it is often recognised as the origin of the concept of sustainable development. It provided a very comprehensive narrative of the environment in the context of political, development and security considerations while reiterating the imperative for new approaches to environmental development, including a holistic, conceptual and institutionally coordinated approach to biodiversity. The Brundtland Report was accompanied by the Report of the WCED Experts Group on Environmental Law which enunciated a more detailed framework of legal principles, rights and responsibilities to undergird environmental protection and sustainable development. Principle 3 is of particular relevance to the CBD. It requires states to:

(a) maintain ecosystems and related ecological processes essential for the functioning of the biosphere in all its diversity . . .
(b) maintain maximum biological diversity by ensuring the survival and promoting the conservation in their natural habitat of all species of flora and fauna, in particular those which are rare, endemic or endangered . . .[45]

Like the Brundtland Report, the Report of the WCED Experts Group on Environmental Law was endorsed and actively promoted by the UNGA. It was followed shortly by the UNEP Executive Director's initiative calling for the rationalisation and general harmonisation of extant international law and policy on biodiversity conservation, which prompted the UNEP Governing Council decision to commence in 1989 the drafting of what was to later crystallise in the CBD in 1992. This initiative happened against the background of elaborate and diverse soft-law interventions, including notably IUCN's World Conservation Strategy as well as the species-specific and other piecemeal treaties, some of which have been identified above.

By the time the CBD was adopted in 1992, the shape and content of the emergent international environmental principles were becoming clearer. Traced back to the Stockholm

---

43 For detailed discussions on these institutional and policy initiatives, see Birnie et al., op. cit., pp. 593–649.
44 World Commission on Environment and Development, *Our Common Future*, Oxford: Oxford University Press, 1987.
45 Birnie et al., op. cit., 2009, p. 606.

Declaration of 1972 and its subsequent elaborations in specific treaties and diverse soft-law initiatives, Jutta Brunnée[46] notes that aside from engineering 'a shift in the predominant focus on transboundary pollution to a conceptual framework with much broader [or global] outlook', Stockholm laid the foundation for the evolution of international environmental law under the following heads: (a) common concerns of humankind;[47] (b) common but differentiated responsibilities of states and stakeholders;[48] (c) sustainable development and intergenerational equity;[49] and (d) the precautionary principle.[50] All the instruments resulting from the UN Conference on Environment and Development (UNCED), including Agenda 21 and the CBD, are generally based on these key principles.

The Convention on Biological Diversity

From the negotiation history of the CBD, which has been explored elsewhere,[51] a few conclusions can be drawn. First, it is clear that the lead-up to the CBD was quite gradual and happened at multiple sites. Second, as is characteristic with international law, most of the key instruments that laid the foundation for the CBD were soft law. Third, the CBD was born at a time when the key principles of IEL had found traction in a significant number of instruments that wholly endorsed the idea of an international collaborative vision for a global environmental strategy.[52]

Perhaps the prime significance of the CBD lies in its status as the first major international environmental instrument to adopt a holistic ecosystem approach to biodiversity conservation. Next to that are the objectives and undergirding strategy of the CBD as articulated under Article 1:

(a) the conservation of biological diversity;
(b) the sustainable use of its components; and
(c) the fair and equitable access to genetic resources as well as fair and equitable sharing of the benefits arising out of their utilisation.

46 J. Brunnée, 'The Stockholm Declaration and the Structure and Process of International Environmental Law', in A. Chircop, T.L. McDorman and S.J. Rolston (ed.) *The Future of Ocean Regime Building: Essays in Tribute to Douglas M. Johnston*, Leiden; Boston: Martinus Nijhoff, 2009, p. 44.
47 See K. Baslar, *The Concept of the Common Heritage of Mankind in International Law*, The Hague: Kluwer Law International, 1998, p. 110.
48 See A.G.M. La Vina, G. Hoff and A. DeRose, *The Successes and Failures of Johannesburg: A Story of Many Summits: A Report on the World Summit on Sustainable Development for Donors and Civil Society Organizations*, World Resources Institute Working Paper (2002), note 6.
49 The principle of intergenerational equity is considered to be an element of sustainable development.
50 See J. D'Argo, 'Precautionary Principle: The "Better Safe than Sorry" Approach', *Greenpeace Synthesis/Regeneration: A Magazine of Green Social Thought* 7:8, 1995. Online. Available HTTP: <www.greens.org/s-r/078/07-54.html> (accessed 8 March 2012).
51 See F. McConnell, *The Biodiversity Convention: A Negotiation History*, The Hague: Kluwer Law International, 1996.
52 For instance, a review of the CBD's preambular paragraphs reflect the sentiments in the Stockholm Declaration, the Brundtland Report, the WCED Export Group Report on International Environmental Law and Agenda 21, to mention a few.

Consistent with key general principles of IEL, specifically common and differentiated responsibilities, the CBD provides for funding and technology transfer schemes to support fair and equitable access and overall distributional equity regarding the benefits of biological diversity.[53]

It has already been noted that in terms of its general language and undergirding ideology, the CBD adopts an instrumentalist and market incentive approach to biodiversity conservation.[54] More than any other instrument before it, the CBD recognises the value of indigenous and local communities and their knowledge systems in biodiversity conservation[55] even though it vests states with the sovereign right to exploit the genetic resources within their jurisdiction.[56] In recognition of the biodiversity conservation as a common concern of humankind, the CBD attempts to balance the interest of users in regard to access with the interest of providers, by elaborating on the principle of ABS.[57]

As a framework convention, the CBD lacks specificity in material respects and uses language such as 'undertake', 'as far as possible and as appropriate', 'promote and encourage', for example. It gives the parties ample flexibility and leverage, allowing national biodiversity conservation policies within the framework of the Convention to be formulated on the basis of vague, subjective and contingent considerations.

The framework model is hardly unique to the CBD.[58] It is pragmatic and not necessarily objectionable; after all, 'the most effective treaties are not necessarily those that are most precisely drafted.'[59] Aside from the usually contentious nature of negotiations on environmental law and policy, the complex nature of environmental issues and the divergent interests of varied stakeholders do not readily lend the resulting instruments to specific and elaborate details, which are often fleshed out in subsequent protocols and programmes of work.

The CBD's programmes of work

As mentioned earlier, a pragmatic way of understanding the influence of the CBD is to explore measures adopted under its programmes of work, resulting protocol(s) and decisions of its Conference of the Parties (COP). Sixteen years after its first meeting, the COP – the principal decision-making body for the CBD – has set the tone for biodiversity conservation by establishing elaborate programmes of work in seven thematic areas: agricultural biodiversity, dry land and sub-humid land biodiversity, forest biodiversity, inland waters biodiversity, island biodiversity, marine and coastal biodiversity and mountain biodiversity. According to the CBD, 'Each programme establishes a vision for, and basic principles to guide future

---

53 *United Nations Convention on Biological Diversity*, Arts 16–21.

54 This is so despite very weak preambular reference to the intrinsic value of biological diversity. The CBD's textual references to the 'sharing of benefits' arising from 'the utilization of genetic resources' are direct examples of its instrumentalist orientation.

55 *United Nations Convention on Biological Diversity*, Art. 8(j).

56 Ibid., Arts 3 and 15(1).

57 Ibid., Arts 8(j), 10(c), and 16; see also the 2002 *Bonn Guidelines on Access to Genetic Resources and Fair and Equitable Sharing of the Benefits Arising out of Their Utilization*. Online. Available HTTP: <www.cbd.int/doc/publications/cbd-bonn-gdls-en.pdf> (accessed 8 March 2012).

58 For example, the Framework Convention on Climate Change is also a framework treaty.

59 Birnie et al., op. cit., p. 614 and note 147 quoting G. Palmer, 'New Ways to Make International Environmental Law', *American Journal of International Law* 86, 1992, 269.

work. They also set out key issues for consideration, identify potential outputs, and suggest a timetable and means for achieving these.'[60]

Also, under the heading of 'cross-cutting issues', the COP 'initiated work on key matters of relevance to all [seven] thematic areas. These cross-cutting issues correspond to the issues addressed in the Convention's substantive provisions in Articles 6 to 20, and provide bridges and links between the thematic programmes.'[61] To date, there are a total of 18 cross-cutting issues, including access and benefit-sharing, biodiversity and development, biodiversity and climate change, and traditional knowledge, innovation and practices – Article 8(j).[62] Overall, pursuant to Article 5, the CBD adopts an international cooperative approach in the implementation of its programmes of work.[63]

In addition to its programmes of work, the CBD has a subsidiary body on scientific, technical and technological advice (SBSTTA)[64] and a number of ad hoc open-ended working groups on specific subject matters. The SBSTTA is a multidisciplinary expert body providing advice to the COP on scientific and technical issues incidental to the implementation of the Convention's objectives.[65] In regard to the working groups, perhaps the most notable ones are those on Biosafety (Article 8(j)) and on ABS. To their credit, the CBD has adopted three important supplementary instruments. The first is the 2000 Cartagena Protocol on Biosafety which aims to 'ensure the safe handling, transport and use of living modified organisms (LMOs) resulting from modern biotechnology that may have adverse effects on biological diversity, taking also into account risks to human health'.[66] The second is the 2002 non-binding Bonn Guidelines on Access to Genetic Resources and Fair and Equitable Sharing of the Benefits Arising out of Their Utilization,[67] which resulted from the work of the working groups on ABS and Article 8(j). The third is the 2010 Nagoya Protocol on ABS explored below.

ABS is an integral part or implementation component of Article 8(j)[68] which requires parties to:

> respect, preserve and maintain knowledge, innovations and practices of indigenous
> and local communities embodying traditional lifestyles relevant for the conservation
> and sustainable use of biological diversity ... and encourage the equitable sharing
> of the benefits arising from the utilization of such knowledge, innovations and
> practices.

---

60 *Convention on Biological Diversity, Thematic Programmes and Cross-Cutting Issues.* Online. Available HTTP: <www.cbd.int/programmes/> (accessed 1 July 2010).
61 Ibid.
62 For the entire list, see ibid.
63 Art. 5 provides: 'Each Contracting Party shall, as far as possible and as appropriate, cooperate with other Contracting Parties, directly or, where appropriate, through competent international organizations, in respect of areas beyond national jurisdiction and on other matters of mutual interest, for the conservation and sustainable use of biological diversity.'
64 *United Nations Convention on Biological Diversity*, Art. 25; see also para. 15 of the preamble thereto.
65 Ibid., Art. 25; see also paras 7 and 9 of the preamble thereto.
66 *Cartagena Protocol on Biosafety to the Convention on Biological Diversity* (29 January 2000) 39 ILM1027. Online. Available HTTP: <http://bch.cbd.int/protocol/text/> (accessed 18 May 2012).
67 See note 57.
68 ABS is also included in other provisions of the CBD. See *United Nations Convention on Biological Diversity*, Arts 10(c) and 15.

Pursuant to the Bonn Guidelines, the CBD has influenced national ABS policies, especially in developing countries. There are to date at least six regional[69] and nearly 100 country-specific ABS laws and regulations.[70] To underscore the complex and interlinked nature of the biodiversity conservation, a survey of the Genetic Resources Action International (GRAIN)'s Biodiversity Resources Law (BRL)[71] database shows that these laws and regulations are expressed in varied domestic regimes such as general environmental law, biodiversity-specific legislation, bio-discovery and bio-prospecting regimes. Others frameworks include wildlife resource conservation, indigenous peoples and indigenous rights laws as well as aspects of plant genetic resources, food and agricultural laws.

Also, at the international level, developing countries have pushed for a framework of prior informed consent and disclosure of origin of genetic resources and, where applicable, traditional knowledge, mandated for patent applications pursuant to the CBD's Bonn ABS Guidelines.[72] Disclosure of origin is a crucial aspect of CBD ABS and has provided a touchstone for linking biodiversity conversation with intellectual property and trade regimes in multiple fora, notably the World Trade Organization (WTO) and the World Intellectual Property Organization (WIPO), through the review of the TRIPS (Trade-Related Aspects of Intellectual Property Rights) Agreement, deliberations on the reviews of relevant patent treaties as part of the WIPO Patent Agenda,[73] and under the auspices of the WIPO

69 They include the African Union Model Law on the Rights of Local Communities, Farmers and Breeders and Access (2000); ASEAN Framework Agreement on Access to Biological Resources (2000); Andean Pact Common Regime on Access to Genetic Resources, Nordic Ministerial Declaration on Access and Rights to Genetic Resources (2003); European Community Directive 98/44 on the Legal Protection of Biotechnological Inventions (1998); The Himalayan Regional Framework Initiative on ABS(2010). For perspective on some of these initiatives, see generally: R. Boza, 'Protecting Andean Traditional Knowledge and Biodiversity Perspectives under the U.S.-Peru Trade Promotion Agreement', *Currents: International Trade Law Journal* 16, 2008, 76; S. Munzer and P.C. Simon, 'Territory, Plants, and Land-Use Rights among the San of South Africa: A Case Study in Regional Biodiversity, Traditional Knowledge and Intellectual Property', *William and Mary Bill of Rights Journal* 17, 2009, 831; K. Kariyawasam, 'Access to Biological Resources and Benefit-Sharing: Exploring a Regional Mechanism to Implement the Convention on Biological Diversity in SAARC Countries', *European Intellectual Property Review* 29, 2007, 325; C.P. Oli, 'Access and Benefit Sharing From Biological Resources and Associated Traditional Knowledge in the HKH Region – Protecting Community Interests', *International Journal of Biodiversity Conservation* 15, 2009, 105. Online. Available HTTP: <www.academicjournals.org/ijbc/PDF/PDF2009/September/Oli. pdf> (accessed 8 March 2012).
70 Convention on Biological Diversity, 'ABS Measures Search Page'. Online. Available HTTP: <http://www.cbd.int/abs/measures/> (accessed 30 April 2012); International Centre for Integrated Mountain Development (ICIMOD), 'Toward an Access and Benefit Sharing Framework Agreement for the Genetic Resources and Traditional Knowledge of the Hindu Kush Himalayan Region', 2010. Online. Available HTTP: <www.icimod.org/abs> (accessed 8 March 2012).
71 Until recently the Genetic Resources Action International (GRAIN) maintained an e-database of Biodiversity Rights Legislation (www.grain.org/brl) from diverse countries and regions, which provided useful resource materials.
72 See note 70; see also C. Oguamanam, 'Patents and Traditional Medicine: Digital Capture, Creative Legal Interventions, and the Dialectics of Knowledge Transformation', *Indiana Journal of Global Legal Studies* 15, 2008, 501.
73 The treaties include: (a) the Patent Cooperation Treaty (PCT), (b) the Patent Law Treaty (PLT) and (c) the Substantive Patent Law Treaty (SPLT). For a general overview of the WIPO Patent Agenda, see S. Musungu and G. Dutfield, *Multilateral Agreements and a TRIPS Plus World: The World Intellectual Property Organization –WIPO*, Quaker United Nations Office, TRIPS Paper #3(2003).

Intergovernmental Committee (IGC) on Intellectual Property and Genetic Resources, Traditional Knowledge and Folklore.[74]

Bowing to the pressure of the 15 mega-biodiverse countries, the World Summit on Sustainable Development (WSSD) in 2002 resolved to commence the negotiation of a binding instrument on ABS which builds on the Bonn Guidelines within the framework of the CBD. After six years of deliberations, the tenth meeting of the Conferences of the Parties to the CBD adopted the text of the Nagoya Protocol on Access to Genetic Resources and the Fair and Equitable Sharing of Benefits Arising from Their Utilization on 29 October 2010.[75] It was expected that the Protocol on ABS would assist in streamlining disparate national laws and create a global framework for clarifying as well as acting a roadmap for implementing state obligations on the subject. Despite initial reservations expressed by critics in regard to the Protocol text, the document would perhaps be one of the major contributions of CBD to a global biodiversity conservation strategy.

The CBD and other biodiversity-related instruments

The birth of the CBD and its Montreal-based secretariat does not necessarily make both the Convention and its secretariat the single instrument and institutional site for cooperative and collaborative global policy and legislative action on biodiversity. Indeed, the CBD was adopted at UNCED, the same platform that adopted Agenda 21, the Non-legally Binding Authoritative Statement of Principles for a Global Consensus on the Management, Conservation and Sustainable Development of All Types of Forests and the Framework Convention on Climate Change – all of these instruments have direct relevance to biodiversity conservation.[76] Post-CBD, international legal schemes relevant to biodiversity conservation have continued to emerge, as the following examples demonstrate. They include the Paris Convention to Combat Desertification (CCD) and Geneva International Tropical Timber Agreement, both of 1994; the 1998 Rotterdam Convention on Prior Informed Consent Procedure for Certain Hazardous Chemicals and Pesticides in International Trade; the 2001 Stockholm Convention on Persistent Organic Pollutants; and the 2004 FAO International Treaty on Plant Genetic Resources for Food and Agriculture (ITPGRFA).

As is evident from its diverse programmes of work and identified cross-cutting issues, the CBD has positioned itself and has been rightly recognised in IEL as a hub for facilitating institutional and regime cross-linkages in national and international biodiversity conservation initiatives. For example, the WSSD approved commencement of negotiation for a binding ABS regime 'within the framework of the Convention on Biological Diversity bearing in mind the Bonn Guidelines'.[77] Also, the ITPGRFA is

---

74 See WIPO, *Intergovernmental Committee*. Online. Available HTTP: <www.wipo.int/tk/en/igc/> (accessed 8 March 2012).
75 See *Nagoya Protocol on Access to Genetic Resources and the Fair and Equitable Sharing of Benefits Arising from Their Utilization*: Online. Available HTTP: <www.cbd.int/abs/text/> (accessed 16 February 2012).
76 One of the cross-cutting issues under the CBD is biodiversity and climate change. Also forest biodiversity is one the CBD's programmes in the seven thematic areas.
77 G. Dutfield, *Protecting Indigenous Knowledge: Pathways to the Future*, Policy Paper Prepared for the International Centre for Trade and Sustainable Development (ICTSD) (2006) at 11 (referring to the decision of the WSSD); See also W.B. Chambers, 'WSSD and International Regime on Access and Benefit Sharing: Is a Protocol the Appropriate Legal Instrument?', *European Community International Environmental Law* 12, 2003, 310.

directly aligned with the objectives of the CBD[78] in the context of sustainable agriculture and food security.

As the CBD continues to grapple with its mandate and to explore the very complex and open-ended nature of biodiversity, its capacity for enhancing institutional collaboration with other established and emerging regimes is continuously being challenged. For example, even before the CBD came into effect and shortly thereafter, there have been parallel international regimes on the management of marine and forest genetic resources which are integral components of the biodiversity conservation regime. One refers to the United Nations Forum on Forests (UNFF), established in 2000[79] and the other refers to the 1982 United Nations Convention on the Law of the Sea (UNCLOS). In regard to the latter, the recent United Nations Informal Consultation Process (ICP) on Oceans and the Law of the Sea identifies marine genetic resources (MGRs) as part of emerging oceans issues.[80] The ICP clearly indicates that MGRs straddle both the biodiversity governance regime under the CBD and the broader oceans governance regime under the UNCLOS.[81]

In regard to the CBD's relationship with other international instruments, especially those not dealing with biodiversity, Article 22(1) provides: 'The provisions of this Convention shall not affect the rights and obligations of any Contracting Party deriving from any existing international agreement, except where the exercise of those rights and obligations would cause a serious damage or threat to biological diversity.' In terms of the CBD's relationship with other existing international instruments on nature conservation, especially those that postdate it, analysts rightly note that:

> It is possible that the concept of bio-diversity as defined in the Convention, could become the 'organizing' or at least 'integrating' concept for relating relevant existing agreements, both to bring them into closer relation with each other, by embodying common concepts, and to the aims of the Biodiversity Convention.[82]

---

78 Art. 1.1. provides: 'The objectives of this Treaty are the conservation and sustainable use of plant genetic resources for food and agriculture and the fair and equitable sharing of the benefits arising out of their use, in harmony with the Convention on Biological Diversity, for sustainable agriculture and food security.' See ITPGRFA, op. cit., note 53.

79 Following the Rio Forest Principles and pursuant to chapter 11 of Agenda 21, the United Nations set up an Intergovernmental Panel on Forests (IPF) which was later replaced by the Intergovernmental Forum on Forests (IFF) to give practical effect to the principles and chapter 11 of Agenda 21. In 2000, the United Nations Economic and Social Council (ECOSOC) established the UN Forum on Forests for effective coordination of diverse state and international commitments to effective management of forests and sustaining the works of the IPF/ IFF.

80 L. Ridgeway, 'Marine Genetic Resources: Outcomes of the United Nations Informal Consultative Process' *International Journal of Marine and Coastal Law*, 24 2009, 309.

81 CBD Art. 22(2) directly accommodates the shared jurisdiction between CBD and UNCLOS. It provides: 'Contracting Parties shall implement this Convention with respect to the marine environment consistently with the rights and obligations of States under the law of the sea.' *United Nations Convention on Biological Diversity*, op. cit., note 11.

82 Birnie et al., op. cit., p. 616.

Conclusion

The idea of integration among global international environmental regimes is gradually but certainly gaining traction.[83] This is evident, in part, in the UNGA's adoption of *Environmental Perspective to the Year 2000 and Beyond*.[84] This major policy document seeks to rectify the concept of environmentally sound development via an appreciation of the importance of cross-sectoral linkages, impacts and coordination of such measures. Consistent with the vision of the perspective instrument, the UNGA declared 2010 the International Year of Biodiversity.

Twenty years after the CBD, the expectations of stemming the unprecedented decline of biodiversity have yet to be realised. Yet again, the CBD is serving as a strategic platform for the United Nations by negotiating a binding ABS regime. The latter is another major step to stem global biodiversity crises. The foundation for this new initiative was laid by the CBD's elaborate programmes of work, active influence in national, regional and international arenas, and its ability to translate or rectify biodiversity issues, especially the idea of ABS across multiple international fora and regimes. Without question, the CBD is an important case study of the imperative and potential for integration amongst international environmental instruments and other relevant and peripheral regimes that are integral aspects of environmentally sound development.

Clearly, the complex nature of biodiversity and its conservation is outside the scope of one single, unified regime. It is hardly surprising that after the CBD came into effect other legal and regulatory instruments and policies that relate to biodiversity conservation have continued to evolve at disparate levels and intersections within and outside the CBD. However, since coming into effect, the CBD has established an elaborate framework for a cross-sectoral and generally collaborative approach to a harmonised and holistic global ecosystem outlook on biodiversity conservation. Despite the lack of progress in global biodiversity conservation, the CBD is unquestionably one of the most effective nexuses for a global environmental strategy. Perhaps it is too early to effectively gauge the Convention's impact on biodiversity conservation.

At present, it would be unrealistic to hinge the hope of salvaging global biodiversity on one instrument. Cleary, the complex subject matter of biodiversity conservation is one that is better tackled by a strategy of integration among biodiversity regimes in the context of the new momentum on the integration of international environmental regimes.[85] Going forward, the CBD has its work cut out, and has, in 20 years of its existence, committed itself to the ongoing exploration of an integrated cross-sectoral approach to biodiversity conservation. The CBD will continue to serve as the hub for international law and policy on biodiversity conservation. That significant role requires the strengthening of the Convention's self-appraisal mechanism and the entrenchment of a constant critical cross-sectoral evaluation of progress in global biodiversity conservation efforts between relevant regimes in mutually re-enforcing ways.

83 For discussions on point, see M. Doelle, 'Integration among Global Environmental Regimes: Lessons Learned From Climate Change', p. 63: Online. Available HTTP: <http://law.dal.ca/Files/ MEL_Institute/Doelle_integration_Johnston_book_chapter.pdf> (accessed 18 March 2012).

84 *Environmental Perspective to the Year 2000 and Beyond*, GA Res. A/RES/42/186, UN GA, 42nd Sess., 96 Plenary Mtg (1987). Online. Available HTTP: <www.un-documents.net/a42r186.htm> (accessed 8 March 2011).

85 For further discussion of treaty congestion and approaches to overcome it see Chapter 36 by D. Anton in this volume.

13

Freshwater, habitats and ecosystems

Douglas E. Fisher

While the Ramsar Convention for the Protection of Wetlands of International Importance was the first habitat-based treaty, much of the recent focus of international attention in the area of freshwater has been on the regulation of watercourses. Attention is only beginning to be given to the interconnectedness of freshwater, habitats and ecosystems. This chapter explores and analyses the context, structure and substantive rules for the conservation and management of freshwater, habitats and ecosystems across the complex range of multilateral environmental agreements.

Introduction

The way in which the sources of freshwater and their interdependent ecosystems are managed is in the first instance a matter for the laws of nation states. But the sources of freshwater and the components of these ecosystems recognise neither these laws nor jurisdictional boundaries. It is trite to observe that these issues over recent years have been increasingly the subject of international and regional cooperation in the context of a set of complex and interrelated normative relationships. While the aspirational goal of these arrangements is that water, land, soil, vegetation, natural habitats and ecosystems should be managed on a coherent, integrated and sustainable basis, the international normative arrangements directed at the outcome of sustainability remain largely fragmented.

The management of freshwater and ecosystems brings together elements of the geosphere and the atmosphere as well as elements of the hydrosphere and the biosphere: in effect the global climate system. The precise relationship between these various elements is no doubt a matter of location and circumstance. The field becomes more complicated when humans become part of these relationships. Water and biota may be preserved as resources of benefit to humans, but exist within their own environments that comprise a series of dependent and related ecosystems. Humans are also part of this environment in just the same way that water and biota are part of the human environment. Humans may be perceived to be the beneficiaries of these relationships, but water, biota and the ecosystems of which they are a part are also beneficiaries.

The quality of these relationships has increasingly become a matter of concern to humans. One of the responses has been to create and implement legal arrangements capable of addressing these concerns. For the last two or three hundred years the focus of the law has been the facilitation of the use and development of natural resources. Towards the end of the nineteenth century and during the twentieth century, protection of the environment and conservation of its natural resources have emerged as a counterpoint to this. More recently these two polarised objectives have been to some extent brought together through the concept of sustainable development.

The interests of humans have always been recognised and protected by a range of legal instruments. To some extent, it may be argued, the interests of nature may be beginning to be recognised and perhaps even protected in various ways by sets of legal arrangements. The arrangements that are beginning to emerge throughout the international legal system need to be analysed in the first instance against the doctrinal context out of which they have emerged.

This chapter explores the international environmental instruments for the governance of freshwater, habitats and ecosystems. The chapter commences with an examination of the doctrinal context in which these instruments are located. Thereafter the grammatical structure and substantive rules are explored and analysed.

The doctrinal context of international instruments for environmental governance

Sovereignty

The most important characteristic of freshwater and related ecosystems is their territoriality. The principle of sovereignty is firmly based upon the control of land and its associated resources within the recognised boundaries of the nation state. However, water and elements of ecosystems are not necessarily confined within these territorial boundaries. More recently, the law has been moving in the direction of a 'sharing of the products' of freshwater and of elements of ecosystems. If the law is moving in this direction, the mechanisms for doing so are the 'numerous limitations' imposed by the law upon the use of territorial as well as of marine resources.

The fundamental limiting principle is now located in Principle 21 of the Stockholm Declaration 1972 and Principle 2 of the Rio Declaration of 1992.[1] Accordingly nation states have the sovereign right to exploit their own resources and the responsibility to ensure that activities within their jurisdiction or control do not cause damage to the environment of other states or of areas beyond the limits of national jurisdiction. The responsibility is limited to environmental damage occurring in the territory of other states or in areas beyond the jurisdiction of the nation state where the activity happened. Significantly it imposes no responsibility for environmental damage occurring within the boundaries of the nation state in question. The responsibility of the nation state recognised in this way is a consequence of the rules that evolved over several decades from the 1940s.[2] The doctrinal developments of international environmental law have arisen largely out of disputes relating to international watercourses and to a lesser extent the ecosystems associated with these watercourses.[3]

---

1 *Stockholm Declaration on the Human Environment* (1972), 11 ILM 1416 ('Stockholm Declaration'); *Rio Declaration on Environment and Development* (1992), 31 ILM 874 ('Rio Declaration').
2 See e.g. T. Stephens, *International Courts and Environmental Protection*, Cambridge: Cambridge University Press, 2009, Chapter 5.
3 For further details of the law of watercourses see A. Rieu-Clarke in Chapter 14 of this volume.

Significantly, the theoretical foundation of these developments has been a reflection of the doctrines of 'limited territorial sovereignty' and 'community of interest'.[4] The former of these doctrines acknowledges the existence of limitations upon the exercise of the rights of territorial sovereignty while the latter reflects the notion of shared resources, which is particularly appropriate not only to water but also to elements of related ecosystems.[5]

Consensual constraints upon sovereignty

Introduction

The power to enter into an agreement is no doubt an exercise of a right of sovereignty but the exercise of that power is subject to one of the other fundamental principles of international law – namely *pacta sunt servanda*. If the agreement contains obligations accepted by the parties, then these are consensual rules. Increasingly, in relation to natural resources and the environment, multilateral agreements impose relatively specific obligations, although these obligations may be qualified rather than absolute. It is the relationship between rights of sovereignty and self-imposed obligations that has become critical. This relationship is particularly significant in the context of shared resources such as freshwater and elements of related ecosystems. This is simply because of their physical mobility. It has been suggested that this approach 'may seem incongruous':

> We should bear in mind the fundamental and generally accepted rule of international law which says that all states are sovereign entities able to exercise sovereign rights over all natural living and non-living resources within their land and sea territory; the notion that states that are under an international legal obligation to protect certain species or habitats within their own territories may seem incongruous.[6]

Multilateral agreements

This perceived incongruity has been addressed through multilateral agreements in a number of different ways. The first is Article 2(3) of the *Conventions on Wetlands of International Importance* 1971 (Ramsar Convention).[7] One of the mechanisms for conserving wetlands is their inclusion in the international list established by this Convention. Article 2(3) provides:

> The inclusion of a wetland in the List does not prejudice the exclusive sovereign rights of the Contracting Party in whose territory the wetland is situated.

---

4 T. Stephens, op. cit., p. 191 referring to A. Rieu-Clarke, *International Law and Sustainable Development: Lessons from the Law of International Watercourse*, London: IWA Publishing, 2005, p. 101.

5 See e.g. D.E. Fisher, *The Law and Governance of Water Resources: The Challenge of Sustainability*, Cheltenham: Edward Elgar, 2009, pp. 189–97.

6 D.M. Ong, 'International Environmental Law Governing Threats to Biological Diversity', in M. Fitzmaurice, D.M. Ong and P. Merkouris (eds) *Research Handbook on International Environmental Law*, Cheltenham: Edward Elgar, 2010, p. 521.

7 *Conventions on Wetlands of International Importance Especially as Waterfowl Habitat*, opened for signature 2 February 1971, 11 ILM 963 (entered into force 21 December 1975) ('Ramsar Convention').

The Convention, as will be seen, contains qualified obligations in relation to listed wetlands. Article 2(3) suggests that how the listed wetland is to be managed to achieve the outcomes stipulated by the Convention is a matter for the state rather than a matter for international normative arrangements.

Article 6(1) of the *Convention Concerning the Protection of the World Cultural and Natural Heritage 1972* (World Heritage Convention)[8] goes somewhat further. It provides:

> Whilst fully respecting the sovereignty of the States on whose territory the cultural and natural heritage . . . is situated, and without prejudice to property rights provided by national legislation, the States Parties to this Convention recognise that such heritage constitutes a world heritage for whose protection it is the duty of the international community as a whole to cooperate.

While there is 'full respect' for the principle of sovereignty, it is linked directly to the recognition of world heritage as a matter of international responsibility. Consistently with this, Article 5 imposes qualified obligations on states to perform functions directed at the outcome of protection. In addition, the obligations of states are similarly without prejudice to property rights recognised by the laws of the states. Accordingly, rights of sovereignty are respected and property rights are not prejudiced by these arrangements.

The *Convention on Biological Diversity 1992* (CBD)[9] recognises in Article 3 the duality of the sovereign right to exploit natural resources and the responsibility to ensure that activities do not cause environmental damage. However, the fundamental concept is based upon jurisdiction. Article 4 provides:

> Subject to the rights of other States . . . the provisions of this Convention apply, in relation to each Contracting Party:
>
> (a) in the case of components of biological diversity, in areas within the limits of its national jurisdiction; and
> (b) in the case of processes and activities, regardless of where their effects occur, carried out under its jurisdiction or control, within the area of its national jurisdiction or beyond the limits of national jurisdiction.

Accordingly the Convention has effect within the territorial jurisdiction of the state and, in the case of transboundary processes and activities, both within and outside it. This approach is 'subject to the rights of other states'. This is a recognition of the rights of sovereignty of other states but coupled, no doubt, with the responsibilities of those states. This Convention, like the others considered above, creates a structure that may be described as a set of contrapuntal relationships between the right of sovereignty and the range of qualified obligations in the Conventions.

---

8 *Convention Concerning the Protection of the World Cultural and Natural Heritage*, opened for signature 16 November 1972, 11 ILM 1358 (entered into force 17 December 1975) ('World Heritage Convention').

9 *Convention on Biological Diversity*, opened for signature 5 June 1992, 31 ILM 818 (entered into force 29 December 1993) ('CBD').

The approach adopted in relation to freshwater resources is much more positive. The *Convention on the Law of the Non-Navigational Uses of International Watercourses* 1997[10] avoids the use of the expression 'sovereignty' except in the context of the duty imposed by Article 8 on watercourse states to cooperate 'on the basis of sovereign equality, territorial integrity, mutual benefit and good faith' with a view to achieving the objectives of the Convention – a reference more to the political context of cooperation rather than its legal context. It is no surprise, therefore, that Article 5 (1) proceeds to state a very positive obligation. In terms:

> Watercourse States shall in their respective territories utilize an international watercourse in an equitable and reasonable manner.

Most importantly of all, the obligation relates quite specifically to activities in the territory of the state in question. The concept of water as a shared resource recognises the interests of other states in how a particular state engages in the use of the watercourse. This positive obligation coupled with the prescribed methodology for its implementation impact considerably upon the way in which the watercourse state may exercise its rights of sovereignty over its natural resources.

The structural framework of an environmental legal system[11]

While it is important to acknowledge the increasing number of restrictions placed upon the exercise of rights of sovereignty by states, it is equally important to analyse the way in which these sets of international arrangements are structured. It has been suggested that the propositions in these international instruments may be classified as either paralegal rules or legal rules and in the form of norms of strategy and norms of operation. Paralegal rules are those that state values and principles without the capacity to be directly enforced legally. These rules inform legal rules which are structured as legally protectable rights and legally enforceable obligations.

It is often perceived to be dangerous to attempt to classify the functions of a legal system. This is no doubt particularly true of the environmental legal system. Nevertheless, it may be possible to explain the functions of the environmental legal system – including the international arrangements – in three ways:

- those facilitating the use and development of the resources of the natural environment;
- those protecting the natural environment from perceived and identified risks of harm; and
- those conserving the existing values of the natural environment both now and in the future.

The legal arrangements relating to freshwater resources, habitats and ecosystems display aspects of each of these three functions. Much depends upon the perspective from which the

---

10 *Convention on the Law of the Non-Navigational Uses of International Watercourses*, opened for signature 21 May 1997, 36 ILM 700 (not yet entered into force).
11 See generally D.E. Fisher, *Australian Environmental Law: Norms, Principles and Rules*, Sydney: Thomson Reuters, 2010, Chapter 1; D.E. Fisher, 'Legal and Paralegal Rules for Biodiversity Conservation: a Sequence of Conceptual, Linguistic and Legal Challenges', in M.I. Jeffery, J. Firestone and K. Bubna-Litic (eds) *Biodiversity Conservation, Law and Livelihoods*, Cambridge: Cambridge University Press, 2008, pp. 94–131.

legal arrangements are formulated. It may be an anthropocentric or an ecocentric perspective. In some cases humans are the principal beneficiary of these arrangements. In other cases nature is the principal beneficiary of these arrangements. Sometimes both are the perceived beneficiaries. Much depends upon how the paralegal rule or the legal rule is structured.

The focus of an international legal instrument and the purported beneficiary of the arrangements are often a reflection of the grammatical and syntactical structure of the provision. For example, what is often described as a principle is stated without reference to any particular person or institution. On the other hand, it is common for specific obligations to be imposed upon identifiable persons and institutions. These include, in the context of international law, states. In this way a statement of principle is of general application in the sense that it confers no rights and imposes no obligations upon anyone in particular but by implication everyone in general. This is on the assumption that such principles are made effective and realised through related sets of directly imposed or implied obligations. This approach is particularly significant to freshwater, habitats and ecosystems. The reason is quite simple. These elements of the natural environment are prospectively conserved for their own intrinsic values as well as – in appropriate circumstances – for their benefits for humans. It is against a framework such as this that the structure of international instruments can be analysed.

The structure of international instruments for freshwater, habitat and ecosystem management

Strategic rules

In this context there are four relevant sets of principles. The first is the Stockholm Declaration 1972.[12] Principles 2 and 5 focus on the benefits accruing to humans from the natural resources of the Earth. Principles 3 and 4 focus on the need for natural resources and nature in general to be conserved. Principle 6 is directed at the protection of the environment from the perceived harmful discharge of toxic and other harmful substances. Significantly, each of these principles is structured grammatically in the same way. The subject of the sentence is either directly or indirectly natural resources or nature. There is no object of the sentence. Each of these principles goes on to state the beneficiary, which may be either humans or the environment. Each of these principles comprises obligations, which are from the point of view of humans passive rather than active, and otherwise the obligation is not imposed upon a state or any other person. In other words it is structured intransitively and passively rather than transitively and actively. According to this analysis the obligation is one that is owed *erga omnes*.

For the most part the World Charter for Nature 1982, the Rio Declaration 1992 and the Forest Principles 1992 are similarly structured. Humans and nature are variously the beneficiaries of these arrangements. This is consistent with the concept of sustainable development that was evolving more formally at that time. Articles 1, 2, 3, 4 and 10 of the World Charter for Nature 1982[13] apply to nature generally and more particularly to elements of nature including freshwater, habitats and ecosystems. Articles 1, 2, 3, and 4 are described as principles while the arrangements in Article 10 are described as rules. The most general provision is Article 1: 'Nature shall be respected and its essential processes shall not be impaired.'

---

12 *Stockholm Declaration on the Human Environment* (1972), 11 ILM 1416 ('Stockholm Declaration').
13 *World Charter for Nature* (1982) GA Res 37/7 (XXXVII), GAOR, 37th Sess, 22 ILM 455.

Nature and its processes are the subject of the sentence and there is no object. The grammatical structure is intransitive and passive. The obligation to respect nature and not to impair its essential processes is thus owed by everyone – *omnes* – and it is not directed at any particular person or state.

The Rio Declaration 1992[14] is a combination of statements of principles in this sense together with statements directed at what states should do. An example of the latter is Principle 13, which requires states to develop national law regarding liability and compensation for the victims of pollution and environmental damage. An example of the former is Principle 3: 'The right to development must be fulfilled so as to equitably meet the developmental and environmental needs of present and future generations.'

In this case, the subject is the right to development; however, the object is the developmental and environmental needs of present and future generations. Principle 2(b) of the Forest Principles 1992[15] is structured in the same way. It provides: 'Forest resources and forest lands should be sustainably managed to meet the social, economic, ecological, cultural and spiritual human needs of present and future generations.' The needs identified include water and habitats and by implication ecosystems.

The significance of the way all of these statements of principle are structured is this. Nature, natural resources and the environment are the subject – both grammatically and substantively – of these statements. There is therefore a clear and unambiguous recognition not only of their value either to themselves or to humans but also of their importance and potential status within the legal system. In other words it may almost be concluded that nature, natural resources and the environment, including freshwater, habitats and ecosystems, enjoy a degree of personality within the law. Clearly their personality is substantially different from the personality of humans within the law. Even if this conclusion is premature, it is the general direction in which the law is moving.

Regulatory rules

Introduction

It is no surprise that multilateral environmental agreements are structured differently. They are concerned less with principles and strategies and more with regulatory rules limiting the activities of states. The principle of sovereignty may continue to remain at the foundations of these arrangements. It is the limitations imposed upon the exercise of the right of sovereignty that are beginning to dominate these legal arrangements. Obligations are imposed upon states parties to the agreements and the beneficiaries of these obligations are variously humans and nature. In terms of grammatical structure, states are the subject of the sentences that comprise these rules while nature, natural resources and the various elements of these are objects of these arrangements. Significantly, however, the obligations imposed in this way are of different kinds. There are obligations, which go to the substance of the rules, about:

- conduct and behaviour;
- the making of plans and decisions;

---

14 *Rio Declaration on Environment and Development* (1992), 31 ILM 874 ('Rio Declaration').
15 *Nonbinding Authoritative Principles for a Global Consensus on the Management, Conservation, and Sustainable Development of all Types of Forests* (1992), 31 ILM 881 ('Forest Principles').

- the achievement of objectives; and
- how to achieve objectives.

Habitats and ecosystems

Before focusing upon the Ramsar Convention[16] five related agreements must be considered:

- the *Convention Concerning the Protection of the World Cultural and Natural Heritage* 1972 (World Heritage Convention);[17]
- the *Convention on International Trade in Endangered Species of Wild Fauna and Flora* 1973 (CITES);[18]
- the *Convention on the Conservation of Migratory Species of Wild Animals* 1979 (CMS);[19]
- the *Convention on Biological Diversity* 1992 (CBD);[20] and
- the *Convention to Combat Desertification* 1994 (CCD).[21]

The 1972 World Heritage Convention[22] includes a definition of natural heritage that is capable of including freshwater, habitats and ecosystems. The essential obligation is to 'ensure that effective and active measures are taken for the protection, conservation and presentation of the cultural and natural heritage'.[23] The obligation is limited in three ways: it is only to endeavour; it is only to do so as far as possible; and to do so as appropriate for each country. However, the range of measures to be taken is extensive. The objective is clear; however, the mechanism for its achievement is limited by these three qualifications.

The approach adopted by CITES and the CMS is quite different. The CITES appendices set out the specific species and specimens of species protected by the Convention. The mechanism for their protection is the regulation of international trade. It involves a complex set of arrangements controlling the import and export of these protected species. The CMS similarly lists endangered migratory species in the appendices. The mechanism contemplated by Article II(3)(c) is an agreement between states with jurisdiction over any part of the range of the migratory species in question.[24] The supporting obligations are twofold. The obligation in Article II(3)(c) is to endeavour to provide immediate protection for migratory species in Appendix 1 and the second in Article II(3)(c) is to endeavour to conclude agreements covering the conservation and management of migratory species in Appendix 2. The obligation in

---

16 Ramsar Convention, op. cit.
17 *Convention Concerning the Protection of the World Cultural and Natural Heritage*, opened for signature 16 November 1972, 11 ILM 1358 (entered into force 17 December 1975) ('World Heritage Convention').
18 *Convention on International Trade in Endangered Species of Wild Fauna and Flora*, opened for signature 3 March 1973, 12 ILM 1088 (entered into force 1 July 1975) ('CITES')
19 *Convention on the Conservation of Migratory Species of Wild Animals*, opened for signature 23 June 1979, 19 ILM 15 (entered into force 1 November 1983) ('CMS').
20 *Convention on Biological Diversity*, opened for signature 5 June 1992, 31 ILM 818 (entered into force 29 December 1993) ('CBD').
21 *Convention to Combat Desertification in Those Countries Experiencing Serious Drought and/or Desertification, Particularly in Africa*, opened for signature 17 June 1994, 33 ILM 1328 (entered into force 26 December 1996) ('CCD').
22 For further details see Chapter 23 by E. Techera in this volume.
23 World Heritage Convention, op. cit., Art. 5(d).
24 Known as range states.

relation to the species listed in Appendix 1 is expanded by Article III(4)(a) to include the conservation and restoration of the habitats of the species dependent upon these habitats. Finally, Article V(1) expects but does not require that the agreement contains within it the ways and means by which the object of restoration of the migratory species to a favourable conservation status can be achieved. Thus CITES relies upon international trade whilst the CMS is based upon agreements between the relevant states.

The structure of the CBD reflects what is emerging as common practice. There is a statement of objectives, a statement of the overarching principle, obligations of performance and obligations of outcome together with a range of provisions about research, information, funding, administration, changes to the arrangements and the settlement of disputes. There are three objectives stated in Article 1:

- the conservation of biological diversity;
- the sustainable use of its components; and
- the fair and equitable sharing of the benefits arising out of the utilisation of genetic resources.

The focus of the first is nature while the focus of the last two is humans. The obligations in Articles 8 and 9 relate to *in situ* and *ex situ* conservation and in Article 10 are directed at the sustainable use of the components of biological diversity. This duality of focus is to some extent reflected in Article 15(2), which states:

> Each Contracting Party shall endeavour to create conditions to facilitate access to genetic resources for environmentally sound uses by other Contracting Parties and not to impose restrictions that run counter to the objectives of this Convention.

In this way the objectives of the Convention remain at the foundation of the edifice constructed by this Convention.

Consistently with common practice, the CCD contains an objective, a set of principles, a number of general obligations and a set of more specific obligations. The principles and the obligations are in many respects procedural. Accordingly the substantive direction of the Convention lies in the objective and the definitions associated with it. The objective is to combat desertification and to mitigate the effects of drought with the ultimate goal of contributing to the achievement of sustainable development. In this way the duality of functions and ultimately of outcomes associated with sustainable development are part of the objective. Article 2(2) indicates how this objective is achieved. This is close to an obligation of performance. It involves:

> Long-term integrated strategies that focus simultaneously on improved productivity of land and the rehabilitation, conservation and sustainable management of land and water resources.

This acknowledges the economic and social implications of sustainable development. What is important, however, is the juxtaposition of the sustainable management of land and water resources. Particularly significant is the definition of land for this purpose. It means:

> The terrestrial bio-productive system that comprises soil, vegetation, other biota, and the ecological and hydrological processes that operate within the system.

This brings together the biological, ecological and hydrological values associated with land as the physical component of the environment. This definition of land thus gives to the Convention a clear conceptual framework that embraces freshwater, habitats and ecosystems and perhaps all aspects of the natural environment. While the obligations in this Convention are somewhat limited in their nature and function, it is the objective coupled with this definition that sets the conceptual framework and strategic direction for the action programmes for combating desertification and mitigating the effects of drought with a view to the achievement of sustainable development.

Conclusion

The way in which the legal instruments are structured reflects the values to be conserved by these arrangements, the priorities involved in conserving those values, how the competing needs of nature and humans may be resolved, the mechanisms and instruments for doing so, and the capacity for them to be protected in the case of rights and enforced in the case of obligations. Nature and the natural environment on the one hand, and humans and the human environment on the other hand, have emerged as both subjects and objects of these arrangements. This has manifested itself not only in terms of the broad structure but also in terms of the grammatical and syntactical arrangements according to which the language comprising these arrangements is composed. The recognition of the interests of humans has been at the forefront of the legal system for a considerable time. The interests of nature have emerged as a counterpoint to the interests of humans. What is evolving is by no means a coherent set of approaches. But at least the structure of these arrangements reveals attempts to accommodate one to the other. If the focus of the rule is humans or a human institution such as the state, then this appears as the subject of the sentence. On the other hand, if nature or elements of the natural environment are the focus of these arrangements, than it similarly appears as the subject of the sentence. In both cases the object of the sentence represents the substantive content of the rule. While humans and their institutions, such as states, exist as a matter of law, nature and the environment do not exist in this way. But what is emerging is a recognition of something in the nature of a status or a personality attached by the legal system to nature and the natural environment.

The substantive rules for freshwater, habitat and ecosystem management

Introduction

In analysing the substantive content of these rules the principal issue for consideration is the objects rather than the subjects of these rules. The objects of these rules comprise essentially a set of limitation rules that restrict the way in which competence rules are exercised.

The principle of sustainable development is intended in theory to bring together the use and development of natural resources and the protection and conservation of the natural environment as a unified concept. But the system remains fragmented and not unified. Accordingly, the way in which freshwater, habitats and ecosystems are managed is governed not by one simple set of arrangements but through provisions in the range of international legal instruments.

Logically, the point of commencement of an analysis of the substantive content would be a discussion of the general principles which point out the direction in which the system is moving or expected to move. This would be followed by a discussion of the detail according to which this happens. However, in this case it is probably the reverse approach which will be more useful. Given that the focus of this discussion is upon freshwater, habitats and ecosystems, it is important to identify a helpful structure for engaging in this analysis. The CITES and the CMS – although important in themselves – are to some extent peripheral to this analysis. The World Heritage Convention protects values that satisfy two eligibility criteria relevant from the point of view of nature. These are outstanding universal value and the point of reference for applying this criterion – aesthetics, science, conservation or natural beauty.

What is natural heritage capable of protection under the Convention is controlled by the definition of natural heritage in Article 2 and the related obligations in Articles 4 and 5. Freshwater, habitats and ecosystems are capable of protection under the Convention to the extent that they fall within these aspects of the definition of natural heritage:

- natural features consisting of biological formations or groups of such formations;
- precisely delineated areas which constitute the habitat of threatened species of animals and plants;
- natural sites or precisely delineated natural areas.

Provided the two criteria for eligibility are satisfied, then protection is realised through the obligations in Articles 4 and 5. Article 4 impliedly recognises an obligation of outcome – to ensure the identification, protection, conservation, preservation and transmission to future generations of the relevant natural heritage. Article 5 imposes a range of qualified obligations linked to this. These relate to policies, services, institutions, studies, research and related activities. Relevantly the most significant is to take a range of measures – including legal measures – necessary for the identification, protection, conservation, presentation and rehabilitation of the natural heritage. The functions contemplated in Article 5(d) are not the same as the functions stated in Article 4. The former includes rehabilitation and the latter includes transmission. In any event the critical functions are protection and conservation. There is no definition of these expressions. However, it is suggested that protection involves protection from perceived and identified risks, while conservation is conservation of the existing values of nature and natural resources on a continuous basis now and in the future. The values protected and conserved by the Convention may be either anthropocentric or ecocentric or perhaps both. In any event freshwater resources, habitats and ecosystems are clearly able to be protected and conserved under the Convention provided they have satisfied the eligibility criteria. The focus is thus protection and conservation and not use and development. Accordingly the concept of sustainable development has no part to play in this Convention.

The concept of land in its extended sense lies at the foundations of the CCD.[25] The substance of the Convention lies in the complex set of definitions together with the objective and its associated obligations. Combating desertification is linked to land-based activities in the context of sustainable development but aimed at the prevention of land degradation, the rehabilitation of degraded land and the reclamation of desertified land. Land extends to soil, vegetation, biota and the ecological and hydrological processes that operate within this terrestrial bio-productive system. The definition of land degradation is thus critical. It means:

---

25 *Convention to Combat Desertification*, op. cit.

> Reduction or loss of the biological or economic productivity and complexity of rainfed cropland, irrigated cropland, or range, pasture, forest and woodlands resulting from the uses of land or from processes arising from human activities.

Accordingly the presence or absence of freshwater, habitats and ecosystems lies at the heart of these definitions. The objective of the Convention is to combat desertification and to mitigate the effects of drought with a view of contributing to the achievement of sustainable development. It is clearly recognised that this involves long-term integrated strategies dealing with – among others – the rehabilitation, conservation and sustainable management of land and water resources. It is the conjunction of land and water resources in this system that is critical – particularly so in view of the extended definition given to land for this purpose. It means effectively that land, water and their associated biological, ecological and hydrological processes must be managed together in a unified and integrated way. The ultimate criterion is the achievement of sustainable development and this Convention goes some way towards creating a framework for doing so in the context of land and water resources and their associated ecosystems.

Focus on wetlands[26]

The earliest and one of the most developed set of arrangements impacting upon freshwater, habitats and ecosystems is the *Convention on Wetlands of International Importance* of 1971.[27] The use of the expression 'wetlands' itself draws attention to the relationship between land and water. The importance attributed to wetlands was originally as waterfowl habitat. Article 1(2) specifically stated that waterfowl are birds ecologically dependent on wetlands. The concept of wetlands thus extends beyond land and water to include the ecosystems of which they are a part. The preamble to the Convention recognised that it was not only waterfowl that were ecologically dependent on wetlands but also a number of other flora and fauna dependent upon habitats such as wetlands. Wetlands for the purposes of the Convention have been defined in this way:

> Areas of marsh, fen, peatland or water, whether natural or artificial, permanent or temporary, with water that is static or flowing, fresh, brackish or salt, including areas of marine water the depth of which at low tide does not exceed 6 metres.

The preamble to the Convention recognised that these areas provide a range of economic, cultural, scientific and recreational services to humans as well as performing valuable functions as regulators of water regimes and as habitats of flora and fauna. While the focus of the Convention is wetlands, it is wetlands within the context of these other values, services and

---

26 See generally A. Gillespie, *Protected Areas and International Environmental Law*, Leiden: Martinus Nijhoff Publishers, 2007, pp. 43, 44, 56, 57, 72–4, 91, 134, 135; M. Bowman, 'Environmental Protection and the Concept of Common Concern of Mankind', in M. Fitzmaurice et al. (eds) op. cit.; D.M. Ong, 'International Environmental Law governing threats to biological diversity', in M. Fitzmaurice et al. (eds) op. cit.; D.E. Fisher, 'Managing Wetlands Sustainably as Ecosystems: the Contribution of the Law (Part 1)', *Water Law* 21, 2010, pp. 19–32.

27 Ramsar Convention, op. cit.

functions. The Convention thus addresses land, water and their ecosystems at least potentially as part of integrated natural systems.

The Convention provides for the management of wetlands in two ways:

- the management of wetlands designated by a state as suitable for inclusion in the list and subsequently included in the List of Wetlands of International Importance; and
- the management of wetlands not included in the list.

Article 2(1) imposes an obligation to designate suitable wetlands for inclusion in the list including an obligation in Article 2(4) for at least one wetland to be so designated. The criteria stated in Article 2(2) relate to the international significance of the wetlands 'in terms of ecology, botany, zoology, limnology or hydrology'. The points of reference are accordingly wide. On the face of it, an ecocentric approach is contemplated rather than an anthropocentric one. In practice considerable emphasis has been placed upon the relationship between the management of wetlands and the management of natural resources impacted upon by the management of wetlands and vice versa: for example, wetlands and agriculture, groundwater, fisheries, coastal zone management, extractive industries, poverty reduction and cultural values.[28]

Wetlands are accordingly managed with reference to relationships that go beyond those that are ecological, botanical, zoological, limnological or hydrological: for example, cultural and social and perhaps even economic perspectives. There arises for analysis, therefore, the nature and the substance of the obligations imposed upon states in relation to the management of wetlands.

The Convention distinguishes between the obligations in relation to listed wetlands and those in relation to wetlands generally. There is the obligation in Article 3(1) to formulate and implement planning so as to promote the conservation of listed wetlands. There is an additional obligation in Article 3(1) to formulate and implement planning so as to promote, as far as possible, the wise use of wetlands in the territory of the state. On the face of it, the obligation of wise use applies to all wetlands in the territory of the state whether listed or not. So the obligation in relation to planning for listed wetlands is twofold: to promote their conservation and as far as possible their wise use. But critically this obligation relates to 'planning' for conservation and for wise use. It does not relate directly to conservation and wise use per se.

Article 4(1) imposes the obligation to promote the conservation of wetlands and waterfowl by establishing reserves on wetlands. There is an additional obligation to provide 'adequately for their wardening'. The adjective 'their' might refer to the wetlands, the waterfowl or the nature reserves. In any event, the expression 'wardening' is unusual. To warden, it would seem, means to take care of or to look after. The obligation to establish nature reserves is an obligation of performance – how to conserve the wetlands and the waterfowl. The obligation in relation to planning is an obligation of outcome. It is ultimately the conservation of the wetlands and their wise use. There is thus no direct obligation to conserve wetlands, to use them wisely or to care for them adequately. Each of these outcomes is prefaced in its own way by the use of a verb such as 'promote' or 'provide'. The only obligation in relation to listed wetlands is to promote their conservation in the context of the planning obligation. The obligation to plan for the wise use of wetlands, the obligation to establish nature reserves for the conservation of wetlands and waterfowl and the obligation to care adequately for wetlands,

---

28 See Resolution VIII. 34 of the 8th Conference of the Parties (COP); C. de Klemm, *The Legal Development of the Ramsar Convention*, Gland: Ramsar Convention Bureau, 1995, Section II, para. 1.

waterfowl and nature reserves apply to all wetlands in the territory of the state whether listed or not. Apart from 'adequate wardening' the Convention depends upon the meaning of the words 'conservation' and 'wise use'.

Both conservation and wise use contain within them the function of use. The Convention itself recognises that ecosystems and humans benefit from the services provided by wetlands. Perhaps conservation recognises the need to protect not only wetlands but also the ecological functions that they perform. To some extent this approach is ecocentric rather than anthropocentric. On the other hand, wise use connotes a human perspective on the benefits provided by wetlands. This tends to suggest an anthropocentric approach. It seems to have been the concept of wise use that has been particularly important in the development of the jurisprudence related to the Convention.

The approach to wise use has changed three times since the coming into force of the Convention. According to one commentator:

> The term 'wise use of wetlands' was interpreted by the First Conference of the Parties at Cagliari in 1980 as involving the maintenance of the ecological character of these areas, which automatically means that they must not be destroyed, altered or polluted.[29]

On the face of it this goes beyond conservation to mean what may be described as absolute preservation. In other words, use for human purposes must not take place. In 1987 sustainable use was included. Thus wise use became 'the sustainable utilisation of wetlands for the benefit of human kind in a way compatible with the maintenance of the natural properties of the ecosystem.'[30] This reflects qualified conservation rather than absolute preservation. The relationship between sustainable use and maintenance of natural properties of ecosystems or between an anthropocentric approach and an ecocentric approach is governed by the adjective 'compatible'. This adjective indicates – perhaps even requires – that the two outcomes of sustainable use and maintenance of ecosystems must be achieved together; in other words, a combination of an anthropocentric and ecocentric approach. Arguably the reference to sustainability points in this direction in any event without further elucidation. Nevertheless, in 1987 for these purposes sustainable utilisation emerged quite clearly as an anthropocentric concept. It was described as:

> Human use of a wetland so that it may yield the greatest continuous benefit to present generations while maintaining its potential to meet the needs and aspirations of future generations.[31]

Finally in 2005 – as a result no doubt of the increasing formalisation of sustainable development within the interstices of international law – wise use emerged as this:

> Wise use of wetlands is the maintenance of their ecological character, achieved through the implementation of ecosystem approaches, within the context of sustainable development.[32]

---

29 de Klemm, op. cit., section II, para. 1
30 See generally Gillespie, *Protected Areas and International Environmental Law*, op. cit., pp. 199, 200.
31 Ibid., Section II, para. 1.
32 Resolution IX.1 Annex A, para. 22. of the 9th COP.

Sustainable development in its current form has thus become the 'context' of wise use. The ecocentric foundations of wise use have been to some extent re-established by reference to the maintenance of the ecological character of wetlands and the implementation of ecosystem approaches. In other words, a modified duality approach has evolved according to which an ecocentric approach applies within the framework of a unified anthropocentric and ecocentric approach.

The use of wetlands for the benefit of humans is undoubtedly an element of these arrangements. But the relationship between the human and non-human perspectives remains somewhat ambiguous. In this way there exists the possibility of competition between the agricultural and the cultural interests in wetlands, on the one hand, and the ecological and hydrological values of wetlands, on the other hand. There is assumed to be some kind of balance between them but how this works in practice is not clear. In any event it must be recalled that the Convention uses the expressions 'conservation' and 'wise use'. They remain the terms of legal significance. The guidelines in relation to wise use[33] are no more than that and they are not in any sense legally binding upon states. Despite the guidelines, Article 3(1) applies the planning obligation so as to deal conjunctively with the promotion of the conservation of wetlands and the promotion of the wise use of wetlands. Whatever is the meaning of wise use, conservation is an essential element of the planning obligation.

Conclusion

The obligations accepted by states under the complex range of multilateral environmental agreements respond to issues on a sectoral and fragmented basis. Freshwater resources, habitats and ecosystems are relevant in a number of different ways and perform a number of functions within these arrangements. The rules in these agreements are structured in different ways and the terminology is diverse. The nature of the obligations varies from those of conduct or behaviour, outcome or performance. In most cases sustainability in one form or another continues to drive the fundamental approach adopted by these agreements. It is difficult for any legal instrument – perhaps especially difficult for international legal instruments – to address sustainability in a way that is informative, explanatory, practical and enforceable.

The above analysis explores some of the rules in these agreements. Do these rules reflect the principles that have been evolving since 1972 and that have generally been accepted by the international community? Most of the principles stated in the Stockholm Declaration 1972 are directed at the protection of the environment and the conservation of its natural resources largely from the perspective of humans. Principles 2 and 5 directly acknowledge the benefits accruing to humans and Principles 3 and 4 similarly by implication. Only Principle 6 seems to contemplate ecosystems directly as the beneficiary of the obligation. Principle 1 of the Rio Declaration 1992 literally places human beings at the centre of concerns for sustainable development. Principle 3 reinforces the importance of the developmental and environmental needs of present and future generations, while Principle 4 postulates protection of the environment as a means of achieving sustainable development. Similarly the Principles on the Management of Forests 1992 are linked to an acknowledgement of their multiple and

---

33 The Ramsar Convention, *Ramsar Handbooks for the Wise Use of Wetlands*. Online. Available HTTP: <http://www.ramsar.org/cda/en/ramsar-pubs-handbooks/main/ramsar/1-30-33_4000_0> (accessed 20 February 2011).

complementary functions and uses. Accordingly forest resources and forest lands are to be sustainably managed to meet the social, economic, ecological, cultural and spiritual human needs of present and future generations. While the services of forests are linked to habitats for wildlife, carbon sinks and carbon reservoirs, the focus is the maintenance of 'their full multiple value' in providing benefits essentially for humans.

It is only the World Charter for Nature 1982[34] that has pointed in a different direction. Nature or aspects of nature are the subject of the general principles stated in Articles 1 to 5. The first three of these articles make no reference to humans. The point of reference is variably nature, all life forms, habitats, ecosystems, and rare and endangered species. Only Article 4 makes any reference to the benefits to be obtained by humans as a result of the functions performed by ecosystems. It provides:

> Ecosystems and organisms, as well as the land, marine and atmospheric resources that are utilised by man shall be managed to achieve and maintain optimum sustainable productivity, but not in such a way as to endanger the integrity of those other ecosystems or species with which they coexist.

In other words, the first three articles focus on the conservation, the protection and the preservation of nature and its elements. Article 4 reintroduces a duality of functions performed by nature and ecosystems. The interest of humans is the achievement and maintenance of optimum sustainable productivity. Clearly it is not maximum productivity that is sustainable; merely the optimum. The use of the expression 'optimum' is no doubt an acknowledgement of the focus upon nature in the first three articles. To paraphrase it: what is indicated is a need to achieve the 'best' way of achieving sustainable development rather than achieving the 'highest' level of development even on a sustainable basis.

The concept of sustainable development has been appearing with increasing rapidity in most if not all of the international legal arrangements for managing the environment and its natural resources. Clearly there is no obligation imposed by international law to achieve sustainable development. But aspects of sustainable development appear interstitially within the fabric of the range of multilateral environmental agreements which we have been considering. However, there is no uniformity of approach; no uniformity of language, structure or outcome. It is a matrix of fragmented and in some cases disjointed rules dealing with specific issues in particular but differentiated ways. Freshwater resources, habitats and ecosystems are capable of protection and conservation within this overall set of arrangements, but clearly there is no one single mechanism for their conservation. While they may be relevant, it is the relationship in strictly grammatical, linguistic and structural terms between freshwater resources, habitats and ecosystems on the one hand and all of the other elements of nature, the natural environment and natural resources on the other hand that is critical in legal terms. In other words, a rule in any of these international legal instruments can be understood and applied only in a practical way in the specific sets of facts and circumstances to which it relates. There is no universal rule that applies to these global issues, which are resolved only by applying the rule to the particular circumstances as they arise in individual locations.

---

34 *World Charter for Nature*, op. cit.

14

International freshwater law

Alistair Rieu-Clarke[*]

International freshwater law has a significant role to play in addressing global water-related issues, including transboundary disputes. This chapter examines the corpus of international freshwater law and how it has evolved to respond to transboundary challenges. The chapter focuses on the relevance and prospects for the Convention on the Law of the Non-Navigational Uses of International Watercourses (UN Watercourses Convention) – the most authoritative statement of international law in this field. The scope, norms, procedures and institutional arrangements are explored as well as the implementation challenges that lie ahead.

Introduction

Water is a central issue in the drive towards sustainable development and global security.[1] However, it is widely believed that 'we are lagging behind in the implementation of the commitments related to water and sanitation, contained in the Millennium Development Goals (MDGs) and other agreed goals in the outcome of the 2002 World Summit on Sustainable Development.'[2] Moreover, the combined forces of the global food, energy and financial crises have made achieving these MDGs ever more challenging.[3] Crucial linkages between water and global security have also been highlighted by UN Secretary-General Ban Ki-Moon, who maintains that 'the challenge of secure, safe and plentiful water for all is one of the most daunting challenges faced by the world today . . . Our experiences tell us that environmental stress due to lack of water may lead to conflict and would be greater in poorer

---

* I am grateful for the research assistance of Jing Lee.

1 P. Wouters, S. Vinogradov and B-O. Magsig, 'Water security, hydrosolidarity and international law: a river runs through it . . .', *Yearbook of International Environmental Law* 19, 2010, 97–134.
2 United Nations Deparatment for Information, 'Sustainable management of water resources vital to achieving anti-poverty goals delegates told, as Generally Assembly high-level dialogue marks World Water Day', 2010. Online. Available HTTP: <http://www.un.org/News/Press/docs/2010/ga10925.doc.htm> (accessed 21 September 2011).
3 United Nations World Water Assessment Programme, *The United Nations World Water Development Report 3: Water in a Changing World*, Paris: UNESCO, 2008, pp. 14–20.

nations.[4] The challenges are therefore acute, but arguably at their greatest where freshwaters defy political boundaries and are shared between states.

In light of the above-mentioned challenges, this chapter seeks to consider the role and relevance of international freshwater law in addressing the water-related issues. More specifically, the chapter will examine international freshwater[5] from a geo-political standpoint, how international law has evolved to respond to transboundary challenges, and the corpus of international freshwater law. Additionally, the chapter examines the relevance and prospects for the Convention on the Law of the Non-Navigational Uses of International Watercourses (UN Watercourses Convention) – the most authoritative statement of international law in this field.

International freshwaters across the world

A total of 145 countries have their territories within at least one of the world's 263 international river basins[6] or 275 transboundary aquifers.[7] These waters encompass almost 50 per cent of the Earth's land surface and 60 per cent of global freshwater flows and are home to around 40 per cent of the world's population.[8] Moreover, through the advent of globalisation and increased international trade, most states rely upon the goods and services derived from such waters, even if they are not directly dependent on them. The question of how to equitably and sustainably govern international freshwaters has proved difficult to address in many regions of the world.

Despite Europe possessing a relatively evolved legal framework for the management of international freshwaters disputes have arisen.[9] For example, a dispute between Hungary and the Slovak Republic relating to a joint barrage system and its environmental impacts remains to this day, despite a case having been decided by the International Court of Justice in 1997.[10] Also within the Danube basin, Romania and Ukraine have disputed the impact of the Bystroe Canal, a navigational channel started in May 2004 that according to Romania threatens the Danube Delta ecosystem.[11]

Africa is home to 64 international river basins, which cover 64 per cent of Africa's surface area, and contain over 90 per cent of the continent's surface resource.[12] In Africa, a drive

---

4 UN News Centre, 'Address as prepared for delivery to the Davos World Economic Forum', 2008. Online. Available HTTP: <www.un.org/apps/news/infocus/sgspeeches/search_full.asp?statID=177> (accessed 21 September 2011).

5 'International freshwater' is taken here to mean surface or groundwater or a combination of the two, which is shared between two or more states.

6 A.T. Wolf, J.A. Natharius, J.J. Danielson, B.S. Ward and J.K. Pender, 'International river basins of the world', *International Journal of Water Resources Development* 15(4), 1999, 387–427.

7 S. Puri and A. Aureli (eds) *Atlas of Transboundary Aquifers*, Paris: UNESCO, 2009.

8 Global International Water Assessment, *Challenges to International Waters – Regional Assessments in a Global Perspective*, Nairobi: UNEP, 2006, p. 20.

9 See generally, A. Rieu-Clarke and A.T. Wolf, *Hydropolitical vulnerability and resilience along international waters – Europe*, Nairobi: UNEP, 2009.

10 *Case concerning the Gabčíkovo-Nagymaros Project (Hungary v Slovakia)*. Online. Available HTTP: <http://www3.icj-cij.org/docket/files/92/7375.pdf> (accessed 21 September 2011).

11 M. Koyano, 'Effective Implementation of International Environmental Agreements: Learning Lessons from the Danube Delta Conflict', in T. Komori and K. Wellens, *Public Interest Rules of International Law*, Surrey: Ashgate, 2009.

12 A.R. Turton, A. Earle, D. Malzbender and P.J. Ashton, 'Hydropolitical Vulnerability and Resilience along Africa's International Waters', in A.T. Wolf (ed.) *Hydropolitical Vulnerability and Resilience along International Waters: Africa*, Nairobi: UNEP, 2005.

towards multilateral approaches to international freshwaters can be seen in the context of the Nile, the longest river in the world.[13] However, pre-existing agreements skewed in favour of a minority of downstream states, as well as climate change, large-scale infrastructure projects and other pressures threaten the ability to find a basin-wide solution.[14]

Across Asia freshwater disputes abound.[15] For example, transboundary water issues came to the forefront when five post-Soviet Central Asian states appeared on the scene in the early 1990s – Kazakhstan, the Kyrgyz Republic, Tajikistan, Turkmenistan and Uzbekistan. Ensuring that the much-depleted waters of the Aral Sea basin are managed sustainably has become a major concern, ultimately intensified by a fragmented legal system and competition between water use upstream (mainly for hydropower) and downstream (irrigation/food production). As noted by Ziganshina, 'food and energy security issues were further complicated by the environmental neglect inherited from the Soviet period when the extensive exploitation of natural resources had incontestable priority over environmental protection'.[16]

Within the context of the Indus Water Treaty a number of conflicts have flared up between India and Pakistan.[17] The latest dispute over India's construction of the Kishanganga hydroelectric project and its alleged negative impact in Pakistan is before the International Court of Arbitration in The Hague.[18]

South America has also witnessed its share of high-profile disputes over water in recent times.[19] Argentina and Uruguay brought a dispute over the Pulp Mills on the River Uruguay to the International Court of Justice (ICJ), the case being decided in 2010.[20] In the same year, Costa Rica instituted proceedings against Nicaragua before the ICJ due to concerns over the environmental impacts of dredging and the construction of a canal in the San Juan River.[21]

The above-mentioned cases merely provide a snapshot of some of the challenges faced by states across the world in sharing their international freshwaters. More extensive analysis is

---

13 D.Z. Mekonnen, 'The Nile Basin Cooperative Framework Agreement negotiations and the adoption of a "water security" paradigm: flight into obscurity or a logical cul-de-sac?', *European Journal of International Law* 21(2), 2010, pp. 421–40.

14 M. Abseno, 'East Africa', in F. Loures and A. Rieu-Clarke (eds) *The UN Watercourses Convention in Force – Strengthening Transboundary Water Management*, London: Earthscan, 2011.

15 See UNEP, *Hydropolitical Vulnerability and Resilience along International Waters – Asia*, Nairobi: UNEP, 2009.

16 D. Ziganshina, 'International water law in Central Asia: the nature of substantive norms and what flows from it', *Asian Journal of International Law*, 2011, 1–24, p. 2, Online. Available HTTP: <http://journals.cambridge.org/action/displayAbstract?fromPage=online&aid=8467139> (accessed 21 September 2011).

17 *The Indus Water Treaty*, opened for signature 19 September 1960 (entered into force 1 April 1960). Online. Available HTTP: <http://siteresources.worldbank.org/INTSOUTHASIA/Resources/223497-1105737253588/IndusWatersTreaty1960.pdf> (accessed 9 November 2011); S. Salman, 'The Baglihar difference and its resolution process – a triumph for the Indus Waters Treaty?' *Water Policy*, 2008, 105–17; N.A. Zawahri, 'India, Pakistan and cooperation along the Indus River system', *Water Policy*, 2009, 1–20.

18 A. Bokhari, 'Setback in the water dispute', Dawn.com, 19 September 2011. Online. Available HTTP: <http://www.dawn.com/2011/09/19/comment-and-analysis-setback-in-the-water-dispute.html> (accessed 11 May 2012).

19 See UNEP, UNA and OSU, *Hydropolitical Vulnerability and Resilience along International Waters – Latin America and the Caribbean*, Nairobi: UNEP, 2007.

20 *Case Concerning Pulp Mills on the River Uruguay* (Argentina v Uruguay) (*Pulp Mills* case). Online. Available HTTP: <http://www.icj-cij.org/docket/files/135/15877.pdf> (accessed 21 September 2011).

21 International Court of Justice Press Release, 'Costa Rica institutes proceedings against Nicaragua and requests the Court to indicate provisional measures', 19 November 2010. Online. Available HTTP: <http://www.icj-cij.org/docket/files/150/16239.pdf> (accessed 21 September 2011).

provided elsewhere;[22] this chapter will focus on the role and relevance of international freshwater law in addressing these challenges.

The evolution of international freshwater law

International freshwater law has a long tradition, with the first international freshwater treaty dating as far back as 2500 BC, when two Sumarian city-states of Lagash and Umma signed an agreement governing the Tigris River.[23] Since this initial agreement, over 3,600 international freshwater agreements have been adopted.[24] The vast majority of those agreements covered navigational issues, which reflects the major use of international freshwaters during the earlier period of treaty evolution.[25] However, the *Atlas of International Freshwater Agreements* identifies a subset of more than 400 agreements signed since 1820 that relate to other uses of international freshwaters, including agriculture, industry, recreation, hydropower, flood control and ecosystem protection.[26] In recent years, international freshwater agreements have shifted away from single-purpose agreements towards the joint management of international waters.[27] Such a trend is reflected in key instruments relating to international freshwaters, including the UN Watercourses Convention, the 1966 Helsinki Rules and the 2001 Berlin Rules, which will be discussed below.[28]

While a significant number of agreements exist serious gaps remain. UN-Water – a body established to coordinate all UN activities related to water – estimates that 158 of the world's 263 international freshwaters lack any type of cooperative management framework, and many others do not have the necessary mechanisms in place to cope with existing and future challenges, such as climate change, population growth and food and energy security.[29] Similarly, Zawahri and Mitchell observe that the existing system is extremely fragmented, with most states preferring to enter bilateral arrangements with their neighbours even when

22 See e.g. A.T. Wolf, 'Conflict and cooperation along international waterways', *Water Policy* 1(2), 1998, 251–65.
23 See generally, S.C. McCaffrey 'The evolution of the Law of International Watercourses', *Austrian Journal of Public International Law* 5(2), 1992, 87–111; E.B. Weiss, *The Evolution of International Water Law*, The Hague: Martinus Nijhoff, 2009; J.W. Dellapenna and J. Gupta, *The Evolution of the Law and Politics of Water*, Berlin: Springer, 2009.
24 M.A. Giordano and A.T. Wolf, 'The World's International Freshwater Agreements: Historical Developments and Future Opportunities', in UNEP, Oregon State University and FAO, *Atlas of International Freshwater Agreements*, Nairobi: UNEP, 2002, p. 6.
25 A. Dinar, S. Dinar, S. McCaffrey and D. McKinney, *Bridges over Water: Understanding Transboundary Water Conflict, Negotiation and Cooperation*, New Jersey: World Scientific Publishing Company, 2007, pp. 58–60.
26 UNEP, Oregon State University and FAO, *Atlas of International Freshwater Agreements*, Nairobi: UNEP, 2002; see also S. Burchi and K. Mechlem, *Groundwater in International Law*, Rome: FAO, 2005.
27 A. Dinar et al., op. cit., pp. 61–3.
28 *Convention on the Law of the Non-Navigational Uses of International Watercourses*, opened for signature 21 May 1997, 36 ILM 700 (not yet entered into force) ('UN Watercourses Convention'); *The Helsinki Rules on the Uses of the Waters of International Rivers* as reprinted in S. Bogdanović, *International Law of Water Resources*, The Hague: Kluwer Law International, 2001, pp. 99–146 ('Helsinki Rules'); *Berlin Rules on Water Resources*. Online. Available HTTP: <http://www.cawater-info.net/library/eng/l/berlin_rules.pdf> (login required; accessed 21 September 2011) ('Berlin Rules'). The latter instruments are discussed in more detail below.
29 UN-Water, *Transboundary Waters: Sharing Benefits, Sharing Responsibilities*. Online. Available HTTP: <http://www.unwater.org/downloads/UNW_TRANSBOUNDARY.pdf> (accessed 21 September 2011).

a particular body of freshwater is shared between more than two states.[30] Such an approach is at variance to conventional wisdom, which calls for an integrated and holistic approach to the management of freshwater.[31]

Despite a general message of fragmentation, it is important to recognise that a number of regional initiatives exist. For instance, within the European context two notable regional instruments apply to international freshwaters: the UN Economic Commission for Europe Convention on the Protection and Use of Transboundary Watercourses and International Lakes, and the EC Water Framework Directive.[32] Additionally, within the Southern African context the Southern African Development Community Revised Protocol on Shared Watercourses governs international freshwaters at a regional level.[33] These regional instruments will be analysed in more detail in the following section.

A further significant feature in the evolution of international freshwater law has been the role of expert groups or epistemic communities. The most notable contribution to the codification and progressive development of international freshwater law has come from the International Law Commission (ILC) under the auspices of the UN General Assembly. The ILC's involvement in international freshwater law originated from a proposal by Bolivia in 1959 for the UN Secretary-General to examine 'the legal problems relating to the utilization and use of international rivers'.[34] Following a report by the UN Secretary-General in 1963, the UN General Assembly recommended that the ILC 'take up the study of the law of the non-navigational uses of international watercourses with a view to its progressive development and codification'.[35]

After 20 years' work and 15 reports by eminent international jurists acting as Special Rapporteurs, the *Draft Articles on the Law of the Non-navigational Uses of International Watercourses* (1994 ILC Draft Articles) were adopted.[36] Upon receipt of the 1994 ILC Draft Articles, the UN General Assembly took the decision to convene a working group to negotiate a Convention on the basis of the draft articles.[37] The working group met on two occasions in 1996 and 1997, prior to the UN Watercourses Convention being adopted on 21 May 1997 by

---

30 N.A. Zawahri and S. McLaughlin Mitchell, 'Fragmented governance in international rivers: negotiating bilateral versus multilateral treaties', *International Studies Quarterly* 55, 2011, 835–58.

31 United Nations, *Agenda 21 – the United Nations Programme for Action From Rio*, paras. 18.1–18.90. Online. Available HTTP: <http://www.un.org/esa/dsd/agenda21/res_agenda21_18.shtml> (accessed 21 September 2011).

32 *Convention on the Protection and Use of Transboundary Watercourses and International Lakes*, opened for signature 17 March 1992, 31 ILM 1312 (entered into force 6 October 1996) ('1992 UN ECE Helsinki Convention'); Directive 2000/60/EC of the European Parliament and the Council of 23 October 2000 establishing a framework for community action in the field of water policy. Online. Available HTTP: <http://ec.europa.eu/environment/water/water-framework/index_en.html> (accessed 9 May 2012) ('EC Water Framework Directive').

33 *Southern Africa Development Community, Revised Protocol on Shared International Watercourses*, opened for signature 7 August 2000, 40 ILM 321 (entered into force 22 September 2003).

34 UN General Assembly Resolution 1401 (XIV), 21 November 1959.

35 *Progressive Development and Codification of the Rules of International Law Relating to International Watercourses*, GA Res 2669 (XXV). Online. Available HTTP: <http://daccess-dds-ny.un.org/doc/RESOLUTION/GEN/NR0/349/34/IMG/NR034934.pdf?OpenElement> or via <http://untreaty.un.org/cod/avl/ha/clnuiw/clnuiw.html> (accessed 21 September 2011).

36 *Draft Articles on the Law of the Non-navigational Uses of International Watercourses* (1994), GA Res 49/52, UN GAOR, 49th Sess. Online. Available HTTP: <http://daccess-dds-ny.un.org/doc/RESOLUTION/GEN/NR0/781/16/IMG/NR078116.pdf?OpenElement> or via <http://untreaty.un.org/cod/avl/ha/clnuiw/clnuiw.html> (accessed 21 September 2011).

37 Ibid.

103 votes in favour, 26 abstentions and 3 votes against.[38] To date, there are 26 contracting states to the Convention, 11 short of the requisite number for the instrument to enter into force.[39] However, despite its non-entry into force, the UN Watercourses Convention remains the most authoritative statement of existing and emerging customary law in the field of international freshwaters and has proved influential in shaping treaty practice.[40] The role and relevance of the Convention will be explored in more detail within the following two sections.

It is also important to recognise the role of two other non–governmental expert bodies, the International Law Association (ILA) and the Institute of International Law (IIL).[41] The IIL's work constitutes the first attempt by an independent expert group to codify rules relating to international freshwaters. This work resulted in the Salzburg Resolution of 1961, which recognised the concept of limited territory sovereignty over international freshwater.[42] In particular, the work of the ILA relating to international freshwaters has proved highly influential.[43] This early work by the ILA culminated in the Helsinki Rules on the Uses of the Waters of International Rivers in 1966.[44] The Helsinki Rules played an important role in shaping subsequent treaty practice, particularly in Africa, and many of the rules and principles found in the Helsinki Rules are reflected in the later UN Watercourses Convention.[45] In addition to the Helsinki Rules, the ILA has examined treaty practice in a number of sub-areas of the law relating to international freshwater.[46] Finally, the ILA sought to develop their work on the codification and progressive development of international freshwater law through the 2004 Berlin Rules on Water Resources.[47] However, the degree to which the latter instrument accurately reflects existing state practice and *opinio juris* is hotly debated.[48]

Finally, the most significant recent development in international freshwater law has been the work of the ILC on the law of transboundary aquifers.[49] In 2009 the ILC presented draft

38 UN Watercourses Convention, which contains the voting record on pages 7 and 8. Online. Available HTTP: <http://www.un.org/ga/search/view_doc.asp?symbol=A/51/PV.99>.
39 *Status of multilateral treaties deposited with the Secretary-General.* Online. Available HTTP: <http://treaties.un.org/Pages/ViewDetails.aspx?src=UNTSONLINE&tabid=2&mtdsg_no=XXVII-12&chapter=27&lang=en#Participants> (accessed 21 September 2011).
40 S.C. McCaffrey, 'The 1997 UN Watercourses Convention: Retrospect and Prospect', *Pacific McGeorge Global Business and Development Law Journal* 21, 2008, 165–74.
41 FAO legal office, *Sources of International Water Law*, Rome: FAO, 2001. Online. Available HTTP: <http://www.fao.org/DOCREP/005/W9549E/w9549e00.htm#Contents> (accessed 21 September 2011).
42 S. Salman, 'The Helsinki Rules, the UN Watercourses Convention and the Berlin Rules: Perspectives on International Water Law', *Water Resources Development* 23(4), 2007, 625–40.
43 C. Bourne, 'The International Law Association's contribution to international water resources law', *Natural Resources Journal* 36, 1996, 155–216.
44 The Helsinki Rules.
45 Salman, 'The Helsinki Rules', op. cit.
46 Bogdanović, op. cit., pp. 147–387.
47 Berlin Rules.
48 ILA Berlin Conference 2004 – Water Resources Committee Report Dissenting Opinion, 9 August 2004. Online. Available HTTP: <http://www.internationalwaterlaw.org/documents/intldocs/ila_berlin_rules_dissent.html> (accessed 21 September 2011). See also Salman, 'The Helsinki Rules', op. cit.
49 An 'aquifer' is defined within the Draft Articles as being 'a permeable water bearing geological formation underlain by a less permeable layer and the water contained in the saturated zone of the formation'. See generally, C. Yamada, 'Codification of the Law of Transboundary Aquifers (Groundwater) by the United Nations', *Water International* 36(5), 2011, 557–65.

articles on the law of transboundary aquifers to the UN General Assembly, with the suggestion that they 'recommend to States concerned to make appropriate bilateral or regional arrangements for the proper management of their transboundary aquifers on the basis of the principles enunciated in the articles'; and 'consider, at a later stage, and in view of the importance of the topic, the elaboration of a convention on the basis of the draft articles'.[50]

The corpus of international freshwater law

The corpus of international freshwater law can be set out under five key elements: scope, substantive norms, procedural obligations, institutional arrangements and dispute settlement mechanisms.[51] However, prior to examining these individual elements, it is important to consider the basis of legal entitlements to international freshwaters.

Throughout the years, alternative claims of entitlement over international freshwaters have been put forward by states – usually in connection with political posturing on a particular dispute with neighbouring riparians. One claim favoured by upstream riparians maintains that a state has unlimited use of the waters of an international freshwater resource situated within its jurisdiction irrespective of the concerns of other watercourse states.[52] The so-called absolute territorial sovereignty principle was made famous by US Attorney-General Judson Harmon within the context of US–Mexico relations pertaining to the Rio Grande.[53] Conversely, other states, usually downstream, have claimed that the principle of absolute territorial integrity should apply; namely that upstream states should not interfere with the natural flow and conditions of an international watercourse.[54]

Given the need to find a balanced approach that satisfies all states, legal entitlements over international freshwaters have tended to be founded upon the doctrine of limited territorial sovereignty, whereby states enjoy equal rights to the utilisation of an international freshwater resource and an obligation to respect the correlative rights of other states sharing the resource.[55] However, it should be noted that while the doctrine of limited territorial sovereignty pervades the corpus of international freshwater law, as described below, many of the disagreements and disputes over the interpretation and application reflect the upstream and downstream stances taken pursuant to the principles of absolute territorial sovereignty and absolute territorial integrity.

50 *The Law of Transboundary Aquifers* (2009), GA Res 63/124, UN GAOR, 63rd Sess. Online. Available HTTP: <http://www.un.org/Docs/journal/asp/ws.asp?m=A/RES/63/124> (accessed 9 May 2012).
51 S. Vinogradov, P. Wouters and P. Jones, *Transforming Potential Conflict into Cooperation Potential: The Role of International Water Law*, Dundee: University of Dundee, 2003. Online. Available HTTP: <http://unesdoc.unesco.org/images/0013/001332/133258e.pdf> (accessed 21 September 2011).
52 See generally, A. Rieu-Clarke, *International Law and Sustainable Development – Lessons from the Law of International Watercourses*, London: IWA Publishing, 2005, pp. 101–3.
53 S.C. McCaffrey, 'The Harmon Doctrine one hundred years later: buried, not praised', *Natural Resources Journal* 36, 1996, 549–90.
54 F.J. Berber, *Rivers in International Law*, London: Stevens & Sons, 1959, pp. 19–22.
55 A. Tanzi and M. Arcari, *The United Nations Convention on the Law of International Watercourses – A Framework for Sharing*, London: Kluwer Law International, 2001, pp. 14–15.

Scope

Scope relates to 'geographical and/or hydrological or hydrographical parameters' and 'the type of uses or activities regulated by an agreement'.[56] Traditional approaches to scope tended to be quite narrow, which reflected both the uses and the scientific understanding of international freshwater resources.

Within the latter half of the last century a broadening of the concept of international freshwaters was witnessed. The 1966 ILA Helsinki Rules, for example, cover 'international drainage basins', which are defined as geographical areas 'extending over two or more states determined by the watershed limits of the system of waters, including surface and underground waters, flowing into a common terminus'.[57] Despite widespread treaty practice, the concept of a 'drainage basin' proved controversial during the work of the ILC because it encompassed both the land and water contained within a particular basin.[58] Ultimately, the UN Watercourses Convention adopted a narrower approach using the term 'watercourse', which was defined as 'a system of surface waters and groundwaters constituting by virtue of their physical relationship a unitary whole and normally flowing into a common terminus'.[59] However, it is important to keep in mind that the definition contained in the UN Watercourses Convention does not preclude land-based activities from being subject to the provisions of the instrument. Under Article 1 it is stipulated that the UN Watercourses Convention is applicable to 'uses of international watercourses *and of their waters* for purposes other than navigation and to measures of protection, preservation and management related to uses of those watercourses and their waters.'[60] The reference to 'international watercourses . . . and their waters' was included in order to cover the situation where waters are diverted away from a particular watercourse.[61] Land-based activities such as the use of such waters to feed an irrigation scheme would therefore still fall within the remit of the Convention.

As noted above, recent treaty practice at a basin level appears to be more amenable to an expansive approach to issues of scope. For example, the 2003 Protocol for the Sustainable Development of Lake Victoria stipulates that the protocol 'shall govern the partner states' cooperation in the sustainable development of Lake Victoria Basin'.[62] 'Lake Victoria Basin' is defined as 'the geographical area extending within the territories of the Partner States determined by the watershed limits of the system of waters, including surface and underground waters flowing into Lake Victoria'.[63]

56 P. Wouters and D. Ziganshina, 'Tackling the Global Water Crisis: Unlocking International Law as Fundamental to the Peaceful Management of the World's Shared Transboundary Waters – Introducing the H2O Paradigm', in Q. Grafton and K. Hussey (eds) *Water Resources Planning and Management: Challenges and Solutions*, Cambridge: Cambridge University Press, 2011, p. 182.

57 The Helsinki Rules, Art. II.

58 *Replies of Governments to the Commission's Questionnaire*, UN Doc A/CN.4/294 and Add. 1. Online. Available HTTP: <http://untreaty.un.org/ilc/documentation/english/a_cn4_294.pdf> (accessed 21 September 2011).

59 UN Watercourses Convention, Art. 2(a).

60 Ibid., Art. 1.

61 A. Tanzi and M. Arcari, op. cit., p. 49.

62 *Protocol for Sustainable Development of Lake Victoria Basin*, opened for signature 29 November 2003, 801 UNTS 101 (entered into force 6 November 1987) Art. 2. Online. Available HTTP: <http://www.internationalwaterlaw.org/documents/regionaldocs/Lake_Victoria_Basin_2003.pdf> (accessed 21 September 2011).

63 *Protocol for Sustainable Development of Lake Victoria Basin*, Art. 1(2).

A slightly nuanced approach to defining scope is offered by the Rhine Convention, which offers a number of definitions according to function.[64] Pursuant to Article 2 the Convention is applicable to 'the Rhine', the 'ground-water interacting with the Rhine', 'the aquatic and terrestrial ecosystems interacting with the Rhine or whose interaction with the Rhine could be re-established', 'the Rhine catchment area, as far as its pollution adversely affects the Rhine' and 'the Rhine catchment area, as far as it is of importance for issues of flood prevention and defence along the Rhine'.[65]

Substantive norms

Substantive norms define the legality of existing, new and planned uses.[66] The principle that states must utilise their international freshwaters in an equitable and reasonable manner is widely accepted as both customary international law and the primary substantive norm of international freshwater law.[67] The applicability of the principles is described by the ILC in the following passage:

> In many cases, the quality and quantity of water in an international watercourse will be sufficient to satisfy the needs of all watercourse states. But where the quantity or quality of the water is such that all the reasonable and beneficial uses of all watercourse states cannot be fully realised, a 'conflict of uses' results. In such a case, international practice recognises that some adjustments or accommodations are required in order to preserve each watercourse state's equality of right. These adjustments or accommodations are to be arrived at on the basis of equity, and can best be achieved on the basis of specific watercourse agreements.[68]

A key aspect of the principle of equitable and reasonable utilisation is that it does not provide for a predetermined priority of uses. The UN Watercourses Convention stipulates that 'no use of an international watercourse enjoys inherent priority', and 'all relevant factors are to be considered together and a conclusion reached on the basis of the whole'.[69] However, the latter statement must be scrutinised on a number of counts.

Firstly, Article 10(2) of the UN Watercourses Convention stipulates that 'special regard' must be given to 'vital human needs', when determining whether a particular use is equitable and reasonable.[70] 'Vital human needs' is defined in the statement of understanding to the Convention so as to mean sufficient water to sustain human life, including both drinking water and water required for the production of food in order to prevent starvation.[71] However, the latter definition leaves certain aspects open to interpretation. By use of the word 'including'

---

64 *Convention on the Protection of the Rhine*, opened for signature 12 April 1999 (entered into force 1 January 2003). Online. Available HTTP: <http://faolex.fao.org/watertreaties/index.htm> (accessed 21 September 2011).
65 Ibid., Art. 2.
66 P. Wouters and D. Tarlock, 'Are shared benefits of international waters an equitable apportionment?', *Colorado Journal of International Environmental Law and Policy* 18, 2007, 523–36.
67 UN Watercourses Convention, Art. 5(1).
68 *Draft Articles on the Law of the Non-navigational Uses of International Watercourses*, op. cit., para. 9.
69 UN Watercourses Convention, Arts 6, 10(1).
70 Ibid., Art. 10(2).
71 UN Watercourses Convention, Statement of Understanding.

the list of uses is clearly intended to be non-exhaustive. What other uses might therefore be included? Would water to sustain livelihoods, such as subsistence farming, be included? Is a certain quality of life recognised? A tighter definition is offered by the ILA Berlin Rules, which describe 'vital human needs' as 'waters used for *immediate* human survival, including drinking, cooking and sanitary needs, as well as water needed for the *immediate* sustenance of a household.'[72]

A second key element in the treatment of vital human needs is the meaning of special regard. Why are vital human needs simply not given priority under Article 10?[73] Some writers have criticised the UN Watercourses Convention on this point.[74] However, interpreting the text of Article 10 in light of the aims and objectives of the principle of equitable and reasonable utilisation, and also accounting for recent development relating to the right to water, it would seem that the criticisms are unduly pessimistic.[75] The use of the term 'special regard' recognises that the so-called 'right to water' should be secured, while also providing a balanced approach. For instance, Article 6 of the UN Watercourses Convention identifies a key factor as being 'the availability of alternatives, of comparable value, to a particular planned or existing use'.[76] A situation may therefore arise where vital human needs might be met by an alternative water source.[77]

A further important qualification to the 'no inherent priority' principle contained within the UN Watercourses Convention comes in the shape of the 'no significant harm' rule. Despite considerable disagreement over which norm should take priority, the 1997 UN Watercourses Convention ultimately sought to find an effective balance between the equitable and reasonable utilisation and no harm principles.[78] Article 7 of the Convention therefore stipulates that

(1) Watercourse states shall, in utilising an international watercourse in their territories, take all appropriate measures to prevent the causing of significant harm to other watercourse states.

(2) Where significant harm nevertheless is caused to another watercourse State, the states whose use causes such harm shall, in the absence of agreement to such use, take all appropriate measures, have due regard for the provisions of articles 5 and 6, in consul-

72 Berlin Rules, Art. 3(20).
73 In contrast, Berlin Rules, Art. 14(2) stipulates that 'States shall first allocate waters to satisfy vital human needs'.
74 E. Hey, 'The Watercourses Convention: to what extent does it provide a basis for regulating uses on international watercourses?', *Review of European Community & International Environmental Law* 7, 1998, 291–300, p. 298; A. Nollkaemper, 'The contribution of the International Law Commission to International Water Law: does it reverse the flight form substance?', *Netherlands Yearbook of International Law* 27, 1996, 39–73.
75 *General Comment No. 15 – The Right to Water (Articles 11 and 12 of the International Covenant on Economic, Social and Cultural Rights, Committee on Economic, Social and Cultural Rights)* (2002), 29th Sess, UN Doc E/C.12/2002/11. See also, *The Human Right to Water and Sanitation* (2010), GA Res 64/292, UN GAOR, 64th Sess. Online. Available HTTP: <http://waterwiki.net/index.php/UN_Human_Rights_Council_Resolution_on_Water_and_Sanitation> (accessed 9 May 2012).
76 UN Watercourses Convention, Art. 6(1)(g).
77 A. Rieu-Clarke, op. cit., pp. 111–15.
78 A.E. Utton, 'Which rule should prevail in international water disputes: that of reasonableness or that of no harm?', *Natural Resources Journal* 36, 1996, 635–41; P.K. Wouters, 'An assessment of recent developments in international watercourse law through the prism of the substantive rules governing use allocation', *Natural Resources Journal* 36, 1996, 417–39.

tation with the affected states, to eliminate or mitigate such harm and, where appropriate, to discuss the question of compensation.

A number of points are worthy of note in the latter provision. First, by the reference to Article 5 and 6, the Convention clearly puts the no significant harm principle beneath the principle of equitable and reasonable utilisation.[79]

Secondly, by the adoption of the term 'all appropriate measures', the obligation placed upon states is one of conduct rather than result. The obligation is therefore seen to be breached where a state 'has intentionally or negligently caused the event which had to be prevented, or has intentionally or negligently not prevented others in its territory from causing that event or has abstained from abating it'.[80] The focus of an alleged breach is likely to rest on whether a state has implemented the necessary administrative, legal and technical measures by which it can fulfil its obligations under the Article.[81]

In terms of the threshold of harm, the 2001 ILC Draft Articles on the Prevention of Transboundary Harm from Hazardous Substances define 'significant' as:

> something more than 'detectable' but need not be at the level of 'serious' or 'substantial'. The harm must lead to a real detrimental effect on matters such as, for example, human health, industry, property, environment or agriculture in other states. Such detrimental effects must be susceptible of being measured by factual and objective standards.

McCaffrey describes paragraph two of Article 7 as 'having all the hallmarks of a hard-won compromise'.[82] Ultimately, the text seeks to find an effective balance between the principles of no harm and equitable and reasonable utilisation.

Finally, a key qualification relating to the principle of equitable and reasonable utilisation concerns the need to protect ecosystems. Article 20 of the UN Watercourses Convention reflects the need to take environmental considerations into account by stipulating that 'watercourse states shall, individually and, where appropriate, jointly, protect and preserve the ecosystems of international watercourses'.[83] This obligation to protect aquatic ecosystems of international watercourses finds increasing support in treaty practice.[84]

Given the above analysis of the substantive norms of international freshwater law, while it could be argued that the overarching principle dictates that states utilise their international freshwater resources in an equitable and reasonable manner, inherent in that notion is the need to, firstly, protect vital human needs consistent with an individual's right to water, and secondly to protect the ecosystems of international watercourses with a view to ensuring the long-term viability of the resource. Such an interpretation also leads to a narrow definition of

79 Salman, 'The Helsinki Rules', op. cit., p. 633.
80 *Draft Articles on the Law of the Non-navigational Uses of International Watercourses*, op. cit., p. 103.
81 *Fourth Report on the Law of the Non-navigational Uses of International Watercourses* (1998), S.C. McCaffrey, Special Rapporteur, UN Doc A/CN.4/412, p. 239. Online. Available HTTP: <http://untreaty.un.org/ilc/documentation/english/a_cn4_412.pdf> (available 21 September 2011).
82 S.C. McCaffrey and M. Sinjela, 'The 1997 United Nations Convention on International Watercourse', *American Journal of International Law* 97, 1998, p. 101.
83 See also UN Watercourses Convention, Arts 5(1) and (2), 6(1)(f), 21, 22, and 23.
84 A. Iza, *International Water Governance: Conservation of Freshwater Ecosystems*, Cambridge: IUCN, 2004; A. Utton and J. Utton, 'The International Law of Minimum Stream Flows', *Colorado Journal of International Environmental Law and Policy* 10, 1999, 7–38.

what 'significant' harm may be permissible, which is likely to be limited to economic, and to some degree social, harm.

Procedural obligations

A strong correlation exists between the substantive norms described above and the procedural obligations. This relationship is summed up by Schachter when he observes that:

> procedural requirements should be regarded as essential to the equitable sharing of water resources. They have particular importance because of the breadth and flexibility of the formulae for equitable use and appropriation. In the absence of hard and precise rules of allocation, there is a relatively greater need for specifying requirements for advance notice, consultation, and decision procedures. Such requirements are, in fact, commonly found in agreements in neighbouring states concerning common lakes and rivers.[85]

Numerous procedural rules can be found in treaty practice relating to international freshwaters. For example, Article 12 of the UN Watercourses Convention, a reflection of customary law,[86] sets out the procedural obligation incumbent upon states to notify each other of planned measures that 'may have a significant adverse effect upon other watercourse states'.[87] Article 12 of the UN Watercourses Convention goes on to require that any notification 'be accompanied by available technical data and information, including the results of any environmental impact assessment'.[88] While this provision may be construed to mean that there is only an obligation to exchange an environmental impact assessment (EIA) where one is available, it would appear that customary law has progressed beyond that. Indeed, the ICJ observed in the recent *Pulp Mills case* that the EIA has 'gained so much acceptance among states that it may now be considered a requirement under general international law to undertake an environmental impact assessment where there is a risk that the proposed industrial activity may have significant adverse impact in a transboundary context, in particular, on a shared resource'.[89] However, it is only at the regional level that one can find details of the form and process that any transboundary EIA might take.[90]

A further feature of the UN Watercourses Convention, commonly found in treaty practice, is the obligation upon states to regularly exchange data and information, 'on the condition of the watercourse, in particular that of a hydrological, meteorological, hydrogeological and ecological nature and related to the water quality as well as related forecasts'.[91] Treaty

---

85 O. Schachter, *Sharing the World's Resources*, New York: Columbia University Press, 1977, p. 398.

86 See e.g. *Convention and Statutes Relating to the Development of the Chad Basin*, opened for signature 22 May 1964, (entered into force 15 September 1964) Art. 5. Online. Available HTTP: <http://www.fao.org/docrep/W7414B/w7414b05.htm> (accessed 21 September 2011); *Agreement Concerning the River Niger Commission and the Navigation and Transport on the River Niger*, opened for signature 25 November 1964, 587 UNTS 19 (entered into force 12 April 1966) Art. 12; *Convention Relating to the Status of the Senegal River*, opened for signature 11 May 1972, IEA 2734 (entered into force 25 May 1973) Art. 4.

87 UN Watercourses Convention, Art. 12.

88 Ibid., Art. 12(1).

89 *Case Concerning Pulp Mills on the River Uruguay*, pp. 60–1.

90 The only instrument that provides a process for the implementation of EIA procedures at the transboundary level is the UN ECE *Convention on Environmental Impact Assessment in a Transboundary Context*, opened for signature 25 February 1991, 30 ILM 800 (entered into force 10 September 1997).

91 UN Watercourses Convention, Art. 9(1).

practice concerning specific international freshwaters tends to provide more details relating to what data and information must be provided, and the manner by which it is exchanged.[92] Central to any system for the regular exchange of data and information will be the establishment of institutional arrangements, as discussed below.

Closely related to the regular exchange of data and information is the need to establish strategies for non-compliance. A prerequisite to such strategies will be reporting requirements concerning the implementation of any agreement. There are several examples of reporting requirements in recent treaty practice. At the regional level, the 2000 Revised SADC (South African Development Community) Protocol requires that watercourse institutions 'provide on a regular basis or as required by the Water Sector Coordinating Unit, all information necessary to assess progress on the implementation of the provisions of . . . [the] Protocol, including the development of their respective agreements'.[93] At the basin level, the 2003 Convention on the Sustainable Management of Lake Tanganyika provides that 'each contracting state shall report periodically . . . on measures that it has taken to implement this Convention and on the effectiveness of these measures in meeting the objective of this Convention'.[94]

Closely aligned to reporting requirements is the need for stakeholders to be involved in the governance of international freshwaters.[95] While international freshwater treaties traditionally tended to focus on state–state relations, to the exclusion of non-state actors with a vested interest within a particular basin, provisions relating to stakeholder participation have been included in more recent treaty practice.[96]

Institutional arrangements

The effective implementation of many of the substantive and procedural norms noted above is almost always contingent on the appropriate institutional arrangements being in place. McCaffrey notes that 'the management of international watercourse systems through joint institutions is not only an increasingly common phenomenon, but also a form of co-operation between watercourse states that is *almost indispensable* if anything approaching optimal utilisation and protection of the system of waters is to be attained'.[97]

---

92 See e.g. *Convention on the Co-operation for the Protection and Sustainable Use of the Waters of the Lusso-Spanish River Basins*, opened for signature 20 November 1998 (entered into force 31 January 2000) ('Lusso-Spanish Agreement'). Online. Available HTTP: <http://faolex.fao.org/watertreaties/index.htm> (accessed 21 September 2011).

93 Southern Africa Development Community, *Revised Protocol on Shared International Watercourses*, Art. 3(c). See also, EC Water Framework Directive, Art. 14; 1992 UN ECE Helsinki Convention, Art. 11.

94 *Convention on the Sustainable Management of Lake Tanganyika*, opened for signature 12 June 2003, Art. 22. See also, *Protocol for Sustainable Development of Lake Victoria Basin*, op. cit., Art. 45.

95 C. Bruch, L. Jansky, M. Nakayama and K.A. Salewicz, *Public Participation in the Governance of International Freshwater Resources*, Tokyo: United Nations University Press, 2005.

96 See, e.g., *Protocol for Sustainable Development of Lake Victoria Basin*, op. cit., Art. 22. See also 1992 UN ECE Helsinki Convention, Art. 16(1); EC Water Framework Directive, Art. 14(1).

97 *Sixth Report on the Law of the Non-navigational Uses of International Watercourses* (1990), S.C. McCaffrey, Special Rapporteur, UN Doc A/CN.4/427, p. 44. Online. Available HTTP: <http://untreaty.un.org/ilc/documentation/english/a_cn4_427.pdf> (accessed 21 September 2011). See also Bogdanović, op. cit., p. 19.

A growing treaty practice establishing joint institutions has therefore evolved.[98] However, despite this general recognition of the need for joint institutions, Dombrovsky only identifies 62 of the world's 263 international river basins as having established international river basin organisations in place.[99] Such figures are alarming, particularly given the role that institutions play in the effective implementation of treaty arrangements and compliance-related strategies.[100]

Dispute settlement mechanisms

Finally, a classic response to resolving non-compliance calls for recourse to judicial and arbitral enforcement, and the law of state responsibility.

Article 33 of the UN Watercourses Convention follows the UN Charter and customary law by stipulating that states are under an obligation to resolve their disputes in a peaceful manner. In addition to the traditional means of dispute settlement, such as negotiation, good offices, mediation, conciliation, arbitration and adjudication, the UN Watercourses Convention also includes the possibility of impartial fact-finding.[101] The latter mechanism obliges states to establish a commission to ascertain the facts, and to identify recommendations deemed appropriate to resolve the disputes. While the states are not obliged to adopt the recommendations, they must consider the findings of the commission in good faith.

Future prospects for the 1997 UN Watercourses Convention

As noted previously, the UN Watercourses Convention is not in force. Given the authoritative nature of the Convention it is worth making a few comments as to its role and relevance, and its prospects for entry into force.[102]

The UN Watercourses Convention gained considerable international support when adopted by the UN General Assembly in 1997. A key question to ask is, therefore, why those 103 votes in favour have not been translated into instruments of ratification, acceptance, approval or accession.

A number of reasons may be behind why the UN Watercourses Convention has not entered into force. One possibility might be 'treaty congestion'.[103] The Convention was

---

98 See e.g. International Joint Commission established under the *Treaty between Great Britain and the United States Relating to Boundary Waters, and Questions Arising between the United States and Canada*, opened for signature 11 January 1909 (entered into force 5 May 1910). Online. Available HTTP: <http://www.ijc.org/rel/agree/water.html> (accessed 21 September 2011).

99 I. Dombrovsky, 'Integration in the Management of International Waters: Economic Perspectives on a Global Policy Discourse', *Global Governance* 14(4), 2008, 455–77, pp. 460–1.

100 *Agreement on the Establishment of the Zambezi Watercourse Commission*, opened for signature 13 July 2004. Online. Available HTTP: <http://www1.eis.gov.bw/EIS/Policies> (accessed 21 September 2011). See UN ECE, *Geneva Strategy and Framework for Monitoring Compliance with Agreements on TransBoundary Waters* (2011), UN Doc MP.WAT/2000/5. Online. Available HTTP: <www.africanwater.org/Documents/compliance_strategy.doc> (accessed 21 September 2011).

101 See also Lusso-Spanish Agreement; *Framework Agreement on the Sava River Basin*, opened for signature 3 December 2002 (entered into force 3 December 2002) Art. 23. Online. Available HTTP: <http://www.savacommission.org/dms/docs/dokumenti/documents_publications/basic_documents/fasrb.pdf> (accessed 21 September 2011).

102 For in-depth analysis, see Loures and Rieu-Clarke, op. cit.

103 E.B. Weiss, 'International environmental law: contemporary issues and the emergence of a new world order', *Georgetown Law Journal* 81, 1993, 675–710, p. 697. See also Chapter 36 by D. Anton in this volume.

adopted at a time when several multilateral environmental agreements and a number of soft-law instruments had been adopted and/or entered into force; which may well have resulted in states feeling reluctant to commit to additional burdens.[104] Closely aligned to the above reason has been the fact that the UN Watercourses Convention has lacked a champion, unlike other instruments that have tended to be promoted by key individual governments, UN bodies or regional organisations. Only in recent years has this lack of support changed, with parts of the international community coming together to promote the Convention, which has had a marked effect on the number of ratifications in the last few years.[105]

Lack of awareness and capacity has also been identified as a key constraint behind the Convention's non-entry into force.[106] A range of surveys conducted by the World Wide Fund for Nature (WWF) and the UNESCO Centre for Water Law Policy & Science, University of Dundee, have demonstrated that across the world more needs to be done to raise awareness of the Convention and examine the likely impacts of implementation at the national level.[107] Low levels of awareness may also be due to the fact that roles and responsibilities for the management of international freshwaters tend to be spread across ministries, such as irrigation and water, law and justice, environment and foreign affairs.

A further factor that may have led to a reluctance of certain states joining the Convention relates to its content. Salman has highlighted a number of different, and sometimes inaccurate, perceptions and interpretations of the Convention.[108] Such misperceptions can only be addressed through increased awareness, training and understanding of international law's function within the context of freshwater, among key stakeholders at global, regional, basin and national levels.

Conclusion

A survey of international freshwater law demonstrates a long tradition of treaty-making, and related practice. Such developments have resulted in a rich body of law covering fundamental aspects of scope, substantive norms, procedural obligations, institutional arrangements and dispute resolution mechanisms. However, much work needs to be done to ensure that this body of law spreads throughout the world's international freshwaters, and, more importantly, is effectively implemented. The fact that the UN Watercourses Convention has yet to enter into force shows that more work is needed to increase awareness, training and understanding of law's role in this increasingly important field of international relations.

---

104 A. Rieu-Clarke and F. Loures, 'Still not in force: should states support the 1997 UN Watercourses Convention?,' *Review of European Community and International Environmental Law* 18(2), 2009, 185–97.
105 See generally, UN Watercourses Convention, op. cit.
106 Rieu-Clarke and Loures, 'Still not in force', op. cit.
107 See 'UN Watercourses Convention Global Initiative'. Online. Available HTTP: <http://www.dundee.ac.uk/water/projects/unwcglobalinitiative/> (accessed 21 September 2011).
108 S. Salman, 'The United Nations Watercourses Convention ten years later: why has its entry into force proven difficult?', *Water International* 32(1), 2007, 1–15, p. 8.

15

Marine environmental law

UNCLOS and fisheries

Rebecca M. Bratspies and Anastasia Telesetsky

The United Nations Convention on the Law of the Sea transformed the jurisdictional zones in the world's oceans and the way in which fisheries are managed. This chapter considers the international legal framework that governs the oceans, focusing on the protection and preservation of the marine environment under the Convention on the Law of the Sea and the management of fisheries, marine habitats and marine biodiversity conservation. Given the imperative of ensuring the protection and sustainable management of marine living resources for livelihoods and food security, this chapter explores innovative approaches to current challenges and the way forward.

Introduction: the state of marine fisheries

The world's oceans are in crisis. There are the perennial problems associated with illegal, unreported, and unregulated fishing (IUU), destructive fishing techniques, and coastal pollution.[1] But now in addition to problems of illegal behaviour, legal fishing activities are taking their toll primarily due to overfishing caused by excess fishing vessel capacity. The most recent Food and Agriculture Organization (FAO) report observes that 32 per cent of fish stocks are depleted and overexploited,[2] and a little over half of the stocks are fully utilised.[3] Recent scientific reports alarmingly suggest that humans are fishing down the food chain in a fashion that may threaten the viability of ocean ecosystems.[4] The warmer, more acidic

---

1 Food and Agriculture Organization, *State of World Fisheries and Aquaculture 2010*. Online. Available HTTP: <http://www.fao.org/docrep/013/i1820e/i1820e.pdf> (accessed 18 January 2012).
2 Among the fully exploited species are the top ten fished species which account for 30 per cent of marine capture fisheries including, for example, tuna, herring and anchovy stocks. FAO, *State of World Fisheries and Aquaculture 2010*, p. 8.
3 Ibid.
4 P. Greenberg, *Four Fish: The Future of the Last Wild Food*, New York: Penguin, 2011; D. Pauly, V. Christensen, S. Guénette, T.J. Pitcher, U.D. Sumaila, C.J. Walters, R. Watson and D. Zeller, 'Towards Sustainability in World Fisheries', *Nature* 418, 2002, 689–95; D. Pauly and M. Palomares, 'Fishing Down Marine Food Web: It Is Far More Pervasive than We Thought', *Bulletin of Marine Science* 76(2), 2005, 197–211.

ocean waters associated with climate change pose a potential threat to coral reefs and to fish migrations.[5] At the same time, aquaculture and coastal developments are putting pressures on critical nursery habitats for many marine species.[6] Thus marine fisheries face growing threats from all directions – the ocean itself is changing in a fashion that undermines biodiversity, even as human consumption of ocean biological resources is intensifying.

These stresses to the marine environment come at a particularly inopportune moment for the hundreds of millions of people dependent on marine fisheries for both their livelihoods and food supply. Indeed, according to the FAO, the per capita reliance on fish as a human food source reached an all-time high in 2008.[7] In short, marine capture fisheries and aquaculture, which now account for nearly two-thirds of the world's food fish supply,[8] are a crucial source of income[9] and food for hundreds of millions of people around the world. Given available technologies, fish production is not distributed equally across continents: Asia produces an average of 2.4 tonnes per person while Europe and North America produce respectively 24 tonnes and 18 tonnes per person.[10]

Governance measures rooted in international law, specifically the 1982 United Nations Convention on the Law of the Sea (UNCLOS), have failed to halt or reverse these trends. The UNCLOS treaty established the overarching framework for states' rights and obligations with respect to a wide range of ocean uses. It is generally considered to be customary law, and thus to bind all states – parties and non-parties alike. As an umbrella treaty, UNCLOS defines jurisdictional zones within the marine environment, and specifies the principles, rights and obligations that apply to various ocean uses. The state obligations laid out in UNCLOS include the responsibility to conserve living resources in the Exclusive Economic Zone (EEZ),[11] to protect and preserve the marine environment,[12] and the obligation to cooperate in conserving living resources of the high seas.[13] Obligations under UNCLOS also require states to take necessary measures 'to protect and preserve rare or fragile ecosystems as well as the habitat of depleted, threatened or endangered species and other forms of marine life'.[14]

Starting with the twentieth-century history of fisheries governance, this chapter discusses major treaty development including UNCLOS – the so-called 'constitution of the oceans'.

---

5 J. Alheit and E. Hagen, 'Long-term Climate Forcing of European Herring and Sardine Population', *Fisheries Oceanography* 6(2), 1997, 130–9.

6 S. Stonich, 'The Environmental Quality and Social Justice Implications of Shrimp Mariculture', *Human Ecology: An Interdisciplinary Journal* 23, 1995, 143, pp. 149–56.

7 Of the 142 million tonnes of fish supplied by both inland and marine capture and aquaculture, 117.8 million tonnes were utilised for human consumption providing 17.2 kilogrammes of fish per capita, which is up one kilogramme from 2004. FAO, *State of World Fisheries and Aquaculture 2010*, p. 3.

8 Ibid.

9 According to the FAO, in 2008, 44.9 million people were directly engaged in either full-time or part-time work in capture fisheries and aquaculture with many of these individuals supporting families (ibid., p. 6). Many more are involved in fish processing, distribution, and marketing. The majority of these individuals (85.5 per cent) are in developing countries, particularly in Asia (ibid., p. 7). Of the 119 million individuals participating both directly and indirectly in small-scale capture fisheries, nearly half of these individuals are women (ibid., p. 10).

10 Ibid., p. 27.

11 *United Nations Convention on the Law of the Sea*, opened for signature 10 December 1982, 1834 UNTS 397 (entered into force 16 November 1994) ('*UNCLOS*') Art. 61.

12 Ibid., Art. 192.

13 Ibid., Arts 117, 118.

14 Ibid., Art. 194(5).

This chapter explores the obligation of states to cooperate and develop conservation and management mechanisms and the enforcement challenges due to the prevalence of vessels flying flags of convenience (FOC). In addition to multilateral and regional efforts through the framework of treaties and regional fisheries management organisations, this chapter reviews key leadership efforts by the FAO to protect threatened marine fisheries. The chapter concludes with an analysis of some of the emerging marine protection themes that will be facing the marine policy decision-makers of the twenty-first century.

Historical multilateral state-based marine fisheries governance

For years, many states did not believe that the ocean fisheries could ever be depleted.[15] By the end of World War II, however, it was becoming abundantly clear that overfishing posed a real threat to the viability of national fisheries. In 1945, US President Harry S. Truman issued an executive proclamation on fisheries calling for better management of coastal fisheries through creations of conservation zones 'in those areas of the high seas [which were measured beginning at three nautical miles] contiguous to the coasts of the United States (US) wherein fisheries activities have been or in the future may be developed and maintained on a substantial scale'.[16]

Truman's proclamation stimulated international interest in creating an international system of shared marine governance. The International Law Commission (ILC) began working in 1949 to codify customary international law regarding ocean management. The ILC prepared four draft conventions, which were adopted at the first United Nations (UN) Conference on the Law of the Sea in 1958, attended by 86 states. The most significant of these was the Convention on Fishing and Conservation of the Living Resources of the High Seas.[17] This convention envisioned only modest changes to the prevailing free-access model of fisheries management and limited its suggested management intervention to the introduction of an 'optimum sustainable yield' for specific commercially valuable fish stocks.[18] State parties to this 1958 Convention further committed to develop domestic law obliging their nationals engaged in fishing on the high seas to implement conservation measures.[19] However, if a party to the 1958 Convention desired to unilaterally apply conservation measures to any area of the high seas adjacent to its territorial sea (which at this time extended three nautical miles from shore), the party was first obligated to try to negotiate a conservation agreement with states whose nationals shared an interest in the particular high-seas fishery.[20] If those negotiations failed to produce an agreement within six months, coastal states could then issue unilateral measures of conservation. However, an objecting state would be free to contest those measures before an international commission.[21]

---

15 L. Juda, *International Law and Ocean Use Management: The Evolution of Ocean Governance*, London: Routledge, 1996, p. 20.
16 H.S. Truman, United States Presidential Proclamation No. 2668, 'Policy of the US with Respect to Coastal Fisheries in Certain Areas of the High Seas', Basic Document No. 6. 1945.
17 *Convention on Fishing and Conservation of the Living Resources of the High Seas*, opened for signature 29 April 1958, 559 UNTS 286 (entered into force 20 March 1966).
18 Ibid., Art. 2.
19 Ibid., Art. 3.
20 Ibid., Art. 4.
21 Ibid., Art. 7(4).

Even though it entered into force in 1966,[22] the 1958 Convention proved burdensome in its application. The treaty relied too heavily on bilateral and regional agreements to monitor high-seas regions, and the tendency of some states to issue flags of convenience undermined the principle of flag state enforcement. Attempts in 1960 to negotiate a second round of international agreements governing the high seas focused on the extent of the territorial sea and fishery limits. After protracted negotiations, the delegates were one vote short. As a result, no new agreements were adopted and the initiative ended in failure. However, international interest in a comprehensive agreement for managing the world's oceans continued to grow. Negotiations began in 1973 for a Third UN Conference on the Law of the Sea with more than 160 participating states. However, there was little international consensus on how to collectively address marine overfishing, and the negotiations dragged on for almost a decade.

By 1982, the negotiating parties had finally reached consensus on an agreement that addressed high-seas overfishing concerns by reimagining marine jurisdictions in a revolutionary manner.[23] To that end, the UNCLOS created new, legally cognisable EEZs that extended 200 nautical miles from the baselines used for measuring the territorial seas. As part of the creation of these EEZs, UNCLOS imposed conservation obligations within the EEZ as well as obligations to conserve living resources on the high seas, and duties to protect and preserve the marine environment from pollution.

Current fisheries management under UNCLOS

The creation of these new, legally distinct EEZs transformed the politics of fishing. These zones created a new legal relationship between coastal states and the 200 nautical miles of ocean adjacent to their shores encompassing the habitat of 95 per cent of the world's commercially exploitable fish.[24] Coastal states were given rights to explore and exploit the EEZ waters with a concomitant responsibility to conserve and manage the living resources within that EEZ.[25] Coastal states agreed to implement measures that would simultaneously maintain existing stocks and restore depleted stocks in order to supply 'maximum sustainable yield, as qualified by relevant environmental and economic factors'.[26]

Under UNCLOS, coastal states were expected to achieve 'optimum utilization' of living resources for both national and foreign fishers.[27] To that end, states were to use 'best scientific evidence' to determine the total allowable catch within their EEZs.[28] Among the methods that coastal states might choose to use to ensure long-term sustainability were closures of

---

22 The treaty currently has 38 parties. Online. Available HTTP: <http://treaties.un.org/doc/publication/mtdsg/volume%20ii/chapter%20xxi/xxi-3.en.pdf> (accessed 18 January 2012).

23 See generally D. Rothwell and T. Stephens, *The International Law of the Sea*, Oxford: Hart Publishing, 2010; R.R. Churchill and A.V. Rowe, *The Law of the Sea*, 3rd edition, Manchester: Manchester University Press, 1988; R. Anand, *Origin and Development of the Law of the Sea: History of International Law*, The Hague: Martinus Nijhoff Publishers, 1982, pp. 175–93.

24 Rothwell and Stephens, op. cit., p. 297.

25 UNCLOS, Art. 56.

26 Ibid., Art. 62. Maximum sustainable yield (MSY) is defined as the highest theoretical yield that can be continually taken from a stock under existing environmental conditions without impacting significantly the reproduction process. C. Finley, *All the Fish in the Sea: Maximum Sustainable Yield and the Failure of Fisheries Management*, Chicago: University of Chicago Press, 2011.

27 UNCLOS, Art. 62(1).

28 Ibid., Art. 61.

fisheries or limiting catch sizes for various species. The critical assumption behind this approach to fisheries management is the possibility of identifying a steady-state equilibrium at which the rate of harvest of a fish population balances the reproduction of the species. If that assumption is correct, it should be possible to set a total allowable catch (TAC) for a fishery that allows harvest of fish in perpetuity. Yet in practice, coastal states pursuing their MSY (maximum sustainable yield) of commercial stocks have continued to overexploit stocks.

The MSY approach to fisheries management is flawed. First, it does not take adequate account of human behaviours and motivations. Fish populations do not exist in a steady state. Recruitment defined as the number of fish surviving to enter a given fishery varies significantly over time, depending on environmental and ecological conditions. However, reducing the TAC to correspond with recruitment fluctuations has serious adverse economic consequences for those who depend on fishing for their livelihood. Thus, there is intense pressure on fisheries managers to keep catch levels constant rather than reducing allowable fishing effort in response to environmental pressures. Under these circumstances, MSY can too easily morph from the absolute limit on a fishery to the official target for fishing effort. Second, MSY-based fisheries management presumes a level of knowledge about marine species that rarely exists,[29] and a level of compliance with catch limits that rarely occurs:[30] IUU fishing, and bycatch, can wreak havoc with careful MSY-oriented planning.[31] Yet pressure to keep catch levels high means that decision-makers rarely have the luxury of adequately accounting for these phenomena. The tradition of open access fisheries further compounds the governance challenges.[32]

Third, coastal states failed to take into consideration 'relevant environmental . . . factors' in calculating MSY by treating commercial fish species as individual species in isolation from both other species and their habitat in spite of obligations under UNCLOS to take into

---

29 C. Ewald and W.K. Wang, 'Sustainable Yields in Fisheries: Uncertainty, Risk-Aversion and Mean-Variance Analysis', *Natural Resources Modeling* 33(3), 2010, 303–23; D. Ludgwig, R. Hilborn and C. Walters, 'Uncertainty, Resource Exploitation and Conservation: Lessons from History', *Science* 260(2), 1993, p. 17; P.A. Larkin, 'An Epitaph for the Concept of Maximum Sustainable Yield', *Transactions of the American Fisheries Society* 106(1), 1977, 1 onwards.

30 C. Smith, 'Addressing Illegal Unreported and Unregulated (IUU) Fishing, International Fisheries Compliance 2004 Conference, Brussels, Belgium, 29–30 September 2004. Online. Available HTTP <http://www.illegal-fishing.info/uploads/OECD-addressing-IUU-Fishing.pdf> (accessed 10 May 2012). Moreover, governments often subsidise unrealistic levels of production in order to avoid social dislocation. WWF, 'Underwriting Overfishing'. Online. Available HTTP: <http://www.worldwildlife.org/what/globalmarkets/fishing/WWFBinaryitem8633.pdf> (accessed 23 January 2012). This phenomenon has also been extensively explored in the context of forest management: R. Repetto and M. Gillis (eds) *Public Policies and the Misuse of Forest Resources*, Cambridge: Cambridge University Press, 1988.

31 The FAO reports that IUU fishing occurs in virtually all fisheries and in many important fisheries may account for a large percentage of the total catch. D.J. Doulman, 'International Plan of Action to Prevent, Deter and Eliminate Illegal, Unreported and Unregulated Fishing', Rome: FAO Fisheries and Aquaculture Department, 20 June 2011. Online. Available HTTP:<http://www.fao.org/fishery/topic/3195/en> (accessed 25 January 2012). The OECD has documented the extent of IUU fishing and proposes ways to eliminate it: High Seas Task Force, 'Closing the Net: Stopping Illegal Fishing on the High Seas', Final Report of the Ministerially-led Task Force on IUU Fishing on the High Seas, March 2006. Online. Available HTTP: <http://www.oecd.org/dataoecd/2/28/39375276.pdf> (accessed 25 January 2012).

32 E. Ostrom, 'A General Framework for Analyzing Sustainability of Social-Ecological Systems', *Science* 325, 2009, 419–22.

account the 'interdependence of stocks'.[33] The growing appreciation of the complexity of marine ecosystems and of inter-species interactions underscores the conceptual problem of basing fisheries management decisions on MSY.[34] Thus, over the past two decades, there has been a growing call to move beyond the current species-based approaches to fisheries to ecosystem-based management.[35] This trend is reflected in international soft-law agreements such as the 1992 Rio Declaration,[36] the 2002 Johannesburg Declaration,[37] the 1995 FAO Code of Conduct for Responsible Fisheries,[38] as well as the activities of various regional fisheries management organisations.[39]

In administrative practice, the reliance on MSY as the current fisheries management approach for most commercial fisheries has meant that state fishery institutions consult with the members of the fishing industry, members of national environmental agencies, and sometimes international research groups to decide sustainable yield numbers and necessary conservation measures. The negotiation processes associated with these groups do not always equitably balance economic and environmental interests. For example, the National Marine Fisheries Service under the Magnuson-Stevens Fishery Conservation and Management Act, the implementing legislation for US ocean management, relies heavily on regional fisheries councils dominated by industry members to set TAC numbers and suggest conservation measures.[40] That said, most states in keeping with their obligations under UNCLOS and customary law to protect marine resources have promulgated through regional fishery management organisations (RFMOs) some conservation measures including minimum and maximum catch sizes, catch quotas for different species, seasonal closures for certain

33 UNCLOS, Art. 61(3).

34 S.M. Garcia, A. Zerbi, C. Aliaume, T. Do Chi and G. Lasserre, 'The Ecosystem Approach to Fisheries: Issues, Terminology, Principles, Institutional Foundations, Implementation and Outlook', Fisheries Technical Paper No. 443, Rome: FAO, 2003. Online. Available FTP: <ftp://ftp.fao.org/docrep/fao/006/y4773e/y4773e00.pdf > (accessed 23 January 2012).

35 *Agenda 21*, Chapter 17, UN Doc. A/CONF.151/26/REV.1(VOL.II). Online. Available HTTP: <http://www.un.org/esa/dsd/agenda21/res_agenda21_17.shtml> (accessed 23 January 2012). See also, *Agreement for the Implementation of the Provisions of the United Nations Convention on the Law of the Sea of 10 December 1982 Relating to the Conservation and Management of Straddling Fish Stocks and Highly Migratory Fish Stocks*, opened for signature 4 December 1995, 2167 UNTS 88 (entered into force 11 December 2001), Arts. 5(d)(e)(f) and (g) ('UN Fish Stocks Agreement').

36 UNCED, *Rio Declaration on Environment and Development* (1992), UN Doc A/CONF.151/26 (Vol. I) ('Rio Declaration'). Online. Available HTTP: <http://www.un.org/documents/ga/conf151/aconf15126-1annex1.htm> (accessed 18 January 2012).

37 *Johannesburg Declaration on Sustainable Development* (2002), UN Doc A/CONF.199/20, pp. 1 5. Online. Available HTTP: <http://www.un.org/esa/sustdev/documents/WSSD_POI_PD/English/POI_PD.htm> (accessed 23 January 2012).

38 FAO Code of Conduct for Responsible Fisheries, Adopted by the 28th Session of the FAO Conference 31 October 1995. Online. Available HTTP: <http://www.fao.org/docrep/005/v9878e/v9878e00.htm> (accessed 18 January 2012).

39 The following RFMOs have competence over not just species but larger ecosystems: Commission on the Conservation of Antarctic Marine Living Resources (CCAMLR), General Fishery Commission for the Mediterranean (GFCM), Northwest Atlantic Fisheries Organization (NAFO) (except sedentary species), North East Atlantic Fisheries Organization (NEAFC) (except sedentary and migratory species), and Southeast Atlantic Fishery Commission (SEAFO).

40 E. Norse, 'Ending the Range Wars on the Last Frontier: Zoning the Sea', in E. Norse and L. Crowder (eds) *Marine Conservation Biology: The Science of Maintaining the Sea's Biodiversity*, Washington DC: Island Press, 2005, p. 431.

fisheries, number of vessels permitted to fish in an area, and type of fishing gear that can be used.[41]

The focus of UNCLOS was predominantly on the EEZ as a means to control overfishing and, to a large extent, it ignored the trickier problems of overfishing on the high seas which have traditionally been open to all. In retrospect, UNCLOS created remarkably little oversight of high seas fisheries, a lack of governance only magnified by the vast reach of this territory and its distance from coasts. Under its discussion of contiguous zones, UNCLOS provides that states which fish for straddling stocks that transit the high seas should directly or through regional organisations agree on measures to protect these stocks.[42] While many conservation measures have been adopted by members of regional fisheries organisations, discussed further below, a number of open registry states who offer flags of convenience have failed to participate in any fishery management organisation conservation measures.[43]

Articles 117 and Article 118 of UNCLOS both address the conservation and management of high-seas marine resources. States are expected to enforce such conservation measures 'as may be necessary for the conservation of the living resources of the high seas'.[44] There is no indication of whether parties collectively decide what is necessary for conservation or simply on a state-by-state basis. The particular challenge with enforcing this language in a meaningful fashion is that very little is known about the high-seas ecosystems in order to rationally guide the conversation about what is 'necessary' for conservation.[45]

Even with the participation of states in both the 1995 Fish Stocks Agreement (described below) and UNCLOS, destructive fishing practices and overexploitation of biological

41 For example, the International Convention for the Conservation of Atlantic Tuna (ICCAT) has set quotas and has imposed fisheries closures and catch size restrictions in a quest to rebuild Bluefin Tuna populations in the Western Atlantic: ICCAT, 'Supplemental Recommendations by ICCAT Concerning the Western Atlantic Bluefin Tuna Rebuilding Program, 10–03 [BFT], 2010. Online. Available HTTP: <http://www.iccat.int/Documents/Recs/compendiopdf-e/2010-03-e.pdf> (accessed 25 January 2012). The Indian Ocean Tuna Commission (IOTC) similarly imposes closure periods, and restricts vessel and gear activities. IOTC, Resolution 10/01 – Timeclosure for Long-Liners in February 2011, IOTC Circular 2011/03, 12 January 2011. Online. Available HTTP: <http://www.iotc.org/files/circulars/2011/03-11%5BE%5D.pdf> (accessed 25 January 2012). A 2007 TRAFFIC report describes all of the many RFMO restrictions imposed on Bigeye Tuna: M. Lack, 'With an eye to the future: Addressing failures in the global management of Bigeye Tuna', *TRAFFIC*, 2011. Online. Available HTTP: <http://www.traffic.org/fisheries/> (accessed 25 January 2012). Coastal states impose a similar array of catch, gear and effort restrictions. Unfortunately, these efforts are often undermined by ineffective enforcement, failure to comply with RFMO-adopted measures, and by IUU fishing from vessels flying flags of convenience.
42 UNCLOS, Art. 63(2).
43 For example, Bolivia, Georgia, Mauritius and Mongolia are all deemed flags of convenience, but have not joined any regional management organisation. It bears mentioning that Bolivia and Mongolia are both land-locked states.
44 UNCLOS, Art. 117.
45 The FAO observed that: 'Most fisheries for these deep-water species are relatively recent and the development of a majority of them has outpaced the ability to provide scientific information and to implement effective management.' J-J. Maguire, M. Sissenwine, J. Csirke and R. Grainger, *State of World Highly Migratory, Straddling and other High Seas Fishery Resources and Associated Species*, Fisheries Technical Paper 495, Rome: Food and Agriculture Organization, 2006, p. 49.

resources on the high seas continue to jeopardise unique and vulnerable ecosystems, like seamounts[46] and cold water coral reefs.[47]

Current enforcement strategies under UNCLOS

In a significant improvement over the 1958 Convention on Fishing, UNCLOS gave coastal states the power to enforce conservation measures, through boarding and inspecting vessels fishing within their EEZ and judicially prosecuting violators.[48] Even with these added capabilities, the current enforcement measures within EEZs lack robustness for a number of reasons. First, many coastal states are not well positioned to enforce conservation measures given the sheer expanse of water to monitor. For many key commercial fisheries, particularly in the Pacific Ocean, the coastal states simply lack the physical and human resources to individually provide any systematic enforcement of their negotiated conservation measures.[49] However, there have been promising developments. In 1992, in response to a lack of resources in the Pacific Ocean, a group of similarly situated small island states, plus Australia, Papua New Guinea and New Zealand, agreed multilaterally in the Niue Treaty to prevent IUU fishing in the South Pacific Region.[50] November 2011 marked a key moment of cooperative success for the Niue Treaty Parties with its largest monitoring and surveillance effort yet, supported by defence forces from Australia, France, New Zealand, and the US.[51]

Second, even those states with adequate resources have found it very difficult to implement their management authority over foreign vessels. A key legal limitation imposed by UNCLOS is the requirement that arrested vessels be promptly released on the posting of a reasonable bond and that states cannot imprison violators of conservation measures unless there is a previous agreement between the flag state and coastal state.[52]

While intended to protect the due process rights of parties, these measures have been interpreted in a manner that frustrates systematic implementation of conservation measures by coastal states. In February 2002, Australia boarded the Russian-flagged fishing vessel *Volga* on the suspicion that the crew had been illegally fishing Patagonian toothfish within the Australian EEZ in violation of Australian conservation measures. Australia seized the boat

---

46 J. Koslow, G.W. Boehlert, J.D.M. Gordon, R.L. Haedrich, P. Lorance and N. Parin, 'Continental Slope and Deep-sea Fisheries: Implications for a Fragile Ecosystem', *ICES Journal of Marine Science* 57, 2000, 548–57.

47 C. Roberts, 'Deep Impact: The Rising Toll of Fishing in the Deep Sea', *TRENDS in Ecology & Evolution* 17(5), 2000, 242–5.

48 UNCLOS, Art. 73(1).

49 K. Barclay and I. Cartwright, 'Governance of Tuna Industries: the Key to Economic Viability and sustainability in the Western and Central Pacific Ocean', *Marine Policy* 20(3), 2007, 348–58.

50 *Niue Treaty of Cooperation in Fisheries Surveillance and Law Enforcement in the South Pacific Region*, opened for signature 9 July 1992, 32 ILM 136 (entered into force 20 May 1993). This treaty has been updated.

51 Surveillance Operation Kurukuru in November 2011 covered an area of roughly 30 million square kilometres – including the exclusive economic zones of the Cook Islands, Federated States of Micronesia, Fiji, Kiribati, Marshall Islands, Nauru, Niue, Palau, Papua New Guinea, Samoa, Solomon Islands, Tokelau, Tonga, Tuvalu and Vanuatu. Pacific News Center News Release, 'Pacific Regional Maritime Surveillance Effort Seeks to Stop Illegal Fishing', 22 November 2011. Online. Available HTTP: <http://www.pacificnewscenter.com/index.php?option=com_content&view= article&id=18840:pacific-regional-maritime-surveillance-effort-seeks-to-stop-illegal- fishing&catid=45:guam-news&Itemid=156> (accessed 18 January 2012).

52 UNCLOS Arts 73(2) and 73(3).

and placed a bond on the vessel with the intention of deterring future illegal activity on the part of the owners. In *Russian Federation v Australia* (the *Volga* case) a majority of the International Tribunal of the Law of the Sea (ITLOS) sided with the flag state and agreed that UNCLOS did not empower states to use the bonds to deter future IUU behaviour.[53]

Moreover, even adequate enforcement cannot suffice to ensure conservation of marine resources as long as more powerful political states are able to override negotiated conservation measures. A recent controversy in the South Pacific illustrates this problem. In protest over the US refusal to compromise preferential fishing rights extracted in exchange for development aid, Papua New Guinea unilaterally withdrew, in April 2011, from the South Pacific Tuna Treaty[54] and walked away from ongoing negotiations for a successor treaty (the existing treaty sunsets in 2013).[55] Papua New Guinea's actions were prompted by the continued exemption of US fishing from regional conservation measures. Specifically, accordingly to the Pacific Islands Forum Fisheries Agency, Papua New Guinea's concerns were that the US vessels, in contrast to both local and other distant water fishing vessels, had no limitations on fishing days and continued to use restricted fishing gear.[56] Worse, the US vessels refused to abide by the prohibition of purse seine gear on the nearby high seas that parties to the 1982 Nauru Agreement Concerning Cooperation in the Management of Fisheries of Common Interest[57] imposed on all other vessels as a condition of fishing within their EEZs.[58] In recent negotiations, the Pacific Island States have refused to make additional conservation concessions to the US and as of January 2012 appeared to be prevailing on these negotiating points.[59] This type of negotiation may mark a shift in power dynamics between distant water fishing nations and states with coastal management interests.

Enforcement of conservation measures for marine fisheries on the high seas under UNCLOS depends almost exclusively on flag state enforcement. This can be problematic when there is no genuine relationship between a vessel's ownership and the coastal state that

---

53 ITLOS, No. 11. (*Russian Federation v Australia*): The '*Volga*' Case (23 December 2002). Available HTTP: <http://www.itlos.org/fileadmin/itlos/documents/cases/case_no_11/Judgment.Volga.E.pdf> (accessed 1 May 2012). Cf Dissenting Opinion by Judge *Ad Hoc* Shearer. Online. Available HTTP: <http://www.itlos.org/fileadmin/itlos/documents/cases/case_no_11/diss.op.Shearer.E.pdf> (accessed 1 May 2012). This raised issues over how the 'prompt release' bonding mechanism in UNCLOS could better promote conservation goals if it deterred IUU fishing by requiring fishers to forfeit a bond or install a vessel monitoring system.

54 *Treaty on Fisheries Between the Governments of Certain Pacific Island States and the Government of the United States*, opened for signature April 2 1987, 26 ILM 1048 (entered into force June 15 1988) Online. Available HTTP: <http://www.jus.uio.no/english/services/library/treaties/08/8-02/south-pacific-tuna.xml> (accessed 18 January 2012) (currently on its third extension).

55 As of January 2012, Papua New Guinea was back at the negotiating table. 'PNG Returns to US Tuna Talks', ABC *Asia Pacific News*, 17 January 2012. Online. Available HTTP: <http://abcasiapacificnews.com/stories/201201/3410080.htm> (accessed 18 January 2012).

56 Pacific Islands Forum Fisheries Agency, A. Hamilton, E. Havice and L. Campling, *Fisheries Trade News* 4(5), 2011. Online. Available HTTP: <http://www.ffa.int/node/459> (accessed 18 January 2012).

57 *Nauru Agreement Concerning the Cooperation in the Management of Fisheries of Common Interest*, opened for signature 11 February 1982, 1833 UNTS 3, 21 ILM 1261 (entered into force 4 December 1982). Online. Available HTTP: <http://www.ffa.int/system/files/%252Fhome/ffaadmin/%252Ffiles/ffa/Nauru%20Agreement.pdf> (accessed 18 January 2012).

58 Pacific Islands Forum Fisheries Agency, *Fisheries Trade News*, op. cit.

59 'Pacific Has Some Wins in Tuna Treaty Talks with US', *Radio Australia*, 19 January 2012. Online transcript. Available HTTP: <http://www.radioaustralia.net.au/pacbeat/stories/201201/s3411645.htm> (accessed 19 January 2012).

has registered the vessel. As noted earlier, many open registry flag states double as flags of convenience, meaning that vessel owners from one state may seek to flag their ships in countries with laxer environmental enforcement measures. Vessels flying flags of convenience exploit a state's lack of ability or interest in asserting oversight jurisdiction. There is a high correlation between being a state that issues flags of convenience and a failure to sign the 1995 Fish Stocks Agreement. Of the 14 FOC states that were responsible for the largest numbers of fishing ships and 9.4 per cent of the vessel tonnage registered with Lloyd's Register of Ships,[60] only six of the countries have signed the Fish Stocks Agreement.[61]

While generally only flag states can board vessels flying their flags, there has been a trend in the past decade for countries to negotiate among themselves bilateral and regional treaties permitting boarding of foreign vessels by non-flag states. Under the 1994 Convention on the Conservation and Management of Pollock Resources in the Central Bering Sea, the six parties to the convention are both permitted to place observers on board foreign ships as well as to board a ship suspected of illegal fishing until the flag state responds.[62] While this may alleviate IUU pressures in some fisheries, the ability of non-flag states to board foreign vessels is the exception and not the rule. These trends may change with more and more bilateral boarding and inspection agreements including a memorandum of agreement between the People's Republic of China and the US to allow for boarding of vessels suspected of illegal drift netting on the high seas.[63]

Fish Stocks Agreement

Chapter 17 of Agenda 21 focused attention on the need for international coordination in managing fishing on the high seas. To that end, the UN General Assembly (UNGA) convened a UN Conference on Straddling Fish Stocks and Highly Migratory Fish Stocks. The resulting Fish Stocks Agreement focuses on improving cooperation in the sustainable management of marine fisheries and has contributed a number of innovations to international fisheries governance.

60 M. Gianni and W. Simpson, *The Changing Nature of High Seas Fishing: How Flags of Convenience Provide Cover for Illegal, Unreported and Unregulated Fishing*, Australian Government Department of Agriculture, Fisheries and Forestry, International Transport Workers' Federation, and WWF International, 2005, pp. 14–15. Online. Available HTTP: <http://www.daff.gov.au/fisheries/iuu/high-seas> (accessed 9 May 2012).

61 Ibid. In 2005, Belize, Bolivia, Cambodia, Cyprus, Equatorial Guinea, Georgia, Honduras, Marshall Islands, Mauritius, Netherlands Antilles, Panama, St Vincent and the Grenadines, Sierra Leone, and Vanuatu issued the most flags of convenience according to Lloyds of London. Only Belize, Cyprus, Marshall Islands, Mauritius, Panama, and St Vincent and the Grenadines are parties to the 1995 Fish Stocks Agreement.

62 *Convention on the Conservation and Management of the Pollock Resources in the Central Bering Sea*, opened for signature 16 June 1994, 34 ILM 67 (entered into force 8 December 1995), Art. XI. Online. Available HTTP: <http://www.afsc.noaa.gov/REFM/CBS/Docs/Convention%20on%20Conservation%20of%20Pollock%20in%20Central%20Bering%20Sea.pdf> (accessed 18 January 2012).

63 United States and People's Republic of China Memorandum of Understanding for Fisheries Enforcement reported in UNGA (1993), Report of the Secretary-General, *Large-scale Pelagic Drift-net Fishing, Unauthorized Fishing in Zones of National Jurisdiction and on the High Seas, Fisheries By-catch and Discards, and other Developments*, UN Doc. A/55/386, 18 September 2000, p. 8, para. 38. Online. Available HTML: <www.un.org/documents/ga/docs/55/a55386.pdf> (accessed 18 January 2012).

Where UNCLOS focused on the optimum utilisation of fish stocks, the Fish Stocks Agreement instead emphasised an ecosystem-based approached to marine conservation. Under Article 5 of the Agreement, states are expected to incorporate a precautionary ecosystem management approach into their efforts to protect living marine resources. In addition, states are expected to rely on the best scientific evidence in calculating allowable catches, to tackle overcapacity in their fishing fleets, to minimise marine and land-based pollution, and to generate and share fishery research. Overall, states are expected to set 'precautionary reference points' to guide both conservation and management goals.[64]

The Agreement emphasised the need for coordination between conservation measures taken by states within their EEZ and practices of fishing nations on the high seas. It represented an international shift from prioritising the short-term interests of the fishing industry to protecting the long-term sustainability of the fish and their habitat. In designing conservation measures, all states were expected to take into account the special needs of coastal fishing communities,[65] and developed states were expected to provide training as well as financial and technical assistance to developing states in order to build capacity in the field of conservation and management of living marine resources.[66] Perhaps most importantly, parties to the Agreement were expected to join any RFMOs that governed the areas where their flagged vessels fish, and to comply with the conservation and management measures adopted by those RFMOs.[67] The idea was to provide RFMOs with new legitimacy. Any states that refused to join an RFMO could be excluded from a fishery. If RFMOs did not exist in a particular marine area, states were directed to cooperate in creating an RFMO to govern their fishing activities.[68]

Enforcement under the Agreement remained primarily with the flag state but regional compliance was enhanced through a mechanism similar to the 1994 Convention on the Conservation and Management of Pollock Resources in the Central Bering Sea. Under the Agreement, all parties operating within an RFMO were permitted to board and inspect fishing vessels flying the flag of any other party to the Fish Stocks Agreement.[69] Perhaps even more importantly, port states were empowered under the Agreement to inspect the fishing gear and catch of any vessel flagged to a party and to prohibit landings if there was evidence that the catch violated conservation measures.[70]

As a separate agreement to UNCLOS, states who were not members of UNCLOS were encouraged to join the Fish Stocks Agreement. The US has joined the Agreement even though it has not yet ratified UNCLOS. As of July 2011, 78 states had ratified the Agreement. While this represents a notable recent development in fishery law, China, the world's highest capacity fishing nation,[71] has yet to join.

---

64 *UN Fish Stocks Agreement*, op. cit., Annex II.
65 Ibid., Art. 11(f).
66 Ibid., Annex 1(1).
67 Ibid., Art. 8(3).
68 Ibid., Art. 8(5).
69 Ibid., Art. 21.
70 Ibid., Art. 23.
71 FAO, *State of World Fisheries and Aquaculture 2010*, p. 13.

Rebecca M. Bratspies and Anastasia Telesetsky

Relationship of the Convention on Biological Diversity to international marine fisheries

Article 22(2) of the Convention on Biological Diversity (CBD)[72] requires that states parties 'implement the Convention with respect to the marine environment consistently with their rights and obligations under the Law of the Sea'. Just as Article 117 of UNCLOS imposes a duty 'to take or to cooperate with other states in taking measures necessary to conservation of the living resources of the high seas', so too does Article 5 of the CBD oblige parties to cooperate 'as far as possible and as appropriate' in the conservation and sustainable use of biological diversity outside areas of national jurisdiction. Moreover, Article 4 of the CBD specifically provides that the obligations imposed under the treaty apply to processes and activities carried out beyond the limits of national jurisdiction. Article 7 requires that states identify processes and activities likely to have significant adverse impacts on the conservation and sustainable use of biodiversity. Thus in principle the CBD provides a basis for governance of fishing activities beyond national jurisdiction.

Yet the CBD's structural shortcomings limit its ability to contribute to help solve the problems of global marine fisheries. For one thing, the CBD imposes few binding obligations on states parties – even the duty to cooperate is limited by what is 'possible and appropriate'. The CBD has neither enforcement mechanisms nor mandatory dispute settlement provisions. The CBD also shares a critical flaw with UNCLOS – the reliance on flag states as the core of its compliance strategy.

Food and Agriculture Organization governance measures to protect marine fisheries

FAO Agreement to Promote Compliance with International Conservation and Management by Fishing Vessels on the High Seas

The 1992 United Nations Conference on Environment and Development's (UNCED) Agenda 21 set out a Programme of Action for Sustainable Development for the Protection of the Oceans and Coastal Areas.[73] It focused world attention on the problems associated with the management of high seas fisheries, particularly the lack of monitoring and enforcement for conservation measures, and the problem of unregulated fishing.[74] Agenda 21 called upon states to take effective action 'to deter reflagging of vessels by their nationals as a means of avoiding compliance with applicable conservation and management measures for fishing activities on the high seas'.[75] Many vessels had discovered, however, that they could get around complying with conservation measures simply by re-registering in countries not party to particular conservation agreements.

In 1993, the FAO responded to this practice of reflagging to avoid conservation obligations by adopting the Agreement to Promote Compliance with International Conservation and

---

72 *Convention on Biological Diversity*, opened for signature 5 June 1992, reprinted in 31 ILM 818 (entered into force 29 December 1993).
73 *Agenda 21*, Chapter 17.
74 Ibid., Chapter 17, para. 45.
75 Ibid., Chapter 17, para. 49.

270

Management by Fishing Vessels on the High Seas.[76] This Agreement was intended to supplement UNCLOS by fleshing out flag state responsibility over high-seas fishing activities of its flagged vessels. In particular, this Agreement targeted the practice of reflagging vessels to avoid compliance with high-seas conservation and management measures. To that end, Article III(1) committed states to ensure that fishing vessels entitled to fly their flags do not undermine the effectiveness of international conservation and management measures. In particular, states agreed to license their high-seas fishing vessels, and to flag only vessels over which the states could exercise control.[77] States also agreed to impose licence conditions that prevent such vessels from undermining the effectiveness of international conservation and management measures.[78] The Agreement further committed states to establishing vessel registries that would collect a standard set of information and would be shared with the FAO.[79]

The Agreement entered into force in 2003 and currently has 39 parties. It has not stopped the practice of reflagging vessels. In the 1950s, approximately 4 per cent of vessels were flying flags of convenience. Today, approximately 60 per cent of vessels are flying flags of convenience.[80]

FAO Code of Conduct for Responsible Fisheries

In 1995, FAO finalised the Code of Conduct for Responsible Fisheries. This soft-law document identified core principles for addressing the problems of unsustainable fishing. Although it shares the limitations inherent in flag state enforcement, the Code of Conduct provided a useful starting place for states and other actors interested in addressing problems of overcapacity, destructive fishing practices and overfishing.

The Code of Conduct ranges beyond the traditional scope of most international fisheries governance schemes. It has provisions governing post-harvest handling of fish,[81] covers aquaculture,[82] and calls for cooperation among all fisheries stakeholders – not just states.[83] The Code declares that all users of living aquatic resources have the obligation to conserve those resources,[84] and embraces a precautionary approach to fisheries management.[85] It calls on all participants in a fishery to join or at least abide by the management plans developed by Regional Fisheries Organisations.[86] Perhaps most importantly, the Code sets out the international standards for identifying and eliminating destructive fishing practices.

76 *Agreement to Promote Compliance with International Conservation and Management by Fishing Vessels on the High Seas*, opened for signature 24 November 1993, 2221 UNTS 120 (entered into force 24 April 2003). Online. Available HTTP: <http://www.fao.org/DOCREP/MEETING/003/X3130m/X3130E00.htm> (accessed 18 January 2012).

77 Ibid., Art. III(2).

78 Ibid., III(5).

79 Ibid., Art. IV.

80 R. George, 'Flying the Flag, Fleeing the State', *New York Times*, 24 April 2011. Online. Available HTTP: <http://www.nytimes.com/2011/04/25/opinion/25george.html> (accessed 18 January 2012).

81 FAO Code of Conduct for Responsible Fisheries, Art. 11.

82 Ibid., Art. 9.

83 Ibid., Art. 4(1).

84 Ibid., Art. 6(1).

85 Ibid., Art. 7.5.

86 Ibid., Art. 7.1.

Thus, the Code of Conduct represents an important attempt to think holistically about fisheries management. It is, however, not a binding agreement complete with sanctions and enforcement provisions. While it represents an important first step toward successful global fisheries management, binding and sanctionable commitments will ultimately be needed as part of any comprehensive solution to the problems of overfishing.

International Plan of Action to Prevent, Deter and Eliminate Illegal Unreported and Unregulated Fishing

In 1999, the FAO began a series of 'International Plans of Action' designed to tackle concrete marine management problems including reducing incidental catch of seabirds, conserving sharks, and restricting fishing overcapacity.[87] In 2001, the FAO Committee on Fisheries, in an effort to further the goals of the Code of Conduct for Responsible Fisheries, adopted the International Plan of Action to Prevent, Deter and Eliminate Illegal, Unreported and Unregulated Fishing (IPOA-IUU). This agreement, drafted in cooperation with the FAO, targets the problem created by a lack of adequate flag state enforcement. It establishes a universal set of comprehensive governance measures targeting IUU fishing.[88] Like the Code of Conduct, the IPOA-IUU emphasises the full participation of all stakeholders, including industry, affected communities, and civil society in addition to states. It emphasises information-sharing as a key means for reducing IUU fishing.

Agreement on Port State Measures

In November 2009, the member states of the FAO adopted the Agreement on Port State Measures[89] as an effort to provide a strong disincentive to IUU fishing by preventing illegally captured fish from entering international markets through ports. Under the terms of the treaty, foreign vessels are expected to request permission from coastal states for port entry and be able to provide copies of authorisations to fish and information about quantities of fish on board.[90] Port states are expected to inspect a certain number of vessels annually to help achieve the goals of the Agreement.[91] Results of the inspection are reported to flag states and to relevant RFMOs.[92] Vessels in violation of fishing management standards will be denied the ability to use the ports of the states who are members of the agreement to land their catch.

---

87 *International Plan of Action for Reducing Incidental Catch of Seabirds in Longline Fisheries* (1999), FAO, Rome, Italy; *International Plan of Action for the Conservation and Management of Sharks* (1999), FAO, Rome, Italy; *International Plan of Action for the Management of Fishing Capacity* (1999), FAO, Rome, Italy.

88 *International Plan of Action to Prevent, Deter and Eliminate Illegal, Unreported and Unregulated Fishing* (2001), FAO Council, Committee on Fisheries, 24th Sess.

89 Agreement on Port State Measures to Prevent, Deter and Eliminate Illegal, Unreported and Unregulated Fishing, Adopted in November 2009, Appendix V of the FAO Council, Hundred and Thirty-seventh Session, Rome, 28 September–2 October 2009, Report of the 88th Session of the Committee on Constitutional and Legal Matters, 23–25 September 2009, CL 137/5, September 2009.

90 Ibid., Art. 8.

91 Ibid., Art. 12.

92 Ibid., Art. 18(1)(a).

As of January 2012, the Agreement had not yet entered into force as a binding agreement but will enter into force when there are 25 signatories.[93]

Future directions

If the oceans are to recover to meet the ongoing needs of both human and non-human species, then states must seek to coordinate their national and international responses. Promising developments include creating legal frameworks for biologically effective marine protected networks, focusing fishing management strategies on ecosystem conservation and restoration, and restricting bottom trawling. A combination of these developments would ensure that the seas are viewed as holistic and complex systems where overexploited species can recover.

Biologically effective networks of marine protected areas

Oceans and seas cover 71 per cent of the Earth, yet while 5 per cent of the terrestrial environment has been designated as reserve or otherwise protected, less than 0.5 per cent of the ocean waters are protected as no-take ocean reserves.[94] As global marine biodiversity plummets, the need for protected marine areas becomes ever more pressing.

In the past, states have established marine protected areas in territorial and EEZ waters. In many instances, these reserves have lacked connectivity or are inadequately sized to be effective in maintaining healthy ecosystems.[95] In other instances, these reserves still continue to allow exploitation of certain fisheries without regard to overall ecosystem impact. The 2010 meeting of the parties for the CBD called upon states to set a target to protect 10 per cent of their waters as marine protected areas by 2020.[96] This target will not be easy to meet even for countries with higher environmental standards. For example, in the US, at present only about 3 per cent of all marine resources are protected in no-take zones, with 95 per cent of those zones being located in one 363,680 sq km reserve in Hawaii, the Papahānaumokuākea Marine National Monument.[97]

Unlike terrestrial areas and EEZs, all of which are within the control of one or more states, wide swathes of the marine environment are designated as high seas and are thus beyond the reach of any state's regulatory authority. There is an urgent need for international cooperation and action to improve conservation and sustainable use of biodiversity in marine

93 'Status of Agreement on Port State Measures to Prevent, Deter and Eliminate Illegal, Unreported and Unregulated Fishing'. Online. Available HTTP: <http://www.fao.org/Legal/treaties/037s-e. htm> (accessed 19 January 2012). (Several states signed but only four have ratified or acceded to the agreement.)

94 Pew Environmental Group, *Global Ocean Legacy*, 2011. Online. Available HTTP: <http://www. pewenvironment.org/campaigns/global-ocean-legacy/id/8589941025/> (accessed 18 January 2012).

95 T. Agardy, G. Notarbartolo di Sciara and P. Christie, 'Mind the gap: Addressing the Shortcomings of Marine Protected Areas through Large Scale Marine Spatial Planning', *Marine Policy* 35, 201, pp. 226–32.

96 CBD, *Strategic Plan for Biodiversity 2011–2020 and Natural Biodiversity Strategies and Action Plans* ('Aichi Targets'), 24 March 2011 UNEP/CBD/RW-BF/4/3, 2011. See Target 11.

97 US National Oceanic and Atmospheric Agency, *Marine Reserves in the United States*, 2011. Online. Available HTTP: <http://www.mpa.gov/pdf/helpful-resources/factsheets/us_marinereserves. pdf> (accessed 18 January 2012).

areas beyond the limits of national jurisdiction through the establishment of further marine protected areas including areas such as seamounts, hydrothermal vents, cold-water corals and other vulnerable high-seas ecosystems.[98] In addition to identifying and legislating for marine protected areas, two promising trends have emerged in response to these challenges: ecosystem-based management and a growing consensus on banning environmentally dangerous fishing techniques.

Ecosystem-based management and restoration

In the past decade, there has been a cognitive shift among fishery managers to focus on an ecosystem approach.[99] Political will has materialised for an 'ecosystem approach to fisheries' as members of the fishing industry are faced with more frequent moratoria and other restrictions on fishing. Governance institutions recognise that deliberate management at an ecosystem level improves long-term fish stock abundance and reduces habitat damage.

Even with this encouraging normative shift among RFMOs and CBD members to protect fisheries, there remains an urgent biological need to focus on a broader 'ecosystem approach to management' of the oceans beyond the current narrow focus on fisheries. There are many other threats to the marine environment besides unsustainable fishing practices that ultimately impact the health of the oceans. In the context of ecosystem-based management, management of the fisheries sector is simply one area of concern if the goal is an overall healthy ecosystem. Issues that have not been addressed systematically across the ecosystem level include operational marine pollution from maritime transport and land-based pollution from agricultural run-off, municipal sewage and coastal tourism.

While states are reflecting on broader policies for ocean health, there is a pressing need for countries to invest immediately in rebuilding ocean stocks and restoring marine habitats. As the World Bank and FAO concluded in their report, *The Sunken Billions*, because of gross mismanagement fisheries are failing to perform as resource assets and are costing the world economy billions by eliminating needed natural resources for future generations.[100] There is no magic formula that can be applied to all ecosystems to provide for effective restoration. Instead fisheries managers in cooperation with colleagues from government land-use planning and environmental institutions must assess what options are available for each ecosystem in light of the specific human threats to the ecosystem. In some areas such as localised fisheries the implementation of individual take quotas may alleviate pressures on fisheries. In other areas such as the high seas, requiring the use of particular low-impact fishing technologies may assist in restoring poorly functioning ecosystems. In still other areas, there may be a need for active restoration through a combination of restocking of marine resources coupled with concerted efforts to implement punitive-based, incentive-based, or some hybrid version of legislation to control chronic pollution sources.

---

98 CBD Decision VII/5 2005, para. 29 and 30. Online. Available HTTP: <http://www.cbd.int/decision/cop/?id=7742> (accessed 18 January 2012).

99 G. Bianchi, 'The Concept of the Ecosystem Approach to Fisheries' in G. Bianchi and H. Skjodal (eds) *The Ecosystem Approach to Fisheries*. Rome: Food and Agriculture Organization, 2008, pp. 20–38.

100 World Bank and FAO, *The Sunken Billions: the Economic Justification for Fisheries Reform*, 2008. Online. Available HTTP: <http://go.worldbank.org/MGUTHSY7U0> (accessed 9 May 2012).

Customary international law to cover bottom trawling

While an ecosystem-based approach to marine management provides a direction it represents an aspiration for shifting current governance practices. Before ecosystem management becomes a policy reality, there is an urgent need to halt certain environmentally devastating practices such as bottom trawling.

In the recent past, states have generated sufficient political will to create customary international law to make drift net fishing illegal. By 1989, a quorum of state parties had recognised that large drift nets, particularly those in the South Pacific, were capturing vast quantities of biodiverse and sometimes endangered bycatch. In response, parties passed a resolution before the UNGA requiring a moratorium on drift net fishing starting on 31 December 1992.[101] The moratorium has subsequently become customary law because of actions taken by numerous key fishing nations. For example, in 1990, the US amended Section 206 of the Magnuson-Stevens Fishery Conservation and Management Act to create a policy to pursue a worldwide ban on drift netting.[102] The EU implemented a drift net ban for certain heavily exploited species such as bluefin tuna and swordfish.[103] The ban has been relatively effective. In 2008, while 24 large-scale drift nets boats were identified in the North Pacific Ocean, only one such drift net boat was identified in 2009.[104]

Given the destructiveness of bottom trawling to non-target species and the interference of the practice in the future of ecosystem-based management, it is hoped that similar customary law will emerge regarding a moratorium on bottom trawling. In 2007 the UNGA[105] passed a resolution requiring RFMOs to implement bottom trawling regulations by the end of 2008 which would provide for an ecosystem approach to management. No moratorium was adopted. While some RFMOs have implemented bottom trawling restrictions, including CCAMLR, NEAFC and the SPRFMO, not all RFMOs have implemented such restrictions. In 2009, the UNGA adopted Resolution 64/72 requesting that states and RFMOs ensure that vessels do not engage in bottom fishing until environmental impact assessments have been carried out.[106]

Conclusion

International fisheries agreements currently place primary reliance on flag state enforcement – a governance structure that has proven itself unable to meet the challenges posed by the combination of overfishing, pollution and climate change. Some of the problems are obvious: many states with large EEZs lack the enforcement and surveillance capacity necessary to properly manage fisheries within those zones. Even the wealthiest states find it difficult to effectively patrol and manage vast marine areas. Added to this problem is the issue of how

101 UNGA, Resolution 46/215, UN Doc A/RES/46/215, (20 December 1991).
102 *Magnuson-Stevens Fishery Conservation and Management Act* 16 USC. §§ 1801–1884.
103 EU, Council Regulation (EC) No 1239/98 laying down certain technical measures for the conservation of fishery resources, Official Journal of the European Communities, 8, June 1998.
104 US Secretary of Commerce. *Report to the Congress of the United States Concerning US Actions Taken On Foreign Large-Scale High Seas Driftnet Fishing*, 2009, p. 7. Online. Available HTTP: <http://www.nmfs.noaa.gov/ia/intlbycatch/docs/congo_09rpt.pdf> (accessed 18 January 2012).
105 UNGA, Resolution 61/105 (2007), UN Doc A/RES/61/105.
106 UNGA, Resolution 64/72 (2010), UN Doc A/RES/64/72.

to conserve and sustainably use biodiversity in marine areas beyond the limits of national jurisdiction.

In addition, UNCLOS falls short in providing the tools to create the governance measures for quality certification and product traceability needed in the ever more globalised fish trade. Thus, new technologies, and new governance measures will be needed if states are to promote transparency, and to foster an ecosystem approach to fisheries management, while also enhancing food security.

The future success of fisheries law in protecting the marine ecosystem depends on creating a more robust governance regime that serves two functions. In addition to boosting existing enforcement efforts to conserve resources, marine governance must be forward-thinking in creating proactive policies and laws that will protect fisheries and marine ecosystems for multiple generations. Some of these laws will need to focus on stopping environmentally devastating practices. Others will need to concentrate on restoring healthy ecosystem functions. While there are daunting challenges posed by ocean acidification and other emerging marine phenomena, there are also opportunities to change human behaviour now to alleviate at least some of the pressures on the marine ecosystem. Political decisions made by this generation will have implications for decades to come and unless this generation wants to be known as the generation that lost the seas, there is much work to be done to restore the oceans.

16

Marine pollution law

*Damien Cremean and Erika J. Techera**

Marine pollution, when and where it occurs, can have disastrous results. It poses a significant and continuing threat to the world's oceans, contributing to environmental degradation of marine areas, depletion of species and damage to the entire ocean ecosystem. This chapter explores the international environmental law relating to marine pollution focusing upon incidental and unintentional discharges from ships as well as the dumping of waste at sea. It will also consider the current governance gaps, emerging challenges and the future of regulation in this area.

Introduction

One learned writer has commented: 'Protection and preservation of the environment are prominent in current world issues.'[1] However, as he also added, concerns 'relating to the marine environment are probably some of the most prominent and most complex'.[2] Marine pollution, when and where it occurs, can have disastrous results – not only for the marine environment itself but also for those dependent on marine resources for food and livelihoods. Indeed, it has been contended that 'it is the sea we must look to if we are to find the resources to feed the rapidly increasing population of the world'.[3]

The marine environment can become polluted via a number of different means including land-based and seabed activities, the deliberate dumping of waste, incidental operational discharges from vessels and installations, and the accidental or unintentional release of oil and other substances from ships. It is perhaps the last of these that has drawn the most public attention and triggered international responses.

Reference need only be made in this regard to the *Exxon Valdez* incident in March 1989. In a pristine marine environment the vessel ran aground and spilled over 40,000 tons (or 10

* The authors are grateful to Emeritus Professor Zada Lipman for comments she provided on an earlier version of this chapter.

1 M.W.D. White, *Australian Marine Pollution Laws*, 2nd edition, Annandale: Federation Press, 2007, p. 1.
2 Ibid.
3 J. Nicholson, *Food from the Sea*, London: Cassell, 1979, p. 1.

million gallons) of crude oil which then spread around the sea and shores.[4] The damage to the environment was extensive and the consequences of that damage are still being felt to the present day. Local communities were devastated by the initial spill and the trauma of the ensuing litigation which followed. This disaster was not isolated and there are other incidents of note including the 1967 *Torrey Canyon* and the 1978 *Amoco Cadiz* accidents. Later there was the Liberian-registered vessel, *The Braer*, which in 1993 spilled its cargo on the shores of the Shetland Islands.[5] After this there was the grounding of *The Sea Empress* at St Ann's Head, Milford Haven, in 1996, and the *Prestige* off the Spanish coast in 2002.[6]

The international community has responded in several ways, including the adoption of a number of conventions. The focus in this chapter will be upon four significant conventions on the subject, which are the *International Convention on Civil Liability for Oil Pollution Damage* 1969 as amended by the 1992 Protocol (CLC);[7] the *Convention on the Prevention of Marine Pollution by Dumping of Wastes and Other Matter* 1972 and 1996 Protocol (London Convention);[8] the *International Convention for the Prevention of Pollution from Ships* 1973 as amended by the 1978 Protocol (MARPOL);[9] and the *International Convention on Salvage* 1989 (Salvage Convention).[10] In between MARPOL and the Salvage Convention a fifth instrument also needs to be included: the United Nations Convention on the Law of the Sea 1982 (UNCLOS). For, as one author says, the 'protection of the marine environment is the subject of a large part of [this] Convention'.[11]

From time to time, however, there have also been other international treaties on the subject of marine pollution. There is, for example, the *International Convention Relating to Intervention on the High Seas in Cases of Oil Pollution Casualties* 1969[12] and the *Convention on Oil Pollution Preparedness, Response and Co-operation* 1990,[13] which obliges state parties to adopt national regimes for rapid and effective response to oil pollution incidents. The *International Convention on Liability and Compensation for Damage in Connection with the Carriage of Hazardous*

---

4 I. Hunter, J. Salzman and D. Zaelke, *International Environmental Law and Policy*, 3rd edition, New York: Foundation Press, 2011, p. 796.

5 For a summary of the volume discharges from each incident see: Oil Spill Solutions, *Tanker Spills Show Declining Trend*. Online. Available HTTP: <www.oilspillsolutions.org/majorspills.htm> (accessed 29 February 2012).

6 For a summary of the history of incidents and responses see International Maritime Organization, *Background*. Online. Available HTTP: <http://www.imo.org/OurWork/Environment/PollutionPrevention/OilPollution/Pages/Background.aspx#2> (accessed 29 February 2012).

7 *International Convention on Civil Liability for Oil Pollution Damage*, opened for signature 29 November 1969, 973 UNTS 3 (entered into force 19 June 1975).

8 Also known as the London Dumping Convention until 1992: *Convention on the Prevention of Marine Pollution by Dumping of Wastes and Other Matter*, opened for signature 29 December 1972, 1046 UNTS 120 (entered into force 15 July 1977).

9 The *International Convention for the Prevention of Pollution from Ships* (1973) and the 1978 *Protocol* are read as a single instrument MARPOL, opened for signature 17 February 1978, 17 ILM 246 (entered into force 2 October 1983).

10 *International Convention on Salvage*, opened for signature 1 July 1989, 1996 UNTS 194 (entered into force 28 April 1989).

11 I. Shearer, 'Current Law of the Sea Issues', in R. Babbage and S. Bateman, *Maritime Change: Issues for Asia*, St Leonards: Allen & Unwin, 1993, p. 61.

12 *International Convention Relating to Intervention on the High Seas in Cases of Oil Pollution Casualties*, opened for signature 29 November 1969, 9 ILM 25 (entered into force 6 May 1975).

13 *Convention on Oil Pollution Preparedness, Response and Co-operation*, opened for signature 30 November 1990, 30 ILM 733 (entered into force 13 May 1995).

and Noxious Substances by Sea 1996, together with a 2010 Protocol,[14] covers not only pollution damage but also the risks of fire and explosion, including loss of life or personal injury and loss of or damage to property. Another example is the *International Convention on Civil Liability for Bunker Oil Pollution Damage* 2001 (Bunkers Convention),[15] which relates to oil spills from ships that are not oil tankers. In addition, there are other treaties which contribute to the protection of the marine environment; for example those governing seabed activities[16] and the environmentally sound deconstruction of ships.[17]

The International Maritime Organization (IMO) is the principal United Nations agency with responsibility for the safety and security of shipping and the prevention of marine pollution by ships.[18] Relevantly, it has established a technical group on marine pollution: the Marine Environmental Protection Committee. It is responsible for many marine pollution treaties including MARPOL and the London Convention,[19] as well as the more recent *Convention on Anti-Fouling Systems* 2001 and the *Ballast Water Convention* 2004, which seek to prevent damage to marine species and the spread of alien species respectively.[20] It has also been influential in the development of important 'soft-law' codes and guidelines that protect the marine environment.[21]

International marine pollution law is thus a complex field which involves a considerable body of law.[22] This chapter, however, will focus upon the five key instruments outlined above. Each of these conventions contributes to securing the marine environment by dealing with marine pollution in a variety of ways. The chapter will explore the major provisions and developments as well as the challenges for the future.

14 *International Convention on Liability and Compensation for Damage in Connection with the Carriage of Hazardous and Noxious Substances by Sea*, opened for signature 3 May 1996, 25 ILM 1406 (not yet in force).

15 *International Convention on Civil Liability for Bunker Oil Pollution Damage*, opened for signature 1 October 2001, 40 ILM 1493 (entered into force 21 November 2008).

16 Article 208 of UNCLOS provides that coastal states shall regulate to prevent, reduce and control pollution from seabed activities within areas of national jurisdiction. Beyond areas of national jurisdiction seabed activities are governed by the International Seabed Authority under Part XI of the UN Convention on the Law of the Sea and the *Agreement Relating to the Implementation of Part XI of the United Nations Convention on the Law of the Sea*. For a summary see P. Sands, *Principles of International Environmental Law*, 2nd edition, Cambridge: Cambridge University Press, 2003, pp. 445–8.

17 For further discussion of the recent *Hong Kong International Convention for the Safe and Environmentally Sound Recycling of Ships* see Chapter 17 by T.G. Puthucherril in this volume. See also Y-C. Chang, N. Wang & O.S. Durak 'Ship Recycling and Marine Pollution' *Marine Pollution Bulletin*, 60, 2010, 1390–6; and Md S. Karim, 'Environmental Pollution from Shipbreaking Industry: International Law and National Legal Response' *Georgetown International Environmental Law Review*, 22, 2010, 185–240.

18 International Maritime Organization. Online. Available HTTP: <www.imo.org> (accessed 29 February 2012). The IMO was created in 1958 and is based in London.

19 International Maritime Organization, *List of IMO Conventions*. Online. Available HTTP: <http://www.imo.org/About/Conventions/ListOfConventions/Pages/Default.aspx> (accessed 29 February 2012).

20 *Convention on Control of Harmful Anti-Fouling Systems on Ships* (2001) and the *Convention for the Control and Management of Ships' Ballast Water* (2004).

21 For example the *Guidelines to Minimize the Transfer of Harmful Aquatic Organisms and Pathogens Through Ballast Water* and *Guidelines on the control and manage of ships' biofouling to minimize the transfer of invasive aquatic species*.

22 For a useful summary of the status of all the IMO Conventions and the percentage of the world's shipping tonnage they cover see: International Maritime Organization, Status of Conventions. Online. Available HTTP: <www.imo.org/About/Conventions/StatusOfConventions/Pages/Default.aspx> (accessed 29 February 2012).

Key international marine pollution conventions

International Convention on Civil Liability for Oil Pollution Damage

The 1969 Convention 'was born of a consciousness of . . . the dangers of oil pollution inherent in the world-wide carriage of oil in bulk by sea'.[23] Also, *inter alia*, of a 'need to ensure that adequate compensation is available to persons who suffer damage caused by pollution resulting from the escape or discharge of oil from ships'.[24] The CLC recites that the states parties are conscious 'of the dangers of pollution posed by the worldwide maritime carriage of oil in bulk' and that they are convinced 'of the need to ensure that adequate compensation is available to persons who suffer damage caused by pollution resulting from the escape or discharge of oil from ships'.[25] To that end it sets up a scheme for those suffering such damage to be able to be compensated.

That scheme, however, was significantly altered by the 1992 Protocol, which amended key elements. A hardening of attitudes towards the menace of oil pollution is evident between 1969 and 1992 as considered in the following examples.

Pollution damage

The limited definition of 'pollution damage' in the CLC was amended in 1992 to include:

(a) loss or damage caused outside the ship by contamination resulting from the escape or discharge of oil from the ship, wherever such escape or discharge may occur, provided that compensation for impairment of the environment other than loss of profit from such impairment shall be limited to costs of reasonable measures of reinstatement actually undertaken or to be undertaken;

(b) the costs of preventive measures and further loss or damage caused by preventive measures.[26]

There is a clear emphasis in this definition on damage to or impairment of the environment which is not evident in the definition of the same expression in the 1969 Convention. Moreover, by virtue of the Protocol, the CLC is not confined to ships 'carrying oil' as it is sufficient that there be contamination resulting from the escape or discharge of oil from a 'ship'. But, as set out below, the ship must be one constructed or adapted for the carriage of oil in bulk as cargo.

Ship

By virtue of the Protocol a 'ship' is defined as:

> any sea-going vessel and any seaborne craft of any type whatsoever constructed or adapted for the carriage of oil in bulk as cargo, provided that a ship capable of carrying oil and other cargoes shall be regarded as a ship only when it is actually carrying oil in

---

23 C. Hill, *Maritime Law*, 4th edition, London: Lloyds of London Press Ltd, 1995, pp. 432.
24 Ibid., p. 433.
25 CLC, Preamble.
26 CLC Protocol, Art. 2(3).

bulk as cargo and during any voyage following such carriage unless it is proved that it has no residues of such carriage of oil in bulk aboard.[27]

In contrast to the definition of 'ship' in the 1969 Convention,[28] a ship need no longer be one which is 'actually carrying oil in bulk as cargo'; it is sufficient if the vessel is one 'constructed or adapted for the carriage of oil in bulk as cargo'. The latter may not be one which is actually carrying oil in bulk as cargo at all, although it may be 'constructed or adapted' to do so. Of course, a ship capable of carrying oil and other cargoes is to be regarded as a ship so constructed or adapted only when it is 'actually' carrying oil in bulk. Escapes of oil from ships that are not oil tankers are dealt with in the Bunkers Convention, as noted above.

Oil

The word 'oil' is defined in the 1992 Protocol as 'any persistent hydrocarbon mineral oil such as crude oil, fuel oil, heavy diesel oil and lubricating oil, whether carried on board a ship as cargo or in the bunkers of such a ship'.[29] This is a wider definition than that contained in the 1969 Convention[30] in that the latter was limited to 'any persistent oil' whereas oil now extends to 'any persistent hydrocarbon mineral oil'. Widening the definition of 'oil' ensures broader coverage of the Convention.

Incident

An 'incident' is defined in the Protocol as 'any occurrence, or series of occurrences having the same origin, which causes pollution damage or creates a grave and imminent threat of causing such damage'.[31] The earlier definition of 'incident' in the 1969 Convention[32] contained no such reference to a 'grave and imminent' threat of damage. Yet inclusion of the threat of damage is clearly important. Furthermore, Article 5 of the Protocol replaces Article IV of the Convention, which now reads:

> When an incident involving two or more ships occurs and pollution damage results therefrom, the owners of all the ships concerned, unless exonerated under Article III, shall be jointly and severally liable for all such damage which is not reasonably separable.

Wherever such escape or discharge may occur

By the 1992 Protocol, the CLC applies:

(a) to pollution damage caused:
    (i) in the territory, including the territorial sea, of a . . . State, and
    (ii) in the exclusive economic zone of a . . . State, established in accordance with international law, or, if a . . . State has not established such a zone, in an area beyond and

---

27 CLC Protocol, Art. 2(1).
28 CLC, Art. 1(1).
29 CLC Protocol, Art. 2(2).
30 CLC, Art. 1(5).
31 CLC Protocol, Art. 2(4).
32 CLC, Art. 1(5).

adjacent to the territorial sea of that State determined by that State in accordance with international law and extending not more than 200 nautical miles from the baseline from which the breadth of its territorial sea is measured;

(b) to preventive measures, wherever taken, to prevent or minimize such damage.[33]

This gives the CLC a much wider application than it had in 1969 when it was stated to 'apply exclusively to pollution damage caused on the territory including the territorial sea of a . . . State and to preventive measures taken to prevent or minimize such damage'.[34] Confining pollution damage to that caused 'on' the territory of a State or in its territorial sea, meant that the CLC did not extend very far at all. As will be seen below, the exclusive economic zone is a much larger area than merely the territorial sea of a state. It is to be noted that preventive measures now qualify, 'wherever taken'.

Loss or damage

Pollution damage is 'loss or damage' as defined by Article 4(1), substituted by the Protocol, except as provided in Articles 4(2) and (3):

> the owner of a ship at the time of an incident, or, where the incident consists of a series of occurrences, at the time of the first such occurrence, shall be liable for any pollution damage caused by oil as a result of the incident.[35]

The intention is clearly for persons to be compensated for loss or damage brought about by a polluting incident. There are, however, several matters of importance which arise in this regard. First, by virtue of the 1992 Protocol,[36] liability is able to be limited by an owner to three million units of account for a ship not exceeding 5,000 units of tonnage and, for other ships, an additional 420 units of account – provided that, in all, the aggregate amount does not exceed 59.7 million units of account. The 'unit of account' is defined in other provisions of the Protocol.[37] This is a considerable advance, as it enhances the limitation of liability provisions in the 1969 Convention which were based on the French currency unit of the franc. So as to give effect to this limitation of liability, the owner is able to constitute a fund[38] for the total amount representing the limits of liability which is distributable among claimants in proportion to the amounts of their established claims.[39]

Some, of course, will be opposed to the notion of limitation of liability, and establishing a limitation fund, in principle. But it does work, particularly in the case of widespread damage, so as to enable all those suffering loss or damage to achieve some recovery. Without it, whoever was first in bringing a legal action could deprive all the others of any chance of compensation, a result which would be unconscionable.

33 CLC Protocol, Art. 3.
34 CLC, Art. 2.
35 See CLC Protocol, Art. 3.
36 CLC Protocol, Art. 6(1).
37 See CLC Protocol, Arts 9(a), (b) and (c).
38 CLC Protocol, Art. 6(2).
39 CLC, Art. 5(4).

Secondly, under the 1969 Convention[40] the ship owner was not entitled to limit liability if the incident occurred 'as a result of [that party's] actual fault or privity'. Now, by virtue of the 1992 Protocol, the owner is not entitled to limit liability 'if it is proved that the pollution damage resulted from his personal act or omission, committed with the intent to cause such damage, or recklessly and with knowledge that such damage would probably result'.[41] In other words, the situations in which a case of disentitlement to limit liability may arise have been broadened.

The third aspect is time limitations. Under Article VIII of the 1969 Convention, which is unchanged by the 1992 Protocol, all rights of compensation are lost 'unless an action is brought . . . within three years from the date when the damage occurred'. This seems unduly restrictive as the right to bring an action may not become clear until well after the three-year period. It is also provided, though, that 'in no case shall an action be brought after six years from the date of the incident which caused the damage'.[42] Once more, this seems overly restrictive – particularly in those cases where damage may be very widespread and continuing to occur, as was the case for example with the *Exxon Valdez*. In such cases, the damage may be continuing well beyond the six-year mark.

Under the 1969 Convention, and it is unchanged by the Protocol, an owner escapes liability upon proving that pollution damage resulted from 'a natural phenomenon of an exceptional inevitable and irresistible character'.[43] In some systems this is known as an 'act of God'. The question may be raised, however, of the exact operation of this exception. Severe weather, which was not anticipated, could fall within it. But why should that be so? At sea, severe weather of all magnitudes arguably should reasonably be expected at all times. Or, at least, it should never be ignored as a realistic possibility.

The compensation scheme created by the CLC, together with the *Convention on the Establishment of an International Fund for Compensation for Oil Pollution Damage* (1971),[44] as amended in 1992, is a critical component of international marine pollution law.[45]

MARPOL

The 1973 Convention recites that the parties are '[c]onscious of the need to preserve the human environment in general and the marine environment in particular'.[46] It is also recognised 'that deliberate, negligent or accidental release of oil and other harmful substances from ships constitutes a serious source of pollution'.[47] Accordingly, by Article 1(1), the parties undertake to give effect to the provisions of the Convention and its annexes in order to

---

40 CLC, Art. 5(2).

41 CLC Protocol, Art. 6(2).

42 CLC, Art. 8.

43 CLC, Art. 3(2)(a).

44 *Convention on the Establishment of an International Fund for Compensation for Oil Pollution Damage*, opened for signature 18 December 1971, 1110 UNTS 57 (entered into force 16 October 1978).

45 The 1971 Fund Convention ceased to be in force in 2002 and was replaced by the 1992 Protocol. The 1971 Fund continues to deal with incidents occurring before 2002. The 1992 Protocol was amended in 2000 to increase the levels of compensation and a further Protocol in 2003 created a Supplementary Fund adding a third tier of compensation: see *International Oil Pollution Compensation Funds*. Online. Available HTTP: <http://www.iopcfund.org/> (accessed 29 February 2012).

46 MARPOL, Preamble.

47 Ibid. MARPOL specifically excludes the dumping of waste, which is dealt with under the London Convention.

prevent the pollution of the marine environment by the discharge of harmful substances or effluents containing such substances.

As amended by 1978 Protocol, MARPOL is the most extensive of the marine pollution conventions relating to discharge of pollutants from ships. It includes discharge standards and technical specifications as well as navigation standards. It is also a treaty which has significant punitive aspects when given the force of law. The master, owner and other persons who cause environmental damage may be charged and the fines may be extensive. Even if a ship complies with the MARPOL requirements, the master and owner are still at risk of being charged under general environmental legislation of a state.[48]

Annex I: oil pollution

Annex I addresses the discharge of oil from ships and imposes a regime under which the discharge of oil overboard, during the normal operations of ships, is strictly controlled. It absorbs the provisions of the original OILPOL 54 (that is, the *International Convention for the Prevention of Pollution of the Sea by Oil*[49]) and extends them enormously. It comprises 37 regulations and several appendices. Regulation 1 and its Appendix 1 define the oils covered – which is practically the whole range but excludes those petrochemicals which come under Annex II. Regulation 1(10) defines 'nearest land' as points to seaward of the baseline from which the territorial sea is established.

From the legal point of view, it is worth highlighting several regulations. Regulation 11 gives the power to enforce port state control and, if the vessel does not comply with Annex I, to detain it until it does. Regulations 15 and 34 relate to the legal requirement about control of oil, and their key provisions are that 'any discharge into the sea of oil or oily mixtures from ships . . . shall be prohibited' unless the regulatory provisions are satisfied. These provisions relate to no discharge in 'special areas' and for other discharges the tanker must be more than 50 miles from the nearest land, proceeding *en route* and the discharge should not exceed 30 litres per nautical mile.[50] Regulation 1(11) defines special areas, which are areas that are particularly at risk and in which no discharges are allowable in the main.

Regulation 4 contains the exceptions to the application of Regulations 15 and 34, which are the defences in fact. These defences apply if the discharge was to secure the safety of the ship or to save life at sea or it resulted from damage to a ship or its equipment provided all reasonable precautions were taken afterwards to prevent or minimise it. This exception does not apply, however, 'if the owner or the master acted either with intent to cause damage, or recklessly and with knowledge that damage would probably result'; or it was approved by the administration to combat another discharge. Annex I applies to all ships by Regulation 2(1) and to fixed and floating drilling rigs, and Regulation 39 equates their responsibilities to non-tankers of 400 tonnes gross tonnage and above.

The rest of Annex I is concerned with details of ships' construction, equipment, record books, forms, calculations to meet these requirements and administrative details. In all it is a long and fairly complex document. Overall, Annex I has been very successful in reducing discharge of oil into the sea.

---

48 White, op. cit., p. 44. For what follows, as an outline of MARPOL's various Annexes, see pp. 45–9.
49 *Convention for the Prevention of Pollution of the Sea by Oil*, opened for signature 12 May 1954, 327 UNTS 3 (entered into force 26 July 1958).
50 There are a number of other provisions which cannot be set out in full here.

Annex II: noxious liquid substances

Annex II addresses the discharge or escape of noxious liquid substances from ships transporting them in bulk, which, in lay terms, could be described as bulk chemicals. This is an annex of growing importance as the tonnages of chemicals transported at sea are rising steadily and chemical tankers are now fairly common. Regulation 1(1) defines 'noxious liquid substance' in terms of a number of categories of the substances (X, Y and Z) and as listed in the International Bulk Chemical Code. 'Nearest land' is defined in similar terms to that in Annex I, as are 'Special Areas'.

It is Regulation 13 that has the enforcement provisions. They are complex and are divided into laws relating to the category of chemicals being carried, as in Appendix 1. There are parallels with the oil regime in Regulations 15 and 34 of Annex I, and, basically, the more toxic categories are prohibited from discharge into the sea unless below the toxic levels laid down. Regulation 3 has the exceptions (defences), which are the usual ones of securing safety of life or property, the discharge resulting from damage to a ship or its equipment or its being approved for combating pollution occurrences.[51] The rest of the lengthy Annex II is devoted to the administration of construction, discharges to facilities ashore, standards for procedures and arrangements and such like.

Annex III: harmful substances in packaged form

Annex III, the first of the optional annexes, addresses the carriage by sea of harmful substances in packaged form. The terms 'harmful substances' and 'packaged form' are both defined in the *International Maritime Dangerous Goods Code* (IMDG Code). States parties are obliged to issue regulations to prohibit the carriage of such substances other than in accordance with Annex III. The Annex sets out a framework for adequate packing, marking, labelling, documentation and stowage of such packages.[52] Basically, Annex III is concerned with bulk shipment of a wide range of substances that may be harmful if discharged into the sea. The Annex III regime also gives some notice to ships' crews and other cargo handlers of the nature of the cargo.

The enforcement provision is in Regulation 1(2), which provides that carriage of harmful substances is prohibited except in accordance with Annex II. The exceptions are in Regulation 7, and are that jettisoning is prohibited except to secure safety of the ship or life at sea, and that washing leaking chemicals overboard should be regulated except where it would impair the safety of the ship. Regulation 8 gives the power for port state control inspections and detention of the ship until it complies with the Regulations.

Annex III has not had a huge impact on shipping – unlike Annex I – but it is of some assistance. It has been more of a support for safety for ships and their crews. For example, a container with unknown and unmarked chemicals that starts to get hot and then to leak highly toxic waste is a major problem for a ship at sea. Any step to avoid or limit such incidents is welcomed by seafarers and all others involved in the transport of goods by sea.

Annex IV: sewage

Annex IV addresses the discharge of sewage from ships on international voyages and it was contentious because there was opposition to the provisions applying to fairly small vessels. As

51 These are the same exceptions as are in Regulation 4 in Annex I.
52 Regulations 1–6.

a result, Annex IV was delayed in achieving sufficient ratifications and it only came into force on 27 September 2003 and then only because some amendments were introduced. The concern was the regulation of what ships were to do with sewage when in restricted waters. For smaller ships it is problem enough, but for the modern large passenger cruise ships carrying thousands of passengers and crew when in ports and bays is a major problem.

The amendment (in Regulation 2(1)) increased the size of the ships to which Annex IV applied to 400 tonnes and above, or to ships below that tonnage certified to carry 15 or more passengers. Only ships engaged in international voyages are caught by it. Annex IV, in Regulation 11, prohibits discharge of sewage into the sea, except:

(a) at a distance of more than three nautical miles from nearest land for comminuted and disinfected sewage or 12 nautical miles for other sewage, provided the ship is under way at more than four knots and the rate of discharge is approved under International Maritime Organization (IMO) standards; or

(b) the ship has an approved sewage treatment plant meeting the operational requirements laid down by the IMO and no effluent is visible in the water; or

(c) the ship is in coastal state waters whose requirements are less stringent than those of Annex IV; or

(d) the discharge is to secure 'the safety of a ship and those onboard or saving life at sea' (Reg 3(1)); or

(e) the discharge results from damage to the ship or its equipment and reasonable precautions were taken before and after the discharge for the purpose of preventing or minimizing it (Reg 3(2)).

It is noted that, like Annexes I and V, the definition of 'nearest land' normally is the baseline of the coastal state, but for the north-east of Australia, for example, it is defined by a series of latitudes and longitudes. The purpose and effect is that the outer edge of the World Heritage listed Great Barrier Reef is the baseline of the land from which is measured the minimum stated distance for discharge of sewage to be permitted.

Under Annex IV by Regulation 12 states parties undertake to ensure provision of facilities at ports and terminals to receive sewage ashore without causing undue delay to the ship. The appendix relates to the relevant international sewage pollution certificate that ships have to carry for entry into port state control regimes.

Annex V: garbage

Annex V strictly regulates the discharge of garbage over the side of a vessel into the sea. It applies to all ships and to fixed or floating platforms. 'Garbage' is defined in Regulation 1(a) as 'all kinds of victual, domestic and operational waste excluding fresh fish and parts thereof, generated during the normal operation of a ship . . .' except those substances covered by other annexes. 'Nearest land' is defined in Regulation 1(2) in the same terms as Annex I, and 'special areas' are also the same as those in Annex I. The discharge of 'all plastics' is totally banned,[53] because they are persistent and not biodegradable, and that of other garbage is regulated so that it is not discharged close to shore. Discharge of dunnage and packing that floats

53 Regulation 3(1)(a).

is prohibited closer than 25 nautical miles offshore and of food wastes to three nautical miles, if comminuted, and otherwise it is 12 miles.[54]

The usual exceptions are provided, namely securing the safety of the ship and those on board, saving life at sea or damage to the ship provided reasonable precautions were taken before and after the discharge.[55] An exception not found in the other annexes is that accidental loss of synthetic fishing nets is a defence under Regulation 6(c) but, once again, all reasonable precautions must have been taken. The remainder of Annex V deals with such matters as shore reception facilities, port state control powers, record keeping and the 'Garbage Record Book'.

Annex VI: air pollution

Annex VI, which was not one of the initial five annexes to MARPOL, regulates air pollution from ships, primarily the composition of bunkers (fuel) and its combustion to ensure that fuel is used which results in restricted amounts of air pollution from the combustion gases. It only came into force on 19 May 2005. It is more detailed than Annexes III to V and, being more recently drafted, has incorporated some aspects not to be found in the earlier annexes.

Any deliberate emissions of ozone-depleting substances are prohibited by Regulation 12(2) unless they come within the provisions of the Regulations, which define and set out the parameters of the fuel that is allowable. Exceptions to this regime are when the emission is necessary for the safety of the ship, saving life at sea, or from a damaged ship when all reasonable precautions have been taken before and after with the exception where the owner or master acted either with intent or recklessly and with knowledge that damage would probably result.[56]

The remainder of the Regulations are concerned with surveys, certification, jurisdiction for port state control regimes and violations and enforcement. Sulphur and nitrogen oxides come in for special mention. Incineration onboard of fuels is regulated by Regulations 16 and 17; governments are to ensure reception facilities are available ashore and offshore platforms are also within the regime. The whole point of Annex VI is that if the quality of the fuel burned in ships is regulated, to restrict sulphur and other noxious chemicals in it, the atmosphere will be cleaner.

It is considered that MARPOL is an effective regime at least in part due to its obligatory technological standards, which have resulted in improvements in ship construction and design.[57]

London Convention[58]

As opposed to the above instruments, which deal with accidental discharges, the London Convention and its Protocol regulate the deliberate dumping of waste at sea.[59] The overall

---

54 Regulation 3(1)(b) and (c).
55 Regulation 6.
56 See Regulation 3.
57 E. Louka, *International Environmental Law: Fairness, Effectiveness, and World Order*, Cambridge: Cambridge University Press, 2006 p. 158.
58 The text of the Convention is online. Available HTTP: <www.imo.org/blast/blastData.asp?doc_id=7521&filename=LC1972.pdf> (accessed 29 February 2012).
59 For a summary of the provisions see Hunter et al., op. cit., pp. 823–7; Louka, op. cit., pp. 148–53; R. Lyster, Z. Lipman, N. Franklin, G. Wiffen and L. Pearson, *Environmental & Planning Law in New South Wales*, 3rd edition, Annandale: Federation Press, 2012, pp. 623–4.

objective of the regime is the prevention of 'pollution of the sea by the dumping of waste and other matter'.[60] It covers the territorial sea and high seas but not internal waters.[61]

Dumping

The Convention includes a wide definition of 'dumping': the 'deliberate disposal at sea' of 'wastes or other matter from vessels, aircraft, platforms or other man-made structures at sea' or the disposal of those structures themselves.[62]

Waste is also defined broadly as 'material and substance of any kind, form or description'.[63] The Convention established three categories of waste and concomitant regulations on their dumping. Highly hazardous waste (listed in Annex I, known as the 'black list') was prohibited from being dumped, except in an emergency and after consultation with states that would be affected.[64] Annex II substances ('grey list') required prior 'special' permit before they could be dumped.[65] All other waste required a prior 'general' permit before it could be disposed of at sea.[66] There were exceptions in circumstances relating to the safety of human life and vessels and other emergency situations which pose an unacceptable risk to human health or where there is no other option.[67]

1996 Protocol

Later developments included a moratorium on the dumping of radioactive waste at sea and resolutions on further limitations on a range of other activities including the disposal of persistent plastics and synthetic materials, incineration at sea, dumping of industrial wastes and the application of the precautionary principle.[68] These developments led to the 1996 Protocol to the London Convention,[69] which updated and replaced the 1992 Convention. Essentially the Protocol strengthened the regime by prohibiting the dumping of all waste with the exception of substances listed in Annex 1.[70] Incineration of waste at sea is prohibited[71] and export of waste to other countries for dumping or incineration is also forbidden.[72]

---

60 London Convention, Art. I.
61 It originally made no mention of the EEZ, having been concluded prior to UNCLOS, but more recent amendments extended its scope in this regard: Louka, op. cit., p. 149. The 1996 Protocol refers to internal waters in Article 7.
62 London Convention, Art. III. But it does not include 'wastes or other matter incidental to, or derived from, the normal operations of' the above structures and equipment.
63 Ibid.
64 London Convention, Art. IV(1)(a).
65 London Convention, Art. IV(1)(b).
66 London Convention, Art. IV(1)(c).
67 London Convention, Art. V.
68 See Sands, op. cit., p. 419.
69 *Protocol to the Convention on the Prevention of Marie Pollution by Dumping of Wastes and Other Matter*, opened for signature 7 November 1996, 36 ILM 1 (entered into force 24 March 2006). The text of the Protocol is online. Available HTTP: <www.imo.org/blast/blastData.asp?doc_id=13203&filename=PROTOCOL%20Amended%202006.doc> (accessed 29 February 2012).
70 London Convention Protocol, Art. 4(1.1). Annex I substances include dredged material, sewage sludge, fish waste, man-made structures, inert inorganic geological material, natural organic material, bulk iron, concrete and similar material and carbon dioxide from processes for sequestration.
71 London Convention Protocol, Art. 5.
72 London Convention Protocol, Art. 6.

With respect to the Annex 1 substances, a permit is required before such substances can be dumped.[73] Parties are to designate a national authority to issue permits for disposal of Annex 1 substances, which is required in addition to keep records of permitted and actual dumping and monitor the condition of the sea.[74] Where possible, more environmentally sound disposal options should be identified, to avoid dumping.[75] In relation to the dumping of other substances a waste assessment procedure is provided in Annex 2.

It calls on the parties to work individually and collectively to 'prevent, reduce and . . . eliminate pollution caused by dumping or incineration at sea'.[76] The Protocol refers to enhancing regional cooperation,[77] encouraging technical cooperation and assistance[78] and promoting the Protocol through international organisations.[79] At the state level each party must report on waste loaded in its territory or onto one of its flagged vessels and the administrative and legislative measures taken to implement the Protocol, as well as their effectiveness.[80]

The Protocol incorporates a more precautionary approach by requiring the adoption of preventative measures where waste is likely to cause harm, 'even where there is no conclusive evidence to prove a causal relation between inputs and their effects'.[81] Exceptions include situations of *force majeure*, where there is a danger to human life or a real threat to vessels.[82] The Protocol also incorporates the polluter pays principle in Article 3, which requires states to ensure that authorised persons bear the cost of preventing and controlling pollution. The Protocol also includes a phase-in period giving states five years to comply with the provisions.

Whilst the Convention and Protocol have been successful at halting unregulated dumping and incineration at sea, significant challenges remain including illegal dumping in deliberate breach of the provisions.[83] Further issues relating to state responsibility for dumping have not been determined.[84]

Law of the Sea Convention

The UNCLOS convention deals with various important matters including delineating a state's territorial sea and contiguous zone. In Part V it also deals with the Exclusive Economic Zone (EEZ). Whereas the territorial sea of a state has a breadth up to a limit of 12 nautical miles measured from the baselines determined by the Convention[85] and the contiguous zone may not extend beyond 24 nautical miles from the baselines from which the breadth of the

---

73 London Convention Protocol, Art. (1.2)
74 London Convention Protocol, Art. 9.
75 London Convention Protocol, Art. 4(1.2).
76 London Convention Protocol, Art. 2.
77 London Convention Protocol, Art. 12.
78 London Convention Protocol, Art. 13.
79 London Convention Protocol, Art. 17.
80 London Convention Protocol, Art. 9(4). The Protocol also refers to the development of compliance procedures: Art. 11.
81 London Convention Protocol, Art. 3.
82 London Convention Protocol, Art. 8.
83 Sands, op. cit., p. 418.
84 P. Birnie, A. Boyle and C. Redgwell, *International Law & the Environment*, 3rd edition, Oxford: Oxford University Press, 2009 p. 431.
85 UNCLOS, Art. 3.

territorial sea is measured,[86] the EEZ is an altogether larger area again. By Article 57 the EEZ of a state 'shall not extend beyond 200 nautical miles from the baselines from which the breadth of the territorial sea is measured'. This, in effect, extends a state far out to sea.

By Article 56(1) of UNCLOS it is provided that:

> In the exclusive economic zone, the coastal state has:
>
> (a) sovereign rights for the purpose of exploring and exploiting, conserving and managing the natural resources, whether living or non-living . . .;
>
> (b) jurisdiction . . . with regard to:
>
> . . . (iii) the protection and preservation of the marine environment.

So it is evident that, in the EEZ, although a coastal state has exclusive authority to be able to do certain things, 'the protection and preservation of the marine environment' is one particular matter in regard to which it has jurisdiction which may be exercised. And this clearly would allow the coastal state to adopt strong laws on the subject to prevent marine pollution.

Many more of the provisions in UNCLOS are aimed at marine protection. The most significant of these, for the purposes of this chapter, are included in Part XII. Article 192 creates a general obligation to protect and preserve the marine environment. Whilst states' rights to exploit natural resources are confirmed,[87] this is balanced with their obligation to take 'all measures . . . that are necessary to prevent, reduce and control pollution of the marine environment from any source, using . . . the best practicable means at their disposal and in accordance with their capabilities' to prevent damage by pollution to other states and areas beyond national jurisdiction.[88] Some further detail is provided in the sub-articles that follow, including that such measures should be 'designed to minimize to the fullest possible extent' the 'release of toxic, harmful or noxious substances' from land-based, atmospheric or dumping, and 'pollution from vessels' and 'installations and devices operating in the marine environment' and those 'used in exploration or exploitation of natural resources of the seabed and subsoil'.[89] Specific mention is made of the need to 'protect and preserve rare or fragile ecosystems as well as the habitat of depleted, threatened or endangered species'.[90] These goals are to be achieved through global and regional cooperation including notification of imminent danger,[91] the preparation of contingency plans,[92] research and exchange of information,[93] and the development of scientific criteria for the development of regulations.[94] Technical assistance and monitoring and assessment are also areas for state cooperation.[95]

Clearly UNCLOS plays an important part in establishing a firm foundation for the future development of marine pollution law, even though it was concluded after some of the most

---

86 UNCLOS, Art. 33(2).
87 UNCLOS, Art. 193.
88 UNCLOS, Arts 194(1) and (2).
89 UNCLOS, Art. 194(3).
90 UNCLOS, Art. 194(5).
91 UNCLOS, Art. 198.
92 UNCLOS, Art. 199.
93 UNCLOS, Art. 200.
94 UNCLOS, Art. 201.
95 UNCLOS, Arts 202–6.

significant international law in this area had already been adopted. In some areas UNCLOS provides quite specific provisions, such as those prohibiting dumping in the territorial sea or the EEZ of a state without consent,[96] and the regulation of vessel-source pollution through the adoption of rules, standards and safe routing systems.[97] But in other places there is less detail, particularly regarding land-based marine pollution, which is perhaps one of the reasons why the law is less developed in this area.

Salvage Convention

A further relevant instrument, where the need to protect the marine environment is given central importance, is the Salvage Convention. The Preamble to that Convention states that the parties recognise the desirability of determining by agreement uniform international rules regarding salvage operations. In that regard, the Preamble notes 'in particular the increased concern for the protection of the environment'. It is also stated that the parties are conscious of 'the major contribution which efficient and timely salvage operations can make to the safety of vessels and other property in danger and to the protection of the environment'. With these in mind, the states parties agree to certain uniform rules regarding salvage operations.

Salvage is the reward payable to those saving life or property at sea. Under the Convention only salvage operations which have had a 'useful result' give rise to a reward.[98] Accordingly, except as otherwise provided, no payment is due under the Convention if salvage operations have had no useful result.[99] The criteria for fixing an award are set out in Article 13. Reward is fixed with a view to encouraging salvage operations.[100] Criteria include the salvaged value of the vessel and other property and 'the skill and efforts of the salvors in preventing or minimizing damage to the environment'.[101] The latter was not, until this Convention, part of salvage law at all. Other criteria include: the measure of success obtained by the salvor; the nature and degree of the danger; the skill and efforts of the salvors in salvaging the vessel, other property and life; the time used and expenses and losses incurred by the salvors; the risk of liability and other risks run by the salvors or their equipment; the promptness of the services rendered; the availability and use of vessels or other equipment intended for salvage operations; and the state of readiness and efficiency of the salvor's equipment and the value thereof.

Apart from preventing or minimising damage to the environment being one of the criteria for reward, provision is made in Article 14 for special compensation in that regard which is intended to give a financial incentive to salvors if they try to protect the marine environment, even if they do not succeed in the salvage. Article 14(1) states:

> If the salvor has carried out salvage operations in respect of a vessel which by itself or its cargo threatened damage to the environment and has failed to earn a reward . . . he shall be entitled to special compensation from the owner of that vessel equivalent to his expenses as herein defined.

96 UNCLOS, Art. 210.
97 UNCLOS, Art. 211.
98 UNCLOS, Art. 12(1).
99 See UNCLOS, Art. 12(2).
100 UNCLOS, Art. 13(1).
101 UNCLOS, Art. 13(1)(b).

Then, by Article 14(2), the Convention provides:

> If . . . the salvor by his salvage operations has prevented or minimized damage to the environment, the special compensation payable by the owner to the salvor . . . may be increased up to a maximum of 30% of the expenses incurred by the salvor. However, the tribunal, if it deems it fair and just to do so and bearing in mind the relevant criteria set out in Article 13, paragraph 1, may increase such special compensation further, but in no event shall the total increase be more than 100% of the expenses incurred by the salvor.

Article 14(3) provides that the salvor's expenses under Articles 14(1) and (2) means the out-of-pocket expenses reasonably incurred by the salvor in the salvage operation and a fair rate for equipment and personnel actually and reasonably used in the salvage operation. Article 14(4) states that the total special compensation shall be paid only if and to the extent that such compensation is greater than any reward recoverable by the salvor under Article 13.

To emphasise the importance of the environment to the Convention, Article 14(5) then goes on to provide:

> If the salvor has been negligent and has thereby failed to prevent or minimize damage to the environment, he may be deprived of the whole or part of any special compensation due under this article.

There is also Part B of the Convention (called the *Common Understanding Concerning Articles 13 and 14 of the Convention*), which reads:

> It is the common understanding of the Conference that, in fixing a reward under article 13 and assessing special compensation under article 14 of the International Convention on Salvage, 1989 the tribunal is under no duty to fix a reward under article 13 up to the maximum salved value of the vessel and other property before assessing the special compensation to be paid under article 13.

In other words, a certain priority is, by this, accorded to assessing special compensation which, in turn, reflects the concern of the Salvage Convention in protection of the marine environment.

Conclusion

From the time of OILPOL 54, if not earlier, the world community has seen a need to take a firm stand against pollution of the sea and, thus, of the marine environment. It has responded with a series of conventions. A number of serious maritime incidents have driven this response.

Those conventions include general obligations to protect and preserve the marine environment, frameworks designed to prevent operational and unintentional releases of pollution from vessels, the regulation of deliberate dumping, and liability and compensation regimes. The most important in terms of civil liability is the CLC as amended by the 1992 Protocol. The significance of MARPOL lies in dealing not only with unintentional vessel-sourced oil pollution but with other kinds of pollution as well. The London Convention and Protocol complement these instruments by regulating the deliberate dumping of waste from ships. Protection of the marine environment, as an international concern, is evident in UNCLOS as well as in the Salvage Convention. Other conventions (such as the Bunkers Convention) have also been noteworthy developments.

Nevertheless, some challenges do remain. First is the issue of failure to implement international law and non-compliance with provisions, particularly by flag states. This is exacerbated by 'flag of convenience' states – countries favoured for ship registration because regulations and enforcement are minimal. Although, as set out above, UNCLOS includes obligations on coastal states to protect and preserve the marine environment, primary regulatory responsibility for vessel construction, design, seaworthiness and safety lies with the state in which a ship is registered – the flag state. Although UNCLOS provides that there should be a 'genuine link' between a ship and its state of registration,[102] this would appear to be aimed at ensuring flag states exercise their responsibility to regulate vessels rather than a test of validity of registration.[103] Many flag of convenience states are influential in the IMO and there has been little progress in addressing the above issue.[104]

Secondly, the CLC, for example, is in need of revision in some areas as there seems little good reason to require legal actions to be brought within three years or no later than six years after the date of an incident. History shows (especially the *Exxon Valdez* disaster) that these periods are far too short. Nor is it at all obvious why an owner should escape liability in the case of a natural phenomenon of 'an exceptional, inevitable and irresistible character'.

Furthermore, not all damage done to the marine environment comes from ships – although much may or does. Land-based pollution, including for example debris, dust and agricultural run-off, impacts significantly on the marine environment. Indeed it has been found that '[l]and-based sources contribute 70 per cent of marine pollution, while maritime transport and dumping-at-sea activities contribute [only] 10 per cent each'.[105] Although UNCLOS called upon states to adopt laws to prevent, reduce and control marine pollution from land-based sources,[106] and the United Nations Environment Programme has implemented the *Global Programme of Action for the Protection of the Marine Environment from Land-based Activities*,[107] there is little hard law at the international level. If the marine environment is to be truly valued and effectively protected, then coastal states, in the next few years, must take serious steps in this regard.

Furthermore, technological advances bring with them novel challenges and risks. For example, seabed activities currently only contribute 1 per cent of marine pollution but this may well increase in the future.[108] International law must develop to meet these new and emerging concerns in ways which do not exacerbate the current fragmented and piecemeal nature of international marine pollution law. Indeed, in time, it may not be too unrealistic to hope for a single convention (perhaps reducing so-called 'treaty congestion'[109]) dealing with all aspects of pollution (on land or on, over or at sea) despoiling or degrading the marine environment.

---

102 UNCLOS, Art. 91.
103 See Birnie et al., op. cit., pp. 400–1 referring to *MV Saiga (No. 2) (Merits)* ITLOS No 2 (1999).
104 Ibid.
105 *Agenda 21* (1992), Report of the UNCED, I, UN Doc A/CONF.151/26/Rev.1. Ch. 17 para. 17.18.
106 UNCLOS, Art. 207.
107 United Nations Environment Programme *Global Programme of Action for the Protection of the Marine Environment from Land-based Activities*. Online. Available HTTP: <www.gpa.depiweb.org/> (accessed 29 February 2012).
108 Louka, op. cit., p. 147.
109 This topic is the subject of D. Anton's Chapter 36 in this volume.

17

Two decades of the Basel Convention

Tony George Puthucherril

This chapter explores the working of the Basel Convention during the past two decades and the extent to which it has been able to resolve the problems associated with the ever increasing generation and unsound management of hazardous wastes. To this end, it probes the relevance of this instrument for a developing economy like Bangladesh. It concludes with an examination of what needs to be done to ensure that the Basel Convention objectives are fulfilled now and in the future.

Introduction

The regulation of the transboundary transport of toxic and dangerous wastes was long based on the international principle of good neighbourliness embodied in the common law maxim of *sic utere tuo ut alienum non laedas*; that is, states are obliged to control activities within their jurisdiction in a manner that does not cause harm to other states.[1] In due course, this principle crystallised into a rule of customary international law and found recognition in several major international environmental law instruments. In the 1980s, owing to rising environmental consciousness in industrialised nations regarding the dangers posed by callous disposal of hazardous and other wastes, there was an overwhelming demand among the general public in these countries to revamp disposal technologies and practices. This resulted in tighter restrictions, which led to an escalation in disposal costs and a consequent shrinkage in the availability of landfill sites. Thus began the international transport of hazardous wastes and international efforts to regulate these transboundary movements.

Unscrupulous traders of toxic wastes in industrialised nations approached developing countries with weak economies, particularly those in Africa and in Eastern Europe, in the search for inexpensive disposal sites. These industrialised nations, which drew benefits from modern economic and technological developments, were unwilling to bear the environmental costs of these advancements and sought to shift these negative externalities to developing countries far away from the place of waste generation. This 'propensity of wealthy,

---

1 K. Kummer, 'The International Regulation of Transboundary Traffic in Hazardous Wastes: The 1989 Basel Convention', *International and Comparative Law Quarterly* 41, 1992, 530.

industrialized nations to export their wastes to poorer, developing nations is a classic and pervading example of international environmental injustice' and is summed up in the phrase 'not in my back yard' (NIMBY).[2] Sheer economics dictated the movement of hazardous wastes since the disposal costs in developing countries were only a fraction of those in the state of generation or other industrialised nations. The fact that developing countries generally had very little or no capacity to process the hazardous wastes, and their environmental standards were also lax or non-existent, facilitated this trade. However, the shipping of hazardous waste to developing countries for disposal in most cases proved costly for the recipient nation. The toxic wastes had high potential to contaminate the environment, jeopardise human health, and, in certain cases, lead to human morbidity. In addition, industrialised nations also resorted to the dumping or incineration of hazardous wastes at sea.[3]

There are several examples of waste transfers that were carried out surreptitiously in flagrant violation of the tenet of good neighbourliness, despite the broad breadth and scope of this principle and other legal instruments, which were to a large extent fragmented and sectoral.[4] 'Garbage barges' laden with hazardous wastes sailed around the world seeking friendly ports and disposal sites where they could dump their dangerous cargo. The *Khian Sea* incident exposed the inadequacies of the then available international legal controls on this matter.

In 1986, the Bahamian-owned *Khian Sea* loaded 28 million pounds of toxic incinerator ash in Philadelphia, USA. The ship unsuccessfully tried to offload its cargo in the Bahamas, and later attempts were also made in the Dominican Republic, Honduras, Costa Rica, Guinea Bissau and in the Cape Verde Islands. Finally, in 1987, it managed to offload a portion of the ash in Haiti. On realising the true nature of the cargo, the authorities there ordered it to leave. Thereafter, the ship sailed to Senegal, Morocco, Yugoslavia, Sri Lanka and Singapore looking for a place to dump its toxic load. Meanwhile, the ship changed its name twice, first to *Felicia*, and thereafter to *Pelacano*. In an attempt to cloak its true identity, its ownership and registration were also changed (first from Liberia to the Bahamas and later to Honduras). Finally, somewhere in the Indian Ocean between Singapore and Sri Lanka, the ash disappeared.[5]

Often, dangerous and toxic cargo was welcomed by corrupt and cash-strapped governments as evidenced in the notorious Koko incident. Between 1987 and 1988, 3,800 tons of hazardous wastes, collected from various European countries and the United States (US) were transported by five ships to Koko, Nigeria. An Italian waste trader persuaded a retired lumber worker to store the wastes in a dirt lot near his home for US$100 a month. The Nigerian authorities were unaware of these transactions, until the matter was brought to their attention by some Nigerian students in Italy.[6] Following a diplomatic stand-off, the Nigerian government compelled the Italian government, and the Italian company that was responsible for the dumping, to remove the toxic waste from Nigeria.

These highly publicised instances of illegal dumping of toxic wastes led to an international outcry and triggered the demand for a comprehensive international legal regime to regulate the export of hazardous wastes and industrial refuse. Under the auspices of the United Nations

2 M.B. Gerrard, 'The Victims of Nimby', *Fordham Urban Law Journal* 21, 1994, 495.
3 For further discussion of the London Convention prohibiting dumping of waste, see Chapter 16 by D. Cremean and E.J. Techera in this volume.
4 K. Kummer, *International Management of Hazardous Wastes*, Oxford: Clarendon Press, 1995, p. 28.
5 M.A. Montgomery, 'Traveling Toxic Trash: an Analysis of the 1989 Basel Convention', *The Fletcher Forum of World Affairs Journal* 14, 1990, 315.
6 S.F. Liu, 'The Koko Incident: Developing International Norms for the Transboundary Movement of Hazardous Waste', *Journal of Natural Resources and Environmental Law* 8, 1993, 121.

Environment Programme (UNEP), negotiations implementing the general principle of good neighbourliness in the context of hazardous waste management culminated in the adoption of the *Basel Convention on the Control of Transboundary Movements of Hazardous Wastes and their Disposal, 1989* (Basel Convention).

This chapter explains the essential features and milestones of the Basel Convention, and reviews the accomplishments and failures of the Convention over its two decades of operation. To put these issues in perspective, the relevance of the Basel Convention to a developing economy, Bangladesh, is also examined. Finally, the conclusion identifies areas that need strengthening if the Basel Convention is to retain its relevance for the future.

The basic tools

In 1981, a group of senior government officials and experts on environmental law were called upon to develop a long-term strategic guidance plan for UNEP in the field of environmental law. The 1982 Montevideo Programme I called on UNEP to prepare principles and guidelines for environmentally sound transport, handling (including storage) and disposal of toxic and dangerous wastes. This initiative culminated in the Cairo Guidelines, which were adopted by UNEP in 1987. Even though these guidelines lacked authority, the Cairo Guidelines highlighted 'major principles of hazardous waste management in rather broad and general terms'.[7]

While adopting the Cairo Guidelines, UNEP also established a working group to draft a global convention to control the transboundary movements of hazardous wastes. The working group had the unwieldy title of 'Ad hoc Working Group of Legal and Technical Experts with a Mandate to Prepare a Global Convention on the Control of Transboundary Movements of Hazardous Wastes'. After years of contentious negotiations, the Conference of Plenipotentiaries on the Global Convention on the Control of Transboundary Movements of Hazardous Wastes convened in 1989 at Basel. At this meeting, 116 countries and a host of non-governmental organisations (NGOs) and international agencies participated, and the final Act of this instrument was presented for consideration. One hundred and four nations signed the Final Act on 22 March 1989 and the Basel Convention came into force from 5 May 1992, after 20 countries formally ratified the agreement.[8]

At present, the Basel Convention has nearly 175 parties and this Convention is a groundbreaking international environmental treaty that recognises the harmful consequences due to the transboundary movement of hazardous wastes, mainly from the developed to the developing world, following 'the path of least resistance'.[9] It provides measures to contain this growing threat to human health and to the environment. The Basel Convention seeks to respond to the growing international concern over the disproportionate environmental burdens borne by developing nations due to the trade in hazardous wastes. Inherently, there is an element of injustice implicit in this relationship. The Basel Convention represents the first comprehensive attempt at the international level to set right the unequal power equation that exists between the different players by regulating the hazardous waste trade. It does not seek to prohibit or restrict the hazardous waste trade; rather the thrust is on providing a set of

7 Kummer, 'The 1989 Basel Convention', op. cit., 533.
8 *Basel Convention on the Control of Transboundary Movements of Hazardous Wastes and their Disposal,* opened for signature 22 March 1989, 1673 UNTS 126 (entered into force 5 May 1992).
9 Kummer, *International Management of Hazardous Wastes*, op. cit., p. 6.

flexible regulatory principles. The underlying principles and basic features of the Basel Convention are discussed below.

The underlying principles

The Basel Convention resonates the principles of environmental justice, sustainable development, promotion of public health, safety and international cooperation. It has three primary objectives, namely to reduce to a minimum the transboundary movements of hazardous and other wastes, consistent with their environmentally sound management; to dispose of hazardous wastes and other wastes as close as possible to their source of generation; and to minimise generation of hazardous wastes in terms of quantity and degree of hazard. Its Preambular Statements, *inter alia*, provide that the Convention aims to 'protect, by strict control, human health and the environment against the adverse effects which may result from the generation and management of hazardous wastes and other wastes'. These goals are to be achieved in two ways. First, the convention seeks to provide enhanced control over the transboundary movement of hazardous and other wastes, so that it may act as an incentive for environmentally sound management (ESM) and reduce the frequency of such movements.[10] Second, the Basel Convention parties are obliged to adopt appropriate measures to minimise the generation of hazardous and other wastes and ensure adequate disposal facilities within the generating state. Such measures will ultimately reduce the transboundary movement of wastes.

Throughout the Convention text, ESM appears as the basic criterion to determine whether a transboundary movement of waste or its disposal conforms to the Basel Convention stipulations. Defined in Article 2(8), ESM is the touchstone of the Convention and it requires the adoption of pragmatic steps to ensure that hazardous or other wastes are managed in a manner that will not jeopardise human health and the environment. The concept of ESM finds concrete expression through a series of 'Technical Guidelines' developed in relation to the management of specific waste streams by the Technical Working Group of the Basel Convention, a subsidiary body to the Conference of the Parties. For instance, in the context of ship deconstruction, ESM is elucidated in the Technical Guidelines on the Environmentally Sound Management of the Full and Partial Dismantling of Ships, 2002.

Primary definitions and major actors

The Basel Convention provides a broad definition of the term hazardous wastes. Since the term 'hazardous' qualifies 'wastes', as a starting point it is necessary to understand what is meant by wastes under the Convention. Wastes are defined as 'substances or objects which are disposed of or are intended to be disposed of or are required to be disposed of by the provisions of national law'.[11] A waste is hazardous if it is listed under Annex I, unless it does not possess any of the characteristics enumerated in Annex III, namely flammability, explosivity, toxicity and eco-toxicity. Wastes that are not covered by this clause can still be considered as hazardous wastes if they are so considered under the national law of the party of export, import or transit.[12] Radioactive wastes and wastes arising from the normal operation of a ship,

10 *Basel Convention*, op. cit., Preamble.
11 Ibid., Art. 2(1).
12 Ibid., Art. 1(1).

which are governed by MARPOL 73/78, are excluded from its ambit.[13] Annexes I and II list the wastes regulated under the Basel Convention (subject to the criteria mentioned in Annex III); Annexes VIII and IX clarify the specific wastes that can be covered by the Convention. Wastes that belong to any category contained in Annex II that are subject to transboundary movement shall be 'other wastes'.[14] These generally include household wastes and their residuals.

As far as the major actors in the trade are concerned, the Basel Convention envisages five natural or legal persons that can be involved in the transport of hazardous wastes. The first is the 'generator', the entity whose activity has produced the wastes or, in cases where this entity is not known, the person who has possession or control over the wastes.[15] The second is the 'exporter' who arranges for the export of hazardous wastes and is under the jurisdiction of the exporting state.[16] The 'carrier' is the performing carrier,[17] while the 'importer' is any person under the jurisdiction of the importing state who imports the hazardous wastes.[18] The final player, the 'disposer', receives the hazardous cargo for disposal.[19] These entities operate in a broad framework where the main drivers are the states of export,[20] import[21] and transit.[22]

Minimising the transboundary movement of hazardous wastes

To minimise transboundary movements, the Basel Convention establishes a system of controls or general responsibilities in relation to the export and import of hazardous waste. To prevent illegal trade, the Basel Convention affirms the sovereign right of a party to unilaterally prohibit the import of hazardous wastes.[23] There is a corresponding obligation on other parties to respect this right.[24] Exports of hazardous wastes are permitted only in cases where the exporting state lacks the technical expertise and capacity for sound disposal or in situations where the waste is required as a raw material for recycling or recovery in the state of import.[25] In all cases, the duty to ensure ESM of the hazardous waste lies solely on the state of export and cannot be transferred to the importing or transit state.[26] In addition, the exporting party is required to prohibit an export if it believes that the wastes will not be managed in accordance with the ESM principles in the intended destination.[27]

Another central feature of the Basel Convention is that it prohibits parties from exporting or importing hazardous or other wastes to or from non-party states.[28] However, Article 11

13 Ibid., Arts 1(3)–(4). For further consideration of MARPOL see Chapter 16 by D. Cremean and E.J. Techera in this volume.
14 Ibid., Art. 1(2).
15 Ibid., Art. 2(18).
16 Ibid., Art. 2(15).
17 Ibid., Art. 2(17).
18 Ibid., Art. 2(16).
19 Ibid., Art. 2(19).
20 Ibid., Art. 2(10).
21 Ibid., Art. 2(11).
22 Ibid., Art. 2(12).
23 Ibid., Preamble.
24 Ibid., Art. 4(1)(b).
25 Ibid., Art. 4(9).
26 Ibid., Art. 4(10).
27 Ibid., Art. 4(2)(e)
28 Ibid., Art. 4(2)(5).

empowers parties to enter into 'bilateral, multilateral, or regional agreements or arrangements' with parties, or even non-parties, for the transboundary movement of hazardous or other waste, provided that such agreements or arrangements do not derogate from the ESM requirements and take into account the interests of developing countries. The Secretariat to the Basel Convention should be notified of such agreements. It is clear that trade with non-parties not undertaken pursuant to Article 11 are prohibited.[29] Article 11 also can be interpreted to support regional agreements initiated by developing nations desiring a total ban on all importation of wastes into their particular region.[30] In this regard, it should be noted that the Basel Convention requires parties to prohibit the export of hazardous wastes to states, particularly developing countries, which belong to an economic or political integration entity that has prohibited by legislation all such imports.[31]

Informed consent and documentation

To enable the importing state to assess the nature of the risks involved in an import, elaborate control measures have been provided for based on the principle of prior informed consent (PIC).[32] For the importing state to make an informed decision, the Basel Convention requires certain information to be provided to it, namely information on the wastes, proposed methods of transportation and disposal, and evidence of a contract between the parties ensuring environmentally sound recycling.[33] Even the prior informed consent of the transit state, irrespective of its party/non-party status, is also required.[34]

For a transboundary movement of hazardous wastes, the Convention contemplates two documents. The first is the 'notification document' by which the exporting states notify, or in the alternative ensure that the generator/exporter notifies, through the competent authority the proposed export and obtain the written consent of both the importing and transit states before the transportation.[35] The next is the 'movement document', which contains information on 14 items, namely declarations by the generator/exporter that the information provided is correct, none of the states involved object to the transport and an overall description of the waste.[36]

Other rules on transboundary movement

Hazardous and other wastes that are intended for transboundary movement should be packaged, labelled and transported in accordance with generally accepted international standards.[37] As may be required by the states of import or transit, the transboundary movement must be covered by insurance, bond or other guarantee.[38] The Basel Convention also

---

29 Ibid., Art. 9(1)(a).
30 L. Widawsky, 'In my Backyard: How Enabling Hazardous Waste Trade to Developing Nations Can Improve the Basel Convention's Ability to Achieve Environmental Justice', *Environmental Law* 38, 2008, 589.
31 *Basel Convention*, op. cit., Art. 4(2)(e).
32 Ibid., Art. 6.
33 Ibid., Annex V A.
34 Ibid., Arts 6(4) and 7.
35 Ibid., Art. 6.
36 Ibid., Annex V B, item 8.
37 Ibid., Art. 7(b).
38 Ibid., Art. 6(11).

establishes rules and procedures on matters relating to liability and compensation for damage during transportation and disposal.[39] Further, only persons authorised by national law can transport or dispose of the hazardous or other wastes, which in effect implies authorisation of recycling facilities.

Duty to reimport and illegal traffic

The Basel Convention disapproves of illegal traffic and establishes a response mechanism to deal with the same. There is provision for reimporting the hazardous waste in cases where the disposal contract stands frustrated.[40] In such cases, the state of export has to ensure that the exporter takes the wastes back if alternative arrangements for its environmentally sound disposal cannot be made. This is also required in cases of non-compliance with the notification and consent requirements; where the consent was obtained through falsification, misrepresentation or fraud; if there is discrepancy between the material particulars in the documents and the transport of the hazardous wastes; or 'deliberate disposal', that is the movement is considered to be illegal traffic.[41] Illegal traffic is a criminal offence and the Basel Convention calls upon parties to initiate steps to introduce appropriate domestic laws to prevent and punish the same.[42]

Management of the Basel Convention

The Basel Convention is managed by a Secretariat which assists parties in identifying illegal traffic, provides assistance to states in cases of emergency and receives and conveys information.[43] Parties provide the Secretariat with information, including an annual national report detailing all movement of wastes pursuant to the Basel Convention, disposal methods, accidents, Article 11 agreements and information pertaining to the breach of the Convention by any party.[44]

Under Article 14, parties to the Convention, can, according to the specific needs of different regions or sub-regions, establish regional or sub-regional centres for training and technology transfer for the management of hazardous and other wastes and the minimisation of their generation. A network of 14 Regional and Coordinating Centres for Capacity Building and Technology Transfer (BCRCs) has been established. The BCRCs are involved in training, dissemination of information, consultation, awareness-raising activities and technology transfer on matters relevant to the implementation of the Basel Convention and to the environmentally sound management of hazardous and other wastes in the countries that they serve.

The Conference of the Parties (COP), which represents the governing body of the Basel Convention, comprises all states parties and reviews and evaluates the implementation of the convention.[45] The COP is empowered to take additional action to achieve the purposes of the convention, to promote harmonization of policies, strategies and measures that seek to minimise harm to human health and to the environment from hazardous and other wastes,

---

39 Ibid., Art. 2.
40 Ibid., Art. 8.
41 Ibid., Art. 9(1).
42 Ibid., Art. 9(5).
43 Ibid., Art. 16.
44 Ibid., Arts 11, 13, 16 and 19.
45 Ibid., Art. 15.

adopt protocols and to establish subsidiary bodies.[46] The tenth meeting of the COP, held at the Cartagena de Indias, Colombia in October 2011, focused on 'prevention, minimization and recovery of wastes' and deliberated on the future roles of the convention.[47]

At the time of its adoption, the Basel Convention was hailed as the broadest and most significant international environmental treaty on the subject of transboundary movement of hazardous wastes. It is the central pillar in a comprehensive package of four environmental treaties dealing with different facets of hazardous waste management, namely the *Rotterdam Convention on the Prior Informed Consent Procedure for Certain Hazardous Chemicals and Pesticides in International Trade 1998* (which regulates the international trade in hazardous chemicals), the *Stockholm Convention on Persistent Organic Pollutants 2001* (which controls chemical substances that persist in the environment) and, finally, the *Protocol to the London Convention on the Prevention of Marine Pollution by Dumping of Waste and Other Matter which replaces the London Dumping Convention 1972* (which deals with the dumping or incineration of wastes at sea).[48] Still, environmentalists and many developing countries condemned the Convention as they felt that it only served to legitimise dumping of toxic waste in developing countries rather than outright criminalisation of it. At each of the COPs, the parties have progressively moved to rectify some of the perceived shortcomings through consensus agreements. Some measures of success have achieved at least at a normative level in addressing some of these concerns. Three measures in particular warrant further scrutiny: the Basel Ban Amendment, the Basel Protocol on Liability and Compensation, and regional arrangements to implement the Convention.

The Basel Ban Amendment

As mentioned above, one of the most serious criticisms against the Basel Convention was that rather than addressing issues of environmental injustice it merely cast a cloak of legitimacy on to a trade that was abhorrent to basic human values of dignity and human rights. Under the Convention, states could now send their hazardous wastes and other industrial residue to developing nations as long as they were parties and the procedures related to prior informed consent were followed. Trade was also permitted between parties and non-parties, provided this was subject to environmentally sound bilateral or multilateral agreements.

At the second meeting of the COP, in 1994, parties sought to address some of these inadequacies by introducing an immediate ban on the export of hazardous wastes for final disposal and of wastes from the Organisation for Economic Co-operation and Development (OECD) to non-OECD countries.[49] As this decision was not incorporated into the Basel Convention text, there were doubts regarding its legal nature. The matter was resolved in 1995, at the third meeting of the COP, when this ban was formally incorporated into the Basel Convention

---

46 Ibid.

47 COP10, *Tenth Meeting of the Conference of the Parties to the Basel Convention*. Online. Available HTTP: <http://www.basel.int/COP10/tabid/1571/Default.aspx> (accessed 8 October 2011).

48 For a consideration of the Stockholm and Rotterdam Conventions see Chapter 18 by Z. Lipman in this volume. For further discussion on the London Convention see Chapter 16 by D. Cremean and E. Techera.

49 Basel Convention on the Control of Transboundary Movements of Hazardous Wastes and their Disposal, *Ban Amendment to the Basel Convention on the Control of Transboundary Movements of Hazardous Wastes and their Disposal Geneva, 22 September 1995*. Online. Available HTTP: <http://www.basel.int/ratif/ban-alpha.htm> (accessed 18 October 2011).

as an amendment.[50] Accordingly, Decision III/1 now bans exports of hazardous wastes intended for final disposal and those for recycling from what are known as Annex VII countries (Basel Convention parties that are members of the EU or OECD and Liechtenstein) to non-Annex VII countries (all other parties to the Convention).[51] Even though it does not use the 'OECD/non-OECD' distinction, in essence, the decision (the so-called Ban Amendment) prohibits the movement of wastes from OECD to non-OECD countries.

Even though the Basel Ban Amendment was welcomed as an important step in the movement towards environmental justice, it met with stiff resistance from several of the industrialised nations, in particular from the US. Despite being a signatory (as early as March 1990), and the US Senate having voted to ratify the Basel Convention, it subsequently reneged on its favourable disposition primarily because of its opposition to the Basel Ban Amendment. Surprisingly, several developing countries also felt that the Ban unfairly deprived them of economic benefits that could flow into their fragile economies from the recovery of materials from hazardous wastes. To come into effect, this amendment requires ratification by three-quarters of the Basel Parties. Thus far, it has not entered into force due to insufficient ratifications.

Basel Protocol on Liability and Compensation

Another criticism against the Basel Convention centred on the absence of a mechanism to assign liability and provide for compensation in case of damages ensuing from the international movement of hazardous and other wastes. As it stands, to assist affected parties on an interim basis, the Basel Convention directs parties to consider the establishment of a 'revolving fund' to respond to emergency situations involving accidents arising from the transboundary movements of hazardous or other wastes or during their disposal.[52]

The Ad Hoc Working Group of Legal and Technical Experts prepared the first draft of a liability protocol in 1993. But it was not until the fifth COP in 1999 that the Basel Protocol on Liability and Compensation was adopted. The Protocol seeks to provide a comprehensive regime to address liability issues and to provide for compensation that is prompt and adequate for any damages consequent to the transboundary movement of hazardous and other wastes and also for incidents that happen due to illegal traffic.[53] The Protocol essentially provides for two types of liability: strict and fault-based.[54] The Protocol also requires notifiers, exporters and importers to carry insurance, bonds or other financial guarantees to cover their liability.[55]

The Protocol acts as a supplement to the Basel Convention and it has to be ratified independently of the Basel Convention to come into force. The Protocol has a total of 13 signatories and the number of parties stands at 10. Pending ratification by 20 parties, the Protocol has not yet entered into force.[56] If this framework does ever come into force, it will emerge as the first international environmental treaty that provides compensation to nations that suffer injury due to the transport in hazardous wastes.

50 Ibid.
51 Ibid.
52 *Basel Convention*, op. cit., Art. 14(2).
53 *Protocol on Liability and Compensation for Damage Resulting from Transboundary Movements of Hazardous Wastes and Their Disposal*, opened for signature 10 December 1999, UN Doc UNEP/CHW.1/WG/1/9/2 (not yet in force), Art. 1.
54 Ibid., Arts 4 and 5.
55 Ibid., Art. 14.
56 *Protocol on Liability and Compensation*, op. cit., Art. 25.

Regional arrangements

Parties can enter into 'bilateral, multilateral, or regional agreements or arrangements' with parties or even non-parties to regulate the transboundary movement of hazardous or other wastes. Such arrangements are premised on the condition that they are not to derogate from the ESM requirements, taking into account the interests of developing countries. Article 3(7) (a) provided the impetus for the development of certain regional regimes for hazardous waste management, the predominant ones being the Bamako Convention and the Lomé Convention.

The members of the Organisation of African Unity (OAU) were dissatisfied with the Basel Convention framework. According to them, it failed to provide for an extensive ban on hazardous waste movements and address the concerns of underdeveloped countries. They opined that, since the Basel Convention arrangements did not emphasise a total ban on the transboundary shipment of hazardous wastes, cash-poor states could potentially be offered sums that would lure them to ignore the disastrous impacts of the hazardous waste trade. Such a situation could potentially turn Africa into a dumping ground for all sorts of hazardous wastes. They believed that the Basel Convention merely legitimised a practice that was essentially 'a crime against Africa and the African people'.[57]

Following nearly two years of intense deliberations, 51 members of the OAU met in Bamako, Mali, in 1991, to adopt the *Bamako Convention on the Ban of the Import to Africa and the Control of Transboundary Movement and Management of Hazardous Wastes within Africa* (Bamako Convention).[58] The Bamako Convention imposes a complete ban on the import of all kinds of hazardous wastes into Africa. Furthermore, all such imports are deemed to be illegal and criminal.[59] It calls upon all parties to take appropriate legal, administrative and other measures to prohibit the import of all hazardous wastes, for any reason, into Africa.[60] Bamako also bans the dumping of hazardous wastes at sea and in internal waters.[61] The transfer of hazardous wastes within and among the African nations is also subjected to certain restrictions.[62] Out of a total of 53 African countries, even though 33 have signed the Bamako Convention, only 24 have ratified the same.

The lack of an effective monitoring and enforcement mechanism, an underdeveloped funding mechanism and the lack of solid commitment among the African states have precluded much of Bamako's anticipated success in reducing dumping of wastes in Africa. Moreover, the Bamako Convention, operating at a regional level, adopted an aggressive posture by insisting on a complete ban on the importation of wastes. This ignores the economic needs of developing nations in Africa who view the recycling industry as providing significant economic opportunities. Consequently, even though this convention was developed to meet the specific requirements of African nations, only a few states have ratified it. A blanket ban on the hazardous waste trade would have had better chances of success had the prohibition been operational at a global level.

---

57 A. Webster-Main, 'Keeping Africa Out of the Global Backyard: A Comparative Study of the Basel and Bamako Conventions', *Environs Environmental Law and Policy Journal* 26, 2002, 65.
58 *Bamako Convention on the Ban of the Import to Africa and the Control of Transboundary Movement and Management of Hazardous Wastes within Africa*, opened for signature 30 January 1991, 30 ILM 773 (entered into force 22 April 1998).
59 Ibid., Art. 4.
60 Ibid.
61 Ibid., Art. 4, para. 2.
62 Ibid, Art. 4, para. 3(n).

In addition there are several other regional instruments that seek to regulate the hazardous wastes trade like the Lomé IV Convention, entered into between the European Community (EC) and the 68 African Caribbean and Pacific (ACP) countries. It agrees, among other things, to completely ban hazardous waste exports from EC to ACP countries.[63] The EC Council Regulation No. 1013/2006 is another regional instrument that aims to strengthen, simplify and specify the procedures for controlling waste shipments to improve environmental protection by including in EC legislation the provisions of the Basel Convention.[64]

The tumultuous two decades of the Basel Convention: the ground covered and space uncovered

At the time of its adoption, the Basel Convention was severely criticised by environmentalists for having legitimised garbage imperialism rather than providing for an outright ban and criminalisation of the toxic trade. However, the fact is that this Convention originated primarily as a compromise between industrialised and developing nations and accordingly its focus was on regulation and on ensuring the safe disposal and minimisation of the transboundary movement of hazardous wastes. Belying the kind of cynicism that prevailed at the time of its adoption, during the past two decades the Basel Convention has evolved considerably and has travelled a long way from its original minimalist approach to emerge as one of the primary international instruments to regulate the trade in hazardous wastes. In this regard, it must be mentioned that during the first decade (1989 to 1999) of its operation, the emphasis was on building a framework to regulate the transboundary movements of hazardous wastes, developing criteria for environmentally sound management, and establishing a control system based on prior written notification. In the second decade (2000 to 2010), emphasis shifted to building on this foundation by seeking the full implementation and enforcement of the different treaty commitments. Essentially spelt out in the Basel Declaration on Environmentally Sound Management, other areas of focus included minimisation of hazardous waste generation, use of cleaner technologies and production methods, reduction in the movement of hazardous and other wastes, prevention and monitoring of illegal traffic, and the further development of regional and sub-regional centres for training and technology transfer. Subsequently, the Strategic Plan developed at the sixth COP in 2002 strengthened these goals and afforded further articulation to these concepts. Composed of three parts, it contains a strategic text and an action table specifying short (2003–4) and mid-to-long-term (2005–10) activities.[65] Some of the major areas of focus for the decade (2000–10) were use of cleaner technologies and production methods, prevention and monitoring of illegal traffic, enhancement of information exchange, and education and awareness raising.[66]

The 1989 Basel Convention is certainly a path-breaking international environmental treaty that provides an opportunity to ensure environmental justice by seeking to rectify the

---

63 *Fourth ACP-EEC Lome Convention*, opened for signature 15 December 1989, 29 ILM 809 (entered into force 1990), Art. 39.

64 'Regulation (EC) No 1013/2006 of the European Parliament and of the Council of 14 June 2006 on Shipments of Waste', *Official Journal of the European Union*, L 190/1. Online. Available HTTP: <http://eur-lex.europa.eu/LexUriServ/LexUriServ.do?uri=OJ:L:2006:190:0001:0098:EN:pdf> (accessed 11 October 2011).

65 *Strategic Plan for the Implementation of the Basel Convention (to 2010)*, Online. Available HTTP: <http://archive.basel.int/meetings/cop/cop6/StPlan.pdf> (accessed 9 May 2012).

66 Ibid.

disproportionate environmental burdens that fall on impoverished developing countries due to the trade in toxic wastes. It strikes a balance between environmental protection and the mandates of free trade. The Basel Convention's emphasis on prior informed consent, the duty on states parties to retrieve exported wastes in certain cases, minimisation of wastes, the proximity principle and the standard of ESM of hazardous wastes play an important role in setting the boundaries within which the hazardous waste trade is to operate.

Despite its positive influences, the Basel regime has not been able to effectively rein in the toxic tide engulfing developing nations. One of the most notorious incidents in recent times unfolded in Côte d'Ivoire, where in 2006 a ship flying the Panama flag, chartered by a Swiss company, Trafigura Beheer BV, offloaded toxic wastes at Abidjan, killing several and injuring more than 30,000. A recent report, entitled 'Waste without Frontiers', compiled by the Basel Secretariat identifies a significant emerging pattern in the waste trade, namely an increase in cross-border movements of hazardous wastes for recycling purposes.

Transboundary movement of hazardous wastes for the purpose of recycling or recovery has long been a controversial subject. It is true that, in certain situations, hazardous wastes may have an economic value. For instance, electronic wastes or e-wastes can be an asset, but, at the same time, they are an enormous problem, since they contain harmful chemicals and substances like lead, mercury, cadmium and zinc.[67] It can be argued that recycling contributes to sustainable development as it helps to conserve natural resources and can considerably reduce the hazard potential of the wastes that are being recycled. Without discounting the merit in such an argument, in practice, recycling in some nations takes place under the most primitive and dangerous conditions as they rarely possess the requisite technological expertise and capacities.

Environmental NGOs have for a long time pointed out that the recycling exception is a dangerous loophole in the Basel Convention. The preamble to the Convention emphasises the significance of recycling and states that the parties to the Convention are 'aware of the need to continue the development and implementation of environmentally sound low-waste . . . recycling options . . .'. The Convention clearly provides that hazardous waste trade will be permitted if 'the wastes in question are required as a raw material for recycling or recovery industries in the state of import . . .'. Thus, the import of recyclable materials is permitted only if the importing country is willing to claim that the materials are required for recycling or reclamation within that country. However, the importing states generally prefer to ignore the environmental risks involved in such imports as they are more concerned with the economic benefits, for example jobs and conservation of resources. Consequently, there is a real possibility and danger of sham recycling. As Katharina Kummer points out, 'The exemption applying to hazardous wastes required for recycling or recovery in the country of destination may encourage fake recycling schemes: recycling may be used as a mere label for exports that would otherwise be prohibited under the Convention.'[68] Given the surge in recycling transactions and the poor state of recycling facilities in developing countries, there is a real possibility and danger that hazardous wastes are being passed off as those intended for recycling.

The problem of hazardous waste generation is now no longer a problem that troubles solely the industrialised world. A large number of nations in the developing world are presently experiencing significant economic growth. The massive industrial development as a result

67 For further discussion of the issue of e-waste, see Chapter 18 by Z. Lipman in this volume.
68 Kummer, *International Management of Hazardous Wastes*, op. cit., p. 56.

of trade liberalisation and globalisation has enhanced purchasing power and increased consumerism. More importantly, rapid industrialisation has also led to the generation of huge quantities of hazardous wastes, which further aggravates the problem of hazardous waste management as these nations are now saddled with not only the wastes that have been imported for 'recycling' but also their own wastes.

Bangladesh and the Basel Convention

Bangladesh is a major importer of hazardous wastes and has suffered considerably due to the toxic waste trade. At the same time, Bangladesh is not an isolated case of a country reeling under the deleterious impacts of the hazardous waste trade. There are several countries in the developing world that are even now willing to accept hazardous wastes for economic benefits despite increasing awareness of the risks. Illegal and sham transactions continue, sometimes beyond the control of state authorities and sometimes even with their connivance, despite the Basel Convention.

Bangladesh is an easy target for industrialised nations who seek to take undue advantage of the economic needs of this developing economy by dumping hazardous wastes. In fact, most of the wastes that enter Bangladesh are primarily intended for recycling purposes. The most sinister form of this toxic recycling commerce is the supposed recycling of decrepit ships that have outlived their utility. End-of-life ships are generally sent to recycling yards in developing countries where they are torn apart for their steel and other usable items. For the past several decades, the shipbreaking industry has been functioning and contributing significantly to the development of Bangladesh by providing employment, steel and, more importantly, revenue to the government. However, the operation of this industry has extracted a heavy price in terms of its environmental and human health impacts. Apart from shipbreaking, toxic recycling in Bangladesh takes other forms including e-wastes. The relevance of the Basel Convention in controlling these waste streams is examined below.

Bangladesh is one of the largest shipbreaking nations in the world and it controls more than 70 per cent of the dismantling business.[69] It is believed that there are nearly 32 shipbreaking yards in operation that are spread out on a 10-kilometre stretch of the Sitakund area of the Chittagong coast. The industry provides valuable steel (providing more than 80 per cent of Bangladesh's steel requirements) in a country that does not have any significant local iron ore resources. More importantly, the shipbreaking industry provides employment to more than 20,000 unskilled workers.

The shipbreaking yards in Bangladesh function in a primitive way and the breaking is generally done in the inter-tidal zone. As a result, there is no possibility to contain the chemicals released when a ship is broken down, which seriously pollutes the marine and coastal environment. The breaking also exposes the workers to harmful chemicals such as polychlorinated biphenyls (PCBs), tributyltin and asbestos, which results in debilitation and ultimately painful death. Being the only country that does not require a gas-free-for-hot-work certificate, Bangladesh is the preferred destination for tankers, which are not pre-cleaned. This has resulted in several explosions that have killed many shipbreakers. Greenpeace estimates that, on average, one shipbreaker dies in the yards every week, and one gets

---

69 T.G. Puthucherril, 'From Shipbreaking to Sustainable Ship Recycling: Evolution of a Legal Regime', in D. Freestone (ed.) *Legal Aspects of Sustainable Development*, Volume V, The Netherlands: Martinus Nijhoff, 2010, p. 27.

injured every day. Another disturbing fact is the large-scale employment of children in the shipbreaking yards.

The shipbreaking industry has vehemently argued that the regulatory ambit of the Basel Convention is restricted only to the transboundary movement of hazardous wastes and that ships are not waste. Moreover, there are certain practical difficulties in applying the Basel Convention tools due to the peculiar features of the shipbreaking industry. For instance, it is difficult to identify an export state in respect of ships that have reached their end-of-life stage. It was to address these concerns that the COP 7 of the Basel Convention urged the International Maritime Organization (IMO) to work towards developing mandatory requirements to ensure environmentally sound management of ship dismantling.

In 2005, the Marine Environment Protection Committee of the IMO started work on developing a legally binding convention, which culminated in the *Hong Kong International Convention for the Safe and Environmentally Sound Recycling of Ships, 2009* (Ship Recycling Convention).[70] Even though the Ship Recycling Convention seeks to effectively address the environmental, occupational health and safety risks related to ship recycling and is a specific treaty on this subject, the Basel Convention still has relevance to shipbreaking. Regulation 3 of the Ship Recycling Convention provides that parties shall take into account relevant and applicable technical standards, recommendations and guidance developed under the Basel Convention. Moreover, it is necessary that the Ship Recycling Convention establish an equivalent level of control similar to that under the Basel Convention. Thus, some of the Basel Convention tools continue to retain their relevance to ship dismantling. These include the proximity principle, ESM, provisions that seek to ensure minimisation of waste material generation and their transboundary movement, ensuring availability of adequate disposal facilities within one's own national boundaries, the obligation not to allow the export of hazardous wastes if the exporting state has reason to believe that the waste will not be managed in an environmentally sound manner, the proper labelling, packaging and transport of hazardous wastes, and the prior informed consent procedure. In addition, the 2002 'Technical Guidelines for Environmentally Sound Management of the Full and Partial Dismantling of Ships' provide guidance to enable ship-dismantling facilities to conduct ship-breaking in an environmentally sound manner.

As mentioned above, shipbreaking represents only one dimension of hazardous wastes dumping that confronts Bangladesh. In recent years, there has been an increase in the quantity of electronic waste that is being dumped in this country. There is also a tendency among developed nations to provide used computers to educational institutions in developing countries like Bangladesh. Officially termed as providing technical support, in reality this is a cost-effective and convenient way for industrialised nations to get rid of obsolete computers. Apart from the inflow of these e-wastes, it is estimated that Bangladesh produces annually about 2.8 million metric tonnes of e-waste. Bangladesh has around 58.36 million active mobile phone subscribers and the total number of personal computers, television sets and refrigerators in use as of 2006 was 600,000, 1,252,000 and 2,200,000 respectively.[71] Even the ship recycling yards produce substantial quantities of e-waste. Most of the recycling of e-waste

---

70 *Hong Kong International Convention for the Safe and Environmentally Sound Recycling of Ships*, opened for signature 1 September 2009, IMO/SR/CONF/45 (not yet entered into force) ('Ship Recycling Convention').

71 P.M. Swift, 'How Can Ship Breaking Become a Sound Industry In its Own Right?', (PowerPoint presentation at the Trade Winds and Mare Forum Shipping China 3–4 March 2005, Shanghai) at slide 14.

takes place in the informal sector, as there is no formal plant in the country to recycle the e-waste in a hazard-free manner. Only a very small portion of these wastes is recycled; the remainder is callously disposed of in landfills, rivers, ponds, drains, lakes and other open spaces. The health consequences of such disposal are severe.

Bangladesh acceded to the Basel Convention in 1993. However, it has yet to ratify the Basel Ban Amendment and the Basel Protocol on Liability and Compensation. Article 4(4) of the Basel Convention requires parties to adopt appropriate legal, administrative and other measures to implement its terms. The Constitution of Bangladesh in its Article 18(1) proclaims improvement of public health as one of the primary duties of the state. This constitutional obligation prompted the government to initiate action to control the trade in hazardous wastes. The *Bangladesh Environment Conservation Act 1985* (ECA) and the *Environment Conservation Rules, 1997* (EC Rules) are the primary laws that give effect to the Basel obligations. The term 'hazardous substance' has been defined in the ECA as a 'substance, the chemical or biochemical properties of which are such that its manufacture, storage, discharge, or unregulated transportation can be harmful to the environment'.[72] The ECA empowers the government to establish the Department of Environment, which is to be headed by a Director General,[73] who, *inter alia*, has the power to give advice or issue directions regarding 'the environmentally sound use, storage, transportation, import and export of a hazardous substance or its components'.[74] Bangladesh has also brought out rules to manage certain specific waste streams such as the *Medical Waste Management Rules, 2008*. The *Bangladesh Import Policy Order 2009–2012*, in its Annexure, specifies the kinds of goods that cannot be imported into Bangladesh. It prohibits the import of any kind of waste into the country.[75]

As part of the requirements mandated by the Basel Convention, Bangladesh has appointed its Secretary to the Ministry of Environment and Forests as National Focal Point and the Director General of the Department of Environment as Competent Authority for the Convention. However, Bangladesh has not yet submitted to the Basel Secretariat any national definition of wastes and hazardous wastes, nor has it provided any list of wastes defined as, or considered to be, hazardous wastes by the national legislation in accordance with the Basel Convention. In addition, Bangladesh has not provided any information to the Basel Secretariat concerning other wastes that would require special consideration while in transboundary movement. It has also reneged on its obligations relating to national reporting, making it difficult to get a fair picture of the ground realities in Bangladesh. Apart from the general environmental laws, Bangladesh as yet does not have comprehensive legislation that gives effect to the Basel Convention provisions. Moreover, the nature of the tools that the present laws prescribe is diffused and is hence inadequate. Consequently, due to the absence of a concrete legal shield, hazardous wastes continue to flow into Bangladeshi territory with very few impediments. It is clear that this country has not undertaken substantial efforts to fulfil its international obligations under the Basel Convention and its constitutional obligations to protect public health.

Bangladesh has as yet not acceded to the Ship Recycling Convention even though, at the time of the adoption of the Convention, it demonstrated a favourable disposition to this instrument. As the Bangladesh delegation observed at the closing session of the conference

---

72 *The Bangladesh Environment Conservation Act 1995* (No 1 of 1995, Bangladesh), s. 2.
73 Ibid., s. 3,
74 Ibid., s. 4.
75 *The Import Policy Order, 2009–2012* (No SRO 22-LAW/2010, Bangladesh).

that led to the adoption of the Convention, 'we have now something which we needed so much for so long to have a smoother sailing of ship recycling.'[76] In sharp contrast, the representative from the Bangladesh Environmental Lawyers Association, who spoke on behalf of Greenpeace International and Friends of the Earth International, noted that the Ship Recycling Convention was 'a profound disappointment for we have sadly missed an opportunity'. Furthermore, she noted that the convention is an 'obsolete relic that ignores . . . environmental and social principles'.[77]

Due to the long-standing public outcry over increasing incidents of gross human rights violations in the shipbreaking yards, the Supreme Court of Bangladesh directed the Ministry of Environment and Forests to frame rules and regulations for the proper handling and management of hazardous materials and wastes, keeping in view the Basel Convention rules.[78] Accordingly, the Ministry recently brought out the draft *Shipbreaking and Hazardous Waste Management Rules 2010*. These rules are yet to be finalised and one hopes that they will embody the core principles enunciated in the Basel Convention and the Ship Recycling Convention. As far as the second waste stream, namely e-waste, is concerned, there is no direct law for its regulation.

While it may be necessary to develop legal frameworks to manage specific waste streams such as e-waste and shipbreaking, it is in Bangladesh's best interests to enact enabling legislation that implements the requirements mandated by the Basel Convention. As a country that often finds itself at the receiving end of the lopsided trade in hazardous wastes, Bangladesh should also initiate steps to ratify the Basel Ban Amendment and the Protocol on Liability and Compensation. In doing so, Bangladesh must assume a leadership role in implementing the Basel Convention regime prescriptions in the South Asian region and demonstrate to its neighbouring countries, who are also victims of the hazardous waste trade (namely India and Pakistan), the importance and the benefits that can accrue to nations that follow a similar path. It would also be in the best interests of these South Asian nations to explore the possibility of a regional agreement to regulate the flow of hazardous wastes into this region.

Conclusion: the future of the Basel Convention

While it is difficult to predict the future of the Basel Convention, it is definitely the pivotal international legal instrument that provides a platform for national governments on which to cooperate to restrict the trade in hazardous wastes. The Basel Convention mechanics have established a system to regulate the transboundary movement of hazardous wastes, and the underlying concept of environmentally sound management of wastes has garnered global acceptance. At the national level, several countries have taken measures to regulate the trade in hazardous wastes and have adopted legislation to give effect to the Basel Convention principles. However, with globalisation and the world economy growing at a brisk pace and with more and more developing nations participating in this development, the cross-border outflow and inflow of goods and wastes have expanded exponentially. In addition, consumerism in the wake of globalisation, coupled with the rapid pace at which technological

---

76 International Maritime Organization, *Statements by Delegations and Observers at the Closing Session of the Conference, Friday, 15 May 2009*. Online. Available HTTP: <http://www.sjofartsverket.se/pages/19514/sr-conf-inf8.pdf> (accessed 15 October 2011).
77 Ibid.
78 *Bangladesh Environmental Lawyers Association v Bangladesh, represented by the Secretary, Ministry of Shipping Bangladesh Secretariat*, Judgment Dated 5 March 2009 and 17 March 2009.

developments unfold, has led to a situation where products, particularly electronic goods, become obsolete very quickly and end up in the waste stream for either disposal or recycling.

Despite its significant milestones over the past two decades, there remain challenges commensurate with economic development and the consequent build-up of industrial residues and other wastes. The Basel Convention has neither been able to make a substantial dent in the generation of hazardous wastes nor has it been able to regulate the movement of hazardous wastes across national borders which, as seen, masquerades as wastes intended for recycling. Perhaps the criticism by environmental NGOs that the Basel Convention subjects parties to conflicting obligations (i.e. on the one hand it speaks about minimisation of waste generation and, on the other, it facilitates waste transportation), that it only legitimises an inherently detestable trade, and that the recycling exception is being abused is fast coming true. The Basel Convention also contains certain exceptions that ensure that the waste trade operates with very few impediments. This situation warrants a revisit of the Basel Ban Amendment and the Protocol on Liability and Compensation. At the tenth COP, a ground-breaking decision was made to revitalise the apparently moribund Ban Amendment by clarifying that the amendment will enter into force once an additional 17 parties have ratified it. However, it has to be noted that even though an absolute ban at the international level may have greater chances of producing tangible results, it may not be in the best interests of both the developing and developed countries. Developing countries may lose access to valuable economic resources, and waste generators in developed countries may continue to be burdened with wastes as they may not have sufficient capacity to dispose of certain kinds of wastes in an environmentally sustainable manner. One of the primary areas of concern in relation to the transboundary movement of hazardous wastes is the need to eliminate sham recycling and ensure that there is adequate capacity in developing countries to recycle waste in an environmentally sound manner. Accordingly, it is necessary that a mechanism be developed under the auspices of the Basel Convention in cooperation with both the states of export and import to ensure that the wastes that are exported are truly wastes that can be recycled and that the recycling takes place in facilities that possess sufficient technical capacity and are authorised to that effect. Similarly, states should also take initiatives to ensure that the Protocol on Liability and Compensation is also brought into force at the earliest opportunity, since its provisions for compensation in cases of injury sustained during the transport of hazardous waste can serve to discipline the hazardous waste industry. Even as the world continues to build a toxic legacy for future generations, our common future lies in ensuring that hazardous waste disposal is not at the expense of destroying human life and limb and polluting the environment.

18

Pollution control and the regulation of chemicals and e-waste

Zada Lipman

Pollution regulation is one of the oldest areas of environmental law. This chapter will provide an overview of key international environmental regimes aimed at the control and management of chemicals. It will also consider how this regime can be designed and/or improved to meet the challenges of an increasingly industrialised world. In particular the issue of recycling and e-waste will be analysed.

Introduction

For many years, the chemical industry has played a major role in scientific advances. This role has increased in the past 40 years as global chemical production has escalated. It is reported that over 63 million organic and inorganic chemicals have been registered to date.[1] Many of these chemicals have contributed greatly to an improved quality of life. Agriculture, health, hygiene, nutrition transport, housing, communications, sport, entertainment and many areas of daily life have been transformed by the development and application of chemical products. However, in some cases these benefits are outweighed by the risks that certain chemicals pose to human health and the environment. The World Health Organization (WHO) has estimated that toxic chemicals are responsible for approximately 355,000 deaths each year, with two-thirds of these deaths occurring in developing countries.[2]

Pesticides are one of the most toxic types of chemicals. Pesticides can adversely impact the long-term survival of major ecosystems and result in loss of biodiversity. They can also have

---

1 Chemical Abstracts Service. Online. Available HTTP: <www.cas.org> (accessed 10 February 2012).
2 World Health Organization, 'Toxic Hazards'. Online. Available HTTP: <www.who.int/heli/risks/toxics/chemicals/en/index.html> (accessed 10 February 2012). The Pesticides Action Network has brought an action against six of the world's major agrochemical companies in the Permanent Peoples' Tribunal, an international opinion tribunal, in December 2011 for promoting use of dangerous pesticides. See 'Permanent Peoples' Tribunal 2011', *The Ecologist*, 16 November 2011. Online. Available HTTP: <www.cbgnetwork.org/4163.html> (accessed 10 February 2012).

significant impacts on human health[3] which were not foreseen when these chemicals were first produced and only become apparent after years of use. Some of the most toxic organic chemicals and pesticides are known as persistent organic pollutants (POPs). They are particularly dangerous to humans and other life and resistant to degradation by chemical, physical or biological means.[4]

Apart from the problems that chemicals pose during their life cycle, disposal can be equally problematic. This has been exacerbated by the emergence of new waste streams, the most outstanding example of which is electronic waste (e-waste).

As the risks associated with chemicals and pesticides have become apparent, more stringent measures have been adopted to regulate their use and disposal, especially in developed countries. In some cases, pesticides have been banned, or their use has been restricted, while disposal options to landfill have become increasingly limited. This has led to an increase in exports of chemicals and hazardous wastes to developing countries where there is less regulation, lower environmental safety requirements and a lack of awareness of the dangers involved. Many of these countries lack the capacity to ensure that recycling is undertaken safely so as to ensure the protection of human health and the environment.

International concerns about the dangers of hazardous chemicals and pesticides and their impact on developing countries has led to the adoption of several international conventions. The first global convention was the *Basel Convention on the Control of Transboundary Movements of Hazardous Wastes and their Disposal 1989* (Basel Convention), which regulates the export of hazardous waste consistent with environmentally sound management principles and subject to a prior informed consent (PIC) procedure.[5] This was followed by two further conventions which regulate the export of certain hazardous chemicals and pesticides, prohibit their generation and institute a PIC procedure: the *Rotterdam Convention on the Prior Informed Consent Procedure for Certain Hazardous Chemicals and Pesticides in International Trade 1998* (Rotterdam Convention)[6] and the *Stockholm Convention on Persistent Organic Pollutants 2001* (Stockholm Convention).[7] These three conventions together provide a 'cradle-to-grave' framework for the environmentally sound management of hazardous chemicals and wastes throughout their life cycles.

This chapter examines the measures that the international community has adopted to deal with hazardous chemicals and pesticides. It discusses the development of the PIC procedure in the *International Code of Conduct on the Distribution and Use of Pesticides*[8] and the *London*

---

3 FAO, *Control of Water Pollution from Agriculture*, Chapter 4, 'Pesticides as Water Pollutants'. Online. Available HTTP: <http://www.fao.org/docrep/w2598e/w2598e07.htm> (accessed 15 November 2011).

4 OECD, 'Environmental Outlook for the Chemicals Industry', OECD 2001, p. 19. Online. Available HTTP: <www.oecd.org/dataoecd/7/45/2375538.pdf> (accessed 15 November 2011).

5 *Basel Convention on the Control of Transboundary Movements of Hazardous Wastes and their Disposal*, opened for signature 22 March 1989, 1673 UNTS 126 (entered into force 5 May 1992).

6 *Convention on the Prior Informed Consent Procedure for Certain Hazardous Chemicals and Pesticides in International Trade*, opened for signature 11 September 1998, 38 ILM 1 (entered into force 24 February 2004).

7 *Stockholm Convention on Persistent Organic Pollutants*, opened for signature 23 May 2001, 40 ILM 532 (entered into force 17 May 2004) (Stockholm Convention).

8 Food and Agriculture Organization (FAO), *International Code of Conduct on the Distribution and Use of Pesticides* (FAO Code), Art. 1(1). Online. Available HTTP: <http://www.fao.org/docrep/x5562E/X5562e0a.htm> (accessed 15 November 2011).

Guidelines for the Exchange of Information on Chemicals in International Trade[9] and its incorporation into a globally binding instrument in the Rotterdam Convention. The chapter then discusses the chemical regime imposed by the Rotterdam and Stockholm Conventions, and assesses its effectiveness.[10] A key focus of the chapter is the special problem of e-waste and an evaluation of the success of the Basel, Rotterdam and Stockholm Conventions in addressing this issue. Finally, product stewardship is considered as a possible solution to some of the challenges of an increasingly industrialised world.

International responses

Most international responses are directed at the protection of developing countries. These initiatives focus on the provision of information and the development of a PIC procedure.

International Code of Conduct on the Distribution and Use of Pesticides

In 1985 the United Nations Food and Agriculture Organization (FAO) introduced the first *International Code of Conduct on the Distribution and Use of Pesticides* (the Code).[11] The Code established voluntary standards of conduct for all public and private entities engaged in the distribution and use of pesticides and provided the first globally accepted standard for pesticide management. It was particularly designed to assist countries which had no national legislation to regulate the risks associated with pesticides.[12] The Code placed the responsibility on governments to regulate the availability, distribution and use of pesticides in their countries.[13] It required pesticide industries to adhere to the provisions of the Code as a standard for the manufacture, distribution and advertising of pesticides.[14] Governments of pesticide-exporting countries were required to provide technical expertise on pesticides to other countries and to ensure that good trading practices were followed in their exports, especially to those countries without adequate legislation.[15]

In 1989 the Code was amended to introduce a PIC procedure.[16] In essence this required that the international shipment of a pesticide that is banned or severely restricted in order to protect human health and the environment should not proceed without the agreement of, or contrary to, the decision of the importing country.[17] Pesticides initially selected were those that were previously banned or severely restricted in at least five countries, as well as pesticide formulations that were acutely toxic. The PIC procedure required a participating government to notify the FAO as soon as possible of any action taken to ban or severely restrict the use or

---

9 UNEP, *London Guidelines for the Exchange of Information on Chemicals in International Trade*. Online. Available HTTP: <http://www.chem.unep.ch/ethics/english/longuien.htm> (accessed 20 November 2011).

10 The Basel Convention is only briefly discussed as it is comprehensively considered by T.G. Puthucherril in Chapter 17 of this volume.

11 FAO Code, op. cit., UN Doc M/R8130. E/8.86/1/1500 (1986).

12 Ibid., Art. 1(1).

13 Ibid., Art. 3(1).

14 Ibid., Art. 3(2).

15 Ibid., Art. 3(3).

16 FAO Conference Res 6/89 (1989) Appendix E. Online. Available HTTP: <http://ufdc.ufl.edu/UF00084642/00001/208j> (accessed 15 November 2011).

17 FAO Code, op cit., Arts 2, 9(7).

handling of a pesticide.[18] If the control actions notified fell within the definitions of the Code, the FAO then provided participating countries with a decision guidance document to assist them in making an informed decision as to whether to permit imports. A database of control actions and decisions was maintained by the FAO and notified to participating governments, who were required to take appropriate measures to ensure they were observed.[19]

Although the Code was approved and reaffirmed at the United Nations Conference on Environment and Development (UNCED),[20] it was not entirely successful in changing pesticide management practices, particularly in developing countries. Although the number of countries without pesticide legislation decreased after the Code was adopted, these countries characteristically did not enforce their legislation, primarily due to a lack of technical expertise or resources. In 2002 it was reported that 'highly hazardous or sub-standard pesticide formulations are still widely sold; and end-users are often insufficiently trained and protected to ensure that pesticides can be handled with minimum risk'.[21] Part of the problem with the Code was that it was voluntary. It was also not clear whether the pesticides included in the PIC procedure were those most responsible for causing health hazards in developing countries.[22] The Code also had 'no reporting mechanism, no monitoring, and no means of enforcement beyond public pressure and self-policing by the parties'.[23]

The Code was radically revised in 2002 to reflect international developments and address persistent pesticide management problems. The revised Code focuses on risk reduction, protection of human and environmental health, and life cycle management. It includes measures to strengthen monitoring and explicitly invites regular feedback on its implementation. The revised Code remains an important framework and reference for pesticide management.[24]

The London Guidelines for the Exchange of Information on Chemicals in International Trade

The United Nations Environment Programme (UNEP) introduced a complementary system to the FAO Code in 1987. The *London Guidelines for the Exchange of Information on Chemicals in International Trade*[25] (London Guidelines) were intended to assist in increasing chemical safety in all countries through the exchange of information on chemicals in international trade.[26] The London Guidelines were voluntary and, with some exceptions, applied to all chemicals, including pesticides. Although they were not specifically prepared for developing countries,

---

18 Ibid., Art. 9(1).
19 Ibid., Art. 9(8), 9(9).
20 *Agenda 21: The United Nations Programme of Action From Rio*, A/Conf.151/26 (1992), Ch. 14.
21 FAO Code, (revised version) adopted by the 123 session of the FAO Council in November 2002, 'Preface'. Online. Available HTTP: <http://www.fao.org/docrep/005/y4544e/y4544e01.htm#bm1> (accessed 15 November 2011).
22 B. Dinham, 'The Success of a Voluntary Code in Reducing Pesticide Hazards in Developing Countries', *Green Global Yearbook*, 1996, p. 34. Online. Available HTTP: <http://www.fni.no/ybiced/96_02_dinham.pdf> (accessed 18 November 2011).
23 Ibid., p. 31.
24 FAO Code (revised version), op. cit.
25 UNEP, London Guidelines, op. cit., UN Doc UNEP/GC, 14/17, Annex IV (1987).
26 Adopted by UNEP Governing Council Decision 14/27 of 27 June 1987, amended by UNEP Governing Decision 15/30 of 25 May 1989.

they provided a framework for establishing procedures for the effective use of information on chemicals in these countries. States with advanced information systems for the safe management of chemicals were required to share their experience with others in need of assistance.[27] States' activities in regard to chemicals were to be conducted in accordance with Principle 21 of the Stockholm Declaration of the UN Conference on the Human Environment.[28] All states were required to strengthen their existing infrastructures and institutions so as to improve control and management of chemicals.[29] The Guidelines also emphasised the importance of technical and financial assistance to enhance decision-making and training in the safe use of chemicals.[30]

The London Guidelines were amended in 1989 to introduce a PIC procedure which operated in a similar manner to that under the FAO Code.[31] States that had banned or severely restricted a chemical were required to notify the International Register of Potentially Toxic Chemicals (IRPTC).[32] If the chemical satisfied the requirements under the Guidelines, a decision guidance document was sent to participating countries who could then decide whether to permit imports.[33] The PIC procedure operated in addition to information exchange and export notification. Countries could participate in the information exchange procedures without participating in the PIC procedure.[34]

In 1992 the FAO and UNEP agreed to cooperate and in 1995 implemented a joint programme on the PIC procedure. This was known as the original PIC procedure and remained in operation until the text of the Rotterdam Convention was adopted in 1998.[35]

The Rotterdam Convention

Background

The voluntary PIC procedures in the FAO Code and London Guidelines were an important initial step in providing information on toxic chemicals. However, their non-binding nature undermined their effectiveness. As a result, the FAO Council and UNEP Governing Council commenced negotiations for a legally binding instrument on PIC procedures. The outcome was the Rotterdam Convention, which was adopted in 1998 and entered into force on 24 February 2004.[36] As at 2011, 143 parties had ratified the Convention.

---

27 UNEP, *London Guidelines*, op. cit., Art. 2(e).
28 Ibid., Art. 2(b). According to Principle 21: 'States have . . . the responsibility to ensure that activities within their jurisdiction or control do not cause damage to the environment of other States or of areas beyond the limits of national jurisdiction': UNCED: Final Documents, 16 June 1972, ILM 11: 1416. This principle is reproduced in Principle 2 of the *Rio Declaration on Environment and Development* (1992), Annex I, UN Doc A/Conf.151/26 (Vol. I) 31 ILM 874 (Rio Declaration).
29 UNEP, *London Guidelines*, op. cit., Art. 2(f).
30 Ibid., Art. 15.
31 UNEP Governing Council Decision 15/30 of 25 May 1989.
32 UNEP *London Guidelines* (amended 1989), Art. 6. Online. Available HTTP: <http://www.chem. unep.ch/ethics/english/longuien.htm> (accessed 23 November 2011).
33 Ibid., Arts 7(2), 7(3).
34 Ibid., Art. 7(1).
35 FAO, 'Guidance to Designated National Authorities on the Operation of the Rotterdam Convention: Introduction and Summary'. Online. Available HTTP: <http://www.fao.org/docrep/007/ y5423e/y5423e02.htm> (accessed 18 November 2011).
36 UNEP, 'Rotterdam Convention: How it was Developed'. Online. Available HTTP: <http://www. pic.int/TheConvention/Overview/Howitwasdeveloped/tabid/1045/language/en-US/Default. aspx> (accessed 18 November 2011).

Objective

The objective of the Rotterdam Convention is:

> to promote shared responsibility and cooperative efforts among Parties in the international trade of certain hazardous chemicals in order to protect human health and the environment from potential harm and to contribute to their environmentally sound use, by facilitating information exchange about their characteristics, by providing for a national decision-making process on their import and export and by disseminating these decisions to Parties.[37]

Chemicals subject to the Convention and the listing process

The chemicals and pesticides subject to the PIC procedure in the Rotterdam Convention are listed in Annex III. These include banned or severely restricted chemicals and severely hazardous pesticide formulations. A 'banned' or 'severely restricted' chemical is more broadly defined than in the FAO Code or London Guidelines. It includes a chemical that has been refused approval for first-time use, or withdrawn from the domestic market, or from the domestic approval process in order to protect human health and the environment.[38] A 'severely hazardous pesticide formulation' refers to 'pesticide formulations that produce severe health or environmental effects observable within a short period of time after single or multiple exposure'.[39] This category of pesticide is included to protect developing countries or a country with an economy in transition, which experiences problems with the pesticide under conditions of use.[40] Certain chemicals are excluded from the scope of the Convention.[41] When the Convention entered into force, 23 chemicals were listed in Annex III, with provision for progressive additions by consensus of the Conference of the Parties (COP). There have been five meetings of the COP since then and a number of additions have been made to Annex III. As at 2011, there were a total of 43 chemicals listed in Annex III, of which 32 are pesticides, including 4 severely hazardous pesticide formulations and 11 industrial chemicals.[42]

The mechanisms for adding chemicals to Article III have been criticised by non-government organisations (NGOs), in particular the requirement for a consensus[43] of the COP to be obtained before the chemical can be listed.[44] This has often resulted in recommendations for

---

37 *Rotterdam Convention on the Prior Informed Consent Procedure for Certain Hazardous Chemicals and Pesticides in International Trade*, opened for signature 10 September 1988, 38 ILM 1 (entered into force 24 February 2004) (Rotterdam Convention) Art. 1.
38 Ibid., Arts 2(b), 2(c).
39 Ibid., Art. 2(d).
40 FAO, 'Guidance to Designated National Authorities on the Operation of the Rotterdam Convention', op. cit.
41 Rotterdam Convention, Art. 3(2).
42 Ibid., Annex III chemicals. Online. Available HTTP: <http://www.pic.int/TheConvention/Chemicals/AnnexIIIChemicals/tabid/1132/language/en-US/Default.aspx> (accessed 20 November 2011).
43 Rotterdam Convention, op. cit., Art. 22(5).
44 Rotterdam Convention Alliance (ROCA), ROCA Position Paper in Preparation of the Rotterdam Convention COP 5. Online. Available HTTP: <http://www.cela.ca/sites/cela.ca/files/Position%20paper%20ROCA92%20%28June%202011%29_0.pdf> (accessed 20 November 2011).

listing being blocked by a small number of parties with a financial interest in maintaining the use and supply of the chemical or pesticide. For example, the Chemical Review Committee has recommended the listing of chrysotile asbestos, which meets all the criteria for listing. However, its listing was blocked at COPs 3, 4 and 5, and it has still not been listed although it results in the death of over 100,000 people each year.[45] This has led to suggestions that the Convention be amended to require a two-thirds majority for listing in Annex III, instead of consensus.[46]

The prior informed consent procedure

The Rotterdam Convention adopts a different procedure to the FAO Code and London Guidelines for determining which chemicals are subject to the PIC procedure. All chemicals[47] in relation to which 'final regulatory action'[48] has been taken to ban or severely restrict their use must be notified to the Secretariat. The notification has to be made no later than 90 days after taking any such action and must include information about the chemical.[49] The Secretariat must forward a summary of the information to all participating parties within six months.[50] Each party is required to appoint a designated national authority to receive information and perform other administrative duties.[51] When at least one notification has been made from two of the seven PIC regions[52] the Secretariat must forward it to the Chemical Review Committee. The Committee then reviews the information and makes a recommendation to the COP as to whether the chemical should be made subject to the PIC procedure and listed in Annex III.[53] The recommendation is accompanied by a decision guidance document providing information about the chemical.[54] Recommendations for listing in Annex III can also be made by a developing country or a country with an economy in transition that is experiencing problems with a pesticide.[55]

Within nine months of receiving a decision guidance document, a response must be made to the Secretariat as to whether to allow imports.[56] A response can be a final decision, detailing legislative or administrative measures on which it is based, to allow imports, refuse imports, or to allow imports on specified conditions. Alternatively, a party may make an interim response that could include a request for further information or for assistance in evaluating

---

45 Ibid.
46 Ibid.
47 'A 'chemical' means 'a substance by itself or in a mixture, whether manufactured or natural, but does not include any living organism. It consists of the following categories: pesticide (including severely hazardous pesticide formulations) and industrial': *Rotterdam Convention*, op. cit., Art. 2(a).
48 'Final regulatory action' is defined as action taken that does not require subsequent regulatory action for the purpose of banning or severely restricting a chemical: ibid., Art. 2(e).
49 Ibid., Art. 5(1).
50 Ibid., Art. 5(3).
51 Ibid., Art. 4.
52 These regions are: Africa, Asia, Europe, Latin America and Caribbean, Near East, North America and the Southwest Pacific.
53 *Rotterdam Convention*, op. cit., Arts 5(5), 5(6).
54 Ibid., Art. 7.
55 Ibid., Art. 6.
56 Ibid., Art. 10(2).

the chemical.[57] If the decision is to refuse imports, or to allow them subject to conditions, the party must ensure that the same restriction is placed on imports from any source, including domestic production for domestic use.[58]

Exporting parties are required to implement appropriate legislative or administrative measures to communicate the responses from importing parties to all persons within their jurisdiction and to ensure that exports do not take place without the prior informed consent of the importing party. Each exporting party is also required to assist importing parties to obtain further information and to strengthen their capacities and capabilities to manage chemicals safely during their life cycle.[59]

Exchange of information

The Rotterdam Convention provides for the exchange of scientific, technical, economic and legal information concerning chemicals.[60] Exports of chemicals are to be appropriately labelled and accompanied by basic health and safety information. Provision is made for protection of confidential information.[61] Parties are also required to provide technical assistance to developing countries and countries with economies in transition, so that they can develop infrastructure and the capacity to manage chemicals throughout their life cycle.[62] Each party is required to introduce national measures, such as chemical registers, initiatives to promote chemical safety, public access to information on chemical handling and accident management and safer alternatives to the chemicals listed in Annex III.[63]

Compliance and dispute settlement

A weakness of the Rotterdam Convention is its failure to include a compliance mechanism. Instead, the COP is required to develop procedures and mechanisms for determining non-compliance and for treatment of parties in non-compliance.[64] A non-compliance committee was established at COP3, but failed to reach agreement on decision-making, trigger mechanisms and punitive measures. Some NGOs have pointed out that a compliance mechanism is fundamental to the success of the Convention, and that as long as no functioning compliance mechanism is in place, no party is forced to implement the provisions of the Convention.[65]

Provision is made for dispute settlement through negotiation, arbitration or submission to the International Court of Justice (ICJ).[66] At COP1 in 2004 Annex VI was adopted, which sets out procedures on arbitration and conciliation.[67]

---

57 Ibid., Art. 10(4).
58 Ibid., Art. 10(9).
59 Ibid., Art. 11(1).
60 Ibid., Art. 14(1).
61 Ibid., Art. 14.
62 Ibid., Art. 16.
63 Ibid., Art. 15.
64 Ibid., Art. 17.
65 Rotterdam Convention Alliance (ROCA), Position Paper in Preparation of the Rotterdam Convention COP 5, op. cit.
66 Rotterdam Convention, op. cit., Art. 20.
67 Decision RC-1/11.

The Stockholm Convention on Persistent Organic Pollutants

Background

Persistent organic pollutants (POPs) are the most dangerous category of pesticides. They are characterised by toxicity, volatility[68] and their capacity to bioaccumulate in the fatty tissues and organs of human beings and animals. Over 90 per cent of human exposure occurs through ingestion of animal products, including milk.[69] Even in low doses, POPs are extremely dangerous to human and animal health.[70]

In 1995 UNEP's Governing Council requested several international bodies to assess 12 of the most dangerous POPs.[71] In 1997, an intergovernmental negotiating committee was established to develop an international legally binding instrument on POPs. The text of the Stockholm Convention was adopted in May 2001 and entered into force in May 2004. The Convention currently has 176 parties.[72]

Objective

The objective of the Convention is set out in Article 1:

> Mindful of the precautionary approach as set forth in Principle 15 of the Rio Declaration on Environment and Development, the objective of this Convention is to protect human health and the environment from persistent organic pollutants.

The objective sets the benchmark by which all action under the Convention should be measured. However, this positive role for precaution is somewhat undermined by the failure to define its role, or to reinforce it in the operational clauses of the Convention.

Intentionally produced POPs

The convention lists chemicals in three Annexes. Annex A chemicals are to be eliminated, Annex B contains chemicals to be restricted, and Annex C calls for the minimisation of intentional releases of certain chemicals.

In relation to intentionally produced POPs, the Convention imposes obligations on parties to take legal and administrative measures to eliminate production, use, import and export of

---

68 Australian Government, *Regulation Impact Statement for the Consideration of the Addition of Nine Chemicals to the Stockholm Convention on POPs'*. Online. Available HTTP: <http://www.environment.gov.au/settlements/chemicals/international/publications/pubs/ris.pdf> (accessed 20 November 2011).

69 Ibid.

70 Ibid.

71 UNEP Governing Council Decision 18/32. The POPs assessed were: aldrin, chlordane, DDT, dieldrin, endrin, heptachlor, mirex, toxaphene and hexachlororbenzene (hexachlorobenzene can be a pesticide, industrial chemical or by-product). It included the by-products: dioxins, furans and polychlorinated biphenyls (polychlorinated biphenyls can be an industrial chemical or by-product).

72 UNEP Governing Council Decision 19/13C; Linkages, 'Summary of the Seventh Meeting of Persistent Organic Pollutants Review Committee of the Stockholm Convention 10–14 October 2011', *Earth Negotiations Bulletin* 15(189), 2011. Online. Available HTTP: <http://www.iisd.ca/vol15/enb15189e.html> (accessed 13 March 2012).

Annex A chemicals. In addition the production and use of Annex B chemicals must be restricted.[73]

Generally, imports and exports of Annex A and B listed chemicals are prohibited, except for environmentally sound disposal or for a use which is permitted for that party under Annex A or B.[74] The same principles apply in relation to exports to non-parties; these are subject to annual certification specifying the intended use of the chemical and a commitment by the non-party to protection of human health and the environment by taking measures to prevent releases and manage stockpiles.[75]

The exemptions detract from the effectiveness of the Convention. The Convention provides for both country-specific exemptions and those applying generally to all chemicals. A register is established for identifying country-specific exemptions.[76] To obtain an exemption, a state may, on becoming a party to the Convention, provide a notification of its intention to register for one or more types of specific exemptions listed in Annex A or B. Exemptions expire after five years, but can be extended for a further five years if the country can justify the need for an extension. Parties that have a specific exemption must take appropriate measures to ensure than any production or use is carried out in a manner that prevents or minimises human exposure and release into the environment.[77] When there are no longer any parties registered for a specific exemption, no new registrations may be made.[78]

In addition, there are a number of general exemptions applying to chemicals and products; for example, the general exemption in Article 3(5) for chemicals used for laboratory-scale research or as a reference standard. A number of additional exemptions are listed in Annexes A and B. These include: chemicals in articles manufactured or already in use prior to the coming into force of the Stockholm Convention and notified to the Secretariat; closed-system site-intermediates (applied only to hexachlorobenzene and DDT); and POPs occurring as unintentional trace contaminants in products and articles.

Unintentional production of POPs

Parties are required to reduce or eliminate releases from unintentional production of POPs listed in Annex C to the convention. There is no immediate requirement for the elimination of these POPs; rather, parties are required at a minimum 'to take measures to reduce the total releases . . . with the goal of their continuing minimization and, *where feasible*, ultimate elimination'.[79] There is a further requirement to develop an action plan to identify, characterise and address the release of these chemicals. Parties are required to promote available, feasible and practical measures that can achieve a realistic and meaningful level of release reduction or source elimination and to promote the development and use of substitute materials.[80] To assist in this process, Annex C lists sources of unintentional POPs and provides general guidance on 'best available techniques' and 'best available practices'.

73 Stockholm Convention, op. cit., Art. 3
74 Ibid., Art. 3(2).
75 Ibid., Art. 3(2).
76 Ibid., Art. 4.
77 Ibid., Art. 3(6).
78 Ibid., Art. 4.
79 Ibid., Art. 5.
80 Ibid., Arts 5(a), (b).

Even if an exemption has been registered, there are still strict controls on the use of certain chemicals, for example polychlorinated biphenyls. Their use is permitted in equipment, such as electrical transformers, capacitors or other receptacles containing liquid stocks, until 2025.[81] This is subject to the percentages and volumes of polychlorinated biphenyls present, as well as labelling, packaging and handling measures to ensure public safety.

Reducing or eliminating releases from stockpiles and wastes

The Stockholm Convention adopts a cradle-to-grave approach to POPs management by requiring stockpiles of wastes to be managed to protect human health and the environment. Parties are required to adopt appropriate strategies for identifying stockpiles containing chemicals listed in Annexes A or B.[82] The Convention specifies how disposal of POPs is to be conducted. Specifically, parties are required to take appropriate measures so that wastes, including products and articles becoming wastes, are:

- handled, collected transported and stored in an environmentally sound manner;
- disposed of in such a way that the POP content is destroyed or irreversibly transformed so that they do not exhibit POPs characteristics, or otherwise disposed of in an environmentally sound manner consistent with international standards and global regimes governing the management of hazardous wastes;
- not permitted to be subjected to disposal operations that may lead to recovery, recycling, reclamation, direct reuse or alternative uses of POPs; and
- not transported across international boundaries without taking into account relevant international standards.[83]

Parties are also required to develop strategies for identifying sites contaminated by POPs, and to carry out any remediation in an environmentally sound manner.[84] The Stockholm Convention does not specify any particular technology that must be used to destroy stockpiles and wastes. However, in considering environmentally safe disposal technology, the COP is required to cooperate with the appropriate bodies of the Basel Convention to determine the methods necessary for environmental sound disposal.

Adding new chemicals to the Annexes

The procedure for listing new chemicals is set out in Article 8 of the Stockholm Convention. Any party can submit a proposal to the Secretariat for a new listing of a chemical in Annexes A, B or C. The proposal must be supported by the information about the chemical specified in Annex D relating to persistence, bioaccumulation, potential for long-range environmental transport and toxicity. If the chemical meets this requirement, the Committee drafts a risk profile taking into account the economic factors in Annex E associated with possible control measures for the chemical. On the basis of the risk profile and risk management evaluation, the Committee then recommends whether the chemical should be considered by the COP

---

81 Ibid., Annex A, Pt 2.
82 Ibid., Art. 6(1).
83 Ibid., Art. 6(1)(d).
84 Ibid.

for listing in Annexes A, B and/or C. The COP then makes the final decision in a precautionary manner as to whether to list the POP, and the annex in which it should be listed, taking into account the recommendation of the Committee and any scientific uncertainty.

The first additions to Annexes A, B and C occurred at COP4 in 2009 when nine new chemicals were included.[85] A further chemical, endosulfan, was added to Annex A at COP5 in 2011.[86] Amendments bind all parties unless the party declared at the time of ratifying the Convention that any additions to Annexes A, B, and C would not apply unless ratified,[87] or if they have notified their intention not to be bound within one year of being informed of the amendment.[88] These provisions distinctly detract from the precautionary approach envisaged by the Convention.

Information exchange

The Stockholm Convention requires parties to facilitate the exchange of information relevant to the reduction or elimination of the production, use and release of POPs, as well as alternatives, including information about the risk. Information supplied is not treated as confidential.[89] Parties are encouraged to provide information to the public and to promote awareness and education programmes about the health and environmental effects of POPs.[90] Further, parties are expected to undertake research, development and monitoring of POPs.[91] Developed countries are required to provide financial assistance to developing countries.[92]

Compliance and dispute settlement

A reporting system is set up whereby parties are required to detail the measures taken to implement the Convention and their effectiveness.[93] Provision is made for a periodic evaluation of the effectiveness of the Convention.[94]

The COP is required to develop mechanisms for determining non-compliance and for treatment of parties in non-compliance.[95] Article 18 requires the COP to adopt arbitration and conciliation procedures to govern the settlement of disputes between parties. This was effected by the adoption of a new Annex G at COP1 in 2005.[96]

85 Stockholm Convention, op. cit., 'Introduction', citing Decisions SC-4/10 to SC 4/18.
86 Linkages, 'Summary of the Seventh Meeting of Persistent Organic Pollutants Review Committee of the Stockholm Convention', op. cit.
87 Stockholm Convention, op. cit., Arts 22(4), 25(4).
88 Ibid., Art. 22(3).
89 Ibid., Art. 9.
90 Ibid., Art. 10.
91 Ibid., Art. 11.
92 Ibid., Art. 13.
93 Ibid., Art. 15.
94 Ibid., Art. 16.
95 Ibid., Art. 18.
96 Decision SC-1/2.

The Basel Convention[97]

The Basel Convention was adopted in 1989 and entered into force in 1992. Its principal concern was to protect developing countries from hazardous waste dumping by industrialised countries. The Convention regulates international movements of hazardous waste through a PIC system and in accordance with the principles of environmentally sound management. It provides the final link in the chain and together with the Stockholm and Rotterdam Conventions creates a cradle-to-grave approach to hazardous waste management.

Only those 'wastes' that are 'hazardous' fall within the scope of the Basel Convention. 'Wastes' are broadly defined to include substances or objects that are intended for disposal.[98] Wastes are designated as 'hazardous' for the purpose of the Convention, unless they do not possess any of the characteristics contained in Annex III.[99] Annex I lists general categories of wastes to be controlled, while hazardous characteristics are listed in Annex III. Annex I classifies waste according to waste streams and constituents, and includes wastes such as polychlorinated biphenyls, lead, mercury and asbestos. The hazardous characteristics listed in Annex III include explosives, flammable liquids and solids, substances liable to spontaneous combustion, and toxic and ecotoxic waste. Wastes are also treated as hazardous if they are listed in Annex II.[100] This includes household wastes and incinerator ash. Wastes defined as hazardous in the national and domestic legislation of the exporting, importing or transit party are also subject to the Convention.[101]

The definition of 'hazardous waste' is complex and creates uncertainty as to which wastes are hazardous for the purposes of the Convention. To clarify this aspect, two lists of wastes were drawn up and adopted as Annexes VIII and IX to the convention. Wastes listed in Annex VIII are presumed hazardous, while those in Annex IX are not.[102]

The Convention focuses on regulating hazardous waste destined for 'disposal'.[103] 'Disposal operations' are broadly defined to include operations leading to final disposal as well as a number of operations that may lead to recovery or recycling.[104] Although the Convention discourages exports of hazardous waste to developing countries, it allows some exports that are required as a raw material for recycling or recovery in the importing country, subject to ensuring its environmentally sound management.[105] The exploitation of this exception by hazardous waste exporters led to a decision to ban exports of all hazardous wastes from Organisation for Economic Co-operation and Development (OECD) countries to non-OECD countries in 1994[106] and to the adoption of the export ban as a new Annex VII in 1995.[107] The amendment prohibits exports of hazardous waste from Annex VII countries (EU, OECD and Liechtenstein) to non-Annex VII countries. The ban applied immediately

97 The operation of the Basel Convention is discussed in detail by T.G. Puthucherril in Chapter 17 of this volume and is only briefly discussed here in the context of e-waste.
98 Basel Convention, op. cit., Art. 2.
99 Ibid., Art. 1(1)(a).
100 Ibid., Art. 1(2).
101 Ibid., Art. 1(1)(b).
102 Decision IV/9.
103 Basel Convention, op. cit., Art. 2.
104 Ibid., Art. 2(4). 'Disposal operations' include the activities specified in Annex IV to the Convention,
105 Ibid., Art. 4(9).
106 Decision II/12, COP2.
107 Decision III/I COP3. A new Art. 4A is proposed to implement the provisions of Annex VII.

to exports of hazardous waste for disposal, while recycling exports were prohibited from December 1997. However, as at 2011 the amendment had not yet come into effect[108] although a number of parties have already informally implemented the ban amendment.[109]

There are indications that the focus of the Convention is shifting from the movement of hazardous waste to its minimisation. At COP8 the parties adopted a Declaration on E-Waste, agreeing *inter alia* to implement measures to promote clean technology and integrated waste management strategies; encourage technology transfer on environmentally sound management of e-waste; improve waste management controls through legislation and diligent enforcement; and prevent and combat illegal trade.[110] At COP10 the parties adopted the Cartagena Declaration, which highlights the importance of reducing the generation of waste amidst a changing perception of waste as a potential resource.[111] The Declaration acknowledges *inter alia* that 'prevention, minimization and recovery of wastes advance the three pillars of sustainable development'.[112] An important initiative at COP10 was to provide for the Ban amendment to come into force for those countries who wish to adhere to it and to introduce a regime for countries who wish to trade in waste to ensure minimisation of risks to human health and the environment.[113]

The special problems posed by e-waste

Over the past 20 years, there has been an upsurge in technological innovation and production of electronic devices such as computers, printers, mobile phones, iPads and other electronic equipment. While initially these devices were confined to the workplace, they have rapidly become an indispensable acquisition for households and individuals in industrialised and industrialising countries. A drawback of these products is that they have a short lifespan and are frequently replaced by new and better models.

E-waste is the most rapidly growing waste stream. A recent study by UNEP estimates global e-waste generation at approximately 40 million tons each year.[114] The study also predicts that by 2020 e-waste from old computers will have risen by 500 per cent in India and by 200 to 400 per cent in South Africa and China, while that from old mobile phones will be 7 times higher in China and 18 times higher in India.[115] E-waste contains a mixture of several hundred components, including valuable products such as silver, gold, palladium,

---

108 As at COP10 in 2011, 17 additional ratifications were required for the amendment to come into effect.

109 Basel Action Network, 'The Basel Ban: A Triumph for Global Environmental Justice', October 2011. Online. Available HTTP: <http://www.ban.org/wp-content/uploads/2011/10/BP1_Oct_2011_Final_Letter.pdf> (accessed 23 November 2011).

110 UNEP/CHW.8/CRP.24.

111 Linkages, 'Summary of the Tenth Meeting of the Conference of the Parties to the Basel Convention', *Earth Negotiations Bulletin* 20(37), 2011. Online. Available HTTP: <http://www.iisd.ca/vol20/enb2037e.html> (accessed 23 November 2011).

112 UNEP/CHW.10/CRP.3/Rev.3.

113 UNEP, 'Historic Agreement Ends 15 year Deadlock over Banning North-South Movements of Hazardous Waste', 25 October 2011. Online. Available HTTP: <http://www.basel.int/>.

114 UNEP: Sustainable Innovation and Technology Transfer Industrial Sector Studies, 'Recycling – from E-Waste to Resources', Final Report July 2009. Online. Available HTTP: <http://ewasteguide.info/files/UNEP_2009_eW2R.PDF> (accessed 25 November 2011).

115 Ibid.

copper and indium. However, e-waste can also be hazardous as it also contains a number of heavy metals and hazardous chemicals. These include beryllium, cadmium, chromium hexavalent, lead, mercury, brominated flame retardants, polyvinyl chloride and orgoteins.[116] Most of these substances are toxic to humans and several are known carcinogens.[117]

E-waste poses serious problems on disposal. Globally, millions of tons of e-waste is being consigned to landfill where it leaches into the ground and water over time, or is released into the atmosphere. The vaporisation of metallic and dimethylene mercury creates a risk of uncontrolled fires with associated health and environmental risks.[118] Consequently, many industrialised countries, such as the European Union, the United States and some Asian nations, have introduced legislation prohibiting the disposal of e-wastes to landfill. Incineration has also been banned in most developed countries because it can result in heavy metals such as lead and cadmium being released into the atmosphere. If the waste contains polyvinyl chloride plastic, POPs such as dioxins and furans are also released.[119]

In most industrialised countries, recycling is now the preferred option for dealing with e-waste. Recycling facilities for e-wastes have been established since the 1990s in most developed countries but are often economically unviable because of high labour costs and environmental restrictions on the disposal of components and residues. In many cases, this has led to the export of large quantities of e-waste to developing countries for disposal or recycling. Less stringent environmental standards and lower labour costs in these countries make exports an economically viable alternative. However, the recycling and disposal of e-waste in developing countries is a serious threat to human health and the environment as these countries often lack the capacity to handle these wastes safely.[120]

Global initiatives to resolve the e-waste problem

International conventions

The Rotterdam, Stockholm and Basel Conventions all regulate a number of constituents of e-waste. The PIC procedures under the Rotterdam Convention apply to chemicals, such as mercury and polychlorinated biphenyls, and exports must not take place without the consent of the importing country. Export of e-waste to developing countries for recycling is also contrary to the obligations imposed by the Stockholm Convention. At COP4 two commercial mixtures of brominated flame retardants, known as pentaBDE and octaBDE, were listed. These chemicals are contained in products such as mobile phones, computers and motor vehicles. Since the Stockholm Convention does not permit wastes that contain POPs to be recovered, recycled,

---

116 Greenpeace International, 'Toxic Tech: Not in our Backyard.' Online. Available HTTP: <http://www.greenpeace.org/international/Global/international/planet-2/report/2008/2/not-in-our-backyard.pdf> (accessed 15 November 2011).

117 Ibid.

118 UNEP: Sustainable Innovation and Technology Transfer Industrial Sector Studies, 'Recycling – from e-Waste to Resources', op. cit.

119 Greenpeace International, 'Where Does E-waste Go?' Online. Available HTTP: <http://www.greenpeace.org/usa/en/campaigns/toxics/hi-tech-highly-toxic/e-waste-goes>(accessed 15 November 2011).

120 See Z. Lipman, 'Economic Growth and Ecological Integrity – the Impact of the Hazardous Waste Trade on the Economy and Environment of Developing Countries', *Environmental Law and Management* 18(5), 2006, 232.

reclaimed or directly re-used, it is problematic as to how products containing these chemicals can be disposed of when they become waste. To deal with this issue, at COP4 an exemption was provided to permit recycling until 2030, but to prohibit exports of such products if they contained levels exceeding those allowed for sale in the exporting country.[121] This compromise may deter exports to developing countries, but a total ban would be preferable.

Of the three conventions, the Basel Convention has the most potential to reduce the movements of e-waste. Among the wastes that are listed as hazardous in Annex VIII and subject to the Convention are a number of constituents of e-waste. Waste electrical and electronic assemblies or scrap are listed as hazardous wastes, as are a number of constituents of computer e-waste such as circuit boards, cathode ray tubes and other electronic boards or components containing lead-based solders and copper beryllium alloys.[122] Thus, exports of whole computers, printers and monitors that contain circuit boards or cathode ray tubes are prohibited under the Basel ban. However, as the ban has not yet come into force, the effectiveness of the Convention to prevent e-waste exports to developing countries is diminished. Indeed, ratification of the ban would not necessarily put an end to the trade, which could continue between states that are not parties to the Convention and between non-Annex VII country parties. There is also the problem of a burgeoning illegal trade in e-waste.

An important recent initiative is the 'synergies' approach which is taking place under the Basel, Rotterdam and Stockholm Conventions. Joint programmes are planned involving all three conventions, in relation to providing technical assistance and promoting global public awareness campaigns on the life cycle management of chemicals and waste.[123]

Technology transfer

Most international initiatives emphasise the importance of information and technology transfer to enable countries to develop the capacity to manage their chemicals and waste in a manner that is safe for human health and the environment.[124] The Basel and Stockholm Conventions both require parties to establish regional and sub-regional centres for capacity-building and technology transfer.[125] Fourteen Basel Convention Regional Centres and 16 Stockholm Convention Regional and Sub-regional Centres have been established.[126] These Centres provide training, information awareness-raising and technology transfer on a range of matters relevant to the Conventions.

There have also been several international e-waste pilot schemes in developing countries and state-of-the-art e-waste recycling facilities have been established. According to UNEP

---

121 Centre for International Environmental Law, 'Nine Chemicals added to Global Toxics Treaty, with Gaping Exemptions,' 11 May 2009. Online. Available HTTP: <http://www.ciel.org/Publications/CIEL_COP4_11May09.pdf> (accessed 25 November 2011).
122 Decision IV/9. The computer wastes noted are listed in Annex VIII to the Basel Convention.
123 UNEP, 'Enhancing Synergies among the Basel Rotterdam and Stockholm Conventions.' Online. Available HTTP: <http://excops.unep.ch/documents/consproc/PPTEnhancingSynergies.pdf> (accessed 25 November 2011).
124 Rotterdam Convention, op. cit., Art. 14 (information exchange), Art. 16 (technical assistance).
125 Basel Convention, op. cit., Art. 14; Stockholm Convention, op. cit., Art. 12.
126 UNEP, 'The Basel Convention Regional and Coordinating Centres at a Glance'. Online. Available HTTP: <http://archive.basel.int/centers/description/BCRCataGlance.pdf>(accessed 9 May 2012); UNEP 'Stockholm Convention Centres'. Online. Available HTTP:<http://chm.pops.int/Implementation/RegionalCentres/TheCentres/tabid/583/Default.aspx>(accessed 23 November 2011).

reports these schemes have not been entirely successful in changing attitudes to informal recycling. This is partly attributable to an uncritical implementation of technology from developed countries without taking local conditions into account. According to UNEP:

> Technology transfer is not merely a simple duplication of technology from developed countries to developing countries. Local situations like available investment, economic conditions, local treatment standards, awareness and education of workers and management level of the recycling chain should be considered when introducing new technology.[127]

Domestic and regional initiatives: product stewardship and extended producer liability schemes

Product stewardship or extended producer liability is an important recent development in waste management and could assist in providing a solution to the e-waste problem. Product stewardship requires all parties in the product chain to share responsibility for the products they produce, handle, purchase, use and discard. This responsibility extends to designers, manufacturers, suppliers, consumers, collectors, processors, transporters and disposers.[128]

Extended producer responsibility is one part of product stewardship but focuses primarily on the producer of the product. It involves producers taking responsibility for the full life cycle of their product and implementing initiatives to reduce resource use, waste generation and environmental impact and enhance post-consumer resource recovery.[129] It includes 'upstream' impacts from choice of materials and manufacturing processes and 'downstream' impacts associated with the use and disposal of products.[130] 'Upstream' aspects focus on the promotion of clean production throughout the manufacturing process. This strategy is in accordance with Agenda 21, which requires states to encourage industry to develop schemes to integrate the cleaner production approach into product design and management practices.[131] Insofar as electronic products are concerned, progress has already been made with the development of a new computer that is free of both polyvinyl chloride and brominated flame retardants, both known POPs.[132] Downstream regulation involves extending the producers' responsibility to the post-consumer stage of the product's life cycle by requiring them to accept responsibility for end-of-life products. According to the OECD, the advantages of transferring the costs of post-consumer impacts to the producers is that it will provide 'powerful incentives for producers to prevent waste generation, reduce the use of potentially

127 UNEP: Sustainable Innovation and Technology Transfer Industrial Sector Studies, 'Recycling – From E-waste to Resources' op. cit., para. 3.6.
128 Government of Western Australia, 'Extended Producer Responsibility Policy Statement,' 29 June 2005, p. 3.
129 Ibid., p. 4.
130 OECD, 'Pollution Prevention and Control Extended Producer Responsibility in the OECD Area Phase 1 Report, Legal and Administrative Approaches in Member Countries and Policy Options for EPR Programs', 'Preface', OECD, 1996. Online. Available HTTP: <http://www.oecd.org/officialdocuments/publicdisplaydocumentpdf/?cote=OCDE/GD(96)48&docLanguage=En> (accessed 28 November 2011).
131 UNCED, *Agenda 21*, op. cit., para. 20(17)(c).
132 Greenpeace International, 'Victory! New Greener Computer Released in India', 4 February 2010. Online. Available HTTP: <http://www.greenpeace.org/international/en/news/features/victory-green-electronic-02032010/> (accessed 26 November 2011).

toxic inputs, design products that are easily recyclable and internalise the costs of waste management into product prices'.[133]

The European Union WEEE directives

A number of extended producer responsibility schemes relating to waste electrical and electronic equipment (WEEE) have been implemented in various countries,[134] particularly in Europe. The scheme adopted by the EU is one of the most comprehensive. In 2002 the EU introduced two directives to specifically address the problem of electrical equipment and e-waste and impose cradle-to-grave responsibility on manufacturers. All EU member states were required to incorporate these directives into national legislation and by 2008 all had done so to a greater or lesser degree.[135]

The Directive on the Restriction of the Use of Certain Hazardous Substances in Electrical and Electronic Equipment[136] requires lead, cadmium, mercury, hexavalent chromium, polybrominated biphenyls and polybrominated diphenyl ethers in electrical and electronic equipment to be substituted by safer alternatives by 1 July 2006. The Directive on Waste Electrical and Electronic Equipment[137] provides for collection schemes where consumers can return their e-waste free of charge. It requires manufacturers of such equipment to take back the appliance at their own expense, recycle it and dispose of the residual waste. Registration is mandatory for all manufacturers.

Despite these measures, it has been reported that only a third of electrical and e-waste is separately collected and appropriately treated. The remainder is either consigned to landfill, inadequately treated or illegally exported.[138] As a result, in 2008, the EU decided to revise Directive 2002/96/EC on electrical and e-waste. The proposed amendments set a new binding target for the collection of electrical and e-waste, which includes non-household waste.

Conclusion

The FAO Code and London Guidelines were important early initiatives in providing information exchange and in developing the PIC system. The Rotterdam, Stockholm and Basel Conventions are the most important internationally binding legal instruments to protect human health and the environment from the dangers associated with hazardous chemicals and pesticides. However, implementation of these Conventions has been difficult. In the case of the Rotterdam and Stockholm Conventions, listing of additional chemicals has proved challenging. The Stockholm Convention has a number of exemptions and the Basel Ban has

---

133 OECD, 'Pollution Prevention and Control Extended Producer Responsibility in the OECD Area Phase 1 Report', op. cit., p. 16.
134 In Australia, manufacturers and importers are liable for disposal costs and material recovery of certain e-waste (*Product Stewardship (Televisions and Computers) Regulations 2011* (Cth)).
135 'The WEEE Directive and its Implementation in the EU', updated September 2009. Online. Available HTTP: <http://www.ecsn-uk.org/Legislation/WEEE/2WEEE%20directive%20&%20implementation%20in%20EU%20sept09v2.pdf> (accessed 2 December 2011).
136 Directive 2002/95/EC.
137 Directive 2002/96/EC.
138 European Commission Environment, 'Recast of the WEEE Directive'. Online. Available HTTP: <http://ec.europa.eu/environment/waste/weee/index_en.htm> (accessed 26 November 2011).

not yet received sufficient ratifications to come into force. Not only has the Basel ban not been observed, but the PIC procedures have not been followed. These problems have been exacerbated by a growing illegal trade in e-waste which necessitates a more careful monitoring of exports and imports. The result is that the capacity of these Conventions to protect human health and the environment from the dangers of chemical and pesticides has been considerably weakened.

An additional global problem is the rapid growth of chemical and electronic production in developing countries. Developed countries should observe their obligations in the Rotterdam, Stockholm and Basel Conventions, to assist developing countries in acquiring the necessary expertise to manage safely any chemicals or hazardous wastes generated domestically. This requires financial assistance and technology transfer. However, experience in developing countries has shown that if these schemes are to be successful, they cannot be transplanted from developed countries without regard to local culture and circumstances.

Clearly, international measures alone are not sufficient to address the problems associated with chemical use and disposal. These measures must to be reinforced by government regulation in developed and developing countries. Developed countries should assume responsibility for waste they have generated instead of exporting it to developing countries. This obligation is reaffirmed in Principle 14 of the Rio Declaration.[139] It is also a fundamental underlying principle in the Basel and Stockholm Conventions. Product stewardship and extended producer responsibility schemes, such as those in the EU, are an important step in achieving this objective. Similar schemes should be adopted in all developed countries and in those developing countries with their own chemical industries.

139 Rio Declaration, op. cit.

19

Air, atmosphere and climate change

Paolo Galizzi

This chapter will briefly analyse customary rules as they apply to atmospheric pollution and will then continue with a more detailed examination of treaty regimes in three selected areas: long-range transboundary air pollution; protection of the ozone layer; and climate change. The chapter will examine these frameworks in terms of the substantive issues they address, as well as the lessons to be learned from each. These three regimes are arguably the most important and provide lessons for both the future regulation of air and atmospheric pollution, and international environmental law as a whole.

Introduction

The regulation of atmospheric pollution is one of the earliest and best-developed areas of international cooperation and regulation in the field of the environment. Atmospheric pollutants, by their very nature, easily cross national boundaries and may cause harmful environmental effects and, as a result, conflicts between states, creating the need for international agreements on how emissions are handled. In addition, some emissions are only problematic upon reaching harmful concentrations in the atmosphere, as in the cases of ozone depletion and climate change, introducing the further complication of allocating how and where reductions should be made and who should pay for them. Tackling these environmental and political crises is a critical challenge for the international community. The nature and evolution of global efforts to address atmospheric pollution are the focus of this chapter. As in other sub-fields of international environmental law, most rules regulating atmospheric pollution are found in treaties. Obviously, international customary rules apply, *mutatis mutandis*, to atmospheric pollution as well. An increasingly important role is also played by soft law.

This chapter will briefly analyse customary rules as they apply to atmospheric pollution and will then continue with a more detailed examination of treaty regimes in three selected areas: long-range transboundary air pollution (LRTAP); protection of the ozone layer; and climate change. The chapter will examine these frameworks in terms of the substantive issues they address, as well as the lessons to be learned from each. These three regimes are arguably the most important and provide lessons for both the future of regulation of atmospheric pollution, and international environmental law as a whole.

Customary law and litigation

One could argue that international environmental law, at least in its modern sense, originated partly from the need to protect the joint atmosphere.[1] One of the earliest cases between states related to transboundary air pollution: the 1941 *Trail Smelter* arbitration award between Canada and the United States (US).[2] The arbitral tribunal's decision laid down what many now consider a fundamental principle of international environmental law: the obligation to prevent transboundary environmental harm.[3] The finding was the precursor of what is now known as Principle 21/2, which holds that states have sovereignty over their natural resources and the responsibility not to cause transboundary environmental harm.[4]

The dispute arose around a Canadian lead and zinc smelting complex in British Columbia that was emitting significant amounts of sulphur dioxide fumes. The US complained that the sulphur dioxide was carried on the winds into Washington State, damaging farmland and forests. Dissatisfied with the recommendations of a joint commission that the two countries had asked to review the issue,[5] the US pushed for the negotiation of a convention under which Canada would pay $350,000 for the damage caused through 1931, and agree to submit the matter to international arbitration. The convention was signed in 1935.[6]

1 Of course, given the inextricable ties between human civilisations and the natural resources on which we depend, rules governing the use of the environment date back centuries to earliest recorded history. While unilateral and bilateral agreements on the preservation of fauna and flora have existed since the mid-1800s, our focus here is on instruments that have been negotiated by the international community as a whole. For a history of environmental regulation, see E.C. Halliday, *An Historical Review of Atmospheric Pollution*, New York: World Health Organization/Columbia University Press, 1961; P. Hawken, *How the Largest Movement in the World Came Into Being and Why No One Saw It Coming*, New York: Viking, 2007.

2 *United States v Canada*, Ad Hoc International Arbitral Tribunal, *1941 UN Reports of International Arbitral Awards 1911*, 1938, p. 1941.

3 Scholars disagree about the importance of this case; see generally R.M. Bratspies and R.A. Miller (eds) *Transboundary Harm in International Law: Lessons from the* Trail Smelter *Arbitration*, Cambridge: Cambridge University Press, 2006.

4 The term 'Principle 21/2' refers to Principle 21 of the *Stockholm Declaration of the United Nations Conference on the Human Environment* (1972), Section I of the *Report of the United Nations Conference on the Human Environment* (1972), UN Doc A/Conf.48/14 and Corr 1, 11 ILM 1416 ('1972 Stockholm Declaration'); and Principle 2 of the *Rio Declaration on Environment and Development* (1992), Annex I, UN Doc A/Conf.151/26 (Vol. I) ('Rio Declaration').

5 Prevailing law at the time held that claims for damage had to be filed in the jurisdiction where the damaged land lay; however, Washington State had no jurisdiction over the Canadian smelter. The matter was initially, therefore, submitted to the International Joint Commission, a commission the two countries had established under a 1909 Boundary Waters treaty. The Commission investigated the situation and, in 1931, issued a report concluding that the smelter had, indeed, caused damage in Washington. The Commission had arrived at an estimate of $350,000 in damage and made several recommendations for reducing emissions going forward. *Trail Smelter Case (United States v Canada)* 3 RIAA 1905, 1911, Trail Smelter Arb. Trib., 1941.

6 *Convention for the Final Settlement of the Difficulties Arising through Complaints of Damage Done in the State of Washington by Fumes Discharged from the Smelter of the Consolidated Mining and Smelting Company* (1935), 162 LNTS 74 ('Trail Smelter Decision').

The arbitral tribunal was charged with devising a solution that was just to both parties, recognising states' interests in both economic activity and environmental integrity.[7] Finding that further damage had been caused to land and improvements in the US since 1932, it awarded damages of $78,000 (US) with interest until paid.[8] Most critically, it also found an:

> adequate basis [to conclude] that, under the principles of international law . . . no State has the right to use or permit the use of its territory in such a manner as to cause injury by fumes in or to the territory of another or the properties or persons therein, when the case is of serious consequence and the injury is established by clear and convincing evidence.[9]

Looking forward then, the tribunal reasoned that further damage might occur in the future if some controls were not placed on the operation of the smelter and, in a ground-breaking move, invoked the obligation to prevent transboundary harm to justify laying down a regulatory regime, including maximum permissible sulphur emissions for the smelter.[10] The purpose was not to shut the smelter down but, rather, to devise restrictions under which it could continue to operate without causing damage in the US. This was a crucial development, signalling that states' duties with respect to serious transboundary harm extend beyond reparations for damage to include an obligation to prevent harm.

A second key principle of international environmental law to have achieved customary law status is the duty to cooperate.[11] Derived from the UN Charter's principle of good-neighbourliness, this duty encompasses, *inter alia*, obligations to share information with, notify and consult with other states in good faith and is asserted in almost every agreement in the field of modern international environmental law.[12] That it has achieved customary law status is hardly in dispute: as the International Tribunal for the Law of the Sea has observed, '[t]he duty to co-operate is a fundamental principle in . . . general international law.'[13]

The Trail Smelter case is probably the most significant dispute that has been decided by an international tribunal. Several other disputes have had the potential to further develop customary obligations in this field but, for varying reasons, did not result in decisions of

---

7 Trail Smelter Decision, p. 9:

> In all the consideration which the Tribunal has given to the problem presented to it, and in all the conclusions which it has reached, it had been guided by that primary purpose of the Convention expressed in the words of Article IV, that the Tribunal 'shall give consideration to the desire of the high contracting parties to reach a solution just to all parties concerned'.

8 Trail Smelter Decision, p. 37.

9 Trail Smelter Decision, p. 62.

10 Trail Smelter Decision, pp. 31–4

11 Prominent formulations of this principle can be found in Principle 24 of the 1972 Stockholm Declaration; and Principle 27 of the Rio Declaration.

12 For a detailed discussion of the meaning and origins of this principle, see P. Sands, *Principles of International Environmental Law*, Cambridge: Cambridge, 2003, pp. 249–51.

13 International Tribunal for the Law of the Sea, *The Mox Plant Case, Republic of Ireland v United Kingdom of Great Britain and Northern Ireland*, Case No. 10 – Request for Provisional Measures, December 3, 2001, para. 82.

such historic weight. Primary examples can be found in the International Court of Justice's jurisprudence on the issue of nuclear testing.

By 1973, all major states with nuclear weapons had signed up to the 1963 *Treaty Banning Nuclear Weapon Tests in the Atmosphere, in Outer Space and Under Water*,[14] except France.[15] France had conducted a series of atmospheric nuclear weapons tests in French Polynesia from 1966 to 1972, and was planning to commence another round in the spring of 1973. In response, Australia and New Zealand filed suit with the International Court of Justice (ICJ), challenging the legality of the tests under international law and asking the Court to order France to cease its testing.[16] As the basis for its claim, Australia asserted several violations of its rights, specifically the right of Australia and its people to be free from atmospheric nuclear weapon tests; the right to sovereignty over its territory and to determine what acts shall take place therein and, in particular, whether Australia and its people shall be exposed to artificial radiation; and, finally, the freedom of the high seas.[17] New Zealand's application was similar but instead of grounding its cause on its own individual rights, it sought to assert rights of 'all members of the international community' to be free from radioactive fallout from nuclear tests and contamination of the air, land and sea.[18]

France chose not to appear in the case, but later issued several unilateral declarations that it would end its testing programme.[19] In response, the Court felt that the desired objectives of Australia and New Zealand's suits had been accomplished and did not proceed with them.[20] When France announced in 1995 that it intended to resume nuclear weapons tests in the South Pacific, New Zealand tried to have the case reopened.[21] The Court declined on the grounds that the original case concerned atmospheric tests, whereas the new tests announced by France were to be underground,[22] so the legality of nuclear testing under international law remains unsettled.

Uncertainly prevails in the related area of liability for nuclear damage, as well. In the aftermath of the Chernobyl accident, not one state has submitted a formal claim in international fora against the USSR for damage from the radioactive fallout, although a few have reserved

---

14 *Treaty Banning Nuclear Weapons Tests in the Atmosphere, in Outer Space and Under Water,* opened for signature 5 August 1963 480 UNTS 43 (entered into force 10 October 1963) ('*Test Ban Treaty*').

15 IAEA Bulletin (1973), *10: Test Ban Treaty,* 5 Aug. 1963 pp. 3, 8, 17 (series of articles commemorating the tenth anniversary of the signing of the Treaty and containing a list of ratifying states from 1963). Online. Available HTTP: <http://www.iaea.org/Publications/Magazines/Bulletin/Bull154/15403500322.pdf> (accessed 31 October 2011).

16 *Nuclear Tests Case (Austr. v. Fr.),* 1974 ICJ Rep. 253; *Nuclear Tests Case (NZ v Fr.),* 1974 ICJ Rep. 457.

17 *Nuclear Tests Case (Austr. v Fr.),* 1974 ICJ Rep. 253, para. 49.

18 *Nuclear Tests Case (NZ v Fr.),* 1974 ICJ Rep. 457, para. 28.

19 *Nuclear Tests Judgment (Austr. v Fr.),* 1974 ICJ Rep., 253, paras 33–47, *Nuclear Tests Judgment (NZ v Fr.),* 1974 ICJ Rep. 457 paras 33–53.

20 *Nuclear Tests Judgment (Austr. v Fr.),* 1974 ICJ Rep., 253, paras 47–62, *Nuclear Tests Judgment (NZ v Fr.),* 1974 ICJ Rep. 457, paras 58–62.

21 The decision disposing of New Zealand's case specified that, while it was not the Court's function to contemplate that France would not comply with its own announcements, New Zealand could request an examination of the situation if the basis for the dismissal of the cases somehow changed. *Nuclear Tests Judgment (NZ v Fr.),* para. 63. New Zealand invoked this statement to ask the Court to reopen the case when France announced it would begin underground nuclear tests in 1995. *Request for Examination of Situation in Accordance with Paragraph 63 of Court's Judgment of 20 December 1974 in the Nuclear Tests (NZ v Fr.),* 1995 ICJ 288, 342, 412.

22 *Nuclear Tests Case (NZ v Fr.),* 1995 ICJ 288, 306.

the right to do so.[23] Nonetheless, a handful did assert that an obligation to compensate for nuclear damage could be established under customary international law,[24] presumably along the lines of the finding in the Trail Smelter case and Principle 21/2, which recognise a general duty to prevent and indemnify transboundary harms. In a 1996 advisory opinion, the International Court of Justice affirmed that this principle has achieved customary law status: 'the general obligation of states to ensure that activities within their jurisdiction and control respect the environment of other states or of areas beyond national control is now part of the corpus of international law relating to the environment.'[25] Questions remain, however, about the level of damage required to trigger the obligation. Some indication may be found in the key treaty regimes that the international community has developed for the protection of the atmosphere.

Long-range transboundary air pollution

Customary rules are, by their very nature, general and incapable of providing very specific guidance. For this reason, states rely on treaties – written agreements that are legally binding upon all states that elect to become parties to the treaty – to set forth their precise rights and responsibilities. In general, international environmental laws in the field of atmospheric pollution follow a common regulatory model:

1) The adoption of a general comprehensive framework; followed later by
2) The adoption of protocols to address more specific topics and obligations.

Parties regularly adopt a preliminary framework convention of very broad and general application and then use it, in turn, to create a forum for the negotiation of more concrete commitments in later protocols.[26] This regulatory technique provides flexibility, in so far as states are free to either take the lead on a particular issue or take more of a wait-and-see approach, and it also enables states to deal with new problems as they arise.

---

23 See e.g. EEC Internal Market Memorandum # 1221, 14 May 1986, at 15 (discussing statements of West German Chancellor Kohl that he would seek reparations from the Soviet Union). For a more detailed discussion of the international response to the accident, see L.A. Malone, 'The Chernobyl Accident: A Case Study in International Law Regulating State Responsibility for Transboundary Nuclear Pollution', *Columbia Journal of Environmental Law* 12, 1987, 203; Tokyo Summit Declaration on the Implications of the Chernobyl Nuclear Accidents (1986), INFCIRC/333, 5 May 1986, reprinted in 'International Organizations and Agreements', 37 *Nuclear Law Bulletin* 37; E.B. Moynagh, 'The Legacy of Chernobyl: Its Significance for the Ukraine and the World', *Boston College Environmental Affairs Law Review* 21, 1994, 709.
24 When the Director General of the International Atomic Energy Agency requested country comments on international liability for damage arising from a nuclear accident back in 1987, 5 of the 32 countries that responded indicated a belief that sufficient customary international law rules and principles existed to establish liability: Canada, Chile, Germany, Guatemala and Thailand. International Atomic Energy Agency document GOV/INF/550 (1987).
25 *Legality of the Threat or Use of Nuclear Weapons*, Advisory Opinion, ICJ Reports 1996, p. 242, Art. 29.
26 The 'comprehensive framework with protocols' approach is borrowed from international human rights law, as exemplified by such frameworks as those surrounding the *International Covenant on Civil and Political Rights*; the *International Covenant on Economic, Social and Cultural Rights*; and the *Convention on the Rights of the Child*.

This model was pioneered by the first major treaty regime on air pollution, which aims to prevent and reduce acid rain.[27] By the early 1970s, acid rain had become a severe problem in Europe, particularly with the acidification of Scandinavian lakes. In 1979, 32 European countries, along with the US and Canada,[28] adopted the *Convention on Long Range Transboundary Air Pollution* (CLRTAP) within the United Nations Economic Commission for Europe.[29] The 1979 Convention sets out a regional framework for countries to cooperate to address the issue of long-distance acid rain.

An important feature of the Convention is its wide scope, in terms of pollution covered. While its title refers to transboundary air pollution, its provisions apply simply to 'air pollution', meaning that its application is not dependent on proof that a pollutant has crossed a state boundary.[30] Furthermore, the definition of air pollution does not include any requirement of a particular type, level or severity of harm, giving the CLRTAP a very broad range of potential applications beyond just acid rain.[31] The Convention calls on the parties to 'limit, and, as far as possible, gradually reduce and prevent air pollution, including long-range transboundary air pollution'.[32] Notably, this obligation contains no specific reduction target or timetable, but rather a soft commitment on the part of the parties to try and lessen air pollution. Obligations to develop policies and strategies are tempered with language that they be compatible with balanced development and economically feasible.[33] Parties are also committed, *inter alia*, to initiate and cooperate on research into and development of new technologies, instruments and models; to exchange information on their domestic emissions and policies; and to notify and consult with one another in the event of significant risk of LRTAP.[34]

Despite the soft nature of the obligations it contains, the CLRTAP has proved very valuable as a framework for cooperation and the development of more specific measures and obligations. It serves as a starting point for research and monitoring of troublesome emissions as well as for coordination, information exchange and consultation between the countries; and has provided the venue for the elaboration of eight protocols since its entry

27 Acid rain is precipitation that contains elevated levels of nitric and sulphuric acids from the combustion of fossil fuels and can acidify water bodies; damage trees, forest soils, building materials and surfaces, statues and sculptures; and degrade visibility and human health. For an in-depth overview of the science of acid rain, see P. Brimblecombe and H. Hara (eds) *Acid Rain – Deposition to Recovery*, New York: Springer, 2010; C.N. Lane, *Acid Rain: Overview and Abstracts*, Hauppuge, NY: Nova Science Publishers, 2003.

28 United Nations Economic Commission for Europe, 'Status of the Convention on Long-range Transboundary Air Pollution and its Related Protocols (as of March 1, 2011)'. Online. Available HTTP: <http://www.unece.org/env/lrtap/status/lrtap_st.html> (accessed 31 Oct. 2011).

29 *Convention on Long Range Transboundary Air Pollution*, opened for signature 13 November 1979, 1302 UNTS 217 (entered into force 16 March 1983) ('CLRTAP').

30 CLRTAP, Art. 2.

31 CLRTAP, Art. 1, para. a.

32 CLRTAP, Art. 2.

33 CLRTAP, Art. 6.

34 CLRTAP, Art. 4.

into force in 1983.[35] Three of the protocols warrant mention here, for innovating a cost-sharing arrangement for scientific monitoring and introducing flexible regulatory techniques and compliance controls that have since become enduring approaches in international environmental law.

The 1984 Geneva Protocol[36] provides for the financing of the joint monitoring programme called for under Articles 9 and 10 of the Convention. The European Monitoring and Evaluation Programme (EMEP) has three main components: gathering emission data, measuring air quality, and modelling atmospheric dispersion.[37] Prior to the agreement of this Protocol, EMEP was reliant on funding from the United Nations Environment Programme (UNEP), which was set to expire in 1984, and voluntary country contributions.[38] Recognising the need for greater and more stable and predictable funding, the Protocol establishes mandatory contributions for all contracting parties and a General Trust Fund into which all contributions are deposited, to cover the annual costs of this vital programme.[39]

The 1991 Geneva Protocol,[40] which deals with emissions of volatile organic compounds (VOCs), is notable for adopting a more flexible alternative to a uniform target for all countries, under which parties have their choice of three different options for reducing their emissions:

(i)   Reduce national annual VOCs emissions levels by at least 30% below 1988 levels or any other annual level from 1984 to 1990 the country may wish;

(ii) Countries that designate tropospheric ozone management areas (TOMAs) have the option of committing to the reductions detailed in (i) for the TOMA alone; and then ensuring that their total national emissions do not exceed 1988 levels by the year 1999; or

---

35 The eight protocols to the 1979 Convention are:
   •   1984 Geneva Protocol on Long-Term Financing of the Cooperative Programme for Monitoring and Evaluation of the Long-Range Transmission of Air Pollutants in Europe;
   •   1985 Helsinki Protocol on the Reduction of Sulphur Emissions or their Transboundary Fluxes by at least 30%;
   •   1988 Sofia Protocol Concerning the Control of Emissions of Nitrogen Oxides or their Transboundary Fluxes;
   •   1991 Geneva Protocol Concerning the Control of Emissions of Volatile Organic Compounds or their Transboundary Fluxes;
   •   1994 Oslo Protocol on Further Reduction of Sulphur Emissions;
   •   1998 Aarhus Protocol on Heavy Metals;
   •   1998 Aarhus Protocol on Persistent Organic Pollutants;
   •   1999 Gothenburg Protocol to Abate Acidification, Eutrophication and Ground-Level Ozone.

36 Protocol to the 1979 LRTAP Convention on Long-term Financing of the Cooperative Programme for Monitoring and Evaluation of the Long-range Transmission of Air Pollutants in Europe, 28 September 1984, United Nations, *Treaty Series*, vol. 1491, p. 167, UN Docs EB.AIR/AC.1/4, Annex and EB.AIR/ CRP.1/Add.4 ('EMEP').

37 CLRTAP, Art. 9.

38 EMEP, preamble, p. 1.

39 EMEP, Art. 1, para. 3; Art. 3 paras 1, 2 and 5.

40 Protocol to the 1979 CLRTAP Convention Concerning the Control of Emissions of Volatile Organic Compounds or their Transboundary Fluxes, opened for signature 18 November 1991, United Nations, Treaty Series, vol. 2001, p. 187 ('Geneva Protocol').

(iii) Countries whose annual emissions in 1988 were below specified thresholds[41] had the further option of just ensuring that their total national emissions do not exceed 1988 levels by the year 1999.[42]

This approach allows the treaty regime to impose commitments based on parties' relative emissions levels and circumstances.

The 1994 Oslo Protocol[43] builds on the flexibility achieved under the VOCs Protocol with minimum targets for each individual country to achieve, according to a staggered timeline of 2000, 2005 and 2010.[44] The individual percentage reductions are based on the actual emissions sources within each country's territory.[45] In place of a uniform inflexible target, these scientifically based targets rely on maps of actual sulphur sources and deposits, thereby maximising both fairness and accuracy. This Protocol also breaks new ground with the establishment of a so-called Implementation Committee to review parties' compliance and implementation of all of the protocols to the 1979 CLRTAP.[46] This exciting development led to the adoption of a full compliance procedure in 1997.[47] As mentioned above, the regulatory legacy of the 1979 Convention is significant, having been among the first instruments in international environmental law to adopt the 'framework convention with protocols' approach. As will be seen, the use of country-specific baselines, targets and timetables is, likewise, replicated in the other two key air pollution regimes designed to protect the ozone layer and combat climate change.

Ozone depletion

Around the same time as evidence was mounting on the dangers of acid rain, scientists were raising alarms about another worrisome environmental problem: depletion of the ozone layer.[48] Like acid rain, ozone depletion is believed to be caused by air pollution – in this case,

---

41 The thresholds were 1988 VOCs emissions lower than 500,000 tons and 20 kilograms per inhabitant and 5 tons per square kilometre. Geneva Protocol, Art. 2, para. 2(c).
42 Geneva Protocol, Art. 2, para. 2(c).
43 Protocol to the 1979 Convention on Long-Range Transboundary Air Pollution on Further Reduction of Sulphur Emissions, 14 June 1994, United Nations, *Treaty Series*, vol. 2030, p. 122; UN Doc EB.AIR/R.84; E/ECE/ENHS/001/2002/l ('Oslo Protocol').
44 Oslo Protocol, Annex II.
45 Oslo Protocol, Art. 8, para. 1.
46 Oslo Protocol, Art. 7.
47 Economic Commission for Europe, Decision 1997/2 Concerning the Implementation Committee, its Structure and Functions and Procedures for Review of Compliance, ECE/EB.AIR/53, 7 January 1998, p. 32.
48 The ozone layer is a layer in the Earth's atmosphere that contains high levels of the colourless gas ozone, and absorbs over 97 per cent of high-frequency ultraviolet light from the sun, sparing the planet's inhabitants from exposure to these potentially damaging rays. By the late 1970s, scientific consensus was growing that the ozone layer was being depleted beyond what normal natural fluctuations could explain, and the primary suspects were two common chemicals: halons, used in fire extinguishers; and chlorofluorocarbons (CFCs), used in aerosol sprays, air conditioners, Styrofoam and solvents. For an in-depth overview of the science of ozone depletion, see Global Ozone Research and Monitoring Project, 'Scientific Assessment of Ozone Depletion: 2010', World Meteorological Organization, Report No. 52, 2010. Online. Available HTTP: <http://www.esrl.noaa.gov/csd/assessments/ozone/2010/chapters/prefaceprologue.pdf> (accessed 2 December 2011).

anthropogenic emissions of chlorofluorocarbons (CFCs) and halons. Unlike acid rain, however, ozone depletion is not a localised problem between neighbouring states; rather, it is a global problem with both producers and users all over the world. Where the CLRTAP had only to address a regional crisis, the ozone regime had to secure buy-in from the whole of the international community, a task of infinitely greater difficulty for the wider range of needs and circumstances that had to be accommodated to achieve consensus. In particular, the ozone negotiations brought to the fore the challenge of reconciling environmental conservation with economic considerations, a rift that cut almost directly along a developed/developing country divide.[49]

By the early 1980s, the US had already acted unilaterally to curb CFCs and was eager for others to follow suit so as not to suffer a disadvantage for not using them. While the Europeans initially expressed scepticism about the scientific evidence, they eventually came on board. The developing countries, however, argued that ozone depletion was largely the result of the historical emissions of the industrialised North, and that it would be unfair to hamper the South's economic growth with burdensome obligations and the outlawing of useful chemicals before they too had a chance to develop. As mentioned above, the reality that ozone-depleting substances threaten the ozone layer equally – regardless of where they are released – meant that any effort to reduce them required a truly global commitment on the part of all states to decrease their production and use, and this meant the developing world had to be brought on board. In March 1985, the international community finally agreed on a framework convention that was similar to the CLRTAP, in so far as it laid out a foundation for countries to meet regularly to review the state and science of the ozone problem, leaving concrete reductions obligations for future protocols. What was different was the special treatment accorded to developing country priorities.

The 1985 *Vienna Convention for the Protection of the Ozone Layer* was the first international treaty focused specifically and exclusively on addressing a global environmental threat.[50] In addition, it is important because it was adopted at a time when the science on ozone depletion was still uncertain: the international community moved forward with efforts to address the problem even though scientific consensus on its causes and solutions was not yet firm. This landmark development unveiled a more precautionary approach to environmental problems that legitimised preventative action to protect the environment. Most critical, however, are its ground-breaking calls for special consideration of the needs of the developing world in the development, exchange and transfer of legal, scientific and technical knowledge. The international regime on the ozone layer is remarkable for the emergence of new and stronger voices from developing countries demanding, and obtaining, a better and fairer bargain in environmental treaties. The principle of common but differentiated responsibility that would be articulated in the Rio Declaration a few years later found one of its earlier concrete applications in this regime.

The Convention establishes a framework of four categories of measures to protect people and the environment from ozone depletion: cooperative monitoring; research; policy development; and implementation of the international regime.[51] As a framework convention, it

---

49 For an in-depth account of the ozone negotiations, see R. Benedick, *Ozone Diplomacy New Directions in Safeguarding the Planet*, Cambridge, MA: Harvard University Press, 1998.

50 *Vienna Convention for the Protection of the Ozone Layer*, opened for signature 22 March 1985, TIAS No 11, 1513 UNTS 293 (entered into force 22 September 1988) ('Vienna Convention') 324.

51 Vienna Convention, Art. 2(2).

imposes no concrete obligations to reduce ozone-depleting substances and, adopting the flexibility of the 1979 CLRTAP, makes states' individual obligations dependent upon their respective means and capabilities, as well as the latest scientific and technological knowledge.[52] To encourage the developing countries to ratify, the treaty also accords special consideration to their needs and situation, and specifies that even the meagre commitments it contains are to be imposed 'in accordance with the means at [countries'] disposal and their capabilities'.[53] With this compromise, the developing countries' participation was secured, providing the needed assistance in meeting their obligations under the Convention and assurances that their participation would not decelerate economic growth and development.

Mere months after the approval of the Convention in 1985, a team of scientists with the British Antarctic Survey published findings of a hole in the ozone layer over Antarctica roughly the size of the continental US.[54] This startling discovery spurred the immediate initiation of negotiations for concrete measures to reduce ozone-depleting substances, leading to the agreement of the *Montreal Protocol on Substances that Deplete the Ozone Layer* in late 1987.[55] Like its parent convention, the Protocol was a ground-breaking instrument with innovative regulatory, institutional and financial arrangements.[56]

While consensus had been achieved on the need to address ozone depletion, the negotiators of the Protocol still had to contend with difficult questions as to where reductions should be made and who should pay for them. In particular, the developing countries remained adamant that they should be able to transition comfortably to alternative chemicals, technologies and industries without any harm to their economies. As a result, the Protocol granted developing countries a ten-year grace period in which they were permitted to increase consumption of the regulated chemicals to meet their 'basic domestic needs', before coming under the Protocol's limitations and reductions on consumption and production.[57] In addition, the Protocol called for the 'provision of subsidies, aid, credits, guarantees or insurance programmes . . . for the use of alternative technology and for substitute products'.[58] Despite these incentives, key developing nations, particularly China and India, still refused to ratify and forced the adoption of several considerable amendments in 1990.[59] The 1990 amendments further revolutionised international environmental regulation, with new approaches to the enduring obstacles of financial assistance, differentiated obligations and compliance incentives.

---

52 Vienna Convention, Art. 2(2), (4).

53 Vienna Convention, Art. 2(2).

54 British Antarctic Survey, 'The Ozone Hole', Natural Environment Research Council Science Briefing, 2010. Online. Available HTTP: <http://www.antarctica.ac.uk/press/journalists/ resources/science/the_ozone_hole_2009.pdf> (accessed 30 November 2011).

55 *Montreal Protocol on Substances that Deplete the Ozone Layer*, opened for signature 16 September 1987, 1522 UNTS 3 (entered into force 1 January 1989) ('Montreal Protocol').

56 For detailed discussion of the Montreal Protocol, see J.T.B. Tripp, 'The UNEP Montreal Protocol: Industrialized and Developing Countries Sharing the Responsibility for Protecting the Stratospheric Ozone Layer', *New York University Journal of International Law and Politics* 20, 1998, 733; J. Lammers, 'Efforts to Develop a Protocol on Chlorofluorocarbons to the Vienna Convention for the Protection of the Ozone Layer', *Hague Yearbook of International Law* 1, 1998, 255.

57 Montreal Protocol, Art. 5(1).

58 Montreal Protocol, Art. 5(3).

59 *Adjustments and Amendments to the Montreal Protocol on Substances That Deplete the Ozone Layer*, opened for signature 29 June 1990, 30 ILM 537 (entered into force 10 August 1992) ('Montreal Amendments').

The 1990 amendments imposed a deadline on the ten-year grace period: in order to benefit from the considerable aid, insurance and subsidies promised, states had to ratify the Protocol by 1 January 1999.[60] At the same time, however, the Protocol was also amended to explicitly tie developing countries' performance to receipt of sufficient financial and technological support from the developed world,[61] and establish a dedicated financial mechanism to coordinate the transfer of funds and technologies.[62] These were landmark developments, conditioning developing states' performance on the satisfaction of support obligations placed on the North and creating an entirely new fund to cover all incremental costs. The governance of the new fund is also significant: it operates under the authority of *all* the parties, and together they decide on its overall policies and select the members of an Executive Committee, which is tasked with developing and monitoring the implementation of the fund, on the basis of balanced representation of the parties.[63] Finally, a new Article was added containing express language calling on the parties to ensure that 'the best available, environmentally safe substitutes and related technologies are expeditiously transferred to the [developing] Parties . . . and that the transfers . . . occur under fair and most favourable conditions'.[64]

These developments reflect the growing recognition in international law on the atmosphere, and on the environment overall, of the close relationship between environmental conservation and development and the need to find approaches to harmonise both. The ozone regime achieved global participation through an optimal combination of impelling incentives and a compelling deadline. The result has been an extremely successful international regime that demonstrates how a well-designed carrot-and-stick approach can marshal universal consensus and compliance.

Climate change

Building on the precautionary approach modelled by the ozone regime, international efforts began in the late 1980s to coordinate research and exchange on another troubling environmental phenomenon: global warming.[65] In 1988, UNEP and the World Meteorological Organization (WMO) established the Intergovernmental Panel on Climate Change (IPCC) to assess the scientific basis for global action to address climate change.[66] In its first report, released in 1990, the IPCC found sufficient scientific consensus to conclude, firstly, that global average temperatures were rising; and, secondly, that these increases were outside the

---

60 Montreal Amendments, Art. 5(1).
61 Montreal Amendments, Art. 5(5).
62 Montreal Amendments, Art. 10(1).
63 Montreal Amendments, Arts 10(4) and (5).
64 Montreal Amendments, Art. 10A.
65 The earth's temperate climate is regulated by atmospheric concentrations of what are known as greenhouse gases (GHGs): gases that allow the sun's visible rays to penetrate the atmosphere, but then trap them when they radiate back off the surface of the planet as heat. As GHG concentrations rise, more heat is trapped, leading to an increase in global average temperatures. In the early days, this phenomenon was termed 'global warming', but this phrase has since been phased out in favour of 'climate change', which encompasses a wider range of variations in the earth's climate patterns beyond temperature rise. For an in-depth overview of the science of climate change, see R.K. Pachauri and A. Reisinger (eds) *Contribution of Working Groups I, II and III to the Fourth Assessment Report of the Intergovernmental Panel on Climate Change,* Geneva: IPCC, 1997.
66 *Protection of Global Climate for Present and Future Generations of Mankind* (1989), GA Res. 43/53, UN GAOR, 43rd Sess, UN Doc A/RES/43/53.

range of natural fluctuations and could be attributed to human activities.[67] As in the case of ozone depletion, these findings were cause for great concern for the health of the planet: scientists cautioned that unchecked increases in greenhouse gas (GHG) levels could have terrible consequences, including rising sea levels, increases in the frequency and severity of extreme weather events, water scarcity and famine.[68] Where ozone depletion involved a set of chemicals used in some packaging and appliances of modern convenience, climate change implicated almost every human activity: the culprit was the burning of the fossil fuels on which humans primarily rely for electricity, transportation and industry. Climate change involves more than the environment: it requires a fundamental change in the global economy. The stakes in the international negotiations on this issue, therefore, could not be higher; indeed, some argue that this regime is among the most crucial in the world.[69]

Shortly following the release of the first IPCC report, an International Negotiating Committee was established under the auspices of the UN General Assembly to negotiate a framework convention on climate change.[70] The negotiations were long and difficult.[71] Climate change exploded the traditional alliances within the developed and developing country blocks. In Vienna and Montreal, the lines had been drawn cleanly along a North/ South divide, but no more. A North/South split still persisted: developing countries argued that climate change was primarily the result of historical emissions from the industrialized North and, therefore, reductions should be imposed there first, so as not to impede the South's ongoing development. Among the developing countries, however, some parties' interests were diametrically opposed: for instance, the small island states that faced submersion from rising sea levels and the oil-producing companies whose exports would collapse if fossil fuel use declined.

Consensus was as hard to come by in the Northern bloc, where the US and Europe clashed over which gases should be regulated and to what extent. Another fundamental disagreement arose around the South's demands that obligations be governed by historical contributions. While the Europeans were prepared to take the lead in reducing emissions, the US insisted that developing country emissions had to be restricted as well, both to protect its own

---

67 IPCC, 'Scientific Assessment of Climate Change', in J.T. Houghton, G.J. Jenkins and J.J. Ephraums (eds) *Contribution of Working Group I to the First Assessment Report of the Intergovernmental Panel on Climate Change*, Cambridge: Cambridge University Press, 1990.

68 Ibid.

69 P.L. Joffe, 'The Dwindling Margin for Error: The Realist Perspective on Global Governance and Global Warming', *Rutgers Journal of Law and Public Policy* 5, 2007, 89; A. Gore, Nobel Peace Prize Lecture, 10 Dec. 2007. Online. Available HTTP: <http://www.nobelprize.org/nobel_prizes/peace/laureates/2007/gore-lecture_en.html> ('We, the human species, are confronting a planetary emergency – a threat to the survival of our civilization that is gathering ominous and destructive potential even as we gather here'); K. Ban, Secretary-General's Message on the International Day for the Preservation of the Ozone Layer, 16 September 2009. Online. Available HTTP: <http://www.un.org/apps/sg/sgstats.asp?nid=4069> ('Without action on climate change, the world faces profound social, economic and environmental disruption').

70 *Protection of Global Climate for Present and Future Generations of Mankind* (1990), GA Res. 45/212, UN GAOR, 45th Sess, UN Doc A/RES/45/212.

71 For an in-depth account of climate politics and negotiations, see US Climate Action Centre, *Copenhagen Climate Negotiations: The Briefing Book*, 2009. Online. Available HTTP: <http://www.usclimatenetwork.org/resource-database/biefingbook_basics.pdf> (accessed 2 December 2011); H. Schroder, *Negotiating the Kyoto Protocol: An Analysis of Negotiation Dynamics in International Negotiations*, London: Lit Verlag, 2001; I.M. Mintzer and J.A. Leonard (eds) *Negotiating Climate Change: The Inside Story of the Rio Convention*, Cambridge: Cambridge University Press, 1994.

industries and to ensure that reductions achieved in the North were not erased by emissions unabated below the Equator. As in the case of the ozone layer, the negotiations were further complicated by the significant scientific uncertainty that remained – no one could say definitively what the climate's critical breaking point for GHG concentrations was or what would happen if that limit was breached – and the debates were very intense. Unable to agree on actual commitments to reduce GHG emissions, the international community agreed a framework treaty, the *United Nations Framework Convention on Climate Change* (UNFCCC), that laid the foundation for stronger action down the road.[72]

The UNFCCC centres on three main principles: the precautionary approach,[73] sustainable development,[74] and a relative newcomer in international environmental law, known as common but differentiated responsibility (CDR).[75] Precaution, familiar from the ozone regime, provides that, where there are threats of serious or irreversible damage, lack of scientific certainty should not preclude cost-effective measures to prevent damage to the environment.[76] Sustainable development calls simply for development that meets the needs of the present without compromising those of future generations.[77] There are two main elements of CDR: first is the recognition of all states' shared interest in and responsibility for protecting the global environment.[78] Second is the recognition that it is also necessary to consider states' individual circumstances: both their contribution to the creation of the environmental problem at hand, and their relative ability to prevent or reduce the threat, in terms of their financial and technological capabilities.[79] Taken together, these three principles formed the basis for the substantive provisions of the Convention.

The UNFCCC sets as its aim the stabilisation of GHGs at levels that would prevent dangerous anthropogenic interference with the planet's climate.[80] To this end, it calls on all nations to, *inter alia*, look into the issue, monitor emissions and share their findings with one another.[81] It then imposes additional obligations on the developed countries only,[82] requiring them to affirmatively 'take the lead' with domestic emissions-reducing policies and measures;[83] commit new and additional funding for the climate regime;[84] assist vulnerable developing countries in meeting the costs of adaptation;[85] and promote, facilitate and finance resource and technology transfers to the developing world, to support them in meeting their commitments under the convention.[86] As under the ozone regime, developing countries'

---

72 United Nations Framework Convention on Climate Change, opened for signature 4 June 1992, 1771 UNTS 107 (entered into force 21 March 1994) ('UNFCCC').
73 UNFCCC, Art. 3, para. 3.
74 UNFCCC, Art. 3, para. 4.
75 UNFCCC, Art. 3, para. 1.
76 Sands, *Principles of International Environmental Law*, op. cit., p. 268.
77 Ibid.
78 Ibid.
79 Ibid.
80 UNFCCC, Art. 2.
81 UNFCCC, Art. 4(1).
82 UNFCCC Annexes I and II, which list the countries that are subject to additional obligations under the Convention, contain the OECD countries and certain so-called 'economies in transition' in Eastern Europe; and then just the OECD countries, respectively.
83 UNFCCC, Art. 4(2)(a).
84 UNFCCC, Art. 4(3).
85 UNFCCC, Art. 4(4).
86 UNFCCC, Art. 4(5).

performance of their obligations is expressly conditioned on receipt of financial and technical support;[87] all parties are required to take into consideration what actions are needed to meet the needs and concerns of the developing world;[88] and a financial mechanism is established to facilitate financial and technological transfers.[89] Soon after the adoption of the Convention, negotiations began on a protocol that would impose concrete GHG emission reduction targets and timetables.

The first and only protocol to the Convention to date, the 1997 *Kyoto Protocol to the United Nations Framework Convention on Climate Change*,[90] is also first in setting country-specific targets in an international instrument and devising a highly innovative and, for some, controversial market-based approach.[91] While the developing countries do not undertake any new commitments beyond their existing monitoring and cooperation obligations under the UNFCCC,[92] the Kyoto Protocol imposes individualised reduction targets for each developed country.[93] The Protocol negotiations involved protracted political weighing of each country's respective emission levels and capacity for cuts, to achieve an overall reduction of 5 per cent below 1990 levels by 2012.[94] Kyoto also laid the foundation for the creation of a global carbon market with the creation of three new market-based mechanisms to enable the international community to reduce emissions in the most efficient and cost-effective ways possible. First, it pioneered an emissions trading mechanism, under which parties can buy and sell emission credits.[95] Then it introduced two other mechanisms that enable developed countries to fund emissions-reducing projects wherever they are least expensive: in other developed countries, under Joint Implementation;[96] and in developing countries, under the Clean Development Mechanism (CDM).[97] Protracted political disagreements that delayed the Protocol's entry into force until 2005[98] and numerous trial-and-error attempts to operationalise its mechanisms have made it difficult to measure the success of the market-based regulation, but it remains an exciting – if still unproven – new approach in international environmental law.[99]

---

87 UNFCCC, Art. 4(7).
88 UNFCCC, Art. 4(8).
89 UNFCCC, Arts 11 and 21. Article 11 specifies that the mechanism should have an 'equitable and balanced representation of all Parties within a transparent system of governance', and refers to interim arrangements in Article 21, which calls for the Global Environment Facility (GEF) to be entrusted with the operation of the financial mechanism on an interim basis. The GEF was restructured to make its membership universal in order to fulfil the Article 11 requirements, and remains the financial mechanism for the UNFCCC as of this writing.
90 *Kyoto Protocol to the United Nations Framework Convention on Climate Change*, opened for signature 10 December 1997, 37 ILM 22 (entered into force 16 February 2005) ('Kyoto Protocol').
91 While a first in international environmental law, the cap-and-trade approach adopted by the protocol was based on a very promising sulphur dioxide trading scheme that had just been developed in the United States. N.O. Keohane, 'Cap-and-Trade is Preferable to a Carbon Tax', in R.B. Stewart, B. Kingsbury and B. Rudyk (eds) *Climate Finance: Regulatory and Funding Strategies for Climate Change*, New York: New York University Press, 2009, p. 58.
92 Kyoto Protocol, Art. 10.
93 Kyoto Protocol, Annex B.
94 Kyoto Protocol, Art. 3(1).
95 Kyoto Protocol, Art. 17.
96 Kyoto Protocol, Art. 6.
97 Kyoto Protocol, Art. 12.
98 Kyoto Protocol, Art. 25.
99 For further consideration of the climate change regime, see Chapter 20 by A. Zahar in this volume.

Looking ahead, negotiations are ongoing for a successor protocol to Kyoto, which is set to expire at the end of 2012. One key issue is the future of the global market approach. While scientific evidence and consensus on the seriousness of climate change has been building the world over, lack of political will has thwarted domestic regulation efforts in key countries and the international regime as well. Even now that several of the major emitters among the developing countries have signalled a willingness to consider reduction commitments, the potential for a truly global market remains very much in the air. In its place, countries are pursuing domestic and regional regimes, a prime example being the European Union's Emission Trading Scheme. California, Japan, China and South Korea have all announced plans to launch their own schemes in the near future, raising the question of whether efforts will end at the national and regional levels, or ever merge into a truly global scheme.

Discussion is also well under way on two new mechanisms: reduced emissions from deforestation and degradation (REDD) and nationally appropriate mitigation actions (NAMAs). The former contemplates assigning a financial value to the carbon stored in forests and offering incentives for countries, particularly those in the developing world, to conserve forest resources, practise sustainable management, and even increase forest stocks,[100] while NAMAs could potentially complement (or replace) the project-based CDM with a mechanism to facilitate financial support and technology transfers for nationwide mitigation standards and initiatives in the developing world. All eyes are now on the Conference of the Parties/Meeting of the Parties, which, it is hoped, will continue to build on the great legacy of international cooperation and innovation in addressing atmospheric pollution, with an agreement on these exciting new mechanisms, as well as a future for the global climate regime as a whole.

Conclusion

The regulation of atmospheric pollution in international law has come a long way, evolving from a few general rules into several complex treaty regimes dealing with some of the most challenging global environmental problems confronting our planet. International rules have shown their ability to effectively address atmospheric pollution with the proven financial and regulatory approaches innovated in the arenas of transboundary air pollution and ozone depletion. At the same time, however, the flagging climate change negotiations point to several potential limitations, particularly when the costs are high and the stakes uncertain. International environmental law is at a critical crossroads: its continuing relevance depends upon its ability to address pressing global environmental challenges. Imaginative ideas and solutions are called for. With the necessary political will, international environmental law can no doubt rise to the challenge.

---

100 REDD is explored further in Chapter 39 by R. Maguire in this volume.

20

The climate change regime

Alexander Zahar

After more than twenty years of development, the international climate change regime has grown into a vast agglomeration of transnational regulation and practice. In the chapter we consider its most salient features: the UN's Framework Convention and Kyoto Protocol and the main institutions that have been created under them. We also ask whether the regime is on track to meet its aim of saving the world from dangerous climate change.

Introduction: a 'global–global' problem

In our response to climate change there has been an expectation that the world's wealthy countries will move in lockstep to solve it. Even developing countries are expected to march in unison, albeit at some distance behind wealthier states. This is unprecedented. Older environmental harms, such as water pollution, deforestation, species' loss or overfishing, are 'global' in the narrow sense that they occur wherever large concentrations of people live. The traditional global–*local* kind of problem can be solved as other local problems are solved, that is, without being concerned about whether the same type of problem is being tackled simultaneously (or instead ignored) in other parts of the world or even in other parts of the same country.

Anthropogenic climate change is in a class of its own because it is an indivisible problem with global causes and effects. Its causes are everywhere. Each person contributes to increasing the concentration of greenhouse gases in the atmosphere simply by being alive (exhaling carbon dioxide, or CO_2), utilising traditional sources of energy, relying on agricultural products, and so on. Emissions from human activity become part of an atmospheric pool and have global climatic consequences. One ton of CO_2 emitted in Angola has the same physical effect as one ton emitted in Australia – it joins an indistinguishable atmospheric whole. These globally dispersed human contributions to the greenhouse effect unite to produce the singular phenomenon of climate change, manifested at a basic physical level through global mean temperature rise and ocean acidification. In turn, these changes produce physical effects everywhere in the world.[1]

1 The only other problem of this kind – tiny by comparison – is the damage to the ozone layer caused by anthropogenic ozone-depleting substances. Ozone-depleting substances consist of a few artificial chemicals produced at well-known locations in a small number of countries. Alternatives to them are readily available.

Table 20.1 Important dates in the global response to climate change

1988: Intergovernmental Panel on Climate Change (IPCC) jointly established by World Meteorological Organization and UN Environment Programme
1990: IPCC First Assessment Report
1992: UNFCCC adopted (9 May)
1994: UNFCCC enters into force (21 March)
1997: Kyoto Protocol adopted (11 December)
2001: Bush Administration withdraws United States from the Kyoto Protocol (March)
2005: Kyoto Protocol enters into force (16 February)
European Union Emissions Trading Scheme (EU ETS) goes into operation
2007: IPCC Fourth Assessment Report.
UNFCCC adoption of Bali Road Map aimed at reaching a new global comprehensive agreement on climate change mitigation by 2009
2008: Start of Kyoto Protocol's first commitment period (2008 to 2012)
2009: Copenhagen Accord, instituting non-binding emission-reduction pledges for the post-2012 period, patched together in closing hours of UNFCCC conference
2011: UNFCCC conference, Durban: European Union and a few other countries agree to a second commitment period under the Kyoto Protocol (2013 to 2017 or 2020; end-date remains to be decided); Canada withdraws from Kyoto Protocol

The logic of the climate change problem has strongly determined the shape of the climate change regime. It helps us understand the regime's achievements as well as its failures. Some of the milestones of that regime are presented in Table 20.1. The purpose of this chapter is to discuss the key elements of the two main pillars of the international climate regime – the UN Framework Convention on Climate Change (UNFCCC) and the Kyoto Protocol. What obligations do these two treaties impose on states? How well have states been complying with their obligations? And what difference has it made for climate change?

State obligations under the Framework Convention

The UNFCCC's preamble states that 'there are many uncertainties in predictions of climate change, particularly with regard to the timing, magnitude and regional patterns thereof'. This was taken almost word for word from the IPCC's first assessment report, dating from 1990.[2] Those were the early days of climate science, when the uncertainties were indeed high compared with the state of our knowledge twenty years later. The IPCC in 1990 expressed 'certainty' on only two points about the physical science of climate change: certainty that a natural greenhouse effect keeps the earth warmer than it would otherwise be; and certainty that emissions resulting from human activity are substantially increasing the atmospheric concentration of CO_2 and other greenhouse gases (GHGs), with the result that the

---

2 Intergovernmental Panel on Climate Change, *First Assessment Report, Vol. 1: Overview and Policymaker Summaries* (World Meteorological Organization, 1990), p. 53.

greenhouse effect could be expected to be enhanced.[3] There was no certainty at that time that the climate had recently warmed or that the warming effect had been caused by human activity. By 2007, though, when the IPCC's fourth assessment report was released, the IPCC could state 'unequivocally' that the climate is warming; it could state with 'very high confidence' that the warming is caused by anthropogenic emissions;[4] and it could state, also with very high confidence, that the warming is strongly affecting terrestrial biological systems.[5]

The Convention's preamble continues with the acknowledgment that 'the global nature of climate change calls for the widest possible cooperation by all countries and their participation in an effective and appropriate international response, in accordance with their common but differentiated responsibilities and respective capabilities and their social and economic conditions.' Reading between the lines, the truly global nature of the climate problem, whose logic we reviewed above, has the effect of retarding mitigation action by willing countries when other countries, which have substantial GHG emissions, favour a business-as-usual approach. When conjoined with a climate-warming problem portrayed as urgent, this logic determines the kind of treaty that comes into being first: an agreement to be signed by *all* states. This agreement necessarily is little more than an unobjectionable shell – a mere *process* for agreeing to concrete actions at a later date. Hence the UNFCCC preamble's emphasis on 'the widest possible cooperation', as opposed to, say, the deepest possible cuts in GHG emissions.

This section focuses on the UNFCCC's substantive part (Articles 2 to 4). To appreciate the state of today's climate change regime it is important to understand this part. The Convention's *objective* is:

> stabilization of greenhouse gas concentrations in the atmosphere at a level that would prevent dangerous anthropogenic interference with the climate system. Such a level should be achieved within a time frame sufficient to allow ecosystems to adapt naturally to climate change, to ensure that food production is not threatened and to enable economic development to proceed in a sustainable manner.

'Stabilization' means the return to a relatively unvarying concentration of CO_2 in the atmosphere (measured in parts per million, or ppm). The concentration of CO_2 in the pre-industrial era (up until the end of the eighteenth century) was relatively unvarying, ranging from 275 to 285 ppm. Following industrialisation, the 10 ppm margin of variation was shattered. In 2005, the CO_2 concentration measured 379 ppm and was rising by about 2 ppm per year.[6] When the effect of all anthropogenic GHGs in the atmosphere is taken into account, the CO_2-equivalent concentration in 2005 was around 455 ppm.[7] Greenhouse gases have thus built up so significantly as to have almost doubled their from the pre-industrial-period.

3 Ibid., p. 53.
4 Intergovernmental Panel on Climate Change, *Climate Change 2007: Synthesis Report* (2007), pp. 30, 37.
5 Ibid., p. 33.
6 Intergovernmental Panel on Climate Change, *Climate Change 2007: The Physical Science Basis: Contribution of Working Group I to the Fourth Assessment Report of the IPCC*, Cambridge: Cambridge University Press, 2007, p. 137.
7 Intergovernmental Panel on Climate Change, *Climate Change 2007: Mitigation of Climate Change: Contribution of Working Group III to the Fourth Assessment Report of the IPCC*, Cambridge: Cambridge University Press, 2007), p. 97.

The Convention provides little practical assistance on the concentration we should aim to 'stabilize' at. The only guidance in the Convention's objective is the imperative to prevent 'dangerous' interference with the climate system. As the IPCC has observed, defining 'dangerous' and the limits to be set for policy purposes 'are complex tasks that can only be partially based on science, as such definitions inherently involve normative judgments'.[8] So, while the UNFCCC's objective does begin to articulate a legal obligation upon states parties (i.e. the obligation to reduce collective emissions), it is an ill-defined obligation.

The UNFCCC's Article 3 ('Principles') may be divided into five principles. It is interesting to reflect on the extent to which they are mutually compatible:

(i)   The parties 'should protect the climate system for the benefit of *present and future generations* of humankind, on the basis of equity'.
(ii) They should do so 'in accordance with their *common but differentiated responsibilities* and respective capabilities. Accordingly, the developed country parties should take the lead in combating climate change'.
(iii) The parties 'should take *precautionary measures* to anticipate, prevent or minimize the causes of climate change and mitigate its adverse effects. Where there are threats of serious or irreversible damage, lack of full scientific certainty should not be used as a reason for postponing such measures, taking into account that policies and measures to deal with climate change should be cost-effective so as to ensure global benefits at the lowest possible cost'.
(iv) The parties 'have a right to, and should, promote sustainable development'; moreover, '*economic development is essential* for adopting measures to address climate change'.
(v)   The parties should 'promote a supportive and *open international economic system*'.

The last of these principles, encouraging open economies, implicitly recognises that global economic openness is far from certain. As the IPCC has put it, 'By 2100 the world will have changed in ways that are difficult to imagine, as difficult as it was at the end of the nineteenth century to imagine the changes of the twentieth century.'[9] This remark was made in the context of the IPCC's development of 'emission scenarios', which have come to assume a central place in research-based and scholarly narratives about the future. The IPCC's four emission scenarios effectively treat as uncertain the extent to which economic globalisation and increased social and cultural interactions will continue over the course of the twenty-first century. Two of the emission scenarios emphasise global economic convergence as well as intensive social and cultural interaction; the other two focus on possible regional developmental pathways that take our societies in a direction of divergence

---

8 Ibid., p. 97. The term 'dangerous climate change' is still in common usage today and is now generally associated with a global mean temperature rise greater than 2 degrees Celsius from pre-industrial levels. See e.g. Australian Climate Commission, *The Critical Decade: Climate Science, Risks and Responses*, Australian Climate Commission, 2011, p. 18.
9 Intergovernmental Panel on Climate Change, Special Report on Emission Scenarios. Online. Available HTTP: <http://www.ipcc.ch/ipccreports/sres/emission/index.php?idp=91#4.2.1> (accessed 2 May 2012).

and traditionalism.[10] These different factors are strongly correlated with differences in the intensity of anthropogenic GHG emissions. But the truth is we do not know what kind of future is in store for us.

The UNFCCC's Article 4, on 'Commitments', has a long and complex structure, summarised in Table 20.2. The article is divided into obligations common to all parties, obligations

Table 20.2 Summary of the main state obligations (and rights) in UNFCCC Art. 4

All parties	Annex I parties	Annex II parties (OECD)
→ → → → → → → → → → → → →*increasing burden*→ → → → → → → → → → → → → →		
• Prepare GHG inventory – but in the case of developing parties only if capacity permits. • Implement, publish, and regularly update national measures to mitigate climate change, as well as measures to facilitate adaptation to climate change, including integrated plans for the management of water resources and agriculture. • Promote sustainable management of GHG sinks/reservoirs including forests and oceans. • Cooperate in scientific research and systematic observation.	• Have in place national mitigation policies and measures limiting anthropogenic GHG emissions and aimed at returning emissions to 1990 levels by 2000. • Periodic detailed report to UNFCCC on above policies and measures, specifying estimated impact on GHG emissions. • Calculation of reported emissions and removals to be scientifically sound.	• Provide new and additional finance to meet costs incurred by developing parties in complying with their reporting obligations. • Same as above for transfer of technology, etc., needed by developing parties to meet the implementation costs of the measures in leftmost column. • Assist developing parties that are particularly vulnerable to the adverse effects of climate change to meet adaptation costs. • Take all steps to facilitate and finance other parties' access to environmentally sound technologies and know-how.

Developing-party rights

• A developing country may request technical and financial support in compiling and communicating information required under the Convention.
• It may propose mitigation/adaptation projects for financing by Annex II parties, including specific technologies needed, with an estimate of consequent benefits.
• The extent to which developing parties implement their commitments will depend on financial resources and transfer of technology from Annex II parties.

10 L. Bernstein, et al., *Climate Change 2007: Synthesis Report*, Geneva: IPCC, 2007, p. 44. Online. Available HTTP: <http://www.ipcc.ch/publications_and_data/publications_ipcc_fourth_assessment_report_synthesis_report.htm> (accessed 2 May 2012).

pertaining only to 'Annex I parties' and obligations exclusive to 'Annex II parties'.[11] Consistently with the Convention's provisions leading up to this point in the treaty text, even the general commitments relating to all parties do not impose equal obligations on all, or demand undifferentiated obedience. They are, instead, subject to the parties' 'common but differentiated responsibilities'.[12]

The Convention requires all states to '[d]evelop, periodically update, [and] publish . . . national inventories of anthropogenic emissions by sources and removals by sinks of all green-house gases . . . using comparable methodologies'.[13] This is the foundation of a complex and influential web of international regulation. It aims to answer the question: what quantity of GHGs does each state emit per annum? Twenty years ago we had no ready or very accurate answer to that question. We will return to this point below.

The commitment in UNFCCC Article 4 that most directly tackles climate change is made by Annex I parties. They must 'limit' their anthropogenic GHG emissions. To limit is not the same as to cut, and a limitation that caps not overall emissions but *the rate of emission growth* is compatible with uninterrupted growth in emissions (albeit at a slower rate).

Having referred somewhat ambiguously to a 'limit', the language of Article 4 becomes diluted to such an extent that the limitation commitment is reduced to a mere aim or aspiration:

> Policies and measures will demonstrate that developed countries are taking the lead in modifying longer-term trends in anthropogenic emissions consistent with the objective of the Convention, recognizing that the *return by the end of the present decade [i.e. by 2000] to earlier levels* of anthropogenic emissions of carbon dioxide and other greenhouse gases . . . would contribute to such modification, and taking into account the differences in these Parties' starting points and approaches . . . the need to maintain strong and sustainable economic growth, available technologies and other individual circumstances, as well as the need for equitable and appropriate contributions by each of these Parties to the global effort regarding that objective.[14]

In the continuation of this Article we learn that the phrase 'earlier levels' of emissions means Annex I emissions as they stood in 1990. Thus the quoted paragraph succeeds in carving out a temporal period in which to test the parties' commitment to 'modify longer-term trends' in their emissions: by the year 2000, the Article implies, Annex I parties should have returned collectively to their 1990 emission levels.

In the event, only seven out of twenty-three OECD/Annex II states were able to do so (Table 20.3). The shaded rows highlight the countries that might be said to have complied with the implied commitment in Article 4 of the UNFCCC to return GHG emissions to 1990 levels by 2000. Note that the years 2008 and 2009 are the first two years of the Kyoto Protocol's first commitment period, discussed in the next section.

---

11 *Annex I* stands for OECD countries (as the membership stood in 1992) and economies making a transition to a market economy (countries of the former Soviet bloc). Annex II is a subset of Annex I, consisting of OECD countries only.

12 *United Nations Framework Convention on Climate Change*, opened for signature 4 June 1992, 31 ILM 854 (entered into force 21 March 1994) ('UNFCCC') Art. 4.

13 UNFCCC, Art. 4(1)(a).

14 UNFCCC, Art. 4(2)(a), emphasis added.

Table 20.3 Greenhouse gas emissions of OECD/Annex II countries (excluding emissions and removals from LULUCF), 1990–2009, in Mt (megatonnes) CO_2 eq. per annum[15]

OECD country	1990	2000	2008	2009	2009 change over 1990 (%)
Australia	418.5	496.3	550.9	545.9	30.4
Austria	78.2	80.5	87.0	80.1	2.4
Belgium	143.3	145.4	135.1	124.4	−13.2
Canada	591.3	717.6	733.7	691.8	17.0
Denmark	69.4	69.3	65.2	62.3	−10.2
Finland	70.4	69.2	70.4	66.3	−5.7
France	565.0	571.0	544.3	522.4	−7.7
Germany	1,248.0	1,042.1	981.1	920.0	−26.3
Greece	104.6	126.2	128.7	122.7	17.4
Iceland	3.4	3.8	4.9	4.6	35.1
Ireland	54.8	67.9	67.8	62.4	13.8
Italy	519.2	551.6	541.7	491.1	−5.4
Japan	1,266.6	1,341.8	1,280.6	1,209.2	−4.5
Luxembourg	12.8	9.8	12.2	11.7	−8.9
Netherlands	212.0	213.2	204.6	199.0	−6.1
New Zealand	59.1	68.4	72.8	70.6	19.4
Norway	49.8	53.4	53.7	51.3	3.1
Portugal	59.4	81.3	78.0	74.7	25.6
Spain	283.2	379.6	404.8	367.5	29.8
Sweden	72.5	69.0	63.6	60.1	−17.2
Switzerland	53.1	52.0	53.4	51.9	−2.2
United Kingdom	779.4	673.5	624.1	570.1	−26.9
United States	6,166.8	7,076.3	7,027.9	6,608.2	7.2
Total	**12,880.8**	**13,959.2**	**13,786.5**	**12,968.3**	**0.7**

A few of the countries in Table 20.3, including the United Kingdom, could boast a consistent downward trend at least partially attributable to government policy. (In the UK's case there was a major shift from coal to less polluting gas-based power generation in the 1990s.)[16] Three of the seven shaded countries (Finland, Luxembourg, and Switzerland) were unable to maintain their downward trend past 2000, their emissions rising again by 2008 only to fall a year later due to the Global Financial Crisis. Most OECD countries, seem to have paid scant regard to the trajectory urged upon them by Article 4 of the Convention. Australia, Canada, and the United States, among others, decisively increased their emissions in the period from 1990 to 2000, with the first two also reporting higher annual emissions in 2008/2009 compared to 2000.

---

15 Adapted from UNFCCC Secretariat, *National Greenhouse Gas Inventory Data for the Period 1990–2009* (16 November 2011), Table 5. 'LULUCF' stands for 'land use, land-use change, and forestry'. The estimation of GHG emissions/removals in the LULUCF sector is relatively uncertain. Moreover, human control over LULUCF emissions/removals is not as complete as in other economic sectors. Hence state GHG emissions are conventionally reported using two sets of numbers, one including the estimated LULUCF contribution and the other excluding it.
16 UNFCCC Secretariat, *Compilation and Synthesis of Fourth National Communications: Executive Summary*, 2007, p. 3.

For twenty years the UNFCCC has defined the international climate change regime. It will probably retain this role for many years to come. While it lacks the specificity of the Kyoto Protocol in the critical area of emission reductions (see below), its ongoing role as a 'framework' for international cooperation is generally accepted.

State obligations under the Kyoto Protocol

Article 17 of the UNFCCC provides for the addition of protocols. The Kyoto Protocol came into force in 2005. It has been ratified by all parties to the UNFCCC except the United States. (Canada withdrew from the Protocol in 2012.) The Kyoto Protocol's most news-worthy feature is its imposition of quantified GHG emission caps on Annex I parties. This occurs in Article 3(1) of the treaty text:

> The Parties included in Annex I shall, individually or jointly, ensure that their aggregate anthropogenic carbon dioxide equivalent emissions of the greenhouse gases listed in Annex A do not exceed their assigned amounts, calculated pursuant to their quantified emission limitation and reduction commitments inscribed in Annex B and in accordance with the provisions of this Article, with a view to reducing their overall emissions of such gases by at least 5 per cent below 1990 levels in the commitment period 2008 to 2012.

This passage has become the most divisive of all provisions of the Kyoto Protocol. The ongoing defence of the Protocol has boiled down to the defence of the idea behind this passage; and the increasingly vocal opposition to the Protocol is simply the rejection of this idea. The idea in question is that those UNFCCC parties that are wealthy and have historically high emissions (developed countries) should accept a legally binding obligation to reduce their emissions over a certain period (in this case 2008 to 2012) by a certain amount ('at least 5 per cent') below a historical benchmark (1990 emissions). All remaining parties (developing countries) are to have no such obligation, but instead generally worded sustainability aims.

The main reason for *opposition* to the idea is that the actual and projected growth in emissions in the unbound group exceeds that of the bound group and renders the effort in the bound group ineffective. The main reason for its *defence* is that without binding emission caps – without compliance mandated by law – each country's emission-control policy will vary unpredictably.

The opposing sides emphasise the 'environmental integrity' of their respective positions. Critics of the Protocol are eager for an alternative because the entrenched negotiating positions have stalled progress.[17] Their critique is difficult to appreciate. For if the Protocol were allowed to evolve over time, incrementally enlarging the group of countries with legally binding emission caps, it could tackle climate change as well as any other arrangement could. Instead, the UNFCCC parties agreed at their conference (COP) in Durban in 2011 to create a new agreement for the post-2020 period outside the framework of the Kyoto Protocol.[18] At this stage it is not known what that agreement might look like.

Article 3 of the Protocol outlines a procedure for the creation of commitment periods additional to the first.[19] The Article provides that party negotiations on a subsequent

---

17 See, e.g., E. Diringer, 'Letting Go of Kyoto', *Nature* 479, 2011, p. 292.
18 UNFCCC, *Decision 2/CP.17, Outcome of the Work of the Ad Hoc Working Group on Long-Term Cooperative Action under the Convention*, 2011.
19 *Kyoto Protocol to the United Nations Framework Convention on Climate Change*, opened for signature 11 December 1997, 2303 UNTS 148 (entered into force 16 February 2005) ('Kyoto Protocol'), Art. 3(9).

commitment period are to be initiated by the CMP (the Protocol's equivalent of the COP) at least seven years before the end of the existing period. As the Protocol went into force in 2005, negotiations on a second commitment period had to be initiated almost immediately.[20] A second commitment period was agreed to at the Durban COP/CMP in 2011.[21]

The Kyoto Protocol is also famous for creating international arrangements designed to help states to more easily meet their domestic emission-reduction obligations. These are the so-called 'flexible mechanisms'. The legal structures put in place to facilitate the mechanisms are some of the most complex of the climate change regime.

The mechanisms create four families of tradable emission allowances: AAUs, ERUs, RMUs, and CERs. Each emission allowance has the same value: 1 ton of CO_2 eq. The four families are distinguished by the rules that govern their creation, use, and lifespan: CERs are created by the Clean Development Mechanism (CDM) under Article 12 of the Protocol (see below); an AAU is the unit that denominates an Annex I party's 'assigned amount' for a commitment period (e.g. Australia's assigned amount of 2,957.6 Mt CO_2 eq. for 2008–2012 equates to about 3 billion AAUs); ERUs are created by the Joint Implementation scheme outlined in Article 6 of the Protocol. The land-use, land-use change, and forestry (LULUCF) sector of an Annex I country, by sequestering carbon, can generate ERUs.

Together, these tradable permits are the currency of the Kyoto Protocol's economy. In a jurisdiction where all GHG emissions are accounted for and controlled, any emission must be backed by a permit. Where a country has excess permits (e.g. AAUs) it may sell them. Where it has excess emissions – 'excess' in both cases being defined relative to a country's commit-ment-period ceiling – it must buy permits. This trading market is not limited to Annex I countries, as CERs are generated exclusively in developing parties for sale to developed parties (as explained below). Thus the Protocol's market is a global one albeit still poorly developed.[22]

Key mechanisms and institutions of the climate change regime

Reporting and verification

Regulation of communication about national actions might not sound like a very exciting area of international law, yet it is a precondition of international collaboration at every higher policy level.

By the fifth COP, in 1999, the UNFCCC parties had agreed to detailed guidelines on reporting.[23] Reporting under the Convention revolves around the following elements, which are compulsory for Annex I parties:

20 See Kyoto Protocol, Ad Hoc Working Group on Further Commitments for Annex I Parties under the Kyoto Protocol (AWG-KP). Online. Available HTTP: <http://unfccc.int/bodies/body/6409.php> (accessed 2 May 2012).
21 Kyoto Protocol, *Decision 1/CMP.7, Outcome of the Work of the Ad Hoc Working Group on Further Commitments for Annex I Parties under the Kyoto Protocol at Its Sixteenth Session*, 2011.
22 The United States, not being a Protocol party, cannot take part.
23 Most of the rules on the regulation of state reporting and compliance under the international regime for climate change are to be found in COP and CMP decisions rather than in the treaties themselves. See UNFCCC, *Decision 1/CP.5, Guidelines for the Preparation of National Communications by Parties Included in Annex I to the Convention, Part II: UNFCCC Reporting Guidelines on National Communications* (1999), and UNFCCC, *Guidelines on Reporting and Review* (1999).

(i) *national communications* by state parties containing information on national GHG emissions, climate-related policies and measures, GHG-emission projections, financial assistance and technology transfer to non-Annex I states, and actions on raising public awareness about climate change;

(ii) *national GHG inventories*, detailing 'activity data', 'emission factors', and the methodologies used to estimate national emissions. Several decisions and guidance documents elaborate this obligation.[24]

National communications are submitted by Annex I parties every four to five years. They are prepared based on agreed reporting guidelines.[25] They are reviewed by Expert Review Teams (ERTs).[26] National GHG inventories are reported annually, on the basis of IPCC methodologies.[27] The inventories are also reviewed by ERTs.[28]

The whole process of national communications and inventories had to be more or less duplicated when the Kyoto Protocol came into effect. The Protocol intensifies the reporting demands on Annex I parties. Under Article 5 of the Protocol, parties are required to establish 'national systems' that facilitate estimation of anthropogenic emissions;[29] and pursuant to Article 7 they must report their emissions regularly.[30] The additional provisions that form part of the Protocol's reporting system are necessary to determine state compliance during a commitment period including compliance with the emission cap.

At Article 8(3), the Protocol calls on ERTs to carry out 'a thorough and comprehensive technical assessment of all aspects' of a state's national system, including its emission inventory. An ERT has the power to 'adjust'[31] a state's reported inventory if it does not agree with the state's accounting of its emissions. This would happen where, for example, the ERT has become aware of an incompleteness in the inventory which the state is refusing to acknowledge. The ERT places itself above the state under review, assuming the authority to correct the quantity of emissions the state is reporting.[32]

---

24 Intergovernmental Panel on Climate Change, *Good Practice Guidance and Uncertainty Management in National Greenhouse Gas Inventories*, Geneva: IPCC, 2000; Intergovernmental Panel on Climate Change, *Revised 1996 IPCC Guidelines for National Greenhouse Gas Inventories*, Geneva: IPCC, 1996; UNFCCC, *Decision 17/CP.8, Guidelines for the Preparation of National Communications from Parties Not Included in Annex I to the Convention*, 2003; UNFCCC, *Decision 18/CP.8, Guidelines for the Preparation of National Communications by Parties Included in Annex I to the Convention, Part I: UNFCCC Reporting Guidelines on Annual Inventories*, 2002; and UNFCCC, *Decision 19/CP.8, UNFCCC Guidelines for the Technical Review of Greenhouse Gas Inventories from Parties Included in Annex I to the Convention*, 2002.

25 UNFCCC, *Decision 4/CP.5*.

26 UNFCCC, *Decision 2/CP.1, Review of First Communications from the Parties Included in Annex I to the Convention*, 1995.

27 UNFCCC, *Decision 18/CP.8*.

28 UNFCCC, *Decision 19/CP.8*.

29 Kyoto Protocol, Art. 5.1. See also Kyoto Protocol, *Decision 19/CMP.1, Guidelines for National Systems under Article 5, Paragraph 1 of the Kyoto Protocol* (30 March 2006).

30 Kyoto Protocol, *Decision 15/CMP.1, Guidelines for the Preparation of the Information Required under Article 7 of the Kyoto Protocol* (30 March 2006).

31 Kyoto Protocol, Art. 5.2. See also Kyoto Protocol, *Decision 20/CMP.1, Good Practice Guidance and Adjustments under Article 5, Paragraph 2 of the Kyoto Protocol* (30 March 2006).

32 For more on the ERT process, see A. Zahar, 'Verifying Greenhouse Gas Emissions of Annex I Parties: Methods We Have and Methods We Want', *Climate Law* 1(3), 2010, 409.

In a 2007 synthesis report based on the fourth national communications of 39 Annex I countries, the UNFCCC Secretariat noted that the parties had generally implemented varied portfolios of policies and measures to mitigate GHG emissions. These included emission-pricing mechanisms (e.g. carbon taxes and, in the energy industries, tradable emission allowances); barrier-reduction policies aimed at overcoming financial and market barriers to the deployment of existing climate-friendly technologies (e.g. feed-in tariffs and green certificates for energy from renewables); energy- and performance-efficiency measures (including regulatory measures and voluntary sectoral commitments for fuel economy in cars); and regulations affecting product and building standards in the residential and commercial sectors.[33]

The synthesis report also found that Annex I parties were increasingly preferring harder (economic and regulatory) instruments over softer (voluntary) instruments to elicit emission reductions. Innovative forms of regulation, in particular tradable certificate systems, were growing more quickly and were more widely in use by 2007 than was the case in years covered by earlier national communications, with the European Union's Emission Trading Scheme standing out for its scale.[34] Parties were increasing their use of 'multilevel governance' – action across several levels of government (local to national) as well as horizontally across governmental departments.[35]

The report also noted shortcomings in the national communications. Annex I countries were not reporting on all the elements of their response to climate change, and not all parties had tried to estimate the actual effects of their policies and measures, in particular on GHG mitigation.[36] By any measure, though, barely a decade into the UNFCCC's life, a sophisticated system of reporting relevant to climate governance had emerged among Annex I states, at a high level of compliance.

Compliance system (Kyoto Protocol)

The Kyoto Protocol's compliance system is adumbrated in Article 18 of the treaty and fleshed out in CMP decisions. It applies only to the Protocol's Annex I parties.[37] The presence of a 'compliance' system in the Protocol is a measure of the strong 'legal force' that the contracting parties wished to impart through the instrument.

The Kyoto Protocol's Compliance Committee became operational in 2006.[38] It is an independent body, whose members and alternate members are sworn to impartiality and conscientiousness in decision-making.[39] The Committee has two branches: the Facilitative Branch and the Enforcement Branch. The mandate of the Facilitative Branch is to provide advice and facilitation to states in implementing the Protocol and to 'promote' compliance by parties with emission limitation commitments. To remedy situations, the Branch is empowered to

---

33 UNFCCC Secretariat, *Compilation and Synthesis Executive Summary*, p. 6.
34 Ibid., p. 7.
35 Ibid., p. 8.
36 Ibid., p. 12.
37 Kyoto Protocol, *Decision 27/CMP.1, Procedures and Mechanisms Relating to Compliance under the Kyoto Protocol* (30 March 2006).
38 Compliance Committee (Kyoto Protocol), *Report on the First Meeting* (29 May 2006).
39 The Kyoto compliance system has been analysed from many angles in J. Brunnée, M. Doelle and L. Rajamani (eds) *Promoting Compliance in an Evolving Climate Regime*, Cambridge: Cambridge University Press, 2011.

provide advice to a state regarding implementation, as well as facilitate financial and technical assistance.[40]

The Enforcement Branch is of quite a different character. It is made up of legal experts. Questions that the Enforcement Branch is limited to dealing with are laid down in the CMP decision containing the Compliance Committee's procedures and mechanisms. The Enforcement Branch is responsible for determining whether an Annex I party is in compliance with:

(a) its quantified emission limitation or reduction commitment [i.e. its emission cap] under Article 3, paragraph 1, of the Protocol;
(b) the methodological and reporting requirements under Article 5, paragraphs 1 and 2, and Article 7, paragraphs 1 and 4, of the Protocol; and
(c) the eligibility requirements under Articles 6 [Joint Implementation], 12 [Clean Development Mechanism] and 17 [international emissions trading] of the Protocol.[41]

In the case of a finding of non-compliance, the Enforcement Branch has to apply 'consequences'. The Branch has no discretion in the application of the consequences at its disposal. In line with its mandate, it must apply the consequences tied to the aforementioned three possible kinds of non-compliance.[42]

The most interesting 'consequence' relates to the situation where a party has failed to comply with its emission cap. In such a case, the Enforcement Branch must deduct 1.3 times the excess tons of CO_2 eq. from the party's assigned amount for the *next* commitment period – imposing, in effect, a penalty of 30 per cent for every ton of excess emissions. A country in non-compliance with its 2008–2012 target has 100 days after the ERT's review of its final emission inventory to make up any shortfall (that is, to buy international credits, in the form of AAUs, CERs, etc.). Thus, this most interesting of issues could not be raised before the Enforcement Branch until at least a year after the end of the first commitment period in 2012. Until then, the power must remain untested.

The initiating action for both branches of the Compliance Committee is a 'question of implementation' raised by an ERT. The Bureau of the Compliance Committee decides whether to assign a question of implementation to the Facilitative Branch or the Enforcement Branch. The Facilitative Branch's powers have remained somewhat theoretical, as the Bureau has never received a question of implementation appropriate for the Facilitative Branch.[43] All questions of implementation to date have been directed to the Enforcement Branch.

In the international climate regime, the Enforcement Branch of the Kyoto Protocol's Compliance Committee is most like a court, in that it hears evidence, follows rules of procedure, is sensitive to due process, and speaks through written decisions. The country under scrutiny by the Enforcement Branch may make written submissions and request a hearing to

---

40 UNFCCC, An Introduction to the Kyoto Protocol Compliance Mechanism. Online. Available HTTP: <http://unfccc.int/kyoto_protocol/compliance/items/3024.php> (accessed 2 May 2012).
41 Kyoto Protocol, *Decision 27/CMP.1*, at Part V(4).
42 Ibid., section XV.
43 The CMP is considering ways to improve the usefulness of the Facilitative Branch; see Compliance Committee (Kyoto Protocol), *Annual Report of the Compliance Committee to the Conference of the Parties Serving as the Meeting of the Parties to the Kyoto Protocol* (3 November 2011), para. 48ff.

present its views. The Branch has the power to call upon expert advice to supplement evidence it has received from the ERT and the state party.[44]

Where non-compliance is found, the Enforcement Branch must make a public declaration of state non-compliance, and must also make public the 'consequences' it has applied. The CMP plenary of the parties can receive an 'appeal' from a state party dissatisfied with a decision of the Enforcement Branch.[45] However, these quasi-appeals are limited to questioning a decision of the Enforcement Branch which relates to emission targets about which the state concerned claims to have been denied due process.[46] If the CMP considers that the state has indeed been treated unfairly, it does not have the authority to decide the question of implementation itself; it must refer it back to the Enforcement Branch.[47]

Oberthür and Lefeber argue that this unusual limitation on the power of states, along with the fact that the CMP is not required to confirm the decisions of either branch of the Compliance Committee on questions of implementation, 'shield[s] the quasi-judicial decision-making of the Committee from political interference'.[48]

Clean Development Mechanism (Kyoto Protocol)

Article 12 of the Kyoto Protocol establishes the CDM as a mechanism for *non*-Annex I parties to achieve sustainable development. In the process, the mechanism assists *Annex I* parties to comply with their emission reduction commitments under the Protocol.[49]

Article 12 creates an Executive Board under the authority of the CMP to supervise the CDM.[50] The Board is effectively the market regulator for CDM offsets. It delegates regulatory functions to other actors, who consequently play quasi-regulatory roles.[51] For example, private 'operational entities' certify emission reductions realised by CDM projects. Here, the Kyoto Protocol differs from the traditional state-centric model of international law. It makes public and private entities subject to the CDM, establishing international bodies that

---

44 See M. Doelle, 'Early Experience with the Kyoto Compliance System: Possible Lessons for MEA Compliance System Design', *Climate Law* 1(2), 2010, 237.

45 S. Oberthür and R. Lefeber, 'Holding Countries to Account: The Kyoto Protocol's Compliance System Revisited after Four Years of Experience', *Climate Law* 1(1), 2010, 133, pp. 150–1.

46 Kyoto Protocol, *Decision 27/CMP.1*, section XI.

47 Ibid., sections XI.3 and XI.4.

48 Oberthür and Lefeber, op. cit., p. 140.

49 The history of the CDM's emergence in the international negotiations has been discussed by several authors. See S. Mathy, J-C. Hourcade and C. de Gouvello, 'Clean Development Mechanism: Leverage for Development?', *Climate Policy* 1, 2001, 251; A. Michaelowa, 'Creating the Foundations for Host Country Participation in the CDM: Experiences and Challenges in CDM Capacity Building', in F. Yamin (ed.) *Climate Change and Carbon Markets – a Handbook of Emission Reduction Mechanisms*, London: Earthscan, 2005; J. Ellisa, H. Winkler, J. Corfee-Morlot and F. Gagnon-Lebrun, 'CDM: Taking Stock and Looking Forward', *Energy Policy* 35(1), 2007, 15; and the articles collected in D. Freestone and C. Streck (eds) *Legal Aspects of Implementing the Kyoto Protocol Mechanisms: Making Kyoto Work*, Oxford: Oxford University Press, 2005, especially D. Freestone, 'The UN Framework Convention on Climate Change, the Kyoto Protocol, and the Kyoto Mechanisms', pp. 3–24.

50 The supervision function is detailed in Kyoto Protocol, *Decision 3/CMP.1, Modalities and Procedures for a Clean Development Mechanism as Defined in Article 12 of the Kyoto Protocol* (30 March 2006), paras 2–4.

51 C. Streck and J. Lin, 'Mobilising Finance for Climate Change Mitigation: Private Sector Involvement in International Carbon Finance Mechanisms', *Melbourne Journal of International Law* 10(1), 2009, 70, p. 73.

administer the Kyoto Protocol mechanisms directly, and entering into relationships with private entities participating in these mechanisms.[52] The relationship between treaty-based international institutions (the CMP, the CDM Executive Board) and a private entity incorporated under state domestic law raises unusual legal issues. In fact, the CDM is a thicket of transnational and what might be called 'trans-scalar' (private-to-international) legal relationships. Private or public project developers create the emission reductions; private or public entities certify them; private or public or international organisations or state sovereigns purchase the emission reduction certificates; public and international bodies oversee their accounting and cancellation; and so on (see Table 20.4.)

The Protocol's Article 12 calls on the CMP to 'elaborate modalities and procedures with the objective of ensuring transparency, efficiency and accountability through independent auditing and verification of [CDM] project activities'.[53] To understand why this is necessary, we need to consider the CDM's logic.

The CDM is a system for the creation of emission *offsets*. This is a key point about the CDM: because it is an offset system, it does not lead to overall emission reductions. It operates to cancel out 'excess' emissions in countries with emission caps. In general, to create an offset, all of the following conditions must be met.

There must be:

(i) a proposed project, which
(ii) itself would not have been realised but for the expected proceeds from the sale of the offsets, and which
(iii) acts as a sink for, or destroys, GHGs, or creates a product or service that substitutes itself for (i.e. displaces) an existing or planned and comparatively more GHG-intensive product or service, and
(iv) the quantity of GHGs removed or avoided through the project is reasonably quantifiable.

The CDM's logic is thus difficult!

The CDM-produced emission reduction is parcelled up into a tradable commodity (CERs) and sold to an Annex I government, or to an industry based in an Annex I country, as an emission allowance.

Against this basic formulation of the CDM's logic we are better able to appreciate the insistence of the Kyoto Protocol that CDM emission reductions are to deliver 'real, measurable, and long-term benefits related to the mitigation of climate change' which 'are additional to any that would occur in the absence of the certified project activity'.[54] We also appreciate the need for a system that verifies and monitors CDM projects. The greater the divergence between the notional 'baseline' (i.e. business as usual) and the emission trajectory realised through the implementation of the CDM project, the greater the value of the project (because the larger the number of CERs issued). The baseline is a counterfactual scenario which by definition cannot be known with certainty; it will always be an estimate. If the baseline is wrongly set (if it has a large margin of error), not only is a CER's value questionable, the

---

52 Ibid., p. 79.
53 Kyoto Protocol, Art. 12(7).
54 Ibid., Art. 12(5).

CDM's environmental integrity suffers. The CDM requires strong regulation to maintain its credibility from an environmental point of view as an offset provider.[55]

Table 20.4 Simplified CDM procedure, from project proposal to CER issuance[56]

Project proposal
The project's compliance with CDM rules is assessed on the basis of the Project Design Document (PDD). The project developer prepares the PDD making use of an approved emission baseline-and-monitoring methodology. Non-CDM finance is usually necessary to cover the up-front costs of project development and initial implementation.
↓

Validation
Validation is the independent assessment of the project's compliance with CDM rules by a Designated Operational Entity (DOE). The DOE is an independent auditor (a private-sector consultant) approved by the CDM Executive Board.
↓

Application for registration
If the DOE determines that the requirements for a CDM project have been met, the DOE, on behalf of the project developer, requests the Executive Board to register the project.
↓

Registration
Registration constitutes formal approval of a CDM project. It is a prerequisite for the verification/certification of the project and issuance of CERs.
↓

Monitoring (ongoing)
The project developer is responsible for monitoring actual emissions of the project (or, where there are no emissions, monitoring the project output which displaces emissions elsewhere), in accordance with the monitoring requirements of the applicable CDM methodology (the 'monitoring plan').
↓

Verification and certification
After a certain period of operation of the project, a DOE verifies that emission reductions have taken place in the amount claimed in the monitoring plan. The verification report is followed by certification, which is the DOE's assurance to the CDM Executive Board that the emission reductions have been verified.
↓

CER issuance
The DOE submits its verification report and certification to the Executive Board with a request for the issuance of CERs. In the normal course of events, the Board will issue CERs on the basis of the DOE's submission. By January 2012, the Board had registered 3,771 projects and issued 826.3 million CERs.[57]
↓

(Continued overleaf)

55 See E. Meijer and J. Werksman, 'Keeping It Clean – Safeguarding the Environmental Integrity of the Clean Development Mechanism', in D. Freestone and C. Streck (eds) *Legal Aspects of Implementing the Kyoto Protocol Mechanisms: Making Kyoto Work*, Oxford: Oxford University Press, 2005, pp. 191–211.
56 See also Kyoto Protocol, *Decision 3/CMP.1*, and Clean Development Mechanism (Kyoto Protocol), *CDM Methodology Booklet*, UNFCCC, 2010, p. 11. For a diagram of the process, see UNFCCC, CDM Project Cycle. Online. Available HTTP: <http://cdm.unfccc.int/Projects/diagram.html> (accessed 2 May 2012).
57 UNFCCC, CDM Home. Online. Available HTTP: <http://cdm.unfccc.int/> (accessed 2 May 2012).

Table 20.4 Continued

Adaptation Fund tax (2%)

Article 12(8) of the Kyoto Protocol provides that proceeds from CDM projects are to be used 'to assist developing country Parties that are particularly vulnerable to the adverse effects of climate change to meet the costs of adaptation'. On this basis, two per cent of CERs issued to a project are redirected to the Protocol's Adaptation Fund.[58]
↓

CER sale

When the CERs are received by the project developer, they are sold in the compliance or voluntary markets. The proceeds fund the ongoing operation of the project or are used to pay back the investor who covered the project's up-front operating costs.

Reducing emissions from deforestation (UNFCCC)

Forests have played a relatively minor role in the international climate change regime to date. The UNFCCC, at Article 4(1)(d), contains only a very general commitment by all parties to the sustainable management, conservation, and enhancement of forests – following which the subject is not taken up again in the treaty text. This is not because the value of forests in climate control is questioned – on the contrary, it is widely appreciated that in sequestering carbon while standing, or releasing carbon dioxide when felled, forests and deforestation have a major impact on climate change. The reason why forest-based mitigation has been very nearly excluded from the international regime has to do with the sheer practical difficulties involved, at every level, in any global effort to protect or augment the world's forests. In this section we focus on efforts now being made, within the framework of the UNFCCC, to agree to a scheme for the reduction of emissions from deforestation and forest degradation in developing countries – the scheme known as REDD.[59]

Assuming that REDD is successfully established, it will, like the CDM, raise money from Annex I investors to purchase emission reductions in developing countries. With REDD, the reductions will be created primarily by deforestation and degradation prevention projects established in developing countries. There is potential for REDD to go even further than anti-deforestation and anti-degradation, potentially generating credits from forest conservation and forest-enhancement activities. This more ambitious form of REDD is known as REDD-plus.[60]

As discussed in the CDM section of this chapter, the generation of emission reductions presupposes proof of two emission trajectories: a counterfactual trajectory which *would have* materialised in the normal course of events (in the absence of the project), and an emission trajectory that factors in the operation of the project. The CDM/REDD logic is the same in this respect. Where REDD differs from the CDM is in its exclusive focus on forests. Also, it is ideologically inclined to conceive of a country's forests holistically, as a single entity. The

---

58 Kyoto Protocol, *Decision 3/CMP.1*, para. 66(a). In June 2011, the share of proceeds from CDM project activities for the Adaptation Fund stood at around US$13 million; see UNFCCC, *Share of Proceeds from the Clean Development Mechanism Project Activities for the Adaptation Fund*. Online. Available HTTP: <http://cdm.unfccc.int/Issuance/SOPByProjectsTable.html> (accessed 9 May 2012).

59 More discussion of these matters will be found in Chapter 39 of this volume by Rowena Maguire.

60 For simplicity, I employ the term REDD to mean both.

CDM, by contrast, has no necessary holistic outlook, operating through a variety of usually piecemeal, unrelated projects, very few of which (less than 1 per cent[61]) are forestry projects.

In the final analysis, what REDD-simpliciter would do is pay people to leave forests alone. Under REDD-plus, it would pay people to look after forests and improve them. Most of the money would ultimately come from Annex I governments, although much of the initial investment would probably come from non-government sources, aiming to create the REDD credits and then sell them on to Annex I governments.

The development of a REDD mechanism was first endorsed by the UNFCCC parties at their conference in Bali in 2007. The task was incorporated into a broad, initially two-year, negotiating track on long-term cooperative action (LCA) outlined in the Bali Action Plan (BAP).[62] The BAP urged parties in the LCA negotiations to consider 'Policy approaches and positive incentives on issues relating to reducing emissions from deforestation and forest degradation in developing countries' (basic REDD), as well as conservation, sustainable management of forests, and enhancement of forest-carbon stocks (REDD-plus).[63] A second decision at Bali gave parties the green light to proceed with REDD-related actions of their own, voluntarily.[64] This decision also tasked the UNFCCC's Subsidiary Body for Scientific and Technological Advice (SBSTA) to commence a programme of work on such methodological issues as the assessment of change in forest cover and associated carbon stocks, methods for setting reference emissions levels (baselines), and methods for demonstrating reduction in emissions from deforestation, as well as reduction in emissions from forest degradation, and so on.[65] Thus, in a kind of pincer movement against the problem, the parties were to find their own way on the ground while the SBSTA went about building the terminological and technical foundations for a universal, centralised system.

The next landmark decision of the UNFCCC parties on REDD was taken at the Cancun COP in 2010.[66] The decision calls on developing parties wanting to participate in the scheme to implement a national action plan, a 'national forest reference emission level', a 'transparent' national system for the monitoring and reporting of REDD activities, and an information system on how several 'safeguards' itemised in the decision would be addressed and adhered to throughout the implementation of REDD activities. These safeguards include respect for the knowledge and rights of indigenous people and ensuring their effective participation.[67] As land tenure issues are central to any scheme that seeks to distribute benefits to people for the protection or improvement of land, the Cancun decision calls on developing countries to clarify the legal status of forest land destined for REDD projects.[68]

In its multilateral manifestation, REDD will be implemented in phases, beginning with the development of national action plans, progressing through capacity-building by means of

---

61 Clean Development Mechanism (Kyoto Protocol), Distribution of Registered Project Activities by Scope. Online. Available HTTP: <http://cdm.unfccc.int/Statistics/Registration/RegisteredProjBy ScopePieChart.html> (accessed 2 May 2012).

62 UNFCCC, *Decision 1/CP.13, Bali Action Plan* (2007), para. 1.

63 Ibid., para. 1(b)(iii).

64 UNFCCC, *Decision 2/CP.13, Reducing Emissions from Deforestation in Developing Countries: Approaches to Stimulate Action* (2007), paras 3–4.

65 Ibid., para. 7(a).

66 UNFCCC, *Decision 1/CP.16, The Cancun Agreements: Outcome of the Work of the Ad Hoc Working Group on Long-Term Cooperative Action under the Convention* (2010), paras 68–79.

67 Ibid., para. 71 and Appendix I.

68 Ibid., para. 72.

demonstration activities, and evolving into broader country-based actions that are measured, reported, and verified.[69] Funding for the early phases of REDD deployment is being sought through bilateral and multilateral channels, as well as private investors, while the financing of the later phases has yet to be worked out.[70] Administratively, REDD is a much larger, riskier, and politically invasive programme than the CDM. 'A future REDD regime should operate at the national level in order to reduce the risk of within-country leakage.'[71] Forests must be protected as wholes, and, for this, the power of the state must be enlisted.[72]

If REDD is realised in its ideal form, it might become a close equivalent of an international convention on forests. Savaresi writes that 'REDD may still present a triple-win solution for climate change, sustainable development, and biodiversity conservation.'[73] It is as yet too early to know whether the regime for REDD will succeed in becoming fully established, or, if it does succeed, what its reputation will be for environmental integrity. Moreover, REDD's success (like the CDM's) depends upon state emission caps and a healthy carbon market. Because 'market-based approaches only work in the context of a constrained system',[74] because no obligatory limits on global emissions have ever been agreed to, and because after 2012 fewer Annex I countries will have obligatory emission caps under the Kyoto Protocol, the carbon market could weaken with time, causing the price of credits to fall and investment in carbon reduction projects and grand schemes like REDD to fall with it.[75]

Finance and technology transfer

This section discusses the climate regime's regulation of the transfer of finance and technology from developed to developing countries in the interests of climate change mitigation and adaptation. Much of the transfer in wealth and knowledge that occurs under this heading is aimed at building up resident expertise in developing countries (capacity-building[76]) and nudging economic development in the direction of greater sustainability (technological leap-frogging). In the context of climate change, aiding sustainability means helping developing countries to cope with the expected climate impacts better than they would have otherwise, that is, with greater 'resilience' and less human suffering, while also *growing their economies*.

Raising money internationally, moving it around the world to wherever it is needed most, in an orderly, fair, and accountable manner, and spending it to procure the desired results of climate change mitigation or adaptation, subject to measurement, reporting, and verification,

---

69 Ibid., para. 73.
70 Ibid., para. 77.
71 C. Parker, A. Mitchell, M. Trivedi and N. Mardas, *Little REDD Book: A Guide to Governmental and Non-Governmental Proposals for Reducing Emissions from Deforestation and Degradation*, Oxford: Global Canopy Programme, 2008, p. 45.
72 See also C. Streck and J. Lin, op. cit., p. 97. See also N.R. Virgilio, S. Marshall, O. Zerbock and C. Holmes, *Reducing Emissions from Deforestation and Degradation (REDD): A Casebook of on-the-ground Experience*, Arlington, VA: The Nature Conservancy, 2010, p. 6.
73 A. Savaresi, 'Forests, Economics, and Climate Change', *Climate Law* 2(3), 2011, 439, p. 446.
74 International Institute for Sustainable Development, 'SB 34 and AWG Highlights: Monday, 13 June 2011', *Earth Negotiations Bulletin* 12 (509), 2011, 1, p. 1.
75 As early as 2010 there was evidence that the global carbon market was flagging. See World Bank, *State and Trends of the Carbon Market 2010*, Washington DC: World Bank, 2011, p. 9.
76 On the UNFCCC's foundational definition of capacity-building, see UNFCCC, *Decision 2/CP.7, Capacity Building in Developing Countries (Non-Annex I Parties)* (21 January 2002); and UNFCCC, *Decision 1/CP.16*, para. 130.

are actions that must be meticulously planned, regulated, and overseen, on a plane that is above that of domestic law, yet engages with it. The money must be able to unlock ideas, know-how, and concrete applications and not trample on human rights or create new threats to society or the environment.

The CDM is itself a mechanism for finance and technology transfer.[77] While it does not have a technology transfer mandate, it contributes to technology transfer by financing emission reduction projects using technologies currently unavailable in host countries.[78] Yet, the CDM's focus is on mitigation rather than adaptation, and its projects have been concentrated in countries where offsets can be most easily, safely, and cheaply produced, not necessarily where finance and technology are needed most. Thus the CDM's vision is limited.

Article 4(3) of the UNFCCC calls on developed countries, and in particular Annex II countries, to assist developing countries through finance and technology transfer (see Table 20.2). It further provides, at 4(4), that the Annex I parties are to assist developing-country parties 'that are particularly vulnerable to the adverse effects of climate change in meeting costs of adaptation' (effects like flood, drought, and desertification). Following this, Article 4(5) states that:

> The developed country Parties . . . shall take all practicable steps to promote, facilitate and finance, as appropriate, the transfer of, or access to, environmentally sound technologies and know-how to other Parties, particularly developing country Parties . . . In this process, the developed country Parties shall support the development and enhancement of endogenous capacities and technologies of developing country Parties.

This is further developed in Article 4(7), which additionally contains an unambiguously stated *quid pro quo*: unless finance and technology can be made to flow from the highly privileged states to the weak and most vulnerable, implementation of other features of the UNFCCC's climate change regime will seize up.

In addition to the above, the UNFCCC, in Articles 11 and 21(3), provides that financial transfers, including funds to enable the transfer of technology, are to be administered by a 'financial mechanism' accountable to the COP. There is no detail in the Convention about how the mechanism would work. The Global Environment Facility (GEF),[79] which was already in existence at the time the UNFCCC was opened for signature, was restructured to play a role under the Convention's financial mechanism.

As to technology transfer in particular, the Convention, at Article 4(1)(h), calls on all parties to 'Promote and cooperate in the full, open and prompt exchange of relevant scientific, technological, technical, socio-economic and legal information related to the climate system and climate change'. The Convention's SBSTA was given the task, among others, of

---

77 The UNFCCC has a web page on the subject: UNFCCC, The *CDM and Technology Transfer*. Online. Available HTTP: <http://cdm.unfccc.int/about/CDM_TT/index.html> (accessed 2 May 2012).
78 UNFCCC, *The Contribution of the Clean Development Mechanism under the Kyoto Protocol to Technology Transfer*, UNFCCC, 2010.
79 On the GEF, see Global Environment Facility, 'What Is the GEF?'. Online. Available HTTP: <http://www.thegef.org/gef/whatisgef> (accessed 2 May 2012); C. Streck, 'The Global Environment Facility – a Role Model for International Governance?', *Global Environmental Politics* 1(2), 2001, 71.

advising the COP 'on the ways and means of promoting development and/or transferring' the relevant technologies to non-Annex I countries.[80]

The legal obligations laid out in the Convention were extended somewhat by the Kyoto Protocol's Articles 10(c) and 11(2)(b). However, little progress was made in these matters prior to the Bali COP in 2007. The Bali Action Plan prioritised:

> Enhanced national/international action on mitigation of climate change, including, *inter alia*, consideration of: . . . (ii) Nationally appropriate mitigation actions by developing country Parties in the context of sustainable development, supported and enabled by technology, financing and capacity-building, in a measurable, reportable and verifiable manner.[81]

The BAP developed the call for 'enhanced action' in finance and technology transfer in relative detail.[82] While this was an advance on the UNFCCC and the text of the Kyoto Protocol, in relation to the central issue of how technological and financial support for developing countries should be generated, governed, and delivered, as well as on technological cooperation, the BAP was still no more than a plan through which subsequent negotiations were to be structured.

At the Copenhagen meeting in December 2009, the parties to the Copenhagen Accord agreed that they would raise money to help poor countries respond to climate change: US$30 billion over the period from 2010 to 2012 (the so-called 'fast-start' finance), rising to US$100 billion *per year* by 2020. It was promised as 'new' money.[83] A year later, at the Cancun COP, the UNFCCC parties reaffirmed the sums promised in the Copenhagen Accord.[84] In exchange for the promise of enhanced financial support, developing countries agreed to implement Nationally Appropriate Mitigation Actions (NAMAs), the effect of which would be a deviation from projected emissions in these countries through to 2020.[85]

The Cancun conference also formalised the existence of two institutions created by the Accord the year before.[86] They are the Green Climate Fund and the Technology Mechanism. The Technology Mechanism is made up of the Technology Executive Committee and the Climate Technology Centre and Network.[87] A large share of the promised international funding is to flow through the Green Climate Fund.[88] The UNFCCC parties have set up a Transitional Committee to develop the operational features of the Fund.[89]

Where will the promised money come from? In December 2009, the UN Secretary-General appointed a High-Level Advisory Group on Climate Change Financing to study potential sources of revenue to meet the Annex I parties' Copenhagen commitments. The

---

80 UNFCCC, Art. 9(2)(c).
81 UNFCCC, *Bali Action Plan*, paras 1(b)(i) and (ii).
82 Ibid., paras 1(d) and 1(e).
83 UNFCCC, *Decision 2/CP.15, Copenhagen Accord* (2009), para. 8 (reiterated in UNFCCC, *Decision 1/CP.16*, paras 95 and 98).
84 UNFCCC, *Decision 1/CP.16*.
85 Ibid., para. 48.
86 See UNFCCC, *Copenhagen Accord*, para. 8 (Copenhagen Green Climate Fund), and para. 11 (Technology Mechanism).
87 UNFCCC, *Decision 1/CP.16*, para. 117.
88 Ibid., para. 100.
89 Ibid., paras 102–12.

Advisory Group concluded that the largest chunk of the promised revenue would have to come from pricing GHG emissions globally:

> Based on a carbon price of US$20–US$25 per ton of CO_2 equivalent, auctions of emission allowances and domestic carbon taxes in developed countries with up to 10 per cent of total revenues allocated for international climate action could potentially mobilize around US$30 billion annually. Without underestimating the difficulties to be resolved, particularly in terms of national sovereignty and incidence on developing countries, approximately US$10 billion annually could be raised from carbon pricing international transportation, assuming no net incidence on developing countries and earmarking between 25 and 50 per cent of total revenues. Up to US$10 billion could be mobilized from other instruments, such as the redeployment of fossil fuel subsidies in developed countries or some form of financial transaction tax, though diverging views will make it difficult to implement this universally.[90]

In the best case, then, the above-listed methods might raise half the annual amount required by 2020 – i.e. US$50 billion out of the US$100 billion per year. The case assumes that cap-and-trade or equivalent systems for raising carbon revenue will soon be established in all major industrialised economies. It requires us to imagine that, for example, the United States will have priced its national emissions by the end of this decade. This is a possibility which, for the moment, seems unlikely.

According to the Advisory Group, the other half of the required amount will have to come from several relatively obscure and speculative sources, as well as from the most obvious of sources: Annex I states' general fiscal revenue (new taxes). About the latter source, the Advisory Group wrote: 'The political acceptability of such sources will depend on national circumstances and on the domestic fiscal environment, which has currently put many developed countries under extreme pressure.'[91]

The sources of finance for the considerable North–South flows promised in Copenhagen and reiterated in Cancun are thus still only a vague and uncertain idea which awaits systematic exploration at the COP level. The Durban COP at the end of 2011 did not make any progress on clarifying longer-term funding sources.

Conclusion: the way the wind blows

The scientific community's verdict on the climate change negotiations is increasingly dismissive. Commenting on the 2011 Durban COP's outcome, Tollefson writes that 'the platform represents an exercise in legalese that does little or nothing to reduce emissions, and defers action for almost a decade.'[92] *Nature*'s editors were even more scathing: 'It takes a certain kind of optimism – or an outbreak of collective Stockholm syndrome – to see the Durban outcome as a significant breakthrough on global warming ... It is clear that the science of climate change and the politics of climate change, which claims

90 M. Zenawi and J. Stoltenberg, *Report of the Secretary-General's High-Level Advisory Group on Climate Change Financing*, Geneva: United Nations, 5 November 2010, pp. 5–6.
91 Ibid., p. 6.
92 J. Tollefson, 'Durban Maps Path to Climate Treaty', *Nature* 480, 2011, p. 299.

to represent it, now inhabit parallel worlds.'[93] One world – the world of politicians and UNFCCC negotiators – is delighted to see a climate change regime still actually in place, hobbling along, making a difference to emissions, however slight. The other world, of climate scientists, sees only the rapidly worsening evidence as measured by their instruments.

Does the history to date of the climate change regime warrant optimism or pessimism about the future? Is it rational to believe that we will 'prevent dangerous anthropogenic interference with the climate system'? One approach to answering this question is to ask how committed we are, realistically, to burning fossil fuels into the future?

Between 1980 and 2007 world primary energy demand,[94] mainly met by fossil fuels, grew by two per cent per year. Under an optimistic scenario in which states take action to *reduce* their dependence on fossil fuel energy, the International Energy Agency (IEA) forecasts continued growth in primary energy demand between 2008 and 2035 at a rate of 1.2 per cent per year, with fossil fuels accounting for more than half of the increase.[95] Under all IEA scenarios, even the most optimistic, fossil fuels remain the dominant energy source in 2035 (the outer year of the projection).[96]

In the most likely IEA case for 2035, oil's share drops to 28 per cent (from 33 per cent in 2008), demand for coal rises through to around 2020 and starts to decline closer to 2035, and demand for natural gas (which has lower carbon emissions per unit of energy) surpasses that of other fossil fuels throughout the period.[97] Under this scenario (which of course must be qualified by our ignorance of many future factors), annual energy-related emissions of GHGs rise from 29 gigatonnes CO_2 eq. in 2008 to 35 gigatonnes in 2035 (a 17 per cent increase).[98] The IEA predicts that 93 per cent of the projected increase in world primary energy demand will be in non-OECD countries.[99] Back in 2000, when the United States was still the world's largest energy user, its energy consumption was twice the size of China's. By 2009, China had overtaken the United States to become the world's largest consumer of energy.[100] China's huge domestic market was, in 2010, underdeveloped, with per capita energy consumption at only one-third of the OECD average.[101] In terms of electricity supply, China is projected to add, in just fifteen years, a generating capacity equivalent to the 2010 installed capacity of the whole of the United States.[102] Most of it will be coal-fired.[103]

Human population growth will continue to outstrip the ability of governments to meet the growing demand for energy, thus maintaining a long tail of unmet energy demand. In 2010, 1.4 billion people (over 20 per cent of the world's population) lacked access to

---

93 Editorial, 'The Mask Slips', *Nature* 480, 2011, p. 292.
94 For the IEA's definition of 'primary energy demand', see International Energy Agency, *World Energy Outlook 2009*, IEA, 2009, p. 670.
95 International Energy Agency, *World Energy Outlook 2010: Executive Summary*, IEA, 2010, pp. 4–5.
96 Ibid., p. 4.
97 Ibid., p. 5.
98 Ibid., p. 11.
99 Ibid., p. 5.
100 Ibid., p. 5.
101 Ibid., p. 5.
102 Ibid., p. 8.
103 A. Petherick, 'Dirty Money', *Nature Climate Change* 2, 2012, p. 73.

electricity.[104] With the population in developing countries expected to grow by many hundreds of millions by 2030, the IEA predicts that, even by that date, 1.2 billion people will still have no access to electricity.[105] For decades ahead, then, there will exist an enormous suppressed demand for energy which gradual increases in wealth will unleash.

Wealth will eventually come to places like Africa. The African population now is mostly poor (the gross national income per capita in sub-Saharan Africa was $1,126 in 2009[106]), poorly governed (many governments in Africa are corrupt and undemocratic),[107] and there are few public services. As a result, the indicators in all areas of life in Africa are miserable:

- child mortality for the continent as a whole during the period from 2005 to 2010 was 82.6 infant deaths per 1,000 live births (compared with 4.1 in Western Europe);[108]
- in sub-Saharan Africa in 2008 life expectancy at birth was only 52 years;[109]
- in the same region in the same year the completion rate for *primary* school was 64 per cent;[110]
- personal security and the rule of law are still a dream for most Africans;[111]
- the development of Africa's agricultural and manufacturing sectors is a 'dismal' twin-failure, according to the International Labour Office;[112]
- persons holding jobs are mostly not occupied in 'decent work' (a technical term): in 2009, 63.7 per cent of those with 'jobs' in Africa's least-developed countries were the working poor (defined by an income not exceeding $1.25 per day);[113]

104 International Energy Agency, *World Energy Outlook 2010*, p. 14. In Kenya and Uganda, for example, only one per cent of the rural households had access to electricity in 2004: S. Karekezi and J. Kimani, 'Have Power Sector Reforms Increased Access to Electricity among the Poor in East Africa?', *Energy for Sustainable Development* 8(4), 2004, p. 10. Having no access to electricity, poor people use LPG where it is affordable, or else fall back on kerosene and charcoal or other biomass; see e.g. G. Bravo, R. Kozulj and R. Landaveri, 'Energy Access in Urban and Peri-Urban Buenos Aires', *Energy for Sustainable Development* 12(4), 2008, 56; S. Karekezi, J. Kimani and O. Onguru, 'Energy Access among the Urban Poor in Kenya', *Energy for Sustainable Development* 12(4), 2008, 38.

105 International Energy Agency, *World Energy Outlook 2010*, p. 14.

106 The World Bank. Online. Available HTTP: <http://data.worldbank.org/region/SSA> (accessed 2 May 2012).

107 According to the Ibrahim Index for 2010, Mauritius was ranked first in governance in Africa with a score of 83/100, Somalia was last with 7.9/100, while about half of all African countries scored below 50 on the scale. Online. Available HTTP: <http://www.moibrahimfoundation.org/en/section/the-ibrahim-index> (accessed 2 May 2012). On corruption in Africa, see also International Labour Office, *Growth, Employment and Decent Work in the Least Developed Countries: Report of the International Labour Office for the Fourth Conference on the Least Developed Countries, Istanbul, 9–13 May 2011*, Geneva: ILO, 2011, pp. 45–6.

108 United Nations, *World Population Prospects: The 2010 Revision*. Online Database. Available HTTP: <http://esa.un.org/unpd/wpp/index.htm> (accessed 9 May 2012).

109 The World Bank. Online. Available HTTP: <http://data.worldbank.org/region/SSA> (accessed 2 May 2012).

110 Ibid.

111 See the Safety and Rule of Law scores in the Ibrahim Index for 2010, according to which 21 of the 53 African countries score below 50 on a scale to 100. Online. Available HTTP: <http://www.moibrahimfoundation.org/en/section/the-ibrahim-index> (accessed 2 May 2012).

112 International Labour Office, *Growth, Employment and Decent Work*, pp. 30–31.

113 Ibid., p. 8.

- only 19.1 per cent of 'employed' persons in those countries were classed by the International Labour Office as employers or wage-and-salary workers, with the remainder (80.9 per cent) falling into the categories of own-account workers and unpaid family workers – that is, vulnerable and low-productivity employment.[114]

Under these conditions, even the simplest environmental problems are not likely to be prioritised or effectively addressed in Africa. The values of the majority of Africa's population are focused on securing improvements to basic services, economic opportunities, and human and political rights – not on the distant and abstract problem of climate change. In 2011, in the uprisings which became known as the Arab Spring, the demands of Arabic-speaking populations in northern Africa were made loud and clear; in essence, they were for jobs and better governance. Mediterranean Africa might be wealthier than the sub-Saharan part (Egypt's GNI per capita in 2009 was $2,070[115] and Tunisia's $3,720[116]), but the north's relative advantage is no cause for contentment in those countries. Their frame of reference is a relatively prosperous and free Europe across the Mediterranean.

Africa's hoped-for transformation into a continent of strong economic growth means *freedom to prosper*. It is a precondition that tells us something about the likely place of environmental values in the transformation.

According to the IEA, whereas a transformation of the global energy system is urgently needed, little is being done to ensure that it happens quickly enough.[117] Non-fossil sources will grow, but all too slowly. Global demand for nuclear power is predicted to increase slightly, with its share rising from 6 per cent in 2008 to 8 per cent in 2035.[118] (This estimate pre-dates the 2011 nuclear disaster in Japan.) The use of renewable energy is forecast to triple in absolute terms by 2035, but this increases its share of primary energy demand only from 7 to 14 per cent.[119] Hydropower (whose infrastructure takes a severe environmental toll) will continue to dominate.[120] This is in contrast with electricity produced from solar photovoltaics, which despite its expected very rapid increase is likely to have a share of only 2 per cent of global energy generation by 2035.[121]

When considering our historical commitment to fossil fuels, and our commitment to continue burning them in steadily increasing quantities well into the future, we may have the experience of a gulf opening up between the reality of our dependence on carbon emissions and the talk of abatement of climate change at international conferences. As of December 2009, the position of most countries officially became one not of preventing global warming, but of avoiding warming in excess of a global average of 2 degrees Celsius above pre-industrial times.[122] As part of the Copenhagen Accord, the world's major economies have

---

114 Ibid., pp. 9, 41.
115 The World Bank. Online. Available HTTP: <http://data.worldbank.org/country/egypt-arab-republic> (accessed 2 May 2012).
116 The World Bank. Online. Available HTTP: <http://data.worldbank.org/country/tunisia> (accessed 2 May 2012).
117 International Energy Agency, *World Energy Outlook 2010*, p. 3.
118 Ibid., p. 5.
119 Ibid., p. 5.
120 Ibid., p. 9.
121 Ibid., p. 9.
122 UNFCCC, *Copenhagen Accord*, para. 2. The two-degree-Celsius target was reaffirmed a year later in a decision of the UNFCCC parties: UNFCCC, *Decision 1/CP.16*, para. 4.

pledged emission reductions for the years following 2012 and up to 2020.[123] Countries are still trying to agree on emission cuts that would put them on a trajectory that keeps warming from exceeding the two-degree ceiling. In the meantime, studies have shown that even if all the pledged cuts were to be fully implemented, the ceiling would still be exceeded.[124] The pledges of the Accord are, in fact, in line with a temperature rise of more than 3.5 degrees.[125]

123 UNFCCC, *Copenhagen Accord*, para. 4. For a compilation of the pledges, see <http://unfccc.int/meetings/cop_15/copenhagen_accord/items/5264.php> (accessed 2 May 2012), and, pursuant to UNFCCC, *Decision 1/CP.16*, para. 36, the revised compilation: Secretariat (UNFCCC), *Compilation of Economy-Wide Emission Reduction Targets to Be Implemented by Parties Included in Annex I to the Convention* (7 June 2011).

124 International Energy Agency, *World Energy Outlook 2010*, p. 3. See also International Energy Agency, 'Prospect of Limiting the Global Increase in Temperature to 2°C Is Getting Bleaker'. Online. Available HTTP: <http://www.iea.org/index_info.asp?id=1959> (accessed 2 May 2012).

125 International Energy Agency, *World Energy Outlook 2010*, p. 11. UNEP's 2011 'emission gap' report notes that for a 'likely' chance to keep temperature increase below two degrees Celsius, the maximum global GHG emission level for 2020 is 44 Gt CO_2 eq. However, according to UNEP, even if the Copenhagen Accord's pledges are met in their most ambitious form, global emissions in 2020 will be 50 Gt – an emission gap of 6 Gt per annum by that stage (with an 11 Gt gap for the low-ambition form); UN Environment Programme, *Bridging the Emissions Gap: A UNEP Synthesis Report*, UNEP, 2011, p. 12.

21

The regulation of space activities and the space environment

Ulrike M. Bohlmann and Steven Freeland

The international legal regulation of outer space has evolved in response to the rapidly expanding activities involving the exploration and use of outer space, beginning at the height of the cold war era. Space law is now an important part of public international law, incorporating significant developments in both space technology and international environmental law. This chapter considers the legal instruments and soft-law principles governing the outer space environment and space activities and explores whether the international law in this area is equipped to deal with the considerable challenges that lie ahead.

Introduction

On 4 October 1957, a Soviet space object, *Sputnik I*, was launched and subsequently orbited the Earth over 1,400 times during the following three-month period. Thus began humankind's adventures in outer space. This milestone heralded the dawn of the space age which, over the ensuing decades, has given rise to the gradual development of fundamental principles that would underpin the legal regulation of the exploration and use of outer space.

The journey of *Sputnik I* highlighted almost immediately some difficult and controversial legal questions, involving previously undetermined concepts. While there had been some (largely) academic scholarship prior to *Sputnik I* regarding the nature and scope of those laws that might be relevant and appropriate in relation to the exploration and use of outer space, these had generally been discussed only at a hypothetical level.[1] However, history changed forever on that day in 1957. All of a sudden, the reality of humankind's aspirations and capabilities with respect to outer space had become apparent, and the world had to react – quickly – to an unprecedented event in an unregulated legal environment, particularly because it was clear that this was just the beginning of what would become an ever increasing

---

1 For a summary of the main academic theories relating to 'space law' in the period prior to the launch of *Sputnik I*, see e.g. F. Lyall and P.B. Larsen, *Space Law: A Treatise*, London: Ashgate, 2009, pp. 3–9.

quest to undertake a wide range of space activities. First and foremost, this necessitated a clarification as to the legal categorisation of outer space for the purposes of international law.[2]

Although the Soviet Union had not sought the permission of any other state to undertake the *Sputnik* mission, there were no significant international protests asserting that this artificial satellite had infringed any country's sovereignty as it circled the Earth. The almost total international (in)action that stemmed from the *Sputnik* mission confirmed that this new frontier for human activity – outer space – did not, from a legal perspective, possess the traditional elements of sovereignty that had already been well established under the binding international law principles that regulated land, sea and air space on Earth. Instead, it was assumed that outer space was to be regarded as an area beyond territorial sovereignty.

Describing the early emergence of this customary international principle in the context of outer space, Judge Manfred Lachs of the International Court of Justice (ICJ) observed in 1969, shortly after the first of the United Nations Space Law Treaties had been finalised, that:

> [t]he first instruments that men sent into outer space traversed the air space of States and circled above them in outer space, yet the launching States sought no permission, nor did the other States protest. This is how the freedom of movement into outer space, and in it, came to be established and recognised as law within a remarkably short period of time.[3]

As such, virtually immediately after humankind had begun its quest to explore and use outer space, a number of foundational principles of the international law of outer space were born – in particular the so-called 'common interest', 'freedom' and 'non-appropriation' principles. These principles were later incorporated into the terms of the United Nations Space Law Treaties,[4] with the result that they also constitute binding conventional rules, codifying what had already amounted to principles of customary international law. In essence, the community of states, including both of the major space-faring states of the time, had accepted that outer space was to be regarded as being similar to a *res communis omnium*.[5]

These fundamental rules underpinning the international law of outer space represent a significant departure from the legal rules relating to air space, which from a legal perspective is categorised as constituting part of the 'territory' of the underlying state. The territorial nature of air space is reflected in the principal air law treaties. For example, reaffirming the principle that had already been acknowledged as early as 1919,[6] the 1944 Convention on International Civil Aviation[7] provides that:

2 For an overview of these and the ensuing developments, see e.g. S. Hobe, 'Historical Background', in S. Hobe, B. Schmidt-Tedd and K-U. Schrogl (eds) *Cologne Commentary on Space Law, Volume I – Outer Space Treaty*, Cologne: Carl Heymanns Verlag, 2009, pp. 4–11, with further references.

3 *North Sea Continental Shelf Cases (Federal Republic of Germany v Denmark and Federal Republic of Germany v The Netherlands)* (Judgment), Dissenting Opinion of Judge Lachs [1969] ICJ Rep 3, 230.

4 See e.g. *Treaty on Principles Governing the Activities of States in the Exploration and Use of Outer Space, including the Moon and Other Celestial Bodies*, opened for signature 27 January 1967, 610 UNTS 205 (entered into force 10 October 1967) ('Outer Space Treaty') Arts I, II.

5 A. Cassese, *International Law*, 2nd edition, Oxford: Oxford University Press, 2005, p. 95.

6 See *Convention on the Regulation of Aerial Navigation*, opened for signature 13 October 1919, 11 LNTS 173 ('Paris Convention').

7 *Convention on International Civil Aviation*, opened for signature 7 December 1944, 15 UNTS 295 (entered into force 4 April 1947) ('Chicago Convention').

[E]very State has complete and exclusive sovereignty over the air space above its territory.[8]

The ICJ has concluded that this characteristic of air space also represents customary international law.[9] As a consequence, civil and commercial aircraft only have certain limited rights to enter the air space of another state,[10] in contrast to the freedom principle relating to outer space.[11]

Thus, even though it would no doubt be relevant in certain respects – indeed, the Outer Space Treaty affirms that activities in space are to be carried on 'in accordance with international law'[12] – the fact that most existing international law at the time had been developed for 'terrestrial' purposes meant that it was not readily or directly applicable in every respect to this new paradigm of human endeavour. Moreover, the non-sovereignty aspect of outer space meant that any then existent national law (which, in any event, did not at that time specifically address space-related issues) would not *prima facie* apply to this frontier, and would not be the appropriate legal basis upon which to establish the initial framework for regulating the conduct of humankind's activities in outer space. It was clear, therefore, that, at the dawn of the development of 'space law', specific international binding rules would be required to address the particular characteristics and legal categorisation of outer space.

In this context, this chapter first sets out the fundamental principles governing the exploration and use of outer space and then proceeds to discuss in more detail the general regulations that apply to the space environment, focusing on specific areas of more pressing concern. On this basis, this chapter concludes that the existing body of international space law does not provide a comprehensive legal framework for the protection of the environment of outer space, nor rigorous environmental standards in relation to the conduct of space activities. It will therefore be necessary to address these concerns in greater detail in order that humankind will be able to expand its endeavours in space.

An overview of the international law of outer space

The negotiations directed towards formalising into conventional form the relevant binding principles relating to the exploration and use of outer space took some time. This was due to a number of reasons, including the unique environment with which it would have to deal, the very significant political and strategic factors at play and the rapid growth of space-related

---

8 Chicago Convention, Art. 1. For the purposes of the Chicago Convention, the territory of a State is regarded as 'the land areas and territorial waters adjacent thereto under the sovereignty, suzerainty, protection or mandate of such State': Chicago Convention, Art. 2.

9 In *Case Concerning Military and Paramilitary Activities in and against Nicaragua (Nicaragua v United States)* (Merits) (Judgment), the court noted that '[t]he principle of respect for territorial sovereignty is also directly infringed by the unauthorized overflight of a State's territory by aircraft belonging to or under the control of the government of another State': [1986] ICJ Rep 14, 128.

10 See Chicago Convention, Arts 5, 6.

11 Of course, any space activities requiring a launch from Earth and/or a return to Earth will also involve a 'use' of air space. In this respect, the law of air space may be relevant to the legal position if, for example, the space object of one state travels through the air space of another state. See also Art. II of the *Convention on International Liability for Damage Caused by Space Objects*, opened for signature 29 March 1972, (entered into force 1 September 1972) which applies *inter alia* to 'aircraft in flight' (i.e. in air space).

12 Outer Space Treaty, Art. III.

technology that followed almost immediately from the *Sputnik* success. Despite the delays, and at times lengthy and fractious negotiations, the law of outer space has developed as an increasingly important discrete corpus of law within the broader realm of general public international law.

This process of evolution has seen the emergence of new rules, and the codification of existing fundamental international legal principles, all of which regulate the exploration and use of outer space. In general terms, these principles have served to allow for the significant improvement of the standard of living for the whole of humanity through the use of space technology – for example, scientific questions concerning environmental protection and climate change issues of the Earth are addressed by fleets of Earth observation satellites; satellite data facilitates relief efforts in regions that suffer natural or technological disaster. The prospects for the future use of outer space offer both tremendous opportunities and challenges for humankind, and law at both the international level, and also now increasingly at the national level, will continue to be at the forefront in this regard.

There is now a substantial body of international and domestic law dealing with many – although not all – aspects of the exploration and use of outer space. These principles are primarily to be found in a number of United Nations sponsored multilateral treaties, United Nations General Assembly Resolutions, a wide range of national legislation, bilateral arrangements and determinations by intergovernmental organisations.

There are five main multilateral treaties that have been finalised through the auspices of the United Nations Committee on the Peaceful Uses of Outer Space (UNCOPUOS), the principal multilateral body involved in the development of international space law.[13] These are:

(i)   1967 Treaty on Principles Governing the Activities of States in the Exploration and Use of Outer Space, including the Moon and other Celestial Bodies;[14]
(ii) 1968 Agreement on the Rescue of Astronauts, the Return of Astronauts and the Return of Objects Launched into Outer Space;[15]
(iii) 1972 Convention on International Liability for Damage Caused by Space Objects;[16]
(iv) 1975 Convention on Registration of Objects Launched into Outer Space;[17] and
(v)   1979 Agreement Governing the Activities of States on the Moon and other Celestial Bodies.[18]

These five treaties deal with various important issues relating to outer space. When assessing them, it is important to also bear in mind that these treaties were formulated in the 'cold war' era, when only a relatively small number of countries had space-faring capability, a situation that has changed over time. In general terms, the international legal principles they contain

---

13 UNCOPUOS was established by the United Nations General Assembly in 1959, shortly after the launch of *Sputnik I*: see *United Nations Committee on the Peaceful Uses of Outer Space* (1959), GA Res 1472(XIV), UN GAOR. It currently has 70 Members, which, according to UNCOPUOS, means that it is 'one of the largest Committees in the United Nations'. Online. Available HTTP: <http://www.unoosa.org/oosa/en/COPUOS/members.html> (accessed 11 August 2011).
14 610 UNTS 205 ('Outer Space Treaty').
15 672 UNTS 119 ('Rescue Agreement').
16 961 UNTS 187 ('Liability Convention').
17 1023 UNTS 15 ('Registration Agreement').
18 1363 UNTS 3 ('Moon Agreement').

provide for the non-appropriation of outer space by any one state, the freedom of the use and exploration of outer space, a liability regime applicable in the case of damage caused by space objects, the safety and rescue of space objects and astronauts, the notification to, and registration of space activities with the United Nations, the scientific investigation and exploitation of the natural resources of outer space, and the settlement of disputes arising from outer space activities.

There are, in addition, five main sets of principles adopted by the United Nations General Assembly (UNGA), each of which relates to specific aspects of the use of outer space. These are:

(i)   1963 Declaration of Legal Principles Governing the Activities of States in the Exploration and Use of Outer Space;[19]
(ii) 1982 Principles Governing the Use by States of Artificial Earth Satellites for International Direct Television Broadcasting;[20]
(iii) 1986 Principles Relating to Remote Sensing of the Earth from Outer Space;[21]
(iv) 1992 Principles Relevant to the Use of Nuclear Power Sources in Outer Space;[22] and
(v)   1996 Declaration on International Cooperation in the Exploration and Use of Outer Space for the Benefit and in the Interest of All States, Taking into Particular Account the Needs of Developing Countries.[23]

These sets of principles provide for the application of international law and the promotion of international cooperation and understanding in space activities, the dissemination and exchange of information through transnational direct television broadcasting via satellites and remote satellite observations of the Earth, and general standards regulating the safe use of nuclear power sources necessary for the exploration and use of outer space.

It is generally agreed that Resolutions of the General Assembly are non-binding,[24] at least within the traditional analysis of the 'sources' of international law[25] specified in Article 38(1)

---

19 *Declaration of Legal Principles Governing the Activities of States in the Exploration and Uses of Outer Space* (1962), GA Res 1962(XVIII), UN GAOR.
20 *Principles Governing the Use by States of Artificial Earth Satellites for International Direct Television Broadcasting* (1982), GA Res 37/92, UN GAOR, 37th Sess, 100th Plen Mtg, UN Doc A/RES/37/92.
21 *Principles Relating to Remote Sensing of the Earth from Outer Space* (1986), GA Res 41/65, UN GAOR, 41st Sess, 95th Plen Mtg, UN Doc A/RES/41/65.
22 *Principles Relevant to the Use of Nuclear Power Sources in Outer Space* (1992), GA Res 47/68, UN GAOR, 47th Sess, 85th Plen Mtg, UN Doc A/RES/47/68 ('Nuclear Power Source Principles').
23 *Declaration on International Cooperation in the Exploration and Use of Outer Space for the Benefit and in the Interest of All States, Taking into Particular Account the Needs of Developing Countries* (1996), GA Res 51/122, UN GAOR, 51st Sess, 83rd Plen Mtg, UN Doc A/RES/51/122.
24 See, e.g., D.J. Harris, *Cases and Materials on International Law*, 6th edition, Andover: Sweet and Maxwell, 2004, pp. 57–61 and the references therein.
25 A growing body of contemporary academic literature that questions the traditional understanding of what constitutes a rule of customary international law has more recently emerged: see e.g. I. Scobbie, 'The Approach to Customary International Law in the Study', in E. Wilmshurst and S. Breau (eds) *Perspectives on the ICRC Study on Customary International Humanitarian Law*, Cambridge: Cambridge University Press, 2007, p. 15 That author (at 24) describes various 'revisionist accounts of custom formation'; see also C. Ochoa, 'The Individual and Customary International Law Formation', *Virginia Journal of International Law* 48, 2007, 119, pp. 135–42.

of the Statute of the International Court of Justice.[26] In the context of the regulation of the use and exploration of outer space, these five sets of principles have largely been considered as constituting 'soft law',[27] although a number of specific provisions may now represent customary international law.[28]

Legal regulation of the space environment – general principles

It is an unfortunate reality that virtually all aspects of the exploration and use of outer space involve elements that are inherently damaging to the space environment – and to the environment of the Earth. Over time, and with the exponential growth of space activities, this has given rise to many (potential) environmental problems relating to space activities, as well as the question of whether, and how, such concerns can and should be addressed within the corpus of the international legal regulation of outer space. Despite the development of those fundamental legal principles referred to above, and the conclusion of the United Nations Space Treaties, it is apparent even from a cursory reading of the basic instruments that the existing body of international space law does not provide a comprehensive legal framework for the protection of the environment of outer space; nor does it specify rigorous environmental standards in relation to the conduct of space activities as they may affect the Earth.

Having said this, it is relevant to note that the United Nations Space Treaties were largely concluded before what has been regarded as the 'environmental movement' relating to activities on Earth had even begun to establish itself, let alone before the development of the significant international environmental law instruments. Even then, the idea that the environment of *outer space* required rigorous regulation was beyond serious consideration, this despite the fact that the need to protect natural celestial environments was at least publically expressed (if not translated into rigorous legal regulation) as being 'among the earliest policies articulated at the dawn of the space age'.[29]

26 1 UNTS 16 (ICJ Statute). It is generally asserted by international law scholars that Article 38(1) of the ICJ Statute lists the so-called 'sources' of international law: see e.g. G. Schwarzenberger, *International Law*, 3rd edition, Volume I, London: Stevens and Sons, 1957, pp. 21–2; Cassese, op. cit., p. 156. Art. 38(1) of the ICJ Statute provides as follows:

The Court, whose function is to decide in accordance with international law such disputes as are submitted to it, shall apply:

a. international conventions, whether general or particular, establishing rules expressly recognized by the contesting states;
b. international custom, as evidence of a general practice accepted as law;
c. the general principles of law recognized by civilized nations;
d. subject to the provisions of Article 59, judicial decisions and the teachings of the most highly qualified publicists of the various nations, as subsidiary means for the determination of rules of law.

27 For a discussion on the use of 'soft-law' instruments in relation to the use and exploration of outer space, see S. Freeland, 'For Better or for Worse? The Use of "Soft Law" within the International Legal Regulation of Outer Space', *Annals of Air and Space Law* 36, 2011.
28 See e.g. R.J. Lee and S. Freeland, 'The Crystallisation of General Assembly Space Declarations into Customary International Law', *Proceedings of the Colloquium on the Law of Outer Space* 46, 2004, 122.
29 L.I. Tennen, 'Evolution of the Planetary Protection Policy: Conflict of Science and Jurisprudence?' *Advances in Space Research* 24, 2004, 2354, p. 2354.

Indeed, the 1972 Stockholm Declaration[30] is generally regarded as the first significant statement of fundamental international principles relating to the protection of the environment.[31] Yet, by the time that the Stockholm Declaration was concluded, the most important fundamental principles relating to the exploration and use of outer space had already been agreed and codified in the Outer Space Treaty and the Liability Convention respectively. Those instruments provided little substance in terms of the protection of the environment, because there was no great concern about the environment of space at the time – why should there have been? – and certainly no appetite to be bound by rigorous environmental protection obligations that might be perceived as impeding the development of the many space activities that were emerging at the time.

However, a number of areas have been considered in the principal space instruments: in terms of the United Nations Space Treaties. The focus has been directed primarily towards the issue of back and forward contamination,[32] and environmental concerns associated with the exploitation of the natural resources of the Moon and other celestial bodies.[33] In addition, there have been a number of soft-law instruments directed *inter alia* towards the use of nuclear power sources in outer space[34] and, in more recent times, of space debris.[35]

Even though these instruments do not directly give rise to internationally binding commitments, they may provide guidance in the assessment of international benchmarks to be considered and applied. In its Advisory Opinion on the *Legality of the Threat or Use of Nuclear Weapons*, the International Court of Justice affirmed:

> the existence of the general obligation of States to ensure that activities within their jurisdiction and control respect the environment of other States or of areas beyond

30 *Declaration of the United Nations Conference on the Human Environment* (1972), UN Doc A/CONF.48/14/Rev.1 ('1972 Stockholm Declaration').

31 R.J. Parsons, 'The Fight to Save the Planet: US Armed Forces, "Greenkeeping", and Enforcement of the Law Pertaining to Environmental Protection During Armed Conflict', *Georgetown International Environmental Law Review* 10, 1998, 441, p. 455.

32 See Outer Space Treaty, Art. IX, which includes the obligation to conduct exploration of outer space, including the Moon and other celestial bodies 'so as to avoid their harmful contamination and also adverse changes in the environment of the Earth resulting from the introduction of extraterrestrial matter . . .'. For a detailed discussion of this provision, see S. Marchisio, 'Article IX', in S. Hobe, B. Schmidt-Tedd and K-U. Schrogl (eds) op. cit., pp. 169–82.

33 See Moon Agreement, Art. 7.

34 See 1992 Nuclear Power Source Principles and United Nations Committee on the Peaceful Uses of Outer Space (UNCOPUOS) Scientific and Technical Sub-Committee and International Atomic Energy Agency (AIEA), *Safety Framework for Nuclear Power Source Applications in Outer Space* (2009). Online. Available HTTP: <http://www.fas.org/nuke/space/iaea-space.pdf> (accessed 17 February 2011).

35 See e.g. *International Cooperation in the Peaceful Uses of Outer Space* (2008), GA Res 62/217, UN GAOR, 62nd Sess, UN Doc A/RES/62/217, which (at para. 26) endorsed *The Space Debris Mitigation Guidelines of the United Nations Committee on the Peaceful Uses of Outer Space* (A/62/20), (at para. 27) agreed that 'the voluntary guidelines for the mitigation of space debris reflect the existing practices as developed by a number of national and international organizations', and (at para. 28) considered it 'essential that Member States pay more attention to the problem of collisions of space objects, including those with nuclear power sources, with space debris, and other aspects of space debris'. See also *International Cooperation in the Peaceful Uses of Outer Space* (2010), GA Res 65/97, UN GAOR, 65th Sess, UN Doc A/RES/65/97, para. 8.

national control is now part of the corpus of international law relating to the environment.[36]

States are therefore obliged to exercise their general right to explore and use outer space, as specified in Article I of the Outer Space Treaty, with due regard also to the protection of the global environment. They have a continuing duty to take appropriate measures to prevent, minimise and control the environmental harm potentially resulting from their space activities, whether these are carried on by governmental agencies or by non-governmental entities.

This continuing duty to take appropriate measures to prevent, minimise and control potential environmental harm equates to an obligation for states to act with due diligence. It is an obligation of conduct rather than of result. Such due diligence necessitates, first, the close monitoring of scientific knowledge, technological developments and standards, and secondly, a prompt transposition of new scientific and technological findings into policies and rules applicable to public and private undertakings.

In this context, internationally agreed guidelines or standards, such as the Committee on Space Research (COSPAR) Planetary Protection Policy,[37] the UN Space Debris Mitigation Guidelines,[38] or the STSC (Scientific and Technical Subcommittee)/IAEA (International Atomic Energy Agency) Safety Framework for Space Nuclear Power Source Applications,[39] take on considerable significance by providing international benchmarks. It is to these specific areas that this chapter now turns.

Legal regulation of the space environment – specific areas of concern

Planetary protection

The seeds for the concept of protection against both forward and backward contamination have been sowed in the second sentence of Article IX of the Outer Space Treaty:

> States Parties to the Treaty shall pursue studies of outer space, including the Moon and other celestial bodies, and conduct exploration of them so as to avoid their harmful contamination and also adverse changes in the environment of the Earth resulting from

---

36 [1996] ICJ Rep 226, para. 29.
37 The current version of the COSPAR Planetary Protection Policy, 20 October 2002, amended up to 24 March 2011, is online. Available HTTP: <cosparhq.cnes.fr/Scistr/PPPolicy%20(24Mar2011).pdf> (accessed 15 September 2011).
38 Adopted by the Scientific and Technical Subcommittee of UNCOPUOS at its 44th session in 2007, A/AC.105/890, para. 99, and endorsed by the *International Cooperation in the Peaceful Uses of Outer Space* (2008), GA Res 62/217, UN GAOR, 62nd Sess, UN Doc A/RES/62/217. Online. Available HTTP: <http://www.unoosa.org/pdf/pres/lsc2009/pres-06.pdf> (accessed 15 September 2011) .
39 UNCOPUOS and the International Atomic Energy Agency (IAEA), 2009, UN Doc A/AC.105/934; for further details, see L. Summerer and U.M. Bohlmann, 'The STSC/IAEA Safety Framework for Space Nuclear Power Source Applications – Influence of Non-binding Recommendations', in I. Marboe (ed.) *Soft Law in Outer Space. The Function of Non-Binding Norms in International Space Law*, Vienna: Böhlau, 2012.

the introduction of extraterrestrial matter and, where necessary, shall adopt appropriate measures for this purpose.[40]

This concept has been transformed into concrete recommendatory guidelines through its implementation in the form of COSPAR's Planetary Protection Guidelines. The Committee on Space Research was established in October 1958 by the International Council of Scientific Unions (ICSU). It is an interdisciplinary scientific committee concerned with scientific research and defines itself as a non-political organisation. Its Panel on Planetary Protection is concerned on the one hand with biological interchange in the conduct of solar system exploration, including possible effects of contamination of planets other than the Earth, and of planetary satellites within the solar system by terrestrial organisms and, on the other hand, with contamination of the Earth by materials returned from outer space carrying potential extraterrestrial organisms.

The planetary protection policy of COSPAR is maintained and promulgated for the reference of space-faring nations, both as an international standard on procedures to avoid organic constituent and biological contamination in space exploration, and also to provide accepted guidelines to aid in compliance with the wording of Article IX of the Outer Space Treaty, as well as other relevant international agreements. The policy bases itself on the statement by DeVincenzi et al. of 1983:

> Although the existence of life elsewhere in the solar system may be unlikely, the conduct of scientific investigations of possible extraterrestrial life forms, precursors, and remnants must not be jeopardized. In addition, the Earth must be protected from the potential hazard posed by extraterrestrial matter carried by a spacecraft returning from another planet. Therefore, for certain space mission/target planet combinations, controls on contamination shall be imposed, in accordance with issuances implementing this policy.[41]

Different categories are established for space mission/target body combinations and respective suggested ranges of requirements, based on the degree of interest they represent for

---

40 Outer Space Treaty, Art. IX in its entirety provides as follows:

> In the exploration and use of outer space, including the Moon and other celestial bodies, States Parties to the Treaty shall be guided by the principle of co-operation and mutual assistance and shall conduct all their activities in outer space, including the Moon and other celestial bodies, with due regard to the corresponding interests of all other States Parties to the Treaty. States Parties to the Treaty shall pursue studies of outer space, including the Moon and other celestial bodies, and conduct exploration of them so as to avoid their harmful contamination and also adverse changes in the environment of the Earth resulting from the introduction of extraterrestrial matter and, where necessary, shall adopt appropriate measures for this purpose. If a State Party to the Treaty has reason to believe that an activity or experiment planned by it or its nationals in outer space, including the Moon and other celestial bodies, would cause potentially harmful interference with activities of other States Parties in the peaceful exploration and use of outer space, including the Moon and other celestial bodies, it shall undertake appropriate international consultations before proceeding with any such activity or experiment. A State Party to the Treaty which has reason to believe that an activity or experiment planned by another State Party in outer space, including the Moon and other celestial bodies, would cause potentially harmful interference with activities in the peaceful exploration and use of outer space, including the Moon and other celestial bodies, may request consultation concerning the activity or experiment.

41 D.L. DeVincenzi, P.D. Stabekis and J.B. Barengoltz, 'A Proposed New Policy for Planetary Protection', *Advances in Space Research* 3, 1983, 13.

an understanding of the process of chemical evolution, or the origin of life.[42] Rather precise technical procedural instructions are proposed for each possible combination. The policy remains flexible, in that it can be updated fairly easily, in order to adapt swiftly to new scientific insights and understanding.[43]

Space-faring nations and the relevant international organisations have made it their declared policy to take into account the COSPAR Planetary Protection Guidelines in the definition of requirements for their respective missions.[44] Although the legal status of these policies remains that of internal documents that do not directly give rise to internationally binding commitments, they may provide guidance in the assessment of international bench-marks that are applicable to any required conditions of 'due diligence'.

The use of nuclear power sources in outer space

The risks associated with the use and application of nuclear power sources (NPS) led to the adoption of the Nuclear Power Source Principles in 1992. Although they do not create binding commitments under general public international law, the Nuclear Power Source Principles do provide some guidance.[45] The preamble of the Nuclear Power Source Principles already recognises that, for some missions in outer space, NPS are particularly suited, or even essential, due to their particular qualities.[46] The first paragraph of Principle 3 of the Nuclear Power Source Principles contains the general provision that:

> [i]n order to minimize the quantity of radioactive material in space and the risks involved, the use of nuclear power sources in outer space shall be restricted to those space missions which cannot be operated by non-nuclear energy sources in a reasonable way.

What factors are to be taken into account, and how to weigh these in order to establish 'reasonableness', is left to the discretion of those states contemplating the use of NPS. What is

42 COSPAR Planetary Protection Policy. Online. Available HTTP: <http://cosparhq.cnes.fr/Scistr/PPPolicy%20(24Mar2011).pdf> (accessed 1 November 2011).

43 See e.g. details of the recent changes incorporated at the 2008 COSPAR Assembly in Montréal in C. Conley and P. Rettberg, 'COSPAR Planetary Protection Policy – Present Status', in M. Hofmann, P. Rettberg and M. Williamson (eds) *IAA 2010 Cosmic Study: Protecting the Environment of Celestial Bodies*, 2010, p. 16 onwards.

44 One prominent example is the NASA Policy Directive NPD 8020.7G, *Biological Contamination Control for Outbound and Inbound Planetary Spacecraft*, Revalidated 25 November 2008. Online. Available HTTP: <http://nodis3.gsfc.nasa.gov/npg_img/N_PD_8020_007G_/N_PD_8020_007G__main.pdf> (accessed 15 September 2011), together with its implementing procedures and guidelines contained in 8020.12D, *Planetary Protection Provisions for Robotic Extraterrestrial Missions*, Effective Date: 20 April 2011. Online. Available HTTP: <http://nodis3.gsfc.nasa.gov/displayDir.cfm?t=NPR&c=8020&s=12D> (accessed 15 September 2011).

45 For a comprehensive analysis of the Principles and their legal significance see D.A. Porras, 'The United Nations Principles Relevant to the Use of Nuclear Power Sources in Outer Space: the significance of a soft law instrument after nearly 20 years in force', in I. Marboe (ed.) op. cit. For a general overview of international law regarding nuclear energy, see M. Elbaradei, E. Nwogugu and J. Rames, 'International law and nuclear energy: overview of the legal framework'. Online. Available HTTP: <http://www.iaea.org/Publications/Magazines/Bulletin/Bull373/37302081625.pdf> (accessed 15 September 2011), where the authors discuss the mix of legally binding rules and agreements on the one hand, and advisory standards and regulations on the other.

46 The intensity of solar radiation decreases exponentially with the distance from the Sun. As a consequence, nuclear power sources constitute the only available option to supply sufficient heat and electricity to spacecraft at the orbit of Jupiter or beyond.

particularly interesting about Section 1 of Principle 3, which lays down 'General goals for radiation protection and nuclear safety', is the fact that it requires not only that individuals, populations and the biosphere be protected against radiological hazards in operational and accidental circumstances, but also that:

> the design and use of NPS shall ensure with high reliability that radioactive material does not cause a significant contamination of outer space.

Sections 2 and 3 of Principle 3 of the Nuclear Power Source Principles proceed to establish specific guidelines for the use of nuclear reactors on the one hand, and radio-isotope generators on the other. Principle 4 stipulates that a launching state (as defined in Principle 2)[47] has to ensure that a thorough and comprehensive safety assessment is conducted, the results of which shall be made publicly available prior to each launch. Furthermore, Principle 5 of the Nuclear Power Source Principles contains provisions as to notification in case of re-entry of satellites with nuclear power sources on board.[48]

The main objective of the 2009 Safety Framework for Nuclear Power Source Applications in Outer Space (2009 Safety Framework)[49] is to:

> protect people and the environment in Earth's biosphere from potential hazards associated with relevant launch, operation and end-of-service phases of space nuclear power source applications.

Neither the extraterrestrial environment, nor humans in outer space, is included within the scope of protection. The 2009 Safety Framework is intended to provide technical guidance only. It has not been drafted as a legally binding instrument. In its preface, it is expressly stated that it is not legally binding under international law, and that it is not a publication in the IAEA Safety Standards Series with the corresponding legal implications,[50] but rather is

---

47 Principle 2 of the Nuclear Power Source Principles provides as follows:

> For the purpose of these Principles, the terms 'launching State' and 'State launching' mean the State which exercises jurisdiction and control over a space object with nuclear power sources on board at a given point in time relevant to the principle concerned.

48 Principle 5 builds on the stipulations of the 1986 Convention on Early Notification of a Nuclear Accident, INFCIRC/335. This duty to inform 'States concerned' and the United Nations Secretary-General is supplemented by the 1987 Convention on Assistance in the Case of a Nuclear Accident or Radiological Emergency, INFCIRC/336. For a detailed discussion on the relationship between the Nuclear Power Source Principles and these Conventions, see M. Benkö, 'Nuklearenergie im Weltraum', in K-H. Böckstiegel (ed.) *Handbuch des Weltraumrechts*, Cologne: Carl Heymanns Verlag, 1991, 457, p. 475.

49 United Nations Committee on the Peaceful Uses of Outer Space and IAEA (2009), UN Doc A/AC.105/934; see also Summerer and Bohlmann, op. cit.

50 According to Article III.A.6. of its Statute, the IAEA is authorised to establish or adopt, in consultation and, where appropriate, in collaboration with the competent organs of the UN and with the specialised agencies concerned, standards of safety for protection of health and minimisation of danger to life and property (including such standards for labour conditions), and to provide for the application of these standards to its own operations as well as to the operations, making use of materials, services, equipment, facilities and information made available by the Agency or at its request or under its control or supervision; and to provide for the application of these standards, at the request of the parties, to operations under any bilateral or multilateral arrangements, or, at the request of a state, to any of that state's activities in the field of atomic energy; see H. Blix, 'The Role of the IAEA in the Development of International Law', *Nordic Journal of International Law* 58, 1989, 231.

intended to complement the IAEA Safety Standards with appropriate guidance concerning the particular aspects resulting from the specific characteristics of space NPS applications compared to NPS applications on Earth. It is a model framework that represents the state of the art in the use of NPS applications in outer space, and transposes this into 'guidance': guidance for government, management and technical guidance.

The guiding principles directed to those governments and relevant international intergovernmental organisations that authorise, approve or conduct space NPS missions addresses not only regulatory aspects, namely the establishment of, and ensuring compliance with, safety policies, requirements and processes, verification of the justification put forward for the use of an NPS, and the establishment of a dedicated, supplementary nuclear launch authorisation process, but also direct governmental activities, such as preparation for emergency preparedness and response.

The guidance for management section addresses all organisations involved with NPS space applications. The technical guidance provided for in the safety framework relates to the design, development and mission phases of space NPS applications, and encompasses key areas for developing and providing a technical basis for authorisation and approval processes, as well as for emergency preparedness and response.

Even though neither the Nuclear Power Source Principles, nor the 2009 Safety Framework give rise to binding commitments, voluntary compliance with the guiding principles they provide seems advisable, since it ensures that space activities involving the use of NPS are carried out in a 'state of the art' manner, thereby fulfilling any due diligence requirements that might be applied.

Space debris

The issue of space debris is a major area for environmental concern, which clearly impacts also upon human safety. For example, on 12 March 2009, the three astronauts aboard the International Space Station (ISS), Americans Mike Fincke and Sandra Magnus and Russian Yuri Lonchakov, were forced to evacuate the main station and remain in the ISS escape vehicle for nine minutes, while a piece of debris about 1 centimetre in length passed by.[51] Had the debris hit and pierced the ISS, it is possible that a fatal loss of air pressure could have ensued. More recently, the six-man crew on the ISS was again forced to take shelter in two *Soyuz* craft on 28 June 2011, when another piece of debris drifted past the station.[52]

Only one month before the March 2009 incident, an operational American commercial satellite (*Iridium 33*) and an inactive Russian communications satellite (*Kosmos 2251*) collided approximately 790 km above the Earth, resulting in the total destruction of both. This was the first time that two intact satellites had collided, and the collision resulted in approximately

---

51 See e.g. M. McKee, 'Debris Threat Prompts Space Station Crew to Evacuate' *New Scientist*. Online. Available HTTP: <http://www.newscientist.com/article/dn16755-debris-threat-prompts-space-station-crew-to-evacuate.html> (accessed 26 July 2011).
52 'Space Debris forces ISS astronauts to evacuate the station'. Online. Available HTTP: <http://thewatchers.adorraeli.com/2011/06/29/space-debris-forces-iss-astronauts-to-evacuate-the-station/> (accessed 26 July 2011).

700 additional pieces of hazardous debris being created, with the potential to cause additional decades-long pollution in space.[53]

Adding to the complexity of the issue, in 2007 and 2008 respectively, both China and the United States proceeded to deliberately destroy their own satellites in space, thus causing additional space debris from the resultant explosions.[54]

According to the United States Space Surveillance Network, 4,765 launches and 251 in-orbit break-ups have led to 16,200 objects being catalogued.[55] Approximately 77 per cent of these objects are in low Earth orbits, 6 per cent are in near-geostationary orbits, 10 per cent in highly eccentric orbits and 7 per cent in other orbits, including GNSS (global navigation satellite system) orbits.[56] Some 20 per cent of the catalogued objects constitute satellites (of which only 6 per cent are operational), 11 per cent are rocket bodies, 5 per cent are mission-related objects and 64 per cent constitute fragments.[57]

Even before the more recent high-profile incidents referred to above, it had been recognised that this environment causes an ever increasing collision hazard for man-made satellites. For this reason, it was decided as early as 1993 to establish among interested space agencies an Inter-Agency Space Debris Coordination Committee (IADC), which is an international governmental forum for the worldwide coordination of activities related to the issues of man-made and natural debris in space. According to its terms of reference:

> [t]he primary purpose of the IADC is to exchange information on space debris research activities between member space agencies, to facilitate opportunities for cooperation in space debris research, to review the progress of ongoing cooperative activities and to identify debris mitigation options.[58]

The IADC Space Debris Mitigation Guidelines[59] were formally adopted by consensus in October 2002 during the Second World Space Congress in Houston, Texas. They:

> describe existing practices that have been identified and evaluated for limiting the generation of space debris in the environment. The Guidelines cover the overall environmental impact of the missions with a focus on the following:

---

53 *NASA orbital debris quarterly news* 13(2), 2009, pp. 1–2. Online. Available HTTP: <http://www.orbitaldebris.jsc.nasa.gov/newsletter/pdfs/ODQNv13i2.pdf> (accessed 1 November 2011); 'Russian and US Satellites Collide', BBC News. Online. Available HTTP: <http://news.bbc.co.uk/2/hi/science/nature/7885051.stm> (accessed 12 March 2012).

54 For background to these two incidents, see S. Freeland, 'The 2008 Russia/China Proposal for a Treaty to Ban Weapons in Space: A Missed Opportunity or an Opening Gambit?', *Proceedings of the Colloquium on the Law of Outer Space* 51, 2008, American Institute of Aeronautics and Astronautics, pp. 261–71.

55 Status as of December 2010.

56 H. Klinkrad, *Space Debris Mitigation Activities at ESA*, Presentation to the Scientific and Legal Subcommittee of the UN Committee on the Peaceful Uses of Outer Space, February 2011. Online. Available HTTP: <http://www.oosa.unvienna.org/pdf/pres/stsc2011/tech-40.pdf> (accessed 1 November 2011).

57 This figure was 41 per cent before the 2007 Chinese *FengYun 1C* ASAT (anti-satellite) test and the 2009 collision between *Iridium 33* and *Kosmos 2251*.

58 Online. Available HTTP: <http://www.iadc-online.org/index.cgi?item=torp> (accessed 15 September 2011).

59 Available in their current version, revision 1 of September 2007. Online. Available HTTP: <http://www.iadc-online.org/index.cgi?item=docs_pub> (accessed 15 September 2011).

(1) Limitation of debris released during normal operations;
(2) Minimisation of the potential for on-orbit break-ups;
(3) Post-mission disposal;
(4) Prevention of on-orbit collisions.[60]

The IADC presented its guidelines to the UNCOPUOS STSC, where they served as a baseline for the development of the UN Space Debris Mitigation Guidelines. In 2007, the UNGA endorsed the Space Debris Mitigation Guidelines as adopted by the UNCOPUOS STSC, and agreed that the voluntary guidelines for the mitigation of space debris reflected the existing practices as developed by a number of national and international organisations.[61] It invited member states to implement those guidelines through relevant national mechanisms.

The document recognises two broad categories of space debris mitigation measures: those that curtail the generation of potentially harmful space debris in the near term – the curtailment of the production of mission-related space debris and the avoidance of break-ups – and those that limit their generation over the longer term – end-of-life procedures that remove decommissioned spacecraft and launch vehicle orbital stages from regions populated by operational spacecraft.

The seven numbered guidelines remain at a generalised level and encourage, on a voluntary basis, actions that would:

(1) limit debris released during normal operations;
(2) minimise the potential for break-ups during operational phases;
(3) limit the probability of accidental collision in orbit;
(4) avoid intentional destruction and other harmful activities;
(5) minimise potential for post-mission break-ups resulting from stored energy;
(6) limit the long-term presence of spacecraft and launch vehicle orbital stages in the low-Earth orbit region after the end of their mission;
(7) limit the long-term interference of spacecraft and launch vehicle orbital stages with geosynchronous region after the end of their mission.[62]

The transformation in character that the guidelines have experienced in their passage from the IADC through to the United Nations system and specifically the UNCOPUOS can easily be attributed to the different composition of the fora, as well as their different focus and scope. Whereas the IADC is an open association of technical entities of space-faring nations, the UN incorporates the representatives of states, both space-faring and non-space-faring. The motivations of the IADC members are far more homogeneous than the different positions of member states of UNCOPUOS. The focus of IADC is very technical, whereas UNCOPUOS is, in addition, more politically influenced, readily taking into account the positions of member states in other debates.

---

60 Section 1 of the guidelines; see also N.L. Johnson, 'Developments in Space Debris Mitigation Policy and Practices', in *Proceedings of the Institution of Mechanical Engineers, Part G, Journal of Aerospace Engineering* 221(6), 2007, pp. 907–9.
61 *International Cooperation in the Peaceful Uses of Outer Space* (2008), GA Res 62/217, UN GAOR, 62nd Sess, UN Doc A/RES/62/217.
62 The document is online. Available HTTP: <http://www.unoosa.org/pdf/publications/st_space_49E.pdf> (accessed 1 November 2011).

It is therefore not surprising that the IADC Guidelines go into much more technical detail than the UN guidelines. Being more easily able to be amended also facilitates this greater emphasis on technical issues. The UN guidelines make a clear reference to the version of the IADC Space Debris Mitigation Guidelines at the time they (the UN guidelines) were themselves published,[63] but they also invite member states and international organisations to:

> refer to the latest version of the IADC space debris mitigation guidelines and other supporting documents, which can be found on the IADC website, . . . for more in-depth descriptions and recommendations pertaining to space debris mitigation measures.[64]

From a legal perspective, neither of the sets of guidelines is binding under international law. Over the years there have also been repeated attempts to bring the subject of space debris onto the agenda of the Legal Subcommittee of UNCOPUOS in one way or another, but so far with only limited success.[65] Member states shy away from any legal discussion of the matter, a behavioural pattern that can also be observed with regard to other subject matters connected to aspects of the sustainability and environmental impacts of space activities. Nevertheless, states and space agencies implement the guidelines, aware of the fact that such implementation serves their own interests in keeping the relevant orbits accessible and useable.[66] However, the point at which they consider themselves ready to commit internationally, in exchange for the same commitment from other states, seems not to have thus far been reached.[67]

Space debris and its cascading effects have been identified as one of the greatest challenges for the long-term sustainability of space activities. Still, the existing international texts as presented above can be characterised as 'soft law' at best. By implementing the guidelines contained in these soft-law instruments via national or agency policies, policy-makers might,

63 As contained in the annex to the *Inter-Agency Space Debris Coordination Committee Space Debris Mitigation Guidelines* (2002), UNCOPUOS, UN Doc A/AC.105/C.1/L.260.
64 Ibid., Chapter 6.
65 The item 'General exchange of information on national mechanisms relating to space debris mitigation measures' has appeared on the Agenda of the Legal Subcommittee of UNCOPUOS since its 48th session in 2009. The latest attempt to give the debate a clear legal impetus was in the form of a Working Paper submitted by the Czech Republic to the Legal Subcommittee of UNCOPUOS proposing as a new agenda item the review of the legal aspects of the Space Debris Mitigation Guidelines of the Committee on the Peaceful Uses of Outer Space, with a view to transforming the Guidelines into a set of principles to be adopted by the General Assembly, UN document A/AC.105/C.2/L.283. This initiative gained support from quite a number of other member states, but could not secure the required consensus in order to give rise to a new agenda item.
66 For example, NASA has developed its Procedural Requirements for Limiting Orbital Debris, NPR 8715.6A. Effective Date 14 May 2009, Expiration Date 14 May 2014. Online. Available HTTP: <http://nodis3.gsfc.nasa.gov/npg_img/N_PR_8715_006A_/N_PR_8715_006A_.pdf> (accessed 15 September 2011), which requires formal assessments and disposition plans.
67 Taking again the NASA Procedural Requirements as an example, one should note that the policy states in its Chapter 1.1.3 that compliance with this NPR meets the guidelines and intent of the following documents (as of the date of this NPR): the US Government Orbital Debris Mitigation Standard Practices and the IADC-0201, Space Debris Mitigation Guidelines. Yet, it is also very clear on its internationally non-binding character: 'This NPR shall not be construed as conferring upon any international body, agency, or committee the right to place upon the U.S. Government or NASA any restrictions or conditions as to its space operations unless required by separate agreement or treaty', Chapter P.1.7.

however, ultimately contribute to the formation of a due diligence standard, if international practice is sufficiently widespread and representative.

Conclusion

In general terms, the existing body of international space law does not provide a comprehensive legal framework for the protection of the environment of outer space, nor does it specify rigorous environmental standards in relation to the conduct of space activities, either in space or on Earth, for example, with respect to launch activities. Moreover, even the rather general obligations relating to environmental aspects of the exploration and use of outer space that are found in the United Nations Space Treaties are not particularly well suited to more recent developments in the exploration and use of outer space. Such concerns will only become more pressing given the likelihood of increased human spaceflight activities, including the proposed advent of a commercial 'space tourism' industry over the coming years and decades.

In addition, the Outer Space Treaty reaffirms that 'international law' applies to 'activities in the exploration and use of outer space'.[68] However, it is not entirely clear how readily the general principles of international law that have been developed primarily in respect of terrestrial activities can be applied to the unique characteristics of space activities, although outer space, as one of the 'areas beyond the limits of national jurisdiction', is considered to be included within the protection of Principle 21 of the 1972 Stockholm Declaration and Principle 2 of the 1992 Rio Declaration on Environment and Development.[69]

To further complicate matters, many space activities are now undertaken by non-governmental commercial entities, which are not *per se* bound by the United Nations Space Treaties,[70] but rather are subject to local laws and the provisions negotiated in commercial launch service contracts, both of which will vary considerably in the particular circumstances.

Yet, as has been indicated above, there are a number of areas related to the space environment that are increasingly giving cause for concern. One obvious area – among several – is that of space debris, which potentially threatens all space activities and, as a consequence, the future of space exploration and use.

To properly address such issues requires close cooperation among all space-faring (and other) states – something that is difficult (though not impossible) given the highly strategic role that space activities play for each state's security, military and commercial interests. Moreover, it is generally agreed that the implementation of binding 'greener' space regulations would significantly increase the costs associated with space activities, at least in the short to medium term. It is not at all clear that space-faring states would be prepared to carry such

---

68 Outer Space Treaty, Art. III.
69 *Declaration of the United Nations Conference on Environment and Development* (1992), UN Doc A/CONF.151/26 (Volume 1), 31 ILM 874 ('Rio Declaration').
70 Outer Space Treaty, Art. VI does, however, provide that:

> States Parties to the Treaty shall bear international responsibility for national activities in outer space, including the Moon and other celestial bodies, whether such activities are carried on by governmental agencies or by non-governmental entities, and for assuring that national activities are carried out in conformity with the provisions set forth in the present Treaty. The activities of non-governmental entities in outer space, including the Moon and other celestial bodies, shall require authorization and continuing supervision by the appropriate State Party to the Treaty.

additional burdens, a situation that is exacerbated further by the current somewhat uncertain state of the world's financial markets and economic outlook.

However, there is a clear commonality of interests in addressing those environmental issues relating to outer space that might unduly impede or restrict humankind's activities in space. The problems will become – if they have not already done so – too large and complex for any one state, or group of states, to be able to deal with alone. The future regulation of outer space necessitates common approaches and commitments. The antecedents of this can already be seen in the form of soft-law instruments that are intended to fill various 'gaps' in the existing corpus of international space law. It is to be hoped that the continuation of this cooperative approach to space law-making will ultimately lead to the codification of new and emerging principles dealing with environmental issues in hard law treaties, with the acceptance of all relevant states. This will complement and expand upon those fundamental rules that already exist in the various United Nations Space Law Treaties.

This is not to ignore the fact that there are many issues that represent considerable challenges as to how international law, incorporating the international legal regulation of outer space, will be able to cope with future activities in space, and their consequences for the outer space environment. The way in which the rules are developed and adapted to meet these challenges will be important not only for outer space itself, but also for future generations living on Earth. This is absolutely necessary for the continued peaceful use of outer space in the future for the benefit of all humankind. Humankind's use of outer space should reflect underlying notions of cooperation and shared benefit, which must remain as the cornerstones in this next phase of human achievement. International law has a crucial part to play in this regard.

22
Nuclear energy and the environment

Abdullah Al Faruque

The linkage between energy and the environment is well established, as any form of power generation will have some effect. Reduction of greenhouse gas emissions remains a dominant factor in future choices about electricity generation. Nuclear energy is one option as it emits only negligible amounts of carbon dioxide. The growing global demand for energy, desire to combat climate change and gradual decline in dependence on fossil fuels have warranted a renewed emphasis on nuclear power. But public concern is increasing due to the potentially catastrophic nature of the risks involved. Thus, safe use of nuclear energy remains a challenge for the international community and the current regime should draw lessons from the recent Fukushima incident.

Introduction

The linkage between energy and the environment is well established and undeniable as the use of any energy source has some effect on the environment, albeit the degree of effect may vary depending on the particular form of energy used. The symbiotic relationship between energy and environment can be further explained by the fact that use of non-renewable sources such as fossil fuels can emit carbon dioxide, which contributes to global warming. The international community is increasingly pursuing energy security and sustainable development through deployment of cleaner, more efficient, and low-carbon energy technologies. Thus, in the energy sector, reduction of greenhouse gas (GHG) emissions remains a driving force and the issue is likely to be the main factor in choices about energy options for electricity generation during the coming decades.

Nuclear energy could be one option for reducing carbon emissions since nuclear power plant operation emits no or negligible amounts of carbon dioxide. Such negligible emission occurs in various stages of the nuclear fuel chain: mining, milling, transport, fuel fabrication, enrichment, reactor construction, decommissioning, and waste management.[1] Nuclear

1 'Reducing Climate Change Impact', IAEA, 7 December 2009. Online. Available. <http://www. iaea.org/newscenter/news/2009/climatechange.html> (accessed 19 March 2012). The 'nuclear fuel cycle' refers to the entire programme from the mining and milling of uranium, through the

393

energy's potential role in reducing GHG emissions and providing for electricity generation will be of central importance.[2] It is precisely in this context that nuclear energy law intersects with international environmental law. This has been reflected in a Massachusetts Institute of Technology (MIT) study, which finds that there are only a few realistic options for reducing carbon dioxide emissions from electricity generation:

- increasing efficiency in electricity generation and use;
- expanding use of renewable energy sources such as wind, solar, biomass, and geothermal;
- capturing carbon dioxide emissions at fossil-fuelled electric generating plants and permanently sequestering the carbon; and
- increasing the use of nuclear power.[3]

The environmental aspects of nuclear power plants and the facilities of the associated fuel cycle are not very different from any other large-scale industrial activity. However, the radioactive materials that are part of the various fuel cycle operations, particularly those radioactive materials generated during the operation of nuclear reactors, have to be strictly controlled.[4]

The growing global demand for energy, the issue of combating climate change and a gradual decline in dependence on fossil fuels have warranted a renewed emphasis on nuclear power. Nuclear energy is currently contributing about 16 per cent of total global electricity production.[5] More than 40 countries have nuclear power plants. Nuclear material and technology is also useful for medicine and agriculture. The main justification for a nuclear revival has been based largely upon two policy priorities: climate change mitigation and security of energy supply.[6] Nuclear energy is often considered as a clean non-renewable energy source in terms of emissions. Nuclear energy is more environmentally friendly than coal, oil or gas from an emission standpoint. The importance of nuclear energy is increasing since it is capable of meeting a significant portion of the energy needs of a country. Thus, nuclear power should be considered as one of the significant options for meeting future world energy needs at low cost and in an environmentally acceptable manner. Nuclear energy has assumed growing significance as emission-free energy in an era of serious concern about global warming.[7]

manufacture of fuel elements for the reactor, transport and reprocessing of irradiated fuel, to the management of wastes produced in all steps of the cycle.

2 E. Bertel and J. Van de Vate, 'Nuclear Energy and the Environmental Debate: The Context of Choices', *IAEA Bulletin* 4, 1995.

3 *The Future of Nuclear Energy, An Inter-disciplinary MIT study*, Cambridge, MA: Massachusetts Institute of Technology, 2003. Online. Available HTTP: <http://web.mit.edu/nuclearpower/pdf/nuclear-power-summary.pdf> (accessed 1 January 2012).

4 A. Hagen, 'Nuclear Power, Man, and the Environment', *IAEA Bulletin* 24(2), 1982, p. 3. Online. Available HTTP: <http://www.iaea.org/Publications/Magazines/Bulletin/Bull242/24204680305.pdf> (accessed 12 March 2012).

5 'Reducing Climate Change Impact', op. cit.

6 P.D. Cameron, 'The Revival of Nuclear Power: An Analysis of the Legal Implications', *Journal of Environmental Law* 19(1), 2007, 71–87.

7 D.C. Rislove, 'Global Warming v Non-Proliferation: The Time has Come for Nations to Reassert their Right to Peaceful Use of Nuclear Energy', *Wisconsin International Law Journal* 24(4), 2007, 1069–98.

Despite these facts, public concern about nuclear energy is increasing. The catastrophic nature of the risk of exposure to radiation from nuclear power plants, which can potentially bring great destruction and untold human suffering to humanity and the environment, makes this risk unacceptable to humanity.[8] The opposition to nuclear power plants has been expressed in the following ways. First, the long-term disposal of radioactive wastes remains a major challenge for the international community. Nuclear power plants create spent nuclear fuel at the reactor site. Spent nuclear fuel is considered high-level waste that can contaminate and degrade land. The resulting nuclear energy wastes can last thousands of years, negatively impacting everything from the land to the oceans. These radioactive wastes therefore pose some danger to present and future generations.

Second, the major concern with nuclear energy is the long-term effects of radiation on the people living near or working in a nuclear power station, the effects of routine radioactive substances and the effects and probability of a large-scale accident. While sources of ionising radiation are essential to modern health care, they can be detrimental to living organisms if the production and the use of radiation sources and radioactive material are not covered by measures to protect individuals exposed to radiation.[9] Ionising radiation and radioactive substances have permanent effects on the environment and the risks associated with radiation exposure can only be restricted, not eliminated entirely.[10]

The third concern is that every operating nuclear power plant poses some risk of a severe accident. The nuclear industry estimates the chances of a severe reactor accident to be about one out of every 10,000 reactor years of operation.[11] Fourth, the mining needed to extract uranium may have some negative environmental impacts. Furthermore, apart from radiation, non-radiological elements, such as different chemicals and equipment used in nuclear fuel cycle facilities, may pose risks. They are the same in many instances as used in other industries but the effects of using these chemicals and equipment in the nuclear power industry may have some further negative impacts on the environment.

Sixth, nuclear power has higher overall lifetime costs compared to natural gas and coal. Seventh, the proliferation of nuclear weapons is another global concern. The current international safeguards regime is inadequate to meet the security challenges of expanded nuclear deployment contemplated in the global growth scenario.[12] Transportation of radioactive material raises another public concern regarding the environmental impacts of such movements. The volume of transportation of radioactive material is increasing rapidly and will continue to increase with the growth of the nuclear power industry.[13] Finally, the possibility of diversion of nuclear material through terrorist acts cannot be ruled out.[14]

8 L.E. Rodríguez-Rivera, 'The Human Right to Environment and the Peaceful Use of Nuclear Energy', *Denver Journal of International Law and Policy* 35(1), 2007, 73–192.
9 C. Stoiber, A. Baer, N. Pelzer and W. Tonhauser, *Handbook on Nuclear Law*, Vienna: International Atomic Energy Agency, 2003, p. 45.
10 Ibid.
11 K.S. Coplan, 'Inter-civilizational Inequities of Nuclear Power Weighed against the Intergenerational Inequities of Carbon Based Energy', *Fordham Environmental Law Review* 17, 2006, p. 227.
12 *The Future of Nuclear Energy*, op. cit.
13 J.U. Ahmed and H.T. Daw, 'Environmental Impacts of the Production and Use of Nuclear Energy: A Summary of the United Nations Environment Programme Study', *IAEA Bulletin* 22(2), 1980, p. 21.
14 E.E. El-Hinnawi, 'Review of the Environmental Impact of Nuclear Energy', *IAEA Bulletin* 20(2), 1978, pp. 39–40.

The aim of this chapter is to highlight the relationship between nuclear energy and the environment, and to focus on the utility of nuclear energy to combat climate change, and the environmental effects of nuclear accidents. This chapter also elaborates upon the relevant provisions of international law and decisions of international courts on the regulation of the use of nuclear energy, legal regimes on management of transboundary movement of radioactive wastes and nuclear safety and liability. Finally, it explores the role of the International Atomic Energy Agency (IAEA) in protecting the environment in its member countries. It concludes that nuclear energy will be considered as the most viable option amongst the sources of renewable energy in the foreseeable future as it produces remarkably little environmental pollution and GHGs. However, global safety standards of nuclear power plants should be further improved, drawing lessons from the recent Fukushima incident in Japan in 2011.

Nuclear energy and the legal regime on climate change

Despite the realisation that nuclear energy is a most valuable tool to counter global climate change, this fact has been ignored in the international legal framework on climate change. Nuclear energy is not mentioned in the United Nations Framework Convention on Climate Change (UNFCCC) 1992 or the Kyoto Protocol 1997. The Kyoto Protocol asks the parties to cooperate in the development and transfer of, or access to, 'environmentally sound' technologies, practices, and processes relevant to climate change. The Protocol calls on parties to implement the Protocol in such a way as to minimise adverse social, economic, and environmental impacts on developing countries. To achieve this end – emissions reductions while achieving sustainable development – parties shall implement or elaborate on policies and measures that include: enhancing energy efficiency; protecting and enhancing GHG sinks; promoting sustainable agriculture; researching, promoting, developing, and increasing the use of 'renewable' forms of energy, CO_2 sequestration; and 'advanced and environmentally sound technologies'.

According to Article 3 of the Kyoto Protocol, developed countries are to refrain from using emission reduction units generated from nuclear facilities to meet their commitments. The rationale appears to be that these two mechanisms should emphasise only renewable energy resources, such as wind, solar, and hydroelectricity.[15] Any rational regime that claims relevancy in addressing global climate change should include nuclear energy as a proven strategy of GHG emission mitigation.[16] It is even claimed by some that, given the tremendous benefits that nuclear energy can bring in combating climate change, the Kyoto Protocol mistakenly excluded nuclear energy from its compliance mechanisms.[17]

Nuclear accidents and their environmental effects

The major accidents that have occurred at nuclear power plants have resulted in severe environmental contamination. Safe use of nuclear energy therefore remains a significant challenge for the international community. Despite the efforts of the current international nuclear safety regime, in the history of nuclear power operation there have been many

15 Ibid.
16 T.J.V. Walsh, 'Turning Our Backs: Kyoto's Mistaken Nuclear Exclusion', *Georgetown International Environmental Law Review* 16(1), 2003, 147–70.
17 Ibid.

accidents, the most serious of which include the accidents at Three Mile Island in March 1979, at Chernobyl in April 1986, and at Fukushima in March 2011. The Chernobyl accident was particularly important in demonstrating the potential international effects of a nuclear power plant accident. The devastating consequences of the Chernobyl incident prompted the international community to take strong regulatory measures to ensure safe and peaceful uses of nuclear energy. In fact, in the light of the accident's significant transboundary consequences, the safety of nuclear power plants had assumed international dimensions. It was recognised that while each state operating a nuclear power plant bears full and unequivocal responsibility for safety, the maintenance of safety was an international responsibility.[18] At the same time, nuclear energy must be used in conformity with basic safety standards.

The Fukushima nuclear accident in Japan, caused by an earthquake on 11 March 2011, resulted in significant emissions of radioactive particles following hydrogen explosions at three reactors. Radioactivity released from the nuclear power plant also affected the marine environment.[19] It also had broader non-environmental effects: after the Fukushima disaster, Germany's government announced that the country is exiting from the nuclear era. Germany plans to shut down all of its nuclear reactors by 2022, ending its reliance on nuclear energy in favour of safer energy from wind, solar, and hydroelectric power.[20] Nuclear power plants generate 23 per cent of Germany's electricity.[21] On the other hand, it must be mentioned that 13 per cent of Germany's electricity is generated from renewable sources.[22] Germany's decision to exit from nuclear energy is a welcome development from an ecological perspective. Although Germany's decision can hardly be emulated by other states, it reflects the fact that there are other viable sources of renewable energies that can be vigorously pursued elsewhere.

International regulation of nuclear risks

The international regulation of nuclear risks consists of both hard-law prescription and soft-law standards designed to achieve the prohibition of nuclear weapon testing, to ensure nuclear safety and international cooperation in the transboundary movement of radioactive wastes, and to establish a nuclear liability regime for environmental pollution or harm.

The first international instrument in the field of nuclear law was the 1963 Nuclear Test Ban Treaty, which prohibits nuclear weapon test explosions in the atmosphere, in outer space, at sea, in Antarctica, or in any circumstances where radioactive debris spreads beyond the territory of the testing state.[23] Thus, it means that tests must be conducted underground and not cause any pollution. However, many nuclear power states are outside the scope of the

---

18 J. Rautenbach, W. Tonhauser and A. Wetherall, *Overview of the International Legal Framework Governing the Safe and Peaceful Uses of Nuclear Energy: Some Practical Steps*, OECD Paper, 2006, p. 13.
19 'Fukushima Daiichi nuclear disaster'. Wikipedia. Online. Available HTTP: <http://en.wikipedia.org/wiki/Fukushima_Daiichi_nuclear_disaster> (accessed 2 May 2012).
20 J. Dempsey and J. Ewing, 'Germany, in Reversal, Will Close Nuclear Plants by 2022', *New York Times*, 30 May 2011. Online. Available HTTP: <http://www.nytimes.com/2011/05/31/world/europe/31germany.html> (accessed 2 May 2012).
21 Ibid.
22 Ibid.
23 *Treaty Banning Nuclear Weapons Tests in the Atmosphere, in Outer Space and Under Water*, opened for signature 5 August 1963, 480 UNTS 43 (entered into force 10 October 1963) ('Partial Nuclear Test Ban Treaty').

treaty and as such the effectiveness of the convention is questionable. In the *Nuclear Tests* case, the International Court of Justice (ICJ) made no determination as to whether atmospheric tests carried out by France violated customary international law. The Court held, however, that France should stop nuclear tests that led to the fall-out of radioactive waste on Australian territory because the French government had committed to conducting no more tests of this kind.[24]

The cataclysmic nature and the environmental risks associated with the use of nuclear weapons was recognised by the ICJ in its 1996 Advisory Opinion on the Legality of the Threat or Use of Nuclear Weapons. The ICJ held that there is no customary or conventional international law on any comprehensive and universal prohibition of the threat or use of nuclear weapons as such. But it placed severe limits on the use of nuclear weapons. The ICJ emphasised that the use of nuclear weapons during armed conflict, as well as the peaceful use of nuclear energy, poses potentially catastrophic threats to all of humanity. The Court recognised that the environment is under daily threat and that the use of nuclear weapons could constitute a catastrophe for the environment. The Court also recognised that the environment is not an abstraction but represents the living space, the quality of life, and the very health of human beings, including generations unborn. By their very nature, nuclear weapons, as they exist today, could release not only immense quantities of heat and energy, but also powerful and prolonged radiation. They have the potential to destroy all civilisation and the entire ecosystem of the planet. The radiation released by a nuclear explosion would affect health, agriculture, natural resources, and demography over a very wide area. Further, the use of nuclear weapons would be a serious danger to future generations.[25]

The ICJ's opinion is a landmark development on the recognition of the environmental consequences of nuclear weapons testing, and limiting methods of warfare which cause long-term and severe damage to the natural environment. However, it missed the opportunity to prohibit the use of nuclear weapons.

Legal regime on management and transboundary movement of radioactive wastes

The purpose of a nuclear waste management system is to ensure the protection of human beings and the environment and to keep the exposure well below the permissible limits. At the domestic level, nuclear law must establish a legislative framework for the safe management of all sources and types of ionising radiation and radioactive wastes. A legislative framework should ensure that individuals, society, and the environment are adequately protected against radiological hazards.[26]

The issue of environmental consequences of radioactive wastes is a major concern for the international community. The Stockholm Conference in 1972 had called for a registry of radioactive emissions and international cooperation on radioactive waste disposal.[27] However, management of radioactive wastes is excluded from the scope of the Basel Convention on Transboundary Movement of Hazardous Wastes, 1989.[28]

---

24 *Nuclear Tests Case (Australia v France)* ICJ, Rep. (1973), 99 (Interim Measures).
25 *Legality of the Threat or Use of Nuclear Weapons*, Advisory Opinion, (1996) ICJ 226, 241–44 (8 July).
26 Ibid., p. 47.
27 A/CONF.48/14/Rev. 1, Rec. 75, Action Plan for the Human Environment.
28 For further consideration of this treaty see Chapter 17 T.G. Puthucherril in this volume.

The London Convention on the Prevention of Pollution by Dumping of Wastes and Other Matter of 1972 does contain provisions aimed at the dumping of radioactive wastes. Article IV of this Convention prohibits the immersion of high-level radioactive wastes or other high-level radioactive matter as unsuitable for dumping at sea.[29] Chapter 22 of Agenda 21 adopted at the Rio Conference[30] addresses the management of radioactive wastes, and takes as its basis for action the radiological and safety risks resulting from radioactive waste.

Chapter 22 of Agenda 21 focuses on four specific activities: promoting policies and practical measures to minimise and limit the generation of radioactive wastes and to provide for their safe processing, conditioning, transportation, and disposal; supporting efforts within the IAEA to develop and apply radioactive waste safety standards or guidelines and codes of practice; promoting safe storage, transportation and disposal; and prompting proper planning of safe and environmentally sound management, including environmental impact assessment (EIA) where appropriate.[31] It also calls for international cooperation to implement the 1990 IAEA Code and keep under review a possible legally binding instrument; and to encourage the 1972 London Convention to complete studies on replacing the voluntary moratorium on low-level radioactive waste disposal at sea by a ban, taking into account the precautionary approach.[32] It also calls upon states not to promote or allow the storage or disposal of high-, intermediate-, or low-level radioactive wastes near the marine environment and not to export radioactive wastes to countries that prohibit the import of such wastes, such as the parties to the 1991 Bamako Convention and the 1989 Lome Convention; and to respect, in accordance with international law, decisions taken by parties to other regional environmental conventions dealing with other aspects of radioactive wastes.[33]

A Joint Convention on the Safety of Spent Fuel and Radioactive Waste Management was adopted in 1997 and it came into force in 2001.[34] The Convention applies both to radioactive waste disposal and spent fuel management. Article 1 recognises the inter-generational implications of nuclear waste, and mandates detailed national reporting requirements. Parties must aim to avoid imposing 'undue burdens' on future generations, including burdens that are greater than those permitted for present generations.[35] It also contains safety measures for transport. It provides that the states parties must develop programmes to ensure that trans-boundary movement is properly authorised and is conducted with prior notification and the consent of the receiving state.[36] It sets out general safety requirements for the management of spent fuel[37] and radioactive waste,[38] the design, siting,[39] and operation of related facilities,[40] and the establishment of a regulatory framework[41] and independent regulatory body.[42]

29 For further discussion of this treaty see Chapter 16 by D. Cremean and E. Techera in this volume.
30 *Agenda 21* (1992), Report of the UN Conference on Environment and Development, Annex II, UN Doc A/Conf.151/26, Chapter 22.
31 Ibid., para. 22.4
32 Ibid., para. 22.5
33 Ibid., para. 22.5 (d) and (e).
34 *Joint Convention on the Safety of Spent Fuel and Radioactive Waste Management* (1997), 36 ILM 1436.
35 Ibid., Art. 4(vii).
36 Ibid., Art. 27.
37 Ibid., Art. 4.
38 Ibid., Art. 11.
39 Ibid., Art. 6.
40 Ibid., Arts 5 and 9.
41 Ibid., Art. 19.
42 Ibid., Art. 20.

More importantly, recognising Antarctica's status, this Convention wholly prohibits storage or disposal of nuclear waste or spent fuel in Antarctica.[43] Article 27 of the Convention also gives binding effect to the main provisions of the IAEA's 1990 Code of Practice on the Transboundary Movement of Radioactive Waste[44] and sets these as minimum standards for national regulation. The Convention states that national law must provide effective protection for individuals, society, and the environment and give due regard to internationally endorsed criteria and standards.[45] Article 24 of the Joint Convention requires parties to implement 'appropriate corrective measures' to control or mitigate accidental releases of radioactivity.

Regarding transboundary movement of nuclear wastes, it provides that waste or spent fuel may only be exported if the state of destination has the requisite capacity to deal with such materials in a manner consistent with the Convention and if it has given its prior informed consent.[46] But the Convention has many shortcomings: first, reprocessing of spent fuel and spent fuel held for reprocessing are included only if the relevant state party so declares. Second, spent fuel or wastes from civilian installations are included only if transported to permanent civilian control, or if the relevant party so declares.[47]

Legal regime on nuclear safety

Non-Proliferation Treaty (NPT) 1968

The Non-Proliferation Treaty (NPT)[48] remains a major instrument to prevent nuclear non-proliferation and to facilitate nuclear safety. It entered into force in 1970. The main purpose of the NPT is to accelerate and enlarge the contribution of atomic energy to peace, health, and prosperity throughout the world. The NPT created two types of states – 'nuclear weapon' and 'non-nuclear weapon' – each responsible for certain differentiated obligations. The Treaty requires nuclear weapon states to avoid the direct and indirect transfer of nuclear weapons or devices to a non–nuclear weapon state and also to not 'assist, encourage or induce' such states in the manufacture or acquisition of nuclear weapons.[49] Furthermore, transfer of material even for peaceful purposes is also restricted. Under Articles I and II of the Treaty, nuclear weapon states agree not to transfer or assist in the development of nuclear weapons or other nuclear explosive devices, and non–nuclear weapon states agree not to receive or seek the same. In exchange, Article IV of the NPT provides that non–nuclear weapon states are granted the inalienable right to develop research, production, and use of nuclear energy for peaceful purposes without discrimination. The non-nuclear states agreed not to acquire nuclear weapons;[50] and to allow verification of that pledge by placing all of their nuclear

---

43 Ibid., Art. 27 (1).
44 IAEA, GC (XXXIV)/939 (1990):30 ILM(1991), 55.
45 *Joint Convention on the Safety of Spent Fuel and Radioactive Waste Management* (1997), 36 ILM 1436, Arts 4(iv) and 11(iv).
46 Ibid., Art. 27(1).
47 P. Birnie and A. Boyle, *International Law and the Environment*, 2nd edition, New York: Oxford University Press, 2002, p. 463.
48 *Treaty on the Non-Proliferation of Nuclear Weapons*, opened for signature 1 July 1968, 21 UST 483, 729. UNTS 161 (entered into force 5 March 1970).
49 Ibid., Art. 1.
50 Ibid., Art. 2.

equipment and facilities under the safeguard system of the IAEA.[51] Parties to the NPT had a right to use nuclear energy for peaceful purposes, and to assist non-nuclear states, mainly developing countries, in gaining nuclear technology.[52] Finally, Article X allows member states to withdraw from the NPT altogether.

The effectiveness of the NPT is, however, questioned in the light of historical and recent events.[53] The main limitations and weaknesses of the present safeguard arrangements which give cause for environmental concern can be summarised as follows: the failure of many states to become parties to the NPT; the inability of safeguards to prevent the transfer of nuclear technology from nuclear power production to the acquisition of nuclear weapons competence; the practical problems of maintaining effective checks on nuclear inventories; the ease with which states can withdraw from the NPT and from most non-NPT safeguards agreements; deficiencies in accounting and warning procedures; and the absence of reliable sanctions to deter division of safeguarded material. Finally, the NPT's broad language allows a state to develop indigenous capacities for the production of fissionable materials or producing and stockpiling such materials or other components that might be used in nuclear weapons. The implications of this tension are that a country can legitimately stockpile nuclear material, withdraw from the NPT using the Article X exit provision, and declare itself a nuclear power.[54]

The Convention on Nuclear Safety 1994

This Convention[55] defines state obligations in general terms regarding operation of nuclear installations. It entered into force on 24 October 1996. The main objectives of the Convention include achieving and maintaining a high level of safety of civil nuclear power plants and related facilities worldwide through the enhancement of national measures and international cooperation; establishing and maintaining effective defences in nuclear installations against potential radiological hazards in order to protect individuals and society and the environment from harmful effects of ionising radiation from such installations; prevention of accidents with radiological consequences; and mitigating such consequences should they occur.[56] The Convention is the first treaty to commit states to control the risks of nuclear energy for environmental protection. It reaffirms the responsibility for nuclear safety rests with the state having jurisdiction over a nuclear installation and requires each party to establish and maintain a national legislative and regulatory framework for the safety of nuclear installations, including a system of licensing, independent inspection, and enforcement of applicable regulations.[57] It is the most significant agreement for improving the safe operation of nuclear power plants.

Again, this Convention has many shortcomings. First, it does not require internationally uniform minimum safety standards. Instead of standards, the Convention requires adherence

---

51 Ibid., Art. 3.
52 Ibid., Art. 5.
53 R. Sieg, 'A Call to Minimize the Use of Nuclear Power in the Twenty-First Century', *Vermont Journal of Environmental Law* 9(2), 2008, 305–70.
54 J.G. Silver, 'The Global Partnership: The Final Blow to the Nuclear Non-Proliferation Regime?', *New York International Law Review* 21(1), 2008, p. 69.
55 *Convention on Nuclear Safety*, opened for signature 20 September 1994, 33 ILM 1514 (entered into force 24 October 1996).
56 Ibid., Art. 1.
57 Ibid., Arts 7–9.

to a broader set of 'safety principles' that cannot be interpreted as standards.[58] Second, the Convention cannot be enforced through sanctions. The Convention is only an 'incentive' instrument. It depends for its effectiveness on a process of peer review. The lack of enforcement power hampers the Convention's usefulness because states have less incentive to adopt safe measures. Third, the vague language gives states wide latitude in implementation and therefore undercuts the assurance of safety. For example, Article 6 of the Convention provides that parties must make all 'reasonably practicable' improvements to upgrade their safety, and that if upgrades are not possible, states are required to shut down the plant 'as soon as practically possible'. Furthermore it lays down that 'The timing of the shutdown may take into account the whole energy context and possible alternatives as well as the social, environmental and economic impact.'[59] These provisions are rather broadly formulated and lack precision to determine these standards. Finally, the Convention's efficacy has been affected by the fact that it was not signed by all states operating nuclear power plants.[60]

Convention on Early Notification of a Nuclear Accident 1986

This Convention[61] entered into force on 27 October 1986. This Convention imposes a duty on a state party to notify other states likely to be affected by transboundary releases of radioactive material.[62] In the case of transboundary radioactive release, this Convention requires immediate notification of IAEA member states and neighbouring states.[63] The information required to be reported includes the accident's location, the amount of radiation released, and the time of the accident. The notification can be made either directly to the potentially affected states or it can be made to the IAEA, which then disseminates the information.[64] The Convention does not, however, cover nuclear accidents involving military facilities.[65]

Convention on Assistance in the Case of Nuclear Accident or Radiological Emergency 1986

This Convention[66] provides for cooperation between member states in the case of a nuclear accident or radiological emergency to minimise its consequences and to protect life, property, and the environment from the effects of radioactive releases. It requires the affected state party to call for assistance from any other state party directly or through the agency,

---

58 K. McMillan, 'Strengthening the International Legal Framework for Nuclear Energy', *Georgetown International Environmental Law Review* 13, 2001, 983–1031.

59 *Convention on Nuclear Safety*, opened for signature 20 September 1994, 33 ILM 1514 (entered into force 24 October 1996), Art. 6

60 Up to 29 June 2011, 74 states were parties to the Convention. Online. Available HTTP: <http://www.iaea.org/Publications/Documents/Conventions/nuclearsafety_status.pdf> (accessed 2 May 2012).

61 *Convention on Early Notification of a Nuclear Accident*, opened for signature 26 September 1986, 1439 UNTS 275 (entered into force 27 October 1986).

62 Ibid., Art. 1.

63 Ibid., Art. 2.

64 Ibid., Arts 4 and 7.

65 Birnie and Boyle, op. cit., p. 471.

66 *Convention on Assistance in the Case of a Nuclear Accident or Radiological Emergency*, opened for signature 26 September 1986, 1457 UNTS 133 (entered into force 26 February 1987).

specifying the scope and type of assistance required.[67] The state party to which the request is made shall notify the requesting state party whether it is in a position to render the assistance requested.[68] The affected state party may call for such assistance from the IAEA.[69] The Convention requires parties to inform the IAEA of their available experts and assistance equipment, and the IAEA uses the information to coordinate equipment, services, potential aid seekers and donors.[70]

Although the Convention does not help prevent accidents, it improves overall nuclear safety by reducing the likelihood of environmental damage resulting from accidents. Safety measures are needed both to prevent and to respond to accidents, because even with perfect safety regulations some accidents may be unavoidable. Therefore, the Convention can minimise international environmental harm caused by nuclear accidents.

Legal regime on nuclear liability

The nuclear liability regime is based first on exceptional risks arising from nuclear activities where common rules may not be appropriate, and, second, the potential transboundary impact of such risks. The liability regime does not, however, address damage that may be caused by radioactive sources outside of a nuclear installation. The international liability regime is primarily contained in two sets of instruments: the IAEA's 1963 Vienna Convention on Civil Liability for Nuclear Damage,[71] which entered into force in 1977 (Vienna Convention), and the OECD's Paris Convention on Third Party Liability in the Field of Nuclear Energy of 1960[72] (Paris Convention), which entered into force in 1968. A Convention on Supplementary Compensation for Nuclear Damage[73] was adopted in 1997 and applies to all states regardless of whether they are parties to any existing nuclear liability Convention. However, the Supplementary Convention is yet to come into force. A Protocol was adopted to the 1963 Vienna Convention in 1997 and came into force in 2003.

The 1963 Vienna Convention and 1960 Paris Convention imposed absolute liability on the operators of nuclear activities.[74] The choice of the operator to channel all liability, rather than any other potential defendant, is based on two grounds: first, to simplify the plaintiff's choice of defendant and establish a clear line of responsibility; and second, the operator of an installation or a ship is usually in the best position to exercise effective responsibility for it.[75] However, the liability was limited in both temporal and financial aspects. As noted above,

---

67 Ibid., Arts 2 (1) and 2(2).

68 Ibid., Art. 2(3).

69 Ibid., Art. 2(6).

70 Ibid., Art. 2(4).

71 *Vienna Convention on Civil Liability for Nuclear Damage*, opened for signature 21 May 1963, 1063 UNTS 266 (entered into force 12 November 1977). Online. Available HTTP: <http://www.iaea.org/Publications/Documents/Infcircs/1996/inf500.shtml> (status available online. HTTP: <http://www.iaea.org/Publications/Documents/Conventions/liability_status.pdf>) (both accessed 2 May 2012).

72 *Convention on Third Party Liability in the Field of Nuclear Energy*, opened for signature 29 July 1960, 956 UNTS 264 (entered into force 1 April 1968). Online. Available HTTP: <http://www.nea.fr/html/law/nlparis_conv.html> (accessed 2 May 2012).

73 The Convention is available online. HTTP: <http://www.iaea.org/Publications/Documents/Conventions/supcomp.html> (accessed 2 May 2012).

74 Birnie and Boyle, op. cit., p. 477.

75 Ibid., pp. 478–9.

liability is channelled exclusively to the operator of the nuclear installation or ship. The conventions make provision for payment up to the prescribed limit of liability, which is supported by compulsory insurance or security held by the operator and guaranteed by state-funded compensation schemes.[76] The conventions cover most of the sources of nuclear damage. But, unlike the 1960 Paris Convention, the Vienna Convention does not limit itself to damage caused in the territory of state parties.[77] It defines nuclear damage as loss of life, any personal injury or any loss of, or damage to, property arising from a nuclear incident.[78] The operator of a nuclear installation is liable for nuclear damage upon proof that the damage has been caused by a nuclear incident.[79]

Both the 1963 Vienna Convention and the 1960 Paris Convention were revised substantially in 1997 and 2004 respectively to address the concerns raised by the Chernobyl incident. The scope of application of the revised conventions has been extended to ensure that more victims will be entitled to compensation than in the past. The 1997 Vienna Protocol[80] broadens the definition of nuclear damage and extends the period during which claims may be brought for loss of life and personal injury.[81] It also explicitly extends the geographical coverage of damage, including damage 'wherever suffered'.[82] For example, it provides for jurisdiction of coastal states over actions incurring nuclear damage during transport if they occurred within the Exclusive Economic Zone (EEZ). The definition of nuclear damage in the 1963 Convention was simply '(i) loss of life, (ii) any personal injury or any loss of, or damage to, property'. But the 1997 Protocol covers costs of reinstatement of the impaired environment provided the impairment is significant and reinstatement measures are actually taken.[83] Compensation for environmental impairment is limited to loss of income deriving from an economic interest in any use or enjoyment of the environment, where the environment was significantly impaired.[84]

Both the 1997 Vienna Protocol and the 2004 Paris Protocol extend the ten-year time limit for claims to 30 years for loss of life and personal injury. On standing, the revised Vienna Convention provides that the state may bring an action on behalf of victims.[85] Liability under the 1997 Vienna Protocol is strict, but there is an exemption for nuclear damage caused by an act of armed conflict, hostilities, civil war, or insurrection.[86]

The current nuclear liability regime has, however, been widely criticised.[87] According to one author, 'The international nuclear liability regime is extremely patchy, complicated and

---

76 Vienna Convention (1963), Art. 6; Paris Convention (1960), Art. 10.
77 '1997 Vienna Convention on Civil Liability for Nuclear Damage and Convention on Supplementary Compensation for Nuclear Damage', 1997-Explanatory Text, Vienna: IAEA, 2007, p. 6.
78 *Vienna Convention*, Art. 1.1(K).
79 Ibid., Arts 2 and 4.
80 *Convention on Supplementary Compensation for Nuclear Damage*, opened for signature 29 September 1997, 36 ILM 1473 (not yet entered into force) ('CSC'). Online. Available HTTP: <http://www.iaea.org/Publications/Documents/Conventions/supcomp.html> (accessed 2 May 2012).
81 '1997 Vienna Convention on Civil Liability for Nuclear Damage and Convention on Supplementary Compensation for Nuclear Damage', 1997-Explanatory Text, Vienna: IAEA, 2007, p. 2.
82 *Vienna Protocol* (1997), Art. I A.
83 Ibid., Arts I.I (K) (iii) to (vii).
84 Ibid., Art. I.I (K)(v).
85 Ibid., Art. 9 A.
86 Ibid., Art. IV.3.
87 See, McMillan, op. cit.; N. Pelzer, 'Learning the Hard Way: Did the Lesson Taught by the Chernobyl Nuclear Accident Contribute to Improving Nuclear Law?' OECD. Online. Available HTTP: <http://www.oecd-nea.org/law/chernobyl/PELZER.pdf> (accessed 2 May 2012).

features sparse participation.'[88] There are also other limitations of the liability regime such as the inadequacies of the system, including the lack of a neutral tribunal, the general requirement that claimants are to file claims in the courts where the nuclear installation is located, and concerns about the neutrality of the applicable law and limitations on recoverable damages.[89]

Any nuclear liability regime should have the following essential elements: absolute liability should govern; limitations should be unlimited in amount; there should be a fair time limit for liability; all responsible parties should bear liability; there should be a back-up fund; claimants should be able to bring claims in a neutral tribunal; the applicable law should be that of the claimant; there should be a broad definition of recoverable damage; and there should be broad provisions on standing and access to justice.[90] Although the recent amendments to the Vienna and Paris Conventions are much appreciated, they contain many exceptions and the amended Protocols enjoy even more sparse participation than the original conventions.[91] Even under the revised system, no neutral tribunal is provided and claimants are generally required to file claims in the courts where the nuclear installation is located.

The IAEA's role in environment protection

The IAEA was established in 1957 by its statute to promote peaceful uses of nuclear energy globally.[92] The IAEA has been instrumental in adopting many legally binding nuclear safety principles and non-binding safety standards. It helps its member states to build national capacity in conducting independent energy and environmental analysis and in developing strategic national energy plans. In order to protect the environment and avoid health hazards, the Agency assists its member states in planning the management and disposal of radioactive wastes, and provides research and scientific support to developing countries at their request. The use of nuclear techniques to help solve pollution problems is well known and is an important contribution to the concept of sustainable development.[93] But the IAEA has only a limited power to act as an international nuclear inspectorate under its statute. Compulsory inspection is possible only where an assistance agreement is in force.[94]

The scope of the IAEA's involvement in the environmental sphere lies in the sustainable use and management of natural resources, the protection and understanding of the environment through nuclear technology, and protecting humans and ecosystems from ionising radiation. The IAEA is actively involved in ensuring the proper operation, closing and decommissioning of nuclear facilities and the proper handling of other radioactive materials, thereby limiting the release of radioactivity into the environment.[95]

88 D.E.J. Currie, 'The Problems and Gaps in the Nuclear Liability Conventions and an Analysis of How an Actual Claim Would be Brought under the Current Existing Treaty Regime in the Event of a Nuclear Accident', *Denver Journal of International Law and Policy* 35(1), 2006, 85–127, p. 85.
89 Ibid.
90 Ibid., p. 87.
91 Ibid.
92 The Statute is available online. HTTP: <http://www.iaea.org/About/statute_text.html> (accessed 2 May 2012).
93 Atomic Energy and the Environment, Fact sheet of IAEA, Vienna: IAEA.
94 Birnie and Boyle, op. cit., p. 458.
95 Atomic Energy and the Environment, IAEA Fact sheets and FAQs. Online. Available HTTP: <http://www.iaea.org/Publications/Factsheets/English/environment.html> (accessed 2 May 2012).

Currently, nuclear technology is applied in the following fields: the monitoring, assessment and protection of air quality; detecting water pollution, increasing the productivity of land; reducing the use of chemicals for agriculture and forestry resources; improving the prediction and understanding of natural phenomena; and managing the marine environment.[96]

Conclusion

Arguably, nuclear energy will be considered as the most viable option amongst the renewable energy options in the foreseeable future as it produces remarkably little environmental pollution and GHG emissions. It is also considered as one of the ways to reduce dependence on coal, oil, and natural gas. However, the operational safety and reliability of nuclear power plants has remained the main concern from an environmental perspective. An environmentally sound nuclear energy regime should address and alleviate safety, waste, and weapons proliferation concerns.

Responsible management of nuclear wastes, more efficient processes for transformation of uranium to energy, and effective and secure technologies for recycling used nuclear fuel are some of the key issues which must be addressed in order to develop sustainable nuclear energy technologies. The current international legal framework for regulating nuclear safety is inadequate. The legal framework should be further improved so that states are responsible under international law for any failure to exercise due diligence over the siting and operation of nuclear facilities and the transport and disposal of nuclear wastes.[97]

Current resistance to nuclear energy is mainly due to public fear of the potential damage that could result from an accident at nuclear installations or during the transport of nuclear material. Although the current nuclear safety regime has led to significant improvements in nuclear safety, there remain serious environmental risks, which mandate an improved international regime. The safety regime should be further developed from drawing lessons from the Fukushima incident so that any nuclear power plant can withstand any natural calamity of catastrophic scale. At the national level, nuclear energy regulatory regimes should be strengthened to reflect the post-Fukushima safety requirement so that the operation of nuclear power plants does not pose an unacceptable level of risk to the environment and humanity.

---

96 A.M. Cetto and W. Burkart, 'Focus on the Environment', *IAEA Bulletin* 49(2). Online. Available HTTP: <http://www.iaea.org/Publications/Magazines/Bulletin/Bull492/49205660610.html> (accessed 2 May 2012).
97 V.P. Nanda and J.M. Van Dyke, 'International Nuclear Law: An Introduction', *Denver Journal of International Law and Policy* 35(1), 2006, 47–65.

23

International cultural heritage law

Erika J. Techera[*]

Good environmental governance requires the protection and preservation of both the natural and cultural environments. This has been recognised by the international community with a number of heritage conventions being adopted over the last forty years. This chapter introduces and explains the seven key global heritage treaties governing tangible heritage sites, moveable cultural property, intangible heritage and underwater cultural heritage. The key provisions are explored as well as remaining challenges including barriers to implementation, armed conflict and the threat of climate change.

Introduction

Heritage is a universal concept and an integral part of all cultures and societies. Its protection is important as it adds 'to our sense of belonging and group identity'.[1] Conventionally heritage has been defined as that which is inherited, although more recently it has come to involve that which is 'worth preserving and sharing with present and future generations'.[2] Heritage is the expression of our past and therefore part of the 'context that makes us human'.[3]

The United Nations Educational, Scientific and Cultural Organization (UNESCO) has described 'culture' as 'the set of distinctive spiritual, material, intellectual and emotional features of society or a social group, and considers that it encompasses, in addition to art and literature, lifestyles, ways of living together, value systems, traditions and beliefs'.[4] 'Cultural heritage' is therefore the expression of this living culture, embodying its 'history, values and beliefs'.[5]

---

[*] The author is very grateful to Danielle N. Techera for research assistance she provided including proofreading of this chapter.
1 G. Aplin, *Heritage: Identification Conservation and Management*, Oxford: Oxford University Press, 2002, p. 4.
2 Ibid., p. 1.
3 Ibid., p. 4.
4 The *UNESCO Universal Declaration on Cultural Diversity*, 2001. Online. Available HTTP: <http://unesdoc.unesco.org/images/0012/001271/127160m.pdf> (accessed 29 February 2012).
5 W. Wendland, 'Intangible Heritage and Intellectual Property: Challenges and Future Prospects', *Museum International* 56(1–2), 2004, 97–107.

Heritage is frequently divided into natural and cultural elements, although this is often artificial as in many cases items fall into both categories; this is particularly the case with indigenous heritage. The focus of this chapter is cultural heritage, which can take many different forms including monumental architecture, prehistoric villages and sacred sites; craftsmanship and works of art; artistic, linguistic and musical expression; traditional knowledge and customary practices. Cultural heritage is commonly classified as tangible or intangible, moveable or immoveable, or other categories such as indigenous, underwater or World Heritage – and it is these classifications that have often been utilised in international law. Nevertheless, more than one category, and thus a combination of laws, may apply in any given situation. For example, items of underwater cultural heritage, once recovered, become moveable cultural heritage. Similarly intangible heritage, such as traditional designs and fabrication techniques, may be utilised to create a tangible heritage object.

Cultural heritage is intrinsically valuable and safeguarding its diversity is 'as necessary for humankind as biodiversity is for nature'.[6] Cultural heritage is not only valuable to those identifying with it as part of their particular culture, as some sites and objects may be of global significance. Importantly, cultural heritage may provide a key to successfully achieving sustainable development and its economic and environmental importance is increasingly being recognised. Heritage may be put to multiple uses: it can provide context for individual lives and group identity, and it may thus be of political value. It can also be economically valuable, for example as the subject of tourism. From an environmental perspective, the inextricable link between cultural and biological diversity is well established, in both the social and natural sciences.[7] Many parts of the world are both culturally and biologically diverse, which is not purely coincidental as traditional natural resource management practices, for example, have contributed to the maintenance of genetic diversity.[8]

International law in this area has developed in direct response to the pressures placed upon heritage sites, objects and elements. The destruction and illicit trade in cultural heritage during and following the World Wars triggered early treaties. But later threats have emerged including population growth, urbanisation and modernisation, development and the homogenising influence of globalisation, and even tourism. These concerns are exacerbated by contemporary challenges such as climate change, which place further stress on both natural and cultural heritage.

The principal intergovernmental organisation (IGO) with responsibility for protecting cultural heritage is UNESCO. Its mandate includes promoting culture and cultural diversity, acting as a forum for and taking an active role in standard setting, awareness raising and capacity building for the safeguarding of cultural heritage. From a legal perspective UNESCO's early work focused on tangible heritage. However, more recently greater attention has been given to a broader range of heritage, including intangible elements. This has led to an increase in the number of heritage treaties as well as other legal instruments and supporting programmes and initiatives.

In total, seven international cultural heritage treaties have now been adopted. One of the earliest international heritage instruments is the *Convention for the Protection of Cultural Property*

---

6 UNESCO *Universal Declaration on Cultural Diversity*, 2001, Art. 1.
7 L. Maffi, 'Biocultural Diversity and Sustainability', in J. Pretty, A. Ball, T. Benton, J. Guivant, D.R. Lee, D. Orr, M. Pfeffer and H. Ward, (eds) *The Sage Handbook of Environment and Society*, London: Sage Publishing, 2007, pp. 267–77.
8 D.A. Posey, 'Introduction: Culture and Nature: The Inextricable Link', in D.A. Posey (ed.) *Cultural and Spiritual Values of Biodiversity*, Nairobi: UNEP, 1999, pp. 1–18.

in the Event of Armed Conflict 1954 (Hague Convention),[9] adopted in the wake of heritage losses during the two World Wars. From the late 1960s, a number of factors combined to prompt further international action: the exposure of illegal excavations and trade in artefacts, pressures brought upon importing states, indigenous peoples' movement to repatriate their heritage items and the growth in organised crime.[10] The next international law development was the *Convention on the Means of Prohibiting the Illicit Import, Export and Transfer of Ownership of Cultural Property* 1970 (UNESCO Convention).[11] Perhaps the most well known of all the heritage treaties is the *Convention for the Protection of the World Cultural and Natural Heritage* which was adopted in 1972 (World Heritage Convention).[12] It is one of the earliest international laws recognising the linkages between nature and culture. Several decades later the *Convention on Stolen or Illegally Exported Cultural Objects* 1995 (UNIDROIT Convention)[13] sought to strengthen the regime for the protection of moveable cultural property. Three further conventions have been adopted and have come into force much more recently. They are the *Convention on the Protection of the Underwater Cultural Heritage* 2001 (Underwater Cultural Heritage Convention),[14] the *Convention on the Safeguarding of Intangible Cultural Heritage* 2003 (Intangible Cultural Heritage Convention)[15] and the *Convention on the Protection and Promotion of the Diversity of Cultural Expressions* 2005 (Convention on Cultural Expression).[16] Together these seven conventions, and their protocols, make up the corpus of international cultural heritage law.

The protection of cultural heritage is an interdisciplinary undertaking involving a range of actors: governments, the private sector (collectors and dealers), institutions (such as museums and galleries) and experts (archivists, heritage and conservation specialists). Legal approaches tend to involve mechanisms for the identification of appropriate heritage (through lists, registers and inventories, for example) underpinned by key concepts such as significance, uniqueness and representativeness. Thereafter a range of mechanisms and techniques are utilised to protect cultural heritage. Heritage law regimes also have an important role to play in encouraging cooperation, providing frameworks for rectification, sanctions and dispute resolution.[17]

International cultural heritage law is thus a contemporary, dynamic and growing field. While it is not possible here to consider each of the global treaties in detail, the aim

---

9 *Hague Convention for the Protection of Cultural Property in the Event of Armed Conflict*, opened for signature 14 May 1954, 249 UNTS 240 (entered into force 7 August 1956).

10 J.A.R. Nafziger, R.K. Paterson and A.D. Renteln, *Cultural Law: International, Comparative and Indigenous*, Cambridge: Cambridge University Press, 2010, p. 249.

11 *Convention on the Means of Prohibiting the Illicit Import, Export and Transfer of Ownership of Cultural Property*, opened for signature 14 November 1970, 823 UNTS 231 (entered into force 24 April 1972).

12 *Convention Concerning the Protection of the World Cultural and Natural Heritage*, opened for signature 16 November 1972, 1037 UNTS 151 (entered into force 7 December 1975).

13 *Convention on Stolen or Illegally Exported Cultural Objects*, opened for signature 24 June 1995, 34 ILM 1322 (entered into force 1 July 1998).

14 *Convention on the Protection of the Underwater Cultural Heritage*, opened for signature 11 February 2001, 51 ILM 40 (entered into force 2 January 2009).

15 *Convention on the Safeguarding of Intangible Cultural Heritage*, opened for signature 17 October 2003, 2368 UNTS 3 (entered into force 20 April 2006).

16 *Convention on the Protection and Promotion of the Diversity of Cultural Expressions*, opened for signature 20 October 2005, 45 ILM 269 (entered into force 18 March 2007).

17 Nafziger et al, op. cit., p. 249.

is to provide an overview of the regimes, their key provisions and application.[18] The remaining challenges and barriers to implementation will be identified and a brief analysis made as to the lessons these treaties offer for the future development of international environmental law.

World Heritage

The World Heritage Convention is arguably the premier international law instrument for the protection of heritage.[19] It was adopted in 1972 amid global concern for the protection of heritage. Following the destruction of cultural heritage during the two World Wars international attention was drawn to protecting cultural sites and objects. The later construction of the Aswan Dam in Egypt, which threatened 22 temples along the Nile Valley, triggered a UNESCO international campaign that eventually led to the adoption of the World Heritage Convention.[20]

The Convention protects those elements of natural and cultural heritage that are of 'outstanding interest' and need to be preserved 'as part of the world heritage of mankind', it being 'incumbent on the international community as a whole to participate in the protection of the cultural and natural heritage of outstanding universal value'.[21]

The goals of the Convention include the identification of sites of outstanding universal value which are then inscribed on the World Heritage List. Thereafter the aim is to ensure their protection through financial support for restoration (via the World Heritage Fund) and maintenance and the recognition of sites in danger (List of World Heritage in Danger). The Convention creates both state obligations and responsibilities for the international community to achieve these goals.

States nominate sites, within their own territorial jurisdiction, for inclusion on the World Heritage List. Those items are placed on the tentative list pending a decision by the World Heritage Committee. The Committee is a sub-group of member states elected for six-year terms. The Committee makes the decision as to listing but is assisted by two external NGOs (non-governmental organisations) – The International Union for Conservation of Nature (IUCN) in relation to natural sites and the International Council on Monuments and Sites (ICOMOS) with respect to cultural sites – which provide expert evaluations of sites. In addition the IGO the International Centre for the Study of the Preservation and Restoration of Cultural Property (ICCROM) advises on restoration and training.

The World Heritage Convention covers natural[22] and cultural heritage, the latter including monuments, groups of buildings and sites.[23] Operational guidelines expand upon these broad

---

18 Some key texts which explore the heritage law regimes and issues in detail include Nafziger, et al, op. cit.; B.T. Hoffman (ed.), *Art and Cultural Heritage: Law, Policy and Practice*, Cambridge: Cambridge University Press, 2006. See also B. Boer and G. Wiffen, *Heritage Law in Australia*, Oxford: Oxford University Press, 2006.

19 The World Heritage Convention has over 186 states parties: UNESCO, *World Heritage Centre*. Online. Available HTTP: <http://whc.unesco.org/> (accessed 29 February 2012).

20 See D. Hunter, J. Salzman and D. Zaelke, *International Environmental Law and Policy*, 3rd edition, New York: Foundation Press, 2011 p. 1128.

21 World Heritage Convention, Preamble.

22 World Heritage Convention, Art. 2.

23 World Heritage Convention, Art. 1.

definitions and provide selection criteria for the assessment and evaluation of sites.[24] Relevantly, a state must be able to show that a site or object will be well managed and legally protected.[25] Thus the preparation of a 'nomination file' is no simple matter. Once they are listed, states are required to take 'effective and active measures' to protect, conserve and present sites including passing appropriate legislation to manage the sites in accordance with World Heritage Convention obligations.[26]

Sites may be placed on the List of World Heritage in Danger if they are in need of special operations for their preservation. This may be for a variety of reasons including natural threats (extreme weather events, natural decay) as well as man-made threats (development, conflict or even lack of adequate management).[27] Although Article 6(3) requires states not to take 'deliberate measures which might damage . . . heritage', no legal consequences are set out. These sites receive priority funding as well as technical assistance. Sites may also be removed from this special list as threats dissipate.

The World Heritage Fund is one of a limited number of specialist funds established under international environmental conventions.[28] It receives its monies from Convention signatories as well as voluntary contributions. Unsurprisingly it is underfunded, but payment of dues is required before a state party can proceed to election on to the World Heritage Committee. Funds are used for preparatory assistance (preparation of tentative lists and training courses), technical cooperation (conservation and management), training (staff and specialist training for identification, protection, conservation, presentation and rehabilitation) as well as emergency assistance (urgent nominations and emergency plans).

Beyond involvement in the World Heritage Committee and contributions to the World Heritage Fund, international obligations include cooperation and education. In relation to the latter states parties are to develop education and information programmes to 'strengthen appreciation and respect by their peoples of the cultural and natural heritage'.[29] This responsibility works in conjunction with the specific state obligation to 'present' World Heritage in drawing attention to the importance of heritage sites and objects, and their outstanding universal values, as well as ensuring their accessibility to the public.[30]

Significantly, the Convention brings together nature and culture, two elements not previously considered in the same instrument. This linkage was strengthened with the broader interpretation of 'combined works of nature and man'[31] as including 'cultural landscapes'[32] which are of outstanding universal value as well as being representative of cultural elements.[33] This development has allowed a greater range of sites to be included within the World Heritage List. However, listing does not automatically ensure protection. Some of the most

---

24 UNESCO World Heritage Centre, *The Operational Guidelines for the Implementation of the World Heritage Convention*. Online. Available HTTP: <http://whc.unesco.org/en/guidelines> (accessed 29 February 2012).
25 Ibid., Part II.F Protection and Management, particularly para. 98.
26 World Heritage Convention, Art. 5.
27 Aplin, op. cit., p. 172.
28 For further consideration of treaty-specific funding see Chapter 9 by J. Wolst in this volume.
29 World Heritage Convention, Art. 27.
30 World Heritage Convention, Art. 4. For a discussion of the background to the inclusion of 'presentation' (which is not defined in the World Heritage Convention) see Boer and Wiffen, op. cit., p. 81.
31 World Heritage Convention, Art. 1.
32 Operational Guidelines, para. 47.
33 Ibid., Annex 3.

pressing current challenges involve natural events (albeit exacerbated by human activity), the most prominent of which is climate change, which has emerged as a significant threat to World Heritage affecting a number of sites and countries. Sea level rise, acidification and extreme weather events all pose risks to both built and natural sites. The World Heritage Committee has undertaken considerable work to review the risks, develop strategies to assist parties and report on managing the effects of climate change.[34]

Intangible cultural heritage

Although UNESCO first began to specifically focus on intangible cultural heritage in 1971, it was not until 1989 that it adopted the *Recommendation on the Safeguarding of Traditional Culture and Folklore*.[35] This was followed by the *Universal Declaration on Cultural Diversity* in 2001 and the *Istanbul Declaration* in 2002. In addition, the Proclamation of the *Masterpieces of the Oral and Intangible Heritage of Humanity*, which commenced in 2001, sought to raise awareness of intangible cultural heritage by drawing public attention to key elements from around the globe. It was with this background that the Intangible Cultural Heritage Convention was adopted in 2003 and came into force in 2006.[36]

The Intangible Cultural Heritage Convention encourages states to identify and protect intangible heritage within their jurisdictions and safeguard it in ways which maintain its functional relevance. It recognises the interdependence of intangible and tangible cultural heritage and natural heritage, threats to its survival, and the important role of communities (particularly indigenous peoples) in the 'production, safeguarding, maintenance and recreation of the intangible cultural heritage'.[37] The aims of the Intangible Cultural Heritage Convention include safeguarding, ensuring respect for, and raising awareness of the importance of intangible cultural heritage and providing international cooperation and assistance.[38] 'Intangible heritage' is defined in the context of five domains: oral traditions and expressions, including language; performing arts; social practices, rituals and festive events; knowledge and practices concerning nature and the universe; and traditional craftsmanship.[39] 'Safeguarding' is defined under Article 2 and focuses on ensuring the viability of the intangible cultural heritage, its transmission and, where necessary, revitalisation. An Intergovernmental Committee is established to promote the goals of the Convention, provide guidance and make recommendations on measures to safeguard intangible cultural heritage, as well as to develop procedures for inclusion of items on the intangible heritage lists.[40] The obligations of states parties are set out

---

34 See UNESCO World Heritage Centre, *Climate Change and World Heritage*. Online. Available HTTP: <http://whc.unesco.org/en/climatechange/> (accessed 29 February 2012).

35 N. Aikawa, 'An Historical Overview of the Preparation of the UNESCO International Convention for the Safeguarding of the Intangible Cultural Heritage', *Museum International*, 5(1–2), 2004, 137–49.

36 For the text of the Convention see UNESCO, *Text of the Convention for the Safeguarding of Intangible Cultural Heritage*. Online. Available HTTP: <http://www.unesco.org/culture/ich/index. php?lg=en&pg=00006> (accessed 29 February 2012). The Convention currently has 142 states parties.

37 Intangible Cultural Heritage Convention, Preamble.

38 Intangible Cultural Heritage Convention, Art. 1.

39 In particular noting that it must be 'recognized' by a community, group or individual and is being 'constantly recreated'; also that it includes associated tangible heritage such as 'cultural spaces' and 'instruments, objects and artefacts': Intangible Cultural Heritage Convention, Art. 2.

40 Intangible Cultural Heritage Convention, Arts 5 and 7.

in Part III and include the identification of intangible heritage within their territories and the preparation of inventories. Intangible cultural heritage is to be identified with the full participation of all stakeholders, and the form of the inventories is left to be determined by individual countries. State obligations include the responsibility to safeguard heritage by developing a national policy, designating a relevant authority, fostering research and adopting legal, technical, financial and administrative measures.[41] The Convention also provides guidance on the ways to facilitate protection, including education, awareness raising and capacity building and the full participation, consent and involvement of communities.[42] Other state obligations include periodic reporting on legislative, regulatory and other measures taken.[43] International obligations include cooperation[44] and assistance[45] as well as specific measures such as the establishment of a Fund for the Safeguarding of the Intangible Cultural Heritage,[46] a Representative List of the Intangible Cultural Heritage of Humanity[47], and a List of Intangible Cultural Heritage in Need of Urgent Safeguarding to ensure the visibility of, and raise awareness about, intangible heritage.[48] Importantly, under Article 18 the Committee selects and promotes programmes, projects and activities for the safeguarding of intangible heritage and includes best-practice means of implementing them. One such initiative is the *Living Human Treasure* programme, which facilitates the transmission of knowledge, skills and the meaning of intangible cultural heritage by states officially recognising persons who possess a high degree of knowledge and skills and assisting them to transmit this information and associated skills to younger generations.[49] UNESCO has sought to build capacity by providing information and resources in relation to inventorying, safeguarding, transmission and protection of intangible heritage. These include, for example, an outline for inventorying heritage, a Register of Good Practices of Language Preservation, a register of NGOs, centres and experts working on safeguarding intangible cultural heritage, a Database of National Cultural Heritage Laws and the Asia–Pacific Database on intangible cultural heritage.[50]

The Intangible Cultural Heritage Convention is innovative in the approach it takes to heritage protection. Two aspects are particularly notable: the emphasis on public participation, community consent and cooperation in the identification and management of intangible cultural heritage; and the focus on the living nature of such heritage and the necessity for its continued relevance, value and practice.[51]

---

41 Particular reference is made to establishing training and documentation institutions and ensuring access to the intangible cultural heritage while respecting customary practices: Intangible Cultural Heritage Convention, Art. 13.
42 Intangible Cultural Heritage Convention, Arts 14 and 15 respectively.
43 Intangible Cultural Heritage Convention, Art. 29.
44 Intangible Cultural Heritage Convention, Art. 19.
45 Intangible Cultural Heritage Convention, Arts 20–4.
46 Intangible Cultural Heritage Convention, Arts 25–8.
47 Such list to include items previously listed as Masterpieces of the Oral and Intangible Heritage of Humanity: Intangible Cultural Heritage Convention, Art. 31.
48 Intangible Cultural Heritage Convention, Arts 16 and 17 respectively.
49 UNESCO, *Encouraging Transmission of ICH: Living Human Treasures*. Online. Available HTTP: <http://www.unesco.org/culture/ich/index.php?lg=en&pg=00061> (accessed 29 February 2012).
50 See UNESCO *Databases*. Online. Available HTTP: <http://www.unesco.org/new/en/culture/themes/movable-heritage-and-museums/illicit-traffic-of-cultural-property/databases/> (accessed 29 February 2012).
51 R. Kurin, 'Safeguarding Intangible Cultural Heritage: Key Factors in Implementing the 2003 Convention', *International Journal of Intangible Heritage*, 2, 2007, 9–20.

The international focus on intangible cultural heritage has continued with the recent adoption of the Convention on Cultural Expression.[52] This Treaty again indicates international concern to protect cultural diversity from the processes of globalisation. It links the protection and promotion of cultural diversity to human rights and refers specifically to a number of international law principles including sovereignty, cooperation and sustainable development.[53] The Convention calls upon states to protect and promote cultural expression through adopting regulations, providing opportunities for cultural activities, goods and services, facilitating cultural industries, encouraging the free exchange of ideas, cultural expressions and activities amongst stakeholders, supporting artists and establishing public institutions and funds.[54] Importantly the Convention acknowledges not only the importance of international cooperation[55] but also the participation of civil society.[56] An International Fund for Cultural Diversity has been established[57] as well as an Intergovernmental Committee for the Protection and Promotion of the Diversity of Cultural Expressions to promote the objectives of the Convention and encourage and monitor implementation.[58]

While the ratification of the Intangible Cultural Heritage Convention may provide opportunities to enhance protection of cultural heritage, there are also some barriers.[59] Intangible heritage in most need of protection is often in those states with indigenous and traditional communities. Many of these countries are developing with limited financial and technical capacity and therefore they may be reluctant to take on new obligations under international law that divert resources from other projects. The Intangible Cultural Heritage Convention requires states to identify heritage, prepare an inventory, establish a national focal point and develop a national policy. Additional treaty obligations such as reporting requirements may be a practical barrier to ratification of international treaties in the region.[60] Drafting legislation is another issue which will likely pose a challenge in the implementation of the Intangible Cultural Heritage Convention. While the UNESCO databases may offer some guidance, it is clear that new laws would need to be drafted for the specific national context. Many developing nations are in a poor position to design or amend legislation as they lack financial resources and an appropriate pool of expertise. A further consideration is the reality in many countries that economic development remains dominant. As noted above, cultural heritage has important economic value and could provide one avenue for sustainable development. While the Intangible Cultural Heritage Convention focuses on maintaining the functional use and relevance of intangible heritage, it does not articulate how this might be achieved in the context of development. To a certain extent the problem has been addressed through the

52 The Convention currently has 100 parties: UNESCO, *Cultural Expressions: Parties to the Convention.* Online. Available HTTP: <http://www.unesco.org/new/en/culture/themes/cultural-diversity/diversity-of-cultural-expressions/the-convention/parties-to-the-convention/> (accessed 29 February 2012).
53 Convention on Cultural Expression, Art. 2. See also Arts 13 and 14 regarding the integration of culture into sustainable development and cooperation for development and also Art. 16 regarding preferential treatment for developing countries.
54 Convention on Cultural Expression, Arts 6 and 7.
55 Convention on Cultural Expression, Art. 12.
56 Convention on Cultural Expression, Art. 11.
57 Convention on Cultural Expression, Art. 18.
58 Convention on Cultural Expression, Art. 23.
59 For a critique of the implementation challenges see Kurin, op. cit.
60 P.I. Jalal, *Pacific Culture and Human Rights: Why Pacific Island Countries Should Ratify International Human Rights Treaties*, Suva: RRRT/UNDP, 2006.

adoption of the *Convention on the Protection and Promotion of the Diversity of Cultural Expressions*, which focuses upon, *inter alia*, the integration of culture in sustainable development through viable cultural industries, activities, goods and services, wider access to global markets and networks, and appropriate collaborations between developed and developing countries.[61] Ratification of both treaties is needed to facilitate the safeguarding of intangible heritage.

Moveable cultural property

Cultural objects are protected by two international treaties:[62] the UNESCO Convention[63] and the UNIDROIT Convention.[64] The UNESCO Convention aims to protect cultural property from illicit or illegal transfer. The Preamble recognises the importance of balancing the need to interchange cultural property for scientific, cultural and educational purposes and the prevention of 'theft, clandestine excavation and illicit export'.[65] The Convention provides that the import, export or transfer of ownership of cultural property is illicit unless conducted in accordance with its articles.[66] It provides for preventative measures, restitution provisions and an international cooperative framework requiring states to address causes, stop current practices and help make reparations.[67]

Cultural property is the product of cultural heritage and is defined widely in the Convention. It can be anything specifically designated by a state as being of importance in the following categories: archaeology, prehistory, history, literature, art or science.[68] The Convention recognises that illicit trade is 'one of the main causes of the impoverishment of the cultural heritage'[69] and calls on states to establish national services to protect and preserve cultural property. Specific measures include the development of laws; establishment of a national inventory of protected cultural property; promotion of scientific research institutions; supervision of excavations; preparation of ethical rules for curators, collectors and dealers;[70] supervision of archaeological works; monitoring of trade and imposition of sanctions; publicising of missing items; and public education about cultural heritage.[71] The Convention requires states to prohibit the import of stolen cultural property and prevent

---

61 Convention on Cultural Expression, Art. 14.
62 In addition to these is the *Hague Convention for the Protection of Cultural Property in the Event of Armed Conflict* 1954 considered further below.
63 UNESCO, *Convention on the Means of Prohibiting and Preventing the Illicit Import, Export and Transfer of Ownership of Cultural Property – 1970*. Online. Available HTTP: <www.unesco.org/new/en/culture/themes/movable-heritage-and-museums/illicit-traffic-of-cultural-property/1970-convention/> (accessed 29 February 2012). The Convention has 121 signatories.
64 UNESCO, *The 1995 UNIDROIT Convention*. Online. Available HTTP: <http://www.unesco.org/new/en/culture/themes/movable-heritage-and-museums/illicit-traffic-of-cultural-property/1995-unidroit-convention/> (accessed 29 February 2012). The Convention has 43 parties.
65 UNESCO Convention, Preamble.
66 UNESCO Convention, Art. 3.
67 UNESCO Convention, Art. 2.
68 UNESCO Convention, Art. 1.
69 UNESCO Convention, Art. 2.
70 UNESCO has developed such a code: UNESCO, *International Code of Ethics for Dealers in Cultural Property*. Online. Available HTTP: <http://portal.unesco.org/culture/en/ev.php-URL_ID=35190&URL_DO=DO_TOPIC&URL_SECTION=201.html> (accessed 29 February 2012).
71 UNESCO Convention, Art. 5.

museums from collecting illegally exported material.[72] Significantly, the Convention provides for the recovery and return of cultural property illicitly exported after the date the Convention came into force provided compensation is paid to any 'innocent purchaser'.[73]

There are a number of concerns surrounding the UNESCO Convention. Although the Convention provides for the payment of compensation it does not resolve the critical issue of the ownership of cultural property that has been transferred to a third party. A further issue is the range of cultural property covered by the Convention. Although extensive, it is clear that some items would fall outside its scope.[74] With the entry into force of the Intangible Cultural Heritage Convention, the processes involved in creating cultural heritage are safeguarded. However, the products of those processes remain at risk if they do not fall under the ambit of the UNESCO Convention. An example would be traditional textiles, which have been made in traditional ways using traditional materials. The final challenge for the UNESCO Convention is domestic implementation, including national legislation, which some states have been reluctant to adopt.[75] To facilitate operationalisation UNESCO has prepared a *Handbook of Legal and Practical Measures against Illicit Trafficking in Cultural Property*,[76] complemented by the database of national legislation.[77]

The UNIDROIT Convention complements the UNESCO Convention. It seeks to harmonise the laws of the different states in relation to the return of cultural property that was stolen or illegally exported. The Convention addresses some of the previously identified concerns, in particular the tension between legitimate owners and buyers in good faith and the ongoing issues of illegal import and export of cultural property. It is an unusual piece of international law as it relates not only to states but also the people involved in transactions relating to moveable cultural property. The Convention permits private entities to bring proceedings in foreign courts to enforce the provisions. Its scope is wider than the UNESCO Convention as it draws specific attention to the loss of significance by an object's removal from a site and the importance of the intact, entire object.[78] Most significantly, it provides that the 'possessor of a cultural object that has been stolen shall return it' even if there is a buyer in good faith.[79] It allows a member state to request a court of another party to order the return of the cultural object.[80] Compensation is only payable if the possessor can show s/he did not know or ought reasonably to have known it was stolen.[81] This is demonstrated by, for example, having an export certificate and through due diligence in tracing the provenance of the item and having undertaken a responsible investigation of authenticity prior to purchase.

---

72 UNESCO Convention, Art. 7.
73 UNESCO Convention, Art. 7(b)(ii).
74 L. Young 'Australian and International Laws on Export Controls for Cultural Heritage'. Paper presented at the *Art Crime: Protecting Art, Protecting Artists and Protecting Consumers Conference*, Australian Institute of Criminology, Sydney, 2–3 December 1999, p. 4.
75 See for example, Young's comments regarding the United Kingdom: ibid., p. 4.
76 UNESCO *Handbook of Legal and Practical Measures against Illicit Trafficking in Cultural Property*, Doc Ref CLT/CH/INS-06/22. Online. Available HTTP: <http://unesdoc.unesco.org/images/0014/001461/146118e.pdf> (accessed 29 February 2012).
77 UNESCO *Database of National Cultural Heritage Laws*. Online. Available HTTP: <http://www.unesco.org/culture/natlaws/index.php?&lng=en> (accessed 29 February 2012).
78 UNIDROIT Convention, Art. 5(3).
79 UNIDROIT Convention, Art. 3. This only applies to items stolen after the Convention entered into force.
80 UNIDROIT Convention, Art. 5.
81 UNIDROIT Convention, Art. 6.

Importantly, a true owner has three years within which to bring a claim, from the time when s/he became aware of the location of the object, and within 50 years of the theft.[82] Therefore, owners of items that might have been acquired many years ago, such as cultural objects taken during World War II, may not be able to make a claim under this Convention. For certain items the time limitation is removed altogether.[83]

Underwater cultural heritage

Underwater cultural heritage is enormously rich and has immense potential in terms of science, history, archaeology and tourism. In recent years, it has attracted increasing attention, driven in part by new technologies which have enabled access to previously unreachable sites. Underwater cultural heritage involves more than shipwrecks and includes, for example, underwater ruins, prehistoric caves and landscapes. These constitute a precious archaeological heritage of significant cultural importance. In particular, as biological material is often much better preserved underwater than on land, due to the lack of oxygen which facilitates deterioration, many of these sites are unique.

Early international law protections were minimal as accessible heritage tended to be found close to shore rather than in international waters. The only notable provisions are in the UN Convention on the Law of the Sea (UNCLOS), which provides that 'all objects of an archaeological and historical nature' found on the seabed beyond national jurisdiction[84] 'shall be preserved or disposed of for the benefit of mankind as a whole', with preferential rights given to the state of cultural, historical and archaeological origin.[85] Furthermore, state obligations include 'the duty to protect objects of an archaeological and historical nature found at sea'.[86]

Although, UNESCO had addressed underwater heritage quite early, in its 1956 *Recommendation on International Principles Applicable to Archaeological Excavation*, this applied only to underwater sites within national jurisdictions. In recognition of the significance of underwater cultural heritage, and the increasing threats it faced, drafting began on a broader international treaty in 1993 and the Underwater Cultural Heritage Convention was adopted in 2001 but only came into force in 2010.[87]

---

82 UNIDROIT Convention, Art. 3.

83 For further discussion see I.A. Stamatoudi, *Cultural Property Law and Restitution: A Commentary to International Conventions and European Union Law*, Cheltenham: Edward Elgar, 2011; L.V. Prott, 'UNESCO and UNIDROIT: 'A Partnership Against Trafficking in Cultural Objects', *Uniform Law Review*, 1, 1996, 59–71.

84 Essentially more than 200 nautical miles from any coastal state.

85 UNCLOS, Art. 149 'Archaeological and historical objects'.

86 UNCLOS, Art. 303 'Archaeological and historical objects found at sea'. The law of salvage and admiralty are specifically preserved and the article makes it clear that this provision is 'without prejudice to other international agreements and rules of international law regarding the protection of objects of an archaeological and historical nature'.

87 UNESCO, *About the Convention on the Protection of the Underwater Cultural Heritage*. Online. Available HTTP: <http://www.unesco.org/new/en/culture/themes/underwater-cultural-heritage/2001-convention/> (accessed 29 February 2012). The Convention currently has 41 state signatories. For an analysis of the Convention see U. Koschtial, 'The 2001 UNESCO Convention on the Protection of the Underwater Cultural Heritage: Advantages and Challenges', *Museum International* 60(4), 2008, 63–9; T.J. Maarleveld, 'How and Why will Underwater Cultural Heritage Benefit from the 2001 Convention?', *Museum International* 60(4), 2008, 50–62. See also S. Drumgoole (ed.) *Legal Protection of the Underwater Cultural Heritage*, London: Kluwer Law International, 1999.

The overall aim of the Convention is 'to ensure and strengthen the protection of underwater cultural heritage'[88] in response to 'increasing commercial exploitation'.[89] The Convention provides for the authorisation of underwater cultural heritage activities by competent authorities. The definition of underwater cultural heritage is drafted broadly to include 'all traces of human existence having a cultural, historical or archaeological character', provided they have been in the water 'for at least 100 years'.[90] The Convention covers vessels, sites, structures, artefacts, human remains 'together with their archaeological and natural context' and prehistoric objects.[91]

Article 2 sets out the objectives and principles. In short, the Convention provides that states should, individually or cooperatively, protect underwater cultural heritage for the benefit of humanity. It stipulates that underwater cultural heritage should not be commercially exploited, nor should it be irretrievably dispersed. However, this is not to be understood as preventing archaeological research or tourist access. Indeed responsible, non-intrusive access is encouraged, recognising that proper respect for human remains should be observed.

The Convention encourages scientific research, training in underwater archaeology and the transfer of technology,[92] cooperation and sharing of information[93] and public education,[94] and generally calls upon states to work together, including through international agreements, to preserve underwater heritage.[95] It requires parties to ensure their nationals give notification of their intention to explore in the exclusive economic zone (EEZ) or on the continental shelf of another state and report when a discovery is made.[96] It is recognised that *in situ* preservation is the first option,[97] but where objects are recovered they shall be 'deposited, conserved and managed' to ensure their long-term preservation.[98] The Convention contains agreed measures on the protection of heritage in areas beyond national jurisdiction.[99] States are required to take measures to regulate their nationals and vessels,[100] including the imposition of sanctions,[101] and procedures for seizure of underwater cultural heritage where necessary.[102] No reservations are permitted.[103]

Of particular note is the Annex to the Convention, entitled *Rules Concerning Activities Directed at Underwater Cultural Heritage*, which is in essence a guide to project management. It confirms that activities may be authorised if they make a 'significant contribution to protection or knowledge or enhancement of'[104] but do not 'adversely affect' underwater cultural

88 Underwater Cultural Heritage Convention Art. 2.
89 Underwater Cultural Heritage Convention, Preamble.
90 Underwater Cultural Heritage Convention Art. 1(a).
91 Ibid. Pipelines, cables and similar installations are excluded: Article 1(b) and (c). See also C. Forrest, 'Defining "Underwater Cultural Heritage", *International Journal of Nautical Archaeology* 31(1), 2002, 3–11.
92 Underwater Cultural Heritage Convention Art. 21.
93 Underwater Cultural Heritage Convention Art. 19.
94 Underwater Cultural Heritage Convention Art. 20.
95 Underwater Cultural Heritage Convention Art. 6.
96 Underwater Cultural Heritage Convention Art. 9.
97 Underwater Cultural Heritage Convention Art. 2(5).
98 Underwater Cultural Heritage Convention Art. 2(6).
99 Underwater Cultural Heritage Convention Art. 12.
100 Underwater Cultural Heritage Convention Art. 16.
101 Underwater Cultural Heritage Convention Art. 17.
102 Underwater Cultural Heritage Convention Art. 18.
103 Underwater Cultural Heritage Convention Art. 30.
104 Underwater Cultural Heritage Convention Annex, Rule 1.

heritage.[105] Rule 2 confirms that commercial exploitation for profit and the irretrievable dispersal of objects is inconsistent with the Convention. Rules 9 to 13 set out how a project is to be designed, including *inter alia* the inclusion of a preliminary evaluation, the qualifications of staff, the methodology and techniques used, environmental and safety policies, a documentation programme and a deposition plan.

The Convention is an important step forward in setting international standards for underwater cultural heritage preservation. It also contributes to capacity building through the inclusion of the Annex. The Convention facilitates research and, for example, tourism, which can incentivise protection and provide livelihoods. But it neither regulates the ownership of heritage, nor does it change the sovereign rights of states. Therefore, it must be implemented in combination with other law.

Armed conflict

Cultural property is at particular risk during armed conflict and may be deliberately attacked, subject to pillage or incidentally damaged during hostilities such as bombing. The first steps towards a global convention were taken in the nineteenth century.[106] But this did not prevent significant damage and destruction during the two World Wars. The subsequent Geneva Convention of 1949 made no specific reference to cultural property or heritage and continuing international concern led to the adoption of the Hague Convention in 1954.[107]

The Convention provides for the protection of cultural property during international or civil wars, including times of occupation.[108] Obligations are placed on both the state in which the property is situated and the attacking or occupying force.[109] Parties are required to instruct their military forces to ensure adherence to the Convention[110] and foster public respect by, for example, disseminating the Convention text.[111]

Cultural property is defined as 'movable or immovable property of great importance to the cultural heritage of every people'.[112] It is identified using a blue and white shield

---

105 Underwater Cultural Heritage Convention Annex, Rule 3.
106 The most significant being the *Lieber Code: Instructions for the Government of Armies of the United States in the Field*, 1863. Online. Available HTTP: <http://www.icrc.org/ihl.nsf/FULL/110?OpenDocument> (accessed 29 February 2012). Followed by the *Convention with respect to the Laws and Customs of War on Land* (Hague, II) 1899 and the *Convention on the Laws and Customs of War on Land* (Hague IV) 1907. These are contemporary protection regimes but there are many earlier examples, including, for example, medieval European protection of churches and seventh-century Islamic protection of monasteries.
107 See further J. Toman, *The Protection of Cultural Property in the Event of Armed Conflict*, Aldershot: Dartmouth Publishing, 1996; K. Hulme, *War Torn Environment: Interpreting the Legal Threshold*, Leiden: Martinus Nijhoff Publishers, 2004; N. Al-Duaij, *Environmental Law of Armed Conflict*, Ardsley: Transnational Publishers, 2004. For an overview of the legal framework see E. Techera, 'Protection of Cultural Heritage in Times of Armed Conflict: The International Legal Framework Revisited', *Macquarie Journal of International and Comparative Environmental Law*, 4(2), 2007, 1–20.
108 Hague Convention, Art. 5.
109 Hague Convention, Art. 4.
110 Hague Convention, Art. 7.
111 Hague Convention, Art. 25.
112 Hague Convention, Art. 1.

emblem[113] and can be given 'general protection' or 'special protection'.[114] 'General protection' requires parties to make preparations in peacetime.[115] Thereafter states must refrain from using their own and other states' cultural property for any purpose likely to expose it to damage or destruction.[116] The only exception is 'military necessity'.[117] Parties must also prohibit, prevent and, if necessary, put a stop to pillage, theft, misappropriation and vandalism of cultural property.[118] There is no military necessity exception in relation to this provision.

Pursuant to Article 8, 'special protection' may be granted to refuges to shelter movable cultural property and centres containing immovable cultural property 'of very great importance'. The property must be away from large industrial centres or any important military objective and is not to be used for military purposes.[119] Once registered, parties must refrain from any act of hostility directed against it. The only exception is 'unavoidable military necessity'.[120] A problem with this wording is that it would not protect buildings, such as museums and art galleries, located in city centres. Therefore, much cultural property remains protected at only the general level.

The most significant problem with the Hague Convention was the lack of any definition of 'military necessity'. Furthermore, there is no Convention body to oversee implementation and no requirement for regular meetings.[121] However, the Convention does include the obligation to report to UNESCO at least once every four years.[122] Article 23 provides for parties to call upon UNESCO for technical assistance, but it has no overriding power to implement the Convention.[123] Article 28 provides for sanctions and the prosecution of offenders but only within the states' 'ordinary criminal jurisdiction'. Breaches of the Convention are not international war crimes and therefore there is no mechanism to bring prosecutions in an international court.

Certain provisions were separated from the Convention and placed in the 1954 Protocol 1 to the Hague Convention. Protocol 1 largely deals with occupation, requiring an occupying

---

113 Hague Convention, Arts 16 and 17. For a detailed discussion of use of the emblem including the marking of destroyed cultural sites see Jan Hladik, 'Marking of Cultural Property with the Distinctive Emblem of the 1954 Hague Convention for the Protection of Cultural Property in the Event of Armed Conflict' *International Review of the Red Cross*, 86(854), 2004, 379–87.

114 Protocol 2 to the Hague Convention 1954 provides for 'enhanced protection', which is discussed further below.

115 Hague Convention, Art. 3.

116 Hague Convention, Art. 4.

117 Hague Convention, Art. 4(2). See further below.

118 Hague Convention, Art. 4(3).

119 Hague Convention, Art. 8(1). Shelters for movable cultural property may be granted special protection wherever they are situated as long as they are unlikely to be damaged by bombs: Hague Convention, Art. 8(2).

120 Hague Convention, Art. 11.

121 Although there is provision for meetings to be convened by UNESCO: Hague Convention, Art. 27.

122 Hague Convention, Art. 26(2).

123 The International Committee of the Red Cross (ICRC) is expected to ensure compliance with the Geneva Convention and its Protocols but has no role in relation to the Hague Convention 1954. See Resolution 11 regarding the protection of cultural property in the event of armed conflict document drawn up by British and German Red Cross Societies and ICRC September 2001. ICRC No. 845 March 2002 pp. 284–5.

state to prevent the export of cultural property,[124] seize all cultural property imported from an occupied territory and return seized property at the close of hostilities.[125] Furthermore, provision is made for payments to third-party legitimate holders of cultural property which is returned, provided they received the property in good faith.[126]

The continued loss of cultural property led to the further consideration of the provisions of the Hague Convention. Four main problems were identified: 'military necessity', limited protection during domestic disputes, a lack of a robust framework of sanctions and the absence of any organising body to administer the Convention. The second Protocol provides for increased pre-planning to protect cultural property. A national inventory must be prepared, emergency measures developed and all moveable cultural property removed from areas likely to be damaged, or adequate protections must be put in place to protect *in situ* property.[127] Furthermore, competent authorities must be established with responsibility for the safeguarding of cultural property. The attacking party has a duty to take all feasible precautions in choosing targets and to ensure that objects likely to be attacked are not protected cultural property. States must refrain from attack if the objective is the destruction of protected cultural property or incidental damage might be suffered that is excessive in relation to the anticipated military advantage.[128]

Protocol 2 established a *Committee for the Protection of Cultural Property in the Event of Armed Conflict* (the Committee), which grants 'enhanced protection'[129] to property of 'the greatest importance to humanity', provided it is already protected under domestic legislation and is not used for military purposes or to shield military sites.[130]

One of the most important advancements is the inclusion of a definition of 'military necessity'. It was agreed that it did not give an unfettered power to damage or destroy cultural property. Cultural property with 'general protection' may be used for purposes likely to endanger it only where there is no feasible alternative to obtain a similar military advantage;[131] for example, where it has, by its use, become a military objective and there is no feasible alternative to obtain a similar military advantage. Two safeguards are provided: an

---

124 Hague Convention, Protocol 1, Art. 1.
125 Hague Convention, Protocol 1, Art. 3.
126 There are several other international agreements that protect cultural heritage in times of armed conflict including the 1977 Protocols I and II to the 1949 Geneva Convention. Protocol I applies to international armed conflict and Protocol II to non-international conflicts. Article 53 of Protocol I prohibits acts of hostility against 'historic monuments, works of art or places of worship' and the use of such objects in support of the military effort or as objects of reprisals. Article 38 prohibits the deliberate misuse of the protective emblem of cultural property. Similarly, Article 16 of Protocol II also prohibits acts of hostility directed against cultural property and the use of such property in support of a military effort. Article 85 of Protocol I provides that the deliberate breach of Article 53, in relation to property granted special protection, resulting in extensive destruction, constitutes a 'grave breach' and therefore a war crime. There is no reciprocal Article in Protocol II: *Protocols Additional to the Geneva Conventions of August 12, 1949 and Relating to the Protection of Victims of International and Non-international Armed Conflicts*, 1125 UNTS 3 (Protocol I) and 1125 UNTS 609 (Protocol II) (entered into force 7 December, 1978); see ICRC *International Humanitarian Law – Treaties & Documents, 1949 Conventions & Additional Protocols*. Online. Available HTTP: <http://www.icrc.org/ihl.nsf/CONVPRES?OpenView> (accessed 29 February 2012).
127 Hague Convention, Protocol 2, Art. 8.
128 Hague Convention, Protocol 2, Art. 7.
129 Hague Convention, Protocol 2, Art. 11.
130 Hague Convention, Protocol 2, Art. 10.
131 Hague Convention, Protocol 2, Art. 6.

officer commanding a force equivalent to a battalion must decide to invoke military necessity and a warning must be given in advance where circumstances permit.[132]

Property granted 'enhanced protection' will lose its special status if, by its use, it becomes a military objective.[133] In those circumstances, it may then be attacked only if that is the only feasible way of terminating such use and measures are taken to minimise damage. The decision must be taken at the highest level of command and a warning must be given in advance of such attack.[134]

Protocol 2 establishes individual criminal responsibility for violations of the Protocol. Attacking cultural property granted 'enhanced protection' is a 'serious violation' and subject to universal jurisdiction. A similar provision is included for cultural property with 'general protection', but only where extensive destruction of such property results.

Overall, Protocol 2 has addressed much of the earlier criticism. The simplified procedure for granting 'enhanced protection' should ensure that more cultural property is protected at this higher level. The greater precision in relation to 'military necessity' and stricter sanctions should also provide a better enforcement mechanism. Whilst the Protocol contains safeguards to protect the sovereignty of states and provides that the primary jurisdiction resides within the territorial state[135] they still represent a major step forward with the inclusion of universal jurisdiction. The Protocol also applies to non-international armed conflicts; therefore, serious violation provisions invoking universal jurisdiction apply to domestic conflicts.[136] However, the retention of this exception will continue to result in military action being taken against cultural property.

The Hague Convention and its protocols provide a valuable legal framework for the protection of cultural property. However, ratifications are relatively low and therefore many states are only subject to limited international obligations contained in other treaties or under customary international law.[137] UNESCO has recognised the continued failure to prevent deliberate damage to cultural property in its *Declaration Concerning the Intentional Destruction of Cultural Heritage* 2003.[138] The Declaration calls upon states to become parties to the Hague Convention and promote the adoption and implementation of legal regimes to protect cultural heritage. The Declaration also calls for states to take all measures to prevent intentional destruction of cultural heritage, wherever it is located, during peacetime activities and when in occupation. The loss, for example, of the Bamiyan Buddhas[139] illustrates that there is little the law can do to protect cultural property from deliberate and wilful destruction, particularly by non-state actors.

---

132 Hague Convention, Protocol 2, Art. 6.
133 Hague Convention, Protocol 2, Art. 14.
134 Hague Convention, Protocol 2, Art. 13.
135 Hague Convention, Protocol 2, Art. 15.
136 Hague Convention, Protocol 2, Art. 22.
137 The HC has 123 parties (including the US which ratified in 2009); P1 has 100 parties and P2 has 61: UNESCO, *Culture: The States Parties*. Online. Available HTTP: <http://www.unesco.org/new/en/culture/themes/movable-heritage-and-museums/armed-conflict-and-heritage/the-states-parties/> (accessed 29 February 2012).
138 The text of the Declaration is online. Available HTTP: <http://portal.unesco.org/en/ev.php-URL_ID=17718&URL_DO=DO_TOPIC&URL_SECTION=201.html> (accessed 29 February 2012).
139 For a discussion of the Taliban's destruction in 2001 of these statues in Afghanistan see K. Wangkeo, 'Monumental Challenges: The Lawfulness of Destroying Cultural Heritage During Peacetime', *Yale Journal of International Law* 28, 2003, 183–274.

Conclusion

It is clear from the above discussion that international heritage law has significantly expanded in recent decades and now covers, at least to some extent, a broad range of heritage items. In the past much of the literature in the field revolved around definitional and terminological issues.[140] Nevertheless, some more substantive issues remain. As with most areas of international law, each of the Conventions relies heavily on state implementation. However, UNESCO has sought to build legal capacity at the domestic level through handbooks,[141] guidelines, programmes[142] and its databases, the most significant of which is the UNESCO Database of National Cultural Heritage Laws.[143]

Beyond these issues a number of new challenges and cross-cutting issues are emerging. Climate change poses both direct and indirect challenges to cultural heritage. Sea-level rise and extreme weather events can directly affect heritage sites and objects. But they also pose risks to intangible heritage and the very survival of some cultures where whole nations may become inundated and displaced from their traditional lands.[144] International law supports indigenous collective rights to practise culture,[145] but much remains to be done to secure indigenous heritage.[146] The protection of bio-cultural heritage[147] and sacred sites[148] are other areas of importance to indigenous peoples. Further concerns surround cultural property originating from indigenous resources, repatriation of indigenous remains and the legal avenues which protect indigenous culture more broadly.[149]

Exploring the body of international heritage law as a whole, it can be seen to encompass a broad mix of regulatory options and innovative practices to protect and safeguard cultural heritage. Each of the treaty regimes examined above adds something to the mix. The Intangible Cultural Heritage Convention incorporates innovative mechanisms which involve local communities and individual holders in practising their cultural heritage to ensure this

---

140 See e.g. L.V. Prott and P.J. O'Keefe, '"Cultural Heritage" or "Cultural Property"?' *International Journal of Cultural Property* 1, 1992, 307–20.

141 UNESCO *Legal and Practical Measures Against Illicit Trafficking in Cultural Property: UNESCO Handbook*, International Standards Section, Division of Cultural Heritage, 2006. Online. Available HTTP: <http://unesdoc.unesco.org/images/0014/001461/146118e.pdf> (accessed 29 February 2012).

142 UNESCO, *Cultural Expression Technical Assistance: Strengthening the System of Governance for Culture in Developing Countries*. Online. Available HTTP: <http://www.unesco.org/new/en/culture/themes/cultural-diversity/diversity-of-cultural-expressions/programmes/technical-assistance/> (accessed 29 February 2012).

143 UNESCO *Databases*. Online. Available HTTP: <http://www.unesco.org/new/en/culture/themes/movable-heritage-and-museums/illicit-traffic-of-cultural-property/databases/> (accessed 29 February 2012).

144 Burkett in Chapter 40 of this volume explores the issues of climate-induced displacement and refugees.

145 For further consideration of indigenous collective rights see Chapter 32 by S. Alam in this volume.

146 T. Chapman '*Corroboree Shield*: A Comparative Historical Analysis of (the Lack of) International, National and State Level Indigenous Cultural Heritage Protection' *Macquarie Journal of International and Comparative Environmental Law*, 5, 2008, 81–96.

147 E. Techera, 'Safeguarding Indigenous Bio-Cultural Heritage in the South Pacific Small Island States' *Policy Matters*, 17, 2010, 29–33.

148 See e.g. B. Verschuuren, R.G. Wild, J. McNeely and G. Oviedo (eds) *Sacred Natural Sites: Conserving Nature and Culture*, London: Earthscan, 2010.

149 See e.g. A.C. Cheng, 'All in the Same Boat? Indigenous Property Rights in Underwater Cultural Heritage', *Houston Journal of International Law* 32(3), 2010, 695–732.

heritage remains alive. The Underwater Cultural Heritage Convention has embedded a project management guide in its Annex which engages with and acknowledges the important role of the private sector and heritage experts in exploration and preservation. This provides guidance on good governance while not stifling non-consumptive uses of heritage through, for example, tourism. The UNIDROIT Convention also addresses private sector concerns through its mechanism to address ownership issues. Even the World Heritage Convention has evolved to include new approaches such as cultural landscapes and serial sites, which assist with holistic conservation and broaden the representativeness of sites listed.

It is therefore clear that cultural heritage law has much to offer other areas of international law, in terms not only of substantive law but also of the tools and processes embedded within the different treaty regimes. The focus of the Intangible Cultural Heritage Convention on the processes that will safeguard heritage, and the establishment of programmes and the incorporation of expert project management in the Underwater Cultural Heritage Convention, both provide valuable models transferrable to other areas. The ongoing evolution of international cultural heritage law is at least in part due to the strong role that UNESCO plays in 'championing' heritage protection. But it is clear that heritage continues to be lost at a rapid rate. As several of the international treaties considered above are relatively new instruments, it remains to be seen whether the innovative mechanisms will be effective at halting the loss of cultural heritage, and thereafter in what other fields they may be employed.

Part IV
Regional environmental law

24

European environmental law

*Elisa Morgera**

This chapter aims to illustrate the development of the environmental law of the European Union (EU) through policy and legislative developments, with a view to emphasising the unique characteristics of the EU legal framework and their relevance from an international environmental law perspective. The objectives and principles of EU environmental law are then discussed, and some of the present challenges facing EU environmental law are identified.

Introduction

There are several reasons why the environmental law of the European Union (EU) makes an interesting topic for international environmental lawyers. First of all, the EU is a prominent international actor, proactively engaged in the development and implementation of international environmental law. For example, the EU is a party to over 40 multilateral environmental agreements (MEAs).[1] This has required changes in the process of international law-making and implementation, to enable the EU as a Regional Economic Integration Organization to participate more effectively in international fora,[2] possibly paving the way for other regional organisations to do so in the future.

In addition, EU environmental law is the most sophisticated example of a regional regime of international environmental law that can be of inspiration (in its successes and short-comings) to other regions establishing free trade agreements.[3] Within MEAs and other

---

* The author is very grateful to Robert Lane, Niamh Nic Shuibhne, Elsa Tsioumani and Soledad Aguilar for their useful comments on an earlier draft of this contribution, and to Gracia Marín Durán for generously sharing her views on EU law along the years of our collaboration.

1 European Commission, 'Multilateral Environmental Agreements to which the EC is a Contracting Party or a Signatory'. Online. Available HTTP: <http://ec.europa.eu/environment/international_issues/pdf/agreements_en.pdf> (accessed 16 March 2012) (although updated only to 2006).

2 L. Kramer, 'Regional Economic Integration Organizations: The European Union as an Example', in D. Bodansky, J. Brunnée and E. Hey (eds) *The Oxford Handbook of International Environmental Law*, Oxford: Oxford University Press, 2007, pp. 853 76.

3 P. Sands, *Principles of International Environmental Law*, Cambridge: Cambridge University Press, 2003, p. 733.

international processes the EU in practice makes a powerful negotiating block, speaking on behalf of its 27 Member States and often of other associated countries[4] and representing the largest provider of official development aid and contributions to UN budgets.[5] Thus, the EU uses its external policies at the multilateral level to increase its influence over the making of international law and policies of international organisations.[6] Furthermore, international environmental law plays a significant role in the bilateral and unilateral external action of the EU, both in its development cooperation and in its political and economic cooperation with neighbouring countries and distant emerging economies.[7]

Significantly, attempts to influence international environmental law by the EU are not confined to its (multilateral or bilateral) external action. The EU is also increasingly using its 'domestic' law-making powers to inspire the development of international environmental law: the most notable case is that of the EU Climate and Energy Package adopted in 2009, which anticipates agreement on a future international climate change regime.[8]

Furthermore, as a 'new legal order of international law' that imposes obligations and confers rights not only on states but also on their nationals,[9] EU environmental law provides additional legal means to ensure prompt and effective implementation of international environmental law at the EU and Member State level (a phenomenon called 'Europeanisation of international law').[10] By becoming part of the EU legal order, international environmental law acquires primacy over conflicting provisions of national law of the EU Member States. In addition, national courts are obliged to interpret provisions of national law in conformity with Europeanised international environmental norms. Equally, EU law itself is to be interpreted in conformity with international environmental instruments to which the EU is a party, so that international environmental instruments and norms can be used in principle to control the validity of EU norms. In addition, enforcement of international environmental law, once included in the EU legal order, can be ensured through the EU-level enforcement procedure against Member States that either do not transpose or fail to actually apply and enforce international treaties concluded by the EU (this may also lead to the imposition of financial penalties). Action for damages brought by individuals against the EU or against

4 For instance, at the UN World Summit the EU spoke on behalf of 36 countries – see E. Morgera and G. Marín Durán, 'The UN 2005 World Summit, the Environment and the EU: Priorities, Promises and Prospects,' *Review of European Community and International Environmental Law* 15, 2006, 1–18.

5 EU@UN website, 'Overview: European Union at the UN'. Online. Available HTTP: <http://www.europa-eu-un.org/articles/articleslist_s88_en.htm> (accessed 3 May 2012).

6 J. Wouters, A. Nollkaemper and E. de Wet, 'Introduction' in Wouters, Nollkaemper and de Wet (eds), *The Europeanization of International Law: The Status of International Law in the EU and its Member States*, The Hague: TMC Asser Press, 2008, p. 7.

7 G. Marín Durán and E. Morgera, *Environmental Integration in the EU's External Relations: Beyond Multilateral Dimensions*, Oxford: Hart Publishing, 2012.

8 H. Vedder, 'Diplomacy by Directive: An Analysis of the International Context of the Emissions Trading Directive', Social Science Research Network, 2009; K. Kulovesi, E. Morgera and M. Muñoz, 'Environmental Integration and the Multi-faceted International Dimensions of EU Law: Unpacking the EU's 2009 Climate and Energy Package', *Common Market Law Review* 48, 2011, 829–91.

9 Case 26/62 *Algemene Transport- en Expeditie Onderneming van Gend en Loos vNederlandse Belastingsadministratie* [1963] ECR 1; Sands, op. cit., p. 734. Note that the Court has no longer used that expression, but rather referred to the EU as a *sui generis* legal system: M. Puder, 'The Rise of Regional Integration Law: Good News for International Environmental Law', *Georgetown International Environmental Law Review* 23, 2011, 165–210, p. 172.

10 Wouters et al., op. cit., pp. 7–11.

Member State authorities for breaches of Europeanised international environmental norms is also in principle possible.[11]

From a comparative perspective, EU environmental law is not only significantly influencing the development of national environmental law in the EU Member States,[12] but also national law beyond its borders: countries in the process of acceding to the EU and also those aspiring to this,[13] as well as those interested in a closer political and economic relationship with the EU, have concluded international treaties providing for the approximation of their environmental laws to those of the EU.[14]

This chapter will illustrate the development of environmental law of the EU with a view to stressing the unique characteristics of the EU legal framework and their relevance from an international environmental law perspective. The chapter will then discuss the objectives and principles of EU environmental law and identify some of its present challenges.

The evolution of EU environmental law

Traditionally, the evolution of EU environmental law is illustrated by successive phases characterised by the entry into force of the treaties that instituted and regulate the EU (the Treaties).[15] This is because the EU can only act, both externally and internally, within the limits of the powers conferred upon it by the Treaties and towards the objectives assigned to it therein (principle of conferral or of attributed competences[16]). While Treaty developments are certainly key elements in the evolution of EU environmental law, other influential factors should also be taken into account: notably, the influence of concurrent developments in international environmental law and the different economic conditions and environmental law traditions of new Member States.[17] It will also be clarified that often Treaty amendments, rather than introducing radically new elements, endorsed developments that had already appeared and crystallised in the practice of the EU.

First phase (1958 to 1972): birth of the EEC and 'incidental'[18] environmental action

The founding Treaty of the European Economic Community (EEC) (Treaty of Rome) entered into force in 1958: it provided for the creation of a single common market in Europe, with a view to preserving and strengthening peace and stability.[19] The common market was

---

11 Ibid., pp. 9–10. On the special legal protection afforded to EU environmental law, see J. Jans and H. Vedder, *European Environmental Law*, Groningen: Europa Law Publishing, 2008, Ch. 5.

12 It has been calculated that around 70 to 80 per cent of national environmental legislation within the EU Member States is adopted as a consequence of EU environmental law (Kramer, op. cit., p. 860.)

13 K. Inglis, 'Enlargement and the Environment *Acquis*,' *Review of European Community and International Environmental Law* 13, 2004, 135–51.

14 Marín Durán and Morgera, 'EU Environmental Law' op. cit.; Wouters et al., op. cit., p. 7.

15 Jans and Vedder, op. cit., pp. 3–9; Sands, op. cit., pp. 740–9. The Treaties are currently the *Treaty of the European Union* (TEU) and the *Treaty on the Functioning of the European Union* (TFEU) [2010] OJ C83/1.

16 TEU, Art. 5.

17 I. von Homeyer, 'The Evolution of EU Environmental Governance', in J. Scott (ed.) *Environmental Protection, European Law and Governance*, Oxford: Oxford University Press, 2009, pp. 1–26.

18 Jans and Vedder, op. cit., p. 3.

19 J. Steiner and L. Woods, *EU Law*, Oxford: Oxford University Press, 2009, p. 1.

based on a customs union, the prohibition of restrictions to the free movement of goods, workers, services and capital among the Member States, a competition policy and a common commercial policy, as well as common policies on agriculture and transport.[20] The same parties to the Treaty of Rome (France, Germany, Italy, Belgium, the Netherlands and Luxembourg) had also signed a 50-year Treaty establishing the European Steel and Coal Community in 1952 and a Treaty establishing the European Atomic Community in 1958. As a result, these European Communities created a 'single, unrestricted Western European market in potential pollutants – steel, iron, coal and nuclear materials, as well as other goods'.[21]

The Treaty of Rome did not contain any reference to the environment, which in retrospect can be considered 'hardly surprising' considering that environmental issues were 'virtually invisible' as a policy concern in the 1950s.[22] Nonetheless, certain 'incidentally environmental' action was taken by the EEC[23] – that is, legislative developments with relevance for environmental protection occurred with a view to attaining the common market.

Second phase (1972 to 1987): emergence of the EEC Environmental Policy

With the convening of the first global summit on environmental protection, the 1972 Stockholm Conference on the Human Environment, the EEC together with the international community identified environmental protection as an issue requiring urgent action.[24] The same year, a Summit of Heads of State of the EEC Member States declared that economic expansion was not an end in itself, but rather the priority was to help attenuate disparities in living conditions, such as improved quality and standard of life: this led to the consideration of 'non-material' values such as environmental protection crucial for the EEC economic objectives to be achieved. The Summit consequently requested the drawing up of an action programme for an EEC environmental policy.[25]

The following year the First Programme of Action of the European Communities on the Environment (1973 to 1976) was adopted:[26] it was a policy declaration setting broad-ranging environmental objectives for the EEC, notably including the search for common solutions to environmental problems with states outside the EEC and international organisations. In effect, the EEC environmental policy and the environmental legislation that was enacted during this second phase following the Programme of Action were not backed by a treaty-based explicit competence for the EEC, but rather on the basis of an extensive interpretation of the provisions of the Rome Treaty.[27]

20 D. Chalmers, G. Davies and G. Monti, *European Union Law*, Cambridge: Cambridge University Press, 2010, p. 12.
21 J. Holder and M. Lee, *Environmental Protection, Law and Policy*, Cambridge: Cambridge University Press, 2007, p. 156.
22 M. Lee, *EU Environmental Law: Challenges, Change and Decision-making*, Oxford: Hart, 2005, p. 1.
23 Jans and Vedder, op. cit., p. 3.
24 von Homeyer, op. cit., p. 2; Sands, op. cit., p. 741; D. McGillivray and J. Holder, 'Locating EC Environmental Law', *Yearbook of European Environmental Law* 2, 2001, 139–71, p. 144 argue that this influence explains the anthropocentric approach of EU Environmental law.
25 Bulletin EC 1972, No. 10.
26 Declaration of the Council of the European Communities and of the representatives of the Governments of the member States meeting in the Council of 22 November 1973 on the programme of action for the European Communities on the environment [1973] OJ C112/1.
27 Jans and Vedder, op. cit., p. 4; Holder and Lee, op. cit., pp. 157–8.

Thus, for the adoption of EEC environmental legislation recourse was made to a Treaty provision allowing the EEC to take legislative action to approximate national laws that directly affect the establishment or functioning of the common market:[28] basically, this was used in cases in which differences in national environmental legislation were considered to have (or were likely to have) a detrimental effect on intra-Community trade and competition.[29] While this practice permitted the adoption of EEC legislation on aquatic pollution, air pollution, industrial hazards and toxic waste, it only allowed environmental law development to the extent permitted by economic considerations. Thus, another legal basis was invoked, namely a Treaty Article empowering the EEC to take the action necessary to attain, in the course of the operation of the common market, one of the objectives of the Community where the Treaty itself has not provided necessary powers (the so-called 'flexibility clause').[30] In addition, a judicially made doctrine of implied powers[31] allowed for broader leeway in environmental law-making by the EEC,[32] as well as enabling the EEC to become a party to multilateral and regional environmental agreements.[33]

In 1985, the Court of Justice sanctioned the possibility of an autonomous environmental policy of the EEC independent of the establishment of the common market.[34] The Court, addressing the question of the validity of certain environmental protection measures conflicting with the free movement of goods, affirmed that the directive had to be interpreted from the perspective of environmental protection, which it declared for the first time to be one of the Community's 'essential objectives'. The Court went on to affirm that environmental protection measures, being of general interest, could justify certain restrictions to the free movement of goods as long as they were non-discriminatory and did not go beyond the inevitable restrictions justified by the pursuit of the objective of environmental protection.[35]

Third phase (1987 to 1993): an explicit legal basis for the EEC environmental policy

The entry into force of the Single European Act (SEA) in 1987 marks the beginning of the third phase of the evolution of the EU environmental policy. The SEA aimed to eliminate remaining barriers to the creation of the single internal market and introduced procedural changes to accelerate decision-making by the EEC.[36] It also extended the sphere of competence of the EEC, introducing for the first time, among others, an explicit legal basis for environmental legislation in the Treaty of Rome by setting the objectives, principles and criteria of the EEC environmental policy.[37] Accordingly, the objectives of EEC action in the

---

28 Article 100 EEC, later 94 EC (now 115 TFEU); see also Case 92-79 *Commission v Italy* [1980] ECR 1115.

29 Jans and Vedder, op. cit., p. 4.

30 Article 235 EEC, later 308 EC (now 352 TFEU).

31 Case C-22/70 *Commission v Council* (AETR) [1971] ECR 263; and *Opinion 1/76 on the Draft Agreement establishing a Laying-up Fund for Inland Waterway Vessels* [1977] ECR 471: for a more detailed explanation, see Marín Durán and Morgera, *Environmental Integration*, op. cit., Ch 1.

32 Jans and Vedder, op. cit., p. 5.

33 Ibid., pp. 58–60.

34 Lee, *EU Environmental Law*, op. cit., p. 16.

35 Case 240/83 *Procureur de la République v Association de Défense des Bruleurs d'huiles usagées* [1983] ECR 531 (ADBHU case).

36 Steiner and Woods, op. cit., p. 6.

37 Post-SEA Art. 130r EEC.

field of the environment were: preserving and improving the quality of the environment, contributing towards the protection of human health, and ensuring a prudent and rational utilisation of natural resources. This was, therefore, a confirmation of the practice of environmental law-making that had developed in the second phase. The powers of the EEC for the protection of the environment were subject to unanimous decision-making by the Council in consultation with the Parliament.

With the joining of the EEC by Spain and Portugal in 1986, Germany and Denmark – countries with traditionally higher environmental standards – insisted on introducing in the Treaty a provision allowing Member States to maintain or introduce more stringent environmental protection measures than might be pursued at EEC level,[38] thereby creating the possibility for a 'two-speed environmental Europe'.[39]

Fourth phase (1993 to 1997): birth of the EU and raising of environmental protection

Following the convening of another major global summit, the 1992 United Nations Conference on Environment and Development in Rio de Janeiro, another phase in the evolution of EU environmental law began. The Treaty of Maastricht, which entered into force in 1993, significantly amended the EEC Treaty, by renaming the EEC the European Community (EC) to reflect a wider purpose than just economic integration, moving into further integration in social and political areas, and providing a separate Treaty for a new entity – the European Union (EU) – representing political cooperation in the areas of foreign and security policy, and justice and home affairs (the so-called second and third pillars). While the distinction between EC and EU became increasingly difficult to draw in practice, the EU was created as an overarching entity that was distinct, but did not formally have a separate legal personality, from the EC. The EU was built upon three pillars: the first pillar embodied by the EC and its supra-national decision-making modalities, while the second and third pillars represented cooperation among the Member States in the EU, based on inter-governmental modalities rather than transfer of sovereign powers. The Treaty of Maastricht also introduced provisions for the creation of a full economic and monetary union.[40]

From an environmental perspective, the Maastricht Treaty for the first time introduced the environment into the overarching provisions of the EC Treaty, by including among the objectives of the EC the 'promotion through the Community of a harmonious and balanced development of economic activities, sustainable and non-inflationary growth respecting the environment'.[41] While the Treaty did not use the expression 'sustainable development', which had been mainstreamed by the Rio Summit, the weaker expressions related to balanced development and sustainable growth were still considered of great political importance.[42]

The Treaty also significantly amended the legal basis on environmental policy, by adding reference to the precautionary principle and the objective of promoting international measures to deal with regional or worldwide environmental problems.[43] In addition, the Treaty of

---

38 M. Soveroski, 'EC Enlargement and the Development of European Environmental Policy: Parallel Histories, Divergent Paths?', *Review of European Community and International Environmental Law* 13, 2004, 127–34.
39 Holder and Lee, op. cit., p. 154.
40 Steiner and Woods, op. cit., p. 7.
41 Post-Maastricht Arts 2 and 3(k) EC. See Jans and Vedder, op. cit., pp. 6–7.
42 Jans and Vedder, op. cit., p. 7.
43 Post-Maastricht Art. 130r(1) EC. See Sands, op. cit., p. 746.

Maastricht established that the general rule for decision-making on environmental policy was qualified majority with certain matters remaining subject to unanimity (which have remained unaltered since and are discussed below).

It should be noted that Sweden, Finland and Austria – states with higher levels of environmental protection than the existing State Members – joined the EU in 1995. Initially it was hoped that a four-year review period would have allowed the revision of EU standards upwards to bring them in line with those of the new Member States. While certain pieces of EU environmental law were amended as a result of this, overall the 'average' EU environmental standards were not raised significantly.[44]

Fifth phase (1997 to 2008): sustainable development in the EU

With the entry into force of the Treaty of Amsterdam in 1997, the EU is believed to have shifted away from a mainly economic organisation to a more political one founded on fundamental rights and principles of liberty, democracy and the rule of law.[45] The Treaty brought about a streamlining of decision-making, mainly focused on the creation of an Area of Freedom, Security and Justice based on the absence of internal border controls for persons, a common policy on asylum, immigration and external border control, a high level of security and access to justice within the EU.[46]

From an environmental perspective, the Treaty of Amsterdam fine-tuned the inclusion of environmental protection and sustainable development in the general clauses of the EC Treaty. It reformulated references to sustainable development among the objectives of the EC as the 'harmonious, balanced and sustainable development of economic activities' and included explicit reference to a 'high level of protection and improvement of the quality of the environment'.[47] It also upgraded a requirement for environmental mainstreaming in other policy areas of the EU ('environmental integration') to a general principle of EU law, rather than a provision confined within the environmental chapter.[48] Finally, the Treaty of Amsterdam established that co-decision was the normal decision-making procedure for environmental policy, thus ensuring a veto power for the European Parliament.[49] This procedure has remained relevant for environmental policy at present, although it has been renamed 'ordinary legislative procedure' by the Treaty of Lisbon (see below).[50]

During this phase the so-called 'big-bang' enlargement of 2004 took place: ten new countries joined the EU from the East and the South. On that occasion, environmental policy formally became an area to be specifically addressed in pre-accession negotiations, given the need for 'upward pressure' to align the environmental protection policy of new Member States with that of the EU.[51] By 2007, the EU had reached its current membership of 27 States: the increased diversity across the Member States has led to more general environmental law-making by the EU.[52]

---

44 Inglis, op. cit., pp. 148–9.
45 Steiner and Woods, op. cit., p. 11.
46 Chalmers et al., op. cit., p. 28.
47 Post-Amsterdam, Art. 2 EC.
48 Post-Amsterdam, Art. 6 EC.
49 Post-Amsterdam, Art. 175 EC. See Jans and Vedder, op. cit., pp. 8–9.
50 TFEU, Art. 294.
51 Soveroski, op. cit., p. 129.
52 Kramer, 'Regional Economic Integration Organization', op. cit., p. 859.

The present: the international relevance of EU environmental law

The most recent Treaty development is the entry into force of the Lisbon Treaty in December 2009: this amended the Treaty of the European Union (TEU), which now includes more general provisions on the mission and values of the EU, its democratic principles, the composition and functions of its institutions and detailed provisions on the EU's external action. The Treaty of Lisbon also significantly amended the EC Treaty, which is renamed the Treaty on the Functioning of the European Union (TFEU), owing to the fact that the EC has been merged with the EU, with the latter having been given an international legal personality.[53] The TEU and TFEU are of equal value.[54]

From an environmental perspective,[55] the Treaty of Lisbon confirmed that the EU shares its competence on environmental protection with the Member States, while it retains exclusive competence with regards to the conservation of marine living resources in the context of the Common Fisheries Policy.[56] With regards to the environmental legal basis, the Treaty of Lisbon singles out climate change as one of the global environmental issues in which the EU is expected to play a significant role at the international level;[57] this actually reflects the political priority attached to this specific environmental problem by the EU since the early 2000s.[58]

As a result of the Treaty of Lisbon, environmental integration is no longer the only mainstreaming requirement included among the general principles of EU law. While it can be argued that this may have decreased its visibility,[59] two new provisions further support environmental integration: one requires integrating animal welfare requirements in certain policy areas,[60] and the other has regard to the need to preserve and improve the environment in the context of the EU energy policy, which is to aim, *inter alia*, at promoting energy efficiency and energy saving and the development of new and renewable forms of energy.[61]

It should also be noted that the Treaty of Lisbon established that the EU Charter of Fundamental Rights (which had been unanimously approved by the European Council in December 2000, albeit with uncertain legal status) has the same legal value as the Treaties.[62] The Charter includes an environmental provision that, significantly, is not framed in rights-based language, but rather provides a policy statement on environmental integration (similar in wording to Article 11 TFEU discussed below).[63]

Possibly the most significant environmental feature of the Treaty of Lisbon, particularly for present purposes, is the emphasis placed on the external dimension of EU environmental

---

53 TEU, Art. 47. Chalmers et al., op. cit., pp. 38–50.

54 TFEU, Art. 1(2); TEU, Art. 1(3).

55 M. Lee, 'The Environmental Implications of the Lisbon Treaty', *Environmental Law Review* 10, 2008, 131–8; H. Vedder, 'The Treaty of Lisbon and European Environmental Policy', Social Science Research Network, 2008.

56 TFEU, Arts 4(2)(e) and 3(1)(d) respectively.

57 Ibid., Art. 191(1).

58 The EU elevated climate change as a priority also in its overall agenda on sustainable development and international cooperation, building upon the UN-driven inclusion of climate change among key threats to global security. Morgera and Marín Durán, 'The 2005 UN Summit', op. cit.

59 Lee, 'The Environmental Integration', op. cit., p. 134; Vedder, 'The Treaty of Lisbon', op. cit., p. 3.

60 Namely in the areas of agriculture, fisheries, transport, internal market, research and technological development and space policies (TFEU, Art. 14).

61 TFEU, Art. 194(1).

62 TEU, Art. 6(1).

63 Charter, [2010] OJ C83/389, Art. 37.

policy. The Treaty introduces an express link between sustainable development and EU external relations, by clarifying that 'in its relations with the wider world, the Union shall . . . contribute to . . . the sustainable development of the Earth'.[64] Furthermore, the Lisbon Treaty underscores the explicit link between environmental protection and external action, clarifying that the EU environmental objectives should guide the general external relations of the EU as well as specifically common foreign and security policy.[65] A new explicit legal basis for the EU external action indeed provides that the EU shall define and pursue common policies and actions, and work for a high degree of cooperation in all fields of international relations, with the specific objective of fostering the sustainable economic, social and environmental development of developing countries, to eradicate poverty; and help to develop international measures to preserve and improve the quality of the environment and the sustainable management of global natural resources, in order to ensure sustainable development.[66]

The objectives of EU environmental law

The Treaty on the Functioning of the EU sets out the objectives of EU environmental policy, its principles and other relevant policy considerations.[67] The objectives are:

> preserving, protecting and improving the quality of the environment; protecting human health; ensuring the prudent and rational utilisation of natural resources; and promoting measures at international level to deal with regional or worldwide environmental problems, and in particular combating climate change.[68]

Given that these objectives are quite broadly defined, it is almost impossible to clearly define the boundaries of EU environmental policy: there is sufficient flexibility for the EU to adapt its environmental policy to new developments and emerging environmental issues, and generally for this provision to be interpreted in a non-restrictive way. In addition, it has been argued that this provision allows the adoption of measures that result directly or indirectly in an improvement of the environment, such as conservation, restoration and repressive, precautionary, preventive and eminently procedural environmental measures.[69]

Ultimately, the substantive limits of EU competence in the area of environmental protection are 'determined on the case-by-case basis by the EU political institutions as they adopt measures in pursuance of the broadly-framed Treaty objectives, whether unilaterally or by concluding international agreements'.[70] The substantive limits of the EU environmental competence (internally and externally) are thus reflected, as they evolve, in the EU 'acquis': the body of common rights and obligations binding upon all the EU Member States arising

---

64 TEU, Art. 3(5).
65 Vedder, 'The Treaty of Lisbon', op. cit., p. 3.
66 TEU, Art. 21(2)(d) and (f). For an in-depth discussion, see E. Morgera (ed.) *The External Environmental Policy of the European Union: EU and International Law Perspectives*, Cambridge: Cambridge University Press, 2012.
67 The latter include: available scientific and technical data; environmental conditions in the various regions of the EU; potential benefits and costs of action or lack of action; economic and social development of the EU as a whole; and the balanced development of its regions (TFEU, Art. 191(3)).
68 TFEU, Art. 191(1).
69 Jans and Vedder, op. cit., pp. 26–35.
70 Marín Durán and Morgera, *Environmental Integration* op. cit., p. 285.

from the content, principles and political objectives of the Treaties; legislation adopted in the application of the Treaties; the case law of the European courts; and international agreements concluded by the EU. In a nutshell, it is the 'growing legal universe' produced by the EU governance system since the launch of its integration process.[71]

While there are no clear substantive limits to the exercise of EU environmental competence, this is still subject to the general principles of proportionality and subsidiarity: under the latter principle, the EU will take action if the objectives of the proposed environmental action cannot be sufficiently achieved by Member States and by reason of the scale or effects of the proposed action, these objectives are better achieved at the EU level.[72] Furthermore, environmental competence is exercised under the decision-making procedures set out by the Treaty. Generally, EU environmental law is subject to the agreement between the Council (acting by qualified-majority voting) and the European Parliament (under the ordinary legislative procedure). In certain specific areas, however, the Treaty requires unanimous decision-making by the Council, namely: provisions primarily of a fiscal nature; measures affecting town and country planning, quantitative management of water resources or affecting, directly or indirectly, the availability of those resources, and land use with the exception of waste management; and measures significantly affecting a Member State's choice between different energy sources and the general structure of its energy supply.[73] These are areas in which Member States wish to retain a higher degree of control because of their politically sensitive nature or concerns about the preservation of national sovereignty.[74]

As indicated above, the environmental competence of the EU is shared with the Member States:[75] thus Member States can exercise their competence only as long as the EU has not exercised its competence, or has decided to cease to exercise it. In this respect, it should be emphasised that the scope of the EU competence vis-à-vis that of the Member States is difficult to determine, as EU environmental policy is subject to continuous evolution.[76] This has important implications on the international scene. As the TFEU states:

> Within their respective spheres of competence, the Union and the Member States shall cooperate with third countries and with the competent international organisations. The arrangements for Union cooperation may be the subject of agreements between the Union and the third parties concerned.
>
> The previous subparagraph shall be without prejudice to Member States' competence to negotiate in international bodies and to conclude international agreements.[77]

In broad approximation, if the EU adopted environmental measures internally, Member States no longer have competence to undertake international obligations that would affect those EU rules, unless the EU measures allowed – which is often the case – Member States to adopt more stringent measures,[78] including in principle the possibility of undertaking more

---

71 Puder, op. cit., p. 179.
72 TEU, Art. 5(3). This principle was initially enshrined in the Treaties with specific regard to environmental policy, and later became a general principle of EU law. See Chalmers et al., op. cit., pp. 363–6.
73 TFEU, Art. 192.
74 Holder and Lee, op. cit., p. 154; McGillivray and Holder, op. cit., p. 145.
75 TFEU, Art. 4(2)(e).
76 Jans and Vedder, op. cit., pp. 61–4.
77 TFEU, Art. 191(4).
78 Jans and Vedder, op. cit., pp. 62–3.

stringent international obligations. This flexibility for Member States, however, is subject to the duty of sincere cooperation enshrined in Article 4(3) TEU, which the Court has interpreted as entailing enforceable substantive and procedural obligations with a view to protecting the unity in the international representation of the EU.[79]

Principles of EU environmental law

The Treaty also identifies the principles that should guide the EU internal and external environmental policy,[80] as a guide both for law-making and for interpretation. The EU legislator, however, has a significant margin of discretion in implementing the principles. The Court has in fact clarified that only in exceptional cases could an EU measure be annulled for insufficient regard to these principles – in cases of manifest error of appraisal by the EU legislature. This was justified on the basis of the need to strike a balance between environmental objectives and principles and of the complexity of the implementation of the environmental policy criteria.[81]

High level of environmental protection

The principle of a 'high' level of protection is considered 'the most important substantive principle of European environmental policy'[82] given its inclusion in the general objectives of the EU.[83]

Nonetheless, the principle is made subject to consideration of the 'diversity of situations in the various regions of the Union'.[84] While a high level of environmental protection cannot be understood as allowing the EU to adopt the lowest common denominator among the Member States' environmental protection measures,[85] the Court of Justice clarified that it does not necessarily have to be the highest that is technically possible.[86] Overall, the principle reflects a moving target – the idea of continuous improvement of the environmental protection standards across the Member States.[87]

Precaution

The precautionary principle has been interpreted by the Commission[88] as a risk management tool that is essential for the achievement of a high level of environmental protection when

---

79 Case C-266/03 *Commission v Luxembourg (re Inland Waterways Agreement)* [2005] ECR I-4805, para. 60 and Case C-433/03 *Commission v Germany (re Inland Waterways Agreement)* [2005] ECR I-6985, para. 66; Case C-246/07 *Commission v Sweden (re POPs Convention)*, judgment 20 April 2010, para. 104. For a discussion, see Marín Durán and Morgera, *Environmental Integration,* op. cit., pp 18–19.
80 TFEU, Art. 191(2).
81 Case C-284/95 *Safety Hi-Tech Srl v S. & T. Srl* [1998] ECR I-4301, para. 37; Jans and Vedder, op. cit., p. 36.
82 Vedder, op. cit., p. 36.
83 TEU, Art. 3(3).
84 TFEU, Art. 191(2).
85 L. Kramer, *EC Environmental Law*, London: Sweet and Maxwell, 2006, pp. 12–13.
86 Case C-284/95 *Safety Hi-Tech Srl. v S. & T. Srl* [1998] ECR I-4301; Jans and Vedder, op. cit., pp. 36 7.
87 Kramer, *EC Environmental Law*, op. cit., p. 12.
88 European Commission, *Guidelines on the Precautionary Principle*, COM(2000)1.

facing unknown risks.[89] To implement the principle, a risk assessment should be as complete as possible given the particular circumstances of the individual case, with a view to establishing precautionary measures that are:

> proportional to the chosen level of protection, non-discriminatory in their application, consistent with similar measures already taken, based on an examination of the potential benefits and costs of action or lack of action, and subject to review in the light of new scientific data.[90]

The trigger of the precautionary principle is a situation where:

> preliminary objective scientific evaluation indicates that there are reasonable grounds for concern that the potentially dangerous effects on the *environment, human, animal or plant health* may be inconsistent with the high level of protection chosen for the [EU].[91]

The Court of Justice held that in the framework of the Habitats Directive,[92] the requirement of an appropriate assessment of the implications of plans or projects that may have significant effects on protected areas is conditional upon the 'probability or the risk' that the plan or project will have significant effects on the site concerned, and that this should be interpreted in a precautionary manner. So an assessment is considered necessary whenever it cannot be excluded that a certain project or plan will have significant effects on the site on the basis of objective information.[93]

Prevention

This principle calls for taking action to protect the environment at an early stage, with a view to preventing damage from occurring rather than repairing it.[94] The main difference from the precautionary principle lies in the availability of data on the existence of a risk, although such a distinction may be difficult to draw in practice. The Court of Justice, for instance, relied on the prevention principle, as well as that of a high level of protection, to review an export ban on British beef adopted in the context of the Common Agricultural Policy because of a possible – rather than certain – risk related to mad cow disease.[95]

Guidance on the application of the principle can be found in the third Environmental Action Programme, which stressed the need to improve information for decision-makers and the public (for instance through monitoring and surveying requirements), introduce

---

89 Puder, op. cit.
90 Commission Guidelines, op. cit., para. 6.
91 Ibid., para. 3.
92 Council Directive (EC) 92/43 on the Conservation of Natural Habitats and of Wild Fauna and Flora [1992] OJ L206/7.
93 Case C-6/04 *Commission v UK* [2005] ECR I-9017, para. 54; Jans and Vedder, op. cit., p. 40.
94 Jans and Vedder, op. cit., pp. 40–2.
95 Case C-157/96 *National Farmers Union* [1998] ECR I-2211, para. 64, although it has been convincingly argued that the precautionary principle rather than the prevention principle was relevant in this case given that the risk was a possibility rather than a certainty: see N. Dhondt, *Integration of Environmental Protection into Other EC Policies; Legal Theory and Practice*, Groningen: Europa Law Publishing, 2003, p. 151.

procedures supporting prompt and informed decision-making on the environment such as environmental impact assessment, and monitor implementation of adopted measures to ensure their adaptation in light of new circumstances or knowledge.[96]

Source principle

The principle provides that environmental damage should be rectified at its source as a priority,[97] and has had particular resonance in the area of waste management. The Court of Justice held that local authorities must take measures necessary to ensure the reception, processing and removal of waste so that it can be disposed of as close as possible to its place of production. This interpretation allowed the Court to consider justified measures that discriminated against waste produced in different areas.[98] In another case, the Court specified that the principle could not serve to justify any restriction on waste exports, but only when the waste in question was harmful to the environment.[99]

Polluter pays

The principle has been interpreted in the EU context so that environmental protection should not in principle depend on the granting of state aid or policies placing the burden on society, and that requirements should not target persons or undertakings for the elimination of pollution that they did not contribute to produce.[100] In the *Standley* case, for instance, the Court of Justice indicated that farmers are not obliged to bear all the costs of pollution by nitrates, but only those caused by their activities, so it is up to authorities to take account of the other sources of pollution and, having regard to the circumstances, avoid imposing on farmers unnecessary costs of eliminating pollution.[101]

Sustainable development

Sustainable development is among the 'objectives' of the EU in both its internal and external action.[102] The EU defined it in a few legal instruments in different ways, thus highlighting that the concept plays out differently in different contexts.[103] The Court of Justice has not engaged in defining the legal implications of sustainable development,[104] but the EU has developed a plethora of policy instruments epitomised by the Sustainable Development

96 Dhondt, op. cit., p. 151.
97 Jans and Vedder, op. cit., pp. 42–3.
98 Case C-2/90 *Commission v Belgium* [1992] ECR I-4431.
99 Case C-209/98 *Sydhavnens Sten & Grus* [2000] ECR I-3743; Jans and Vedder, op. cit., pp. 43–5.
100 Jans and Vedder, op. cit., pp. 43–5.
101 Case C-293/97 *Standley* [1999] ECR I-2603, paras 46–52; L. Kramer, 'Environmental Justice in the European Court of Justice', in J. Ebbesson and P. Okowa (eds) *Environmental Law and Justice in Context*, Cambridge: Cambridge University Press, 2009, 195–210, p. 202.
102 TEU, Arts 3(3) and (5), and 21(2)(f).
103 McGillivray and Holder, op. cit., p. 150.
104 Case C-371/98 *R v Secretary of State for Environment, Transport and the Regions, ex parte First Corporate Shipping* [2000] ECR-I 9235; McGillivray and Holder, op. cit., p. 151.

Strategy.[105] Views on the role of sustainable development in EU environmental law remain divided: Lee underscores the potential of sustainable development to stimulate debate in the EU, privileging participatory processes to allow the balancing of different interests where environmental protection competes with other imperative public interests;[106] while Kramer criticises the inflationary use of sustainable development by the EU as a separate concept from environmental protection.[107]

Environmental integration

Environmental integration is included among the general principles of EU law and framed in clearly mandatory wording. According to Article 11 TFEU, environmental integration demands that 'Environmental protection requirements must be integrated into the definition and implementation of the Union policies and activities, in particular with a view to promoting sustainable development.' The 'requirements' that are the object of this obligation are those included in Articles 2 and 191 TFEU, namely the objectives, principles and criteria of the EU environmental policy discussed above.[108] Environmental integration is to occur in all policies of the EU,[109] internal and external ones, both at the stage of the framing of these policies ('definition' therefore includes every stage of the EU legislative processes: definition of policy objectives, as well as preparation, proposal and adoption of policies and legislation, and their revision); and at the stage of their 'implementation' (which includes the adoption of further implementing acts, adoption of decisions outside the legislative process, and enforcement).[110]

Environmental integration therefore functions as a requirement for legislative action, as well as an interpretative tool of primary and secondary legislation outside the environmental field (external integration),[111] which requires that the environmental objectives, principles and criteria are 'applied' in other policy areas in the same way as they must be applied in the environmental policy: that is, that other policy areas must 'pursue' the environmental objectives, 'aim at' or 'be based on' the environmental principles, and 'take account of' the environmental criteria.[112] The requirement also entails EU environmental law itself being interpreted broadly, in light of the environmental objectives, principles and criteria of Article (191 TFEU), even when these objectives, principles or criteria are not explicitly incorporated in the specific piece of secondary legislation (internal integration).[113]

Overall, the environmental integration requirement has an *amplifying* effect on EU environmental policy, in that it requires the systematic pursuance of environmental objectives,

---

105 European Commission, *A Sustainable Europe for a Better World. A European Union Strategy for Sustainable Development*, COM(2001) 264; and Goteborg European Council Conclusions (15–16 June 2001). This was complemented by European Commission, *Towards a Global Partnership for Sustainable Development*, COM(2002) 82, on the external dimension. For a discussion, see L. Kramer, 'Sustainable Development in the EC', in H. Bugge and C. Voigt (eds) *Sustainable Development in International and National Law*, Groningen: Europa Law Publishing, 2008, pp. 377–96.
106 Lee, *EU Environmental Law*, op. cit., p. 47.
107 Kramer, 'Sustainable Development', op. cit., pp. 391–3.
108 Jans and Vedder, op. cit., p. 17.
109 Ibid.
110 Dhondt, op. cit., pp. 45–53.
111 Jans and Vedder, op. cit., p. 17.
112 Dhondt, op. cit., p. 84.
113 Ibid., p. 179.

principles and criteria in all EU policies and actions.[114] The requirement has resulted in significant legislative developments, in terms of 'greening' other areas of EU law (such as the Common Agricultural Policy, Common Fisheries Policy, Common Transport Policy)[115] as well as in the recourse to an 'integrationist' approach in the development of EU environmental law (relying, for instance, on environmental impact assessment, strategic environmental assessment, and integrated pollution prevention and control).[116] Its influence is also significant in relation to EU external relations, as evidenced by the insertion of several environmental integration clauses in cooperation and trade agreements between the EU and third countries, the conduct of sustainability impact assessments before the conclusion of trade agreements, and the consideration of environmental requirements in the definition and implementation of legislation on external funding.[117]

Conclusion

European Union environmental law is an interesting object of study both as a possible source of inspiration for other states and regional organisations, and for its impacts on the development and implementation of international environmental law. The environmental law of the EU has been a testing ground for principles and innovative regulatory techniques, and has been increasingly marked by further experimentalism, harnessing the pluralism across Member States, different levels of government as well as different groups of stakeholders.[118]

Nonetheless, significant challenges face EU environmental law. While the EU continues to use its domestic and external legislative action to support the implementation of international environmental law and influence its development, it is not yet possible to assert that these complex strategies have yielded positive results. The limited success of the EU strategy at the Copenhagen Climate Change Conference in 2009, for instance, has provided a hard lesson for the EU.[119]

Internal shortcomings also undermine the credibility of the EU as a model and global actor. One major challenge is certainly the problematic 'implementation gap', that is the continuous lack of compliance with and enforcement of EU environmental law by the Member States.[120] Another is the 'appalling' lack of data on the environment, in particular the lack of ex-post evaluation of the effectiveness of existing measures, which leads Kramer

114 Ibid., p. 109.
115 For a succinct assessment, see Kramer, *EC Environmental Law*, op. cit.; for a more detailed assessment, see Dhondt, op. cit., Part III.
116 McGillivray and Holder, op. cit., p. 154.
117 Marín Durán and Morgera, *Environmental Integration*,op. cit.
118 J. Scott and J. Holder, 'Law and New Environmental Governance in the European Union', in J. Scott and G. de Búrca (eds) *Law and New Governance in the EU and the US*, Oxford: Hart Publishing, 2006, pp. 215–42; I. von Homeyer, 'Emerging Experimentalism in EU Environmental Governance', in C. Sabel and J. Seitlin (eds) *Experimentalist Governance in the European Union: Towards a New Architecture?*, Oxford: Oxford University Press, 2010, pp. 121–50.
119 European Commission Staff Working Document, 2009 Environment Policy Review, SEC(2010)975, 3, where it is stated that 'the results in Copenhagen fell short of the European Union's goal . . .'.
120 Lee, *EU Environmental Law*, op. cit., Ch. 3; Jans and Vedder, op. cit., Ch. 4.

to conclude that EU environmental policy is based on assumptions rather than hard facts.[121] Finally, the 'structural imbalance concerning access to courts' in environmental matters at the level of both national courts and EU judiciary, particularly for environmental NGOs concerned with environmental damage,[122] does not reflect well on the EU as a self-proclaimed environmental leader. Whether the EU will succeed in gradually transforming these challenges into opportunities for further innovation is yet another reason to continue to study the evolution of EU environmental law.

---

121 Kramer, 'Sustainable Development', op. cit., p. 393.
122 Kramer, 'EC Environmental Law', op. cit., pp. 209–10. This is based on a restrictive interpretation of the criteria for standing by the European courts (see Communication to the Aarhus Convention Compliance Committee ACCC/C/2008/32, 2008; in particular, the Compliance Committee's Findings and Recommendations (2011) UN Doc. ECE/MP.PP/C.1/2011/4/Add.1) and the lack of progress on a 2003 legislative proposal for ensuring access to justice in environmental matters at the Member State level (European Commission, *Proposal for a Directive on Access to Justice in Environmental Matters*, COM(2003) 624).

25

The Americas' environmental and sustainable development law

Marie-Claire Cordonier Segger* and Renée Gift

This chapter explores and evaluates regional environmental law in the Americas, canvassing the unique approaches that the region has taken to address environmental protection and sustainable development. It explores regional environmental and sustainable development law and policy, examines the Organization of American States and the Inter-American Forum on Environmental Law, as well as cooperation through sub-regional institutions. It also includes reference to trade agreements that contain important commitments on sustainable development, relevant provisions of investment treaties, and environment and sustainable development aspects of the inter-American human rights system. It concludes with the challenges and opportunities to strengthen environmental management and sustainable development in the Americas.

Introduction

The 35 sovereign countries of the Americas share more than two connected continents and their islands. They depend on good-faith collaboration for stewardship of great ecological and hydrological systems, chains of important geographical features, interlinked cultural, social and biological commonalities and diversities, and many environmental and sustainable development challenges.[1] To promote sustainable development of these unique and important natural resources, and the protection of these ecological systems, their countries cooperate through various hemispheric institutions such as the Organization of American States (OAS), through five sub-regional institutions covering North America, Central America, the

* Marie-Claire Cordonier Segger extends warmest thanks to Renée Gift, CISDL Legal Researcher, for her excellent insights, writing and research skills, and for her invaluable assistance in the elaboration of this chapter.

1 M-C. Cordonier Segger, M. Araya, A.K. Gonzáles-Lützenkirchen, N. Lucas, M.B. Muños, J.Z. Taurel, H. Blanco and M.L. Reynal, *Ecological Rules and Sustainability in the Americas*, IISD/UNEP/OAS, 2004; D. Esty and C. Deere (eds) *Greening the Americas*, Cambridge, MA: MIT Press, 2005; UNEP (2010) *Latin America and the Caribbean Environmental Outlook (GEO-Latin America and the Caribbean 3)*. Online. Available HTTP: <http://www.unep.org/geo/pdfs/GEOLAC_3_ENGLISH.pdf> (accessed 3 May 2012).

Caribbean, the Andes and South America, along with other specific instruments.[2] The North American bloc covers Canada, the United States and Mexico; Central America includes Belize, Costa Rica, El Salvador, Guatemala, Honduras, Nicaragua and Panama; the Andean Region consists of Columbia, Bolivia, Peru, Ecuador and Venezuela; the Southern Cone covers Chile, Argentina, Brazil, Paraguay and Uruguay; and the Caribbean region includes Antigua and Barbuda, Barbados, Cuba,[3] Dominica, the Dominican Republic, Grenada, Guyana, Haiti, Jamaica, St Kitts and Nevis, St Lucia, St Vincent and the Grenadines, the Bahamas, Suriname and Trinidad and Tobago. Together, they represent all major climatic regions and form an interdependent web of ecosystems through the vast array of forests, mountains, watersheds and oceans that they share.

These regions are among the most biologically diverse on the planet.[4] Six of its countries – Brazil, Colombia, Ecuador, Mexico, Peru and Venezuela – are considered mega-diverse.[5] The region holds almost one-half of the world's tropical forests, 33 per cent of its total mammals, 35 per cent of its reptilian species, 41 per cent of its birds and 50 per cent of its amphibians. The Caribbean alone is home to 11 percent of the world's coral reefs.[6] Many of its species are endemic to those regions, as in the Caribbean where 50 per cent of the plant life is unique.[7]

Many major ecosystems are shared by more than one country, and this presents a particular challenge for environmental protection in the Americas. The interrelation of ecosystems and habitats throughout the Americas causes great vulnerability to the impacts of transboundary harms. For instance, many migratory species, with habitats that cross several countries, rely on the collaborative conservation efforts of many states to ensure protection.[8] However, all 35 countries of the Americas have specific priorities at each political moment, complicating

2 Cordonier Segger et al., op. cit.
3 OAS AG/RES. 2438 (XXXIX-O/09).
4 UNEP (2010) *State of Biodiversity in Latin America and the Caribbean*, p. 1. Online. Available HTTP: <http://www.unep.org/DEC/PDF/LatinAmerica_StateofBiodiv.pdf> (accessed 3 May 2012).
5 Ibid., p. 64.
6 UNEP/CARICOM/UWI (2004) *Caribbean Environmental Outlook, Special Edition for the Mauritius International Meeting for the 10-year Review of the Barbados Programme of Action for the Sustainable Development of Small Island States*, p. 52. Online. Available HTTP: <http://www.unep.org/geo/pdfs/Caribbean_EO_final.pdf> (accessed 3 May 2012).
7 Ibid.
8 For example, the North American waterfowl population relies on the cooperation of Canada, the United States and Mexico through the North American Waterfowl Management Plan (NAWM) to protect coastal and inland wetland habitats with an aim of restoring waterfowl populations (see UNEP (2007) *Global Environmental Outlook GEO4, Environment for Development*, p. 36. Online. Available HTTP: <http://www.unep.org/geo/GEO4/report/GEO-4_Report_Full_en.pdf> (accessed 3 May 2012). In the Latin American region, the planned construction of the Madeira River dams in the Brazilian Amazon and Bolivia will have particularly devastating impacts on the gilded catfish, a species which holds tremendous ecological and economic importance in Colombia, Bolivia and Peru, as well as in Brazil and Bolivia (see Friends of the Earth Brazil (2007) *The Amazon River's Largest Tributary is Under Threat*, Amigos da Terra Brasil, ECOA. Online. Available HTTP: <http://www.foei.org/en/get-involved/take-action/pdfs/RIO_MADEIRA.pdf> (accessed 3 May 2012).

matters.[9] Each country is also influenced by its own unique cultural, political and social traditions, with differences of governance and languages, including a rich diversity of indigenous languages.[10]

The Americas share important environment and sustainable development challenges.[11] Common concerns include deforestation, biodiversity loss and destruction of habitat, rapid urbanisation with attendant environmental and social challenges, protection of oceans and coastal ecosystems, stewardship of rivers, pollution and waste control, and other issues. Further pressing sustainable development matters include climate change mitigation and adaptation,[12] the shift to clean and renewable energy sources,[13] sustainable use of biological resources and technologies,[14] the need to better enforce laws and regulations for sustainable resources management,[15] food security[16] and changing patterns of consumption.[17] It is a difficult agenda, and one that has been canvassed in hemispheric and sub-regional cooperation processes, including a series of high-level summits, as well as the development of a soft-law 'Agenda 21' for the Americas[18] and five sub-regional sets of action plans.[19]

For these reasons, among others, the Americas have been demonstrably supportive of international environmental regulation and management efforts. In 2011, participation in 14 major multilateral environmental agreements (MEAs) by Latin American and Caribbean states (in the form of ratification, accession, acceptance or approval) stood at

9   The Americas produce a unique example of how varied the challenges for each country tend to be. For example, countries like Argentina, Chile, Ecuador, Mexico and Venezuela are highly dependent on fossil fuels, while Costa Rica and Paraguay use more renewable energy. In other countries, fuelwood remains an important energy source. For countries such as Argentina and Uruguay, where the urban population rests at 90 per cent, urbanisation presents acute cross-cutting environmental management issues, unlike in Guyana and St Lucia, where the urban population represents less than 28 per cent of the total. Many Latin American countries containing vast areas of rainforest landscape and shared freshwater basins face terrestrial biodiversity preservation challenges, while the Caribbean counterparts deal with marine fisheries management issues, unprecedented coral bleaching events and overall coastal degradation. Contrastingly, in North America, excessive energy consumption and carbon dioxide emissions, and freshwater quality and quantity concerns, are some of its most pressing environmental concerns. See UNEP (2007), op. cit., Chapter 6.
10 The Index of Biocultural Diversity (IBCD) estimates there to be more than 1,500 languages spoken in the Americas. Of the nine countries which contain the highest number of languages, Brazil, Mexico, Columbia, Ecuador, Peru and Venezuela represent more than half. See UNESCO (2009) *UNESCO World Report, Investing in Cultural Diversity and Intercultural Dialogue* at p. 74. Online. Available HTTP: <http://unesdoc.unesco.org/images/0018/001852/185202e.pdf> (accessed 3 May 2012). See also UNEP (2010), op. cit., p. 24 which discusses the environmental complexity of the LAC as a result of its colourful and varied history.
11 Cordonier Segger et al., op. cit., pp. 11–12.
12 UNEP (2010), op. cit., pp. 40–3, 160–2; UNEP (2007), op. cit., pp. 254–8.
13 UNEP (2007), op. cit., p. 257.
14 UNEP (2010), op. cit., pp. 328–9.
15 Ibid., p. 323.
16 The intensification of agricultural activities to ensure food security has fed directly into a number of other environmental issues, such as pollution of groundwater and coastal areas.
17 UNEP (2010), op. cit., pp. 27–9.
18 *Agenda 21: A Programme for Action for Sustainable Development*, Report of the UN Conference on Environment and Development, Annex II, 12 August 1992, UN Doc A./Conf. 151/26 (Vol II–IV).
19 See generally Cordonier Segger et al., op. cit.

86.1 per cent and 75 per cent in North America.[20] The vast majority of countries in the Americas have national legislation that expressly incorporates environmental protection and conservation measures into its domestic law.[21] The number of marine and terrestrial protected areas in Latin America and the Caribbean increased more than twofold between 1990 and 2011.[22] Overall, there have been considerable advances towards the implementation of environmental and sustainable development in the Americas and this trend continues today.

Regional responses to these challenges have been spurred by a commonality in environmental challenges faced. Such challenges include the management of the use of natural resources, the management of migratory species and populations, and the conservation of shared ecosystems.[23] In many cases, the coordination of efforts has been facilitated by the operation of already existing regional trade and integration blocs. In others, cooperation on sustainable development challenges, including harmonisation of MEA implementation, is facilitated by institutions established by existing Free Trade Agreements (FTAs).

One such institution is the North American Agreement on Environmental Cooperation (NAAEC),[24] which was established by the Parties to the North American Free Trade Agreement (NAFTA). The NAAEC establishes a regional body, the Commission for Environmental Cooperation (CEC), which works to coordinate the efforts of the United States, Canada and Mexico to achieve their domestic, regional and international environment and sustainable development objectives.

Elsewhere in the Americas, collaboration on environmental and sustainable development programmes and instruments has been established by further sub-regional institutions. The Andean Community (CAN),[25] the Central American Commission for Environment and Development (CCAD),[26] the Southern American Common Market

20 UNEP (2011) *UNEP Year Book, Emerging Issues in Our Global Environment*, p. 70. Online. Available HTTP: <http://www.unep.org/yearbook/2011/> (accessed 3 May 2012).
21 Inter-American Forum on Environmental Law (FIDA), *Environmental Legislation*. Online. Available HTTP: <http://www.oas.org/dsd/FIDA/laws/database.htm> (accessed 3 May 2012).
22 UNEP (2010), op. cit., p. 1. See also ECLAC (2010), Chapter 3, 'Environmental Statistics' in *Statistical Yearbook for Latin America and the Caribbean*, p. 184. Online. Available HTTP: <http://www.eclac.org/publicaciones/xml/7/42167/LCG2483b_3.pdf>; ECLAC (2006), Chapter 3, 'Statistics on Natural Resources and the Environment', *Statistical Yearbook for Latin America and the Caribbean*, p. 322. Online. Available HTTP: <http://www.eclac.org/publicaciones/xml/4/28074/LCG2332B_3.pdf> (both accessed 3 May 2012).
23 Cordonier Segger et al., op. cit., p. 32.
24 *North American Agreement on Environmental Cooperation*, Sept. 9 and Sept. 13, 1993, 32 ILM 1480. Online. Available HTTP: <http://www.cec.org/Page.asp?PageID=1226&ContentID=&SiteNodeID=567&BL_ExpandID= 154> (accessed 3 May 2012).
25 Also known as the *Comunidad Andina* (CAN), the body was established by the Cartagena Agreement in 1969. See Andean Subregional Integration Agreement, 26 May 1969. Online. Available HTTP: <http://www.sice.oas.org/trade/JUNAC/Decisiones/dec563e.asp> (accessed 3 May 2012). For more details about CAN, see 'About Us', *Comunidad Andina*. Online. Available HTTP: <http://www.comunidadandina.org/ingles/who.htm> (accessed 3 May 2012).
26 Also known as the Comisión Centroamericana de Ambiente y Desarrollo (CCAD), it was established by the Central American Agreement for the Protection of the Environment on 14 June 1990. Online. Available HTTP: <http://www.sica.int/busqueda/busqueda_archivo.aspx?Archivo= conv_7590_2_17042006.pdf> (accessed 3 May 2012).

(MERCOSUR)[27] and the Caribbean Community (CARICOM)[28] have facilitated the development of a number of regional programmes and subsidiary bodies to address common environmental and sustainable development challenges, and to implement MEAs and other international treaties on sustainable development.

Several hemispheric institutions such as the OAS, the United Nations Environment Programme's (UNEP) two regional offices (the Regional Office for North America based in Washington, and the Regional Office for Latin America and the Caribbean based in Panama City), as well as other inter-American secretariats and instruments, lead valiant attempts to coordinate the activities of regional bodies in focusing efforts, providing information resources and supporting coherent decision-making and implementation of international obligations. Given the myriad elements of environmental management and sustainable development,[29] as well as the size of the challenges,[30] inter-linkages between specialised bodies and institutions can significantly increase the effectiveness and relevance of integrated regional strategies.[31]

Principal environment and sustainable development challenges

The nature of hemispheric collaboration and collective action taken by the Americas can only be understood by the varied sustainable development challenges and environmental pressures they face. Air quality is a major problem in the developing countries of the Americas and particularly in urbanised areas. In North America, high greenhouse gas (GHG) emissions as a result of heavy fossil fuel dependence continue to contribute to overall climate change and its associated problems. Unsustainable human development practices have resulted in widespread destruction of natural terrestrial and marine habitat, leading to huge biodiversity losses. These practices include unregulated urban sprawl and the significant expansion of agricultural activity which, in addition to ecosystem destruction, has caused land degradation and desertification. The following briefly illustrates the problems currently faced by the Americas according to atmosphere; forests and biodiversity; land, desertification and agriculture; and oceans, rivers and freshwater.

Atmosphere

Air pollution as a result of human-induced factors is one of the most significant adverse impacts on human health. The problem exists especially in cities and rapid urbanisation, especially in developing countries, has exacerbated the problem by putting an even larger

27 Also known as the Mercado Común del Sur (MERCOSUR), the body was established by the Treaty of Asunción, 26 March 1991. Online. Available HTTP: <http://www.sice.oas.org/Trade/MRCSR/MRCSRTOC.ASP>. For more information about the MERCOSUR, see 'Acerca del MERCOSUR'. Online. Available HTTP: <http://www.mercosur.int/t_generic.jsp?contentid=655&site=1&channel=secretaria&seccion=2> (both accessed 3 May 2012).

28 The Revised Treaty of Chaguaramas Establishing the Caribbean Community came into force in 2001. Online. Available HTTP: <http://www.caricom.org/jsp/community/revised_treaty-text.pdf>. For more information on the Caribbean Community (CARICOM), see *CARICOM Secretariat*. Online. Available HTTP: <http://www.caricom.org/index.jsp> (both accessed 3 May 2012).

29 UNEP (2007), op. cit., Chapter 1, p. 3.

30 Ibid.

31 Cordonier Segger et al., op. cit., p. 1.

number of people at risk. Particulate matter is the most important air pollutant, and atmospheric levels in many urban areas already exceed established standards of human safety. Indoor air pollution arising from the burning of biomass, kerosene or coal for cooking is responsible for over 1.6 million premature deaths and disproportionally affects women and children.[32] Poor indoor air quality is of particular concern in developing countries. In developed countries, outdoor particulates and tropospheric ozone have had their greatest impacts on agricultural productivity and natural ecosystem functioning. The accumulation of persistent organic pollutants (POPs) and mercury in the food chain is a global problem.

Climate change as a result of rising global GHG emissions is gaining recognition in the Americas. Unprecedented rises in GHGs, CO_2 and methane in particular, since the nineteenth century, have already caused significant disturbances to global weather patterns, sea levels and proper ecosystem functioning. High-consumption lifestyles requiring greater energy use, an increased need for industry/manufacturing, in addition to worldwide deforestation, account for more than 60 per cent of all GHG emissions.[33] North America alone contributes to 25 per cent of global energy-related GHG emissions.[34] Developing countries are most impacted, and are already facing massive adaptation challenges. Unpredictable weather patterns resulting in extremes of drought or storms have had huge negative impacts on agricultural-based societies and have wreaked havoc in poorer countries. Low-lying small-island states are at great risk from sea level rise.

The thinning of the ozone layer was a further atmospheric challenge. However, due to the tremendous efforts of the international community to phase out CFCs (chlorofluorocarbons) and reduce overall the consumption and production of other ozone-depleting substances (ODS), certain levels of ozone depletion have halted.[35] Such efforts are clearly linked to commitments made under the Montreal Protocol on Substances that Deplete the Ozone Layer. Today, the ozone layer is recovering, albeit slowly. Use and production of hydro-chlorofluorocarbons (HCFCs) and hydrofluorocarbons (HFCs) has not yet been phased out and usage exemptions and incidences of illegal use still exist.[36]

Forests and biodiversity

Extreme levels of biodiversity loss driven by population growth and increased consumption[37] continue to be a major global problem, already resulting in mass species extinction,[38] disruption of ecosystems[39] and loss of genetic diversity.[40] In North America, over 380 species were

---

32 UNEP (2007), *GEO Fact Sheet 3, The Air That We Breathe*. Online. Available HTTP: <http://www.unep.org/geo/GEO4/media/fact_sheets/Fact_Sheet_3_Air.pdf> (accessed 3 May 2012).
33 UNEP (2011), *Keeping Track of Our Changing Environment, From Rio to Rio+20 (1992–2012)*, p. 24. Online. Available HTTP: <http://www.unep.org/geo/pdfs/Keeping_Track.pdf> (accessed 3 May 2012).
34 UNEP (2007), op. cit., p. 256.
35 UNEP (2011), ft. 40, op. cit., p. 26.
36 UNEP (2011), ft. 26, op. cit. p. 62.
37 UNEP (2007), ft. 10, op. cit., p. 167.
38 Ibid., p. 162, where it states that '[t]he current rate of biodiversity loss suggests that a sixth major extinction due to human activities is underway.'
39 Ibid.
40 Ibid., p. 165.

listed as endangered, threatened or of special concern in Canada, while in the United States over 1,231 species were listed as endangered or threatened.[41]

The two largest problems contributing to biodiversity loss in North America are wetland destruction and bio-invasion.[42] Wetland conservation is of particular importance in North America, since about a third of its threatened and endangered species depend on wetland habitat for survival.[43] Prior to the 1970s, government programmes encouraged the conversion of wetlands into agricultural and industrial sites, resulting in the loss of more than one-half its original wetland habitat.[44] Agricultural expansion alone was responsible for between 85 and 87 per cent of overall wetland losses.[45] Since the 1980s, significant national and regional efforts have been made to protect and restore wetlands.[46] Internationally, both Canada and the United States are parties to the Ramsar Convention and have together listed 67 sites as Wetlands of International Importance. Though much has been done to stem wetland loss and promote its conservation, habitat loss due to human activities still continues, requiring continuous review and updating of current conservation programmes.

Bio-invasion, or the influx of alien and invasive species as a result of human activity, is another important problem in North America. The zebra mussel is a major example of such a species that has wreaked havoc on natural ecosystems since it was introduced in 1980 in ballast water from cargo ships. Alien aquatic species are expected to contribute to the extinction of native freshwater species in North America at a rate of 4 per cent over the next century.[47] Increasing international trade, which has created more opportunities for alien invasive species to be introduced, and climate change, which has opened up warmer, more hospitable environments, previously uninhabitable for alien species, are drivers of the problem of bio-invasion.[48]

In Latin America and the Caribbean (LAC), which contains the world's greatest biodiversity,[49] there is the most to lose from deforestation, land degradation, land-use change, marine pollution and ecosystem loss.[50] According to UNEP reports, 41 per cent of threatened endemic plants worldwide are in the tropical Andes, about 30 per cent are in Meso-America and the Caribbean, and 26 per cent are in the Brazilian Atlantic Forest and Cerrado.[51] Though the region contains 23 per cent of the world's forest cover, average global annual forest loss was the highest in Latin America and the Caribbean between 2000 and 2005, accounting for 66 per cent of the worldwide forest cover loss.[52] Evidence shows that the greatest contributor to terrestrial biodiversity loss in LAC is the growth of large-scale commercial agriculture,[53]

41 UNEP (2002) *North America's Environment, A Thirty-Year State of the Environment and Policy Retrospective*, p. 31.
42 Ibid., p. 33.
43 Ibid., pp. 33–4.
44 Ibid.
45 Ibid.
46 Ibid., pp. 34–8.
47 Ibid., p. 40.
48 Ibid., p. 42.
49 Twenty per cent of all of the recognised ecoregions in the world; see UNEP (2010), op. cit., p. 94.
50 UNEP (2007), op. cit., p. 245. Also, 5 of the 20 countries with the greatest number of endangered species of fauna, and 7 of the 20 countries with the greatest number of endangered plant species, are in LAC: UNEP (2010), op. cit., p. 101.
51 Ibid., UNEP (2007), p. 248.
52 Ibid., p. 246.
53 UNEP (2010), op. cit., p. 101.

which is responsible for almost one-half of the deforestation in the region.[54] The problem is most acute in South and Central America, where large areas of forest are removed to make way for roads which facilitate the expansion of agriculture, but also encourage illegal logging.[55]

Coastal degradation and pollution affects marine biodiversity in LAC. In the Caribbean alone, 30 per cent of coral reefs have either been decimated or are at serious risk, and without drastic action, estimates are that 20 per cent more will be lost over the next 10 to 30 years.[56] The main drivers of this problem are overfishing, sedimentation and run-off of hazardous chemicals, nutrients and waste, and land-use change. Overfishing affects approximately 60 per cent of Caribbean reefs.[57] Though wetlands perform valuable services to the marine ecosystem, they continue to be destroyed at an unprecedented rate in LAC[58] to make way for urban development in coastal areas, the expansion of tourism and aquaculture development.[59] Added to this, pollution from untreated sewage[60] and agricultural and industrial run-off causes eutrophication, which destroys corals and other marine life. Approximately 36 per cent of the Caribbean's coral reefs are within 2 kilometres of the coast and they are therefore highly susceptible to impacts from coastal activities.[61]

Land, desertification and agriculture

Urbanisation is one of the most significant contributors to land degradation in the Americas today, and has had some of the most adverse impacts on air and water quality, coastal and marine ecosystem health, and wildlife habitat. According to 2011 data, in North America 82 per cent of its population live in urban areas, and in LAC this figure is 79 per cent.[62]

In North America, the problem has been exacerbated by urban sprawl, marked by the concentration of low-density residential development in rural or previously undeveloped areas just on the outskirts of urban centres. In 2000, urban sprawl exceeded the rate of population growth and three of the world's ten most sprawling urban areas were situated in Canada.[63] Low-density residential development even further beyond the urban fringe, separated by natural areas and known as exurban sprawl, is yet another concern. Sprawl has contributed to the increase in car use and the length of time taken to commute, which have thereby increased dependency on fuel and carbon emissions produced. Sprawl is also accompanied by massive infrastructural and commercial development, further pressuring stressed natural rural environments and fragmenting forests, wetlands and other wildlife habitats. From 1982 to 1997, almost 50 per cent of annual net wetland loss was as a result of urban development.[64] Run-off

54 UNEP (2010), op. cit., p 5.
55 Ibid.
56 Ibid., pp 3–4.
57 UNEP (2007), op. cit., p. 170.
58 For example, in St Lucia, where it has been reported that hotel development is directly responsible for 50 per cent of its mangrove loss; see UNEP (2010), op. cit., p. 123.
59 UNEP (2010), op. cit., pp. 123–33.
60 In the Latin American and Caribbean region, about 86 per cent of the sewage enters untreated into rivers and oceans; in the Caribbean, the figure stands at 80–90 per cent; ibid., p. 129.
61 Ibid., p. 131.
62 World Urbanization Prospects: The 2011 Revision Population Database, Online. Available HTTP: <http://esa.un.org/unpd/wup/Analytical-Figures/Fig_1.htm> (accessed 16 May 2012).
63 UNEP (2007), op. cit., p. 258.
64 Ibid., p. 259.

from roads and sewers does not replenish the groundwater but instead flows into and contaminates water bodies with pollutants.

Urbanisation in LAC shares many of the same impacts as it does in North America. However, problems such as the lack of basic sanitation and sewage infrastructure, haphazard solid waste disposal strategies[65] and unplanned development, that do not exist to such a large extent in the North American region, cause urbanisation to have an even greater impact on the environments in LAC. In many cities throughout LAC, urban waste water flows untreated into water sources.[66] Solid waste management plans are not sufficient to deal with the problems of massive waste generation associated with rapid urbanisation, and as a result 23 per cent of the solid waste actually collected is not properly disposed of.[67] Most solid waste is therefore dumped in watercourses, on roadsides, or is burned, polluting the land, atmosphere and water sources.

Increasing pressures from growing populations and globalisation have encouraged the growth of the agricultural sector in the Americas. An expansion in agricultural productivity has meant more intense farming activity, and this mainly has been in the form of greater pesticide use and multiple cropping. Unsustainable, commercial agricultural practices now replace traditional farming activities, and the this has caused exacerbated soil and wind erosion, sedimentation of waterways and overall land degradation.[68] Pesticide use is also a major concern throughout the Americas. North America uses 36 per cent of the world's pesticides, and as a result constitutes the largest global pesticide consumer.[69] Though enhanced controls in North America have stemmed the increase in pesticide use over the years, many pesticides contain POPs, toxic chemicals which bio-accumulate for many years before breaking down, interfering with natural ecosystems and threatening human health. In LAC, agricultural activities additionally fuel problems such as deforestation, as natural forested areas are converted to arable or grazing land to support a growing global demand for food products.[70]

Mining is also one of the most polluting activities in LAC, resulting in erosion, destruction of natural areas and contamination of water bodies. In many areas, national legislation to regulate the industry is too lax to be of any success, and serves as no real disincentive to investment.[71]

Oceans, rivers and freshwater

Anthropogenic pollution is a significant contributor to coastal and freshwater area degradation in the Americas. Extensive use of agro-chemical products such as pesticides or fertiliser contaminates surface run-off, creating a mixture of heavy metals, toxic chemicals, solid waste and other pollutants, which eventually flows into surface water[72] and oceans alike.[73] In LAC, run-off from open-pit mining containing toxic chemicals contributes to a substantial part of

---

65 UNEP (2010), op. cit., pp. 158–9.
66 Ibid., p. 156.
67 UNEP (2007), op. cit., p. 244.
68 Ibid., pp. 90–6.
69 Ibid., p. 97.
70 UNEP (2010), op. cit., pp. 64–6, 77–8.
71 Ibid., pp. 68–9.
72 UNEP (2002), op. cit., pp. 71–2; UNEP (2010), op. cit. pp. 114–15.
73 UNEP (2010), op. cit., pp. 129–30.

the contamination of groundwater.[74] In North America, the growing number and scale of confined animal feeding operations (CAFOs) add significant amounts of nutrients into the water system.[75] Many of these contaminants persist in the environment for many years before being broken down, therefore making their use and control imperative in protecting the long-term viability of natural ecosystems. Anthropogenic pollution has also had major adverse impacts on fish stocks and coral reef health.[76]

In LAC such problems are compounded by the lack of national policies to regulate, monitor or control such activities, or preserve natural resources.[77] Fish stocks are undergoing massive decline as a result of overfishing, unsustainable fishing practices, lack of regulation and control, and pollution. Coral reef populations have been similarly affected by such activities, and as a result have been said to have demonstrated the most severe recent increase in extinction.[78]

The Americas' sub-regional environmental and sustainable development cooperation responses

Many countries of the Americas have adopted sub-regional or bilateral environmental agreements (REAs) as part of their international environmental management framework, and new treaties are also being developed to secure sustainable development in key sectors. Such REAs are commonly formed in response to shared sub-regional environmental concerns over floods and fires, transboundary pollution of air and water, desertification and land-use policies, lack of regional environmental standards and the need for shared ecosystem management regimes.[79] Many of the REAs now in existence have come about as a result of efforts made by regional integration institutions.

North American environmental cooperation

The NAAEC was the first organisation of its kind to establish a framework to address environmental concerns and ensure sustainable development as a parallel to the intensification of bilateral trade within the region. The agreement requires parties to promote the development of environmental law and education in their respective countries and establish mechanisms for government monitoring and enforcement. It establishes a Commission for Environmental Cooperation (CEC) to oversee and support such matters, make recommendations to encourage parties to achieve their environmental goals, and hear submissions from third parties on issues where state parties fail to effectively enforce their environmental laws.

One of the region's most successful conservation initiatives has been the North American Waterfowl Management Plan in 1986, involving the United States, Canada and Mexico.[80] The main objective of the Plan is to recover waterfowl populations by restoring and managing

---

74 Ibid., p. 115.
75 UNEP (2007), op. cit., p. 262.
76 UNEP (2010), op. cit., pp. 124–5; UNEP/CARICOM/UWI (2004), op. cit., p. 61.
77 This is especially compared to national strategies in North America that have curbed and in some cases, actually improved areas of degraded water quality. See UNEP (2007), op. cit., pp. 263–4. Most coastal areas in LAC are not Marine Protected Areas (MPAs) and lack any management plan. See UNEP (2010), op. cit., pp. 121–2.
78 UNEP (2010), op. cit., p. 4.
79 Cordonier Segger et al., op. cit., p. 21.
80 Mexico became a signatory to the North American Waterfowl Management Plan in 1994.

wetland ecosystems. The Plan is assessed and updated every five years by the North American Waterfowl Management Plan Committee. In 1998, an update to the Plan established a biologically based planning strategy which would take into consideration the overall ecosystem conditions necessary for the habitat of waterfowl and other wetland-associated species.[81] It also provided for a more broad-based approach by collaborating with all stakeholder groups for information and resources. Though the Plan has been extremely successful in mitigating or halting the decline of several waterfowl populations throughout North America, its periodic updates struggle to deal with growing pressures from agricultural development, pollution and invasive species.[82]

In 2001, the New England Governors (NEG) and the Eastern Canadian Premiers (ECP) established a Climate Change Action Plan (CCAP) which outlines specific GHG-reduction goals and sets timelines for their fulfilment. The CCAP represents the first international, multi-jurisdictional climate initiative of its type in the world.[83] Since its implementation, several climate programmes have been created in all New England states and Eastern Canadian provinces.

The NEG/ECP Climate Change Steering Committee (CCSC) periodically assesses the parties' activities under the CCAP, reviews targets and creates new strategies aimed at dealing with climate change and adaptation.

Caribbean environmental cooperation

The Caribbean has made significant strides in the use of regional integration and cooperation in implementing programmes and establishing information clearinghouses with the aim of facilitating MEA compliance. The Caribbean Community (CARICOM)[84] was established as a regional coordinating bloc to increase trade, economic development and cooperation among Commonwealth Caribbean heads of government. Since then, much of the current regional efforts to implement MEA requirements can be attributed to the creation of the 1994 Barbados Programme of Action (BPOA) during the first CARICOM Ministerial Conference on the Environment.

The BPOA was monumental in facilitating the development of regional organisations and action plans focused on environmental management throughout the Caribbean. The Small Island Developing States Network (SIDSnet) came as a direct follow-up to the BPOA and its primary function is to support the sustainable development of Small Island Developing States (SIDS) through enhanced information and communication technology. There are 23 SIDS in the Latin American and Caribbean region.

The Caribbean Action Plan (CAP) is another major regional environmental programme, established in 1981, which eventually led to the adoption of the Convention for the Protection

81 *Expanding the Vision, 1998 Update, North American Waterfowl Management Plan.* Online. Available HTTP: <http://www.fws.gov/birdhabitat/NAWMP/files/NAWMP1998.pdf> (accessed 3 May 2012).

82 *North American Waterfowl Management Plan: Strengthening the Biological Foundation, 2004 Implementation Framework.* Online. Available HTTP: <http://www.fws.gov/birdhabitat/NAWMP/files/ImplementationFramework.pdf> (accessed 3 May 2012).

83 New England Governors' Conference, Inc., 'NEG/ECP Climate Change Program'. Online. Available HTTP: <http://negc.org/main/?do=page&id=39> (accessed 3 May 2012).

84 Its members are Antigua and Barbuda, the Bahamas, Barbados, Belize, Dominica, Grenada, Guyana, Haiti, Jamaica, Montserrat, St Lucia, St Kitts and Nevis, St Vincent and the Grenadines, and Trinidad and Tobago.

and Development of the Marine Environment of the Wider Caribbean Region (Cartagena Convention) in 1983. The Convention is supplemented by three protocols addressing specific environmental issues, namely oil spills, specially protected areas and wildlife and land-based sources and activities of marine pollution. The CAP led to the creation of the Caribbean Environmental Programme (CEP), which provides the programmatic framework for the Cartagena Convention. It is one of the UNEP-administered Regional Seas Programmes. The Cartagena Convention and its associated protocols are unique to the Latin American and Caribbean region and collectively have been extremely effective in facilitating member parties in implementing their obligations under MEAs such as the Convention on Biological Diversity and the International Convention for the Prevention of Pollution from Ships (MARPOL).

The Caribbean Community Climate Change Centre (CCCCC) acts as the region's coordinating response centre and implementation body on the United Nations Framework Convention on Climate Change (UNFCCC). It advises the CARICOM on climate change and adaptation-related issues and liaises with the Alliance of Small Island States (AOSIS) to assist SIDS in developing sustainable energy resources. Initially, the organisation's efforts to build climate change adaptation capacity in the Caribbean region stemmed from an OAS and CARICOM collaboration in 1997 known as the Caribbean Planning for Adaptation to Climate Change Project (CPACC). The CPACC was directly inspired by the BPOA and was the CCCCC's first project to further UNFCCC implementation in the Caribbean. Since its completion, the CPACC has been succeeded by the Adaptation to Climate Change in the Caribbean Project (ACCC), Mainstreaming and Adaptation to Climate Change (MACC), Special Program on Adaptation to Climate Change (SPACC), and most recently Enhancing Capacity for Adaptation to Climate Change (ECACC).

The Organisation of Eastern Caribbean States (OECS)[85] has also done a significant amount of work in the development of regional MEA collaboration and implementation in the region. Attached to the OECS is an Environment and Sustainable Development Unit whose responsibility is to assist member states 'in all matters pertaining to the sustainable use of natural resources to ensure the sustainability of livelihoods of the peoples of the OECS'.[86] In 2000, the OECS adopted the St George's Declaration, which contains 21 principles on environmental sustainability, which are continuously referenced by the organisation and its member states as a guide to environmental management planning. Its principles include a commitment to integrate regional and national development programmes with environmental factors, and to coordinate its work with the international community. The OECS launched its first Climate Change project called 'Reducing risk to human and natural assets resulting from climate change' (RRACC) in July 2011, targeted at implementing adaptation strategies as well as developing a database of critical climate change information needs.[87]

85 Its members are Anguilla, Antigua and Barbuda, the British Virgin Islands, the Commonwealth of Dominica, Grenada, Montserrat, Saint Lucia, St Christopher (St Kitts) and Nevis and St Vincent and the Grenadines.
86 For information about the Environment and Sustainable Development Unit, see OECS, 'About ESDU'. Online. Available HTTP: <http://www.oecs.org/esdu/about-esdu> (accessed 3 May 2012).
87 OECS, 'First OECS Climate Change Project launched'. Online. Available HTTP: <http://www.oecs.org/esdu/esdu-news/787-first-oecs-climate-change-project-launched> (accessed 3 May 2012).

Central American environmental cooperation

The Central American Alliance for Sustainable Development (ALIDES) was the first major initiative in the region to establish a comprehensive initiative to address sustainable development in Central America. It established a framework for regional action, eventually leading to the development of the Central American Commission for Environment and Development (CCAD), which is the implementing body for the ALIDES and represents the environmental arm of the regional integration body known as the Central American Integration System (SICA).[88] The main goal of the CCAD is to strengthen the national authorities and regulations on environmental management. Many of its initiatives promote compliance with responsibilities under the Convention on Biological Diversity (CBD). The principal coordinating instrument of the CCAD is the Central American Environmental Plan (PARCA), which is reviewed periodically. One of its strategic objectives is the integration of regional environmental management by strengthening regional and national implementation and the coordination of institutional action.[89] The CCAD has also established regional environmental integration programmes such as the Regional Strategy for the Conservation and Sustainable Use of Biodiversity in Mesoamerica (ERB), which acts as an information-gathering body on biodiversity in Mesoamerica, as well a coordinator between political and institutional activities on biodiversity issues.

The Environmental Cooperation Commission (ECC) also operates in the Central American region and acts as the supervising body over the region's CAFTA-DR Environmental Cooperation Program (ECP). The ECC was established by the Environmental Cooperation Agreement (ECA) which was signed by parties to the US–Dominican Republic–Central American Free Trade Agreement (CAFTA-DR) after having recognised the need to incorporate environmental concerns into the regional trade agenda. Of the ECP's four main strategy areas, one includes institutional strengthening and biodiversity and conservation. An example of its activities is the establishment of a Regional Pollutant Release and Transfer Register (PRTR). The CCAD coordinates with the ECC to collect and monitor information on pollutants from all member states and ensure compliance with emissions standards.[90]

Andean environmental cooperation

The creation of the Andean Community (CAN)[91] in 1969 through the Cartagena Agreement and subsequently the Trujillo Protocol marked the region's initial steps towards integration in the Andes. An Andean Integration System serves as an inter-linkage between the several regional bodies and institutions of the CAN. In 2001, the Andean Community of

88 The member states of the Central American Integration System (SICA) are Belize, Costa Rica, El Salvador, Guatemala, Honduras, Nicaragua and Panama.
89 CCAD (2009), *Central American Environmental Plan (PARCA 2010–2014)*, p. 16. Online. Available HTTP:<http://www.sica.int/busqueda/busqueda_archivo.aspx?Archivo=pres_47436_1_12032010.pdf> (accessed 3 May 2012).
90 CAFTA-DR Environmental Cooperation Program. Online. Available HTTP: <http://www.caftadr-environment.org/top_menu/countries/Regional/A_re_activitiy_snapshot_polutant_release.html> (accessed 3 May 2012).
91 The members of the Andean Community (CAN) are Bolivia, Ecuador, Peru and Columbia. Venezuela joined the Agreement in 1973 but later withdrew in 2006. Chile was also a member from 1969 until 1976.

Environmental Authorities (CAAAM) approved the 'Guidelines for Environmental Management and Sustainable Development in the Andean Community', spurring regional collaboration efforts on environmental management and sustainable development. Shortly thereafter, CAN also approved a Regional Biodiversity Strategy for Andean countries. Both developments eventually led to the creation of an Andean Environmental Agenda (AEA). The AEA is a regional integrated plan of action to deal with environmental and sustainable development matters using agreed-upon short- and medium-term actions.[92] It outlines biodiversity, climate change and water resources as the main regional issues and identifies capacity building for trade, environmental and sustainable development; environmental education; and sustainable production and consumption as cross-cutting concerns. The AEA continues to be instrumental in facilitating implementation of MEA responsibilities throughout that region.[93]

Another major regional institution is CONDESAN (Consortium for the Sustainable Development of the Andean Eco-region), which facilitates horizontal integration among various governmental and non-governmental stakeholders involved in the promotion of sustainable development in the Andean region.[94] CONDESAN conducts research and advances dialogue on regional environmental issues, and partners with the CAAAM in implementing the AEA. It has also established InfoAndina, which facilitates the dissemination of information and the preparation of mailing lists and publications and serves as a news portal for CONDESAN activities.

South American environmental cooperation

The Southern American Common Market (MERCOSUR)[95] was initially established primarily to facilitate economic development among its member states, though over time it has developed into a regional integration institution for social and sustainable development in the Southern American states. The 2001 MERCOSUR Framework Agreement on the Environment marked the institution's first significant step in coordinating a regional response to environmental management. Its main purposes were: (a) to incorporate environmental considerations and sustainable development into the coordination of sectoral policies and decision-making within the MERCOSUR; and (b) to fulfil responsibilities under international environmental agreements, and implement measures to cooperate on the establishment of environmental policies and the harmonisation of environmental legislation.

Since the inception of the Framework Agreement on the Environment, the MERCOSUR has created a number of subsequent agreements and policies on environmental management. Among such policies are the Environmental Management of Chemical Substances and

---

92 CAN (2007), *Andean Environmental Agenda 2006–2010*, 2nd edition, p. 2. Online. Available HTTP: <http://www.comunidadandina.org/public/libro_54.htm> (accessed 3 May 2012).
93 Responses include programmes such as the implementation of the Andean Strategy on Climate Change and the Regional Biodiversity Strategy.
94 BioOne (2009), *CONDESAN: An Innovative and Multi-institutional Andean Platform in Continuing Evolution*, p. 356. Online. Available HTTP: <http://www.bioone.org/doi/abs/10.1659/mrd.mp013> (accessed 3 May 2012).
95 The Mercado Común del Sur (MERCOSUR) was established by the Treaty of Asunción in 1990, and its members are Argentina, Brazil, Paraguay and Uruguay.

Products: Action Plan of MERCOSUR (2006),[96] which focuses on the regulation of mercury and pesticides, management of contaminated sites and implementation of the Globally Harmonized System (GHS) of Classification and Labelling of Chemicals.

Most recently, the MERCOSUR and the European Union have partnered to implement an ambitious ECONORMAS-MERCOSUR programme aimed at building capacity in member states to enhance environmental protection and sustainable resource management efforts. Renewable energy is also an increasing priority area in the MERCOSUR, and is currently being addressed by member states under a 2007 Action Plan for Cooperation on Biofuels, as well as under an initiative to develop nuclear power in Argentina and Brazil.[97]

Building further hemispheric environmental collaboration

The UNEP Regional Office for Latin America and the Caribbean (ROLAC) is a branch of its Division of Regional Cooperation (DRC) that works closely with 33 countries of the region, to assist regional efforts to implement UNEP's work programme, based on UNEP-identified priority areas. It partners with existing regional bodies such as CAN, CCAD, OECS[98] and CARICOM, as well as national institutions, to facilitate these goals, which include the provision of technical and financial assistance and support for projects to build capacity on MEA implementation and legislative drafting, and to compile information to track MEA activity and compliance in the region. The North American equivalent of this body is the Regional Office for North America (RONA). Its mission is to foster cooperation on environmental issues between North America and the international community by collaborating with regional stakeholders throughout all levels of society. Like ROLAC, RONA also collects and disseminates information on the region's activities to stakeholders and undertakes public education programmes on international environmental issues.

The Organization of American States (OAS) brings together the 35 independent states of the Americas. Its Department of Sustainable Development (DSD) was established to ensure that environmental management and sustainable development are a priority for member states and it supports activities that translate these developments into local action. Notably, the DSD serves as the secretariat for the Inter-American Forum on Environmental Law (FIDA), which operates a database to track, exchange and organise information on the development of environmental legislation at the national level in member states, and to support all such efforts to promote MEA compliance.

The OAS is also the secretariat for the annual Summit of the Americas meeting, where heads of state and government meet to discuss matters of common importance and establish commitments to address regional issues; FIDA is one such initiative that emerged from the 1996 Summit of the Americas for Sustainable Development. Similarly, the Inter-American

96 ECLAC (2010), *Sustainable Development in Latin America and The Caribbean: Trends, Progress, and Challenges in Sustainable Consumption and Production, Mining, Transport, Chemicals and Waste Management Report to The Eighteenth Session of the Commission on Sustainable Development of The United Nations*, pp. 20, 73.

97 EU (2011), *EU External Action – Mid-Term Review and Regional Indicative Programme for 2011–2013*, pp. 10–11. Online. Available HTTP: <http://www.eeas.europa.eu/mercosur/rsp/11_13_mtr_en.pdf> (accessed 3 May 2012).

98 UNEP Division of Environmental Conventions, *Development of a Framework for Harmonized Legislation to Implement Biodiversity-Related MEAs*. Online. Available HTTP: <http://www.unep.org/DEC/Support/Cross_Cutting/Biodiv_Leg.asp> (accessed 3 May 2012).

Biodiversity Information Network (IABIN) was also established as a result of the 1996 Summit, and its purpose is to promote greater coordination among Western Hemispheric countries in the collection, sharing and use of biodiversity information relevant to decision-making and education.[99]

Partly due to the efforts of these regional institutions, there are a number of further important environmental cooperation instruments and regimes that have been created to assist in the management of transboundary resources, or in a collaborative response to a common concern. These include treaties and instruments for joint management of rivers and other freshwater bodies,[100] treaties for coastal and marine ecosystem protection,[101] treaties for the common protection and sustainable development of transboundary forest or other terrestrial ecosystems,[102] and several inter-American conventions to address particular concerns.[103]

99 For an overview of IABIN, see 'IABIN overview'. Online. Available HTTP: <http://www.iabin-us.org/about_iabin/overview.html> (accessed 3 May 2012).

100 For example, the establishment of the International Joint Commission (IJC) under the Boundary Waters Treaty of 1909, to assess, monitor, report and resolve disputes concerning lakes and rivers along the Canada-United States border. The IJC eventually established the Great Lakes Water Quality Agreement of 1978 to restore and maintain the chemical, physical and biological integrity of the Great Lakes Basin Ecosystem. Online. Available HTTP: <http://www.ijc.org/rel/agree/quality.html> (accessed 3 May 2012).

101 For example, the Mesoamerican Barrier Reef System (MBRS) Project, which covers Belize, Honduras, Guatemala and Mexico, the goal of which is to coordinate the protection of the unique Mesoamerican Barrier Reef ecosystem, and to assist participating countries in strengthening and harmonising national policies, regulations and institutional arrangements for the conservation and sustainable use of that ecosystem. For more information, see IUCN, 'Conservation and Sustainable Use of the Mesoamerican Barrier Reef System Project'. Online. Available HTTP: <http://www.tbpa.net/page.php?ndx=66> (accessed 3 May 2012).

102 For example, the Amazon Cooperation Treaty Organization (ACTO) established by the Amazon Cooperation Treaty (ACT), 3 July 1978, to which Bolivia, Brazil, Colombia, Ecuador, Guyana, Peru, Suriname and Venezuela are parties, is aimed at promoting joint actions towards the harmonious development of the Amazon Basin. For more information, see OTCA, 'Projects and Programs'. Online. Available HTTP: <http://www.otca.org.br/en/exped_jovem.php> (accessed 3 May 2012). Another example is the Regional Environmental Program for Central America (PROARCA), which supports the conservation and sustainable management of biologically important and diverse areas in the Mesoamerican Biological Corridor (Central America and Mexico). PROARCA's three main components are aimed at Coastal Resource Management, Protected Area Management, and Environmental Protection and Legislation activities. For more information see USAID, 'USAID Regional Environmental Program for Central America (PROARCA).' Online. Available HTTP: <http://www.usaid.gov/locations/latin_america_caribbean/environment/proarca.html> (accessed 3 May 2012).

103 For example, the Pacific Salmon Treaty, signed by the governments of Canada and the United States to implement the Pacific Salmon Commission, the purpose of which is to oversee programmes to prevent over-fishing and protect salmon habitat. For more information see PSC, 'About the Commission'. Online. Available HTTP: <http://www.psc.org/about.htm> (accessed 3 May 2012). Another example is the formation of the North American Plant Protection Organization (NAPPO) through the NAPPO Cooperative Agreement, 17 October 2004 (a supplement to the North American Plant Protection Agreement). NAPPO's mandate is to 'encourage cooperative efforts among the member countries to prevent the entry, establishment and spread of quarantine pests and to limit the economic impact of regulated non-quarantine pests while facilitating international trade in plants, plant products and other regulated articles; and to encourage and participate in similar hemispheric and global cooperative efforts,' Article III, NAPPO Constitution and By-Laws. For more information, see NAPPO, Official Documents. Online. Available HTTP: <http://www.nappo.org/en/?sv=&category=Official%20Documents&title=Official%20Documents> (accessed 3 May 2012).

A number of FTAs, including between North America, Central America and the Andean countries, also contain commitments for sustainable development and the environment. Between 2000 and 2011, the Unites States entered into trade agreements with Peru (Peru Trade Promotion Agreement),[104] Chile (United States–Chile Free Trade Agreement),[105] and most notably the Dominican Republic and the following Central American bloc of countries: Costa Rica, El Salvador, Guatemala, Honduras, and Nicaragua (CAFTA-DR).[106] In Canada, since the 1997 Chile–Canada Free Trade Agreement, Canada has also entered into several FTAs between 2000 and 2011, namely the Canada–Costa Rica Free Trade Agreement, Canada–Colombia Free Trade Agreement, and the Canada–Peru Free Trade Agreement.[107] Like the NAAEC, these agreements contain parallel environmental agreements or incorporate environmental concerns into the structure of the agreement itself.

The European Union has recently signed on to a new generation of Economic Partnership Agreements, containing important sub-regional provisions on the environment, and sustainable development as 'Partnerships for Sustainable Development'. Characterised by political dialogue and sub-regional sustainable development cooperation, as well as enhancement of trade, these treaties include the EU–CARIFORUM Economic Partnership Agreement[108], the EU–Central America Economic Partnership Agreement[109] and the EU–Colombia–Peru Economic Partnership Agreement.[110] An EU–MERCOSUR FTA is also currently being negotiated.[111] These economic treaties have important environmental and sustainable development cooperation components, which include commitments to collaborate in developing carbon markets, renewable energy, organic agriculture, sustainable use of biological resources, and other efforts.

---

104 The United States–Peru Trade Promotion Agreement, 12 April 2006 establishes an Environmental Affairs Council, the goal of which is to implement the Environmental Chapter of the Agreement, which includes ensuring enforcement of national environmental legislation. See Article 18.6, United States–Peru Trade Promotion Agreement. Online. Available HTTP: <http://www.ustr.gov/trade-agreements/free-trade-agreements/peru-tpa/final-text> (accessed 3 May 2012).

105 Article 19.3 of the United States–Chile Free Trade Agreement, 1 January 2004. Online. Available HTTP: <http://www.ustr.gov/trade-agreements/free-trade-agreements/chile-fta/final-text> (accessed 3 May 2012). This establishes an Environmental Affairs Council to oversee environmental issues arising between member parties, and to address such issues, whilst promoting full public participation.

106 See also, OAS Foreign Trade Information System (SICE) United States of America: Trade Agreements. Online. Available HTTP: <http://www.sice.oas.org/ctyindex/USA/USAagreements_e.asp> (accessed 3 May 2012).

107 OAS Foreign Trade Information System (SICE) Canada: Trade Agreements. Online. Available HTTP: <http://www.sice.oas.org/ctyindex/CAN/CANagreements_e.asp> (accessed 3 May 2012).

108 The EU–CARIFORUM Economic Partnership Agreement entered into force on 29 December 2008. Online. Available HTTP: <http://trade.ec.europa.eu/doclib/docs/2008/february/tradoc_137971.pdf> (accessed 3 May 2012).

109 Also known as the EU–Central America Association Agreement, it was signed between the EU and the Central American countries of Costa Rica, El Salvador, Guatemala, Honduras, Nicaragua and Panama on 22 March 2011. Online. Available HTTP: <http://trade.ec.europa.eu/doclib/press/index.cfm?id=689> (accessed 3 May 2012).

110 The Trade Agreement between the European Union and Colombia and Peru was signed in April 2011. Online. Available HTTP: <http://trade.ec.europa.eu/doclib/press/index.cfm?id=691> (accessed 3 May 2012).

111 For more information, see European Commission, 'Trade: Regions: Mercosur'. Online. Available HTTP: <http://ec.europa.eu/trade/creating-opportunities/bilateral-relations/regions/mercosur/> (accessed 3 May 2012).

Conclusion

Among the 35 countries of the Americas there exist many good reasons to collaborate on care of the environment and sustainable development. It is a massive task, and for effective stewardship of significant ecological and hydrological systems, a great deal remains to be done to address the many environmental and sustainable development challenges.[112]

Countries currently cooperate through various hemispheric institutions such as the OAS and through five sub-regional institutions covering North America, Central America, the Caribbean, the Andes and South America, along with other specific instruments, in order to secure sustainable development of these unique and important natural resources and the protection of these ecological systems.

In terms of environmental cooperation for the protection of ecosystems and the control of pollution, perhaps the most pressing and least effectively addressed challenges include defor-estation, biodiversity loss and destruction of habitat for migratory species and populations, rapid urbanisation with attendant environmental and social challenges, protection of oceans and coastal ecosystems, and stewardship of rivers, pollution and waste control.[113] Further pressing sustainable development matters include climate change mitigation and adaptation,[114] the shift to clean and renewable energy sources,[115] sustainable use of biological resources and technologies,[116] the need to better enforce laws and regulations for sustainable resources management,[117] and changing patterns of consumption.[118] It is a difficult agenda. In many cases, the coordination of efforts has been facilitated by the operation of already existing regional trade and integration blocs. In others, cooperation on sustainable development chal-lenges, including harmonisation of MEA implementation, is facilitated by institutions estab-lished by existing FTAs. While treaties and other instruments exist at many levels, there remain pressing legal and institutional challenges to secure faithful implementation of these commitments.

Pressing regime implementation challenges include the need for scientific research and data, the need for greatly increased capacity and resources (including reliable financing), the need for integrated and mutually supportive law and policy-making among economic, social and environmental bodies (including the elaboration of new sustainable development law where appropriate) and the need for reliable compliance mechanisms for monitoring, enforce-ment and dispute settlement. This agenda, while difficult, is certainly worthwhile. Some progress has been made in recent decades, but a great deal more is needed.

112 Cordonier Segger et al., op. cit.
113 Ibid., p. 14.
114 UNEP (2010), op. cit., pp. 40–3, 160–2; UNEP (2007), op. cit., pp. 251–3.
115 UNEP (2007), op. cit., p. 257.
116 UNEP (2010), op. cit., pp. 328–9.
117 Ibid., p. 323.
118 Ibid., pp. 27–9.

26

South East Asian environmental legal governance

Koh Kheng-Lian and Md Saiful Karim

South East Asian nations share many similar environmental issues to those in other parts of the world. The Association of South East Asian Nations (ASEAN) envisions a green and clean region. However, effective environmental governance has not been fully achieved. This chapter evaluates recent development in South East Asia including the implementation of legal frameworks and a governance system to meet changing circumstances. It is argued that there are still many political, policy and other challenges in South East Asia, and if the ASEAN vision for a green and clean region is to be realised, there is still much that needs to be done.

Introduction

Environmental governance may be defined as the regulatory process through which different actors and stakeholders influence the process of environmental conservation.[1] The process works through the action and interaction of state and non-state actors.[2] It includes *inter alia* institutions, policies and laws. However, this term may convey different meanings in different contexts. This chapter predominantly focuses on legal aspects of environmental governance in the Association of South East Asian Nations (ASEAN).

Established in 1967, ASEAN consists of ten Member States, namely Brunei, Cambodia, Indonesia, Laos, Myanmar, Malaysia, the Philippines, Singapore, Thailand and Vietnam.[3] Its members range from economies in transition to developing and developed economies. There are two main legal traditions represented – the common law and the civil law, or a hybrid of the two. Many of its members have had different colonial rulers. The ASEAN association has a combined area of approximately 4.47 million square kilometres and a population of

---

1 M.C. Lemos and A. Agrawal, 'Environmental Governance' *Annual Review of Environment and Resources* 11, 2006, pp. 297, 298.
2 Ibid.
3 The ASEAN Declaration (Bangkok Declaration), Bangkok, 8 August 1967. Online. Available HTTP: <http://www.aseansec.org/1212.htm> (accessed 22 November 2011). The founder members were Indonesia, Malaysia, the Philippines, Singapore and Thailand.

approximately 580 million.[4] Some of its Member States are very rich in biodiversity and natural resources. The region is blessed with a number of diverse and unique ecosystems including the Mekong River Basin, Ha Long Bay and Lake Toba. In the first 40 years ASEAN has been operated as a coalition of nations without its own international legal personality and legally binding constitutional instrument. In 2007, the ASEAN Charter was adopted as the constitutional document.[5] It entered into force on 15 December 2008 and bestowed an international legal personality upon the organisation.[6]

The region shares many environmental issues in common with those in other parts of the world, such as biodiversity loss, climate change, transboundary pollution and zoonotic diseases. Environmental matters are dealt with within one of three pillars or communities namely, the ASEAN Socio-Cultural Community (ASCC), ASEAN Political Security Community (APSC) and ASEAN Economic Community (AEC); these are three of the five documents in the Roadmap of an ASEAN Community (2009–2015). In addition there are numerous binding and non-binding environmental instruments covering general and sectoral areas including biodiversity and natural resources, forestry, transboundary pollution, water resources, marine pollution, zoonotic diseases, energy, climate change and environmental emergency response.[7]

As yet, ASEAN has not fully achieved effective environmental governance for sustainable development but is working towards it. As will be discussed, environmental governance in ASEAN, including regional institutions and the law and policy framework, is not very effective in solving critical transboundary environmental issues involving state responsibility.

The ASEAN Vision 2020 of 15 December 1997 states that to realise its vision of 'a community of caring societies' there is a need, *inter alia*, to establish 'a clean and green ASEAN with fully established mechanisms for sustainable development to ensure the protection of the region's environment, the sustainability of its natural resources, and the high quality of life of its peoples'.[8] In 1997, ASEAN members pledged to bring this vision into reality. Since then ASEAN's strong commitment[9] has led it to aim at accelerating the establishment of the ASEAN Community by 2015 (instead of 2020).[10] Ensuring effective environmental governance is a critical step to achieving a clean and green ASEAN with fully established mechanisms for sustainable development as envisioned by the ASEAN Vision 2020.

As a sub-regional organisation, ASEAN has two main roles in ensuring environmental protection; first, to deal with environmental issues of common concern in the region, with

4 United Nations Environment Programme (UNEP), *Fourth ASEAN State of the Environment Report 2009*. Online. Available HTTP: <http://www.aseansec.org/publications/SoER4-Report.pdf> (accessed 22 November 2011).
5 *Charter of the Association of Southeast Asian Nations*. Online. Available HTTP: <http://www.aseansec.org/21069.pdf> (accessed 22 November 2011 (hereinafter ASEAN Charter).
6 Lin Chun Hung, 'ASEAN Charter: Deeper Regional Integration under International Law?' (2010) 9 *Chinese Journal of International Law* 821, pp. 824–6.
7 For a comprehensive list see Koh Kheng-Lian, *ASEAN Environmental Law, Policy and Governance Selected Documents* (Vol. I), Hackensack, NJ: World Scientific, 2009 and Koh Kheng-Lian, *ASEAN Environmental Law, Policy and Governance Selected Documents* (Vol. II, forthcoming 2012, 'Hackensack, NJ: World Scientific').
8 ASEAN Vision 2020. Online. Available HTTP: <http://www.aseansec.org/1814.htm> (accessed 22 November 2011).
9 See also the Declaration of the ASEAN Concord II of 2003. Online. Available HTTP: <http://www.aseansec.org/15159.htm> (accessed 22 November 2011).
10 Cebu Declaration on the Acceleration of the Establishment of an ASEAN Community by 2015. Online. Available HTTP: <http://www.aseansec.org/19260.htm> (accessed 22 November 2011).

linkages from global and national/provincial levels. Second, to supplement, facilitate and support global efforts, particularly in the implementation of Multinational Environmental Agreements (MEAs). The two are not mutually exclusive. This chapter evaluates ASEAN's environmental legal governance in the 'ASEAN Way' of decision-making; the environmental governance structure; and some case studies on environmental governance.

The 'ASEAN Way' of decision-making – a possible inroad?

Until recently, due to a lack of a central bureaucracy and for historical reasons, decision-making among the ASEAN Member States has been by consensus or *musyawarah*,[11] commonly known as the 'ASEAN Way'. The ASEAN Way emphasised three basic norms: first, non-interference in other states' affairs; second, consensus and non-binding plans avoiding treaties and legalistic rules; and finally using national institutions and actions, rather than creating a strong central bureaucracy.[12] This approach may be criticised because it is slow and lacks legal backing, but it did serve a purpose of engendering trust among its members, to bring about cooperation. However, as ASEAN has matured, the question is whether a bolder approach should be taken.

While critiquing the ASEAN Way, we need to appreciate the complex legal, economic and social-cultural dimensions of wider East Asia and the historical baggage of each of the Member States. The ASEAN Way has enabled members to build mutual trust and confidence, and progress at 'a pace comfortable to all'.[13] Confidence-building through the gentle *musyawarah* was previously considered the only way. The founding members – Indonesia, Malaysia, the Philippines, Singapore and Thailand – had not always had the best of political relationships and there were even hostile periods. For example, in 1963, Indonesia mounted a *konfrontasi* (confrontation) against Singapore when it joined Malaya to form Malaysia, as Indonesia thought that it was a 'colonial' plot to marginalise Indonesia. Even today, ASEAN members still have occasional spats with one another, as seen in the recent border dispute between Cambodia and Thailand at the Preah Vihear temple.[14] Part of Preah Vihear temple reportedly collapsed after a Thai bombardment in February 2011.[15] This led to Cambodia filing an application in the International Court of Justice (ICJ) on 2 May 2011, requesting interpretation of the 1962 Judgment and also for the urgent indication of provisional measures.[16]

---

11 *Musyawarah dan mufakat* is a Malay custom of decision-making through consultation and consensus. See generally S. Narine, *Explaining ASEAN: Regionalism in Southeast Asia*, Boulder: Lynne Rienner Publishers, 2002.

12 See generally Koh Kheng-Lian and N.A. Robinson, 'Strengthening Sustainable Development in Regional Inter-Governmental Governance: Lessons from the "ASEAN Way"' *Singapore Journal of International and Comparative Law* 6, 2002, p. 640.

13 R.C. Severino, *Southeast Asia in Search of an ASEAN Community: Insights from the Former ASEAN Secretary-General*, Singapore: Institute of Southeast Asian Studies, 2006, p. 18.

14 In 1962 the International Court of Justice (ICJ) recognised Cambodia's claim to it and it was recently designated a UNESCO World Heritage site: *Temple of Preah Vihear (Cambodia v Thailand) (Merits)* [1962] ICJ Rep 6.

15 BBC News, 'Thai-Cambodia clashes "damage Preah Vihear temple"'. Online. Available HTTP: <http://www.bbc.co.uk/news/world-asia-pacific-12377626> (accessed 22 November 2011).

16 *Request for interpretation of the Judgment of 15 June 1962 in the case concerning the Temple of Preah Vihear (Cambodia v Thailand)*. Online. Available HTTP· <http://www.icj-cij.org/docket/index.php?p1=3&p2=3&k=46&case=151> (accessed 22 November 2011).

Since the establishment of ASEAN, there has been no open warfare – peace and security has been maintained, despite fault lines. While there are virtues in the ASEAN Way, there are also setbacks. An example is the persistent and uncompromising application of the principle of state sovereignty and the principle of non-interference with internal affairs.[17] One practical significance of the ASEAN Way is the extent to which it balances national and regional interests. The late S. Rajaratnam, then Foreign Minister of Singapore and founder member of ASEAN, made these insightful remarks at the establishment of the Bangkok Declaration in 1967:

> We must think not only of our national interests but posit them against regional interests: that is a new way of thinking about our problems. And that is two different things and sometimes they can conflict. Secondly, we must also accept the fact, if we are really serious about it, that regional existence means painful adjustments to those practices and thinking in our respective countries. We must make these painful and difficult adjustments. If we are not going to do that, then regionalism remains a Utopia.[18]

His words ring true even after 45 years, even though a new era of closer cooperation emerged in 2007 through a revamped environmental governance architecture under the ASEAN Charter.[19] While the ASEAN Charter introduced a refined and expanded governance system, perhaps the greatest stumbling block to effective decision-making is the application of the principle of sovereignty and non-interference which have been embedded in the Charter. 'National interests', as Rajaratnam so rightly observed, must be posited against 'regional interests'. Can an inroad be made into the ASEAN Way by the recalibration of this principle? If recalibration cannot be done, as this was rejected by the ASEAN Charter, would another pathway lie in the non-traditional security (NTS) approach for transboundary challenges under section II, B.4 of the APSC Blueprint? This has been comprehensively considered by in a number of papers[20] and hence will not be dealt with here. Suffice it to say that in appropriate contexts, such as where human security is threatened (e.g. transboundary challenges such as avian flu or climatic disasters), the concept of human security provides a deliberative space for the invocation of the NTS approach which calls for 'shared responsibility' among Member States. The concept of 'shared responsibility' involves giving up some sovereignty for the common good of all. This approach can be viewed as a contravention of the principles of sovereignty and non-intervention under the ASEAN Charter or it can be

---

17 See the *Indonesian Haze* case study later in this chapter.
18 Speech given at the First Ministerial Meeting of the Association of South East Asia (ASEAN) held on Tuesday 8 August 1967, at the Ministry of Foreign Affairs, Bangkok (emphasis added).
19 Singapore Declaration on the ASEAN Charter. Online. Available HTTP: <http://www.aseansec. org/21233> (accessed 22 November 2011); T. Koh, W. Woon, A. Tan and C. Sze-Wei, 'The ASEAN Charter'. Online. Available HTTP: <http://www.csis.org/media/csis/pubs/pac0733a. pdf> (accessed 22 November 2011).
20 Koh Kheng-Lian, 'Framing New and Emerging Transboundary Environmental Challenges: Impact on the ASEAN Way and Environmental Governance', paper presented at the 2nd CILS Conference 2011, International Conference on ASEAN's Role in Sustainability Development, Faculty of Law, Universitas Gadjah Mada, Indonesia, 21 and 22 November 2011; Koh Kheng-Lian, 'The Discourse of Environmental Security in the ASEAN Context' in B. Jessup and K. Rubenstein (eds) *Environmental Discourses in Public and International Law*, Cambridge: Cambridge University Press, 2012; Koh Kheng-Lian, 'Transboundary and Global Environmental Issues: the Role of ASEAN' *Transnational Environmental Law* 1, 2012, pp. 67–82.

considered as an exception or circumvention. How the principle of sovereignty and that of non-intervention are played out in environmental governance will be examined using the Indonesian Haze as an example in a later part of this chapter.

ASEAN environmental governance

The ASEAN environmental governance structure has been evolving over the last 34 years, since the establishment of the ASEAN Sub-regional Environmental Programme in 1978, and has over the years had accretions to deal with global, regional and national environmental issues.

ASEAN environmental governance in the pre-ASEAN Charter era

When ASEAN was established in 1967, the word 'environment' did not appear in the ASEAN Declaration as the regional formation was mainly for political (security) and economic reasons. The ASEAN environmental agenda began in 1976 after the Stockholm Conference when the United Nations Economic and Social Commission for Asia and the Pacific (UNESCAP) sent a team to the five founding ASEAN Member States (namely Indonesia, Malaysia, the Philippines, Singapore and Thailand) to determine the then six priority areas in terms of the environment formulated in the ASEAN Environmental Programmes (ASEPs) (Phases I to III), 1978 to 1992, namely Environmental Management including Environmental Impact Assessment; Nature Conservation and Terrestrial Ecosystems; Marine Environment; Industry and Environment; Environmental Education and Training; and Environmental Information.

The next stage was not only to update the ASEPs but also to respond to the recommendations of Agenda 21 requiring priority action in ASEAN. This became the ASEAN Strategic Plan of Action on the Environment (ASPAE), 1994–98 as well as the ASEAN Hanoi Plan of Action (HPA), 1999–2004; and the ASEAN Vientiane Action Programme, 2004–10. These cover the environmental priority areas in the ASEAN and can be considered a continuum from 1978 to the year 2010, with refinements at different stages. As for the HPA, it focused on a number of factors aimed at bringing about ASEAN's progress on regional cooperation/integration. These include strengthening coordination among member countries, laying down completion dates for urgent issues such as the Indonesia Haze and identifying crucial environmental issues.[21]

The ASEAN policy guidelines are set out at various times in soft-law instruments to assist member countries in formulating their environmental policies and also to develop harmonisation of environmental law within the region. The Manila Declaration on the ASEAN Environment, 1981 aimed to ensure, as far as practicable, that environmental considerations are taken into account in development efforts, both ongoing and in the future.[22] The Declaration encourages the enactment and enforcement of environmental protection measures in the ASEAN countries.

21 C.F. Habito, F.T. Aldaba and O.M. Templo, *An Assessment Study on the Progress of ASEAN Regional Integration: The Ha Noi Plan of Action Toward ASEAN Vision 2020* (ASEAN Secretariat: 2004).
22 ASEAN, Manila Declaration on the ASEAN Environment Manila, 30 April 1981. Online. Available HTTP: <http://www.aseansec.org/6077.htm> (accessed 2 February 2012).

465

The commitment of ASEAN to promote regional cooperation to achieve sustainable development was reiterated in the Preamble to the Jakarta Resolution on Sustainable Development, 1987.[23] It recognised both that the development processes in ASEAN must be accelerated to meet growing needs and provide a quality of life, and that these processes could only be sustained if the natural resources were not degraded. It stressed the utilisation of natural resources to meet the needs of the present and future generations, and called for an integrated approach. The Preamble underlined that ASEAN members were intensely aware that international and regional cooperation should be heightened and that it was the duty of states to develop sustainable development in terms of the Stockholm Declaration and other environmental law instruments.

Other policy guidelines laid down by ASEAN have been used in the formulation of various programmes and plans of action. Thus, for example, before formulating ASPAE, in July 1993 at its fourth meeting in Bangkok, ASEAN senior environmental officials reviewed past policies, some of which were still legitimate. The policy guidelines contained in a number of ASEAN soft-law instruments had in fact been reflected in Phase 1 of ASEP way back in 1978.[24] These and other ASEAN instruments on policy imperatives for a transition to sustainable environment and development focused on incorporating environmental factors into economic evaluations.

The institutional framework for ASEAN's environmental governance structure has been evolving since 1978. It has focal points in each Member State, forming a comprehensive network. As environmental issues have become more complex and complicated and as ASEAN's mandate in environmental matters has expanded in tandem with the global mandate, the current governance has proved to be inadequate in terms of structure and the limited mandate given to personnel.

The Secretariat that serves ASEAN is based in Jakarta. The governance structure has undergone refinements over the years. There were originally six ASEAN Working Groups on environment: Marine Environment; Environmental Management including Environment Impact Assessment; Nature Conservation and Terrestrial Ecosystems; Industry and Environment; Environment Education and Training; and Environmental Information. In 1998, these were reorganised and refined to three. However, in recent years, three more working groups have been added: the Working Group on Environmentally Sustainable Cities, the Working Group on Water Resources Management and the Conference of the Parties Committee (COM) under the COP (Conference of the Parties) to the ASEAN Haze Agreement and the Technical Working Groups which have replaced the Haze Technical Task Force.[25]

Apart from the various ASEAN Working Groups directly relating to the environment, the ASEAN Sectoral Ministerial Bodies[26] also deal directly or indirectly with the environment. These include the ASEAN Ministers on Energy Meeting; ASEAN Ministerial Meeting on

---

23 ASEAN, Jakarta Resolution on Sustainable Development Jakarta, 30 October 1987. Online. Available HTTP: <http://www.aseansec.org/6081.htm > (accessed 2 February 2012).

24 These were those in the Manila Declaration on the ASEAN environment 1981, Bangkok Declaration on the ASEAN Environment 1984: Jakarta Resolution on Sustainable Development 1987; Kuala Lumpur Accord on Environment and Development 1990.

25 A. Sunchindah, 'The ASEAN Approach to Regional Environmental Management'. Online. Available HTTP: <http://www.aseansec.org/2838.htm> (accessed 2 February 2012).

26 ASEAN, ASEAN Sectoral Ministerial Bodies. Online. Available HTTP: <http://www.asean.org/21071.pdf> (accessed 2 February 2012).

Disaster Management; ASEAN Health Ministers Meeting; ASEAN Ministers on Rural Development; ASEAN Ministers Meeting on Agriculture and Forestry; ASEAN Ministers on Energy Meeting; ASEAN Specialised Meteorological Centre; and the Conference of the Parties to the ASEAN Agreement on Transboundary Haze Pollution (COP). A Committee under the COP to the ASEAN Agreement on Transboundary Pollution was also established.

The ASEAN Centre for Biodiversity (ACB) (located in Los Banos, Philippines) was established by ASEAN under the Agreement on the Establishment of the ASEAN Centre for Biodiversity in 2005.[27] The purpose as set out in Article 2 is to facilitate cooperation and coordination among its members on the conservation and sustainable use of biological diversity and the fair and equitable sharing of benefits arising from the use of such biodiversity in the region. The predecessor of the ACB was the ASEAN Regional Centre for Biodiversity Conservation (ARCBC) established jointly by ASEAN and the European Union from 1999 to 2004. The ACB promotes the exchange of relevant knowledge, thus helping national, intra-ASEAN and international needs and commitments to be fulfilled. It is served by focal points in the Member States to advance its objectives and take into consideration developments at the global level. It encourages and enables ASEAN member countries to meet the UN Millennium Development Goals[28] in achieving a reduction in the rate of biodiversity loss by 2010.

The pre-ASEAN Charter environmental governance architecture was inadequate to cope with the increasingly integrated and interdependent, regional and international world in which ASEAN would like to play a pivotal role. This includes dealing with transnational environmental issues. The ASEAN Charter has made significant changes to its governance system, including environmental governance. The next section elaborates upon the environmental governance structure under the ASEAN Charter.

The ASEAN Charter: new horizon of environmental legal governance

The purposes of the ASEAN Charter include the promotion of sustainable development, the sustainability of its natural resources, the preservation of its cultural heritage and achieving a high quality of life for its peoples.[29] To make for effective governance, some new organisational structures were introduced while some existing ones were replaced or refined to take into account the increased role of ASEAN at the global, regional and national levels. This answers the call of ASEAN in its report to the World Summit on Sustainable Development (WSSD) to streamline the sustainable development governance framework at the international level.

The major restructuring of governance was the establishment of the ASEAN Coordinating Council, which coordinates the three ASEAN Community Councils (each of which deals with the mutually reinforcing three pillars to enhance policy coherence, efficiency and cooperation). This restructure was against the background of ASEAN's increased role and centrality, not only in the ASEAN region but also in Asia and the world. As a region, ASEAN

27 Agreement on the Establishment of the ASEAN Centre for Biodiversity. Online. Available HTTP: <http://www.aseansec.org/acb_copy.pdf> (accessed 2 February 2012).
28 UNICEF, UN Millennium Development Goals. Online. Available HTTP: <http://www.unicef.org/statistics/index_24304.html> (accessed 2 February 2012).
29 ASEAN Charter, Art. 1(9).

has to increase its participatory role in shaping international issues as well as its own. The Group of Eminent Persons (EPG) established in 2005 to draft the ASEAN Charter was to 'consider bold and visionary ideas to strengthen ASEAN'.[30] After 40 years of history ASEAN had reached a critical turning point. To move forward and to remain the driving force in regional cooperation, it had to have a legal framework, a sophisticated governance system – including a strong reporting system – and an effective secretariat with monitoring powers, among other things. It needed to address the growing challenges and opportunities of regional integration and Asia's widening links with the rest of the world.[31]

A significant addition to the governance structure is the establishment of the ASEAN Human Rights Body[32] under the Charter. At the 14th ASEAN Summit, a Task Force was established to draft the Terms of Reference for the High Level Panel on Human Rights.

In the pre-ASEAN Charter, the ASEAN Secretariat and the role of the Secretary-General were limited.[33] The Charter vested the Secretary-General, together with two Deputy Secretaries-General, with more powers and they are expected to play a greater role in stepping up regional integration and international collaboration and cooperation. One disappointing feature of the Charter is that the recommendation of the EPG for a calibration of decision-making was not accepted. The ASEAN Way is retained[34] but Article 2(g) speaks of 'enhanced consultations on matters seriously affecting the common interest of ASEAN'. This sounds like 'flexible engagement' or 'enhanced interaction'. Article 5(2) also calls upon Member States to take measures and adopt legislation to effectively implement the provisions of the Charter and to comply with all obligations of membership. Ambassador Tommy Koh (one of the drafters of the Charter) and others said, 'It [the ASEAN Way] will be supplemented by a new culture of adherence to rules.'[35]

The pace of environmental developments has been exponential and because we share the same stratosphere and biosphere, we are all connected, and what happens in one part of the world will very likely affect other parts of the world. The strengthening of environmental governance under the ASEAN Charter will enable ASEAN to meet future environmental challenges. These were outlined in the 13th ASEAN Summit which adopted the ASEAN Plus Three Cooperation Work Plan (2007–17),[36] which calls for closer cooperation in the area of environment and sustainable development to address concerns relating to transboundary pollution, biodiversity and water resources.

As noted earlier, the ASEAN Charter committed to intensifying community-building through enhanced regional cooperation and integration, in particular by establishing an ASEAN Community comprising APSC, ASCC and AEC.[37] Environmental conservation is a cross-cutting issue which is relevant for all three pillars of ASEAN community-building. To achieve the goal of the establishment of an ASEAN Community, three blueprints were

---

30 ASEAN Report of the Eminent Persons Group on the ASEAN Charter. Online. Available HTTP: <http://www.aseansec.org/19247.pdf> (accessed 22 November 2011).
31 Ibid.
32 ASEAN Charter, Article 14.
33 For example, there were no powers to monitor performance.
34 ASEAN Charter, Article 20.
35 Tommy Koh et al, 'The ASEAN Charter'. Online. Available HTTP: <http://csis.org/files/media/csis/pubs/pac0733a.pdf> (accessed 22 November 2011).
36 ASEAN Plus Three Cooperation Work Plan. Online. Available HTTP: <http://www.aseansec.org/21104.pdf> (accessed 22 November 2011).
37 ASEAN Charter, preamble and Art. 9.

developed – APSC,[38] ASCC[39] and AEC.[40] Environmental governance is mainly included in the ASCC Blueprint which elaborated different aspects of ensuring environmental sustainability including addressing global environmental issues; managing and preventing transboundary environmental pollution; and promoting sustainable development through environmental education and public participation.[41] In 2011, ASEAN adopted a Roadmap for the Attainment of the Millennium Development Goals.[42] This Roadmap acknowledged the need for enhancing environmental sustainability within the ASCC Blueprint.[43]

Moreover, the APSC Blueprint is also highly relevant for environmental legal governance. According to the APSC Blueprint:

> In building a cohesive, peaceful and resilient Political Security Community, ASEAN subscribes to the principle of comprehensive security, which goes beyond the requirements of traditional security but also takes into account non-traditional aspects vital to regional and national resilience, such as the economic, socio-cultural, and environmental dimensions of development.[44]

The APSC Blueprint introduced an NTS approach by acknowledging the multidimensional impacts of environmental sustainability in the process of regional integration. While the three pillars are mutually reinforcing, the promotion of an ASEAN Community and broadening of understanding of 'security' offers greater scope for environmental law and policy development. It also offers opportunities to strengthen the position of ASEAN as a bridge between public international legal systems. Transboundary environmental challenges under APSC have opened the door to new and emerging environmental issues to be framed which are both state- and human-centric. This is particularly significant at a time when ASEAN and the world are experiencing unprecedented environmental issues that require the enhanced coordination and cooperation not only of ASEAN but across the globe.

In conclusion, the role of environmental sustainability in enhancing regional integration and cooperation has been highlighted in the APSC and ASCC Blueprints. The ASCC Blueprint has identified a number of environmental issues including combating transboundary environmental pollution; combating transboundary movement of hazardous wastes; capacity-building; enhancing public awareness; strengthening law enforcement; and promoting environmentally sustainable practices, as well as the implementation of the ASEAN Agreement on Transboundary Haze Pollution as its strategic objective to achieve the ASCC Blueprint.[45] Moreover, the APSC Blueprint recognised environmental dimensions of development as a critical NTS issue for the ASEAN Political Security Community.

---

38 ASEAN Political-Security Community Blueprint. Online. Available HTTP: <http://www. aseansec.org/5187-18.pdf> (accessed 22 December 2011) ('APSC Blueprint').
39 ASEAN Socio-Cultural Community Blueprint. Online. Available HTTP: <http://www.aseansec. org/5187-19.pdf > (accessed 22 December 2011) ('ASCC Blueprint').
40 ASEAN Economic Community Blueprint. Online. Available HTTP: <http://www.asean. org/21083.pdf> (accessed 22 December 2011).
41 Ibid.
42 ASEAN Roadmap for the Attainment of the Millennium Development Goals. Online. Available HTTP: <http://www.aseansec.org/documents/19th%20summit/MDG-Roadmap.pdf> (accessed 14 January 2012).
43 Ibid.
44 APSC Blueprint, op.cit.
45 ASCC Blueprint, op. cit., 14.

Case studies on ASEAN environmental legal governance

This section covers only three case studies as it is not possible to consider all the work of ASEAN in numerous environmental instruments. Three case studies will be presented on the Indonesian Haze; the ASEAN Heritage Parks; and the ASEAN Statement on CITES (Convention on International Trade in Endangered Species of Wild Fauna and Flora) and the ASEAN Wildlife Law Enforcement Network (ASEAN-WEN). These case studies will be used to examine how the existing environmental governance systems of ASEAN have been successful in solving regional transboundary environmental problems as well as ensuring conservation of the natural recourses of the region.

The Indonesian Haze: the stumbling blocks in ASEAN environmental governance

In 1997 and 1998, the ASEAN region suffered an unprecedented health and environmental catastrophe due to a choking haze created by a massive forest fire in Indonesia. It is estimated that the total losses from the fire could be as high as US$5–6 billion after taking into account the loss of trees and other natural resources as well as the long-term impacts on human health. In recent years, the El Niño Southern Oscillation (ENSO)[46] has played the role of catalyst in many forest fires, but the facts suggest that almost all large-scale forest fires in the ASEAN region over the last 20 years have been the result of anthropogenic intervention.[47] Some of those with vested interests blame lightning strikes, asserting that the haze problem is not a man-made disaster.[48] Indonesia has yet to take any effective measures; hence the threat of haze has remained at the same level since initial discussions.

As the haze problem is largely man-made, it could be controlled by changing human behaviour. On the basis of this underlying philosophy ASEAN initiated a number of regional initiatives for combating forest fire and haze.[49] However, the situation forced the ten ASEAN Member States to conclude a legally binding Agreement on Transboundary Haze Pollution in June 2002.[50] The Agreement came into force on 25 November 2003 after being ratified by Singapore, Malaysia, Myanmar, Brunei, Vietnam, Thailand and the Lao People's Democratic Republic, but not Indonesia.

The ASEAN Haze Agreement seeks to institutionalise and enhance existing measures and to offer legal support that may facilitate regional and international assistance in efficiently addressing the transboundary haze catastrophe.[51] It begins by reaffirming the Parties' commitment to the previous non-legally binding instruments, and affirming the Parties' willingness to further strengthen international cooperation to develop national policies, and to coordinate national action for preventing and monitoring transboundary haze pollution through the

---

46 A cyclical climatological phenomenon.
47 ASEAN and ADB, 'The Problem: Region-Wide Fires and Haze'. Online. Available HTTP: <http://www.fire.uni-freiburg.de/se_asia/projects/asean.html> (accessed 22 November 2011).
48 I.P. Anderson and M.R. Bowen, 'Fire Zones and the Threat to the Wetlands of Sumatra, Indonesia'. Online. Available HTTP: <http://www.fire.uni-freiburg.de/se_asia/projects/ffpcp/FFPCP-14-Firezone-Threat-Wetlands-Sumatra.pdf > (accessed 22 November 2011).
49 See generally D.S. Jones, 'ASEAN and Transboundary Haze Pollution in Southeast Asia', *Asia Europe Journal* 4, 2006, p. 431.
50 ASEAN Agreement on Transboundary Haze Pollution (Kuala Lumpur, 10 June 2002). Online. Available HTTP: <http://www.aseansec.org/pdf/agr_haze.pdf> (accessed 22 November 2011).
51 ASEAN Cooperation on Environment. Online. Available HTTP: <http://www.aseansec.org/8914.htm> (accessed 22 November 2011).

exchange of information, consultation, research and monitoring. The Parties also indicate strong willingness to undertake individual and joint action to solve the problem by applying environmentally sound policies, practices and technologies and to strengthen national and regional capabilities.[52]

The Agreement's main objective is prevention, mitigation and monitoring of transboundary haze pollution through concerted national efforts and intensified regional and international cooperation in the overall context of sustainable development.[53] In fulfilling this objective, parties will be guided by the sovereign right to exploit their own resources pursuant to their own environmental and developmental policies, and the responsibility to ensure that activities within their jurisdiction or control do not cause damage to the environment and harm human health in other states or in areas beyond the limits of national jurisdiction. The principles of cooperation, precautionary measures, ecologically sound and sustainable management of natural resources, and participation of stakeholders are all duly recognised as guiding principles for attaining the objectives of the agreement.[54] But some legal experts are of the opinion that all these principles have been deliberately framed in nonmandatory language and therefore may not be able to create legally binding norms.[55] The Agreement introduced detailed provisions for monitoring, assessment, prevention and response; technical cooperation and scientific research; and institutional and procedural arrangements.[56]

In pursuing its objective, the Agreement calls on Parties to cooperate in developing and implementing measures to prevent and monitor transboundary haze pollution. Each country also commits to responding promptly to a request for relevant information or consultations sought by an affected state or states, when any transboundary haze pollution originates within its territory. Parties have also agreed to take legislative, administrative and other measures to implement their obligations under this Agreement. The Agreement includes no provision for sanctions or penalties if any party fails to comply with these general obligations, suggesting that states may ultimately treat these general obligations as non-binding.[57]

Major concerns have been identified, as a result of the absence of sanctions for noncompliance of the agreements, weak dispute resolution systems and non-concessions of state sovereignty. In particular, the Agreement's restriction of dispute resolution to include only consultation and negotiation fails to provide any remedy for suffering parties if the consultation and negotiation process fails.[58] This reflects, in some ways, traditional ASEAN hypersensitivity to creating state responsibility and stringent enforceable legal obligations.[59] In one way, it may close the door on an international arbitral or judicial system, but it does not prevent states from seeking dispute resolution by other means, given that this Agreement

---

52 See ASEAN Haze Agreement, Preamble.
53 Ibid., Art. 2.
54 Ibid., Art. 3.
55 A.K-J. Tan, 'The ASEAN Agreement on Transboundary Haze Pollution: Prospects for Compliance and Effectiveness in Post-Suharto Indonesia' *New York University Environmental Law Journal* 13, 2006, 647, p. 662.
56 Md S. Karim, 'Future of the Haze Agreement – Is the Glass Half Empty or Half Full?', *Environmental Policy and Law* 38, 2008, p. 328.
57 Tan, op. cit., pp. 663–4; ASEAN Haze Agreement, Art. 4.
58 ASEAN Haze Agreement, Art. 27; Tan, op. cit., pp. 663–5.
59 See generally J. Cotton, 'The "Haze" over Southeast Asia: Challenging the ASEAN Mode of Regional Engagement' *Pacific Affairs* 72, 1999, p. 331.

specifically states that it shall in no way affect the rights and obligations of any party with regard to any existing treaty, convention or agreement to which it is a party.[60] Another criticism that could be raised is that the Agreement failed to introduce any positive obligation to impose penalties and failed to incorporate provision for sanctions. This is not necessarily a great obstacle to the future effectiveness of the Agreement as 'any breach of an engagement involves an obligation to make reparation'.[61]

Before this upsetting haze problem, ASEAN had gained a reputation as one of the most vibrant regional organisations for its outstanding contributions to political and economic development. Many researchers see this achievement as a direct outcome of cooperation for building stable relations among nations, popularly known, as discussed above, as the 'ASEAN Way'.[62] But due to increasing external and internal factors, ASEAN is gradually moving towards more legalised regional economic integration and hence ASEAN countries are relinquishing the orthodox concept of state sovereignty. Unlike rule-based economic integration, ASEAN nations are not ready to create an effective rule-based environmental regime in South East Asia.[63]

In the pre-haze era, ASEAN's environmental instruments were largely dominated by non-binding declarations and action plans or programmes, although such a situation is not unusual in the context of the environment for various reasons.[64] However, there was one exception: the 1985 Agreement on the Conservation of Nature and Natural Resources. In this agreement, sustainable development was adopted as a goal and several ambitious joint and individual state actions were envisaged, and wide-ranging policy targets were provided which have not, as yet, entered into force.[65] The Indonesian Haze not only brought unprecedented misery to the environment and people of South East Asia but also showed the flaws in the widely practised 'pollute first, clean up later' approach. Although ASEAN achievements in economic development are, on the whole, quite remarkable, ASEAN nations responded to the global environmental protection movement with several reservations.[66] Moreover, the haze problem evolved at a time when there was a downward trend in economic growth in some parts of ASEAN. This downward trend in the region's economy also played a catalytic role in the haze problem.[67]

The geopolitical reality was that other ASEAN nations, led by Singapore and Malaysia, have had to initiate regional action to prevent haze pollution, focusing on helping Indonesia rather than blaming it for the situation. While President Suharto publicly regretted the haze

---

60 ASEAN Haze Agreement, Art. 26; Tan, op. cit., pp. 659–65.
61 *Chorzow Factory Case* [1927] PCIJ Ser. A, No. 9, 21; P. Sands, *Principles of International Environmental Law*, 2nd edition, Cambridge: Cambridge University Press, 2003, p. 873.
62 S.S.C. Tay, 'Southeast Asian Fires: The Challenge for International Environmental Law and Sustainable Development', *Georgetown International Environmental Law Review* 11, 1999, 241, p. 255.
63 See generally K.K. Mulqueeny, 'Regionalism, Economic Integration in ASEAN: What Space for Environmental Sustainability?' *Asia Pacific Journal of Environmental Law* 8, 2004, p. 5.
64 E.B. Weiss, 'New Directions in International Environmental Law' in D. Craig, N. Robinson and Koh Kheng-Lian (eds) *Capacity Building for Environmental Law in the Asian and Pacific Region*, Volume I, Manila: Asian Development Bank, 2002, p. 9.
65 Y. Usui, 'An Evolving Path of Regionalism: The Construction of an Environmental Acquis in the EEC and ASEAN'. Online. Available HTTP: <http://project.iss.u-tokyo.ac.jp/crep/pdf/2006ic/2006ic_D9.pdf> (accessed 22 November 2011).
66 Tay, op. cit., p. 253.
67 J. Mayer, 'Transboundary Perspectives on Managing Indonesia's Fires', *Journal of Environment and Development* 15, 2006, 202, p. 204.

pollution, his government accepted only moral, rather than legal, responsibility.[68] The enforcement deficiency found in international legal systems is another catalyst for this approach. An insightful look at the ASEAN Haze Agreement will reveal that each and every sentence of this agreement reflects the inevitable geopolitical reality that cooperation rather than blame is the best path to positive results. However, the success of the ASEAN Haze Agreement is almost entirely dependent on whether it will be successful in bringing Indonesia on board.

Another obstacle to effective governance illustrated by this case study is that extraneous factors have been brought to bear on the haze issues. On 20 October 2006 the prime minister of Singapore approached the Indonesian delegation at the United Nations General Assembly (UNGA) meeting to issue an ASEAN Statement on the haze, in order to seek financial and technical assistance.[69] An Indonesian representative stated that the haze was an internal problem and Indonesia did not want any interference with its internal affairs.[70] After this incident Indonesia abruptly refused to sell sand and granite to Singapore and also raised the question of the drafting of the extradition treaty between the two countries. It was reported that some ministers in Jakarta appeared to suggest that the ban was a way of punishing it for its sluggish behaviour in negotiations on border delineation and extradition treaties.[71]

The debate surrounding the haze problem illustrates the long-standing conflict between 'national interests' and 'regional interests' confronting ASEAN. Nevertheless, adoption and ratification of the ASEAN Haze Agreement indicates the growing role of ASEAN in rule-based environmental governance in the region. However, Indonesian reluctance in joining the treaty indicates the infectiveness of the ASEAN Way in the establishment of an effective environmental governance system. Moreover, the choice to house the ASEAN Haze Agreement under the ASCC Blueprint, rather than under the NTS aspects of the APSC Blueprint, shows the traditional ASEAN hypersensitivity in dealing with politically sensitive issues.

ASEAN Heritage Parks

The ASEAN Heritage Parks (AHPs) provide an interesting study of ASEAN environmental governance. Under the Declaration of the ASEAN Heritage Parks 2003,[72] all ASEAN Member States have to designate at least one ASEAN Heritage Park; there are now 30 such parks.[73] The Declaration facilitates the implementation of the Convention on Biological

---

68 D. Rosenberg, 'Environmental Pollution around the South China Sea: Developing a Regional Response to a Regional Problem'. Online. Available HTTP: <https://digitalcollections.anu.edu.au/bitstream/1885/40977/3/rmap_wp20.pdf> (accessed 22 November 2011).

69 'Haze: Balls on UN table, Indonesia upset'. Online. Available HTTP: <http://www.jeffooi.com/2006/11/haze_balls_on_un_table_and_ind.php> (accessed 22 November 2011).

70 *The Straits Times*, 4 November 2006; see also, *The Straits Times*, 'ASEAN needs help to tackle haze: PM: international expertise needed to help nip problem in the bud', 6 November 2006; *The Straits Times*, 'Embassy: Jakarta prefers to solve haze within ASEAN', 9 November 2006.

71 *The Straits Times*, 'Indonesia's Sand Ban: Spore's vulnerable side exposed', 6 April 2007.

72 Declaration of the ASEAN Heritage Parks. Online. Available HTTP: <http://www.aseansec.org/15524.htm> (accessed 22 November 2011).

73 Factsheet: ASEAN Heritage Parks. Online. Available HTTP: <http://www.news.gov.sg/public/sgpc/en/media_releases/agencies/nparks/press_release/P-20111019-1/AttachmentPar/00/file/Factsheet-%20Asean%20Heritage%20Parks.pdf> (accessed 22 December 2011).

Diversity (CBD),[74] the World Heritage Convention[75]and the Ramsar Convention.[76] It has only been over the last 13 years or so that ASEAN has taken an interest in developing it further. The concept of AHPs[77] was first introduced by the then ASEAN Expert Group on Environment in 1978.

The AHPs are protected areas of high conservation importance preserving in total a complete spectrum of representative ecosystems of the ASEAN region. There were various stages in their development, beginning in 1978.[78] After the United Nations Conference on Environment and Development (UNCED) in 1992,[79] the global community was determined to reduce biodiversity loss and ASEAN member countries that had ratified the biodiversity conventions such as CBD, Ramsar and the World Heritage Convention were expected to implement them. As a regional organisation, ASEAN has facilitated their implementation. The ASEAN Working Group on Nature Conservation has changed its nomenclature to reflect the focus on biodiversity of the CBD and other biodiversity MEAs. It was renamed the ASEAN Working Group on Nature Conservation and Biodiversity (AWGNCB). Another significant development was the strengthening of ASEAN's governance network on bio-diversity with the establishment of the ASEAN Regional Centre for Biodiversity Conser-vation (ARCBC) from 1999 to 2004, and in 2005 the establishment of the ACB. The ACB together with the AWGNCB and the national focal points in each of the ten Member States are working to significantly reduce biodiversity loss.[80]

In June 2010, the ACB organised the third ASEAN Heritage Parks Conference.[81] The Conference aimed to promote the effective management of AHPs and to identify areas for cooperation among AHP managers and partners.[82] It developed a network of AHP managers for the exchange of learning and experiences among managers as well as to create greater awareness of the AHPs.[83] The conference adopted a Regional Work Plan for AHPs, high-lighting a number of important issues such as: resource assessment and monitoring including species identification and habitat management; ecotourism; law enforcement; information-sharing, communications and outreach; and exchange programmes and study tours.[84]

74 *Convention on Biological Diversity*, opened for signature 5 June 1992, 1760 UNTS 79 (entered into force 29 December 1993) ('CBD').
75 *Convention Concerning the Protection of the World Cultural and Natural Heritage*, opened for signature 16 November 1972, 1037 UNTS 151 (entered into force 17 December 1975) (World Heritage Convention).
76 *Convention on Wetlands of International Importance Especially as Waterfowl Habitat*, opened for signature 2 February 1971, 996 UNTS 245 (entered into force 21 December 1975) (Ramsar Convention).
77 Koh Kheng-Lian, 'Land Stewardship and the Law: ASEAN Heritage Parks and Transboundary Biodiversity Conservation' in N.J. Chalifour, P. Kameri-Mbote, L.H. Lye and J.R. Nolon (eds) *Land Use Law for Sustainable Development*, Ottawa: IUCN Academy of Environmental Law, 2006, p. 352.
78 A. Sunchindah, 'ASEAN initiatives in protected areas management, presented at the Second Regional Forum for Southeast Asia of the IUCN WCPA' (1999).
79 United Nations Conference on Environment and Development. Online. Available HTTP: <http://www.un.org/geninfo/bp/enviro.html> (accessed 22 November 2011).
80 WSSD, *Plan of Implementation*. Online. Available HTTP: <http://www.un.org/jsummit/html/documents/summit_docs/2309_planfinal.htm> (accessed 22 November 2011).
81 ASEAN Centre for Biodiversity, *The ASEAN Heritage Parks: A Journey to the Natural Wonders of Southeast Asia*, Laguna: ASEAN Centre for Biodiversity, 2010.
82 Ibid., pp. 6–7
83 Ibid.
84 Ibid.

Recently, the ASEAN nations and the Republic of Korea signed an agreement for ensuring sustainable forest management through enhancing forest laws and enforcement, sustainable forest product development and utilisation, wildlife conservation and protection of the livelihoods of forest communities and indigenous people.[85]

This case study shows that, as the role of ASEAN expands to facilitate the implementation of MEAs, its governance structure can develop in tandem. It is also an example where Member States have demonstrated some degree of success in an ASEAN initiative. One reason may be that many of the Member States have ratified some of the MEAs on biological diversity, and this initiative acted as a catalyst for implementation.

ASEAN Statement on CITES and ASEAN Wildlife Law Enforcement Network

Environmental governance of a particular region has a global focus because regional environmental governance is part of global environmental governance.[86] In this case study we will examine the implementation of MEAs in ASEAN using the Convention on International Trade in Endangered Species of Wild Fauna and Flora (CITES)[87] as an example. All ASEAN Member States have ratified CITES. At the thirteenth COP meeting of CITES held in Bangkok between 2 and 14 October 2004, it was noted that South East Asia's illegal trade was rife.[88] ASEAN issued the 'ASEAN Statement on CITES'[89] on 11 October 2004, highlighting six key areas of cooperation. Subsequently, the ASEAN Regional Action Plan on Trade in Wild Fauna and Flora 2005–2010 ('the Plan')[90] was launched at the Special Meeting of the ASEAN Ministers Responsible for the Implementation of CITES, on 1 December 2005, in Bangkok. Pursuant to this Plan, the ASEAN Wildlife Law Enforcement Network (ASEAN-WEN) was established to promote networking among enforcement authorities in ASEAN and non-ASEAN regions to combat illegal trade in wildlife. This involves intelligence-sharing, reviewing weak laws and coordinating enforcement action.[91] Subsequently, ASEAN-WEN has become the largest wildlife law enforcement network in the world and its membership includes relevant governmental, intergovernmental and non-governmental organisations in ASEAN and non-ASEAN countries, and also international organisations. It is open to CITES, TRAFFIC (the wildlife trade monitoring network), WildAid (an NGO which aims to end the illegal wildlife trade), customs, police, prosecutors, specialised governmental wildlife law enforcement organisations and other relevant national law enforcement

---

85 ASEAN, 'Advancing Forestry Cooperation in International Year of Forest 2011'. Online. Available HTTP: <http://www.aseansec.org/26733.htm> (accessed 13 January 2012).

86 This aspect has been endorsed in the recently adopted *Bali Declaration on ASEAN Community in A Global Community of Nations*. Online. Available HTTP: <http://www.aseansec.org/documents/19th%20summit/Bali%20Concord%20III.pdf> (accessed 14 January 2012).

87 *Convention on International Trade in Endangered Species of Wild Fauna and Flora*, opened for signature 3 March 1973, 999 UNTS 243 (entered into force 1 July 1975) ('CITES').

88 ASEAN Statement on CITES. Online. Available HTTP: <http://www.aseansec.org/16470.htm> (accessed 22 November 2011); J. Lin, 'Tackling Southeast Asia's Illegal Wildlife Trade' *Singapore Year Book of International Law* 9, 2005, p. 191.

89 ASEAN Statement on CITES, ibid.

90 ASEAN Regional Action Plan on Trade in Wild Fauna and Flora, 2005–2010. Online. Available HTTP: <http://www.asean.org/17753.pdf > (accessed 22 November 2011).

91 ASEAN, 'Asian Nations Launch Regional Plan to Smash Wildlife Smuggling Rings', 11 October 2004. Online. Available HTTP: <http://www.aseansec.org/afp/75p.htm> (accessed 22 November 2011).

agencies. It is significant that it actively engages civil society by raising awareness of issues of legality and sustainability.[92]

From the viewpoint of environmental legal governance, ASEAN-WEN has attained a number of milestones. The ASEAN–WEN Support Program Assessment Report dated 10 April 2008[93] noted the increased support from civil societies. This would be further strengthened through public awareness and in developing a network of civil society organisations to support and collaborate with ASEAN-WEN. Some of the challenges of civil societies were noted in the report. This includes cultural differences between them and government law agencies, and even among different civil societies themselves. Indeed, there are some great cultural divides among the different countries in ASEAN and non-ASEAN regions in terms of wildlife trade. There is, for example, great interest in traditional medicine relating to wildlife parts not only in the ASEAN countries but also in China and even in the United States of America.[94] Work is underway to develop greater civil society support through outreach activities and to identify current NGO programmes and increase strategic leveraging across organisations involving NGOs, civil societies and the private sector. In this context (as in other settings), the role of NGOs and civil societies is vital.

The ASEAN–WEN network also provides an example of cooperation and coordination of regional and state-level environmental governance among ASEAN countries (as well as non-ASEAN countries). It even extends to international cooperation, making it a global network for the countering of illegal trade in endangered species. Thus, its regional crime task force network of transnational enforcement includes national agencies such as customs, police and civil societies, as well as international agencies. This mechanism is an 'Interpol' of wildlife trade. Thus ASEAN-WEN is the first globalised governance network initiated by ASEAN to implement and enforce an MEA.[95] It is a fine example of global environmental governance, one which would have made the dream of Esty and Ivanova come true, when they said:

> Today's global environmental governance challenge thus requires a more virtual structure with a multi-institutional foundation capable of drawing in a wide array of underlying disciplines through governments, the private sector, NGOs, and global public policies networks.[96]

Also, ASEAN–WEN has the potential to expand. For the moment it is too early to gauge its full impact. The policy challenges are that with multiple stakeholders, each with its own

92 ASEAN Action Plan on Wildlife Trade. Online. Available HTTP: <http://www.indianjungles. com/280505.htm> (accessed 22 November 2011).
93 ASEAN-WEN Support Program Assessment Report. Online. Available HTTP: <http://www. aseanwen.org/newscenter_typepopup.php?newsID=31> (accessed 1 September 2008); see also J. Silver's speech, ASEAN WEN Presentation of Survey Results, 19 October 2006, Phnom Penh. Online. Available HTTP: <http://cambodia.usembassy.gov/sp_101906b.html> (accessed 1 September 2008).
94 ABC, US second only to China in illegal wildlife trade: official. Online. Available HTTP: <http:// www.abc.net.au/news/2008–06–10/us-second-only-to-china-in-illegal-wildlife-trade/2466308> (accessed 22 November 2011).
95 ASEAN Report to the World Summit on Sustainable Development, 26 August to 4 September 2002: Jakarta ASEAN Secretariat. Online. Available HTTP: <http://www.aseansec.org/pdf/ WSSD.pdf> (accessed 22 November 2011).
96 D.C. Esty and M.H. Ivanova, 'The Road Ahead: Conclusions and Action Agenda', in D.C. Esty and M.H. Ivanova (eds) *Global Environmental Governance: Options & Opportunities*, New Haven: Yale School of Forestry and Environmental Studies, 2002, pp. 225, 229.

agenda, cooperation problems can be posed. The challenge is to conduct research into the synergies and conflicts of these stakeholders because trade in endangered species is a multi-million dollar business, as lucrative as trafficking in drugs, if not more so. In the ASEAN–WEN Support Program Assessment Report 2008 it was noted that the global wildlife trade has an estimated value of eight to ten billion US dollars a year (with future estimates of $20 billion a year). Therefore, it is one of the most lucrative black market trades.

In the ASEAN Statement 2004 and, following that in 2005, ASEAN-WEN has inspired some Member States to amend their laws to reflect the objectives of the Statement. Singapore was the first to do so. In 2006 it amended its Endangered Species (Import and Export) Act[97] to enhance its penalties on CITES – for listed wildlife, for example, a fine of SGD$50,000 is imposed per scheduled species (up to an aggregate of SGD$500,000) and a term of imprisonment of up to two years. The fine applies to each animal or plant protected under the CITES which is seized, and is capped at $500,000. Previously, offenders were fined according to species, and not the number seized. Singapore's amendments have set a regional precedent against wildlife smuggling.[98] Singapore is a member of ASEAN-WEN and it is sharing its intelligence network and is providing capacity-building to facilitate cross-border collaboration to counter the illegal wildlife trade.

A number of milestones have been achieved by ASEAN-WEN in enhancing environmental governance. It has inspired increased support to remove illegal trade from civil society.[99] It is an example of cooperation between different ASEAN countries and beyond and has become a global network for the enforcement of sanctions against illegal trade in endangered species.

Conclusion

There are still many political, policy and other challenges to governance for environmental sustainability in ASEAN, though recent years have seen the development of legal frameworks aimed at a green and clean ASEAN with an adequate governance system to meet changing circumstances. If the ASEAN Vision is to be realised, there is still much that needs to be done. It cannot be gainsaid that political will is critical. This requires a focus on solving environmental issues and should not be sidetracked by an uncompromising application of state sovereignty and non-intervention, or extraneous issues, as the Indonesian Haze case so aptly demonstrated. It is suggested that ASEAN should recalibrate its approach to align these concepts with Principle 7 of the Rio Declaration on the common responsibilities of states for sustainable development. It should adopt a policy of 'flexible' or 'enhanced' engagement in dealing with environmental issues of common interest such as transboundary pollution by allowing members to cooperate more closely in, for example, imposing trade sanctions on unsustainable products or require eco-labelling. A recalibrated approach could also regulate unsustainable practices in clearing land. In this regard some inroads should be made into the consensus process in the ASEAN Way. Or perhaps the more recent NTS approach

97 *Endangered Species (Import and Export) Act*, Chapter 92, Singapore Statutes Online. Available HTTP: <http://statutes.agc.gov.sg/> (accessed 22 November 2011).

98 Asian Turtle Conservation Network, 'Singapore's Harsh Penalties Set Regional Precedent Against Wildlife Smuggling', 18 June 2006. Online. Available HTTP: <http://www.asianturtlenetwork. org/library/news_articles/Singapore_Harsh_Penalties_Set_Regional_Precedent_Against_ Wildlife_Smuggling.html> (accessed 22 November 2011).

99 ASEAN-WEN Support Program Assessment Report, op. cit.

can open the door to circumventing the inveterate application of state sovereignty and non-intervention principles in the context of transnational challenges.

To further develop effective environmental governance for sustainable development, there should be a new, 'fourth' ASEAN pillar. Currently, environment is subsumed under the third ASEAN pillar – the ASCC Blueprint. Environmental problems today are more complex and cross-cutting and although the socio-cultural dimension is important, by subsuming it under this pillar, the environment is being marginalised. The new fourth pillar to be devoted to the environment should include cross-cutting issues. One such example is the environmental implications of free trade agreements, for example the ASEAN Free Trade Area[100] and those that the ASEAN bloc has concluded with non-ASEAN countries. What the policy measures are that would encourage the integration of environmental factors in all these trade agreements is not very explicit. Another example is the potential problem of environmentally forced migration, which can be brought about by extreme weather conditions, floods and sea level rise due to climate change, resulting in people leaving their villages, townships and even countries. The ASEAN Charter has strengthened the environmental governance framework but unless environmental and cross-cutting issues are clearly set out, these concerns may not be taken up at the institutional level.

Over the last 34 years, since ASEAN put the environment on its agenda, there have been progressive developments in the ASEAN environmental legal framework, though slow and laggardly at times. The time has come for ASEAN to take a more robust role in bringing the environment agenda and legal governance forward. This chapter gives only a broad-brush overview of the challenges and opportunities and more research needs to be done on a continuous basis to track the scoreboard of good environmental legal governance in the region.

---

100 ASEAN Free Trade Area. Online. Available HTTP: <http://www.aseansec.org/12039.htm> (accessed 22 November 2011).

27

International environmental law and Australia and New Zealand

*Cameron Holley**

This chapter considers the implementation of international environmental law in Australia and New Zealand. It examines the legal and regulatory frameworks that have developed in response to some of the most influential, complex and challenging international environmental issues, including ecologically sustainable development, biodiversity and climate change. It therefore highlights and provides a succinct overview of some of the fundamental and recent developments in mainstream environmental law in Australia and New Zealand engendered by international environmental law.

Introduction

A comprehensive examination of international environmental law requires us to cast our gaze beyond interstate negotiations and regimes, to consider how international law interacts with domestic-level systems.[1] Indeed, with the recent growth in global public good problems like climate change and declining biodiversity, there has been burgeoning interest in exploring international regulatory responses that foster more productive interaction with lower-level domestic systems and agents.[2] Simultaneously, at domestic levels, there has been a growing focus on the 'embeddedness' of local and regional regulatory institutions within international

* The research was partially funded by a Macquarie University New Staff Grant through Macquarie University and the National Centre for Groundwater Research and Training. I am grateful for the research assistance of Guy Dwyer, and for the helpful comments on the paper by Erika Techera.

1 J. Speth and P. Haas, *Global Environmental Governance*, Delhi: Pearson and Longman, 2006, p. 3.

2 F. Biermann, 'Beyond the Intergovernmental Regime: Recent Trends in Global Carbon Governance', *Current Opinion in Environmental Sustainability* 2, 2010, pp. 284–6; L. Andonova and R. Mitchell, 'The Rescaling of Global Environmental Politics', *Annual Review of Environment and Resources* 35, 2010, pp. 255, 264; C. Okereke, H. Bulkeley and H. Schroeder, 'Conceptualizing Climate Governance Beyond the International Regime', *Global Environmental Politics* 9(1), 2009, pp. 58–78; L. Godden and J. Peel, *Environmental Law Scientific, Policy and Regulatory Dimensions*, Melbourne: Oxford University Press, 2009, pp. 331–79; Speth and Hass, op. cit., p. 3.

architectures and the interaction between these different systems.[3] It is within this context, and with an interest in illuminating the relationship between international environmental law and domestic legal practice, that this chapter is situated. Its particular focus is on how key aspects of international environmental law and governance have influenced and been integrated with the domestic regimes of Australia and New Zealand.

As will be seen below, developments in international environmental law have had wide-ranging and significant impacts on environmental law and policy in both nations.[4] However, as a single chapter, the discussion inevitably cannot explore the interplay between international environmental law and the two domestic regimes in their entirety. It does not seek to offer an exhaustive overview of either nation's domestic environmental law framework,[5] nor a detailed discussion on the role of either nation in developing international environmental law.[6] The chapter's primary concern is the influence of international environmental law on key elements of Australia and New Zealand's domestic environmental regimes. The analysis is mainly confined to those areas of international law that have had the most direct influence on the Australian and New Zealand context, namely international environmental treaties and conventions.[7]

The chapter is organized as follows. First the chapter frames its analysis by briefly outlining the basic legal structure and arrangements of Australia and New Zealand. It then provides an overview and critical analysis of some of the key environmental law and policy regimes in both countries that have evolved in response to international environmental law developments. Of particular concern will be the legal and regulatory frameworks that have developed in response to some of the most influential, complex and challenging international environmental issues, namely ecologically sustainable development, biodiversity and climate change. The discussion flags recent and emerging developments in these and other areas of environmental law, before concluding.

National legal arrangements for implementing international environmental law

As countries with a similar English genealogy, the legal structures of Australia and New Zealand share a number of familial traits. For example, both are Commonwealth constitutional

3 D. Rothwell and B. Boer, 'From Franklin to Berlin: The Internationalization of Australian Environmental Law and Policy', *Sydney Law Review* 17, 1995, pp. 242–77; P. Taylor, 'The Global Perspective: Convergence of International and Municipal Law', in K. Bosselmann and D. Grinlinton (eds.) *Environmental Law for a Sustainable Society*, Auckland: NZCEL, 2002, pp. 123–43; F. Biermann, M. Betsill, J. Gupta, N. Kanie, L. Lebel, D. Liverman, H. Schroeder, B. Siebenhuner and R. Zondervan, 'Earth System Governance: A Research Framework', *International Environmental Agreements: Politics, Law and Economics* 10(4), 2010, pp. 277–98; Speth and Haas, op. cit., p. 3.

4 G. Bates, *Environmental Law in Australia*, Chatswood: LexisNexis Butterworths, 2010, p. 111; D. Nolan (ed.), *Environment and Resource Management Law*, 4th edition, Wellington: LexisNexis, 2011; K. Keith, 'The Impact of International Law on New Zealand Law', *Waikato Law Review* 6, 1998, pp. 1, 7–8.

5 For further on Australia see e.g. Bates op. cit., D. Fisher, *Australian Environmental Law: Norms Principles and Rules*, 2nd edition, Pyrmont: Lawbook, 2010. On New Zealand, see e.g. Nolan, op. cit., R. Harris (ed.), *Handbook of Environmental Law*, Wellington: Royal Forest and Bird Society, 2004.

6 For an early overview see e.g. B. Boer, R. Ramsay and D. Rothwell, *International Environmental Law in the Asia Pacific*, London: Kluwer Law International, 1998, pp. 268–71; Rothwell and Boer, op. cit., pp. 245–6; S. Blay, R. Piotrowicz and M. Tsamenyi (eds.), *Public International Law: An Australian Perspective*, 2nd edition, Melbourne: Oxford University Press, 2005.

7 Godden and Peel, op. cit., p. 340; Fisher, op. cit., p. 73.

monarchies (although New Zealand's constitution is uncodified).[8] Both also rely on a system of judge-made common law. While Australia is a federation, with a federal government and eight states and territories, New Zealand is a unitary government. Yet, despite this different structure, both nations have devolved significant environmental responsibilities to lower levels of government. In New Zealand, this includes regional and district councils that have been established under central legislation.[9] In Australia's case, significant responsibility for the environment and natural resources are held by both state governments (pursuant to the Australian Constitution) and local councils (established under state legislation and constitutions).[10]

National governments naturally have played a prominent role in international environmental law. Indeed, in both countries they have primary responsibility for representing their nation on the international stage, entering into and ratifying environmental treaties and ensuring the terms are fulfilled.[11] In Australia, the federal system complicates this process, with the Commonwealth having agreed to notify and consult with affected states in the negotiation, joining and implementation of agreements and to include states in negotiations if appropriate.[12]

It is important to note, however, that there is no automatic application of international environmental law in either country. Certainly, both nations remain answerable to the international community for their performance under ratified treaties and both are subject generally to international customary law.[13] However, domestic law is determined by democratically elected parliaments. Thus to be given effect, international environmental law must be translated into local law and policy by legislatures.[14]

Notably, the courts in both countries are prepared to interpret domestic legislation in a way that fulfils legal responsibilities and ensures consistency with international law.[15] Further, the courts have been willing to draw on international law in appropriate circumstances for the purposes of development and interpretation of judge-made common law.[16] Specialist

---

8 See e.g. *Australian Constitution*. There are many relevant acts in New Zealand, but see e.g. *The Constitution Act 1986* (NZ) and *Treaty of Waitangi Act 1975* (NZ).

9 See, e.g. *Local Government Act 2002* (NZ), s 21. *Resource Management Act 1991* (NZ), ss 30, 31.

10 *Australian Constitution*, s 51, 52, 90, 106, 107. Local government is established pursuant to state statutes and constitutions. See e.g. *Local Government Act 1993* (NSW), ss 21, 204, 219. *Constitution Act 1902* (NSW), s 51. Other states and territories have similar constitution and/or self-government Acts. For further, see Bates, op. cit., pp. 126–7.

11 For further on this and relevant references, see Bates, op. cit., p. 111. Keith, op. cit., pp. 15–19.

12 *Intergovernmental Agreement on the Environment 1992*, Arts 2.3.2, 2.5.2; R. Lyster, Z. Lipman, N. Franklin, G. Wiffen and L. Pearson, *Environmental and Planning Law in New South Wales*, Sydney: Federation Press, 2009, pp. 16–17, 20.

13 Keith, op. cit., p. 15–19; P. Taylor, 'International Law and the New Zealand Environment', in R. Harris (ed.) *Handbook of Environmental Law*, Wellington: Royal Forest and Bird Society, 2004, p. 528. Rothwell and Boer, op. cit., pp. 242–5.

14 Bates, op. cit., p. 98, Taylor, op. cit., p. 528.

15 This is where relevant and where statutory language permits. In New Zealand see e.g. *van Gorkon v Attorney General* [1977] 1 NZLR 535; *Tavita v Minister of Immigration* [1994] 2 NZLR 257; *Federated Farmers of New Zealand (Inc) v New Zealand Post* [1990–92] 3 NZBORR 339; *New Zealand Air Line Pilots' Association v Attorney-General* [1997] 3 NZLR 269, 289. In Australia see e.g. *Brown v Forestry of Tasmania* (No. 4) (2006) 157 FCR 1; *Newcrest Mining (WA) Ltd v Commonwealth* (1997) 147 ALR 42; *Minister for Environment and Heritage v Queensland Conservation Council Inc* [2004] FCAFC 190; *Acts Interpretation Act 1901* (Cth) s 15AB(2)(d); Godden and Peel, op. cit., p. 349; D. Williams, *Environmental and Resource Management Law*, Wellington: Butterworths, 1997, pp. 45–6.

16 See e.g. *Mabo v Queensland (no 2)* (1992) 175 CLR 1 at 42 per Brennan J; Bates, op. cit, p. 99; Godden and Peel, pp. 44, 349; Williams, op. cit., p. 45.

environmental courts have similarly been influenced by principles of international law and policy.[17] However, if domestic law in either nation does not reflect international obligations, the substance of those obligations is generally not enforceable in the courts.[18] In particular, specifically seeking to invalidate or obtain a remedy for breach or failure to enact or administer legislation to protect the environment, where there is a duty to do so under a convention, is beyond the jurisdiction of domestic courts in either nation.[19]

Having outlined some of the basic environmental legal arrangements and principles for both Australia and New Zealand, the next section turns to discuss the influence of international environmental law on legislation and regulatory arrangements in both nations.

National responses to international environmental law

Environmental law in both Australia and New Zealand has only been viewed as a defined body of legal principle and regulatory practice since the 1970s.[20] Prior to this time, environmental controls and protections in both nations consisted of little more than technically focused urban planning controls and relatively ad hoc environmental protections provided through judge-made common law (e.g. actions in nuisance, negligence and trespass).[21] Environmental legislation and innovative environmental regulatory practice[22] has since proliferated in both countries, largely in response to the growth of international conventions and treaties on the environment.[23]

Indeed, on the international stage, both national governments have had a close working relationship, in part because of their neighbouring geographical location in the South Pacific. For example, both countries were parties to the Nuclear Tests dispute, which they brought before the International Court of Justice in 1974 against France's atmospheric nuclear tests in

17 In New Zealand, see e.g. *Mighty River Power Ltd v Waikato Regional Council* (23 and 24 October 2001) EC A 146/2001. For further discussion, including counterexamples of the Environment Court being hesitant towards the use of international instruments see A. Kerr, 'Untapped Potential: Administrative Law and International Environmental Obligations', *NZJPIL* 6, 2008, vol. 6, 81, 87–9. In Australia see e.g. the discussion of the precautionary principle in *Leatch v National Parks and Wildlife Service (NSW)* (1993) 81 LGERA 270 at 281, 282. Note, however, that Justice Stein avoided the question of the incorporation of international law into domestic law per se, and instead found that the precautionary principle was based on 'common sense'. For further discussion see Bates, op. cit., p. 100; Godden and Peel, op. cit, p. 350.

18 *Minister for Immigration and Ethnic Affairs v Teoh* (1995) 183 CLR 273. *Re Minister for Immigration and Multicultural Affairs, Ex parte Lam* (2003) 214 CLR 1; *Federated Farmers of New Zealand (Inc) v New Zealand Post* [1990–92] 3 NZBORR 339; *Ashby v Minister of Immigration* [1981] 1 NZLR 222; *Khan v Branch Manager of NZ Immigration Services* (High Court, Hamilton M 335/94, 11 August 1995). Further see W. Lacey, 'A Prelude to the Demise of Teoh: the High Court Decision in *Re Minister for Immigration and Multicultural Affairs; Ex Parte Lam*', *Sydney Law Review* 26, 2004, pp. 131, 156; Williams, op. cit., p. 47; Bates, op. cit., p. 98; Godden and Peel, op. cit., p. 351; Taylor, op. cit., p. 528.

19 See also *Horta v Commonwealth* (1994) 181 CLR 183; Fisher, op. cit., p. 73; Williams, op. cit., pp. 45–6; Kerr, op. cit., pp. 83–5.

20 See e.g. N. Gunningham and C. Holley, *Bringing the 'R' Word Back: Regulation, Environment Protection and NRM*, Canberra: Academy of Social Sciences in Australia, 2010; Lyster et al., op. cit., pp. 1, 13.

21 Ibid, pp. 2–12; Williams, op. cit., pp. 8–14.

22 C. Holley, N. Gunningham and C. Shearing, *The New Environmental Governance*, Abingdon: Earthscan, 2011.

23 Boer et al., op. cit., pp. 265–83.

the South Pacific.[24] New Zealand and Australia were also strong supporters of a range of marine and other environmental treaties within the Southern Ocean,[25] Southwest Pacific[26] and Antarctica.[27] Other national responses to major international environmental law developments are discussed below, commencing with Australia.

Australian implementation of international environmental law

An exhaustive review of Australia's responses to developments in international environmental law is beyond this section.[28] However, Table 27.1 provides an overview of some of the main

Table 27.1 Key international environmental treaties and Australian national legislation[29]

Relevant international treaties	Commonwealth legislation
Convention on Territorial Sea and the Contiguous Zone; Convention on Continental Shelf	Sea and Submerged Lands Act 1973
Agreement between the Netherlands and Australia concerning old Dutch shipwrecks	Historic Shipwrecks Act 1976
Protocol on Environmental Protection to the Antarctic Treaty; Convention for the Conservation of Antarctic Seals	Antarctic Treaty (Environment Protection) Act 1980
Convention relating to Intervention on the High Seas in Cases of Oil Pollution Casualties; Protocols relating to Intervention on the High Seas in relation to Pollution by Substances other than Oil	Protection of the Sea (Powers of Intervention) Act 1981

(Continued overleaf)

24 *Nuclear Tests (Australia and New Zealand v France)* (1974) ICJ Rep 253. Separate campaigns were conducted again in the 1990s. See P. Sands, *Principles of International Environmental Law*, 2nd edition, Melbourne: Cambridge University Press, 2003, pp. 319–21; Godden and Peel, op. cit., p. 335; Boer et al., op. cit., p. 268.

25 See, e.g. *International Convention on the Regulation of Whaling*, opened for signature 2 December 1946, 161 UNTS 72 (entered into force 10 November 1948). *Convention on the Conservation of Southern Blue Fin Tuna*, opened for signature 10 May 1993, 1819 UNTS 360 (entered into force 30 May 1994).

26 *Convention for the Prohibition of Fishing with Long Driftnets in the South Pacific*, opened for signature 24 November 1989, 29 ILM 1454 (entered into force 17 May 1991) ('Wellington Convention'); *South Pacific Nuclear Free Zone Treaty* (1985) 24 ILM 1442; *Convention for the Protection of Natural Resources and Environment of the South Pacific Region*, opened for signature 25 November 1986, 26 ILM 38 (entered into force 22 August 1990) ('Noumea Convention').

27 *Antarctic Treaty*, opened for signature 1 December 1959, 402 UNTS 71 (entered into force 23 June 1961); *Convention on the Conservation of Antarctic Marine Living Resources*, opened for signature 1 August 1980, 19 ILM 841 (entered into force 7 April 1982) (CCAMLR); Protocol to the Antarctic Treaty on Environmental Protection (1991) 30 ILM 1461. For further discussion on these issues see E. Techera, *Marine Environmental Governance: From International Law to Local Practice*, New York: Routledge, 2011, pp. 63–95, 269–70; N. Klein, 'Whales and Tuna: The Past and Future of Litigation between Australia and Japan', *Georgetown International Environmental Law Review* 21(2), 2009, pp. 143–217; Taylor, op. cit., p. 537; Rothwell and Boer, op. cit., p. 255–8; Boer et al., op. cit., pp. 265–83.

28 For further see Boer et al., op. cit., pp. 271–9.

29 Based on Bates, op. cit., pp. 113–14. For a full list of treaties see *Australian Treaties Database*, online. Available HTTP: <http://www.dfat.gov.au/treaties/index.html> (accessed 4 November 2011).

Table 27.1 Continued

Relevant international treaties	Commonwealth legislation
Convention on Civil Liability for Oil Pollution Damage	Protection of the Sea (Civil Liability) Act 1981
Convention on Civil Liability for Oil Pollution Damage	Environment Protection (Sea Dumping) Act 1981
Convention on the Conservation of Antarctic Marine Living Resources	Antarctic Marine Living Resources Conservation Act 1981
Convention for the Prevention of Pollution from Ships	Protection of the Sea (Prevention of Pollution from Ships) Act 1983
Basel Convention on the Control of Transboundary Movements of Hazardous Wastes and their Disposal	Hazardous Waste (Regulation of Exports and Imports) Act 1989
Vienna Convention for the Protection of the Ozone Layer	Ozone Protection and Synthetic Greenhouse Gas Management Act 1989
Convention on the World Cultural and National Heritage; Convention on the Conservation of Migratory Species of Wild Animals; Ramsar Convention on Wetlands of International Importance; Conventional on International Trade in Endangered Species; Convention on Biological Diversity	Environment Protection and Biodiversity Conservation Act 1999[30]
International Convention on Civil Liability for Bunker Oil Pollution Damage 2001	Protection of the Sea (Civil Liability for Bunker Oil Pollution Damage) Act 2008
Ramsar Convention on Wetlands of International Importance; The Convention on Biological Diversity;[31]	Water Act 2007
United Nations Framework Convention on Climate Change; Kyoto Protocol	National Greenhouse and Energy Reporting Act 2007
United Nations Framework Convention on Climate Change; Kyoto Protocol	Clean Energy Act 2011 and associated Acts in the Clean Energy Legislative Package

pieces of domestic legislation and the relevant corresponding international environmental conventions. The following discussion concentrates in greater depth on some of the more prominent Australian environmental laws that have been spurred by key international environmental law developments. This includes consideration of four key issues for the Australian and global communities, namely World Heritage, sustainable development, biodiversity and climate change. While the discussion touches on the actions of state and local government and non-governmental agents, the national government remains the main focus of this analysis because of its significant role and responsibilities regarding implementing international environmental law in Australia.

30 Note that this Act also reflects other international environmental obligations. For further discussion see A. Hawke, *The Australian Environment Act – Report of the Independent Review of the Environment Protection and Biodiversity Conservation Act 1999*, Canberra: Australian Government, 2009, p. 12.
31 Other relevant treaties and declarations can be found in *Water Act 2007* (Cth), s 4.

World Heritage

Australia was an international leader in implementing the 1972 Convention Concerning the Protection of the World Cultural and Natural Heritage (the World Heritage Convention).[32] Indeed, Australia was the first nation to legislate for a specific World Heritage management regime under its flagship legislation known as the *World Heritage Properties Conservation Act 1983* (Cth) (World Heritage Act).[33] The domestic implementation of the World Heritage Act quickly became one of most controversial, yet important, environmental law developments in Australia.[34] In particular, constitutional challenges by state governments against the Commonwealth's exercise of power under the World Heritage Act represent some of the most significant environmental cases in Australia's history.[35]

Before discussing these cases, it is important to briefly appreciate Australia's constitutional distribution of powers.[36] The Australian Constitution confers a number of exclusive powers on the Commonwealth government;[37] however, the primary powers of relevance to implementing international treaties arise under section 51 of the Constitution. Of the 39 heads of power articulated, none of these relate to the environment per se.[38]

Certainly, a number of these powers have been held to enable the Commonwealth to protect *aspects* of the Australian environment. Of particular relevance to international environmental law are heads of power with respect to international and interstate trade and commerce (which have allowed for the regulation of the impacts of mining),[39] fisheries (which enable the Federal Government to regulate fisheries in Australian waters beyond state-controlled coastal zones)[40] and foreign and domestic trading of financial corporations (which have enabled the regulation of the environmental impacts of Australian corporations' trading activities).[41]

However, to date, arguably the most important head of power for federal implementation of international environmental obligations has been the 'external affairs' power.[42] The scope

---

32 *Convention Concerning the Protection of the World Cultural and Natural Heritage (Paris)*, opened for signature 16 November 1972, 1037 UNTS 151 (entered into force 17 December 1975).

33 D. Haigh, 'Australian World Heritage, the Constitution and International Law', *Environmental and Planning Law Journal* 22, 2005, p. 385.

34 For further information about Australia's world heritage properties see Australia's World Heritage. Online. Available HTTP: <http://www.environment.gov.au/heritage/about/world/index.html> (accessed 4 November 2011); Haigh, op. cit.

35 Other relevant and important domestic case law has developed around ocean management, the continental shelf and territorial sea. See e.g. *New South Wales v Commonwealth* (1975) 8 ALR 1; *Seas and Submerged Lands Act 1973* (Cth), s 16; *Coastal Waters (State Title) Act 1980* (Cth); *Coastal Waters (State Powers) Act 1980* (Cth); Bates, op. cit., pp. 121–2.

36 Boer et al., op. cit., p. 266.

37 See, e.g. *Australian Constitution*, ss 52, 90; Bates, op. cit., p. 127.

38 Note, however, *Australian Constitution*, s 100 regarding rights of states and their residents to access water from rivers.

39 *Australian Constitution* s 51(i); *Murphyores Inc v Commonwealth* (1976) 136 CLR 1.

40 *Australian Constitution*, s 51(x). See e.g. *Fisheries Management Act 1991* (Cth), ss 5, 10. B. Walrut, 'The Legislative Powers of the Commonwealth and States Affecting Aquaculture', *Environmental and Planning Law Journal* 19, 2002, 415. Bates, op. cit., p. 123.

41 This also includes non-trading activities carried out for the purposes of engaging in trade. *Australian Constitution* s 51(xx); see *NSW v Commonwealth* (2006) 229 CLR 1; Godden and Peel, op. cit., pp. 130–2.

42 *Australian Constitution*, s 51(xxxix); Bates, op. cit., pp. 105–6.

of this power was determined in the seminal case of *Commonwealth v Tasmania* (the Tasmanian Dam Case).[43] The case was concerned with the validity of the World Heritage Act, which had been enacted by the Commonwealth to prevent the Tasmanian state government from constructing a dam on the Gordon River, in what was then the World Heritage-nominated Western Tasmanian Wilderness National Parks. The High Court held that the legislation was a valid exercise of the Commonwealth power under the external affairs power and the prohibitions contained in the legislation were appropriate to the Commonwealth carrying out its international obligations under the World Heritage Convention.[44]

This and subsequent progressive conflicts[45] motivated both the states and the Commonwealth to seek more cooperative solutions to domestic World Heritage management, as well as domestic environmental governance more generally. Central mechanisms for achieving this cooperation have included site-specific legislation and policy for World Heritage properties,[46] as well as agreements and legislation designed to facilitate sharing of responsibility for World Heritage sites.

One such agreement was the *Intergovernmental Agreement on the Environment 1992*, which lay the foundation for Australia to adopt a more cooperative approach to federalism. Among other things, it recognized that although the states effectively had primary responsibility for environmental issues in their jurisdiction, the Commonwealth has a legitimate role in respect of national environmental issues. These national issues include foreign policy and international obligations (such as under the World Heritage Convention), as well as environmental effects reaching beyond one state and/or into the marine environment.[47]

However, consistent with the cooperative intent of the *Intergovernmental Agreement on the Environment*, these national roles are typically underpinned by a process of consultation with the states.[48] These cooperative policy commitments were given effect in what is now the primary piece of Commonwealth environmental legislation, namely the *Environment Protection and Biodiversity Conservation Act 1999* (Cth) (EPBC Act).[49] The EPBC Act replaced the World Heritage Act in 1999.[50] Despite criticism from many environmental groups at the time,[51] the

---

43 *Commonwealth v Tasmania* [1983] HCA 21; (1983) 158 CLR 1. For further on the Tasmanian Dam case, its significance and subsequent developments see J. Peel and L. Godden, 'Australia Environmental Management: A "Dams" Story', *UNSW Law Journal* 28(3), 2005, p. 668.

44 For further discussion see Bates, op. cit., pp. 109–14; Boer et al., op. cit., pp. 276–7.

45 *Richardson v Forestry Commission* [1988] HCA 10; (1988) 164 CLR 261; *Lemonthyme and Southern Forests (Commission of Inquiry) Act 1987* (Cth); *Queensland v Commonwealth* (1989) 167 CLR 232; *Minister for Arts, Heritage and Environment v Peko-Wallsend* (1987) 75 ALR 218; Boer et al., op. cit., pp. 276–8; Bates, op. cit., pp. 111–12.

46 *Great Barrier Reef Marine Park Act 1975* (Cth). See also Australian Government and State of Queensland, *Reef Water Quality Protection Plan 2009*, Brisbane: Reef Water Quality Protection Plan Secretariat, 2009.

47 *Intergovernmental Agreement on the Environment 1992*, Art. 2.2.1. However, as noted above, the Commonwealth has undertaken to consult with the states before committing to any international agreements. See Bates, op. cit., pp. 141–2.

48 *Intergovernmental Agreement on the Environment 1992*, Art. 2.5.2. For further, see Lyster et al., op. cit., p. 17; Bates, op. cit., p. 111.

49 Godden and Peel, op. cit., p. 75.

50 See also *Aboriginal and Torres Strait Islanders Heritage Protection Act 1984* (Cth).

51 Australian Conservation Foundation, including peak environment groups in most Australian States. It was supported by the World Wildlife Fund, Tasmanian Conservation Council and the Queensland Conservation Council. For further see Haigh, op. cit., p. 388. For background see M. Kennedy, N. Beynon, A. Graham and J. Pittock, 'Development and Implementation of Conservation Law in Australia', *RECIEL* 10(3), 2001, p. 296.

EPBC Act was heralded as delivering an improved, consolidated and more comprehensive Commonwealth environmental legal regime.[52]

In addition to setting out processes of nomination and development of management plans for World Heritage properties,[53] the EPBC Act gives the Commonwealth and its agencies responsibilities for protecting heritage properties on the basis of the values for which they have been listed.[54] This protection occurs primarily[55] through a process of prescribed environmental assessment and approval of development that is likely to have a significant impact on World Heritage values. As discussed below, this environmental assessment process also applies to other matters of international environmental significance.

Despite some success (e.g. in relation to offence provisions) and the relatively compressive management regime for World Heritage sites established under the EPBC Act,[56] a number of its features have been subject to criticism. For example, although World Heritage property management plans developed under the Act apply to a specific listed place, some scholars have argued that the regime's emphasis on *values* (and retaining those values via the management of sites) fails to adequately implement the World Heritage Convention and its requirements for managing World Heritage *property* as an area per se.[57] Others have argued that the Australian regime has failed to advance a system for effective identification and protection of indigenous tangible and intangible heritage of World Heritage sites,[58] not least because Australia has yet to ratify the related *Convention for the Safeguarding of the Intangible Cultural Heritage*.[59]

More broadly, recent independent reviews of the EPBC Act have pointed to the overly prescriptive, resource-intensive and onerous process of developing heritage management plans, which themselves do not enable recognition of more flexible or alternative management

---

52 This was particularly in regard to the other repealed Commonwealth legislation, including the *Environment Protection (Impact of Proposals) Act 1974* (Cth) and the *Endangered Species Protection Act 1992* (Cth).

53 The Commonwealth is also responsible for managing properties via management plans (that are, *inter alia*, not inconsistent with the obligations under the World Heritage Convention), for all world heritage properties that are within commonwealth areas. Where the area is within state or territory then the federal government must ensure that an appropriate plan is prepared and implemented in cooperation with the state and/or territory. See *Environment Protection and Biodiversity Conservation Act 1999* (Cth), ss 13, 14, 314, 315 (nomination, listing and declaration), 316 (within commonwealth areas) 320, 321 (with state and territory lands). Note also that State Management Plans may also be accredited under bilateral agreements pursuant to section 46 of the *Environment Protection and Biodiversity Conservation Act 1999* (Cth). See Bates, op. cit.; Godden and Peel, op. cit.

54 *Environment Protection Biodiversity Conservation Act 1999* (Cth), s 12(1); Haigh, op. cit., pp. 388, 392; Bates, op. cit., p. 423.

55 For other means of protection see e.g. *Environment Protection and Biodiversity Conservation Act 1999* (Cth), ss 322, 324; Bates, op. cit., p. 423.

56 See e.g. C. McGrath, 'Flying Foxes, Dams and Whales: Using Federal Environmental Laws in the Public Interest', *Environmental and Planning Law Journal* 25, 2008, pp. 324–59; Godden and Peel, op. cit., pp. 108–10, 133–4; Bates, op. cit., p. 422.

57 Haigh, op. cit., pp. 389, 895; see also Hawke, op. cit., p. 173.

58 I. Connolly, 'Can the World Heritage Convention be Adequately Implemented in Australia without Australia becoming a Party to the Intangible Heritage Convention?', *Environmental and Planning Law Journal* 24, 2007, pp. 198, 209; *Aboriginal and Torres Strait Islanders Heritage Protection Act 1984* (Cth).

59 *Convention for the Safeguarding of the Intangible Cultural Heritage* (Paris), opened for signature 17 October 2003 (entered into force on 20 April 2006); Connolly, op. cit., p. 209.

arrangements that may achieve equivalent or superior heritage outcomes.[60] In response, a number of recently proposed reforms to the EPBC Act aim,[61] *inter alia*, to allow more tailored management arrangements that can vary according to different circumstances, provided the arrangements meet Commonwealth standards.[62] These changes will arguably bring Australia more in line with the considerable flexibility in management systems and mechanisms recognized under the UNESCO *Operational Guidelines for the Implementation of the World Heritage Convention.*[63]

Cooperative responses to UNCED and other international environmental obligations

As was the case in the World Heritage context, a hallmark of Australia's response to broader international environmental law developments has been its attempts to implement a cooperative approach to environmental regulation. Notwithstanding recent tensions between state and Commonwealth governments on transboundary water management issues,[64] an exemplar of Australian governmental cooperation was its response to the 1992 United Nations Conference on Environment and Development. Following the adoption of the Rio Declaration[65] and Agenda 21,[66] much of Australia's federal and state environmental policy and legislation has now come to reflect these documents and the concept of sustainable development.[67] In particular, state governments, courts and tribunals[68] play an important role in developing integrated approaches to development, pollution and environmental management so as to promote sustainable development.[69]

Important to achieving this success was the fact that all levels of Australian government adopted two important national guiding documents, namely: (i) the *National Strategy for*

---

60 Hawke, op. cit., p. 178.
61 The government is also producing new guidelines for listed World Heritage properties and listed national heritage places, which outline constraints and types of actions likely to have a significant impact. Australian Government, *Australian Government Response to the Report of the Independent Review of the Environment Protection and Biodiversity Conservation Act 1999*, Canberra: Australian Government, 2011, p. 54. Online. Available HTTP: <http://www.environment.gov.au/epbc/publications/pubs/epbc-review-govt-response.pdf> (accessed 4 November 2011).
62 Ibid, p. 63.
63 Ibid. UNESCO, *Operational Guidelines for the Implementation of the World Heritage Convention*, Paris: UNESCO World Heritage Centre, 2008.
64 In particular, the reliance by the Water Act 2007 (Cth) on the external affairs power has been subject to some debate. For further see The Senate, Legal and Constitutional Affairs References Committee, *A Balancing Act: Provisions of the Water Act 2007*, Canberra: Australian Government, 2011, pp. 45–9, 61–8, 73; D. Connell and R. Quentin Grafton (eds.) *Basin Futures: Water Reform in the Murray-Darling Basin*, Canberra: ANU E-Press, 2011; Godden and Peel, op. cit., p. 74.
65 *Rio Declaration on Environment and Development,* Report of the United Nations Conference on Environment and Development, UN Doc A/CONF.151/6/Rev.1 (1992) ('Rio Declaration').
66 *Agenda 21,* Report of the UNCED, *I*, UN Doc A/CONF. 151/26/Rev.1, 1992 ('Agenda 21').
67 See e.g. Lyster et al., op. cit., pp. 23–5; G. Bates, 'Legal Perspectives', in S. Dovers and S. Wild River (eds.) *Managing Australia's Environment*, Annandale: Federation Press, 2003, pp. 292–4; Techera, op. cit., pp. 12–45.
68 This is particularly in the context of planning and development control legislations. See e.g. *BGP Properties Pty Limited v Lake Macquarie City Council* [2004] NSWLEC 399; *Telstra Corporation Limited v Hornsby Shire Council* [2006] NSWLEC 133.
69 See e.g. *Environmental Planning and Assessment Act 1979* (NSW), s 79C, 91; Bates, op. cit., pp. 293–4; G. Bates, *Environmental Law in Australia*, op. cit., p. 100.

Ecologically Sustainable Development (ESD) 1992, which provided a framework for governments to cooperatively make decisions and take actions to pursue ESD in Australia;[70] and (ii) the *Intergovernmental Agreement on the Environment 1992*, which similarly included the commitment to ESD principles.[71]

Under the Intergovernmental Agreement on the Environment, coordinated responses to international environmental obligations have been structured and implemented through a range of ministerial councils, consisting of Ministers from national, state and territory governments.[72] It is often through these councils and committees that Australia has produced national policies and strategies to coordinate action across all levels of government in addressing international environmental obligations. In addition to the National Strategy on ESD noted above, some of the most relevant to Australia's various international environmental obligations include the Oceans Policy,[73] National Forests Policy,[74] Australian Weeds Strategy (relevant to invasive species)[75] and a National Cooperative Approach to Integrated Coastal Zone Management.[76]

Two further vital non-statutory coordinating strategies and programmes have been pursued by Australia in response to its ratification of the Convention on Biological Diversity (CBD).[77] The first seeks to respond to the fact that the Commonwealth[78] and state governments[79] have separate systems for listing and managing protected reserves (both marine and terrestrial). Accordingly, since 1992, Australia has been developing and investing in a terrestrial national reserves system and strategy[80] that seeks to ensure these separate regimes (along

---

70 *National Strategy for Ecologically Sustainable Development*, Ecologically Sustainable Development Steering Committee (endorsed by the Council of Australian Governments), 1992.

71 *Intergovernmental Agreement on the Environment 1992*.

72 *Intergovernmental Agreement on the Environment 1992*, para. 2.5.4.2; Lyster et al., op. cit., pp. 18–20. There have also been a number of standing committees and speciality committees on issues such as world heritage and natural resource management. See Bates, op. cit.

73 Australian Government, *Australia's Oceans Policy*, Canberra: Australian Government, 1998.

74 Australian Government, *National Forest Policy Statement*, Canberra: Australian Government, 1992.

75 Natural Resource Management Ministerial Council, *Australian Weeds Strategy – A National Strategy for Weed Management in Australia*, Canberra: Australian Government, 2006, pp. 9, 18.

76 Natural Resource Management Ministerial Council, *National Cooperative Approach to Integrated Coastal Zone Management – Framework and Implementation Plan*, Canberra: Australian Government, 2006. See also Bates, op. cit., p. 137.

77 *Intergovernmental Agreement on the Environment 1992*, sch 9.

78 The Act also enables conservation agreements to be made between the government and person for the purposes of, *inter alia*, protecting and conserving biodiversity outside of Commonwealth reserves. See e.g. *Environment Protection and Biodiversity Conservation Act 1999* (Cth) ss 24, 304, 305, 343–352. *Environmental Protection and Biodiversity Conservation Regulations 2000* (Cth), sch 8, pt 2. See also discussion of world heritage and RAMSAR wetlands above.

79 States and territories also maintain protected areas. See e.g. *National Parks and Wildlife Act 1974* (NSW); *Marine Parks Act 1997* (NSW), s 3; *Fisheries Management Act 1994* (NSW), s 194; *Wilderness Act 1987* (NSW); *Nature Conservation Act 1992* (Qld); Bates, op. cit.

80 See National Reserve System Task Group, *Australia's Strategy for Australia's National Reserve System 2009–2030*, Canberra: Australian Government, 2009. See also investment and actions to support the national reserves system via the 'Caring for our Country' programme: L. Robins and P. Kanowski, ' "Crying for our Country": Eight Ways in Which "Caring for our Country" has Undermined Australia's Regional Model for Natural Resource Management', *Australasian Journal of Environmental Management* 18(2), 2011, pp. 88–108. See also *Intergovernmental Agreement on the Environment* 1992, sch 9 cl 13; L. Byrne, 'Crown Land and Protected Areas', in D. Farrier and P. Stein (eds) *The Environmental Law Handbook*, 5th edition, Pyrmont: Thomson Reuters, 2011, p. 113; L. Ogle, 'Biodiversity', in D. Farrier and P. Stein (eds) *The Environmental Law Handbook*, 5th edition, Pyrmont: Thomson Reuters, 2011, p. 470.

with Indigenous Protected Areas)[81] cover a sample of all Australia's diverse ecosystems, plants and animals. A National Representative System of Marine Protected Areas has since complemented this terrestrial system.[82]

However, despite long-standing commitments to achieve a framework of consistency between state and Commonwealth protected area management, harmony between the two is yet to be fully achieved.[83] Indeed, as was recently pointed out by a group of concerned scientists, a number of bioregions remain poorly represented in both the national reserve system and the national marine protected area system; and marine protected area networks are compromised by low levels of protection and sometimes poor surveillance.[84]

The second vital coordinating mechanism for Australia's implementation of the CBD has been the *National Strategy for the Conservation of Australia's Biological Diversity 1996* (the Biodiversity Strategy). This strategy adopted the same priorities for conservation as the CBD, embodied principles of ESD and aimed to protect biological diversity and maintain ecological processes and systems.[85] In some ways a far-sighted document, the strength of the Biodiversity Strategy was a national approach to conserving biodiversity that spurred important corresponding efforts at state and local levels to achieve significant advances in biodiversity conservation in Australia.[86]

However, over the last decade, reviews have identified a range of weaknesses in this flagship national strategy including an over-reliance on broad statements of intent that failed to provide clear direction and thus undermined implementation efforts at lower state and local levels.[87] Furthermore, the Biodiversity Strategy set only broad qualitative objectives, making it difficult to objectively measure achievement and performance.[88]

In an effort to provide greater clarity, ten priority outcomes were subsequently produced under the *National Objectives and Targets for Biodiversity Conservation 2001–2005*.[89] Nevertheless,

81 Further see P. Havemann, D. Thiriet, H. Marsh and C. Jones, 'Traditional Use of Marine Resources Agreements and Dugong Hunting in the Great Barrier Reef World Heritage Area', *Environmental and Planning Law Journal* 22, 2005, pp. 258–60.

82 ANZECC Taskforce on Marine Protected Areas, *Guidelines for Establishing the National Representative System of Marine Protected Areas*, Canberra: Environment Australia 1998, p. 5; Bates, op. cit., p. 419.

83 For a discussion in a NSW context see S. Hickie, 'Managing Recreation, Conservation and Economy: A Critical Appraisal of the New South Wales Marine Parks Amendment Act 2008', *Environmental and Planning Law Journal* 26, 2009, p. 61.

84 A. Arthington and J. Nevill, 'Australia's Biodiversity Conservation Strategy 2010–2020: Scientists' letter of concern', *Ecological Management and Restoration* 10(2), 2009, pp. 78–81; J. Nevill and T. Ward 'The National Representative System of Marine Protected Areas: Comment on Recent Progress', *Ecological Management and Restoration* 10(3), 2009, pp. 228–31; M. Taylor, P. Sattler, J. Fitzsimons, C. Curnow, D. Beaver, L. Gibson and G. Llewellyn, *Building Nature's Safety Net 2011: The State of Protected Areas for Australia's Ecosystems and Wildlife*, Sydney: WWF-Australia, 2011.

85 For an overview of the strategy see F. Dawson, 'Analysing the Goals of Biodiversity Conservation: Scientific, Policy and Legal Perspectives', *Environmental and Planning Law Journal* 21(6), 2004, pp. 18–22. See also *Australia's Biodiversity Conservation Strategy 2010–2030*, Canberra: Australian Government, 2010, p. 31; Boer et al., op. cit., p. 276.

86 See e.g. Arthington and Nevill, op. cit., pp. 78–83; Australian Local Government Association in conjunction with Biological Diversity Advisory Council, *National Local Government Biodiversity Strategy* (1998).

87 Arthington and Nevill, op. cit., p. 78; Dawson, op. cit., pp. 19–20.

88 Australian Government, *Australia's Biodiversity Conservation Strategy 2010–2030*, pp. 31–2.

89 Australian Government, *The National Objectives and Targets for Biodiversity Conservation 2001–2005*, Canberra: Australian Government, 2001.

coordinated implementation of these targets across the nation was never achieved due to a lack of agreement on the specific targets by all state and territory jurisdictions.[90] Moreover, as time passed, the Biodiversity Strategy itself lacked a response to modern threats to biodiversity, including vulnerability due to climate change.[91]

In response to these problems, a new Biodiversity Conservation Strategy was recently developed. Earlier drafts of the new Strategy were widely criticized, and questions remain as to whether it will be sufficiently supported with funding, and coordinated legislative implementation, to achieve successful outcomes.[92] Even so, the new Strategy appears to take some steps towards addressing historic weaknesses by setting out three specific priorities for action ('Engaging all Australians; Building ecosystem resilience in a changing climate; and Getting measurable results') and ten measurable national targets to be achieved by 2015.[93]

An important additional result of the new Biodiversity Strategy is the opportunity it offers to renew attention on aligning the extensive legislative priorities and actions of state governments within the broader national context, so as to successfully respond to Australia's international obligations.[94] Particularly important in this regard will be aligning existing biodiversity-focused state regimes, including state biodiversity strategies, threatened and invasive species policy and legislation (which contain prescribed controls for landowners and resource managers),[95] native vegetation regulation,[96] local planning controls (which require environmental assessment and approvals for removing native vegetation)[97] and regional natural resource management planning and investment.[98]

Of course, aligning legislative action on biodiversity and other environmental issues of international importance is never an easy task within a federal system. Indeed, even with coordination mechanisms such as ministerial councils and national strategies, inevitable

90 Dawson, op. cit., p. 21; Australian Government, *Australia's Biodiversity Conservation Strategy 2010–2030*, pp. 31–2; Clear Horizon, *Evaluation of the Victorian Biodiversity Strategy, Summary Report*, Melbourne: Clear Horizon, 2007, p. 4.

91 The strategy also lacked a number of modern management responses, such as landscape context, and a whole-of-ecosystem management approach. See discussion and studies cited in Australian Government, *Australia's Biodiversity Conservation Strategy 2010–2030*, p. 32.

92 Ogle, op. cit., p. 469; Arthington and Nevill, op. cit.

93 *Australia's Biodiversity Conservation Strategy 2010–2030*.

94 Ibid, p. 69.

95 See e.g. *Threatened Species Conservation Act 1995* (NSW), *Nature Conservation Act 1992* (Qld); *National Parks and Wildlife Act 1972* (SA); *Wildlife Act 1975* (Vic); M. Burgman, T. Walshe, L. Godden and P. Martin, 'Designing Regulation for Conservation and Biosecurity', *Australasian Journal of Natural Resources Law and Policy* 13(1), 2009, pp. 93, 96.

96 See e.g. C. McGrath, 'Editorial comment: End of Broadscale Clearing In Queensland', *Environmental and Planning Law Journal* 24, 2007, 5; Ogle, op. cit., pp. 520–31; Bates, op. cit., p. 453.

97 See e.g. Ogle, op. cit., pp. 514–20; Bates, op. cit., pp. 47, 454, 469; R. Blomquist, 'Protecting Nature "Down Under": An American Law Professor's View of Australia's Implementation of the Convention of Biological Diversity: Laws, Policies, Programs, Institutions and Plans 1992–2000', *Dickinson Journal of Environmental Law and Policy* 9, 2000, pp. 227, 324.

98 M. Lane, B. Taylor and C. Robinson (eds.) *Contested Country*, Collingwood: CSIRO, 2009; C. Holley, 'Removing the Thorn from New Governance's Side: Examining the Emergence of Collaboration in Practice and the Roles for Law, Nested Institutions and Trust', *Environmental Law Reporter* 40(7), 2010, p. 10656.

conflicts between overlapping state and federal environmental legislation can arise. Recognizing this fact, the *Intergovernmental Agreement on the Environment* suggested that having the Commonwealth accrediting state processes and according full faith and credit to the results could avoid such conflict.[99] This commitment to accreditation was subsequently given effect via the EPBC Act and its environmental assessment process for development proposals.

The EPBC Act establishes a process of referral, assessment and approval that is intended to provide protection for 'matters of national environmental significance' (MNES).[100] Apart from World Heritage (discussed above),[101] MNES largely represent legal responsibilities the Commonwealth already has under international law by reason of ratification of international conventions.[102] These include: national heritage places;[103] declared Ramsar wetlands of international importance;[104] nationally listed threatened species and ecological communities;[105] nationally listed migratory species;[106] nuclear actions;[107] the Commonwealth marine environment;[108] and the Great Barrier Reef Marine Park.[109]

Under the Act, a process is established for assessing the environmental impacts (e.g. environmental impact assessment)[110] of certain actions (e.g. projects and proposals)[111] which are likely to have significant impacts on these MNES.[112] The Federal Minister must then decide whether or not to approve the action, taking into account a range of factors, including the principles of ESD and the precautionary principle.[113]

This assessment process operates concurrently with environmental impact assessment legislation in states and territories.[114] However, where a project requires federal assessment it may be assessed under state or territory legislation that has gone through an accreditation

99 *Intergovernmental Agreement on the Environment 1992*, para. 2.5; Godden and Peel, op. cit., pp. 74–5.
100 See e.g. J. Johnson, 'Commonwealth Environmental Assessment and Approval' in D. Farrier and P. Stein (eds) *The Environmental Law Handbook*, 5th edition, Pyrmont: Thomson Reuters, 2011, pp. 274–303.
101 *Environment Protection and Biodiversity Conservation Act 1999* (Cth) s 12.
102 See e.g. Bates, op. cit., p. 143.
103 *Environment Protection and Biodiversity Conservation Act 1999* (Cth) s 15B.
104 *Environment Protection and Biodiversity Conservation Act 1999* (Cth) s 16.
105 *Environment Protection and Biodiversity Conservation Act 1999* (Cth) s 18.
106 *Environment Protection and Biodiversity Conservation Act 1999* (Cth) s 20.
107 *Environment Protection and Biodiversity Conservation Act 1999* (Cth) s 21.
108 *Environment Protection and Biodiversity Conservation Act 1999* (Cth) s 23.
109 *Environment Protection and Biodiversity Conservation Act 1999* (Cth) s 24B. For further discussion of the effectiveness of EPBCA in protecting these MNES see A. Macintosh, 'Why the Environment Protection and Biodiversity Conservation Act's Referral, Assessment and Approval Process is Failing to Achieve its Environmental Objectives', *Environmental and Planning Law Journal* 21, 2004, p. 288.
110 *Environment Protection and Biodiversity Conservation Act 1999* (Cth) s 87.
111 *Environment Protection and Biodiversity Conservation Act 1999* (Cth) s 67, 67A, 75.
112 *Environment Protection and Biodiversity Conservation Act 1999* (Cth) ss 82, 527E.
113 *Environment Protection and Biodiversity Conservation Act 1999* (Cth) s 130, 133, 136–140A, 391. Note that there are some exceptions to actions that require approval. For example if the action is undertaken in accordance with the *Great Barrier Reef Marine Park Act 1975* (Cth): *Environment Protection and Biodiversity Conservation Act 1999* (Cth) s 43. For further exceptions see *Environment Protection and Biodiversity Conservation Act 1999* (Cth) ss 29–32, 32, 38–42, 159–164. See also Johnson, op. cit.; Bates, op. cit., pp. 146–7.
114 *Environment Protection and Biodiversity Conservation Act 1999* (Cth) s 10. Godden and Peel, op. cit., pp. 74–6.

processes (on a one-off[115] or permanent basis[116]).[117] While the accreditation process can provide opportunities for the Commonwealth to raise the environmental standards of its state partners, the process has been widely criticized as complex and having failed to achieve significant gains in the standards set for assessments.[118] Concerns of bias have also been raised about the devolution of assessment to states, particularly because it may allow a state agency to be responsible for assessing a state government project.[119] These issues in turn have led some to suggest the accreditation process undermines the Federal Government's central responsibility to effectively implement its international obligations.[120]

More broadly, a number of related concerns have also been raised regarding the implementation of international obligations via the EPBC Act's referral and assessment process. For instance, a number of commentators have argued that the EPBC Act should include a broader vision of matters of national environmental significance, such that its processes protect significant impacts on a much broader range of international obligations, particularly greenhouse gas (GHG) reduction.[121] Other concerns relate to the range of actions that are exempt from regulation under the assessment process, including forestry operations that occur in accordance with a regional forest agreement.[122] Perhaps of even greater concern are claims that the EPBC Act has allowed for the continued degradation of Ramsar wetlands because, *inter alia*, its regime does not regulate the continuation of uses on land and water that were lawful prior to the EPBC Act's proclamation. Nor does the Act incorporate the full range of Australian obligations under the Ramsar Convention.[123] One recent report even indicated that a number of Australian Ramsar sites had no management plan or planning document completed or being developed.[124]

115 *Environment Protection and Biodiversity Conservation Act 1999* (Cth) s 87(4).

116 These include bilateral agreements – approval bilaterals or assessment bilateral: *Environment Protection and Biodiversity Conservation Act 1999* (Cth) ss 46, 47. See also *Environment Protection and Biodiversity Conservation Regulations 2000*, sch 1.

117 Godden and Peel, op. cit., pp. 75–6. *Environment Protection and Biodiversity Conservation Act 1999* (Cth) ss 48, 50.

118 C. McGrath 'The QLD Bilateral', *Queensland Environmental Practice Reporter* 8, 2002–3, p. 145; L. Ogle, 'The Environment Protection and Biodiversity Conservation Act 1999 (Cth): How Workable is it?', *Environmental and Planning Law Journal* 17, 2000, p. 468; Hawke, op. cit., p. 66, 69; Godden and Peel, op. cit., pp. 74–6.

119 Hawke, op. cit., p. 66; Godden and Peel, op. cit., pp. 74–6.

120 Godden and Peel, op. cit., pp. 76–9 discussing *Wilderness Society Inc v Turnbull, Minister for the Environment and Water Resources* (2007) 158 LGERA 134; (2008) 157 LGERA 413.

121 See e.g. R. Lyster and A. Bradbrook, *Energy Law and the Environment*, Port Melbourne: Cambridge University Press, 2006, pp. 92–5; Kennedy et al., op. cit.; Bates, op. cit., p. 144; L. Godden and J. Peel, 'The Environment Protection and Biodiversity Conservation Act 1999 (Cth): Dark Sides of Virtue', *Melbourne University Law Review* 31, 2007, 106, pp. 116–17.

122 Kennedy et al., op. cit., p. 303. Note that forest assessment undertaken under regional agreements constitutes a form of assessment and approval rather than an exemption per se from the Act. See Hawke, op. cit., p. 22; Johnson, op. cit, p. 285.

123 J. Pittock, M. Finlayson, A. Gardner and C. McKay, 'Changing Character: The Ramsar Convention on Wetlands and Climate Change in the Murray-Darling Basin, Australia', *Environmental and Planning Law Journal* 27, 2010, 401, pp. 407–8.

124 BMT WBM, *Ramsar Snapshot Study – Final Report*, Brisbane: BMT WBM, 2007, pp. 3-31–3-32; Hawke, op. cit., p. 187. See also V. Prahalad and L. Kriwoken, 'Implementation of the Ramsar Convention on Wetlands in Tasmania', *Australia, Journal of International Wildlife Law and Policy* 13(3), 2010, 205, pp. 211–21.

In addition to these weaknesses, there have been related concerns regarding the effectiveness of the EPBC Act as Australia's primary national legislative response to the CBD (although national quarantine legislation also plays an increasingly prominent role).[125] In addition to the referral and assessment process,[126] the EPBC Act regime contributes to biodiversity conservation via, *inter alia*,[127] establishing a system for identifying and managing reserves,[128] the regulation of wildlife trade,[129] listing threatened species and the preparation and implementation of recovery plans.[130]

While these controls have made some progress in advancing biodiversity conservation by identifying species at risk and addressing evident threats, there are substantial limits to the effectiveness of these federal laws and their interaction with state threatened species regimes.[131] These limits include differing eligibility criteria at a national and state level, which can produce inconsistency in listing and the protection provided,[132] as well as the limits of species-focused listing processes to capture cumulative and interactive impacts of multiple threatening processes.[133]

These and other limitations of the EPBC Act have been explored in a recent ten-year review of the legislation,[134] which identified both the regime's strengths (e.g. various avenues for public participation in decision-making process) as well as its weaknesses.[135] This has led to 71 recommendations being made for reform.[136] The Commonwealth's recent response included

---

125 *Quarantine Act 1908* (Cth). See also R. Beale, J. Fairbrother, A. Inglis and D. Trebeck, *The Independent Review of Australia's Quarantine and Biosecurity Arrangements Report to the Australian Government*, Canberra: Australian Government, 2008; Burgman et al., op. cit., p. 96; Ogle, op. cit.; Kennedy, op. cit.

126 Pittock et al., op. cit., p. 408; Kennedy et al., op. cit., p. 305.

127 The Act is also responsible for managing migratory species and actions in Commonwealth areas and listing key threatening processes that threaten native species or ecological communities. See Byrne, op. cit., pp. 122–43; Bates, op. cit., p. 494.

128 See e.g. *Environment Protection and Biodiversity Conservation Act 1999* (Cth) ss 24, 304, 305, 343–52; *Environmental Protection and Biodiversity Conservation Regulations 2000* (Cth), sch 8, pt 2.

129 *Environment Protection and Biodiversity Conservation Act 1999* (Cth) ss 303BA–303GY; T. Hewitt, 'Implementation and Enforcement of the Convention on International Trade in Endangered Species of Wild Fauna and Flora in the South Pacific Region: Management and Scientific Authorities', *Queensland University of Technology Law and Justice Journal* 2, 2002, p. 98.

130 See e.g. *Environment Protection and Biodiversity Conservation Act 1999* (Cth) ss 178, 179, 181, 182, 186, 187; R. Beeton and C. McGrath, 'Developing an Approach to the Listing of Ecological Communities to Achieve Conservation Outcomes', *Australian Journal of Natural Resource Law and Policy* 13(1), 2009, p. 61; M. Palmer, 'Turtle Power Down Under The Sea?: Comparative Domestic And International Legal Protection Of Marine Turtles By Australia And The United States', *Georgia Journal of International and Comparative Law* 37, 2008–9, p. 115; Godden and Peel, op. cit., pp. 170, 341–2; Bates, op. cit., pp. 409–435.

131 Burgman et al., op. cit., p. 95.

132 M. Jenkins and A. Gardner, 'Conservation of Biodiversity through the Listing of Threatened Species and Ecological Communities: A Comparative Review', *The Australasian Journal of Natural Resources Law and Policy* 10(1), 2005, pp. 1, 3–4; Department of Sustainability, Environment, Water, Population and Communities, *Reforming National Environment Law: An Overview*, Canberra: Australian Government, 2011, p. 15.

133 Burgman et al., op. cit., p. 95.

134 *Environment Protection and Biodiversity Conservation Act 1999* (Cth) s 522A.

135 Note that the Hawke review recommends changes to the public participation process, but points out that participation avenues were strongly supported by public submissions. Hawke, op. cit., pp. 9, 256–60; Macintosh, op. cit., p. 9; McGrath, 'Flying Foxes', op.cit., p. 353.

136 Hawke, op. cit.

a broad package of reforms for Australia's national environmental laws, which importantly purport to be better for the environment, better for business and to lead to better cooperation. Key elements of the reform package that will likely have a significant impact on Australia's approach to meeting international environmental obligations, include the following:[137]

(i)   new national standards for accrediting environmental assessment and approval processes to ensure Commonwealth and state systems are better aligned for delivering on international obligations;
(ii) a new biodiversity policy, designed to complement the new Biodiversity Strategy and describe the role of the Australian Government;
(iii) improving the listing of species for protection by producing a single national list of threatened species and ecological communities to reduce inconsistencies between jurisdictions; and
(iv) identifying and protecting ecosystems of national significance through regional environment plans, strategic assessments and/or conservation agreements that stand to offer a more proactive and potentially more holistic approach to conserving Australia's environmental assets in the long term, rather than waiting until threats from specific developments become significant.[138]

Australian responses to climate change

Having touched on Australia's management of World Heritage, and various legislative and cooperative policy approaches to regulating biodiversity and ESD, we come to the final but perhaps most significant of international environmental law challenges, namely climate change. Despite ratifying the UN Framework Convention on Climate Change (UNFCCC) following the UNCED, and subsequently holding numerous domestic inquiries into Australia's response to climate change, the national government has historically been reticent to regulate on climate change.[139] This is despite the fact that the national government arguably has more than sufficient constitutional powers to allow it to introduce climate regulation,[140] and that the government has direct international responsibilities to protect the world's largest World Heritage Area (the Great Barrier Reef), which has been shown to be in direct peril from global warming.[141]

---

137 Further see Department of Sustainability, Environment, Water, Population and Communities, op. cit.
138 Note that marine reserves have already begun this process. Department of Sustainability, Environment, Water, Population and Communities, op. cit.
139 For overview see generally T. Bonyhady and P. Christoff (eds), *Climate Law in Australia*, Sydney: Federation Press, 2007; R. Rayfuse, 'Drowning our Sorrows to Secure a Carbon Free Future? Some International Legal Considerations Relating to Sequestering Carbon by Fertilising the Oceans', *UNSW Law Journal* 31, 2008, p. 919.
140 See e.g. J. Peel 'The Role of Climate Change Litigation in Australia's Response to Global Warming', *Environmental and Planning Law Journal* 24, 2007, 90, p. 104; Godden and Peel, op. cit., p. 348; A. Huggins, 'Protecting World Heritage Sites from the Adverse Impacts of Climate Change: Obligations for States Parties to the World Heritage Convention', *Australian International Law Journal* 14, 2007, p. 121.
141 P Marshall, *GBR Coral Bleaching Response Program*, Townsville: GBRMPA, 2003, p. 1; Havemann et al., op. cit., p. 263.

During the period of minimal national action on climate change, state-based regimes began to fill the regulatory void, including establishing their own GHG abatement scheme.[142] Simultaneously, there was growth in litigation on climate change under state (and to a lesser extent Commonwealth) planning and pollution regulatory frameworks relating to environmental impacts of generation and transmission of electricity.[143] To date, there has been little firm opinion emerging from this case law as to when, and to what extent, the potential climate change impacts of developments are to be considered by regulatory decision-makers.

It was not until 2007 that Australia ratified the Kyoto Protocol, introduced reforms that increased Australia's renewable energy target[144] and began to develop new climate pollution reduction mechanisms.[145] An important input into national government policy was Professor Garnaut's Review, which recommended medium- to long-term policy options for Australia's response to the challenge of climate change.[146] The initial response to this advice came in the form of a 'Carbon Pollution Reduction Scheme' (CPRS). Despite this initial policy momentum, the government deferred the CPRS to at least 2013, due to slow global control efforts and domestic political difficulty.[147] This deferral was followed by a national election in 2010 and a further deferral of an emissions trading scheme until 2015. However, following the establishment of a Multi-Party Climate Change Committee to explore options for implementing a carbon price,[148] the Clean Energy Agreement was produced, which set out a

142 See e.g. *Electricity Supply Act 1995* (NSW) Part 8A. National Emissions Trading Taskforce, *Possible Design for a National Greenhouse Gas*, NETT, 2006. Further see R. Lyster, 'Australia's Clean Energy Future Package: Are We There Yet?', *Environmental and Planning Law Journal* 28, 2011, p. 446; R. Lyster, 'Australia's Clean Energy Future Package: Are we there yet?', Sydney Law School Research Paper No. 11/85, 2011. Online Available HTTP: <http://ssrn.com/abstract=1954238> (viewed 4 November 2011); R. Bullmore, 'Energy', in D. Farrier and P. Stein (eds.) *The Environmental Law Handbook*, 5th edition, Pyrmont: Thomson Reuters, 2011, pp. 415–7; Godden and Peel, op. cit., pp. 368–9.

143 See e.g. *Greenpeace Australia Limited v Redbank Power Company Pty Ltd and Singleton Council* (1994) 84 LGERA 143; *Australian Conservation Foundation v La Trobe City Council* (2004) 140 LGERA 100; *Wildlife Preservation Society of Queensland Proserpine/Whitsunday Branch Inc v Minister for the Environment and Heritage* (2006) 232 ALR 510; *Gray v Minister for Planning* (2006) 152 LGERA 258; *Anvil Hill Project Watch Association Inc v Minister for the Environment and Water Resources* [2007] FCA 1480; *Re Xstrata Coal Queensland Pty Ltd and Ors* [2007] QLRT 33; *Minister for Planning v Walker* [2008] NSWCA 224, (2008) 161 LGERA 423; *Aldous v Greater Taree City Council* [2009] NSWLEC 17.

144 This expanded the target to 20 per cent of electricity from renewable sources by 2020. For further see Bullmore, op. cit., pp. 418–20.

145 Godden and Peel, op. cit., pp. 370–1.

146 R. Garnut, *The Garnut Climate Change Review Final Report*, Port Melbourne: Cambridge University Press, 2008; R. Garnut, *The Garnut Review 2011 Australia in the Global Response to Climate Change*, Port Melbourne: Cambridge University Press, 2011.

147 See R. Lyster, 'The Australian Carbon Pollution Reduction Scheme: What Role for Complementary Emissions Reduction Regulatory Measures?', *UNSW Law Journal* 31(3), 2008, pp. 880–93. See *Carbon Pollution Reduction Scheme*. Online. Available HTTP: <http://www.aph.gov.au/About_Parliament/Parliamentary_Departments/Parliamentary_Library/Browse_by_Topic/ClimateChange/Governance/Domestic/national/cprs> (accessed 24 April 2012). L. Nielson, J. Styles, A. Talberg and J. Tomaras, 'Carbon Pollution Reduction Scheme 2009 (No. 2)', Bills Digest, No. 59, 2009–2010, 29 October 2009, Canberra: Parliamentary Library. See also the *National Greenhouse Energy Reporting Act 2007* (Cth).

148 See Multi-Party Climate Change Committee. Online. Available HTTP: <http://www.climate change.gov.au/government/initiatives/mpccc.aspx> (accessed 4 November 2010).

framework for reforms to move Australia toward 'a clean energy future' by putting a price on carbon pollution.[149]

The Clean Energy Agreement led to the introduction of a package of 19 bills into the Federal parliament in 2011; and these were made into law later that year. The principal Act is the *Clean Energy Act 2011* (Cth), which seeks to reduce emissions by 80 per cent compared with 2000 levels by 2050.[150] The administration for the *Clean Energy Act 2011* was set to commence in mid-2012, under which around 500 of the biggest polluters in Australia will need to buy and surrender to the government a permit for every tonne of carbon pollution they produce.[151] For the first three years, a carbon price will be fixed like a tax, before moving to an emissions trading scheme in 2015. As part of the support package accompanying these reforms farmers and land managers will be encouraged to pursue climate change action and enhance biodiversity through new funding initiatives and measures.[152] This includes the Carbon Farming Initiative, which is the first of its kind in the world to provide domestic offsets from the land sector.[153] This involves a scheme for the issue of carbon credit units in relation to eligible offsets projects, which include sequestration and emissions avoidance projects.[154]

The Clean Energy package of bills also establishes new regulatory and governance bodies, including the Clean Energy Regulator (which will regulate the carbon pricing mechanism),[155] the Climate Change Authority (to provide independent reviews and advice on the Australian government's policies for reducing carbon pollution)[156] and the Land Sector Carbon and Biodiversity Board (to provide advice to the government on the implementation of various land sector measures).[157]

Given the unsuccessful attempts in the past to put a price on carbon, exactly whether this new package of reforms will play out successfully in practice remains to be seen. As commentators have pointed out, the recent Federal Opposition's pledge to dismantle the package and all of the associated agencies means that Australia may yet continue to flounder in seeking to respond to international obligations on climate change.[158] Even so, there will no doubt be increasing attention on other emerging, but vital issues in climate change governance, including the increasing private sector presence in climate marine sequestration projects in and around Australia.[159]

---

149 Multiparty Climate Change Committee, *Clean Energy Agreement*, Canberra: Australian Government, 2011.

150 *Clean Energy Act 2011* (Cth), s 3; Lyster, op. cit., p. 2.

151 Australian Government, *Securing a Clean Energy Future – the Australian Government's Climate Change Plan*, Canberra: Australian Government, 2011, p. vii. See also 'Clean Energy bills receive Royal Assent', Canberra; Australian Government. Online. Available HTTP: <http://www.cleanenergyfuture.gov.au/clean-energy-bills-receive-royal-assent> (accessed 25 January 2012).

152 Ibid. This also includes a new Biodiversity Fund.

153 Lyster, op. cit., p. 34.

154 *Carbon Credits (Carbon Farming Initiative) Act 2011* (Cth). Lyster, op. cit., p. 34.

155 *Clean Energy Regulator Act 2011* (Cth), ss 11–13, 16–19. Lyster, op. cit., pp. 32–33.

156 *Climate Change Authority Act 2011* (Cth) ss 3, 10–13, 16–18. Lyster, op. cit., pp. 32–33.

157 *Climate Change Authority Act 2011* (Cth), ss 61–6. See generally *Clean Energy Legislative Package*, online. Available HTTP: <http://www.climatechange.gov.au/en/government/clean-energy-future/legislation.aspx> (accessed 24 April 2012).

158 Lyster, op. cit., p. 35.

159 See e.g. Y. Carr, 'The International Legal Issues Relating to the Facilitation of Sub-Seabed CO_2 Sequestration Projects in Australia' *Australian International Law Journal* 14, 2007, p. 137; Rayfuse, op. cit., pp. 921–2, 928.

New Zealand's implementation of international environmental law

Like Australia, New Zealand has actively adopted and implemented a range of international environmental conventions and treaties. Some of New Zealand's key responses to developments in international environmental law are summarized in Table 27.2.[160] In the following, the chapter will provide a general overview of some of the more prominent domestic legal developments spurred by international environmental law including consideration of three key issues for New Zealand and the globe: sustainable development, biodiversity and climate change.

Table 27.2 Key international environmental treaties and New Zealand national legislation[161]

Relevant international treaties	Legislation[162]
Vienna Convention for the Protection of the Ozone Layer	Ozone Layer Protection Act 1996
Convention on Biological Diversity; Convention on the Conservation of Migratory Species of Wild Animals; Kyoto Protocol; UN Framework Convention on Climate Change; UN Convention on the Law of the Sea	Resource Management Act 1991[163]
International Convention for the Prevention of Pollution from Ships; Convention on the Prevention of Marine Pollution by Dumping of Wastes and Other Matter	Maritime Transport Act 1994[164]
Convention on Biological Diversity	Biosecurity Act 1993
Convention on Biological Diversity	Hazardous Substances and New Organisms Act 1996
Convention on the Conservation of Migratory Species of Wild Animals	Wildlife Act 1953
Convention on the Conservation of Migratory Species of Wild Animals; International Convention for the Regulation of Whaling and the Protocol to the International Convention for the Regulation of Whaling	Marine Reserves Act 1971;[165] Marine Mammals Protection Act 1978

160 Boer et al., op. cit., p. 271.
161 This table is based on information from Taylor, op. cit. For a full list of treaties see *MEAs in Force.* Online. Available HTTP: <http://www.mfe.govt.nz/laws/meas/meas-in-force.html> (accessed 4 November 2011).
162 The legislation listed has only partial responsibility in some instances and may be supplemented by national policies and strategies, such as under the *Resource Management Act 1991* (NZ). See Taylor, op. cit.
163 The RMA also has responsibilities for, *inter alia*, the International Convention for the Prevention of Pollution from Ships and the Convention on the Prevention of Marine Pollution by Dumping of Wastes and Other Matter. It also regulates hazardous wastes.
164 The *Resource Management (Marine Pollution) Regulations 1998* (NZ) also control New Zealand's obligations under the London Dumping Convention and MARPOL. See Taylor, op. cit., p. 539.
165 A review was initiated in 2000, and a bill introduced in 2002. For further see *Review of the Marine Reserves Act 1971.* Online. Available HTTP: <http://doc.govt.nz/publications/conservation/marine-and-coastal/marine-protected-areas/review-of-the-marine-reserves-act-1971/> (accessed 4 November 2011).

Convention on International Trade in Endangered Species	Trade in Endangered Species Act 1989
Convention on the World Cultural and National Heritage	National Parks Act 1980
Convention on the Conservation of Antarctic Marine Living Resources	Antarctic Marine Living Resources Act 1981
UN Convention on the Law of the Sea	Continental Shelf Act 1964; Territorial Sea, Contiguous Zone, and Exclusive Economic Zone Act 1977
Protocol on Environmental Protection to the Antarctic Treaty (The Madrid Protocol)	Antarctica (Environment Protection) Act 1994
South Pacific Nuclear Free Zone Treaty; Treaty on the Non-Proliferation of Nuclear Weapons	New Zealand Nuclear Free Zone Disarmament and Arms Control Act 1987
Convention for the Prohibition of Fishing with Long Driftnets in the South Pacific	Driftnet Prohibition Act 1991
United Nations Fish Stocks Agreement; United Nations Convention of the Law of the Sea	Fisheries Act 1996; Driftnet Prohibition Act 1991
United Nations Convention on the Law of the Sea	Proposed Exclusive Economic Zone and Continental Shelf (Environmental Effects) Bill
United Nations Framework Convention on Climate Change; Kyoto Protocol	Energy Efficiency and Conservation Act 2000; Climate Change Response Act 2002

UNCED and multi-level regulation under the Resource Management Act 1991

As with Australia, a defining element of New Zealand's response to international environmental law was the development of a raft of environmental legislation and policy following the UNCED. Indeed, the majority of New Zealand's legislation is largely in accordance with the principles of sustainable development and Agenda 21.[166] Not least, elements of ESD underpin the primary piece of environmental legislation in New Zealand, the *Resource Management Act 1991* (RMA), which regulates water and natural resource management activities on land and in the territorial sea out to 12 nautical miles.[167]

Given the centrality of the RMA to New Zealand's domestic environmental law framework, the following discussion zeroes in on this Act to critically evaluate its incorporation of

166 Historical policy documents included the New Zealand Government, *Environment 2010 Strategy*, Wellington: Ministry for the Environment, 1995; New Zealand Government, *Sustainable Development for New Zealand: Programme of Action*, Wellington: Department of the Prime Minister and Cabinet, 2003. Key pieces of legislation for achieving ESD are the *Resource Management Act 1991* (NZ), s 5 and *Local Government Act 2002* (NZ), s 3 discussed below. For further discussion on other legislation see P. Taylor and J. Yates, 'Background Paper on Environmental Sustainability in New Zealand: Sustainable Development in General – Institutional and Legislative Frameworks'. Online. Available HTTP: <http://www.pce.parliament.nz/assets/Uploads/Reports/pdf/legal.pdf> (accessed 4 November 2011).
167 *Resource Management Act 1991* (NZ), s 5; Williams, op. cit., p. v.; I. Carlman, 'The Resource Management Act 1991 Through External Eyes', *New Zealand Journal of Environmental Law* 11, 2007, pp. 181–93.

ESD principles, and to highlight some of the key international obligations implemented through this important piece of legislation.

When it was enacted, the RMA was widely hailed as a pioneering piece of international legislation for advancing sustainability.[168] Its emphasis on sustainable management of the biophysical environment, the integration and coordination of actions of multiple government agencies, and the location of most decision-making at the local level (via regional and district councils) were particularly praised.[169] Under the RMA regime, ministers were responsible for preparing various national policy statements and standards,[170] while regional councils were given the primary decision-making responsibilities, including resource consent decision-making (a form of licensing for issues such as discharges and water)[171] and the development of regional plans.[172] At the 'territorial' level of government, councils were charged with implementation measures under district plans.[173]

Despite the initial fanfare at the time of its introduction, more recent scrutiny has questioned whether the RMA makes sustainable development operational.[174] For instance, the Parliamentary Commissioner for the Environment has suggested that, notwithstanding the introduction of the RMA, New Zealand has not addressed sustainable development in a coordinated and meaningful fashion, and that in many respects it may be performing poorly in comparison with other developed countries.[175] A variety of scholars and policy-makers have also pointed to a substantial gap between the aspirations of the RMA and its achievements, identifying a range of specific shortcomings, including imprecision in its central goal of sustainable management.[176] Freeman, for example, argues that while the RMA prioritized sustainability in planning and resource management, it did not seek to promote sustainable development per se, but only the 'narrower notion' of sustainable

168 P. Memon and B. Gleeson, 'Towards a New Planning Paradigm? Reflections on New Zealand's Resource Management Act', *Environment and Planning B: Planning and Design* 22(1), 1995, pp. 109–24.

169 Boer et al., op. cit., p. 279; N. Gunningham, *Innovative Governance and Regulatory Design: Managing Water Resources*, Lincoln: Landcare Research, 2008, p. 22. Online. Available HTTP: <http://www.landcareresearch.co.nz/publications/researchpubs/water_gunningham_LC0708137.pdf> (accessed 4 November 2011).

170 See e.g. *Resource Management Act 1991* (NZ), ss 24, 43, 46.

171 *Resource Management Act 1991* (NZ), s 87, s 88, sch 4.

172 *Resource Management Act 1991* (NZ), ss 63–70. Note that the RMA also requires regional councils to recognize and provide for the relationship of Maori with the environment and to take into account the principles of the Treaty of Waitangi (hereinafter the Treaty). The Treaty sets a framework in relation to resource ownership – both in terms of the treaty itself and in relation to the iwi or hapū's customary authority exercised in an identified area incorporated in the *Resource Management Act 1991* (NZ), ss 6, 8.

173 Carlman, op. cit., p. 195.

174 Ibid.

175 Parliamentary Commissioner for the Environment (PCE), *Creating our Future: Sustainable Development for New Zealand*, Wellington: PCE, 2002, p. 3.

176 R. Harris and H. Atkins, 'Planning Law: The RMA and Related Development; and Local Authority Legislation' in R. Harris (ed.) *Handbook of Environmental Law*, Wellington: Royal Forest and Bird Protection Society of New Zealand, 2004, pp. 56–76; B. Pardy, 'Planning for Serfdom: Resource Management and the Rule of Law', *New Zealand Law Journal*, 1997, pp. 69–72; M. Bellingham, 'Biodiversity and Sustainability: Theory, Framework and the Legislation' in R. Harris (ed.) *Handbook of Environmental Law*, Wellington: Royal Forest and Bird Protection Society of New Zealand, 2004, p. 385; Taylor, op. cit., p. 527; Gunningham, *Innovative Governance*, op. cit., pp. 14–15.

management, which focused on natural and physical resources and offered no guidance on critical sustainability issues such as economic development, social development, justice and equity.[177]

There has accordingly been a contemporary lack of enthusiasm for the RMA's philosophy and a shift in emphasis, particularly with the enactment of the *Local Government Act 2002* (LGA).[178] This Act requires regional and territorial governments to play a broad role in promoting the social, economic, environmental and cultural well-being of their communities, taking a sustainable development approach.[179] The LGA expressly requires councils to achieve sustainable development (as defined by community outcomes) through government, industry and community collaboration, and these can be used in tandem with the provisions for regulating sustainable management under the RMA.[180] Even so, recent assessments of programs implemented in line with the LGA mandate suggest that, unless they are properly supported, there will be distinct limits to the ability of such collaborative approaches to achieve sustainable outcomes.[181]

Beyond the LGA and issues relating to ESD, the RMA framework was also designed to provide various, albeit largely discretionary, opportunities for implementing and incorporating international environmental law obligations into domestic environmental decision-making. Some of the primary avenues are outlined below, before their implementation is critically evaluated.[182]

First, international environmental law can be incorporated via national policy statements under the RMA. Policy statements can be developed by a national government to set objectives and policies on matters of national significance so as to guide RMA decisions.[183] In considering whether it is desirable to prepare a national policy statement, the minister can have regard to, *inter alia*, New Zealand's interests and obligations in maintaining or enhancing aspects of the national or global environment.[184] A related process is the compulsory *National Coastal Policy Statement 2010*, which sets objectives and policies about the implementation of New Zealand's international obligations affecting the coastal environment, including biodiversity, biosecurity and impacts of climate change.[185]

Akin to national policy statements, a second means for incorporating international law under the RMA are national standards, which relate to issues such as air quality and drinking water.[186] These standards can incorporate requirements, or recommended practices of international or national organizations.[187]

177 C. Freeman, 'Sustainable Development from Rhetoric to Practice? A New Zealand Perspective', *International Planning Studies* 9, 2004, 307, p. 311.
178 Gunningham, *Innovative Governance*, op. cit.
179 *Local Government Act 2002* (NZ), s 3.
180 *Local Government Act 2002* (NZ), ss 10, 14, 76–81, 91–2. K. Palmer, 'Local Government Law and Resource Management', *NZ Law Review*, 2004, pp. 751, 752–6. B. Jenkins, *Canterbury Strategic Water Study: Briefing Document to Canterbury Mayoral Forum*, Christchurch: ECan, 2007, p. 2.
181 C. Holley and N. Gunningham, 'Natural Resources, New Governance and Legal Regulation: When Does Collaboration Work?', *New Zealand Universities Law Review* 24, 2011, pp. 309–27.
182 Taylor, op. cit., pp. 529–30. See also *Resource Management Act 1991* (NZ), s 360(2B).
183 *Resource Management Act 1991* (NZ), ss 45–55; Bellingham, op. cit., pp. 387–8.
184 *Resource Management Act 1991* (NZ) s 45(2)(b).
185 *Resource Management Act 1991* (NZ), s 58(f). *New Zealand Coastal Policy Statement 2010 Factsheet*, Wellington: Department of Conservation, 2011.
186 *Resource Management Act 1991* (NZ) ss 43, 44.
187 *Resource Management Act 1991* (NZ) schedule 1AA (1).

In addition to national standards, the RMA empowers the minister to 'call in' resource consent applications of national significance.[188] In determining whether a matter is of national significance the minister can consider whether the proposal affects, is likely to affect or is relevant to New Zealand's international obligations to the global environment.[189]

Beyond national-level policy and decisions, a fourth and final avenue for incorporating international environmental law into domestic decision-making is via the resource consent application process. In making a decision on an application (e.g. to take water from a stream), the consent authority (e.g. a regional council) is to have regard, *inter alia* to any other matter considered relevant and reasonably necessary to determine the application. This can include treaties, to the extent that it informs the decision-maker about the environmental context.[190]

Despite these various means for integrating and incorporating international obligations into New Zealand's domestic environmental law, there have been a number of shortfalls in the implementation of the RMA that have constrained these opportunities. In particular, the importance of national standards has been understated in the RMA, with concerns expressed that the 'central government has abrogated its responsibility' to provide national guidance and policy direction.[191]

Indeed, the absence of national direction over the last decade, particularly on key international obligations regarding biodiversity, climate change and the marine environment, has resulted in attempts to supplement the RMA and other legislation with 'strategies'.[192] These strategies included the New Zealand Biodiversity Strategy[193] and Climate Strategy,[194] which set out principles to guide both local authorities in the development of their district and regional plans, and central government in developing national polices. Nevertheless, in the absence of formal RMA statutory documents like national policy statements and standards, it has generally proven difficult for local decision-makers to draw effectively upon and implement international commitments and developments.[195]

Fortunately, in very recent times the New Zealand national government has reinvigorated its RMA policies.[196] The government has committed to reviewing the

---

188 *Resource Management Act 1991* (NZ) s 142.
189 *Resource Management Act 1991* (NZ) s 142(3)(a)(iv).
190 Taylor, op. cit., p. 530; *Resource Management Act 1991* (NZ) s 104(1).
191 K. Bosselmann and D. Grinlinton (eds) *Environmental Law for a Sustainable Society*. Auckland: New Zealand Centre for Environmental Law, 2002, p. 37; Gunningham, *Innovative Governance*, op. cit.; Carlman, op. cit., p. 201.
192 Taylor, op. cit., p. 529.
193 This set four goals: to involve communities and individuals in biodiversity conservation, to protect Māori interests, to maintain and restore natural ecosystems and to maintain the genetic resources of introduced species. The Strategy applied to terrestrial and marine environments. See Bellingham, op. cit., pp. 387–8; A.G.P. Midence, 'Protected Areas Strategy: An Overview of New Zealand and Guatemala', *New Zealand Journal of Environmental Law* 9, 2005, p. 91; R. Bess, 'Maintaining a Balance between Resource Utilisation and Protection of the Marine Environment in New Zealand', *Marine Policy* 34, 2010, 690, p. 694.
194 This included a focus on net carbon dioxide emissions, forest planting, energy efficiency and renewable energy and the role of local government and the development of a comprehensive long-term response to climate change. See Boer et al., op. cit., p. 279.
195 Taylor and Yates, op. cit., p. 11.
196 In addition to those discussed above, see also the National Policy Statement on Electricity Transmission and ongoing consideration being given to National Policy Statement on Urban Design. Online. Available HTTP: <http://www.mfe.govt.nz/rma/central/nps/index.html> (accessed 4 November 2011).

RMA,[197] and has released new national policy statements for renewable electricity generation, freshwater and a proposed indigenous biodiversity policy statement. Each has an important role for the future integration of international law into New Zealand's domestic framework.

For instance, the National Policy Statement on Freshwater[198] aims to contribute to the management of biodiversity (including threatened and at risk species) and protecting the significant values of wetlands from drainage and/or contamination. It does so by setting a consistent, nationwide regulatory framework for establishing water quality and quantity limits to govern the allocation and use of freshwater.[199] Local authorities in turn are required to relevantly amend regional policy statements and plans to give effect to the statement.[200]

The statement on freshwater is partly complemented by the proposed National Policy Statement on Indigenous Biodiversity.[201] This statement will contribute to implementing the CBD by providing for the protection of the habitat of threatened and at risk species (including in rivers and lakes). It will do so by listing criteria for identifying areas of indigenous vegetation and habitats of indigenous animals that have been recognized as being rare and/or threatened at a national level.[202] Under this statement, district and regional plans will be required to identify these areas of significant biodiversity and manage the effects of activities through district and regional plans and resource consent decisions (or be satisfied that effects are managed by other methods) to ensure there is no net loss of significant indigenous biodiversity.[203]

While the proposed policy and the existing Biodiversity Strategy will ensure that the domestic implementation of the CBD[204] is primarily through the resource consent process, it is important to note that there are a number of other regulatory frameworks that contribute to biodiversity protection in New Zealand. These include the *Biosecurity Act 1993* (NZ)[205] and

---

197 The first phase involved reducing the cost and time frame for the resource consent process and improving the regional planning process: see *Resource Management (Simplifying and Streamlining) Amendment Act 2009* (NZ). The more complex second phase of the review aims to have central government provide better direction for regional councils and improved alignment of the RMA with existing legislation. See Bess, op. cit., p. 696.

198 The New Zealand Coastal Policy Statement 2010 also contains policies in relation to water quality in the coastal environment and is to be implemented in coordination with the national policy statement on freshwater. *National Policy Statement on Freshwater Management*, gazetted 12 May 2011, p. 4. Note also that the Land and Water forum continue to work on related policy issues, See *Freshwater Reform: Fresh Start for Fresh Water*. Online. Available HTTP: <http://www.mfe.govt.nz/issues/water/freshwater/fresh-start-for-fresh-water/index.html> (accessed 4 November 2011).

199 *National Policy Statement on Freshwater Management*, gazetted 12 May 2011, p. 6.

200 *National Policy Statement on Freshwater Management*, gazetted 12 May 2011, pp. 7, 9. *National Policy Statement (NPS) for Freshwater Management 2011*. Online. Available HTTP: <http://www.mfe.govt.nz/rma/central/nps/freshwater-management.html> (accessed 4 November 2011).

201 *Proposed National Policy Statement on Indigenous Biodiversity*. Online. Available HTTP: <http://www.mfe.govt.nz/publications/biodiversity/indigenous-biodiversity/index.html> (accessed 4 November 2011).

202 *Proposed National Policy Statement on Indigenous Biodiversity*, 2011, pp. 1–2

203 Ibid, p. 6.

204 Ibid, p. 1–2.

205 This Act is currently under review as of 2010. Further see *Amendments to the Biosecurity Act 1993*. Online. Available HTTP: <http://www.biosecurity.govt.nz/biosec/pol/biosecurity-act-review> (accessed 4 November 2011). See also *Hazardous Substances and New Organisms Act 1996*.

a network of protected areas under the *Conservation Act 1987* (NZ), *National Parks Act 1980* (NZ), *Reserves Act 1977* (NZ) and *Marine Reserves Act 1971* (NZ).[206]

Beyond biodiversity obligations, the National Policy Statement on Renewable Energy Generation also provides an important response under the RMA to the risks of climate change.[207] Specifically, it supports New Zealand's renewable electricity target of 90 per cent of electricity from renewable sources by 2025, by giving planning and direction to resource consent decision-makers and local authorities on the benefits and need for provision of renewable electricity generation (which can reduce GHG caused by the production and use of energy).[208]

Even with this new policy statement, the issue of climate change and New Zealand's obligations under the UNFCCC and Kyoto Protocol remains a complex issue for resource consent decision-making under the RMA.[209] This process, in addition to New Zealand's emerging climate change regime, is explored further below.

Climate change: RMA and New Zealand's emissions trading scheme

The relevance of international climate change obligations under the RMA consent process has received considerable administrative and judicial consideration.[210] One of the first examinations of climate change issues was administrative in nature and arose in 1993, following a proposal to build a 400-megawatt combined cycle power station (with an estimated 1.5 million tonnes per annum of carbon dioxide emissions).[211] The proposal was 'called in' by the Minister under the RMA and subject to a Board of Inquiry on the grounds that it would have a likely effect on New Zealand's ability to meet its obligations under the UNFCCC.[212] In ultimately approving the air discharge permit the Minister considered whether the application would affect New Zealand's international commitments, and sought to ensure actions were taken to mitigate the effects on any increase in carbon dioxide emissions.[213] Since this time, numerous decisions relating to applications for expansion of power stations and discharge permits have raised Kyoto Protocol issues.[214] However, there remained a lack of clarity as to the relevance of climate change impacts as a consideration under the RMA for consent authorities.[215]

206 See Midence, op. cit., p. 106.

207 *National Policy Statement for Renewable Electricity Generation 2011*, gazetted 14 April 2011, p. 3.

208 It covers all renewable electricity generation types, hydro, wind, geothermal, solar, biomass, and marine. *National Policy Statement for Renewable Electricity Generation 2011*, gazetted 14 April 2011, pp. 3–4.

209 B. Richardson, 'Kyoto Protocol to the United Nations Framework Convention on Climate Change', *New Zealand Journal of Environmental Law* 2(2), 1998, pp. 249–62.

210 K. Bosselmann, J. Fuller, and J. Salinger (eds) *Climate Change in New Zealand: Scientific and Legal Assessments*, Auckland: New Zealand Centre for Environmental Law, 2002; Kerr, op. cit., pp. 87–93.

211 Boer et al., op. cit., p. 281.

212 Taylor, op. cit., p. 533; Boer et al., op. cit., p. 281.

213 Boer et al., op. cit., p. 281–2.

214 Taylor, op. cit., pp. 530, 533.

215 See *Environmental Defence Society (Inc) v Auckland Regional Council* [2002] NZRMA 492; E. Steane and T. Weeks, 'Climate Change and the RMA: Implications of *Greenpeace New Zealand Inc v Genesis Power Ltd*', *Resource Management Journal*, 2009, 1, p. 5.

A suite of energy and climate change-focused RMA reforms followed in 2004,[216] and judicial attention quickly came to focus on the newly inserted section 104E.[217] This section prohibited consent authorities from considering the effect of GHG on climate change in discharge and coastal permit applications, 'except to the extent that the use and development of renewable energy enables a reduction in the discharge into air of greenhouse gases'.[218] Following a number of earlier decisions interpreting section 104E, the majority of the Supreme Court handed down a decision in the so-called *Genesis* case that found this exception applies only to applications that involve the use of renewable sources of energy production.[219] Despite settling the interpretation of section 104E, there are areas where the role of the RMA in addressing climate change continues to remain unsettled, not least whether indirect emissions (e.g. end use of fuels exported oversees) fall under the remit of the RMA.[220]

Beyond the contested role of the RMA in governing climate change, New Zealand's response to the UNFCCC and Kyoto Protocol historically involved a voluntary approach, principally though its Climate Strategy. However, New Zealand has gradually developed a legislative framework. Pursuant to the Kyoto Protocol, New Zealand has an obligation to reduce its GHG levels back to 1990 levels by 2012 or else pay for any excess.[221] After a series of Climate Change Policy Options statements, the *Climate Change Response Act 2002* was passed. A key feature of the Act included gross emissions being 'netted out' against absorption sinks and a least-cost approach by using sinks and coordinated domestic and global trading regimes.[222]

More recently, New Zealand has developed the New Zealand Emissions Trading Scheme (NZETS), established by the *Climate Change Response (Emissions Trading) Amendment Act 2008*.[223] This framework puts a price on emissions and requires certain participants to account

---

216 This included the insertion of new matters into s 7 of the RMA, which provide that a consent authority is required to have particular regard to (i) the effects of climate change; and (ii) the benefits to be derived from the use and development of renewable energy. Ibid. *Resource Management (Energy and Climate Change) Amendment Act 2004* (NZ). B. Barton, 'Renewable Energy in New Zealand', *Journal of Energy and Natural Resources Law* 23, 2005, 141, pp. 150–1.

217 *Resource Management Act 1991* (NZ) ss 7, 104E.

218 *Resource Management Act 1991* (NZ) ss 7, 104E.

219 As opposed to having regard to the effects on climate change of discharges into the air of GHGs to the extent that such effects may be compared against the effects of an equivalent renewable energy proposal, which would reduce GHG discharges. See *Greenpeace New Zealand v Northland Regional Council* [2007] NZRMA 87; *Greenpeace New Zealand Inc v Genesis Power Ltd* SC 94/2007 [2008] NZSC 112. See also G. Thatcher, Supreme Court Registrar, *Media Release, Greenpeace New Zealand Inc v Genesis Power Ltd SC 94/2007* [2008] NZSC 112, Supreme Court of NZ, 19 December 2008; Steane and Weeks, op. cit., p. 2.

220 Note also that there are a variety of resource consent applications that may not trigger s 104E but that climate change considerations may still be relevant. For further see Steane and Weeks, op. cit., pp. 4–5.

221 D. Nolan and B. Matheson, 'New Zealand: The International Comparative Legal Guide to Environment and Climate Change Law', *Global Legal Group*, 2011, p. 289.

222 Taylor, op. cit., p. 531.

223 T. Moyes, 'Greenhouse Gas Emissions Trading in New Zealand: Trailblazing Comprehensive Cap and Trade', *Ecology Law Quarterly* 35, 2008, p. 911. L. Te Aho, 'Contemporary Issues in Maori Law and Society: The Tangled Web of Treaty Settlements Emissions Trading, Central North Island Forests, and the Waikato River', *Waikato Law Review* 16, 2008, p. 229; Nolan and Matheson, op. cit., p. 284.

for the emissions they produce by purchasing and surrendering emission units.[224] Units are purchased from the government, or from other participants who have units to trade. This includes forestry emissions,[225] which made New Zealand one of the first countries in the world to have covered this area (as well as agriculture) in their domestic trading regime.[226] Notably, the NZETS is still an emerging market, and precisely how it will play out is a highly complex matter, turning on numerous factors, both internal and external to New Zealand.[227] In particular, a review of the NZETS, undertaken in 2011, is likely to affect policy approaches and the market in the future.[228]

A final noteworthy development regarding climate change in New Zealand has been the recent progress on legislation to govern marine energy generation and carbon capture developments, as well as other potential environmental risks like petroleum exploration and seabed mining, in New Zealand's Exclusive Economic Zone (EEZ).[229] This represents an important development both domestically and internationally because historically New Zealand has had no means to assess and regulate the environmental effects of many activities beyond 12 nautical miles off its coast.

Certainty, within those 12 miles, New Zealand has had relative success implementing international agreements relevant to the marine environment,[230] including fisheries management via a quota management system and tradable quotas.[231] Although often disputed by green NGOs, New Zealand is an often-cited world example of how fish stocks can be sustainably managed.[232] Nevertheless, beyond 12 nautical miles significant regulatory gaps had persisted and the proposed *Exclusive Economic Zone and Continental Shelf (Environmental Effects) Bill*[233] seeks to fill these gaps by identifying activity categories that will be regulated

224 *Climate Change Response Act 2002* (NZ), ss 54, 63.
225 *Climate Change Response Act 2002* (NZ), ss 68, 70–86F, Part 5.
226 P. Lough and A. Cameron, 'Forestry in the New Zealand Emissions Trading Scheme: Design and Prospects for Success', *Carbon Climate Law Review* 3, 2008, pp. 281, 282; J. Lennox and R. van Nieuwkoop, 'Output-based Allocations and Revenue Recycling: Implications for the New Zealand Emissions Trading Scheme', *Energy Policy* 38(12), 2010, pp. 7861–72; A. Daigneault, S. Greenhalgh and O. Samarasinghe, 'Estimated Impacts of New Zealand Agriculture Climate Policy: A Tale of Two Catchments', paper presented at New Zealand Agricultural and Resource Economics Society, 2011 Conference, Nelson, August 2011.
227 S. Perdan and A. Azapagic, 'Carbon Trading: Current Schemes and Future Developments', *Energy Policy* 39, 2011, 6040, p. 6046; Moyes, op. cit., p. 965.
228 Emissions Trading Scheme Review Panel, *Doing New Zealand's Fair Share – Emissions Trading Scheme Review 2011: Final Report*, Wellington: Ministry for the Environment, 2011, p. 17; Nolan and Matheson, op. cit.
229 Bess, op. cit., p. 695.
230 Taylor op. cit., pp. 537–40. Parliamentary Commissioner for the Environment, *Setting the Course for a Sustainable Future: the Management of New Zealand's Marine Environment*, Wellington: Parliamentary Commissioner for the Environment, 1999.
231 *Ministry of Fisheries v Yoshimura and Urata* (Unreported, District Court, Dunedin, O'Driscoll DCJ, 17 January 2005); Judge T.J. Broadmore, 'International Law And National Law Enforcement – A Regional Example. Sentencing for Fisheries Offending in the New Zealand District Court', *Australia and New Zealand Maritime Law Journal* 24, 2010, p. 1. This has included a major commercial fisheries settlement made with all Māori in recognition of the loss of their fishing rights under the *Treaty of Waitangi*. For further information see Havemann op. cit., pp. 278–9.
232 Broadmore, op. cit., p. 11.
233 Introduced to Parliament on 24 August 2011.

through rules that define 'effect thresholds' levels of harm and apply a consent application process.[234]

Conclusion

In many respects Australia and New Zealand have been leaders in implementing international environmental law.[235] From the above it is clear that international environmental law has had a significant influence on domestic regimes in both nations. It has been at the heart of legislative and policy reforms of both countries on the environment, spurring action on ESD, biodiversity, natural heritage and climate change.

Even so, there are weaknesses, as well as key issues on which more work could be done to ensure consistency with and more effective implementation of international environmental law obligations. One common problem for both nations has been ineffective legal cooperation and integration between different levels of government (federal and state in Australia and central and local in New Zealand) and the significant impediments this imposes on implementing international law obligations in both nations. Indeed, despite recent reforms designed to improve coordination, it is clear that weak systems of accreditation under the EPBC Act in Australia, and the limited role of national policy statements and standards under the RMA in New Zealand, have undermined efforts to achieve a whole of government response to international environmental issues.

The record of both countries on climate change has also been relatively slow, particularly in Australia. National responses to climate change, however, are now occurring, and the review of New Zealand's emissions trading scheme and Australia's new Clean Energy reform package will be important developments to examine in the near future. Both nations have also made concerted efforts to respond to the CBD; however, existing weaknesses in the strategies and listing process in Australia, and policy gaps in New Zealand, have led to recent reforms in this area. As both countries continue to embark on these and other domestic environmental law reforms, there appears to be little doubt that international legal measures to protect the environment will continue to have an important influence on environmental law in both nations.[236]

---

234 Interim measures are currently in place and the legislation will not come into effect until a complete set of regulations is developed (to establish the legislation's management system of rules and standards) in 2012. See Bess, op. cit., p. 695; *Exclusive Economic Zone and Continental Shelf (Environmental Effects) Bill 2011*, Digest No. 1923, 2011; *Protecting New Zealand's Exclusive Economic Zone*. Online. Available HTTP: <http://www.mfe.govt.nz/issues/oceans/current-work/index.html> (accessed 4 November 2011).
235 See Boer et al., op. cit., p. 283.
236 Boer et al., op. cit., p. 282.

28

Environmental law in Africa

Michael Kidd

The African continent is a region of the world where the biological and cultural diversity is matched by a varied array of approaches taken to environmental governance. This chapter examines African membership of key international environmental treaties, as well as trends in national approaches to address environmental issues, for example through commitments given to environmental protection in national constitutions. It also explores and analyses the particular challenges to implementation in this region of the world, including civil unrest and poaching, and considers the initiatives that have been taken and those that remain for the future.

Introduction

Africa is the continent with the highest number of states: 54.[1] It is often categorised into distinctive regions. North Africa comprises states that are often regarded as being as much Arab as African, with the states in this region all belonging to the Arab League, Arabic and French being the dominant languages. This part of the continent is also associated with the Sahara Desert. The rest of the continent is often referred to as sub-Saharan Africa, and is further divided into West Africa, Central Africa, East Africa and Southern Africa. West Africa contains a combination of former British and French colonies and consequently one finds a mix of civil law and common law in the region. East Africa is primarily Anglophone and common law, being largely former British colonies. Central Africa was primarily colonised by Belgium and France, and has civil law systems. Southern Africa was mainly colonised by Britain and is characterised by a predominance of common law systems. The continent can be (roughly) divided into Francophone Africa with civil law systems and Anglophone Africa with common law systems, with some exceptions such as former Portuguese colonies such as Angola and Mozambique.

Africa is a continent simultaneously blessed with enormous biodiversity and unspoilt wilderness, yet also facing environmental problems that resonate on the world stage. At the time of writing, millions of Somali people are in need of humanitarian assistance due to

---

1 This includes South Sudan, which became independent on 9 July 2011.

famine.[2] Internationally, climate change is probably the environmental problem with the highest profile currently, and if climate change is not kept within acceptable levels, Africa will be one of the worst-affected areas. Yet there are other severe environmental problems in Africa, such as biodiversity loss, desertification, deforestation and water shortages. Many of these problems cannot be separated from human crises, particularly poverty. According to the 2010 United Nations Human Development Index (HDI), 35 of the 54 African countries are ranked as countries with low human development.[3] Of the 20 bottom HDI countries, only one is not African. Similarly, of the 48 United Nations-recognised 'least developed countries', 33 are in Africa.[4] It is not surprising, then, that the New Partnership for Africa's Development (NEPAD) has linked two defining features of the region – poverty and the environment – in its Environmental Action Plan.[5]

This factual context indicates clearly that international environmental law has a critical role to play in Africa. This chapter considers the role of international environmental law on the continent and its effects within individual nations. It is evident in overview that Africa is a significant participant in international environmental law and there is considerable environmental law on paper in African domestic legal systems. Yet the implementation of environmental law is often weak, with the result that environmental degradation is continuing apace.

The chapter commences by considering African participation in multilateral environmental agreements (MEAs). This is followed by considering the role played by human rights in pursuit of a healthy environment in Africa. The next section considers international environmental legal instruments with a particularly African flavour. The remainder of the chapter considers several themes relating to environmental conservation and sustainable development, within the context of the operation of international environmental law in Africa. These themes are not intended to cover all environmental issues. They are, of necessity, somewhat selective but sufficiently representative of regional issues that it is possible to paint a general picture of international environmental law in Africa.

Membership of multilateral environmental agreements by African states

An examination of participation by African states in several of the most prominent MEAs reveals that this is substantial. Table 28.1 below shows that, of the selected MEAs, participation by African states is in the magnitude of approximately 85 per cent or higher.[6]

---

2 See e.g. Food and Agriculture Organization of the United Nations (FAO), 'Famine spreads further in Somalia'. Online. Available HTTP: <http://www.fao.org/news/story/en/item/89101/icode/> (accessed 30 November 2011).
3 United Nations Development Programme, (2011) *Human Development Index – 2011 Rankings*. Online. Available HTTP: <http://hdr.undp.org/en/statistics/> (accessed 30 November 2011). There are at least two countries that are not ranked (Eritrea and Somalia) that would probably also be ranked as 'low' if all information were available.
4 United Nations Office of the High Representative for the Least Developed Countries, Landlocked Developing Countries and the Small Island Developing States (UN-OHRLLS), 'List of Least Developed Countries'. Online. Available HTTP: <http://www.unohrlls.org/en/ldc/25/> (accessed 30 November 2011).
5 United Nations Environment Programme (UNEP), (2003) *Action Plan of the Environment Initiative of the New Partnership for Africa's Development*. Online. Available HTTP: <http://www.uneca.org/unregionalconsultations/documents/NEPAD%20Action%20Plan%20-%20environment.pdf> (accessed 30 November 2011).
6 In respect of those that are in force.

Table 28.1 Participation by African states in prominent MEAs

Name of convention	Number of African states parties	African states not parties[7]
Basel Convention on Transboundary Movement of Hazardous Waste	49	Angola, Sao Tome and Principe, Sierra Leone, Zimbabwe.
Bonn Convention on Migratory Species	42	Botswana, Central African Republic, Comoros, Lesotho, Malawi, Namibia, Sierra Leone, Sudan, Swaziland, Zambia, Zimbabwe.
Convention on Biological Diversity (CBD)	53	
Convention on International Trade in Endangered Species (CITES)	52	Angola.
International Maritime Organisation[8]	44	Non-maritime states.[9]
Ramsar Convention on Wetlands	47	Angola, Eritrea, Ethiopia, Somalia, Swaziland, Zimbabwe.
Rotterdam Convention on Prior Informed Consent	45	Algeria, Central African Republic, Comoros, Egypt, Sao Tome and Principe, Sierra Leone, Zimbabwe.
Stockholm Convention on Persistent Organic Pollutants	51	Equatorial Guinea, Zimbabwe.
United Nations Convention on the Law of the Sea (UNCLOS)	45	Burundi, Central African Republic, Eritrea, Ethiopia, Libya, Niger, Rwanda, Swaziland.
United Nations Convention on the Non-navigational Uses of International Watercourses[10]	8	All except Burkina Faso, Guinea-Bissau, Libya, Morocco, Namibia, Nigeria, South Africa and Tunisia.
United Nations Convention to Combat Desertification (UNCCD)	52	Libya.
United Nations Framework Convention on Climate Change (UNFCCC)	49	Libya, Seychelles, Swaziland, Tunisia.
Vienna Convention for the Protection of the Ozone Layer and Montreal Protocol	53	
World Heritage Convention	52	Somalia.

While it is beyond the scope of this chapter to consider in detail the extent to which international environmental law is incorporated in the domestic law of African countries, general trends are apparent. First, however, the extent to which African countries recognise that humans have a right to a healthy environment sets an overarching framework within which

7 South Sudan is a member of none of these conventions as it is too new to have become a party.
8 This entails membership of the MARPOL Convention and the London Convention.
9 All African maritime states are members, as well as some non-maritime states (e.g. Uganda, Zimbabwe).
10 Not yet in force.

the individual themes of environmental conservation, and the laws and institutions addressing them, can be evaluated.

Environmental rights in Africa

Environmental rights, by which is meant rights of humans to an environment that is healthy, are generally well entrenched in Africa. At the continental level, the African Charter on Human and Peoples' Rights of 1981[11] was the first international human rights instrument to include an 'environmental right'.[12] The Charter provides in Article 24 that 'All peoples shall have the right to a general satisfactory environment favourable to their development'. In the *Ogoniland* decision of the African Commission on Human and Peoples' Rights,[13] Article 24 (among other rights) took centre stage. The case concerned complaints that oil production activities had caused environmental degradation and adverse health effects on the Ogoni people. In finding that the government of Nigeria had infringed both Article 24 as well as several other rights in the Charter (including Article 16, which protects the right to health), the Commission observed that Article 24 'requires the State to take reasonable and other measures to prevent pollution and ecological degradation, to promote conservation, and to secure an ecologically sustainable development and use of natural resources'.[14] Moreover, the Commission added:

> Government compliance with the spirit of Articles 16 and 24 of the African Charter must also include ordering or at least permitting independent scientific monitoring of threatened environments, requiring and publicising environmental and social impact studies prior to any major industrial development, undertaking appropriate monitoring and providing information to those communities exposed to hazardous materials and activities and providing meaningful opportunities for individuals to be heard and to participate in the development decisions affecting their communities.[15]

A further important dictum of the Commission was to the effect that it was clear that 'collective rights, environmental rights, and economic and social rights are essential elements of human rights in Africa'.[16] Shelton describes the *Ogoniland* case as a 'landmark', not only because it is the first case decided by an international human rights body that involved the environmental right, but also because of the 'Commission's articulation of the duties of governments in Africa to monitor and control the activities of multinational corporations'.[17]

---

11 *African Charter on Human and Peoples' Rights*, 27 June 1981, 1520 UNTS 217, 21 ILM 59 (entered into force 21 October 1986. Convention text online. Available HHTP: <http://www.africa-union.org/official_documents/treaties_%20conventions_%20protocols/banjul%20charter.pdf> (accessed 30 November 2011).

12 Dinah Shelton, 'Decision regarding Communication 155/96 (Social and Economic Rights Action Center/Center for Economic and Social Rights v Nigeria)', *American Journal of International Law* 96, 2002, p. 941.

13 Decision regarding Communication 155/96 (*Social and Economic Rights Action Center/Center for Economic and Social Rights v Nigeria*), Case No. ACHPR/COMM/A044/1 (2002). Online. Available HTTP: <http://www.cesr.org/downloads/AfricanCommissionDecision.pdf> (accessed 30 November 2011). For discussion, see Shelton, op. cit., and Kaniye SA Ebuku, 'The right to a satisfactory environment and the African Commission', *African Human Rights Law Journal* 3, 2003, 149.

14 Para. 52.

15 Para. 53.

16 Para. 68.

17 Shelton, op. cit., p. 941.

The decision also highlights that environmental law subject to Article 24 is not merely a reactive 'command and control' type of mechanism, but that it involves proactive involvement in development planning.

At the national level, Bruch et al. observed in 2000 that:

> African nations figure prominently among nations worldwide in incorporating environmental provisions into their constitutions, if not necessarily in their application. In fact, at least 32 countries in Africa (approximately two-thirds) have some constitutional provisions ensuring the right to a healthy environment.[18]

Since 2000, several Constitutions in Africa have been amended or replaced, and now at least 35 African countries have constitutional environmental rights, whether fundamental justiciable rights (such as in Mali and South Africa) or directive principles of state policy (as in Nigeria and Swaziland). Of those African countries not constitutionally recognising environmental rights, most do protect the right to life, which can be (and has been) interpreted to incorporate the right to a healthy environment.[19]

Although constitutional provisions are common, it was observed in 2000 that there was a 'marked dearth of cases interpreting and applying them'.[20] Eleven years later, there are some (but not many) decisions of domestic courts that address environmental rights. In Nigeria, in *Gani Fawehinmi v Abacha*,[21] the Court of Appeal was faced with the question of whether the rights in the African Charter on Human and People's Rights (in particular the environmental right in Article 24) were justiciable in a Nigerian Court. The Charter had been enacted into Nigerian national law, and the Court held that it was superior to a domestic decree. This was important because the environmental provision in section 20 of the Nigerian Constitution of 1989 is not justiciable.[22]

It has been suggested that Tanzania appears to be the first African nation where courts have upheld environmental protection within the ambit of the right to life,[23] in *Joseph D Kessy and others v The City Council of Dar es Salaam*.[24] A similar decision was reached in Kenya in *Waweru v Republic*.[25] In South Africa, the Constitutional Court has invoked the environmental right in section 24 of the Constitution of the Republic of South Africa, 1996 in two cases. In both *Fuel Retailers Association of Southern Africa v Director-General: Environmental Management, Department of Agriculture, Conservation and Environment, Mpumalanga Province*,[26]

---

18 C. Bruch, W. Coker and C. Van Arsdale, 'Breathing life into fundamental principles: Implementing Constitutional environmental protections in Africa', *South African Journal of Environmental Law and Policy* 7(21), 2000, p. 34.

19 See Bruch et al., op. cit., p. 33.

20 Ibid., p. 39.

21 (1996) 9 NWLR part 475, p. 710. Online. Available HTTP: <http://www.nigeria-law.org/General%20Sanni%20Abacha%20&%20Ors%20%20V%20%20Chief%20Gani%20Fawehinmi.htm> (accessed 30 November 2011).

22 L. Atsegbua, 'Environmental rights, pipeline vandalisation and conflict resolution in Nigeria', *International Energy Law and Taxation Review*, 2001, p. 89.

23 P. Kameri-Mbote and C. Odote, 'Courts as champions of sustainable development: Lessons from East Africa', *Sustainable Development Law and Policy* 10, 2009, p. 34.

24 High Court of Tanzania, Civil Case No. 29 of 1998 (unreported).

25 (2006) 1 KLR 677–700 (HCK) (Kenya).

26 2007 (6) SA 4 (CC).

and *Member of the Executive Council, Department of Agriculture, Conservation and Environment v HTF Developers (Pty) Ltd*[27] the Court has followed the international law relating to sustainable development in reaching decisions that upheld the environmental right in section 24. In the *Fuel Retailers* case, the Court stated that:

> The importance of the protection of the environment cannot be gainsaid. Its protection is vital to the enjoyment of the other rights contained in the Bill of Rights; indeed, it is vital to life itself. It must therefore be protected for the benefit of the present and future generations. The present generation holds the earth in trust for the next generation. This trusteeship position carries with it the responsibility to look after the environment. It is the duty of the Court to ensure that this responsibility is carried out.[28]

It is of some concern, however, that there is so little jurisprudence in African courts dealing with the human right to a healthy environment.

MEAs with a particular African focus

There are several MEAs with a particular focus on Africa. Those that most clearly fall into this category are the United Nations Convention to Combat Desertification in Countries Experiencing Serious Drought and/or Desertification, Particularly in Africa (UNCCD), the Bamako Convention on the Ban of the Import into Africa and the Control of Transboundary Movement and Management of Hazardous Wastes within Africa (Bamako Convention), and the African Convention on the Conservation of Nature and Natural Resources. There are numerous other regional conventions, some of which are mentioned in the consideration of the subject themes below.

The UN Convention to Combat Desertification

The UNCCD had its roots in a severe drought and consequent famine in the Sahel area of West Africa in the early 1970s, which led to the establishment of the UN Conference on Desertification in 1977. In the early 1990s, there was initial resistance to the adoption of a new global treaty on desertification. Since most countries suffering from the threat of desertification are poor countries, developed states were concerned that adoption of a convention would increase pressure on them for more official development assistance.[29] Nevertheless, following a change of position by the USA, the European Union followed and the Convention became a reality.[30] The negotiations at the Earth Summit in Rio de Janeiro in 1992 led to a decision to adopt a convention and the UNCCD was adopted in 1994.[31]

---

27 2008 (2) SA 319 (CC).
28 Para. 102.
29 B. Kjellen, 'The role of the Desertification Convention in the early 21st Century', *Environmental Policy and Law* 40(4), 2010, p. 149.
30 Ibid.
31 See A. Jamal, 'The United Nations Convention to Combat Desertification in those Countries Experiencing Serious Drought and/or Desertification, Particularly in Africa; Implementing Agenda 21', *RECIEL* 6, 1997, p. 1.

As the full name of the UNCCD suggests, desertification has its greatest impact in Africa.[32] There are 16 African least-developed countries that have the majority of their agricultural lands in semi-arid regions which are subject to the threat of desertification.[33] The UNCCD contains regional implementation annexes, and the Annex for Africa is the most detailed and comprehensive. It requires African country parties to prepare National Action Programmes (NAPs), one of the key instruments of the UNCCD.[34] By February 2008, 41 African countries had adopted NAPs.[35] There are also five Sub-regional Action Programmes (for example, the Permanent Inter-State Committee for Drought Control in the Sahel) and a regional action plan being developed. In order to address desertification, these plans have to be implemented. Because desertification does not operate in a vacuum, action plans must be 'effectively linked to poverty reduction and investment strategies'.[36] Much of the potential of the Convention is still to be realised, possibly due in part to funding deficiencies.[37] Funding, therefore, is a central feature of the ten-year strategic plan and framework to enhance the implementation of the Convention.[38] It has also been suggested that the UNCCD could be strengthened by beefing up its enforcement mechanisms,[39] but this might not be feasible as the flexible current wording of the Convention is clearly the outcome of compromise negotiations and the dynamics are not likely to be different in the case of the suggested amendment of the Convention.

The flexible nature of the 'responsibilities' established by the Convention lies at the heart of another perceived problem with the UNCCD, one which at first glance appears to be a positive feature. The emphasis on 'bottom-up' solutions to problems of desertification, argue Tal and Cohen,[40] may serve to address the symptoms of land degradation rather than the underlying causes (such as, for example, erosion from cultivation, overgrazing, deforestation and water mismanagement). The UNCCD requires in Article 5(e) that signatories must 'provide an enabling environment by strengthening, as appropriate, relevant existing legislation and, where they do not exist, enacting new laws and establishing long-term policies and action programmes'. Yet:

> to date there has been no serious effort by UNCCD-affiliated institutions to encourage enactment of strong and proven legal regimes to combat desertification. Relevant legislation that has been adopted is often quite unrelated to the UNCCD per se.[41]

---

32 L.C. Clark, 'A call to restructure existing international environmental law in light of Africa's renaissance: The United Nations Convention to Combat Desertification and the New Partnership for Africa's Development (NEPAD)', *Seattle University Law Review* 27, 2003, pp. 525–6.

33 Secretariat of the UNCCD and the Common Fund for Commodities, (2009) *African Drylands Commodity Atlas.* Online. Available HTTP: <http://www.unccd.int/Lists/SiteDocumentLibrary/Publications/Atlas%20web.pdf> (accessed 15 May 2012).

34 Article 6 of Annex I: Regional Implementation Annex for Africa.

35 UNCCD, 'Action Programmes'. Online. Available HTTP: <http://www.unccd.int/en/regional-access/Pages/regionalprofiles.aspx?region=Africa&ctx=pro> (accessed 15 May 2012).

36 UNCCD, *Fact Sheet: Combating Desertification in Africa.* Online. Available HTTP: <http://www.unccd.int/Lists/SiteDocumentLibrary/Publications/Fact_sheet_11eng.pdf> (accessed 15 May 2012).

37 Kjellen, op. cit., p. 152. See also Clark, op. cit., p. 540.

38 Decision 3/COP 8. ICCD/COP(8)/16/Add.1.

39 Clark, op. cit., p. 556.

40 A. Tal and J.A. Cohen, 'Bringing "top-down" to "bottom-up": A new role for environmental legislation in combating desertification', *Harvard Environmental Law Review* 31, 2007, p. 163.

41 Ibid., p. 169.

There was also apparently inadequate progress in alignment of NAPs to existing environmental policies,[42] a situation that does not appear to have improved. It is important that African countries consider the role that national legislation can play in addressing desertification as well as seriously pursuing the co-ordination of NAPs with other environmental and land-use policies. While it is easy for lack of progress to be blamed on absence of funding, this should not be used as an excuse for inertia.

Kjellen points out that the positioning of the Convention is being made within the general framework of global efforts at tackling climate change and human threats to ecosystems. In setting the UNCCD in its global context, 'relating it to the effects of climate change on land degradation and food security in already vulnerable regions, we realise that it is part of a broader picture, involving security concerns, migration and other realities of our time'.[43] These observations resonate clearly in respect of the 2011 famine in Somalia, which demonstrates the importance of continuing efforts to ensure the effective implementation of the UNCCD in Africa.

The Bamako Convention

Following incidents such as the dumping of toxic waste in Koko, Nigeria, in 1988,[44] developing countries, particularly African countries, acquired a heightened awareness about their vulnerability to dumping of wastes from the developed world and an associated determination to address the problem.[45] Although the Basel Convention[46] had its roots in the problems of dumping of hazardous wastes in developing countries, African countries felt that the Basel Convention did not go far enough in meeting their concerns.[47] In particular, African countries were in favour of a prohibition on the import of hazardous wastes into the continent, feeling that regulated movement under Basel was open to circumvention. Consequently, African countries under the auspices of the Organisation of African Unity (OAU) adopted the Bamako Convention on 30 January 1991. It entered into force on 22 April 1998. As of February 2010, there were 24 ratifications, somewhat short of the 33 countries that had signed the Convention initially.[48]

While the Convention has been hailed as symbolising the 'proclivity of African states to act regionally in preventing the export of hazardous waste to the African continent',[49]

---

42 UNCCD, 'UN Maps New Ways to Mainstream Desertification', 12 May 2005. Online. Available HTTP: <http://archive.unccd.int/publicinfo/pressrel/showpressrel.php?pr=press12_05_05> (accessed 15 May 2012).

43 Ibid.

44 S.G. Ogbodo, 'Environmental protection in Nigeria: Two decades after the Koko incident', *Annual Survey of International and Comparative Law* 15, 2009, p. 1.

45 J.R. Kitt, 'Waste exports to the developing world: A global response', *Georgetown International Environmental Law Review* 7, 1995, p. 500; C.N. Eze, 'The Bamako Convention on the Ban on the Import into Africa and the Control of the Transboundary Movement and Management of Hazardous Wastes within Africa: A milestone in environmental protection?', *African Journal of International and Comparative Law* 15, 2007, p. 214.

46 Examined further by T.G. Puthucherril in Chapter 17 of this volume.

47 Eze, op.cit., p. 214.

48 See list at <http://www.africa-union.org/root/au/documents/treaties/List/Bamako%20Convention. pdf> (accessed 30 November 2011).

49 A. Webster-Main, 'Keeping Africa out of the global backyard: A comparative study of the Basel and Bamako Conventions', *Environs Environmental Law and Policy Journal* 26, 2002, p. 67.

there are signs that the Convention is largely a paper instrument at present. It has been suggested, quite rightly, that the 2006 dumping of hazardous waste in Côte d'Ivoire that killed eight people and led to thousands more requiring medical treatment[50] 'raises some fundamental questions on the effectiveness' of the Bamako Convention.[51] Writing in 2007, Eze states that the Convention's 'effective implementation remains to be seen',[52] an observation reinforced by the lack of any reported activities by either the Bamako Secretariat or the Conference of the Parties. In fact, the African Union is still playing the role of Secretariat for the Convention. Pratt observed in 2011 (albeit relying on the authority of Kitt's 1995 paper) that:

> Bamako countries simply lacked the capacity to effectively implement the provisions and domestically prevent toxic waste colonialism within their borders; as a result, the application of Bamako became quite limited.[53]

Since Bamako does go further than the Basel Convention in protecting African countries from the scourge of unregulated export of toxic waste, it is potentially a very beneficial instrument in the African context. Yet it seems plain that the Bamako Convention is not being implemented properly and much work remains to be done on improving this. Judging by the relative paucity of literature on the current implementation of the Convention, there is clearly a need for further research in this area, with a view to improving the Convention's implementation.

The Revised African Convention on the Conservation of Nature and Natural Resources 2003

In 1968, the original convention of this name (the Algiers Convention) was adopted under the auspices of the OAU. Ratified by 30 African states, it laid an important path for newly independent nations in the sphere of conservation of natural resources. The convention involved African states in the articulation of 'the principles of sustainable development and respect for the environment as a common heritage or public good before they became more commonly acknowledged, even within the UN context'.[54] Due, however, to shortcomings in institutional structure and the lack of compliance and enforcement mechanisms, it became necessary to revise the Convention.[55] The revised convention was adopted in Maputo by the African Union in July 2003 and 'now assumes the status of a framework environmental treaty

50 United Nations News Centre, 'Deadly toxic waste dumping in Côte d'Ivoire clearly a crime – UN environmental agency', 29 September 2006.
51 Eze, op. cit., p. 210.
52 Ibid., p. 228.
53 L.A.W. Pratt, 'Decreasing dirty dumping? A reevaluation of toxic waste colonialism and the global management of transboundary hazardous waste', *Texas Environmental Law Journal* 41, 2011, p. 165.
54 T. Maluwa, 'The OAU/African Union and international law: Mapping new boundaries or revising old terrain?', *American Society of International Law Proceedings* 98, 2004, p. 234.
55 C.O. Okidi, 'Concept, function and structure of environmental law', in C.O. Okidi, P. Kameri-Mbote and M. Apech (eds) *Environmental Governance in Kenya*, Nairobi: East African Educational Publishers, 2008, p. 45; B. Chaytor, 'Editorial', *RECIEL* 6, 1997, p. iii.

for Africa'.[56] As of April 2012[57] there were eight ratifications, seven short of what is required for it to enter into force. As with the Bamako Convention, then, the Algiers-Maputo Convention is another case of potential as yet unfulfilled.

Selected environmental themes

In this section, various subject themes relevant to international environmental law are considered. Through this discussion, the intention is to indicate thematically the role of international environmental law and its implementation in Africa, and consequently its strengths and shortcomings.

Biodiversity generally

According to the United Nations Environment Programme (UNEP):

> Africa is home to some one quarter of the world's 4,700 mammal species, including 79 species of antelope. It also has more than 2,000 species of birds – one fifth of the world's total – and at least 2,000 species of fish, alongside 950 amphibian species. The African mainland harbours between 40,000 and 60,000 plant species and about 100,000 known species of insects, spiders and other arachnids. Eight of the world's 34 biodiversity hotspots are in Africa.[58]

The last fact is particularly pertinent in consideration of biodiversity in Africa: hotspots are simultaneously the richest and most threatened reservoirs of animal and plant life on Earth.[59] All African countries[60] are parties to the Convention on Biological Diversity (CBD) and, in 2010, 49 African countries had national biodiversity strategies and action plans.[61] At the time of writing, 46 countries had submitted their Fourth National Report, as required by the CBD.

This demonstrates, by and large, that there is widespread formal compliance with the CBD by African states parties, but the crucial question is the extent to which the objectives of the CBD are being met in Africa. The *Global Biodiversity Outlook* (GBO3) makes it clear that the underlying causes of biodiversity loss (habitat change, overexploitation, pollution, invasive alien species and climate change) have not been addressed.[62] Despite the presence of biodiversity strategies and action plans, these have not been sufficiently integrated into

---

56 Okidi, op. cit., p. 46.
57 The latest available information provided on the African Union website. Online. Available HTTP: <http://www.au.int/en/sites/default/files/Revised%20-%20Nature%20and%20Natural%20Resources_0.pdf> (accessed 15 May 2012).
58 UNEP (2010) *State of Biodiversity in Africa*, p. 3. Online. Available HTTP: <http://www.unep.org/DEC/PDF/State%20of%20biodiversity%20in%20Africa.pdf> (accessed 30 November 2011).
59 Conservation International, 'Biodiversity Hotspots'. Online. Available HTTP: <http://www.biodiversityhotspots.org/Pages/default.aspx> (accessed 30 November 2011).
60 Other than South Sudan.
61 UNEP, *State of Biodiversity in Africa*, op. cit., p. 2.
62 Secretariat of the Convention on Biological Diversity, *Global Biodiversity Outlook 3*, 2010. Online. Available HTTP: <http://gbo3.cbd.int/> (accessed 30 November 2011).

national policies.[63] Part of the reason for this may be financial and technical limitations in developing countries.[64] The issue of 'mainstreaming' biodiversity planning mirrors a similar problem observed in respect of NAPs for desertification, discussed above. There are some positive developments, however. For example, both the number and extent of protected areas, terrestrial and marine, have been expanded in Africa.[65]

Further aspects relating to conservation and sustainable use of biodiversity will be raised in some of the sections below. As for access and benefit-sharing in Africa, UNEP reports that there has been little progress:

> because of reluctance from user countries to share benefits. In addition, many African Governments lack regulations on bioprospecting, resulting in the unregulated exploitation of their biological and genetic resources. They have recognized that, without a legal framework, it will be difficult to provide controlled and legally secure access to potential users of locally available biological and genetic resources.[66]

It is hoped that the decisions taken at Nagoya, particularly the adoption of the Protocol on Access to Genetic Resources and Fair and Equitable Sharing of Benefits arising from their Utilisation (the Nagoya Protocol), will assist in addressing this.

Ramsar and World Heritage Sites under threat

One of the manners in which biodiversity loss can be retarded is by protection of habitat and one of the main ways in which this can be achieved is through the establishment and effective management of protected areas. Wetlands, ecosystems that are critical for biodiversity, are well recognised in Africa under the auspices of the Convention on Wetlands of International Importance (Ramsar Convention). There are 304 Wetlands of International Importance designated in Africa under the Ramsar Convention – 50 in Algeria alone. Given the social and political unrest that arises from time to time in Africa (more chronically in some places than others), one might expect that several of the African Ramsar sites might be suffering from poor management and subsequent threats to their vitality. The official position, however, is that only eight sites in Africa are on the Montreux Record of wetlands whose ecological character is or has changed, most of which are in countries that are relatively stable (or have been until recently).

Another important internationally recognised 'protected area' is the World Heritage Site under the World Heritage Convention.[67] Sites may be designated as World Heritage Sites either for their cultural or natural attributes (or both), so many of these sites would have a role to play in the conservation of biodiversity. In Africa, 13 'natural' Heritage Sites are on the List of World Heritage in Danger.[68] Common threats to most of these sites are poaching and agricultural expansion.[69] Whereas there was no clear correlation between Ramsar sites under

---

63 M.J. Ortiz, 'Aichi biodiversity targets on direct and indirect drivers of biodiversity loss', *Environmental Law Review* 13, 2011, p. 100.

64 Ibid. See also Secretariat of the CBD, *Global Biodiversity Outlook 3*, op. cit., p. 7.

65 UNEP, *State of Biodiversity in Africa*, op. cit., p. 2.

66 Ibid.

67 For further details of the Convention see Chapter 23 by E. Techera in this volume.

68 List available online. Available HTTP: <http://whc.unesco.org/pg.cfm?cid=86> (accessed 30 November 2011).

69 Details of individual sites can be accessed from the site referred to in the previous footnote.

threat and the political instability of their host areas, this is different in respect of the World Heritage Sites. More than half of the sites are in areas where there is political instability. For example, there is a programme in the Democratic Republic of Congo to address the threat to five of that country's natural sites due largely to the severe political and social instability in the Great Lakes region.[70]

It is probably trite to observe that a protected area (not only a World Heritage Site) on paper is of little value if it is not effectively managed. Such management would entail aspects such as the imposition of land management measures and control of poaching, encroachment by communities carrying out agriculture and grazing, and deforestation. This, however, requires resources (financial and technical) that are often in short supply in many African countries. These deficiencies are obviously exacerbated in cases where political instability makes it difficult, if not impossible, to carry out 'normal' management practices. It is also important that protected areas management in Africa engages with, and accommodates as far as possible, community land-use practices in order to avoid conflict and adverse impact on the protected area. One way in which this can be pursued is to include poverty alleviation aspects in protected area management plans where this is possible.[71]

Forests

Forests are not only an important component of biological diversity in their own right, but are also an important habitat.[72] Africa's forests are important from a global point of view: in 2010, the estimated forest area in Africa accounted for about 17 per cent of global forest area and 23 per cent of the total land area in the region.[73] About a quarter of the world's tropical forests are in Africa. There was a reduction in the rate of net forest loss in the region, from 4.0 million hectares per year in the decade from 1990 to 2000 to 3.4 million hectares per year during the period from 2000 to 2010.[74] This equates to approximately 0.15 per cent of total forest coverage. Deforestation is an important environmental threat in Africa and is subject to international law efforts in various spheres.

In 2007, the seventh meeting of the United Nations Forum on Forests (UNFF) adopted the Non-Legally Binding Instrument on All Types of Forests.[75] In its Multi-Year Programme of Work (2007 to 2015), the implementation of the instrument is identified as the main task. One of the issues likely to affect implementation is the provision of finance to developing countries.[76] It is also pertinent to recognise that the issue of forests, in the absence of achievement of a binding MEA, has been considerably subsumed under climate change initiatives

70 World Heritage Convention Secretariat, 'Rescuing the Congo's natural world heritage'. Online. Available HTTP: <http://whc.unesco.org/en/news/700/> (accessed 30 November 2011).
71 R.C. Gardner, K.D. Connolly and A. Bamba, 'African wetlands of international importance: Assessment of benefits associated with designations under the Ramsar Convention', *Georgetown International Environmental Law Review* 21, 2009, pp. 292–3.
72 See M. Kidd, 'Forest issues in Africa', *International Law-making and Diplomacy Review*, 2005, p. 189.
73 Food and Agriculture Organization, *State of the World's Forests 2011*, 2011, p. 3.
74 Ibid., p. 4.
75 Online. Available HTTP: <http://www.un.org/esa/forests/pdf/session_documents/unff7/UNFF7_NLBI_draft.pdf> (accessed 30 November 2011).
76 K. Kunzmann, 'The Non-Legally Binding Instrument on Sustainable Management of All Types of Forests – Towards a legal regime for sustainable forest management?', *German Law Journal* 9, 2008, p. 987.

relating to Reducing Emissions from Deforestation and Degradation (REDD).[77] Forests would also fall within the purview of the CBD, and individual species of endangered trees are addressed by the Convention on International Trade in Endangered Species (CITES).[78] Overall, international law efforts at addressing deforestation in Africa could fairly be characterised as a work in progress. This mirrors the global situation, where international efforts thus far have resulted only in a non-binding international instrument.

Bushmeat

The hunting and trade in bushmeat (the meat of wild animals) is a particular threat to biodiversity in central Africa.[79] While for many Africans the hunting and consumption of bushmeat would be a traditional practice and a primary source of protein, the practice has now become commercialised and is clearly unsustainable. There are even situations where poverty is causing people who have not used bushmeat before to turn to it now.[80] In many instances either the hunting or the trade (or both) is illegal under domestic laws. This is an area for concern, with particular geographical focus on central Africa, for both the CBD and CITES (insofar as bushmeat is traded across borders). Both conventions have bodies working on bushmeat: the CBD Liaison Group on Bushmeat[81] and the CITES Central Africa Bushmeat Working Group.[82] Recent joint meetings of the bodies have resulted in a series of recommendations, including the examination of formalising markets within a milieu of sustainable use, and insisting on appropriate law enforcement. If one considers various familiar themes that are present in the recommendations, it is possible to conclude that the challenges facing those combating the bushmeat crisis, as with most other environmental problems in Africa, revolve around resources and capacity.

The ivory trade

One of the 'flagship' environmental issues in Africa is the ivory trade and its regulation by CITES. This has been a major issue in COP (Conference of the Parties) discussions leading up to and since the decision in 1989 to list the elephant in Appendix I (effectively prohibiting the international trade in elephant and elephant products, including ivory).[83] Currently, the ivory trade is still prohibited. The CITES programme for Monitoring the Illegal Killing of

77 See e.g. A. Long, 'Global climate governance to enhance biodiversity and well-being: Integrating non-state networks and public international law in tropical forests', *Environmental Law* 41, 2011, p. 95.
78 For example, several species of ebony are on Appendix III at the instance of Madagascar.
79 A.E. Kohn and H.E. Eves, 'The African bushmeat crisis: A case for global partnership', *Environs Environmental Law and Policy Journal* 30, 2007, p. 247.
80 Maggie Fox, 'Finding No Fish, Ghanaians Turn to Bushmeat', *Planet Ark*, 15 November 2004. Online. Available HTTP: <http://www.planetark.com/avantgo/dailynewsstory.cfm?newsid=28148> (accessed 30 September 2011).
81 Details available online. Available HTTP: <http://www.cbd.int> and <http://www.cbd.int/doc/?meeting=LGB-01> (accessed 30 November 2011).
82 Details available online. Available HTTP: <http://bushmeat.org/about_bctf/engaging_with_key_decision_makers/cites_summary>. See also <http://www.cites.org/eng/prog/bushmeat.shtml> (both sites accessed 30 November 2011).
83 See M. Kidd and M. Cowling, 'CITES and the African Elephant', in B. Chaytor and K.R. Gray, *International Environmental Law and Policy in Africa*, Dordrecht: Kluwer, 2003, p. 49.

Elephants (MIKE) reported in March 2010 for CITES COP 15 that elephant poaching levels declined or remained stable between 2002 and 2006, followed by a steep increase, peaking in 2008, and a decline in 2009.[84] More recently, MIKE reported that 2010 saw the highest levels of elephant poaching since 2002, with central Africa being of high concern.[85] The response from the CITES Secretariat has been to launch a donor fund with a target of $100 million over the next three years to 'enhance law enforcement capacity and secure the long-term survival of African elephant populations'.[86]

It is interesting to consider the intention to raise funds for elephant conservation in the light of elephant poaching trends identified by MIKE. In short, countries that have low government effectiveness and with low human development have higher levels of elephant poaching, and 'poaching rates decline as government effectiveness and the Human Development Index increase'.[87] In addition, 'based on the limited evidence available, no relationship can be inferred between CITES decisions and levels and trends of poaching as estimated by the Proportion of Illegally Killed Elephants'.[88] This corresponds with the observation made several times earlier in this chapter that capacity and resource constraints often lie at the centre of the failure to implement international environmental law and consequently the failure to address environmental degradation.

Rhinoceros poaching

A similar problem to the illegal hunting of elephants for ivory has recently manifested itself at a level that is becoming alarming – the poaching of rhinoceros for their horns. The situation has been described as 'almost out of control'.[89] Most rhinoceros species are on CITES Appendix I and cannot be legally traded internationally. The South African government has reported to CITES that:

> a total of 174 rhino have been illegally killed in that country alone during the first six months of 2011. Poaching levels in South Africa have risen dramatically in recent years: 13 rhinos poached in 2007, 83 in 2008, 122 in 2009 and 330 in 2010. A total of 122 suspected rhino poachers have been arrested in South Africa since January 2011, 60 of them in the Kruger National Park, which is the protected area that has suffered the biggest losses.[90]

While recognising that rhinoceros poaching is a global trend, not just a South African one, the fact that illegal rhinoceros hunting in South Africa is becoming difficult to combat illustrates that not all environmental problems in Africa revolve around capacity and resource

---

84 CITES Secretariat, *Monitoring of Illegal Hunting in Elephant Range States*, March 2010, CoP15 Doc. 44.2 (Rev. 1), p. 20.
85 CITES Secretariat, 'African elephant fund launched at CITES meeting', 19 August 2011. Online. Available HTTP: <http://www.cites.org/eng/news/press/2011/20110819_SC61.php> (accessed 30 November 2011).
86 Ibid.
87 CITES Secretariat, *Monitoring of Illegal Hunting*, op. cit., p. 22.
88 Ibid.
89 CITES Secretariat, 'African elephant fund', op. cit.
90 South African Report to CITES Secretariat (2011). Online. Available HTTP: <http://www.cites.org/common/com/SC/61/E61i-02.pdf> (accessed 30 November 2011).

constraints, or have their roots in poverty. The Kruger National Park is well resourced and well managed (at least relative to many other protected areas in Africa) and yet is battling to contend with rhinoceros poaching. Clearly there are other issues that warrant consideration in this context, including the legalisation of trade in rhinoceros horn and efforts at combating the demand for rhinoceros horn, which is mostly East Asian in origin.[91] South Africa and Vietnam have recently agreed to fight rhinoceros poaching and South Africa also intends to meet with China and Thailand.[92]

Coastal and marine aspects

Africa has two instruments falling under the aegis of the UNEP Regional Seas Programme.[93] The Convention for the Protection, Management and Development of the Marine and Coastal Environment of the Eastern African Region (the Nairobi Convention) was adopted in 1985 and came into force in 1996. In essence, the Convention provides a legal framework for the cooperation of parties aimed at addressing issues relating to coastal and marine environmental problems, from East to Southern Africa.[94] The Convention for Co-operation in the Protection and Development of the Marine and Coastal Environment of the West and Central African Region (Abidjan Convention) 1981 entered into force in 1984. It has basically the same objectives as the Nairobi Convention but for the opposite coast of the continent.[95] There is little information in the public domain evaluating the effectiveness of these instruments, but both conventions are clearly active judging by the activities appearing on their websites.

The effectiveness of marine and coastal instruments in Africa cannot be underestimated as the threats to the African marine environment are growing. Not only is there increasing minerals exploitation in marine areas,[96] but illegal fishing in African waters is reportedly leading to poverty and piracy, particularly off West Africa.[97]

Climate change

According to data provided by the US Energy Information Administration,[98] in 2009 Africa produced 1,122 million metric tons of carbon dioxide out of a world total of 30,452 million

---

91 WWF, 'Rhino poaching in South Africa reaches all-time high', 12 January 2011. Online. Available HTTP: <http://www.worldwildlife.org/who/media/press/2011/WWFPresitem19251.html> (accessed 30 November 2011).
92 J. Kew, 'South Africa, Vietnam Agree to Work to Stem Rhino Poaching', *Business Week*, 28 September 2011. Online. Available HTTP: <http://www.businessweek.com/news/2011-09-28/south-africa-vietnam-agree-to-work-to-stem-rhino-poaching.html> (accessed 30 November 2011).
93 Okidi, op. cit., p. 47.
94 See Convention website online. Available HTTP: <http://www.unep.org/NairobiConvention/index.asp> (accessed 30 November 2011).
95 See Convention website online. Available HTTP: <http://www.unep.org/AbidjanConvention/index.asp> (accessed 30 November 2011).
96 See, e.g., C.J. Moreno, 'Oil and gas exploration and production in the Gulf of Guinea: Can the new Gulf be green?' *Houston Journal of International Law* 31, 2009, p. 419.
97 Anon, 'Illegal European fishing contributing to poverty and piracy in Africa', *Ecologist*, 20 April 2011.
98 US Energy Information Administration, 'International Energy Statistics'. Online. Available HTTP: <http://www.eia.gov/cfapps/ipdbproject/IEDIndex3.cfm?rid=90&pid=44&aid=8> (accessed 30 November 2011).

tons – 3.28 per cent of the total. Although Africa is a very small contributor to global emissions, it is nevertheless an important player in international climate change negotiations, not least because Africa is likely to be among the worst-affected regions by climate change.

In climate change negotiations, Africa usually presents a common front.[99] In September 2011, leading up to the UN Framework Convention on Climate Change (UNFCCC) COP 17 to be held in Durban, South Africa, the African Ministers for the Environment met for the Fourth Special Session of the African Ministerial Conference on the Environment (AMCEN) and adopted the Bamako Declaration, which endorsed the African Common Position as the basis for negotiations at COP 17.[100] The Declaration reportedly stresses that the UNFCCC and its Kyoto Protocol 'still constitute the fundamental global framework on climate change and requires full and effective implementation'.[101] It is likely, too, that the common position will emphasise that developed countries be required to undertake ambitious mitigation efforts, insist on the centrality of concrete adaptation implementation, and require financing and technological support.

While African countries have not had to implement climate change commitments as yet, due to the principle of common but differentiated responsibilities, and are still not intending to commit to mandatory mitigation targets, several have agreed to nationally appropriate mitigation actions following association with the Copenhagen Accord of 2009. South Africa is ranked twelfth internationally for CO_2 emissions in 2009 and produces about 40 per cent of Africa's total CO_2 emissions. It has pledged a (conditional) 34 per cent reduction in greenhouse gas (GHG) emissions from business as usual by 2020 and 42 per cent by 2025. This is conditional on 'the provision of financial resources, the transfer of technology and capacity building support by developed countries . . . [and] . . . requires the finalisation of an ambitious, fair, effective and binding multilateral Agreement'. This is not much different from the African Common Position outlined above.

Transboundary water management

According to UNEP:

> There are 677 lakes in Africa, of which 88 are principal lakes. Africa has also some 80 transboundary rivers and lake basins, and the catchment areas of the 17 largest exceed 100,000 square kilometres. The largest freshwater lake in Africa and the second largest in the world is Lake Victoria.[102]

Transboundary water management is therefore an important feature of international environmental law on the continent. There are several instruments in this sphere: for example, the East African Community: Protocol for Sustainable Development of Lake Victoria Basin 2003; the Lake Victoria Fisheries Organisation 1994; and the South African Development Community (SADC) Protocol on Shared Watercourses. Probably the most

---

99 See e.g. M. Kidd, *Environmental Law*, Cape Town: Juta, 2011, pp. 325–6.
100 International Institute for Sustainable Development (IISD), 'AMCEN Special Session endorses African Common Climate Position', 19 September 2011.
101 Ibid.
102 UNEP, *State of Biodiversity in Africa*, op. cit., p. 7.

high-profile shared watercourse in Africa is the Nile. This is not only because it is the longest river in the world, but because it presents an extremely complex set of physical, political and legal factors that make a solution that is mutually acceptable to all Nile basin states extremely difficult. None of the Nile basin countries is a party to the UN Convention on Non-navigational Uses of International Watercourses and there still appears to be some way to go towards an agreement relating to the use of the Nile's waters.[103] In contrast, there are agreements for many of the other major African basins, for example the Agreement on the Establishment of the Zambezi Watercourse Commission (ZAMCOM) in 2004[104] and the International Commission for the Congo-Oubangui-Sangha Basin (CICOS).[105] Given the shortage of water in many parts of the continent, strong agreements on transboundary water resources are a prerequisite for peaceful development in Africa and continued efforts need to be made in this direction.

Environmental impact assessment

In 1999, Maluwa observed that commentators on African environmental law in the 1970s had observed various inadequacies 'that continue to characterize the legal and legislative landscape in most African countries today'.[106] He asserted that there was a bias towards use-oriented legislation characterising environmental policy-making in all African states.[107] By this he was referring to rule-based 'command and control' type mechanisms, instead of resource- or management-oriented laws. Is this still the case? While command and control may still be the dominant regulatory paradigm in Africa, there has been progress to more proactive regulation. This is evidenced in part by the widespread planning initiatives (in desertification and biodiversity at least) outlined above. It is also demonstrated by increasing incorporation of environmental impact assessment (EIA) legislation in African countries.

Wood stated in 2003 that EIA was not mandatory in many African countries and that 'the enactment of appropriate legislation there is now almost universally regarded as a crucial first step'.[108] In 2005, the Economic Commission for Africa noted that 18 out of 23 African countries in its study had enabling EIA legislation.[109] Although there are positive developments in this regard, EIA practice is still deficient in many respects and it is important to remember that the existence of legislation does not in itself guarantee good practice. Kakonge has identified problems in EIA practice in sub-Saharan Africa relating to lack of finance and human resources, inadequate public participation and data inadequacy. He also suggested that

---

103 See E. Kasimbazi, 'The principle of equitable utilisation and its implications for water resources management in the Nile basin', Unpublished PhD thesis, University of KwaZulu-Natal, 2008.

104 Commission website online. Available HTTP: <http://www.icp-confluence-sadc.org/rbo/66> (accessed 30 November 2011).

105 Commission website online. Available HTTP: <http://www.cicos.info/siteweb/> (accessed 30 November 2011) (in French).

106 T. Maluwa, *International Law in Post-Colonial Africa*, Dordrecht: Kluwer, 1999, p. 317.

107 Ibid., p. 318.

108 C. Wood, 'Environmental impact assessment in developing countries: An overview', Unpublished conference paper, 2003, p. 8.

109 Economic Commission for Africa, *Review of the Application of Environmental Impact Assessment in Selected African Countries*, 2005.

existing enforcement mechanisms need to be strengthened.[110] These themes are not unique to EIA, as suggested elsewhere in this chapter.

Conclusion

It is plain that there is widespread pursuit of the international environmental law agenda in Africa. It is encouraging that environmental planning has taken place in most countries. The challenge remains to coordinate these plans with other environmental plans, as well as with initiatives to alleviate poverty and economic development strategies. Moreover, the plans have to be put into operation by the adoption of appropriate policies and laws. Where countries have developed environmental law consistent with or in pursuance of international environmental law, implementation is often lacking. In 1999, Maluwa suggested that there were two major factors influencing the fact that laws on paper had not arrested environmental degradation: inadequacy of enforcement machinery and lack of standards and controls for maintaining environmental quality.[111] While he was relying on 1982 authority for this assertion, this observation still rings true for many African countries.

While in some countries weak implementation is due to political instability, in other countries there are often problems of government weakness, whether due to corruption, lack of political will or capacity constraints. It is clear from the above analysis that there are often financial constraints, although African countries must avoid doing nothing for want of funding. Finance can assist with a dilemma that lies at the heart of many African environmental concerns, particularly in respect of the conservation of biodiversity. International environmental law aimed at conserving biodiversity is based on the idea that biodiversity is an asset for the world as a whole, and yet components of that biodiversity are found within individual states. International insistence on conservation of biodiversity within individual nation states can run into conflict with issues of state sovereignty. Moreover, many developing countries are receiving a mixed message. While components of biodiversity (species, for example) are to be preserved for the benefit of the entire planet, conservation efforts are seen to be the responsibility of a particular country because those species are found there. This kind of thinking will not promote conservation efforts in developing countries, particularly those that are worst resourced. This would suggest that finance needs to be targeted to address this dilemma.

The above observations may well be criticised as vague generalisations. Unfortunately, in researching this topic it became apparent that there is a relative dearth of literature on the subject of the implementation of international law in Africa. Of the literature that does exist, conclusions are frequently somewhat glib and often based on authorities that are themselves dated. As a result, the concluding remarks made above are, to an extent, based on a process of adding two and two and getting four. It would be surprising, however, if the true overview position were much different from what has been suggested here. This caveat, however, does offer a suggestion for further study. In 1997, Chaytor quoted Okidi as suggesting that:

110 J.O. Kakonge, 'Environmental Planning in Sub-Saharan Africa: Environmental Impact Assessment at the Crossroads', Working Paper Number 9, Yale School of Forestry and Environmental Studies, 2006.
111 Maluwa, *International Law in Post-Colonial Africa*, op. cit., p. 318.

A useful exercise would be to carry out detailed studies in respect of each treaty on environmental protection in Africa, in order to ascertain the position of each state on implementation of the agreement generally or on specific provisions.[112]

This view, in many respects, holds true almost fifteen years later. The somewhat vague picture outlined above can be considerably improved by further research along the lines suggested by Okidi. This will not be a purely academic exercise, since highlighting both success stories and shortcomings is likely to be of comparative value in improving the implementation of international environmental law in African countries.

112 Chaytor, 'Editorial', op. cit.

29

Polar law and good governance

Elizabeth Burleson

This chapter explores the existing governance arrangements in the Antarctic and Arctic, examines emerging polar coordination, the challenges that lie ahead, and a way forward.

Introduction

Antarctica is a continent surrounded by a sea, while the Arctic is a sea surrounded by continents. Both the Arctic and Antarctic are fragile polar ecosystems, yet the lack of a permanent human population in Antarctica has facilitated a more straightforward legal framework than has been achieved in the Arctic. Nothing comparable to the freezing of Antarctic sovereignty claims exists in Arctic governance. While there are distinct geopolitical sensitivity thresholds in the Arctic and Antarctic, strengthening cooperation at all levels and across all sectors can enhance overall good governance.

Emerging polar law is interdisciplinary at the intersection of law, policy, politics, and science. Cross-cutting issues that come into play when addressing polar law include domestic and international environmental law generally and climate and biodiversity law in particular. Human rights law,[1] state constitutional law, and maritime law also impact upon polar decision-making.[2] Transcending inertia can facilitate inclusive ecosystem governance within a meaningful timeframe. The emerging consensus on enhancing polar governance can stimulate effective decision-making that is both equitable and reasonable.[3] This chapter will explore

---

1 E. Burleson, 'Climate Change Displacement to Refuge', *Journal of Environmental Law and Litigation* 25, 2010, p. 35; *United Nations Framework Convention on Climate Change*, opened for signature 4 June 1992, 1771 UNTS 107 (entered into force 21 March 1994); *Convention on Biological Diversity*, opened for signature 5 June 1992, 31 ILM 818, 825 (entered into force 29 December 1993).

2 N. Loukacheva (ed.) *Polar Law Textbook*, Copenhagen: Nordic Council of Ministers, 2010, p. 215. Online. Available HTTP: <http://www.norden.org/en/publications/publikationer/2010-538> (accessed 9 May 2012).

3 E. Burleson, 'Equitable and Reasonable Use of Water in the Euphrates-Tigris River Basin', *Environmental Law Reporter News & Analysis* 35, 2005, p. 10041.

the governance regimes that exist in both the Antarctic and Arctic regions. It will assess the Antarctic Treaty System, ask what lessons can be learned regarding common pool resources, and analyse law of the sea and related measures. It will consider such substantive areas as natural resource management as well as procedural opportunities for inclusive governance structures. Enhancing good governance can occur through trust-building forums that bring together stakeholders to share information and make sensible decisions regarding sustainable development.

Antarctic Treaty System

The Antarctic Treaty System (ATS) includes the Antarctic Treaty[4] and its related agreements. The ATS froze sovereignty claims and established the continent as a zone of peace and a scientific reserve south of 60°S latitude.[5] Its origins are found in the first International Geophysical Year (IGY) in 1957–58 in which more than 65 nations participated. By that time Chile, Argentina, the United Kingdom, Australia, New Zealand, Norway, and France had claimed sovereignty over regions of Antarctica. The Soviet Union and the United States had Antarctic scientific research stations but had not made territorial claims nor recognised the claims of others.[6] The countries which became the 12 original signatories of the Treaty participated in Antarctic cooperation during the 1957–58 IGY and attended the Treaty negotiation conference.[7] This unprecedented cooperation led to the Antarctic Treaty, which came into force in 1961.[8]

Calling for 'preservation and conservation of living resources in Antarctica',[9] Antarctic Treaty Article 9 mandates member states to meet periodically, share information, and agree upon measures to further the Treaty. Parties have adopted over 200 recommendations at these consultative meetings.[10]

Beyond making recommendations under the Treaty, states entered into three additional international treaties: the 1972 Convention for the Conservation of Antarctic Seals;[11] the 1980 Convention on the Conservation of Antarctic Marine Living Resources;[12] and the 1988

---

4 *Antarctic Treaty*, opened for signature 1 December 1959, 12 UST 794 (entered into force 23 June 1961), Art. 4(2).
5 South of 60°S latitude is a generally accepted boundary for the Antarctic (despite CCAMLR use of the Antarctic convergence).
6 Loukacheva (ed.), op. cit., p. 32.
7 Argentina, Australia, Belgium, Chile, France, Japan, New Zealand, Norway, South Africa, Soviet Union, the UK and the US.
8 K. Kraft Sloan and D. Hik, 'International Polar Year as a Catalyst For Sustaining Arctic Research', *Sustainable Development Law and Policy* 8, 2008, p. 4.
9 *Antarctic Treaty*, opened for signature 1 December 1959, 12 UST 794 (entered into force 23 June 1961), Art. 9(1)(f).
10 Resolutions online. Available HTTP: <http://www.ats.aq/devAS/info_finalrep.aspx?lang=e&menu=2> (accessed 4 May 2012).
11 *Convention for the Conservation of Antarctic Seals*, opened for signature 1 June 1972, 11 ILM 251 (entered into force 11 March 1978).
12 *Convention on the Conservation of Antarctic Marine Living Resources*, opened for signature on 1 August 1980, 19 ILM 841 (entered into force on 7 April 1982) (CCAMLR); see E.J. Molenaar, 'CCAMLR and Southern Ocean Fisheries', *International Journal of Marine and Coastal Law* 16, 2001, p. 465.

Convention on the Regulation of Antarctic Mineral Resource Activities[13] – ratified primarily by Consultative Parties.[14] After Australia and France abandoned the latter in favour of greater conservation,[15] states concluded the Madrid Protocol on Environmental Protection to the Antarctic Treaty prohibiting mining.[16]

Since 2004 Argentina has hosted the Antarctic Treaty Secretariat. Any state wishing to become a Consultative Party, with full rights under the Treaty, must conduct substantial research activity in Antarctica.[17] The original 12 signatories and 16 states that have demonstrated sufficient scientific research constitute the Consultative Parties that can make decisions in Antarctic Treaty Consultative Meetings. Non-consultative member states can attend but are not able to participate in decision-making. Given the substantial expense of conducting research, a two-tier status has emerged with largely rich states able to vote as Consultative Parties and poorer states left with non-consultative status and no voting rights.

Despite room for improvement, the ATS has successfully diffused a volatile sovereignty conflict and achieved continental ecosystem preservation on an unprecedented scale. The Antarctic Treaty refrains from recognising, disputing, or establishing sovereignty.[18] It preserves the continent 'for peaceful purposes only; military activity, such as weapons testing, is prohibited but military personnel and equipment may be used for scientific research or any other peaceful purpose'.[19] It calls for continued global scientific cooperation[20] and information sharing.[21] It protects the environment by banning nuclear explosions or disposal of radioactive wastes.[22] Further, the Madrid Protocol on Environmental Protection to the Antarctic Treaty (1991) prohibits some mineral development and introduces annexes on marine pollution, fauna and flora, environmental impact assessments, waste management, and protected areas. The Protocol also prohibits non-scientific mineral activities and introduces liability arising from environmental emergencies. These aspects of the Madrid Protocol will be compared to Arctic resource management in the following sections.[23]

---

13 *Convention on the Regulation of Antarctic Mineral Resource Activities*, opened for signature June 1988, 27 ILM 868. CRAMRA has not entered into force. See D.R. Rothwell, 'The Antarctic Treaty System: Resource Development, Environmental Protection or Disintegration?' *Arctic* 43(3), 1990, p. 284. Yet, given the 50-year review under Article 25(2) of the 1991 Protocol, the mineral ban under CRAMRA Article 7 would have a remote chance of emerging into a mineral resource regime; see D.W. Floren, 'Antarctic Mining Regimes: An Appreciation of the Attainable', *Journal of Environmental Law and Litigation* 16, 2001, p. 467; see also J.J. Ward, 'Black Gold in a White Wilderness – Antarctic Oil: The Past, Present and Potential of a Region in Need of Sovereign Environmental Stewardship', *Journal of Land Use and Environmental Law* 13, 1998, p. 363.
14 Loukacheva (ed.), op. cit., pp. 33–4.
15 See D.R. Rothwell, 'Polar Environmental Protection and International Law: The 1991 Antarctic Protocol', *EJIL* 11(3), 2000, pp. 591–614; D. Bodansky, 'What's So Bad about Unilateral Action to Protect the Environment?' *European Journal of International Law* 11(2), 2000, p. 345.
16 *Protocol on Environmental Protection to the Antarctic Treaty*, opened for signature 4 October 1991, 30 ILM 1455 (entered into force 15 January 1998).
17 *Antarctic Treaty*, opened for signature 1 December 1959, 12 UST 794 (entered into force 23 June 1961), Art. 9(2).
18 Ibid., Art. 4.
19 Ibid., Art. 1.
20 Ibid., Art. 2.
21 Ibid., Art. 3.
22 Ibid., Art. 5.
23 Only the latter has yet to come into force.

Polar natural resource governance generally and an emerging Arctic framework

Where polar oil and gas exploration presents common pool resource gaming, one entity's extraction of non-renewable resources increases natural resource scarcity and costs to other entities that have to seek more remote resources.[24] In the context of marine pollution, the common pool problem occurs when entities place a larger pollution burden on the common pool than the pool can sustain. This lowers the value of the resource and raises costs to find alternatives to the ecosystem services once accessible from the common pool. For instance, traditional subsistence foods and the public health of Arctic communities are adversely impacted by the negative externalities of energy extraction and global persistent organic pollutants. Whether discussing Hardin's sheep grazing a public grassy field[25] or polar resource extraction, absent incentives for polluters to internalise the cost of negative externalities, negative impacts on fragile polar regions are unlikely to be minimised. Yet, Elinor Ostrom notes that cooperation can overcome the race to overexploit a natural resource irrespective of the interests of others.[26] Antarctic cooperation has been built upon the freezing of sovereignty claims. This approach has not resonated with Arctic coastal states that have significant populations and economic investments in the Arctic. Nevertheless, applying Ostrom's cooperative approach to the Arctic, governance structures layered on top of private natural resource use could facilitate environmentally sound multilateral, multi-resource use.[27]

Since there are no permanent human populations in Antarctica, states have been able to agree upon environmental provisions without regard to impacts on tribal or non-tribal local communities. While fewer than 30 states have ratified the Madrid Protocol, the international community has largely adhered to an 'aesthetic and scientific' priority for Antarctic activities;[28] a ban on mineral resources use beyond scientific research;[29] environmental assessment studies for all activities;[30] a Committee for Environmental Protection;[31] state emergency response preparation;[32] and dispute resolution provisions.[33]

Similarly, Antarctic governance benefits from the 1982 Convention on the Conservation of Antarctic Marine Living Resources (CCAMLR),[34] part of the Antarctic Treaty System

---

24 G. Hardin, 'The Tragedy of the Commons', *Science* 162, 1968, p. 1243.
25 Ibid.
26 E. Ostrom, *Governing the Commons: The Evolution of Institutions for Collective Action*, Cambridge: Cambridge University Press, 1990 (encouraging resource appropriators to participate in decision-making).
27 E.A. Posner and A.O. Sykes, 'Economic Foundations of the Law of the Sea', *American Journal of International Law* 104, 2010, 569, p. 574 (2010) ('The economic theory of international law suggests that the primary function of international law, whether customary or treaty law, is to ameliorate international externalities').
28 *Protocol on Environmental Protection to the Antarctic Treaty*, opened for signature 4 October 1951 (entered into force 15 January 1998) ('Madrid Protocol'), Art. 3.
29 Ibid., Art. 7. (In contrast, the *Convention on the Regulation of Antarctic Mineral Resource Activities* would have regulated mining pursuant to an international organisation.)
30 Ibid., Art. 8.
31 Ibid., Art. 11.
32 Ibid., Art. 15.
33 Ibid., Arts 18–20.
34 The *Convention on the Conservation of Antarctic Marine Living Resources* ('CCAMLR') came into force in 1982, as part of the Antarctic Treaty System, in pursuance of the provisions of Article IX of the Treaty.

that protects marine life and addresses activities that can have a negative impact on marine life. Article 2 specifically clarifies that conservation encompasses maintaining a sound ecological relationship among harvested, dependent, and related populations. Article 2 also covers effects on marine life as a result of associated activities on the marine ecosystem and environmental changes. Energy extraction would generally be at odds with such conservation and thus CCAMLR provides an important means by which to protect the Antarctic ecosystem. Implementing CCAMLR requires extensive development of appropriate analytical methods to collect sufficient scientific information.[35] The Convention calls upon states to use a 'precautionary' approach to minimise adverse impacts in the face of uncertainty.[36] Using an ecosystem approach, the CCAMLR Commission coordinates activities with other decision-making bodies within the ATS framework. The International Polar Year provided an opportunity to coordinate polar research generally and climate research in particular.[37] The Antarctic Treaty Meeting of Experts (ATME) on climate change and implications for Antarctic management and governance agreed to focus upon the implications of climate change for Antarctica.[38]

Turning to the Arctic, a third of remaining global hydrocarbon reserves appear to be north of the Arctic Circle under less than 500 metres of water and within clear national jurisdictions.[39] Additional resources appear to lie in disputed territorial areas, where delineation of continental shelves is under way. Eight states have territorial claims – the five Arctic coastal states (Canada, Denmark, Norway, Russia, and the United States) and three others (Iceland, Finland, and Sweden). While many conflicting claims have been resolved, melting ice due to climate change is opening up areas where states seek to extend continental shelf activity.[40] With millions of Russians within the Arctic Circle and a substantial Arctic military, Russia is the largest stakeholder in the region.[41] Building on the numerous calls for scientific cooperation throughout the United Nations Convention on the Law of the Sea (UNCLOS),[42] countries are beginning to work together to expand relevant baseline data. This provides a foundation upon which ecosystem-based, integrated management can occur. Mapping, combining information into a shared database, and deciding upon a single method of analysis can facilitate coordinated interpretations and even a boundary agreement prior to submitting information.[43] Entering into multilateral

---

35 Online. Available HTTP: <http://www.ccamlr.org/pu/e/gen-intro.htm> (accessed 4 May 2012).
36 Ibid.
37 *International Polar Year 2007–2009.* Online. Available HTTP: <http://www.ipy.org/> (accessed 4 May 2012).
38 *Antarctic Treaty Meeting of Experts.* Online. Available HTTP: <http://atme2010.npolar.no/en/> (accessed 9 May 2012).
39 B. Baker, 'Law, Science, And The Continental Shelf: The Russian Federation And The Promise Of Arctic Cooperation', *American University International Law Review* 25, 2010, 251, p. 257.
40 R.M. Bratspies, 'Human Rights and Arctic Resources', *Southwestern Journal of International Law* 15, 2009, p. 265.
41 Baker, op. cit., p. 251.
42 *United Nations Convention on the Law of the Sea* (UNCLOS), opened for signature 10 December 1982, 21 ILM 1261 (entered into force 16 November 1994), Arts 194, 197, 200, 204, 206, and 234; P. Allott, 'Power Sharing in the Law of the Sea', *American Journal of International Law* 77, 1983, pp. 18–20.
43 M.A. Allain, 'Canada's Claim to the Arctic: a Study in Overlapping Claims to the Outer Continental Shelf', *Journal of Maritime Law and Commerce* 42, 2011, 1, p. 37.

agreements and increasing polar inclusive governance and funding can address environment and development challenges going forward.

A number of provisions of UNCLOS are relevant to Arctic governance. Article 76 established a process for resolving conflicting continental shelf claims.[44] Annex II of UNCLOS requires states to make submissions within ten years of ratification.[45] Once states submit claims to the Commission on the Limits of the Continental Shelf, the latter can proceed with approval of and reconciling claims.[46] Article 122 encourages regional sea cooperation, emphasising coordination on such multilateral concerns as natural resource management. Together with the International Maritime Organization[47] and Arctic Council,[48] the above provide a loose Arctic legal framework.

While Article 193 of UNCLOS recognises states' rights to mineral resources, Article 192 sets forth states' duties to protect marine ecosystems. Article 234 authorises Arctic coastal states to enforce shipping environmental protection provisions for such ice-covered waters as the Northwest Passage.[49] Nonetheless, there are substantial gaps in this loose Arctic legal framework including disagreement as to the status of the Northwest Passage as an international strait or historic internal waters of Canada; the absence of the United States in the UNCLOS dispute resolution procedures regarding the Northwest Passage due to its failure to ratify the Convention; and general uncertainty as to the extent to which given states can extend into newly accessible regions of the Arctic.

Arctic coastal states seek to frame Arctic governance narrowly, based upon territorial sovereignty. In 2008 the five Arctic coastal states met in Greenland without including the three other Arctic states or other stakeholders.[50] The Ilulissat Declaration[51] that the Arctic coastal states crafted demonstrates strong Arctic coastal state consensus that UNCLOS should be the framework for the Arctic. While the Arctic coastal states may prefer a status quo law-of-the-sea-based path forward, UNCLOS does not mention indigenous peoples. The international human rights regime, on the other hand, does recognise indigenous rights and is part of the fabric with which stakeholders can weave inclusive Arctic governance.[52] International law recognises individuals and groups as subjects of international law with rights. UN General Assembly adoption of the United Nations Declaration on the Rights of Indigenous Peoples brings with it the opportunity to redefine the governance relationship among indigenous

---

44 UNCLOS, Art. 76.
45 Ibid., Annex II Art. 4.
46 Ibid., Annex II Art. 76.
47 See IMO, online. Available HTTP: <http://www.imo.org/> (accessed 4 May 2012).
48 See Arctic Council, online. Available HTTP: <www.arctic-council.org/> (accessed 4 May 2012).
49 UNCLOS, Art. 234.
50 Indigenous Portal, *Ilulissat Declaration from the Arctic Ocean Conference*, 24 June 2008. Online. Available HTTP: <http://www.indigenousportal.com/Politics/The-Ilulissat-declaration-from-the-Artic-Ocean-Conference.html> (accessed 4 May 2012).
51 Arctic Council, *Ilulissat Declaration* 2, Ilulissat, Greenland, 2008. Online Available HTTP: <http://www.oceanlaw.org/downloads/arctic/Ilulissat_Declaration.pdf> (accessed 9 May 2012); see also T. Koivurova, 'Limits and Possibilities of the Arctic Council in a Rapidly Changing Scene of Arctic Governance' Polar Record 7, 2009, Cambridge University Press.
52 P. Stephens, 'Applying Human Rights Norms to Climate Change: the Elusive Remedy', *Colorado Journal of International Environmental Law and Policy* 21, 2010, p. 49; see also E. Park, 'Searching For A Voice: The Indigenous People In Polar Regions', *Sustainable Development Law & Policy* 8, 2008, p. 30.

peoples and the rest of the international community.[53] The need for protection of indigenous territory is already recognised and falls within provisions set forth by the International Covenant on Civil and Political Rights,[54] the International Convention on the Elimination of All Forms of Racial Discrimination,[55] and Protocol 1 of the European Convention on Human Rights.[56] International minority rights standards also apply to indigenous peoples in minority situations within modern nation states. Irrespective of sovereignty claims under UNCLOS, international law provides an emerging legal framework with which to enhance inclusive decision-making.

In the Arctic, Denmark's recognition of Greenland's right to self-determination and natural resource devolution is an encouraging sign for inclusive governance.[57] In contrast to Greenlanders, many Arctic indigenous communities have yet to regain self-determination recognition generally and jurisdiction over land/resources in particular. The Alaska Native Claims Settlement Act of 1971 (ANCSA) exemplifies domestic state law impacting indigenous rights to self-determination[58] where full, effective, and meaningful participation and consent were not applied. It is also worth noting that only Denmark and Norway have ratified the International Labour Organization (ILO) Convention No. 169 concerning Indigenous and Tribal Peoples in Independent Countries.[59]

Climate risks to tribes are both physical and cultural as traditional livelihoods retreat with the ice. Even urban indigenous individuals face a disproportionate risk to the general population of most states given their relative lack of financial resources.[60] The international community has looked to indigenous communities for traditional knowledge.[61] Prior informed consent, acknowledging native research contributions, active participation in research as well

---

53 *United Nations Declaration on the Rights of Indigenous Peoples* (2007), GA Res 61/259, UN GAOR, 61st Sess, 49th Supp, UN Doc A/Res/61/259; *Petition to the Inter American Commission on Human Rights Seeking Relief from Violations Resulting from Global Warming Caused by Acts and Omissions of the U.S.* 1 (7 Dec 2005). Online. Available HTTP: <http://inuitcircumpolar.com/files/uploads/icc-files/FINALPetitionICC.pdf>; see also Organization of American States, *American Convention on Human Rights* (1969), OASTS No. 36, 1144 UNTS 123, Art. 29; Organization of American States, *American Declaration on the Rights and Duties of Man* (1948), OAS Res XXX, OAS Off Rec OEA/Ser.L./V/I.4 Rev; *Convention on Access to Information, Public Participation in Decision-Making and Access to Justice in Environmental Matters*, opened for signature 25 June 1998, 38 ILM 517 (entered into force 30 October 2001).

54 *International Covenant on Civil and Political Rights*, opened for signature 16 December 1966, 999 UNTS 171 (entered into force 23 March 1976), Art. 1.

55 *International Convention on the Elimination of All Forms of Racial Discrimination*, opened for signature 7 March 1966, 659–60 UNTS 195 (entered into force 4 January 1969), Arts 1, 5.

56 *Protocol to the Convention for the Protection of Human Rights and Fundamental Freedoms*, opened for signature 20 March 1952, 213 UNTS 262 (entered into force 1 November 1998), Art. 1; T. Koivurova, 'Jurisprudence of the European Court of Human Rights Regarding Indigenous Peoples: Retrospect and Prospects', *International Journal on Minority and Group Rights* 18, 2011, pp. 1–37.

57 G. Alfredsson, 'Human Rights and Indigenous Rights', in Loukacheva (ed.) op. cit., p. 160.

58 Ibid., p. 202.

59 *ILO Convention (No. 169) Concerning Indigenous and Tribal Peoples in Independent Countries*, opened for signature 27 June 1989 (entered into force 5 September 1991). Online. Available HTTP: <http://www.ilo.org/ilolex/cgi-lex/convde.pl?C169> (accessed 4 May 2012); G. Alfredsson, op. cit., p. 157

60 G. Alfredsson, 'Human Rights and Indigenous Rights', in Loukacheva (ed.) op. cit., pp. 147–70 ('the relocation of the village of Newtok is expected to cost as much as $130 million').

61 Ibid.

as sharing research outcomes with indigenous communities can go a long way to enhance understanding of the Arctic.[62] Canada's Oceans Act has begun this process by mandating indigenous cooperation, facilitating traditional knowledge-sharing in ocean ecosystem assessment.[63] Similarly, the Yukon River Inter-Tribal Watershed Council (YRITWC) exemplifies an indigenous-led initiative that provides a best-practice model.[64]

Learning polar lessons about common pool resources

International law has regulated Antarctic environmental protection while national environmental laws have regulated much of the Arctic beyond the international high seas and deep seabed.[65] Antarctic cooperation has also resulted in more hard international law while Arctic cooperation has thus far come primarily in the form of such softer measures as the declarations establishing the Arctic Council. Yet, the Arctic Council has recently established a permanent secretariat in its last ministerial meeting in Nuuk, Greenland in May 2011 as well as adopting the first legally binding agreement on search and rescue.[66]

Can the Arctic and Antarctic regimes borrow anything from one another? At the beginning of this chapter, this author described ways in which an emerging Arctic framework can build upon the strong species and habitat treaties that make up the ATS. For instance, the Arctic can benefit from the best practice established by the Madrid Protocol's restriction on mineral extraction and environmental impact assessments for all activities. In return, the ATS can benefit from growing Arctic Council understanding of climate and persistent organic pollutants. Similarly, Timo Koivurova explains that the Arctic Council can 'benefit from the long-standing high-quality environmental protection regime created for Antarctica'[67] while the ATS can join the Arctic Council's efforts to highlight the need for comprehensive climate change mitigation, adaptation, environmentally sound technology transfer, and funding in polar regions.[68]

Due to atmospheric circulation and ocean currents both polar regions have become persistent organic pollutant sinks and have suffered from global problems produced beyond these regions. Internalising such externalities as pollution can best be accomplished through robust environmental provisions at the source of the pollution. The Arctic Council has been a strong public health advocate, addressing the bio-magnification of persistent organic pollutants and contamination of traditional foods.[69] The Arctic Council's work to highlight the profound impact of polar chemical contamination provides a model with which other

---

62 Ibid.
63 *Oceans Act*, RSC, ch. 31, §§29, 33, 42j (Can.).
64 D.S. Dorough, 'Inuit of Alaska: Current Issues', in Loukacheva (ed.) op. cit., p. 208.
65 Loukacheva (ed.), op. cit., 36.
66 T. Koivurova and D. VanderZwaag, 'The Arctic Council at 10 Years: Retrospect and Prospects', *University of British Columbia Law Review* 40(1), 2007, pp. 121–94.
67 T. Koivurova, 'Environmental Protecion in the Arctic and Antarctica' in Loukacheva (ed.) op. cit., pp. 23–44, p. 40.
68 E. Burleson, 'Climate Change Consensus: Emerging International Law', *William & Mary Environmental Law & Policy Review* 34, 2010, p. 558; Loukacheva, op. cit., p. 40 (discussing the precautionary approach taken in Antarctica).
69 E. Burleson and S. Dodson, 'Arctic Justice: Addressing Persistent Organic Pollutants', *Law and Inequality*, 30, 2012, 57. Draft located online. Available HTTP: <http://works.bepress.com/cgi/viewcontent.cgi?article=1037&context=elizabeth_burleson> (accessed 4 May 2012).

international entities, including the ATS, can affect global sustainable development decision-making.[70]

Many countries deal with polar issues together. Furthermore, such Arctic states as the USA, Norway, Sweden, Finland, and Russia are Consultative Parties in the ATS while Denmark and Canada hold non-consultative status.[71] The polar regimes held a joint Antarctic Treaty and Arctic Council meeting at the end of the International Polar Year 2009, issuing the Washington Declaration on the International Polar Year and Polar Science.[72] They agreed to cooperate to review scientific findings and coordinate information sharing.[73]

As polar routes expand, new shipping routes may tempt those seeking shorter transit durations.[74] Yet, unsettled claims, a dearth of navigational aids, and harsh conditions still deter rapid development. Building upon existing governance structures and addressing the centre of the Arctic Ocean first may be useful means by which to build collective political will. One inclusive approach that addresses global interests in the high seas and deep seabed involves negotiation of a polar ocean protocol to UNCLOS,[75] as UNCLOS provides a framework with which to identify and resolve competing resource claims and free rider problems among states. Integrating inclusive, ecosystem-adaptive management can enhance polar good governance.

Remaining challenges to such an approach include the focus on delineating polar claims. The status of the Northwest Passage (as an international strait or Canadian internal waters) provides a case in point.[76]

Timo Koivurova and Erik Molenaar have identified various substantive and procedural gaps in Arctic governance. Regarding procedure, Arctic states are jeopardising global polar interests through their unwillingness to cooperate under UNCLOS, its related Fish Stocks Agreement,[77] or customary international law. In addition, despite willingness to recognise much of the law of the sea as customary international law, the failure of the United States to ratify the 1982 UNCLOS precludes full use of its dispute settlement mechanism under

70 Arctic Contaminants Action Program. Online. Available HTTP: <http://www.arctic-council.org/index.php/en/acap> (accessed 19 March 2012); See also ATS pollution measures. Online. Available HTTP: <http://www.ats.aq/e/ep_marine.htm> (accessed 19 March 2012).

71 Loukacheva, op. cit., p. 41.

72 Ibid.

73 *Antarctic Treaty – Arctic Council Joint Meeting Washington Ministerial Declaration on the International Polar Year and Polar Science*, Communiqué, Bureau of Oceans and International Environmental and Scientific Affairs, April 2009. Online. Available HTTP: <http://www.state.gov/e/oes/rls/other/2009/121340.htm> (accessed 9 May 2012).

74 See e.g. P. Reynolds, *Russia Ahead in Arctic 'Gold Rush'*, BBC News, 1 August 2007. Online. Available HTTP: <http://news.bbc.co.uk/2/hi/in_depth/6925853.stm> (accessed 19 March 2012); M.E. Rosen, 'Energy Independence and Climate Change: the Economic and National Security Consequences of Failing to Act', *University of Richmond Law Review* 44, 2010, p. 977; S. Ashfaq, 'Something For Everyone: Why the United States Should Ratify the Law of the Sea Treaty', *Journal of Transnational Law & Policy* 19, 2010, p. 357.

75 J. McGlade, *Speech at Arctic Frontiers Conference*, Tromsø, 9 January 2007. Online Available HTTP: <http://www.eea.europa.eu/pressroom/speeches/23-01-2007>.

76 UNCLOS, Art. 234.

77 *Agreement for the Implementation of the Provisions of the United Nations Convention of the Law of the Sea of 10 December 1982 Relating to the Conservation and Management of Straddling Fish Stocks and Highly Migratory Fish Stocks* (1995), Conference on Straddling Fish Stocks and Highly Migratory Fish Stocks, 6th Sess, UN Doc A/ CONF 164/37, 34 ILM 1542.

Part XV. Nevertheless, new or existing competent international organisations should play a role in facilitating conflict resolution in the face of rapid environmental change and economic development. As to substantive regulatory gaps, such emerging maritime activities as floating energy installations, CO_2 sequestration, tourism, and piracy lack multi-sectoral integrated ecosystem management. Comprehensive environmental impact assessments and other regulatory tools would enhance Arctic governance.

Regional marine environmental protection models for Arctic decision-makers to consider include: (1) the OSPAR Commission of the OSPAR Convention for the Protection of the marine Environment of the North-East Atlantic;[78] (2) the Helsinki Commission of the Helsinki Convention for the Baltic Sea;[79] (3) other regimes resulting from the Regional Seas Programme of the United Nations Environment Programme;[80] and (4) Antarctic Treaty Consultative Meetings of the Antarctic Treaty.[81] Arctic decision-makers can look to these models to fill enhanced procedural governance as well as flesh out substantive regulatory provisions.

The Convention for the Protection of the Marine Environment of the North-East Atlantic (OSPAR)[82] exemplifies ecosystem regional marine protection and can play a direct as well as indirect role in Arctic governance. It directly obligates member Arctic states to implement protection measures and indirectly provides a model with which Arctic good governance may be expanded. One option would be for OSPAR to become the umbrella framework to protect the Arctic marine environment. States that have signed up to OSPAR can unanimously invite new members to join the Convention.[83] If it is politically infeasible for OSPAR membership to expand to all Arctic stakeholders, best practices can be borrowed from OSPAR and applied to the Arctic. While the Arctic Council has conducted crucial scientific studies, effectively responding to emerging environmental and natural resource use challenges can best be facilitated through a commission/council with a secretariat that can enact binding decisions in light of the polluter pays principle, precautionary principle, and best environmental practices principle.[84] Annex III of OSPAR addresses offshore pollution and the OSPAR Commission has already adopted mandatory provisions to reduce offshore pollution.[85] Annex V of OSPAR addresses the establishment of marine protected areas.[86]

78 *Convention for the Protection of the Marine Environment of the North-East Atlantic*, opened for signature 22 September 1992, 32 ILM 1069 (entered into force 25 March 1998).
79 *Convention on the Protection of the Marine Environment of the Baltic Sea Area*, opened for signature 9 April 1992 (entered into force 17 January 2000).
80 *United Nations Environment Programme Regional Seas Programmes*. Online. Available HTTP: <www.unep.org/regionalseas> (accessed 4 May 2012).
81 *ATCM*. Online. Available HTTP: <http://www.ats.aq/e/ats_meetings_atcm.htm> (accessed 4 May 2012).
82 Convention for the Protection of the Marine Environment of the North-East Atlantic (OSPAR), Paris, 22 September 1992, preamble. In force 25 March 1998. Online. Available HTTP: <www.ospar.org/>. Annex V, Sintra, 23 September 1998. In force 30 August 2000. OSPAR jurisdiction extends to the North-East Atlantic sector of the Arctic Ocean.
83 Ibid., Art. 27(2).
84 Ibid., Art. 2(2).
85 *OSPAR Decision 9/3 on the Disposal of Disused Offshore Installations*. Online. Available HTTP: <http://www.ospar.org/documents/DBASE/DECRECS/Decisions/od98-03e.doc> (accessed 4 May 2012); K.N. Casper, 'Oil and Gas Development in the Arctic: Softening of Ice Demands Hardening of International Law', *Nat. Resources J.* 49, 2009, p. 848.
86 OSPAR, Annex V, Art. 2.

The OSPAR Commission has integrated climate change and offshore oil and gas analysis into its overall work. The Arctic marine environment constitutes a substantial part of OSPAR jurisdiction and its expansion to the Arctic at large may provide the most effective protection of the fragile Arctic region.

All of the Arctic states have ratified the International Convention on Oil Pollution Preparedness, Response, and Co-operation (OPRC) calling for oil pollution emergency plans,[87] pollution event reporting to coastal authorities,[88] and assistance in the event of an oil pollution incident.[89] Taking precautionary and polluter pays principles[90] into account, OPRC parties[91] and the International Maritime Organization facilitate compliance[92] through adoption of regulations,[93] reporting,[94] cooperation, and collaboration.[95]

The OPRC Convention addresses the narrow field of oil pollution, not attempting to cover fisheries, navigation, or other areas in need of Arctic coordination. While it addresses the Arctic, in scope it may not be sufficiently focused upon unique polar vulnerabilities. Given the relative success of layering the 1995 United Nations Agreement on Straddling and Highly Migratory Fish Stocks[96] on UNCLOS, Arctic stakeholders should try to negotiate an offshore energy instrument with which the US can participate despite US non-party status in UNCLOS. This could be an UNCLOS protocol-like agreement, a free-standing multilateral agreement on Arctic energy, or some hybrid. Whether to centre consensus building upon a theme such as energy or a region such as the Arctic is not as important as beginning the process of trying to strengthen protection before economic activity advances beyond the ecosystem's capacity to cope.

To maximise Arctic ecosystem protection, 'special area' status should be extended to the Arctic under Annex I of MARPOL (the International Convention for the Prevention of Pollution from Ships) 73/78, discussed below.[97] Another option involves expanding the membership and area covered by OSPAR. While the nature and scope of the instrument may depend upon geopolitical constraints, there appears to be widespread recognition on the following: (1) Arctic governance strengthening constitutes a global public good; (2) Arctic stakeholders can build upon cooperation to date; (3) Human rights, energy, natural resources, and other sensitive topics can be broached through inclusive ecosystem decision-making forums. Some of these non-exclusive points may have broader support than others. Yet, climate and energy consensus building provides the catalyst with which to transcend isolationism to enhance good governance in the Arctic.

---

87 Ibid., Art. 3(2).
88 Ibid., Art. 4(1)(a).
89 Ibid., Art. 7.
90 Ibid., preamble.
91 Ibid., Art. 2(6).
92 Ibid., Art. 12(2).
93 Ibid., Art. 3(1)(a).
94 Ibid., Art. 4(2).
95 Ibid., Art. 8(1).
96 *Agreement for the Implementation of the Provisions of the United Nations Convention of the Law of the Sea of 10 December 1982 Relating to the Conservation and Management of Straddling Fish Stocks and Highly Migratory Fish Stocks* (1995), Conference on Straddling Fish Stocks and Highly Migratory Fish Stocks, 6th Sess, UN Doc A/ CONF 164/37, 34 ILM 1542.
97 *International Convention for the Prevention of Pollution from Ships*, opened for signature 2 November 1973, 1340 UNTS 61 (entered into force 2 October 1983) as modified by the Protocol of 1978 ('MARPOL 73/78') Art. 16.

Elizabeth Burleson

The European Union's (EU) Marine Strategy Framework Directive (MSFD)[98] marks a departure from a sector-by-sector approach to the regulation of maritime activities.[99] Legally the Directive is based upon ecosystem protection.[100] Directives require a given outcome but leave member states the flexibility with which to carry out the Directive.

Conceptually the Directive is based upon (1) the precautionary principle; (2) the principle that preventive action should be taken; (3) the polluter pays principle; and (4) the principle that pollution should be reduced at its source. Given that most marine pollution originates from inland sources, the MSFD and the EU Water Framework Directive[101] are integrated – using a natural resource methodology based upon cooperative, scientific, adaptive coordination at regional levels. The MSFD seeks to fulfil the EU's UNCLOS obligation to take all measures that are necessary to prevent, reduce, and control pollution of the marine environment.[102]

The MSFD preamble states that 'the serious environmental concerns, in particular those due to climate change, relating to the Arctic waters, a neighbouring marine environment of particular importance for the Community, need to be assessed by the Community institutions and may require action to ensure the environmental protection of the Arctic'.[103] The EU has begun integrating Arctic matters into EU policies and negotiations,[104] including with Norway and Iceland on how the MSFD will be integrated into the European Economic Area Agreement's coverage of the Arctic Ocean.[105]

The International Convention for the Prevention of Pollution from Ships (MARPOL 73/78) currently applies to oil and gas exploration and exploitation in the Arctic.[106] All five Arctic coastal states have ratified MARPOL 73/78, which addresses energy in that fixed or floating platforms are included in the definition of ships.[107] Nevertheless, the shallow Arctic

98 Directive 2008/56/EC of the European Parliament and of the Council of 17 June 2008 establishing a framework for community action in the field of marine environmental policy, Marine Strategy Framework Directive, OJ L 164/19, 25 June 2008.
99 R. Long, 'The Marine Strategy Framework Directive: A New European Approach to the Regulation of the Marine Environment, Marine Natural Resources and Marine Ecological Services', Journal of Energy and Natural Resources Law 29(1), 2011, p. 2.
100 Furthermore, assessment and monitoring under the MSFD must be coordinated with that of the Habitats and Birds Directives. Article 13(4) of Directive 2008/56/EC. Council Directive 92/43/EEC of 21 May 1992 on the conservation of natural habitats and of wild fauna and flora, OJ L 206, 22 July 1992, p 7. Directive as last amended by Directive 2006/105/EC (OJ L 363, 20 December 2006, p. 368). Council Directive 2009/147/EC of the European Parliament and of the Council of 30 November 2009 on the conservation of wild birds, OJ 2010 L20/7.
101 Directive 2000/60/EC of the European Parliament and of the Council of 23 October 2000 establishing a framework for Community action in the field of water policy, OJ L 327, 22 December 2000, 1. Directive as last amended by Directive 2008/32/EC (OJ L 81, 20 March 2008, p. 60).
102 UNCLOS, Arts 194, 195.
103 Recital 42 of Directive 2008/56/EC.
104 Communication from the Commission to the Council and the European Parliament, on The European Union and the Arctic Region, COM, (2008) 763 final, Brussels, 20 November 2008; Council of the European Union conclusions on Arctic issues, Brussels, 8 December 2009. Online. Available HTTP: <http://eur-lex.europa.eu/LexUriServ/LexUriServ.do?uri=COM:2008:0763:FIN:EN:pdf> (accessed 9 May 2012).
105 Communication from the Commission to the Council and the European Parliament on The European Union and the Arctic Region, COM, (2008) 763 final, Brussels, 20 November 2008 at 11; see also Long, op. cit., p. 1.
106 MARPOL 73/78, preamble.
107 Ibid., Art. 2(4).

Ocean floor is not sufficiently mapped and single-hulled container ships pose a serious risk of spilling oil or hazardous chemicals. Global cooperation is needed to prevent such events given the impracticability of remediation. States lack the capacity to mitigate and respond to temperate oil and gas disaster areas, let alone chronic and catastrophic Arctic contamination. Furthermore, the Arctic Council's Arctic Offshore Oil and Gas Guidelines[108] remain voluntary and do not address the reality that technologies do not exist to clean up polar oil spills.

There should be agreement on substantial levels of funding with which to understand scientific baseline conditions and environmental impacts of both successful and unsuccessful oil and gas activities. Funding discussions should also include the amount that will go towards insurance to fully compensate injured parties and mitigate environmental impacts of disasters. Drilling should not get out in front of fiscal and technological capacity to respond to disasters.[109] The design, execution, and outcome of monitoring programmes should be transparent and involve active civil society participation. Legally required environmental and safety reviews should occur at the planning stage of energy development.[110] Existing provisions can be amended to facilitate multi-scale governmental cooperative regulation. Permitting should involve adequate timeframes within which to review proposed operations as well as adequate funding with which to carry out such reviews.[111]

Conclusion

One of the best practices of the Antarctic regime that could be implemented in the Arctic involves the listing of 'special areas'.[112] Antarctica is a special area known to be vulnerable to pollution. The Arctic is similarly fragile and could benefit from comprehensive designation as a special area where certain activities are prohibited except for minor and well-defined exceptions.[113]

Good governance of energy resources remains embryonic, and regulatory capture a real risk. However, international, tribal, state, and civil society coordination of imminent polar energy generation through ongoing efforts to implement best practices may help to address existing problems.[114]

Open and transparent decision-making facilitates trust and the capacity to coordinate ongoing multi-natural resource sustainable development as well as occasional disaster responses among an array of polar stakeholders. As Norse and Amos note, 'When disseminated publicly, the analyses of skilled nongovernmental observers can provide crucial perspective and a useful reality check on powerful economic interests and government.'[115]

108 *Arctic Council, Protection of the Arctic Marine Environment (PAME), Arctic Offshore Oil and Gas Guidelines* § 1.5 (10 October 2002).

109 E.A. Norse and J. Amos, 'Ilulissat Declaration, and Policy Implications of the Deepwater Horizon Oil and Gas Disaster', *ELR News and Analysis* 40, 2010, p. 11071; R.O. Brooks, 'The Gulf Oil Spill: The Road Not Taken', *Albany Law Review* 74, 2010–2011, p. 489.

110 S. Kalen, R.M. Seidemann, J.G. Wilkins and M.K. Terrell, 'Lingering Relevance of the Coastal Zone Management Act to Energy Development in our Nation's Coastal Waters?', *Tulane Environmental Law Journal* 24, 2010, p. 106.

111 Norse and Amos, op. cit., p. 11072 (including monitoring active and abandoned infrastructure).

112 Ibid., Annexes I, V (as amended 17 March 1992).

113 Ibid., Annex I, reg. 1(10). See also Existing Particularly Sensitive Sea Areas (PSSA).

114 Norse and Amos, op. cit., p. 11070.

115 Ibid., p. 11058.

Scientific understanding and economic recognition of ecosystem services continue to gain broad support but are at risk of being outstripped by industry capacity for rapid expansion of extraction activities beyond the public sector's current regulatory capacity.[116] Crafting a sound energy policy involves informed public discourse regarding the following: whether energy operations should be permitted; what should be the scope of full environmental review and adequate contingency plans; who decides and who bears the risk of energy extraction; what are current pollution levels; who is responsible for minimising pollution; and how can coordinated oversight become most effective at preserving fragile ecosystems?[117]

The five Arctic coastal states belong to the Conference of the Parliamentarians of the Arctic Region,[118] Spitsbergen Treaty,[119] North Atlantic Coastguard Forum,[120] MARPOL,[121] and other multilateral agreements. National legislation applicable in the Arctic includes the US National Environmental Policy Act,[122] Endangered Species Act,[123] and the Canadian Arctic Waters Pollution Prevention Act.[124] The IMO (International Maritime Organization) has developed the IMO Guidelines for Ships Operating in Arctic Ice-covered Waters.[125] Efforts are under way to make the IMO 2009 polar code legally binding.[126]

This chapter has considered the ATS and polar lessons on common pool resources. The law of the sea and related measures provide a broad framework that can be supplemented by further substantive polar region natural resource management and inclusive polar region governance. Integrating inclusive, ecosystem-adaptive management can enhance good governance.

116 Z.J.B. Plater, 'Learning From Disasters: Twenty-One Years After the Exxon Valdez Oil Spill, Will Reactions to the Deepwater Horizon Blowout Finally Address the Systemic Flaws Revealed in Alaska?' *ELR News & Analysis* 40, 2010, p. 11044.
117 Norse and Amos, op. cit., p. 11071.
118 Conference of Arctic Parliamentarians. Online. Available HTTP: <http://www.arcticparl.org/> (accessed 4 May 2012).
119 The Arctic Governance Project, *Arctic Governance in an Era of Transformative Change: Critical Questions, Governance Principles, Ways Forward*, 14 April 2010, p. 4.
120 North Atlantic Coast Guard Forum. Online. Available HTTP: <http://www.ccg-gcc.gc.ca/e0003559> (accessed 4 May 2012).
121 *International Convention for the Prevention of Pollution from Ships*, opened for signature 2 November 1973, 1340 UNTS 61 (entered into force 2 October 1983) as modified by the Protocol of 1978 ('MARPOL 73/78').
122 The US Congress enacted NEPA in order to require federal agencies to incorporate environmental assessment into the decision-making process. 42 USC § 4331(a).
123 *Endangered Species Act* 1973 (7 US § 136, 16 USC § 1531 onwards, ESA). Online. Available HTTP: <http://www.epa.gov/regulations/laws/esa.html> (accessed 4 May 2012) (e.g. protecting polar bears as a threatened species).
124 *Arctic Waters Pollution Prevention Act*, RSC 1985, c. A-12 (Can.).
125 *IMO Guidelines for Ships Operating in Arctic Ice-covered Waters*. Online. Available HTTP: <http://www.fni.no/doc&pdf/FNI-R0207.pdf> (accessed 4 May 2012).
126 IMO, 'Mandatory Polar Code further developed'. Online. Available HTTP: <http://www.imo.org/mediacentre/meetingsummaries/de/pages/de-54th-session.aspx> (accessed 4 May 2012) ('The move to develop a mandatory Code follows the adoption by the IMO Assembly, in 2009, of Guidelines for ships operating in polar waters'). See also *Guidelines for Ships Operating in Polar Waters* (2009), IMO Res, 26th Sess, UN Doc A 26/Res.1024. Online. Available HTTP: <http://www.arcticportal.org/images/stories/Arctic_Shipping_Portlet/A.102426_Guidelines_for_ships_operating_in_polar_waters.pdf> (accessed 4 May 2012).

Preserving 10 per cent of the Earth's surface, the ATS has successfully protected Antarctica to date.[127] While political will among the Arctic states is currently lacking with regard to establishing a global polar code,[128] some or all of an ATS model may eventually meet the collective needs of stakeholders in the Arctic. As climate change renders the Arctic unrecognisable to its native inhabitants and governance becomes an ever-pressing matter of international security, good governance appears elusive. Yet, inclusive decision-making forums can build trust. Global cooperation in the face of unprecedented environmental and security challenges remains a sensible path forward.

Can supplementing the existing polycentric Arctic loose framework with a new multilateral regime enhance Arctic governance? If so, does it make sense to agree upon a sectoral or comprehensive approach? Given the contemporary geopolitical pulse, a starting point might be to build consensus regarding the central Arctic Ocean that is emerging as the ice cap melts. Irrespective of Arctic state efforts to expand continental claims, the centre of the Arctic still represents high seas and seabeds that are global commons.

Regarding substantive good governance, the first question should be whether to drill for oil and gas, given the substantial carbon dioxide, methane, and other GHG (greenhouse gas) emissions that result from such industrial operations.[129] Answering this question requires robust life-cycle analyses of the spectrum of energy sources. A broad array of assessments that include wind, wave, solar, and geothermal options both on and off shore should be part of an informed, transparent examination of the risks and advantages of polar energy generation.

Procedural good governance might be achieved by introducing multi-scale government and diverse stakeholder participation into polar decision-making. This can be done by scaling up involvement by civil society, including establishing regional citizen advisory councils with subpoena power into energy extraction and transportation oversight.[130] Transcending the one-industry-versus-one-agency governance model by introducing pluralism into the process of crafting sound energy policies can enhance polar governance.

Enhancing governance involves inclusive decision-making at all levels and across all sectors. Issues such as sovereignty and oil exploration are clearly controversial. Addressing them in an integrated and straightforward manner can build trust among stakeholders with which to strengthen good governance.

---

127 Although Shackelford notes that 'Argentina's claim could bring the ATS and UNCLOS into conflict', he further explains that Article IV of the Antarctic Treaty prohibits Antarctic Shelf claims via UNCLOS Art, 76; S.J. Shackelford, 'Was Selden Right?: the Expansion of Closed Seas and its Consequences', *Stanford Journal of International Law* 47, 2011, p. 44.
128 The Arctic Governance Project, op. cit., p. 18.
129 Norse and Amos, p. 11064.
130 Plater, op. cit., p. 11046 (building on the post *Exxon Valdez* spill requirement that the oil industry fund independent watchdog citizen oversight councils).

Part V
Cross-cutting issues

30

International trade rules and environmental effects

Indira Carr

International trade is widely seen by environmentalists as an opposing force. However, the adoption of the General Agreement on Tariffs and Trade (GATT) 1994 and subsequent disputes on the trade and environment interface indicate that environment-related issues are now approached in a sensitive manner by the World Trade Organization (WTO). This chapter commences with a brief account of the theory that has promoted free trade in modern times and examines the Tuna-Dolphin dispute by way of background. The chapter then considers GATT 1994 and the disputes under it, before concluding with an examination of the environment-focused provisions in other WTO agreements.

Introduction

This chapter examines the current approach to the environment in the World Trade Organization (WTO) Agreements,[1] in particular the *General Agreement on Tariffs and Trade* (GATT) 1994 in order to see whether the initial conflict between what is widely perceived to be two opposing regimes of free trade and environment has been resolved in the developing case law post GATT 1994. Before proceeding with an examination of the developments post GATT 1994, by way of context, a brief account of the theory that has promoted free trade in modern times is provided in the next section. This is followed with an analysis of the Tuna-Dolphin dispute under GATT 1947[2] which was instrumental in the vociferous debate between the environmentalists and the free trade promoters. Thereafter this chapter concentrates on the developments after the Tuna-Dolphin dispute. The aim in examining the GATT 1994, the WTO Preamble and the subsequent trade-related environment measures disputes, is to

---

1 The other agreements that are annexed to the umbrella agreement include General Agreement on Trade in Services (GATS); Agreement on Technical Barriers to Trade (TBT); Agreement on Sanitary and Phytosanitary Measures (SPS); Trade-Related Aspects of Intellectual Property Rights (TRIPS) and Agreement on Agriculture.
2 *General Agreement on Tariffs and Trade*, opened for signature 30 October 1947, 55 UNTS 187 (ended 31 December 1995) ('GATT 1947').

establish whether the free trade philosophy as enshrined in the GATT 1994 is interpreted in a manner that is sensitive to and takes within its equation environmental protection. The concluding section examines in brief the environment-focused provisions in the other WTO agreements.

It must be added that there are other regional trade agreements such as the North American Free Trade Agreement 1993 (NAFTA) and MERCOSUR Treaty Establishing the Southern Common Market 1991 where there is scope to explore the trade versus environment conflict. This chapter, for reasons of space, focuses on the GATT 1947, GATT 1994 and the other WTO agreements since a large number of states are WTO members.

The promotion of free trade

The Second World War left the world in tatters and it was widely felt that free trade between nations would bring about prosperity and peace in the world such that there would be no repetition of the destruction and gross inhumanities that people had endured. The view that free flow of goods across borders would result in friendship and consequently peace is not new. The long peaceful period, for instance, after the Battle of Waterloo is often attributed to 'the international flow of commodities and ideas'.[3] In more recent times similar links between trade and peace have been promoted by political scientists[4] and economists.[5] The reasons given for this close link are that conflict undermines trade, which in turn damages the economic growth and prosperity of the state; it therefore makes sense to continue trading and not have conflicts. Of course it is always possible to point to conflicts that have erupted between friendly nations after long periods of trade and resulting peace. Some of these conflicts may be attributed to internal power struggles that could find their expression in external conflict. It is not the intention here to explore the merits and demerits of liberalism. The purpose of mentioning this link between trade, peace and prosperity is to state that the framers of the GATT 1947 were influenced by this liberalist ideology.

The Second World War was instrumental in ushering in the era of free trade, resulting in the GATT adopted in 1947, which came into effect on 1 January 1948. The GATT promoted free trade through the principles of non-discrimination (expressed as the Most Favoured Nation obligation)[6] and the elimination of quantitative restrictions such as export/import licences, quotas or other measures.[7]

Trade between nations and the link between trade and economic growth are neither recent nor novel developments. The existence of trade routes such as the Silk Route[8] and

---

3 G. Blainey, *The Causes of War*, New York: Free Press, 1973.
4 R. Cooper, *The Economics of Interdependence: Economic Policy in the Atlantic Community*, New York: McGraw-Hill, 1968; K.R.J. Nye, *Transnational Relations and World Politics*, Cambridge, MA: Harvard University Press, 1972. M.W. Doyle, 'Liberalism and World Politics', *The American Political Science Review* 80(4), 1986, 1151–69.
5 K. Boulding, 'Towards a Pure Theory of Threat Systems', *American Economic Review* 53, 1966, 424–34.
6 This principle is found in Arts I and III. Article I requires that a contracting party (CP) should treat all CPs alike such that where a trade advantage has been granted by one CP to another CP it should be granted equally to other CPs. Article III requires that no discrimination be made between imported products and domestically produced like products.
7 Art. XI.
8 Refers to the combination of ancient land and sea routes connecting East, Southern and Western Asia with the Mediterranean and North Africa.

the Amber Route[9] crossing boundaries and continents is ample evidence that international trade is not a recent phenomenon. The link between economic growth and trade was realised and exploited widely between the fifteenth and eighteenth centuries. The Venetians and Genoese traders with commercial acumen accumulated huge wealth by buying goods at low prices in one port and selling them at high prices at another. This period also saw the emergence of a new form of mercantile venture through corporations. The East India Company established under the Royal Charter in 1600 by Queen Elizabeth I,[10] the Dutch East Indies Company[11] and the Swedish East Indies Company[12] are some examples. Trade, mainly in spices, silk, opium and saltpetre between the East and the West, thrived and helped in the economic growth of the European states. However, mercantilism, which was essentially protectionist, was the prevailing view in Europe during the seventeenth and eighteenth centuries. Mercantilism argued for strict regulation that encouraged exports and domestic manufacture of goods rather than cheaper imports.

Mercantilism, however, had its opponents and Adam Smith (1723–90) put forward his theory (often called the theory of absolute advantage) establishing that mercantilism would not enable economic growth. And it is to Adam Smith that the modern free trade philosophy owes much. Comparing the state to a household Adam Smith, wrote:

> It is the maxim of every prudent master of a family, never to attempt to make at home what it will cost him more to make than to buy. The tailor does not attempt to make his own shoes, but buys them of the shoemaker. The shoemaker does not attempt to make his own clothes, but employs a tailor . . . All of them find it in their interest to employ their whole industry in a way in which they have some advantage over their neighbours, and to purchase with a part of its produce or what is the same thing, with the price of a part of it, whatever else they have occasion for.
>
> What is prudence in the conduct of every private family, can scarce be folly in that of a great kingdom. If a foreign country can supply us with a commodity cheaper than we ourselves can make it, better buy it of them with some part of the produce of our own industry, employed in a way in which we have some advantage.[13]

To explain by way of illustration, according to Adam Smith, if State X is efficient in producing wheat and State Y in manufacturing fertilisers, and assuming that X needs fertilisers and Y needs wheat, then X and Y should concentrate on what they are good at and trade in the two products, which would be advantageous to both. That is, X should export wheat to Y and import fertilisers from Y, and Y should import wheat from X and export fertilisers to X.

There are, however, some problems with Smith's absolute advantage theory. What if a state does not have an absolute advantage in any of its goods or services over its trading

---

9   Refers to the route which connected Europe to Africa and was used for the amber trade.
10 This company was also imparted with powers to make laws and tax the locals. There were other corporations that were given charters for trading activities in specific countries – for instance the Levant Company for trading in Russia and the Morocco Company for trading in Morocco. For more on the origins of corporations see J.P. Davis, *Corporations: A Study of the Origin and Development of Great Business Combinations and their Relation to the Authority of the State*, New York: Capricorn Books, 1961.
11 This was established in 1602 and is often said to be the first multinational company.
12 This was established in 1731.
13 A. Smith, The *Wealth of Nations*, New York: Modern Library Edition, 1937, p. 424.

partners? David Ricardo (1772–1823) offered his theory of comparative advantage and he illustrated his theory thus. England takes 100 men to produce cloth and 120 men to produce wine whereas Portugal produces cloth with the efforts of 90 workers and the wine with 80 workers. In the production of both wine and cloth Portugal enjoys a position of absolute advantage when compared to England. However, in Ricardo's view trade would still be mutually advantageous if England imported wine produced by the efforts of 80 workers and Portugal imported cloth made by the effort of 100 workers from England. Both Portugal and England would benefit. Portugal would have gained from the efforts of her 80 workers that which would have taken 90 of her workers to produce and England would have gained from the efforts of her 100 workers that which would have taken 120 workers to produce. For Ricardo a country should focus on specialising in producing and exporting that in which it has a comparative advantage and importing that where it has a comparative disadvantage.

As with any theory there are a number of omissions in Ricardo's theory. It does not, for instance, take into account the relationship of costs to scale of operation and costs of labour (production of cloth) versus cost of land use (production of wine). A revised theory that builds these factors into the comparative advantage theory was offered by Heckscher and Ohlin and this theory is known as the Factor Proportions Theory or the Heckscher-Ohlin Theorem. This theory has been criticised on a number of counts, for instance for assuming that all countries have access to identical technologies and for not taking into account intra-industry trade.[14] Regardless of these criticisms, for the purposes of this chapter, suffice it to say that the theory of comparative advantage is the foundation on which the regulation of international trade in modern times rests. It underpins the ideologies of free trade reflected in the GATT 1947 and continues to this day in the form of GATT 1994.[15]

However, in the context of current concerns about environmental degradation as a result of rampant exploitation of natural resources such as fossil fuels, deforestation and pollution, the important question is: should free trade be promoted at all costs? How does GATT deal with this issue? Did the drafters of GATT include environmental aspects within the instrument?

The GATT 1947 primarily seemed to promote the exploitation of resources with prosperity as the objective since its Preamble in part read:

> [r]ecognising that their relations in the field of trade and economic endeavour should be conducted with a view to raising standards of living, ensuring full employment and a large and steadily growing volume of real income and effective demand, developing the full use of resources of the world and expanding the production and exchange of goods . . .

While the above may be said to be perfectly reasonable, since achieving economic growth leading to prosperity was the aim at the time GATT 1947 was drafted, the publication of a book in 1962 'triggered a greater public awareness and understanding of environmental

---

14 For further on this see A.O. Sykes, 'Comparative Advantage and the Normative Economics of International Trade Policy', *Journal of International Economic Law* 1(1), 1988, 49–82; H.G. Grubel and P.J. Lloyd, *Intra-Industry Trade: The Theory and Measurement of Trade in Differentiated Products*, London: Macmillan, 1975.

15 This is set out in Annex 1A to the WTO Agreement. It contains many of the key provisions of GATT 1947.

issues'.[16] The book was *Silent Spring* by Rachel Carson,[17] which highlighted the devastating effects of pesticides, in particular DDT,[18] on the environment and the depletion of wildlife. Carson's work was instrumental in harnessing the movement towards environmental protection by politicians, intellectuals and policy-makers. And since the 1960s the international community has been adopting a plethora of regional and international treaties focusing on the environment and conservation of wildlife.[19] It was generally felt that there were sufficient safeguards in the GATT 1947 in respect of environmental protection within its Article XX exceptions regardless of the ambitions expressed in its Preamble. But these views were to be undermined with the Tuna-Dolphin dispute brought before the GATT Panel, which showed the potential for conflict between free trade and environmental values and the usefulness of the exceptions in respect of conservation measures, human and animal life, and plant life as expressed in Articles XX(b) and (g).[20]

Tuna-Dolphin disputes under GATT 1947

The first Tuna-Dolphin dispute (Tuna-Dolphin I)[21] arose when the United States (US) imposed an embargo on the import of commercial yellowfin tuna and tuna products caught using the purse seine method in the Eastern Tropical Pacific under the *Marine Mammal Protection Act 1972* (as revised in 1988 and 1990) (MMPA). Section 101(a)(2) of the said legislation prohibits the importation of fish products from countries which have commercial fishing technology that results in the incidental killing of, or serious injury to, ocean mammals in excess of the US standards. Section 102(a)(2)(b) prohibits the importation of yellowfin

---

16 Senator G. Mitchell in the United States Senate, 3 August 1987, 'A resolution to express the sense of the Senate that Rachel Carson is recognised on the twenty fifth anniversary of her book "Silent Spring" for her outstanding contribution to public awareness and understanding of environmental issues.'

17 R. Carson, *Silent Spring*, Boston: Houghton Mifflin, 1962.

18 Dichlorodiphenyltrichloroethane. The use of DDT except for malaria control was banned by the *Stockholm Convention on Persistent Organic Pollutants*, opened for signature 23 May 2001, UN Doc UNEP/. POPS/CONF/4, App. 11 (entered into force 17 May 2004).

19 Sweden called for an international conference on the environment which resulted in the United Nations Conference on the Human Environment in 1972. The proposal made in the Conference resulted in the setting up of the United Nations Environment Programme (UNEP). For further on the report of the conference see L.B. Sohn, 'The Stockholm Declaration on the Human Environment', *Harvard International Law Journal* 14, 1973, 423–515. Some of the well-known treaties from the 1970s and 1980s include the *Convention on the International Trade in Endangered Species* 1973, the *Vienna Convention for the Protection of the Ozone Layer* 1985 and *Basel Convention on the Control of Transboundary Movements of Hazardous Waste* 1989.

20 Article XX states:

> Subject to the requirement that such measures are not applied in a manner which would constitute a means of arbitrary or unjustifiable discrimination between countries where the same conditions prevail, or a disguised restriction on international trade, nothing in this Agreement shall be construed to prevent the adoption or enforcement by any contracting party of measures:
>
> . . .
>
> (b) necessary to protect human, animal or plant life or health . . .
> (g) relating to the conservation of exhaustible natural resources if such measures are made effective in conjunction with restrictions on domestic production or consumption . . .

21 Panel Report, United States – Restrictions on Imports of Tuna, GATT Doc. DS21/R (3 September 1991).

tuna and tuna products using the purse seine method unless the exporting country has regulations that control the incidental taking of mammals comparable with those of the US. The embargo affected Mexico, which claimed that the US measure was a quantitative restriction and thus breached Article XI of GATT.[22] The US defended its measures on the basis of Articles III(4)[23] and XX(b) and (g). The US stated that the treatment accorded to the Mexican Tuna was not less favourable than that accorded to like products of national origin. The Panel concluded that Article III focused on the characteristics of the product and not on the method of production. Article III(4), the Panel said, called for the 'comparison of imported tuna as a product with that of domestic tuna as a product' and they could not see how tuna as a product could be affected by the method of production. The product/process distinction was therefore irrelevant.[24]

As for Article XX(b),[25] the US argued that the objective of the MMPA was the preservation of animal life, the MMPA was the only measure they had at their disposal and the GATT exception should be read in a manner that would endorse the import ban of products caught outside their territorial waters. The Panel concluded that Article XX(b) did not have an extra-jurisdictional effect and that the US was unable to demonstrate that their measure was necessary for the protection of dolphins. The word 'necessary' was interpreted extremely restrictively and the US interpretation of 'necessary' as 'needed' did not have any impact on the Panel. As for the argument by the US that the measures were primarily aimed at the protection of dolphins,[26] in raising the Article XX(g) exception the Panel could not see how the measures could be primarily aimed at conservation of dolphins. It was impossible for Mexico to tell with certainty whether her conservation policies met the US standards during a specific period since the tolerance level during a specific period was to be calculated in terms of the US incidental dolphin taking recorded during the same period. The Panel also stated that Article XX(g) did not have extra-jurisdictional effect since to give such an interpretation could result in each contracting party 'determin[ing] the conservation policies from which other contracting policies could not deviate without jeopardising their rights under the General Agreement'.[27] The Panel concluded that the US embargo was in breach of Article XI(1) and could not be justified on the basis of Articles XX(b) and (g).

22 Article XI permits quantitative restrictions through tariffs but not non-tariff restrictions such as quotas or import/export permits.

23 Article III(4) states:

> The products of the territory of any contracting party imported into the territory of any other contracting party shall be accorded treatment no less favourable than that accorded to like products of national origin in respect of all laws, regulation and requirements affecting their internal sale, offering for sale, purchase, transportation, distribution or use.

24 For more on this distinction and the criticisms see R. Howse and D. Regan, 'The Product/Process Distinction – An Illusory Basis for Disciplining Unilateralism' *European Journal of International Law* 11, 2000, 249–89; S. Charnovitz, 'The Law of "PPMs" in the WTO: Debunking the Myth of Illegality' *Yale Journal of International Law* 27, 2000, 59–110. See also J.L. Nissen, 'Achieving a Balance between Trade and the Environment: The Need to Amend he WTO/GATT to include Multilateral Environmental Agreement' *Law and Policy in International Business* 28, 1996–1997, 901–28.

25 See note 20 above for the wording of Art. XX(b).

26 The US were relying on the interpretation given to 'relating to the conservation of exhaustible natural resources' in *Canada – Measures Affecting Exports of Unprocessed Herring and Salmon*, adopted 22 March 1988, BISD 355/98, 114, para. 4.6.

27 Ibid., para. 5.32.

The Panel Report was not adopted since no request for adoption was made. This was possibly due to the NAFTA negotiations that were taking place at the time between the US and other North American states. Subsequent to Tuna-Dolphin I the European Community (EC) and the Netherlands brought a complaint to the GATT Panel (Tuna-Dolphin II)[28] saying that the 'intermediary nation embargo' or secondary embargo was in breach of GATT since the US legislation prohibited the import of yellowfin tuna or products from any country that could not certify that it had not imported products from a state that was the subject of a direct embargo in the preceding six months. The conclusions of the Tuna-Dolphin II Panel were no different from that of the Tuna-Dolphin I Panel. These two cases made a huge impact on environmentalists. The product/process distinction and the emphasis on physical characteristics were criticised for their short-sightedness. The suggestion that the US should have explored other avenues such as international cooperation was seen as naive since international agreements take time and the Panel's lack of interest in instituting change through their interpretation of Article XX(b) and (g), taking into account the strong consensus of environmental protection, was seen as strongly endorsing the widely held view in the environmentalist camp that free trade, regardless of the environmental costs, was the primary and only goal for GATT. This view, however, is questionable since the exceptions would not have been included in the first place in the GATT 1947 had the instrument been purely trade-oriented.

It must also be pointed out that the Panel were concerned about interpreting Article XX widely, the reason being that such an interpretation would restrict trade to states that had identical or equivalent regulations in place, which would undermine the Most Favoured Nation principle embodied in the GATT. In short, it was felt that their broad interpretation was likely to fuel a trade war that would undermine the foundations of the GATT.

The WTO, GATT 1994 and subsequent cases

The worldwide publicity caused by the Tuna-Dolphin disputes was at a time when the Uruguay Round of trade negotiations was taking place.[29] It would only be right to expect that the balance between trade and environment would be addressed and the negotiations would have revisited the various exceptions contained in Article XX of GATT 1947 with a view to clarifying various issues such as the product/process methods in the context of like products and the meaning of 'necessary', and the relationship between GATT and the multilateral environmental agreements (MEAs) of which there were plenty. Many of the critics felt that these reforms would rectify any issues there were in dealing with trade-related environment measures.[30] Unfortunately these widely floated ideas, to reconcile free trade with environment, were not taken on board. The wording of Article XX remained unchanged in the GATT 1994, attached as Annex I to the WTO Agreement. The Preamble of the WTO Agreement itself made specific reference to environmental protection. The relevant part of the Preamble reads:

---

28 Panel Report, *United States – Restrictions on Imports of Tuna*, GATT Doc. DS29/R (1994).

29 This Round, involving negotiations on various issues including intellectual property and trade in services, lasted from 1986 to 1994.

30 B. Chaytor and J. Cameron, 'The Treatment of Environmental Considerations in the World Trading Organisation', *Yearbook of International Co-operation on Environment and Development*, 1999/2000, 55–64.

relations in the field of trade and economic endeavour should be conducted with a view to raising standards of living, ensuring full employment and a large and steadily growing volume of real income and effective demand, and expanding the production of trade in goods and services, while allowing the optimal use of the world's resources in accordance with the objective of sustainable development, seeking both to protect and preserve the environment and to enhance the means for doing so in a manner consistent with the needs and concerns at different levels of economic development . . .[31]

This emphasis could be seen in positive terms since it indicates that environmental protection was a concern that the free trade promoters had taken into account, as well as the need for striking a balance between the use of resources and the preservation of the environment. It must also be said that this Preamble is different from the Preamble to the GATT 1947, which focuses on 'ensuring full employment. .. growing of real income . . . [and] developing the full use of the resources of the world . . .'. There is no mention of sustainability or continuity by ensuring that the world we inhabit is preserved for future generations. The entire emphasis of the GATT 1947 is human-centric, showing no inter-generational or cross-species sympathies since it encourages the full exploitation of resources.

The first dispute to be heard after the formation of the WTO, *United States – Standards for Reformulated and Conventional Gasoline*[32] (US Gasoline), did not endorse the new optimism that may have pervaded those who wanted environmental protection to be firmly entrenched in the free trade agenda. In this case the US promulgated Gasoline Rules under the *Clean Air Act 1963* (as amended in 1990), which allowed only gasoline of specified cleanliness to be sold to consumers in high-pollution areas in the country. The statutory baseline assigned affected importers of gasoline and Venezuela and Brazil complained that the Rules were in violation of Article III of GATT 1994, the wording of which was no different from GATT 1947. The US justified them on the basis of Article XX exceptions. The Panel concluded that the statutory baseline was discriminatory since the importer would be required to provide gasoline of a higher quality than that provided by a domestic producer who used an individual refinery baseline. The Panel's reasoning reflects, to a great extent, the reasoning of the Tuna-Dolphin panels. It was widely felt that despite the wording of the Preamble of the WTO Agreement, environmental issues had had no impact on the GATT panels. This, however, is perhaps a misplaced criticism since there was a softening towards and recognition of environmental issues even though the conclusions may not have gone the way the US wanted. The Appellate Body recognised the importance of coordinating trade and environment policies and noted that the language of the Preamble did add 'colour, texture and shading' to the interpretation of agreements annexed to the WTO Agreement.[33] They

---

31 *The Final Act Embodying the Results of the Uruguay Round of Multinational Trade Agreements* (1994), 1867 UNTS 14, 33 ILM 1143.
32 Panel Report WT/DS2R, January 1996; Report of the Appellate Body WT/DS2/AB/R, April 1996.
33 The use of this phrase has attracted criticism. Among the critics are S. Gaines, 'The WTO's Reading of the GATT Article XX Chapeau: A Disguised Restriction on Environmental Measures', *University of Pennsylvania Journal of International Economic Law* 22(4), 2001, 739–862, p. 836, who says such phrases reduce the importance of environment objectives. It must be added that Gaines' article is vigorously arguing for the justification for unilateral action in environmental matters and the need for the WTO to allow such measures.

also openly stated that they were in no way questioning the authority of a state to pursue environmental objectives.[34]

That the environment is a relevant factor has been endorsed further by cases subsequent to US Gasoline. The facts of *United States − Important Prohibitions of Certain Shrimp and Shrimp Products*[35] (Shrimp-Turtle) are not unlike those of the Tuna-Dolphin cases. The US banned the import of shrimp and shrimp products that were harvested using technology that would affect sea turtles.[36] The complainants were India, Malaysia, Pakistan and Thailand and yet again the US raised the Article XX exceptions. During the course of the hearing, however, a number of points emerged. For instance, the US had unilaterally imposed the embargo and had not engaged in serious negotiations to conclude bilateral or multilateral agreements for the preservation of sea turtles. There was also no transparency or procedural fairness in the certification process, in that there were no formal procedures for a country applying for certification to be heard, or for that matter to respond, to arguments made against them during the certification process.[37] The Appellate Body was very clear in agreeing that the measures served the environmental objective recognised as legitimate under Article XX(g). However, the way the US had applied the measures amounted to unjustifiable and arbitrary discrimination contrary to the chapeau of Article XX. It is very clear from the Appellate Body Report that environmental concerns were being taken seriously. Its generous interpretation of 'resources' to include living or non-living things, and that they need not be rare or endangered for them to be 'exhaustible', lends support to the view that the panels were taking a genuinely inclusive approach in the interpretation of environment-related provisions in the GATT 1994. As in US Gasoline, in the Shrimp-Turtle matter the Appellate Body stated what they were not deciding in the appeal. The paragraphs preceding the Finding and Conclusions of the Appellate Body Report said:

> [W]e wish to underscore what we have not decided in this appeal. We have not decided that the protection and the preservation of the environment is of no importance

---

34 The last paragraph of Section V, Appellate Body Report WT/DS2/AB/R, April 1996 states:

> It is of some importance that the Appellate Body point out what this does *not* mean. It does not mean or imply that the ability of any WTO Member to take measures to control air pollution or, more generally, to protect the environment is at issue. This would be to ignore the fact that Article XX of the *General Agreement* contains provisions designed to permit important state interests – including the protection of human health, as well as the conservation of exhaustible natural resources – to find expression. The provisions of Article XX were not changed as a result of the Uruguay Round of Multilateral Trade Negotiations. Indeed in the preamble to the WTO Agreement and in the *Decision of Trade and Environment* [adopted by Ministers at the Meeting of the Trade Negotiations Committee in Marrakesh on April 14, 1994], there is specific acknowledgement to be found about the importance of co-ordinating policies on trade and environment. WTO members have a large measure of autonomy to determine their own policies on the environment (including its relationship with trade), their environmental objectives and the environmental legislation they enact and they implement. So far as concerns the WTO, that autonomy is circumscribed only by the need to respect the requirement of the *General Agreement* and other covered agreements.

35 Report of the Panel WT/DS58/R May 1998 and Appellate Body Report WT/DS58/AB/R October 1998.

36 Prohibition under section 609 of Public Law 101-162 16 United States Code § 1537.

37 See WT/DS58/AB/R October 1998, paras 166–72, 180–3.

to the Members of the WTO. Clearly it is. We have not decided that the sovereign nations that are Members States of the WTO cannot adopt effective measures to protect endangered species, such as sea turtles. Clearly they can and should. And we have not decided that sovereign states should not act together bilaterally, plurilaterally or multilaterally, either within the WTO or in other international fora, to protect endangered species or to otherwise protect the environment. Clearly, they should and do.

What we have decided is simply this: although the measure of the United States in dispute in this appeal serves as an environmental objective recognised as legitimate under paragraph (g) of Article XX of the GATT 1994, this measure has been applied by the United States in a manner which constitutes an arbitrary and unjustifiable discrimination between Members of the WTO, contrary to the requirements of the chapeau of Article XX.

The Shrimp-Turtle dispute helped make clear what a state, interested in protecting marine resources, must not do in order for it not to fall foul of the WTO provisions when banning imports of products on environmental grounds from other countries. It must, for instance, make sure that its procedures are fair and make serious efforts to procure a bilateral or multilateral agreement rather than adopting unilateral measures.

At this juncture, in support of the WTO, it must be said that the Appellate Body did make frequent references to developments in environmental law, thus exhibiting a sensitivity to environmental issues. This certainly was not that apparent in the Tuna–Dolphin disputes.[38]

Two further disputes relating to trade and environment have been heard by the WTO since the Shrimp-Turtle matter. The question then is: have these disputes advanced the more inclusive agenda apparent in Shrimp-Turtle, or is there a return to the old ways of thinking found in Tuna-Dolphin? It would be fair, from an objective standpoint, to say that there is certainly a broadening of interpretation of problematic words and phrases in Article XX as the following discussion exhibits. While the reasoning may not be as tidy or clear-cut as some lawyers might expect, this should not detract attention from the Panel's sophisticated approach in dealing with trade-related environment measures in a mature and careful manner.

In *European Communities – Measures Affecting Asbestos and Asbestos-Containing Products Asbestos*[39] (EC Asbestos) the French Government prohibited the manufacture, sale and import of asbestos since it was a highly toxic material harmful to human health. Canada, the second largest producer of asbestos, complained to the WTO. The EC contended that it was hazardous not only to workers exposed to the materials but also to the general population. Canada argued that a distinction ought to be drawn between chrysotile asbestos fibres and chrysotile that had been 'encapsulated in a cement matrix', as the latter stopped any fibres being released, and that the imposed ban was contrary to GATT Articles III(4) and XI. The EC argued otherwise. The Appellate Body examined the issue of like products and came to the conclusion it was appropriate to take into account the risks associated with chrysotile fibres when examining the likeness of products and that the physical properties were of themselves

---

38 See G. van Claster 'Faites Vos Jeux – Regulatory Autonomy and the World Trade Organisation after *Brazil Tyres*', *Journal of Environmental Law* 20(10), 2008, 121–36.
39 WT/DS135/AB/R 12 March 2001.

insufficient to establish likeness.[40] Neither did taking the health risks into account when looking at establishing the likeness of products nullify the effect of Article XX(b).[41] As for the word 'necessary' that had been restrictively interpreted in the Tuna-Dolphin cases, the Appellate Body in the present case construed it as 'reasonably available', thus introducing an element of flexibility. The Appellate Body introduced the 'weighing and balancing approach' that had been developed in *Korea – Measures Affecting Import of Fresh, Chilled and Frozen Beef*[42] (Korea Beef). According to this approach the question of whether a measure is 'necessary' requires a series of factors to be taken into account and these include 'the contribution made by the compliance measure to the enforcement of the law or regulation at issue, the importance of the common interests or values protected by that law or regulation and the accompanying impact of the law or regulation on imports or exports'.[43] In applying this approach to the dispute under consideration, the Appellate Body concluded that the objective pursued by the measure, the preservation of human life and health, was vital and important in the highest degree and that the EC had demonstrated a *prima facie* case that there was no 'reasonably available alternative'.[44]

An argument was made by Canada that the EC should have quantified the risk associated with chrysotile cement and could not simply rely on hypotheses.[45] However, the Appellate Body was of the view that Article XX(b) does not impose an obligation to quantify the risk to human life or health and that the pathologies associated with chrysotile were of such a serious nature that the EC was not relying on mere hypotheses.[46]

The 'weighing and balancing' approach developed in Korea Beef and adopted in EC Asbestos seems to have established itself in disputes involving Article XX as indicated by *Brazil – Measures Affecting Imports of Retreaded Tyres*[47] (Brazil Tyres). This dispute concerned the banning of import of retreaded tyres by Brazil on the grounds of protection of human, animal or plant life or health. Once again the word 'necessary' in Article XX(b) was analysed. The Appellate Body took the view that the word was not limited to that which is 'indispensable'. It went on to say that:

> in order to determine whether a measure is 'necessary' within the meaning of Art XX(b) . . . a panel must consider the relevant factors, particularly the importance of the interests and values at stake, the extent of the contribution to the achievement of the measure's objectives, and its trade restrictiveness. If this analysis yields a preliminary conclusion

---

40 Ibid., para. 122. In para. 113 the Appellate Body said:

> [A]s we have said, in examining the 'likeness' of products, panels must evaluate *all* of the relevant evidence. We are very much of the view that evidence relating to the health risks associated with a product may be pertinent in an examination of 'likeness' under Art III:4 of the GATT 1994. We do not, however, consider that the evidence relating to the health risks associated with chrysotile asbestos fibres need be examined under a *separate* criterion, because we believe that this evidence can be evaluated under the existing criteria of physical properties, and of consumers' tastes and habits . . .

41 Ibid., para. 115.
42 WT/DS161/AB/R 10 January 2001, para. 166.
43 Ibid., para. 164.
44 Ibid., paras 172–5.
45 Ibid., para. 165.
46 Ibid., para. 167.
47 Appellate Body Report WT/DS332/AB/R 3 December 2007.

that the measure is necessary, this result must be confirmed by comparing the measure with possible alternatives, which may be less trade restrictive while providing an equivalent contribution to the achievement of the object. . . . It is through this process that a panel determines whether a measure is necessary.[48]

The adoption of this 'weighing and balancing' approach does not, however, mean that the importance of the chapeau to Article XX has been overlooked or in any way diminished. The link between the chapeau and the sub-paragraphs of Article XX was highlighted by the Appellate Body when it said that there is:

arbitrary and unjustifiable discrimination within the meaning of chapeau of Article XX, when a Member seeks to justify the discrimination resulting from the application of its measure by a rationale that bears no relationship to the accomplishment of the objective that falls within the purview of one of the paragraphs of Article XX, or goes against this objective.[49]

These four cases, relating to the trade and environment interface, indicate that the allegations that were made about the intolerance of the promoters of free trade towards the environment cannot be advanced meaningfully. The WTO seems to have taken a sensitive approach in the interpretation of 'necessary'. The Appellate Body has repeatedly acknowledged that, in reaching a decision on whether an import ban can be justified on the basis of Article XX exceptions, they are involved in (1) the weighing and balancing of relevant factors and assessing the measure taken by the state with possible alternatives, and (2) considering whether possible alternatives could help in achieving the environmental or health objectives that a state has aimed to meet with the trade-restrictive measures it has taken. The relevant factors that are taken into account are certainly wide-ranging, from physical characteristics to consumer tastes and behaviour, thus indicating an openness towards a flexible approach. This is in complete contrast to the rigid interpretation that was applied in the Tuna-Dolphin Case. Admittedly there are still issues as to what phrases such as 'equivalent contribution' mean and whether the Panel engages in a cost–benefit analysis in its weighing and balancing test.[50] These are sound criticisms, but the nature of the circumstances for adopting trade-related environment measures are inevitably context-dependent and against this background the Appellate Body can do no more than provide a general description of what it means by the 'weighing and balancing' test. While this approach may not meet the demands of those who wish the WTO to give precedence to environmental issues, it must be admitted that the

---

48 Ibid., para. 178.
49 Ibid., para. 246. Of course the use of phrases such as 'material contribution' and 'marginal contribution' has prompted commentators to say that 'the use of the word "material" surely implies a factual, quantitative analysis': G. van Claster, 'Faites Vos Jeux – Regulatory Autonomy and the World Trade Organisation after *Brazil Tyres*' *Journal of Environmental Law* 20 (1), 2008, 121–36, p. 136. However, others have argued otherwise. See D. Regan, 'The Meaning of "Necessary" in GATT Article XX and GATS Article XIV: The Myth of Cost-benefit Balancing', *World Trade Review* 6, 2007, 347–69. See also G. Kapetarian, 'A Critique of the WTO Jurisprudence in "Necessity"', *International & Comparative Law Quarterly*, 2010, 89–127; See also S. Thomas, 'Trade and Environment under WTO Rules after the Appellate Body Report in *Brazil-retreaded Tyres*', *Journal of International Commercial Law and Technology* 4(1), 2009, 42–9.
50 Ibid.

WTO has moved in the right direction by taking environmental concerns into the equation when examining the trade-related environment measures.

The WTO approach to trade and environment is an expansive one that seeks to accommodate the value systems of both free trade and the environment that were initially perceived to be opposing values. It is doing this in a balanced fashion. It must be appreciated that the sole promotion of the environmental agenda and its whole-hearted adoption, without taking into account the importance of trade for economic growth, will result in developmental stagnation. This would not only undermine the goals set in the WTO Agreement but also the poverty reduction goal set by the Millennium Development Goals. It is certainly not the case that the trade promoters and the environmentalists are at opposite ends of the spectrum as they were made out to be following the Tuna-Dolphin cases. It is apparent from the recent decisions emanating from the WTO that there is some degree of convergence between the free trade promoters and the environmentalists. Without doubt, trade – and thus economic growth and human prosperity – remain an important part of the WTO, but they have shown through their decisions that they are willing to balance the trade interests with state measures that are addressed to protect the environment or health.

Conclusion

Before concluding this chapter brief mention must be made of a number of other WTO agreements that also address measures to protect human, animal or plant life or health. These are the *Agreement on the Application Sanitary and Phytosanitary Agreement Measures* (SPS Agreement) and the *Agreement on Technical Barriers to Trade* (TBT Agreement). The SPS Agreement applies only to measures directed at protecting the risks arising from, for instance, the entry of disease-causing organisms, additives or toxins, diseases carried by animals, plants or products thereof or to prevent or limit other damage from the entry, establishment or spread of pests.[51] The TBT Agreement's focus is on documents dealing with:

> product characteristics or their related processes and production methods, including the applicable administrative provisions, with which compliance is mandatory. It may also include or deal exclusively with terminology, symbols, packaging, marking or labelling requirements as they apply to a product, process or production method.[52]

There is some degree of convergence between these two agreements and GATT 1994, and there is some ambiguity as to whether the SPS Agreement or the TBT Agreements will be applied when there is a challenge, for instance, on the basis of both the GATT 1994 and the SPS Agreement. The SPS Agreement in its Preamble states that it aims to elaborate rules on the application of Article XX(b), and there is a similarity of approach in that both require that the policy adopted towards health is necessary. However, the SPS Agreement goes further in requiring measures to be consistent and scientifically based, thus laying down further criteria.[53]

---

51 For the full definition of the phrase 'sanitary and phytosanitary measure' see the *Agreement on the Application of Sanitary and Phytosanitary Agreement Measures*, Uruguay Round Agreement (entered into force 1995), Annex A.1.

52 *Agreement on the Application of Sanitary and Phytosanitary Agreement Measures*, Uruguay Round Agreement (entered into force 1995), Annex I.1.

53 Ibid., Arts 2(1), 2(2), 5(5).

As to the TBT Agreement, an opportunity for a GATT Panel did arise in EC Asbestos but the Panel decided not to examine Canada's four claims under the TBT Agreement. The Appellate Body, however, reversed the findings in section 8.72(a) of the Panel Report that the TBT Agreement 'does not apply to the part of the Decree relating to the ban on imports of asbestos and asbestos-containing products since it did not constitute a "technical regulation" within the meaning of Annex 1.1 to the TBT Agreement'.[54] The Appellate Body did not, however, go on to analyse the TBT Agreement[55] but observed that:

> not *all* internal measures covered by Article III (4) of the GATT 1994 'affecting [the] sale, offering for sale, purchase, transportation or distribution or use' of a product are necessarily 'technical regulation' under the TBT Agreement. Rather, we rule only that this particular measure, the Decree at stake, falls within the definition of a 'technical regulation' given in Annex 1.1. of that Agreement.[56]

There are other ambiguities in the trade environment interface, for instance the issue of the relationship of the suite of WTO agreements with MEAs that also include trade restriction provisions.[57] There is no provision that is comparable to that found in the NAFTA, which provides that a number of MEAs such as the Montreal Protocol take precedence over the NAFTA. Commentators have talked about revising various provisions in the GATT 1994, for instance Article XX, to make way for MEAs, but these are perhaps long-term solutions. In the short term the panels could use their innovative techniques of interpretation to accommodate MEAs. After all, the Shrimp-Turtle Panel did state that the US should have considered the possibility of multilateral agreements before imposing a ban on imports. Also the WTO Panels could use Article 31(3) of the *Vienna Convention on Law of Treaties* effectively to give precedence to MEAs, since it requires that when interpreting a treaty subsequent practice, legal treaties and relevant rules of international law have to be taken into account.

There is still a great deal of work to be done on a case-by-case basis by the panels hearing trade disputes at different levels. The important thing to remember is that the trade–environment interface is a complex one, but it is possible to reconcile the two fields by adopting a sensitive and pragmatic approach that does not at the same time forget the need to achieve a balance. As Mike Moore, the ex-Director-General of the WTO has said, 'Trade and environment need not be contradictory forces but can indeed be complementary.'[58] Indeed, regardless of the sceptics,[59] the WTO dispute settlement body has shown that there is meaningful engagement between trade and environment issues.

54 *European Communities – Measures Affecting Asbestos and Asbestos-containing Products*, EC Asbestos WT/DS135/AB/R, para. 76
55 Ibid., para. 78.
56 Ibid., para. 77.
57 D. Brack, 'The Shrimp-Turtle Case: Implications for the Multilateral Environmental Agreement', *Yearbook of International Law* 9, 1998, 13–19.
58 Press Release, 'Trade Liberalisation Reinforces the Need for Environmental Co-operation', 8 October 1999.
59 See e.g. S.E. Gaines 'The WTO's Reading of the GATT Article XX Chapeau: A Disguised Restriction on Environmental Measures' *University of Pennsylvania Journal of International Economic Law* (8), 2001, 739–862.

31

International investment agreements and sustainable development

Future pathways

*Markus W. Gehring and Avidan Kent**

The relationship between foreign direct investment (FDI) and sustainable development can be described as 'dual-natured'. On the one hand, the activity of Transnational Corporations (TNCs) can, and often does, promote certain aspects of sustainable development. On the other hand, it has been argued by many that TNCs' activities can also frustrate sustainable development goals. Moreover, ignoring sustainable development issues can be bad for business. Therefore, there is much to gain by the integration of sustainable development and FDI policies. This chapter reviews the procedural and substantive dimensions of international investment agreements and the tools available to integrate sustainable development goals within them, as well as the challenges faced by policy-makers in this field.

Introduction

The concept of 'sustainable development' has been recognised by the world's nations in a line of international documents and global events.[1] While many have attempted to define this term,[2] perhaps the most commonly accepted definition is the one proposed almost 25 years ago by the Brundtland Report, in which it was described as 'development that meets the needs of the present without compromising the ability of future generations to meet their

---

* With special thanks to Erika Arban and Misha Benjamin for invaluable research assistance and to SSHRC for contributing financially to this project. This chapter shares thoughts with previous work of the authors.

1 See *inter alia The Rio Declaration on Environment and Development*, UN GAOR (1992) UN Doc. A/CONF.151/26. Online. Available HTTP: <www.un.org/documents/ga/conf151/aconf15126-1annex1.htm> (accessed 19 December 2011) ('*Rio Declaration on Environment and Development*'); *Johannesburg Declaration on Sustainable Development* (2002), UN Doc. A/CONF/199/20; *Doha Ministerial Declaration*, Ministerial Conference, Fourth Session, 14 November 2001, WTO Doc. WT/MIN(01)/DEC/W/1. For a more detailed review, see M.C. Cordonier Segger and A. Khalfan, *Sustainable Development Law: Principles, Practices and Prospects*, Oxford: Oxford University Press, 2004, pp. 3–4.

2 Cordonier Segger and Khalfan, op. cit., pp. 3–4.

own needs'.[3] In essence, the ultimate objective of sustainable development is the integration of economic development with environmental protection and social well-being.[4] Sir Elihu Lauterpacht has recently explained in this respect:

> Sustainable development, therefore, represents a commitment to a different kind of economic development, one that focuses on achieving important improvements in the opportunities and quality of life without jeopardizing the interests of future generations.[5]

Foreign Direct Investment (FDI), as defined by the Organisation for Economic Co-operation and Development (OECD), 'reflects the objective of establishing a lasting interest by a resident enterprise in one economy (direct investor) in an enterprise (direct investment enterprise) that is resident in an economy other than that of the direct investor'.[6] It is usually assumed that such investments include several features, such as the transfer of funds, long-term activity, at least partial participation of the investor in the management of the project, and business risk.[7] The promotion of FDI is regulated mainly by international investment agreements (IIAs). These treaties are designed to provide security and certainty for foreign investors, in order to promote FDI, with the object of achieving the ultimate goal of development.

The relationship between FDI and sustainable development can be described as 'dual-natured'.[8] On the one hand, the activity of Transnational Corporations (TNCs) can, and often does, promote certain aspects of sustainable development. This is evident in fields such as climate change, poverty eradication and labour standards. The activity of TNCs, for example, supports the transfer of technology and knowledge, the creation of jobs and increases in productivity. On the other hand, it has been argued by many that TNCs' activities can also frustrate sustainable development goals. For example, the UN 'Special Representative of the Secretary-General on the issues of human rights and transnational corporations' revealed serious allegations of violations of a wide range of human rights by TNCs.[9] Similarly, some

---

3 World Commission on Environment and Development (WCED), *Our Common Future*, New York: Oxford University Press, 1987. Online. Available HTTP: <http://www.un-documents.net/wced-ocf.htm> (accessed 7 May 2012).

4 Cordonier Segger and Khalfan, op. cit., p. 103.

5 Sir Elihu Lauterpacht, in his foreword to M.C. Cordonier Segger, M. Gehring and A. Newcombe (eds) *Sustainable Development in World Investment Law*. Alphen aan den Rijn: Kluwer Law International, 2010.

6 Secretary-General of the OECD, *OECD Benchmark Definition of Foreign Direct Investment*, 4th edn. Paris: OECD, 2008. Online. Available HTTP: <http://www.oecd.org/dataoecd/26/50/40193734.pdf> (accessed 19 December 2011) ('OECD Benchmark Definition of Foreign Direct Investment'), at para. 117.

7 R. Dolzer and C. Schreuer, *Principles of International Investment Law*, New York: Oxford University Press, 2008, p. 60.

8 This term was recently used to describe the more specific relationship between FDI and climate change; see United Nations Conference on Trade and Development, *World Investment Report 2010, Investing in a Low Carbon Economy*, New York: United Nations Publications, 2010 ('UNCTAD Report 2010') p. 136.

9 Report of the Special Representative of the Secretary-General on the issue of human rights and transnational corporations and other business enterprises: J.ArJ.K Ruggie, *Promotion and Protection of all Human Rights, Civil, Political, Economic, Social and Cultural Rights, Including the Right to Development* (2008) UN Doc A/HRC/8/5/Add.2. Online. Available HTTP: <www2.ohchr.org/english/bodies/hrcouncil/8session/reports.htm> (accessed 19 December 2011).

FDI also adversely affect the environment. The establishment of coal-based power plants is one such example.[10]

The relationship between FDI and sustainable development is therefore two-sided. While FDI can support sustainable development, sustainable development can also support the interests of TNCs. The great economic potential embedded in the prospect of a 'green economy' is indeed noticeable.[11] For example, in the context of climate change, according to some estimation the demand for emission credits may reach 100 billion US dollars by 2050.[12] An increase in the demand for low-carbon technologies is therefore expected, and consequently also great economic gains to the owners of these technologies. Moreover, ignoring sustainable development issues can be bad for businesses. For example, as identified by the Stern Report, the effects of climate change are expected to damage economic growth and disrupt the economy 'on a scale similar to those associated with the great wars and the economic depression of the first half of the twentieth century'.[13]

It can be understood, therefore, that there is much to gain by the integration of sustainable development and FDI policies. Such integration can take place in several fora. For example, it has been suggested that the protection offered by IIAs should be integrated within the Kyoto Protocol's flexible mechanisms, as a means to promote low-carbon investments.[14] But, as stated by Sussman, in light of the complex questions climate change negotiators already must face, adding the negotiation over a multilateral investment agreement into this process seems impractical.[15] Moreover, past attempts to conclude investment treaties in multilateral frameworks (the OECD, or the WTO for example) raise even more doubts as to the viability of this idea.

Another, perhaps more practical possibility, would be to integrate sustainable development goals into IIAs. As explained in this chapter, the integration of sustainable development in IIAs can take place on several levels. First, sustainable development objectives can be integrated before the conclusion of IIAs. For example, impact assessment mechanisms can assist decision-makers in understanding the impact, whether positive or negative, an investment treaty may have on sustainable development objectives. Second, sustainable development can be integrated within the procedural dimensions of IIAs' dispute settlement mechanisms. For example, the principle of public participation, as phrased by the International Law Association's

10 See e.g. the factual background of the Vattenfall case, *Vattenfall AB, Vattenfall Europe AG, Vattenfall Europe Generation AG and Co. KG (Sweden and Europe) v The Federal Republic of Germany*, (Award) ('2011') ICSID Case No. ARB/09/6 (ECT).

11 See e.g. C. Kauffmann and C. Tébar Less, *Transition to a Low-carbon Economy: Public Goals and Corporate Practices*, Paris: OECD, 2010. Online. Available HTTP: <http://www.oecd.org/data-oecd/40/52/45513642.pdf> (accessed 19 December 2011) ('OECD, 'Transition to a low-carbon economy"), at paras. 105–109.

12 UNFCCC, *Investment and Financial Flows to Address Climate Change*, 2007. Online. Available HTTP: <http://unfccc.int/cooperation_and_support/financial_mechanism/items/4053.php> (accessed 19 December 2011) ('UNFCCC 2007') at para. 637.

13 N. Stern, *The Stern Review on the Economics of Climate Change*, submitted on 30 October 2006. Online. Available HTTP: <http://webarchive.nationalarchives.gov.uk/+/http://www.hm-treasury.gov.uk/stern_review_report.htm> (accessed 19 December 2011) ('The Stern Review'), at ii.

14 E. Sussman, 'The Energy Charter Treaty's Investor Protection Provisions: Potential to Foster Solutions to Global Warming and Promote Sustainable Development', in Cordonier Segger et al., op. cit., p. 513, p. 528.

15 Ibid. p. 529.

New Delhi Declaration of Principles of International Law Relating to Sustainable Development,[16] can be integrated through the inclusion of the public's right to submit *amicus curiae* briefs in investment disputes, or by allowing free access to documents. Lastly, sustainable development can be integrated within the substantive provisions of IIAs. For example, the substantive rules of IIAs can be phrased in a manner that does not restrict states from enacting environmental or social laws. Moreover, IIAs can also be designed so as to actively promote sustainable investment. This can be achieved, *inter alia*, by creating a privileged business environment for these investments.

According to the concept of sustainable development, when states are embarking on new IIA negotiations they should take three dimensions into account: economic development, social development, and environmental protection. While there is a widespread consensus on the need for sustainable development, most will also agree that FDI is a key component of any development agenda. However, although the concept of sustainable development has been enshrined as an explicit objective in several binding international treaties, it is at the core of the mandate of many international organisations, and it is also the subject of various soft-law declarations and standards, sustainable development remains challenging to include in new IIAs.[17]

This chapter explains how sustainable development objectives can be integrated into international investment law. It reviews both the procedural and the substantive dimensions of sustainable development and IIAs, the tools available for states in order to integrate sustainable development goals into their IIAs, and the challenges faced by policy-makers when making policy choices in this field.

Sustainable development in the drafting of IIAs: procedural dimension

Impact assessment as a new dimension[18]

Foreign direct investment can bring social, economic, and environmental benefits to countries. Indeed, FDIs have a positive impact on such issues as income growth, modernisation, employment, and productivity.[19] Yet without careful crafting, investment agreements can frustrate sustainable development objectives and create potential conflicts between the commercial, social, and environmental goals.[20] Moreover, well-drafted agreements can achieve more than their inherent goals. For example, trade and investment agreements can, at least potentially, also support and promote climate change, or poverty eradication

---

16 International Law Association, *New Delhi Declaration of Principles of International Law Relating to Sustainable Development, Netherlands International Law Review* 49(2), 2002, 299 ('New Delhi Declaration').

17 K. Gordon, 'International Investment Agreements: A Survey of Environmental, Labour and Anti-corruption Issues', in *International Investment Law: Understanding Concepts and Tracking Innovations*, Paris: OECD, 2008. Online. Available HTTP: <www.oecd.org/dataoecd/3/5/40471550.pdf> (accessed 19 December 2011).

18 This section draws on M. Gehring, 'Impact Assessments of Investment Treaties', in Cordonier Segger et al., op. cit., p. 149 ('Gehring').

19 OECD, Committee on International Investment and Multinational Enterprises, *Foreign Direct Investment for Development: Maximising Benefits, Minimising Costs*, Paris: OECD, 2002. Online. Available HTTP: <http://www.oecd.org/dataoecd/47/51/1959815.pdf> (accessed 19 December 2011) ('OECD, "FDI for development" ').

20 For a review of the potential conflicts, see Cordonier Segger et al., op. cit.

objectives. One way to avoid potential conflicts on the one hand, and promote possible synergies on the other, is the use of impact assessment mechanisms.[21]

Impact assessments are comprehensive independent studies in which the future impact of negotiated agreements is assessed. In the past, the focus of these mechanisms was limited to the environmental effects of trade agreements. These assessments are known as Environmental Impact Assessments (EIAs). Nowadays, however, the scope of impact assessments is increasingly expanding. For example, some impact assessments are specifically designed to review the impact of international trade or foreign investments on human rights.[22]

More widely, and in accordance with the 'holistic' concept of sustainable development,[23] some impact assessment mechanisms attempt to provide a fuller picture, by assessing the economic, environmental, and social implications of investment and trade agreements. For example, the EU Commission *Handbook* on this topic proposes the examination of such issues as energy use, poverty, gender equality, external debt, public health, living conditions, access to education, labour standards, unemployment and more.[24] These wider assessments are known as Sustainability Impact Assessments (SIAs).

Impact assessment mechanisms can be found at both the domestic and international levels. At the national level, domestic environmental and planning laws require the impact assessment of major projects. At the international level, some trade and investment negotiations include requirements for assessing the impact negotiated agreements might have on sustainable development. For example, as part of the EU–Canada negotiations of a Comprehensive Economic and Trade Agreement (CETA), SIAs were prepared so as to assess the impact of both international trade and investment on economic, social, and environmental issues.[25]

Impact assessments of trade agreements often follow these four steps:[26] (a) the 'screening and scoping' phase. In this stage the relevant issues are framed, and the measures that are most

21 For a more detailed review of this topic, see Gehring, op. cit.
22 For a detailed review, see J. Harrison and A. Goller, 'Trade and Human Rights: What Does "Impact Assessment" Have to Offer?', *Human Rights Law Review* 8(4), 2008, 587. For an example of impact assessment of for foreign investment, see Rights and Democracy, *Human Right Impact Assessments for Foreign Investment Projects: Learning from Community Experience in the Philippines, Tibet, the Democratic Republic of Congo, Argentina, and Peru*, Montreal: Rights and Democracy, 2007. Online. Available HTTP: <www.dd-rd.ca/site/_PDF/publications/globalization/hria/full%20report_may_2007.pdf> (accessed 19 December 2011) ('Rights and Democracy, "Human Rights Impact Assessments for Foreign Investment Projects" ').
23 The EU Commission's 'Impact Assessment Guidelines' indeed mention that one of the objectives of impact assessments, is to ensure coherence and consistency with the EU's sustainable development strategies. See in European Commission, *Impact Assessment Guidelines*, 15 January 2009, SEC(2009)92. Online. Available HTTP: <http://ec.europa.eu/governance/impact/commission_guidelines/docs/iag_2009_en.pdf> (accessed 19 December 2011) ('EU Impact Assessment Guidelines'), p. 6.
24 European Commission, External Trade, *Handbook for Sustainability Impact Assessment*, 2006. Online. Available HTTP: <http://trade.ec.europa.eu/doclib/docs/2006/march/tradoc_127974.pdf> (accessed 19 December 2011) ('EU Handbook for Sustainability Impact Assessment'), pp. 52–6.
25 See a report commissioned by the European Commission, *A Trade SIA Relating to the Negotiation of a Comprehensive Economic and Trade Agreement (CETA) Between the EU and Canada*, Final Report, June 2011. Online. Available HTTP: <http://www.eucanada-sia.org/docs/EU-Canada_SIA_Final_Report.pdf> (accessed 19 December 2011) ('EU–Canada SIA'). On investment, see p. 337.
26 The exact classification varies between one jurisdiction and another. However, in essence these stages are mostly similar. For example, for the EU classification of these stages, see the *EU Handbook for Sustainability Impact Assessment*, op. cit., p. 12, 17–19, or EU Impact Assessment Guidelines, op. cit., p. 7. For a more detailed review of the classification proposed in this chapter, see Gehring, op. cit., pp. 154–5.

likely to impact the environment (or broader issues in the case of SIAs) are identified. This step often includes expert meetings and public consultations; (b) the next stage is the initial review. In this phase the potential impact of the negotiated agreement (or, more accurately, of the measures identified in the first step) on the environment (or on issues such as social well-being, in the case of SIAs) are identified. The scope of this examination varies from one mechanism to another. While in certain countries only local effects are examined (Canada, for example), in other jurisdictions transboundary and global effects are also assessed (the EU, for example); (c) following the initial review, a preliminary assessment is often published. The purpose of this review is to inform the negotiators about the projected impacts of trade liberalisation in the identified areas; (d) lastly, an *ex post* final assessment is prepared following the conclusion of the negotiations and after the final text of the agreement has been concluded. The final assessment outlines how some negotiating positions might have changed due to the content of the preliminary assessment, as well as the trade-offs and balances made between economic liberalisation and environmental protection.

The use of SIAs can promote sustainable development goals in several ways. As in the field of international trade, when applied to foreign investments SIAs allow negotiators to identify aspects of agreements that require mitigation or enhancement measures, in order to achieve the fullest benefits of investment.[27] By assessing economic, environmental, and social impacts of potential measures, decision-makers have a better idea of the advantages and disadvantages of each proposal. Thus SIAs allow decision-makers to fully understand the synergies between the different fields, and how one policy can support another. Alternatively, by addressing more than just environmental or economic aspects, SIAs equip decision-makers with better tools to perform the trade-offs that are necessary in places where the promotion of one policy inherently frustrates the goals of another. Lastly, where the public is effectively invited to take part in this process, SIAs also increase the democratic legitimacy and the quality of negotiated agreements.

The use of impact assessment mechanisms has increased in recent years. The following section provides a brief overview of the approaches to impact assessment mechanisms applied by Canada, the United States (US), and the European Union in the field of international trade.[28] Some of these are also applicable to foreign investment arising in the specific context of FTAs (free trade agreements).

Canada

Canada's first foray into impact assessment of investment came at the end of the WTO Uruguay Round in 1994, when it carried out an *ex post* environmental review of the Round's Agreements.[29] In 1999, the Liberal Government introduced the internally binding 'Strategic Environmental Assessment of Plans and Policies (SEA)', a directive mandating that every government policy should be assessed for its environmental impact prior to implementation.[30]

---

27 For a detailed review of SIAs, see Gehring, op. cit., p. 145.
28 For a more detailed review, see Gehring, op. cit., pp. 156–68.
29 The Government of Canada, *Uruguay Round of Multilateral Trade Negotiations: Canadian Environmental Review*, Ottawa, 1994.
30 See Foreign Affairs and International Trade Canada, *Framework for Conducting Environmental Assessments of Trade Negotiations*, February 2001. Online. Available HTTP: <http://www.international.gc.ca/trade-agreements-accords-commerciaux/ds/Environment.aspx?lang=enandview=d> (accessed 19 December 2011).

In February 2001, the Cabinet adopted the *Environmental Assessment of Trade Negotiations* as the stand-alone assessment tool.[31] This EA (environmental assessment) focuses almost entirely on environmental issues. However, despite this limited focus, the Canadian government refers to this instrument as an indispensable decision-making tool for the promotion of sustainable development by engaging representatives from other levels of government, the public, the private sector, and non-governmental organisations in the process.[32]

The process of EAs includes six phases:[33] (1) Notice of Intent, in which the purpose of the proposed negotiations is explained; (2) Initial EA, which is equivalent to the 'scoping' phase, as explained above; (3) Initial EA Report, issued during the negotiations and identifying potential environmental impacts; (4) where likely significant impacts are identified, a Draft EA will be prepared and more detailed assessment will be made; (5) the final EA Report is issued with the conclusion of the negotiations; (6) follow-up and monitoring will be performed following the conclusion of the negotiations.

Although offering the right balance between public participation and innovation, one limitation in this Canadian EA methodology is that it focuses only on the environmental impacts within Canada, without explicitly requiring the assessment of social and developmental concerns. Furthermore, this procedure eschews any investigation of the environmental impacts on the trading partner or potential implications on a global level.[34] The Canadian EA was used, *inter alia*, as part of the trade negotiations with the Andean Community (2008) and with Panama (2009).[35] In both cases it was concluded that the environmental consequences for Canada resulting from the trade flow and foreign investment in Canada would be negligible.[36] Also, the assessments did not consider the effects of the negotiations on either Panama or the Andean Community, nor was a more regional approach to the EA considered (see below). With regard to public participation, although it is still limited, it nonetheless provides members of civil society with insights into at least the economic rationale of trade liberalisation negotiations.[37]

United States

In practice, Environmental Reviews (ERs) have been performed in the US since 1992 when the NAFTA (North American Free Trade Agreement) was negotiated and

---

31 Ibid.
32 Foreign Affairs and International Trade Canada, *Handbook for Conducting Environmental Assessments of Trade Negotiations*, March 2008. Online. Available HTTP: <http://www.international.gc.ca/enviro/assets/pdfs/EnvironA/overview/handbook-e.pdf> (accessed 19 December 2011) ('Handbook for Conducting Environmental Assessments of Trade Negotiations').
33 *Framework for Conducting Environmental Assessments of Trade Negotiations*, op. cit., pp. 8–9.
34 Gehring, op. cit., p. 158.
35 For Canadian Environmental Assessments, see Foreign Affairs and International Trade Canada, *Canada's Environmental Assessment Framework for Trade Negotiations*. Online. Available HTTP: <http://www.international.gc.ca/trade-agreements-accords-commerciaux/env/env-ea.aspx?lang=enandmenu_id=2andview=d> (accessed 8 March 2012).
36 See *Initial Environmental Assessment Report of the Canada-Andean Community Free Trade Negotiations*. Online. Available HTTP: <http://www.international.gc.ca/trade-agreements-accords-commerciaux/agr-acc/andean-andin/ea-toc.aspx?view=d> (accessed 16 May 2012); See *Initial Environmental Assessment Report of the Canada-Panama Free Trade Negotiations*. Online. Available HTTP: <http://www.international.gc.ca/trade-agreements-accords-commerciaux/agr-acc/ea-panama.aspx?lang=engandview=d> (accessed 19 December 2011).
37 Gehring, op. cit., p. 159.

reviewed.[38] However, it was only in 1999 that President Clinton signed an executive order codifying ERs as an internally binding assessment obligation for trade negotiations.[39] Like the Canadian EAs, US ERs are conducted as *ex ante* procedures and are laden with public participation requirements.[40] Indeed there is evidence that ERs engage with parts of the civil society, particularly academia, and some recommendations made in the ERs are carefully evaluated and considered by negotiators.

Similarly to Canadian EAs, US ERs look mainly to domestic impacts and foreign impacts that may affect the US. It should be noted, however, that where 'appropriate and prudent', ERs may also assess global and transboundary environmental impacts.[41] Again, like Canadian EAs, US ERs are concerned primarily with environmental issues. The use of ERs has included the Central American Free Trade Agreement (CAFTA), the US–Andean FTA, the US–Panama FTA, and the US–Chile FTA.[42]

The European Union

In the EU, the scope of assessment of investment chapters of FTAs is broader than in the US and Canada, in terms of both subject matter and jurisdiction. The EU has established SIA mechanisms seeking to identify potential social, economic, and environmental impacts, placing these SIAs at the vanguard of impact assessment tools, being a fully integrated instrument which also includes recommendations for enhancement and mitigation, if relevant.[43] The SIAs also include an important public participation component. Indeed the establishment of SIAs mechanisms by the EU Trade Commissioner at the time, Pascal Lamy, was explained as a response to civil society pressure and growing suspicions towards economic globalisation, as was demonstrated in the negotiations over the OECD Multilateral Agreement on Investment and the 1999 WTO Ministerial Conference in Seattle.[44]

---

38 See US Environmental Protection Agency, 'Environmental Reviews of Trade and Investment Agreements'. Online. Available HTTP: <http://www.epa.gov/international/trade/reviews.html> (accessed 19 December 2011).

39 Executive Order 13141 of November 16, 1999 'Environmental Reviews of Trade Agreements'. Online. Available HTTP: <http://ceq.hss.doe.gov/nepa/regs/eos/eo13141.html> (accessed 19 December 2011).

40 See United States Trade Representative and Council on Environmental Quality, *Guidelines for implementation of Executive Order 13141, Environmental Review of Trade Agreements*, December 2000. Online. Available HTTP: <http://www.ustr.gov/sites/default/files/guidelines%20for%2013141.pdf> (accessed 19 December 2011).

41 Article 5(b) of Executive Order 13141, op. cit.

42 ERs conducted by the US can be found at the United States Trade Representative's website. Online: Available HTTP: <http://www.ustr.gov/trade-topics/environment/environmental-reviews> (accessed 19 December 2011).

43 Gehring, op. cit., p. 164.

44 T. Ruddy and L. Hilty, 'Impact Assessment and Policy Learning in the European Commission', *Environmental Impact Assessment Review* 28(2–3), 2008, p. 90, p. 94. The OECD Multilateral Agreement on Investment (OECD MAI) and the 1999 WTO Ministerial Conference in Seattle were both highly influenced by intense pressure applied by civil-society organisations. This pressure led to the 'Battle in Seattle' events, and partly also to the failure of the OECD MAI negotiations (see review in Jürgen Kurtz, 'NGOs, the Internet and International Economic Policy Making: The Failure of the OECD Multilateral Agreement on Investment' *Melbourne Journal of International Law* 3, 2002, 213).

The SIAs consist of the following phases: screening, scoping, preliminary sustainability assessment, and mitigation and enhancement analysis.[45] As already mentioned, these phases include opportunities for public participation and consultation with civil society organisations.[46] Unlike the Canadian and US impact assessment mechanisms, the SIA methodology is not limited to the impact within the EU, but aims at exploring the impact within trading partners as well. According to some, about 80 per cent of the impacts studied by European SIAs are expected to take place outside of the EU.[47] *Inter alia*, SIAs were used in the ambit of EU–MERCOSUR trade negotiations and EU–Mediterranean FTAs.[48]

The dispute resolution process

Another procedural aspect that can be relevant for sustainable development is the body of procedural rules according to which investor–state arbitrations are being held. The investor–state dispute settlement mechanism is often criticised for being held away from the public eye.[49] The chosen dispute settlement model adopted by most investment agreements – the commercial arbitration model[50] – indeed opts for a discreet method of adjudication. The reasons for this choice are understandable: the commercial arbitration model, at least theoretically, ensures an efficient, non-politicised, professional, and easily enforceable form of dispute settlement. Additionally, this model allows investors to distance disputes from the control of host states and the reach of biased, or simply overly-patriotic, domestic courts.

It is argued, however, that the public nature of investment disputes,[51] and the possibility of improving the quality and legitimacy of investment awards, require certain modifications to this model. The following section explains that through increased open process and by adhering to the sustainable development principle of public participation, wider perspectives, that go beyond the immediate commercial dispute, can be assimilated into this process.

Public participation in investment disputes

The concept of public participation in decision-making processes was recognised in many international documents.[52] In 1992, this concept was declared as a 'principle' in

---

45 *EU Handbook for Sustainability Impact Assessment*, op. cit., p. 8.

46 Ibid., p. 49.

47 Ruddy and Hilty, op. cit., p. 91.

48 The SIAs conducted by the EU can be found at the European Commission's website. Online. Available HTTP: <http://ec.europa.eu/trade/analysis/sustainability-impact-assessments/assessments/> (accessed 19 December 2011).

49 See e.g. J. Wouters and N. Hachez, 'The Institutionalization of Investment Arbitration and Sustainable Development', in Cordonier Segger et al., op. cit., pp. 615, 627; *Public Statement on the International Investment Regime*, 31 August 2010. Online. Available HTTP: <http://www.osgoode.yorku.ca/public_statement> (accessed 19 December 2011) ('Public Statement').

50 For further reading on the nature and characters of investment treaty arbitration, see Z. Douglas, *Investment Treaty Arbitration*, Cambridge: Cambridge University Press, 2008.

51 G. Van Harten and M. Loughlin, 'Investment Treaty Arbitration as a Species of Global Administrative Law' *European Journal of International Law* 17(1), 2006, 121.

52 See e.g. *Universal Declaration of Human Rights* (1948), GA Res. 217(III), UN GAOR, 3rd Sess, 13th Supp, UN Doc A/810, Art. 21(1); *UN Declaration on Social Progress and Development* (1969), UN GAOR, 24th Sess, UN Doc A/RES/24/2542, Art. 5. Online. Available HTTP: <www.un-documents.net/a24r2542.htm> (accessed 19 December 2011) ('UN Declaration on Social Progress and Development').

international sustainable development law by the *Rio Declaration on Environment and Development* (Rio Declaration).[53] In essence, the principle of public participation includes: (a) the public's right to participate in decision-making processes in which sustainable development issues are involved; and (b) an effective access to information so as to ensure the quality of the public's participation.[54] This principle is mostly derived from the public's right to actively participate in decisions that affect their lives, and as part of the people's right to express their opinion. More recently, this principle has also been regarded as a means to ensure good governance and a high quality of decisions.[55] Although designed for decision-making processes and not for adversarial forms of adjudication, it is argued that this principle can and should be assimilated into investor–state dispute settlement mechanisms.

Investment disputes are often public in nature. The measures scrutinised by investment tribunals are mostly administrative[56] and can involve subject matters such as financial, social, or environmental regulation. For example, in numerous cases filed against Argentina investors have challenged emergency measures put in place by the state in order to address the catastrophic financial crisis it endured during the early 2000s. This crisis, it should be remembered, involved *inter alia* questions of poverty, security, and public health.[57] These issues, as argued by some, were not always adequately addressed by investment tribunals.[58]

Moreover, the compensation claimed by investors is paid from taxpayers' money. Considering the high sums involved in these cases (Argentina's potential liability in investment cases litigated against it was estimated, at a certain point in time, to be as high as 8 billion US dollars[59]), and the effect these can have on a state's budget, the public's interest in these cases is obvious.

It can be seen, therefore, that investment disputes potentially affect the public's living reality. But where the public is not entitled to follow, critique, participate, or even to know

---

53 Rio Declaration on Environment and Development, op. cit.
54 Usually, this principle includes also a requirement to enable access to judicial and administrative procedures, in order to enable claims for compensation. This part, however, is less relevant for this chapter.
55 See e.g. *Aarhus Convention on Access to Information, Public Participation in Decision Making and Access to Justice in Environmental Matters*. See *Convention on Access to Information, Public Participation in Decision Making and Access to Justice in Environmental Matters*, UN Doc. ECE/CEP43, 25 June, 1998 (Aarhus Convention).
56 See relevant critique in Van Harten and Loughlin, op. cit.
57 During the Argentinian financial crisis almost half of the Argentine population was living below the poverty line. Due to high prices, medications became overly expensive for large sections of the population, hospitals suffered shortages of supplies, about a quarter of the population was not able to afford even a minimal food supply, and due to looting and rioting curfews were imposed by the government. See the review of these issues in *LG and E v Argentine Republic* (Decision on Liability), ('2006') ICSID Case No. ARB/02/1, at paras 232–5.
58 See critique by J. Taillant and J. Bonnitcha, 'International Investment Law and Human Rights', in Cordonier Segger et al., op. cit., pp. 67–8.
59 Estimation made by Gabriel Bottini from the Office of the Attorney General, Republic of Argentina, as quoted in W. Burke-White and A. von Staden, 'Investment Protection in Extraordinary Times: The Interpretation and Application of Non-Precluded Measures Provisions in Bilateral Investment Treaties', *Virginia Journal of International Law* 48(2), 2008, 307, p. 311. Burke-While and von Staden mention that other estimations regarding Argentina's potential liability are up to USD 80 billion.

about the existence of these disputes,[60] serious questions of legitimacy and accountability should be raised. This fact was indeed emphasised by several investment tribunals.[61] It is important, therefore, to ensure that the dispute settlement process will not overlook non-commercial interests, especially where either states or investors ignore them.

Implementing the principle of public participation can help in this respect. It can ensure that all stakeholders will be heard, and enforce standards of transparency in tribunals in which public matters are being deliberated. Moreover, public participation in investment disputes can also improve the quality of investment awards.[62] Public participation can present arbitrators with wider perspectives or information that was not available or known to them. It can also bring to arbitrators' attention the voices of unrepresented stakeholders, whose interests may not coincide with those of the state. Decision-making processes in which effective public participation is permitted, therefore, are likely to be more accurate and comprehensive.[63]

Investor–state arbitration procedural rules on public participation

It should be remembered in this respect that arbitrators are permitted to hear and consider only those issues and claims that were asked of and presented to them by the parties.[64] The focus of this discussion, therefore, should concentrate on the arbitration procedural rules and the ways these have been read by investment tribunals. These rules, in general, allow some place for public participation. Mostly, rules of arbitration permit arbitrators to accept *amicus curiae* briefs from the public.[65] Access to information (to the arbitration's documents, for

---

60 In 2008, among known UNCITRAL arbitrations (not all investor–state arbitration are known to the public), a quarter of the awards were not released to the public. See F. Ortino, 'External Transparency of Investment Awards', *Society of International Economic Law (SIEL) Inaugural Conference Paper*, 2008. Online. Available HTTP: <http://papers.ssrn.com/sol3/papers.cfm?abstract_id=1159899> (accessed 19 December 2011).

61 *Biwater Gauff (Tanzania) Ltd. v United Republic of Tanzania* (Procedural Order No 5), ('2007') ICSID Case No ARB/05/22, (International Centre for Settlement of Investment Disputes), ('*Biwater Gauff*, 2007') at para. 51; *Suez, Sociedad General de Aguas de Barcelona S.A. and Vivendi Universal S.A v Argentine Republic* (Order in Response to a Petition for Transparency and Participation as *Amicus Curiae*) ('2005') ICSID Case No. ARB/03/19, (International Centre for Settlement of Investment Disputes) ('*Suez*') at para. 22.

62 The notion according to which public participation improves the quality of decisions was recognised, *inter alia*, in the preamble to the Aarhus Convention, op. cit.

63 Indeed, for these reasons 'public participation' was recognised as a principle in sustainable development law on more than one occasion. See e.g. Principle 10 of the *Rio Declaration on Environment and Development*, op. cit., and Principle 5 of the New Delhi Declaration.

64 A fundamental principle of the 'arbitration' model is that arbitrators' mandate is determined by the parties. In the case of investment treaty arbitration, arbitrators' mandate is often decided in investment treaties or investment agreements.

65 See e.g. the ICSID Rules of Arbitration as amended in 2006, or the practice of investment tribunals under the UNCITRAL Rules of Arbitration, as demonstrated in several NAFTA cases; see e.g. *United Parcel Services of America Inc. v Canada* (Decision of the Tribunal on Petitions for Intervention and Participation as Amici Curiae), ('2001') UNCITRAL, ('*UPS, Amici Curiae Decision*'); *Methanex Corporation v United States of America* (Decision of the tribunal on petitions from third persons to intervene as 'Amici Curiae'), ('2001') UNCITRAL (North American Free Trade Agreement) ('*Methanex Amici Curiae decision*'). See also a statement made by the NAFTA Free Trade Commission in this respect, NAFTA Free Trade Commission, 'Statement of the Free Trade Commission on non-disputing party participation' (2003). Online. Available HTTP: <http://www.international.gc.ca/trade-agreements-accords-commerciaux/assets/pdfs/Nondisputing-en.pdf> (accessed 19 December 2011), (NAFTA Statement).

example), however, is still largely restricted and in most cases depends on the parties' consent to make such information public. Similarly, access to arbitration hearings is also often restricted.[66] On several occasions, third parties have also requested the right to actively participate in the dispute by raising legal claims and to defend their interests before the tribunal.[67] These requests, however, were all denied.

Although in recent years some changes have been made in order to improve aspects such as transparency and public participation,[68] the full application of the public participation principle is still far from a reality. For example, effective access to arbitration documents or hearings is relatively restricted,[69] despite the fact that allowing such access can enhance the quality of submitted *amicus curiae* briefs. Measures such as the making of investment disputes known to the public, the publication of arbitration documents, or allowing public access to hearings, are often denied.

To conclude, it is argued that the principle of public participation should be, if not completely assimilated into investment treaties, at least better balanced against other rationales of the investor–state dispute settlement mechanism. It is believed that the measures suggested above, if refined and adjusted to the context of investment arbitration, will undermine conflicting values such as efficiency only to a certain extent (if at all). In light of their potential advantages, they should be considered by states.

Sustainable development in the drafting of IIAs: substantive dimension

From a sustainable development perspective, the main challenge faced by treaty negotiators is to balance the conflicting interests present in the essence of foreign investments. Treaty negotiators, for example, must design tools which will promote sustainable investments by providing them a secure and stable business environment. On the other hand, they also

---

66 See e.g. Rule 32 of the ICSID Rules of Arbitration and Article 28 of the UNCITRAL Rules of Arbitration.

67 See e.g. *Aguas del Tunari S.A. v Republic of Bolivia* (Petition of La Coordinadora para la defensa del Agua Y Vida and others, to the arbitral Tribunal), ICSID Case No. ARB/02/3. Online. Available HTTP: <http://ita.law.uvic.ca/documents/Aguaaboliviapetition.pdf> (accessed 19 December 2011) ('*Tunari, Petition*'); *United Parcel Services of America Inc. v Canada* (Decision of the Tribunal on Petitions for Intervention and Participation as Amici Curiae) ('2001') UNCITRAL, ('*UPS, Amici Curiae Decision*').

68 See e.g. the 2006 amendments made in the ICSID Arbitration Rules; or Articles 10.20–10.21 of the Central America – Dominican Republic – United States FTA (CAFTA-DR).

69 Regarding access to hearings, see Article 28 of the UNCITRAL Arbitration Rules (as revised in 2010) and Rule 32 of the ICSID Arbitration Rules. Regarding access to documents, ICSID tribunals denied such access on several occasions, see e.g. *AES Summit Generation Limited and AES-Tisza Erömü Kft. v Republic of Hungary* (Award), ('2010') ICSID Case No. ARB/07/22 ('*AES*') at para. 3.22. See also UNCITRAL tribunals, e.g. *V.G. Gallo v Government of Canada* (Procedural Order No. 1) ('2008') UNCITRAL, ('*V.G. Gallo*') at para. 38. The one exception for this rule is the Piero Foresti Arbitration (under ICSID rules), in which the Tribunal allowed access to information. The case, however, was discontinued before the non–disputing parties had the chance to view these documents; see *Piero Foresti, Laura de Carli and others v Republic of South Africa* (Letter from the Tribunal to the Parties, from 5 October 2009) ('2009'), ICSID Case No ARB/05/22, (International Centre for Settlement of Investment Disputes), ('*Foresti*') at para. 2.2–3.

need to secure ample regulatory flexibility so states will be able to reform and adapt their policies.

Although increasing,[70] the explicit presence of sustainable development objectives in investment treaties remains relatively low.[71] The following section discusses some of the examples offered by IIAs' substantive rules in order to address sustainable development objectives. It should be mentioned that this is not an exhaustive list of possible solutions. In fact, the complex nature of sustainable development requires many different approaches to the numerous issues embedded in this concept. Indeed, what is right for climate change will not necessarily work for smoking prevention or biodiversity. However, the cases reviewed below can be used as a point of departure, from which more complex solutions can be developed.

Preambular language

One, albeit uncommon,[72] solution adopted by states is the inclusion of references to sustainable development objectives in preambles to IIAs. The importance of preambular language can be understood from Article 31(2) of the 1969 *Vienna Convention on the Law of Treaties* ('VCLT'), according to which the context and the purpose of a treaty is to be derived *inter alia* from the treaty's preamble.[73] In light of the different interpretations given to legal terms such as 'expropriation', 'legitimate expectations', and 'like-circumstances', and the effects these can have on sustainable development objectives,[74] the role preambular language can fulfil is significant.[75]

Preambular references can be made either directly to the concept of sustainable development as a whole, or to a specific issue such as climate change, labour standards, health, or human rights. There are several ways in which states refer to sustainable development objectives in their preambles. First, states can declare sustainable development to be a specific objective of the treaty. For example, the Canadian Model Foreign Investment Protection Agreement (FIPA) states in its preamble that:

> the promotion and the protection of investments of investors of one Party in the territory of the other Party will be conductive to the stimulation of mutually beneficial business

---

70 K. Gordon and J. Pohl, 'Environmental Concerns in International Investment Agreements: a survey', *OECD Working Papers on International Investment*, 2011, No. 2011/1. Online. Available HTTP: <www.oecd.org/dataoecd/50/12/48083618.pdf> (accessed 19 December 2011) p. 8.

71 See K. Gordon, 'International Investment Agreements: A Survey of Environmental, Labour and Anti-corruption Issues', in *International Investment Law: Understanding Concepts and Tracking Innovations* (Paris: OECD, 2008). Online. Available HTTP: <www.oecd.org/dataoecd/3/5/40471550.pdf> (accessed 19 December 2011) ('Gordon') in Annex 3.A1.

72 A. Newcombe, 'Sustainable Development and Investment Treaty Law', *Journal of World Investment and Trade* 8, 2007, 357.

73 *Vienna Convention on the Law of Treaties*, opened for signature 23 May 1969, 1155 UNTS 1980 ('VCLT') Art. 31(2).

74 For a review of these terms and their relations to sustainable development, see Cordonier-Segger et al. (eds) op. cit.

75 M.C. Cordonier Segger and A. Newcombe, 'An Integrated Agenda for Sustainable Development in International Investment Law', in Cordonier Segger et al. (eds) op. cit., p. 126.

activity, to the development of economic cooperation between them and to the promotion of sustainable development.[76]

Similarly, the Parties to the NAFTA express in its preamble their determination both to promote sustainable development in general and to address many of the topics which are included under this definition, such as environmental objectives and economic development.[77] Similar examples can be found in the preamble to the Common Market for Eastern and Southern Africa (COMESA) investment agreement,[78] and several Canadian IIAs.[79] Some agreements also refer to more specific issues, such as the promotion of climate change objectives.[80]

A second type of preambular language, while not referring to sustainable development as a treaty objective *per se*, imposes upon parties an obligation to behave consistently with this principle. This type of language can be found in US IIAs. The preamble to the US–Rwanda IIA, for example, defines as treaty objectives *inter alia* the promotion of economic cooperation, the stimulation of private investment, and the creation of a stable business environment. It continues, however, by stating that the Parties are: '*Desiring* to achieve these objectives in a manner consistent with the protection of health, safety, and the environment, and the promotion of internationally recognised labor rights.'[81]

A third example of preambular language can be defined as 'non-derogation' language. This language can be found in many of the IIAs signed by states such as Finland, the Netherlands, Japan and the US.[82] According to these references, the treaty's objectives (often economic in nature) are to be achieved without relaxing regulatory standards in fields such as the environment, health, or safety.

Lastly, on very rare occasions references to sustainable development treaties can be found in the preamble to IIAs. Such references can be found in model treaties which are not in use, such as the International Institute for Sustainable Development's Model BIT (bilateral investment treaty), in which references to numerous treaties have been made,[83] or the Norway 2007 Model BIT,[84] in which a reference to the United Nations Charter and the Universal

---

76 *Canada Model Foreign Investment Promotion and Protection Agreement* (2004). Online. Available HTTP: <www.international.gc.ca/trade-agreements-accords-commerciaux/agr-acc/fipa-apie/index.aspx> (accessed 19 December 2011) ('Canada Model FIPA').

77 *North American Free Trade Agreement*, opened for signature 17 December 1992, 32 ILM 1480 (entered into force 1 January 1994) (NAFTA).

78 Common Market for Eastern and Southern Africa, *Investment Agreement for the COMESA Common Investment Area* (2007) (COMESA).

79 See e.g. the *Canada-Peru IIA* (2006) and the *Canada–Jordan IIA* (2009).

80 See e.g. the preamble to the *Japan–Switzerland FTA* (2009).

81 See similar language in the US 2004 Model BIT, and the *US–Uruguay BIT* (2006).

82 See e.g. *Finland–Ethiopia BIT* (2006); *Finland–Armenia BIT* (2004), *Netherlands–Suriname BIT* (2005); *Netherlands–Burundi BIT* (2007), *US–Mozambique BIT* (1998); *US–Jordan BIT* (2003); *US–Bahrain BIT* (2001), *Japan–Korea BIT* (2002); *Japan–Vietnam BIT* (2003).

83 The IISD Model BIT includes *inter alia* references to the 1992 *Rio Declaration on Environment and Development*; the 2002 *World Summit on Sustainable Development and the Millennium Development Goals* and the *OECD Guidelines for Multinational Enterprises*. See H. Mann et al. 'IISD Model International Agreement on Investment for Sustainable Development', 2005. Online. Available HTTP: <http://italaw.com/documents/investment_model_int_agreement.pdf> (accessed 19 December 2011) ('IISD Model BIT').

84 2007 Norway Draft Model BIT. Online. Available HTTP: <www.asil.org/ilib080421.cfm#t1> (accessed 19 December 2011).

Declaration of Human Rights can be found. More relevant examples can be found in the preamble to the Singapore–EFTA FTA (which includes investment protection), in which the parties reaffirm 'their commitment to the principles set out in the United Nations Charter and the Universal Declaration of Human Rights',[85] and in the Energy Charter Treaty, in which the parties are '[r]ecalling the United Nations Framework Convention on Climate Change, the Convention on Long-Range Transboundary Air Pollution and its protocols, and other international environmental agreements with energy-related aspects'.[86]

Exceptions and reservations

Another way in which states attempt to promote sustainable development objectives is the use of exceptions and reservations in IIAs. Like almost any international agreement, IIAs impose certain restrains on states' regulatory flexibility. Through the use of exceptions, states ensure that their ability to regulate certain fields will not be restricted by investment treaties.

Exceptions in IIAs appear in several forms. First, some IIAs include provisions that allow for treaty reservations, which are sector-specific carve-outs from treaty obligations. For example, Annex I of the Canada–Peru FIPA includes a list of sectors that are exempted from the IIAs' substantive rules.[87] Second, a few IIAs adopt general exceptions provisions, modelled on Article XX of the General Agreement on Tariffs and Trade (GATT). These general exceptions exclude from the scope of IIAs measures relating to the protection of, *inter alia*, 'human, animal, or plant life or health', or to the conservation of exhaustible natural resources. As in Article XX of the GATT, these exceptions are subject to non-discriminatory treatment and should not be used as disguised restrictions for investment or trade.[88]

Third, several IIAs include what was described by some as 'non-precluded measures' (NPMs).[89] These NPMs are intended to exempt certain subject areas (e.g. public health, public security, morality) form the scope of the treaty, or from specific treaty obligation. For example, the protocol following the Germany–Bangladesh BIT states: 'Measures that have to be taken for reasons of public security and order, public health or morality shall not be deemed "treatment less favourable" within the meaning of Article 2.'[90]

Exceptions, at least in theory, can promote sustainable development objectives. Their main contribution in this respect is by preventing conflicts between investment rules and sustainable development regulation. The recent Philip Morris claims made against Australia and Uruguay following their anti-smoking regulations (mainly plain-packaging rules) is an excellent example of a case in which general exceptions would have been helpful.[91]

85 *Free Trade Agreements between the EFTA States and Singapore* (2002).
86 *Energy Charter Treaty*, opened for signature 17 Dec. 1994, 34 ILM 360, 385 ('ECT').
87 See e.g. Article 9 of the *Canada–Peru FIPA* (2003).
88 For examples and detailed discussion, see A. Newcombe, 'General Exceptions in International Investment Agreements' in Cordonier Segger et al. (eds) op. cit., p. 356 ('Newcombe "General Exceptions" '), p. 358.
89 Burke-White and von Staden, op. cit.; Newcombe 'General Exceptions', op. cit., p. 358.
90 *Germany–Bangladesh BIT*; See example for general exclusion in Article X at the *US–Panama BIT* (1982).
91 *FTR Holding SA, Philip Morris Products S.A. and Abal Hermanos S.A. v Oriental Republic of Uruguay*, ICSID Case No. ARB/10/7; *Philip Morris Asia Limited v Australia* (Written Notification of Claim), ('2011') UNCITRAL. Online. Available HTTP: <http://italaw.com/documents/PhilipMorrisAsiaLimited_v_Australia_NotificationOfClaim_22Jun2011.pdf> (accessed 19 December 2011).

However, the authors believe that the use of exceptions should be made with care. First, exceptions should not be overly inclusive. While they may be useful in certain cases of public health, human rights, or treatment granted to indigenous people, they may actually frustrate the objectives of fields such as climate change in which private investments are badly needed. Alternatively, as stated by Newcombe, in several cases tribunals have already approved the view that measures aimed at the protection of public policy objectives do not breach investment treaty obligations. Providing a closed list of protected areas will therefore simply limit the scope of what can be considered as *bona fide* public policy objectives.[92]

Language clarifications

A third tool available for states in order to promote sustainable development objectives can be described as 'language clarification' provisions, or 'improved definitions'. The field of international investment law relies on several standards of protection, most notably 'fair and equitable treatment', non-discriminatory treatment (including 'national treatment' and 'most-favoured nation treatment'), and protection from unlawful expropriation. The definition of each of these standards includes many legal tests, most of which rely on the interpretation of legal terms. For example, the 'national treatment' standard relies on arbitrators' interpretation of what may constitute 'like circumstances'. Similarly, the 'fair and equitable treatment' standard relies, among other things, on the tribunal's interpretation of what investors may 'legitimately expect' when making their investment. Other questions which tribunals dispute include the role of a state's intentions (whether *bona fide* or *mala fide*) when expropriating investor's property.

All of these questions, and the manner in which tribunals chose to answer them, can affect sustainable development.[93] For example, by deciding that carbon footprints are irrelevant for what may constitute 'like circumstances', states' attempts to differentiate between low-carbon and carbon-intensive producers (for example, by imposing carbon taxes) can be viewed as a violation of the non-discrimination rules. By clarifying the language used in treaties, states can avoid such conflicts.

Indeed, in recent years states have become aware of these potential conflicts and have aimed to clarify legal terms.[94] Most notably, some states have made clarifications with respect to the terms 'expropriation' and 'indirect expropriation', perhaps due to the wide meaning some tribunals have read into them.[95] The ASEAN–Australia–New Zealand FTA, for example, emphasises with respect to 'expropriation':[96]

---

92 Newcombe, 'General Exceptions', op. cit., pp. 357–8.
93 For a detailed review of the potential issues that may arise out of these questions, see Cordonier Segger et al. (eds) op. cit.
94 See examples in M. Malik, 'Recent Developments in International Investment Agreements: Negotiations and Disputes', *IV Annual Forum for Developing Country Investment Negotiators, Background Papers*, 2010. Online. Available HTTP: <www.iisd.org/pdf/2011/dci_2010_recent_developments_iias.pdf> (accessed 19 December 2011) pp. 4–5.
95 The Metalclad Tribunal, for example, has stated that 'expropriation under NAFTA includes not only open, deliberate and acknowledged takings of property, such as outright seizure or formal or obligatory transfer of title in favour of the host State, but also covert or incidental interference with the use of property which has the effect of depriving the owner, in whole or in significant part, of the use or reasonably-to-be-expected economic benefit of property even if not necessarily to the obvious benefit of the host State'. *Metalclad Corporation v Mexico*, ('2000') ICSID Case No. ARB(AF)97/1 (NAFTA) ('*Metalclad*') at para. 103.
96 Annex on Expropriation and Compensation, Article 4, *ASEAN–Australian–New Zealand FTA*.

Non-discriminatory regulatory actions by a Party that are designed and applied to achieve legitimate public welfare objectives, such as the protection of public health, safety, and the environment do not constitute expropriation of the type referred to in Paragraph 2(b).

Similar clarifications can also be found, *inter alia*, in Canadian and US IIAs, and the COMESA investment agreement.[97] With respect to the term 'indirect expropriation', it is stressed under the US–Uruguay BIT that:[98]

Except in rare circumstances, non-discriminatory regulatory actions by a Party that are designed and applied to protect legitimate public welfare objectives, such as public health, safety, and the environment, do not constitute indirect expropriations.

Language clarifications can also be found more generally. As mentioned above, commitment to rules of international law implies a certain loss of regulatory flexibility. In some cases, states provides clarifications as to what is included in this 'loss' of regulatory flexibility, and what is not. Article 10.12 of the US–Chile FTA ('Investment and Environment') for instance, clarifies that environmental regulation shall not be limited by the investment rules prescribed in this agreement. It is stated:[99]

Nothing in this Chapter shall be construed to prevent a Party from adopting, maintaining, or enforcing any measure otherwise consistent with this Chapter that it considers appropriate to ensure that investment activity in its territory is undertaken in a manner sensitive to environmental concerns.

Similar language concerning the term 'expropriation' can also be found in IIAs signed by other states.[100] Other potential language clarifications can be made in future treaties as well. For example, it can be emphasised that a specific state commitment is needed in order to establish investors' 'legitimate expectations',[101] and that the mere change in regulation (subject to good faith and non-discrimination) should not be considered as a breach of such. Furthermore, it can also be clarified that environmental issues, human rights, or social considerations, when applied in order to protect such interest, should be considered as part of the 'like-circumstances' legal test.

---

97 See in Common Market for Eastern and Southern Africa, *Investment Agreement for the COMESA Common Investment Area* (2007) (COMESA) at Article 20(8); Annex 811 ('Indirect expropriation') of the *Canada–Colombia FTA* (2008); for US IIAs, see the next footnote.

98 Annex B, Article 4(b) of the *US-Uruguay BIT*. See also Annex 10-D of Chapter 10, Article 4(b) *US–Chile FTA*.

99 Article 10.12 of the *US–Chile FTA*.

100 See e.g. Article VII(4) of the *Belgium/Luxembourg–Colombia BIT* (2009); Article G-14 of the *Canada–Chile FTA* (1996).

101 This approach was adopted by several investment tribunals. See e.g. *Total S.A. v Argentine Republic* (Decision on Liability) ('2010'), ICSID Case No. ARB/04/01 ('*Total S.A.*') at para. 117; *Grand River Enterprises Six Nations, Ltd., et al. v United States of America* (Award), ('2011') UNCITRAL (NAFTA) ('*Grand River*') at para. 141; *Glamis Gold, Ltd. v The United States of America*, (Award), ('2009') UNCITRAL (NAFTA) ('*Glamis Gold*') at paras 766–7; *Joseph Charles Lemire v Ukraine* (Decision on Jurisdiction and Liability) ('2010') ICSID Case No. ARB/06/18 ('*Lemire*, Decision on Jurisdiction and Liability') at para. 284.

Language clarifications can also be made with respect to the term 'investment'. The 'Salini test', for example, requires 'contribution, a certain duration of performance of the contract and participation in the risks of transaction' in order to establish 'investment'.[102] Recently, it was doubted by a certain prominent scholar whether investment in cigarettes should be considered as 'investment'.[103] This suggestion was made following the recent Philip Morris investment claims, and the doubts whether investment in cigarettes actually promoted states' development. While this proposition is certainly appealing, it is not without fault. Most notably, this proposition leaves investors in doubt as to whether their investment is, or is not, covered by the investment treaty, until such time as an investment tribunal makes the determination. The term 'contribution' is wide and vague, and by itself does not allow investors to know in advance whether their investment is to be considered as 'contributing' (and thus covered by the IIA) or not. While agreeing with the general idea, according to which only investments that promote sustainable development should be covered by investment agreements, the authors believe that such a determination should be made *ex ante*, before the investment is made, and not *ex post facto*, only after a dispute has arisen. This is required for reasons of predictability and transparency. Furthermore, decisions as to the investment's contribution should be made by professional bodies, and not by arbitrators, who are not suited to making such determinations. It is argued, therefore, that decisions as to the contributing nature of an investment should be made by impact assessment mechanisms, or any other pre-investment examination.

In order to conclude this section, a word of caution is required. States should not forget that private investments are crucial for sustainable development, and that a stable legal and business environment is essential for their promotion. States should therefore be wary of turning language clarifications into overly sweeping exclusions. States should identify those legal tests which could potentially affect sustainable development goals, and refine them so as to achieve a delicate balance between the need to provide a stable business environment, on the one hand, and to allow sufficient regulatory flexibility on the other.

Corporate social responsibility

Another layer in which IIAs can promote sustainable development objectives is by the use of Corporate Social Responsibility (CSR). The modern concept of CSR can be traced back to the 1950s, when CSR was defined as 'obligations of businessmen to pursue those policies, to make those decisions, or to follow those lines of action which are desirable in terms of the objectives and values of our society'.[104] Although nowadays some debate still takes place on the exact definition of CSR,[105] for the purposes of this chapter the words of Judge Gontheir will suffice:

---

102 *Salini Costruttori S.p.A. and Italstrade S.p.A. v Morocco*, (Decision on Jurisdiction), ('2001') ICSID Case No. ARB/00/4, at para. 52.

103 This remark was made by one of the senior speakers in a conference held at Leiden University, 'The Interaction of International Investment Law with Other Fields of Public International Law', 8–9 April 2011.

104 H.R. Bowen, *Social Responsibility and Accountability*, New York: Harper and Row, 1953, as cited in A. Carroll, 'Corporate Social Responsibility: Evolution of a Definitional Construct', *Business and Society* 38(3), 1999, 268 p. 270.

105 P. Muchlinski, *Multinational Enterprises and the Law*, New York: Oxford University Press, 2007, p. 101.

[CSR] generally embodies the notion that a corporation must act in a responsible manner with regard to the environment, community and the society in which it operates. In its most basic form, CSR emphasizes an approach to corporate governance and operations that integrates and balances the self-interests of the corporation, and those of its investors, with the concerns and interests of the public.[106]

Perhaps the most eminent example of a CSR code is the OECD Guidelines for Multinational Enterprises ('the OECD Guidelines'), which have been described by some as an 'emerging consensus on the social obligations of MNEs [multinational enterprises]'.[107] The OECD Guidelines represent a comprehensive code of conduct, including voluntary standards for environment, employment, combating bribery, science, competition, and taxation.[108] A more recent example, albeit one that focuses exclusively on human rights, is the 2011 'principles for responsible contracts' that were formulated by John Ruggie, the Special Representative of the Secretary-General on the issue of human rights and transnational corporations and other business enterprises.[109] These principles include *inter alia* the planning and management of potential adverse impacts on human rights, project operating standards, community engagement, and grievance mechanisms.

The vast majority of CSR norms can be considered as 'soft law', as they are voluntary and rely on self-governance. This, however, does not make them ineffective. Soft-law mechanisms often include other 'sticks and carrots' besides the threat of legal action.[110] In some cases CSR 'soft law' norms have indeed proven successful in enforcing higher standards of social responsibility.[111]

The activity of foreign investors, as discussed above, can impact social, economic, and environmental issues. But while some governments are equipped with the means to regulate and control these effects, others are not. This situation can be aggravated where states are eager to attract foreign investment and consequently are willing to ignore the adverse effects on issues like human rights or the environment. Furthermore, the existence of governmental corruption, or the mere inability to enforce high standards of regulation, can result in the exploitative behaviour of foreign multinationals. All of these scenarios are the result of inefficient enforcement of high standards of corporate social 'behaviour' on foreign investors. The role CSR can play in this respect is evident. By adhering to external norms, on top of, or in place of, the norms imposed by host states, higher standards of behaviour can be

106 C.D. Gonthier, 'Foreword', in M. Kerr, R. Janda and C. Pitts (eds) *Corporate Social Responsibility: A Legal Analysis*, Ontario: LexisNexis, 2009, as cited in J. Hepburn and V. Kuuya, 'Corporate Social Responsibility and Investment Treaties', in Cordonier Segger et al. (eds) op. cit., p. 585.
107 Muchlinski, op. cit., p. 103.
108 OECD, *OECD Guidelines for Multinational Enterprises*. Online. Available HTTP: <www.oecd.org/daf/investment/guidelines> (accessed 19 December 2011).
109 UN Human Rights Council, *Report of the Special Representative of the Secretary-General on the issue of human rights and transnational corporations and other business enterprises*, UN GAOR, 17th Session, Agenda item 3, UN Doc. A/HRC/17/31/Add.3 (2011). Online. Available HTTP: <http://www.ohchr.org/Documents/Issues/Business/A.HRC.17.31.Add.3.pdf> (accessed 19 December 2011) ('Ruggie, "Principles for responsible contracts" ').
110 R. Ghafele and A. Mercer, 'Not Starting in Sixth Gear: An Assessment of the UN Global Compact's Use of Soft Law as a Global Governance Structure for Corporate Social Responsibility', *UC Davies Journal of International Law and Policy* 17, 2010, 41.
111 J. Conley and C. Williams, 'Global Banks as Global Sustainability Regulators?: The Equator Principles', *Law and Policy* 33(4), 2011, 542.

achieved. Furthermore, following CSR principles such as those proposed by John Ruggie[112] will assist foreign investors to plan and avoid potential conflicts and enhance their acceptance by the local community.

These CSR norms can be imported into IIAs in several ways. First, several of the provisions already discussed in this chapter can be designed to enforce (as 'hard law') higher standards of social activity.[113] With respect to self-governed 'soft law' norms, these can be mentioned in the preambles to IIAs and serve as a source for treaty interpretation. The preamble to the Canada–Peru FTA, for example, 'encourages' enterprises to respect CSR norms. A more comprehensive example can be found in the preamble to the IISD (International Institute for Sustainable Development) Model BIT, where one of its aims is described as:

> Affirming the progressive development of international law and policy on the relation-ships between multinational enterprises and host governments as seen in such interna-tional instruments as the ILO Tripartite Declaration on Multinational Enterprises and Social Policy; the OECD Guidelines for Multinational Enterprises; and the United Nations' Norms and Responsibilities of Transnational Corporations and Other Business Enterprises with Regard to Human Rights.[114]

Furthermore, IIAs can also include more specific treaty provisions with respect to CSR. The IISD Model BIT, for example, includes a CSR provision (Article 16), according to which foreign investors must adhere to a list of CSR codes and guidelines. Another possi-bility is an *ex ante* review of the investors' CSR policies and their suitability for desig-nated projects. The implementation of such a review may be prescribed as a precondition for certain types of investments, especially for those that were identified as sensitive by SIAs. Alternatively, as implied by Article 13.6(2) of the EU–Korea FTA (which specifically refers also to FDI), states can also grant preferential treatment to investors who comply with CSR obligations.[115] If such a strategy is to be adopted, states should adjust other treaty provisions, such as the non-discrimination provisions, for example, in order to ensure that CSR-based preferential treatment will not be considered as a treaty violation.

Interesting developments in this respect can be found in the evolving EU policy of inter-national investment law. Pursuant to the entry into force of the Treaty of Lisbon, FDI has been integrated into the EU common commercial policy. While the formulation of the EU's future investment policy is still ongoing, it may be predicted that the inclusion of CSR in this policy is highly likely. First, the EU's latest FTAs with Korea, and with Colombia and Peru, mention CSR standards as a means to promote sustainable development goals.[116] Second, in two recent Resolutions the European Parliament expressed its will to see CSR provisions

---

112 Ruggie, 'Principles for responsible contracts', op. cit. For example, Ruggie suggests maintaining community engagement and establishing 'grievance mechanisms', to which individuals and local communities will be able to approach.
113 See a review in Hepburn and Kuuya, op. cit., p. 599-600.
114 IISD Model BIT, op. cit.
115 Hepburn and Kuuya, op. cit., p. 609.
116 In both cases FDI are specifically mentioned. See Art. 13.6 of the *EU–Korea FTA*, and Art. 271 of the *EU–Colombia Peru FTA*.

incorporated into future investment and trade agreements.[117] Most notably, in its Resolution on the future European international investment policy it was stated that the Parliament is calling 'for a corporate social responsibility clause and effective social and environmental clauses to be included in every FTA the EU signs'.[118] Similar recognition was also made by the European Council, in its 'conclusion on a comprehensive European international investment policy' from 2010.[119]

Interaction with sustainable development treaties

Another aspect that should be addressed in future IIAs in order to promote sustainable development is the interaction between IIAs and Multilateral Environmental Agreements. As mentioned above, FDIs interact with numerous other subject matters. Investors' activity can therefore both promote and frustrate the objectives of other treaties. International Relations (IR) scholars refer to this situation as 'institutional interaction'.[120] Gehring and Oberthür, for example, identify 'behavioural interaction' as a situation under which the rules of one institution[121] imposes behavioural changes on its members, which consequently affect the effectiveness of other institutions. The phenomenon of 'regulatory chill' can serve as an example in this respect, as restrictions imposed by investment treaties can 'chill' states from promoting the objectives of other institutions (climate change objectives, for example).[122] Similarly, 'impact level' interaction is a situation in which externalities created by one institution affect the ultimate target of another institution. For example, increased low-carbon investments and the enhanced transfer of technologies that they bring can be seen as externalities of IIAs,

---

117 European Parliament, *European Parliament resolution of 25 November on corporate social responsibility in international trade agreements*, 2010. Online. Available HTTP: <http://www.europarl.europa.eu/sides/getDoc.do?type=TAandlanguage=ENandreference=P7-TA-2010-0446> (accessed 19 December 2011); European Parliament, *European Parliament resolution of 6 April 2011 on the future European international investment policy*, 2011. Online. Available HTTP: <http://www.europarl.europa.eu/sides/getDoc.do?type=TA&reference=P7-TA-2011-0141&language=EN> (accessed 19 December 2011) ('EU Parliament resolution on the future European international investment policy').

118 Ibid.

119 Council of the European Union, *Conclusion on a comprehensive European international investment policy*, 3041st Foreign Affairs Council Meeting, Luxemburg, 25 October 2010. Online. Available HTTP: <www.consilium.europa.eu/uedocs/cms_data/docs/pressdata/EN/foraff/117328.pdf> (accessed 19 December 2011), in para. 16.

120 See e.g. T. Gehring and S. Oberthür, 'The Causal Mechanisms of Interaction between International Institutions', *European Journal of International Relations* 15, 2009, 125; O. Stokke, 'The Interplay of International Regimes: Putting Effectiveness Theory to Work', FNI Report 14/2001, 2001. Online. Available HTTP: <http://www.fni.no/doc&pdf/FNI-R1401.pdf> (accessed 19 December 2011).

121 The reader should note that the IR definition of 'institutions' is perhaps comparable to what lawyers often (mistakenly) define as 'regimes', a definition which is wider, and much less formal, than that of 'organisations' such as the World Trade Organization, or the United Nations. An often sited definition of institutions was provided by Keohane: 'persistent and connected set of rules (formal or informal) that prescribe behavioural roles, constrain activity, and shape expectations'. See in R. Keohane, 'International Institutions: Two Approaches', *International Studies Quarterly* 32(4), 1988, 379, p. 383.

122 See review by F. Baetens, 'Foreign Investment Law and Climate Change: Legal Conflicts Arising from Implementing the Kyoto Protocol through Private Investment' *Sustainable Development Law on Climate Change Working Paper Series*, 2010, p. 11.

which in turn promote the ultimate target of the United Nations Framework Convention on Climate Change (UNFCCC).[123]

The main challenge in this respect is to ensure that IIAs will promote the objectives of sustainable development treaties (i.e. environmental treaties, human rights treaties, etc.). Currently, IIAs hardly ever explicitly address the objectives of other treaties. Rare examples can be found *inter alia* in the preamble to the Energy Charter Treaty (ECT), Article 104 of the NAFTA, Article I(6) of the Belgium–Luxembourg–Colombia BIT, and in model treaties like the IISD Model BIT.[124] Implicitly, however, it can be argued that the measures discussed above (exceptions, reservations, language clarifications, etc.) are aimed also to ensure that states' ability to promote the objectives of sustainable development treaties will not be frustrated by the rules of IIAs.

Although IIAs have not yet posed fundamental challenges to other regimes, there have been a certain amount of disputes, both at the WTO and in the investment law systems, directly related to sustainable development. For example, in *Vattenfall v Germany*[125] the Swedish state-owned company Vattenfall challenged regulations imposed on its coal-fired power plant located near Hamburg, which imposed more onerous measures on the plant compared to those originally guaranteed. These measures were enacted after the 2008 elections, when the Green Party had entered power in a coalition in the Hamburg municipal government, and were partly justified by the fact that coal-fired plants affected climate change. Vattenfall claimed violation of the Energy Charter Treaty[126] (which mandates that investments be accorded fair and equitable treatment, and not suffer unreasonable impairment) and sought 1.4 billion Euros in damages.

Following Vattenfall's legal actions, the German federal government agreed to a settlement according to which the required permits for Vattenfall's operation would be granted. Furthermore, Vattenfall was released from earlier commitments to reduce environmental damage.[127] While the exact reasons for the government's motivation to settle this case are not known to the authors, it can be assumed that the prospect of paying 1.4 billion Euros in compensation 'chilled' the government's desire to stop the construction and the operation of this power plant. This case represents an example of climate-related disputes that could become popular in the future, and it may demonstrate that it is possible for IIA provisions to frustrate the objectives of climate change treaties.

What kind of treaty measures are being applied by states in order to address institutional interactions? Largely, as can be seen from the reviews above, states have focused their attention on avoiding conflicts. This can be viewed as a 'defensive' strategy, according to which

---

123 *United Nations Framework Convention on Climate Change*, opened for signatures 4 June 1992, 1771 UNTS 107 (entered into force 21 March 1994).
124 The preamble to the ECT includes reference to the *United Nations Framework Convention on Climate Change, the Convention on Long-Range Transboundary Air Pollution* 'and other international environmental agreements with energy-related aspects'. Art. 104 of the NAFTA includes references to *Convention on International Trade in Endangered Species of Wild Fauna and Flora; the Montreal Protocol on Substances that Deplete the Ozone Layer; the Basel Convention on the Control of Transboundary Movements of Hazardous Wastes and Their Disposal*, Article I(6) of the *Belgium–Luxembourg–Colombia BIT* includes reference to the *International Labour Organization Declaration on Fundamental Principles and Rights at Work.*
125 *Vattenfall*, op. cit.
126 *ECT*, op. cit.
127 *Vattenfall*, op. cit.

states mainly attempt to ensure that one treaty will not frustrate the objectives of another. For example, Article 104 of the NAFTA instructs that in the event of legal conflicts between the NAFTA and a list of environmental treaties, the latter shall prevail. More commonly, as stated above, exceptions and reservation provide the same solution, as they exclude certain fields from the scope of IIAs and *de facto* prioritise these subject matters over the need to protect foreign investments. States' motivation to apply this 'defensive' strategy is obvious; such action prevents future legal claims by investors.

It should be noted, however, that institutional interaction can also result in synergies: the promotion of one treaty's objectives through the provisions of another. States, it is argued, should devote more attention to creative investment provisions, such as may actually promote sustainable development objectives rather than just ensure the avoidance of future conflicts. In trade law, for example, the concept of 'green goods and services' prescribes that, by reducing tariffs for specific goods and services, states can promote climate change objectives. This is an example of how one treaty's provisions can actively promote the objectives of another. In light of the potential embedded in FDI for the promotion of sustainable development objectives, similar concepts should also be developed within IIAs.

Conclusion

Modern IIAs offer greater possibilities to balance different public policy objectives. This is mainly due to the growing concern of the parties involved in the negotiation of the agreements regarding the widespread impact that these instruments can have, not only on the environment but also on trade, labour conditions, health issues, and so on. This chapter has reviewed some of the tools states may find useful when attempting to incorporate sustainable development objectives into their IIAs. It has been explained that the challenge faced by treaty-drafters is multi-layered, as states must strike a balance between the need to secure ample regulatory flexibility, on the one hand, and to create a stable, transparent, and inviting business environment on the other. These tools, it was emphasised, should be developed and refined in order to maximise the potential embedded in FDI for supporting sustainable development.

In order to conclude this chapter, three final remarks should be made. First, the essence of the term 'sustainable development' lies in the desired balance between economic, social, and environmental concerns. All three pillars are important, and all should be taken into consideration. This is what distinguishes 'sustainable development' from pure environmental or economic approaches. Following this view, it is argued that states should apply some of the discussed measures with caution, and only after a careful review of their *full* implications. For example, it may be that the easiest way to prevent future conflicts actually frustrates potential synergies. The use of exceptions, for example, may hinder foreign investments and thus frustrate technology transfer or the creation of new jobs.

Second, the concept of 'sustainable development' includes numerous interests, with almost everyone requiring different balances and different treatment. Therefore, IIAs should avoid using 'one size fits all' solutions for sustainable development as a whole. For example, it would be wrong to address the interaction between economic development and climate change mitigation with the same legal tools used for the interaction between human rights and economic development. More detailed IIAs should therefore be promoted.

Lastly, IIAs should focus more on potential synergies with other treaties. At the moment, IIAs (where these actually refer to other treaties or policies) apply a 'defensive' strategy, according to which emphasis is placed on preventing conflicts and avoiding future claims by investors. There are hardly any IIAs in which the ultimate goals of another treaty are actively promoted.[128] It could be that this is mainly due to the tool often applied by IIAs – investment protection – in which the potential to promote certain types of investment is rather limited (although not non-existent). Perhaps a conceptual change should be made and other tools which are based on incentives, such as those applied by the Kyoto Protocol flexible mechanism for example, should also be developed in order to prioritise certain types of investments.

128 A very limited implementation of this concept can be found in the *Energy Charter Protocol on Energy Efficiency and Related Environmental aspects (Annex 3 to the Final Act of the European Energy Charter Conference).*

32

Collective indigenous rights and the environment

Shawkat Alam

This chapter outlines the connections between Indigenous peoples and their environments, and how this relationship impacts upon the realisation of their collective human rights. It explores the emergence of the notion of collective rights, and highlights the interdependence of the right to self-determination, land rights and cultural rights. It analyses existing international law and uses the example of climate change to examine the impact of environmental damage on Indigenous peoples' rights. It is concluded that a searching reappraisal of current approaches to Indigenous peoples' rights is necessary, and recognition of the unique vulnerability of indigenous collective rights to environmental degradation needs greater international attention.

Introduction

This chapter outlines the connections between Indigenous peoples, their collective rights, and their relationships with the environment. It shows that environmental destruction has particular implications for Indigenous peoples' rights, due to their close affiliation with the land. This chapter will first briefly outline the evolution of the rights of Indigenous peoples. Secondly, it discusses the meaning of collective rights, and specifically concentrates on self-determination, land rights, and culture. Finally, it uses the example of climate change to examine the impact of environmental destruction on Indigenous peoples' rights in a specific context. It will be concluded that a searching reappraisal of current approaches to Indigenous peoples' rights is necessary, and that the particular vulnerability of these communities to environmental degradation and climate change is a pressing issue which requires international attention.

Indigenous peoples' rights and environmental destruction

Indigenous has been defined as 'aboriginal, or first peoples, of a region'.[1] Traditionally, Indigenous peoples struggled for recognition of their rights, especially due to the process of

---

1 K. Lehmann, 'To Define or Not to Define: The Definitional Debate Revisited', *American Indian Law Review* 31, 2006/2007, 509–29, p. 514.

colonisation, and the application of concepts such as *terra nullius* (land belonging to no one).[2] Colonialism attempted to label Indigenous peoples as inferior beings, and subjected them to a particular religion and way of life.[3] However, due to the introduction of international law instruments, such as the United Nations Declaration on the Rights of Indigenous Peoples (UNDRIP), there has been a shift towards the formal recognition of the importance of Indigenous communities, culture, self-determination, participation, and land use.[4] These changes began developing alongside the era of decolonisation, which occurred in the post-World War II period.[5]

International law

Initially, the rights-based movement was concerned only with individual rights, rather than the collective rights of Indigenous communities. For example, the International Convention on the Elimination of All Forms of Racial Discrimination concentrated on rights and equality of all persons.[6] Furthermore, the International Covenant on Civil and Political Rights outlined the importance of minority culture (Article 27).[7] However, in the 1980s a specific focus on the rights of Indigenous peoples began.[8] This was exemplified in 1989 by the 'only internationally binding instrument specifically designed to protect the rights of indigenous peoples': the International Labour Organization Convention Number 169 on Indigenous and Tribal Peoples (ILO 169).[9] This convention emphasises the equality of rights of Indigenous peoples in relation to land (ownership and use), culture, and governance[10] and was considered the most prominent international law instrument protecting the rights of Indigenous people until 2007, when the UNDRIP was adopted. Despite being 'soft law', the UNDRIP is now considered the main international law instrument that concerns the rights of Indigenous peoples.[11] Accordingly, the UNDRIP is the key focus of this chapter. Nevertheless, the UNDRIP did not develop without

2 R. Bratspies and R. Miller, 'Introduction', *American Indian Law Review* 31, 2006/2007, 253–6, p. 253.

3 R. Gordon, 'Saving Failed States: Sometimes a Neocolonialist Notion', *American University Journal of International Law and Policy* 19, 1997, 903–74, pp. 929–40; J.H. Elliott, *Empire of the Atlantic World: Britain and Spain in America 1492–1830*, New Haven: Yale University Press, 2006, p. 85.

4 Bratspies and Miller, op. cit., p. 253; *United Nations Declaration on the Rights of Indigenous Peoples*, UNGA Res 61/295, UN GAOR, Plen Comm, 61st Sess, 107th plen mtg, Agenda Item 68, Supp No 49, UN Doc A/Res/61/259 (13 September 2007), Annex I.

5 Bratspies and Miller, op. cit., p. 254.

6 *International Convention on the Elimination of All Forms of Racial Discrimination*, opened for signature 7 March 1966, 660 UNTS 195 (entered into force 4 January 1969); S. James Anaya, 'Indigenous Peoples and Their Mark on the International Legal System', *American Indian Law Review* 31, 2006/2007, 257–72, p. 259.

7 *International Covenant on Civil and Political Rights* (ICCPR), opened for signature 16 December 1966, 999 UNTS 171 (entered into force 23 March 1976).

8 Anaya, op. cit., p. 259.

9 M. Barelli, 'The Interplay between Global and Regional Human Rights Systems in the Construction of the Indigenous Rights Regime', *Human Rights Quarterly* 32, 2010, 951–79, p. 955.

10 *United Nations Declaration on the Rights of Indigenous Peoples* (2007), GA Res 61/259, UN GAOR, 61st Sess, 49th Supp, UN Doc A/Res/61/295, Annex I; *Convention Concerning Indigenous and Tribal Peoples in Independent Countries*, 72 ILO Official Bull. 59 (entered into force 5 September 1991) preamble ('ILO 169'); Anaya, op. cit., pp. 260–1; See also, A. Xanthaki, *Indigenous Rights and United Nations Standards: Self-determination, Culture and Land*, Cambridge: Cambridge University Press, 2007, p. 70.

11 Barelli, op. cit., p. 957.

criticism, particularly because rights, such as self-determination, were seen as a threat to sovereignty.[12] Furthermore, UNDRIP represented a broader shift from individual-based rights to collective rights,[13] and therefore was seen to question the 'Western individualistic conception of human rights'.[14] Indeed, the 'collective essence' of the UNDRIP text is 'established in the very first articles by recognizing rights to indigenous *peoples*'.[15] Despite these criticisms, the introduction of the UNDRIP resulted in a consideration of specific collective rights, such as self-determination, culture, and land rights (examined below).[16]

Environmental degradation

A key barrier to the recognition of the collective rights of Indigenous peoples is their unique connection to their surrounding environment. In fact it has been stated that 'environmental damage commonly confers benefits on some while inflicting harm on others'.[17] For example, Indigenous peoples may be dependent on land, and the resources that it provides, and exploitation of these resources can impact their health, livelihood, culture, and spiritual connection to the land.[18] In other words, '[f]or indigenous peoples, environmental degradation is not just an "unfortunate but necessary byproduct of economic growth", it is a significant threat to their lives and culture.'[19] However, the connections between environmental destruction and the violation of collective rights is complicated by the scale of the impact, the specific connections of the Indigenous peoples to the land, and their relationship with the 'so-called exploiters' of resources.[20] It follows that environmental destruction is inherently connected to socio-economic status.[21] This has been recently emphasised by the Human Development Report (2011), which states that:

> the most disadvantaged people carry a double burden of deprivation . . . [m]ore vulnerable to the wider effects of environmental degradation, they must also cope with threats to their immediate environment posed by indoor air pollution, dirty water and unimproved sanitation.[22]

However, Shelton suggests that the acknowledgment of human rights in relation to environmental degradation ensures that:

---

12 Ibid., p. 956.
13 Xanthaki, op. cit., p. 71.
14 Barelli op. cit., pp. 956–7.
15 Xanthaki, op. cit., p. 71 (emphasis in original).
16 *United Nations Declaration on the Rights of Indigenous People*, op. cit., Annex I.
17 S. Stewart, 'A Limited Future: The Alien Tort Claims Act Impacting Environmental Rights: Reconciling Past Possibilities with Future Limitations', *American Indian Law Review* 31, 2006/2007, 743–62, pp. 751–2.
18 Ibid., p. 752.
19 Ibid., pp. 751–2.
20 Ibid., pp. 753–5.
21 C.G. Gonzalez, 'An Environmental Justice Critique of Comparative Advantage: Indigenous Peoples, Trade Policy, and the Mexican Neoliberal Economic Reforms', *University of Pennsylvania Journal of International Law* 32, 2011, 723–803, p. 728; R. Guha, *Environmentalism: A Global History*, New York: Longman, 2000, p. 105.
22 United Nations Development Programme, *Human Development Report 2011: Sustainability and Equity: A Better Future for All*, New York: Palgrave Macmillan, 2007, p. 5.

the environment does not deteriorate to the point where the human right to life, the right to health, the right to a family and a private life, the right to culture, the right to safe drinking water, or other human rights are seriously impaired.[23]

What are collective rights?

Collective rights are often affiliated with Indigenous peoples, as they are defined as rights held by groups – 'a collection of persons that one would identify as the same group even under some conditions in which some or all of the individual persons in the group changed'.[24] It follows that collective rights are connected to a community or group, which is often of minority status.[25] However, it has been argued that the 'recognition of collectivities and collective rights is one of the most contested in international law and politics'.[26] Indeed, as previously mentioned, this concept of collective rights can be seen to conflict with Western ideas of individual freedom and liberty.[27] It is axiomatic that some favour assimilation over collective rights, due to concerns over difference, conflict, and societal divisions.[28] However, others see difference as present within society irrespective of policies.[29] Furthermore, collective rights have been seen to foster tolerance, and diversity of culture and knowledge.[30] To this end, many Indigenous peoples view the recognition of their cultural rights as 'of paramount importance'[31] or 'as a token of respect towards their identity and communities as well as the only way for their survival and development'.[32] The recognition of indigenous collective rights in international law is an important step; such acknowledgement, however, does not mean that 'in every case indigenous collective rights will prevail over individual rights of members of indigenous communities';[33] it does mean, though, that 'indigenous communities and their cultures will be better protected from violations of their rights'.[34]

United Nations Declaration on the Rights of Indigenous Peoples (UNDRIP)

As previously mentioned, the UNDRIP particularly endorses the rights of Indigenous peoples 'as a collective or as individuals' (Article 1).[35] In terms of collective rights it focuses

23 D. Shelton, 'Environmental Rights', in P. Alston (ed.) *Peoples' Rights*, New York: Oxford University Press, 2001, p. 187.
24 D.G. Newman, 'Theorizing Collective Indigenous Rights', *American Indian Law Review* 31, 2006/2007, 273–90, pp. 280–81.
25 Y. Dinstein, 'Collective Human Rights of Peoples and Minorities', *International and Comparative Law Quarterly* 25, 1976, 102–20, pp. 102–3.
26 Xanthaki, op. cit., p. 13.
27 R.N. Clinton, 'The Rights of Indigenous Peoples as Collective Group Rights', *Arizona Law Review* 32, 1990, 739–48, p. 740.
28 D. Sanders, 'Collective Rights', *Human Rights Quarterly* 13, 1991, 368–86, p. 375.
29 Ibid.
30 Ibid.
31 United Nations Sub-Commission, 'Indigenous Peoples Preparatory Meeting: Comments on the First Revised Text of the Draft Declaration on Rights of Indigenous Peoples', July 1989, UN Doc E/CN.4/Sub.2/AC.4/1990/3/Add.2.
32 Xanthaki, op. cit., p. 13.
33 Ibid., p. 39.
34 Ibid.
35 *United Nations Declaration on the Rights of Indigenous Peoples*, op. cit., Annex I, Art. 1.

on three key elements. The first is self-determination, the second is land rights, and the third is culture. First, self-determination is explicitly outlined in Articles 3 and 4.[36] Article 3 emphasises that Indigenous peoples have the unique right to develop politically, economically, socially, and culturally.[37] Article 4 expands on this provision by asserting that 'Indigenous peoples . . . have the right to autonomy or self-government in matters relating to their internal and local affairs, as well as ways and means for financing their autonomous functions'.[38] Also, Article 5 outlines that 'Indigenous peoples have the right to maintain and strengthen their distinct political, legal, economic, social and cultural institutions, while retaining their right to participate fully, if they so choose, in the political, economic, social and cultural life of the State'.[39] Furthermore, Article 7 outlines that Indigenous people should be able to live in peace, free from fear of genocide or removal of children,[40] and Article 8 states that 'Indigenous peoples and individuals have the right not to be subjected to forced assimilation or destruction of their culture'.[41] Article 14 also emphasises 'the right to establish and control . . . educational systems', which reinforces their own governance abilities. Lastly, Article 18 outlines the importance of participation of Indigenous peoples 'in decision-making in matters which would affect their rights'.[42] It follows that self-determination is a collective right that concerns the empowerment and unique place of Indigenous societies.

Secondly, Articles 8 and 9 show that Indigenous people should not be deprived of their land, nor should they be removed by force.[43] The UNDRIP provisions surrounding land rights largely reflect 'the rights already recognised in ILO Convention No. 169 but take them further'. For instance, it is recognised that Indigenous peoples have a particular 'spiritual relationship' with land that must be maintained.[44] It follows that 'Indigenous peoples have the right to lands, territories and resources which they have traditionally owned, occupied or otherwise used or acquired'.[45] This means that states are required to 'give legal recognition and protection to these lands, territories and resources'.[46]

Lastly, UNDRIP recognises the importance of culture to Indigenous people. For example, Article 11 emphasises the importance of 'cultural traditions and customs' (elements of self-determination), and Article 12 (also elements of self-determination) states that 'Indigenous peoples have the right to manifest, practice, develop and teach their spiritual and religious traditions, customs and ceremonies', as well as maintain privacy, use 'ceremonial objects' and undertake 'repatriation of their human remains'.[47] Further, the importance of 'passing on' culture 'to future generations' is emphasised in Article 13,[48] and Article 31 indicates that culture must be able to be maintained.[49] While the above discussion outlines only some Articles relevant to self-determination, land rights, and culture, it is apparent that UNDRIP

36 Ibid., Annex I, Arts 3–4.
37 Ibid., Annex I, Art. 3.
38 Ibid., Annex I, Art. 4.
39 Ibid., Annex I, Art. 5.
40 Ibid., Annex I, Art. 7.
41 Ibid., Annex I, Art. 8.
42 Ibid., Annex I, Art. 18.
43 Ibid., Annex I, Arts 8–9.
44 Ibid., Annex I, Art. 25.
45 Ibid., Annex I, Art. 26(1).
46 Ibid., Annex I, Art. 26(3).
47 Ibid., Annex I, Arts 11–2.
48 Ibid., Annex I, Art. 13.
49 Ibid., Annex I, Art. 31.

is an amalgamation of these ideas and values. The implications of each, in the context of environmental destruction, will be further explored in this chapter.

Self-determination

Aside from being central to Indigenous collective rights recognised under UNDRIP, '[t]he right to self-determination is one of the fundamental principles of international law.'[50] However, in a new development in the recognition of self-determination as a right other than to an individual, UNDRIP 'is the first international human rights instrument to expressly recognize the right to self-determination to a sub-state group'.[51] In other words, self-determination questions sovereignty of states, though it does not go as far as to allow secession.[52] However, there is difficulty defining the concept of self-determination. In fact, Miller suggests that 'international lawyers understand that no one quite knows what the right to self-determination means – or worse, everyone knows what the right to self-determination means to *them*'.[53] Nevertheless, Knop argues that UNDRIP contains three key elements of self-determination.[54] They include that Indigenous peoples are distinct, that self-determination 'guarantees fundamental human rights', and that it ensures political participation 'in the' state.[55]

While self-determination is recognised in other international law instruments, such as the United Nations Charter (Articles 1 and 5), the International Covenant on Civil and Political Rights (Article 1), and the Covenant on Economic, Social and Cultural Rights (Article 1), the UNDRIP differs because the right is particularly focused on Indigenous peoples.[56] The above discussion outlines that the vast majority of UNDRIP is related to self-determination, though the key elements are found in Articles 3, 4, 5, 8, 11, 12, 14, and 18.[57] Article 3, which

---

50 J. Neumann, *Human Rights and Climate Change: International Human Rights as an Instrument for Measures of Equalization?* (Master Thesis, 2010, GRIN Verlag) p. 18; See also the *International Covenant on Economic, Social and Cultural Rights, International Covenant on Civil and Political Rights* and *Optional Protocol to the International Covenant on Civil and Political Rights* (1966), UNGA Res 2200(XXI) A, UN GAOR, 21st Sess, 16th Supp, UN Doc A/RES/2200(XXI)A, Annex, Art. 1(a) and Art. 1(1) (respective covenants):

> All peoples have the right of self-determination. By virtue of that right they freely determine their political status and freely pursue their economic, social and cultural development.

51 Barelli, op. cit., p. 959.
52 Ibid; R.A. Miller, 'Collective Discursive Democracy as the Indigenous Right to Self-Determination', *American Indian Law Review* 31, 2006/2007, 341–73, pp. 345, 348.
53 Miller, op. cit., p. 344.
54 Ibid., p. 351.
55 Ibid.
56 *Charter of the United Nations* (1945), 1 UNTS XVI, Arts 1, 5; *International Covenant on Economic, Social and Cultural Rights, International Covenant on Civil and Political Rights* and *Optional Protocol to the International Covenant on Civil and Political Rights* (1966), UNGA Res 2200(XXI) A, UN GAOR, 21st Sess, 16th Supp, UN Doc A/RES/2200(XXI)A, Annex, Art. 1(a) and Art. 1(1) (respective covenants); E. Cirkovic, 'Self-Determination and Indigenous Peoples in International Law', *American Indian Law Review* 31, 2006/2007, 375–400, pp. 375–6, 390–1; *United Nations Declaration on the Rights of Indigenous Peoples*, op. cit., Annex I.
57 *United Nations Declaration on the Rights of Indigenous Peoples*, op. cit., Annex I, Arts 3, 4, 5, 8, 11, 12, 14, 18; W.A. Wastewin, 'Cultural and Economic Self-Determination for Tribal Peoples in the United States Supported by the UN Declaration on the Rights of Indigenous Peoples', *Pace Environmental Law Review* 28, 2010–2011, 357–65, p. 358.

recognises the right to self-determination, has been referred to as the 'heart of the Declaration',[58] and the right to self-determination has also been named by some as a 'pre-requisite for the full enjoyment of all human rights of indigenous peoples'.[59]

Australian Indigenous peoples

Perhaps inconstant with the Indigenous peoples' collective right to self-determination is the fact that '[t]he vast majority [of Indigenous communities] lack political power at the national or even the regional level'.[60] Historically, this has been true in the Australian context, for example. Indeed, Indigenous Australians were not recognised as citizens or counted in the census until a successful referendum in 1967. While many Aboriginal people could vote in the Federal elections, not all Indigenous people were afforded the right to vote until 1983, when the Commonwealth Electoral Act was amended to remove optional enrolment for Indigenous people, removing all discrimination based on race in the Australian electoral system.[61] While this example reflects the individual rights of Indigenous Australians, it highlights that Indigenous communities are underrepresented in government, perhaps because of their lack of recognition, historically.

It is axiomatic that such communities have had difficulties in pursuing their right to self-determination; that is, enjoying their right to full recognition of their own laws and customs, institutions for the management of land and natural resources, and land tenure systems.[62] The approach of the Australian government over the course of the past century has been a policy of assimilation rather than any attempt at understanding the Indigenous communities' laws, customs, or traditions. These policies have in the past gone to such extremes as the removal of Indigenous children from their families, to be raised by a 'white' family, and be indoctrinated into a Europeanised Australian culture. Such children are now known in Australia as the 'Stolen Generation'.[63] While ostensibly such policies have been officially abandoned in Australian politics, and since the 1990s a so-called reconciliation approach has been preferred, there are still extensive limits to the pursuit of Indigenous self-determination. This has most starkly been demonstrated in Australia's recent history with the Northern Territory Intervention in 2007. This intervention came as a result of reports of child abuse in Indigenous communities in the Northern Territory. It resulted in a series of restrictive policies being applied to these communities, including restrictions related to alcohol, the imposition of limits on Indigenous land rights in the area, and the suspension of the Racial Discrimination Act 1975 (Cth).

---

58 *United Nations Declaration on the Rights of Indigenous Peoples*, op. cit., Annex I, Art. 3; Statement of the Representative of the Chittagong Hill Tracts Peace Campaign in Report of the Working Group established in accordance with Commission on Human Rights Resolution 1995/32, UN Doc. E/CN.4/1997/102 (1996), para. 339, in Xanthaki, op. cit., p. 131.

59 Report of 1995 Commission Working Group, E/CN.4/1996/84 (1996), para. 51, in Xanthaki op. cit., p. 131.

60 R.K. Hitchcock, 'International Human Rights, the Environment, and Indigenous Peoples', *Colorado Journal of International Environmental Law and Policy* 5, 1994, 1–22, p. 5.

61 Commonwealth Electoral Legislation Amendment Bill 1983, *Explanatory Memorandum*: Online. Available HTTP: <http://www.aph.gov.au/binaries/library/pubs/explanmem/docs/1983commonwealthelectorallegislationamndtbillem.pdf> (accessed 11 May 2012).

62 Hitchcock, op. cit., p. 11.

63 For an extended discussion of Australian Indigenous policy, see e.g. A. Armitage, *Comparing the Policy of Aboriginal Assimilation: Australia, Canada and New Zealand*, Vancouver: UBC Press, 1995.

Land rights

The second key connection between Indigenous peoples' collective rights and environmental destruction is found in land rights. Indigenous peoples place significant emphasis on land rights, as it represents not only their self-determination but also their ability to survive.[64] The large number of references to land rights in UNDRIP is a reflection of the emphasis made by the United Nations treaty bodies on 'prevailing discrimination of indigenous land rights' (see Articles 8, 9, 25 and 26 as previously mentioned).[65] Wastewin emphasises that Indigenous peoples are inherently linked to the land through all aspects of their life.[66] She goes on to state that 'Cultural and Economic Self-determination is recognition of our responsibilities and obligations to Mother Earth as we build prosperous, good lives for our people'.[67] It is for this reason that Wastewin suggests that 'legal trickery . . . restrains the relationship between the Tribes and Mother Earth'.[68] However, despite these criticisms, Wastewin sees the UNDRIP as a step forward, as it connects Indigenous peoples' lives with rights.[69] In order to show the importance of these connections, some examples will be discussed.

Awas Tingni v Nicaragua

A key example of particular importance is that of *Awas Tingni v Nicaragua*.[70] As explained by Anaya and Grossman, the Awas Tingni is a community found on the coast of Nicaragua, which was particularly impacted by a decision made by 'the Nicaraguan government' to allow the logging of 43,000 hectares of forest.[71] Due to concerns raised by the World Wildlife Fund, the Nicaraguan Government decided that an agreement should be reached with the Awas Tingni people.[72] This was to ensure that the Awas Tingni people were heard during the negotiation process, and to make sure that environmental destruction was minimised.[73] The resulting agreement stated that the people would be economically compensated, and that traditional land would be legally recognised.[74] However, during this time the Nicaraguan government was concurrently granting further logging of 63,000 hectares to another corporation.[75] Accordingly, in view of the inadequate responses given to the concerns of the Awas Tingni people, they eventually approached the 'Inter-American Commission' based on

64 Barelli, op. cit., pp. 959–60.
65 *United Nations Declaration on the Rights of Indigenous Peoples*, op. cit., Annex I, arts 8, 9, 25 and 26; Xanthaki, op. cit., p. 117, citing as an example, 'Concluding Observations of the Human Rights Committee, Columbia', UN Doc. CCPR/CO/80/COL of 26 May 2004, para. 20.
66 Wastewin, op. cit., p. 362.
67 Ibid., pp. 362–3.
68 Ibid., p. 363.
69 Ibid., p. 364.
70 *The Mayagna (Sumo) Awas Tingni Community v Nicaragua*, Judgment of 31 August 2001, Inter-Am. Ct HR, (Ser. C) No. 79 (2001).
71 S.J. Anaya and C. Grossman, 'The Case of *Awas Tingni v Nicaragua*: A New Step in the International Law of Indigenous Peoples', *Arizona Journal of International and Comparative Law* 19, 2002, 1–15, pp. 1, 3.
72 Ibid., p. 3.
73 Ibid.
74 Ibid.
75 Ibid., p. 4.

the allegations that property and cultural rights were adversely impacted by the agreement.[76] In order to support their claims, maps of traditional land were developed.[77]

Once the case proceeded to the Inter-American Court, the Nicaraguan Government argued that the Awas Tingni had no ancestral claim (the village at the time dated 'to the 1940s'), and that the area being claimed was larger than required.[78] However, it was found that the Awas Tingni people did in fact have a relationship with the land, and an entitlement to it as property.[79] In other words, the agreements had been made against the land rights held by the Awas Tingni people.[80] This included 'a violation of the right to property', which is necessary for Indigenous peoples to continue to maintain their customs and culture.[81] It follows that the Inter-American Court required the Nicaraguan government to invest US $50,000 'in works or services of collective interest for the benefit of the Awas Tingni Community', and US $30,000 for costs.[82] This case is therefore of prominent importance as it is 'the first legally binding decision by an international tribunal to uphold the collective land and resource rights by indigenous peoples in the face of a state's failure to do so'.[83]

Endorois case

The case of *Endorois Welfare Council v Kenya* is another relevant example endorsing the importance of land rights with respect to Indigenous peoples.[84] This case arose in the context of the African Commission on Human and Peoples' Rights, rather than the UNDRIP, but it nonetheless still represents the importance of land rights to Indigenous people, and the subsequent connections that such rights have with environmental issues.[85] The Endorois community was initially located in Kenya, next to Lake Bogoria, though due to the creation of a nature reserve they were evicted in 1973.[86] This eviction occurred without consideration of land rights, without any participation of the community, and without 'benefit-sharing' or compensation.[87] Following the eviction of the Endorois community, members of the community

---

76 Ibid., pp. 4–5.
77 Ibid., p. 6.
78 Ibid., p. 9, citing Reply of the Republic of Nicaragua to the Complaint Presented Before the Inter-American Court of Human Rights in the Case of the Mayagna Community of Awas Tingni, pp. 101–27; Final Written Arguments of the Republic of Nicaragua on the Merits of the Issue (Case No. 11.577 – Mayagna Community of Awas Tingni), reproduced in their entirety, pp. 369–78.
79 Ibid., pp. 1, 12; *The Mayagna (Sumo) Awas Tingni Community v. Nicaragua*, Judgment of 31 August 2001, op. cit., [151].
80 Anaya and Grossman, op. cit., pp. 12–3.
81 Ibid., p. 12.
82 Ibid., p. 14; *The Mayagna (Sumo) Awas Tingni Community v. Nicaragua*, Judgment of 31 August 2001, op. cit., [167]–[169].
83 Ibid., p. 2.
84 *Center for Minority Rights Development (Kenya) and Minority Rights Group International on behalf of the Endorois Welfare Council vs. Kenya*, African Court for Human and Peoples' Rights, Case No. 276/2003.
85 C. Morel, 'Conservation and Indigenous Peoples' Rights: Must One Necessarily Come at the Expense of the Other?' in IUCN-CEESP (ed.) *Exploring the Right to Diversity in Conservation Law, Policy, and Practice, Policy Matters* 17, 2010, 174–81, p. 174. See generally, *Center for Minority Rights Development (Kenya) and Minority Rights Group International on behalf of the Endorois Welfare Council vs. Kenya*, op. cit..
86 Ibid.
87 Ibid.

were considered trespassers if they utilised the land for spiritual and medicinal reasons.[88] This case therefore highlights the importance of the land for cultural, social, and economic factors.[89] However, instead of representing environmental destruction, it shows a conflict between environmental protection (the nature reserve) and collective rights (in this case, land rights). According to Morel, the African Commission on Human and Peoples' Rights addressed this particular conflict by recognising 'the Endorois' ownership over their ancestral land and its restitution', their 'right to development', and 'the community's natural resources'.[90] In other words, the decision to evict the Endorois was seen as acting contrary to their land rights.[91] Interestingly, the judgment in this case went as far as to indicate that Indigenous peoples should not only be able to access land, but they should be able to make use of and manage the land.[92]

A further issue that the *Endorois* case examined was the connection between land rights and 'natural resources', specifically the existence of rubies.[93] While initial mining was halted due to a lack of consultation with the Endorois people, the African Commission did not go so far as to suggest that the 'natural resources' were owned by the Endorois people.[94] Nevertheless, there was recognition of the importance of 'natural resources' to the people for economic and socio-cultural reasons.[95] In other words, the African Commission showed the connections between environmental destruction and impacts on the land rights of Indigenous people.[96] It did this by emphasising that sovereignty of the state must only prevail if urgent or necessary.[97] It stated:

> Few, if any, limitations on indigenous resource rights are appropriate, because the indig-
> enous ownership of the resources is associated with the most important and fundamental
> human rights, including the right to life, food, the right to self-determination, to shelter,
> and the right to exist as a people.[98]

The overlap between environmental destruction – which is often caused by natural resource exploitation – and rights is clearly represented by this case. While the case occurred before the UNDRIP, the same concepts are apparent. Overall, the *Endorois* case highlights the importance of recognising collective rights when making decisions about environmental policies.

---

88 Ibid.
89 Ibid., pp. 174–5.
90 Ibid., p. 175 (quotations); *Center for Minority Rights Development (Kenya) and Minority Rights Group International on behalf of the Endorois Welfare Council vs. Kenya*, op. cit. [298], recommendations.
91 Morel, op. cit., p. 175.
92 *Center for Minority Rights Development (Kenya) and Minority Rights Group International on behalf of the Endorois Welfare Council vs. Kenya*, op. cit. [204]; Morel, op. cit., p. 177.
93 *Center for Minority Rights Development (Kenya) and Minority Rights Group International on behalf of the Endorois Welfare Council vs. Kenya*, op. cit. [124]; Morel, op. cit., p. 178.
94 *Center for Minority Rights Development (Kenya) and Minority Rights Group International on behalf of the Endorois Welfare Council vs. Kenya*, op. cit. [260]; Morel, op. cit., p. 178.
95 Ibid.
96 Ibid.
97 *Center for Minority Rights Development (Kenya) and Minority Rights Group International on behalf of the Endorois Welfare Council vs. Kenya*, op. cit., [212] quoting E-I. Daes, 'Indigenous Peoples' Right to Land and Natural Resources' in N. Ghanea and A. Xanthaki (eds) *Minorities, Peoples and Self-Determination*, Leiden: Martinus Nijhoff Publishers, 2005.
98 Ibid; Morel, op. cit., p. 178.

Shoshone

Another example of particular relevance to both self-determination and land rights is that of the Shoshone people. While the Shoshone people have specific connections to the land, located particularly in the wide area from southern Idaho, through eastern Nevada, to the Mojave Desert of California, corporations have also been particularly interested in the land for its abundance of gold, water, and geothermal energy, and the possibilities of nuclear waste disposal and military undertakings in the same area.[99] However, the Inter-American Commission on Human Rights in 2002 issued a final report once again emphasising the connection between collective rights and environmental destruction, by finding the United States of America to be 'in violation of rights to property, due process and equality under the law'.[100] Subsequently, in 2006, the United Nations Committee on the Elimination of Racial Discrimination 'publicly issued a full decision against the United States'.[101] The decision went as far as to encourage the US to 'freeze', 'desist', and 'stop' current and anticipated actions against the Western Shoshone People of the Western Shoshone Nation.[102]

The long-standing, entrenched cultural belief that Indigenous peoples have natural and close ties with the land is the reason why economic justifications for the use of the land, which are often argued by the government and corporations, are almost always at odds with the spiritual attachment to the land of Indigenous populations. The US Government adopted a number of legislative measures that would directly and unequivocally prejudice the rights of the Shoshone people. One commentator notes that the laws enacted by the US Government, and passed by former President Bush and Congress:

> [c]onfirm[ed] Western Shoshone predictions about massive federal land giveaways . . . the House Resources Budget Reconciliation Package was amended in late 2005 to include what one leading Congressman dubbed 'a blazing fire sale of federal lands to domestic and international corporate interests'.[103]

The Shoshone case study highlights the tension between different stakeholders striving to achieve different goals: the government aiming to maximise economic development, corporations focused on maximising the profitability of their companies by attempting to privatise the Shoshone people's land, and finally, Indigenous communities trying to live in harmony with their land, and practise their traditional culture. Carrie Dann's quote that follows adds perspective to the Shoshone people's position in this tension, and a stance that is indeed indicative of the collective beliefs of many Indigenous communities. Dann stated:

---

99 J.A. Fishel, 'United States Called to Task on Indigenous Rights: The Western Shoshone Struggle and Success at the International Level', *American Indian Law Review* 31, 2006/2007, 619–50, pp. 619, 624, 633, 646.

100 Ibid., p. 620.

101 Ibid., p. 621, citing Decision 1 (68) (*United States of America*), UN ESCOR, CERD, 68th Sess, UN Doc CERD/C/USA/DEC/I (11 April 2006) [10].

102 Ibid., [10].

103 Fishel, op. cit., p. 632, citing US Representative Nick J Rahall, II, *Extension of Remarks, An Assault on America's Public Lands: The Hardrock Mining Provisions of the Resources Committee's Budget Reconciliation Package* (3 November 2005): Online. Available HTTP. <www.house.gov/list/press/ii00_democrats/mininglawcrremarks.pdf> (accessed 29 December 2011).

We were taught that we were placed here as caretakers of the lands, the animals, all the living things – those things that cannot speak for themselves in this human language. We, the two-legged ones, were placed here with that responsibility. We see the four most sacred things as the land, the air, the water and the sun (l.a.w.s.). Without any one of these things there would be no life. This is our religion – our spirituality – and defines who we are as a people.[104]

Culture

In some respects culture is not a separate category, as it is inherently connected to self-determination and land rights, especially insofar as Indigenous culture has a special connection with the land. However, cultural rights are fundamentally important to Indigenous communities. Indeed, the widespread belief, from the perspective of Indigenous people, that culture is fundamentally important is articulated powerfully by the following quote: 'Our knowledge, our cultures and our languages belong to us, they are what makes us who we are.'[105] It follows that, as previously mentioned, culture is such an important collective right that it is separately addressed in the UNDRIP.[106] Most notably, Articles 11, 12, and 13 reinforce the undertaking of 'cultural traditions', and the importance of this for 'future generations'.[107] Moreover, Article 31 emphasises the importance of maintaining these cultural connections.[108] Furthermore, Article 15 entitles Indigenous peoples 'to the dignity and diversity of their *cultures*, traditions, histories and aspirations reflected in education and public information'[109] and 'urges states to take effective measures to promote tolerance, understanding and good relations with all segments of society'.[110] The UNDRIP does, however, recognise that 'indigenous peoples [have] the control to determine their own cultural revolution'.[111] Despite this recognition, however, particularly in the USA there are issues with Indigenous peoples' names, culture, artwork, symbols, and knowledge being commercially exploited.

---

104 Fishel, op. cit., p. 624, citing Corpwatch, *Barrick's Dirty Secrets: An Alternative Annual Report* 14 (2007): Online. Available HTTP: <http://protestbarrick.net/downloads/barrick_report.pdf> (accessed 29 December 2011).

105 Statement of the Federation of Independent Aboriginal Education Providers in 'Review of Developments pertaining to the Promotion and Protection of Human Rights and Fundamental Freedoms of Indigenous People: Indigenous Peoples', Note by the Secretariat on Information Received from Intergovernmental Organisations and Indigenous Peoples, UN Doc. E/CN.4/Sub.2/AC.4/1998, p. 8, para. [2], cited in Xanthaki, op. cit., p. 14.

106 The right to culture is also acknowledged as an individual right: See Article 27 ICCPR; and Article 15 *International Covenant on Economic, Social and Cultural Rights*, opened for signature 16 December 1966, 993 UNTS 3 (entered into force 3 January 1976).

107 *United Nations Declaration on the Rights of Indigenous Peoples*, op. cit., Annex I, Arts 11, 12, 13.

108 Ibid., Annex I, Art. 31.

109 Ibid., Annex I, Art. 15.

110 Xanthaki, op. cit., p. 115.

111 Ibid., p. 115, stating in footnote 99: 'As evidenced by recognising the "future" as well as present and past manifestations of cultures in Article 11, the right to indigenous peoples to "develop their own indigenous decision-making institutions" in Article 18 and the references to the non-economic development in Articles 20, 23, 29, 31, 32, 34 and 36.'

The importance of recognising cultural rights was explained by UN Special Rapporteur Danilo Turk, when he stated:

> The centrality of the right to culture is obvious, for instance, with regard to the rights of indigenous peoples. Without affording full guarantees for their cultural rights, including the right not to assimilate and the right to cultural autonomy, the protection offered to indigenous peoples by other rights can become practically meaningless.[112]

The following example highlights the importance of this right in the practical sense, given the tension between competing rights of government, indigenous peoples, and the corporate sector.

Lihirian People of Papua New Guinea

Papua New Guinea is a geologically rich nation, and consequently mining has been an important part of the country's economic growth and industrial development. However, the government must be aware of its policies and law, and their indirect effects on the local Indigenous populations. Indeed, 'Papua New Guinea is almost 100 per cent Indigenous, having over 800 different local tribes . . . Nevertheless, common resources such as minerals and water are state-owned by law.'[113]

For the Lihirian people, environmental degradation has been a major concern. Environmental damage and destruction is largely caused by the extractive industries, particularly mining companies who have shifted their operations to Papua New Guinea because of the rich resources available. The tension between mining companies, the government, and Indigenous peoples grew in the 1980s and 1990s, resulting in complaints, law suits, and even bloodshed between locals and miners.[114]

In terms of the legal framework within Papua New Guinea, the Mining Act (1992) establishes that the state owns all minerals at six feet or more below the earth.[115] Accordingly, even if 'local indigenous people own the land there is a conflict of interest with the state's ownership of minerals below it'.[116] Moreover, all of the water in Papua New Guinea is also state-owned. This puts the government in a unique position of being able to issue licenses for the use of water – either for 'domestic or industrial use, or for the disposal of waste or for the diversion for industrial purposes or for storage such as dams for hydropower generation'.[117]

---

112 D. Turk. 'The Realization of Economic, Social and Cultural Rights', *Final report submitted by Mr. Danilo Turk, Special Rapporteur*, to the Sub-Commission on Prevention of Discrimination and Protection of Minorities, of the United Nations Commission on Human Rights, 3 July 1992, UN Doc. E/CN.4/Sub.2/1992/16), 198, cited in E. Ward, *Indigenous Peoples between Human Rights and Environmental Protection*, Danish Centre for Human Rights, 1993.

113 *A Case Study on Indigenous People, Extractive Industries and the World Bank: Papua New Guinea*, Presented at the workshop on 'Indigenous Peoples, the Extractive Industries and the World Bank', Exeter College, University of Oxford, UK, 14–15 April 2003, p. 4. Online. Available HTTP: <http://www.forestpeoples.org/sites/fpp/files/publication/2010/08/eirinternatwshoppngcaseapr03eng.pdf> (accessed 7 May 2012).

114 Ibid., p. 7.

115 *Mining Act* (1992), s. 5.

116 *A Case Study on Indigenous People, Extractive Industries and the World Bank: Papua New Guinea*, op. cit., p. 8.

117 Ibid., p. 8.

A particularly noteworthy example within Papua New Guinea where social and cultural challenges have arisen is on Lihir Island, where the lifestyle and cultural influences on the local Indigenous population 'has changed dramatically since the mining began'[118] and there has been a rapid transition in both the physical and social environment'.[119] Traditionally, the Lihirian people, as is the case with the majority of Papua New Guineans, have relied on subsistence farming for their livelihood. That is, they 'grow and harvest food from gardens and get protein from hunting in the bush and water for their family's consumption'.[120] However, since the mine has 'brought a sudden transitional change from subsistence to a monetary-based lifestyle',[121] this has forced a cultural shift within the Indigenous community. Many local Indigenous people 'still feel strongly about the loss of traditional values and their simple way of life'.[122]

Due to this rapid development and resulting environmental degradation, 'Several cultur- ally and socially important areas such as hot springs, graveyards, and even villages, are being transformed into construction sites to support the mine.'[123] With specific reference to social and cultural implications of such change, one author has noted that:

> Social problems trail alongside the industry as it enters into very remote areas, where there are people with very limited exposure to so-called civilisation. This causes sudden transitional changes that are sometimes very detrimental to the people's traditions and cultures. Respect for elders and women are no longer in existence. Womanising, marriage break-ups, new diseases, alcoholism and drug abuse are introduced and on the rise in our innocent communities.[124]

It is evident that culture is a fundamental aspect of Indigenous communities. Accordingly, it is clear that economic development that occurs at an unsustainable pace, without con- sideration for the environment and social and cultural implications, is likely to be detrimental to local Indigenous peoples in the longer term. This underscores the importance of the connection between sustainable development and the collective rights of Indigenous peoples. As such, long-term damage to the earth's atmosphere and environmental degradation gener- ally, is likely to have long-term implications for groups of people who value, and indeed rely on, their close connection to the environment.

The impact of climate change on Indigenous peoples' rights

This section will discuss how climate change effects the above three collective rights (self-determination, land rights, and culture) of Indigenous populations. The reason why climate change and environmental damage can have far-reaching implications on the rights of Indigenous peoples has been concisely explained by Julia Neumann. She states that:

---

118 Ibid., p. 13.
119 Ibid.
120 Ibid., p. 14.
121 Ibid.
122 Ibid., p. 15.
123 Ibid., p. 17.
124 Ibid., p. 19.

The special relationship and close linkage between indigenous people's way of life and their land has long been recognised. Indigenous people quite often suffer the most from environmental affects since in a lot of cases they inhabit the world's most vulnerable ecosystems and are highly dependent on their habitat's functionality and balance.[125]

It has therefore been stated that 'sustained material growth destroys ecosystems, impoverishes the planet, diminishes the human spirit, and visits violence upon whole poor communities'.[126] When speaking in broad terms, it is logical that if indigenous populations often inhabit vulnerable environmental areas, these groups are most likely to first experience some of the more extreme effects of climate change. Moreover, the unique close interrelationship that Indigenous communities share with the land often means that not only are they likely to be the first to experience the effects of climate change, but they are also more likely to suffer from more extreme consequences of such environmental damage, as the land and the environment are an integral part of their community.

In order to place the connections between collective rights and environmental destruction in context, it is useful to examine the topic of climate change. Hunter, Salzman, and Zaelke outline that climate change will not only be an issue for collective rights, but also for the right 'to life, health, habitation, culture, [and] equality before the law'.[127] In fact, the *Report of the United Nations Office of the High Commissioner for Human Rights on the Relationship between Human Rights and Climate Change* generally outlines the connections between climate change and human rights.[128] It suggests that climate change will impact life, due to increased severity and frequency of diseases, floods, heatwaves, storms, droughts, and fires.[129] Furthermore it will impact food and water availability, which is of particular concern for those Indigenous people that rely on the land for survival.[130] It may also result in increased health issues due to disease, malnutrition, reduced water availability, and adverse impacts on housing because of storm surge and sea level rise.[131]

Of particular significance to Indigenous peoples, however, is the predicted impact on self-determination.[132] It is suggested that 'While the right to self-determination is a collective right held by peoples rather than individuals, its realization is an essential condition for the effective enjoyment of individual human rights'.[133] It follows that climate change may result

125 Neumann, op. cit., p. 19, citing, S.C. Aminazadeh, 'Moral Imperative: The Human Rights Implications of Climate Change', *Hastings International and Comparative Law Review* 30, 2007, 231–66, pp. 254f.

126 W.E. Rees and L. Westra, 'When Consumption Does Violence: Can There be Sustainability and Environmental Justice in a Resource-limited World?', in J. Agyeman, R.D. Bullard and B. Evans (eds) *Just Sustainabilities: Development in an Unequal World*, Cambridge, MA: MIT Press, 2003, p. 107.

127 D. Hunter, J. Salzman and D. Zaelke, *International Environmental Law and Policy*, 4th edition, New York: Foundation Press, 2010, p. 1343.

128 *Report of the United Nations Office of the High Commissioner for Human Rights on the Relationship between Human Rights and Climate Change*, A/HRC/10/61, 15 January 2009: Online. Available HTTP: <http://www.ohchr.org/EN/Issues/HRAndClimateChange/Pages/Study.aspx> (accessed 11 May 2012); See also, Hunter et al., op. cit., pp. 1343–50.

129 *Report of the United Nations Office of the High Commissioner for Human Rights*, op. cit., p. 9.

130 Ibid., pp. 9–11.

131 Ibid., pp. 12–3.

132 Ibid., pp. 14–5.

133 Ibid., p. 14.

in threats to 'traditional territories and sources of livelihood'.[134] This is because Indigenous peoples often 'live in marginal lands and fragile ecosystems which are particularly sensitive to alterations in the physical environment'.[135] This threat is especially the case for peoples such as the Inuit, and those that live in 'low–lying island States'.[136]

Despite these threats, Indigenous peoples have unsuccessfully requested an Ad Hoc Working Group on Indigenous Peoples and Climate Change within the UNFCCC (United Nations Framework Convention on Climate Change) framework.[137] Consistent with the concerns of Indigenous peoples that climate change will affect their collective rights, the *Milan Declaration of the Sixth International Indigenous Peoples Forum on Climate Change 2003* outlines that:

> All development projects within indigenous ancestral territories must respect our fundamental rights to lands, territories, self-determination and ensure our right to our prior and informed consent. Sinks project [*sic*] do not contribute to climate change mitigation and sustainable development. The modalities and procedures for afforestation and reforestation project activities under the CDM [clean development mechanism] do not respect and guarantee our right to lands, territories and self-determination.[138]

Furthermore, the *Permanent Forum on Indigenous Issues, Declaration* merely highlights the impact of climate change on Indigenous peoples' rights.[139] It states that:

> The United Nations Declaration on the Rights of Indigenous Peoples should serve as a key and binding framework in the formulation of plans for development and should be considered fundamental in all processes related to climate change at the local, national, regional and global levels.[140]

It also suggests that stakeholders, such as states, organisations under the umbrella of the United Nations, and financial bodies, should provide the necessary financial and technological support to ensure that Indigenous peoples can maintain collective rights, such as self-determination, land rights, and culture.[141] It follows that there has been some development with respect to international instruments in the realms of climate change and Indigenous rights, though these developments have been limited. The following example of the Inuit people highlights the overlaps between climate change and human rights.

---

134 Ibid.
135 Ibid., p. 17.
136 Ibid.
137 Hunter et al., op. cit., p. 1353.
138 Ibid; *Milan Declaration of the Sixth International Indigenous Peoples Forum on Climate Change 2003*, UNSW Indigenous Law Centre (2011): Online. Available HTTP: <http://www.ilc.unsw.edu.au/sites/ilc.unsw.edu.au/files/mdocs/milan%20declaration.pdf> (accessed 29 December 2011).
139 Hunter et al., op. cit., p. 1353; United Nations Economic and Social Council, *Permanent Forum on Indigenous Issues: Report of the Seventh Session (21 April-2 May 2008) E/2008/43/E/C.19/2008/13* (2008) United Nations: Online. Available HTTP: <http://daccess-dds-ny.un.org/doc/UNDOC/GEN/N08/338/82/PDF/N0833882.pdf?OpenElement> (accessed 29 December 2011).
140 United Nations Economic and Social Council, *Permanent Forum on Indigenous Issues: Report of the Seventh Session*, op. cit., p. 4 (accessed 29 December 2011).
141 Ibid.

The Inuit

The impacts of climate change are complex, though they are of particular concern for the Inuit people living in the Arctic. The Arctic region refers to the area surrounding the North Pole and comprises the Arctic Ocean and the territory of eight states: Canada, Denmark (including Greenland), Finland, Iceland, Norway, Russia, Sweden, and the United States. The area is largely characterised by a harsh climate with short summers, extremely low temperatures and the presence of permafrost. This area is vulnerable to melting ice and sea-level rise, and it is due to this vulnerability that the Inuit are concerned about their future livelihoods, food supply, and culture.[142] A (failed) petition to the Inter-American Commission on Human Rights (2005) emphasised these concerns by stating that the USA was not adequately addressing greenhouse gas (GHG) emissions.[143] In fact, the petition outlined that climate change was impacting particular rights of the Inuit.[144] These included the:

> right to enjoy the benefits of their culture, the right to use and enjoy lands they have traditionally occupied, their right to use and enjoy their personal property, the right to the preservation of health, the right to life, physical integrity, and security, the right to their own means of subsistence, and their rights to residence and movement and inviolability of the home.[145]

Watt-Cloutier outlines that, while the petition is not legally enforceable, it has a moral basis that aims to educate and connect the various Inuit groups.[146] However, the key issue with this type of environmental degradation is that, unlike logging or oil extraction, the cause and effect of GHG emissions is across space and time.[147] It follows that once again there is a conflict between collective rights and sovereignty, though it is complicated by the need to address climate change as a global problem.[148] However, it must also be emphasised that not only could climate change impact the human rights of Indigenous people, it may result in their 'very existence' being threatened.[149]

It seems that a complexity of the connection between climate change and Indigenous collective rights in this instance is the temporal, longer-term implications of the destruction of the environment. As such, since few immediate effects are evident, policy-makers and law reformers are reluctant to rely on science as a justification to hinder economic development (by, for example, limiting industrial growth by requiring certain environment-friendly conditions). This is a valid criticism. However, it is argued that this short-term perception of the interaction between Indigenous collective rights and climate change is potentially

142 H.M. Osofsky, 'The Inuit Petition as a Bridge? Beyond Dialectics of Climate Change and Indigenous Peoples' Rights', *American Indian Law Review* 31, 2006/2007, 675–98, p. 675.

143 Ibid., p. 684.

144 Ibid., pp. 685–7.

145 Ibid., pp. 685–6.

146 Ibid., pp. 686–7, citing S. Watt-Cloutier, Chair, *Presentation at the Eleventh Conference of Parties to the UN Framework Convention on Climate Change: The Climate Change Petition by the Inuit Circumpolar Conference to the Inter-American Commission on Human Rights*, Inuit Circumpolar Conference, Montreal, 7 December 2005.

147 Ibid., p. 688.

148 Ibid., pp. 689–90.

149 S. Rahman and G.E. Schafft, 'Climate Change and Human Rights in Bangladesh', *Anthropology News* 51, 2010, 30–1, p. 31.

threatening the sustainability of these communities. Since the rights to self-determination, lands, and cultural rights are so fundamental to Indigenous populations, a failure by governments to regulate industry and slow the degradation of the environment and destruction of the atmosphere will have far-reaching long-term implications on the very existence of some such populations.

It is these longer-term, big-picture impacts of climate change that concern the Inuit people, and with good reason. This point is illustrated by Watt-Cloutier, who contrasts the legal technicalities of the dispute with the broader picture and the implications of environmental damage. The following quote highlights the importance of policies that are often made by people who are not directly affected by them, and how the livelihood of Indigenous peoples are dependent on the apparently non-existent foresight of such policy-makers. Watt-Cloutier asserted:

> I have attended three COPs [Climate Change Conferences]. People rush from meeting to meeting arguing about all sorts of narrow technical points. The bigger picture, the cultural picture, the human picture is being lost. Climate change is not about bureaucrats scurrying around. It is about families, parents, children, and the lives we lead in our communities in the broader environment. We have to regain this perspective if climate change is to be stopped.
>
> Inuit understand these connections because we remain a people of the land, ice, and snow. This is why, for us, climate change is an issue of our right to exist as an Indigenous people. How can we stand up for ourselves and help others do the same?[150]

Indeed, the far-reaching effects that climate change is likely to have on the collective rights of Indigenous peoples are not limited to the Inuit people.

Conclusion

Indigenous communities hold a special relationship with their land. As a result they are particularly and uniquely affected by environmental destruction and the effects of climate change. This relationship to their environment also demonstrates the interconnected nature of their rights. In particular self-determination, land rights, and cultural rights are all heavily interdependent, and any attempts at protection or promotion of these rights must be cognisant of that fact. Likewise, Indigenous peoples' particular vulnerabilities to climate change are also in need of greater recognition. Thus far, developments in this field have been extremely limited. The rights to self-determination, lands, and cultural integrity are fundamental to any community, but for Indigenous populations these rights are inherently tied to the environment around them. If that environment is threatened, or risks becoming fundamentally changed in the long term, as is the case with climate change, then these basic and interdependent collective rights are themselves seriously threatened as well. What is needed now is a searching reappraisal of existing models of approaching climate change and Indigenous people, with a focus on the interdependence of the collective rights on which Indigenous peoples' heritage and future both depend.

---

150 Watt-Cloutier, op. cit., cited in Osofsky, op. cit., p. 697.

33

Global constitutional environmental rights

James R. May and Erin Daly

This chapter addresses the worldwide phenomenon of constitutional environmental rights. Constitutional provisions from roughly ninety countries embed individualised rights to some form of healthy, adequate or quality environment, and the list is growing. Domestic courts and international tribunals are enforcing constitutionally enshrined environmental rights with growing frequency, recognising basic human rights to clean water, air, and land, and environmental opportunity. This chapter concludes that courts are increasingly taking seriously the challenge of enforcing both substantive and procedural constitutional environmental rights, to the benefit of constitutional law generally and environmental rights in particular.

Introduction

This chapter addresses the worldwide phenomenon of constitutional environmental rights. About seventy-five countries worldwide constitutionally embed individualised rights to some form of healthy, adequate or quality environment.[1] Domestic courts and international tribunals are enforcing constitutionally enshrined environmental rights with growing frequency,[2] recognising basic human rights to clean water, air, and land, and environmental opportunity.[3]

Constitutional protection for environmental rights

Of the nearly 200 constitutions currently in effect, nearly three-quarters refer in one way or another to the need for environmental protection. The list spans the globe: Africa, the Middle

---

1 J. May, 'Constituting Fundamental Environmental Rights Worldwide', *Pace Environmental Law Review* 23, 2006, p. 113; Cf. D. Boyd, *The Environmental Rights Revolution*, Vancouver: UBC Press, 2012, p. 59.
2 J. May and E. Daly, 'Vindicating Constitutionally Entrenched Environmental Rights Worldwide', *Oregon Review of International Law* 11, 2010, p. 365.
3 S. Kravchenko and J. Bonine, *Human Rights and the Environment: Cases, Law and Policy*, Durham, NC: Carolina Academic Press, 2008.

East, Western Europe, the former Soviet bloc, Latin America, Oceania.[4] The list is also diverse politically, including countries with civil, common law, Islamic, Native American, and other traditions.[5] And yet, it is nearly impossible to draw general conclusions about the nature of these rights: countries with cultures and histories as diverse as those found in Kenya, Thailand, and Bolivia are among the most generous in according environmental rights. Moreover, space limitations preclude deep analysis of the way environmental rights play out in any particular country or in all. Nonetheless, this chapter provides an overview of the global trends that we are seeing in the vindication of constitutional environmental rights. Domestic constitutions tend to reflect environmental norms in one of four ways:[6] (1) as a policy directive, (2) as a procedural right or duty, (3) as an explicit substantive right, or (4) as an implicit substantive right derived from another enumerated right, such as a 'right to life'.[7] Policy directives are intended to influence governmental decision-making but are generally not directly judicially enforceable. Recent examples include provisions from the constitutions of Uruguay in 2004 ('The protection of the environment is of common interest')[8] and Qatar in 2006 ('The State endeavours to protect the environment and its natural balance, to achieve comprehensive and sustainable development for all generations').[9] Still, constitutional policy directives can be instrumental in providing the kinds of environmental norms that loomed large, for example, in saving Greece's famed Acheloos River from being dammed beyond recognition.[10]

Environmental procedural rights normally involve requirements for environmental assessment, access to information, or rights to petition or participate.[11] Some recent examples of

---

4 Ibid.

5 *Constitutional Environmental Rights in Africa*, Washington: Environmental Law Institute, 2008.

6 T. Hayward, *Constitutional Environmental Rights*, Oxford: Oxford University Press, 2005, pp. 72–92; May, op. cit., 115, citing C. Bruch, W. Coker and C. Van Arsdale, 'Constitutional Environmental Law: Giving Force to Fundamental Principles in Africa', *Columbia Journal of Environmental Law* 26, 2001, pp. 131–2.

7 May and Daly, op. cit., p. 373. Professor Glazewski divides domestic constitutional environmental provisions into those that (1) confer a human right, (2) direct policy, and (3) impose a duty. J. Glazewski, 'The Environment, Human Rights and a New South African Constitution', *South African Journal of Human Rights* 167, 1991, pp. 173–5.

8 *Constitución Política de la República Oriental del Uruguay de 1967 con reformas hasta 2004* § II, ch. II, Art. 47. In 2004, the Constitution was amended to state that 'water is a natural resource essential to life', and that access to piped water and sanitation services are 'fundamental human rights'.

9 *Permanent Constitution of the State of Qatar* pt. II, Art. 33.

10 O. Houck, 'A Case of Sustainable Development: The River God and the Forest at the End of the World', *Tulsa Law Review* 44, 2008, pp. 286–7; O. Houck, *Taking Back Eden: Eight Environmental Cases that Changed the World*, Washington: Island Press, 2009, pp. 131–50 (Archeloos story, with pictures).

11 W. Onzivu, 'International Environmental Law, The Public's Health, and Domestic Environmental Governance in Developing Countries', *American University International Law Review* 597, 2006, p. 672; B. Cramer, 'The Human Right to Information, the Environment and Information About the Environment: From the Universal Declaration to the AARHUS Convention', *Communication Law and Policy*, 2009, pp. 73–4; G. Bandi, 'The Right to Environment in Theory and Practice: The Hungarian Experience', *Connecticut Journal of International Law* 8, 1993, pp. 450–65; Hayward, op. cit., pp. 200–203.

Bolivia in 2009,[12] Kosovo in 2008,[13] and Thailand in 2004[14] join about thirty other nations in constitutionally guaranteeing procedural environmental rights.

About seventy-five countries have included or added constitutional provisions that expressly recognise a right to a quality environment.[15] Recent examples include Ecuador in 2007 ('Right to live in an environment that is healthy and ecologically balanced'),[16] France in 2005 ('Everyone has the right to live in a balanced and health-friendly environment'),[17] Afghanistan in 2004 (right to 'prosperous life and sound living environment for all inhabitants of this land'),[18] Rwanda (right of 'every citizen . . . to a healthy and satisfying environment'),[19] and South Africa in 1996 ('everyone has the right to an environment that is not harmful to their health or well-being').[20] Most of these provisions require significant elucidation. The term 'environment' is rarely if ever explained, so that it is not clear whether it includes air, water, soil, or any combination of these. Nor is the scope of the right delimited or defined, so that it will be left up to the courts to determine what it means for the environment to be 'healthful' or 'balanced' and by whose perspective those qualities should be measured. Even from these few examples, moreover, the range of concerns that attaches to substantive environmental rights can be gleaned: in some countries, the guarantee seems to be for the benefit of people's health or their prosperity, while in others, the right seems to run to nature itself. The breadth of these provisions, which is typical for environmental rights generally, leaves a wide berth for judicial discretion.

Even where they are not explicitly mentioned or where judicial enforcement has been withheld, courts have read environmental rights into constitutions. Courts in Southern Asia have led the way, inferring environmental rights from some other constitutionally entrenched

12 World Resources Institute, *Bolivia's New Pro-Environment Constitution* (2009). Online. Available HTTP: <http://projects.wri.org/node/1206> (accessed 7 May 2012) (describing environmental rights provisions in the new constitution, including public participation in environmental decision-making).

13 *Kosovo Constitution*, Arts 52(2) and (3): '2. Everyone should be provided an opportunity to be heard by public institutions and have their opinions considered on issues that impact the environment in which they live. 3. The impact on the environment shall be considered by public institutions in their decision making processes.' Online. Available HTTP: <http://www.kushtetutakosoves.info/?cid=2,250> (accessed 16 May 2012)

14 *Ra tta'tamma noon Ha'eng Raatcha anaaja'k Tai* [Constitution] Pt. 12, § 67 (Thail.):

> Any project or activity which may seriously affect the quality of the environment, natural resources and biological diversity shall not be permitted, unless its impacts on the quality of the environment and on health of the people in the communities have been studied and evaluated and consultation with the public and interested parties have been organized, and opinions of an independent organization, consisting of representatives from private environmental and health organizations and from higher education institutions providing studies in the field of environment, natural resources or health, have been obtained prior to the operation of such project or activity.

15 May, op. cit., p. 129; Boyd, op. cit., p. 59; EarthJustice, *Environmental Rights Report 2008*. Online. Available HTTP: <http://www.earthjustice.org/library/reports/2008-environmental-rights-report.pdf> (accessed 7 May 2012).

16 *Constitución Política de la República del Ecuador*, title II, ch. 2, Art. 14.

17 1958 Const. title XVII Art. 1 (Fr.) (Charter of the Environment, 2004).

18 *Constitution of Afghanistan*, preamble.

19 *Constitution of the Republic of Rwanda*, Art. 49.

20 *South African Constitution* 1996 ch. 2, Art. 24. Even in South Africa, where volumes have been written about the writing of the constitution, relatively little attention has been paid to this provision. See H. Ebrahim, *The Soul of a Nation*, Oxford: Oxford University Press, 1999. See also *Constitution of Argentina* pt. 1, ch. II, Art. 41.

right, most commonly a 'right to life'.[21] Most notably, as discussed below, the highest courts in India,[22] Pakistan,[23] Bangladesh, and Nepal have each read a constitutional 'right to life' in tandem with directive principles aimed at promoting environmental policy to embody substantive environmental rights.[24]

What is an actionable 'right' to the 'environment'?

What is the 'environment'?

The 'environment' is a very broad concept. In the landmark Philippine case, *Minors Oposa v Factoran*, the Philippine Supreme Court observed that:

> the environment, environmental heritage and preservation of nature, of which the Constitution speaks and which it secures and protects, is everything which naturally surrounds us and that permits the development of life, and it refers to the atmosphere as it does to the land and its waters, to the flora and fauna, all of which comprise nature, with its ecological systems of balance between organisms and the environment in which they live.[25]

Indeed, by definition, the 'environment' is everything around us. It affects our lives, dignity, health, housing, access to food and water, livelihood, and so on. In *Fundepublico v Mayor of Bugalagrande*, the Constitutional Court of Colombia wrote that '[i]t should be recognized that a healthy environment is a *sina qua non* condition for life itself and that no right could be exercised in a deeply altered environment.'[26]

What is an actionable violation of an environmental right?

If constitutional environmental rights are understood in this broad way, then courts must ask what constitutes a violation. Whereas every other right is designed to benefit people – the holders of constitutional rights – environmental rights may also be understood to protect the flora and fauna, and even the oceans and forests themselves.

The Supreme Court of Chile seems to have recognised that harm to the environment itself (and not just to the people who enjoy it) is sufficient to trigger the court's jurisdiction. In

21 Bruch et al., op. cit.
22 S. Chubai, 'Environmental Law of India', in *International Environmental Law and Regulation*, Ind-1, § 2.2; B. Hill, S. Wolfson and N. Targ, 'Human Rights and the Environment: A Synopsis and Some Predictions', *Georgetown International Environmental Law Review* 16, 2004, p. 382. For a helpful discussion of these environmental rights in India, see M. Anderson, 'Individual Rights to Environmental Protection in India', in M. Anderson and A. Boyle (eds) *Human Rights Approaches to Environmental Protection*, Oxford: Oxford University Press, 1996, pp. 199–225.
23 For discussion of environmental rights in Pakistan, see M. Lau, 'Islam and Judicial Activism: Public Interest Litigation and Environmental Protection in the Islamic Republic of Pakistan', in Anderson and Boyle, op. cit., pp. 285–302.
24 Bruch et al., op. cit., pp. 166–7 (discussing constitutional interpretation in Tanzania, India, Pakistan, Bangladesh, Nepal, Columbia, Ecuador, Costa Rica, and some countries in Africa).
25 *Minors Oposa v Factoran Jr.*, GR No. 10183, 224 SCRA 792 (July 30, 1993). (Phil.), *reprinted in* 33 ILM 173, 175 (1994) (Feliciano, J., concurring) ('*Minors Oposa*').
26 *Fundepublico v Mayor of Bugalagrande y otros*, Interlocutorio #032, (Tulua, 19 December 1991) (Colom.) ('*Fundepublico*'), in D. Shelton and A. Kiss, *Judicial Handbook on Environmental Law*, UNEP, 2005, p. 7.

Pedro Flores v Corporación del Cobre, Codelco, Division Salvador, the Court found judicially cognizable harm in:

> the daily accumulation of thousands of tons of contaminants . . . producing the ecological destruction of all forms of marine life in hundreds of square kilometers . . . a devastation that blossoms over the whole coastal area of the National Park Pan de Azucar, with which dies a piece of Chile.[27]

Recognition of this kind of damage, without requiring evidence of specific harm to a specific individual, not only increases the likelihood of success of the plaintiff's claim, but it also reduces the plaintiffs' costs and, consequently, encourages more claims: it is much less expensive to show that the defendant's actions caused harm to the environment than that they injured the specific plaintiff.

Courts have found that harm to the environment *is* harm to the people who would enjoy it. In an extraordinary decision in 1997 relying on the environmental rights provision of the constitution, the Chilean court stopped a huge logging project at the bottom of the world. In what is commonly referred to as the *Trillium* decision, the court held that the Chilean government's approval of the Rio Condor Project, the US-based Trillium Corporation's $350 million project to log 270,000 hectares of pristine forests in Tierra del Fuego at the southern tip of South America, violated certain citizens' constitutional environmental 'right to live in an environment free from contamination'.[28] The Court said that this provision required 'the maintenance of the original conditions of natural resources' and was designed to keep 'human intervention to a minimum'.[29]

In *Fundación Natura v Petro Ecuador*, the Ecuadorian court turned to a constitutional right to live in a 'healthy' environment when it upheld a civil verdict concluding that Petro Ecuador's production of leaded fuel violated federal law.[30] In *Arco Iris v Instituto Ecuatoriano de Mineria*, the court concluded that the company's degradation of Podocarpus National Park was 'a threat to the environmental human right of the inhabitants of the provinces of Loja and Zamora Chinchipe to have an area which ensures the natural and continuous provision of water, air humidity, oxygenation and recreation'.[31] These cases assume that harm to the environment is harm to the people who live nearby, but because they do not engage in rigorous analysis, the limits of the principle remain ill-defined.

Courts in post-communist countries in Eastern Europe have also implemented newly minted constitutional environmental rights provisions so as to protect the environment. The constitutional court of Hungary seems to have been the first in Central and Eastern Europe

---

27 *Pedro Flores v Codelco, División Salvador*, Rol. 2.052 (Sup. Ct. Chile, 23 June 1988) ('*Pedro Flores*'), translated in *Georgetown International Environmental Law Review* 2, 251, p. 253 (1989) (Claudia C. Bohorquez trans.). For a discussion on the Supreme Court of Chile see May and Daly, op. cit., p. 392.

28 '*Trillium Case*', Decision No. 2.732–96, at 8, Sup. Ct. of Chile, (Mar. 19, 1997) ('*Trillium*'). Online. Available HTTP: <http://www.elaw.org/node/1310> (accessed 7 May 2012). Houck, *Taking Back Eden*, op. cit., pp. 151–74 (story behind the *Trillium* case, with pictures). See generally, May and Daly, op. cit., p. 392.

29 *Trillium*, para. 12.

30 Case Nos. 377/90, 378/90, 379/90, 380/90 combined, *Fundacion Natura v Petroecuador*, [Tribunal of Constitutional Guarantees] Resolution No. 230-92-CP (15 October 1992).

31 Case No. 224/90, *Arco Iris v Instituto Ecuatoriano de Mineria*, [Constitutional Court of Ecuador] Judgment No. 054-93-CP, translated in Bruch et al., op. cit., p. 26.

to give force to this type of provision.[32] In *Case 28/1994*, the court held that the Hungarian legislature's efforts to sell for cultivation previously nationalised forested lands under the former communist regime would be unconstitutional, finding that it violated the constitutional environmental rights residing in the Hungarian Constitution.[33] The Court rejected the state's justification for the repeal, reasoning that 'The right to a healthy environment guaranteed the physical conditions necessary to enforce the right to human life [and that] extraordinary resolve was called for in establishing legislative guarantees for the right.'[34] Thus, it held that once the state created a baseline of environmental protection, it could not thereafter degrade it.[35]

The amorphousness of the very definition of environmental harms means that the harms alleged are not purely private harms but may be shared by the community, the nation, or, in fact, the world now and in future generations. Environmental litigation may often in fact invert the normal expectations relating to the roles of public and private parties. Whereas traditional constitutional rights litigation pits the private individual against the public authority, environmental litigation often pits members of the public against a private entity (thus invoking the principle of the horizontal application of constitutional rights and obligations). Moreover, in many of these cases, private individuals are asserting public rights, whereas the government (through lenient regulation and licensing) is facilitating private gain.[36]

Parties

Given the amorphous contours of environmental rights, courts' inclination in some circumstances to read constitutional texts broadly in this area, and the far-reaching ramifications of rulings in these cases, it is critical to understand environmental rights in terms both of the harms to the putative plaintiffs and of the actions of the putative defendants. In some jurisdictions, the restrictions are in the very definition of the environmental right: the Constitutional Court of Turkey has interpreted the constitutional provision that 'Everyone has the right to live in a healthy, balanced environment'[37] to permit solely facial challenges to legislation,

---

32 Bandi, op. cit., p. 449 ('[T]he right to an environment may serve as a possible basis for legal action only in the procedure of the Constitutional Court. Only this court is authorized to revise legal provisions based upon constitutionality. The general courts rarely use a constitutional right as a reference in cases.'). The relevant constitutional provisions can be found in *A Magyar Köztársaság Alkotmánya* [Constitution] ch. I, Art. 18 ('The Republic of Hungary recognizes and shall implement the individual's right to a healthy environment.'), Art. 70/D(2) (requiring State to implement this right 'through . . . protection of the . . . natural environment'.).

33 MK. Case No. 1994/Decision 28 (*Hungary Constitution* Ct. 1994); S. Kravchenko, 'Citizen Enforcement of Environmental Law in Eastern Europe', *Widener Law Review* 10, 2004, p. 484 (calling it 'a remarkable case.'); S. Stec, 'Ecological Rights Advancing the Rule of Law in Eastern Europe', *Journal of Environmental Law and Litigation* 13, 1998, pp. 320–1. The Court also held that violation of environmental rights ran afoul of the constitution's 'right to life'. See C. Dupre, *Importing the Law in Post-Communist Transitions*, Oxford: Hart Publishing, 2003, pp. 69, 73–4.

34 *Alkotmánybíróság* [MK] [Constitutional Law Court] Case No. 1994/Decision 28, p. 14.

35 Ibid., pp. 1–3. This has been described as enforcing a 'third generation' right. See Dupre, op. cit., p. 69.

36 *Minors Oposa*, p. 173 (government revoked timber licenses); Kravchenko and Bonine, op. cit., p. 79 (referring to Hungary helping to sell off forests to private interests).

37 *Türkiye Cumhuriyeti Anayasasi* [Turk. Repub. Const.] pt. II, ch. III, Art. 56.

notwithstanding its orbit with other 'Social and Economic Rights and Duties'.[38] And Spain's constitutional 'right to enjoy an environment suitable for the development of the person,'[39] falls outside the actionable private 'rights' the constitution otherwise guarantees.[40] In other jurisdictions, constitutions and constitutional traditions limit the cohort of people who can sue to enforce constitutional rights, and environmental rights in particular. Namibia's environmental rights provision may only be enforced by an ombudsman,[41] and citizens of Cameroon are not allowed to pursue environmental rights before the country's constitutional court,[42] to give a couple of examples.

Who can vindicate a violation?

In some countries, courts have been willing to expand the universe of possible plaintiffs precisely to enhance the control that the people (via the courts) have over the government. In many Latin American countries, courts have allowed *amparo* actions (or *acciones de inconstitucionalidad*), which permit any citizen to enforce constitutional rights.[43] In *Proterra v Ferroaleaciones San Ramon S.A.*, the Supreme Court of Peru allowed open standing to enforce entrenched environmental rights.[44] Courts in Argentina have also found broadly enforceable its constitutional guarantee that 'All inhabitants enjoy the right to a healthful, balanced environment fit for human development, so that productive activities satisfy current needs without compromising those of future generations.'[45] In 1993, the Supreme Court of Argentina observed that 'The right to live in a healthy and balanced environment is a fundamental attribute of people. Any aggression to the environment ends up becoming a threat to life itself and to the psychological and physical integrity of the person.'[46] And in *Sociedad de Fomento Barrio Félix v Camet y Otros*, the court accepted a plaintiff's claim that the environmental right includes the right to enjoy an ocean view.[47]

38 E. Brandl and H. Bungert, 'Constitutional Entrenchment of Environmental Protection: A Comparative Analysis of Experiences Abroad', *Harvard Environmental Law Review* 16, 1992, p. 72.
39 Constitución [C.E.] title I, ch. III, Art. 45.
40 Brandl and Bungert, op. cit., p. 65 (noting that the provision 'is not enforceable through a constitutional complaint brought by an individual' but must be brought by a state-appointed ombudsman); A. Herrero de la Fuente, in J. Ebbesson (ed.) *Access to Justice in Environmental Matters in the EU*, Kluwer Law International, 2002, pp. 421, 442) ('The right to an adequate environment . . . is not understood as a fundamental right, but rather as a leading principle for social and economic politics').
41 E. Brown Weiss, D. Magraw and P. Szasz, *International Environmental Law and Policy*, New York: Aspen, 1998, p. 417.
42 Bruch et al., op. cit., p. 139.
43 An *acción de amparo* is a cause of action to enforce constitutional rights, used widely throughout the Spanish-speaking world. Houck, 'Sustainable Development', op. cit., p. 306.
44 *Proterra v Ferroaleaciones San Ramon S.A.*, Judgment No. 1156-90 (Sup. Ct. Peru, 19 November, 1992), cited in Bruch et al., op. cit., p. 27 (footnote omitted). See May and Daly, op. cit., p. 393.
45 *Constitution of Argentina*, pt. 1, ch. II, Art. 41.
46 *Irazu Margarita v Copetro S.A.*, Camara Civil y Comercial de la Plata, Ruling of 10 May 1993, in Shelton and Kiss, op. cit., p. 7. *Accord* Asociación Para la Protección de Medio Ambiente y Educacion Ecologica '18 de Octubre' v Aguas Argentinas S.A. & otros, Fed. Appellate Tribunal of La Plata (2003); *Kattan, Alberto et al. v Nat'l Gov't, Juzgado Nacional de la Instancia en lo Contenciosoadministrativo Federal.* No. 2, Ruling of 10 May 1983, La Ley, 1983-D, 576. See also, *Constitution of Argentina*, pt. 1, ch. II, § 41.
47 Shelton and Kiss, op. cit., p. 7, citing *Sociedad de Fomento Barrio Félix v Camet y Otros*); see also *Irazu Margarita v Copetro S.A.*, Camara Civil y Comercial de la Plata, Ruling of 10 May 1993.

This expanded form of standing obviously benefits the plaintiff class, to the detriment of the defendant class, both private and public. The Chilean Supreme Court's jurisprudence in this regard has been exemplary. In the 1988 case of *Pedro Flores*, the Court upheld a constitutional environmental right 'to live in an environment free from contamination',[48] in a lawsuit that aimed to stop the deposition of copper mill tailings onto Chilean beaches to protect marine life. Likewise, in *Comunidad de Chañaral v Codeco División el Saldor*, the Court upheld the right of a farmer to bring a constitutional right to life claim to enjoin the drainage of Lake Chungará.[49]

Perhaps even more remarkable than the work of the Latin American courts is that of courts in India, Pakistan, Bangladesh, and Nepal, which have embraced constitutional environmental principles even in the absence of explicit constitutional authority. These courts have recognised a form of open standing to vindicate environmental harms on behalf of the public interest under the auspices of other constitutional rights, including a 'right to life'.[50]

Who can be sued?

The question of identifying proper defendants may turn on the proper definition of the right but it is further complicated because it implicates questions of sovereignty, immunity, extraterritoriality, and the horizontal application of constitutional rights. Most significant environmental claims arise out of a mixture of public and private wrong-doing so that it is often difficult to identify the responsible party. In the *Eurogold* case, the Turkish government allowed the giant French mining conglomerate to use cyanide heap-leaching to mine gold and other metals from a centuries-old olive-growing region in Turkey.[51] After government-paid loggers began to remove olive trees, olive farmers claimed that the government's licence contravened Turkey's new constitutional environmental right 'to live in a healthy, balanced environment'.[52] Turkey's highest administrative court agreed, assigning responsibility to the government, thereby stopping the operation in its tracks.[53]

Courts have also held private parties accountable for violations of constitutionally embedded environmental rights provisions. In another celebrated case, a court in Costa Rica invoked the country's fundamental environmental rights provision to stop a transnational banana company from clear-cutting approximately 700 hectares – including a nesting habitat for the endangered green macaw – near the Tortuguero National Park.[54]

Remedies

In most constitutional litigation, the question of remedies is relatively straightforward. Even in some environmental cases, where the defendant's action caused the plaintiff's injury, the

---

48 Bruch et al., op. cit., p. 134.
49 Hill et al., op. cit., p. 387; May and Daly, op. cit., pp. 392, 418.
50 See discussion within text at accompanying notes 73 onwards.
51 A. Sachs, 'What Do Human Rights Have To Do With Environmental Protection? Everything', *Sierra Magazine*, November–December 1997. Online. Available HTTP: <http://www.sierraclub.org/sierra/199711/humanrights.asp> (accessed 7 May 2012).
52 *Türkiye Cumhuriyeti Anayasasi* [Turk. Repub. Const.], pt. II, ch. III, Art. 56.
53 Sachs, op. cit.
54 Bruch et al., op. cit., p. 26; Environment Law Alliance Worldwide (E-Law), *Valuing Biodiversity in Costa Rica* (July 1999). Online. Available HTTP: <http://www.elaw.org/node/866> (accessed 7 May 2012). See generally May and Daly, op. cit., p. 394 (discussing the Costa Rica court's enforcement of right).

court can order the defendant to cease or to pay damages sufficient to cover the costs of medical care or the loss of employment income, for instance. While this requires careful assessment of damages, experts are usually available to quantify the harm, and the remedy is routinely enforced: if the defendant does not cease its activities or refuses to pay, it can be held in contempt of court. But even these apparently simple orders can be problematic in environmental rights cases, often tempting courts to fashion more elaborate remedial orders. In one Colombian case, where toxic fumes emanated from an open pit, defendants were required 'to remediate the site and to pay past and future medical expenses to those who became sick'.[55]

The more common environmental cases are far more challenging because the harm is irremediable. In *Metropolitan Manila Development Authority v Concerned Residents of Manila Bay*, the Philippine Supreme Court upheld a request for multifaceted injunctive relief to prevent massive pollution discharges from choking Manila Bay and to clean and protect it for the benefit of future generations.[56] In upholding the lower court's grant of injunctive relief, the court insisted on the obligations of the petitioners 'to future generations of Filipinos to keep the waters of the Manila Bay clean and clear as humanly as possible. Anything less would be a betrayal of the trust reposed in them.'[57] Notwithstanding this strikingly non-legalistic language, the court's message was clear: those in a position to care for the environment must take responsibility for it, as a matter of constitutional law, if not also as a matter of moral obligation to 'future generations'.

In some environmental cases, fashioning a remedy can be even more complex than ascertaining liability. In Nepal, the court prohibited the use of diesel trucks in Kathmandu in the name of environmental rights.[58] Similarly, the Dhaka High Court in Bangladesh 'ordered the Government to convert petrol and diesel engines in government-owned vehicles to gas-fueled engines'.[59] In a case from India, the court recognised that 'closure of tanneries may bring unemployment [and] loss of revenue', and it made the policy judgment that 'life, health, and ecology have greater importance to the people',[60] even though those who rely on the tanneries for their livelihood may not have made the same calculation. Environmental cases almost invariably present difficult and far-reaching policy choices that are challenging to judicial resolution. And often, when a government changes its policy to enhance the environment, it is private individuals who bear the burden.[61]

---

55 *Corte Constitucional*, Chamber of Civil and Agrarian Appeals, 19 November 1997, *Castrillon Vega v Federación Nacional de Algodoneros y Corporacion Autonoma Regional del Cesar (CORPOCESAR) / Acción de Tutela* Case No. 4577 (Colom.), discussed in Kravchenko and Bonine, op. cit., p. 70.

56 *Metro. Manila Dev. Auth. v Concerned Residents of Manila Bay*, G.R. Nos. 171947-48 (S.C., 18 December, 2008) (Phil.).

57 Ibid.

58 *Advocate Kedar Bhakta Shrestha v HMG, Dep't of Transp. Mgmt.*, Writ No. 3109 of 1999 (Nepal), in UN Environment Programme [UNEP], *Compendium of Summaries of Judicial Decisions in Environment-Related Cases* 2005, pp. 90, 134 ('*UNEP Summaries*').

59 P. Hassan and A. Azfar, 'Securing Environmental Rights Through Public Interest Litigation in South Asia', *Virginia Environmental Law Journal* 22, 2004, p. 244.

60 *M.C. Mehta v Union of India*, A.I.R. (1987) 4 SCC 463 (India).

61 *Yogi Narahari Nath & Others v Honourable Prime Minister Girija Prasad Koirala & Others*, 33 NLR 1955 (SC Nepal) in *UNEP Summaries*, op. cit., at 134 (environmental rights prevailed over establishment of medical college).

Justiciability: are courts receptive to constitutional environmental rights?

Vindicating environmental rights presents even more fundamental questions of policy choices. In some ways, environmental rights are similar to other social and economic rights that are routinely vindicated in the world's courts in that remedying their violation often entails expenditure of significant resources. But environmental rights often pit the human rights claims against each other. Protecting the environment can help preserve the way of life for some, but it can impair the way of life for others.

The problem is one of proportion requiring careful balancing, as is indicated by the language in the Philippine Constitution requiring that the State 'protect and advance the right of the people to a balanced and healthful ecology'.[62] Recognising the need for proportion and context, the Supreme Court of Nepal has said: 'It is beyond doubt that industry is the foundation of development of the country. Both the country and society need development; however, it is essential to maintain an environmental balance along with industry.'[63] Other courts have drawn the line where the environmental degradation seems neglectful[64] or vindictive.[65]

The judgement of how to balance the competing claims is one that should typically be done politically and not judicially. But as the Chief Justice of India has said, 'it has fallen frequently to the judiciary to protect environmental interests, due to sketchy input from the legislature, and laxity on the part of the administration.'[66] In *Clean Air Foundation v Hong Kong Special Administrative Region*, the government had prohibited the sale of diesel fuel, but not its use or importation, and plaintiffs had alleged that this contributed to soot levels nearly three times higher than those of New York City, which violated their constitutionally guaranteed rights to health and life.[67] Although the Court of First Instance agreed that the plaintiffs had made a *prima facie* case, it found the matter to be essentially one of policy consigned to the political process, observing: 'How possibly can this court decide that this decision fails to reach a fair balance between the duty Government has to protect the right to life and the duty it has to protect the social and economic well-being of the Territory? It cannot do so. . . .'[68] And as the Hong Kong court remarked in *Ng Ngau Chai v Town Planning Bd*: 'I fully sympathise with . . . concerns about the deteriorating quality of the environment . . . But the Court can only apply law. The Judiciary cannot manage the environment. That is the role of the

---

62 *Const.* (1987) Art. II, § 16 (Phil.) ('The State shall protect and advance the right of the people to a balanced and healthful ecology in accord with the rhythm and harmony of nature.'),

63 *Dhungel v Godawari Marble Indus.*, WP 35/1992 (SC Nepal, 31 October, 1995) (*en banc*), reprinted in Kravchenko and Bonine, op. cit., pp. 96–7.

64 See e.g. *Defensoria de Menores Nro 3 v Poder Ejecutivo Municipal*, Agreement 5, Superior Justice Court. Neuquen, 2 March 1999. (Arg.) (Court required State Government to provide 100 litres of drinkable water per day to each individual member of the families living in the rural colony of Valentina Norte who were drinking water polluted with hydrocarbons).

65 See e.g. *Soc. and Econ. Rights Action Ctr. v Nigeria, Commc'n* 155/96, African Commission on Human and Peoples' Rights (27 October, 2001). Online. Available HTTP: <http://www.cesr.org/downloads/AfricanCommissionDecision.pdf> (accessed 7 May 2012).

66 B.N. Kirpal, Chief Justice, Supreme Court of India, 'M.C. Bhandari Memorial Lecture: Environmental Justice in India' (2002), in 7 SCC 1 (2002). Online. Available HTTP: <http://www.ebc-india.com/lawyer/articles/2002v7a1.htm> (accessed 7 May 2012).

67 *Clean Air Foundation Ltd. & Another v Gov't of H.K.*, 2007 WL 1824740, #pg 29, 30, [2007] HKEC 1356, HCAL 35/2007 (CFI).

68 Ibid., para. 42.

69 *Ng Ngau Chai v Town Planning Bd* [2007] HCAL 64/2007 (HK, quoted in *Clean Air Found. et al. v Gov't of Hong Kong SAR*, [2007] HKEC 1356, HCAL 35/2007 (CFI), available at 2007 WL 1824740, n. 9.

Executive.'[69] But of course, staying out of the fray has substantive consequences that sustain the continued deterioration of the environment.

The result is under-enforcement of constitutional environmental rights in most countries, including in Brazil, Ecuador, and the former Soviet bloc. In other countries, environmental rights provisions are expressed so insipidly as to be thought too weak to be worth litigating.[70] Constitutionally entrenched environmental rights provisions in sub-national state constitutions in the US have fared only slightly better in court.[71] Courts in most states have been reluctant to enforce these provisions, except in Hawaii and Montana.[72]

The most notable exceptions are where courts have found that environmental damage or degradation implicates other enumerated constitutional rights, most commonly the right to life. The Supreme Court of India was one of the first to find that a 'right to life' embeds a right to a quality environment.[73] In *Subhash Kumar v State of Bihar*, the plaintiffs sought to stop tanneries from discharging pollutants into the Ganges River.[74] While the Court dismissed the action for lack of standing, it found that the discharges were sufficient to make the river unfit for drinking and irrigation, which could violate the constitutionally protected 'right to life' which 'includes the right of enjoyment of pollution-free water and air for full enjoyment of life'.[75] Subsequently in *M.C. Mehta v Union of India*, as noted above, the Court ordered the tanneries to shut down unless effluent was first subjected to pretreatment processes approved by the governing environmental agency.

The Supreme Court of Pakistan has also held that environmental rights are embedded within that country's constitutional 'right to life'. In *In re: Human Rights Case (Environment Pollution in Balochistan)*, the Court took judicial notice of a newspaper report that 'business tycoons are making attempts to purchase coastal area of Balochistan and convert it into a dumping ground' for nuclear and highly hazardous waste.[76] The Court ordered the agency charged with implementing environmental laws in the area to monitor land allocations in the affected area and forbid such use.[77] In *West Pakistan Salt Miners v Directors of Industries and Mineral Development*, the Court upheld a claim that the right to life included a right to water

---

70 T. Ankersen, 'Shared Knowledge, Shared Jurisprudence: Learning to Speak Environmental Law Creole (Criollo)', *Tulane Environmental Law Journal* 16, 2003, p. 826 ('Cuba's environmental constitutional language also appears relatively weak and is framed in terms of state duties (*deberes*). It does not appear to confer defensible individual or collective rights').

71 M.E. Cusack, 'Judicial Interpretation of State Constitutional Rights to a Healthful Environment', *Boston College Environmental Affairs Law Review* 20, 1993, p. 181. Among the different types of environmental amendments to state constitutions are 'those granting citizens the right to a healthful environment; public policy statements concerning preservation of natural resources; financial provisions for environmental programs; and clauses that restrict the environmental prerogatives of state legislatures'; Hill et al., op. cit., p. 390.

72 *Mont. Const.* Art. II, § 3; see generally B. Wilson, 'State Constitutional Environmental Rights and Judicial Activism: Is the Big Sky Falling?', *Emory Law Journal* 53, 2004, p. 627.

73 *Bandhua Mukti Morcha v Union of India*, (1984) 3 SCC 161 (interpreting *India Const.* Art. 21) and *Charan Lal Sahu v Union of India*, AIR 1990 SC 1480, both discussed in Shelton and Kiss, op. cit., p. 8.

74 *Subhash Kumar v State of Bihar*, AIR 1991 SC 420 in *UNEP Summaries*, op. cit. 58, p. 104. See May and Daly, op. cit., p. 400.

75 Ibid.

76 Human Rights Case No. 31-K/92(Q), PLD 1994 S. C. 102 (1992), in UNEP, *Compendium of Judicial Decisions in Matters Related to Environment: National Decisions*, vol. I, 1998, p. 280 ('*UNEP Compendium*').

77 Ibid., p. 281.

free from contamination from mining activities: 'The right to have unpolluted water is the right of every person wherever he lives.'[78]

The Supreme Court of Bangladesh has also followed suit. In *Mohiuddin Farooque v Bangladesh*, the petitioner alleged that the implementation of a substantial flood control plan would so disrupt the affected community's life, property, and environmental security as to violate a constitutional 'right to life'.[79] While the Supreme Court of Bangladesh held that the Constitution's guarantee of a 'right to life' included environmental rights, it dismissed the action, reasoning that petitioners were not 'person[s] aggrieved' within the meaning of the Constitution.[80]

The trend is also evident in other regions. The Constitutional Court of Colombia has read a constitutional 'right to life' as encompassing a substantive right to a healthy environment.[81] In *Maria Elena Burgos v Municipality of Campoalegre (Huila)*, the Court upheld a lower court's order to destroy pig stalls that caused neighbours to fall ill with respiratory distress and fever, finding an actionable violation of the country's fundamental environmental right encompassed in a right to life.[82] And in *Victor Ramon Castrillon Vega v Federacio National de Algodoneros*, the Court found that emissions of toxic fumes from an open pit contravened a constitutional right to life and ordered a company to remediate the pit and pay medical expenses.[83] In reaching these results, the Court has conceived the right to the environment as 'a group of basic conditions surrounding man, which define his life as a member of the community and allow his biological and individual survival'.[84] Thus, environmental rights exist 'side by side with fundamental rights such as liberty, equality and necessary conditions for people's life . . . [W]e can state that the right to the environment is a right fundamental to the existence of humanity.'[85] Hence, even in *Jose Cuesta Novoa v Secretary of Public Health of Bogota*, which confirmed on procedural ground a lower court's dismissal of an effort to enforce environment rights, the Court still recognised that a right to life includes environmental protections.[86]

The Philippine Constitutional Court has gone beyond even the broad constitutional text. In the celebrated case of *Minors Oposa v Factoran*, attorney, writer, and law professor Tony

---

78 1994 SCMR 2061 (S.C. Pak.), in *UNEP Compendium*, op. cit., p. 282. See also *Ms. Shehla Zia et al. v WAPDA*, PLD 1994 S.C. 693, in *UNEP Compendium*, op. cit., p. 323 (constitutional right to life provides cause of action for electromagnetic hazards associated with construction of power plant and power grid).

79 *Dr. Mohiuddin Farooque v Bangladesh*, 48 Dir 1996 (SC Bangl. App. Div., Civ.) ('*Farooque*'), in *UNEP Summaries*, op. cit., p. 90.

80 Hassan and Azfar, op. cit., p. 242.

81 The Colombian Constitution also includes environmental rights: 'Every individual has the right to enjoy a healthy environment.' *Constitución Política de la República de Columbia de* 1991, title II, ch. III, Art. 79.

82 *María Elena Burgos v Municipality of Campoalegre (Huila)* (Const. Ct. Colom. 27 February, 1997) in *UNEP Summaries*, op. cit., p. 79. See May and Daly, op. cit., pp. 403–404 (discussing Constitutional Court of Columbia).

83 Hill et al., op. cit., p. 386.

84 A. Fabra and E. Arnal, 'Review of Jurisprudence on Human Rights and the Environment in Latin America', Joint UNEP–OHCHR Expert Seminar on Human Rights and the Environment, Background Paper No. 6 (2002). Online. Available HTTP: <http://www2.ohchr.org/english/issues/environment/environ/bp6.htm> (accessed 16 May 2012) (describing right as a 'fundamental human right') (citing *Fundepublico*, cited in Shelton and Kiss, op. cit., p. 7).

85 Ibid. (citing case of *Antonio Mauricio Monroy Cespedes*).

86 *José Cuesta Novoa v the Sec'y of Pub. Health of Bogota* (Const. Ct. Colom. 17 May, 1995) in *UNEP Summaries*, op. cit., p. 77.

Oposa filed a lawsuit on behalf of his children, his friends' children, and generations to come to 'prevent the misappropriation or impairment' of Philippine rainforests and 'arrest the unabated hemorrhage of the country's vital life-support systems and continued rape of Mother Earth'.[87] At one time, the Philippines contained nearly 100 million acres of verdant, ancient forests.[88] By the 1990s, commercial logging had reduced this by about 99 per cent.[89] The plaintiffs claimed that the government's continued issuance of timber licensing agreements violated the country's recently minted constitutional directive that, *inter alia*, 'The State shall protect and advance the right of the people to a balanced and healthful ecology in accord with the rhythm and harmony of nature.'[90] In a sweeping pronouncement and in language that bears attention, the Court determined that rights to a quality environment are enforceable whether or not they are textually expressed. 'As a matter of fact,' the Court said, 'these basic rights need not even be written in the Constitution for they are assumed to exist from the inception of humankind.' Nonetheless, including them in a constitution is not for naught. According to the Court, environmental rights are now explicitly mentioned in the constitution:

> because of the well-founded fear of its framers that unless the rights to a balanced and healthful ecology and to health are mandated as state policies by the Constitution itself, thereby highlighting their continuing importance and imposing upon the state a solemn obligation to preserve the first and protect and advance the second, the day would not be too far when all else would be lost not only for the present generation, but also for those to come – generations which stand to inherit nothing but parched earth incapable of sustaining life.[91]

Conclusion

It is perhaps not surprising that, although constitutions have textually protected substantive environmental rights for decades, courts are only now beginning to embrace the challenge of defining and enforcing them. Among the challenges of litigating constitutional environmental rights are those relating to the scope of the right, the appropriate litigants, and the fashioning of legally acceptable and judicially enforceable remedies. The complexities are not simply matters of definition – if the constitutional text would only demarcate more clearly the boundaries of the 'environment' – or of settling the precedent – if the relevant jurisprudence clearly indicated who may sue on the basis of what kind of injury. Rather, they inhere in the nature of environmental rights, especially at the constitutional level.

The experience that courts have had in trying to make sense of and take seriously constitutional environmental rights reveals another lesson which, when learned, may significantly enrich the praxis of constitutional law generally. No judicial order can resolve the problems of environmental degradation or climate change; in many cases, the most that a court can do is galvanise the political process to take environmental protection seriously. But this, in and of itself, is worth the effort to vindicate constitutional environmental rights.

87 *Minors Oposa*, op. cit., p. 176.
88 Ibid., p. 179; O. Houck, 'Light from the Trees, The Stories of Minors Oposa and the Russian Forest Cases', *Georgetown International Environmental Law Review* 19, 2007, p. 326 ('Houck II'). See generally, Houck, *Taking Back Eden*, op. cit. pp. 43–60 (2009) (story behind Minors Oposa).
89 Houck II, op. cit., p. 326.
90 *Minors Oposa*, op. cit., pp. 180–81; *Phillipines Const.* (1987), Art. II, §§ 15–16.
91 Ibid.

34

Protection of the environment during armed conflict

Susan Breau

One of the concerns of international humanitarian law is lack of enforcement of customary and treaty rules on protection of the environment during armed conflict. Environmental degradation may be a priority issue for the international community but the same cannot be said for addressing environmental damage during wars. This chapter assesses the effectiveness of treaty and customary international law rules with respect to the environment and armed conflict. It argues that investigation of the conflict in Kosovo illustrates the weakness of the treaty regime. This chapter argues that it is customary humanitarian law which offers hope for environmental protection in armed conflict.

Introduction

One of the most troublesome areas of international humanitarian law is the lack of enforcement of customary and treaty rules on the protection of the environment during armed conflict. It is an understatement to say that the environment is not protected sufficiently in times of wars. The detritus of a conflict can remain in the environment for several generations after it has ended, posing a threat to the civilian population. An excellent example is in Northern France, where more than 90 years since the end of the First World War unexploded bombs are still being discovered in farmers' fields. As Bouvier argues, 'some battlefields of the First and Second Wars, to give only two examples, remain unfit for cultivation or dangerous to the population because of the unexploded devices (especially mines) and projectiles still embedded in the soil.'[1]

This chapter reviews the treaty regimes and customary international law rules with respect to the environment and assesses their effectiveness. The first section will discuss the development of the applicable treaty regime and uses the investigation of the conflict in Kosovo as an example of the weakness of the current treaty regime. The second section will review the customary law regime in light of the influential and recent International Committee of the

---

1 A. Bouvier, 'Protection of the Natural Environment in Time of Armed Conflict', *International Review of the Red Cross*, No. 285, 1991, p. 138. Online. Available HTTP: <http://www.icrc.org/eng/resources/documents/misc/57jmau.htm> (accessed 10 March 2012).

Red Cross (ICRC) Customary Humanitarian Law study.[2] In the next part the sparse amount of case law concerning environmental protection in armed conflict will be discussed. Finally, the United Nations Environmental Programme (UNEP) report will be reviewed which recommends changes to the current legal regime and evaluates the possibility of those changes being implemented. Although environmental degradation is a high-priority issue for the international community, the same cannot be said for the damage caused to the environment during armed conflict.

Treaties with respect to the environment and armed conflict

Environmental protection was not addressed in early humanitarian law treaties but there were cardinal principles expressed in these instruments that have relevance. The *Hague Convention IV* of 1907 Article 22 specified that 'right of belligerents to adopt means of injuring the enemy is not unlimited'.[3] Secondly, the 1925 *Protocol for the Prohibition of the Use in War of Asphyxiating, Poisonous or Other Gases, and of Bacteriological Methods of Warfare* prohibited the use of gas in warfare.[4] As gas can remain in the environment for a lengthy period of time the ban on gas in itself would provide some environmental protection. As Brantz stated in her study of trench warfare during the First World War, 'Gas represented a new weapons technology that did not kill directly but altered the environment in such a way as to make it uninhabitable.'[5] In a similar vein the 1972 *Convention on the Prohibition of the Development, Production and Stockpiling of Bacteriological (Biological) and Toxin Weapons and their Destruction* was adopted. This Convention prohibits the development, production, stockpiling or any other possession of microbial agents, toxins and weapons.[6] Once again it protects the environment from weapons that would cause significant harm, particularly to the natural environment which would also be poisoned by these weapons. In a similar way to chemical weapons, biological weapons can leave materials in the environment for some period to come.[7] The fourth *Geneva Convention* (of 1949) *Relative to the Protection of Civilian Persons* does not contain any provisions with respect to protection of the environment.[8]

It was not until the 1970s that the international community turned its attention specifically to conflict and the environment. There are three separate sources of treaty law on environmental protection during armed conflict. The first and most important is the *Convention*

---

2 J-M Henckaerts and L. Doswald-Beck (eds) *Customary International Humanitarian Law*, Cambridge: Cambridge University Press, 2005 (the 'Study').

3 *Regulations Respecting the Laws and Customs of War on Land, to the Convention (IV) Respecting the Laws and Customs of War on Land*, opened for signature 18 October 1907, UKTS 9, Cd.5030 (entered into force 26 January 1910).

4 *Protocol for the Prohibition of the Use of Asphyxiating or Other Gases, and of Bacteriological Methods of Warfare*, opened for signature 17 June 1925 (entered into force 8 February 1928) ('Geneva Protocol').

5 D. Brantz, 'Environments of Death' in C. Clossman (ed.) *War and the Environment: Military Destruction in the Modern Age*, College Station: Texas A& M University Press, 2009, p. 81.

6 *Convention on the Prohibition of the Development, Production and Stockpiling of Bacteriological (Biological) and Toxin Weapons and their Destruction*, opened for signature 10 April 1972 (entered into force 26 March 1975) ('Biological Weapons, Convention'), Art. 1.

7 E. Eitzen, 'Use of Biological Weapons', in *Medical Aspects of Chemical and Biological Warfare*, Washington DC: Office of The Surgeon General, Borden Institute, Walter Reed Army Medical Center, 1997, pp. 437–50.

8 *Geneva Convention IV Relative to the Protection of Civilian Persons in Time of War*, opened for signature 12 August 1949, 75 UNTS (entered into force 21 October 1950), 287–417.

on the Prohibition of Military and any other Hostile Use of Environmental Modification Techniques, 1976 (known as the ENMOD Convention).[9] This treaty was drafted as a result of the significant environmental damage caused by the use by the United States of such chemicals as napalm during the Vietnam War. Furthermore, the use of the toxic herbicide 'Agent Orange' and the deforestation and chemical contamination that resulted had sparked an international outcry.[10] The goal of this treaty is the prohibition of the use of environmental modification techniques as a means of warfare. Article 1 of the Convention states:

> Each State Party to this Convention undertakes not to engage in military or any other hostile use of environmental modification techniques having widespread, long-lasting or severe effects as the means of destruction, damage or injury to any other State Party.

In submitting the text of the ENMOD Convention to the General Assembly, the UN Conference of the Committee on Disarmament submitted a list of understandings on the three factors of the test in Article 1 for breach of the convention. 'Widespread' is defined to encompass several hundred square kilometres, 'long-lasting' is to last for several months and 'severe' is to involve serious or significant disruption or harm to human life, natural and economic resources or other assets.[11] If any one of these three thresholds is met then the ENMOD convention is breached.[12] The Convention applies to any hostile use of environmental modification techniques. Although this treaty is in force, regrettably there are only 73 states parties.

The second instrument is limited to specific instances of international armed conflict but has obtained great international acceptance and many of its provisions are part of customary international law. This is the *Protocol Additional to the Geneva Conventions* of 12 August 1949, and relating to the *Protection of Victims of International Armed Conflicts* of 8 June 1977. It contains two pertinent articles: 35(3) and 55. Article 35(3) specifies that 'It is prohibited to employ methods or means of warfare which are intended, or may be expected, to cause widespread, long-term and severe damage to the natural environment', and Article 55 sets out that:

> 1. Care shall be taken in warfare to protect the natural environment against widespread, long-term and severe damage. This protection includes a prohibition of the use of methods or means of warfare which are intended or may be expected to cause such damage to the natural environment and thereby to prejudice the health or survival of the population.
> 2. Attacks against the natural environment by way of reprisals are prohibited.[13]

These articles contain the same threefold test as ENMOD except that the terms are 'widespread, long-term and severe damage', which indicates that all three elements must be present

---

9 *United Nations Convention on the Prohibition of Military or Any Other Hostile Use of Environmental Modification Techniques (ENMOD)*, opened for signature 18 May 1977, 16 ILM (entered into force 5 October 1978), 88–94.

10 United Nations Environmental Programme, *Protecting the Environment during Armed Conflict*, Nairobi: UNEP, 2009, p. 8.

11 A.P.V. Rogers, *Law on the Battlefield*, Manchester: Manchester University Press, 1996, p. 110.

12 S. Oeter, 'Methods and Means of Combat', in D. Fleck (ed.) *The Handbook of Humanitarian Law in Armed Conflict*, Oxford: Oxford University Press, 1995, p. 117.

13 *Protocol Additional to the Geneva Conventions of 12 August 1949, and Relating to the Protection of Victims of International Armed Conflicts*, opened for signature 8 June 1977, 16 ILM (entered into force 7 December 1978), 1391–441.

Susan Breau

for a finding of environmental damage rather than one of the three.[14] This is a significant difference from ENMOD and is clearly a less onerous obligation on those countries which are states parties only to this Convention.

Another important provision of Additional Protocol I is Article 56, which prohibits attacks against works or installations containing dangerous forces, such as dams, dykes and nuclear generating stations. Regrettably this provision does not include oil fields and petrochemical plants. The 'dangerous forces' refers primarily to dangers to human beings but also could mean the risk of environmental harm from the release of substances, particularly of nuclear substances from nuclear power stations. This provision is also included in Article 15 of the *Additional Protocol II Relating to the Protection of Victims of Non-International Armed Conflict* of 1977, thus extending this protection to non-international armed conflict but not to internal disturbances.[15]

The third treaty source is Protocol III to the 1980 *Convention on Certain Conventional Weapons* (CWC), which prohibits incendiary attacks on forests or other kinds of plant cover, unless they are concealing combatants or military objectives.[16] The preamble to the CWC itself states that 'it is prohibited to employ methods or means of warfare which are intended, or may be expected, to cause widespread, long-term and severe damage to the natural environment'.[17] An amendment to Article 1 of the Convention introduced in 2001 extends the application to non-international armed conflict.[18]

There are two other treaties that provide important benefits to the environment: the *Ottawa Landmines Convention* and the *Convention on Cluster Munitions*, which would eliminate a large body of weaponry left behind after conflict.[19] The problem with these conventions is the level of acceptance by the international community. Unlike the four Geneva Conventions none of these treaties has achieved universal ratification and therefore there is an argument to be made as to whether the provisions are customary. Clearly treaties abolishing certain kinds of weapons are not customary unless it can be shown that there is widespread and uniform state practice and *opinio juris*.[20]

The treaties discussed above have been subject to extensive scrutiny, especially in the wake of the 1990 to 1991 Gulf War as it resulted in extensive pollution due to the destruction of over 600 oil wells in Kuwait by the retreating Iraqi army. In 1992 the UN General Assembly passed Resolution 47/37, which urged Member States to 'take all measures to ensure compliance with the existing international law applicable to the protection of environment in times

14 Rogers, op. cit., p. 15.
15 *Protocol Additional to the Geneva Conventions, and Relating to the Protection of Victims of Non-International Armed Conflicts*, opened for signature 8 June 1977, 16 ILM (entered into force 7 December 1978), 1442–9.
16 *Protocol III on Prohibitions or Restrictions on the Use of Mines, Booby-Traps and Other Devices to the 1980 United Nations Convention on Prohibitions or Restrictions on the Use of Certain Conventional Weapons Which May Be Deemed to Be Excessively Injurious or to Have Indiscriminate Effects*, opened for signature 10 April 1981, 19 ILM 1529 (entered into force 2 December 1983).
17 Ibid.
18 Article 1 of the CWC amended at 2nd Review Conference, 21 December 2001.
19 *Convention on the Prohibition of the Use, Stockpiling, Production and Transfer of Anti-Personnel Mines and on their Destruction*, opened for signature 3 December 1997 (entered into force 1 March 1999) ('Ottawa Treaty'); and the *Convention on Cluster Munitions*, opened for signature 3 December 2008 (entered into force 1 August 2010).
20 *North Sea Continental Shelf Cases (Federal Republic of Germany/Denmark; Federal Republic of Germany/Netherlands)* Judgment of 20 February 1969, [1969] ICJ Reports 3.

of armed conflict'.[21] It also urged states to take steps to incorporate the provisions of international law applicable to the protection of the environment into their military manuals.[22]

In 1994 the ICRC issued a set of guidelines that summarised the existing international rules on protection of the environment in armed conflict.[23] The guidelines specified that the general principles of international law applicable in armed conflict such as the principle of distinction and proportionality provide protection of the environment as only a military objective may be attacked and no methods or means of warfare which cause excessive damage shall be employed. Although, as Gasser argues, guidelines are neither an international treaty nor a draft for a codification exercise, they are a tool for making the existing treaty provisions better known to those who must comply with them in the course of military operations.[24] These guidelines were targeted at the drafters of military manuals, who could incorporate these rules. The specific rules on the environment were:

(8) Destruction of the environment not justified by military necessity violates international humanitarian law. Under certain circumstances such destruction is punishable as a grave breach of international humanitarian law.
(9) The general prohibition to destroy civilian objects, unless such destruction is justified by military necessity, also protects the environment.

Listed under this prohibition are: forests and plants; objects indispensable to the survival of the civilian population; attacks on works or installations containing dangerous forces; attacks on historic monuments.

(10) The indiscriminate laying of landmines is prohibited.
(11) Care shall be taken in warfare to protect and preserve the natural environment.
(12) The military or any hostile use of environmental modification techniques having widespread, long-lasting or severe effects as the means of destruction, damage, or injury to any other State party is prohibited.
(13) Attacks against the natural environment by way of reprisals are prohibited for States party to Protocol I.[25]

These rules were all based in existing treaty law which includes the CWC, ENMOD and Additional Protocol I and II. A real difficulty in the rules was the lack of ratification of ENMOD and Additional Protocols I and II by many belligerent states. It has to be noted that the ICRC on this occasion was attempting to introduce the more easily enforceable ENMOD standard rather than the Additional Protocol I cumulative test.

Furthermore, the Rome Statute establishing the International Criminal Court criminalises destruction of the environment under its Article 8 War Crimes provision based on the

21 *Protection of the Environment in Times of Armed Conflict* (1992), GA Res 47/37, UN GAOR, 47th Sess, 49th Supp, UN Doc A/47/49.
22 Ibid.
23 ICRC, 'Guidelines for Military Manuals and Instructions on the Protection of the Environment in Times of Armed Conflict', *International Revue of the Red Cross* 311, 1996, p. 230.
24 H-P. Gasser, 'For Better Protection of the Natural Environment in Armed Conflict: A Proposal for Action', *American Journal of International Law* 89, 1995, p. 641.
25 ICRC, 'Guidelines for Military', op. cit.

Susan Breau

cumulative standard (as in Article 35 of Additional Protocol I rather than ENMOD). The section states:

> A serious violation of international humanitarian law includes:
>
> (iv)   Intentionally launching an attack in the knowledge that such attack will cause incidental loss of life or injury to civilians or damage to civilian objects or widespread, long-term and severe damage to the natural environment which would be clearly excessive in relation to the concrete and direct overall military advantage anticipated.
> (xvii) Employing poison or poisoned weapons;
> (xviii) Employing asphyxiating, poisonous or other gases, and all analogous liquids, materials or devices.[26]

In spite of these treaty obligations and the ICRC guidelines, the conduct of the conflict in Kosovo in 1999 highlighted the lack of enforceability of these treaty provisions as the course of the conflict had severe environmental ramifications, particularly with respect to targeting of industrial facilities, the use of cluster munitions and the use of depleted uranium in weaponry. Uniquely, this conflict was subject to a comprehensive assessment with respect to the damage to the environment from two sources. Firstly, the report of the Prosecutor in the International Criminal Tribunal for Yugoslavia (ICTY) (into whether charges should result from the NATO bombing of Yugoslavia) considered the allegation that the NATO campaign damaged the environment, especially with the use of depleted uranium and the targeting of industrial facilities such as chemical plants and oil installations.[27] The report concluded that the NATO campaign had damaged the environment as the attacks on the chemical plants and oil installations resulted in the release of pollutants. The report stated that Article 55 may be part of customary international law as at the time neither the US nor France had ratified Additional Protocol I.[28] However, the report concluded that Articles 35(3) and 55 have a very high threshold of application and that their conditions for application were extremely stringent and their scope and content imprecise. The report concluded that it would be extremely difficult to develop a *prima facie* case on the basis of these provisions. Even on the general test of proportionality the committee advising the Prosecutor concluded that the Office of the Prosecutor should not commend an investigation into the collateral environmental damage caused by the NATO bombing campaign.[29] This was the same conclusion with respect to the use of depleted uranium and cluster munitions as neither was specifically prohibited in treaty or customary law.[30]

The UNEP also established a Balkan Task Force to look into the Kosovo campaign. The international scientific teams examined several areas, such as the environmental consequences

26 *Rome Statute of the International Criminal Court*, opened for signature 17 July 1998, 2187 UNTS 90 (entered into force 1 July 2002).
27 ICTY, Office of the Prosecutor, *Final Report to the Prosecutor by the Committee Established to Review the NATO Bombing Campaign against the Federal Republic of Yugoslavia*, ('Prosecutor's Report'). Online. Available HTTP: <http://www.icty.org/x/file/About/OTP/otp_report_nato_bombing_en.pdf> (accessed 4 August 2010).
28 Ibid., p. 6. France has since ratified the Convention.
29 Ibid., pp. 8–9.
30 Ibid., p. 9.

of air strikes on industrial sites, including the attacks on the Pancevo and Novi Sad oil refineries, attacks on petrochemical industries and the possible use of depleted uranium weapons. The key conclusions were that the Kosovo conflict did not cause an environmental catastrophe affecting the Balkans regions. The second conclusion was that pollution detected at some sites was serious and could pose a threat to human health. The third was that environmental hotspots requiring immediate action were identified including Novi Sad, Kragujevac, Bor and Pancevo, where the environmental damage was as a result of the conflict. Therefore, the results of the mission found significant areas of pollution. The agency recommended that the international community should assist with the clean-up efforts, as there was urgent humanitarian need.[31] In their recommendations on depleted uranium, the agencies recommended that NATO confirm how and where it was used and that the World Health Organization make 'a thorough review of the effects on health of medium-and long-term exposure to depleted uranium'.[32]

The key conclusion is the fact that reliance on the significantly onerous test established in Articles 35 and 55 of widespread, long-term and severe damage to the natural environment meant that a conclusion could not be reached of criminality in Kosovo. The Prosecutor did not apply the easier alternate test contained in either ENMOD or the ICRC guidelines.

Customary humanitarian law

Given the lack of universal acceptance of the environmental protection treaty provisions, it is important to examine universally binding[33] customary international law. In 2005, the ICRC concluded its ground-breaking study of customary humanitarian law undertaken by a group of humanitarian law experts. These experts reviewed the proposed customary rules under rigorous conditions, testing state practice and *opinio juris*.[34] The study proposed a series of customary rules relating to protecting the environment in armed conflict. Of all the rules analysed those respecting the environment were probably the most controversial. The first rule relevant to environmental protection is that with respect to works and installations containing dangerous forces. Rule 42 states:

> Particular care must be taken if works and installations containing dangerous forces, namely dams, dykes and nuclear electrical generating stations, and other installations located at or in their vicinity are attacked, in order to avoid the release of dangerous forces and consequent severe losses among the civilian population.[35]

The Rule does not repeat the extensive provision in Article 56 of Additional Protocol I cited above.

A critical piece of evidence against Article 56 having customary status is the reservations to Additional Protocol I made by both the United Kingdom and France with respect to Article 56. Their reservations state that they could not grant absolute protection to works and installations

---

31 United Nations Environmental Programme, *The Kosovo Conflict: Consequences for the Environment & Human Settlements*, Nairobi: UNEP, 1999, see 10 and Recommendations 72–9.

32 Ibid., p. 76.

33 Save for persistent objector states to a particular rule.

34 'Study', op. cit., Vol. 1.

35 Ibid., Vol. I.

containing dangerous forces which were military objectives but would take precautions to avoid severe collateral losses.[36] However, in contrast, the volume on practice concerning this proposed rule provides extensive citations, including numerous references to military manuals. The quotations from the military manuals of Israel and of the United States are particularly informative as they were not and are not now parties to Additional Protocol I. First of all, Israel's manual states that although Article 56 is not binding, it is 'nevertheless widely accepted as a binding provision' and such an attack would lead to the unleashing of destructive forces 'resulting in tens of thousands of civilian victims, and therefore it is forbidden'.[37] The *US Air Force Pamphlet, Air Force Commander's Handbook* and the *US Naval Handbook* and supplement all contain language confirming the restraint doctrine and the avoidance of excessive civilian casualties in adherence to the principle of proportionality. It must be noted that the environment did not feature in these commentaries.

The volume on practice also contains extensive citation of national legislation confirming penalisation in national criminal law of attacks on these types of installations. It has to be noted that most of the states concerned are parties to Additional Protocols I and II. However, there is support for the customary status of this rule in the section on other national practice. First of all the report on the practice of China recalls that in 1938 the Nationalist government decided to bomb a dam on the Yellow River to use the water to halt the Japanese offensive. The floods caused many casualties and the Communist government later condemned this method of warfare.[38] The practice of Colombia (not a party to Additional Protocol II which contains a similar prohibition in Article 15) consists of a statement of the Presidency of the Colombian Republic in 1994 that it would not occur to any sensible military officer to bomb a dam in order to dislodge guerrillas and thus cause a deluge that would sweep away the inhabitants.[39] Indonesia was and is not a party to either Additional Protocol I or II and yet the report on the practice of Indonesia states that installations containing dangerous forces could not be attacked as long as they were not used for military purposes.[40] None of the practice particularly mentions environmental damage caused by these attacks but it can be assumed that large-scale flooding will damage the environment for many years to come.

Further support for this Rule's customary status could be found in the practice materials of Iran and Iraq in relation to their armed conflict from 1980 to 1988. During this conflict Iran denied that it had attacked a power station at Ducan Dam and stated that it considered the protection of nuclear plants to be part of customary international law. Iraq, according to Iran, had attacked one of their nuclear plants at Bushehr. Iraq's practice manual cited a letter to the UN Secretary General complaining of US attacks in the Saddam Dam area and a letter from the President of Iraq to the World Association for Peace and Life against Nuclear War in 1983, condemning attacks on peaceful nuclear installations as tantamount to an attack by nuclear weapons.[41]

The practice of Pakistan, another state not a party to Additional Protocol I, is also very informative. During the wars with India in 1965 and 1971 Pakistan refrained from striking against installations that contained dangerous forces. In response to rumours that India was planning to attack Pakistan's nuclear facilities, Pakistan took a very stern position.

---

36 Ibid., Vol. I, 140 and Vol. II, Part 1, 815.
37 Ibid., Vol. II, Part 1, 820–21.
38 Ibid., 830.
39 Ibid., 830–31.
40 Ibid., 832.
41 Ibid., 832.

Finally, there is in the study an extensive analysis of the practice of the United States. There is a reference to a significant piece of practice during the Vietnam War. In 1972 the US planned to attack a hydroelectric plant which included a dam; if the dam had been breached, as many as 23,000 civilians could have died. The plant was authorised to be attacked by President Nixon but using laser-guided bombs, because that gave a 90 per cent chance that the dam would not be breached. This is an example of the proportionality principle being utilised with respect to dangerous forces. The statements of the US officials cited from 1987 through 1997 clearly indicate that they did not consider that there were any restrictions on attack against works and installations containing dangerous forces but their actual practice and military manuals reveal a use of proportionality particularly directed at these targets.[42]

The extensive and thorough analysis of state practice conducted by the ICRC leads to the conclusion that Rule 42 is customary in internal and international armed conflict.[43] It is the practice of non-states parties to Additional Protocol I that supports, at the very least, precautions in attacking installations containing dangerous forces. The Rule does not attempt to reflect the absolute prohibition in Article 56 of Additional Protocol I but supports an analysis which is based on the customary rule of proportionality. As Aldrich, the principle drafter of Article 56, states:

> This standard is reasonable and is a formulation I would have been satisfied to use in Protocol I, but it would have been unacceptable then at the conference to a group of States led by Switzerland and the Netherlands.[44]

There are three rules proposed in the study that directly relate to environmental damage. Firstly, Rule 43 of the ICRC customary humanitarian law study states:

> The general principles on the conduct of hostilities apply to the natural environment:
>
> A. No part of the natural environment may be attacked, unless it is a military objective.
> B. Destruction of any part of the natural environment is prohibited, unless required by imperative military necessity.
> C. Launching an attack against a military objective which may be expected to cause incidental damage to the environment which would be excessive in relation to the concrete and direct military advantage anticipated is prohibited.[45]

Rule 43 has two aspects:

(1) the umbrella notion that the natural environment is included within the rules and principles governing the conduct of hostilities; and
(2) sub-rules A–C which extend the remit of the established rules and principles of humanitarian law to include the natural environment.[46]

42 Ibid., 834–6.
43 S. Breau, 'Protected Persons and Objects', in E. Wilmshurst and S. Breau (eds) *Perspectives on the ICRC Study on Customary International Humanitarian Law*, Cambridge: Cambridge University Press, 2007, p. 197.
44 G.H. Aldrich, 'Customary International Humanitarian Law – an Interpretation on Behalf of the ICRC', *British Yearbook of International Law* 76, 2006, p. 513.
45 'Study', op. cit., Vol. 1, 143.
46 K. Hulme, 'Natural Environment', in Wilmshurst and Breau (eds.), op. cit., p. 207.

International Environmental Law scholar Karen Hulme is not prepared to agree that 43 (B) is customary, arguing that it is superfluous in relation to Rule 50 which states:

> The destruction or seizure of the property of an adversary is prohibited, unless required by imperative military necessity.[47]

However, she agrees that Rule 43(C) restates the rule of proportionality with respect to the environment and argues that it is 'universally accepted that the principle of proportionality applies equally to the environment as it does to other civilian objects'. She would have suggested that the rule be reworded to:

> Launching an attack against a military objective which may be expected to cause incidental damage to the *environment, civilians and civilian objects, or a combination thereof,* which would be excessive in relation to the concrete and direct military advantage anticipated is prohibited.[48]

The next important customary rule is Rule 44(1), which states:

> Methods and means of warfare must be employed with due regard to the protection and preservation of the natural environment.[49]

The United Kingdom Military Manual[50] reflects this recognition and refers to Article 35(3) as providing direct protection to the environment.[51]

The next rule of relevance is 44(2):

> In the conduct of military operations, all feasible precautions must be taken to avoid, and in any event to minimise, incidental damage to the environment.[52]

There is no controversy with the customary nature of this provision as with the next provision, Rule 44(3):

> Lack of scientific certainty as to the effects on the environment of certain military operations does not absolve a party to the conflict from taking such precautions.[53]

The last rule with specific reference to the environment and perhaps the most significant in the study is Rule 45, which is similar to Articles 35 and 55 of Additional Protocol I. More than any other it is this rule which is critical in protection of the environment in armed

---

47 Ibid., p. 215.
48 Ibid., p. 216.
49 'Study', op. cit., Vol. 1,147.
50 United Kingdom Ministry of Defence, *Manual of the Law of Armed Conflict*, Oxford: Oxford University Press, 2004, para. 5.29.
51 Ibid.
52 'Study', op. cit., Vol 1, 147; see also the IHRC Customary International Humanitarian Law Database for Rule 45. Online. Available HTTP: <http://www.icrc.org/customary-ihl/eng/docs/v2_rul_rule45> (accessed 23 August 2010).
53 'Study', op. cit., Vol 1, 147.

conflict, which potentially binds non-parties to Additional Protocol I. This rule is divided into two parts:

> Rule 45(1)
> The use of methods or means of warfare that are intended, or may be expected, to cause widespread, long-term and severe damage to the natural environment is prohibited.
>
> Rule 45(2)
> Destruction of the natural environment may not be used as a weapon.[54]

In the case of this rule, Hulme indicates that the evidence to support part (1) as customary is not 'entirely convincing' even though the wording is almost identical to Article 35(3). She argues that this was new law in 1977 and she is not convinced by the inclusion in 23 military manuals that this provision is now customary as they are 'in fact only training manuals and do not necessarily reflect binding legal obligations on those States'.[55] However, one can disagree with Hulme in examining both the commentary in Volume I and the practice in Volume II, as the evidence given in the study is compelling. Evidence is provided of the above provision being outlined in military manuals of 20 states, albeit only the United States and Kenya were not parties to Additional Protocol I when the manuals were drafted (Kenya later became a party). The provisions in those manuals surely are reflective of the position of the military in this issue, an important part of state practice. Furthermore, the study outlines that 21 states have criminalised the violation of Rule 45(1), which is surely significant practice. At the very least it can be argued to be an emerging norm. Importantly, the study also discusses the *Nuclear Weapons Case*, where nine states 'indicated in their submissions . . . that they considered the rule [in Articles 35(3) and 55(1)] to be customary',[56] and seven 'other States appeared to be of the view that these rules are customary . . .'.[57] Hulme dismisses this contention as not all states were unequivocal and the case itself did not confirm the rule to be customary. However, this evidence should be taken together with the military manuals and points to an emergence of custom. With respect to the second part of the rule, Hulme accepts that there 'would appear to be some evidence to suggest that States may view as custom a duty not to use environmental destruction as a tactic or instrument of war'.[58]

Jean-Marie Henckaerts, one of the authors of this pivotal study, had earlier written an article on the environment and armed conflict. In this article he argued that the conclusions of the customary law study were that damage to the environment in violation of the principle of proportionality and damage to the environment not justified by military necessity were prohibited in both international and non-international armed conflict. He, however, conceded that the humanitarian treaty law protecting the environment is more limited with respect to non-international armed conflict and that it would be left to customary rules to fill the gaps.[59]

---

54 Ibid., 151.
55 Hulme, op. cit., p. 230.
56 'Study', op. cit., Vol. 1, 151.
57 Ibid., 52, fn 56.
58 Ibid., 234.
59 J-M. Henckaerts, 'Towards Better Protection for the Environment in Armed Conflict: Recent Developments in International Humanitarian Law', *RECEIL* 9, 2000, p. 18.

Dinstein points out an important overriding consideration that an attack against a military objective is liable to produce 'legitimate collateral damage to the environment'.[60] However, he is not prepared to accept that the articles contained in either the ENMOD Convention or Protocol I were customary in nature. He argues that some intentional and direct damage to the environment is not covered by either treaty and consequently is still permissible.[61] This surely cannot be correct in light of the comprehensive analysis conducted by the ICRC study.

Another important source that examines customary law in relation to the controversial area of non-international armed conflict is the *Manual for Non-International Armed Conflict* drafted by three eminent humanitarian law scholars.[62] Interestingly, they examined the provisions for the environment from Additional Protocol I as possibly applicable to non-international armed conflict as follows:

> Damage to the natural environment during military operations must not be excessive in relation to the military advantage anticipated from those operations.

> 1. Articles 35.3 and 55 of Additional Protocol I, which address damage to the natural environment in terms of 'widespread, long-term, and severe damage' in the context of international armed conflict, have not been accepted as customary international law in either international or non-international armed conflict. However, the natural environment is a civilian object. As such, parts of the environment benefit from all the rules regarding protection of civilian objects. Like other civilian objects, they may become military objectives by virtue of their nature, location, purpose or use (see Rule 1.1.4).[63]

Although not accepting that Articles 35, 55 of Additional Protocol I are customary, they do acknowledge that within the general rules regarding protection of civilian objects environmental provisions are applicable to non-international armed conflict.

On the basis of academic opinion including Hulme, Dinstein and the *Manual for Non-International Armed Conflict*, it is evident that the author of this chapter may well be in the minority in arguing that Articles 35(3) and 55 in Additional Protocol I are part of customary international law. However, it is urged on scholars and practitioners alike to assess the practice contained in the study, which seems to support the customary nature of all the environmental rules set out in this chapter.

Environmental law rules generally

International environmental law includes general principles binding on states that are applicable in armed conflict. The first of these is the obligation on states to avoid causing environmental damage beyond their borders.[64] The second principle is the obligation on states to

---

60 Y. Dinstein, 'Protection of the Environment in International Armed Conflict', *Max Planck Yearbook of United Nations Law* 5, 2001, p. 525.
61 Ibid., p. 549.
62 M.N. Schmitt, C.H.B. Garraway and Y. Dinstein, *The Manual on the Law of Non-International Armed Conflict: With Commentary*, San Remo: International Institute of Humanitarian Law, 2006.
63 Ibid., 59–60.
64 Principle No. 21 of the Declaration of Stockholm adopted 16 June 1972.

respect the environment in general.[65] A third principle, derived from international human rights law, is the right to a healthy environment.[66] Finally there is a principle in the Rio Declaration which might not yet be customary law but is applicable. Principle 24 declared that 'Warfare is inherently destructive of sustainable development. States shall therefore respect international law providing protection of the environment in armed conflict and cooperate in its further development if necessary.'[67] All of these principles taken together with the rules of customary humanitarian law provide further support to the less widely ratified treaty provisions.

Case law applying the legal standards

There is a scarcity of case law applying the customary and treaty law on protection of the environment in armed conflict. The *Advisory Opinion on Nuclear Weapons* addressed the possible environmental damage of nuclear weapons. The court confirmed there was a 'general obligation of States to ensure that activities within their jurisdiction or control respect the environment of other States or areas beyond national control' and that obligation was part of the corpus of international law.[68] This principle, known as the Trail Smelter Principle, had been confirmed in the 1972 Stockholm Declaration and the 1992 Rio Declaration. The Tribunal in the *Trail Smelter* case between Canada and the United States held that no state had the right to use or permit the use of its territory in such a manner as to cause injury by fumes in or to the territory of another state. Importantly, a regime of control to prevent further damage by the smelter had to be instituted in Canada.[69] This vital principle was confirmed in the *Advisory Opinion on Nuclear Weapons* to be part of customary international law. Second, the International Court of Justice instructed states to account for environmental considerations when determining what constituted necessary and proportionate levels of military action. Third, although the Court did not find that possession of nuclear weapons in themselves was unlawful, it did hold that nuclear weapons 'would generally be contrary to the rules of international law applicable in armed conflict, and in particular the rules and principles of humanitarian law'.[70]

The United Nations Compensation Commission, established to adjudicate claims of compensation relating to the 1990 to 1991 Gulf War, awarded damages in two categories: claims for environmental damage and the depletion of natural resources in the Persian Gulf region, including those resulting from oil-well fires and the discharge of oil into the sea. It also assessed claims for costs incurred by governments outside of the region in providing assistance to countries that were directly affected by the environmental damage. Of the 168 claims brought within this category, 109 were awarded compensation for a total of

---

65 Principle No. 2 of the Declaration of Stockholm adopted 16 June 1972.

66 See for example the *Need to ensure a healthy environment for the well-being of individuals* (1990), GA Res 45/94, UN GAOR, 45th Sess, 49th Supp, UN Doc A/45/94, which states that all individuals are entitled to live in an environment adequate for their health and well-being.

67 United Nations Conference on Environment and Development, *Rio Declaration on Environment and Development* (1992), UN Doc A/CONF.151/26 (Vol.I), Principle 24.

68 *Legality of the threat or use of nuclear weapons advisory opinion*, Advisory Opinion of 8 July 1996, [1996] *ICJ Reports* 226, para. 29.

69 *Trail Smelter Case, United States of America v Canada* (1938 and 1941) *Volume III RIAA*, pp. 1905–82.

70 Ibid., para. 105.

$5.3 billion (US). The approach by the Security Council in Resolution 687, creating a body in charge of evaluating and compensating wartime environmental damage, is one that was studied in the UNEP report on reform of the law in this area.[71]

There is another example of considering environmental damage in international criminal jurisprudence. The Prosecutor, in his application for a warrant of arrest against President Omar Al-Bashir of Sudan, alleged, as part of the charge of genocide against the Fur, Masalit, and Zaghawa ethnic groups, the creating of conditions of life calculated to bring about their physical destruction resulting from severe environmental degradation and depletion of natural resources which 'were designed to destroy the very means of survival of the groups'.[72] Thus the Prosecutor was inviting the Court to recognise that environmental degradation in Darfur could constitute an underlying act of genocide. Regrettably the Court dismissed the genocide claim but invited the Prosecutor to submit more evidence.[73] There was an interesting dissenting opinion by Judge Usacka, who concluded that the groups outlined above were subjected to conditions 'calculated to bring about the destruction of the group'. She suggested that the charge of genocide must be 'analysed in the context of Darfur's harsh terrain, in which water and food sources are naturally scarce'. She would have supported the charge of genocide based on the general destruction of the means of survival, which include food supplies, food sources and shelter in addition to the destruction of the water sources.[74]

UNEP report and recommendations for reform of law in this area

In November 2009 the UNEP released a study, *Protecting the Environment during Armed Conflict*, which contained a number of recommendations for changes in the legal regime. The report inventoried and analysed the relevant provisions not only within international humanitarian law but also within international criminal law, international environmental law and international human rights law.[75] As a result of this analysis recommendations were made about steps that should be taken by various international and national actors to ensure the 'expansion, implementation and enforcement of a more effective legal framework' to protect the environment in both international and non-international armed conflict.

The first recommendation accords with much of the academic analysis in this area. It was that:

> The terms *widespread, long-term and severe* within Articles 35 and 55 of Additional Protocol I to the 1949 Geneva Convention should be clearly defined.

The report stated that a starting point would be to use the precedents set by the 1976 ENMOD Convention. Firstly, widespread would encompass an area on the scale of several hundred square kilometres; secondly, long-term would be for a period of months, or approximately a season, and severe would be 'significant disruption or harm to human life, natural economic resources or other assets'.[76]

---

71 UNEP, *Protecting the Environment during Armed Conflict*, op. cit., pp. 27–8.
72 *Situation in Darfur*, ICC-02/05-157-AnxA, Public Redacted Version of the Prosecution's Application under Article 58, 14 July 2008, para. 31.
73 *Prosecutor v Omar Al-Bashir*, ICC-02/05-01/09-3. Decision on the Prosecution's Application for a Warrant of Arrest against Omar Hassan Ahmad Al-Bashir, 4 March 2009.
74 Separate and Partly Dissenting Opinion of Judge Anita Usacka, para. 1.
75 UNEP, *Protecting the Environment during Armed Conflict*, op. cit., p. 9.
76 Ibid., 52.

The second recommendation of the study was that the ICRC *Guidelines on the Protection of the Environment during Armed Conflict* 1994 require urgent updating. This could well be a 'soft law' method of clarifying those gaps that it might not be possible to address by a treaty regime. Such guidelines could then be recommended for inclusion in national military manuals which govern the conduct of armed forces in conflict. The report suggests that the revised guidelines should:

- explain how damage to the environment affects human health, livelihoods and security, and undermines effective peace building;
- define key terms such as 'widespread', 'long-lasting' and 'severe';
- address the continued application of international environmental law during armed conflict;
- explain how damage to the environment can be considered a criminal offence under international criminal law, enforceable in both international and national courts; and
- examine protection of the environment and natural resources in the context of non-international armed conflict.[77]

Another key recommendation directed that the International Law Commission should examine existing international law for the protection of the environment during armed conflict and recommend how it can be clarified, codified and expanded. The examination was suggested to include among others:

- an inventory of the legal provisions and the identification of gaps and barriers to enforcement; and
- an exploration of options for clarifying and codifying this body of law.[78]

Other important recommendations were that a permanent UN body be established to monitor violations and address compensation for environmental damage and that the international community should consider strengthening the role of the Permanent Court of Arbitration to address disputes related to environmental damage during armed conflict.[79]

A separate key recommendation suggested that a new legal instrument is needed for 'place-based protection of critical natural resources and areas of ecological importance during armed conflicts'. Within this instrument would be the provision that critical natural resources and areas of ecological importance would be delineated and designated as demilitarised zones. Parties to the conflict would be prohibited from conducting military operations within these zones. This instrument should include protection for watersheds, groundwater aquifers, agricultural and grazing lands, parks, natural forests and the habitat of endangered species.[80]

Although these recommendations are meritorious, having a truly enforceable treaty-based regime in this area is difficult given the lack of ratifications by the major powers of the regime that already exists. In London in 1995 a radical proposal was discussed, the drafting of a 'Fifth Geneva Convention on the Protection of the Environment in Time of Armed Conflict'; but this did not find strong backing.[81] A more fruitful avenue might be to consider the customary

---

77 Ibid., 52–53.
78 Ibid., 53.
79 Ibid.
80 Ibid., 54.
81 Gasser, op. cit., p. 639.

international law regime that may already bind all countries, and consider an enforcement mechanism similar to the UN Compensation Commission established after the first Gulf War.

Conclusion

The conclusion to this analysis is a familiar one in international law. It can be argued that there is a body of customary and treaty law applicable to the protection of the environment in armed conflict but that it is not enforced. Sadly it is very unlikely that a new treaty will be negotiated given the lack of ratifications of ENMOD. It is therefore necessary to fall back on the customary status of the rules set out in Articles 35, 55 and 56 of Additional Protocol 1. These rules may have already reached the status of customary international law but this is not a unanimous viewpoint in academic literature. However, the ICRC customary humanitarian law study is a tremendous boost to the customary status of environmental protection obligations in armed conflict.

Nevertheless, what is truly tragic is that within the enumerated international law standards the only one that can truly be argued to be customary is the almost impossibly high standard of widespread, long-term and severe damage caused to the environment by an armed conflict. It is clear from the analysis conducted on the Kosovo conflict by the Prosecutor of the ICTY that this standard may be impossible to reach unless there is catastrophic environmental damage. The UNEP report is an important first step in arguing for more consistent enforcement and clarification of the standards, but it will be some time before the environment is truly protected within armed conflict.

35

International disaster law

*Michael Eburn**

An expected consequence of climate change will be more frequent and severe natural hazard events such as storms, floods and wildfires, while rising sea levels will increase vulnerability to storm surge and tsunami. This chapter will explore the current state of international law governing the response to disasters and the range of recurring problems and issues in managing this international response (both from governments and the non-government sector). The chapter will consider the role of international conventions and standards and other proposed solutions to facilitate rapid and appropriate responses to natural hazard events.

Introduction

Climate change is expected to lead to more and more severe natural hazard events.[1] Natural hazard events are not, however, disasters. An extreme flood, storm or wildfire does not qualify as a disaster unless it impacts upon a vulnerable population:

> A disaster occurs when a disaster agent exposes the vulnerability of a group or groups in such a way that their lives are directly threatened or sufficient harm has been done to economic and social structures, inevitably undermining their ability to survive.[2]

Climate and environmental change will not only increase the number and severity of hazard events or 'disaster agents' but can also impact upon vulnerability. For example, rising sea levels and coastal erosion may bring larger populations closer to the coastal edge, making

---

* This chapter is based on work completed for the author's PhD thesis, 'Australia's International Disaster Response – Laws, Rules and Principles' (2009, Monash University).

1 R. Garnaut, *The Garnaut Review 2011*, Cambridge: Cambridge University Press, 2011, p 6; see also R.K. Pachauri and A. Reisinger (eds) *Climate Change 2007: Synthesis Report. Contribution of Working Groups I, II and III to the Fourth Assessment Report of the Intergovernmental Panel on Climate Change*, Geneva: IPCC and Climate Commission, *The Critical Decade; Climate Science, Risks and Responses*, Canberra: Commonwealth of Australia, [2,4].

2 R.C. Kent, *Anatomy of Disaster Relief: The International Network in Action*, London: Pinter, 1987, p. 4.

them more vulnerable to events such as storm surge or tsunami. It is expected, therefore, that climate change will see more extreme hazard events impacting upon larger populations – in short, more, and more severe, natural *disasters*.

Individuals, non-government organisations (NGOs), civil society and other countries come to the aid of neighbouring states that have been struck by natural disasters. In principle, international aid should be supplied solely on the basis of need. The delivery of international aid is, however, *ad hoc*, unpredictable, often inappropriate, and sometimes delivered in a high-handed way without due regard to local sensitivities or needs by organisations of varying ability, capacity and integrity.[3]

Aid can come in the form of specialised government services such as urban search and rescue and field medical teams, while NGOs also bring particular skills expertise or ability to provide services to affected sub-groups or in the form of donated food, clothes and other relief goods sent from around the world as a sign of goodwill and human solidarity. Such assistance is not always beneficial and affected countries can be overwhelmed dealing with the inflow of aid workers and relief supplies that may, or may not, be appropriate for local conditions or reflect what is needed to respond to the particular event. Other problems include aid being delayed due to administrative bottlenecks and the imposition of import fees, charges and duties. Aid workers may have trouble accessing the necessary permission to enter the affected country, to practise their profession or to bring with them essential supplies. Affected countries may not wish to ask for international aid or the international community may be unwilling to assist. In addition, most calls for international financial assistance are undersubscribed.[4]

The problems experienced by providers of international aid and disaster relief have not gone unnoticed. The International Federation of Red Cross and Red Crescent Societies (IFRC) conducted an extensive review of the experience of international disaster relief providers and identified a number of areas where common problems were experienced. Those were:

(a) initiation and termination of the international response;
(b) goods and equipment (including issues of inappropriate aid and delays in getting humanitarian supplies into an affected country due to customs, transport or administrative barriers);
(c) personnel (including issuing visas and recognition of professional qualifications);
(d) transport and movement around the disaster area;
(e) operational matters (such as establishing an office, opening bank accounts and employing staff);
(f) quality and accountability; and
(g) the coordination of international responders.[5]

---

3 See Kent, op. cit.; R. Falk, 'Human Rights, Humanitarian Assistance and the Sovereignty of States', p. 27, K.N. Awoonor, 'The Concerns of Recipient Nations', p. 63, A.A. Farah, 'Responding to Emergencies: A View from Within', p. 259, all in K.M. Cahill (ed.) *A Framework for Survival: Health, Human Rights, and Humanitarian Assistance in Conflicts and Disasters*, New York: Basic Books, 1993.
4 D. Fisher, *Law and Legal Issues in International Disaster Response: a Desk Study*, Geneva: International Red Cross, 2007, pp. 13–14.
5 Ibid., pp. 4–6.

Identifying these problems was not new; the problems with international disaster response 'have been described year after year . . . [but] the same problems keep reappearing in emergency responses'.[6] The question remains, 'How can these issues be most effectively addressed?' The answer lies in both international law and, more importantly, in the domestic laws of disaster affected states. This chapter will review international law that applies to the delivery of disaster assistance and identify gaps and shortfalls in the current regulatory regime. It will consider whether international law requires states to offer, or accept, immediate disaster relief assistance. The limits on the ability of international law to effectively regulate the delivery of quality aid will be shown. The discussion will introduce the Red Cross/Red Crescent *Guidelines for the Domestic Facilitation and Regulation of International Disaster Relief and Initial Recovery* and it will be argued that the real solutions to the problems in international disaster assistance lie in domestic rather than international law.

Key concepts, principles and laws

Recognition of, and respect for, state sovereignty remains the key principle in this area of international law. Responding to disasters is a matter that is essentially for the government of the affected state. It is up to that state to determine if international assistance is required, what form of assistance they will accept and from whom they will accept assistance.

As the discussion below will show, there are no universal international legal standards applicable to the delivery of international disaster relief or the quality of relief to be provided. A number of non-binding international instruments, such as United Nations (UN) resolutions, and resolutions of international organisations such as the International Red Cross, encourage states to plan for disasters and disaster response, including the management of an international response. International aid agencies may be committed to delivering assistance that meets one or more sets of minimum standards,[7] but these standards are not mandated by international law. Without clear standards of what should be done in an emergency, 'the disaster victim is at the mercy of the vagaries of humanitarian response, political calculation, indifference or ignorance.'[8]

International conventions

There is no single binding, universal international convention setting out the rights or obligations of states when responding to disasters, or affirming the right of affected populations to receive disaster relief, either from their own government or from international relief providers. Nonetheless, there is relevant international law – first, the general principles of human rights law will impose obligations upon states to protect the rights of their citizens, rights that can

---

6 J. Telford, J. Cosgrave and R. Houghton, *Joint Evaluation of the International Response to the Indian Ocean Tsunami: Synthesis Report*, London: Tsunami Evaluation Coalition, 2006, p. 106.

7 See e.g. *The Sphere Project*. Online. Available HTTP: <http://www.sphereproject.org/> (accessed 2 September 2011); Humanitarian Accountability Partnership – International, *The 2010 HAP Standard in Accountability and Quality Management*. Online. Available HTTP: <http://www.hapinternational.org/projects/standard/hap-2010-standard.aspx> (accessed 2 September 2011); *The Code of Conduct for the International Red Cross and Red Crescent Movement and Non-Governmental Organisations (NGOs) in Disaster Relief*, Geneva: International Federation of Red Cross and Red Crescent Societies, 1995.

8 M. Hoffman, 'Towards an International Disaster Response Law' in *World Disasters Report 2000*, Geneva: International Federation of Red Cross and Red Crescent Societies, 2000, p. 146.

be significantly affected by the consequences of a disaster. Second, even though there is no single binding, universal convention there are specific conventions that facilitate particular types of disaster relief, disaster relief in response to particular hazards and regional relief arrangements. Finally other areas of law, for example international humanitarian law, may have consequential impact upon the rights of disaster victims. These issues are explored, in turn, below.

Civil, political, economic, social and cultural rights

The *International Covenant on Civil and Political Rights*[9] and the *International Covenant on Economic, Social and Cultural Rights*[10] give legal effect to the rights that are accepted by the international community and expressed in the *Universal Declaration of Human Rights*.[11] These covenants give substance to the right to life,[12] a right to work in safe conditions,[13] the right to social security,[14] and an obligation to protect the family and to provide special protection for new mothers and children.[15] It is stated that it is 'the right of everyone to [enjoy] an adequate standard of living for himself and his family, including adequate food, clothing and housing'.[16]

State signatories to the *Covenant on Economic, Social and Cultural Rights* have obligations to 'take steps, individually and through international assistance'[17] to allow the population to realise their rights. Under the *Covenant on Civil and Political Rights* the parties have agreed 'to ensure to all individuals within its territory and subject to its jurisdiction the rights recognized in the present Covenant'.[18] A natural disaster can have an impact upon the rights protected by these covenants by causing death, dislocation, destruction of homes and livelihoods and the spread of disease. Where this happens and the affected population is not provided adequate assistance by their own government, then the affected state is not abiding by its obligations.

Alleging a state failure to adhere to human rights conventions, or a failure to adequately protect human rights, is time-consuming and complex. Aggrieved parties can complain to the relevant tribunal established under human rights conventions[19] but only after they have exhausted all local procedures to remedy the alleged violation. It follows that such a procedure will have little practical application during the response to a natural disaster. An

---

9 *International Covenant on Civil and Political Rights*, opened for signature 16 December 1966, 999 UNTS 171 (entered into force 23 March 1976).
10 *International Covenant on Economic, Social and Cultural Rights*, opened for signature 16 December 1966, 993 UNTS 3 (entered into force 3 January 1976).
11 *Universal Declaration of Human Rights* (1948), GA Res 217(III), 3rd sess, 183rd plen mtg, UN Doc A/RES/217(III).
12 *Covenant on Civil and Political Rights*, Art. 6.
13 *Covenant on Economic, Social and Cultural Rights*, Art. 7(ii)(b).
14 Ibid., Art. 9.
15 Ibid., Art. 10.
16 Ibid., Art. 11.
17 Ibid., Art. 2(1).
18 *Covenant on Civil and Political Rights*, Art. 2(1).
19 The Human Rights Committee, the Committee on the Elimination of Racial Discrimination, the Committee against Torture or the Committee on the Elimination of Discrimination against Women; Office of the United Nations High Commissioner for Human Rights, *Human Rights Treaty Bodies – Individual Communications* Online. Available HTTP: <http://www2.ohchr.org/english/bodies/petitions/individual.htm> (accessed 5 September 2011).

individual impacted by a natural hazard event is unlikely to have the resources to seek local or international remedies for human rights violations and will have more immediate priorities. Action after the event, to allege that the response was flawed or that individuals or groups missed out on disaster assistance because of their race or political affiliation, may be important but will not bring immediate assistance at the time of the disaster.

The international community does recognise an obligation to step in to protect human rights where a population is exposed to large-scale loss of life or economic disruption either as a result of a direct action, or omission, by their government. This 'responsibility to protect' is discussed, below, where it is argued that this, too, has limited application in the context of a natural disaster.

Specific disaster conventions

There are some specific international conventions that impose obligations upon parties during a disaster but these are limited by the type of disaster or the type of response, or are regional in nature, rather than imposing universal obligations.

Examples of conventions that are limited by the type of disaster include the convention requiring seafarers and coastal states to go to the aid of people in distress at sea[20] and the convention on providing and receiving international assistance in the event of a nuclear accident.[21] The nuclear accident convention provides that any state that needs assistance to deal with a nuclear accident may call for that assistance,[22] specifying the assistance required.[23] A party receiving such a request must then consider whether or not it is able to assist.[24]

Conventions that may apply to any disaster but are limited in their scope include the *International Convention on the Simplification and Harmonization of Customs Procedures*,[25] which provides that a state receiving disaster assistance should have in place procedures to allow for simplified documentation and should provide that the inspection of the imported relief consignment will take place only in exceptional circumstances. Where an inspection is required, provision should be made to allow it to take place away from the normal customs office and outside normal office hours.[26] Relief consignments should be admitted duty and tax free.[27]

---

20 Relevant conventions are the *International Convention for the Safety of Life at Sea*, opened for signature 1 November 1974, 1184 UNTS 2 (entered into force 25 May 1980); *International Convention on Salvage*, opened for signature 28 April 1989, 1996 UNTS 194 (entered into force 14 July 1996); *International Convention on maritime search and rescue*, opened for signature 27 April 1979, [1986] ATS 29 (entered into force 22 June 1985).

21 *Convention on Assistance in the Case of a Nuclear Accident or Radiological Emergency*, opened for signature 26 September 1986, [1987] ATS 15 (entered into force 26 February 1987).

22 Ibid., [2(1)].

23 Ibid., [2(2)].

24 Ibid., [2(3)].

25 *International Convention on the Simplification and Harmonization of Customs Procedures*, opened for signature 18 May 1973, [1975] ATS 12 (entered into force 25 September 1974) as amended by the *Protocol of Amendment to the International Convention on the Simplification and Harmonization of Customs Procedures of 18 May 1973*, opened for signature 26 June 1999, [2006] ATS 22 (entered into force 3 February 2006).

26 Ibid., Annex J5(3).

27 Ibid., Annex J5(6).

Parties to the *Convention on the Facilitation of International Maritime Traffic*[28] have agreed to facilitate the 'arrival and departure of vessels engaged in natural disaster relief work'[29] and 'the entry and clearance of persons and cargo arriving' in those vessels.[30] Similar provisions are found in the *Civil Aviation Convention*[31] relating to the entry, departure and transit of relief flights and the early entry clearance for people and goods arriving on relief flights.

The *Tampere Convention on the Provision of Telecommunication Resources for Disaster Mitigation and Relief Operations*[32] is a genuine multilateral, multi-hazard disaster treaty but is, by its very nature, limited to the provision and operation of telecommunications equipment.

There are some other regional, multilateral and bilateral disaster agreements that are in place. The *Agreement Establishing the Caribbean Disaster Emergency Management Agency (CDEMA)*[33] and the *ASEAN Agreement on Disaster Management and Emergency Response*[34] provide for the sharing of resources and cooperation across the region in the event of a natural disaster, including provisions to facilitate interstate assistance and movement across national boundaries following a disaster.

As examples of bilateral agreements, Germany and Denmark have agreed to 'provide mutual assistance in the event of disasters or serious accidents'[35] and Australia and Indonesia have an agreement on Security Cooperation that includes cooperation in emergency response.[36]

There are, therefore, a myriad of international conventions that have some impact upon international disaster assistance. Universal human rights obligations may impose obligations upon countries, but they may be of little practical assistance at the actual time of a natural disaster. Where there are specific conventions designed to facilitate international disaster assistance, they are limited either by the type of assistance (for example, telecommunications), the type of disasters (for example, accidents at sea and nuclear accidents) or only apply bilaterally or within a region.

Geneva Conventions

Apart from specific disaster-related conventions other areas of international law may impact upon the rights of affected peoples and the obligations of states parties. One example of this

28 *Convention on Facilitation of International Maritime Traffic*, opened for signature 9 April 1965, [1986] ATS 12 (entered into force 5 March 1967).
29 Ibid., [5.11].
30 Ibid., [5.12].
31 *Convention on International Civil Aviation*, opened for signature 7 December 1944, [1957] ATS 5 (entered into force 4 April 1947), Annex 9.
32 *Tampere Convention on the Provision of Telecommunication Resources for Disaster Mitigation and Relief Operations*, opened for signature 18 June 1998, UNTS 2296 (entered into force 8 January 2005).
33 *Agreement Establishing the Caribbean Disaster Emergency Management Agency,* opened for signature 26 February 1991, UNTS 2256 (entered into force 19 May 1992).
34 *ASEAN Agreement on Disaster Management and Emergency Response*, opened for signature 26 July 2005 (entered into force 24 December 2009).
35 *Agreement between the Federal Republic of Germany and the Kingdom of Denmark on Mutual Assistance in the Event of Disasters or Serious Accidents*, Denmark–Germany, signed 16 May 1985, 1523 UNTS 109 (entered into force 1 August 1988).
36 *Agreement between Australia and the Republic of Indonesia on the Framework for Security Cooperation*, Australia–Indonesia, signed 13 November 2006, [2008] ATS 3 (entered into force 7 February 2008), [18]–[19].

ancillary impact can be found in international humanitarian law (or the law of armed conflict).[37] Provisions in the fourth Geneva Convention and *Additional Protocol I*[38] impose obligations upon parties to armed conflicts to provide relief to civilian populations. They must accept offers of international assistance where they are unable to adequately provide for the population in an occupied territory;[39] they must allow the free entry of relief goods and facilitate the distribution of those goods;[40] they must allow the Red Cross movement and other humanitarian organisations to perform their work with the affected populations;[41] they must respect civil defence organisations not only from the occupied country but also from other countries and allow them to perform their civil defence tasks.[42] Those provisions would impose obligations upon parties to an armed conflict should a natural disaster impact upon the affected population.

It remains the case, however, that there are no 'comprehensive rules of international law binding on states through treaties and customary international law'[43] setting out the responsibility of states to protect their own population or assist others, or to facilitate international assistance by setting out how requests for assistance are to be made, how needs are to be assessed and met, when and how foreign aid agencies are to be allowed to access disaster-affected populations and the like.

Customary international law

To determine if state behaviour reflects a rule of customary international law:

> two conditions must be fulfilled. Not only must the acts concerned amount to a settled practice, but they must also be such, or be carried out in such a way, as to be evidence of a belief that this practice is rendered obligatory by the existence of a rule of law requiring it. . . . The States concerned must therefore feel that they are confirming to what amounts to a legal obligation. The frequency, or even habitual character of the acts is not in itself enough.[44]

Although states frequently, or even habitually, respond to requests for international assistance, statements made by the international community in the forum of the UN, and academic

---

37 International humanitarian law is established both by customary law; see J-M. Henckaerts and L. Doswald-Beck (eds) *Customary International Humanitarian Law*, Cambridge: Cambridge University Press, 2008; and by convention, in particular the four Geneva Conventions and their additional protocols.

38 *Convention (IV) relative to the Protection of Civilian Persons in Time of War*, opened for signature 12 August 1949, 75 UNTS 288 (entered into force 21 October 1950) and *Protocol Additional to the Geneva Conventions of 12 August 1949, and relating to the Protection of Victims of International Armed Conflicts (Protocol I)*, opened for signature 8 June 1977, 1125 UNTS 4 (entered into force 7 December 1978).

39 *Protocol I*, [70(1)].

40 *Convention (IV)*, [59]–[61]; *Protocol I*, [70(2)].

41 *Convention (IV)*, [63]; *Protocol I*, [81].

42 *Protocol I*, [62]–[64].

43 D.P. Fidler, 'Disaster Relief and Governance After the Indian Ocean Tsunami: What Role for International Law?' *Melbourne Journal of International Law* 6, 2005, 458, p. 472.

44 *North Sea Continental Shelf cases (FRG v Denmark; FRG v The Netherlands)* (1969) 41 ILR 29 in E. Heinze and M. Fitzmaurice, *Landmark Cases in Public International Law*, London: Kluwer Law International, 1998, p. 77.

commentary, do not suggest that this is due to a belief that such actions are required by international law.

Resolutions and the role of the United Nations

Resolutions of the UN General Assembly have directed the Secretary-General to develop and improve the organisation's ability to respond to a disaster.[45] United Nations resolutions have reiterated that the key principle in disaster relief is national sovereignty. In December 1991, the UN General Assembly:

- restated that the principles of humanity, neutrality and impartiality were fundamental principles governing the delivery of international aid;[46] but
- reaffirmed the paramount issue of sovereignty and that aid should only be delivered at the request of the affected government;[47]
- called upon states to work with intergovernmental organisations (IGOs) and NGOs and to facilitate their access to affected populations;[48] and
- called upon neighbouring states to facilitate the transhipment of relief supplies.[49]

Further resolutions[50] have reaffirmed the UN's commitment to this Resolution[51] and therefore the role of sovereignty, while continuing to urge the international community of states and non-government actors to work together to better coordinate the response to natural disasters.

Nothing in the UN resolutions suggests that the law has moved to impose an obligation upon states to accept international assistance or to come to the aid of their neighbours. In fact an 'analysis of General Assembly resolutions on disasters from 1981 until 2002 reveals an increasingly explicit emphasis on sovereignty'.[52] There is nothing in the UN resolutions that could suggest that the members of the UN are of the view that providing assistance to another state is a requirement of international law.

Macalister-Smith states:

---

45 *Assistance in Cases of Natural Disaster*, GA Res 2034(XX) UN GAOR 20th sess, 1390th plen mtg, UN Doc A/RES/2034(XX) (1964); *Strengthening the Capacity of the United Nations System to Respond to Natural Disasters and Other Disaster Situations*, GA Res 36/225, UN GAOR 36th sess, 103rd plen mtg, UN Doc A/RES/36/225 (1981); *Humanitarian Assistance to Victims of Natural Disasters and Similar Emergency Situations*, GA Res 43/131, UN GAOR 43rd sess, 75th plen mtg, UN Doc A/RES/43/131 (1988).

46 *Strengthening of the Coordination of Humanitarian Emergency Assistance of the United Nations*, GA Res 46/182, UN GAOR, 46th sess, 78th plen mtg, Annex [2], UN Doc A/RES/46/182 (1991).

47 Ibid., Annex [3] and Annex [4].

48 Ibid., Annex [5] and Annex [6].

49 Ibid., Annex [7].

50 *International Cooperation on Humanitarian Assistance in the Field of Natural Disasters, from Relief to Development*, GA Res 64/251, UN GAOR, 64th sess, 69th plen mtg, UN Doc A/RES/64/251 (2010); *Strengthening of the Coordination of Emergency Humanitarian Assistance of the United Nations*, GA Res 65/133, UN GAOR, 65th sess, 67th plen mtg, UN Doc A/RES/65/133 (2010).

51 *Strengthening of the Coordination of Humanitarian Emergency Assistance of the United Nations*, GA Res 46/182, UN GAOR, 46th sess, 78th plen mtg, Annex [2], UN Doc A/RES/46/182 (1991).

52 Fidler, op. cit., p. 472.

It should be apparent that the individual nature of at least some disaster situations, the uncertainty as to the general character of humanitarian practices and, above all, the influence of political factors in relief, work firmly against the crystallization of particular customary international rules in this area.[53]

Fidler argues:

> Concerns and controversies about advocacy for a right of humanitarian intervention grounded in a 'responsibility to protect' reinforce the reticence of many states to bind themselves to rules concerning disaster relief. . . .
>
> Assisting states do not want legally binding obligations to pay for the significant costs that in-depth disaster governance presents for many countries. States facing potentially adverse effects from disasters will likewise stress sovereignty in the face of a potential avalanche of demands from the international community on preparing for, protecting against, and responding to natural disasters.[54]

Although states do come to the aid of others, there is no evidence that this is due to a belief that requesting, accepting or providing assistance is a legal obligation. In the absence of any *opinio juris*, there can be no suggestion that the provision of international assistance is required by customary international law.

The responsibility to protect

The international community has recognised that there is shared 'responsibility to protect' persons affected by conflict and, possibly, disasters. That responsibility may, in extreme circumstances, be exercised without the consent of the affected state. The *International Commission on Intervention and State Sovereignty* argued that international intervention may be justified where there are:

> overwhelming natural or environmental catastrophes, where the State concerned is either unwilling or unable to cope, or call for assistance, and significant loss of life is occurring or threatened.[55]

The UN General Assembly has given only limited support to the principle of the responsibility to protect. It restricted its endorsement to cases where the affected population was subject to 'genocide, war crimes, ethnic cleansing and crimes against humanity', expressly excluding any reference to natural disasters.[56]

Even if the principle of the 'responsibility to protect' was extended to an international commitment to provide assistance to disaster-affected communities, that action, in the

---

53 P. Macalister-Smith, *International Humanitarian Assistance: Disaster Relief Actions in International Law and Organization*, Dordrecht: Martinus Nijhoff, 1985, p. 54.
54 Fidler, op. cit., p. 472.
55 The International Commission on Intervention and State Sovereignty, *The Responsibility to Protect*, Ottawa: International Development Research Centre, 2001, [4.20].
56 *2005 World Summit Outcome*, GA Res 1/60, UN GAOR, 60th sess, 8th plen mtg, UN Doc A/RES/60/1 (2005).

absence of the consent of the affected state, could only be justified in the most extreme circumstances. The mere presence of a natural hazard (earthquake, flood, storm, wildfire and so on) would not be sufficient. The hazard would have to have an impact upon the affected community in such a significant way that it causes, or threatens to cause, a massive loss of life or threat to health. Furthermore, the government of the affected state would have to be unwilling or unable to respond to that event and the delivery of aid or assistance must be truly humanitarian, that is based solely on the needs of the population.

The general principles of law recognised by civilised nations

Another source of international law, identified in the *Statute of the International Court of Justice*, is 'the general principles of law recognized by civilized nations'.[57] Brownlie argues that this provision allows the Court to borrow from domestic law the principles and reasoning that would assist the development of interstate relations.[58] If the national laws of 'civilized nations'[59] impose a widely recognised legal duty to rescue, then that duty could, if it 'would assist the development of interstate relations',[60] be borrowed and applied to states as part of international law.

A duty to come to the aid of other people is not a principle universally recognised in domestic law. It is traditionally said that common law countries, such as Australia, the United Kingdom, the United States and Canada, do not have a legal duty to rescue,[61] whereas the civil law countries, such as most European countries, do.[62] While there may be specific exceptions,[63] it can be accepted as a statement of general principle. In international law there are examples where a duty to assist others is imposed,[64] but the fact that these international duties exist does not establish a general rule that one state must provide aid to another. It may be argued that the various treaties establishing such a duty 'could be seen as a reflection of a lack in general international law of an equivalent norm'.[65] The fact that treaties create a duty on limited parties (for example coastal states), and in limited circumstances, certainly does not support an argument that the international community has accepted a universal, legal obligation to go to another state's aid.

---

57 *Statute of the International Court of Justice 1945* (Int) Art. 38(1)(c).
58 I. Brownlie, *Principles of Public International Law*, 6th edition, Oxford: Oxford University Press, 2003, p. 16.
59 *Statute of the International Court of Justice 1945* (Int) Art. 38(1)(c).
60 Brownlie, op. cit., p. 16.
61 A. McCall-Smith, 'The Duty to Rescue and the Common Law', in M.A. Menlowe and A. McCall-Smith (eds) *The Duty to Rescue: The Jurisprudence of Aid*, Aldershot: Dartmouth Publishing, 1993, p. 55.
62 A. Cadoppi, 'Failure to Rescue and the Continental Criminal Law', in M.A. Menlowe and A. McCall-Smith (eds) *The Duty to Rescue: The Jurisprudence of Aid*, Aldershot: Dartmouth Publishing, 1993, p. 93.
63 For example, *Criminal Code Act 1983* (NT) s 155.
64 See e.g. the *International Convention for the Safety of Life at Sea*, opened for signature 1 November 1974, UNTS 1184 (entered into force 25 May 1980); *International Convention on Salvage*, opened for signature 28 April 1989, UNTS 1953 (entered into force 14 July 1996); *International Convention on Maritime Search and Rescue*, opened for signature 27 April 1979, [1986] ATS 29 (entered into force 22 June 1985).
65 N. Nordstrom, 'Managing Transboundary Environmental Accidents: The State Duty to Inform', in D.D. Caron and C. Leben (eds) *The International Aspects of Natural and Industrial Catastrophes*, The Hague: Martinus Nijhoff, 2001, pp. 376–7.

What follows, from the discussion above, is that it is the responsibility of the affected state to manage the response to a disaster, leaving them, generally speaking, free to seek international assistance as they see fit; and it is the sovereign right of states to offer only that assistance that they wish to offer. There is no universal obligation imposed by international law that requires states to make assistance available.[66]

The importance of domestic laws

The absence of specific, universal international obligations may not be as significant an issue as it appears. The international community does respond to disasters across the world. The international response to events such as the 2003 Iranian earthquake,[67] the 2004 Boxing Day South East Asian Tsunami[68] and the 2011 Japanese earthquake and tsunami[69] are well known.

Although there are problems with international aid delivery, the solution may lie in domestic rather than international law. Fidler argues that:

> the direct role of international law with respect to policy on natural disasters will not grow significantly. . . . [T]he policy focus for the foreseeable future will involve political dynamics that make states hesitant to negotiate and accept far-reaching treaties that impose legally binding responsibilities with respect to disaster preparedness, protection, and response.[70]

The Red Cross/Red Crescent guidelines for international disaster response law

The International Federation of Red Cross and Red Crescent Societies has developed guidelines to allow countries to assess their domestic laws to facilitate international disaster assistance and to avoid the problems identified above. The *Guidelines for the Domestic Facilitation and Regulation of International Disaster Relief and Initial Recovery Assistance* ('the IDRL Guidelines') are intended to be used by states 'as a tool to examine their own legal, institutional and policy frameworks'[71] to determine if they are ready to deal with an influx of international disaster relief and/or to deliver aid should that be required.

The IDRL Guidelines urge the international community and states that are likely to need aid, or to send aid, to ensure that aid priorities are calculated on the basis of need alone, and that relief efforts are responsive to the needs of the affected community and in particular

66 See also V. Bannon, 'Rethinking Legal Mechanisms for Access and Facilitation of International Disaster Response in Cases of Natural Disaster', Master of Laws thesis, University of Melbourne, 2004, pp. 43–73; B. Okere and E.M. Makawa, 'Global Solidarity and the International Response to Disasters', in D.D Caron and C. Leben (eds) *The International Aspects of Natural and Industrial Catastrophes*, The Hague: Martinus Nijhoff, 2001, pp. 436–41.

67 BBC News, *Iran earthquake kills thousands*, 26 December 2003. Online. Available HTTP: <http://news.bbc.co.uk/2/hi/3348613.stm> (accessed 3 November 2011).

68 Telford et al., op. cit.

69 'Humanitarian response to the 2011 Tōhoku earthquake and tsunami', Wikipedia. Online. Available HTTP: <http://en.wikipedia.org/wiki/Humanitarian_response_to_the_2011_T%C5%8Dhoku_earthquake_and_tsunami> (accessed 3 November 2011).

70 Fidler, op. cit., p. 473.

71 *Guidelines for the Domestic Facilitation and Regulation of International Disaster Relief and Initial Recovery Assistance*, Geneva: International Federation of Red Cross and Red Crescent Societies, 2007, p. 9.

vulnerable groups within that community. Furthermore, the Guidelines recommend that actions be coordinated, that relief efforts meet minimum quality standards and services are provided by competent personnel with the involvement of the affected community.[72] They further recommend that where states provide aid by funding third-party organisations, they should take steps to ensure that the funded organisations comply with the principles[73] that are summed up by the words 'humanity, neutrality and impartiality'.[74]

A critical question when receiving disaster assistance is determining who should be allowed to provide aid. The IDRL Guidelines recommend that the necessary legal facilities to allow aid providers to operate, for example by recognising qualifications and allowing them to operate an office, should be extended to:

- assisting states (which would include state agencies such as defence or civil defence organisations);[75]
- humanitarian organisations that meet pre-established and published criteria, including a willingness to ensure that their aid is delivered on the basis of the overriding principles of 'humanity, neutrality and impartiality';[76] and as a corollary to this provision, states should have well-established procedures to allow for potential humanitarian actors to apply for the necessary legal facilities;[77] and
- other organisations that can assist 'such as private companies providing charitable relief, provided this does not negatively affect operations of assisting humanitarian organizations or assisting States'.[78]

There is no predominating and internationally recognised system to identify organisations that are effective, competent and accountable in the delivery of aid.[79] Some organisations, such as the Red Cross, have long-established histories and reputations that may reassure affected nations that they will be competent to provide the assistance that they promise, but others arise out of necessity where people simply observe the disaster, realise that they can assist and a new NGO is created.

It has been argued that a global system of 'accreditation and certification' should be in place to allow organisations that can demonstrate they have in place procedures to ensure that they are competent and accountable to be listed on an approved register of international providers.[80]

---

72 Ibid., [4(3)].
73 Ibid., [5(1)].
74 *Humanitarian Assistance to Victims of Natural Disasters and Similar Emergency Situations* (1988), GA Res 43/131, UN GAOR 43rd sess, 75th plen mtg, UN Doc A/RES/43/131.
75 Ibid., [13].
76 *Humanitarian Assistance to Victims of Natural Disasters and Similar Emergency Situations* (1988), GA Res 43/131, UN GAOR 43rd sess, 75th plen mtg, UN Doc A/RES/43/131; *Guidelines for the Domestic Facilitation and Regulation of International Disaster Relief and Initial Recovery Assistance*, [14(2)].
77 *Guidelines for the Domestic Facilitation and Regulation of International Disaster Relief and Initial Recovery Assistance*, [14(4)].
78 Ibid., [15].
79 Even though there are a number of schemes that set minimum standards in disaster relief, they are all voluntary and none is the primary or internationally adopted standard; see e.g. *The Sphere Project*, op. cit.; Humanitarian Accountability Partnership – International, *The 2010 HAP Standard in Accountability and Quality Management*, op. cit.; *The Code of Conduct for the International Red Cross and Red Crescent Movement and Non-Governmental Organisations (NGOs) in Disaster Relief*, op. cit.
80 Telford et al., op. cit., pp 120–21.

Such a system is, however, impractical; the limited mandate of the UN and the desire of NGOs to remain independent, including independent of an inherently political organisation like the United Nations, means that the UN is not seen as a suitable organisation to manage such a process. There is, however, no other entity that would appear able to fill the role of endorsing appropriate aid agencies. Further, an accreditation scheme necessarily excludes new NGOs that may arise in response to a particular incident and be able to provide a valuable service, but who have not had the time to commit themselves to particular standards or undergo an accreditation process.

It follows that deciding where aid should come from remains a matter for the affected state. States suffering from the impact of a disaster must decide whether they will restrict access to agencies with pre-established roles and relationships or throw their international borders open to all comers.

Having determined who is eligible to provide aid and assistance, preferably well before the impact of any hazard, the IDRL Guidelines urge affected states to:

- grant visas and permits without cost and without delay;
- recognise professional qualifications;
- facilitate freedom of movement to and about the disaster area;[81]
- exempt relief goods from all duties, tariffs, fees and import and export restrictions;
- avoid unnecessary inspection of incoming relief goods and, where inspection is required, ensure that it is done as a matter of priority;
- have in place arrangements to allow inspection and import clearance to take place at any time and anywhere;
- consider whether normal restrictions on the importation of food and the normal requirements to fumigate or quarantine food imports can be relaxed or waived;[82]
- recognise the registration of motor vehicles, boats and aircraft brought in by assisting agencies and allow them to be operated without being registered or issued with domestic registration or number plates;[83]
- allow assisting agencies to import and use their own telecommunications equipment and allocate the necessary frequencies and bandwidth to allow them to operate their communications devices;[84]
- facilitate the arrival of foreign relief aircraft, ships and vehicles and allow them to arrive, carry out their relief work and depart without the usual fees and charges such as landing fees at international airports and port fees at sea ports.[85] Aircraft operated by assisting agencies should be allowed to operate freely in the affected country;[86]
- grant whatever authority is required to allow assisting agencies to operate in the affected country. This would include providing necessary legal status to allow them to 'open bank accounts, enter into contracts and leases, acquire and dispose of property and instigate

---

81 *Guidelines for the Domestic Facilitation and Regulation of International Disaster Relief and Initial Recovery Assistance*, [16)].
82 Ibid., [18(4)].
83 Ibid., [18(1)].
84 Ibid., [18(2)].
85 Ibid., [19(1)].
86 Ibid., [19(2)].

legal proceedings',[87] and to employ local staff.[88] Assisting organisations should be free to import and export relief funds without regard to domestic currency restrictions;[89]

- exempt humanitarian relief agencies from all taxes including 'value-added' or goods and services taxes;[90]
- provide security for relief workers, relief supplies and for the premises and equipment used by relief agencies and assisting states;[91]
- ensure that all domestic agencies that are required to operate to facilitate disaster relief are open for extended hours during the disaster relief operations;[92] and
- assist in meeting the costs of disaster relief by waiving fees and charges and by providing domestic transport, the use of buildings and land free of charge and providing any 'cargo handling equipment and logistic support', without charge.[93]

Although they do not have the force of law, the IDRL Guidelines have been recognised by the UN and countries have been encouraged to 'take further steps to strengthen operational and legal frameworks for international disaster relief, taking into account the Guidelines, as appropriate'.[94]

Emerging issues, prospective research agenda and recommendations for law reform

The key issue in international disaster assistance remains, as it has been since at least 1932,[95] to ensure that disaster assistance is delivered on the basis of need rather than *ad hoc* generosity.[96] Concerns about the *ad hoc* and unpredictable nature of international disaster assistance were expressed by the United Nations Economic and Social Council when deliberating on the UN first formal resolution on disaster relief[97] and in subsequent resolutions as well as the resolutions of the International Red Cross and other non-government actors. Resolving the complex legal issues to ensure that aid is delivered when required, and on the basis of need alone, remains the ultimate objective for law reform in this area.

---

87 Ibid., [20(1)].
88 Ibid., [20(3)].
89 Ibid., [20(2)].
90 Ibid., [21].
91 Ibid., [22].
92 Ibid., [23].
93 Ibid., [24(2)].
94 *Strengthening of the Coordination of Emergency Humanitarian Assistance of the United Nations* (2010), GA Res 65/133, UN GAOR, 65th sess, 67th plen mtg, UN Doc A/RES/65/133, Art. 11.
95 *Convention and Statute Establishing an International Relief Union*, opened for signature 12 July 1927, CXXXV (1932–1933) LNTS 247 (entered into force 27 December 1932).
96 The International Relief Union was established to manage the international response to disasters so that donations to affected countries did not depend upon the generosity of donor states and individuals. The Union only provided operational assistance following earthquakes in 1934 and 1935 but was otherwise hampered by political concerns. The Union continued, at least in theory, following the establishment of the United Nations, but efforts to revive it were unsuccessful and the Union's assets and functions were finally transferred to the United Nations Economic and Social Council in 1967; P. Macalister-Smith, 'The International Relief Union: Reflections on the Convention Establishing an International Relief Union of July 12, 1927' *Tijdschrift voor Rechtsgeschiedenis* 54, 1986, 363, pp. 370–2.
97 *Assistance in Cases of Natural Disaster* (1964), GA Res 2034(XX) UN GAOR 20th sess, 1390th plen mtg, UN Doc A/RES/2034(XX).

Failing resolution of this 'holy grail' a number of legal issues exist that will benefit from further research and debate. A key emerging issue in the area of international emergency response will be the impact of climate change on the size and frequency of natural disasters and the foreseeable increased demand for international assistance. Climate change may make low-lying island nations and coastal areas uninhabitable and will require the community of nations to consider how affected populations will be moved and rehoused. The development of 'climate change refugees' will highlight the increasing overlap between the law governing refugees, internally displaced persons[98] and disaster relief.[99]

In order to minimise the impact of hazards on populations, and to reduce the calls for international assistance, the international community is encouraging governments to take steps to make their populations more resilient. The *Hyogo Framework for Action 2005–2015*[100] is intended to assist countries to incorporate disaster planning and reduce vulnerability, thereby decreasing the severity of the impact of natural hazards and the demands for international assistance. Vulnerable states will benefit from further research to assist them to reduce vulnerability through accurate risk assessment, improved local laws, efficient response agencies and appropriate land-use planning. Adapting to the likely impact of climate change is essential if communities are to be protected from hazards, rather than being left to be rescued when the hazard strikes.

Further work on the extent of the 'responsibility to protect' is also required. Following the impact of Cyclone Nargis on Burma in 2008 there were calls for the international community to intervene due to the failure of the government to allow foreign aid agencies to access the community and provide disaster relief.[101] Notwithstanding the failure of the UN General Assembly to include natural disasters in the circumstances that trigger the 'responsibility to protect' there is likely to be pressure to intervene if similar circumstances were to arise again. The limitation of the 'responsibility to protect' is likely to be tested and require further exploration and elaboration in the future.

Conclusion

This chapter has discussed the emerging area of international disaster response law. The question of when and how countries should respond to the needs of others affected by natural calamities has been a core concern of the international community since at least the time of the League of Nations. Notwithstanding this, the primary issue remains the same: how to ensure that aid is delivered quickly and on the basis of need and that disaster-affected

98 United Nations Office for the Coordination of Humanitarian Affairs. *Guiding Principles on Internal Displacement*, 2nd edn., 2004. Online. Available HTTP: <http://www.brookings.edu/fp/ projects/idp/resources/GPEnglish.pdf> (accessed 5 September 2011).

99 For further discussion of the issue of environmental refugees, see Chapter 40 by M. Burkett in this volume.

100 The ten-year action plan was adopted by 168 Member States of the United Nations at the World Disaster Reduction Conference, 2005; United Nations International Strategy for Disaster Reduction. *Hyogo Framework for Action*. Online. Available HTTP: <http://www.unisdr.org/we/ coordinate/hfa> (accessed 3 November 2011).

101 G. Evans, 'Facing Up to Our Responsibilities.' *The Guardian* 12 May 2008. Online. Available HTTP: <http://www.guardian.co.uk/commentisfree/2008/may/12/facinguptoourresponsbilities> (accessed 3 November 2011); French Embassy. *Burma – Cyclone Nargis*. Online. Available HTTP: <http://www.ambafrance-uk.org/Bernard-Kouchner-on-Burma-disaster.html> (accessed 3 November 2011).

populations are not relieved only when it is politically opportune or where the Western media takes a significant interest in the event.

Many steps have been taken to improve the coordination of the international response to disasters, to facilitate the delivery of aid and to ensure that aid that is provided meets some level of acceptable minimum standards. The basic problem, entrenched as it is in the concept of state sovereignty, remains. State sovereignty allows affected states to determine if and when they will call for aid, and from whom they will accept assistance, and leaves donor states free to offer help if and when, and on what terms that they choose.

Civil society through NGOs and IGOs has moved a long way to fill the gap by being willing to provide assistance and being prepared to offer aid even before it is asked. Some NGOs argue that they have a right to access affected populations regardless of the wishes of the affected government.[102] These arguments are not generally accepted but they do reflect the constant pressure on governments to ensure that affected populations are given the assistance that is on offer.

With more and more severe natural hazard events predicted to occur as a result of climate change, the need to regularise and make disaster assistance efficient and predictable will become more pressing.

---

102 In particular Médecins Sans Frontières, Aide Médicale Internationale and Médecins du Monde; Y. Beigbeder, *The Role and Status of International Humanitarian Volunteers and Organizations: The Right and Duty to Humanitarian Assistance*, Dordrecht: Martinus Nijhoff, 1991; R. Brauman, 'The Médecins sans Frontières Experience', in K.M. Cahill (ed.) *A Framework for Survival: Health, Human Rights, and Humanitarian Assistance in Conflicts and Disasters*, New York: Basic Books, 1993, p. 202.

Part VI
Contemporary and future challenges

36

"Treaty congestion" in contemporary international environmental law

Donald K. Anton

The rapid expansion of international environmental law in recent decades has led to what some commentators have termed "treaty congestion". Arguably the number of international instruments has hampered implementation. In particular, the lack of coordination in the face of proliferation and the lack of capacity challenge the operationalization of international environmental obligations by necessary and sufficient laws, policies, programs and plans. This contribution considers the issue of treaty congestion, and makes suggestions for how it might be overcome.

Introduction

Looking back now, the rapid growth of international environmental conventional norms that took place over roughly the last thirty years of the twentieth century is striking. Few fields have burst on the scene with as much unplanned fecundity. John Lawrence Hargrove was perhaps the only one who thought to ask in 1971, near the beginning of the modern international environmental law enterprise, "How much international law-making is required" to protect the global environment?[1] Answers were few, if any.

Instead, the standard account tells of a piecemeal and *ad hoc* development of international environmental law as a response to particular crises and new challenges and problems.[2] As treaties increased in number and international environmental law-making gathered steam, just keeping up to date required (and still requires) concerted effort. More significantly, the rapid growth of the law posed "treaty congestion" problems for states and the international system. This contribution is designed to provide, in short compass, a current review of treaty congestion, focusing in particular on its capacity and normative challenges.

---

1 J.L. Hargrove (ed.) *Law, Institutions and The Global Environment*, NY/Leiden: Oceana Publications/ A.W. Sijthoff, 1971, p. 170.
2 United Nations Environment Programme (UNEP), *Training Manual on International Environmental Law*, Nairobi: UNEP, 2006, p. 23.

The phenomenon of treaty congestion

Overwhelmed by treaties

The essence of treaty congestion lies in the appearance of too much law, too fast. For international environmental law, the normative proliferation took place in plain view and was contemporaneously chronicled in an array of treaty collections. Starting in the mid-1970s – and continuing with increasing frequency – an impressive host of general and specialized compilations of the multiplying numbers of multilateral environmental agreements appeared.[3] As is well known, by the late 1990s it was estimated that over 1,000 different international environmental legal instruments (hard and soft)[4] and 139 different major international environmental treaties[5] were in existence.

As this normative proliferation took place, one was reminded of Cicero's teaching, *summum ius summa iniuria* ("the more law, the less justice").[6] It also became apparent that the increasing number of treaties and subjects of international environmental obligation posed practical and normative concerns. These concerns were neatly encapsulated in a 1993 critique of contemporary international environmental law by Edith Brown Weiss.[7]

Brown Weiss identified that the surfeit of international environmental law could constitute too much of a good thing. She showed that it is possible that a swiftly expanding corpus of international environmental law might create two major problems. First, as a practical matter, a large number of new international environmental treaties might overwhelm the capacity of states to monitor, implement, and comply with a plethora of new obligations.[8] As a result, states might find that the impressive edifice of law they had created would prove ineffective in ameliorating the environmental problems addressed.[9] Second, and more normatively troubling, Brown Weiss highlighted that a large, growing, and uncoordinated body of international environmental law posed a danger of inconsistent obligations, overlapping norms, gaps in coverage, and outright duplication.[10]

Brown Weiss coined the term "treaty congestion" as a way to explain these capacity and normative problems.[11] She argued, however, that the solution to treaty congestion did not necessarily lie in slowing the process of norm creation, but rather in making the process more manageable and efficient.[12] Since Brown Weiss wrote, the phenomenon of treaty congestion has been widely observed and has garnered notable scholarly and professional attention. It has

---

3 See the extensive sources cited in an expanded online version of this chapter. D.K. Anton, ' "Treaty Congestion" in Contemporary International Environmental Law', nn. 5–7. Online. Available HTTP: <http://papers.ssrn.com/sol3/papers.cfm?abstract_id=1988579> (hereafter 'Anton Extended Version').
4 E.B. Weiss, 'Understanding Compliance with International Environmental Agreements: The Baker's Dozen Myths', *University of Richmond Law Review*, 1999, vol. 32, p. 1555.
5 United Nations Environment Programme (UNEP), *Register of International Treaties*, UN Doc. UNEP/GC.15/Inf.2 (1989).
6 Cicero, *De Officiis* (Walter Miller, trans.), Cambridge, MA: Harvard University Press, 1913, Bk I, p. 33.
7 E.B. Weiss, 'International Environmental Law: Contemporary Issues and the Emergence of a New World Order', *Georgetown Law Journal*, 1993, vol. 81, 675, pp. 697–702.
8 Ibid.
9 Ibid. See also 'Anton Extended Version', n. 15.
10 Ibid.
11 Ibid., n. 697.
12 Weiss, 'Contemporary Issues', op. cit., p. 697 n. 147. See also 'Anton Extended Version', n 18.

been treated in a variety of monographs[13] and is repeatedly mentioned in a voluminous periodic literature.[14]

A diminishing normative proliferation?

It should be noted that since approximately 2002 the negotiation and adoption of major global
and regional environmental agreements has seemingly slowed. This diminishing trend in
environmental treaty negotiation and adoption has been especially noticeable since 2005. The
International Environmental Agreements (IEA) Database Project reports the appearance of
only seventeen new multilateral agreements (and ten protocols) over the last seven years.[15] This
is striking when compared with 348 multilateral treaties and 149 protocols in the years between
1970 and 2004, an average of roughly 100 combined instruments every five years until 2005
– approximately three times more output every five years previous to the last seven.[16]

After three decades of international cooperation in establishing treaties, principles and
institutions, a noticeable shift towards implementation has taken place.[17] This was promi-
nently reflected in the Plan of Implementation produced at the 2002 World Summit on
Sustainable Development.[18] It is also evinced in the increasing adoption of protocols to
existing international environmental treaties to provide more operational detail. It could be
that this shift of resources to implementation has staunched norm creation, at least to a degree.
However, despite this apparent lessening in environmental norm creation, treaty congestion
remains a live aspect of international environmental law. A vast corpus of international environmental law exists that still challenges the capacity for effective implementation and poses
at least a latent potential for conflict.

Treaty congestion and the capacity challenge

Treaty congestion, especially when proliferating treaties are widely ratified, is invariably
accompanied by treaty over-commitment for significant numbers of states. Over-commitment
has been a feature of contemporary international environmental law and seriously challenges
the capacity of states to implement and comply with their international obligations. This is
especially so for states without the requisite human, institutional, and technological resources
to deal effectively, if at all, with expanding obligations. Of course, state compliance with
international environmental obligations is a necessary (if not always a sufficient) condition of
effectiveness in most cases – either in terms of fixing the environmental problem addressed or
in successfully changing state behavior in relation to treaty norms.[19]

---

13 See citations in 'Anton Extended Version', n. 19.
14 Ibid., n. 20.
15 See IEA Database Search Results, 'Multilateral Environmental Agreements for the period from
    2005 to 2011 (inclusive)'. Online. Available HTTP: <http://iea.uoregon.edu/> (accessed 8 May
    2012).
16 Ibid.
17 See C. Bruch and E. Mrema, 'UNEP Guidelines and Manual on Compliance with and Enforcement
    of Multilateral Environmental Agreements', *Proceedings of the Seventh International Conference on
    Environmental Compliance and Enforcement*, vol. 1, 2005, p. 1.
18 *Johannesburg Plan of Implementation of the World Summit for Sustainable Development*, UN Doc A/Conf
    199/20 (2002).
19 For detailed discussions of the meanings of implementation and compliance, especially as they are
    tied to effectiveness, see 'Anton Extended Version', n. 28.

Donald K. Anton

Over-commitment caused by treaty congestion poses a number of capacity challenges. Three in particular have been the source of concern for international environmental law. First, as noted, the basic ability to *comply* with substantive obligations is undermined by an unmanageable number of commitments. Second, as treaty bodies and institutions proliferate along with the growing corpus of conventions, the capacity of states to meaningfully *participate* in institutional activities to advance their interests is eroded. Third, the ability of states to adequately *monitor and report* on the implementation of their obligations, as international environmental treaties increasingly require, is hampered by treaty congestion. These capacity challenges can be conceptualized as substantive compliance challenges, institutional participation challenges, and monitoring and reporting process challenges. Each of these capacity challenges is explored below, along with strategies the international community has employed to help meet them.

Substantive compliance challenges

Substantive compliance challenges involve treaty congestion impediments that thwart the fulfillment of agreed environmental obligations with fundamental environmental outcomes – that is preventing pollution, reducing emissions, conserving biological diversity, protecting world heritage.[20] At bottom, these impediments stem from a lack of human, financial, and technological resources required to effectively implement obligations.[21] The lack of necessary financial and human capability virtually assures that compliance will be deficient.[22]

Even with a robust capacity, however, often additional impediments exist and effective implementation requires a variety of related abilities. These include the ability of a state: (i) to overcome domestic institutional weaknesses in political structures and legal frameworks; (ii) to remove market impediments; (iii) to provide missing incentives or remove perverse incentives; (iv) to effectively manage and coordinate across treaty obligations; (v) to effectively incorporate public participation and private sector involvement; and (vi) to access reliable and necessary information.[23] These capacity challenges are compounded by the complexity of a tangled web of multiple environmental regimes.[24]

Institutional challenges

Treaty congestion has greatly expanded the number of international environmental institutions that place demands on the attention and resources of states.[25] These institutions include

---

20 See generally *Bali Strategic Plan for Technology Support and Capacity Building*, Governing Council of the United Nations Environment Programme, Note by the Executive-Director, UN Doc UNEP/GC.23/6/Add.1 (23 December 2004).

21 D. Freestone, 'The Challenge of Implementation: Some Concluding Notes', in A. Boyle and D. Freestone (eds) *International Law and Sustainable Development*, Oxford: Oxford University Press, 1999, p. 360.

22 See M. Jänicke and H. Weidner, 'Summary: Global Environmental Policy Learning', in M. Jänicke and H. Weidner (eds) *National Environmental Policies: A Comparative Study of Capacity-Building*, Berlin: Springer, 1997, p. 309.

23 R.T. Watson, J.A. Dixon, S.P. Hamburg, A.C. Janetos and R.H. Moss, *Protecting Our Planet, Securing Our Future: Linkages Among Global Environmental Issues and Human Needs*, UNEP, US NASA, World Bank, 1998, p. 57.

24 P. Sand, *Lessons Learned in Global Environmental Governance*, Washington DC: World Resources Institute, 1990, p. 35.

25 See B.H. Desai, *Institutionalizing International Environmental Law*, Ardsley, NY: Transnational Publishers, 2004, pp. 279–80.

an array of treaty bodies – a plethora of regime-specific secretariats, conferences/meetings of parties, subsidiary bodies, non-compliance mechanisms, and working groups – created by the expanding treaty universe. These treaty bodies make significant capacity and expertise demands on states to engage in further normative development, internal and external compliance monitoring, decision-making regarding regime-specific projects, and decision-making regarding disputes.[26] The demands have continued to grow and have resulted in what has been called "institutional overload"[27] – the requirement of extensive and intensive party participation beyond capacity.[28] The institutional demands created by environmental treaty bodies are exacerbated by competing demands that come from other international institutions.[29]

Because treaty bodies and institutions exist independently of each other and are largely uncoordinated, the institutional framework is subject to significant administrative inefficacies. Consider, for instance, the burden imposed on states in terms of human and financial resources just to participate in institutional meetings. The number of meetings that require attendance is enormous. The timing of meetings is largely happenstance. The venues of meetings stretch around the globe. In 2010, for instance, it was reported that there were 63 major institutional and diplomatic meetings in a host of locations.[30]

Assuming attendance is possible, effective participation in these bodies imposes additional significant demands on the administrative capacity of states. The expertise required to be an effective participant is significant and treaty congestion has spread resources thin.[31] Of course, non-participation or perfunctory participation in institutional decision-making, compliance, and implementation activities compromises the ability of a state to promote its own interests. Just as importantly, it potentially deprives the institution or regime of ideas or additional options (possibly the best ones) that it might have had available if greater participation had been possible.

Monitoring and reporting process challenges

Perhaps the most immediate practical challenge that treaty congestion has raised is the way it can diminish the capacity of states to monitor and report on the implementation of the myriad environmental obligations established over the last 40 years.[32] Without an

26 See E. Hey, 'International Institutions' in D. Bodansky, J. Brunnee, and E. Hey (eds) *The Oxford Handbook of International Environmental Law*, Oxford: Oxford University Press, 2007, p. 749.

27 M.A. Levy, R.O. Keohane and P.M. Haas, 'Improving the Effectiveness of International Environmental Insitutions', in P.M. Haas, R.O. Keohane and M.A. Levy (eds) *Institutions for Earth: Sources of Effective International Environmental Protection*, Cambridge, MA: MIT Press, pp. 421–2.

28 A. Chayes and A.H. Chayes, *The New Sovereignty: Compliance with International Regulatory Agreements*, Cambridge, MA: Harvard University Press, 1995, p. 283.

29 P. Birnie, A. Boyle and C. Redgwell, *International Law and the Environment*, 3rd edn, Oxford: Oxford University Press, 2009, pp. 58–100.

30 See e.g. meetings covered by International Institute for Sustainable Development (IISD) Reporting Services in 2010. Online. Available HTTP: <http://www.iisd.ca/meetings/2010.html> (accessed 8 May 2012).

31 Preparatory Committee for the United Nations Conference on Sustainable Development, Second Session, *Objective and Themes of the United Nations Conference on Sustainable Development, Report of the Secretary-General*, UN Doc. A/CONF.216/PC/7 (22 December 2010), para. 108.

32 Cf. L. Gündling, 'Compliance Assistance in International Environmental Law: Capacity-Building Through Financial and Technology Transfer', *Zeitschrift für Ausländisches Öffentliches Recht und Völkerrecht*, vol. 56, 1996, p. 796.

international institutional authority to implement and monitor the treaty performance of states, obligations to monitor and report on activities related to implementation of and compliance with conventional requirements are now commonly imposed on states as an internal supervisory technique.[33] The proliferation of environmental reporting obligations under different treaties (in addition to non-environmental reporting obligations) can significantly overburden the administrative capacity of a state to accurately report or, indeed, to report at all.[34]

Capacity is challenged by the large number of monitoring and reporting requirements and significant differences in those requirements across regimes.[35] It is well known that even with the best of intentions, states – and developing states in particular – often lack, again, the human and financial resources to effectively superintend what are often voluminous international environmental commitments.[36] Even where commitments are not overwhelming, a lack of environmental expertise and management skills may still make implementation difficult.[37] As a result, states challenged by capacity have been found to limit their ratification to "general declaratory instruments not involving active participation [or] operational aspects" of technical implementation.[38]

Because subject matter varies greatly across environmental treaties, monitoring and reporting requirements demand a significant range of technology and expertise.[39] For instance, monitoring and reporting requirements can range from gathering and interpreting complex statistical details on production, imports, and exports under the Montreal Protocol on Substances that Deplete the Ozone Layer[40] and the Convention on Persistent Organic Pollutants[41] to accounting for all aspects of transboundary trade and disposal of hazardous wastes, including information on the grant of permits (including criteria) under the Basel Convention on the Control of Transboundary Movements of Hazardous Wastes.[42]

One of the most frequent concerns expressed in relation to implementation and compliance is a lack of human and administrative resources and expertise. In such circumstances, institutions need to be designed (and/or redesigned) to assist in upgrading capacity[43] and to

---

33 R. Wolfrum, 'Means of Ensuring Compliance with and Enforcement of International Environmental Law', *Recueil des Cours*, vol. 272, 1998, p. 37.

34 A. Kiss, 'Reporting Obligations and Assessment of Reports', in U. Beyerlin, P-T. Stoll and R. Wolfrum (eds) *Ensuring Compliance with Multilateral Environmental Agreements: A Dialogue Between Practitioners and Academia*, Leiden: Martinus Nijhoff, 2006, p. 245.

35 G. Loibl, 'Reporting and Information Systems in International Environmental Agreements as a Means for Dispute Prevention – The Role of "International Institutions" ', *Non-State Actors and International Law*, vol. 5, 2005, pp. 13, 15–16.

36 H. Mainhardt, 'Capacity-Building Strategies in Support of Multilateral Environmental Agreements', in L.E. Suskind, W. Moomaw, K. Gallagher and E. Corell (eds) *Reforming the International Enviornmental Treaty-Making System*, Cambridge, MA: PON Books, 2001, p. 183.

37 Ibid.

38 P. Sand (ed.) *The Effectiveness of International Environmental Agreements*, Cambridge: Grotius Publications Ltd, 1992, p. 11.

39 See e.g. P. Sands, *Principles of International Environmental Law*, Cambridge: Cambridge University Press, 2003, 2d ed., pp. 832–8.

40 *Montreal Protocol on Substances that Deplete the Ozone Layer*, Art. 7, UNTS, vol. 1522, p. 3 (as amended in 1990, 1992 and 1999).

41 *Convention on Persistent Organic Pollutants*, Art. 15, ILM, vol. 40, p. 532.

42 *Convention on the Control of Transboundary Movements of Hazardous Wastes*, Art. 13, UNTS, vol. 1673, p. 125.

43 P. Sand, 'Institution-building to Assist Compliance with International Environmental Law: Perspectives', *Zeitschrift für Ausländisches Öffentliches Recht und Völkerrecht*, vol. 56, 1996, pp. 774–95.

increase efficiencies in international administration, coordination, and integration across environmental regimes.[44]

Addressing the capacity challenge

Building capacity

Capacity-building measures are used as incentives to promote participation in international environmental regimes and to assist overburdened, resource-poor states in complying with and implementing international environmental obligations.[45] Whether these capacity-building incentives have been developed exclusively in response to treaty congestion is, however, doubtful. Well-worn and frequently copied provisions existed before treaty congestion prompted developed states to "offer assistance with inventories, reporting, training, and an empty promise of technology transfer".[46] Nevertheless, with the advent of treaty congestion, financing and effective transfer of technology became much more a focus for negotiations between developed and developing states.[47] By 1992, the "new and equitable global partnership" for sustainable development[48] was dependent on "new and additional financial resources" and "access to environmentally sound technologies" for developing states.[49]

David Freestone has highlighted research demonstrating that a large range of capacity is crucially dependent on adequate funding.[50] Building on the growing financing and technology focus, developing countries have insisted on provisions in several treaties that seek to condition the fulfillment of their environmental obligations on the receipt of financial and technological support needed to build capacity in order to meet commitments.[51] Conditionality aside, however, "financial and technical assistance is a necessary, but clearly insufficient, condition to promote capacity."[52] Indeed, some evidence suggests international financial assistance often fails to drive the environmental policy goals it is designed to accomplish.[53] It certainly is not as easy

---

44 F. Biermann, 'The Emerging Debate on the Need for a World Environment Organization: A Commentary', *Global Environmental Politics*, vol. 1, 2001, pp. 45–55.

45 H.K. Jacobson and E.B. Weiss, 'Assessing the Record and Designing Strategies to Engage Countries', in E.B. Weiss and H.K. Jacobson (eds) *Engaging Countries: Strengthening Compliance with International Environmental Accords*, Cambridge, MA: MIT Press, 1998, p. 546.

46 Mainhardt, op. cit., pp. 184–5.

47 Freestone, op. cit., p. 360.

48 Preamble, para. 3, *Rio Declaration on Environment and Development*, Report of the United Nations Conference on Environment and Development, vol. 1, UN Doc. A/CONF.151/26/Rev.1 (Vol. I) (New York: United Nations, 1993), p. 3.

49 'Overview of Agenda 21 and Implementation Mechanisms', Report of the Secretary-General, UN Doc. A/CONF.151/PC/100/Add.1, reprinted in Nicholas A. Robinson (ed.), *Agenda 21 and the UNCED Proceedings*, vol. 1, (New York: Oceana Publications Inc.), at p. 54.

50 Freestone, op. cit., pp. 361–2.

51 See e.g. *Montreal Protocol on Substances that Deplete the Ozone Layer*, Art. 5(5), as amended by *Amendments to the Montreal Protocol on Substances that Deplete the Ozone Layer*, Art. 1(P), Annex II of the Report of the Second Meeting of the Parties, UN Doc. UNEP/OzL.Pro.2/3 (29 June 1990); *United Nations Framework Convention on Climate Change* (UNFCCC), Art. 4 (7), UNTS, vol. 1771, p. 107; Art. 20(4), *Convention on Biological Diversity*, UNTS, vol. 1760, p. 142.

52 M.A. Drumbl, 'Does Sharing Know Its Limits? Thoughts on Implementing International Environmental Agreements', *Virginia Environmental Law Journal*, vol. 18, 1999, p. 287.

53 E.R. DeSombre, 'Encouraging Participation in International Environmental Agreements', in Ho-Won Jeong (ed.) *Global Environmental Policies: Institutions and Procedures*, Basingstoke: Palgrave, 2011, pp. 203–205.

as "leap-frogging" dirty technology that money and access to technology on favorable terms may allow.[54] Instead, real and long-lasting improvements in human and technological capacity require a much broader approach that also successfully addresses structural deficiencies, institutional weaknesses, managerial hurdles, and problems in capacity retention.[55] Capacity-building must be integrated in new governance structures at the global level.

At the treaty level, it has been suggested that every instrument ought to establish a holistic "capacity-building management unit" (CBMU).[56] It is true that the CBMU would add another treaty body to the existing mix. However, unlike the treaty bodies already mentioned, a CBMU would not be a challenge or drain on capacity; just the opposite. It would be responsible for determining capacity-building needs and effectively enhancing participation and implementation across the regime.[57] In other words, a CBMU's function is to ensure ultimate self-reliance and provide assistance in achieving that goal. Of course, a CBMU would need to be sufficiently resourced, including an ability to provide funding and technology on a recurrent basis if necessary.

Enhancing institutional efficiencies

The fragmented, uncoordinated, and underfunded nature of global environmental governance by international institutions,[58] such as it is, poses another significant challenge raised by treaty congestion. As new institutions created by new treaties have proliferated, the need to coordinate supervisory responsibilities and administrative requirements has grown.[59] While a loose set of some cooperative arrangements between some institutions exists, an extensive literature has grown up around advancing international reform that entails a host of institutional proposals.[60]

One central idea is the need to simplify and streamline. In order to accomplish this, the creation of an overarching and unified organization for the environment has been urged. It is postulated that such an organization would reduce the burdens of institutional overload on states by eliminating overlap and redundancy and increasing efficiency. It is also argued that a global environmental organization would have enhanced standing and resources, leading to greater effectiveness.[61]

The most recent work on institutional and governance reform is bound up with the 2012 United Nations Conference on Sustainable Development (UNCSD) (Rio+20). One of the two

54 Drumbl, op. cit., p. 287.
55 D. Fairman and M. Ross, 'Old Fads, New Lessons: Learning from Economic Development Assistance', in R.O. Keohane and M.A. Levy (eds) *Institutions for Environmental Aid*, Cambridge, MA: MIT Press, 1996, pp. 29, 41–5.
56 Mainhardt, op. cit., pp. 188–91.
57 Ibid.
58 See G.C. Bryner, *From Promises to Performance: Achieving Global Environmental Goals*, New York/London: W.W. Norton & Co., 1997, chapter 4.
59 E.R. DeSombre, *Global Environmental Institutions*, Abingdon: Routledge, 2006, p. 2.
60 For a good collection of proposals see D. Hunter, J. Salzman and D. Zaelke, *International Environmental Law and Policy*, New York: Foundation Press, 3rd edn, 2007, pp. 234–48. For more detail see Anton Extended Version, n. 80.
61 The various models of reform and arguments pro and con are extensively canvassed in F. Biermann and S. Bauer (eds) *A World Environment Organization: Solution or Threat for Effective Environmental Governance?*, Aldershot/Burlington: Ashgate, 2005.

major themes of UNCSD will be "the institutional framework for sustainable development".[62] During the preparatory process for the Conference, UNEP was involved on a number of fronts, including convening the Consultative Group of Ministers or High-level Representatives on International Environmental Governance which produced the *Nairobi–Helsinki Outcome* in November 2010.[63] The *Outcome* focuses the international community's attention on six institutional/governance issues: (i) strengthening capacity in the "science–policy interface" to facilitate cooperation in management, analysis, use, and exchange of environmental information; (ii) developing a system-wide strategy for the environment in the UN system to "increase effectiveness, efficiency and coherence"; (iii) locating synergies between international environmental treaties in order to jointly deliver "common multilateral environmental agreement services with the aim of making them more efficient"; (iv) creating a stronger link between policy-making and financing; (v) developing a system-wide capacity-building network "to ensure a responsive and cohesive approach to meeting country needs"; and (vi) strengthening engagement at the regional level by "increasing the capacity of UNEP regional offices".[64]

The Consultative Group also recognized in the *Outcome* the need to further develop five options for broader institutional reform previously identified by UNEP. These options include: (i) enhancing UNEP; (ii) establishing a new umbrella organization for sustainable development, (iii) establishing a specialized agency such as a world environment organization, (iv) reforming ECOSOC (the Economic and Social Council) and the CSD (Commission for Sustainable Development); or (v) enhancing institutional reforms and streamlining existing structures.[65] It remains to be seen what the institutional/governance outcome of UNCSD will be. However, following the second UNCSD preparatory commission in March 2011, Steven Bernstein and Jutta Brunnée were retained to prepare a consultant report on *Options for Broader Reform of the Institutional Framework for Sustainable Development* (IFSD).[66] It assesses the structural, legal, and financial implications of options for reform identified in the *Nairobi–Helsinki Outcome*. Perhaps most importantly for treaty congestion, the IFSD report places significant attention on ways and means to enhance capacity and emphasizes the need to simplify and streamline the current institutional framework.

Treaty congestion and normative challenges

The large and heterogeneous collection of international environmental treaties and the corpus of law they contain pose normative challenges. The great expansion of international environmental norms raises the prospect that different norms governing the same issue will run up against each other in conflict and incoherence.

---

62 GA Res. 64/236, UN Doc. A/RES/64/236 (24 December 2009), at para. 20(a).
63 UNEP Governing Council Decision SS.XI/1, UN Doc. UNEP GC/SS.XI/1 (26 February 2010); *Nairobi–Helsinki Outcome*, Second Meeting of the Consultative Group of Ministers or High Representatives on International Environmental Governance, Espoo, Finland, 21–23 November 2010. Online. Available HTTP: <http://www.unep.org/environmentalgovernance/Portals/8/documents/Events/NairobiHelsinkifinaloutcomeedited.pdf> (accessed 8 May 2012).
64 Ibid., para. 7.
65 Ibid., paras 11–13.
66 The IFSD analysis. Online. Available HTTP: <http://www.uncsd2012.org/rio20/content/documents/322IFSD%20FIVE%20OPTIONS%20REPORT%20-%20FINAL%20VERSION%201%20NOV%20for%20posting.pdf> (accessed 8 May 2012).

Overlap and conflict

Brown Weiss highlighted that treaty congestion has the potential to create a conflict of norms because of the overlap of substance and coverage of different treaty regimes.[67] Much of the normative overlap has been without incident and is, perhaps, mostly benign.[68] However, the potential for serious conflict tends to undermine overall effectiveness by creating uncertainty about interpretation and application and because international law can only imperfectly resolve such conflicts.[69]

Institutional competition

Institutional proliferation can be viewed as a form of congestion creating rivalries over competence and jurisdiction.[70] This sort of competition can take place between treaty bodies or the adjudicative fora available under a growing number of international environmental treaties.[71] Normative overlap and the potential conflict in interpretation has been of greatest concern, even though accommodation is perhaps more common.

Take the well-known potential for friction between World Trade Organization (WTO) norms and various international environmental treaties, for example.[72] The provisions of the Montreal Protocol on Substances that Deplete the Ozone Layer[73] restrict trade with non-parties[74] and appear to offend prohibitions on quantitative restrictions and discrimination between like products established by the 1994 General Agreement on Tariffs and Trade (GATT)[75] – a situation ripe for conflict. However, a GATT trade expert and the Secretariat of the Montreal Protocol expressed compatible views that the restrictions were justified GATT exceptions and that the exceptions' "disguised restrictions" limitation did not apply.[76]

Similarly, in the *MOX Plant* litigation, four different actions were launched in different jurisdictions (three by Ireland and one by the European Commission),[77] under four different

---

67 Weiss, 'Contemporary Issues', op. cit., pp. 699–700.
68 T. Stephens, *International Courts and Environmental Protection*, Cambridge: Cambridge University Press, 2009, p. 272.
69 R. Wolfrum and N. Matz, *Conflicts in International Environmental Law*, Berlin: Springer, 2003, p. 3.
70 T. Gehring, 'Treaty-Making and Treaty Evolution', in D. Bodansky, J. Brunnee and E. Hey (eds) *The Oxford Handbook of International Environmental Law*, Oxford: Oxford University Press, 2007, pp. 475–6.
71 C.P.R. Romano, *The Peaceful Settlement of International Disputes: A Pragmatic Approach*, The Hague/London/Boston: Kluwer Law International, 2000, pp. 91–2.
72 See e.g. P.K. Rao, *The World Trade Organization and the Environment*, New York: St Martin's Press, 2000.
73 UNTS, vol. 1522, p. 3.
74 Ibid., Arts 4 and 4A (as amended).
75 General Agreement on Tariffs and Trade (revised to 1994), UNTS, vol. 55, p. 187, reprinted as amended, GATT Secretariat, *Legal Instruments – Results of the Uruguay Round*, Geneva, Switzerland: GATT Secretariat, 1994.
76 See R.E. Benedick, *Ozone Diplomacy: New Directions in Safeguarding the Planet*, Cambridge, MA: Harvard University Press, 1991, p. 91; D. Pruzin, 'Ozone Depletion: Trade Measures Under Montreal Pact Justified, Secretariat Tells Trade Body', *International Environment Daily*, Washington DC: Bureau of National Affairs, 30 June 1999.
77 The four judicial bodies concerned with the matter included the International Tribunal for the Law of the Sea (ITLOS), an UNCLOS Annex VII arbitral tribunal (under the auspices of the Permanent Court of Arbitration (PCA)), an arbitral tribunal convened under the Convention for the Protection of the Marine Environment of the North East Atlantic (OSPAR Convention) (under ICSID auspices), and the European Court of Justice. For relevant disposition of the cases, see 'Anton Expanded Version' at n. 100.

regimes,[78] against the United Kingdom over activities associated with a nuclear reprocessing plant located on the Irish Sea in north-west England.[79] An underlying jurisdictional tension ran throughout the litigation but was resolved without contradictory jurisprudence.

The initial action started in June 2001 with a request by Ireland for the establishment of an arbitral tribunal under the OSPAR Convention. Ireland claimed the UK had violated OSPAR by failing to provide access to information on the MOX plant as required by Article 9. In October 2001, Ireland commenced Annex VII proceedings under UNCLOS against the UK, asserting more direct environmental breaches under a number of the Convention's marine environmental protection provisions. Ireland also foreshadowed that it intended to commence action in the European Court of Justice (ECJ) for alleged breaches of the EC Treaty and EURATOM treaty. On 15 November 2001, pending the constitution of the UNCLOS Annex VII arbitral tribunal (and one month before the plant was due to be commissioned), Ireland requested the indication of provisional measures by ITLOS against the UK. It was determined by ITLOS that the Annex VII tribunal had *prima facie* jurisdiction and the provisional measures were prescribed on 3 December 2001. In July 2003, the OSPAR arbitral tribunal found in favor of the United Kingdom. In the meantime, before Ireland could act in the ECJ, the European Commission successfully initiated action against Ireland in the same court, asserting that the Irish claims pending before the UNCLOS Annex VII tribunal violated the exclusive jurisdiction of the ECJ.

Three interesting competing institutional aspects of jurisdiction were in high relief in this litigation. First, the wide choice of litigation options available to Ireland allowed a certain degree of strategic "forum shopping" for remedies tailored to needs (i.e. for information, for provisional measures, and for prevention of environmental harm). One can see little harm in this case, but one can easily imagine situations where an applicant's expediency might be used to thwart justice.[80]

Second, whenever ITLOS prescribes provisional measures in a case whose merits are to be decided by arbitration under Part XV of UNCLOS, differing views and tensions about merits jurisdiction are possible. In the *MOX Plant* litigation both ITLOS and the arbitral tribunal were in accord about the presence of merits jurisdiction. But this is not invariable and one is reminded of the prescription of provisional measures after finding *prima facie* jurisdiction in the *Southern Bluefin Tuna* dispute by ITLOS[81] and the subsequent dismissal of the same case for want of jurisdiction by the Annex VII tribunal.[82]

Third, if the UNCLOS Annex VII tribunal had not suspended the hearing of the merits until the ECJ could rule on competence and then terminated the proceedings with consent of the parties, real conflict over jurisdiction could have become live. Indeed, the possibility of an inconsistent ECJ judgment and Annex VII award was present. For now, though, it appears

---

78 United Nations Convention on the Law of the Sea, UNTS, vol. 1833, p. 3; OSPAR Convention, reprinted in ILM, 1993, vol. 32, p. 1069; Treaty Establishing the European Economic Community (EC Treaty),UNTS, vol. 298, p. 11 (as amended); Treaty Establishing the European Atomic Energy Authority (EURATOM treaty), *UNTS*, vol. 298, p. 169 (as amended).

79 For an overview see N. Lavranos, 'Epilogue in the MOX Plant Dispute: An End Without Findings', *European Energy and Environmental Law Review*, 2009, vol. 18, p. 180.

80 Stephens, op. cit., pp. 275–9.

81 Southern Bluefin Tuna Cases (*New Zealand v Japan; Australia v Japan*) (Cases Nos 3 & 4), ITLOS, Order of 27 August 1999 (provisional measures), reprinted in ILM, 1999, vol. 38, p. 1634.

82 Southern Bluefin Tuna Case (*Australia and New Zealand v Japan*), Annex VII Arbitral Award on Jurisdiction and Admissibility, August 4, 2000, reprinted in ILM, 2000, vol. 39, p. 1359.

that the ECJ has exclusive jurisdiction over EC members in cases that may overlap with treaties that have higher environmental standards than the EC Treaty.

These two examples highlight the potential for institutional conflict that treaty congestion can create. When one considers the vast institutional environmental structure in place, it appears, though, that these institutions operate with a basic level of at least understanding co-existence. What are needed now are more formal structures of coordination to allow for faster progress in meeting the challenge of international environmental problems.

Normative conflict

Outside of institutional proliferation, the normative aspect of treaty congestion, in particular, has been increasingly analyzed under the banner of "fragmentation"[83] or, in older parlance, "conflicts"[84] in international law. The recognition of the basic problem, however, goes back to at least the Congresses of Vienna.[85] By the early twentieth century international jurisprudence had started to confront the issue[86] and scholarship about normative conflict begins with the advent, in significant numbers, of major multilateral treaties[87] and the appearance of the Draft Articles on the Law of Treaties.[88]

In the contemporary world of international environmental law, treaty congestion has meant that the international community faces topic-specific and specialized regimes in greater and greater numbers at sub-regional, regional, and global levels. This is coupled with nominal vertical coordination in the international legal system and the appearance of so-called functionally "self-contained" systems.[89] Functionally isolated normative regimes can be seen to challenge the coherence of an international legal system. They also heighten the possibility of conflict between international environmental legal norms applicable to the same act or omission and across different subject matter areas of international law such as human rights, trade and investment law, the laws of war and humanitarian law, and others. International law does not currently provide an adequate means for the satisfactory resolution of conflict beyond the limited operation of Articles 30, 53, and 59 of the 1969 Vienna Convention on the Law of Treaties.[90]

83 See the extensive sources cited in 'Anton Extended Version', n. 106.
84 Ibid., at n. 107.
85 See G. Binder, *Treaty Conflict and Political Contradiction: The Dialectic of Duplicity*, New York/Connecticut/London: Praeger, 1988, chapter 3.
86 Ibid.
87 See e.g., C.W. Jenks, 'The Conflict of Law-Making Treaties', *British Yearbook of International Law*, 1953, vol. 30, p. 401; P. Cobbett, *Cases on International Law*, 1947, vol. 1 Peace, p. 368; Q. Wright, 'Conflicts Between International Law and Treaties', *American Journal of International Law*, 1917, vol. 11, p. 566.
88 See Report on the Law of Treaties, *Yearbook of the International Law Commission*, 1953, vol. II, pp. 156–9, UN Doc. A/CN.4/63 (1953); Second Report on the Law of Treaties, *Yearbook of the International Law Commission*, 1954, vol. II, pp. 133–9, UN Doc. A/CN.4/87 and Corr.1 (1954); Third Report on the Law of Treaties, *Yearbook of the International Law Commission*, 1958, vol. II, pp. 41–5, UN Doc. A/CN.4/115 and Corr.1 (1958); Fourth Report on the Law of Treaties, *Yearbook of the International Law Commission*, 1959, vol. II, pp. 61–2, UN Doc. A/CN.4/120 (1959).
89 See *Prosecutor v Tadic*, Case No. IT-94-1-I, Decision on Defense Motion for Interlocutory Appeal on Jurisdiction, 11 (2 October 1995), reprinted in ILM, 1996, vol. 35, pp. 32, 39.
90 UNTS, vol. 1155, p. 331. See D.R. Rothwell, 'Relationship Between the Environmental Protocol and UNEP Instruments', in D. Vidas (ed.) *Implementing the Environmental Protection Regime for the Antarctic*, Dordrecht: Kluwer Academic Publishers, 2000, pp. 230–32.

Conflict, or potential conflict, between competing international environmental norms can be resolved in a number of ways. First and no doubt hardest, it is possible, in theory at least, for states to establish a general hierarchy of treaties or norms, as a matter of positive law, in which treaties are ranked according to their objects and normative content. This model of reconciliation focuses on areas of regulation as such and ranks them in order of importance. The more important the norm or goal at stake, the more priority it has.[91] This, of course, is precisely what the policy-oriented New Haven school aspires to achieve with the value of human dignity as polestar.[92]

If such a value-laden exercise was possible, whether environmental protection would be accorded a high-level trumping value in this sort of hierarchy is questionable. Moreover, a formal fix by states does not appear on the foreseeable horizon. In this situation and in a structurally horizontal legal world of treaty congestion it seems that the ideas of cross-fertilization and legal pluralism may assist in bolstering environmental protection at institutional centers (the likely site of the most intense competition) and normative margins (at least as between competing environmental norms).

Cross-fertilization and legal pluralism

Cross-fertilization

Cross-fertilization can assist treaty congestion to overcome the anxiety created by the isolation of the norms and institutions of diverse, functionally oriented regimes – the isolation of so-called "self-contained systems". Cross-fertilization provides the potential for the infusion of concepts, principles, and rules from one area of law into another.[93] Cross-fertilization occurs when new legal solutions to existing problems are proffered using rules or principles from other areas of international law. Cross-fertilization may result in the creation of new or the adaptation of existing legal principles, norms, and rules. Law, in this sense of transplantation from one field of law to another (or, indeed, from one legal system to another),[94] is parasitical. It is much like how a living language appropriates outside nomenclature and grammar for its own.[95] Optimally, cross-fertilization uses and embroiders on extrinsic material in order to adapt and thrive. It "shows an assimilative power which, to all appearance, grows by what it feeds on".[96]

---

91 Such normative hierarchies are well anchored in municipal legal systems. See R. Pound, 'Hierarchy of Sources and Forms in Different Systems of Law', *Tulane Law Review*, 1933, vol. 7, p. 475.

92 M.S. McDougal, H.D. Lasswell and W.M. Reisman, 'The World Constitutive Process of Authoritative Decision', in M.S. McDougal and W.M. Reisman (eds) *International Law Essays: A Supplement to International Law in Contemporary Perspective*, Mineola, NY: Foundation Press, 1981, pp. 191, 201.

93 See J. Fawcett, 'Cross-Fertilization in Private International Law', *Current Legal Problems*, 2000, vol. 53, p. 303 (defining cross-fertilization as the process by which 'rules in one area of . . . international law influence the rules in another area'.)

94 For a variety of reasons, legal transplants do not always go well or take as anticipated. See e.g. W.L. Andreen, 'Environmental Law and International Assistance: The Challenge of Strengthening Environmental Law in the Developing World', *Columbia Journal of Environmental Law*, 2000, vol. 25, pp. 17, 26–32.

95 See L.M. Friedman, *A History of American Law*, New York: Simon & Schuster, 1973, pp. 13–14.

96 F. Pollock, *The Genius of the Common Law*, New York: Columbia University Press, 1912, p. 77.

In international law, the use of cross-fertilization as a technique or stratagem harks back to the legal system's natural law foundations.[97] An attentive reading, for instance, of the authorities and sources employed by Franciscus de Vitoria in his 1532 *De Indis recenter inventis relectio prior*, or Alberico Gentili in his 1598 *De iure belli libri tres*, or Grotius in his 1625 *De jure belli ac pacis libri tres*, shows the free use of precepts and ideas from the Old and New Testament, Aristotle, the "Fathers of the Church", theologians, canonists, glossators, and commentators. In medieval Europe, in an age without modern national legal systems, "[c]ross-fertilization was the order of the day, because the law was seen as a vast treasure house from which kings and nations could pick and choose what suited them."[98]

Before the close of World War II, cross-fertilization took place, for the most part, within largely self-contained legal systems, and occasionally families of legal systems.[99] Following World War II, and with increasing frequency since, the judicial borrowing across fields, jurisdictions, and even disciplines has continued apace.[100]

Cross-fertilization in the international legal system must account for the consensual nature of international law. This makes borrowing and applying rules of decision outside of consent more difficult. Major multilateral agreements sometimes allow for cross-fertilization in one form or another.[101] However, Article 31(3)(c) of the Convention on the Law of Treaties is more generally relevant. This provision allows for consideration of "any relevant rules of international law applicable in the relations between the parties".[102] This is important not as a matter of hierarchy or priority in case of conflict, but as a matter of cross-fertilization by interpretation.[103] Provided an outside norm is relevant and applicable, other rules of international law outside the treaty have an informative, possibly mediating, role to play when taken into account as required by the law of treaties. This, of course, does not dictate environmentally friendly results even when relevant and applicable environmental norms are brought to bear under Article 31(3)(c). It does mean, however, that at least such a result is possible.

Legal pluralism

Legal pluralism can be thought of as the counterpart to cross-fertilization. It accepts an institutional and normative fragmentation with the multiplicity of competing institutions

---

97 See generally, P. Allott, *The Health of Nations*, Cambridge, Cambridge University Press, 2002, pp. 410–11.

98 R.C. van Caenegem, *European Law in the Past and the Future: Unity and Diversity over Two Millennia*, Cambridge: Cambridge University Press, 2002, pp. 1–2.

99 R. David and J.E.C. Brierley, *Major Legal Systems in the World Today: An Introduction to the Comparative Study of Law*, London: Stevens & Sons, 3rd ed., 1985, p. 25; D. Williams, 'Courts and Globalization, *Indiana Journal of Global Legal Studies*, 2004, vol. 3, pp. 57, 66.

100 See e.g. F.G. Jacobs, 'Judicial Dialogue and the Cross-Fertilization of Legal Systems: The European Court of Justice', *Texas International Law Journal*, vol. 38, p. 547.

101 See e.g. *Understanding on Rules and Procedures Governing the Settlement of Disputes*, Art. 3.2, Annex 2 to the Agreement Establishing the World Trade Organization, UNTS, vol. 1867, p. 401; Arts 293, 297(1)(b), 301, 304, UNCLOS, UNTS, vol. 1833, p. 3.

102 UNTS, vol. 1155, pp. 331, 340.

103 See C. Brown, 'The Cross-Fertilization of Principles Relating to Procedure and Remedies in the Jurisprudence of International Courts and Tribunals', *Loyala of Los Angeles International and Comparative Law Review*, 2008, vol. 30, pp. 219, 232–3; P. Sands, 'Treaty, Custom and the Cross-Fertilization of International Law', *Yale Human Rights & Development Law Journal*, 1998, vol. 1, pp. 85, 102–105.

brought forth by treaty congestion. However, instead of seeing only disadvantage in such a situation, legal pluralism embraces the diffusion of power that competing institutions entail.[104]

If all or most normative and institutional control is unitary and rests at the centre of a system, then very limited (perhaps only one) opportunity exists to influence activities, decisions, policies, programs, and so on. Disenchantment with outcomes can be much more profound and lasting in such a system. In a more normatively and institutionally variegated system, like the present one, disenchantment with outcomes will still arise. But these disappointments have the potential to be offset by other outcomes at other centers of power and decision-making involved in international environmental issues.

So long as this diffuse power operates within the basic framework of international law, then diversity and difference can be healthy for international law. Anne-Marie Slaughter writes about this diversity as a principle of "legitimate difference", which "enshrines pluralism as a basis for, rather than a bar to, regulatory cooperation, leaving open the possibility of further convergence . . . but not requiring it".[105]

In a world of treaty congestion accompanied by fragmentation, legal pluralism offers the possibility of a development of international law to improve conditions on Earth through interaction by a wide range of institutions engaged in the international law enterprise. Legitimate differences and the dialogue enabled by cross-fertilization in interpretation, application, and development of international law might even lead to better decisions[106] and strengthen compliance.[107]

Conclusion

Treaty congestion has been a fact of modern international law for a number of decades. As greater international cooperation is required to address global problems, the need for more law to implement cooperation accompanies. The response to fragmentation and conflict arising from the proliferation of norms that accompanies environmental treaty congestion has ranged from that of the despairingly alarmist to the overly optimistic. Between these extremes it is necessary to accept that a realistic appraisal must take account of the current limitations imposed by the international legal system.

While improving governance structures and coordination functions may help improve the situation, those with strong environmental values must be on guard to limit the extent of environmentally unfavorable interpretation and application of competing norms. It is likewise important to attempt to ensure that the institutional treatment of environmental norms first of all takes place, and secondly, adheres to the environmental purpose and objective of the norms. It is inevitable that there will be failures and disappointments, but increased coordination and synergies across normative boundaries and enhanced capacity-building will help minimize them.

---

104 See W.T. Worster, 'Competition and Comity in the Fragmentation of International Law, *Brooklyn Journal of International Law*, 2008, vol. 34, p. 119.
105 A-M. Slaughter, *A New World Order*, Princeton, NJ: Princeton University Press, 2004, p. 249.
106 Worster, op. cit., p. 141
107 W. Burke-White, 'International Legal Pluralism', *Michigan Journal of International Law*, 2004, vol. 25, pp. 963, 978–9.

37

Sustainable development and international environmental law

Klaus Bosselmann

Sustainable development has emerged as the dominant theme in environmental governance. Yet its definition remains ambiguous. It is argued that an interpretation of 'sustainable development' as 'ecologically sustainable development' is supported by history and academic scholarship. For example, the concept of sustainability has been known for hundreds of years, is consistent with the Brundtland Report and more recent publications including 'Harmony with Nature' of the UN Secretary General. Ecologically sustainable development provides clear guidance for the further development of international environmental law: from (reductionist) environmental law to (integrative) sustainability law. These issues will be explored in this chapter.

Introduction

The concept of sustainable development has entered international environmental law through the *Rio Declaration* and *Agenda 21*, both adopted at the 1992 Earth Summit. It has since been referred to in numerous soft-law documents and treaties, but still lacks a legally binding definition. Essentially, sustainable development relates the concern for the carrying capacity of Earth's natural systems to the concern for economic and social developments. The exact relationship between these two concerns is the subject of ongoing ethical and political debate, yet is crucially important for the legal quality and enforceability of the concept.

While the composite term 'sustainable development' is relatively new, the underlying idea of sustainability is not. Societies and civilizations have always altered their physical environments (landscapes, waterways, vegetation, wildlife) to their advantage and were often confronted with environmental problems such as droughts, floods, desertification, erosion or loss of vegetation and species. Continued success and development were dependent on living sustainably with nature. This has not changed over time. However, the environmental problems of the past were localized and often temporary, allowing for adjustments through space (moving on) and time (easing pressure). Today's environmental problems are global, inter-related and dynamic. In an overpopulated world with ever-increasing demands on natural resources the adjustments of the past are no longer available. The only option left is to live sustainably within the limits of ecological systems, whether local or global. This is the challenge of sustainable development. As nature knows no boundaries, the legal challenge is to regulate economic and social development at all levels (local, regional and global) in a manner that respects ecological limitations.

This chapter explores the political and legal importance of sustainable development in the context of international environmental law. The environmental core of sustainable development, i.e. to understand sustainability as the protection of ecological integrity, has hardly been recognized, leaving the concept shapeless, nebulous and vague. Recognizing the environmental core ('sustainability') will be vital to make sustainable development relevant in international policy, governance and law.

Meaning of sustainable development

Sustainable development is not legally defined. At present, neither international law nor domestic laws prescribe a way to resolve conflicting priorities between the social, economic and environmental concerns involved. In many instances sustainable development seems to be accomplished when everything is taken care of – the environment is protected, the economy is developed and social equity is achieved. Such a view assumes that the three objectives are not in conflict with each other and can be achieved simultaneously. To date the notion of sustainable development appears to resist definition and avoid the hard questions. This may explain its ongoing attraction within the UN system and among states. It is not surprising, therefore, that the Rio+20 Summit in June 2012, despite its declared ambition to rekindle the sustainable development discourse, did not actually aim for clarification and codification of the concept.

Some commentators see wisdom in keeping legal definitions open. Dan Tarlock, for example, asserts: 'Environmental impact assessment, polluter pays, precaution, and sustainable development are useful starting points but they can only serve as guideposts to structure a dynamic, but inevitably ad hoc, decision making process.'[1] A widespread assumption is, in fact, that environmental decision-making must be subject-specific; that different subjects (air, water, pesticides, energy, etc.) require different regimes and that the outcomes should meet the expectations of many, if not all, 'stakeholders'. Such pragmatism makes it almost impossible to think of sustainable development as a general principle or rule.

On the other hand, law and society are not principally opposed to absolutes of this nature. For example, criminal law protects absolutes such as life, health, well-being, integrity, freedom and property. They cannot be compromised. Consequently, harming a person or property carries penalties, but not harming the environment. There is no general rule not to harm the environment. Laws may prohibit specific activities like felling a tree or killing an animal without reason[2] or building a house without resource consent, but these are exceptions to the basic right to use the environment in its various forms. In their accumulation, existing user rights result in large-scale destruction of the global environment.[3] At the time of its inception

---

1 A.D. Tarlock, 'Is There a There There in Environmental Law?', *Journal of Land Use & Environmental Law* 19, 2004, 213–53, p. 219.
2 Although under most animal welfare laws, this would be permissible so long as the animal is killed in a 'humane' manner without suffering that would constitute 'cruelty'. No justification per se is required.
3 Often referred to as the 'tragedy of the commons'.

in the 1987 *Brundtland Report*,[4] the notion of sustainable development was meant to overcome the environment-destroying nature of dominant policies, laws and practices.

The Report contains a statement that became commonly referred to as a definition:

> Sustainable development is development that meets the needs of the present without compromising the ability of future generations to meet their own needs.[5]

However, the sentence immediately following this statement is of equal importance and ought to be considered simultaneously:

> It [i.e. sustainable development] contains within it two key concepts:
>
> - the concept of 'needs', in particular the essential needs of the world's poor, to which overriding priority should be given; and
> - the idea of limitations imposed by the state of technology and social organization on the environment's ability to meet present and future needs.[6]

The 'environment's ability' seems the forgotten part of the definition, yet only with some sense of what the needs of future generations might be would it be possible to operationalize the basic concern behind the idea of sustainable development.

While the first key concept of the *Brundtland* description refers to the development problem ('needs'), the second key concept refers to the sustainability problem ('environment's ability'). How then can 'needs' and the 'environment's ability' be understood?

There is no obvious reason to assume that only basic material needs are meant, such as healthy living conditions or protection from poverty. With equal justification one could include immaterial needs such as freedom, security, education or justice, and protection from ever-increasing debts that countries are presently producing. All these and many other things that we do today to meet our 'needs' potentially have some effect of 'compromising the ability of future generations to meet their own needs'. What does matter, however, is the distinction between those forms of development that perceivably do not compromise the ability of future generations and those that do. In the former group are developments towards healthier living conditions, freedom from poverty, access to education, material security and so on. In the latter group are the very same developments except for their unsustainable nature. What is crucial is *how* needs are being met. This puts the focus on the sustainability of ecological systems. Nothing can ever be developed for the benefit of humanity (now and in the future) if it threatens the very living conditions that all humanity depends on.

In other words, human needs ('development') and the 'environment's ability' are intrinsically linked: no development without keeping the environment sustainable. If the sustainability of ecological systems is paramount, it sets a non-negotiable absolute to any form of development. This interpretation prohibits compromises or trade-offs between the 'economy' and the 'environment'. This interpretation is usually referred to as 'strong' (as opposed to 'weak') sustainable development. It is more correct, however, to think of genuine sustainable

4 World Commission on Environment and Development, *Our Common Future*, Oxford: Oxford University Press, 1987 (*Brundtland Report*).
5 Ibid, p. 65
6 Ibid.

development as opposed to watered-down versions merely promoting an undefined 'integration' of social, economic and environmental concerns. Origins, history and conceptualization of sustainability prior to the *Brundtland Report*[7] clearly show that there can only ever be one meaning of *sustainable* development, not two to choose from.

At this point, it should also become clear how severely hampered anthropocentric approaches to sustainable development are. They attempt the impossible. How could a future-oriented concept of needs ever be practical if based on anything other than respect and care for ecological sustainability? Anthropocentric motivations are riddled with uncertainties with respect to what human needs are, what the needs of future generations will be and what the needs of the non-human world may be. The unqualified focus on human needs leaves speculation about the future wide open, ranging from a planet without nature to a planet without humans. In our age of the Anthropocene it is not beyond imagination that humans may, one day, aim for an artificial environment to completely substitute the natural environment. Such a view spells ecological suicide ('ecocide')[8] as it overlooks a simple truth, namely the interrelatedness of all life across the boundaries between humans and non-humans.

Respect for Earth and life in all its diversity[9] is a far better guide into the future. It allows for a more practical focus on essentials that are common to all life, that is the ability to exist, reproduce and evolve. These essentials call for the preservation of conditions that have proven to be favourable in the past. And while predictions of such conditions for future life are far from reliable, it is wise to preserve what has proven successful rather than trying to create unknown new conditions.

From an ecological point of view, anthropocentric conceptions of the future are difficult to justify. Edith Brown Weiss, the eminent proponent of intergenerational equity,[10] has never attempted to exclude the welfare of nature from our thinking about future generations. Her three principles of intergenerational equity involve the preservation of options, quality and access.[11] The first principle is 'to conserve the diversity of the natural and cultural resource base', the second 'to maintain the quality of the planet' and the third to provide 'equitable rights of access to the legacy of the past'.[12] While this third principle is anthropocentric in character, the former two describe duties towards the community of life. There is certainly no suggestion in Brown Weiss's concept to be only concerned with the welfare of humans.[13] According to Ulrich Beyerlin, 'much speaks in favour of conceiving the intergenerational

---

7 K. Bosselmann, *The Principle of Sustainability*, Aldershot/UK: Ashgate, 2008, pp. 10–26.
8 P. Higgins, *Eradicating Ecocide: Laws and Governance to Stop the Destruction of the Planet* London: Shepheard-Walwyn, 2010.
9 Principle 1, *The Earth Charter*. Online. Available HTTP: <http://www.earthcharterinaction.org/content/pages/Read-the-Charter.html> (accessed 19 April 2012).
10 E.B. Weiss, *In Fairness to Future Generations: International Law, Common Patrimony and Intergenerational Equity*, United Nations University Press, 1989, pp. 17 onwards.
11 E.B. Weiss (1990), 'Intergenerational Justice and International Law', in S. Busuttil, E. Agius, P.S. Inglott and T. Macelli (eds) *Our Responsibilities to Future Generations*, Malta: Foundation for International Studies, 1998, pp. 98 onwards.
12 Ibid.
13 K. Bosselmann, 'A Legal Framework for Sustainable Development', in K. Bosselmann and D. Grinlinton (eds.) *Environmental Law for a Sustainable Society*, Auckland: New Zealand Centre for Environmental Law, 2002, vol. 1, pp. vii–ix, 151.

component of sustainable development in eco-centric terms'.[14] He concludes: '[a]s intergenerational equity is inseparably intertwined with intra-generational equity, the concept of sustainable development in its entirety must be perceived as both anthropocentric and eco-centric in nature.'[15]

Other commentators have made the same point, thus challenging the widely held view that sustainable development reflects anthropocentrism and trade-offs between environmental, economic and social interests.[16] The fundamental importance of the environment is not contingent on an ecological approach to sustainable development. The economic approach may emphasize material prosperity, but can nevertheless be formulated on the basis of ecological sustainability. World Bank economist Roberto Repetto wrote:

> The core idea of sustainability is that current decisions should not impair the prospects for maintaining or improving future living standards. This implies that our economic systems should be managed so that we can live off the dividends of our resources.[17]

Two other economists from the World Bank, Mohan Munasinghe and Ernst Lutz, define sustainable development as 'an approach that will permit continuing improvements in the quality of life with a lower intensity of resource use, thereby leaving behind for future generations an undiminished or even enhanced stock of natural resources and other assets'.[18]

Clearly, the preservation of the natural stock determines the ability to meet the needs of present and future generations.

The eco-centric component of sustainable development is indeed crucial for making the concept operable. If we perceive human needs without regard to ecological reality, we are at risk of losing the ground under our feet. Against this reality, any talk about the equal importance of development and environment, the 'two-scale model', 'three-pillar model' or 'magic triangle', reveals outdated, ideologically motivated thinking. Concerns for social justice and economic prosperity are vital, yet secondary compared to the functioning of the Earth's ecological systems as the basis of any human prosperity. Hence, ecological sustainability is foundational for development and not a mere 'pillar'.

As a consequence, despite the ambiguity of the *Brundtland Report*'s reception in the literature and international documents, it would be wrong to conclude that the principle of

---

14 U. Beyerlin, 'Bridging the North–South Divide in International Environmental Law', *Zeitschrift für ausländisches und öffentliches Recht* 66, 2006, 263–75; see also U. Beyerlin and T. Marauhn, *International Environmental Law*, Oxford: Hart Publishing, 2011, p. 77. Further, E. Agius, 'Towards a Relational Theory of Intergenerational Ethics', in S. Busuttil, E. Agius, P.S. Inglott and T. Macelli (eds.) *Our Responsibilities to Future Generations*, Malta: Foundation for International Studies, 1998, p. 87; and P. Taylor, *An Ecological Approach to International Law*, London/New York: Routledge, 1998, pp. 281–2.

15 Beyerlin, 'Bridging the North–South Divide', op. cit.

16 See B. Boer, 'Implementation of International Sustainability at a National Level', in K. Ginther, E. Denters and P.J.I.M. de Waart (eds.) *Sustainable Development and Good Governance*, Dordrecht/Boston: Kluwer Academic Publishers, 1995, pp. 111–13; Taylor, op. cit., pp. 325–7, 348–9; A. Gillespie, *International Law, Policy and Ethics*, Oxford: Oxford University Press, 1997, pp. 2–5, 127–8; and (with less clarity) P. Birnie and A. Boyle, *International Law and the Environment*, 2nd edition, Oxford: Oxford University Press, 2002, pp. 44–7.

17 R. Repetto, *World Enough and Time*, New Haven: Yale University Press, 1986.

18 M. Munansinghe and E. Lutz, *Environmental-Economic Evaluation of Projects and Policies for Sustainable Development*, Environment Working Paper No. 42, World Bank, 1991.

sustainability has lost its contours. To the contrary, international environmental law has always been informed by it.

International agreements on sustainable development

A few years after the *Brundtland Report*, the *World Conservation Strategy*[19] was revised. The 1991 document *Caring for the Earth. A Strategy for Sustainable Living*[20] incorporated the *Brundtland Report*, but did not lose track of the core meaning of sustainable development. It describes the purpose of sustainable development as improving the quality of human life while living within the carrying capacity of the Earth's ecosystems.[21] *Caring for the Earth* contains two distinct requirements: one is the commitment to a new ethic based on respect and care for one another and for the Earth; the other is integration of conservation and development.[22] The document warns us not to lose the focus of sustainability when it is used in combination with other words such as 'use', 'yield', 'development', 'management', 'economy' and 'society'.[23]

1992 Rio Earth Summit

Until 1992, there was no apparent rift between *strong* and *weak sustainability*. Wherever the term 'sustainability' was used, it had the meaning of ecological sustainability, and where the term 'sustainable development' was used, the principle of sustainability was implied. A rift emerged, however, in June 1992 during the Rio UN Conference on Environment and Development (UNCED). Symbolically visible in the fortress-type venue of the official Earth Summit, where states negotiated, and the beachside venue of the Global Forum, where civil society groups met, the sustainability agendas differed considerably. The 160 participating states left any commitment to sustainable development to two soft-law documents, the *Rio Declaration on Environment and Development*[24] and *Agenda 21*,[25] both stressing the interconnectedness of environmental, social and economic concerns. Civil society, on the other hand, emphasized ecological sustainability as the key to dealing with social and economic concerns. Several hundred NGOs (non-governmental organizations) negotiated fifteen so-called

---

19 International Union for the Conservation of Nature and Natural Resources (IUCN) (ed.) *World Conservation Strategy: Living Resource Conservation for Sustainable Development*, Gland, Switzerland: IUCN, 1980.

20 International Union for the Conservation of Nature and Natural Resources (IUCN), World Wide Fund for Nature (WWF) and United Nations Environment Programme (UNEP), *Caring for the Earth: A Strategy for Sustainable Living*, Gland, Switzerland: IUCN, 1991.

21 Ibid, pp. 3–4.

22 Boer, op. cit., pp. 111, 113.

23 IUCN, WWF and UNEP, *Caring for the Earth*, op. cit.

24 *Rio Declaration on Environment and Development*, Report of the UN Conference on Environment and Development, Annex I, 12 August 1992, UN Doc A/Conf. 151/26 (Vol. I) (Rio Declaration); see Taylor, op. cit., pp. 324–7, 379–81.

25 *Agenda 21: A Programme for Action for Sustainable Development*, Report of the UN Conference on Environment and Development, Annex II, 12 August 1992, UN Doc A./Conf. 151/26 (Vols II–IV).

'alternative treaties', among them the *Earth Charter*[26] as an alternate to the *Rio Declaration*. Ecological sustainability was referred to as central to everything, poverty eradication, socio-economic development, human rights and peace.

The *Earth Charter* was not only responding to the *Rio Declaration*, but to the entire preparatory process for UNCED. Following the *Brundtland Report* with its call for a 'new charter' that 'should prescribe new norms for states and state behaviour to maintain livelihoods and life on our shared planet',[27] several preparatory meetings in 1990 and 1991 identified the elements for an *Earth Charter* to be agreed upon by states. However, a few months before the Rio Summit, at the fourth and last Preparatory Committee (PrepCom), it became clear that intergovernmental agreement could not be reached. States moved away from the idea of a charter with its emphasis on ecological sustainability and eventually adopted the *Rio Declaration*[28] instead.[29]

This is not to say, however, that the concept of sustainability was dismissed. The *Rio Declaration* just lacked definitions for sustainable development or sustainability, instead favouring a comprehensive description of political issues involved. A careful interpretation shows that the *Rio Declaration* did not promote the three-pillars model that was heralded by many post-Rio commentators. Principle 4 of the *Declaration* states that 'in order to achieve sustainable development, environmental protection shall constitute an integral part of the development process and cannot be considered in isolation from it'. Thus, a mere undefined idea of integration was perceived as a sufficient modus operandi of sustainable development. However, Principle 4 can also be interpreted in a strong sense: the development process can only be pursued through preserving its ecological basis.

The *Declaration* mentions the right to development (Principle 3),[30] the integrative approach (Principle 4) and the indispensable task of poverty alleviation (Principle 5) as key aspects of sustainable development. The relative prominence of the right to development and poverty alleviation are clearly meant to acknowledge the special needs of developing countries. However, this does not diminish the importance of ecological sustainability. The *Declaration* does not allow industrialized states to compromise the principle of sustainability for the sake of pursuing their economic prosperity and social development.[31] The developing states participating in Rio did not insist on their right to development to allow multinational corporations of rich states to develop more quickly and effectively. The political implication merely is to not expect sustainability measures from developing states with the same urgency as can be expected from developed states that have affected the Earth's ecological integrity to a much higher degree.

---

26 The Rio Earth Charter was followed-up by the 1994 initiative of Maurice Strong, Chair of the Earth Council, and Mikhail Gorbachev, President of Green Cross International. The new initiative led to a worldwide process of consultation with the eventual launch of the *Earth Charter* in 2000. See M. Vilela, 'Building Consensus on Shared Values. History and Provenance of the Earth Charter', in P.B. Corcoran (ed.) *The Earth Charter in Action. Toward a Sustainable World*, Amsterdam: KIT, 2005, pp. 17 onwards.

27 *Brundtland Report*, op. cit., p. 332.

28 *Rio Declaration*, op. cit.

29 Vilela, op. cit., p. 18.

30 The proximity to the Brundtland definition with its 'needs' concept is obvious in the wording: '(t)he right to development must be fulfilled so as to equitably meet developmental and environmental needs of present and future generations.'

31 D. Murswiek, 'Nachhaltigkeit – Probleme der rechtlichen Umsetzung eines umweltpolitischen Leitbildes', *Natur und Recht*, 2002, 641–5.

Klaus Bosselmann

Essentially, the *Rio Declaration* attempted to find a solution to the distribution problem that the global ecological crisis has created. This attempt may have been incomplete and not very satisfactory; however, it can hardly be argued that the principle of sustainability had been dismissed or replaced by something else.[32] To the contrary, Principles 3 and 4 confirm its existence: even economic development in developing countries must not compromise the ability of future generations to meet their needs.[33] If the right to development could only be exercised by violating this principle of sustainability because of developed countries' overburdening of the environment, then *these* countries need to reduce their overburdening in order to preserve the development chances of developing countries. It follows that ecological sustainability is paramount in the developing world, and even more so in the developed world.

The other Rio soft-law document, *Agenda 21*, confirms this interpretation of the *Declaration*. *Agenda 21* provides a comprehensive plan for strategies and programmes to reverse the effects of environmental degradation and promote sustainable development. Its text comprises four sections beginning with 'social and economic development' (including poverty alleviation, consumption patterns and integration) and 'conservation and management of resources for development' (including the atmosphere and biosphere).[34] As in the *Declaration*, the signatories of *Agenda 21* agreed on a number of principles and concepts, but left a definition and the details of commitments of the developed world to further negotiations on treaties, institutions[35] and laws. In the case of *Agenda 21*, this expectation was not unreasonable. At least civil society, particularly local governments and educational institutions, used *Agenda 21* as a genuine blueprint for actions toward sustainable development.

The general legacy of Rio, however, is one of unfinished business. With the absence of a binding treaty and clear definitions, an important opportunity was lost. In the closing statement of UNCED, Secretary General Maurice Strong said:

> We have a profoundly important *Declaration*, but it must continue to evolve towards what many of us hope will be an *Earth Charter* that could be finally sanctioned on the fiftieth anniversary of the United Nations in 1995.[36]

Maurice Strong went on to initiate a worldwide campaign for an *Earth Charter*. Created by several thousand civil society groups, but without direct input from states, the *Earth Charter* was eventually launched at the Peace Palace in The Hague in 2000. It represents a broader consensus on the principle of sustainability than has ever been achieved before. The responsibility was now on the states to respond to the challenge.

32 See P. Sands, *Principles of Internationale Environmental Law*, 2nd edition, Cambridge: Cambridge University Press, 2003, p. 259. That the *Rio Declaration* did not replace or narrow down the principle of sustainability is also concluded, for example, by Murswiek, op. cit., pp. 4–6; R. Schmidt and H. Müller, *Einführung in das Umweltrecht*, 6th edition, Munich: Beck, 2001, para. 7.
33 U. Beyerlin, 'The Concept of Sustainable Development', in R. Wolfrum (ed.) *Enforcing Environmental Standards: Economic Mechanisms as Viable Means?*, Berlin: Springer, 1996, pp. 95, 104–105.
34 Section 3 deals with 'strengthening the role of major groups'; Section 4 with 'means of implementation'.
35 For example, the UN Commission for Sustainable Development (CSD) initiated and monitored national strategies for sustainable development and programmes for sustainability indicators to measure progress.
36 Quoted by Vilela, op. cit., p. 18.

Shortly after the launch, more than a thousand NGOs at the Millennium NGO Forum endorsed the *Earth Charter* and recommended that the UN Millennium Summit recognize and support the document. While this did not happen, the *UN Millennium Declaration*[37] does, for the first time in two decades, reaffirm the principle of 'respect for nature' as among the 'fundamental values essential to international relations'.[38] It also identifies freedom, equality, solidarity, tolerance and shared responsibility as fundamental values and calls for a 'new ethic'. In addition, the *Millennium Development Goals*[39] associated with the declaration are entirely consistent with the *Earth Charter*.[40]

2002 Johannesburg Summit on Sustainable Development

Next came the 2002 World Summit on Sustainable Development (WSSD) in Johannesburg. At the opening, the Secretary General, South African President Mbeki, referred to the *Earth Charter* as a central document to guide the Summit's negotiations. The draft *Johannesburg Declaration* contained specific reference to the *Charter* and called for a commitment to the values and principles outlined there. However, the final version had this reference removed following last-minute objections, mainly from the United States.[41] As had happened ten years earlier, before UNCED, several PrepComs to the WSSD had recognized the *Earth Charter*'s key importance, and as before, states again moved away from a firm commitment to the principle of sustainability.

The key outcomes of the WSSD, the *Johannesburg Declaration on Sustainable Development*[42] and the *Johannesburg Plan of Implementation*,[43] failed to define sustainable development. They did, however, express support for the principle of ecological sustainability, albeit in an indirect manner. The *Declaration* commits to sustainable development and building a humane, equitable and caring global society cognizant of the need for human dignity for all. Paragraph 6 uses language almost identical to the *Earth Charter's* Preamble:

> From this continent, the cradle of humanity, we declare, through the Plan of Implementation of the World Summit on Sustainable Development and the present declaration, our responsibility to one another, to the greater community of life and to our children.

This statement is the first time that an international law document has made an explicit reference to the community of life. This affirmation deepens the meaning of respect for

---

37 *United Nations Millennium Declaration*, GA Res. 55/2, UN GAOR, 55th sess., 8th plen. mtg., UN Doc A/Res/55/2 (2000).
38 The *Earth Charter* preamble reads: 'We must join together to bring forth a sustainable society founded on respect for nature, universal human rights, economic justice, and a culture of peace.'
39 See *Millennium Declaration*, op. cit.
40 S. Rockefeller, 'The Transition to Sustainability', in P.B. Corcoran (ed.) *The Earth Charter in Action. Toward a Sustainable World*, Amsterdam: KIT, 2005, pp. 165, 167.
41 Ibid.
42 *Johannesburg Declaration on Sustainable Development*, Report of the World Summit on Sustainable Development, Chapter 1, Resolution 1, UN Doc A/Conf. 199/20. Online. Available HTTP: <http://www.un.org/esa/sustdev/documents/WSSD_POI_PD/English/POI_PD.htm>.
43 Plan of Implementation of the World Summit on Sustainable Development, Report of the World Summit on Sustainable Development, Chapter 1, Resolution 2, UN Doc A./Conf. 199/20 ('*Johannesburg Plan of Implementation*'). Online. Available HTTP: <http://www.un.org/esa/sustdev/documents/WSSD_POI_PD/English/POIToc.htm>.

nature. At the same time, it is reflective not only of the *Earth Charter*'s recognition that people are members of the Earth's community of life, but also the acknowledgement that non-human species are worthy of moral considerations. In other words, non-human species as members of the greater community of life have intrinsic value as well as instrumental value.[44]

While the *Declaration* is reflective of some of the ethics underpinning ecological sustainability, the *Plan of Implementation* acknowledges, for the first time, 'the importance of ethics for sustainable development'.[45] To this end, both soft-law documents reveal a heightened sense of ecological responsibility. Their *travaux préparatoires* and actual texts do not signal a specific commitment to the principle of sustainability; however, they do indicate a search for adopting it. If responsibilities are no longer limited to the social and economic side of sustainable development, but are inclusive of 'the greater community of life', then the formal recognition of the principle of sustainability becomes a distinct possibility. It all depends on how the 'ethics for sustainable development' is understood and applied.

Preceding the Johannesburg Summit was an effort by the International Law Association (ILA) to identify the key legal principles relevant to sustainable development. The 2002 *New Delhi Declaration on the Principles of International Law Related to Sustainable Development*[46] adopted seven such principles: (1) the duty of states to ensure sustainable use of natural resources; (2) the principle of equity and the eradication of poverty; (3) the principle of common but differentiated responsibilities; (4) the principle of the precautionary approach to human health, natural resources and ecosystems; (5) the principle of public participation and access to information and justice; (6) the principle of good governance; and (7) the principle of integration and interrelationship, in particular in relation to human rights and social, economic and environmental objectives.

With respect to this last principle, the *Declaration* explains that it 'reflects the interdependence of social, economic, financial, environmental and human rights aspects of principles and rules of international law', further that 'states should strive to resolve apparent conflict between competing economic, financial, social and environmental considerations', and finally that 'the above principles are interrelated and each of them should be construed in the context of the other principles of this Declaration'.[47] This suggests that there is no overall prime principle to guide the others. However, the first principle of sustainable use could be seen as having such a function if interpreted as a reflection of the principle of sustainability.

The content and limitations of the principle of sustainable use are uncertain under international law. On the one hand, there is the well-established right to permanent sovereignty over natural resources to which Principle 21 of the *Stockholm Declaration* and Principle 2 of the *Rio Declaration* added certain restrictions with respect to transboundary effects. On the other hand, the significance of this rule is far from clear. Commentators tend to give the duty of states not to harm the environment or, termed positively, the duty to manage natural resources in a sustainable manner, a certain prominence. Some consider this duty a 'central tenet of

---

44 See Principles 1 and 15 of the *Earth Charter*; Rockefeller, op. cit., p. 167.
45 *Johannesburg Plan of Implementation*, op. cit., para. 6.
46 *New Delhi Declaration on the Principles of International Law Related to Sustainable Development*, London: ILA resolution 3/2002.
47 Ibid.

international environmental law',[48] while others speak of a 'nascent responsibility'.[49] As will be discussed later, the interpretation of sustainable use depends on the ethics of sustainable development and the general importance of the principle of sustainability.

Towards the 2012 Rio Conference

The period since the 2002 WSSD is marked by several international resolutions to endorse the *Earth Charter*.[50] In 2003, the UNESCO General Conference recognized the *Earth Charter* as an important framework for sustainable development and affirmed member states' intention to use the *Earth Charter* 'as an educational instrument, particularly in the framework of the United Nations Decade on Education for Sustainable Development' (2005 to 2014).[51] The 2005 International Implementation Scheme for the UN Decade affirms that the Charter 'provides an excellent example of an inclusive vision of the fundamental principles for building a just, sustainable, and peaceful world'.[52]

In 2004, the IUCN World Conservation Congress adopted a resolution that 'endorses the Earth Charter as an inspirational expression of civil society's vision', 'recognises . . . the Earth Charter as an ethical guide for IUCN policy', seeks to 'implement its principles through the IUCN Programme' and encourages member states 'to determine the role the Earth Charter can play as a policy guide within their own spheres of responsibility'.[53] With only the United States opposing the resolution and 67 of 77 member states plus 800 NGOs supporting it, the *Earth Charter* gained further recognition as expressing a consensus within the international community.

Such consensus does not, at present, amount to soft-law recognition, nor is there a consensus among states on the *Earth Charter*'s values and principles. However, the increased international recognition marks 'a significant, even if very gradual, shift in humanity's ethical awareness'.[54] Considering the ethical commitments of the Johannesburg documents and the recognized moral authority of the *Earth Charter*, the ethics of sustainability are more appreciated today than ten or fifteen years ago. It therefore becomes possible to adequately describe the core meaning of 'sustainable development'.

However, the immediate prospects for reaching such a consensus are not good. The UN Conference on Sustainable Development in June 2012 (Rio+20) aims for a 'renewed political commitment to sustainable development'[55] around the themes 'green economy within the context of sustainable development and poverty eradication' and 'institutional framework for

---

48 M-C. Cordonier Segger and A. Khalfan, *Sustainable Development Law: Principles, Practices and Prospects*, Oxford: Oxford University Press, 2004, 112 with reference to Sands, op. cit.

49 N. Schrijver, *Sovereignty over Natural Resources: Balancing Rights and Duties*, Cambridge: Cambridge University Press, 1997, pp. 390–2.

50 K. Bosselmann, 'Earth Charter', in R. Wolfrum (ed.) *Max Planck Encyclopedia of Public International Law*, Oxford: Oxford University Press, 2009.

51 UNESCO, 'UNESCO's Support for the Earth Charter' in UNESCO *Records of the General Conference 32nd session Paris, 29 September to 17 October 2003*, Paris: UNESCO, 2003, vol.1, p. 35.

52 UNESCO, 'Education for Sustainable Development: Highlights on DESD Progress to Date', April 2007, p. 1.

53 International Union for the Conservation of Nature and Natural Resources, *Endorsement of the Earth Charter*, Res.WCC 3.022 (2004).

54 Rockefeller, op. cit., p. 167.

55 UN Conference on Sustainable Development, *The Future We Want*, 2012. Online Available HTTP: <http://www.uncsd2012.org/rio20/index.php?menu=17> (accessed 19 April 2012).

sustainable development'.[56] However, a rethink of the concept of sustainable development itself is not on the agenda. Nor are there, at present, initiatives towards a definition or legally binding agreement on sustainable development. As the gap between global civil society and the UN system (favouring the weak three-pillar model) remains unchanged, we are left with keeping the sustainability discourse alive. If followed through, it will show that policies modelled around economic growth and policies modelled around sustainability are irreconcilable. A well-defined concept of sustainable development would have to be modelled around ecological sustainability at its core.[57]

Conclusion

Since 1972, and especially since 1992, sustainability seems to have lost its contours. Its popularization in the composite term 'sustainable development' created an invitation to use it for all sorts of objectives purported to be desirable, such as 'sustainable economy', 'sustainable growth' and 'sustainable jobs', for example. Many of these terminological constructs have no relation to the original meaning of sustainability. If, for example, corporate managers stress economic sustainability as a legitimate goal next to ecological efficiency, chances are that they mean economic efficiency, but certainly not ecological sustainability. Economist Wilfred Beckerman was only slightly cynical when he wrote his article: 'How Would You Like Your "Sustainability", Sir? Weak or Strong?'[58]

But does the inflationary use of sustainability reduce its significance for the meaning and importance of sustainable development in international environmental law? Not if we focus on the historical, ethical and legal context in which the term has been used. There is clear evidence to suggest that sustainability remains foundational to the meaning of sustainable development.

Following on from the 1972 *Stockholm Declaration*, the 1980 *World Conservation Strategy* and the 1982 *World Charter of Nature*, the 1987 *Brundtland Report* shaped its new concept of sustainable development around the known notion of sustainability. It did so by demanding global, long-term economic justice without sacrificing the Earth's ecological integrity. There may be many problems with a one-size-fits-all formula for solving the world's problems, but referring to sustainability is not one of them. It is the best term to capture the ecological challenges that human societies, time and again, have had to face.

Ecological sustainability was embedded in the *Brundtland Report* on sustainable development and, more importantly, in the 1992 *Rio Declaration*. While it is true that this document and the other more recent soft-law documents on sustainable development contain political compromises and only general descriptions, it is also true that they are concerned with ecological sustainability. In fact, if today the concept of sustainable development is recognized

---

56 Ibid.
57 For the implications of this concept with respect to Rio+20, see K. Bosselmann, P. Brown and B. Mackey, *Enabling a Flourishing Earth: Challenges for the Green Economy, Opportunities for Global Governance*, 2011. Online. Available HTTP: <http://www.stakeholderforum.org/sf/index.php/our-publications/governance-papers/266-sdg-thinkpieces>. Beyerlin and Marauhn rightly observe that 'giving ecology general preponderance over development ... hardly reflects the current state of thinking in international environmental and developmental relations and doctrine', but rather 'points to an ambitious long-term goal', op. cit., pp. 78, 79.
58 W. Beckerman, ' "How Would You Like Your 'Sustainability', Sir? Weak or Strong?" A Reply to My Critics', *Environmental Values* 5, 1995, p. 169.

as a principle of international law, it owes its main reason, namely its operational quality, to the principle of sustainability. Without it sustainable development (requiring the integration of environmental, social and economic goals) could not be made operable. This is critical for recognizing it as a legal norm. In other words, the concept of sustainable development can only perform its normative functions in so far as it incorporates the idea of ecological sustainability.

The continued existence of the principle of sustainability has two important consequences. The first is that sustainable development is given meaning and direction. For developed states there is no free choice between three equally relevant political objectives, but only one available option: any use of natural resources has to be sustainable. Goals such as economic prosperity and social justice are secondary in the sense that they can only be pursued without threatening the Earth's ecological systems. Developing countries do not have the same responsibility. The principle of 'common but differentiated responsibilities', as defined in the *Rio Declaration*, affirmed in the UN *Framework Convention on Climate Change* and repeated six times in the *Johannesburg Plan of Implementation*, means that developed countries bear a special burden of responsibility for reducing and eliminating unsustainable patterns of production and consumption.

The second consequence is that existing treaties, laws and legal principles need to be interpreted in the light of the principle of sustainability. It provides crucial guidance for the interpretation of legal norms and sets the benchmark for understanding justice, human rights and state sovereignty. In doing so, sustainability represents the foundational concept of emerging 'sustainability law' based on ecological justice, human rights and institutions.[59]

59 Bosselmann, *The Principle of Sustainability*, op. cit.

38

International responsibility and liability for environmental harm

Robert V. Percival

The law of international responsibility and liability for environmental harm is a complicated mix of customary law, sparse precedents from arbitral or judicial panels, liability provisions in international agreements, and domestic law. There is wide agreement on a few long-standing principles, but these have not yielded clear rules for resolving specific conflicts over transboundary environmental harm. This chapter will explore the evolution of law in this area, including recent developments and future challenges. Examining first the history of these developments, this chapter explores contemporary developments including the International Law Commission's work, the European Union's directive and various civil liability regimes.

Introduction

The law of international responsibility and liability for environmental harm is a complicated mix of customary law, sparse precedents from arbitral or judicial panels, liability provisions in international agreements, and domestic law. There is wide agreement on a few long-standing principles, but these have not yielded clear rules for resolving specific conflicts over transboundary environmental harm. Perhaps the most influential precedent has been the *Trail Smelter* arbitration, which drew on principles of the ancient common law of nuisance to address a transboundary pollution dispute between the United States and Canada.[1] More recently the International Law Commission has worked to develop principles of state responsibility for environmental harm.[2] In addition more specific international civil liability regimes have been established by treaty for particular high-risk activities such as those involving nuclear materials or the production and transportation of oil.

This chapter will explore the evolution of law in this area, including recent developments and future challenges. After reviewing the history of customary international law and the

---

1 *Trail Smelter* (1941) 3 R.Int'l Arb. Awards 1911, 1963.
2 International Law Commission, *Summary: International Liability for Injurious Consequences arising out of Acts not Prohibited by International Law.* Online. Available HTTP: <http://untreaty.un.org/ilc/summaries/9.htm> (accessed 16 March 2012).

Trail Smelter arbitration, the chapter examines contemporary developments. These include the International Law Commission's work on principles of international responsibility for environmental harm, the European Union's directive on liability for environmental harm and various civil liability regimes.

Trail Smelter and the evolution of customary international law

The *Trail Smelter* case involved claims that emissions of sulphur dioxide from a smelter in Trail, British Columbia, Canada, had caused property damage across the US border in the state of Washington. Pursuant to the Boundary Waters Treaty of 1909,[3] the United States and Canada established an arbitral tribunal to resolve the dispute. On 11 March 1941, the tribunal issued its final decision. It recognised that a state 'owes at all times a duty to protect other States against injurious acts by individuals from within its jurisdiction'.[4] Finding no international law precedent involving pollution, the tribunal turned to decisions of the US Supreme Court involving transboundary pollution disputes between states. In particular the tribunal found the Court's 1907 decision in *Georgia v Tennessee Copper Co.* to be especially useful. Writing for the Court majority in this case, Justice Oliver Wendell Holmes had declared that 'It is a fair and reasonable demand on the part of a sovereign that the air over its territory should not be polluted on a great scale by sulphurous acid gas'.[5] The Court eventually issued an injunction to control transboundary pollution from a copper smelter in one state to protect crops in another.[6]

Relying on this precedent the *Trail Smelter* tribunal declared:

> under the principles of international law, as well as of the law of the United States, no State has the right to use or permit the use of its territory in such a manner as to cause injury by fumes in or to the territory of another or the properties or persons therein, when the case is of serious consequence and the injury is established by clear and convincing evidence.[7]

The *Trail Smelter* decision has served as an important precedent for the development of principles of international responsibility for environmental harm. The first comprehensive effort to articulate these principles occurred in 1972 when representatives from 114 nations gathered in Stockholm for the first global environmental summit – the United Nations Conference on the Human Environment. At the conference they unanimously agreed on a declaration of principles of environmental law, the *Stockholm Declaration on the Human Environment*. Principle 21 states that:

> States have, in accordance with the Charter of the United Nations and the principles of international law, the sovereign right to exploit their own resources pursuant to their own environmental policies, and the responsibility to ensure that activities within their jurisdiction or control do not cause damage to the environment of other States or of areas beyond the limits of national jurisdiction.[8]

---

3 36 Stat. 2448, T.S. No. 548, 12 Bevans 319.
4 *Trail Smelter* (1941) 3 R.Int'l Arb. Awards 1911, 1963.
5 *Georgia v Tennessee Copper Co.*, 206 US 230, 238 (1907).
6 *Georgia v Tennessee Copper Co.*, 237 US 474 (1915).
7 *Trail Smelter* (1941) 3 R.Int'l Arb. Awards 1911, 1965.
8 *Declaration of the United Nations Conference on the Human Environment* (1972), Principle 21.

This Declaration gave international recognition to a principle rooted in ancient Roman law, the British common law of private nuisance, and the US federal common law of public nuisance articulated in *Georgia v Tennessee Copper*.[9] Expressed as the Latin maxim *sic utere tuo ut alienum non laedas*, the principle – that no one has the right to use their property in a manner that causes harm to another – is now widely known as the '*sic utere* principle'. The *Trail Smelter* decision and Stockholm Declaration extended this principle to establish state responsibility to prevent transboundary harm.

Yet the *sic utere* principle offers little guidance concerning how to resolve specific transboundary pollution disputes. It does not address what threshold level of significance environmental damage must have to be actionable, how causation is to be proven, or what degree of fault, if any, a polluter must exhibit to be held liable. Thus, the Stockholm Declaration urged the development of more specific principles of liability for environmental harm. Principle 22 of the Stockholm Declaration states:

> States shall cooperate to develop further the international law regarding liability and compensation for the victims of pollution and other environmental damage caused by activities within the jurisdiction or control of such States to areas beyond their jurisdiction.[10]

Principle 21 of the Stockholm Declaration has been incorporated in general terms into several multilateral treaties, including the 1980 *United Nations Convention on the Law of the Sea*, the *Vienna Convention for Protection of the Ozone Layer*, and the 1992 *Convention on Biological Diversity*. However, scant progress has been made in reaching agreement on more specific principles of liability for transboundary environmental harm. Despite widespread transboundary radiation damage from the 1986 Chernobyl nuclear accident, no state was held liable and no compensation was paid. As Lakshman Guruswamy noted in 1994, 'Thus far it does not appear that states are willing to engage in the delicate process of defining the conditions and scope of international responsibility for environmental damage.'[11]

In 1987 the Third Restatement of Foreign Relations described the concept of state responsibility for environmental harm as 'rooted in customary international law'.[12] It summarised state responsibility for environmental harm in the following terms:

> (1) A state is obligated to take such measures as may be necessary, to the extent practicable under the circumstances, to ensure that activities within its jurisdiction or control
>
>   (a) conform to generally accepted international rules and standards for the prevention, reduction, and control of injury to the environment of another state or of areas beyond the limits of national jurisdiction; and
>
>   (b) are conducted so as not to cause significant injury to the environment of another state or of areas beyond the limits of national jurisdiction.'[13]

---

9 As explained by Lord Holt in 1702 in *Tenant v Goldwin*: 'every man must so use his own as not to damnify another'. (1704), 92 Eng. Rep. 222, 224 (KB).
10 *Declaration of the United Nations Conference on the Human Environment* (1972), Principle 22.
11 L. Guruswamy, G. Palmer and B. Weston, *International Environmental Law and World Order*, 1st edition, St Paul: West Publishing, 1994, p. 327.
12 2 Restatement (Third) of Foreign Relations Law of the US 100 (1987) § 601.
13 2 Restatement (Third) of Foreign Relations Law of the US 100 (1987).

Note that the Restatement provides that states are responsible for both their own activities and those of individuals or corporations that operate under their jurisdiction. It also provides that states are liable not only for breaches of the above obligations, but also for any significant injury that such violations cause to the environment, property or persons in other states.

In 1992, 20 years after the Stockholm Conference, the 172 governments participating in the United Nations Conference on Environment and Development in Rio de Janeiro reaffirmed the concept of state responsibility for transboundary environmental harm. In language that tracks Principle 21 of the Stockholm Declaration, Principle 2 of the *Rio Declaration on Environment and Development* states:

> States have, in accordance with the Charter of the United Nations and the principles of international law, the sovereign right to exploit their own resources pursuant to their own environmental and developmental policies, and the responsibility to insure that activities within their jurisdiction or control do not cause damage to the environment of other states or of areas beyond the limits of national jurisdiction.[14]

Notice that the Rio Declaration's discussion of sovereign rights refers to both environmental and *developmental* policies. Although this has led some commentators to view Rio's Principle 2 as weakening the force of Stockholm's Principle 22,[15] its statement of state responsibility to avoid transboundary harm remains intact.

Principle 13 of the Rio Declaration reaffirms the pledge made in Stockholm's Principle 22 to develop global norms of state responsibility for environmental harm and more specific international standards of liability and compensation. However, it also reflects growing frustration with the lack of progress toward this end by pledging more expeditious and determined efforts. Principle 13 of the Rio Declaration states:

> States shall develop national law regarding liability and compensation for the victims of pollution and other environmental damage. States shall also cooperate in an expeditious and more determined manner to develop further international law regarding liability and compensation for adverse effects of environmental damage caused by activities within their jurisdiction or control to areas beyond their jurisdiction.[16]

Despite the failure to reach agreement on generally applicable standards of liability and compensation for environmental harm, the principle of state responsibility for transboundary harm is now accepted as part of customary international law. In its 1996 Advisory Opinion on the Legality of the Threat or Use of Nuclear Weapons, the International Court of Justice (ICJ) referred to it as 'part of the corpus of international law on the environment'.[17] One year later in its 1997 judgment on the Gabčíkovo–Nagymaros Project, the ICJ again endorsed the principle of state responsibility for transboundary harm while referring for the first time to 'sustainable development' as an emerging concept reflecting the 'need to reconcile economic development with protection of the environment'.[18] There is considerable debate concerning

---

14 *Rio Declaration on Environment and Development* (1992), Principle 2.
15 L. Guruswamy, *International Environmental Law*, 3rd edition, St Paul: Thomson/West, 2007, p. 46.
16 *Rio Declaration on Environment and Development* (1992), Principle 13.
17 International Court of Justice, 1996 ICJ 226, paras 29, 140.
18 Gabčíkovo–Nagymaros Project, 1997 ICJ 7, at 41, para. 53.

whether the concept of 'sustainable development' has normative legal force. But there is broad acceptance of the principle of state responsibility for transboundary environmental harm.[19]

The International Law Commission and state responsibility

The focus of efforts to develop more specific international standards of liability and compensation for environmental harm has been the International Law Commission (ILC). The ILC was established in 1947 by the General Assembly of the United Nations.[20] Arising out of their work on state responsibility and following a recommendation by the General Assembly, the ILC began discussions on 'international liability for injurious consequences arising out of acts not prohibited by international law'.[21] From the time of the initial discussions in the late 1970s through the early 1980s, five draft articles were proposed by the Special Rapporteur; however, no decision was taken to refer them to the Drafting Committee.[22] The discussions about liability did not stop, and a number of reports were released on the topic throughout the 1980s.[23] Finally, in 1992 a Working Group was formed to research and report on the possibility of establishing an international liability scheme.[24]

On the Working Group's recommendation as to the scope and approach to be taken in the future, the Commission decided to continue work on the topic in two stages – prevention of transboundary harm, and remedial measures.[25] In 1997 the Commission determined that these two issues should be dealt with separately and that the issue of prevention should be researched first, as a considerable amount of progress had already been made on the topic.[26] Since this decision, the ILC has released two relevant documents. The first, the *Draft Articles on Prevention of Transboundary Harm from Hazardous Activities*, was published in 2001. The second, the *Draft Principles on the Allocation of Loss in the Case of Transboundary Harm Arising out of Hazardous Activities*, was published in 2006.

Draft Articles on Prevention of Transboundary Harm from Hazardous Activities

After its forty-ninth session in 1997, the ILC proceeded with its work on the 'prevention' portion of the liability topic.[27] A Working Group was established in 1998 to determine

19 P-M. Dupuy, 'Formation of Customary International Law and General Principles', in D. Bodansky, J. Brunnee and E. Hey (eds) *The Oxford Handbook of International Environmental Law*, Oxford: Oxford University Press, 2007, p. 452.
20 International Law Commission (ILC), Introduction: Origin and background of the development and codification of international law. Online. Available HTTP: <http://untreaty.un.org/ilc/ilcintro.htm> (accessed 16 March 2012).
21 ILC, Summary: International Liability for Injurious Consequences arising out of Acts not Prohibited by International Law. Online. Available HTTP: <http://untreaty.un.org/ilc/summaries/9.htm> (accessed 16 March 2012).
22 Ibid.
23 ILC, Analytical Guide: International Liability for Injurious Consequences arising out of Acts not Prohibited by International Law. Online. Available HTTP: <(http://untreaty.un.org/ilc/guide/9.htm>(accessed 16 March 2012).
24 Ibid.
25 ILC, Summary: International Liability for Injurious Consequences arising out of Acts not Prohibited by International Law, op. cit.
26 Ibid.
27 ILC, Summary: Prevention of transboundary damage from hazardous activities. Online. Available HTTP: <http://untreaty.un.org/ilc/summaries/9_7.htm> (accessed 16 March 2012).

whether a set of draft articles recommended to the Commission in 1996 appropriately represented 'the principles of procedure and content of the duty of prevention'.[28] Based on the Working Group's discussions, a revised text was referred to the Drafting Committee, who submitted a report to the ILC. The Commission reviewed the report and adopted a set of seventeen draft articles on prevention of transboundary damage from hazardous activities.

The Commission formed a Working Group in 2000 to review comments and observations made by states. As a result of the Working Group's review, the Special Rapporteur presented a report, which the Commission considered before referring the draft articles contained in the report to the Drafting Committee. In 2001, the Commission adopted the final text of the *Draft Articles on Prevention of Transboundary Harm from Hazardous Activities* and submitted them to the General Assembly. In their submission of the final draft, the Commission 'recommended that the General Assembly elaborate a convention on the basis of the draft articles'.[29]

The *Draft Articles on Prevention of Transboundary Harm from Hazardous Activities* direct states to cooperate to accommodate their mutual interests, taking into account the interests of other states:

> The articles deal with the concepts of prevention in the context of authorization and regulation of hazardous activities which pose a significant risk of transboundary harm. Prevention in this sense, as a procedure or as a duty, deals with the phase prior to the situation where significant harm or damage might actually occur, requiring States concerned to invoke remedial or compensatory measures, which often involve issues concerning liability.[30]

The scope of the draft articles on prevention encompasses internationally acceptable activities 'carried out in the territory or otherwise under the jurisdiction or control of a State'[31] that 'involve a risk of causing significant transboundary harm through their physical consequences'.[32] The ILC did not develop a specific list of activities to be covered by the draft articles on prevention because it felt that risk is 'primarily a function of the particular application, the specific context and the manner of operation' rather than simply from the existence of an activity.[33]

The commentary to Article 1 emphasises that the activities that trigger a preventive obligation must involve a 'risk of causing significant transboundary harm' due to the physical consequences of the activity.[34] The ILC recognises that the term 'significant' can be ambiguous. Their clarifying formulation is that '"significant" is something more than "detectable" but need not be at the level of "serious" or "substantial" '.[35]

Article 3 on prevention together with Article 4 on cooperation provide the 'basic foundation' of the draft articles on prevention. Article 3 articulates that states of origin (i.e. where transboundary harm originates) should take all necessary measures in order to prevent

28 Ibid.
29 Ibid.
30 Ibid., p. 148.
31 Ibid., pp. 152, 149.
32 Ibid., p. 149.
33 Ibid., pp. 149–50.
34 Ibid., pp. 150–51.
35 Ibid., p. 152.

significant transboundary harm or at least to minimise the risk. Article 4 expresses the need for all states concerned to cooperate with one another in good faith in order to prevent significant transboundary harm from occurring or at least to minimise the risk.

The draft articles emphasise that the state of origin should notify affected states about potential risks, cooperate if a state likely to be affected feels that there is a risk of harm that they have not been notified about, develop contingency plans for responding to emergencies with states likely affected by potential risks, and immediately notify affected states when there is an emergency. Additionally, states are to enter into consultations or negotiations at the request of any party involved in order to resolve issues, settle disputes expeditiously through peaceful means, exchange relevant and available information with one another, and provide the likely affected public with relevant information related to the 'risky' activity[36]. However, 'data or information vital to the national security of the State of origin or to the protection of industrial secrets or concerning intellectual property may be withheld' as long as the state of origin is cooperating in good faith.[37]

While duties to notify and consult are generally considered to be procedural obligations, compliance with them should not relieve a state of liability for damage caused by transboundary pollution. The ILC views the duty not to cause such damage as unconditional.

Draft Principles on the Allocation of Loss in the Case of Transboundary Harm Arising Out of Hazardous Activities

In 2006 the ILC released eight *Draft Principles on the Allocation of Loss in the Case of Transboundary Harm Arising out of Hazardous Activities*, which it described as a 'non-binding declaration'.[38] The Preamble to the principles emphasises the importance of the Rio Declaration and the *Draft Articles on the Prevention of Transboundary Harm from Hazardous Activities*.[39] It notes that environmental harm often does not stay within state borders and that individuals who suffer harm should be able to obtain quick and ample compensation.[40]

The principles are intended to apply to any hazardous or ultra-hazardous activity, involving at least 'a risk of causing significant transboundary harm'.[41] They focus on the consequences of activities, not whether the activities are legal or not, and on damages caused despite an actor's due diligence.[42] The threshold for damage is 'significant' damage, which is defined as 'something more than "detectable" but not necessarily "serious" or "substantial".'[43]

Principle 4 provides that states should take all needed actions to ensure that prompt and adequate compensation is available as a result of damage caused by activities located within their territory or under their control. Principle 4 also states that the actions should include the imposition of liability on the operator or other responsible parties, that the liability should not require proof of fault, and that all conditions to such liability shall be consistent with the purposes of the draft principles. The commentary indicates that it is not always the 'operators'

---

36 Ibid., p. 165.
37 Ibid., pp. 166–7.
38 *Report of the International Law Commission* (2006), UN GAOR, 58th Sess, UN Doc A/61/10, p. 111.
39 Ibid., p. 114.
40 Ibid., pp. 114–16.
41 Ibid.
42 Ibid., p. 118.
43 Ibid., p. 123.

who should be liable, but rather 'the party with the most effective control of the risk at the time of the accident or [that] has the ability to provide compensation'.[44] Although several recently negotiated treaties provide for strict liability, Principle 4 concludes that activities that are not dangerous but still carry a risk of causing significant harm might be better dealt with if liability is linked to fault or negligence.[45]

Principle 4 specifies additional measures that states should take. First, states should require operators 'to establish and maintain financial security such as insurance bonds, or other financial guarantees to cover claims'.[46] Next, where appropriate, states should require industry-wide compensation funds to be set up at the national level. Finally, where the above measures are not enough, the state of origin should make sure that additional financial resources are made available. This does not mandate that the state of origin must use government money to provide prompt and adequate compensation, but only that there be sufficient financial resources available to provide it.[47]

As noted in the Third Restatement of Foreign Relations, the Stockholm Conference on the Human Environment was unable to achieve consensus on the scope of the obligation for a state to notify and consult other states concerning activities that might cause it significant injury. The Restatement noted that 'such an obligation is generally accepted, as long as it does not cause inordinate delays in development projects'.[48] Principle 5 of the ILC's draft principles states that the state of origin should provide prompt notification to all states that might be affected when an incident occurs and to ensure that proper response measures are taken. It also specifies that the state of origin should confer with and seek the assistance of all affected states to mitigate, and if possible to eliminate, the effects of transboundary damage.[49]

Principle 6 directs states to ensure that their courts have proper jurisdiction and competence to address claims arising from transboundary damage caused by hazardous activities located within the state. Victims are to be given the same access to prompt, adequate and effective remedies in the state of origin that victims within the state of origin receive 'without prejudice to the right of the victims to seek remedies other than those available in the State of origin'. It allows states to provide recourse to claims in international settlement procedures so long as they are swift and inexpensive, and to establish settlement boards or claims commissions between the state of origin and the affected state to deal with the various claims.[50]

The draft principles on allocation of loss were adopted by the ILC at its 58th session and submitted to the General Assembly. The Commission recommended that the Assembly endorse the draft principles on allocation of loss by a resolution and urged states to take national and international action to implement them. The General Assembly, at its 61st session, after receiving the report of the Commission, acknowledged the principles and commended them to the attention of governments. The General Assembly considered the issue again in the 65th session of the United Nations in December 2010. Again it commended the draft text to governments without prejudice to any future actions that may be taken on the subject.[51]

---

44 Ibid., p. 155.
45 Ibid., p. 156.
46 Ibid., p. 151.
47 Ibid., p. 165.
48 American Law Institute (1987), *Restatement Third of Foreign Relations* § 601 Comment e.
49 Ibid.
50 Ibid., p. 177.
51 (2010), UN GAOR 65/28, paras 1–2, UN Doc A/RES/65/28.

European Union Liability Directives

In the absence of effective international enforcement mechanisms, domestic law remains the most important vehicle for implementation of liability norms for environmental harm. The regional initiative that has been most influential in shaping domestic law is that of the European Union (EU). The European Commission (EC) has directed member states of the EU to establish more effective domestic liability schemes to prevent and to remedy environmental damage. The EU environmental directives 'impose levels of minimum harmonization on member states by setting environmental standards that are subsequently enforced by the member states' authorities on individuals'.[52] Member states retain discretion concerning the form and method of implementation so long as the directive's desired result is achieved.

Directive 2004/35 on Environmental Liability With Regard to the Prevention and Remedying of Environmental Damage

In April 2004 the EC adopted Directive 2004/35 on Environmental Liability with Regard to The Prevention and Remedying of Environmental Damage.[53] Addressed to all member states of the European Union,[54] the purpose of the Environmental Liability Directive 'is to establish a framework of environmental liability based on the "polluter pays" principle, to prevent and remedy environmental damage'.[55] The 'polluter pays' principle provides that an operator that causes environmental damage or creates an imminent threat of damage should 'bear the cost of the necessary preventative or remedial measures'. It is reflected in Principle 16 of the Rio Declaration, which provides that:

> National authorities should endeavor to promote the internalization of environmental costs and the use of economic instruments, taking into account the approach that the polluter should, in principle, bear the cost of pollution, with due regard to the public interest and without distorting international trade and investment.[56]

The EC Directive adopts the 'polluter pays' principle by articulating as a 'fundamental principle':

> that an operator whose activity has caused environmental damage or the imminent threat of such damage is to be held financially liable, in order to induce operators to adopt

---

52 J.A.W. van Zeben, 'The Untapped Potential of Horizontal Private Enforcement Within European Environmental Law', *Geo. Int'l Envtl. L. Rev.* 22, 2010, 241, p. 242; see *Treaty of Amsterdam Amending the Treaty on European Union*, the *Treaties Establishing the European Communities and Related Acts*, Art. 249, 2 October, 1997, 1997 OJ (C 340) 1 ('A directive shall be binding, as to the result to be achieved, upon each Member State to which it is addressed, but shall leave to the national authorities the choice of forms and methods').
53 Council Directive 2004/35, Environmental Liability with Regard to the Prevention and Remedying of Environmental Damage, Art. 21, 2004 O.J. (L 143) 56 ('2004 Directive'). Online. Available HTTP: <http://eur-lex.europa.eu/LexUriServ/LexUriServ.do?uri=OJ:L:2004:143:0056:0075:EN:PDF> (accessed 16 March 2012).
54 Ibid.
55 Ibid., Art. 1.
56 *Rio Declaration on Environment and Development* (1992), Principle 16.

measures and develop practices to minimise the risks of environmental damage so that their exposure to financial liabilities is reduced.[57]

Where a member state's competent authority acts instead of the operator, the authority is directed to ensure that any costs incurred are recovered from the operator.

The Directive does not prevent member states from maintaining or enacting more stringent provisions[58] but does require them to designate a 'competent authority' to fulfil the Directive's purpose.[59] Additionally, the Directive instructs member states to 'encourage the development of financial security instruments and markets . . . with the aim of enabling operators to use financial guarantees to cover their responsibilities under this Directive'.[60]

To redress environmental damage, the Directive provides for two types of liability schemes. The first is a strict liability scheme that applies to specific economic activities listed in Annex III of the Directive. For harm caused by these activities the operator may be held liable without proof of fault.[61] The second is a fault-based liability scheme that applies to all activities that are not listed in Annex III of the Directive. It only applies, however, where the damage (or imminent threat of damage) is to species or natural habitats protected by Community legislation. The operator is liable only if he is at fault or negligent.[62] In either scheme, 'the operator shall bear the costs for the prevention and remedial actions taken pursuant to this Directive.'[63] Should transboundary damage occur, member states are directed to cooperate and to communicate with one another in order to effectively achieve the purpose of the Directive, allowing affected member states to recover costs for preventive or remedial actions.[64]

The Directive provides exemptions from liability for certain types of environmental damage. These include environmental damage:

- resulting from an act of armed conflict or unavoidable natural phenomenon;
- arising from an incident in which liability or compensation is within the scope of the International Conventions listed in Annex IV;
- for which the operator has limited his liability in accordance with national legislation implementing the Convention on Limitation of Liability for Maritime Claims or the Strasbourg Convention on Limitation of Liability in Inland Navigation;
- caused by nuclear risks or activities covered by the Treaty establishing the European Atomic Energy Community or by activities where liability or compensation is within the scope of the international instruments included in Annex V;
- that is not caused by 'pollution of a diffuse character, where it is possible to establish a causal link between the damage and the activities of individual operators'; and
- caused by activities whose main purpose is to serve national defence or international security or activities protecting from natural disasters.[65]

---

57 2004 Directive, preamble 2.
58 Ibid., Art. 16.
59 Ibid., Art. 11.
60 Ibid., Art. 14.
61 Ibid., Art. 3, para. 1(a).
62 Ibid., Art. 3, para. 1(b).
63 Ibid., Art. 8
64 Ibid., preamble 28, Art. 15.
65 Ibid., Art. 4.

Recovery by private parties for environmental damage to private property is excluded from the scope of the 2004 Directive.[66] Private parties may seek recourse under Article 12's 'Request for Action' and Article 13's 'Review Procedures'.[67] The owner of the damaged property may request that the competent authority take action and be consulted about the level of damage and the form of remedial measures. Alternatively, the owner has access to the court system or an able reviewer to challenge the competent authority's actions. However, access may be barred or limited if national legislation is in place regulating access to justice or if administrative procedures must be exhausted prior to judicial proceedings

Member states were to implement the provisions in the Directive by April 2007.[68] The EC, per Article 14(2) of the Directive, reported on the implementation effectiveness of the Directive on 12 October 2010.[69] Only four member states – Italy, Lithuania, Latvia and Hungary – met the 2007 deadline. As a result, the EC started infringement procedures against 23 member states. The EC eventually referred a number of non-complying countries to the European Court of Justice. In 2008 and 2009, seven member states – France, Finland, Slovenia, Luxembourg, Greece, Austria and the UK – received judgments against them.[70] By October 2010, all Member States had fully transposed the Directive except for Austria and Finland.[71]

EC Criminal Liability Directive

Criminal liability for those who cause environmental harm is still a relatively new concept outside of the US. In November 2008 the EC issued a Directive on The Protection of The Environment Through Criminal Law. The objective of the Directive is to impose criminal liability on certain behaviour that is seriously harmful to the environment. 'In order to achieve effective protection of the environment, there is a particular need for more dissuasive penalties for environmentally harmful activities, which typically cause or are likely to cause substantial damage.'[72]

The Directive provides a list of environmental offences that must be considered criminal offences by all member states, when unlawful and committed intentionally or with at least serious negligence.[73] Additionally, the Directive deems that inciting, aiding and abetting the commission of the listed offences is punishable as a criminal offence.[74] The Directive requires member states to ensure that parties can be held liable for offences committed for their benefit

66 Ibid., Preamble 14, Art. 3, para. 3; van Zeben, op. cit., p. 264.
67 2004 Directive, op. cit., Arts 12–13.
68 Ibid., Art. 19, para. 1.
69 Ibid., Art. 14, para. 2.
70 European Commission, *Report From the Commission to the Council, the European Parliament, the European Economic and Social Committee and the Committee of the Regions, Under Article 14(2) of Directive 2004/35/CE on the Environmental Liability with Regard to the Prevention and Remedying of Environmental Damage*, COM, 2010, 581, p. 3.
71 European Commission, *Study on the Implementation Effectiveness of the Environmental Liability Directive (ELD) and Related Financial Security Issues*, 070307/2008/516353/ETU/G.1, 2009, p. 25.
72 Council Directive 2008/99/EC, *Protection of the Environment through Criminal Law*, preamble 5, 2008 O.J. (L 328) 28 ('2008 Directive'). Online. Available HTTP: <http://eur-lex.europa.eu/LexUriServ/LexUriServ.do?uri=OJ:L:2008:328:0028:0037:EN:pdf> (accessed 16 March 2012).
73 Ibid., Art. 3.
74 Ibid., Art. 4.

and that the commission of the offences is subject to effective, proportionate and dissuasive criminal sanctions.[75]

Environmental liability provisions in treaties

Several treaties incorporate liability provisions reflecting the *sic utere* principle, but most of them remain handicapped by the difficulty of defining what harm is actionable and how much proof of causation is required. Out of more than a dozen multilateral agreements addressing transboundary environmental problems[76] only five have entered into force[77] and all of these address liability for either oil spills or nuclear accidents, where causation is rarely an issue. A few were enacted in response to the April 1986 Chernobyl nuclear accident, the worst nuclear accident in history, which is often cited to illustrate the inadequacy of existing international norms on state responsibility for transboundary environmental harm because no nation asserted any liability claims.[78] Effective global liability rules 'are the Yeti of international environmental law – pursued for years, sometimes spotted in rough outlines, but remarkably elusive in practice'.[79] Civil liability treaties governing transnational environmental harm remain 'unadopted orphans in international environmental law'.[80]

Among the multilateral environmental agreements that include liability provisions are the *Basel Convention*, the *International Convention on Liability and Compensation for Damage in Connection with the Carriage of Hazardous and Noxious Substances (HNS) by Sea*, and the *International Convention on Civil Liability for Bunker Oil Pollution Damage*. Conventions on liability for nuclear releases include the 1997 *Vienna Convention on Liability for Nuclear Damage* and the *Convention on Third Party Liability in the Field of Nuclear Energy*.

75 Ibid., Arts 6–7.
76 These include: the *Paris Convention on Third Party Liability in the Field of Nuclear Energy*, the *Convention on Liability of Operators of Nuclear Ships*, the *Vienna Convention on Civil Liability for Nuclear Damage*, the *Convention on Civil Liability for Oil Pollution Damage*, the *Convention on Civil Liability for Damage Caused During Carriage of Dangerous Goods*, the *International Maritime Organization Convention on Civil Liability for Oil Pollution Damage*, the *International Convention on the Establishment of an International Fund for Oil Pollution Damage*, the *Lugano Convention on Civil Liability for Damage Resulting from Activities Dangerous to the Environment*, the *International Maritime Organization Convention on Liability and Compensation in Connection with Carriage of Hazardous and Noxious Substances by Sea*, the *Basel Protocol on Liability and Compensation for Damage Resulting from Transboundary Movement of Hazardous Wastes*, the *International Maritime Organization Convention on Civil Liability for Bunker Oil Pollution Damage*, and the *UNECE Protocol on Civil Liability and Compensation for Damage Caused by the Transboundary Effects of Industrial Accidents on Transboundary Waters*. N. Sachs, 'Beyond the Liability Wall: Strengthening Tort Remedies in International Environmental Law,' *UCLAL Rev.* 55, 2008, 837, pp. 854–7.
77 *Paris Convention on Third Party Liability in the Field of Nuclear Energy*, *Vienna Convention on Civil Liability for Nuclear Damage*, *International Maritime Organization Convention on Civil Liability for Oil Pollution Damage*, *International Convention on the Establishment of an International Fund for Oil Pollution Damage*, *International Maritime Organization Convention on Civil Liability for Bunker Oil Pollution Damage*.
78 See E.B. Weiss, S. McCaffrey, D. McGraw and A.D. Tarlock, *International Environmental Law and Policy*, 2nd edition, New York: Foundation Press, 2007, pp. 419–23. They note that the Chernobyl accident contributed to the adoption of the *Convention on Early Notification of a Nuclear Accident*, opened for signature 26 September 1986, 25 ILM 1391 (entered into force 18 November 1986) and the *Convention on Assistance in the Case of a Nuclear Accident or Radiological Emergency*, opened for signature 26 September 26 1986, 25 ILM 1377 (entered into force 18 November 1986).
79 Sachs, op. cit., p. 839.
80 Ibid.

The Basel Liability Protocol seeks to establish a compensation regime for harm caused by the export of hazardous waste. The protocol holds exporters of hazardous waste strictly liable for such damage, but caps this liability while imposing generous time limits on the filing of claims.

The 1969 *International Convention on Civil Liability for Oil Pollution Damage* has been one of the most successful treaties providing for liability for transboundary harm. Several hundreds of millions of dollars of compensation has been paid for claims made pursuant to this convention. To recover for economic losses, parties must demonstrate that they were directly affected by the pollution. Punitive damages are not available under this convention. The 1993 Lugano Convention sought to establish a liability regime for broader categories of transboundary environmental harm, but it has never entered into force in part because of its incorporation of unlimited liability provisions.

Treaties vary in the standard of liability they adopt for environmental harm. As noted in the Third Restatement of Foreign Relations, some provide for balancing the significance of the environmental harm against the economic importance of the activity that causes it. An example of this is the 1971 *Agreement Concerning Frontier Rivers between Finland and Sweden*, which contains the following provision:

> Where the construction would result in a substantial deterioration in the living conditions of the population or cause a permanent change in natural conditions such as might entail substantially diminished comfort for people living in the vicinity or a significant nature conservancy loss or where significant public interests would be otherwise prejudiced, the construction shall be permitted only if it is of particular importance for the economy or for the locality or from some other public standpoint.[81]

Some treaties impose strict liability for environmental harm without regard to fault. For example, because the launching of space objects is considered an abnormally dangerous activity, the 1972 *Convention on International Liability for Damage Caused by Space Objects* provides that the launching state is 'absolutely liable to pay compensation for damage caused by its space object on the surface of the earth or to aircraft in flight'.[82]

Despite a trend toward incorporating liability regimes in multilateral treaties, outside of the context of oil spills there have been very few instances where compensation for environmental harm has been efficiently delivered. Recovery for harm to ecosystems has been difficult to obtain, as has recovery for damages to the global commons.

Equal access to domestic remedies

In the absence of an effective liability regime under international law for most environmental damage, domestic courts are an important vehicle of redress. Thus, the Third Restatement of Foreign Relations emphasises the importance of providing foreigners injured by domestic actors with equal access to domestic remedies. Section 602(2) provides that:

---

81 *Agreement Concerning Frontier Rivers between Finland and Sweden* (1971), 825 UNTS 191, 282, Ch. 3, Art. 3(2).
82 *Convention on International Liability for Damage Caused by Space Objects* (1972), Art. 2, 24 UST 2389, TIAS No. 7762, 961 UNTS 187.

> Where pollution originating in a state has caused significant injury to persons outside that state, or has created a significant risk of such injury, the state of origin is obligated to accord to the person injured or exposed to such risk access to the same judicial or administrative remedies as are available in similar circumstances to persons within the state.[83]

Spurred in part by the aftermath of the *Trail Smelter* controversy, seven US states and three Canadian provinces have adopted the *Uniform Transboundary Pollution Reciprocal Access Act*.[84]

In the US the *Alien Tort Statute* has expressly allowed foreigners to sue in US federal courts for violations of 'the law of nations'.[85] Using the *Alien Tort Statute*, residents of the Oriente region of Ecuador sued Texaco in 1993 for severe pollution caused by oil drilling operations in Ecuador during the 1970s. Texaco initially persuaded a federal trial court in New York to dismiss the litigation on the ground of *forum non conveniens*. But this dismissal was reversed on appeal in *Jota v Texaco, Inc.*[86] The appellate court held that the district court should not have used the doctrine of *forum non conveniens* to dismiss the case without at least requiring the company to submit to Ecuador's jurisdiction. In subsequent litigation the court affirmed the dismissal of the suit only on the condition that Texaco submit to the jurisdiction of the Ecuadoran courts.[87] This dismissal was widely viewed as Texaco's escape from liability. However, in May 2003 the case was refiled in Ecuador by 48 residents of the afflicted Oriente region, which changed this perception. After eight years of litigation in the Ecuadoran courts, in February 2011 the plaintiffs obtained a judgment against Texaco's new corporate parent, Chevron, of $18 billion for compensation and remediation.

Chevron is now seeking to block enforcement of the judgment by claiming it is the product of fraud. Chevron has filed suit against the Ecuadoran plaintiffs and their lawyers in the federal court in New York under the *Racketeer Influenced and Corrupt Organizations (RICO) Act*. Chevron alleges that the 'ultimate aim' of the litigation in Ecuador is to 'create enough pressure on Chevron in the United States to extort it into paying to stop the campaign against it'.[88] Chevron seeks a judicial declaration that the Ecuador court's judgment is fraudulent and unenforceable. As noted by one of the US judges hearing these claims, Chevron's statements make a striking contrast to the arguments its predecessor used in seeking a dismissal from the US court on grounds of *forums non conveniens*.[89] How the courts of other countries respond to the plaintiffs' efforts to enforce the judgment against Chevron will help shape norms of reciprocity for the enforcement of judgments in other cases of environmental damage by multinational corporations.

---

83 American Law Institute (1987), Restatement (Third) of Foreign Relations §602(2).
84 9C ULA 392-98 (1982).
85 28 USC §1350. The *Alien Tort Statute*, which was adopted as part of the *Judiciary Act* 1789, gives federal courts jurisdiction to hear a civil action by 'an alien for a tort only, committed in violation of the law of nations or a treaty of the United States'.
86 157 F.3d 153 (2d Cir. 1998).
87 *Aguinda v Texaco, Inc.*, 303 F.3d 470 (2d Cir. 2002),
88 See *Chevron Corp v Steven Donziger et al.*, US District Court for the Southern District of New York, No. 11-CV-0691. The complaint can be viewed online. Available HTTP: <http://www.scribd.com/collections/2839203/2-1-11-Fraud-and-RICO-Case> (accessed 16 March 2012).
89 See *In re application of Chevron*, 2010 WL 1801526 (SDNY, 20 May 2010) paras 12–13 (noting that Chevron 'extolled the virtues of the Ecuadorian legal system while the plaintiffs questioned its abilities and rectitude' during Chevron's earlier request for dismissal, and suggesting that the change to a more plaintiff-friendly national government may have something to do with this role reversal).

Conclusion

The norm of state responsibility for transboundary environmental harm has been widely accepted by the nations of the world and by international tribunals hearing environmental cases. But international law has failed to develop efficient liability and compensation regimes for most forms of global environmental harm, despite pledges to do so in Stockholm in 1972 and Rio in 1992. Multilateral treaties have established liability regimes applicable to harm caused by certain types of pollutants, such as oil and nuclear materials, with some success. But for more diffuse forms of environmental harm that are difficult to trace to specific polluters, liability regimes have proved ineffectual. Thus, the focus of efforts to redress global environmental harm appears to be shifting away from top-down approaches embodied in multilateral agreements in favour of more bottom-up, ad hoc approaches including transparency initiatives that are changing the behaviour of multinational corporations.

39

Deforestation, REDD and international law

Rowena Maguire

International environmental law governing conservation and management of forests has been largely limited to soft-law instruments. Nevertheless, increasing attention has been given to forest issues, most recently in the context of the climate change regime and the Reducing Emissions from Deforestation and Degradation (REDD) mechanism. The current law impacting upon the protection of forests and the contribution of emissions from deforestation will be considered in this chapter. The way forward will be explored, including the current options being considered for the post-Kyoto period.

Introduction

Forest regulation has historically proved challenging due to the wide range of values associated with forest areas. Reduced Emissions from Deforestation and Degradation (REDD) is a new mechanism that is driving global policy and investment in sustainable forest management and related activities. There are a range of hurdles for REDD to overcome in order for the mechanism to achieve the dual goals of contributing to global mitigation efforts and improving the quality of forest environments for local communities and ecological purposes. These obstacles include political impediments which must be addressed to ensure that REDD policies operate to recognise and protect all stakeholder interests associated with forest areas. Other challenges include designing polices that address methodological concerns associated with accounting for forest carbon, while keeping these policies clear and simple for implementation purposes. From a legal perspective, the biggest hurdle to overcome in the development of REDD policy is linked to reform of land tenure and the appropriate recognition of all interests within forest areas. The REDD policy is a popular one from a carbon mitigation perspective as globally forest degradation and deforestation accounts for around 20 per cent of global emissions and it is estimated that forests store 50 per cent of terrestrial carbon.[1]

---

1 A. Shvidenko, C.V. Barner and R. Persson, (2005), Chapter 21, 'Forest and Woodland Systems' in *Millennium Ecosystem Assessment*, 605. Online. Available HTTP: <http://www.maweb.org/documents/document.290.aspx.pdf> (accessed 9 May 2012).

Different terminology is used to describe REDD activities. This chapter will use the term REDD as this is the term referred to within the United Nations Framework Convention on Climate Change (UNFCCC) Conference of the Parties (COP) decisions. The scope of a legally binding instrument on REDD could take any of the following formations:

- RED: Reducing emissions from (gross) deforestation. This option only includes changes from 'forest' to 'non-forest' land cover types.[2]
- REDD: as above plus forest degradation, or the shifts to lower carbon-stock densities within the forest.[3]
- REDD+: as above, the term plus includes afforestation, poverty alleviation, biodiversity conservation and improved forest governance.[4]
- REDD++: as above, but also includes emissions from other land conversion (e.g. agriculture).[5]

Negotiations on REDD are occurring within the UNFCCC regime.[6] Negotiations within the UNFCCC regime are working towards the development of a legally binding instrument which defines REDD targets, policies and methodologies. Outside of UNFCCC REDD negotiations other REDD activities are taking place within REDD-specific institutions (for example the United Nations (UN) REDD Programme and Forest Carbon Partnership Facility) which focus on the implementation issues by conducting demonstration activities.

This chapter examines the development of REDD commitments within the UNFCCC regime. In order to understand the debates around REDD it is necessary to understand the context in which international forestry regulation takes place. The chapter begins with a brief summary of the international law concerning forestry, noting that there is currently no legally binding instrument applicable to all forest estates and areas. This is followed by an examination of the global forest policy developments made by the United Nations Forum on Forests (UNFF) and its predecessor bodies. The key instruments created by the UNFF and the shortcomings of the regime are discussed. The chapter then moves to consider regulation of forest activities by the UNFCCC framework. The UNFCCC, the Kyoto Protocol and other guidelines dealing with forest carbon sinks and sources are examined in order to understand the approach of the UNFCCC in dealing with forest-related issues. The chapter then moves to discuss the development of REDD policy by focusing on developments as they are recorded in COP decisions.

---

2 P.A. Minang, S. Jungcurt, V. Meadu and D. Murphy, (2009) 'THE REDD Negotiations: Moving into Copenhagen', *International Institute for Sustainable Development* 4. Online. Available HTTP: <http://www.iisd.org/pdf/2009/redd_negotiations.pdf> (accessed 14 December 2011).

3 Ibid.

4 B. Blom, T. Sunderland and D. Murdiyarso, 'Getting REDD to Work Locally: Lessons Learned from Integrated Conservation and Development Projects', *Environmental Science and Policy* 13(2), 2010, 164–172, p. 165.

5 Ibid.

6 For a concise summary of REDD negotiations see: C. Parker and A. Mitchell, *The Little REDD+ Book: An updated guide to governmental and non-governmental proposal for reducing emission from deforestation and degradation*, Global Canopy Program, 2009. Online. Available HTTP: <http://unfccc.int/files/methods_science/redd/application/pdf/the_little_redd_book_dec_08.pdf> (accessed 14 December 2011).

The role of demonstration REDD bodies is also explored in order to raise some of the methodological issues that arise when implementing REDD projects. The chapter concludes by noting the challenges that REDD policy must overcome (governance, tenure and corruption-related issues) and considers potential regulation of forests by the UNFCCC post 2012.

International law concerning forests

There are no legally binding international obligations to ensure that forests are managed sustainably. Negotiations at the international level concerning forest rights and responsibilities have always been politically charged.[7] The concept of state sovereignty gives states a number of rights to use natural resources found within their borders. States have been unwilling to negotiate binding commitments limiting their sovereign use of natural resources when the natural resource in question contributes to the state's economy and the livelihoods of local people. A quote from Mickelson is useful in explaining the sovereignty concerns linked with the development of a legally binding instrument:

> An essential difficulty that arises in the context of developing a forests convention, is that of avoiding the perception that such an agreement constitutes an infringement of sovereignty. In fact, if an instrument on forests is qualitatively different from previous international instruments in the environmental area it is precisely because its potential impact on sovereignty over resources appears to be much more direct.[8]

The negotiation of binding international instruments regulating forest use and management is particularly challenging due to the number of different values associated with forest areas. There are a number of anthropocentric values that compete for legal recognition and protection within forest areas. Typically most forest areas will be valued for one of the following reasons: their ability to provide economic benefits through the sale of timber and other forest products; their role in ensuring ecological function and integrity; and the contribution that forests make socially to local and global populations.[9] The challenge in creating international legally binding obligations in this area is not the design of a system which has the capacity to balance and recognise each forest value and identify the most appropriate value to recognise in a given instance. The real challenge lies in creating an instrument that is politically acceptable to states while seeking to ensure that forests are managed sustainably.

7 For an excellent summary of international forestry negotiations see D. Humphreys, *Logjam: Deforestation and the Crisis of Global Governance*, London: Earthscan, 2006; and R. Tarasofsky (ed.) (1999) *Assessing the International Forest Regime*, IUCN Environmental Law Centre. Online. Available HTTP: <http://weavingaweb.org/pdfdocuments/EPLP37EN.pdf> (accessed 14 December 2011).

8 K. Mickelson, 'Seeing the Forest, the Trees and the People: Coming to Terms with Developing Perspectives on the Proposed Global Forest Regime', in S. Johnson (ed.) *Global Forests and International Environmental Law*, Kluwer Law International, 1996, p. 248.

9 J. Bishop and N. Landell-Mills, 'Forest Environmental Services: An Overview', in S. Pagiola, J. Bishop and N. Landell-Mills (eds) *Selling Forest Environmental Services: Market-based Mechanisms for Conservation and Development*, London: Earthscan, 2004, p. 16.

Rowena Maguire

International institutions involved in forestry regulation

The United Nations Forum on Forests (UNFF) is the key body within the UN structure charged with regulating forest use and management. This body has been unable to deal effectively with the political issues surrounding forest regulation.[10] Lack of progress by the UNFF has led to the development of a number of alternative international forestry institutions and regulatory approaches. As a result, global forest regulation is patched together by different international bodies regulating individual forest values. A number of UN bodies play a role in forestry regulation, and Table 39.1 summarises the dominant UN institutions and instruments playing a role in global forest regulation. This chapter will focus on the regulation carried out by the UNFF and climate change regime.

Table 39.1 Regulation by United Nations institutions

Institution	Key forest instruments
United Nations Forum on Forests	Non-Legally Binding Authoritative Statement of Principles for a Global Consensus on the Management, Conservation and Sustainable Development of all Types of Forests (1992)
	Intergovernmental Panel on Forests/Intergovernmental Forum on Forests Proposals for Action (1995–2000).
	Non-Legally Binding Instrument on all types of Forests (2007)
International Climate Change Regime	Land-Use, Land-Use Change and Forestry Guidelines Decision 11/CP.7 2001
	CDM Forest Credit Guidelines Decision 14/CP.10 2004
	REDD policy (in development)
World Bank	The World Bank Forest Strategy 2002
Food and Agriculture Organization (Forestry)	FAO Ministerial Meeting on Forest Declaration: 1995, 1999, 2005
	Voluntary Code on Fire Management 2007
	Voluntary Code on Responsible Management of Planted Forests 2007
	State of the World's Forest Annual Report
International Tropical Timber Organization	International Tropical Timber Agreement 1994
	International Tropical Timber Agreement 2006
International Wetlands Regime	Convention on Wetlands of International Importance especially as Waterfowl Habitat 1971
International Biological Diversity Regime	Convention on Biological Diversity 1992
	Forest Biological Diversity COP 6 Decision V1/22 2002
International Desertification Regime	United Nations Convention to Combat Desertification 1994

10 For political analysis on the operation of the United Nations Forum on Forests, see generally Humphreys, op. cit.

Regulation by the United Nations Forum on Forests

The UNFF is the only international institution that focuses solely on forest issues. Predecessor bodies to the UNFF include the Intergovernmental Panel on Forestry, which operated from 1995 to 1997, and the International Forum on Forestry, which operated from 1997 to 2000. Both of these international forest institutions carried out similar roles to the UNFF, namely the provision of an international platform for forest negotiations.

In 2000, the UNFF was created under ECOSOC (Economic and Social Council) Resolution 2000/35. At the commencement of the forum's reign, it was envisaged that the body would continue in operation until 2005. In 2005, at the seventh session of the UNFF, a new forest instrument was drafted. In addition to this, a multi-year programme of work was also drafted to implement this new forest instrument. This multi-year programme of work has had the effect of informally continuing the operation of the forum until 2015. No formal negotiations took place to extend the duration of the forum; however, it seems that the parties have accepted that the forum will operate until the end of 2015.[11]

The forum is inclusive of all 'forest values', including productive and protective forest areas and all types of forest biome (such as tropical, boreal, native and plantation forest forms). The forum focuses on the concept of sustainable forest management, which recognises the ecological, social and economic values attributed to forest areas.[12] Because sustainable forest management involves the recognition of all forest values/services, the application of this concept often leads to conflict and/or confusion as the recognition of one forest value may be incompatible with the recognition of another. This difficulty has been identified and dealt with through the evolution of sustainable forest management methodologies and implementation tools.[13]

The UNFF and its predecessor bodies created the following legal instruments:

- Non-legally binding Authoritative Statement of Principles for a Global Consensus on the Management, Conservation and Sustainable Development of all Types of Forests 1992 (Forest Principles 1992).
- Intergovernmental Panel on Forests/Intergovernmental Forum on Forests Proposals for action (1995–2000).
- Non-legally binding Instrument on all Types of Forests 2007 (*Forest Principles 2007*).

There is a common understanding within international forestry networks, domestic policy counterparts and academic circles that the *Forest Principles 1992* were largely ignored by domestic regimes.[14] The subsequent proposals for action created between 1995 and 2000 were an attempt to address the lack of domestic implementation of the *Forest Principles 1992*. The proposals recommended that parties develop National Forest Policies to evaluate progress

---

11 United Nations Forum on Forests, *Multi-Year Programme of Work 2007–2015*. Online. Available HTTP: <http://www.un.org/esa/forests/multi-year-work.html> (accessed 14 December 2011).
12 G. Hickey, 'Evaluating Sustainable Forest Management', *Ecological Indicators* 8, 2008, 109–14, p. 111.
13 F. Cubbage, P. Harou and E. Sills, 'Policy Instruments to Enhance Multi-functional Forest Management', *Forest Policy and Economics* 9, 2007, 833–51.
14 J. Innes and K. Er, 'Global Forest Regulation in the Ten Years after the Rio Conference', *Trends in Ecology and Evolution 9, 2002, 115* and I. Visseren-Hamakers and P. Glasbergen, 'Partnerships in Forest Governance' *Global Environmental Change* 17, 2007, 408–20.

towards achieving SFM (sustainable forest management) at the domestic level.[15] National Forest Policies were to be developed at the domestic level taking into consideration the following:

- consistency of National Forest Policy with national, sub-national or local polices and strategies and international agreements where appropriate;
- partnership and participatory mechanisms to involve interested parties;
- recognition and respect for customary and traditional rights of indigenous people and local communities;
- examination of land tenure arrangements in connection with forestry activities;
- the utilization of an ecosystem approach that integrates the conservation of biological diversity and the sustainable use of biological resources; and
- the creation of a system that considerers the adequate provision and valuation of forest goods and services.[16]

Countries are not required to report to any particular body regarding the development and implementation of their National Forest Policy. Despite this, most countries have adopted some form of National Forest Policy to regulate and measure domestic forest use.[17] The widespread use of National Forest Policies is celebrated as one of the main achievements of the international dialogue on forests.[18]

The UNFF was formed to implement the proposals for action generated by the Intergovernmental Panel on Forests and the Intergovernmental Forum on Forests. The purpose behind the creation of the *Forest Principles* (2007) was to strengthen political commitment and action at all levels to implement effective sustainable management of all types of forests.[19] The instrument sets out four global forest goals:

(1) Reverse the loss of forest cover worldwide through SFM, including protection, restoration, afforestation and reforestation and increasing efforts to prevent forest degradation.
(2) Enhance forest-based economic, social and environmental benefits, including by improving the livelihoods of forest-dependent people;
(3) Increase significantly the area of protected forests worldwide and other areas of sustainably managed forests, as well as the proportion of forest products from sustainably managed forests;

15 This article contains an overview of the different international institutional perspectives on the role and purpose of National Forest Programmes: T. Michaelsen, L. Ljungmann, M.H. El-Lekany, P. Hyttinen, K. Giesen, M. Kaiser and E. von Zitzewitz, 'Hot Spot in the Field: National Forest Programmes – a New Instrument within Old Conflicts of the Forestry Sector', *Forest Policy and Economics* 1, 2000, 95–106.
16 United Nations Forum on Forests, *IPF Proposal for Action*. Online. Available HTTP: <http://www.un.org/esa/forests/pdf/ipf-iff-proposalsforaction.pdf> (accessed 14 December 2011). See Principle 17 (a).
17 Food and Agriculture Organisation, *National Forest Programmes*. Online. Available HTTP: <http://www.fao.org/forestry/nfp/en/> (accessed 14 December 2011).
18 National Forest Programme Facility (FAO), *Understanding National Forest Programmes: Guidance for Practitioners (2006)*. Online. Available HTTP: <http://www.fao.org/forestry/13533-0d0e0d879a9f3e-fc6ca9f847cd6ebb654.pdf> (accessed 14 December 2011).
19 United Nations Forum on Forestry, Report of the seventh session, *Non-legally binding instrument on all types of forests*, E/2007/42 E/cn.18/2007/18, Principle 1(a).

(4) Reverse the decline in official development assistance for SFM and mobilise significantly increased, new and additional financial resources from all sources for the implementation of sustainable forest management.[20]

In 2005, a report was prepared reviewing the effectiveness of the international arrangement on forests[21] using information from voluntarily submitted reports and questionnaires from countries and other organisations on the implementation of the proposals for action. The second section of the report collated responses on the overall effectiveness of the international arrangement on forests. Switzerland suggested that resolutions negotiated during Forum sessions have had limited impact on the implementation of proposals for action and that UNFF sessions did not prompt action for implementation.[22] The European Union suggested that formal forest policy development at the global level has been hindered by a lack of participation and a policy implementation instrument.[23] Conversely, Norway suggested that the proposals for action had enhanced policy development and dialogue at the international level and contributed to European collaboration on forest policy. Norway did, however, note that the effects of the proposals for action on policy development and dialogue at the domestic level were less obvious.[24]

The third part of the report summarised achievements and challenges for international forest regulation. Generally, there was consensus that the greatest level of achievement had been made through advances in national forest policy formulation, extending stakeholder engagement and the development of criteria and indicators. Weaknesses of the international arrangements on forests included failure of the regime to: address deforestation and illegal forestry practices; assist in the development of domestic institutional forestry frameworks; create sectoral links with other national policy processes; and create a mechanism to value forests' non-market values.[25] The report also revealed that many of responses noted the lack of a legally binding instrument concerning the use of the world's forests as a weakness undermining the success of the regime.

The lack of success by the UNFF and predecessor bodies has seen forest regulation encapsulated within the international climate change regime through the REDD dialogue. The development and implementation of REDD policy and activities is supported by the UNFF. The four global goals of the *Forest Principles 2007* will stand a much greater chance of implementation as a result of the REDD dialogue. In particular, REDD will assist with goal four in mobilising significantly increased, new and additional financial resources for sustainable forest management.[26] However, REDD will not be immune from the challenges associated

---

20 Ibid., Art. IV.
21 Department of Economic Secretariat of the United Nations Forum on Forestry (2005), *Review of the Effectiveness of the International Arrangement on Forests*, CN.18/2005/6.
22 Ibid., 66.
23 Ibid., 73.
24 Ibid., 74.
25 Ibid., 97.
26 REDD credits accounted for 33 per cent of all forest carbon credits sold in voluntary markets in 2010; see D. Diaz, K. Hamilton and E. Johnson (2011), *State of the Forest Carbon Markets 2011: From Canopy to Currency*, Ecosystem Marketplace. Online. Available HTTP: <http://forest-trends.org/publication_details.php?publicationID=2963> (accessed 14 December 2011). On the role of compliance versus voluntary forest markets, see R. Maguire, 'Opportunities for Forest Finance: Compliance and Voluntary Markets', *Carbon and Climate Law Review* 1, 2011, 100–23.

with regulating forest use and management and the success of the REDD regime will be dependent upon its learning from the experiences of bodies like the UNFF and others in dealing with the various stakeholder interests associated with forest areas.

Forest regulation within the climate change regime

Discussions about the role that forests should play in mitigation have taken place since the inception of the climate change regime. The term 'climate change regime' is used in this chapter to refer to the governance arrangements that exist to support the implementation of the UNFCCC. This includes a combination of the laws,[27] institutions[28] and processes.[29] The climate change regime is primarily concerned with the contributions that forests make as sinks or sources of greenhouse gas (GHG) emissions. Forest practices can be modified to reduce their 'source value' of emissions (for example employing more sustainable harvesting and silviculture practices). Forests are also regulated by the regime for their sink values (their ability to absorb GHG emissions). Presently afforestation and reforestation activities are dealt with under the Kyoto Protocol (though countries are not required to account for sink or source emissions from these activities).[30] Activities to avoid or reduce deforestation are not included within the ambit of the Kyoto Protocol, which is resulting in the development of a separate instrument on deforestation (REDD). The particulars of this regulation will be explored in greater detail below.

The following climate change instruments touch on or directly address forest carbon issues:

- The United Nations Framework Convention on Climate Change (UNFCCC)
- The Kyoto Protocol
  - Land Use, Land-Use Change and Forestry Guidelines
  - Clean Development Mechanism Forest Credit Guidelines
- REDD Instrument (instrument in development to deal with deforestation)

United Nations Framework Convention on Climate Change

Article 4 (d) of the UNFCCC creates an obligation on parties to promote sustainable management of all sinks of emissions. Forests are specially mentioned as a resource to be managed for this purpose and reading of this text alone suggests that the management of forest areas should focus on enhancing the carbon value of forests ahead of other economic, ecological or social interests associated with the forest area. Forest-dependent developing countries are given special recognition under the Convention within Article 4(8)(c), which requires parties to

---

27 For example the *United Nations Framework Convention on Climate Change*, opened for signature 4 June 1992, 1771 UNTS 107 (entered into force 21 March 1994) and the *Kyoto Protocol to the United Nations Framework Convention on Climate Change*, opened for signature 11 December 1997, 2303 UNTS 148 (entered into force 16 February 2005).
28 For example: The Subsidiary Body for Scientific and Technological Advice and The Intergovernmental Panel on Climate Change.
29 Formal negotiations with the regime take place through Conference of the Parties (COP) decisions.
30 Articles 3 and 4 of the Kyoto Protocol allows parties to opt in or opt out of accounting for land use practices contributing as a sink or source of emissions.

consider the impact of the Convention's obligations on developing countries with forested areas. It encourages the transfer of funding, insurance and technology to these countries to assist in addressing the adverse impact of climate change within forest estates and/or the impact of implementation of response measures within forest estates. While this obligation to assist countries in conserving forests as GHG sinks has been in existence since the creation of the UNFCCC in 1992, this obligation was largely ignored until the COP negotiations in Bali in 2007 when REDD negotiations commenced.

Kyoto Protocol

Article 3 of the Kyoto Protocol defines the role of forests in climate change mitigation. Under Article 3 parties to the Protocol are given the option of including domestic forest activities within their emission calculations. If parties opt to include forest activities within their carbon accounting they must include both sink and source forest activities. The inclusion of forest activities within the Kyoto regime proved to be controversial due to a number of methodological concerns related to calculating a baseline, scale, permanence, additionality, dealing with system leakages and double counting.

- Baseline: this is the hypothetical reference which represents the volume of GHGs that would have been emitted if the project had not occurred. Governments need to create, implement and enforce domestic policies and law to reduce deforestation against a baseline.[31] It is, however, difficult to set a baseline when there is limited or incomplete data on deforestation.
- Scale: concern that forest projects are cheaper to implement compared with clean/renewable energy projects and the inclusion of forest projects acting as a disincentive against investment in energy projects.
- Permanence: the issue being the scientific uncertainty surrounding the duration and level of carbon sequestered in forests, soils and other vegetation.[32] From a legal perspective it is necessary to ensure that carbon is stored in the forest for perpetuity, despite transfer in title. Legal instruments that can be utilised in this respect include leases, licenses, acquiring forestry concessions, entry into stewardship agreements or legislative measures, which continue for the entire permanence period.[33]
- Additionality: this concept ensures that credits are only given for practices which go above business as usual. Concern surrounded the issue that forest credits would be created to reward parties who undertook no additional carbon reduction activities.

31 R. O'Sullivan and C. Streck, 'Conservation Carbon: A New Voluntary Market Mechanism to Protect Forests', *Carbon and Climate Law Review* 3, 2008, 312–21, p. 316.

32 Means which can be used to account for non-permanence; these include various insurance options, renewal or temporary crediting, and banking carbon credits as a risk buffer. See I. Fry, 'Twists and Turns in the Jungle: Exploring the Evolution of Land Use, Land-Use Change and Forestry Decisions within the Kyoto Protocol', *Review of European Community and International Environmental Law* 11(2), 2002, 159–68, p. 161.

33 J. Crittenden and M. Wilder, 'Brining the Forest to Market: Structuring Avoided Deforestation Projects', *Carbon and Climate Law Review* 3, 2008, 273–81, p. 279.

- Leakage: the concern being that improved forest activity in one area may result in unsustainable practice taking place in another area.[34] A purchaser of voluntary offsets will be particularly concerned about leakage issues to ensure that it does not jeopardise the veracity of any environmental claims that have been made on the basis of the offsets purchased.[35]
- Double counting: this may occur where credits are being sold to more than one purchaser.[36]

Land use, land use change and forestry guidelines

Parties to UNFCCC were concerned that forest credits lacked legitimacy compared with energy-generated credits. Furthermore there was concern that forest credits allowed parties to continue polluting activities by offsetting polluting activities as opposed to firm action to address the activities causing emissions.[37] In order to overcome the controversy of including forest activities within domestic accounting regimes the Land-Use, Land-Use Change and Forestry Guidelines (LULUCFG) were prepared by the Intergovernmental Panel on Climate Change (IPCC) in 2003.[38] In 2006 the IPCC updated its Guidelines for National Greenhouse Gas Inventories to include a chapter on 'Agriculture, Forestry and other Land Use' (material in this chapter is reflective of the LULUCFG).[39] It is worth noting that the LULUCFG do not include activities aimed at reducing forest degradation and deforestation; they only allow for reforestation or afforestation activities. Most states have opted not to include sink and source values of forest activities within national accounting frameworks as the reporting requirements within the LULUCFG are viewed as being onerous in this regard.[40]

At the COP meeting in Cancun in 2010 the LULUCFG were revisited and Annex 1 parties were requested to submit information on their forest management systems to be reviewed by an independent panel for verification.[41] Parties were requested to provide information on areas under forest management, emissions and removal from forest management, forest characteristics (age, structure and rotation length), historical and assumed harvesting

---

34 Certain developing nations may prove to have superior capacity conditions for implementing Kyoto forest projects and, as such, deforestation activities may then be transferred to countries with weaker capacity – resulting in no net global gain in emission reductions. See M. Jung, 'The Role of Forestry Projects in the Clean Development Mechanism', *Environmental Science and Policy* 8, 2005, 87–104.
35 Crittenden and Wilder, op. cit., p. 278.
36 R. Maguire, 'Legal Issues in the Design and Implementation of Environmental Offset and Environmental Trading Frameworks', *Queensland Environmental Practice Reporter* 14(64), 2008–2009, 53–61.
37 Legitimacy concerns arise as to the scientific complexity, insufficient data on forest coverage and challenge of monitoring forests activities. See C. Streck, 'Forests, Carbon Markets and Avoided Deforestation: Legal Implications', *Carbon and Climate Law Review* 3, 2008, 239–48, p. 242.
38 Intergovernmental Panel on Climate Change, (2003) 'Good Practice Guidance for Land-Use, Land-Use Change and Forestry'. Online. Available HTTP: <http://www.ipcc-nggip.iges.or.jp/public/gpglulucf/gpglulucf_contents.html> (accessed 14 December 2011).
39 Intergovernmental Panel on Climate Change, *IPCC Guidelines of National Greenhouse Gas Inventories*. Online. Available HTTP: <http://www.ipcc-nggip.iges.or.jp/public/2006gl/index.html> (accessed 14 December 2011).
40 For more detailed consideration on this issue see Fry, op. cit., p. 159.
41 *United Nations Framework Convention on Climate Change*, Decision 2/CMP.6, 'The Cancun Agreements: Land use, land use change and forestry', FCCC/KP/CMP2010/12/Add.1.

rates, harvested wood products and disturbances in the context of *force majeure*. Parties were also required to provide a description about domestic policies adopted and implemented in regard to forest management. The information provided by Annex 1 parties was to be independently reviewed and a report produced for the COP meeting in Durban in 2012.

Clean Development Mechanism

A number of special rules were introduced for forest Clean Development Mechanism (CDM) projects.[42] The most significant difference between CDM forest projects and energy-related CDM projects is the temporary nature of the forest credits. There are two categories of forest CDM:

- Temporary certified emission reduction credits (replaced every five years); and
- Long-term certified emission reduction credits (lifespan of 60 years but must be verified every five years).[43]

The CDM forest credits can only be generated from afforestation and reforestation activities, again excluding reduced forest degradation and deforestation activities. The temporary nature of forest credits has made investments in forest projects under the CDM unattractive to investors and as such there has been limited use of the CDM special rules for forest projects.[44] Climate change instruments on afforestation and reforestation have seen limited application to date. It is believed by many that the REDD policy will have a much greater influence on global forest carbon management in the developing country context.[45] Furthermore, recent moves by the COP to reconsider the LULUCFG may see increased attention being directed to forest management for Annex 1 parties as a means for mitigation under a post-2012 regime.

Second commitment period – forest policy

The 2011 UNFCCC negotiations held in Durban clarified the role of forest sink and source activities for the second commitment period. Decision CMP.7 (Land use, Land-use change and Forestry)[46] suggests that parties will have mandatory obligations to report upon forest sink and source GHG emissions in the second commitment period. This is a significant change from the first commitment, which allowed parties to opt in or opt out of reporting upon land-use-related sink and/or source activities.

---

42 For more information see P. Graichen, 'Can Forestry Gain from Emissions Trading? Rules Governing Sinks Projects Under the UNFCCC and the EU Emissions Trading System', *Review of the European Community and International Environmental Law* 14(1), 2005, 11–18.

43 K. Rosenbaum, D. Schone and A. Mekouar, 'Climate Change and the Forest Sector: Possible national and subnational legislation', FAO Working Paper No 144, Food and Agriculture Organization of the United Nations, 2004, p. 17.

44 For a discussion on the implementation of CDM forest projects see J.E. Henman, S.P. Hamburg and A.A. Salazar Vega, 'Feasibility and Barrier to Entry for Small-Scale CDM Forest Carbon Projects: A Case Study from the Northeastern Peruvian Amazon', *Carbon and Climate Law Review* 3, 2008, 254–64.

45 O'Sullivan and Streck, op. cit.

46 CMP is the acronym used to designate decisions emerging from the Conference of the Parties serving as a meeting of the Parties to the Kyoto Protocol.

Decision CMP.7 clarifies the types of forest activities that can be included within existing implementation mechanisms. Noteworthy changes include:

- Deforestation activities to be included within the ambit of Article 3 and 4 of the Kyoto Protocol. This means that countries will be able to account for avoided deforestation activities undertaken domestically.[47]
- Carbon stored in harvested wood products to be recognised in the second commitment period.[48]

Decision CMP.7 also confirms that afforestation and reforestation projects will remain as eligible activities under the CDM in the second commitment period. It seems that deforestation will not be amalgamated into the CDM and that a separate policy on REDD will deal with deforestation-related activities undertaken by Annex I parties in partner or host countries.

REDD policy development

The REDD policy has evolved over a number of COP negotiations. The first time that REDD reached the COP negotiation platform was in 2005 at the 11th Meeting of the COP in Montreal, when Costa Rica and Papua New Guinea[49] submitted a proposal entitled 'Reducing emissions from deforestation in developing countries: approaches to stimulate action'. The submission made a compelling case as to why emissions from deforestation must be included within climate regulation and demonstrated that the climate change regime had authority to create policy on deforestation under the convention. The proposal suggested the creation of an optional protocol to the UNFCCC dealing with deforestation or in the alternative expanding the definition of forest activities under the LULUCFG. It was suggested that the methodological issues preventing the development of REDD policy be referred to the Subsidiary Body for Scientific and Technical Advice (SBSTA)[50] for further investigation. This proposal received broad support and began the impetus for the development of an international policy within the climate change regime to reduce emissions from deforestation – referred to at that point in time as RED.

COP13 Bali 2007

The SBSTA provided reports on the methodological issues associated with recognising deforestation activities at a number of SBSTA sessions (the SBSTA 25th session (Nairobi 2006), 26th session (Bonn, 2007) and 27th session (Bali, 2007)). These SBSTA reports led to

---

47 *United Nations Framework Convention on Climate Change*, Decision CMP.7 (2011), Art. 2. Online. Available HTTP: <http://unfccc.int/files/meetings/durban_nov_2011/decisions/application/pdf/awgkp_lulucf.pdf>.
48 Ibid., Art. 16.
49 Supported by eight other countries: Bolivia, Central African Republic, Chile, Congo, Costa Rica, Democratic Republic of the Congo, Dominican Republic and Nicaragua.
50 This body is established under Article 9 of the UNFCCC. The purpose of the SBSTA is to provide the COP with timely information and advice on scientific and technological matters relating to the convention. This body is comprised of government representatives who are competent in their relevant field of expertise.

a decision at COP13 in Bali in 2007 to formally include RED on the policy agenda. The COP decision encouraged parties to undertake RED demonstration activities, leading to formal approval for the pilot RED projects that started to take place across the globe[51] and multiple requests for the mobilisation of finance to support efforts to address deforestation. The COP decision also provided some guidance on how such activities were to occur:

(1) Demonstration activities to occur with the approval of the host Party.
(2) Estimates of reductions or increases in emissions should be founded on results-based, demonstrable, transparent and verifiable data and estimated consistently over time.
(3) Parties are encouraged to use the LULUCFG as the basis for estimating and monitoring emissions.
(4) Emission reduction from national demonstration activities should be assessed on the basis of national emissions from deforestation and forest degradation.
(5) Sub-national demonstration activities should be assessed within the boundary used for demonstration and for associated displacement of emissions.
(6) Reductions in emissions or increases resulting from the demonstration activity should be based on historical emissions, taking into account national circumstances.
(7) Sub-national approaches, where applied, should constitute a step towards the development of national approaches, reference levels and estimates.
(8) Demonstration activities should be consistent with sustainable forest management, noting *inter alia*, the relevant provisions of the UNFF, the UNCCD (United Nations Convention to Combat Desertification) and the CBD.
(9) Experiences in implementing activities should be reported and made available via the Web platform.
(10) Reporting on demonstration activities should include a description of the activities and their effectiveness, and may include other information.
(11) Independent expert review is encouraged.

There has been much contention over the development of RED policy and the consideration of indigenous groups and forest dwellers' community interest in forest estates where such activities are taking place.[52] Principle 1 requires that the host country provide approval for such activities to occur, but unless there is free prior informed consent of the group whose forest area is to be part of RED activities, there is concern that such initiatives may overlook indigenous and local interests in forest areas.[53] There is a moral obligation on the part of the global community to design RED in a way that is equitable for poor, forest-dwelling communities. The objective of a funded forest programme should be to provide local communities and governments with the support, technology and financial assistance necessary to

51 *United Nations Framework Convention on Climate Change*, Decision 2/CP.13, 'Reducing emissions from deforestation in developing countries: approaches to stimulate action', FCCC/CP/2007/6/ Add.1. Online. Available HTTP: <http://unfccc.int/resource/docs/2007/cop13/eng/06a01. pdf#page=8> (accessed 14 December 2011).
52 T. Griffiths, (2008) *Seeing 'REDD'? Forests, Climate Change Mitigation and the Rights of Indigenous Peoples and Local Communities*, Forest Peoples Programme, p. 27. Online. Available HTTP: <http:// www.forestpeoples.org/sites/fpp/files/publication/2010/08/seeingreddupdatedraft3dec08eng. pdf> (accessed 14 December 2011).
53 R. Hiraldo and T. Tanner, 'Forest Voices: Competing Narratives over REDD+', *IDS Bulletin* 42, 2011, 42–51.

sustainably manage their natural environment and to improve their own livelihoods thorough the sale of carbon and other ecosystem products. In order for such projects to be considered equitable it is essential to ensure that carbon payments do in fact flow through to local communities and farmers and that this process is not impeded through corrupt governance practices.[54]

Principles 2 to 7 provide some guidance on the methodological issues associated with forest activities. It is interesting that a distinction is drawn between national and sub-national forest activities and the means by which displacement is to be dealt with in each of these instances. Most RED demonstration activities would currently fall within the sub-national category, which means that those in charge of implementing such pilot studies must be careful to ensure that sustainable forest management in the project area is not leading to forestation degradation or deforestation in another region. Principle 8 could be seen as implying that RED activities are not to be governed purely on the basis of managing the forest carbon value alone and that all other values/services associated with the forest area must also be recognised. Such an interpretation is made on the basis of the inclusion of the term 'sustainable forest management' and reference to other international instruments concerned with the regulation and protection of ecological and social forest values.

COP15 Copenhagen 2009

The COP negotiations at Copenhagen in 2009 were considered to be a failure by many. However, one of the positive stories to emerge from this session was a further decision by the COP concerning REDD. This decision was responsible for changing the acronym of policy in this area from RED to REDD,[55] which has the effect of including activities that prevented forest degradation within the scope of the programme. Decision 4/CP.15 is entitled 'Methodological guidance for activities relating to reducing emissions from deforestation and forest degradation and the role of conservation, sustainable management of forests and enhancement of forest carbon stocks in developing countries', which of itself can be seen as a positive indication of the regime's intention to focus upon the recognition of all forest values.

This COP decision requested developing country parties to report upon the following issues:

- To identify the drivers of deforestation resulting in emissions and also the means to address these drivers; and
- To identify activities within the country that result in reduced emissions and increased removals, and stabilisation of forest carbon stocks.

Developing countries were also requested to develop a transparent national forest monitoring system that uses a combination of remote sensing and ground-based forest carbon inventory approaches. It is not overtly recognised within the text that developing countries parties may lack technical and other capacity to carry out this assessment, but, despite it not being expressly called for, a number of international bodies with an interest in REDD have stepped forward

---

54 Crittenden and Wilder, op. cit., p. 280.
55 REDD is the current acronym used to discuss the proposal, but RED is the correct term to use when referring to the concept's original status in COP documents.

to assist countries in meeting this requirement (referred to as demonstrating institutions).[56] The decision also calls for increased coordination in policy developments and from all international organisations, non-governmental organisations and other stakeholders working in these areas to prevent duplication and enhance synergy among efforts. In particular the decision encourages effective engagement of indigenous people and local communities in monitoring and reporting, but this clearly falls short of ensuring that indigenous people and local communities have consented to and benefit from the project.

COP16 Cancun 2010

The Cancun negotiations provided clarification on the nature and processes required for REDD+ activities. The Cancun COP report provides in paragraph 70 the types of REDD+ activities encouraged, paragraph 71 requests developing countries to develop certain systems and capacities to implement these activities, and Annex I of the agreement sets out a number of REDD+ safeguards.[57] The REDD+ activities encouraged under paragraph 70 are: reducing emissions from deforestation; reducing emission from forest degradation; conservation of carbon stocks; sustainable management of forests; and enhancement of forest carbon stocks. The types of REDD+ activities are therefore much broader then the forest activities provided for under the LULUCFG and the CDM forest guidelines.

Paragraph 71 requests developing countries parties to establish (in accordance with national circumstances) the following systems and capacities: national strategy plan; a national forest emission level or forest reference level; a robust and transparent national forest monitoring system; and a system on how safeguards are to be addressed while respecting sovereignty. The activities described under paragraph 71 are the types of activities being funded by REDD+ demonstration bodies (discussed in more detail below) in order to prepare developing countries to participate in the REDD+ regime. The Durban COP negotiations stated that forest reference emission levels and/or forest reference levels should be expressed in tonnes of carbon dioxide equivalent per year, as a benchmark for assessing each country's performance in implementing REDD+ activities from paragraph 70.[58]

The Annex I safeguards build on the guidance provided at Bali and require the following conditions to be addressed in REDD+ projects:

(1) The activities referred to in paragraph 70 of this decision should:
  (a) contribute to the achievement of the objective set out in Article 2 of the Convention;
  (b) contribute to the fulfilment of the commitments set out in Article 4, paragraph 3, of the Convention;
  (c) be country-driven and be considered options available to Parties;
  (d) be consistent with the objective of environmental integrity and take into account the multiple functions of forests and other ecosystems;

56 See C. Potvin and A. Bovarnick, 'Reducing Emissions from Deforestation and Forest Degradation in Developing Countries: Key Actors, Negotiations and Actions', *Carbon and Climate Law Review* 3, 2008, 264–73, p. 268.

57 Report of the Conference of the Parties on its sixteenth session, FCCC/CP/2010/7/Add.1.

58 Conference of the Parties Draft Decision /CP.17 'Guidance on systems for providing information on how safeguards are addressed and respected modalities relating to forest reference emission levels and forest reference levels as referred to in decision 1/CP.17', para. 7.

    (e) be undertaken in accordance with national development priorities, objectives and circumstances and capabilities and should respect sovereignty;

    (f) be consistent with Parties' national sustainable development needs and goals;

    (g) be implemented in the context of sustainable development and reducing poverty, while responding to climate change;

    (h) be consistent with the adaptation needs of the country;

    (i) be supported by adequate and predictable financial and technology support, including support for capacity-building;

    (j) be results-based;

    (k) promote sustainable management of forests.

(2) When undertaking the activities referred to in paragraph 70 of this decision, the following safeguards should be promoted and supported:

    (a) that actions complement or are consistent with the objectives of national forest programmes and relevant international conventions and agreements;

    (b) transparent and effective national forest governance structures, taking into account national legislation and sovereignty;

    (c) respect for the knowledge and rights of indigenous peoples and members of local communities, by taking into account relevant international obligations, national circumstances and laws, and noting that the UN General Assembly has adopted the UN Declaration on the Rights of Indigenous Peoples;

    (d) the full and effective participation of relevant stakeholders, in particular indigenous peoples and local communities, in the actions referred to in paragraphs 70 and 72 of this decision;

    (e) that actions are consistent with the conservation of natural forests and biological diversity, ensuring that the actions referred to in paragraph 70 of this decision are not used for the conversion of natural forests, but are instead used to incentivise the protection and conservation of natural forests and their ecosystem services, and to enhance other social and environmental benefits;

    (f) actions to address the risks of reversals;

    (g) actions to reduce displacement of emissions.

Demonstrating institutions

The UN REDD platform identifies two institutions as playing a large role in the implementation of demonstration REDD activities. These two bodies are the Forest Carbon Partnership Facility (FCPF) and the UN REDD Programme. The FCPF is housed within the World Bank's Carbon Finance unit and became operational in 2008.[59] The main objective of the FCPF is to provide technical assistance which supports countries to build national strategies and systems for REDD. Support by the FCPF is made through the use of two mechanisms: the Readiness Fund and the Carbon Fund. The UN REDD Programme was also launched in 2008 and brings together expertise from the Food and Agriculture Organization of the United Nations (FAO), the United Nations Development Programme (UNDP) and the

59 The website of the Forest Carbon Partnership Facility is online. Available: <http://www.forestcarbonpartnership.org/fcp/> (accessed 8 May 2012).

United Nations Environment Programme (UNEP).[60] The UN REDD programme differs from the FCFP approach in that it actively promotes the informed and meaningful involvement of all stakeholders, including indigenous and forest-dependent communities, in REDD implementation.

The FCPF and the UN REDD Programme have jointly prepared two reports examining the different safeguard policies implemented by REDD-demonstrating institutions and the various regulatory tools used by REDD demonstrating bodies. The review on safeguard mechanisms compares the policies of the FCFP, UN REDD-Programme and REDD+ Social and Environmental Standards to determine how each of these bodies considers the social and environmental implications of REDD activities.[61] The report recommends the development of overarching international principles to guide national programmes on appropriate safeguards and recommends the use of international environmental principles as the basis for the development for such principles. This recommendation is made after finding that, while the bodies examined share some commonalties in their approaches, there is considerable overlap in the scope of issues addressed by each body and differences in the level of detail or standards required under each approach.

The report on the different regulatory instruments for REDD compares the use of Payment for Ecosystem Services (PES) schemes, Participatory Forestry Management (PFM) approaches and the Forest Concession Management approach.[62] The report finds that each approach is a valid tool, concluding that PES and PFM approaches provide the best outcomes for sustainability and equity, whereas forest concession approaches offer efficiency advantages while states build capacity to implement PES and PFM. The report further recommends the devolution of certain decision-making powers with respect to forests to local governments and a focus within all mechanisms on the prioritisation of poor and marginalised groups in order to ensure that REDD regulatory tools operate effectively and equitably.

REDD challenges and future policy directions

Integrity of REDD Schemes

There are still a number of challenges to be overcome before investments made in REDD projects achieve positive environmental, social and economic outcomes. Ensuring the integrity of REDD systems is essential to facilitate long-term investment and progress in achieving global sustainable forest management. A major impediment in the implementation of REDD activities will be overcoming corrupt practices that are historically embedded in many forest regulatory systems. Corruption 'is linked to the failure of states to achieve the goals they set themselves for the very simple reason that the power, people and resources allocated to

---

60 The website of the UNREDD programme is online. Available HTTP: <http://www.un-redd.org/> (accessed 8 May 2012).

61 N. Moss and R. Nussbaum, (2011) 'A Review of three REDD+ Safeguards Initiatives' Forest Carbon Partnership Facility and UN REDD Programme. Online. Available HTTP: <http://reddpluspartnership.org/29785−0e1d064b96b75dfb79469cf0d86708dda.pdf> (accessed 14 December 2011).

62 J. Costenbader, (2011) 'REDD+ Benefit Sharing: A Comparative Assessment of Three National Policy Approaches' Forest Carbon Partnership Facility and UN REDD Programme. Online. Available HTTP: <http://www.uncclearn.org/sites/www.uncclearn.org/files/wb93.pdf> (accessed 14 December 2011).

achieving those goals are used for other purposes'.[63] Within REDD frameworks there are a number of stakeholder interests and there is great potential for conflicts to arise between different interest groups. A report analysing the operation of the REDD markets concludes that the bulk of the benefits from forest carbon investment will not make its way to indigenous groups and local communities and that a great deal of funds invested in REDD will end up in the pockets of institutions and individuals regulating such investments.[64]

Corruption within regulatory frameworks can be classed as being collusive or non-collusive in nature. Collusive corruption involves situations where forestry officers and the private sector collude to engage in questionable activities; while in non-collusive corruption, forestry officers act against the private sectors, for example by demanding a bribe be paid before allowing a legal activity to take place.[65] The following general factors have been identified as leading to corruption within the forestry sectors (these factors vary across geographic regions, states, cultures, economies and administrative capacity):

- The existence of bribes encourages those involved in forest regulation to participate in corruption.
- Forest enforcers being paid low salaries and waiting a long time for promotion act as disincentives for honest work.
- Forest enforcers lack sufficient resources to carry out their responsibilities (vehicles, technology, office space not in functional condition).
- The agency may lack procedures to ensure that actions of employees are transparent and accountable.
- Close relationships between people working in the forestry sector – the forest officer may have friends or family with private forest interests.
- Forest enforcers may work in a culture of corruption, where in order to avoid hostile workplaces and/or threats of violence to them or their family, they participate in questionable practices.

Combating corruption and promoting integrity requires a combination of state institutions and agencies (courts, parliament, police, legal practitioners), state watchdog agencies, non-governmental organisations, enforceable norms and incentive mechanisms to encourage integrity.[66] It would be unrealistic to assume that REDD investments alone will be a sufficient enough incentive to overcome corrupt practices in forest estates. In instances where corruption is resource-born, such as low salaries and lack of equipment, REDD investments will be able to address these issues directly, assuming that money makes its way to the appropriate stakeholders. In instances where there is a culture of corruption it will be much more difficult for REDD to ensure transparent and accountable systems resulting in good favourable environmental and social outcomes for local communities.

---

63 C. Sampford, 'Global Transparency: Fighting Corruption for a Sustainable Future', Proceedings of the 14th International Anti-Corruption Conference, Bangkok, Thailand, 10–13 November, 2009.
64 The Munden Project, (2011) 'REDD and Forest Carbon: Market Based Critique and Recommendations'. Online. Available HTTP: <http://www.rightsandresources.org/documents/files/doc_2215.pdf> (accessed 14 December 2011).
65 M. Miller, 'Persistent Illegal Logging in Costa Rica: The Role of Corruption among Forestry Regulators', *Journal of Environment and Development* 20(1), 2011, 50–68, p. 51.
66 Sampford, op. cit.

Land tenure

> The underlying rationale for linking tenure with sustainable forest management is the common assumption that secure tenure provides incentives for people to invest time and resources into forest management. Underlying this assumption is the idea that people will look after forest resources if they can benefit from them.[67]

All REDD instruments and demonstrating bodies recognise the importance of forest tenure considerations in REDD project areas. In many potential REDD project and pilot study sites, there are usually issues associated with identifying who owns the land, who has rights to use the land and who has rights to benefit from the land. The FAO has prepared a report on reforming forest tenure, which creates ten principles for forest tenure reform processes.[68] The report finds that radical changes in tenure reform are often associated with major political events such as revolutions and wars as opposed to reform by technocrats and civil society. This finding suggests that REDD efforts to reform forest tenure may not on their own carry sufficient weight to ensure appropriate tenure reform. It recommends that forest tenure reform be implemented as part of a holistic and integrated reform agenda, supported by related forest policy, legislation and institutional arrangements and that importantly it should not be limited to recognising or granting title and usufruct rights. This is a recommendation that REDD-demonstrating institutions should follow, otherwise it is possible that in the great enthusiasm to get REDD projects up and running, forest tenure reform processes will focus upon the granting of individual entitlements, without ensuring that a broader policy setting exists to support the creation of new rights.

Principle 4 of the FAO Report on Reforming Forest Tenure deals with the operation of REDD projects in areas regulated by customary law and recommends that relevant customary tenure systems be identified, recognised and incorporated into regulatory frameworks. This is an extremely relevant recommendation as many areas in which REDD projects will be carried out will be regulated under plural legal systems and it is very possible that there will be conflicts between interests recognised under customary legal systems and those recognised under state legislation. The report also highlights the role that tenure reform can have in human rights processes, particularly for indigenous groups seeking recognition of their custodial lands. Another useful recommendation is to design compliance procedures that are as simple as possible to minimise transaction costs and maximise the regulatory framework's enabling effects. The REDD demonstration institutions must heed the recommendations made by the FAO and set realistic goals and targets in relation to forest tenure reforms possible under REDD investment.

REDD, reforestation and afforestation policy post 2012

It is not yet clear how climate change instruments on deforestation, afforestation and reforestation will be structured under a 2012 regime. Different forest activities may well continue

---

67 Food and Agriculture Organization, (2011) 'Reforming Forest Tenure: Issues, Principles and Process', *FAO Forestry Paper* 165. Online. Available HTTP: <http://www.fao.org/docrep/014/i2185e/i2185e00.pdf> (accessed 14 December 2011). Also see on issues of property rights and environmental markets, R. Maguire and A. Phillips, 'The Role of Property Law on Environmental Management', *Environment and Planning Law Journal* 28(4), 2011, 215–42.

68 Ibid.

to be regulated under individual instruments, though it would seem more efficient to have all forest activities regulated under a common framework. It is likely that climate mitigation instruments will introduce mandatory reporting requirements for the domestic management of forest sink/source activities.[69] The existing LULUCFG are likely to be used as the basis for development of obligations in this regard. The role that forests play in mitigation seems to be a less controversial topic then it was in 1997 and is perceived as being a less political move than making significant cuts to emissions from other sources. As such, parties may take on higher obligations in relation to managing emissions from forest areas.

It is certain that REDD policy will play a dominant role in international forest regulation for the foreseeable future, and that a significant amount of capital will be invested in REDD projects in the coming years. It is likely that the development of a legally binding REDD instrument will occur at the same time as the renegotiation of a post-Kyoto Protocol, and that REDD may sit as a separate policy instrument within the post-2012 framework, though there is potential for it to be part of a redefined CDM instrument.[70] Adaptation policy will play a much more significant role in the post-2012 regime and forests may be seen as a means of addressing coastal erosion, preventing landslides and regulating climatic conditions. Forest enhancement in coastal areas and areas subject to natural disasters may also be seen as a priority within adaptation planning frameworks.

Conclusion

The REDD initiative instrument is different to earlier global initiatives concerning forestry. This is because it provides an economic benefit for forest conservation and circumvents sovereignty-based concerns by making involvement with the instrument voluntary but politically attractive; if parties want to share in REDD financial investments they decide to comply with the management standards prescribed by the regime. It is evident that REDD has the potential to become the most prominent international tool for forest regulation and to raise the political platform of forest conservation and management at a global level. The success of REDD will be measured by its ability to deliver upon environmental, social and economic factors, and developing indicators of success against these three criteria will be essential to ensure continued investment and development. The implementation of REDD activities will face significant hurdles in trying to ensure that carbon mitigation, the social and economic well-being of local forest communities and the interests of investors are all appropriately recognised and balanced within each project site. Legally the biggest challenges will be ensuring that indigenous/community interest groups' rights are protected by REDD instruments and in trying to address integrity system and land tenure reform in areas of REDD activities. The rapid growth and interest in REDD policy demonstrates that forest conservation, and improving the lives of those dependent upon forest areas, is an area of interest to multiple stakeholders. It is to be hoped that REDD can live up to these large expectations and deliver improved outcomes for global forest conservation and livelihood standards for forest communities and indigenous groups.

69 This prediction is supported by the CMP.7 decision on Land-Use, Land-Use Change Forestry Decision, op. cit.
70 The CMP.7 decision on Land-Use, Land-Use Change Forestry Decision suggests that REDD will sit as a separate instrument.

40

Climate refugees

Maxine Burkett

Climate change disproportionately impacts vulnerable communities globally. For some of the most vulnerable, these impacts will force them to move within and across borders, challenging international law to provide a coordinated and just means for migration. This chapter explores the phenomenon of 'climate-induced migration', identifies the sociological and legal uncertainties that surround it, and suggests areas of further research to respond appropriately to the emerging crisis.

Introduction

Individuals and communities displaced by an environmental shock have long been subjects of uncertainty in international law. Though referred to as 'environmental refugees' in popular discourse, this categorisation as 'refugee' has little support in existing law. The same uncertain categorisation is true for those displaced by climate change-related impacts, commonly labelled 'climate refugees'. As early as 1990, the Intergovernmental Panel on Climate Change (IPCC) stated that 'one of the gravest effects of climate change may be those on human migration'.[1] Unsurprisingly, as climate change impacts become more evident and worsen, the movement of peoples due to sudden- and slow-onset climate-related events require an appropriate legal response, particularly because those who are most vulnerable to this type of movement typically are the least responsible for anthropogenic climate change. This chapter explores the phenomenon of 'climate-induced migration',[2] identifies the sociological and legal uncertainties that surround it, and suggests areas of further research to respond appropriately to the emerging crisis. Perhaps more than any other area of international environmental law, the issues raised by climate-induced migration are the most complex, with no clear resolution.

---

1 IPCC, 'First Assessment Report', Contribution of Working Group II to the First Assessment Report of the Intergovernmental Panel on Climate Change (Potential Impacts of Climate Change), 1990, p. 103, para. 5.0.10.
2 Because the term 'climate refugee' does not have a clear legal status, as discussed in greater detail below, scholars, researchers, and some political voices employ proxy terms such as 'climate-induced migration', 'climate migrants' or 'the climate-displaced' to describe the phenomenon and those affected. The latter two terms are used interchangeably in this chapter.

Exploration of key concepts, principles and laws

Climate forecasts and climate-induced migration – facts and figures

Stronger and more frequent hydro-meteorological and climatological events are the hallmark of anthropogenic climate change. There has been a marked increase in both sudden-onset events, such as storms and flooding, as well as slow-onset events like sea-level rise and drought with attendant desertification.[3] Indeed, more volatile weather may be 'the new normal'.[4] Heightened disaster risk, social upheaval, and increased violence are possible results of this new normal, with poorer regions and countries among the most vulnerable. This section briefly describes the relevant climate change impacts and their influence on the phenomenon of climate-induced migration.

Current observation suggests that the changing climate has already caused significant displacement. Migration, as defined by the International Organization for Migration, is a process of population movement, either across an international border or within a state.[5] There is significant speculation regarding who might move and from which locations. Indeed, the substantial populations that live along the coastlines are most cited 'hotspots' for climate migration, such as the vast low-lying regions of Bangladesh.[6] Though the numbers and their derivation are highly controversial, as described below, assessments of vulnerable regions and the populations they host suggest that climate-related impacts might displace hundreds of millions throughout the globe over the next few decades. There is also evidence that adverse impacts of climate change are already contributing to the increased rate of domestic migration and relocation from rural areas and outlying islands to urban centres.[7] These kinds of environmental disturbances 'push' people to migrate and may be responsible for mass population movements in the Sahel region of Africa and areas in South America and the Middle East, among other places.[8] They may also have the ancillary effect of further provoking geopolitical tensions. For example, there is already opposition in some countries to accept climate-induced migrants, as evidenced in India's plan to erect a barrier at its border with Bangladesh to prevent entry of 'terrorists and illegal immigrants'.[9]

Due to the generally multi-causal nature of migration, it is difficult to know, or forecast, the true number of people who will migrate due to climate change. That has not inhibited efforts to try, with mixed results. Estimates of future environmental migrants vary by a factor of 40, with figures ranging from 25 million to 1 billion people, depending in part on the

---

3 Norwegian Refugee Council, 'Climate Changed: People Displaced', NRC Reports, 2009, p. 5.
4 Ibid.
5 International Organization for Migration, *Glossary on Migration*.
6 F. Laczko and C. Aghazarm, 'Introduction and Overview: Enhancing the Knowledge Base', in F. Laczko and C. Aghazarm (eds) *Environment and Climate Change: Assessing the Evidence*, International Organization for Migration, 2009 (stating that 44 per cent of the world's population lives within 150 km of the coast); D.C. Roy, 'Vulnerability and Population Displacements due to Climate-induced Disasters in Coastal Bangladesh', in M. Leighton, X. Shen and K. Warner (eds) *Climate Change and Migration: Rethinking Policies for Adaptation and Disaster Risk Reduction*, SOURCE, Publication Series of UNU-EHS, No. 15/2011. (Almost 40 million people live in coastal areas of Bangladesh, which is particularly vulnerable to coastal storms and surge.)
7 'Climate Change and its possible security implications', Report of the Secretary-General, A/64/150 and Corr. 1 (11 September 2009), p. 16.
8 Ibid., p. 17.
9 Roy, 'Vulnerability and Population Displacements', op. cit., p. 30.

IPCC emissions scenario employed. The most commonly cited number of environmental migrants by 2050, however, is 200 million.[10] Though this number is ubiquitous, it is speculative.[11] There is some evidence, however, that there are substantial and alarming numbers of current climate-displaced persons, warranting a coordinated response from the international community. For example, the findings of a joint report of the United Nations (UN) and prominent international displacement and refugee organisations found that in 2008 alone climate-related, sudden-onset natural disasters displaced more than 20 million people.[12] These numbers suggest that the number of displaced will rise with the increased frequency and severity of extreme weather. A much larger number may move due to gradual deterioration of their environment.[13]

Climate impacts generally will amplify existing social vulnerability, challenging the assumption that climate change will lead directly to migration. Many scholars have described migration as a social phenomenon in which environmental factors, such as a changing climate, may create an initial 'push' to migrate, but socio-political and economic causes are the underlying sources of vulnerability that may have more to do with why people ultimately move.[14] In other words, the individual's or community's ability to adapt to environmental changes may be a greater determinant of climate-induced migration than a particular sudden- or slow-onset event. Underlying social vulnerability, then, may determine if an individual or community can avail itself of the luxury to migrate.[15] Indeed, the financial resources and/or community networks in destination locations needed to migrate, particularly across borders, will limit many poor and landless from ever moving in the first place.[16]

For some migrants, however, staying may not be possible irrespective of their current socio-economic status. While climate forecasters deem small-islanders as among the most vulnerable to climate change impacts, a subset of small-islanders also face the spectre of permanent loss of state territory rendering them migrants without a home country.[17] In the

10 N. Stern, *The Economics of Climate Change: The Stern Review*, 'Part II: Impacts of CC on Growth and Development', 2006, p. 56. Online. Available HTTP: <http://webarchive.nationalarchives.gov.uk/+/http://www.hm-treasury.gov.uk/stern_review_report.htm> (accessed 16 May 2012).

11 See discussion below in the section headed 'Uncertainty, multi-causality, and political lethargy'.

12 OCHA/IDMC, 'Monitoring disaster displacement in the context of climate change – Findings of a study by the United Nations Office for the Coordination of Humanitarian Affairs and the Internal Displacement Monitoring Centre', 2009. Online. Available HTTP: <http://www.internal-displacement.org/8025708F004CFA06/(httpPublications)/451D224B41C04246C12576390031FF63?OpenDocument> (accessed 16 May 2012). Estimates on numbers displaced by natural disasters appear to be more robust and less controversial. F. Gemenne, 'Why the Numbers Don't Add Up: A Review of Estimates and Predictions of People Displaced by Environmental Changes', *Global Environmental Change* 21(1), 2011, p. 3.

13 *Compendium of IOM's Activities in Migration, Climate Change and the Environment*, International Organization for Migration.

14 M.A.M. Lueck, in Leighton et al. (eds) *Climate Change and Migration*, op. cit.

15 *Compendium of IOM's Activities in Migration*, op. cit., p. 20.

16 P. Boncour, 'The Moment of Truth – Adapting to Climate Change', *Migration*, 2009, p. 4.

17 N. Mimura, L. Nurse, R.F. McLean, J. Agard, L. Briguglio, P. Lefale, R. Payet and G. Sem, 'Small Islands', *Climate Change 2008: Impacts, Adaptation and Vulnerability. Contribution of Working Group II to the Fourth Assessment Report of the Intergovernmental Panel on Climate Change*, M.L. Parry, O.F. Canziani, J.P. Palutikof, P.J. van der Linden and C.E. Hanson (eds), Cambridge: Cambridge University Press, 2007, p. 697 (describing island abandonment as an extreme example of the ultimate impacts of sea-level rise on small islands).

Caribbean and the Pacific islands, more than half of the population resides within a mile of the shore and '[a]lmost without exception, international airports, roads and capital cities in the small islands of the Indian and Pacific Oceans and the Caribbean are sited along the coast, or on tiny coral islands'.[18] Further, under most scenarios, climate change will likely seriously compromise water resources in small islands and heavily impact their coral reefs and fisheries.[19] Climate change impacts will also very likely adversely affect subsistence and commercial agriculture on these islands.[20] Though they are responsible for less than one per cent of global greenhouse gases, small islands are already expending scarce resources on strategies to adapt to growing climate threats.[21] Migration of entire communities is one of the adaptation strategies that island and atoll nations like the Maldives must contemplate.[22]

There are existing examples of island abandonment within and across borders.[23] Further, elaborate resettlement schemes to accommodate these migrants are in their nascent stages, though climate forecasts suggest that this should be a significant area of rapid development for the international community.[24] This kind of relocation and resettlement raises thorny legal questions that are particularly distressing to islanders. As expressed by Ronald Jumeau, Seychelles Ambassador to the United Nations and the United States:

> When we relocate, what happens to the resources you may have on the seabed? . . . When you relocate and you lose your country, what happens? What's your status in the country you relocate to? Who are you? Do you have a government there? Government of what? There hasn't been a government of refugees before.[25]

Uncertainty, multi-causality, and political lethargy

There are a number of areas of uncertainty surrounding the size, scope, and legal ramifications of the climate migration phenomenon. These uncertainties may in part account for the very little attention the international community has heretofore given to the emerging issue. This section further explores the controversy surrounding the calculation of the number of climate-displaced, including the multi-causal nature of the phenomenon, and the ambiguity as to the legal status of those displaced. It concludes by maintaining that, in spite of the uncertainty in size and cause, climate change will provoke significant social upheaval through migration, warranting investigation of the appropriate legal mechanisms for coordinating

---

18 Ibid., p. 689.
19 Ibid.
20 Ibid.
21 Ibid.
22 BBC News, 'Plan for new Maldives homeland', 11 November 2008. Online. Available HTTP: <http://news.bbc.co.uk/go/pr/fr/-/2/hi/south_asia/7719501.stm> (accessed 19 March 2012). Vulnerable atoll nations include the Maldives, the Republic of the Marshall Islands, Tuvalu, Tokelau and Kiribati.
23 Mimura et al., op. cit., pp. 707–708.
24 Ibid., p. 708 (citing ongoing resettlement schemes for Kiribati and the Maldives); UN General Assembly, 'Climate change and its possible security implications', A/64/350, 11 September 2009, p. 16; S. Leckie, 'Climate-related Disasters and Displacement: Homes for Lost Homes, Lands for Lost Lands', in J.M. Guzman, G. Martine, G. McGranahan, D. Schensul and C. Tacoli (eds) *Population Dynamics and Climate Change*, UNFPA and IIED, 2009, p. 123.
25 'Seychelles Sink as Climate Change Advances', National Public Radio, 22 September 2010.

migration within and across international borders and ensuring necessary rights protection for those who will migrate.

The single greatest controversy around the issue of climate-induced migration is predicting how many will move. Though 200 to 250 million is a popular number, as discussed above, arriving at that number required 'heroic extrapolations'.[26] A thorough survey of the numbers derived and the supporting methodology (or lack thereof) demonstrates the incredible divergence in numbers cited – from 10 million to 25 million to 200 million, and one enormous outlier of 1 billion.[27] The timescales used are also inconsistent and confusing. While many use 2050 as a benchmark year for which to make a prediction, others have used 2010. None have been clear as to whether they are describing the stock or flow – or both – of climate migrants.[28] Due to the myriad uncertainties in the extent and magnitude of future climate change, coupled with the multiple contexts and perceptions of climate threats, a reliable number of migrants may elude researchers indefinitely.[29]

Scholars have speculated that clear numbers are necessary both to raise awareness of the emerging crisis and to incite decision-makers at all scales to respond swiftly and appropriately for the benefit of potential migrants and others that this kind of migration may impact.[30] Yet, settling on appropriate numbers and time-scales, particularly for slow-onset changes, plagues scholars. In fact, it has produced an ongoing rift between so-called 'maximalists' – those who assume that environmental change is a major driver of migration and displacement and whose estimates tend to be greater – and 'minimalists' – those who tend to insist on the multi-causality of migration.[31] Because environmental factors are one of many factors influencing migration, the minimalists maintain, it is unclear how much climate change will tip an individual's or community's long-term decision or immediate need to move. The absence of comprehensive studies on this point challenges the assumption that climate change will lead to migration in a linear way.[32] This is a conceptual challenge for most migration scenarios – though for small-atoll nations, for example, the causal relationship is far more

26 R. Morris, 'What Happens When Your Country Drowns', *Mother Jones*, 2009 (citing Oxford ecologist Norman Myer's concession, and describing the absence of a vetted scientific methodology).

27 See generally, Gemenne, op. cit.

28 Ibid. The stock estimates of migrants describe the people who have been displaced because of environmental factors but have returned or resettled elsewhere. Ibid., p. 3. The flow estimates describe the number of migrants on the move at a given moment in time.

29 D. Kniveton, C. Smith, R. Black and K. Schmidt-Verkerk, 'Challenges and Approaches to Measuring the Migration-Environment Nexus', in F. Laczko and C. Aghazarm (eds) *Environment and Climate Change: Assessing the Evidence*, International Organization for Migration, 2009, p. 18.

30 See e.g. Gemenne, op. cit., p. 6. Impacted communities include those that experience displacement, those to which migrants immigrate, and those who would suffer the loss of diverted, scarce resources to meet their needs, such as existing political refugees.

31 Ibid; A. Naik, 'Migration and Natural Disasters', in F. Laczko and C. Aghazarm (eds) *Environment and Climate Change: Assessing the Evidence*, International Organization for Migration, 2009, p. 253.

32 J. McAdam, 'Environmental Migration Governance', University of New South Wales Faculty of Law Research Series, 2009, p. 5; C. Tacoli, 'Crisis or Adaptation? Migration and Climate Change in a Context of High Mobility', in J.M. Guzman, G. Martine, G. McGranahan, D. Schensul and C. Tacoli (eds) *Population Dynamics and Climate Change*, UNFPA and IIED, 2009, p. 107.

straightforward.[33] Further, the absence of a 'consensual definition' of 'climate-induced migration', and the migrants it seeks to describe, has meant that different numbers can refer to different realities.[34]

This lack of appropriate nomenclature also results in a dangerous absence of clear legal recognition and the benefits and obligations such recognition might confer. By delimiting rights and obligations, definitions serve an important instrumental purpose,[35] particularly to determine appropriate legal mechanisms for protecting those who might indeed fall into the category of climate-induced migrant and to identify the relevant legal avenues that require further exploration. Accordingly, while the 'refugee' appellation may have political and sociological valence,[36] the absence of legal weight to the popular term 'environmental or climate refugee' is a real and formidable hurdle in finding and developing appropriate responses at the national and international scales.

There is some degree of consensus, however, in the understanding that the number and severity of natural disasters will increase with knock-on effects on the numbers of people displaced,[37] a phenomenon for which there are more reliable numbers and greater empirical linearity. Particularly troubling for those seeking clarity and swift action in this arena, however, will continue to be the cross-cutting complexity of climate-induced migration. Indeed, climate-induced migration implicates several spheres of governance and their relevant institutions, including migration and asylum law, environmental law, international development law, and human rights and humanitarian law, among others.[38] Because of its cross-cutting nature, it can continue to evade focused attention because no one policy

33 See M. Burkett, 'The Nation Ex-Situ: On Climate Change, Deterritorialized Nationhood, and the Post-Climate Era', *Climate Law*, 2011; R. Zetter, 'The Role of Legal and Normative Frameworks for the Protection of Environmentally Displaced People', in F. Laczko and C. Aghazam (eds) *Migration, Environment and Climate Change: Assessing the Evidence*, op. cit., p. 396 (suggesting that cases may exist where environmental change will be so dramatic and so all-encompassing of livelihoods that, regardless of livelihood strategies or socially constructed differences in wealth, most or all inhabitants of impacted areas will be forced to migrate; such people would be easily identifiable because of the direct link between severe environmental change and migration generated by the scale of impact).

34 Gemenne, op. cit. For example, does it describe temporary displacement, permanent local displacement, permanent internal displacement, permanent regional displacement, permanent inter-continental displacement. Leckie, op. cit., pp. 122–3 (defining each and stating that each of the five categories has different policy and legal implications for governments, the people concerned, and the international agencies tasked with assisting).

35 McAdam, op. cit., p. 7. 'Legal definitions bind States in ways that descriptive labels cannot': Ibid.

36 'A refugee can be defined in three ways: legally (as stipulated in national or international law); politically (as interpreted to meet political exigencies), and sociologically (as reflecting an empirical reality)': A. Lopez, 'The Protection of Environmentally-Displaced Persons in International Law', *Environmental Law* 37, 2007, 365, p. 367, n. 7 (citing A. Suhrke, 'Global Refugee Movements and Strategies of Response', in M.M. Kriz (ed.) *U.S. Immigration Policy: Global and Domestic Issues*, 1983, pp. 157–62.

37 Naik, op. cit., p. 248.

38 McAdam, op. cit., p. 23. This also implicates national security, indigenous rights and property law, for example. Leckie identifies five different categories of displacement climate change impacts might effect and emphasizes that each has different policy and legal implications for governments, the people concerned, and the international agencies tasked with assisting climate-induced migration to find durable solutions. Leckie, op. cit., pp. 122–3 (the five broad categories are temporary displacement, permanent local displacement, permanent internal displacement, permanent regional displacement, and permanent inter-continental displacement).

community is obliged to respond, nor can migrants hold any one entity accountable for its failure to respond.[39]

Relevant law and policy

The multi-causal nature of the climate migration phenomenon, coupled with the reluctance for existing policy regimes to take the mantle, arguably militates in favour of creating a new regime.[40] There have been equally strong calls, however, to explore existing instruments that might easily address the issue.[41] The current climate regime has been an obvious policy space for exploration. However, neither the landmark UN Framework Convention on Climate Change (UNFCC) nor the binding Kyoto Protocol acknowledge migration issues.[42] It was not until the Cancun Adaptation Framework in 2010 that the international community affirmatively recognised the importance of addressing the impacts of climate-induced migration and displacement, with yet to be determined influence on actual international policy.[43] The Framework Convention's few successes overall suggest that other avenues may more effectively protect migrants. This section identifies the main alternatives, and their possibilities and pitfalls.

Human rights law – and the numerous human rights instruments, norms, conventions and covenants dealing with forced displacement[44] – has been the primary alternative focus for potential law and policy remedies. Generally speaking, human rights law sets out minimum standards of treatment of individuals that a host state must observe.[45] A human rights frame for the climate-displaced suggests that each person displaced has a remedy available to him or her that respects, protects, and fulfils his or her rights as recognised under relevant international law.[46] Indeed, the governments of the atoll nations of Kiribati, the Maldives, and Tuvalu have been the most vocal in their appeal to human rights as a way to frame their experience of dangerous anthropogenic climate change.[47] The erosion of livelihoods and the threats to territorial existence of a number of low-lying island states implicate the rights to adequate housing and self-determination, respectively.[48] Further, as climate change becomes ever more dangerous, legal norms protecting rights to life, health, and food, among others, become particularly relevant.

39 P. Boncour and B. Burson, 'Climate Change and Migration in the South Pacific Region: Policy Perspectives', Institute for Policy Studies, Position Paper, 2009, p. 6.
40 See e.g. B. Docherty and T. Giannini, 'Confronting a Rising Tide: A Proposal for a Convention on Climate Change Refugees', *Harvard Environmental Law Review* 33, 2010, 349, pp. 357, 359. These proposals and the equally strong dissent are discussed below.
41 Zetter, op. cit., pp. 395–6.
42 Other elements of the UNFCC may arguably require a prompt and adequate response to climate-induced migration. In particular, adherence to the precautionary principle, reflected in Article 3 of the Convention, would require acting to avoid unnecessary delay in taking action to contain the threats of climate-induced migration. See Human Rights Council, Annual Report of the United Nations High Commissioner for Human Rights and Reports of the Office of the High Commissioner and the Secretary General, 'Report of the Office of the United Nations High Commissioner for Human Rights on the relationship between climate change and human rights,' A/HRC/10/6, 15 January 2009, p. 19.
43 Cancun Adaptation Framework, para. 14(f).
44 See generally, Zetter, op. cit.
45 Ibid.
46 See generally, Leckie, op. cit., p. 119.
47 Ibid.
48 Human Rights Council, 'Report on the relationship between climate change and human rights', pp. 13–14.

In addition to these more general rights appeals, the instruments related to migration and refugees have been of particular interest. Many scholars deem refugee law to be particularly relevant, even if ultimately unavailing. The 1951 *Convention Relating to the Status of Refugees*[49] and its 1967 *Protocol*[50] provide protection for those who have been forcibly displaced due to persecution and conflict. Article 1.A.2 of the Convention provides a definition of 'refugee' that arguably excludes those displaced by environmental factors. The term 'refugee' applies to any person who 'owing to well-founded fear of being persecuted for reasons of race, religion, nationality, membership of a particular social group or political opinion, is outside the country of his nationality and is unable or, owing to such fear, is unwilling to avail himself of the protection of that country'.[51] Interpretations of the 1951 Convention,[52] a product of the post–World War II proliferation of human rights law and related protection instruments, find that it seeks to protect people from the well-founded fear of state-sponsored persecution. Though the scope of the Convention has expanded since its inception, there are significant differences in the plight of the climate-displaced than what is currently recognised. Notably, the element of state-sponsored persecution on account of some kind of membership is absent. This may be insurmountable for those arguing that climate-induced migration falls under traditional refugee law, particularly because there is no consensus to amend the Convention to include them. Moreover, creative interpretations to include climate-induced migration might result in a significant disservice to the climate-displaced as well as traditional refugees, both of whom would now have to compete for finite resources amid growing international fatigue regarding cross-border movement.

While including environmental triggers in the refugee determination might add greater complexity and confusion with little tangible result, there may be avenues for protection through the *Guiding Principles on Internal Displacement*.[53] Because the greater balance of climate-induced migration will occur within countries, the principles regarding internally displaced persons appear to be a more promising protection framework. The *Guiding Principles* provide a normative framework for providing protection to the internally displaced. They define internally displaced persons (IDP) as 'persons or groups of persons who have been forced or obliged to flee or to leave their homes or places of habitual residence, in particular as a result of or in order to avoid the effects of *natural* or *human-made disasters* and who have not crossed an internationally recognized State border'.[54] The *Guiding Principles* effectively entitle IDPs to the same freedoms as other persons within their country,[55] including the full range of human rights guarantees given by a respective state.[56] Further, the principles acknowledge environmental triggers with the explicit recognition of disasters. The UN has clarified that the *Guiding Principles* cover all forms of climate change displacement, including

49 *Convention Relating to the Status of Refugees*, opened for signature 28 July 1951, 189 UNTS 150 (entered into force 22 April 1954).
50 *Protocol Relating to the Status of Refugees*, opened for signature 31 January 1967, 606 UNTS 267 (entered into force 4 October 1967).
51 *Convention Relating to the Status of Refugees*, Art. 1.
52 N. Hall, 'Climate Change and Organizational Change in UNHCR', in Leighton et al. (eds) *Climate Change and Migration*, op. cit., pp. 106–107.
53 E/CN.4/1998/53/Add.2, 11 February 1998.
54 Ibid., p. 5 (emphasis added).
55 Zetter, op. cit., p. 419.
56 Human Rights Council, Annual Report of the United Nations High Commissioner for Human Rights and Reports of the Office of the High Commissioner and the Secretary General, 'Report of the Office of the United Nations High Commissioner for Human Rights on the relationship between climate change and human rights,' A/HRC/10/6, 15 January 2009, p. 19.

those from slow-onset changes, such as drought.[57] The *Guiding Principles* are more promising only in theory, however, because they are neither binding nor enforceable. Further, many governments have not incorporated the principles into their national laws and their application has not been consistent across vulnerable communities.[58] Incorporation of the *Guiding Principles* into national laws may be a helpful first step for protection of IDPs.

The principle of non-refoulement is one other avenue that may provide protection for climate-induced displacement. In fact, in a Report of the Security-General on the possible security implications of climate change, the report states that arguably Article 33(1) of the 1951 Convention, on non-refoulement, prohibits a state from forcing people who move owing to environmental factors to return to the original state, or deny them entry at the border, if their life would be threatened as a result. The report concedes that this does not provide for an indefinite right to stay in the host state, limiting protections for those migrants permanently displaced from their homes. Further, a *prima facie* reading of the text suggests that the nature of the refugees' displacement is still dispositive – the Convention affords protection to the refugee expelled or refouled 'on account of his race, religion, nationality, membership of a particular social group or political opinion'.[59] Even if creative interpretation expanded this protection, the doctrine is too narrow to deal adequately with the circumstances of the climate-induced migrant.

This is also true for the international protections for stateless persons. These protections are not squarely relevant to the circumstances of island nation states that face the decreasing habitability of their territory, for example. As discussed in greater detail below, the current protections are too narrow, leaving significant questions for international law unresolved. In sum, there remains a significant gap in protection for cross-border climate migrants, particularly for those who are permanently displaced.

Unresolved questions of law and policy: new regimes, resettlement rights and statelessness

A new regime

With the absence of coherent and comprehensive legal avenues for the climate-displaced, there have been numerous calls for creating a regime specifically addressing the circumstances of climate-induced migration. There have been a few comprehensive proposals for creating an international protection mechanism, including one spearheaded by the Maldivian government.[60]

---

57 V. Kolmannskog, 'Climate Changed: People Displaced', Norwegian Refugee Council, 2009. Parallel regional instruments are also promising, including the African Union Convention for the Protection and Assistance of Internally Displaced Persons in Africa, 2009. See generally, Zetter, op. cit.

58 Leighton et al. (eds), *Climate Change and Migration: Rethinking Policies for Adaptation and Disaster Risk Reduction*, op. cit., p. 20.

59 *Convention Relating to the Status of Refugees*, Art. 33(1).

60 'Protocol on environmental refugees: Recognition of environmental refugees in the 1951 Convention and 1967 protocol relating to the status of refugees', cited in F. Biermann and I. Boas, 'Preparing for a Warmer World: Towards a Global Governance System to Protect Climate Refugees', Global Governance Working Paper, No 33, 2007, pp. 18–19 (describing draft text and elements produced at the meeting); see also, D. Hogkinson, T. Burton, S. Dawkins, L. Young and A. Coram, 'Towards a Convention for Persons Displaced by Climate Change: Key Issues and Preliminary Responses', *The New Critic*, Issue 8, September 2008 (describing a proposed draft 'Convention for Persons Displaced by Climate Change').

This section describes two of the more elaborated proposals as well as the arguments of their detractors.

Arguing that the people forced to leave their homes due to the 'grim consequences' of climate change deserve equal protection to those who fear political persecution, Bierman and Boas propose extending the notion of 'refugee' as a step toward a global governance system to protect 'climate refugees'.[61] They define 'climate refugees' as 'people who have to leave their habitats, immediately or in the near future, because of sudden or gradual alterations in their natural environment related to at least one of three impacts of climate change: sea-level rise, extreme weather events, and drought and water scarcity'.[62] The problem of multi-causality of migration is a surmountable hurdle in their view. While acknowledging the many reasons victims of storms, drought, and water scarcity might move, they stress resolution of these ambiguities through a political process, rather than an '*a priori*' exclusion of a large group of people from the climate refugee definition. Indeed, the authors choose the three 'direct, largely undisputed climate change impacts' when tailoring their definitions. Importantly, Bierman and Boas see an extension of the refugee definition under the 1951 Convention to be politically infeasible and likely ineffective. Instead, they affirmatively propose a global adaptation governance architecture to recognise, protect, and support the resettlement of climate refugees that accounts for the impossibility of their return, the collectivity and predictability of their flight, and the special moral and possible legal responsibilities of the largest emitters.[63] The key elements of their proposal are a Protocol on Recognition, Protection, and Resettlement of Climate Refugees, a new legal instrument under the UNFCCC (United Nations Framework Convention on Climate Change) specifically tailored to the needs of climate refugees, and the Climate Refugee and Resettlement Fund, a separate funding mechanism to facilitate the execution of the resettlement.

Docherty and Giannini propose a stand-alone convention to confront the issue of climate refugees who must migrate across national borders.[64] They define 'climate change refugee' as 'an individual who is forced to flee his or her home and to relocate temporarily or permanently across a national boundary as the result of sudden or gradual environmental disruption that is consistent with climate change and to which humans more likely than not contributed'.[65] Key to their definition is the capacity for advances in science to enable a more accurate determination of which events climate change has caused and, accordingly, which migration event is related. The proposed instrument would contain nine components organised around three broader categories: guarantees of assistance, shared responsibility, and administration of the instrument.[66] Guarantees of assistance would include standards for making 'climate change refugee' status determinations, human rights protections and humanitarian aid. Docherty and Giannini detail the shared responsibilities and attendant mechanisms to facilitate executing the obligations of host states, home states and the international community. Finally, a global fund, a coordinating agency, and a body of science experts would facilitate efficient, while scientifically rigorous, administration of the larger instrument and its component parts.

There is significant scepticism regarding the likelihood of the international community embracing a new regime of any kind. The international community has demonstrated a

61 Biermann and Boas, op. cit., p. 8.
62 Ibid.
63 Ibid., p. 16.
64 Docherty and Giannini, op. cit., p. 349.
65 Ibid., p. 361.
66 Ibid., pp. 373–89.

reluctance to negotiate new conventions or ensure the success of existing climate treaties, much less address climate-induced migration in any committed or coordinated way.[67] Zetter and McAdam suggest that there are affirmative drawbacks to a new regime. Zetter argues that, among other things, perceiving climate change impacts as migration drivers promotes the impression that there is a separate category of protection claims, which would favour migrations over the larger number of individuals who will not or cannot migrate. Indeed, a more fruitful avenue, according to Zetter, may be 'adapting and reconfiguring' existing protection norms and legislative frameworks.[68] McAdam contends that the absence of a definition for climate refugees may actually allow for more flexible responses. For example, certain people may be able to relocate through regional migration schemes that operate independent of climate drivers, such as labour migration schemes like New Zealand's Pacific Access Category.[69] If a treaty does become the main focus of international policy development, McAdam argues, attention may shift to 'more immediate, alternative and additional responses that may enable people to remain in their homes for as long as possible . . . or to move safely within their own countries, or to migrate in a planned manner over time'.[70] The absence of sufficient empirical understandings, as detailed above, further risks the international community acting at a level of generality that does not ensure optimal policy responses at scales most relevant to migration.[71] It may be that regionally based, bilateral or multilateral migration agreements are the most effective avenues for responding to the specifics of migration in a changing climate.

Resettlement rights

The challenges that the climate-displaced may encounter in host states are also of great concern.[72] Involuntary relocation and resettlement rarely improve the migrant's quality of life.[73] Further, empirical evidence suggests that displacement in the aftermath of natural disasters exacerbates 'pre-existing patterns of discrimination'.[74] The result is that already marginalised groups are further at risk of human rights abuses, including unequal access to humanitarian assistance, sexual and gender-based violence, and/or difficulties with restitution or compensation for lost property.[75] Clearly articulated resettlement rights would help to guard against the proliferation of these risks.

Beyond remedial and reparative measures, the international community should undertake affirmative efforts to ensure that the displaced are not significantly worse off in the process of framing a resettlement framework once they have immigrated to the host state. The relevant bodies should invite the participation of those at risk of climate-induced migration at the start

---

67 Hall, op. cit., p. 111.
68 Zetter, op. cit., p. 425.
69 McAdam, op. cit., pp. 7, 30–31.
70 J. McAdam, 'Swimming Against the Tide: Why a Climate Change Displacement Treaty is Not the Answer', *International Journal of Refugee Law*. 23, 2011, 2, p. 5.
71 See ibid. and McAdam, 'Environmental Migration Governance', op. cit., p. 8.
72 See UN General Assembly, 'Climate Change and its possible security implications', op. cit., p. 8.
73 NRC, 'Climate Changed: People Displaced', op. cit., p. 12.
74 'Forced Displacement in the Context of Climate Change: Challenges for States Under International Law', submitted by the Office of the United Nations High Commissioner for Refugees (UNHCR) in cooperation with NRC, the Representative of the Secretary General on the Human Rights of Internally Displaced Persons and the United Nations University, 19 May 2009, p. 8.
75 Ibid.

of any discussion regarding intervention measures. Together they would work to forestall the need to move, but also coordinate evacuation, relocation and resettlement, and possible return decisions and design, if return is viable for the migrant.[76] Once resettled in the host state, the relevant authorities must resolve citizenship questions. Current labour arrangement schemes may be instructive here.[77] Nevertheless, this latter point of immigration and full integration into a host state may be particularly thorny if the home state is no longer inhabitable and resettlement is, therefore, permanent.

Statelessness

For the Maldives, Tuvalu, Kiribati, and the Marshall Islands – atoll nation states that risk losing habitable territory through either seawater inundation and/or overtopping due to sea-level rise – their status as states, with its attendant benefits, are at risk. This scenario is truly unprecedented for international law.[78] As enumerated in the Restatement (Third) of Foreign Relations and the *Montevideo Convention*, international law generally regards a 'State' to have four key elements. Criteria for statehood include (i) a permanent population; (ii) a defined territory; (iii) a functioning government; and (iv) the capacity to enter into relations with other states.[79] When island states are no longer inhabited and the population is permanently displaced to other countries due to the loss of defined territory, it is unclear whether those citizens will become stateless persons under international law or landless citizens of a state that no longer exists.[80]

The international personality of states, particularly their creation and disappearance, is one of the most complex areas of law. There are international law regimes that govern issues of deprivation of nationality following the succession of a state, for example. There are none, however, that govern circumstances in which no successor state exists and the predecessor state has been rendered uninhabitable or has physically disappeared.[81] There is evidence, however, that while statehood is a legal concept with a determinate content, it may be sufficiently flexible to embrace novel approaches to address the circumstances of atoll nations.[82]

---

76 NRC, 'Climate Changed: People Displaced', p. 11.
77 See F. Thornton, 'Regional Labour Migration as Adaptation to Climate Change: Option in the Pacific', in Leighton et al. (eds) *Climate Change and Migration: Rethinking Policies for Adaptation and Disaster Risk Reduction*, op. cit.
78 See generally, Burkett, op. cit., p. 1; 'Climate Change and Statelessness: An Overview', submitted by United Nations High Commissioner for Refugees (UNHCR) supported by IOM and NRC to the UNFCCC, 15 May 2009. Online. Available HTTP: <http://www.unhcr.org/refworld/docid/4a2d189d3.html> (accessed 16 March 2012).
79 Restatement (Third) of Foreign Relations 201; Montevideo Convention on the Rights and Duties of States Art. 1, 26 December 1933, 49 Stat. 3097, 3 Bevans 145. See generally, J. Crawford, *The Creation of States in International Law*, 2nd edition, Oxford: Oxford University Press, 2006.
80 See Zetter, op. cit., p. 428. Further, the current statelessness treaties are generally poorly ratified and implemented, disfavouring reliance on them to address the circumstances of small islands. McAdam, 'Environmental Migration Governance', op. cit., p. 17 (citing the *Convention relating to the Status of Stateless Persons* (adopted 9/28/54) 360 UNTS 1171, Art. 1(1): 'For the purpose of this Convention, the term "stateless person" means a person who is not considered as a national by any State under the operation of its law').
81 See UNHCR, 'Climate Change and Statelessness: An Overview', op. cit., p. 28.
82 Crawford, op. cit., p. 718.

Notably, substantial changes in territory, population, or government, or even a combination of all three, do not necessarily extinguish a state.[83] In fact, in the period since the signing of the UN Charter, there have been very few cases of state extinction and almost no cases of involuntary extinction. That possibility for flexibility, coupled with the strong presumption that favours the continuity and disfavours the extinction of an established state,[84] suggests that acceptance of creative interpretations of law to recognise the continued existence of a state is plausible. Existing proposals suggest the maintenance of a discrete population in some portion of the compromised territory to formal international recognition of deterritorialised states.[85] Nonetheless, further research as well as early engagement of small islands is necessary as a matter of rights protection, regional peace and security, and the sovereignty of threatened nations.[86]

Conclusion

There are myriad legal questions raised by climate-induced migration. Clarity on some of the foundational elements of the phenomenon, such as accurate numbers and a better understanding of migration's primary drivers in a changing climate, might need to precede further development of appropriate law and policy. To the extent that there is a near-term risk of significant climate-induced migration, however, unknotting the legal tangles becomes more urgent.

In the near term, therefore, displacement monitoring and streamlined data-gathering is essential.[87] This would include the design of a common working definition as well as developing local research capability.[88] Research within the appropriate and clearly stated time and spatial scales – for example, forecasts detailing the movement of x millions each year in y region – will allow for multilateral, comprehensive agreements that detail to where the affected populations could move with the appropriate legal protections. While there is greater predictability in the plight of small atoll nations, the question of statelessness still requires significant attention and clarification. Finally, the extent to which the international community fails to bring emissions under control will affect how greatly climate change impacts all communities, especially the most vulnerable to extremes. Any near-term initiation of concerted law reform, to both the current international and climate change legal regime, will indicate the extent to which the globe can effectively accommodate a great reshuffling of human habitation.

83 Ibid., p. 700.
84 UNHCR, 'Climate Change and Statelessness' (stating that to the extent that statelessness is foreseeable, efforts should focus on preventing it from arising, consistent with the principle of prevention of statelessness recognised in international law as a corollary to right to a nationality); J. McAdam, ' "Disappearing States", Statelessness and the Boundaries of International Law', in J. McAdam (ed.) *Climate Change and Displacement: Multidisciplinary Perspectives*, Oxford/Portland, OR: Hart, 2010.
85 See J.G. Stoutenburg, 'When Do States Disappear? Thresholds of Effective Statehood and the Continued Recognition of "Deterritorialized" Island States', Conference Proceedings of 'Threatened Island Nations: Legal Implications of Rising Seas and a Changing Climate', Center for Climate Change Law, Columbia Law School, New York, 23 May 2011; R. Rayfuse, 'W(h)ither Tuvalu? International Law and Disappearing States', 2009, University of New South Wales Faculty of Law Research Series; Burkett, op. cit.
86 UN General Assembly, 'Climate change and its possible security implications', A/64/350, 11 September 2009, pp. 1, 16.
87 See generally, Gemenne, op. cit.
88 Ibid., p. 6.

Bibliography

Books and journal artices

Abbott, K.W. and Snidal, D., 'Hard and Soft Law in International Governance', *International Organization* 54(3), 2000, 421.

Abseno, M., 'East Africa', in F. Loures and A. Rieu-Clarke (eds) *The UN Watercourses Convention in Force – Strengthening Transboundary Water Management*, London: Earthscan, 2011.

Agardy, T., Notarbartolo di Sciara, G. and Christie, P., 'Mind the Gap: Addressing the Shortcomings of Marine Protected Areas through Large Scale Marine Spatial Planning', *Marine Policy* 35(2), 2011, 226.

Agius, E., 'Towards a Relational Theory of Intergenerational Ethics', in S. Busuttil, E. Agius, P.S. Inglott and T. Macelli (eds) *Our Responsibilities to Future Generations*, Malta: Foundation for International Studies, 1998.

Ahmed, J.U. and Daw, H.T., 'Environmental Impacts of the Production and Use of Nuclear Energy: A Summary of the United Nations Environment Programme Study', *IAEA Bulletin* 22(2), 1980.

Aikawa, N., 'An Historical Overview of the Preparation of the UNESCO International Convention for the Safeguarding of the Intangible Cultural Heritage', *Museum International* 5(1–2), 2004, 137.

Aldrich, G.H., 'Customary International Humanitarian Law – an Interpretation on Behalf of the ICRC', *British Yearbook of International Law* 76, 2006.

Al-Duaij, N., *Environmental Law of Armed Conflict*, Ardsley: Transnational Publishers, 2004.

Alfredsson, G., 'Human Rights and Indigenous Rights', in Loukacheva, N. (ed.) *Polar Law Textbook*, Copenhagen: Nordic Council of Ministers, 2010.

Alheit, J. and Hagen, E., 'Long-term climate forcing of European herring and sardine populations.' *Fisheries Oceanography* 6(2), 1997, 130.

Alkon, A.H. and Agyeman, J., 'Introduction: The Food Movement as Polyculture', in A.H. Alkon and J. Agyeman (eds) *Cultivating Food Justice: Race, Class, and Sustainability*, Cambridge, MA: MIT Press, 2011.

Allain, M.A., 'Canada's Claim to the Arctic: a Study in Overlapping Claims to the Outer Continental Shelf', *Journal of Maritime Law and Commerce* 42, 2011, 1.

Allott, P., *The Health of Nations*, Cambridge, Cambridge University Press, 2002.

Allott, P., 'Power Sharing in the Law of the Sea', *American Journal of International Law* 77(1), 1983, 1.

Aminazadeh, S.C., 'Moral Imperative: The Human Rights Implications of Climate Change', *Hastings International and Comparative Law Review* 30, 2007, 231.

Amnesty International, The UN Human Rights Norms for Business: Towards Legal Accountability, London: Amnesty International Publications, 2004.

Anand R., *International Environmental Justice: A North–South Dimension*, Burlington: Ashgate, 2004.

Anand R., *Origin and Development of the Law of the Sea: History of International Law*, The Hague: Martinus Nijhoff Publishers, 1982.

Anaya, S.J., 'Indigenous Peoples and Their Mark on the International Legal System', *American Indian Law Review* 31, 2006/2007, 257.

Anaya, S.J. and Grossman, C., 'The Case of *Awas Tingni v Nicaragua*: A New Step in the International Law of Indigenous Peoples', *Arizona Journal of International and Comparative Law* 19, 2002, 1.

Anderson, D., 'Law-Making Processes in the UN System – Some Impressions', *Max Planck UN Law* 2, 1998, 23.

Anderson, I.P. and Bowen, M.R., 'Fire Zones and the Threat to the Wetlands of Sumatra, Indonesia'. Online. Available HTTP: <http://www.fire.uni-freiburg.de/se_asia/projects/ffpcp/FFPCP-14-Firezone-Threat-Wetlands-Sumatra.pdf> (accessed 22 November 2011).

Anderson, M. 'Human Rights Approaches to Environmental Protection: An Overview', in M. Anderson and A. Boyle (eds) *Human Rights Approaches to Environmental Protection*, Oxford: Oxford University Press, 1996.

Anderson, M. 'Individual Rights to Environmental Protection in India', in M. Anderson and A. Boyle (eds) *Human Rights Approaches to Environmental Protection*, Oxford: Oxford University Press, 1996.

Andonova, L. and Mitchell, R., 'The Rescaling of Global Environmental Politics', *Annual Review of Environment and Resources* 35, 2010, 255.

Andresen, S., 'The Effectiveness of UN Environmental Institutions', *International Environmental Agreements* 7, 2007, 317.

Andresen, S. and Hey, E., 'The Effectiveness and Legitimacy of International Environmental Institutions', *International Environmental Agreements* 5, 2006, 211.

Ankersen, T., 'Shared Knowledge, Shared Jurisprudence: Learning to Speak Environmental Law Creole (Criollo)', *Tulane Environmental Law Journal* 16, 2003.

Anon, 'Illegal European fishing contributing to poverty and piracy in Africa', *Ecologist*, 20 April 2011.

Anton, D., 'Seabed Mining: Advisory Opinion on Responsibility and Liability' *Environmental Policy and Law* 41, 2011, 60.

Anton, D., Kohout, J. and Pain, N., 'Nationalizing Environmental Protection in Australia: The International Dimensions', *Environmental Law* 23, 1993, 763–83. Online. Available HTTP: <http://www.ciesin.org/docs/010-567/010-567.html> (accessed 23 November 2011).

Anton, D.K. ' "Treaty Congestion" in Contemporary International Environmental Law'. Online. Available HTTP: <http://papers.ssrn.com/sol3/papers.cfm?abstract_id=1988579> (accessed 8 May 2012).

ANZECC Taskforce on Marine Protected Areas, *Guidelines for Establishing the National Representative System of Marine Protected Areas*, Canberra: Environment Australia, 1998.

Aplin, G., *Heritage: Identification Conservation and Management*, Oxford: Oxford University Press, 2002.

Arezzo, E., 'Struggling Around the Natural Divide: The Protection of Tangible and Intangible Indigenous Property', *Cardozo Arts & Entertainment Law Journal* 25(1), 2007, 367.

Armitage, A., *Comparing the Policy of Aboriginal Assimilation: Australia, Canada and New Zealand*, Vancouver: University of British Columbia Press, 1995.

Arthington, A. and Nevill, J., 'Australia's Biodiversity Conservation Strategy 2010 – 2020: Scientists' letter of concern', *Ecological Management and Restoration* 10(2), 2009, 78.

ASEAN Centre for Biodiversity, *The ASEAN Heritage Parks: A Journey to the Natural Wonders of Southeast Asia*, Laguna: ASEAN Centre for Biodiversity, 2010.

Ashfaq, S., 'Something For Everyone: Why the United States Should Ratify the Law of the Sea Treaty', *Journal of Transnational Law & Policy* 19(2), 2010, 357.

Asian Development Bank, *What is Governance? Governance in Asia: From Crisis to Opportunity*, Bangkok, ADB: 1999.

Atsegbua, L., 'Environmental rights, pipeline vandalisation and conflict resolution in Nigeria', *International Energy Law and Taxation Review*, 2001.

Australian Climate Commission, *The Critical Decade: Climate Science, Risks and Responses*, Australian Climate Commission, 2011.

Australian Government and State of Queensland, *Reef Water Quality Protection Plan 2009*, Brisbane: Reef Water Quality Protection Plan Secretariat, 2009.

Australian Government, *Australia's Biodiversity Conservation Strategy 2010–2030*, Canberra, Australian Government, 2010.

Australian Government, *Australia's Oceans Policy*, Canberra: Australian Government, 1998.

Australian Government, *Australian Government Response to the Report of the Independent Review of the Environment Protection and Biodiversity Conservation Act 1999*, Canberra: Australian Government, 2011.

Australian Government, *National Forest Policy Statement*, Canberra: Australian Government, 1992.

Australian Government, *Regulation Impact Statement for the Consideration of the Addition of Nine Chemicals to the Stockholm Convention on POPs*. Online. Available HTTP: <http://www.environment.gov.au/settlements/chemicals/international/publications/pubs/ris.pdf> (accessed 20 November 2011).

Australian Government, *Securing a Clean Energy Future – the Australian Government's Climate Change Plan*, Canberra: Australian Government, 2011, p. vii. Online. Available HTTP: <http://www.cleanenergyfuture.gov.au/clean-energy-bills-receive-royal-assent/> (accessed 25 January 2012).

Australian Government, *The National Objectives and Targets for Biodiversity Conservation 2001–2005*, Canberra: Australian Government, 2001.

Awoonor, K.N., 'The Concerns of Recipient Nations', in K.M. Cahill (ed.) *A Framework for Survival: Health, Human Rights, and Humanitarian Assistance in Conflicts and Disasters*, New York: Basic Books, 1993.

Baetens, F., 'Foreign Investment Law and Climate Change: Legal Conflicts Arising from Implementing the Kyoto Protocol through Private Investment', *Sustainable Development Law on Climate Change Working Paper Series*, 2010.

Baker, B., 'Law, Science, And The Continental Shelf: The Russian Federation And The Promise Of Arctic Cooperation', *American University International Law Review* 25, 2010, 251.

Baldwin, M., 'The Santa Barbara Oil Spill', *University of Colorado Law Review* 42, 1970–71, 33.

Ball, S. and Bell, S., *Environmental Law*, 2nd edition, Delhi: Universal Law Publishing, 1994.

Ban, K., *Secretary-General's Message on the International Day for the Preservation of the Ozone Layer*, 16 September 2009. Online. Available HTTP: <http://www.un.org/apps/sg/sgstats.asp?nid=4069>.

Bandi, G., 'The Right to Environment in Theory and Practice: The Hungarian Experience', *Connecticut Journal of International Law* 8(2), 1933, 439.

Barclay, K. and Cartwright, I., 'Governance of Tuna Industries: the Key to Economic Viability and Sustainability in the Western and Central Pacific Ocean', *Marine Policy* 20(3), 2007, 348.

Barelli, M., 'The Interplay between Global and Regional Human Rights Systems in the Construction of the Indigenous Rights Regime', *Human Rights Quarterly* 32, 2010, 951.

Barnes, A.J., 'The Growing International Dimension to Environmental Issues', *Columbia Journal of Environmental Law* 13, 1988, 389.

Barnes, R., *Property Rights and Natural Resources*, Oxford: Hart Publishing, 2009.

Barsh, L.R., 'Indigenous Peoples in the 1990s: From Object to Subject of International Law', *Harvard Human Rights Journal* 33, 1994, reprinted in L. Watters (ed.) *Indigenous Peoples, the Environment and Law*, Durham, NC: Carolina Academic Press, 2004.

Barton, B., 'Renewable Energy in New Zealand', *Journal of Energy and Natural Resources Law* 23, 2005, 141.

Baslar, K., *The Concept of the Common Heritage of Mankind in International Law*, The Hague: Kluwer Law International, 1998.

Bates, G., *Environmental Law in Australia*, Chatswood: LexisNexis Butterworths, 2010.

Bates, G., 'Legal Perspectives', in S. Dovers and S. Wild River (eds) *Managing Australia's Environment*, Annandale: Federation Press, 2003.

Battiste, M. and Henderson, J., *Protecting Indigenous Knowledge and Heritage: A Global Challenge*, Saskatoon: Purich, 2000.

Beale, R., Fairbrother, J., Inglis, A. and Trebeck, D., *The Independent Review of Australia's Quarantine and Biosecurity Arrangements Report to the Australian Government*, Canberra: Australian Government, 2008.

Beckerman, W., ' "How Would You Like Your 'Sustainability', Sir? Weak or Strong?" A Reply to My Critics', *Environmental Values* 5, 1995, 169.

Beeton, R. and McGrath, C., 'Developing an Approach to the Listing of Ecological Communities to Achieve Conservation Outcomes', *Australian Journal of Natural Resource Law and Policy* 13(1), 2009, 61.

Beigbeder, Y., *The Role and Status of International Humanitarian Volunteers and Organizations: The Right and Duty to Humanitarian Assistance*, Dordrecht: Martinus Nijhoff, 1991.

Bellingham, M., 'Biodiversity and Sustainability: Theory, Framework and the Legislation', in R. Harris (ed.) *Handbook of Environmental Law*, Wellington: Royal Forest and Bird Protection Society of New Zealand 2004.

Benedick, R.E., *Ozone Diplomacy: New Directions in Safeguarding the Planet*, Cambridge, MA: Harvard University Press, 1991 (2nd edition 1998).

Benkö, M., 'Nuklearenergie im Weltraum', in K-H. Böckstiegel (ed.) *Handbuch des Weltraumrechts*, Cologne: Carl Heymanns Verlag, 1991.

Berber, F.J., *Rivers in International Law*, London: Stevens & Sons, 1959.

Berkes, F., 'Commons in a Multilevel World', *International Journal of the Commons* 2, 2008, 1.

Bernstein, L., Bosch, P., Canziani, O., Zhenlin, C., Christ, R., Davidson, O., Hare, W., Huq, S., Karoly, D., Kattsov, V., Kundzewicz, Z., Jian, L., Lohmann, U., Manning, M., Matsuno, T., Menne, B., Metz, B., Mirza, M., Nicholls, N., Nurse, L., Pachauri, R., Palutikof, J., Parry, M., Dahe, Q., Ravindranath, N., Reisinger, R., Ren, J., Riahi, K., Rosenzweig, C., Rusticucci, M., Schneider, S., Sokona, Y., Solomon, S., Stott, P., Stouffer, R., Sugiyama, T., Swart, R., Tirpak, D., Vogel, C. and Yohe, G., *Climate Change 2007: Synthesis Report*, Geneva: IPCC, 2007.

Berry, M. and Nelson, A., 'Steering Sustainability: What, When, and Why', in A. Nelson (ed.) *Steering Sustainability in an Urbanizing World: Policy Practice and Performance*, Aldershot: Ashgate, 2007.

Bertel, E. and Van de Vate, J., 'Nuclear Energy and the Environmental Debate: the Context of Choices', *IAEA Bulletin* 4, 1995.

Bess, R., 'Maintaining a Balance between Resource Utilisation and Protection of the Marine Environment in New Zealand', *Marine Policy* 34, 2010, 690.

Betsill, M.M. and Corell, E., 'NGO Influence in International Environmental Negotiations: A Framework for Analysis', *Global Environmental Politics* 1, 2001, 4.

Beyerlin, U., 'Bridging the North–South Divide in International Environmental Law', *Zeitschrift für ausländisches und öffentliches Recht* 66, 2006, 263.

Beyerlin, U., 'The Concept of Sustainable Development', in R. Wolfrum (ed.) *Enforcing Environmental Standards: Economic Mechanisms as Viable Means?*, Berlin: Springer, 1996.

Beyerlin, U. and Marauhn, T., *International Environmental Law*, Oxford: Hart Publishing, 2011.

Bhagwati, J., 'Trade and the Environment: The False Conflict?', in D. Zaelke, R. Housman and P. Orbach (eds) *Trade and the Environment: Law, Economics and Policy*, Washington DC: Island Press, 1995.

Biagiotti, I., 'Emerging Corporate Actors in Environment and Trade Governance: New Vision and Challenge for Norm-setting Processes', in S. Thoyer and B. Martimort-Asso (eds) *Participation for Sustainability in Trade*, Aldershot: Ashgate Publishing, 2007.

Bianchi, G., 'The Concept of the Ecosystem Approach to Fisheries' in G. Bianchi and H. Skjodal (eds) *The Ecosystem Approach to Fisheries*. Rome: Food and Agriculture Organization, 2008.

Biermann, F., 'Beyond the Intergovernmental Regime: Recent Trends in Global Carbon Governance', *Current Opinion in Environmental Sustainability* 2, 2010, 284.

Biermann, F., 'The Emerging Debate on the Need for a World Environment Organization: A Commentary', *Global Environmental Politics* 1, 2001, 45.

Biermann, F., 'Strengthening Green Global Governance in a Disparate World Society. Would a World Environment Organisation Benefit the South?', *International Environmental Agreements: Politics, Law and Economics*, 2002, 297.

Biermann, F. and Bauer, S. (eds) *A World Environment Organization: Solution or Threat for Effective Environmental Governance?*, Aldershot/Burlington: Ashgate, 2005.

Biermann, F., Betsill, M., Gupta, J., Kanie, N., Lebel, L., Liverman, D., Schroeder, H., Siebenhuner, B. and Zondervan, R., 'Earth System Governance: A Research Framework', *International Environmental Agreements: Politics, Law and Economics* 10(4), 2010, 277.

Biermann, F. and Boas, I., 'Preparing for a Warmer World: Towards a Global Governance System to Protect Climate Refugees', *Global Governance Working Paper* No. 33, 2007.

Binder, G., *Treaty Conflict and Political Contradiction: The Dialectic of Duplicity*, New York/Connecticut/London: Praeger, 1988.

Birnie, P.W. and Boyle, A.E., *International Law and the Environment*, reprint 1994, Oxford: Clarendon Press, 1992.

Birnie, P.W. and Boyle, A.E., *International Law and the Environment*, 2nd edition, Oxford: Oxford University Press, 2002.

Birnie, P.W., Boyle, A.E. and Redgwell, C., *International Law and the Environment*, 3rd edition, Oxford: Oxford University Press, 2009.

Bishop, J. and Landell-Mills, N., 'Forest Environmental Services: An Overview', in S. Pagiola, J. Bishop and N. Landell-Mills (eds) *Selling Forest Environmental Services: Market-based Mechanisms for Conservation and Development*, London: Earthscan, 2004.

Blainey, G., *The Causes of War*, New York: Free Press, 1973.

Blakeney, M., *Legal Aspects of the Transfer of Technology to Developing Countries*, Oxford: ESC, 1989.

Blanco, E. and Razzaque, J., 'Ecosystem Services and Human Well-being in a Globalized World: Assessing the Role of Law', *Human Rights Quarterly* 31(3), 2009, 692.

Blanco, E. and Razzaque, J., *Globalisation and Natural Resources Law*, Cheltenham: Edward Elgar, 2011, 131.

Blay, S., Piotrowicz, R. and Tsamenyi, M. (eds), *Public International Law: An Australian Perspective*, 2nd edition, Melbourne: Oxford University Press, 2005.

Blix, H., 'The Role of the IAEA in the Development of International Law', *Nordic Journal of International Law* 58, 1989, 231.

Blom, B., Sunderland T. and Murdiyarso, D., 'Getting REDD to Work Locally: Lessons Learned from Integrated Conservation and Development Projects', *Environmental Science and Policy* 13 (2), 2010, 164.

Blomquist, R., 'Protecting Nature "Down Under": An American Law Professor's View of Australia's Implementation of the Convention of Biological Diversity – Laws, Policies, Programs, Institutions and Plans 1992–2000', *Dickinson Journal of Environmental Law and Policy* 9, 2000, 227.

Bodansky, D., *The Art and Craft of International Environmental Law*, Cambridge, MA: Harvard University Press, 2011.

Bodansky, D., 'The Copenhagen Climate Change Conference: A Post-Mortem', *American Journal of International Law* 104, 2010, 231. Online. Available HTTP: <http://papers.ssrn.com/sol3/papers.cfm?abstract_id=1553167> (accessed 26 July 2010).

Bodansky, D., 'Customary (And Not So Customary) International Environmental Law', *Indiana Journal of Global Legal Studies* 3(1), 1995, 106.

Bodansky, D., 'The Legitimacy of International Governance: A Coming Challenge for International Law?', *American Journal of International Law* 93(3), 1999, 596.

Bodansky, D., 'What's So Bad about Unilateral Action to Protect the Environment?' *European Journal of International Law* 11(2), 2000, 339.

Boer, B., 'Implementation of International Sustainability at a National Level', in K. Ginther, E. Denters and P.J.I.M. de Waart (eds) *Sustainable Development and Good Governance*, Dordrecht/Boston: Kluwer Academic Publishers, 1995, pp. 111–13.

Boer, B. and Wiffen, G., *Heritage Law in Australia*, Oxford: Oxford University Press, 2006.

Boer, B., Ramsay, R. and Rothwell, D., *International Environmental Law in the Asia Pacific*, London: Kluwer Law International, 1998.

Bogdanović, S., *International Law of Water Resources*, The Hague: Kluwer Law International, 2001.

Boisson de Chazournes, L., 'The Global Environment Facility (GEF): A Unique and Crucial Institution', *Review of European Community and International Environmental Law*, 14(3), 2005, 193.

Boncour, P., 'The Moment of Truth – Adapting to Climate Change', *Migration*, 2009.

Boncour, P. and Burson, B., 'Climate Change and Migration in the South Pacific Region: Policy Perspectives', Institute for Policy Studies, Position Paper, 2009.

Bonyhady, T. and Christoff, P. (eds) *Climate Law in Australia*, Sydney: Federation Press, 2007.

Bosselmann, K., 'Earth Charter', in R. Wolfrum (ed.) *Max Planck Encyclopedia of Public International Law*, Oxford: Oxford University Press, 2009.

Bosselmann, K., 'A Legal Framework for Sustainable Development', in K. Bosselmann and D. Grinlinton (eds) *Environmental Law for a Sustainable Society*, Auckland: New Zealand Centre for Environmental Law, 2002.

Bosselmann, K., *The Principle of Sustainability*, Aldershot: Ashgate, 2008.

Bosselmann, K., 'The Right to Self-Determination and International Environmental Law: An Integrative Approach', *New Zealand Journal of Environmental Law* 1, 1997, 1.

Bosselmann, K. and Grinlinton, D. (eds) *Environmental Law for a Sustainable Society*. Auckland: New Zealand Centre for Environmental Law, 2002.

Bosselmann, K., Brown, P. and Mackey, B., *Enabling a Flourishing Earth: Challenges for the Green Economy, Opportunities for Global Governance*, 2011. Online. Available HTTP: <http://www.stakeholderforum.org/sf/index.php/our-publications/governance-papers/266-sdg-thinkpieces> (accessed 19 April 2012).

Bosselmann, K., Fuller, J. and Salinger, J. (eds) *Climate Change in New Zealand: Scientific and Legal Assessments*, Auckland: New Zealand Centre for Environmental Law, 2002.

Boulding, K., 'Towards a Pure Theory of Threat Systems', *American Economic Review* 53, 1966, 424.

Bourne, C., 'The International Law Association's contribution to international water resources law', *Natural Resources Journal* 36, 1996, 155.

Bouvier, A., 'Protection of the Natural Environment in Time of Armed Conflict', *International Review of the Red Cross*, No. 285, 1991. Online. Available HTTP: <http://www.icrc.org/eng/resources/documents/misc/57jmau.htm> (accessed 10 March 2012).

Bowen, H.R., *Social Responsibility and Accountability*, New York: Harper and Row, 1953.

Bowman, M., 'Environmental Protection and the Concept of Common Concern of Mankind', in M. Fitzmaurice, D.M. Ong and P. Merkouris (eds) *Research Handbook on International Environmental Law*, Cheltenham: Edward Elgar, 2010.

Boyd, D., *The Environmental Rights Revolution*, Vancouver: UBC Press, 2012.

Boyle, A., 'Human Rights or Environmental Rights? A Reassessment', *Fordham Environmental Law Review* 18, 2007, 471.

Boyle, A., 'The Role of International Human Rights Law in the Protection of the Environment', in A. Boyle (ed.) *Human Rights Approaches to Environmental Protection*, Oxford: Oxford University Press, 1996.

Boyle, A. and Chimkin, C.M., *The Making of International Law*, Oxford: Oxford University Press, 2007.

Boza, R., 'Protecting Andean Traditional Knowledge and Biodiversity Perspectives under the, US–Peru Trade Promotion Agreement', *Currents: International Trade Law Journal* 16, 2008, 76.

Brack, D., 'The Shrimp-Turtle Case: Implications for the Multilateral Environmental Agreement', *Yearbook of International Law* 9, 1998.

Brandl, E. and Bungert, H., 'Constitutional Entrenchment of Environmental Protection: A Comparative Analysis of Experiences Abroad', *Harvard Environmental Law Review* 16(1), 1992, 1.

Brandl, E. and Bungert, H., 'Constitutional Entrenchment of Environmental Protection: A Comparative Analysis of Experiences Abroad', *Harvard Environmental Law Review* 16, 1992.

Brantz, D., 'Environments of Death', in C. Clossman (ed.) *War and the Environment: Military Destruction in the Modern Age*, College Station: Texas A & M University Press, 2009.

Bratspies, R.M., 'Human Rights and Arctic Resources', *Southwestern Journal of International Law* 15, 2009.

Bratspies, R.M. and Miller, R.A., 'Introduction', *American Indian Law Review* 31, 2006/2007, 253.

Bratspies, R.M. and Miller, R.A. (eds) *Transboundary Harm in International Law: Lessons from the Trail Smelter Arbitration*, Cambridge: Cambridge University Press, 2006.

Brauman, R., 'The Médecins sans Frontières Experience', in K.M. Cahill (ed.) *A Framework for Survival: Health, Human Rights, and Humanitarian Assistance in Conflicts and Disasters*, New York: Basic Books, 1993.

Bravo, G., Kozulj, R. and Landaveri, R., 'Energy Access in Urban and Peri-Urban Buenos Aires', *Energy for Sustainable Development* 12(4), 2008.

Breau, S., 'Protected Persons and Objects', in E. Wilmshurst and S. Breau (eds) *Perspectives on the ICRC Study on Customary International Humanitarian Law*, Cambridge: Cambridge University Press, 2007, p. 197.

Brimblecombe, P. and Hara, H. (eds) *Acid Rain – Deposition to Recovery*, New York: Springer, 2010.

British Antarctic Survey, 'The Ozone Hole', Natural Environment Research Council Science Briefing, 2010. Online. Available HTTP: <http://www.antarctica.ac.uk/press/journalists/resources/science/the_ozone_hole_2009.pdf> (accessed 30 November 2011).

Broadmore, T.J., 'International Law and National Law Enforcement – A Regional Example. Sentencing for Fisheries Offending in the New Zealand District Court', *Australia and New Zealand Maritime Law Journal* 24, 2010, 1.

Brooks, R.O., 'The Gulf Oil Spill: The Road Not Taken', *Albany Law Review* 74(1), 2010, 489.

Brown, C., 'The Cross-Fertilization of Principles Relating to Procedure and Remedies in the Jurisprudence of International Courts and Tribunals', *Loyala of Los Angeles International and Comparative Law Review*, 30, 2008, 219.

Brown, C., 'The Settlement of Disputes Arising in Flexibility Mechanism Transactions under the Kyoto Protocol' *Arbitration International* 21, 2005, 361.

Brown, M.F., 'Can Culture be Copyrighted', *Current Anthropology* 39, 1998, 193.

Brownlie, I., *Principles of Public International Law*, 6th edition, Oxford: Oxford University Press, 2003.

Bruch, C., *Constitutional Environmental Law: Giving Force to Fundamental Principles in Africa*, 2nd edition, Washington DC: Environmental Law Institute.

Bruch, C. and Mrema, E., 'UNEP Guidelines and Manual on Compliance with and Enforcement of Multilateral Environmental Agreements', *Proceedings of the Seventh International Conference on Environmental Compliance and Enforcement* 1, 2005.

Bruch, C., Coker, W. and Van Arsdale, C., 'Breathing life into fundamental principles: Implementing Constitutional environmental protections in Africa', *South African Journal of Environmental Law and Policy* 7(21), 2000, 34.

Bruch, C., Coker, W. and Van Arsdale, C., 'Constitutional Environmental Law: Giving Force to Fundamental Principles in Africa', *Columbia Journal of Environmental Law* 26, 2001.

Bruch, C., Jansky, L., Nakayama, M. and Salewicz, K.A., *Public Participation in the Governance of International Freshwater Resources*, Tokyo: United Nations University Press, 2005.

Brunnée, J., 'Climate change, global environmental justice and international environmental law', in J. Ebbesson and P. Okowa (eds) *Environmental Law and Justice in Context*, Cambridge: Cambridge University Press, 2009.

Brunnée, J., 'Reweaving the Fabric of International Law? Patterns of Consent in Environmental Framework Agreements', in R. Wolfrum and V. Roben (eds) *Developments of International Law in Treaty Making*, Berlin: Springer, 2005.

Brunnée, J., 'The Stockholm Declaration and the Structure and Process of International Environmental Law', in A. Chircop, T.L. McDorman and S.J. Rolston (ed.) *The Future of Ocean Regime Building: Essays in Tribute to Douglas M. Johnston*, Leiden; Boston: Martinus Nijhoff, 2009.

Brunnée, J., Doelle, M. and Rajamani, L. (eds) *Promoting Compliance in an Evolving Climate Regime*, Cambridge: Cambridge University Press, 2011.

Bruno, K. and Karliner, J., 'The UN's Global Compact, Corporate Accountability and the Johannesburg Earth Summit', *Development* 45, 2002, 33.

Bryner, G.C., *From Promises to Performance: Achieving Global Environmental Goals*, New York/London:, W.W. Norton & Co., 1997.

Bullard, R.D., 'Environmental Justice in the Twenty-First Century' in R.D. Bullard (ed.) *The Quest for Environmental Justice: Human Rights and the Politics of Pollution*. San Francisco: Sierra Club Books, 2005.

Bullmore, R., 'Energy', in D. Farrier and P. Stein (eds) *The Environmental Law Handbook*, 5th edition, Pyrmont: Thomson Reuters, 2011.

Burchi, S. and Mechlem, K., *Groundwater in International Law*, Rome: FAO, 2005.

Burgman, M., Walshe, T., Godden, L. and Martin, P., 'Designing Regulation for Conservation and Biosecurity', *Australasian Journal of Natural Resources Law and Policy* 13(1), 2009, 93.

Burkett, M., 'Climate Reparations', *Melbourne Journal of International Law* 10(2), 2009, 509.

Burkett, M., 'The Nation Ex-Situ: On Climate Change, Deterritorialized Nationhood, and the Post-Climate Era', *Climate Law*, 2, 2011, 345.

Burleson, E., 'Climate Change Consensus: Emerging International Law', *Wm. & Mary Envtl., L. & Policy Rev.* 34, 2010.

Burleson, E., 'Climate Change Displacement to Refuge', *Journal of Environmental Law and Litigation* 25, 2010.

Burleson, E., 'Equitable and Reasonable Use of Water in the Euphrates-Tigris River Basin', *Environmental Law Reporter News & Analysis* 35, 2005.

Burleson, E. and Dodson, S., 'Arctic Justice: Addressing Persistent Organic Pollutants', *Law and Inequality*, 30, 2012, 57.

Byrne, L., 'Crown Land and Protected Areas', in D. Farrier and P. Stein (eds) *The Environmental Law Handbook*, 5th edition, Pyrmont: Thomson Reuters, 2011.

Cadoppi, A., 'Failure to Rescue and the Continental Criminal Law', in M.A. Menlowe and A. McCall-Smith (eds) *The Duty to Rescue: The Jurisprudence of Aid*, Aldershot: Dartmouth Publishing, 1993.

Calder, F. and Culverwell, M., *Following up the WSSD Commitments on Corporate Responsibility & Accountability*, London: Royal Institute of International Affairs, 2004.

Caldwell, L.K., *International Environmental Policy: Emergence and Dimensions*, Durham, NC: Duke University Press, 1984.

Camenzuli, L.K., 'The Development of International Environmental Law at the Multilateral Environmental Agreements' Conference of the Parties and its validity'. Online. Available HTTP: <http://cmsdata.iucn.org/downloads/cel10_camenzuli.pdf> (accessed 23 November 2011).

Cameron, J. and Abouchar, J., 'The Status of the Precautionary Principle in International Law', in D. Freestone and E. Hey (eds) *The Precautionary Principle and International Law: The Challenge of Implementation*, The Hague: Kluwer Law International, 1996.

Cameron, P.D., 'The Revival of Nuclear Power: An Analysis of the Legal Implications', *Journal of Environmental Law* 19(1), 2007, 71.

Carlman, I., 'The Resource Management Act 1991 Through External Eyes', *New Zealand Journal of Environmental Law* 11, 2007.

Carroll, A., 'Corporate Social Responsibility: Evolution of a Definitional Construct', *Business and Society* 38(3), 1999, 268.

Carson, R., *Silent Spring*, Boston: Houghton Mifflin Company, 1962.

Casper, K.N., 'Oil and Gas Development in the Arctic: Softening of Ice Demands Hardening of International Law', *Natural Resources Journal* 49, 2009.

Cassels, J., 'Judicial Activism and Public Interest Litigation in India: Attempting the Impossible?', *American Journal of Comparative Law* 37, 1989.

Cassese, A., *International Law*, 2nd edition, Oxford: Oxford University Press, 2005.

Centre for International Environmental Law, 'Nine Chemicals added to Global Toxics Treaty, with Gaping Exemptions,' 11 May 2009. Online. Available HTTP: <http://www.ciel.org/Publications/CIEL_COP4_11May09.pdf> (accessed 25 November 2011).

Cetto, A.M. and Burkart, W., 'Focus on the Environment', *IAEA Bulletin* 49(2). Online. Available HTTP: <http://www.iaea.org/Publications/Magazines/Bulletin/Bull492/49205660610.html> (accessed 2 May 2012).

Chalmers, D., Davies, G. and Monti, G., *European Union Law*, Cambridge: Cambridge University Press, 2010.

Chambers, W.B. and Green, J.F. (eds) *Reforming International Environmental Governance: From Institutional Limits to Innovative Reforms*, Tokyo: United Nations University Press, 2005.

Chang, H., 'The East Asian Development Experience', in H. Chang (ed.) *Rethinking Development Economics*, London / New York: Anthem Press, 2003.

Chang, H., *Kicking Away the Ladder: Development Strategy in Historical Perspective*, London / New York: Anthem Press, 2002.

Chapman, T., '*Corroboree Shield*: A Comparative Historical Analysis of (the Lack of) International, National and State Level Indigenous Cultural Heritage Protection' *Macquarie Journal of International and Comparative Environmental Law* 5, 2008, 81.

Charnovitz, S., 'The Law of "PPMs" in the WTO: Debunking the Myth of Illegality' *Yale Journal of International Law* 27, 2000, 59.

Charnovitz, S., 'A World Environment Organization', *Columbia Journal of Environmental Law* 27, 2002, 323.

Chayes, A. and Chayes, A.H., *The New Sovereignty: Compliance with International Regulatory Agreements*, Cambridge, MA: Harvard University Press, 1995.

Chaytor, B. and Cameron, J., 'The Treatment of Environmental Considerations in the World Trading Organisation', *Yearbook of International Co-operation on Environment and Development*, 1999/2000, 55.

Cheng, A.C., 'All in the Same Boat? Indigenous Property Rights in Underwater Cultural Heritage', *Houston Journal of International Law* 32(3), 2010, 695.

Chimni, B.S., 'International Institutions Today: An Imperial Global State in the Making', *European Journal of International Law* 15, 2004, 26.

Chimni, B.S., 'WTO and Environment: Shrimp-Turtle and EC-Hormones Cases', *Economic and Political Weekly*, 2000, 1752.

Churchill, R. and Ulfstein, G., 'Autonomous Institutional Arrangements in Multilateral Environmental Agreements: A Little-Noticed Phenomenon in International Law', *American Journal of International Law* 94, 2000, 623.

Churchill, R.R., 'Environmental Rights in Existing Human Rights Treaties', in A. Boyle and M. Anderson (eds) *Human Rights Approaches to Environmental Protection*, Oxford: Oxford University Press, 1996.

Churchill, R.R. and Rowe, A.V., *The Law of the Sea*, 3rd edition, Manchester: Manchester University Press, 1988.

Cicero, *De Officiis* (Walter Miller, trans.), Cambridge, MA: Harvard University Press, 1913.

Cirkovic, E., 'Self-Determination and Indigenous Peoples in International Law', *American Indian Law Review* 31, 2006/2007, 375.

Clark, L.C., 'A call to restructure existing international environmental law in light of Africa's renaissance: The United Nations Convention to Combat Desertification and the New Partnership for Africa's Development (NEPAD)', *Seattle University Law Review* 27, 2003.

Clear Horizon, *Evaluation of the Victorian Biodiversity Strategy, Summary Report*, Melbourne: Clear Horizon, 2007.

Clinton, R.N., 'The Rights of Indigenous Peoples as Collective Group Rights', *Arizona Law Review* 32, 1990, 739.

Cobbett, P., *Cases on International Law*, 1947, Volume 1.

Code of Conduct for the International Red Cross and Red Crescent Movement and Non-Governmental Organisations (NGOs) in Disaster Relief, Geneva: International Federation of Red Cross and Red Crescent Societies, 1995.

Coffey, C. and Newcombe, J., *The Polluter Pays Principle and Fisheries: The Role of Taxes and Charges*, London: Institute for European Environmental Policy. Online. Available HTTP: <http://www.ieep.eu/assets/238/thepolluterpaysprincipleandfisheries.pdf > (accessed 27 April 2012).

Cole, L. and Foster, S., *From the Ground Up: Environmental Racism and the Rise of the Environmental Justice Movement*, New York: New York University Press, 2001

Conant, J., 'Massive UN Supported African Palm Plantations Leading to Oppression Kidnapping and Murder', (2011) *Rainforest Rescue*. Online. Available HTTP: <http://www.rainforest-rescue.org/news/3319/massive-un-supported-african-palm-plantations-leading-to-oppression-kidnapping-and-murder> (accessed 19 February 2012).

Conley, C. and Rettberg, P., 'COSPAR Planetary Protection Policy – Present Status', in M. Hofmann, P. Rettberg and M. Williamson (eds) *IAA 2010 Cosmic Study: Protecting the Environment of Celestial Bodies*, 2010.

Conley, J. and Williams, C., 'Global Banks as Global Sustainability Regulators?: The Equator Principles', *Law and Policy* 33(4), 2011, 542.

Connell, D. and Quentin Grafton, R. (eds) *Basin Futures: Water Reform in the Murray-Darling Basin*, Canberra: ANU E-Press, 2011.

Connolly, I., 'Can the World Heritage Convention be Adequately Implemented in Australia without Australia becoming a Party to the Intangible Heritage Convention?', *Environmental and Planning Law Journal* 24, 2007.

Coonrod, S., 'The United Nations Code of Conduct for Transnational Corporations', *Harvard International Law Journal* 18, 1977, 273.

Cooper, R., *The Economics of Interdependence: Economic Policy in the Atlantic Community*, New York: McGraw-Hill, 1968.

Coplan, K.S., 'Inter-civilizational Inequities of Nuclear Power Weighed against the Intergenerational Inequities of Carbon Based Energy', *Fordham Environmental Law Review* 17, 2006.

Cordonier Segger, M.C. and Khalfan, A., *Sustainable Development Law: Principles, Practices and Prospects*, Oxford: Oxford University Press, 2004.

Cordonier Segger, M.C. and Newcombe, A., 'An Integrated Agenda for Sustainable Development in International Investment Law', in M.C. Cordonier Segger, M. Gehring and A. Newcombe (eds) *Sustainable Development in World Investment Law*, Alphen aan den Rijn: Kluwer Law International, 2011.

Cordonier Segger, M.C., Araya, M., Gonzáles-Lützenkirchen, A.K., Lucas, N., Muños, M.B., Taurel, J.Z., Blanco, H. and Reynal, M.L., *Ecological Rules and Sustainability in the Americas*, IISD/UNEP/OAS, 2004.

Costenbader, J., 'REDD+ Benefit Sharing: A Comparative Assessment of Three National Policy Approaches', Forest Carbon Partnership Facility and UN REDD Programme (2011). Online. Available HTTP: <http://www.uncclearn.org/sites/www.uncclearn.org/files/wb93.pdf> (accessed 14 December 2011).

Cotton, J., 'The "Haze" over Southeast Asia: Challenging the ASEAN Mode of Regional Engagement' *Pacific Affairs* 72, 1999.

Craig, D., Robinson, N. and Koh, K-L. (eds) *Capacity Building for Environmental Law in the Asian and Pacific Region: Approaches and Resources*, Manila: Asian Development Bank, 2003.

Craik, N., *The International Law of Environmental Impact Assessment: Process, Substance and Integration*, Cambridge: Cambridge University Press, 2008.

Cramer, B., 'The Human Right to Information, the Environment and Information About the Environment: From the Universal Declaration to the AARHUS Convention', *Communication Law and Policy*, 2009.

Crittenden, J. and Wilder, M., 'Brining the Forest to Market: Structuring Avoided Deforestation Projects', *Carbon and Climate Law Review* 3, 2008, 273.

Crozier, M., Huntington, S. and Watanuki, J., *The Crisis of Democracy: Report on the Governability of Democracies to the Trilateral Commission*, New York: New York University Press, 1975.

Cubbage, F., Harou, P. and Sills, E., 'Policy Instruments to Enhance Multi-functional Forest Management', *Forest Policy and Economics* 9, 2007, 833.

Currie, D.E.J., 'The Problems and Gaps in the Nuclear Liability Conventions and an Analysis of How an Actual Claim Would be Brought under the Current Existing Treaty Regime in the Event of a Nuclear Accident', *Denver Journal of International Law and Policy* 35(1), 2006, 85.

Cusack, M.E., 'Judicial Interpretation of State Constitutional Rights to a Healthful Environment', *Boston College Environmental Affairs Law Review* 20, 1993.

Cypher, J.M. and Dietz, J.L., *The Process of Economic Development*, London / New York: Routledge, 1997.

D'Amato, A., *The Concept of Custom in International Law*, New York: Cornell University Press, 1971.

D'Argo, J., 'Precautionary Principle: The 'Better Safe than Sorry' Approach', *Greenpeace Synthesis/ Regeneration: A Magazine of Green Social Thought* 7:8, 1995. Online. Available HTTP: <www.greens. org/s-r/078/07-54.html> (accessed 8 March 2012).

Daes, E.I., 'Indigenous Peoples' Right to Land and Natural Resources', in N. Ghanea and A. Xanthaki, (ed.) *Minorities, Peoples and Self-Determination*, Leiden: Martinus Nijhoff Publishers, 2005.

Daigneault, A., Greenhalgh, S. and Samarasinghe, O., 'Estimated Impacts of New Zealand Agriculture Climate Policy: A Tale of Two Catchments', paper presented at New Zealand Agricultural and Resource Economics Society, 2011 Conference, Nelson, August 2011.

Dalai-Clayton, B. and Sadler, B., *Strategic Environmental Assessment: A Sourcebook and Reference Guide to International Experience*, London: Earthscan, 2005.

Damrosch, L.F., Henkin, L., Smit, H. and Murphy, S.D., *International Law, Cases, and Materials*, St Paul: Thomson/West, 2009.

David, R. and Brierley, J.E.C., *Major Legal Systems in the World Today: An Introduction to the Comparative Study of Law*, 3rd edition, London: Stevens & Sons, 1985.

Davis, J.P., *Corporations: A Study of the Origin and Development of Great Business Combinations and their Relation to the Authority of the State*, New York: Capricorn Books, 1961.

Dawson, F., 'Analysing the Goals of Biodiversity Conservation: Scientific, Policy and Legal Perspectives', *Environmental and Planning Law Journal* 21(6), 2004.

De Jonge, A., *Transnational Corporations and International Law: Accountability in the Global Business Environment*, Cheltenham: Edward Elgar, 2011.

de Klemm, C., *The Legal Development of the Ramsar Convention*, Gland: Ramsar Convention Bureau, 1995.

Dejeant-Pons, M., "Human Rights to Environmental Procedural Rights," in M. Anderson and A. Boyle (eds) *Human Rights Approaches to Environmental Protection*, Oxford: Oxford University Press, 1996.

Dellapenna, J.W. and Gupta, J., *The Evolution of the Law and Politics of Water*, Berlin: Springer, 2009.

Department of Economic Secretariat of the United Nations Forum on Forestry (2005), *Review of the Effectiveness of the International Arrangement on Forests*, CN.18/2005/6.

Department of Sustainability, Environment, Water, Population and Communities, *Reforming National Environment Law: An Overview*, Canberra: Australian Government, 2011.

Dernbach, J. (ed.) *Agenda for a Sustainable America*, Washington DC: Environmental Law Institute, 2009.

Desai, B.H., *Institutionalizing International Environmental Law*, Ardsley, NY: Transnational Publishers, 2004.

DeSombre, E.R., 'Encouraging Participation in International Environmental Agreements', in Ho-Won Jeong (ed.) *Global Environmental Policies: Institutions and Procedures*, Basingstoke: Palgrave, 2011.

DeSombre, E.R., *Global Environmental Institutions*, Abingdon: Routledge, 2006.

DeSombre, E. and Kauffman, J., 'The Montreal Protocol Multilateral Fund: Partial Success Story', in R.O. Keohane and M.A. Levy (eds) *Institutions for Environmental Aid: Pitfalls and Promise*, Cambridge, MA: MIT Press.

DeVincenzi, D.L., Stabekis, P.D. and Barengoltz, J.B., 'A Proposed New Policy for Planetary Protection', *Advances in Space Research* 3, 1983, 13.

Dharmadhikari, D.M., 'Environment – Problems and Solutions', *AIR Journal* 90, 2003, 161.

Dhavan, R., 'Whose Law? Whose interest?', in J. Cooper and R. Dhavan (eds) *Public Interest Law*, Oxford: Blackwell, 1986.

Dhondt, N., *Integration of Environmental Protection into Other EC Policies; Legal Theory and Practice*, Groningen: Europa Law Publishing, 2003.

Diaz, D., Hamilton, K. and Johnson, E., (2011) *State of the Forest Carbon Markets 2011: From Canopy to Currency*, Ecosystem Marketplace. Online. Available HTTP: <.http://forest-trends.org/publication_details.php?publicationID=2963> (accessed 14 December 2011).

Dinar, A., Dinar, S., McCaffrey, S. and McKinney, D., *Bridges over Water: Understanding Transboundary Water Conflict, Negotiation and Cooperation*, New Jersey: World Scientific Publishing Company, 2007.

Dinham, B., 'The Success of a Voluntary Code in Reducing Pesticide Hazards in Developing Countries', *Green Global Yearbook*, 1996. Online. Available HTTP: <http://www.fni.no/ybiced/96_02_dinham.pdf> (accessed 18 November 2011).

Diringer, E., 'Letting Go of Kyoto', *Nature* 479, 2011, 291.

Docherty, B. and Giannini, T., 'Confronting a Rising Tide: A Proposal for a Convention on Climate Change Refugees', *Harvard Environmental Law Review* 33, 2010, 349.

Doelle, M., 'Early Experience with the Kyoto Compliance System: Possible Lessons for MEA Compliance System Design', *Climate Law* 1(2), 2010, 237.

Doelle, M., 'Integration among Global Environmental Regimes: Lessons Learned From Climate Change'. Online. Available HTTP: <http://law.dal.ca/Files/MEL_Institute/Doelle_integration_Johnston_book_chapter.pdf> (accessed 18 March 2012).

Dolzer, R. and Schreuer, C., *Principles of International Investment Law*, New York: Oxford University Press, 2008.

Dombrovsky, I., 'Integration in the Management of International Waters: Economic Perspectives on a Global Policy Discourse', *Global Governance* 14(4), 2008, 455.

Dorough, D.S., 'Inuit of Alaska: Current Issues', in Loukacheva, N. (ed.) *Polar Law Textbook*, Copenhagen: Nordic Council of Ministers, 2010.

Dorsen, N., Baer, S., Sajo, A. and Rosenfeld, M., *Comparative Constitutionalism, Cases and Materials*, St Paul, MN: West, 2003.

Doulman, D.J., 'International Plan of Action to Prevent, Deter and Eliminate Illegal, Unreported and Unregulated Fishing', Rome: FAO Fisheries and Aquaculture Department, 2011. Online. Available: <http://www.fao.org/fishery/topic/3195/en> (accessed 25 January 2012).

Doyle, M.W., 'Liberalism and World Politics' *American Political Science Review* 80(4), 1986, 1151.

Drahos, P., 'Indigenous Knowledge, Intellectual Property and Biopiracy: Is a Global Bio-collecting Society the Answer', *European Intellectual Property Law Review* 22, 2000.

Drexhage, J. and Murphy, D., 'From Brundtland to Rio 2012', *International Institute for Sustainable Development Background Paper prepared for consideration by the High Level Panel on Global Sustainability at its first meeting*, 2010. Online. Available HTTP: <http://www.un.org/wcm/webdav/site/climatechange/shared/gsp/docs/GSP1-6_Background%20on%20Sustainable%20Devt.pdf> (accessed 19 February 2012).

Drumbl, M., 'Actors and Law-making in International Environmental Law', in M. Fitzmaurice, D.M. Ong and P. Merkouris (eds) *Research Handbook on International Environmental Law*, Cheltenham: Edward Elgar, 2010.

Drumbl, M.A., 'Does Sharing Know Its Limits? Thoughts on Implementing International Environmental Agreements', *Virginia Environmental Law Journal* 18, 1999.

Drumgoole, S. (ed.) *Legal Protection of the Underwater Cultural Heritage*, London: Kluwer Law International, 1999.

Dupre, C., *Importing the Law in Post-Communist Transitions*, Oxford: Hart Publishing, 2003.

Dupuy, P-M., 'Formation of Customary International Law and General Principles', in D. Bodansky, J. Brunnée and E. Hey (eds) *The Oxford Handbook of International Environmental Law*, Oxford: Oxford University Press, 2007.

Dupuy, P.M., 'Soft Law and the International Law of the Environment', *Michigan Journal of International Law* 12, 1991.

Dupuy, P.M., *L'unité de l'ordre juridique international*, Leiden: Martinus Nijhoff Publishers, 2003.

Durst, P.B., Brown, C., Tacio, H.D. and Ishikawa, M. (eds) *In Search of Excellence: Exemplary Forest Management in Asia and the Pacific*, Bangkok: Food and Agriculture Organisation, 2005.

Dutfield, G., *Protecting Indigenous Knowledge: Pathways to the Future*, Policy Paper Prepared for the International Centre for Trade and Sustainable Development (ICTSD), 2006.

Dutfield, G., *Protecting Traditional Knowledge: Pathways to the Future*, ICTSD Issue Paper, No. 6, 2006.

Ebbesson, J., 'The Notion of Public Participation in International Environmental Law', *Yearbook of International Environmental Law* 8, 1997.

Ebrahim, H., *The Soul of a Nation*, Oxford: Oxford University Press, 1999.

Eckersley, R., 'The Big Chill: The WTO and Multilateral Environmental Agreements' (2004) *Global Environmental Politics* 4, 24.

ECLAC, Chapter 3, 'Statistics on Natural Resources and the Environment', *Statistical Yearbook for Latin America and the Caribbean*, 2006. Online. Available HTTP: <http://www.eclac.org/publicaciones/xml/4/28074/LCG2332B_3.pdf> (accessed 3 May 2012).

Economic Commission for Africa, *Review of the Application of Environmental Impact Assessment in Selected African Countries*, 2005.

Eitzen, E., 'Use of Biological Weapons', in *Medical Aspects of Chemical and Biological Warfare*, Washington, D.C.: Office of The Surgeon General, Borden Institute, Walter Reed Army Medical Center, 1997.

Elbaradei, M., Nwogugu, E. and Rames, J., 'International Law and Nuclear Energy: Overview of the Legal Framework'. Online. Available HTTP: <http://www.iaea.org/Publications/Magazines/Bulletin/Bull373/37302081625.pdf> (accessed 15 September 2011).

El-Hinnawi, E.E., 'Review of the Environmental Impact of Nuclear Energy', *IAEA Bulletin* 20(2), 1978.

Ellerman, A.D. and Buchner, B.K., 'The European Union Emissions Trading Scheme: Origins, Allocations, and Early Results', *Environmental Economics and Policy* 1(1), 2007, 66.

Elliott, J.H., *Empires of the Atlantic World: Britain and Spain in America 1492–1830*, New Haven: Yale University Press, 2006.

Ellis, J. and FitzGerald, A., 'The Precautionary Principle in International Law: Lessons from Fuller's Internal Morality', *McGill Law Journal* 49, 2004, 780. Online. Available HTTP: <http://lawjournal.mcgill.ca/documents/Ellis_and_FitzGerald.pdf> (accessed 23 November 2011).

Ellisa, J., Winkler, H., Corfee-Morlot, J. and Gagnon-Lebrun, F., 'CDM: Taking Stock and Looking Forward', *Energy Policy* 35(1), 2007, 15.

Emissions Trading Scheme Review Panel, *Doing New Zealand's Fair Share – Emissions Trading Scheme Review 2011: Final Report*, Wellington: Ministry for the Environment, 2011.

Esty, D. and Deere, C. (eds) *Greening the Americas*, Cambridge, MA: MIT Press, 2005.

Esty, D.C. and Ivanova, M.H., 'The Road Ahead: Conclusions and Action Agenda', in D.C. Esty and M.H. Ivanova (eds) *Global Environmental Governance: Options & Opportunities*, New Haven: Yale School of Forestry and Environmental Studies, 2002.

Ewald, C. and Wang, W.K., 'Sustainable Yields in Fisheries: Uncertainty, Risk-Aversion and Mean-Variance Analysis', *Natural Resources Modelling* 33(3), 2010.

Eze, C.N., 'The Bamako Convention on the Ban on the Import into Africa and the Control of the Transboundary Movement and Management of Hazardous Wastes within Africa: A milestone in environmental protection?', *African Journal of International and Comparative Law* 15, 2007.

Fabra, A. and Arnal, E., 'Review of Jurisprudence on Human Rights and the Environment in Latin America', Joint UNEP-OHCHR Expert Seminar on Human Rights and the Environment, Background Paper No. 6 (2002). Online. Available HTTP: <http://www2.ohchr.org/english/issues/environment/environ/bp6.htm> (accessed 7 May 2012).

Fairman, D. and Ross, M., 'Old Fads, New Lessons: Learning from Economic Development Assistance', in R.O. Keohane and M.A. Levy (eds) *Institutions for Environmental Aid*, Cambridge, MA: MIT Press, 1996.

Falk, R., 'Human Rights, Humanitarian Assistance and the Sovereignty of States', in K.M. Cahill (ed.) *A Framework for Survival: Health, Human Rights, and Humanitarian Assistance in Conflicts and Disasters*, New York: Basic Books, 1993.

Falk, R., 'The Second Cycle of Ecological Urgency: An Environmental Justice Perspective' in J. Ebbesson and P. Okowa (eds) *Environmental Law and Justice in Context*, Cambridge: Cambridge University Press, 2009

FAO, Voluntary Guidelines to Support the Progressive Realisation of the Right to Adequate Food in the Context of National Food Security (2004), Report of the 30th Session of the Committee on World Food Security, Rome.

Farah, A.A., 'Responding to Emergencies: A View from Within', in K.M. Cahill (ed.) *A Framework for Survival: Health, Human Rights, and Humanitarian Assistance in Conflicts and Disasters*, New York: Basic Books, 1993.

Fatouros, A.A., 'Looking for an International Legal Framework for Transnational Corporations', in A.A. Fatouros (ed.) *Transnational Corporations: The International Legal Framework*, London: Routledge, 1994.

Fawcett, J., 'Cross-Fertilization in Private International Law', *Current Legal Problems* 53, 2000.

Fecenko, M.J., *Biotechnology Law: Corporate-Commercial Practice*, Toronto: Butterworths, 2002.

Fernandez, J., 'State Constitutions, Environmental Rights Provisions, and the Doctrine of Self-Execution: A Political Question?', *Harvard Environmental Law Review* 17, 1993.

Fidler, D.P., 'Disaster Relief and Governance After the Indian Ocean Tsunami: What Role for International Law?' *Melbourne Journal of International Law* 6, 2005, 458.

Finley, C., *All the Fish in the Sea: Maximum Sustainable Yield and the Failure of Fisheries Management*, Chicago: University of Chicago Press, 2011.

Fishel, J.A., 'United States Called to Task on Indigenous Rights: The Western Shoshone Struggle and Success at the International Level', *American Indian Law Review* 31, 2006/2007, 619.

Fisher, D., *Australian Environmental Law: Norms Principles and Rules*, 2nd edition, Pyrmont: Lawbook, 2010.

Fisher, D., *Law and Legal Issues in International Disaster Response: a Desk Study*, Geneva: International Red Cross, 2007.

Fisher, D.E., *Australian Environmental Law: Norms, Principles and Rules*, Sydney: Thomson Reuters, 2010.

Fisher, D.E., *The Law and Governance of Water Resources: The Challenge of Sustainability*, Cheltenham: Edward Elgar, 2009.

Fisher, D.E., 'Legal and Paralegal Rules for Biodiversity Conservation: a Sequence of Conceptual, Linguistic and Legal Challenges', in M.I. Jeffery, J. Firestone and K. Bubna-Litic (eds) *Biodiversity Conservation, Law and Livelihoods*, Cambridge: Cambridge University Press, 2008.

Fisher, D.E., 'Managing Wetlands Sustainably as Ecosystems: the Contribution of the Law (Part 1)', *Water Law* 21, 2010.

Fitzmaurice, M., *Contemporary Issues in International Environmental Law*, Cheltenham: Edward Elgar, 2009.

Fitzmaurice, M., 'Environmental justice through international complaint procedures? Comparing the Aarhus Convention and the North American Agreement on Environmental Cooperation', in J. Ebbesson and P. Okowa (eds) *Environmental Law and Justice in Context*, Cambridge: Cambridge University Press, 2009.

Fitzmaurice, M., 'Some Reflections on Public Participation in Environmental Matters as a Human Right in International Law', *Non-State Actors & International Law* 2, 2002.

Flavin, C. and Gardner, G., 'China, India, and the New World Order', in Worldwatch Institute, *State of the World 2006: Special Focus: India and China*, New York: W. W. Norton and Company, 2006.

Floren, D.W., 'Antarctic Mining Regimes: An Appreciation of the Attainable', *Journal of Environmental Law and Litigation* 16, 2001.

Forrest, C., 'Defining "underwater cultural heritage"', *International Journal of Nautical Archaeology* 31(1), 2002, 3.

Foti, J., de Silva, L., McGray, H., Shaffer, L., Talbot, J. and Werksman, J., *Voice and Choice: Opening the Door to Environmental Democracy*, Washington DC: World Resources Institute, 2008.

Francioni, F., 'International Codes of Conduct for Multinational Enterprises: An Alternative Approach', *Italian Yearbook of International Law* 3, 1977, 143.

Freeland S., 'For Better or for Worse? The Use of "Soft Law" within the International Legal Regulation of Outer Space', *Annals of Air and Space Law* 36, 2011.

Freeland S., 'The 2008 Russia/China Proposal for a Treaty to Ban Weapons in Space: A Missed Opportunity or an Opening Gambit?', *Proceedings of the Colloquium on the Law of Outer Space* 51, American Institute of Aeronautics and Astronautics, 2008.

Freeman, C., 'Sustainable Development from Rhetoric to Practice? A New Zealand Perspective', *International Planning Studies* 9, 2004, 307.

Freestone, D., 'The Challenge of Implementation: Some Concluding Notes', in A. Boyle and D. Freestone (eds) *International Law and Sustainable Development*, Oxford: Oxford University Press, 1999.

Freestone, D. 'The Precautionary Principle', in R. Churchill and D. Freestone (eds) *International Law and Global Climate Change*, London: Graham and Trotman, 1991;

Freestone, D. and Hey, E., 'Origins and Development of the Precautionary Principle', in D. Freestone and E. Hey (eds) *The Precautionary Principle and International Law: The Challenge of Implementation*, The Hague: Kluwer Law International, 1996.

Freestone, D. and Streck, C. (eds) *Legal Aspects of Implementing the Kyoto Protocol Mechanisms: Making Kyoto Work*, Oxford: Oxford University Press, 2005.

French, D., *International Law and Policy on Sustainable Development*, Manchester: Manchester University Press, 2004.

French, D., 'Sustainable Development and the Instinctive Imperative of Justice in the Global Order', in D. French (ed.) *Global Justice and Sustainable Development*, Leiden: Martinus Nijhoff Publishers, 2010.

743

French, D. (ed.) *Global Justice and Sustainable Development*, Leiden: Martinus Nijhoff, 2010.

Friedman, L.M., *A History of American Law*, New York: Simon & Schuster, 1973.

Fry, I., 'Twists and Turns in the Jungle: Exploring the Evolution of Land Use, Land-Use Change and Forestry Decisions within the Kyoto Protocol', *Review of European Community and International Environmental Law* 11(2), 2002, 159.

Fuller, L., 'The Form and Limits of Adjudication', *Harvard Law Review* 92, 1978, 353.

Gaines, S., 'The WTO's Reading of the GATT Article XX Chapeau: A Disguised Restriction on Environmental Measures', *University of Pennsylvania Journal of International Economic Law* 22 (4), 2001.

Garcia, F.J., 'Beyond Special and Differential Treatment', *Boston College International and Comparative Law Review* 27, 2004.

Garcia, S.M., Zerbi, A., Aliaume, C., Do Chi, T. and Lasserre, G., 'The Ecosystem Approach to Fisheries: Issues, Terminology, Principles, Institutional Foundations, Implementation and Outlook', Fisheries Technical Paper No. 443, Rome: FAO, 2003. Online. Available: <ftp://ftp.fao.org/docrep/fao/006/y4773e/y4773e00.pdf > (accessed 23 January 2012).

Gardner, R.C., Connolly, K.D. and Bamba, A., 'African wetlands of international importance: Assessment of benefits associated with designations under the Ramsar Convention', *Georgetown International Environmental Law Review* 21, 2009.

Garnut, R., *The Garnut Climate Change Review Final Report*, Port Melbourne: Cambridge University Press, 2008.

Garnaut, R., *The Garnaut Review 2011*, Cambridge: Cambridge University Press, 2011.

Garnut, R., *The Garnut Review 2011: Australia in the Global Response to Climate Change*, Port Melbourne: Cambridge University Press, 2011.

Gasser H-P., 'For Better Protection of the Natural Environment in Armed Conflict: A Proposal for Action', *American Journal of International Law* 89, 1995.

Gehring, M., 'Impact Assessments of Investment Treaties', in M. C. Cordonier Segger, M. Gehring and A. Newcombe (eds) *Sustainable Development in World Investment Law*, Alphen aan den Rijn: Kluwer Law International, 2011.

Gehring, T., 'International Dynamic Regimes: Dynamic Sectoral Legal Systems', *Yearbook of International Environmental Law*, 1, 1990, 35–49, pp. 35–36.

Gehring, T., 'Treaty-Making and Treaty Evolution', in D. Bodansky, J. Brunnée, and E. Hey (eds) *The Oxford Handbook of International Environmental Law*, Oxford: Oxford University Press, 2007.

Gehring, T. and Oberthür, S., 'The Causal Mechanisms of Interaction between International Institutions', *European Journal of International Relations* 15, 2009, 125.

Gemenne, F., 'Why the Numbers Don't Add Up: A Review of Estimates and Predictions of People Displaced by Environmental Changes', *Global Environmental Change* 21(1), 2011.

Gentry, B.S. and Esty, D.C., 'Private Capital Flows: New and Additional Resources for Sustainable Development', in J.A. Miller and J. Coppock (eds) *Bridges to Sustainability: Business and Government Working Together for a Better Environment*, Yale School of Forestry & Environmental Studies Bulletin 101, 1997, 18.

George, R., 'Flying the Flag, Fleeing the State', *New York Times*, 24 April 2011. Online. Available: <http://www.nytimes.com/2011/04/25/opinion/25george.html> (accessed 18 January 2012).

Gerrard, M.B., 'The victims of Nimby', *Fordham Urban Law Journal* 21, 1994, 495.

Ghafele, R. and Mercer, A., 'Not Starting in Sixth Gear: An Assessment of the UN Global Compact's Use of Soft Law as a Global Governance Structure for Corporate Social Responsibility', *UC Davies Journal of International Law and Policy* 17, 2010, 41.

Gianni, M. and Simpson, W., *The Changing Nature of High Seas Fishing: How Flags of Convenience Provide Cover for Illegal, Unreported and Unregulated Fishing*, Australian Government Department of Agriculture, Fisheries and Forestry, International Transport Workers' Federation, and WWF International, 2005. Online. Available: <http://www.daff.gov.au/fisheries/iuu/high-seas> (accessed 9 May 2012).

Gillespie, A., *International Law, Policy and Ethics*, Oxford: Oxford University Press, 1997.

Gillespie, A., *Protected Areas and International Environmental Law*, Leiden: Martinus Nijhoff Publishers, 2007.

Giordano, M.A. and Wolf, A.T., 'The World's International Freshwater Agreements: Historical Developments and Future Opportunities', in UNEP, Oregon State University and FAO, *Atlas of International Freshwater Agreements*, Nairobi: UNEP, 2002.

Glazewski, J., 'The Environment, Human Rights and a New South African Constitution', *South African Journal of Human Rights* 167, 1991.

Gleckman, H., 'Transnational Corporations' Strategic Responses to "Sustainable Development"', in H.O. Bergenses, G. Parmann and Ø.B. Thommessen (eds) *Green Globe Yearbook of International Cooperation on Environment and Development*, Oxford: Oxford University Press, 1995.

Global International Water Assessment, *Challenges to International Waters – Regional Assessments in a Global Perspective*, Nairobi: UNEP, 2006.

Global Ozone Research and Monitoring Project, 'Scientific Assessment of Ozone Depletion: 2010', World Meteorological Organization, Report No. 52, 2010. Online. Available HTTP: <http://www.esrl.noaa.gov/csd/assessments/ozone/2010/chapters/prefaceprologue.pdf> (accessed 2 December 2011).

Godden, L. and Peel, J., *Environmental Law Scientific, Policy and Regulatory Dimensions*, Melbourne: Oxford University Press, 2009.

Godden, L. and Peel, J., 'The Environment Protection and Biodiversity Conservation Act 1999 (Cth): Dark Sides of Virtue', *Melbourne University Law Review* 31, 2007, 106.

Gonthier, C.D., 'Foreword', in M. Kerr, R. Janda and C. Pitts (eds) *Corporate Social Responsibility: A Legal Analysis*, Ontario: LexisNexis, 2009.

Gonzalez, C., 'Beyond Eco-Imperialism: An Environmental Justice Critique of Free Trade', *Denver University Law Review* 78, 2001, 979.

Gonzalez, C.G., 'China in Latin America: Law, Economics, and Sustainable Development', *Environmental Law Reporter* 40, 2010, 10171.

Gonzalez, C.G., 'An Environmental Justice Critique of Comparative Advantage: Indigenous Peoples, Trade Policy, and the Mexican Neoliberal Economic Reforms', *University of Pennsylvania Journal of International Law* 32, 2011, 723.

Gonzalez, C.G., 'Genetically Modified Organisms and Justice: The International Environmental Justice Implications of Biotechnology', *Georgetown International Environmental Law Review* 19, 2007, 595.

Gonzalez, C.G., 'Trade Liberalization, Food Security, and the Environment: The Neoliberal Threat to Sustainable Rural Development', *Transnational Law & Contemporary Problems* 14(2), 2004, 219.

Gordon, K., 'International Investment Agreements: A Survey of Environmental, Labour and Anti-corruption Issues', in *International Investment Law: Understanding Concepts and Tracking Innovations*, Paris: OECD, 2008. Online. Available HTTP: <www.oecd.org/dataoecd/3/5/40471550.pdf> (accessed 19 December 2011).

Gordon, K. and Pohl, J., 'Environmental Concerns in International Investment Agreements: a survey', *OECD Working Papers on International Investment*, 2011, No. 2011/1. Online. Available HTTP: <www.oecd.org/dataoecd/50/12/48083618.pdf> (accessed 19 December 2011)

Gordon, R., 'Climate Change and the Poorest Nations: Further Reflections on Global Inequality', *University of Colorado Law Review* 78, 2007.

Gordon, R., 'The Dawn of a New, New International Economic Order?' *Law and Contemporary Problems* 72, 2009.

Gordon, R., 'Saving Failed States: Sometimes a Neocolonialist Notion', *American University Journal of International Law and Policy* 19, 1997, 903.

Gordon, R. and Sylvester, J.H., 'Deconstructing Development', *Wisconsin International Law Journal* 22, 2004.

Gore, A., Nobel Peace Prize Lecture, 10 December 2007. Online. Available HTTP: <http://www.nobelprize.org/nobel_prizes/peace/laureates/2007/gore-lecture_en.html>.

Government of Canada, *Uruguay Round of Multilateral Trade Negotiations: Canadian Environmental Review*, Ottawa, 1994.

Government of Western Australia, 'Extended Producer Responsibility Policy Statement,' 29 June 2005.

Graichen, P., 'Can Forestry Gain from Emissions Trading? Rules Governing Sinks Projects Under the UNFCCC and the EU Emissions Trading System', *Review of the European Community and International Environmental Law* 14(1), 2005, 11.

Greenberg, P., *Four Fish: The Future of the Last Wild Food*, New York: Penguin, 2011.

Griffiths, T., (2008) *Seeing 'REDD'? Forests, Climate Change Mitigation and the Rights of Indigenous Peoples and Local Communities*, Forest Peoples Programme. Online. Available HTTP: <http://www.forestpeoples.org/sites/fpp/files/publication/2010/08/seeingreddupdatedraft3dec08eng.pdf> (accessed 14 December 2011).

Gross, L., 'The Peace of Westphalia, 1648–1948', *American Journal of International Law* 42(1), 1948.

Grossman, D., 'Tort based climate litigation', in W.C.G. Burns and H. Osofsky (eds) *Adjudicating Climate Change: State, National and International Approaches*, Cambridge: Cambridge University Press, 2009.

Grossman, G. and Krueger, A., 'Environmental Impacts of a North American Free Trade Agreement', Washington DC: NBER Working Paper No. 3914, 1991.

Grubel, H.G. and Lloyd, P.J., *Intra-Industry Trade: The Theory and Measurement of Trade in Differentiated Products*, London: Macmillan, 1975.

Gudynas, E., 'Más allá del nuevo extractivismo: transiciones sostenibles y alternativas al desarrollo', in F. Wanderley (ed.) *El desarrollo en cuestión. Reflexiones desde América Latina*, La Paz, Bolivia: Oxfam, 2011.

Guha, R., *Environmentalism: A Global History*, New York: Longman, 2000.

Guha, R. and Martinez-Alier, J., *Varieties of Environmentalism: Essays North and South*, London: Earthscan, 1997.

Guidelines for the Domestic Facilitation and Regulation of International Disaster Relief and Initial Recovery Assistance, Geneva: International Federation of Red Cross and Red Crescent Societies, 2007.

Gündling, L., 'Compliance Assistance in International Environmental Law: Capacity-Building Through Financial and Technology Transfer', *Zeitschrift für Ausländisches Öffentliches Recht und Völkerrecht*, vol. 56, 1996.

Gunningham, N., *Innovative Governance and Regulatory Design: Managing Water Resources*, Lincoln: Landcare Research, 2008. Online. Available HTTP: <http://www.landcareresearch.co.nz/publications/researchpubs/water_gunningham_LC0708137.pdf> (accessed 4 November 2011).

Gunningham, N. and Holley, C., *Bringing the 'R' Word Back: Regulation, Environment Protection and NRM*, Canberra: Academy of Social Sciences in Australia, 2010.

Guruswamy, L., 'Energy Justice and Sustainable Development', *Colorado Journal of International Environmental Law and Policy* 12, 2010.

Guruswamy, L., *International Environmental Law*, 3rd edition, St Paul: Thomson/West, 2007.

Guruswamy, L., Palmer, G. and Weston, B., *International Environmental Law and World Order*, 1st edition, St Paul: West Publishing, 1994.

Guzman, A.T. and Meyer, T.L., *Explaining Soft Law*, American Society of International Law. Online. Available HTTP: <http://www.asil.org/files/guzman.pdf> (accessed 20 November 2011).

Habito, C.F., Aldaba, F.T. and Templo, O.M., *An Assessment Study on the Progress of ASEAN Regional Integration: The Ha Noi Plan of Action Toward ASEAN Vision 2020* (ASEAN Secretariat: 2004).

Hagen, A., 'Nuclear Power, Man, and the Environment', *IAEA Bulletin* 24(2), 1982. Online. Available HTTP: <http://www.iaea.org/Publications/Magazines/Bulletin/Bull242/24204680305.pdf> (accessed 12 March 2012).

Haigh, D., 'Australian World Heritage, the Constitution and International Law', *Environmental and Planning Law Journal* 22, 2005.

Hall, N., 'Climate Change and Organizational Change in UNHCR', in M. Leighton, X. Shen and K. Warner, (eds) *Climate Change and Migration: Rethinking Policies for Adaptation and Disaster Risk Reduction*.

Halliday, E.C., *An Historical Review of Atmospheric Pollution*, New York: World Health Organization/Columbia University Press, 1961.

Halvorssen, A., *Equality Among Unequals in International Environmental Law – Differential Treatment for Developing Countries*, Boulder: Westview Press, 1999.

Hamilton, A., Havice, E. and Campling, L., *Fisheries Trade News* 4(5), 2011. Online. Available HTTP: <http://www.ffa.int/node/459> (accessed 18 January 2012).

Hanna, S., Folke, C. and Mäler K-G. (eds) *Rights to Nature*, Washington DC: Island Press, 1996.

Hansen, M., 'Environmental Regulation of Transnational Corporations', in P. Utting (ed.) *The Greening of Business in Developing Countries*, London: Zed Books in association with UNRISD, 2002.

Hansen, P. and Aranda, V., 'An Emerging International Framework for Transnational Corporations', *Fordham International Law Journal* 14, 1990, 881.

Hardin, G., 'The Tragedy of the Commons', *Science* 162, 1968.

Hargrove, J.L. (ed.) *Law, Institutions and the Global Environment*, NY/Leiden: Oceana Publications/A.W. Sijthoff, 1971.

Harris, D.J., *Cases and Materials on International Law*, 6th edition, Andover: Sweet and Maxwell, 2004.

Harris, R. (ed.) *Handbook of Environmental Law*, Wellington: Royal Forest and Bird Society, 2004.

Harris, R. and Atkins, H., 'Planning Law: The RMA and Related Development; and Local Authority Legislation' in R. Harris (ed.) *Handbook of Environmental Law*, Wellington: Royal Forest and Bird Protection Society of New Zealand 2004.

Harrison, J. and Goller, A., 'Trade and Human Rights: What Does "Impact Assessment" Have to Offer?', *Human Rights Law Review* 8(4), 2008, 587.

Harvey, D., *A Brief History of Neoliberalism*, Oxford: Oxford University Press, 2005.

Harvey, D., *The Conditions of Postmodernity*, London: Basil Blackwell, 1989.

Hassan, P. and Azfar, A., 'Securing Environmental Rights through Public Interest Litigation in South Asia', *Virginia Environmental Law Journal* 22, 2004.

Havemann, P., Thiriet, D., Marsh, H. and Jones, C., 'Traditional Use of Marine Resources Agreements and Dugong Hunting in the Great Barrier Reef World Heritage Area', *Environmental and Planning Law Journal* 22, 2005.

Hawke, A., *The Australian Environment Act – Report of the Independent Review of the Environment Protection and Biodiversity Conservation Act 1999*, Canberra: Australian Government, 2009.

Hawken, P., *How the Largest Movement in the World Came Into Being and Why No One Saw It Coming*, New York: Viking, 2007.

Haya, B., McCully, P. and Pearson, B., 'Damming the Dams: Why Big Hydro Is Ruining the Clean Development Mechanism', (2002) *International Rivers Network/CDM Watch*. Online. Available HTTP: <http://unfccc.int/cop8/se/kiosk/cm2.pdf> (accessed 19 February 2012).

Hayward, T., *Constitutional Environmental Rights*, Oxford: Oxford University Press, 2005.

Heald, P.J., 'The Rhetoric of Biopiracy', *Cardozo Journal of International and Comparative Law* 11, 2003, 519.

Heinze, E. and Fitzmaurice, M., *Landmark Cases in Public International Law*, London: Kluwer Law International, 1998.

Henckaerts, J-M., 'Towards Better Protection for the Environment in Armed Conflict: Recent Developments in International Humanitarian Law', *RECEIL* 9, 2000.

Henckaerts, J-M and Doswald-Beck, L. (eds) *Customary International Humanitarian Law*, Cambridge: Cambridge University Press, 2005.

Henckaerts, J-M. and Doswald-Beck, L. (eds) *Customary International Humanitarian Law*, Cambridge: Cambridge University Press, 2008.

Henman, J.E., Hamburg, S.P. and Salazar Vega, A.A., 'Feasibility and Barrier to Entry for Small-Scale CDM Forest Carbon Projects: A Case Study from the Northeastern Peruvian Amazon', *Carbon and Climate Law Review* 3, 2008, 254.

Herrera Izaguirre, J.A., 'International Law and GMOS: Can the Precautionary Principle Protect Biological Diversity', *Boletin Mexicano de Derecho Comparado* 11, 2007, 97. Online. Available HTTP: <http://www.estig.ipbeja.pt/ ac_direito/HerreraIz.pdf > (accessed 26 April 2012).

Herrero de la Fuente, A., in J. Ebbesson (ed.) *Access to Justice in Environmental Matters in the EU*, Kluwer Law International, 2002.

Hewitt, T., 'Implementation and Enforcement of the Convention on International Trade in Endangered Species of Wild Fauna and Flora in the South Pacific Region: Management and Scientific Authorities', *Queensland University of Technology Law and Justice Journal* 2, 2002.

Hey, E., 'International Institutions' in D. Bodansky, J. Brunnée, and E. Hey (eds) *The Oxford Handbook of International Environmental Law*, Oxford: Oxford University Press, 2007.

Hey, E., 'The Watercourses Convention: To What Extent Does it Provide a Basis for Regulating Uses on International Watercourses?', *Review of European Community & International Environmental Law* 7, 1998, 291.

Hickey, G., 'Evaluating Sustainable Forest Management', *Ecological Indicators* 8, 2008, 109.

Hickie, S., 'Managing Recreation, Conservation and Economy: A Critical Appraisal of the New South Wales Marine Parks Amendment Act 2008', *Environmental and Planning Law Journal* 26, 2009.

Hicks, R.L., Parks, B.C., Roberts, J.T. and Tierney, M.J., *Greening Aid? Understanding the Environmental Impacts of Developing Assistance*, Oxford: Oxford University Press, 2008.

Higgins, P., *Eradicating Ecocide: Laws and Governance to Stop the Destruction of the Planet*, London: Shepheard-Walwyn Publ., 2010.

Higgins, R., 'Natural Resources in the Case Law of the International Court', in A. Boyle and D. Freestone, *International Law and Sustainable Development: Past Achievements and Future Challenges*, Oxford: Oxford University Press, 1999.

Higgins, R., *Problems and Process: International Law and How We Use It*, Oxford and New York: Clarendon Press/Oxford University Press, 1994/5.

Hill, B., Wolfson, S. and Targ, N., 'Human Rights and the Environment: A Synopsis and Some Predictions', *Georgetown International Environmental Law Review* 16, 2004.

Hill, C., *Maritime Law*, 4th edition, London: Lloyds of London Press Ltd, 1995.

Hillemanns, C.F., 'UN Norms on the Responsibility of Transnational Corporations and Other Business Enterprises with Regard to Human Rights', *German Law Journal* 4, 2003, 1065.

Hiraldo, R. and Tanner, T., 'Forest Voices: Competing Narratives over REDD+', *IDS Bulletin* 42, 2011, 42.

Hiskes, R., 'The Right to a Green Future: Human Rights, Environmentalism, and Intergenerational Justice', *Human Rights Quarterly* 27, 2005.

Hitchcock, R.K., 'International Human Rights, the Environment, and Indigenous Peoples', *Colorado Journal of International Environmental Law and Policy* 5, 1994, 1.

Hladik, J., 'Marking of Cultural Property with the Distinctive Emblem of the 1954 Hague Convention for the Protection of Cultural Property in the Event of Armed Conflict', *International Review of the Red Cross*, 86(854), 2004.

Hobe, S., 'Historical Background', in S. Hobe, B. Schmidt-Tedd and K-U. Schrogl (eds) *Cologne Commentary on Space Law, Volume I – Outer Space Treaty*, Cologne: Carl Heymanns Verlag, 2009.

Hodkova, I., 'Is There a Right to a Healthy Environment in the International Legal Order?', *Connecticut Journal of International Law* 7, 1991.

Hoffman, B.T. (ed.), *Art and Cultural Heritage: Law, Policy and Practice*, Cambridge: Cambridge University Press, 2006.

Hoffman, M., 'Towards an International Disaster Response Law' in *World Disasters Report 2000*, Geneva: International Federation of Red Cross and Red Crescent Societies, 2000.

Hogkinson, D., Burton, T., Dawkins, S., Young, L. and Coram, A., 'Towards a Convention for Persons Displaced by Climate Change: Key Issues and Preliminary Responses', *New Critic* 8, 2008.

Holder, J., *Environmental Assessment: the Regulation of Decision Making*, Oxford: Oxford University Press, 2005.

Holder, J. and Lee, M., *Environmental Protection, Law and Policy*, Cambridge: Cambridge University Press, 2007.

Holley, C., 'Removing the Thorn from New Governance's Side: Examining the Emergence of Collaboration in Practice and the Roles for Law, Nested Institutions and Trust', *Environmental Law Reporter* 40(7), 2010.

Holley, C. and Gunningham, N., 'Natural Resources, New Governance and Legal Regulation: When Does Collaboration Work?', *New Zealand Universities Law Review* 24, 2011.

Holley, C., Gunningham, N. and Shearing, C., *The New Environmental Governance*, Abingdon: Earthscan, 2011.

Hosein, H., 'Unsettling: Bhopal and the Resolution of International Disputes Involving an Environmental Disaster', *Boston College International and Comparative Law Review* 16, 1993, 285.

Hossay, P., *Unsustainable: A Primer for Global Environmental and Social Justice*, London and New York: Zed Books, 2006.

Houck, O., 'A Case of Sustainable Development: The River God and the Forest at the End of the World', *Tulsa Law Review* 44, 2008.

Houck, O., 'Light from the Trees: The Stories of Minors Oposa and the Russian Forest Cases', *Georgetown International Environmental Law Review* 19, 2007.

Houck, O., *Taking Back Eden: Eight Environmental Cases that Changed the World*, Washington: Island Press, 2009.

Howse, R. and Regan, D., 'The Product/Process Distinction – An Illusory Basis for Disciplining Unilateralism' *European Journal of International Law* 11, 2000, 249.

Huggins, A., 'Protecting World Heritage Sites from the Adverse Impacts of Climate Change: Obligations for States Parties to the World Heritage Convention', *Australian International Law Journal* 14, 2007.

Hulme, K., 'Natural Environment', in E. Wilmshurst and S. Breau (eds) *Perspectives on the ICRC Study on Customary International Humanitarian Law*, Cambridge: Cambridge University Press, 2007.

Hulme, K., *War Torn Environment: Interpreting the Legal Threshold*, Leiden: Martinus Nijhoff Publishers, 2004.

Humphreys, D., *Logjam: Deforestation and the Crisis of Global Governance*, London: Earthscan, 2006.

Huner, J., 'The Multilateral Agreement on Investment and the Review of the OECD Guidelines for Multinational Enterprises', in M.T. Kamminga and S. Zia-Zarifi (eds) *Liability of Multinational Corporations under International Law*, The Hague: Kluwer Law International, 2000.

Hunter, D., 'Using the World Bank Inspection Panel to Defend the Interests of Project-Affected People', *Chicago Journal of International Law* 4, 2003, 201.

Hunter, D., Salzman, J. and Zaelke, D., *International Environmental Law and Policy*, 3rd edition, NSW Australia: Foundation Press, 2007.

Hunter, D., Salzman, J. and Zaelke, D., *International Environmental Law and Policy*, 4th edition, New York: Foundation Press, 2011.

ICRC, 'Guidelines for Military Manuals and Instructions on the Protection of the Environment in Times of Armed Conflict', *International Revue of the Red Cross* 311, 1996.

Inglis, K., 'Enlargement and the Environment *Acquis*,' *Review of European Community and International Environmental Law* 13, 2004, 135.

Innes, J. and Er, K., 'Global Forest Regulation in the Ten Years after the Rio Conference', *Trends in Ecology and Evolution* 9, 2002, 445.

Intergovernmental Panel on Climate Change (IPCC), 'First Assessment Report', Contribution of Working Group II to the First Assessment Report of the Intergovernmental Panel on Climate Change (Potential Impacts of Climate Change), 1990.

Intergovernmental Panel on Climate Change (IPCC), 'Scientific Assessment of Climate Change', in J.T. Houghton, G.J. Jenkins and J.J. Ephraums (eds) *Contribution of Working Group I to the First Assessment Report of the Intergovernmental Panel on Climate Change*, Cambridge: Cambridge University Press, 1990.

International Commission on Intervention and State Sovereignty, *The Responsibility to Protect*, Ottawa: International Development Research Centre, 2001.

International Energy Agency, *World Energy Outlook 2009*, International Energy Agency, 2009.

International Energy Agency, *World Energy Outlook 2010: Executive Summary*, International Energy Agency, 2010.

International Institute for Sustainable Development, 'SB 34 and AWG Highlights: Monday, 13 June 2011', *Earth Negotiations Bulletin* 12 (509), 2011, 1.

International Labour Office, *Growth, Employment and Decent Work in the Least Developed Countries: Report of the International Labour Office for the Fourth Conference on the Least Developed Countries, Istanbul, 9–13 May 2011*, Geneva: ILO, 2011.

International Law Association, 'New Delhi Declaration of Principles of International Law Relating to Sustainable Development', *Netherlands International Law Review* 49(2), 2002, 299.

International Union for the Conservation of Nature and Natural Resources (IUCN) (ed.) *World Conservation Strategy: Living Resource Conservation for Sustainable Development*, Gland, Switzerland: IUCN, 1980.

International Union for the Conservation of Nature and Natural Resources (IUCN), World Wide Fund for Nature (WWF) and United Nations Environment Programme (UNEP), *Caring for the Earth: A Strategy for Sustainable Living*, Gland, Switzerland: IUCN, 1991.

Ismail, F., 'Rediscovering the Role of Developing Countries in GATT Before the Doha Round', *Law and Development Review* 1, 2008.

IUCN – World Conservation Union, *Guide to Preparing and Implementing National Sustainable Development Strategies and Other Multi-sectoral Environmental and Development Strategies*, prepared by the IUCN's Commission on Environment Strategies Working Group on Strategies for Sustainability, the IUCN Secretariat and the Environment Planning Group of the IIED, pre-publication review Draft 1993.

IUCN Inter-Commission Task Force on Indigenous Peoples, *Indigenous Peoples and Sustainability: Cases and Actions*, Utrecht: International Books, 1997.

IUCN, UNEP and WWF, *World Conservation Strategy: Living Resource Conservation for Sustainable Development*, Gland: International Union for the Conservation of Nature and Natural Resources, 1980.

Iza, A., *International Water Governance: Conservation of Freshwater Ecosystems*, Cambridge: IUCN, 2004.

Jacobs, F.G., 'Judicial Dialogue and the Cross-Fertilization of Legal Systems: The European Court of Justice', *Texas International Law Journal*. 38.

Jacobson, H.K. and Weiss, E.B., 'Assessing the Record and Designing Strategies to Engage Countries', in E.B. Weiss and H.K. Jacobson (eds) *Engaging Countries: Strengthening Compliance with International Environmental Accords*, Cambridge, MA: MIT Press, 1998.

Jalal, P.I., *Pacific Culture and Human Rights: Why Pacific Island Countries Should Ratify International Human Rights Treaties*, Suva: RRRT/UNDP, 2006.

Jamal, A., 'The United Nations Convention to Combat Desertification in those Countries Experiencing Serious Drought and/or Desertification, Particularly in Africa; Implementing Agenda 21', *RECIEL* 6, 1997.

Jänicke, M. and Weidner, H., 'Summary: Global Environmental Policy Learning', in M. Jänicke and H. Weidner (eds) *National Environmental Policies: A Comparative Study of Capacity-Building*, Berlin: Springer, 1997.

Jans, J. and Vedder, H., *European Environmental Law*, Groningen: Europa Law Publishing, 2008.

Janusz, B., 'The Framework Convention for the Protection of the Marine Environment of the Caspian Sea', *Chinese Journal of International Law* 4(1), 2005.

Jeffrey, M.I., 'Intervenor Funding as Key to Effective Citizen Participation in Environmental Decision-Making', *Arizona Journal of International and Comparative Law* 19, 2002.

Jena, K.C., 'Ecology and Environmental Protection Movements: A Brief Conspectus', *AIR Journal* 92, 2005, 288.

Jenkins, B., *Canterbury Strategic Water Study: Briefing Document to Canterbury Mayoral Forum*, Christchurch: ECan, 2007.

Jenkins, M. and Gardner, A., 'Conservation of Biodiversity through the Listing of Threatened Species and Ecological Communities – A Comparative Review', *The Australasian Journal of Natural Resources Law and Policy* 10(1), 2005.

Jenks, C.W., 'The Conflict of Law-Making Treaties', *British Yearbook of International Law* 30, 1953, 401;

Jennings, R. and Watts, A. (eds) *Oppenheim's International Law*, 9th edition, Boston: Addison Wesley Publishing, 1996.

Jessup, B. and Rubenstein, K. (eds) *Environmental Discourses in International and Public Law*, Cambridge: Cambridge University Press, 2011.

Joffe, P.L., 'The Dwindling Margin for Error: The Realist Perspective on Global Governance and Global Warming', *Rutgers Journal of Law and Public Policy* 5, 2007, 89.

Johnson, J., 'Commonwealth Environmental Assessment and Approval', in D. Farrier and P. Stein (eds) *The Environmental Law Handbook*, 5th edition, Pyrmont: Thomson Reuters, 2011.

Johnson, N.L., 'Developments in space debris mitigation policy and practices', in *Proceedings of the Institution of Mechanical Engineers, Part G, Journal of Aerospace Engineering* 221(6), 2007.

Johnson, S., *The Earth Summit: The United Nations Conference on Environment and Development (UNCED)*, London: Kluwer Law International, 1993.

Johnson, S.P., *The Earth Summit: The United Nations Conference on Environment and Development (UNCED)*, Dordrecht: Martinus Nijhoff, 1992.

Johnston, D.M., 'Fishery Diplomacy and Science and the Judicial Function', *Yearbook of International Environmental Law* 10, 1999, 33.

Jones, D.S., 'ASEAN and Transboundary Haze Pollution in Southeast Asia', *Asia Europe Journal* 4, 2006.

Juda, L., *International Law and Ocean Use Management: The Evolution of Ocean Governance*, London: Routledge, 1996.

Jung, M., 'The Role of Forestry Projects in the Clean Development Mechanism', *Environmental Science and Policy* 8, 2005.

Kakonge, J.O., 'Environmental Planning in Sub-Saharan Africa: Environmental Impact Assessment at the Crossroads', Working Paper Number 9, Yale School of Forestry and Environmental Studies, 2006.

Kalen, S., Seidemann, R.M., Wilkins, J.G. and Terrell, M.K., 'Lingering Relevance of the Coastal Zone Management Act to Energy Development in our Nation's Coastal Waters?', *Tulane Environmental Law Journal* 24, 2010.

Kameri-Mbote, P. and Odote, C., 'Courts as champions of sustainable development: Lessons from East Africa', *Sustainable Development Law and Policy* 10, 2009.

Kapetarian, G., 'A Critique of the WTO Jurisprudence in "necessity"', *International & Comparative Law Quarterly*, 2010, 89.

Karekezi, S. and Kimani, J., 'Have Power Sector Reforms Increased Access to Electricity among the Poor in East Africa?', *Energy for Sustainable Development* 8(4), 2004, 10.

Karekezi, S., Kimani, J. and Onguru, O., 'Energy Access among the Urban Poor in Kenya', *Energy for Sustainable Development* 12(4), 2008, 38.

Karim, Md., S., 'Environmental Pollution from Shipbreaking Industry: International Law and National Legal Response' *Georgetown International Environmental Law Review* 22, 2010, 185.

Karim, Md., S., 'Future of the Haze Agreement – Is the Glass Half Empty or Half Full?', *Environmental Policy and Law* 38, 2008.

Kariyawasam, K., 'Access to Biological Resources and Benefit-Sharing: Exploring a Regional Mechanism to Implement the Convention on Biological Diversity in SAARC Countries', *European Intellectual Property Review* 29, 2007, 325.

Karousakis, K., 'Joint Implementation: Current Issues and Emerging Challenges', 2006. Online. Available HTTP: <http://www.oecd.org/dataoecd/45/32/37672335.pdf> (accessed 19 February 2012).

Kasimbazi, E., 'The principle of equitable utilisation and its implications for water resources management in the Nile basin', Unpublished PhD thesis, University of KwaZulu-Natal, 2008.

Kathmandu to Copenhagen: A Regional Climate Change Conference, Nepal, 2009.

Kauffmann, C. and Tébar Less, C., *Transition to a Low-carbon Economy: Public Goals and Corporate Practices*, Paris: OECD, 2010. Online. Available HTTP: <http://www.oecd.org/dataoecd/40/52/45513642.pdf> (accessed 19 December 2011).

Keith, K., 'The Impact of International Law on New Zealand Law', *Waikato Law Review* 6, 1998.

Kelly, J.P., 'The Seduction of the Appellate Body: Shrimp/Sea Turtle I and II and the Proper Role of States in WTO Governance', *Cornell International Law Journal* 38, 2005.

Kelsey, J., *Rolling Back the State: Privatisation of Power in Aotearoa/New Zealand* Wellington: Bridget Williams Books, 1993.

Kennedy, M., Beynon, N., Graham, A. and Pittock, J., 'Development and Implementation of Conservation Law in Australia', *RECIEL* 10(3), 2001.

Kent, R.C., *Anatomy of Disaster Relief: The International Network in Action*, London: Pinter, 1987.

Keohane, N.O., 'Cap-and-Trade is Preferable to a Carbon Tax', in R.B. Stewart, B. Kingsbury and B. Rudyk (eds) *Climate Finance: Regulatory and Funding Strategies for Climate Change*, New York: New York University Press, 2009.

Keohane, R., 'International Institutions: Two Approaches', *International Studies Quarterly* 32(4), 1988, 379.

Kerr, A., 'Untapped Potential: Administrative Law and International Environmental Obligations', *NZJPIL* 6, 2008.

Kidd, M., *Environmental Law*, Cape Town: Juta, 2011.

Kidd, M., 'Forest issues in Africa', *International Law-making and Diplomacy Review*, 2005.

Kidd, M. and Cowling, M., 'CITES and the African Elephant', in B. Chaytor and K.R. Gray, *International Environmental Law and Policy in Africa*, Dordrecht: Kluwer, 2003.

Kirpal, B.N., Chief Justice, Supreme Court of India, 'M.C. Bhandari Memorial Lecture: Environmental Justice in India' (2002), in 7, SCC 1 (2002). Online. Available HTTP: <http://www.ebc-india.com/lawyer/articles/ 2002v7a1.htm> (accessed ? May 2012).

Kiss, A., *Introduction to International Environmental Law*, 2nd edition, Geneva: United Nations Institute for Training and Research, 2005.

Kiss, A., 'Reporting Obligations and Assessment of Reports', in U. Beyerlin, P-T. Stoll and R. Wolfrum (eds) *Ensuring Compliance with Multilateral Environmental Agreements: A Dialogue Between Practitioners and Academia*, The Netherlands: Martinus Nijhoff, 2006.

Kiss, A. and Shelton, D., *International Environmental Law*, 2nd edition, Ardsley: Transnational Publishers, 2000.

Kitt, J.R., 'Waste exports to the developing world: A global response', *Georgetown International Environmental Law Review* 7, 1995.

Kjellen, B., 'The role of the Desertification Convention in the early 21st Century', *Environmental Policy and Law* 40(4), 2010.

Klabbers, J., *An Introduction to International Institutional Law*, Cambridge: Cambridge University Press, 2004.

Klein, N., 'Settlement of International Environmental Disputes', in M. Fitzmaurice, D.M. Ong and P. Merkouris (eds) *Research Handbook on International Environmental Law*, Cheltenham: Edward Elgar, 2010, 379.

Klein, N., 'Whales and Tuna: The Past and Future of Litigation between Australia and Japan', *Georgetown International Environmental Law Review* 21(2), 2009.

Kline, J.M., 'Business Codes of Conduct in a Global Political Economy', in O.F. Williams (ed.) *Global Codes of Conduct: An Idea Whose Time Has Come*, Indiana: University of Notre Dame Press, 2000.

Klinkrad, H., *Space Debris Mitigation Activities at ESA*, Presentation to the Scientific and Legal Subcommittee of the UN Committee on the Peaceful Uses of Outer Space, February 2011. Online. Available HTTP: <http://www.oosa.unvienna.org/pdf/pres/stsc2011/tech-40.pdf> (accessed 1 November 2011).

Kniveton, D., Smith, C., Black, R. and Schmidt-Verkerk, K., 'Challenges and Approaches to Measuring the Migration-Environment Nexus', in F. Laczko and C. Aghazarm (eds) *Environment and Climate Change: Assessing the Evidence*, International Organization for Migration, 2009.

Knox, J., 'Climate Change and Human Rights Law', *Virginia Journal of International Law* 50, 2009.

Knox, J.H., 'The Neglected Lessons of the NAFTA Environmental Regime', *Wake Forest Law Review* 45, 2010.

Koh, K.L., 'Framing New and Emerging Transboundary Environmental Challenges: Impact on the ASEAN Way and Environmental Governance', paper presented at the 2nd CILS Conference 2011, International Conference on ASEAN's Role in Sustainability Development, Faculty of Law, Universitas Gadjah Mada, Indonesia, 21 and 22 November 2011;

Koh, K.L., 'Land Stewardship and the Law: ASEAN Heritage Parks and Transboundary Biodiversity Conservation' in N.J. Chalifour, P. Kameri-Mbote, L.H. Lye and J.R. Nolon (eds) *Land Use Law for Sustainable Development*, Ottawa: IUCN Academy of Environmental Law, 2006.

Koh, K.L., 'The Discourse of Environmental Security in the ASEAN Context' in B. Jessup and K. Rubenstein (eds) *Environmental Discourses in Public and International Law*, Cambridge: Cambridge University Press, 2012.

Koh, K.L., 'Transboundary and Global Environmental Issues: the Role of ASEAN' Transnational Environmental Law 1, 2012, 1–16.

Koh, K.L., *ASEAN Environmental Law, Policy and Governance Selected Documents* (Vol. I), Hackensack, NJ: World Scientific, 2009.

Koh, K.L., *ASEAN Environmental Law, Policy and Governance Selected Documents* (Vol. II, forthcoming 2012).

Koh, K.L., and Robinson, N.A., 'Strengthening Sustainable Development in Regional Inter-Governmental Governance: Lessons from the 'ASEAN Way'' *Singapore Journal of International and Comparative Law* 6, 2002.

Koh, T., Woon, W., Tan, A. and Sze-Wei, C., 'The ASEAN Charter'. Online. Available HTTP: <http://www.csis.org/media/csis/pubs/pac0733a.pdf> (accessed 22 November 2011).

Kohn, A.E. and Eves, H.E., 'The African bushmeat crisis: A case for global partnership', *Environs Environmental Law and Policy Journal* 30, 2007.

Koivurova, T., 'Jurisprudence of the European Court of Human Rights Regarding Indigenous Peoples: Retrospect and Prospects', *International Journal on Minority and Group Rights* 18, 2011.

Koivurova, T., 'Limits and Possibilities of the Arctic Council in a Rapidly Changing Scene of Arctic Governance', Polar Record 7, 2009, Cambridge University Press.

Koivurova, T. and VanderZwaag, D., 'The Arctic Council at 10 Years: Retrospect and Prospects', *University of British Columbia Law Review* 40(1), 2007.

Koskenniemi, M., 'Peaceful Settlement of Environmental Disputes' *Nordic Journal of International Law* 60, 1991.

Koslow, J., Boehlert, G.W., Gordon, J.D.M., Haedrich, R.L., Lorance, P. and Parin, N., 'Continental Slope and Deep-sea Fisheries: Implications for a Fragile Ecosystem', *ICES Journal of Marine Science* 57, 2000, 548.

Kovar, J.D., 'A Short Guide to the Rio Declaration', *University of Colorado Journal of International Environmental Law and Policy* 4, 1993.

Koyano, M., 'Effective Implementation of International Environmental Agreements: Learning Lessons from the Danube Delta Conflict', in T. Komori and K. Wellens, *Public Interest Rules of International Law*, Surrey: Ashgate, 2009.

Kraft Sloan, K. and Hik, D., 'International Polar Year as a Catalyst For Sustaining Arctic Research', *Sustainable Development Law and Policy* 8, 2008.

Kramer, L., *EC Environmental Law*, London: Sweet and Maxwell, 2006.

Kramer, L., 'Environmental Justice in the European Court of Justice', in J. Ebbesson and P. Okowa (eds) *Environmental Law and Justice in Context*, Cambridge: Cambridge University Press, 2009, 195.

Kramer, L., 'The EU: a Regional Model?', in G. Winter (ed.) *Multilevel Governance of Global Environmental Change*, Cambridge: Cambridge University Press, 2006.

Kramer, L., 'The Implementation of Community Environmental Directives Within Member States: Some Implications of Direct Effect Doctrine', *Journal of Environmental Law* 3, 1991, 39.

752

Kramer, L., 'Regional Economic International Organizations: The European Union as an Example', in D. Bodansky, J. Brunnée and E. Hey (eds) *The Oxford Handbook of International Environmental Law*, Oxford: Oxford University Press, 2007.

Kramer, L., 'Sustainable Development in the EC', in H. Bugge and C. Voigt (eds) *Sustainable Development in International and National Law*, Groningen: Europa Law Publishing, 2008, 377.

Krasner, S.D., 'Power Structures and Regional Development Banks', *International Organization* 35, 1981, 303.

Kravchenko, S., 'The Aarhus Convention and Innovations in Compliance with Multilateral Environmental Agreements', *University of Colorado Journal of International Environmental Law and Policy* 18, 2007.

Kravchenko, S., 'Citizen Enforcement of Environmental Law in Eastern Europe', *Widener Law Review* 10, 2004.

Kravchenko, S., 'The Myth of Public Participation in a World of Poverty', *Tulane Environmental Law Journal* 23, 2009.

Kravchenko, S. and Bonine, J., *Human Rights and the Environment: Cases, Law and Policy*, Durham, NC: Carolina Academic Press, 2008.

Kuehn, R.R., 'A Taxonomy of Environmental Justice', *Environmental Law Reporter* 30, 2000.

Kulovesi, K., Morgera, E. and Muñoz, M., 'Environmental Integration and the Multi-faceted International Dimensions of EU Law: Unpacking the EU's 2009 Climate and Energy Package', *Common Market Law Review* 48, 2011.

Kummer, K., *International Management of Hazardous Wastes*, Oxford: Clarendon Press, 1995.

Kummer, K., 'The International Regulation of Transboundary Traffic in Hazardous Wastes: The 1989 Basel Convention', *International and Comparative Law Quarterly* 41, 1992, 530.

Kunzmann, K., 'The Non-Legally Binding Instrument on Sustainable Management of All Types of Forests – Towards a legal regime for sustainable forest management?', *German Law Journal* 9, 2008.

Kurin, R., 'Safeguarding Intangible Cultural Heritage: Key Factors in Implementing the 2003 Convention', *International Journal of Intangible Heritage*, 2, 2007.

La Vina, A.G.M., Hoff, G. and DeRose, A., *The Successes and Failures of Johannesburg: A Story of Many Summits: A Report on the World Summit on Sustainable Development for Donors and Civil Society Organizations*, World Resources Institute Working Paper (2002).

Lack, M., 'With an eye to the future: Addressing failures in the global management of Bigeye Tuna', *TRAFFIC*, 2011. Online. Available HTTP: <http://www.traffic.org/fisheries/> (accessed 25 January 2012).

Laczko, F. and Aghazarm, C., 'Introduction and Overview: Enhancing the Knowledge Base', in F. Laczko and C. Aghazarm (eds) *Environment and Climate Change: Assessing the Evidence*, International Organization for Migration, 2009.

Lake, R., 'Finance for the Global Environment: the Effectiveness of the GEF as the Financial Mechanism to the Convention on Biological Diversity', *Review of European Community & International Environmental Law* 7, 1998.

Lammers, J., 'Efforts to Develop a Protocol on Chlorofluorocarbons to the Vienna Convention for the Protection of the Ozone Layer', *Hague Yearbook of International Law* 1, 1998, 255.

Lane, C.N., *Acid Rain: Overview and Abstracts*, Hauppuge, New York: Nova Science Publishers, 2003.

Lane, M., Taylor, B. and Robinson, C. (eds) *Contested Country*, Collingwood: CSIRO, 2009.

Larkin, P.A., 'An Epitaph for the Concept of Maximum Sustainable Yield', *Transactions of the American Fisheries Society* 106(1), 1977, 1.

Lau, M., 'Islam and Judicial Activism: Public Interest Litigation and Environmental Protection in the Islamic Republic of Pakistan', in M. Anderson and A. Boyle (eds) *Human Rights Approaches to Environmental Protection*, Oxford: Oxford University Press, 1996.

Lauterpacht, E., 'Foreword', in M.C. Cordonier Segger, M. Gehring and A. Newcombe (eds) *Sustainable Development in World Investment Law*. Alphen aan den Rijn: Kluwer Law International, 2010.

Lavranos, N., 'Epilogue in the Mox Plant Dispute: An End Without Findings', *European Energy and Environmental Law Review* 18, 2009.

Leckie, S., 'Climate-related Disasters and Displacement: Homes for Lost Homes, Lands for Lost Lands', in J.M. Guzman, G. Martine, G. McGranahan, D. Schensul and C. Tacoli (eds) *Population Dynamics and Climate Change*, UNFPA and IIED, 2009.

Lee, M., 'The Environmental Implications of the Lisbon Treaty', *Environmental Law Review* 10, 2008, 131.

Lee, M., *EU Environmental Law: Challenges, Change and Decision-making*, Oxford: Hart, 2005.

Lee, R.J. and Freeland S., 'The Crystallisation of General Assembly Space Declarations into Customary International Law', *Proceedings of the Colloquium on the Law of Outer Space* 46, 2004, 122.

Lee, Y.S., *Reclaiming Development in the World Trading System*. Cambridge: Cambridge University Press, 2006

Lefeber, R., 'Creative Legal Engineering', *Leiden Journal of International Law* 13, 2000, 1.

Lehmann, K., 'To Define or Not to Define: The Definitional Debate Revisited', *American Indian Law Review* 31, 2006/2007, 509.

Leighton, M., Shen, X. and Warner, K. (eds), *Climate Change and Migration: Rethinking Policies for Adaptation and Disaster Risk Reduction*, Publication Series of United Nations University, No. 15/2011.

Lemos, M.C. and Agrawal, A., 'Environmental Governance' *Annual Review of Environment and Resources* 11, 2006.

Lennox, J. and van Nieuwkoop, R., 'Output-based Allocations and Revenue Recycling: Implications for the New Zealand Emissions Trading Scheme', *Energy Policy* 38(12), 2010, 7861.

Leonard, H.J. and Morrell, D., 'Emergence of Environmental Concern in Developing Countries: A Political Perspective', *Stanford Journal of International Law* 17, 1981, 281.

Leonard, L.L., 'Recent Negotiations Toward the International Regulation of Whaling', *American Journal of International Law* 35, 1941.

Levy, M.A., Keohane, R.O. and Haas, P.M., 'Improving the Effectiveness of International Environmental Insitutions', in P.M. Haas, R.O. Keohane and M.A. Levy (eds) *Institutions for Earth: Sources of Effective International Environmental Protection*, Cambridge, MA: MIT Press.

Lin, C.H., 'ASEAN Charter: Deeper Regional Integration under International Law?' (2010) *Chinese Journal of International Law* 9, 821.

Lin, J., 'Tackling Southeast Asia's Illegal Wildlife Trade' *Singapore Year Book of International Law* 9, 2005.

Linkages, 'Summary of the Seventh Meeting of Persistent Organic Pollutants Review Committee of the Stockholm Convention 10–14 October 2011', *Earth Negotiations Bulletin* 15(189), 2011. Online. Available HTTP: <http://www.iisd.ca/chemical/pops/poprc7/> (accessed 13 March 2012).

Linkages, 'Summary of the Tenth Meeting of the Conference of the Parties to the Basel Convention', *Earth Negotiations Bulletin* 20(37), 2011. Online. Available HTTP: <http://www.iisd.ca/vol15/enb15189e.html> (accessed 23 November 2011).

Liu, S.F., 'The Koko Incident: Developing International Norms for the Transboundary Movement of Hazardous Waste', *Journal of Natural Resources and Environmental Law* 8, 1993, 121.

Loibl, G., 'Reporting and Information Systems in International Environmental Agreements as a Means for Dispute Prevention – The Role of "International Institutions"', *Non-State Actors and International Law* 5, 2005, 13.

Long, A., 'Global climate governance to enhance biodiversity and well-being: Integrating non-state networks and public international law in tropical forests', *Environmental Law* 41, 2011, 95.

Long, R., 'The Marine Strategy Framework Directive: A New European Approach to the Regulation of the Marine Environment, Marine Natural Resources and Marine Ecological Services', *Journal of Energy and Natural Resources Law* 29(1), 2011.

Lopez, A., 'The Protection of Environmentally-Displaced Persons in International Law', *Environmental Law* 37, 2007, 365.

Lough, P. and Cameron, A., 'Forestry in the New Zealand Emissions Trading Scheme: Design and Prospects for Success', *Carbon Climate Law Review* 3, 2008.

Louka, E., *International Environmental Law: Fairness, Effectiveness, and World Order*, Cambridge: Cambridge University Press, 2006.

Loukacheva, N. (ed.) *Polar Law Textbook*, Copenhagen: Nordic Council of Ministers, 2010. Online. Available HTTP: <http://www.norden.org/en/publications/publikationer/2010-538> (accessed 9 May 2012).

Ludgwig, D., Hilborn, R. and Walters, C., 'Uncertainty, Resource Exploitation and Conservation: Lessons from History', *Science* 260(2), 1993.

Lueck, M.A.M., in Michelle Leighton, Xiaomeng Shen and Koko Warner (eds) *Climate Change and Migration: Rethinking Policies for Adaptation and Disaster Risk Reduction*, Publication Series of UNU-EHS, No. 15/2011.

Lyall, F. and Larsen, P.B., *Space Law: A Treatise*, London: Ashgate Publishing, 2009.

Lyster, R., 'Australia's Clean Energy Future Package: Are We There Yet?', *Environmental and Planning Law Journal* 28, 2011.

Lyster, R., 'Australia's Clean Energy Future Package: Are We There Yet?', Sydney Law School Research Paper No. 11/85, 2011. Online Available HTTP: <http://ssrn.com/abstract=1954238> (viewed 4 November 2011).

Lyster, R. 'The Australian Carbon Pollution Reduction Scheme: What Role for Complementary Emissions Reduction Regulatory Measures?', *UNSW Law Journal* 31(3), 2008.

Lyster, R. and Bradbrook, A., *Energy Law and the Environment*, Port Melbourne: Cambridge University Press, 2006.

Lyster, R., Lipman, Z., Franklin, N., Wiffen, G. and Pearson, L., *Environmental and Planning Law in New South Wales*, Sydney: Federation Press, 2009.

Lyster, R., Lipman, Z., Franklin, N., Wiffen, G. and Pearson, L., *Environmental & Planning Law in New South Wales*, 3rd edition, Annandale: Federation Press, 2012.

Maarleveld, T.J., 'How and Why will Underwater Cultural Heritage Benefit from the 2001 Convention?', *Museum International* 60(4), 2008, 50.

Macalister-Smith, P., *International Humanitarian Assistance: Disaster Relief Actions in International Law and Organization*, Dordrecht: Martinus Nijhoff, 1985.

Macalister-Smith, P., 'The International Relief Union: Reflections on the Convention Establishing an International Relief Union of July 12, 1927' *Tijdschrift voor Rechtsgeschiedenis* 54, 1986, 363.

Macintosh, A., 'Why the Environment Protection and Biodiversity Conservation Act's Referral, Assessment and Approval Process is Failing to Achieve its Environmental Objectives', *Environmental and Planning Law Journal* 21, 2004, 288.

Mackenzie, R., Romano, C., Shany, Y. and Sands, P., *The Manual on International Courts and Tribunals*, 2nd edition, Oxford: Oxford University Press, 2010.

Maffi, L., 'Biocultural Diversity and Sustainability', in J. Pretty, A. Ball, T. Benton, J. Guivant, D.R. Lee, D. Orr, M. Pfeffer and H. Ward, (eds) *The Sage Handbook of Environment and Society*, London: Sage Publishing, 2007.

Maguire J-J., Sissenwine, M., Csirke, J. and Grainger, R., *State of World Highly Migratory, Straddling and other High Seas Fishery Resources and Associated Species*, Fisheries Technical Paper 495, Rome: Food and Agriculture Organization, 2006.

Maguire, R., 'Legal Issues in the Design and Implementation of Environmental Offset and Environmental Trading Frameworks', *Queensland Environmental Practice Reporter* 14(64), 2008–2009, 53.

Maguire, R., 'Opportunities for Forest Finance: Compliance and Voluntary Markets', *Carbon and Climate Law Review* 1, 2011, 100.

Maguire, R. and Phillips, A., 'The Role of Property Law on Environmental Management', *Environment and Planning Law Journal* 28(4), 2011.

Mainhardt, H., 'Capacity-Building Strategies in Support of Multilateral Environmental Agreements', in L.E. Suskind, W. Moomaw, K. Gallagher and E. Corell (eds) *Reforming the International Enviornmental Treaty-Making System*, Cambridge, MA: PON Books, 2001.

Malik, M., 'Recent Developments in International Investment Agreements: Negotiations and Disputes', *IV Annual Forum for Developing Country Investment Negotiators, Background Papers*, 2010. Online. Available HTTP: <www.iisd.org/pdf/2011/dci_2010_recent_developments_iias.pdf> (accessed 19 December 2011)

Malone, L.A., 'The Chernobyl Accident: A Case Study in International Law Regulating State Responsibility for Transboundary Nuclear Pollution', *Columbia Journal of Environmental Law* 12, 1987, 203.

Maluwa, T., *International Law in Post-Colonial Africa*, Dordrecht: Kluwer, 1999.

Maluwa, T., 'The OAU/African Union and international law: Mapping new boundaries or revising old terrain?', *American Society of International Law Proceedings* 98, 2004.

Mann, H., von Moltke, K., Peterson, L.E. and Cosbey, A. (2005), *International Institute for Sustainable Development Model International Agreement for Sustainable Development*. Online. Available HTTP: <http://www.iisd.org/pdf/2005/investment_model_int_agreement.pdf>

Marceau, G. and Stilwell, M., 'Practical Suggestions for *Amicus Curiae* Briefs before WTO Adjudicating Bodies', *Journal of International Economic Law* 4, 2001, 161.

Space Law, Volume I – Outer Space Treaty, Cologne: Carl Heymanns Verlag, 2009.

Marín Durán, G. and Morgera, E., *Environmental Integration in the EU's External Relations: Beyond Multilateral Dimensions*, Oxford: Hart Publishing, 2012.

Marsh, G.P., *Man and Nature, or, Physical Geography as Modified by Human Action*, New York: Charles Scribner and Co, 1867.

Marshall, P., *GBR Coral Bleaching Response Program*, Townsville: GBRMPA, 2003.

Martin, G. and Vermeylen, S., 'Intellectual Property, Indigenous Knowledge and Biodiversity', *Capitalism, Nature, Socialism* 26, 2005, 27.

Martinez-Alier, J., *The Environmentalism of the Poor: A Study of Ecological Conflicts and Valuation*, Chelthenham: Edward Elgar, 2002.

Mathy, S., Hourcade J-C. and de Gouvello, C., 'Clean Development Mechanism: Leverage for Development?', *Climate Policy* 1, 2001, 251.

Matz, N., 'Environmental Financing and Coherence of Financial Mechanisms in International Environmental Agreements', *Max Planck Yearbook of United Nations Law* 6, 2002, 473.

Matz, N., 'Financial Institutions between Effectiveness and Legitimacy – A Legal Analysis of the World Bank, Global Environment Facility and Prototype Carbon Fund', *International Environmental Agreements* 5, 2005, 265.

Matz-Lück, N., 'Framework Conventions as a Regulatory Tool', *Goettingen Journal of International Law* 1(3), 2009, 440.

May, J., 'Constituting Fundamental Environmental Rights Worldwide', *Pace Environmental Law Review* 23, 2006.

May, J., 'The North American Symposium on the Judiciary and Environmental Law: Constituting Fundamental Environmental Rights Worldwide', *Pace Environmental Law Review* 23, 2005/2006.

May, J., 'Of Development, daVinci and Domestic Legislation: The Prospects for Sustainable Development in Asia and its Untapped Potential in the United States', *Widener Law Symposium Journal* 3, 1998.

May, J.R. and Daly, E., 'Vindicating Constitutionally Entrenched Environmental Rights Worldwide', *Oregon Review of International Law* 11, 2010.

Mayer, J., 'Transboundary Perspectives on Managing Indonesia's Fires', *Journal of Environment and Development* 15, 2006, 202.

McAdam, J., '"Disappearing States", Statelessness and the Boundaries of International Law', in J. McAdam (ed.) *Climate Change and Displacement: Multidisciplinary Perspectives*, Oxford/Portland, OR: Hart, 2010.

McAdam, J., 'Environmental Migration Governance', University of New South Wales Faculty of Law Research Series, 2009.

McAdam, J., 'Swimming Against the Tide: Why a Climate Change Displacement Treaty is Not the Answer', *Internationall Journal of Refugee Law* 23, 2011, 2.

McCaffrey, S.C., 'The 1997 UN Watercourses Convention: Retrospect and Prospect', *Pacific McGeorge Global Business and Development Law Journal* 21, 2008, 165.

McCaffrey, S.C., 'The evolution of the Law of International Watercourses', *Austrian Journal of Public International Law* 5(2), 1992, 87.

McCaffrey, S.C., 'The Harmon Doctrine one hundred years later: buried, not praised', *Natural Resources Journal* 36, 1996, 549.

McCaffrey, S.C. and Sinjela, M., 'The 1997 United Nations Convention on International Watercourse', *American Journal of International Law* 97, 1998.

McCall-Smith, A., 'The Duty to Rescue and the Common Law', in M.A. Menlowe and A. McCall-Smith (eds) *The Duty to Rescue: The Jurisprudence of Aid*, Aldershot: Dartmouth Publishing, 1993.

McConnell, F., *The Biodiversity Convention: A Negotiation History*, The Hague: Kluwer Law International, 1996.

McCorquodale, R. and Simons, P., 'Responsibility Beyond Borders: State Responsibility for Extraterritorial Violations by Corporations of International Human Rights Law', *Modern Law Review* 70, 2007.

McDougal, M.S., Lasswell, H.D. and Reisman, W.M., 'The World Constitutive Process of Authoritative Decision', in M.S. McDougal and W.M. Reisman (eds) *International Law Essays: A Supplement to International Law in Contemporary Perspective*, Mineola, NY: Foundation Press, 1981.

McGillivray, D. and Holder, J., 'Locating EC Environmental Law', *Yearbook of European Environmental Law* 2, 2001.

McGlade, J., Speech, *Arctic Frontiers Conference*, Tromsø, 23 January. 2007. Online Available HTTP: <http://www.eea.europa.eu/pressroom/speeches/23-01-2007> (accessed 9 May 2012).

McGrath, C., 'Editorial comment – End of Broadscale Clearing In Queensland', *Environmental and Planning Law Journal* 24, 2007, 5.

McGrath, C., 'Flying Foxes, Dams and Whales: Using Federal Environmental Laws in the Public Interest', *Environmental and Planning Law Journal* 25, 2008, 324.

McGrath, C., 'The QLD Bilateral', *Queensland Environmental Practice Reporter* 8, 2002–2003.

McIntyre, O. and Mosedale, T., 'The Precautionary principle as a Norm of Customary International Law', *Journal of Environmental Law*, 1997.

McKee, M., 'Debris Threat Prompts Space Station Crew to Evacuate' *New Scientist*. Online. Available HTTP: <http://www.newscientist.com/article/dn16755-debris-threat-prompts-space-station-crew-to-evacuate.html> (accessed 26 July 2011).

McLaren, D., 'Environmental Space, Equity and the Ecological Debt', in A.H. Alkon and J. Agyeman (eds) *Cultivating Food Justice: Race, Class, and Sustainability*, Cambridge, MA: MIT Press, 2011.

McMillan, K., 'Strengthening the International Legal Framework for Nuclear Energy', *Georgetown International Environmental Law Review* 13, 2001, 983.

McNeely, J.A., *Conserving the World's Biological Diversity*, Washington DC: IUCN, 1990.

Meijer, E. and Werksman, J., 'Keeping It Clean – Safeguarding the Environmental Integrity of the Clean Development Mechanism', in D. Freestone and C. Streck (eds) *Legal Aspects of Implementing the Kyoto Protocol Mechanisms: Making Kyoto Work*, Oxford: Oxford University Press, 2005.

Mekonnen, D.Z., 'The Nile Basin Cooperative Framework Agreement negotiations and the adoption of a "water security" paradigm: flight into obscurity or a logical cul-de-sac?', *European Journal of International Law* 21(2), 2010.

Memon, P. and Gleeson, B., 'Towards a New Planning Paradigm? Reflections on New Zealand's Resource Management Act', *Environment and Planning B: Planning and Design* 22(1), 1995.

Merrills, J.G., 'Environmental Protection and Human Rights: Conceptual Aspects', in M. Anderson and A. Boyle (eds) *Human Rights Approaches to Environmental Protection*, Oxford: Oxford University Press, 1996.

Mgbeoji, I., *Global Biopiracy: Patents, Plants and Indigenous Knowledge*, Vancouver: UBC Press, 2005.

Mgbeoji, I., 'Patents and Traditional Knowledge of Uses of Plants: Is a Communal Patent Regime Part of the Solution to the Scourge of Biopiracy?' *Indiana Journal of Global Legal Studies* 9, 2001.

Michaelowa, A., 'Creating the Foundations for Host Country Participation in the CDM: Experiences and Challenges in CDM Capacity Building', in F. Yamin (ed.) *Climate Change and Carbon Markets – a Handbook of Emission Reduction Mechanisms*, London: Earthscan, 2005.

Michaelsen, T., Ljungmann, L., El-Lekany, M.H., Hyttinen, P., Giesen, K., Kaiser, M. and von Zitzewitz, E., 'Hot Spot in the Field: National Forest Programmes – a New Instrument within Old Conflicts of the Forestry Sector', *Forest Policy and Economics* 1, 2000, 95.

Mickelson, K., 'Competing narratives of justice in North-South environmental relations: the case of ozone layer depletion', in J. Ebbesson and P. Okowa (eds) *Environmental Law and Justice in Context*, Cambridge: Cambridge University Press, 2009.

Mickelson, K., 'Leading Towards a Level Playing Field, Repaying Ecological Debt, or Making Environmental Space: Three Stories about International Environmental Cooperation', *Osgoode Hall Law Journal* 43, 2005.

Mickelson, K., 'Seeing the Forest, the Trees and the People: Coming to Terms with Developing Perspectives on the Proposed Global Forest Regime', in S. Johnson (ed.) *Global Forests and International Environmental Law*, Kluwer Law International, 1996.

Mickelson, K., 'South, North, International Environmental Law, and International Environmental Lawyers', *Yearbook of International Environmental Law*, 2000.

Midence, A.G.P., 'Protected Areas Strategy: An Overview of New Zealand and Guatemala', *New Zealand Journal of Environmental Law* 9, 2005, 91.

Millennium Ecosystem Assessment, *Health Synthesis*, World Health Organization, 2005.

Miller, M., 'Persistent Illegal Logging in Costa Rica: The Role of Corruption among Forestry Regulators', *Journal of Environment and Development* 20(1), 2011, 50.

Miller, R.A., 'Collective Discursive Democracy as the Indigenous Right to Self-Determination', *American Indian Law Review* 31, 2006/2007, 341.

Mimura, N., Nurse, L., McLean, R.F., Agard, J., Briguglio, L., Lefale, P., Payet, R. and Sem, G., 'Small Islands', *Climate Change 2008: Impacts, Adaptation and Vulnerability. Contribution of Working Group II to the Fourth Assessment Report of the Intergovernmental Panel on Climate Change*, M.L. Parry, O.F. Canziani, J.P. Palutikof, P.J. van der Linden and C.E. Hanson (eds), Cambridge: Cambridge University Press, 2007.

Minang, P.A., Jungcurt, S., Meadu, V. and Murphy, D., (2009) 'The REDD Negotiations: Moving into Copenhagen', *International Institute for Sustainable Development* 4. Online. Available HTTP: <http://www.iisd.org/pdf/2009/redd_negotiations.pdf> (accessed 14 December 2011).

Mintzer, I.M. and Leonard, J.A. (eds) *Negotiating Climate Change: The Inside Story of the Rio Convention*, Cambridge: Cambridge University Press, 1994.

Miranda, L.A., 'Indigenous Peoples as International Lawmakers', *University of Pennsylvania Journal of International Law* 32(1), 2010.

MIT, *The Future of Nuclear Energy*, An Inter-disciplinary MIT study, MA: Massachusetts Institute of Technology, 2003. Online. Available HTTP: <http://web.mit.edu/nuclearpower/pdf/nuclearpower-summary.pdf> (accessed 1 January 2012).

Mitchell, R., 'Compliance Theory: An Overview', in J. Cameron, J. Werksman and P. Roderick, *Improving Compliance with International Environmental Law*, London: Earthscan, 1996.

Molenaar, E.J., 'CCAMLR and Southern Ocean Fisheries', *International Journal of Marine and Coastal Law* 16, 2001.

Montgomery, M.A., 'Traveling Toxic Trash: an Analysis of the 1989 Basel Convention', *The Fletcher Forum of World Affairs Journal* 14, 1990, 315.

Morel, C., 'Conservation and Indigenous Peoples' Rights: Must One Necessarily Come at the Expense of the Other?' in IUCN–CEESP (ed.) *Exploring the Right to Diversity in Conservation Law, Policy, and Practice, Policy Matters* 17, 2010, 174.

Moreno, C.J., 'Oil and gas exploration and production in the Gulf of Guinea: Can the new Gulf be green?' *Houston Journal of International Law* 31, 2009, 419.

Morgera, E., *Corporate Accountability in International Law*, Oxford: Oxford University Press, 2009.

Morgera, E., (2010) *Expert Report Corporate Responsibility to Respect Human Rights in the Environmental Sphere*, Commission-funded project, University of Edinburgh. Available HTTP: <http://www.law.ed.ac.uk/euenterpriseslf/documents/files/CSR Environment.pdf> (accessed 28 December 2011).

Morgera, E. (ed.) *The External Environmental Action of the European Union: EU and International Law Perspectives*, Cambridge: Cambridge University Press, 2012.

Morgera, E., 'From Corporate Social Responsibility to Accountability Mechanisms', in P.M. Dupuy and J. Vinales (eds) *Protecting the Environment in the XXIst Century – The Role of the Private Sector*, Cambridge: Cambridge University Press, forthcoming 2012.

Morgera, E. and Marín Durán, G., 'The UN 2005 World Summit, the Environment and the EU: Priorities, Promises and Prospects,' *Review of European Community and International Environmental Law* 15, 2006.

Morris, R., 'What Happens When Your Country Drowns', *Mother Jones*, 2009.

Moss, N. and Nussbaum, R., (2011) *'A Review of three REDD+ Safeguards Initiatives'* Forest Carbon Partnership Facility and UN REDD Programme. Online. Available HTTP: <http://reddpluspartnership.org/29785-0e1d064b96b75dfb79469cf0d86708dda.pdf> (accessed 14 December 2011).

Moyes, T., 'Greenhouse Gas Emissions Trading in New Zealand: Trailblazing Comprehensive Cap and Trade', *Ecology Law Quarterly* 35, 2008.

Moynagh, E.B., 'The Legacy of Chernobyl: Its Significance for the Ukraine and the World', *Boston College Environmental Affairs Law Review* 21, 1994.

Muchlinski, P., 'Attempts to Extend the Accountability of Transnational Corporations: The Role of UNCTAD', in M.T. Kamminga and S. Zia-Zarifi (eds) Liability of Multinational Corporations under International Law, The Hague: Kluwer Law International, 2000.

Muchlinski, P., *Multinational Enterprises and the Law*, New York: Oxford University Press, 2007.

Mulqueeny, K.K., 'Regionalism, Economic Integration in ASEAN: What Space for Environmental Sustainability?' *Asia Pacific Journal of Environmental Law* 8, 2004.

Multiparty Climate Change Committee, *Clean Energy Agreement*, Canberra: Australian Government, 2011.

Munansinghe, M. and Lutz, E., *Environmental-Economic Evaluation of Projects and Policies for Sustainable Development*, Environment Working Paper No. 42, World Bank, 1991.

Munzer, S. and Simon, P.C., 'Territory, Plants, and Land-Use Rights among the San of South Africa: A Case Study in Regional Biodiversity, Traditional Knowledge and Intellectual Property', *William and Mary Bill of Rights Journal* 17, 2009, 831.

Murswiek, D., 'Nachhaltigkeit – Probleme der rechtlichen Umsetzung eines umweltpolitischen Leitbildes', *Natur und Recht*, 2002.

Mushkat, R., 'The Principle of Public Participation: A Selective Asia-Pacific Perspective', in N. Schrijver and F. Weiss (eds) *International Law and Sustainable Development: Principles and Practice*, Boston/Leiden: Martinus Nijhoff Publishers, 2004.

Musungu, S. and Dutfield, G., *Multilateral Agreements and a TRIPS Plus World: The World Intellectual Property Organization –WIPO* Quaker United Nations Office, TRIPS Paper #3, 2003.

Nafziger, J.A.R., Paterson, R.K. and Renteln, A.D., *Cultural Law: International, Comparative and Indigenous*, Cambridge: Cambridge University Press, 2010.

Naik, A., 'Migration and Natural Disasters', in F. Laczko and C. Aghazarm (eds) *Environment and Climate Change: Assessing the Evidence*, International Organization for Migration, 2009, 253.

Narine, S., *Explaining ASEAN: Regionalism in Southeast Asia*, Colorado: Lynne Rienner Pub., 2002.

National Emissions Trading Taskforce, *Possible Design for a National Greenhouse Gas*, NETT, 2006.

National Reserve System Task Group, *Australia's Strategy for Australia's National Reserve System 2009–2030*, Canberra: Australian Government, 2009.

Natural Resource Management Ministerial Council, *Australian Weeds Strategy – A National Strategy for Weed Management in Australia*, Canberra: Australian Government, 2006.

Natural Resource Management Ministerial Council, *National Cooperative Approach to Integrated Coastal Zone Management – Framework and Implementation Plan*, Canberra: Australian Government, 2006.

Nature, 'The Mask Slips' (Editorial), *Nature* 480, 2011, 292.

Neumann, J., *Human Rights and Climate Change: International Human Rights as an Instrument for Measures of Equalization?*, Master Thesis, 2010, GRIN Verlag.

Nevill, J. and Ward, T., 'The National Representative System of Marine Protected Areas: Comment on Recent Progress' *Ecological Management and Restoration* 10(3), 2009.

New Zealand Coastal Policy Statement 2010 Factsheet, Wellington: Department of Conservation, 2011.

New Zealand Government, *Environment 2010 Strategy*, Wellington: Ministry for the Environment, 1995.

New Zealand Government, *Sustainable Development for New Zealand: Programme of Action*, Wellington: Department of the Prime Minister and Cabinet, 2003.

Newcombe, A., 'General Exceptions in International Investment Agreements' in M.C. Cordonier Segger, M. Gehring and A. Newcombe (eds) *Sustainable Development in World Investment Law*, Alphen aan den Rijn: Kluwer Law International, 2011.

Newcombe, A., 'Sustainable Development and Investment Treaty Law', *Journal of World Investment and Trade* 8, 2007, 357.

Newman, D.G., 'Theorizing Collective Indigenous Rights', *American Indian Law Review* 31, 2006/2007, 273.

Ngugi, J., 'The "Curse" of Ecological Interdependence: Africa, Climate Change and Social Justice', in W.H. Rodgers, Jr and M. Robinson-Dorn (eds) *Climate Change: A Reader*, Durham, NC: Carolina Academic Press, 2011.

Ngugi, J., 'The Decolonization–Modernization Interface and the Plight of Indigenous Peoples in Post-Colonial Development Discourse in Africa', *Wisconsin International Law Journal* 20, 2002.

Nicholson, J., *Food from the Sea*, London: Cassell Ltd, 1979.

Nielson, L., Styles, J., Talberg, A. and Tomaras, J., 'Carbon Pollution Reduction Scheme 2009 (No. 2)', Bills Digest, No. 59, 2009–2010, 29 October 2009, Canberra: Parliamentary Library.

Nissen, J.L., 'Achieving a Balance between Trade and the Environment: The Need to Amend he WTO/GATT to include Multilateral Environmental Agreement' *Law and Policy in International Business* 28, 1996–1997, 901.

Nolan, D. (ed.), *Environment and Resource Management Law*, 4th edition, Wellington: LexisNexis, 2011.

Nolan, D. and Matheson, B., 'New Zealand: The International Comparative Legal Guide to Environment and Climate Change Law', *Global Legal Group*, 2011.

Nollkaemper, A., 'The contribution of the International Law Commission to International Water Law: does it reverse the flight form substance?', *Netherlands Yearbook of International Law* 27, 1996, 39.

Nollkaemper, A., 'Responsibility of Transnational Corporations in International Environmental Law: Three Perspectives', in G. Winter (ed.) *Multilevel Governance of Global Environmental Change: Perspectives from Science, Sociology and the Law*, Cambridge: Cambridge University Press, 2006, 186.

Nordström, H. and Vaughan, S., *Trade and Environment*, Special Studies 4, World Trade Organization, 1999.

Nordstrom, N., 'Managing Transboundary Environmental Accidents: The State Duty to Inform', in D.D. Caron and C. Leben (eds) *The International Aspects of Natural and Industrial Catastrophes*, The Hague: Martinus Nijhoff, 2001.

Norse, E., 'Ending the Range Wars on the Last Frontier: Zoning the Sea', in E. Norse and L. Crowder (eds) *Marine Conservation Biology: The Science of Maintaining the Sea's Biodiversity*, Washington DC: Island Press, 2005.

Norse, E.A. and Amos, J., 'Ilulissat Declaration, and Policy Implications of the Deepwater Horizon Oil and Gas Disaster', *ELR News and Analysis* 40, 2010.

Nye, K.R.J., *Transnational Relations and World Politics*, Cambridge, MA: Harvard University Press, 1972.

Oberthur, S. and Gehring, T., 'Reforming International Environmental Governance. An Institutionalist Critique of the Proposal for a World Environmental Organisation', *International Environmental Agreements. Politics, Law and Economics* 4, 2004, 359.

Oberthür, S. and Lefeber, R., 'Holding Countries to Account: The Kyoto Protocol's Compliance System Revisited after Four Years of Experience', *Climate Law* 1(1), 2010, 133.

Ochoa, C., 'The Individual and Customary International Law Formation', *Virginia Journal of International Law* 48, 2007, 119.

Oeter, S., 'Methods and Means of Combat', in D. Fleck (ed.) *The Handbook of Humanitarian Law in Armed Conflict*, Oxford: Oxford University Press, 1995.

Ogbodo, S.G., 'Environmental protection in Nigeria: Two decades after the Koko incident', *Annual Survey of International and Comparative Law* 15, 2009, 1.

Ogle, L., 'Biodiversity', in D. Farrier and P. Stein (eds) *The Environmental Law Handbook*, 5th edition, Pyrmont: Thomson Reuters, 2011.

Ogle, L. 'The Environment Protection and Biodiversity Conservation Act 1999 (Cth): How Workable is it?', *Environmental and Planning Law Journal* 17, 2000, 468.

Oguamanam, C., 'Agro-Biodiversity and Food Security: Biotechnology and Traditional Agricultural Practices at the Periphery of International Intellectual Property Regime Complex', *Michigan State Law Review* 215, 2007, 222.

Oguamanam, C., 'Canada: Time to Take Access and Benefit Sharing Over Genetic Resources Seriously', *University of New Brunswick Law Journal* 60, 2010, 139.

Oguamanam, C., *International Law and Indigenous Knowledge: Intellectual Property, Plant Biodiversity, and Traditional Medicine*, Toronto: University of Toronto Press, 2006.

Oguamanam, C., 'Local Knowledge as a Trapped Knowledge: Intellectual Property, Culture, Power and Politics', *Journal of World Intellectual Property* 11, 2008, 29.

Oguamanam, C., 'Patents and Traditional Medicine: Digital Capture, Creative Legal Interventions, and the Dialectics of Knowledge Transformation', *Indiana Journal of Global Legal Studies* 15, 2008, 501.

Okere, B. and Makawa, E.M., 'Global Solidarity and the International Response to Disasters', in D.D. Caron and C. Leben (eds) *The International Aspects of Natural and Industrial Catastrophes*, The Hague: Martinus Nijhoff, 2001.

Okereke, C., Bulkeley, H. and Schroeder, H., 'Conceptualizing Climate Governance Beyond the International Regime', *Global Environmental Politics* 9(1), 2009.

Okidi, C.O., 'Concept, function and structure of environmental law', in C.O. Okidi, P. Kameri-Mbote and M. Apech (eds) *Environmental Governance in Kenya*, Nairobi: East African Educational Publishers, 2008.

Ong, D.M., 'International Environmental Law Governing Threats to Biological Diversity', in M. Fitzmaurice, D.M. Ong and P. Merkouris (eds) *Research Handbook on International Environmental Law*, Cheltenham: Edward Elgar, 2010.

Ortino, F., 'External Transparency of Investment Awards', *Society of International Economic Law (SIEL) Inaugural Conference Paper*, 2008. Online. Available HTTP: <http://papers.ssrn.com/sol3/papers.cfm?abstract_id=1159899> (accessed 19 December 2011).

Ortiz, M.J., 'Aichi biodiversity targets on direct and indirect drivers of biodiversity loss', *Environmental Law Review* 13, 2011.

Osofsky, H.M., 'The Inuit Petition as a Bridge? Beyond Dialectics of Climate Change and Indigenous Peoples' Rights', *American Indian Law Review* 31, 2006/2007, 675.

Osofsky, H.M., 'Learning from Environmental Justice: A New Model for International Environmental Rights', *Stanford Environmental Law Journal* 24, 2005, 71.

Ostrom, E., 'A General Framework for Analyzing Sustainability of Social-Ecological Systems', *Science* 325, 2009, 419.

Ostrom, E., *Governing the Commons: The Evolution of Institutions for Collective Action*, Cambridge: Cambridge University Press, 1990.

O'Sullivan, R. and Streck, C., 'Conservation Carbon: A New Voluntary Market Mechanism to Protect Forests', *Carbon and Climate Law Review* 3, 2008.

Overland J., 'A Multi-Faceted Journey: Globalisation, Transnational Corporations, and Corporate Social Responsibility', in S. Alam, N. Klein and J. Overland (eds) *Globalisation and the Quest for Social and Environmental Justice: the Relevance of International Law in an Evolving World Order*, New York: Routledge, 2011.

Pachauri, R.K. and Reisinger, A. (eds) *Climate Change 2007: Synthesis Report. Contribution of Working Groups I, II and III to the Fourth Assessment Report of the Intergovernmental Panel on Climate Change*, Geneva: IPCC and Climate Commission, *The Critical Decade; Climate Science, Risks and Responses*, Canberra: Commonwealth of Australia.

Pachauri, R.K. and Reisinger, A. (eds) *Contribution of Working Groups I, II and III to the Fourth Assessment Report of the Intergovernmental Panel on Climate Change*, Geneva: IPCC, 1997.

Pallemaerts, M., 'The Human Right to a Healthy Environment as a Substantive Right', in M. Déjeant-Pons and M. Pallemaerts (eds) *Human Rights and the Environment*, Brussels: Council of Europe Publishing, 2002.

Palmer, G., 'New Ways to Make International Environmental Law' *American Journal of International Law* 86, 1992, 259.

Palmer, K., 'Local Government Law and Resource Management', *NZ Law Review*, 2004, 751.

Palmer, M., 'Turtle Power Down Under The Sea?: Comparative Domestic and International Legal Protection Of Marine Turtles By Australia And The United States', *Georgia Journal of International and Comparative Law* 37, 2008–2009.

Panjabi, R.K.L., *The Earth Summit at Rio: Politics, Economics, and the Environment*, New England: Northeastern University Press, 1997.

Pardy, B., 'Planning for Serfdom: Resource Management and the Rule of Law', *New Zealand Law Journal*, 1997, 69.

Park, E., 'Searching For A Voice: The Indigenous People In Polar Regions', *Sustainable Development Law & Policy* 8, 2008.

Parker, C. and Mitchell, A., *The Little REDD+ Book: An updated guide to governmental and non-governmental proposal for reducing emission from deforestation and degradation*, Global Canopy Program, 2009. Online. Available HTTP: <http://unfccc.int/files/methods_science/redd/application/pdf/the_little_redd_book_dec_08.pdf> (accessed 14 December 2011).

Parker, C., Mitchell, A., Trivedi, M. and Mardas, N., *Little REDD Book: A Guide to Governmental and Non-Governmental Proposals for Reducing Emissions from Deforestation and Degradation*, Oxford: Global Canopy Programme, 2008.

Parliamentary Commissioner for the Environment (PCE), *Creating our Future: Sustainable Development for New Zealand*, Wellington: PCE, 2002.

Parliamentary Commissioner for the Environment, *Setting the Course for a Sustainable Future: the Management of New Zealand's Marine Environment*, Wellington: Parliamentary Commissioner for the Environment, 1999.

Parsons, R.J., 'The Fight to Save the Planet:, US Armed Forces, "Greenkeeping", and Enforcement of the Law Pertaining to Environmental Protection During Armed Conflict', *Georgetown International Environmental Law Review* 10, 1998, 441.

Pauly, D. and Palomares, M., 'Fishing Down Marine Food Web: It Is Far More Pervasive than We Thought' *Bulletin of Marine Science* 76(2), 2005, 197.

Pauly, D., Christensen, V., Guénette, S., Pitcher, T.J., Sumaila, U.D., Walters, C.J., Watson, R. and Zeller, D., 'Towards Sustainability in World Fisheries', *Nature* 418, 2002, 689.

Pauwelyn, J., 'Judicial Mechanisms: Is There a Need for a World Environment Court?', in W.B. Chambers and J.F. Green (eds) *Reforming International Environmental Governance: From Institutional Limits to Innovative Reforms*, Tokyo: United Nations University Press, 2005.

Peel, J., 'The Role of Climate Change Litigation in Australia's Response to Global Warming', *Environmental and Planning Law Journal* 24, 2007, 90.

Peel, J. and Godden, L., 'Australia Environmental Management: A "Dams" Story', *UNSW Law Journal* 28(3), 2005.

Peet, R., *Unholy Trinity: The IMF, World Bank and WTO*. London and New York: Zed Books, 2003.

Pellow, D.N., *Resisting Global Toxics: Transnational Movements for Environmental Justice*, Cambridge, MA: MIT Press, 2007.

Pelzer, N., 'Learning the Hard Way: Did the Lesson Taught by the Chernobyl Nuclear Accident Contribute to Improving Nuclear Law?'. Online. Available: <http://www.oecd-nea.org/law/chernobyl/PELZER.pdf> (accessed 2 May 2012).

Perdan, S. and Azapagic, A., 'Carbon Trading: Current Schemes and Future Developments', *Energy Policy* 39, 2011, 6040.

Persson, Å., 'Environmental Policy Integration and Bilateral Development Assistance: Challenges and Opportunities with an Evolving Governance Framework', *International Environmental Agreements* 9, 2009, 409.

Petherick, A., 'Dirty Money', *Nature Climate Change* 2, 2012, 72.

Petkova, E., Maurer, C., Henninger, N. and Irwin, F., *Closing the Gap: Information, Participation, and Justice in Decision-making for the Environment*, Washington DC: World Resources Institute, 2002.

Pittock, J., Finlayson, M., Gardner, A. and McKay, C., 'Changing Character: The Ramsar Convention on Wetlands and Climate Change in the Murray-Darling Basin, Australia', *Environmental and Planning Law Journal* 27, 2010, 401.

Pollock, F., *The Genius of the Common Law*, New York: Columbia University Press, 1912.

Pontin, B., 'Environmental Rights under the UK's "Intermediate Constitution"', *Natural Resources & Environment* 17, 2002.

Porras, D.A., 'The United Nations Principles Relevant to the Use of Nuclear Power Sources in Outer Space: the Significance of a Soft Law Instrument after nearly 20 Years in Force', in I. Marboe (ed.) *Soft Law in Outer Space. The Function of Non-Binding Norms in International Space Law*, Vienna: Böhlau, 2012.

Posey, D.A., *Cultural and Spiritual Values of Biodiversity*, Nairobi: United Nations Environment Programme, 1999.

Posey, D.A., 'Introduction: Culture and Nature – The Inextricable Link', in D.A. Posey (ed.) *Cultural and Spiritual Values of Biodiversity*, Nairobi: UNEP, 1999.

Posner, E.A., 'Climate Change and International Human Rights Litigation: A Critical Appraisal', *University of Pennsylvania Law Review* 155, 2007.

Posner, E.A. and Sykes, A.O., 'Economic Foundations of the Law of the Sea', *American Journal of International Law* 104, 2010, 569.

Potvin, C. and Bovarnick, A., 'Reducing Emissions from Deforestation and Forest Degradation in Developing Countries: Key Actors, Negotiations and Actions', *Carbon and Climate Law Review* 3, 2008, 264.

Pratt, L.A.W., 'Decreasing dirty dumping? A reevaluation of toxic waste colonialism and the global management of transboundary hazardous waste', *Texas Environmental Law Journal* 41, 2011.

Pring, G. and Noe, S.Y., 'The Emerging International Law of Public Participation Affecting Global Mining, Energy and Resource Development', in D.N. Zillman, A. Lucas and G. Pring (eds) *Human Rights in Natural Resource Development: Public Participation in the Sustainable Development of Mining and Energy Resources*, Oxford: Oxford University Press, 2002.

Prott, L.V., 'UNESCO and UNIDROIT: 'A Partnership Against Trafficking in Cultural Objects', *Uniform Law Review*, 1, 1996, 59.

Prott, L.V. and O'Keefe, P.J., ' "Cultural Heritage" or "Cultural Property"?' *International Journal of Cultural Property* 1, 1992, 307.

Pruzin, D., 'Ozone Depletion: Trade Measures Under Montreal Pact Justified, Secretariat Tells Trade Body', *International Environment Daily*, Washington DC: Bureau of National Affairs, 1999.

Puder, M., 'The Rise of Regional Integration Law: Good News for International Environmental Law', *Georgetown International Environmental Law Review* 23, 2011, 165.

Puri, S. and Aureli, A. (eds) *Atlas of Transboundary Aquifers*, Paris: UNESCO, 2009.

Puthucherril, T.G., 'From Shipbreaking to Sustainable Ship Recycling: Evolution of a Legal Regime', in D. Freestone (ed.) *Legal Aspects of Sustainable Development*, Volume V, The Netherlands: Martinus Nijhoff, 2010.

Rahall, N.J., *Extension of Remarks, An Assault on America's Public Lands: The Hardrock Mining Provisions of the Resources Committee's Budget Reconciliation Package* (3 November, 2005). Online. Available HTTP: <www.house.gov/list/press/ii00_democrats/mininglawcrremarks.pdf> (accessed 29 December 2011).

Rahman, S. and Schafft, G.E., 'Climate Change and Human Rights in Bangladesh', *Anthropology News* 51, 2010, 30.

Rajagopal, B., 'International Law and Social Movements: Challenges of Theorizing Resistance', *Columbia Journal of Transnational Law* 41, 2003, 409.

Rajamani, L., *Differential Treatment in International Environmental Law*, Oxford: Oxford University Press, 2006.

Rao, A.S., 'Enforcement of Environmental Laws', *AIR Journal* 88, 2001, 222.

Rao, M., 'Equity in a Global Public Goods Framework', in I. Kaul, I. Grunberg and M.A. Stern (eds) *Global Public Goods: International Cooperation in the 21st Century*, New York: Oxford University Press, 1999.

Rao, P.K. *The World Trade Organization and the Environment*, New York: St Martin's Press, Inc., 2000.

Rathgeber, T., 'UN Norms on the Responsibilities of Transnational Corporations', Friedrich-Ebert-Stiftung Occasional Geneva Papers, N. 22, 2006.

Rautenbach, J., Tonhauser, W. and Wetherall, A., *Overview of the International Legal Framework Governing the Safe and Peaceful Uses of Nuclear Energy: Some Practical Steps*, OECD Paper, 2006.

Raven, P.H. and McNeely, J.A., 'Biological Extinction: Its Scope and Meaning for Us', in L.D. Guruswamy and J.A. McNeely *Protection of Global Biodiversity: Converging Strategies*, Durham: Duke University Press, 1988.

Rayfuse, R., 'Drowning our Sorrows to Secure a Carbon Free Future? Some International Legal Considerations Relating to Sequestering Carbon by Fertilising the Oceans', *UNSW Law Journal* 31, 2008.

Rayfuse, R., 'W(h)ither Tuvalu? International Law and Disappearing States', University of New South Wales Faculty of Law Research Series, 2009.

Razzaque, J., 'Implementing International Procedural Rights and Obligations: Serving the Environment and Poor Communities', in T. Bigg and D. Satterthwaite (eds) *How to Make Poverty History – The Central Role of Local Organisations in Meeting the MDGs*, London: International Institute for Economic Development, 2005, 175.

Razzaque, J., 'Linking Human Rights, Environment and Development: Experience from Litigation in South Asia', *Fordham Journal of Environmental Law* 18(3), 2007, 587. World Resources Institute, Partnership for Principle 10. Online. Available HTTP: <www.pp10.org> (accessed 24 April 2012).

Razzaque, J., 'Participatory Rights in Natural Resource Management: Role of the Communities in South Asia', in J. Ebbesson and P. Okowa (eds) *Environmental Law and Justice in Context*, Cambridge: Cambridge University Press, 2009.

Razzaque, J., *Public Interest Environmental Litigation in India, Pakistan and Bangladesh*, The Hague: Kluwer, 2004.

Razzaque, J., 'Public Participation in Water Governance', in J. Dellapenna and J Gupta (eds) *The Evolution of Law and Politics of Water*, Dordrecht: Springer, 2008.

Regan, D., 'The Meaning of 'Necessary' in GATT Article XX and GATS Article XIV: The Myth of Cost-benefit Balancing', *World Trade Review* 6, 2007, 347.

Renn, O., Webler, T. and Wiedemann, P. (eds) *Fairness and Competence in Citizen Participation: Evaluating Models for Environmental Discourse*, Dordrecht: Kluwer, 1995.

Repetto, R., *World Enough and Time*, New Haven: Yale University Press, 1986.

Repetto, R. and Gillis, M. (eds) *Public Policies and the Misuse of Forest Resources*, Cambridge: Cambridge University Press, 1988.

Reynolds, P., *Russia Ahead in Arctic 'Gold Rush,'* BBC News, 1 August 2007. Online. Available HTTP: <http://news.bbc.co.uk/2/hi/in_depth/6925853.stm> (accessed 4 May 2012).

Richardson, B., 'Indigenous Peoples, International Law and Sustainability', *Review of European Community and International Environmental Law and Policy* 10, 2001, 1.

Richardson, B., 'Kyoto Protocol to the United Nations Framework Convention on Climate Change', *New Zealand Journal of Environmental Law* 2(2), 1998, 249.

Richardson, B. and Razzaque, J., 'Public Participation in the Environmental Decision-making', in B.J. Richardson and S. Wood (eds) *Environmental Law for Sustainability*, London: Hart Publishing, 2006, 165.

Ridgeway, L., 'Marine Genetic Resources: Outcomes of the United Nations Informal Consultative Process' *International Journal of Marine and Coastal Law*, 24, 2009, 309.

Rieu-Clarke, A., *International Law and Sustainable Development: Lessons from the Law of International Watercourses*, London: IWA Publishing, 2005.

Rieu-Clarke, A. and Loures, F., 'Still not in force: should states support the 1997 UN Watercourses Convention?,' *Review of European Community and International Environmental Law* 18(2), 2009, 185.

Rieu-Clarke, A. and Wolf, A.T., *Hydropolitical vulnerability and resilience along international waters – Europe*, Nairobi: UNEP, 2009.

Rislove, D.C., 'Global Warming v Non-Proliferation: The Time has Come for Nations to Reassert their Right to Peaceful Use of Nuclear Energy', *Wisconsin International Law Journal* 24(4), 2007, 1069.

Roberts, A. and Kingsbury, B. (eds) *United Nations, Divided World. The UN's Role in International Relations*, Oxford: Oxford University Press, 1993.

Roberts, C., 'Deep Impact: The Rising Toll of Fishing in the Deep Sea', *TRENDS in Ecology & Evolution* 17(5), 2000, 242.

Roberts, J.T. and Parks, B.C., *A Climate of Injustice: Global Inequality, North–South Politics, and Climate Policy*, Cambridge, MA: MIT Press, 2007.

Robins, L. and Kanowski, P., ' "Crying for our Country": Eight Ways in Which "Caring for our Country" has Undermined Australia's Regional Model for Natural Resource Management', *Australasian Journal of Environmental Management* 18(2), 2011.

Rockefeller, S., 'The Transition to Sustainability', in P.B. Corcoran (ed.) *The Earth Charter in Action. Toward a Sustainable World*, Amsterdam: KIT, 2005.

Rodríguez-Garavito, C.A. and Arenas, L.C., 'Indigenous Rights, Transnational Activism, and Legal Mobilisation', in B. de Sousa-Santos and C.A. Rodríguez-Garavito (eds) *Law and Globalisation from Below*, Cambridge: Cambridge University Press, 2005.

Rodríguez-Rivera, L.E., 'The Human Right to Environment and the Peaceful Use of Nuclear Energy', *Denver Journal of International Law and Policy* 35(1), 2007.

Rogers, A.P.V., *Law on the Battlefield*, Manchester: Manchester University Press, 1996.

Romano, C.P.R., 'International Dispute Settlement', in D. Bodansky, J. Brunnée and E. Hey (eds) *The Oxford Handbook of International Environmental Law*, Oxford: Oxford University Press, 2007, 1036.

Romano, C.P.R., *The Peaceful Settlement of International Disputes: A Pragmatic Approach*, The Hague/London/Boston: Kluwer Law International, 2000.

Rosemann, N., 'The UN Norms on Corporate Human Rights Responsibilities: An Innovating Instrument to Strengthen Business' Human Rights Performance', Friedrich-Ebert-Stiftung Occasional Geneva Papers, N. 20, 2005.

Rosen, M.E., 'Energy Independence and Climate Change: the Economic and National Security Consequences of Failing to Act', *University of Richmond Law Review* 44, 2010.

Rosenbaum, K., Schone, D. and Mekouar, A., 'Climate Change and the Forest Sector: Possible national and subnational legislation', FAO Working Paper No 144, Food and Agriculture Organization of the United Nations, 2004.

Rosenberg, D., Environmental Pollution around the South China Sea: Developing a Regional Response to a Regional Problem. Online. Available HTTP: <https://digitalcollections.anu.edu.au/bitstream/1885/40977/3/rmap_wp20.pdf> (accessed 22 November 2011).

Rosenne, S., *Practice and Method of International Law*, New York: Oceania, 1984.

Rosso Grossman, M., 'Agriculture and Polluter Pays Principle', *Netherlands Comparative Law Association*. Online. Available HTTP: <http://www.ejcl.org/113/article113-15.pdf> (accessed 17 March 2012).

Rothwell, D.R., 'The Antarctic Treaty System: Resource Development, Environmental Protection or Disintegration?' *Arctic* 43(3), 1990, 284.

Rothwell, D.R., 'Polar Environmental Protection and International Law: The 1991 Antarctic Protocol', *EJIL* 11(3), 2000.

Rothwell, D.R., 'Relationship Between the Environmental Protocol and UNEP Instruments', in D. Vidas (ed.) *Implementing the Environmental Protection Regime for the Antarctic*, Dordrecht: Kluwer Academic Publishers, 2000.

Rothwell, D. and Boer, B., 'From Franklin to Berlin: The Internationalization of Australian Environmental Law and Policy', *Sydney Law Review* 17, 1995 , 242.

Rothwell, D.R. and Stephens, T., *The International Law of the Sea*, Oxford: Hart Publishing, 2010.

Roy, D.C., 'Vulnerability and Population Displacements due to Climate-induced Disasters in Coastal Bangladesh', in M. Leighton, X. Shen, and K. Warner (eds) *Climate Change and Migration: Rethinking Policies for Adaptation and Disaster Risk Reduction*, SOURCE, Publication Series of UNU-EHS, No. 15/2011.

Rubin, S.J., 'Transnational Corporations and International Codes of Conduct: a Study of the Relationship between International Legal Cooperation and Economic Development', *American University Journal of International Law and Policy* 10, 1994–1995, 1275.

Ruddy, T. and Hilty, L., 'Impact Assessment and Policy Learning in the European Commission', *Environmental Impact Assessment Review* 28(2–3), 2008.

Ruggie, J., *Promotion and Protection of all Human Rights, Civil, Political, Economic, Social and Cultural Rights, Including the Right to Development* (2008) UN Doc A/HRC/8/5/Add.2. Online. Available HTTP: <www2.ohchr.org/english/bodies/hrcouncil/8session/reports.htm> (accessed 19 December 2011).

Ruhl, J.B., 'Climate Change Adaptation and the Structural Transformation of Environmental Law', *Environmental Law* 40, 2010.

Rustiala, K., 'The Participatory Revolution in International Environmental Law', *Harvard Environmental Law Review* 21, 1997, 537.

Sachs, A., 'What Do Human Rights Have To Do With Environmental Protection? Everything', *Sierra Magazine*, 1997. Online. Available HTTP: <http://www.sierraclub.org/sierra/199711/humanrights. asp> (accessed 9 May 2012).

Sachs, N., 'Beyond the Liability Wall: Strengthening Tort Remedies in International Environmental Law,', *UCLA Law Review* 55, 2008, 837, P. 839.

Sachs, W. and Santorius, T. (eds) *Fair Future: Resource Conflicts, Security and Global Justice*, London/New York: Zed Books, 2007.

Salman, M.A., 'The Helsinki Rules, the UN Watercourses Convention and the Berlin Rules: Perspectives on International Water Law', *Water Resources Development* 23(4), 2007, 525.

Salman, S., 'The Baglihar difference and its resolution process – a triumph for the Indus Waters Treaty?' *Water Policy*, 2008, 105.

Salman, S., 'The Helsinki Rules, the UN Watercourses Convention and the Berlin Rules: Perspectives on International Water Law', *Water Resources Development* 23(4), 2007, 625.

Salman, S., 'The United Nations Watercourses Convention Ten Years Later: Why Has Its Entry Into Force Proven Difficult?', *Water International* 32(1), 2007, 1.

Sampford, C., 'Global Transparency: Fighting Corruption for a Sustainable Future', Proceedings of the 14th International Anti-Corruption Conference, Bangkok, Thailand 10–13 November, 2009.

Sand, P. (ed.) *The Effectiveness of International Environmental Agreements*, Cambridge: Grotius Publications, 1992.

Sand, P., 'Institution-building to Assist Compliance with International Environmental Law: Perspectives', *Zeitschrift für Ausländisches Öffentliches Recht und Völkerrecht* 56, 1996.

Sand, P., *Lessons Learned in Global Environmental Governance*, Washington DC: World Resources Institute, 1990.

Sanders, D., 'Collective Rights', *Human Rights Quarterly* 13, 1991, 368.

Sandin, P., *The Precautionary Principle: From Theory to Practice*, Stockholm, 2002. Online. Available HTTP: <http://kth.diva-portal.org/smash/get/diva2:7408/FULLTEXT01> (accessed 23 November 2011).

Sands, P., *Principles of International Environmental Law I: Frameworks, Standards and Implementation*, 2nd edition, Cambridge: Cambridge University Press, 2003.

Sands, P., 'Treaty, Custom and the Cross-Fertilization of International Law', *Yale Human Rights & Development Law Journal* 1, 1998, 85.

Sands, P. and MacKenzie, R., 'Guidelines for Negotiating and Drafting Dispute Settlement Clauses for International Environmental Agreements', in International Bureau of the Permanent Court of Arbitration (ed.) *International Investments and Protection of the Environment*, Leiden: Kluwer, 2001, 305.

Sauvant, K.P. and Aranda, V., 'The International Legal Framework for Transnational Corporations', in A.A. Fatouros (ed.) *Transnational Corporations: The International Legal Framework*, London: Routledge, 1994.

Savaresi, A. 'Forests, Economics, and Climate Change', *Climate Law* 2(3), 2011, 439.

Sax, J., 'The Search for Environmental Rights', *Journal of Land Use and Environmental Law* 6, 1990.

Schachter, O., *Sharing the World's Resources*, New York: Columbia University Press, 1977.

Schachter, O., *International Law in Theory and Practice*, Dordrecht: Martinus Nijhoff Publishers, 1991.

Schermers, H.G and Blokker, N.M, *International Institutional Law. Unity Within Diversity*, Leiden: Martinus Nijhoff Publishers, 2004.

Schmidt, R. and Müller, H., *Einführung in das Umweltrecht*, 6th edition, Munich: Beck, 2001.

Schmitt, M.N., Garraway, C.H.B. and Dinstein, Y., *The Manual on the Law of Non-International Armed Conflict: With Commentary*, San Remo: International Institute of Humanitarian Law, 2006.

Schrijver, N., *Sovereignty over Natural Resources: Balancing Rights and Duties*, Cambridge: Cambridge University Press, 1997.

Schroder, H., *Negotiating the Kyoto Protocol: An Analysis of Negotiation Dynamics in International Negotiations*, London: Lit Verlag, 2001.

Schwarzenberger, G., *International Law*, 3rd edition, Volume I, London: Stevens and Sons, 1957.

Scobbie, I., 'The Approach to Customary International Law in the Study', in E. Wilmshurst and S. Breau (eds) *Perspectives on the ICRC Study on Customary International Humanitarian Law*, Cambridge: Cambridge University Press, 2007.

Scott, J. and Holder, J., 'Law and New Environmental Governance in the European Union', in J. Scott and G. de Búrca (eds) *Law and New Governance in the EU and the US*, Oxford: Hart Publishing, 2006.

Secretary-General's High-Level Panel on UN System-Wide Coherence in the Areas of Development, Humanitarian Assistance, and the Environment, *Delivering as One. Report of the Secretary-General's High-Level Panel*, New York: United Nations, 2006.

Secretary-General of the OECD, *OECD Benchmark Definition of Foreign Direct Investment*, 4th edition, Paris: OECD, 2008. Online. Available HTTP: <http://www.oecd.org/dataoecd/26/50/40193734. pdf> (accessed 19 December 2011).

Senate, Legal and Constitutional Affairs References Committee, *A Balancing Act: Provisions of the Water Act 2007*, Canberra: Australian Government, 2011.

Severino, R.C., *Southeast Asia in Search of an ASEAN Community: Insights from the Former ASEAN Secretary-General*, Singapore: Institute of Southeast Asian Studies, 2006.

Shackelford, S.J., 'Was Selden Right?: the Expansion of Closed Seas and its Consequences', *Stanford Journal of International Law* 47, 2011.

Shaughnessy, M., 'The United Nations Global Compact and the Continuing Debate about the Effectiveness of Corporate Voluntary Codes of Conduct', *Colorado Journal of International Environmental Law and Policy Yearbook*, 2000.

Shaw, M., *International Law*, Cambridge: Cambridge University Press, 2008.

Shearer, I., 'Current Law of the Sea Issues', in R. Babbage and S. Bateman, *Maritime Change: Issues for Asia*, St Leonards: Allen & Unwin, 1993.

Shelton, D., 'Decision regarding Communication 155/96 (Social and Economic Rights Action Center/Center for Economic and Social Rights v Nigeria)', *American Journal of International Law* 96, 2002, 937.

Shelton, D., 'Describing the Elephant: International Justice and Environmental Law', in J. Ebbesson and P. Okowa (eds) *Environmental Law and Justice in Context*, Cambridge: Cambridge University Press, 2009.

Shelton, D., 'The Environmental Jurisprudence of International Human Rights Tribunals', in R. Picolotti and J.D. Taillant (eds) *Linking Human Rights and the Environment*, Tucson: University of Arizona Press, 2003.

Shelton, D., 'Environmental Rights and Brazil's Obligations in the Inter-American Human Rights System', *George Washington International Law Review* 40, 2009.

Shelton, D., 'Environmental Rights', in P. Alston (ed.) *Peoples' Rights*, New York: Oxford University Press, 2001, 187.

Shelton, D., 'Human Rights, Environmental Rights, and the Right to the Environment', 28 *Stanford Journal of International Law* 28, 1991, 103.

Shelton, D., 'The Utility and Limits of Codes of Conduct for the Protection of the Environment', in A. Kiss, D. Shelton and K. Ishibashi (eds) *Economic Globalization and Compliance with International Environmental Agreements*, The Hague: Kluwer Law International, 2003.

Shvidenko, A., Barner, C.V. and Persson, R., (2005) Chapter 21, 'Forest and Woodland Systems' in *Millennium Ecosystem Assessment*. Online. Available HTTP: <http://www.maweb.org/documents/document.290.aspx.pdf> (accessed 9 May 2012).

Sieg, R., 'A Call to Minimize the Use of Nuclear Power in the Twenty-First Century', *Vermont Journal of Environmental Law* 9(2), 2008, 305.

Silver, J., Speech, ASEAN WEN Presentation of Survey Results, 19 October 2006, Phnom Phem. Online. Available HTTP: <http://cambodia.usembassy.gov/sp_101906b.html> (accessed 1 September 2008).

Silver, J.G., 'The Global Partnership: The Final Blow to the Nuclear Non-Proliferation Regime?', *New York International Law Review* 21(1), 2008.

Simms, A., *Ecological Debt: The Health of the Planet & the Wealth of Nations*, London: Pluto Press, 2005.

Sinden, A., 'Power and Responsibility: Why Human Rights Should Address Corporate Environmental Wrongs', in D. McBarnet, A. Voiculescu and T. Campbell (eds) *The New Corporate Accountability: Corporate Social Responsibility and the Law*, Cambridge: Cambridge University Press, 2009.

Slaughter A-M., *A New World Order*, Princeton, NJ: Princeton University Press, 2004.

Smets, H., 'The Polluter Pays Principle in the Early 1990's', in L. Campiglio, L. Pineschi, D. Siniscalco and T. Treves (eds) *The Environment After Rio: International Law and Economics*, London: Martinus Nijhoff, 1994.

Smith, A., The *Wealth of Nations*, New York: Modern Library Edition, 1937.

Smith, C., 'Addressing Illegal Unreported and Unregulated (IUU) Fishing, International Fisheries Compliance 2004 Conference, Brussels, Belgium, 29–30 September 2004. Online. Available:

HTTP <http://www.illegal-fishing.info/uploads/OECD-addressing-IUU-Fishing.pdf> (accessed 10 May 2012).

Sohn, J. (ed.) *Development Without Conflict: The Business Case for Community Consent*, Washington DC: World Resources Institute, 2007.

Sohn, L.B., 'The Stockholm Declaration on the Human Environment', *Harvard International Law Journal* 14, 1973, 423.

Sornarajah, M., *The International Law on Foreign Investment*, Cambridge: Cambridge University Press, 2004.

Soveroski, M., 'EC Enlargement and the Development of European Environmental Policy: Parallel Histories, Divergent Paths?', *Review of European Community and International Environmental Law* 13, 2004, 127.

Spector, B.I., 'International Environmental Negotiation: Insights for Practice', *The Processes of International Negotiation Project*, Executive Report (ER-21), 1992. Online. Available HTTP: <http://www.iiasa.ac.at/Admin/PUB/Documents/ER-92-021.pdf> (accessed 06 December 2011).

Speth, J.G., *The Bridge at the Edge of the World: Capitalism, the Environment, and Crossing from Crisis to Sustainability*, New Haven: Yale University Press, 2008.

Speth, J. and Haas, P., *Global Environmental Governance*, Delhi: Pearson and Longman, 2006.

Stamatoudi, I.A., *Cultural Property Law and Restitution: A Commentary to International Conventions and European Union Law*, Cheltenham: Edward Elgar, 2011.

Stavenhagen, R., 'Indigenous Peoples and the State in Latin America: An Ongoing Debate', in R. Sieder (ed.) *Multiculturalism in Latin America: Indigenous Rights, Diversity and Democracy*, New York: Palgrave Macmillan, 2002.

Steane, E. and Weeks, T., 'Climate Change and the RMA: Implications of *Greenpeace New Zealand Inc v Genesis Power Ltd*', *Resource Management Journal*, 2009, 1.

Stec, S., 'Ecological Rights Advancing the Rule of Law in Eastern Europe', *Journal of Environmental Law and Litigation* 13, 1998, 275.

Steele, J., 'Participation and Deliberation in Environmental Law: Exploring and Problem-Solving Approach', *Oxford Journal of Legal Studies* 21, 2001, 437.

Steiner, J. and Woods, L., *EU Law*, Oxford: Oxford University Press, 2009.

Stephens, P., 'Applying Human Rights Norms to Climate Change: the Elusive Remedy', *Colorado Journal of International Environmental Law and Policy* 21, 2010.

Stephens, T., 'International Courts and Climate Change: Progression, Regression and Administration', in R. Lyster (ed.) *In the Wilds of Climate Change Law*, Brisbane: Australian Academic Press, 2010.

Stephens, T., *International Courts and Environmental Protection*, Cambridge: Cambridge University Press, 2009.

Stern, N., *The Economics of Climate Change: The Stern Review*, 'Part II: Impacts of CC on Growth and Development', 2006. Online. Available HTTP: <http://webarchive.nationalarchives.gov.uk/+/http://www.hm-treasury.gov.uk/stern_review_report.htm> (accessed 16 May 2012).

Stern, N., *The Stern Review on the Economics of Climate Change*, submitted on 30 October 2006. Online. Available HTTP: <webarchive.nationalarchives.gov.uk/+/http://www.hm-treasury.gov.uk/stern_review_report.htm> (accessed 19 December 2011).

Stewart, S., 'A Limited Future: The Alien Tort Claims Act Impacting Environmental Rights: Reconciling Past Possibilities with Future Limitations', *American Indian Law Review* 31, 2006/2007, 743.

Stoiber, C., Baer, A., Pelzer, N. and Tonhauser, W., *Handbook on Nuclear Law*, Vienna: International Atomic Energy Agency, 2003.

Stokke, O., 'The Interplay of International Regimes: Putting Effectiveness Theory to Work', FNI Report 14/2001, 2001. Online. Available HTTP: <www.fni.no/docandpdf/FNI-R1401.pdf> (accessed 19 December 2011).

Stone, C.D., 'Common But Differentiated Responsibilities in International Law', *American Journal of International Law* 98, 2004, 276.

Stone, C.D., 'Should Trees Have Standing? – Toward Legal Rights for Natural Objects', *Southern California Law Review* 45, 1972, 450.

Stonich, S., 'The Environmental Quality and Social Justice Implications of Shrimp Mariculture.' *Human Ecology: An Interdisciplinary Journal* 23, 1995, 143.

Stoutenburg, J.G., 'When Do States Disappear? Thresholds of Effective Statehood and the Continued Recognition of "Deterritorialized" Island States', Conference Proceedings of 'Threatened Island Nations: Legal Implications of Rising Seas and a Changing Climate', Center for Climate Change Law, Columbia Law School, New York, 23 May 2011.

Streck, C., 'The Global Environment Facility – a Role Model for International Governance?', *Global Environmental Politics* 1(2), 2001, 71.

Streck, C., 'Forests, Carbon Markets and Avoided Deforestation: Legal Implications', *Carbon and Climate Law Review* 3, 2008, 239.

Streck, C., 'The World Summit on Sustainable Development: Partnerships as the New Tool in Environmental Governance', *Yearbook of International Environmental Law* 13, 2003, 63.

Streck, C. and Lin, J., 'Mobilising Finance for Climate Change Mitigation: Private Sector Involvement in International Carbon Finance Mechanisms', *Melbourne Journal of International Law* 10(1), 2009, 70.

Suagee, D.N., 'Tribal Self-Determination and Environmental Federalism: Cultural Values as a Force for Sustainability', *Widener Law Symposium* 3, 1998.

Summerer, L. and Bohlmann, U.M., 'The STSC/IAEA Safety Framework for Space Nuclear Power Source Applications – Influence of Non-binding Recommendations', in I. Marboe (ed.) *Soft Law in Outer Space. The Function of Non-Binding Norms in International Space Law*, Vienna: Böhlau, 2012.

Sunchindah, A., The ASEAN Approach to Regional Environmental Management. Online. Available HTTP: <http://www.aseansec.org/2838.htm> (accessed 2 February 2012).

Sunchindah, A., 'ASEAN initiatives in protected areas management', presented at the Second Regional Forum for Southeast Asia of the IUCN WCPA (1999).

Sunstein, C.R., 'Beyond the Precautionary Principle', *University of Pennsylvania Law Review* 1(151), 2003, 1003. Online. Available HTTP: <http://sciencepolicy.colorado.edu/students/envs_5000/sunstein_2003.pdf> (accessed 23 November 2011).

Sussman, E., 'The Energy Charter Treaty's Investor Protection Provisions: Potential to Foster Solutions to Global Warming and Promote Sustainable Development', in M.C. Cordonier Segger, M. Gehring and A. Newcombe (eds) *Sustainable Development in World Investment Law*, Alphen aan den Rijn: Kluwer Law International, 2011.

Swift, P.M., 'How Can Ship Breaking Become a Sound Industry In its Own Right?', PowerPoint presentation at the Trade Winds and Mare Forum Shipping China, 3–4 March 2005, Shanghai.

Sykes, A.O., 'Comparative Advantage and the Normative Economics of International Trade Policy', *Journal of International Economic Law* 1(1), 1988, 49.

Symposium, 'Earth Rights and Responsibilities: Human Rights and Environmental Protection', *Yale Journal of International Law* 18, 1993.

Tacoli, C., 'Crisis or Adaptation? Migration and Climate Change in a Context of High Mobility,' in J.M. Guzman, G. Martine, G. McGranahan, D. Schensul and C. Tacoli (eds) *Population Dynamics and Climate Change*, UNFPA and IIED, 2009, 107.

Taillant, J. and Bonnitcha, J., 'International Investment Law and Human Rights', in M.C. Cordonier Segger, M. Gehring and A. Newcombe (eds) *Sustainable Development in World Investment Law*, Alphen aan den Rijn: Kluwer Law International, 2011.

Tal, A. and Cohen, J.A., 'Bringing "top-down" to "bottom-up": A new role for environmental legislation in combating desertification', *Harvard Environmental Law Review* 31, 2007, 163.

Tan, A.K-J., 'The ASEAN Agreement on Transboundary Haze Pollution: Prospects for Compliance and Effectiveness in Post-Suharto Indonesia' *New York University Environmental Law Journal* 13, 2006, 647.

Tanzi, A. and Arcari, M., *The United Nations Convention on the Law of International Watercourses – A Framework for Sharing*, London: Kluwer Law International, 2001.

Tarasofsky, R. (ed.) (1999) *Assessing the International Forest Regime*, IUCN Environmental Law Centre. Online. Available HTTP: <http://weavingaweb.org/pdfdocuments/EPLP37EN.pdf> (accessed 14 December 2011).

Tarlock, A.D., 'Is There a There There in Environmental Law?', *Journal of Land Use & Environmental Law* 19, 2004, 213.

Tarlock, D., 'The Role of Non-Governmental Organizations in the Development of International Environmental Law', contribution to the Chicago-Kent Dedication symposium 'Environmental Law', *Chi-Kent L Rev* 68, 1992–1993, 61.

Tay, S.S.C., 'Southeast Asian Fires: The Challenge for International Environmental Law and Sustainable Development', *Georgetown International Environmental Law Review* 11, 1999, 241.

Taylor, M., Sattler, P., Fitzsimons, J., Curnow, C., Beaver, D., Gibson, L. and Llewellyn, G., *Building Nature's Safety Net 2011: The State of Protected Areas for Australia's Ecosystems and Wildlife*, Sydney: WWF-Australia, 2011.

Taylor, P., *An Ecological Approach to International Law*, London/New York: Routledge, 1998.

Taylor, P., 'The Global Perspective: Convergence of International and Municipal Law', in K. Bosselmann and D. Grinlinton (eds) *Environmental Law for a Sustainable Society*, Auckland: NZCEL, 2002.

Taylor, P., 'International Law and the New Zealand Environment', in R. Harris (ed.) *Handbook of Environmental Law*, Wellington: Royal Forest and Bird Society, 2004.

Taylor, P. and Yates, J., 'Background Paper on Environmental Sustainability in New Zealand. Sustainable Development in General – Institutional and Legislative Frameworks'. Online. Available HTTP: <http://www.pce.parliament.nz/assets/Uploads/Reports/pdf/legal.pdf>.

Te Aho, L., 'Contemporary Issues in Maori Law and Society: The Tangled Web of Treaty Settlements Emissions Trading, Central North Island Forests, and the Waikato River', *Waikato Law Review* 16, 2008, 229.

Techera, E.J., *Marine Environmental Governance: From International Law to Local Practice*, New York: Routledge, 2011.

Techera, E., 'Protection of Cultural Heritage in Times of Armed Conflict: The International Legal Framework Revisited', *Macquarie Journal of International and Comparative Environmental Law* 4(2), 2007, 1.

Techera, E., 'Safeguarding Indigenous Bio-Cultural Heritage in the South Pacific Small Island States' *Policy Matters* 17, 2010, 29.

Telford, J., Cosgrave, J. and Houghton, R., *Joint Evaluation of the International Response to the Indian Ocean Tsunami: Synthesis Report*, London: Tsunami Evaluation Coalition, 2006.

Tennen, L.I., 'Evolution of the Planetary Protection Policy: Conflict of Science and Jurisprudence?', *Advances in Space Research* 24, 2004, 2354.

Thomas, S., 'Trade and Environment under WTO Rules after the Appellate Body Report in *Brazil-retreated Tyres*', *Journal of International Commercial Law and Technology* 4(1), 2009.

Thorme, M., 'Establishing Environment as a Human Right', *Denver Journal of International Law and Policy* 19, 1991.

Thornton, F., 'Regional Labour Migration as Adaptation to Climate Change: Option in the Pacific', in M. Leighton, X. Shen and K. Warner (eds) *Climate Change and Migration: Rethinking Policies for Adaptation and Disaster Risk Reduction*.

Thurer, D., 'The Emergence of Non-governmental Organizations and Transnational Enterprises in International Law and the Changing Role of the State', in R. Hofmann and N. Geissler (eds) *Non-State Actors as New Subjects of International Law*, Berlin: Duncker & Humblot, 1999.

Tokyo Summit Declaration on the Implications of the Chernobyl Nuclear Accidents (1986), INFCIRC/333, May 5, 1986, reprinted in 'International Organizations and Agreements', *Nuclear Law Bulletin* 37.

Tolba, M., *Global Environmental Diplomacy*, Cambridge, MA: MIT Press, 1998.

Tolentino, A.S., 'Legislative Reform for Good Governance through Popular Participation in the Sustainable Development of Wetlands', *Bulletin on APEC Marine Resources Conservation* 4(4), 2002.

Tollefson, J., 'Durban Maps Path to Climate Treaty', *Nature* 480, 2011, 299.

Toman, J., *The Protection of Cultural Property in the Event of Armed Conflict*, Aldershot: Dartmouth Publishing, 1996.

Tomuschat, C., 'International Liability for Injurious Consequences Arising out of Acts Not Prohibited by International Law: The Work of the International Law Commission', in F. Francioni and T. Scovazzi (eds) *International Responsibility for Environmental Harm*, London: Graham & Trotman, 1991.

Tripp, J.T.B., 'The UNEP Montreal Protocol: Industrialized and Developing Countries Sharing the Responsibility for Protecting the Stratospheric Ozone Layer', *New York University Journal of International Law and Politics* 20, 1998, 733.

Truman, H.S., *United States Presidential Proclamation No. 2668,* 'Policy of the US with Respect to Coastal Fisheries in Certain Areas of the High Seas', Basic Document No. 6. 1945.

Tunkin, G., 'Is General International Law Customary Law Only?', *European Journal of International Law* 4, 1993.

Turk, D., 'The Realization of Economic, Social and Cultural Rights', *Final report submitted by Mr. Danilo Turk, Special Rapporteur*, to the Sub-Commission on Prevention of Discrimination and Protection of Minorities, of the United Nations Commission on Human Rights, 3 July 1992, UN Doc. E/CN.4/Sub.2/1992/16), 198.

Turner, S., *A Substantive Environmental Right: An Examination of the Legal Obligations of Decision-makers Towards the Environment*, The Hague: Kluwer Law International, 2008.

Turton, A.R., Earle, A., Malzbender, D. and Ashton, P.J., 'Hydropolitical Vulnerability and Resilience along Africa's International Waters', in A.T. Wolf (ed.) *Hydropolitical Vulnerability and Resilience along International Waters: Africa*, Nairobi: UNEP, 2005.

Udemgba, S., 'The Precautionary and Differentiated Responsibility Principles in the Climate Change Context', Master of Law Thesis, 2005, University of Saskatchewan, Canada. Online. Available HTTP: <http://library.usask.ca/theses/available/etd-09132005-171902/unrestricted/LLMTHESIS.pdf> (accessed 27 April 2012).

Ulfstein, G., 'International Framework for Environmental Decision-making', in M. Fitzmaurice, D.M. Ong and P. Merkouris (eds) *Research Handbook on International Environmental Law*, Cheltenham: Edgar Elgar, 2010.

UN Commission on Global Governance, *Our Global Neighbourhood*, Oxford: Oxford University Press, 1995.

UN Department of Economic and Social Affairs, *Participatory Governance and the Millennium Development Goals*, New York, 2008.

United Kingdom Ministry of Defence, *Manual of the Law of Armed Conflict*, Oxford: Oxford University Press, 2004.

United Nations Conference on Trade and Development, *World Investment Report 2010, Investing in a Low Carbon Economy*, New York: United Nations Publications, 2010.

United Nations Development Programme (UNDP), *Human Development Report 2011: Sustainability and Equity: A Better Future for All*, New York: Palgrave Macmillan, 2011.

United Nations Development Programme (UNDP), *Human Development Report 2011: Sustainability and Equity: A Better Future for All*, New York: Palgrave Macmillan, 2007.

United Nations Environment Programme (UNEP), *Bridging the Emissions Gap: A UNEP Synthesis Report*, UNEP, 2011.

United Nations Environment Programme (UNEP), *Compendium of Judicial Decisions in Matters Related to Environment: National Decisions*, vol. I, 1998.

United Nations Environment Programme (UNEP), *Guidelines for the Development of National Legislation on Access to Information, Public Participation and Access to Justice in Environmental Matters* (2010), Decision SS.XI/5, part, A.

United Nations Environment Programme (UNEP), *Hydropolitical Vulernability and Resilience along International Waters – Asia*, Nairobi: UNEP, 2009.

United Nations Environment Programme (UNEP), *The Kosovo Conflict: Consequences for the Environment & Human Settlements*, Nairobi: UNEP, 1999.

United Nations Environment Programme (UNEP), *Manual on Compliance with and Enforcement of Multilateral Environmental Agreements*, 2006.

United Nations Environment Programme (UNEP), *Protecting the Environment during Armed Conflict*, Nairobi: UNEP, 2009.

United Nations Environment Programme (UNEP), Division of Environmental Policy Development and Law, *Training Manual on International Environmental Law*, Nairobi: Publishing Section of UNON, 2006.

United Nations Environment Programme (UNEP), *United Nations Environment Programme Annual Report 2010*, Nairobi: UNEP, 2010.

United Nations Environment Programme (UNEP), Oregon State University and FAO, *Atlas of International Freshwater Agreements*, Nairobi: UNEP, 2002.

United Nations Environment Programme (UNEP), UNA and OSU, *Hydropolitical Vulnerability and Resilience along International Waters – Latin America and the Caribbean*, Nairobi: UNEP, 2007.

United Nations Framework Convention on Climate Change (UNFCCC), *The Contribution of the Clean Development Mechanism under the Kyoto Protocol to Technology Transfer*, UNFCCC, 2010.

United Nations World Water Assessment Programme, *The United Nations World Water Development Report 3: Water in a Changing World*, Paris: UNESCO, 2008.

Utting, P., 'The Global Compact: Why All the Fuss?', *UN Chronicle* 40, 2003, 1.

Utton, A.E., 'Which rule should prevail in international water disputes: that of reasonableness or that of no harm?', *Natural Resources Journal* 36, 1996, 635.

Utton, A. and Utton, J., 'The International Law of Minimum Stream Flows', *Colorado Journal of International Environmental Law and Policy* 10, 1999.

van Caenegem, R.C., *European Law in the Past and the Future: Unity and Diversity over Two Millennia*, Cambridge: Cambridge University Press, 2002.

van Claster, G., 'Faites Vos Jeux – Regulatory Autonomy and the World Trade Organisation after *Brazil Tyres*', *Journal of Environmental Law* 20(10), 2008.

van de Kerkhof, M., 'The Trail Smelter Case Re-examined: Examining the Development of National Procedural Mechanisms to Resolve a Trail Smelter Type Dispute', *Merkourios – International and European Environmental Law* 27(73), 2011.

van der Gaag, P., 'OECD Guidelines for Multinational Enterprises: Corporate Accountability in a Liberalised Economy?' Online. Available HTTP: <http://www.oecdwatch.org/docs/paper%20 NC%20IUCN.pdf> (accessed 10 April 2008).

Van Dyke, J.M., *The Evolution and International Acceptance of the Precautionary Principle*. Online. Available HTTP: <http://mmc.gov/sound/internationalwrkshp/pdf/vandyke.pdf> (accessed 23 November 2011).

Van Harten, G. and Loughlin, M., 'Investment Treaty Arbitration as a Species of Global Administrative Law' *European Journal of International Law* 17(1), 2006, 121.

van Zeben, J.A.W., 'The Untapped Potential of Horizontal Private Enforcement Within European Environmental Law', *Georgetown International Environmental Law Review* 22, 2010, 241.

Vedder, H., 'Diplomacy by Directive: An Analysis of the International Context of the Emissions Trading Directive', Social Science Research Network, 2009.

Vedder, H., 'The Treaty of Lisbon and European Environmental Policy', Social Science Research Network, 2008.

Verschuuren, B., Wild, R.G., McNeely, J. and Oviedo, G. (eds) *Sacred Natural Sites: Conserving Nature and Culture*, London: Earthscan, 2010.

Vilela, M., 'Building Consensus on Shared Values. History and Provenance of the Earth Charter', in P.B. Corcoran (ed.) *The Earth Charter in Action. Toward a Sustainable World*, Amsterdam: KIT, 2005.

Vinogradov, S., Wouters, P. and Jones, P., *Transforming Potential Conflict into Cooperation Potential: The Role of International Water Law*, Dundee: University of Dundee, 2003. Online. Available HTTP: <http://unesdoc.unesco.org/images/0013/001332/133258e.pdf> (accessed 21 September 2011).

Virgilio, N.R., Marshall, S., Zerbock, O. and Holmes, C., *Reducing Emissions from Deforestation and Degradation (REDD): A Casebook of on-the-ground Experience*, Arlington, VA: The Nature Conservancy, 2010.

Visseren-Hamakers, I. and Glasbergen, P., 'Partnerships in forest governance' *Global Environmental Change* 17, 2007, 408.

von Homeyer, I., 'Emerging Experimentalism in EU Environmental Governance', in C. Sabel and J. Seitlin (eds) *Experimentalist Governance in the European Union: Towards a New Architecture?*, Oxford: Oxford University Press, 2010, 121.

von Homeyer, I., 'The Evolution of EU Environmental Governance', in J. Scott (ed.) *Environmental Protection, European Law and Governance*, Oxford: Oxford University Press, 2009.

Vonada, R., Herbert, T. and Waage, S., *Introduction to Payments for Ecosystem Services: A Reference Book for Uganda*, Uganda: National Environment Management Authority, 2011.

Wagenbaur, R., 'The European Community's Policy on Implementation of Environmental Directives', *Fordham International Law Journal* 14, 1990, 455.

Waldmann, R.J., *Regulating International Business through Codes of Conduct*, Washington DC: American Enterprise Institute for Public Policy Research, 1980.

Walrut, B., 'The Legislative Powers of the Commonwealth and States Affecting Aquaculture', *Environmental and Planning Law Journal* 19, 2002, 415.

Walsh, T.J.V., 'Turning Our Backs: Kyoto's Mistaken Nuclear Exclusion', *Georgetown International Environmental Law Review* 16(1), 2003, 147.

Wangkeo, K., 'Monumental Challenges: The Lawfulness of Destroying Cultural Heritage During Peacetime', *Yale Journal of International Law* 28, 2003, 183.

Ward, E., *Indigenous Peoples between Human Rights and Environmental Protection*, Danish Centre for Human Rights, 1993.

Ward, J.J., 'Black Gold in a White Wilderness – Antarctic Oil: The Past, Present and Potential of a Region in Need of Sovereign Environmental Stewardship', *Journal of Land Use and Environmental Law* 13, 1998.

Watson, R.T., Dixon, J.A., Hamburg, S.P., Janetos, A.C. and Moss, R.H., *Protecting Our Planet, Securing Our Future: Linkages Among Global Environmental Issues and Human Needs*, UNEP, US NASA, World Bank, 1998.

Watt-Cloutier, S., Chair, *Presentation at the Eleventh Conference of Parties to the UN Framework Convention on Climate Change: The Climate Change Petition by the Inuit Circumpolar Conference to the Inter-American Commission on Human Rights*, Inuit Circumpolar Conference, Montreal, 7 December 2005.

Webster-Main, A., 'Keeping Africa Out of the Global Backyard: A Comparative Study of the Basel and Bamako Conventions', *Environs Environmental Law and Policy Journal* 26, 2002, 65.

Weil, P., 'Toward Relative Normativity in International Law', *American Journal of International Law* 77, 1983.

Weiss, E.B., 'The Emerging Structure of International Environmental Law', in N.J. Vig and R.S. Axelrod (eds) *The Global Environment Institutions, Law and Policy*, London: Earthscan, 1999.

Weiss, E.B., 'Environmental Equity: The Imperative for the Twenty-First Century', *in* W. Lang (ed.) *Sustainable Development and International Law*, London: Graham & Trotman\M. Nijhoff, 1995.

Weiss, E.B., *The Evolution of International Water Law*, The Hague: Martinus Nijhoff, 2009.

Weiss, E.B., *In Fairness to Future Generations: International Law, Common Patrimony, and Intergenerational Equity*, New York: Transnational Publishers, 1988.

Weiss, E.B., 'Intergenerational Justice and International Law', in S. Busuttil, E. Agius, P.S. Inglott and T. Macelli (eds) *Our Responsibilities to Future Generations*, Malta: Foundation for International Studies, 1998.

Weiss, E.B., 'International Environmental Law: Contemporary Issues and the Emergence of a New World Order', *Georgetown Law Journal* 81, 1993, 675.

Weiss, E.B., 'New Directions in International Environmental Law', in D. Craig, N. Robinson and Koh, K.L. (eds) *Capacity Building for Environmental Law in the Asian and Pacific Region*, Volume I, Manila: Asian Development Bank, 2002.

Weiss, E.B., 'Understanding Compliance with International Environmental Agreements: The Baker's Dozen Myths', *University of Richmond Law Review* 32, 1999, 1555.

Weiss, E.B., Magraw, D. and Szasz, P., *International Environmental Law and Policy*, New York: Aspen, 1998.

Weiss, E.B., McCaffrey, S., McGraw, D. and Tarlock, A.D., *International Environmental Law and Policy*, 2nd edition, New York: Foundation Press, 2007.

Weissbrodt, D. and Kruger, M., 'Norms on the Responsibilities of Transnational Corporations and Other Business Enterprises with regard to Human Rights', *American Journal of International Law* 97, 2003, 901.

Wells, A., Luttrell, C., Brown, D. and Bird, N., 'Public Goods and Private Rights: The Illegal Logging Debate and the Rights of the Poor', London: Overseas Development Institute Forestry Briefings, 2006.

Werksman, J., 'Consolidating Governance of the Global Commons: Insights from the GEF', *Yearbook of International Environmental Law* 47(6), 1995, 27.

White, M.W.D., *Australian Marine Pollution Laws*, 2nd edition, Annandale: Federation Press, 2007.

Widawsky, L., 'In my Backyard: How Enabling Hazardous Waste Trade to Developing Nations Can Improve the Basel Convention's Ability to Achieve Environmental Justice', *Environmental Law* 38, 2008, 589.

Wijen, F., Zoetman, K. and Pieters, J. (eds) *A Handbook of Globalisation and Environmental Policy: National Government Intervention in a Global Arena*, Cheltenham: Edward Elgar, 2005.

Williams, D., 'Courts and Globalization, *Indiana Journal of Global Legal Studies* 3, 2004, 57.

Williams, D., *Environmental and Resource Management Law*, Wellington: Butterworths, 1997.

Wilson, A. and Guéneau, S., *Enhancing the Compatibility of Market-based Policy Instruments for Sustainable Forest Management*, Paris: Institute of Sustainable Development and International Relations, 2004.

Wilson, B., 'State Constitutional Environmental Rights and Judicial Activism: Is the Big Sky Falling?', *Emory Law Journal* 53, 2004, 627.

Wirth, D.A., 'Re-examining Decision-Making Processes in International Environmental Law' *Iowa Law Review* 79, 1994, 769.

Wolf, A.T., 'Conflict and cooperation along international waterways', *Water Policy* 1(2), 1998, 251.

Wolf, A.T., Natharius, J.A., Danielson, J.J., Ward, B.S. and Pender, J.K., 'International river basins of the world', *International Journal of Water Resources Development* 15(4), 1999, 387.

Wolfrum, R., 'Means of Ensuring Compliance with and Enforcement of International Environmental Law', *Recueil des Cours* 272, 1998, 29.

Wolfrum, R. and Matz, N., *Conflicts in International Environmental Law*, Berlin: Springer, 2003.

Wood, C., 'Environmental impact assessment in developing countries: An overview', Unpublished conference paper, 2003.

Wood, P.M., *Biodiversity and Democracy: Re-Thinking Society and Nature*, Vancouver: UBC Press, 2000.

Woolf, H., Jowell, J. and Le Sueur, A.P., *De Smith, Woolf and Jowell's Principles of Judicial Review*, London: Sweet and Maxwell, 1999.

Wouters, J. and Hachez, N., 'The Institutionalization of Investment Arbitration and Sustainable Development', in M.C. Cordonier Segger, M. Gehring and A. Newcombe (eds) *Sustainable Development in World Investment Law*, Alphen aan den Rijn: Kluwer Law International, 2011.

Wouters, J., Nollkaemper, A. and de Wet, E. (eds) *Introduction to The Europeanization of International Law: The Status of International Law in the EU and its Member States*, The Hague: TMC Asser Press, 2008.

Wouters, P.K., 'An assessment of recent developments in international watercourse law through the prism of the substantive rules governing use allocation', *Natural Resources Journal* 36, 1996, 417.

Wouters, P. and Tarlock, D., 'Are shared benefits of international waters an equitable apportionment?', *Colorado Journal of International Environmental Law and Policy* 18, 2007, 523.

Wouters, P. and Ziganshina, D., 'Tackling the Global Water Crisis: Unlocking International Law as Fundamental to the Peaceful Management of the World's Shared Transboundary Waters – Introducing the H2O Paradigm', in Q. Grafton and K. Hussey (eds) *Water Resources Planning and Management: Challenges and Solutions*, Cambridge: Cambridge University Press, 2011.

Wouters, P., Vinogradov, S. and Magsig B-O., 'Water security, hydrosolidarity and international law: a river runs through it . . .', *Yearbook of International Environmental Law* 19, 2010, 97.

Wright, C., 'Setting Standards for Responsible Banking: Examining the Role of the International Finance Corporation in the Emergence of the Equator Principles', in F. Biermann, B. Siebenhüner and A. Schreyrögg (eds) *International Organizations in Global Environmental Governance*, Abingdon: Routledge, 2009.

Wright, Q., 'Conflicts Between International Law and Treaties', *American Journal of International Law* 11(3), 1917, 566.

Xanthaki, A., *Indigenous Rights and United Nations Standards: Self-determination, Culture and Land* Cambridge: Cambridge University Press, 2007.

Yamada, C., 'Codification of the Law of Transboundary Aquifers (Groundwater) by the United Nations', *Water International* 36(5), 2011, 557.

Yang, T., 'The Effectiveness of the NAFTA Environmental Side Agreement's Citizen Submission Process: A Case Study of Metales y Derivados', *University of Colorado Law Review*, 2005.

Yang, T., 'International Environmental Protection: Human Rights and the North–South Divide', in K.H. Mutz, G. Bryner and D. Kenney (eds) *Justice and Natural Resources: Concepts, Strategies and Applications*, Washington DC: Island Press, 2002.

Yang, T. and Percival, R., 'The Emergence of Global Environmental Law', *Ecology Law Quarterly* 36, 2009.

Young, L., 'Australian and International Laws on Export Controls for Cultural Heritage'. Paper presented at the *Art Crime Protecting Art, Protecting Artists and Protecting Consumers Conference*, Australian Institute of Criminology, Sydney, 2–3 December 1999.

Young, O.R., Berkhout, F., Gallopin, G.C., Janssen, M.A., Ostrom, E. and van der Leeuw, S., 'The Globalisation of Socio-Ecological Systems: An Agenda for Scientific Research', *Global Environmental Change* 16, 2006, 308.

Zahar, A., 'Verifying Greenhouse Gas Emissions of Annex I Parties: Methods We Have and Methods We Want', *Climate Law* 1(3), 2010, 409.

Zammit, A., *Development at Risk. Rethinking UN-Business Partnerships*, Geneva: UNRISD, 2003.

Zawahri, N.A., 'India, Pakistan and cooperation along the Indus River system', *Water Policy*, 2009.

Zawahri, N.A. and McLaughlin Mitchell, S., 'Fragmented governance in international rivers: negotiating bilateral versus multilateral treaties', *International Studies Quarterly* 55, 2011, 835.

Zenawi, M. and Stoltenberg, J., *Report of the Secretary-General's High-Level Advisory Group on Climate Change Financing*, Geneva: United Nations, 2010.

Zerbe, N., 'Biodiversity, Ownership, and Indigenous Knowledge: Exploring Legal Frameworks for Community, Farmers, and Intellectual Property Rights in Africa', *Ecological Economics* 53, 2005.

Zetter, R., 'The Role of Legal and Normative Frameworks for the Protection of Environmentally Displaced People', in F. Laczko and C. Aghazam (eds) *Migration, Environment and Climate Change: Assessing the Evidence*, International Organization for Migration, 2009.

Ziganshina, D., 'International water law in Central Asia: the nature of substantive norms and what flows from it', *Asian Journal of International Law*, 2011, 1. Online. Available HTTP: <http://journals.cambridge.org/action/displayAbstract?fromPage=online&aid=8467139> (accessed 21 September 2011).

International documents, agreements and conventions

Adjustments and Amendments to the Montreal Protocol on Substances That Deplete the Ozone Layer, opened for signature 29 June 1990, 30 ILM 537 (entered into force 10 August 1992).

African Charter on Human and Peoples' Rights, 27 June 1981, 1520 UNTS 217, 21 ILM 59 (entered into force 21 October 1986.

African Convention on the Conservation of Nature and Natural Resources, opened for signature 15 September 1968, CAB/LEG/24. Online. Available HTTP: <http://www.paxafrica.org/documents/resources/african-union-documents/african-convention-on-the-conservation-of-nature-and-natural-resources-algiers-convention-1968/view> (accessed 8 July 2010).

Agenda 21: A Programme for Action for Sustainable Development (1992), Report of the UN Conference on Environment and Development, UN Doc A./Conf. 151/26.

Agreement between Australia and the Republic of Indonesia on the Framework for Security Cooperation, Australia–Indonesia, signed 13 November 2006, [2008] ATS 3 (entered into force 7 February 2008).

Agreement between the Federal Republic of Germany and the Kingdom of Denmark on Mutual Assistance in the Event of Disasters or Serious Accidents, Denmark–Germany, signed 16 May 1985, 1523 UNTS 109 (entered into force 1 August 1988).

Agreement Concerning Frontier Rivers between Finland and Sweden (1971), Finland–Sweden, 825 UNTS 191.

Agreement Concerning the River Niger Commission and the Navigation and Transport on the River Niger, opened for signature 25 November 1964, 587 UNTS 19 (entered into force 12 April 1966).

Agreement Establishing the Caribbean Disaster Emergency Management Agency, opened for signature 26 February 1991, UNTS 2256 (entered into force 19 May 1992).

Agreement Establishing the European Bank for Reconstruction and Development, signed on 29 May 1990 (entered into force 29 March 1991)

Agreement for the Implementation of the Provisions of the United Nations Convention on the Law of the Sea of 10 December 1982 Relating to the Conservation and Management of Straddling Fish Stocks and Highly Migratory Fish Stocks, opened for signature 4 December 1995, 2167 UNTS 88 (entered into force 11 December 2001).

Agreement on Port State Measures to Prevent, Deter and Eliminate Illegal, Unreported and Unregulated Fishing, opened for signature November 2009, 137th Sess, Committee on Constitutional and Legal Matters, 88th Sess, FAO Doc CL 137/5.

Agreement on the Application of Sanitary and Phyto-sanitary Agreement Measures, Uruguay Round Agreement (entered into force 1995).

Agreement on the Establishment of the ASEAN Centre for Biodiversity 2005. Online. Available HTTP: <http://www.aseansec.org/acb_copy.pdf> (accessed 2 February 2012).

Agreement on the Establishment of the Zambezi Watercourse Commission, opened for signature 13 July 2004. Online. Available HTTP: <http://www1.eis.gov.bw/EIS/Policies> (accessed 21 September 2011).

Agreement to Promote Compliance with International Conservation and Management by Fishing Vessels on the High Seas, opened for signature 24 November 1993, 2221 UNTS 120 (entered into force 24 April 2003). Online. Available HTTP: <http://www.fao.org/DOCREP/MEETING/003/X3130m/X3130E00.HTM> (accessed 18 January 2012).

American Convention on Human Rights, 21 November 1969, OAS Treaty Series No 36, 1144 UNTS 123 (entered into force 18 July 1978).

Antarctic Treaty, opened for signature 1 December 1959, 12 UST 794, (entered into force 23 June 1961).

ASEAN Agreement on Disaster Management and Emergency Response, opened for signature 26 July 2005 (entered into force 24 December 2009).

Assistance in Cases of Natural Disaster (1964), UNGA Res 2034(XX) UN GAOR 20th Sess, 1390th Plen Mtg, UN Doc A/RES/2034(XX).

Bali Strategic Plan for Technology Support and Capacity Building, Governing Council of the United Nations Environment Programme, Note by the Executive-Director, UN Doc UNEP/GC.23/6/Add.1 (23 December 2004).

Bamako Convention on the Ban of the Import to Africa and the Control of Transboundary Movement and Management of Hazardous Wastes within Africa, opened for signature 30 January 1991, 30 ILM 773 (entry into force 22 April 1998).

Basel Convention on the Control of Transboundary Movement of Hazardous Wastes and their Disposal, opened for signature 22 March 1989, 28 ILM 657 (entered into force 5 May 1992).

Bergen Ministerial Declaration on Sustainable Development (1990), The Hague, UN Doc A/CONF.151/PC/10. Online. Available HTTP: <http://www.seas-at-risk.org/1mages/1990%20Hague%20Declaration.pdf> (accessed 23 November 2011).

Canada – Measures Affecting Exports of Unprocessed Herring and Salmon, adopted 22 March 1988, BISD 355/98, 114.

Cartagena Protocol on Biosafety, opened for signature 29 January 2000, 39 ILM 1027 (entered into force 11 September 2003). Online. Available HTTP: <http://bch.cbd.int/protocol/text/> (accessed 18 May 2012).

CBD, *Strategic Plan for Biodiversity 2011–2020 and Natural Biodiversity Strategies and Action Plans* (Aichi Targets), 24 March 2011 UNEP/CBD/RW-BF/4/3, 2011.

CITES Secretariat, *Monitoring of Illegal Hunting in Elephant Range States*, March 2010, CoP15 Doc. 44.2 (Rev. 1).

Communication by the Commission: Analysis of options to move beyond 20% greenhouse gas emission reductions and assessing the risk of carbon leakage, Brussels, (2010).

Communication from the Commission on the Precautionary Principle. Online. Available HTTP: <http://ec.europa.eu/dgs/health_consumer/library/pub/pub07_en.pdf> (accessed 23 November 2011).

Communication from the Commission to the Council and the European Parliament, on The European Union and the Arctic Region, COM, (2008) 763 final, Brussels, 20 November 2008. Online. Available HTTP: <http://eur-lex.europa.eu/LexUriServ/LexUriServ.do?uri=COM:2008:0763:FIN:EN:pdf> (accessed 9 May 2012).

Convention and Statute Establishing an International Relief Union, opened for signature 12 July 1927, 1932–1933 LNTS 247 (entered into force 27 December 1932).

Convention and Statutes Relating to the Development of the Chad Basin, opened for signature 22 May 1964 (entered into force 15 September 1964). Online. Available HTTP: <http://www.fao.org/docrep/W7414B/w7414b05.htm> (accessed 21 September 2011).

Convention between France and Great Britain relative to Fisheries, France-Great Britain, opened for signature 11 November 1867, XXI IPE 1.

Convention between the United States, Great Britain, Russia and Japan for the Preservation and Protection of Fur Seals, opened for signature 7 July 1911. Online. Available HTTP: <http://docs.lib.noaa.gov/noaa_documents/NOS/ORR/TM_NOS_ORR/TM_NOS-ORR_17/HTML/Pribilof_html/Documents/THE_FUR_SEAL_TREATY_OF_1911.pdf> (accessed 9 May 2012).

Convention Concerning Indigenous and Tribal Peoples in Independent Countries, 72 ILO Official Bulletin 59 (entered into force 5 September 1991).

Convention Concerning the Protection of the World Cultural and Natural Heritage, opened for signature 16 November 1972, 11 ILM 1358 (entered into force 17 December 1975).

Convention for the Conservation of Antarctic Seals, opened for signature 1 June 1972, 11 ILM 251 (entered into force 11 March 1978).

Convention for the Conservation of Southern Bluefin Tuna, opened for signature 10 May 1993, 1819 UNTS 359 (entered into force 20 May 1994).

Convention for the Final Settlement of the Difficulties Arising through Complaints of Damage Done in the State of Washington by Fumes Discharged from the Smelter of the Consolidated Mining and Smelting Company (1935), 162 LNTS 74.

Convention for the Physical Protection of Nuclear Material, opened for signature 3 March 1980, 1456 UNTS 124 (entered into force 8 February 1987).

Convention for the Prevention of Pollution of the Sea by Oil, opened for signature 12 May 1954, 327 UNTS 3 (entered into force 26 July 1958).

Convention for the Prohibition of Fishing with Long Driftnets in the South Pacific, opened for signature 24 November 1989, 29 ILM 1454 (entered into force 17 May 1991).

Convention for the Protection of Natural Resources and Environment of the South Pacific Region, opened for signature 25 November 1986, 26 ILM 38 (entered into force 22 August 1990).

Convention for the Protection of the Marine Environment of the North-East Atlantic, opened for signature 22 September 1992, 32 ILM 1069 (entered into force 25 March 1998).

Convention for the Regulation of Whaling, opened for signature 24 September 1931, 155 LNTS 351.

Convention on Access to Information, Public Participation in Decision-Making and Access to Justice in Environmental Matters, opened for signature on 25 June 1998, 38 ILM 517 (entered into force 30 October 2001).

Convention on Assistance in the Case of a Nuclear Accident or Radiological Emergency, opened for signature 26 September 1986, 1457 UNTS 133 (entered into force 26 February 1987).

Convention on Biological Diversity, opened for signature 5 June 1992, 31 ILM 818 (entered into force 29 December 1993).

Convention on Civil Liability for Nuclear Damage, opened for signature 21 May 1963, 1063 UNTS 265 (entered into force 12 November 1977).

Convention on Cluster Munitions, opened for signature 3 December 2008 (entered into force 1 August 2010).

Convention on Early Notification of a Nuclear Accident, opened for signature 26 September 1986, 1439 UNTS 275, 25 ILM 1391 (entered into force 27 October 1986).

Convention on Environmental Impact Assessment in a Transboundary Context, opened for signature 25 February 1991, 1989 UNTS 309 (entered into force 10 September 1997).

Convention on Facilitation of International Maritime Traffic, opened for signature 9 April 1965, [1986] ATS 12 (entered into force 5 March 1967).

Convention on Fishing and Conservation of the Living Resources of the High Seas, opened for signature 29 April 1958, 559 UNTS 286 (entered into force 20 March 1966).

Convention on International Civil Aviation, opened for signature 7 December 1944, 15 UNTS 295 (entered into force 4 April 1947).

Convention on International Liability for Damage Caused by Space Objects, opened for signature 29 March 1972 (entered into force 1 September 1972).

Convention on International Trade in Endangered Species of Wild Fauna and Flora, opened for signature 3 March 1973, 12 ILM 1088 (entered into force 1 July 1975).

Convention on Jurisdiction and Enforcement of Judgments in Civil and Commercial Matters, opened for signature 27 September 1968 8 ILM 229 (entered into force 1 February 1973).

Convention on Long-Range Transboundary Air Pollution, opened for signature 13 November 1979, 1302 UNTS 217 (entered into force 16 March 1983).

Convention on Nuclear Safety, opened for signature 20 September 1994, 33 ILM 1514 (entered into force 24 October 1996).

Convention on Oil Pollution Preparedness, Response and Co-operation, opened for signature 30 November 1990, 30 ILM 733 (entered into force 13 May 1995).

Convention on Stolen or Illegally Exported Cultural Objects, opened for signature 24 June 1995, 34 ILM 1322 (entered into force 1 July 1998).

Convention on Supplementary Compensation for Nuclear Damage, opened for signature 29 September 1997, 36 ILM 1473 (not yet entered into force). Online. Available HTTP: <http://www.iaea.org/Publications/Documents/Conventions/supcomp.html> (accessed 11 May 2012).

Convention on the Conservation and Management of the Pollock Resources in the Central Bering Sea, opened for signature 16 June 1994, 34 ILM 67 (entered into force 8 December 1995).

Convention on the Conservation of Antarctic Marine Living Resources, opened for signature on 1 August 1980, 19 ILM 841 (entered into force 7 April 1982).

Convention on the Conservation of Migratory Species of Wild Animals, opened for signature 23 June 1979, 19 ILM 15 (entered into force 1 November 1983).

Convention on the Conservation of Southern Blue Fin Tuna, opened for signature 10 May 1993, 1819 UNTS 360 (entered into force 30 May 1994).

Convention on the Conservation of Antarctic Marine Living Resources, opened for signature 1 August 1980. Online. Available HTTP: <www.ccamlr.org/pu/e/e_pubs/bd/pt1.pdf> (accessed 8 March 2012);

Convention on the Continental Shelf, opened for signature 29 April 1958, 499 UNTS 311 (entered into force 10 June 1964).

Convention on the Control of Transboundary Movements of Hazardous Wastes and their Disposal (Basel) 22 March 1989, 28 ILM 657 (entered into force 5 May 1992).

Convention on the Co-operation for the Protection and Sustainable Use of the Waters of the Lusso-Spanish River Basins, opened for signature 20 November 1998 (entered into force 31 January 2000). Online. Available HTTP: <http://faolex.fao.org/watertreaties/index.htm> (accessed 21 September 2011).

Convention on the Establishment of an International Fund for Compensation for Oil Pollution Damage, opened for signature 18 December 1971, 1110 UNTS 57 (entered into force 16 October 1978).

Convention on the High Seas, opened for signature 29 April 1958, 450 UNTS 82 (entered into force 30 September 1962).

Convention on the Law of the Non-Navigational Uses of International Watercourses, opened for signature 21 May 1997, 36 ILM 700 (not yet in force).

Convention on the Means of Prohibiting the Illicit Import, Export and Transfer of Ownership of Cultural Property, opened for signature 14 November 1970, 823 UNTS 231 (entered into force 24 April 1972).

Convention on the Non-Navigational Uses of International Watercourses, opened for signature 21 May 1997, 36 ILM 700 (has not entered into force).

Convention on the Prevention of Marine Pollution by Dumping of Wastes and Other Matter, opened for signature 29 December 1972, 26 UST 2403, 1046 UNTS 120 (entered into force 15 July 1977).

Convention on the Prior Informed Consent Procedure for Certain Hazardous Chemicals and Pesticides in International Trade, opened for signature 10 September 1998, 38 ILM 1 (entered into force 24 February 2004).

Convention on the Prohibition of the Development, Production and Stockpiling of Bacteriological (Biological) and Toxin Weapons and their Destruction, opened for signature 10 April 1972, (entered into force 26 March 1975).

Convention on the Prohibition of the Use, Stockpiling, Production and Transfer of Anti-Personnel Mines and on their Destruction, opened for signature 3 December 1997 (entered into force 1 March 1999).

Convention on the Protection and Promotion of the Diversity of Cultural Expressions, opened for signature 20 October 2005, 45 ILM 269 (entered into force March 18 2007).

Convention on the Protection and Use of Transboundary Watercourses and International Lakes, opened for signature 17 March 1992, 31 ILM 1312 (entered into force 6 October 1996).

Convention on the Protection of the Marine Environment of the Baltic Sea Area, opened for signature 9 April 1992, 13 ILM 546 (entered into force 17 January 2000) ('Helsinki Convention'). Online. Available HTTP: <http://www.helcom.fi/stc/files/Convention/Conv0704.pdf> (accessed 17 February 2012).

Convention on the Protection of the Rhine, opened for signature 12 April 1999 (entered into force 1 January 2003). Online. Available HTTP: <http://faolex.fao.org/watertreaties/index.htm> (accessed 21 September 2011).

Convention on the Protection of the Underwater Cultural Heritage, opened for signature 11 February 2001, 51 ILM 40 (entered into force on 2 January 2009).

Convention on the Regulation of Aerial Navigation, opened for signature 13 October 1919, 11 LNTS 173.

Convention on the Regulation of Antarctic Mineral Resource Activities, opened for signature June 1988, 27 ILM 868 (not yet entered into force).

Convention on the Safeguarding of Intangible Cultural Heritage, opened for signature 17 October 2003, 2368 UNTS 3 (entered into force 20 April 2006).

Convention on the Sustainable Management of Lake Tanganyika, opened for signature 12 June 2003.

Convention on the Transboundary Effects of Industrial Accidents, opened for signature 18 March 1992, 32 ILM 1330 (entered into force 19 April 2000). Online. Available HTTP: <http://sedac.ciesin.org/entri/texts/industrial.accidents.1992.html> (accessed 17 February 2012).

Convention on Third Party Liability in the Field of Nuclear Energy, opened for signature 29 July 1960, 956 UNTS 264 (entered into force 1 April 1968). Online. Available HTTP: <http://www.nea.fr/html/law/nlparis_conv.html> (accessed 2 May 2012).

Convention on Wetlands of International Importance especially as Waterfowl Habitat (Ramsar), opened for signature 2 February 1971, 996 UNTS 245, 11 ILM 963 (entered into force 21 December 1975).

Convention Relating to the Status of the Senegal River, opened for signature 11 May 1972, IEA 2734 (entered into force 25 May 1973).

Convention to Combat Desertification in Those Countries Experiencing Serious Drought and/or Desertification, Particularly in Africa, opened for signature 17 June 1994, 33 ILM 1328 (entered into force 26 December 1996).

Convention to Protect Birds Useful to Agriculture, opened for signature 19 March 1902. Online. Available HTTP: <http://eelink.net/~asilwildlife/bird_1902.html> (accessed 8 July 2010).

Cooperation for the Sustainable Development of the Mekong River Basin, opened for signature 5 April 1995, 2069 UNTS 3 (entered into force 5 April 1995).

COSPAR Planetary Protection Policy, 20 October 2002, amended up to 24 March 2011, is online. Available HTTP: <cosparhq.cnes.fr/Scistr/PPPolicy%20(24Mar2011).pdf> (accessed 15 September 2011).

Council Directive (EC) 92/43 on the Conservation of Natural Habitats and of Wild Fauna and Flora [1992] OJ L206/7.

Council Directive 2008/99/EC, *Protection of the Environment through Criminal Law*, preamble 5, 2008 O.J. (L 328) 28 (2008 Directive). Online. Available HTTP: <http://eur-lex.europa.eu/LexUriServ/LexUriServ.do?uri=OJ:L:2008:328:0028:0037:EN:PDF> (accessed 19 March 2012).

Declaration of Environmental Policies and Procedures Relating to Economic Development, opened for signature 1 February 1980, 19 ILM 524.

Declaration of Legal Principles Governing the Activities of States in the Exploration and Uses of Outer Space (1962), UNGA Res 1962(XVIII), UN GAOR.

Declaration of the United Nations Conference on the Human Environment (1973), UN Doc A/CONF.48/14/Rev. 1.

Declaration on the Rights of Indigenous Peoples (2007), UNGA Res 295, UN GAOR, 61st Sess, 107th Plen Mtg, UN Doc A/Res/295.

Directive 2000/60/EC of the European Parliament and of the Council of 23 October 2000 establishing a framework for Community action in the field of water policy (2000), OJL 327.

Directive 2000/60/EC of the European Parliament and the Council of 23 October 2000 establishing a framework for community action in the field of water policy. Online. Available HTTP: <http://eur-lex.europa.eu/LexUriServ/LexUriServ.do?uri=CELEX:32000L0060:EN:NOT> (accessed 21 September 2011).

Directive 2003/87/EC the European Parliament and the of the Council of 13 October 2003 establishing a scheme for greenhouse gas emission allowance trading within the Community and amending Council Directive 96/61/EC, OJ L 275, 25 October 2003.

Directive 2004/101/EC of the European Parliament and the of the Council of 27 October 2004 amending Directive 2003/87/EC establishing a scheme for greenhouse gas emission allowance trading within the Community, in respect of the Kyoto Protocol's project mechanisms, OJ L 338/18, 13 November 2004.

Directive 2008/56/EC of the European Parliament and of the Council of 17 June 2008 establishing a framework for community action in the field of marine environmental policy, Marine Strategy Framework Directive, OJ L 164/19, 25 June 2008.

Directive 2009/29/EC of the European Parliament and the of the Council of 23 April 2009 amending Directive 2003/87/EC so as to improve and extend the greenhouse gas emission allowance trading scheme of the Community, OJ L 140/63, 5 June 2009.

Doha Ministerial Declaration, Ministerial Conference, Fourth Session, 14 November 2001, WTO Doc. WT/MIN(01)/DEC/W/1.

Draft Articles on the Law of the Non-navigational Uses of International Watercourses (1994), GA Res 49/52, UN GAOR, 49th Sess.

ECE Convention on Environmental Impact Assessment in a Transboundary Context, opened for signature 25 February 1991, 30 ILM 800 (entered into force 10 September 1997).

EC Measures Concerning Meat and Meat Products (the *Hormones Case*), WTO Doc. WT/DS48/AB/R (6 January 1998).

Economic and Social Council, *Prevention of Discrimination and Protection of Indigenous Peoples and Minorities* (2001), E/CN.4/Sub.2/2001/21.

Economic Commission for Europe, *Decision 1997/2 Concerning the Implementation Committee, its Structure and Functions and Procedures for Review of Compliance*, ECE/EB.AIR/53, 7 January 1998.

Economic Commission for Europe, *Global and Regional Developments on Issues Related to Principle 10 of the Rio Declaration on Environment and Development* (2008), ECE/MP.PP/2008/8.

Economic Commission for Europe, *Implementation Report Submitted by the United Kingdom* (2008), ECE/MP.PP/IR/2008/GBR.

Economic Commission for Europe, *Rio plus Aarhus – 20 years on: Bearing fruit and looking forward* (2011), ECE/MP.PP/2011/CRP.4/rev. 1.

Economic Commission for Europe, *Synthesis Report on the Status of Implementation of the Convention* (2008), ECE/MP.PP/2008/4. Online. Available HTTP: <http://www.unece.org/env/documents/2008/pp/mop3/ece_mp_pp_2008_4_e.pdf> (accesed 11 May 2012).

Economic Commission for Europe, *Synthesis report on the status of implementation of the Convention* (2008), ECE/MP.PP/2008/4.

ECOSOC, *Follow-up to the United Nations Conference on Environment and Development as related to Transnational Corporations: Report of the Secretary-General* (1993), UN Doc E/C.10/1993/7.

ECOSOC, *Report of the UN Secretary-General: Transnational Corporations and Issues Relating to the Environment* (1991), UN Doc E/C.10/1991/3.

Environmental Perspective to the Year 2000 and Beyond, GA Res. A/RES/42/186,UN GA, 42nd Sess, 96th Plen Mtg, (1987).

EU-CARIFORUM Economic Partnership Agreement, entered into force 29 December 2008. Online. Available HTTP: <http://trade.ec.europa.eu/doclib/docs/2008/february/tradoc_137971.pdf> (accessed 19 March 2012).

European Commission for Europe, *Synthesis Report on the Status of Implementation of the Convention* (2008), ECE/MP.PP/2008/4.

European Commission, *Report From the Commission to the Council, the European Parliament, the European Economic and Social Committee and the Committee of the Regions, Under Article 14(2) of Directive 2004/35/ CE on the Environmental Liability with Regard to the Prevention and Remedying of Environmental Damage*, COM, 2010, 581.

European Commission, *Study on the Implementation Effectiveness of the Environmental Liability Directive (ELD) and Related Financial Security Issues*, 070307/2008/516353/ETU/G.1, 2009.

European Communities – Measures Affecting Asbestos and Asbestos-containing Products, EC Asbestos WT/ DS135/AB/R.

European Communities – Measures Affecting the Approval and Marketing of Biotech Products, WTO Docs WT/ DS291/R, WT/DS292/R, WT/DS293/R (2006) (report of the Panel).

European Community Directive 98/44 on the Legal Protection of Biotechnological Inventions (1998).

European Convention for the Protection of Human Rights and Fundamental Freedoms, 4 November 1950, 213 UNTS 222 (entered into force 3 September 1953).

European Parliament, *European Parliament resolution of 25 November on corporate social responsibility in international trade agreements*. 2010. Online. Available HTTP: <http://www.europarl.europa.eu/sides/ getDoc.do?type=TAandlanguage=ENandreference=P7-TA-2010-0446> (accessed 19 December 2011).

European Parliament, *European Parliament resolution of 6 April 2011 on the future European international investment policy*, 2011. Online. Available HTTP: <www.europarl.europa.eu/sides/getDoc. do?type=TAandreference=P7-TA-2011-0141andlanguage=EN> (accessed 19 December 2011).

Fifteenth Conference of the Parties to the United Nations Framework Convention on Climate Change, *Copenhagen Accord*, Decision 2/CP.15 in *Report of the Conference of the Parties in its Fifteenth Session*, addendum one, part two, UN Doc FCCC/CP/2009/11/Add.1.

Final Act Embodying the Results of the Uruguay Round of Multinational Trade Agreements (1994), 1867 UNTS 14, 33 ILM 1143.

Final report on the Human Rights and the Environment for the Sub-Commission on Prevention of Discrimination and Protection of Minorities (1994), E/CN.4/Sub.2/1994/9.

Fragmentation of International Law: Difficulties Arising from the Diversification and Expansion of International Law: Report of the Study Group of the International Law Commission, Finalised by Chairman M. Koskenniemi ILC, UN Doc. A/CN.4/L.682.

Framework Agreement on the Sava River Basin, opened for signature 3 December 2002 (entered into force 3 December 2002).

General Agreement on Tariffs and Trade, opened for signature 30 October 1947, 55 UNTS 187 (entered into force 1 January 1948).

General Comment No. 15 – The Right to Water (Articles 11 and 12 of the International Covenant on Economic, Social and Cultural Rights, Committee on Economic, Social and Cultural Rights) (2002), 29th Sess, UN Doc E/C.12/2002/11.

Geneva Convention (IV) relative to the Protection of Civilian Persons in Time of War, opened for signature 12 August 1949, 75 UNTS 288 (entered into force 21 October 1950).

Geneva Protocol (III) on Prohibitions or Restrictions on the Use of Mines, Booby-Traps and Other Devices to the 1980 United Nations Convention on Prohibitions or Restrictions on the Use of Certain Conventional Weapons Which May Be Deemed to Be Excessively Injurious or to Have Indiscriminate Effects, opened for signature 10 April 1981, 19 ILM 1529 (entered into force 2 December 1983).

Guidelines for Ships Operating in Polar Waters (2009), IMO Res, 26th Sess, UN Doc A 26/Res.1024. Online. Available HTTP: <http://www.arcticportal.org/images/stories/Arctic_Shipping_ Portlet/A.102426_Guidelines_for_ships_operating_in_polar_waters.pdf> (accessed 11 May 2012).

Hague Convention for the Protection of Cultural Property in the Event of Armed Conflict, opened for signature 14 May 1954, 249 UNTS 240 (entered into force 7 August 1956).

Hong Kong International Convention for the Safe and Environmentally Sound Recycling of Ships, opened for signature 1 September 2009, IMO/SR/CONF/45 (not yet in force).

HRC, *Report of the Special Representative of the Secretary-General on the issue of Human Rights and Transnational Corporations and Other Business Enterprises: Protect, Respect and Remedy: A Framework for Business and Human Rights* (2008), UN Doc A/HRC/8/35.

Human Rights and Transnational Corporations and Other Business Enterprises (2005), UNCHR Res 2005/69; (2011), HRC Res 17/4.

Humanitarian Assistance to Victims of Natural Disasters and Similar Emergency Situations, GA Res 43/131, UN GAOR 43rd Sess, 75th Plen Mtg, UN Doc A/RES/43/131 (1988).

ILO Convention (No. 169) Concerning Indigenous and Tribal Peoples in Independent Countries, opened for signature 27 June 1989, (entered into force 5 September 1991). Online. Available HTTP: <http://www.ilo.org/ilolex/cgi-lex/convde.pl?C169> (accessed 11 May 2012).

Implementation Agreement for Part XI of the UNCLOS, opened for signature 28 July 1994, 1836 UNTS 42 (entered into force 28 July 1996).

Indus Water Treaty, opened for signature 19 September 1960 (entered into force 1 April 1960).

Institutional and Financial Arrangements for International Cooperation (1972), UNGA Res 2997, 27 UN GAOR Supp. No. 30, UN Doc A/8730.

Institutional arrangements to follow up the United Nations Conference on Environment and Development, A/RES/47/191. Online. Available HTTP: <http://www.un.org/documents/ga/res/47/ares47-191.htm> (accessed 11 May 2012).

Inter-Agency Space Debris Coordination Committee Space Debris Mitigation Guidelines (2002), UNCOPUOS, UN Doc A/AC.105/C.1/L.260.

Intergovernmental Panel on Climate Change, *Climate Change 2007: The Physical Science Basis: Contribution of Working Group I to the Fourth Assessment Report of the IPCC*, Cambridge: Cambridge University Press, 2007.

Intergovernmental Panel on Climate Change, *First Assessment Report, Vol. 1: Overview and Policymaker Summaries* (World Meteorological Organization, 1990).

Intergovernmental Panel on Climate Change, *Good Practice Guidance and Uncertainty Management in National Greenhouse Gas Inventories*, Geneva: IPCC, 2000.

Intergovernmental Panel on Climate Change, *IPCC Guidelines of National Greenhouse Gas Inventories*. Online. Available HTTP: <http://www.ipcc-nggip.iges.or.jp/public/2006gl/index.html> (accessed 14 December 2011).

Intergovernmental Panel on Climate Change, *Revised 1996 IPCC Guidelines for National Greenhouse Gas Inventories*, Geneva: IPCC, 1996.

Intergovernmental Panel on Climate Change, *Special Report on Emission Scenarios*. Online. Available HTTP: <http://www.ipcc.ch/ipccreports/sres/emission/index.php?idp=91#4.2.1> (accessed 11 May 2012).

Interim Report of the Special Representative of the Secretary-General on the Issue of Human Rights and Transnational Corporations and other Business Enterprises (2006), UN Doc E/CN.4/2006/97.

International Convention for the Prevention of Pollution from Ships, opened for signature 2 November 1973, 1340 UNTS 61 (entered into force 2 October 1983) as modified by the Protocol of 1978.

International Convention for the Prevention of Pollution of the Sea by Oil, opened for signature 12 May 1954, 327 UNTS 3 (entered into force 2 October 1983).

International Convention for the Safety of Life at Sea, opened for signature 1 November 1974, UNTS 1184 (entered into force 25 May 1980).

International Convention on Civil Liability for Bunker Oil Pollution Damage, opened for signature 1 October 2001, 40 ILM 1493 (entered into force 21 November 2008).

International Convention on Civil Liability for Oil Pollution Damage, opened for signature 29 November 1969, 973 UNTS 3 (entered into force 19 June 1975).

International Convention on Liability and Compensation for Damage in Connection with the Carriage of Hazardous and Noxious Substances by Sea, opened for signature 3 May 1996, 25 ILM 1406 (not yet in force).

International Convention on Maritime Search and Rescue, opened for signature 27 April 1979, [1986] ATS 29 (entered into force 22 June 1985).

International Convention on Oil Pollution, Preparedness, Response and Cooperation, opened for signature 30 November 1990, 30 ILM 733 (entered into force 13 May 1995).

International Convention on Salvage, opened for signature 28 April 1989, UNTS 1953 (entered into force 14 July 1996).

International Convention on the Elimination of All Forms of Racial Discrimination, opened for signature 7 March 1966, 660 UNTS 195 (entered into force 4 January 1969).

International Convention on the Establishment of an International Fund for Compensation for Oil Pollution Damage, opened for signature 18 December 1971 (entered into force 16 October 1978) (as superseded by the *1992 Protocol*; amended by the *2000 Amendments*; supplemented by the *2003 Protocol*, opened for signature 16 May 2003, entered into force 3 March 2005).

International Convention on the Simplification and Harmonization of Customs Procedures, opened for signature 18 May 1973, [1975] ATS 12 (entered into force 25 September 1974) as amended by the *Protocol of Amendment to the International Convention on the Simplification and Harmonization of Customs Procedures of 18 May 1973*, opened for signature 26 June 1999, [2006] ATS 22 (entered into force 3 February 2006).

International Convention Relating to Intervention on the High Seas in Cases of Oil Pollution Casualties, opened for signature 29 November 1969, 9 ILM 25 (entered into force 6 May 1975).

International Cooperation in the Peaceful Uses of Outer Space (2008), GA Res 62/217, UN GAOR, 62nd Sess, UN Doc A/RES/62/217.

International Cooperation in the Peaceful Uses of Outer Space (2010), GA Res 65/97, UN GAOR, 65th Sess, UN Doc A/RES/65/97.

International Cooperation on Humanitarian Assistance in the Field of Natural Disasters, from Relief to Development (2010), GA Res 64/251, UN GAOR, 64th Sess, 69th Plen Mtg, UN Doc A/RES/64/251.

International Covenant on Civil and Political Rights, opened for signature 16 December 1966, 999 UNTS 171 (entered into force 23 March 1976).

International Covenant on Economic, Social and Cultural Rights, opened for signature 16 December 1966, 993 UNTS 3 (entered into force 3 January 1976).

International Plan of Action to Prevent, Deter and Eliminate Illegal, Unreported and Unregulated Fishing (2001), FAO Council, Committee on Fisheries, 24th Sess.

International Treaty on Plant Genetic Resources for Food and Agriculture, opened for Signature 3 November 2001, FAO Res. 3/2003. Online: Available HTTP: <http://www.fao.org/legal/treaties/033t-e.htm> (accessed 18 May 2012).

International Union for the Conservation of Nature and Natural Resources, *Endorsement of the Earth Charter*, Res WCC 3.022 (2004).

Johannesburg Declaration on Sustainable Development (2002), UN Doc A/CONF.199/20, pp. 1–5. Online. Available HTTP: <http://www.un.org/esa/sustdev/documents/WSSD_POI_PD/English/POI_PD.htm> (accessed 23 January 2012).

Johannesburg Plan of Implementation of the World Summit for Sustainable Development (2002), UN Doc A/Conf 199/20.

Joint Convention on the Safety of Spent Fuel and Radioactive Waste Management, 5 September 1997, 36 ILM 1436 (entered into force 18 June 2011).

Kyoto Protocol to the United Nations Framework Convention on Climate Change, opened for signature 11 December 1997, 2303 UNTS 148 (entered into force 16 February 2005).

Lome Convention, opened for signature 15 December 1989, 29 ILM 809 (entered into force 1990).

Mandate of the Special Representative of the Secretary-General on the issue of human rights and transnational corporations and other business enterprises (2008), HRC Res 8/7.

Marrakesh Agreement Establishing the World Trade Organisation, opened for signature 15 April 1994, 1869 UNTS 190 (entered into force 1 January 1995).

Montevideo Programme for the Development and Periodic Review of Environmental Law (1981), Ad Hoc Meeting of Senior Government Officials Expert in Environmental Law, Montevideo, Decision 10/21 of Governing Council of UNEP.

Montreal Protocol on Substances that Deplete the Ozone Layer, opened for signature 16 September 1987, 1522 UNTS 3 (entered into force 1 January 1989).

National Policy Statement on Electricity Transmission and ongoing consideration being given to National Policy Statement on Urban Design. Online. Available HTTP: <http://www.mfe.govt.nz/rma/central/nps/index.html> (accessed 4 November 2011).

Nauru Agreement Concerning the Cooperation in the Management of Fisheries of Common Interest, opened for signature 11 February 1982, 1833 UNTS 3, 21 ILM 1261 (entered into force 4 December 1982).

Need to ensure a healthy environment for the well-being of individuals (1990), UNGA Res 45/94, UN GAOR, 45th Sess, 49Ath Supp, UN Doc A/45/94.

Niue Treaty of Cooperation in Fisheries Surveillance and Law Enforcement in the South Pacific Region, opened for signature 9 July 1992, 32 ILM 136 (entered into force 20 May 1993).

Nonbinding Authoritative Principles for a Global Consensus on the Management, Conservation, and Sustainable Development of all Types of Forests, opened for signature 13 June 1992, 31 ILM 881.

Non-legally binding instrument on all types of forests (2008), GA Res, UN GAOR, A/RES/62/98.

North American Agreement on Environmental Cooperation, Sept. 9 and Sept. 13, 1993, 32 ILM 1480. Online. Available HTTP: <http://www.cec.org/Page.asp?PageID=1226&ContentID=&SiteNodeID=567&BL_ExpandID=154> (accessed 11 May 2012).

North American Free Trade Agreement, opened for signature 17 December 1992, 32 ILM 1480 (entered into force 1 January 1994).

Nusa Dua Declaration (2010), UNEP/GCSS.XI/L.6.

Organisation for Economic Co-Operation and Development, *Recommendation of the Council on Measures Required to Facilitate the Environmental Assessment of Development Assistance Projects and Programmes* (1986), C(86)26/FINAL.

Organization of American States, *American Convention on Human Rights* (1969), OASTS No. 36, 1144 UNTS 123.

Organization of American States, *American Declaration on the Rights and Duties of Man* (1948), OAS Res XXX, OAS Off Rec OEA/Ser.L./V/I.4 Rev.

OSPAR Convention for the Protection of the Marine Environment of the North East Atlantic, opened for signature 22 September 1992, 32 ILM 1069 (entered into force 25 March 1998). Online. Available HTTP: <http://www.ospar.org/html_documents/ospar/html/OSPAR_Convention_e_updated_text_2007.pdf> (accessed 17 February 2012).

Panel Report, *United States – Restrictions on Imports of Tuna*, GATT Doc. DS29/R (1994).

Permanent Sovereignty over Natural Resources (1962), GA Res 1803 (XVII), 17 UN GAOR Supp (no 17) 15, UN Doc A/5217.

Pollution Release and Transfer Registers Protocol, opened for signature 21 May 2003 at an extraordinary meeting of the MOP, Kiev (entered into force 8 October 2008).

Preparatory Committee for the United Nations Conference on Sustainable Development, Second Session, *Objective and Themes of the United Nations Conference on Sustainable Development, Report of the Secretary-General*, UN Doc A/CONF.216/PC/7 (22 December 2010).

Principles Governing the Use by States of Artificial Earth Satellites for International Direct Television Broadcasting (1982), GA Res 37/92, UN GAOR, 37th Sess, 100th Plen Mtg, UN Doc A/RES/37/92.

Principles Relating to Remote Sensing of the Earth from Outer Space (1986), GA Res 41/65, UN GAOR, 41st Sess, 95th Plen Mtg, UN Doc A/RES/41/65.

Principles Relevant to the Use of Nuclear Power Sources in Outer Space (1992), GA Res 47/68, UN GAOR, 47th Sess, 85th Plen Mtg, UN Doc A/RES/47/68.

Progressive Development and Codification of the Rules of International Law Relating to International Watercourses, GA Res 2669 (XXV). Online. Available HTTP: <http://daccess-dds-ny.un.org/doc/RESOLUTION/GEN/NR0/349/34/IMG/NR034934.pdf?OpenElement> (accessed 21 September 2011).

Protection of Global Climate for Present and Future Generations of Mankind (1989), GA Res. 43/53, UN GAOR, 43rd Sess, UN Doc A/RES/43/53.

Protection of the Environment in Times of Armed Conflict (1992), GA Res 47/37, UN GAOR, 47th Sess, 49th Supp, UN Doc A/47/49.

Protocol for Sustainable Development of Lake Victoria Basin, opened for signature 12 December 1985, 801 UNTS 101 (entered into force 6 November 1987).

Protocol for the Prohibition of the Use of Asphyxiating or Other Gases, and of Bacteriological Methods of Warfare, opened for signature 17 June 1925 (entered into force 8 February 1928).

Protocol on Environmental Protection to the Antarctic Treaty, opened for signature 4 October 1991, 30 ILM 1455 (entered into force 15 January 1998).

Protocol on Water and Health to the 1992 Convention on the Protection and Use of Transboundary Watercourses and International Lakes, opened for signature 17 June 1999 (entered into force 4 August 2005).

Protocol to the 1979 Convention on Long-Range Transboundary Air Pollution on Further Reduction of Sulphur Emissions, 14 June 1994, 2030 UNTS 122, UN Doc EB.AIR/R.84.

Protocol to the 1979 LRTAP Convention Concerning the Control of Emissions of Volatile Organic Compounds or their Transboundary Fluxes, opened for signature 18 November 1991, 2001 UNTS 187.

Protocol to the 1979 LRTAP Convention on Long-term Financing of the Cooperative Programme for Monitoring and Evaluation of the Long-range Transmission of Air Pollutants of Air Pollutants in Europe, opened for signature 28 September 1984, 1491 UNTS 167, UN Docs EB.AIR/AC.1/4, Annex and EB.AIR/ CRP.1/Add.4.

Protocol on Environmental Protection to the Antarctic Treaty (Madrid) 4 October 1991, 30 ILM 1461 (entered into force 14 January 1998).

Protocol to the Convention for the Protection of Human Rights and Fundamental Freedoms, opened for signature 20 March 1952, 213 UNTS 262 (entered into force 1 November 1998).

Protocol to the Convention on the Prevention of Marie Pollution by Dumping of Wastes and Other Matter, opened for signature 7 November 1996, 36 ILM 1 (entered into force 24 March 2006).

Protocols Additional to the Geneva Conventions of August 12, 1949 and Relating to the Protection of Victims of International and Non-international Armed Conflicts, 1125 UNTS 3 (Protocol I) and 1125 UNTS 609 (Protocol II) (entered into force 7 December, 1978).

Regulations Respecting the Laws and Customs of War on Land, to the Convention (IV) Respecting the Laws and Customs of War on Land, opened for signature 18 October 1907, UKTS 9, Cd.5030 (entered into force 26 January 1910).

Report of the Group of Eminent Persons, The Impact of Multinational Corporations on the Development Process and on International Relations (1974), UN Doc E/5500/Add.1.

Report of the Secretary General on the Environment and Human Settlements (1999) UNGA Res 53/242, 53rd session, Agenda item 30, A/RES/53/242.

Report of the Special Representative of the Secretary-General on the Issue of Human Rights and Transnational Corporations and Other Business Enterprises, Protect, Respect and Remedy: A Framework for Business and Human Rights (2008), UN Doc A/HRC/8/35.

Report of the Special Representative of the Secretary-General on the Issue of Human Rights and Transnational Corporations and Other Business Enterprises: Mapping International Standards of Responsibility and Accountability for Corporate Acts (2007), UN Doc A/HRC/4/35.

Report of the Special Representative of the Secretary-General on the Issue of Human Rights and Transnational Corporations and Other Business Enterprises, Business and Human Rights: Towards Operationalizing the 'Protect, Respect and Remedy' Framework (2009), UN Doc. A/HRC/11/13.

Report of the United Nations Office of the High Commissioner for Human Rights on the Relationship between Climate Change and Human Rights, A/HRC/10/61, 15 January 2009: Online. Available HTTP: <http://www.ohchr.org/EN/Issues/HRAndClimateChange/Pages/Study.aspx> (accessed 11 May 2012).

Report of the World Summit on Sustainable Development, 26 August – 4 September 2002, A/CONF.199/20. Online. Available HTTP: <http://daccess-dds-ny.un.org/doc/UNDOC/GEN/N02/636/93/PDF/N0263693.pdf?OpenElement> (accessed 26 July 2010).

Report on Indigenous Peoples' Permanent Sovereignty over Natural Resources, Special Rapporteur of the Commission on Human Rights (2004), E/CN.4/Sub.2/2004/30.

Report on the Law of Treaties, *Yearbook of the International Law Commission* (1953), UN Doc. A/CN.4/63.

Rio Declaration on Environment and Development (1992), Report of the UN Conference on Environment and Development, UN Doc A/CONF.151/26 (vol. I), reprinted in 31 ILM 874.

Rome Declaration on World Food Security (1996), FAO, Report of the World Food Summit, WFS96/Rep.

Rome Statute of the International Criminal Court, opened for signature 17 July 1998, 2187 UNTS 90 (entered into force 1 July 2002).

Rotterdam Convention on the Prior Informed Consent Procedure for Certain Hazardous Chemicals and Pesticides in International Trade, opened for signature 10 September 1998, 38 ILM 1 (entered into force 24 February 2004).

'Second Report on the Law of Treaties', *Yearbook of the International Law Commission* (1954), UN Doc. A/CN.4/87 and Corr.1 (1954).

Secretariat on Information Received from Intergovernmental Organisations and Indigenous Peoples, *Review of Developments pertaining to the Promotion and Protection of Human Rights and Fundamental Freedoms of Indigenous People: Indigenous Peoples*, UN Doc E/CN.4/Sub.2/AC.4/1998.

Sixth Report on the Law of the Non-navigational Uses of International Watercourses (1990), S.C. McCaffrey, Special Raporteur, UN Doc A/CN.4/427. Online. Available HTTP: <http://untreaty.un.org/ilc/documentation/english/a_cn4_427.pdf> (accessed 21 September 2011).

Southern Africa Development Community, Revised Protocol on Shared International Watercourses, opened for signature 7 August 2000, 40 ILM 321 (entered into force 22 September 2003).

Statement of the Representative of the Chittagong Hill Tracts Peace Campaign in Report of the Working Group established in accordance with Commission on Human Rights Resolution 1995/32 (1996), UN Doc. E/CN.4/1997/102.

Status of the Environment Fund and Other Sources of Funding of the UNDP, 25th Session of the Governing Council/Global Ministerial Forum (2009), Nairobi, UNEP/GC.25.INF/5.

Statute of the International Court of Justice, adopted in 1920, which later was attached to the Charter of the United Nations, adopted in 1945. The text of the Statute is online. Available HTTP: <http://www.icj-cij.org/documents/index.php?p1=4&p2=2&p3=0> (accessed 10 October 2011).

Statute of the River Uruguay, opened for signature 26 February 1975, 1295 UNTS 340 (entered into force 18 September 1976).

Stockholm Convention on Persistent Organic Pollutants, opened for signature 23 May 2001, 40 ILM 532 (entered into force 17 May 2004).

Strategic Plan for the Implementation of the Basel Convention (to 2010), Online. Available HTTP: <http://archive.basel.int/meetings/cop/cop6/StPlan.pdf> (accessed 9 May 2012).

Strengthening of the Coordination of Emergency Humanitarian Assistance of the United Nations (2010), GA Res 65/133, UN GAOR, 65th Sess, 67th Plen Mtg, UN Doc A/RES/65/133.

Strengthening the Capacity of the United Nations System to Respond to Natural Disasters and Other Disaster Situations (1981), GA Res 36/225, UN GAOR 36th Sess, 103rd Plen Mtg, UN Doc A/RES/36/225.

Tampere Convention on the Provision of Telecommunication Resources for Disaster Mitigation and Relief Operations, opened for signature 18 June 1998, UNTS 2296 (entered into force 8 January 2005).

The Human Right to Water and Sanitation (2010), GA Res 64/292, UN GAOR, 64th Sess. Online. Available HTTP: <http://waterwiki.net/index.php/UN_Human_Rights_Council_Resolution_on_Water_and_Sanitation> (accessed 9 May 2012).

The Law of Transboundary Aquifers (2009), GA Res 63/124, UN GAOR, 63rd Sess. Online. Available HTTP: <http://www.un.org/Docs/journal/asp/ws.asp?m=A/RES/63/124> (accessed 9 May 2012).

Third Report on the Law of Treaties (1958), *Yearbook of the International Law Commission*, 1958, vol. II, pp. 41–45, UN Doc A/CN.4/115.

Towards Global Partnership (2007) UNGA Res 62/211.

Towards Global Partnership (2009) UNGA Res 64/223.

Treaty Banning Nuclear Weapons Tests in the Atmosphere, in Outer Space and Under Water, opened for signature 5 August 1963, 480 UNTS 43 (entered into force 10 October 1963).

Treaty between Great Britain and the United States Relating to Boundary Waters, and Questions Arising between the United States and Canada, Great Britain-United States, opened for signature 11 January 1909, 11 IPE 5704 (entered into force 5 May 1910).

Treaty Establishing the European Atomic Energy Authority, opened for signature 25 March 1957, 298 UNTS 169 (entered into force 1 January 1958) (as amended).

Treaty Establishing the European Economic Community, opened for signature 25 March 1957, 298 UNTS 11 (entered into force 1 January 1958) (as amended).

Treaty on Fisheries between the Governments of Certain Pacific Island States and the Government of the United States, opened for signature 2 April 1987, 26 ILM 1048 (entered into force 15 June 1988).

Treaty on Principles Governing the Activities of States in the Exploration and Use of Outer Space, including the Moon and Other Celestial Bodies, opened for signature 27 January 1967, 610 UNTS 205 (entered into force 10 October 1967).

Treaty on the Non-Proliferation of Nuclear Weapons, opened for signature 1 July 1968, 21 UST 483, 729. UNTS 161 (entered into force 5 March 1970).

UNCTC, 'Business and the UNCED Process', *Activities of Transnational Corporations and Management Division and its Joint Units: Follow-up to the UN Conference on Environment and Development as related to Transnational Corporations* (1993), UN Doc E/C.10/1993/7.

UNEP Governing Council, *Decision SS.XI/1*, UN Doc UNEP GC/SS.XI/1 (26 February 2010).

UNEP Governing Council, *Introductory Statement by the Executive Director* (11 February 1975) UNEP/GC/31, UNEP/GC/31/Add 1, UNEP/GC/31/Add 2, UNEP/GC/31/Add 3.

UNESCO, 'UNESCO's Support for the Earth Charter' in UNESCO *Records of the General Conference 32nd session Paris, 29 September to 17 October 2003*, Paris: UNESCO, 2003.

UNESCO, *Operational Guidelines for the Implementation of the World Heritage Convention*, Paris: UNESCO World Heritage Centre, 2008.

UNFCCC Conference of the Parties Fifteenth session (2009), Copenhagen, 7–18 December 2009, FCCC/CP/2009/L.7.

UNFCCC Secretariat, *Compilation and Synthesis of Fourth National Communications: Executive Summary*, 2007.

UNFCCC Secretariat, *National Greenhouse Gas Inventory Data for the Period 1990–2009* (2011).

UNFCCC, *Decision 2/CP.17, the Cancun Agreements: Outcome of the Work of the Ad Hoc Working Group on Long-Term Cooperative Action under the Convention* (2011).

UNFCCC, *Decision 17/CP.8, Guidelines for the Preparation of National Communications from Parties Not Included in Annex I to the Convention*, 2003.

UNFCCC, *Decision 18/CP.8, Guidelines for the Preparation of National Communications by Parties Included in Annex I to the Convention, Part I: UNFCCC Reporting Guidelines on Annual Inventories*, 2002.

UNFCCC, *Decision 19/CP.8, UNFCCC Guidelines for the Technical Review of Greenhouse Gas Inventories from Parties Included in Annex I to the Convention*, 2002.

UNFCCC, *Decision 2/CP.1, Review of First Communications from the Parties Included in Annex I to the Convention*, 1995.

UNFCCC, *Decision 2/CP.13, Reducing Emissions from Deforestation in Developing Countries: Approaches to Stimulate Action* (2007).

UNFCCC, *Decision 2/CP.15, Copenhagen Accord* (2009).

UNFCCC, *Decision 2/CP.7, Capacity Building in Developing Countries (Non-Annex I Parties)* (2002).

United Nations Convention on the Law of the Sea, opened for signature 10 December 1982, 21 ILM 1261 (entered into force 16 November 1994).

United Nations Convention on the Prohibition of Military or Any Other Hostile Use of Environmental Modification Techniques, opened for signature 18 May 1977, 16 ILM 88 (entered into force 5 October 1978).

United Nations Framework Convention on Climate Change, opened for signature 4 June 1992, 1771 UNTS 107 (entered into force 21 March 1994).

United Nations Declaration on Social Progress and Development (1969), UN GAOR, 24th Sess, UN Doc A/RES/24/2542. Online. Available HTTP: <www.un-documents.net/a24r2542.htm> (accessed 19 December 2011).

United Nations Economic and Social Council, *Open-Ended Working Group on the Review of Arrangements for Consultations with Non-Governmental Organizations* (1994), Report of the Secretary-General, UN Doc E/AC.70/1994/5.

United Nations Economic Commission for Europe, *Aarhus Convention on Access to Information, Public Participation in Decision-Making and Access to Justice in Environmental Matters* (1998), UN Doc ECE/CEP/43.

United Nations Environment Programme (UNEP), *Register of International Treaties* (1989), UN Doc UNEP/GC.15/Inf.2.

United Nations Forum on Forestry, Report of the seventh session, *Non-legally binding instrument on all types of forests*, E/2007/42 E/cn.18/2007/18.

United Nations General Assembly Resolution on the Financial Crises (2011), UNGA Res 63/303, UN GAOR, UN Doc A/RES/63/303.

United Nations Human Rights Council, *Report of the Special Representative of the Secretary-General on the issue of human rights and transnational corporations and other business enterprises* (2011), UN GAOR, 17th Session, Agenda item 3, UN Doc. A/HRC/17/31/Add.3. Online. Available HTTP: <http://www.ohchr.org/Documents/Issues/Business/A.HRC.17.31.Add.3.pdf> (accessed 19 December 2011).

United Nations Millennium Declaration, UNGA Res. 55/2, UN GAOR, 55th Sess, 8th Plen Mtg, UN Doc A/Res/55/2 (2000).

United Nations Special Representative on Human Rights and Business Enterprises, *Guiding Principles on Business and Human Rights to implement the UN Protect, Respect and Remedy Framework* (2011), UN Doc A/HRC/17/31.

United Nations Sub-Commission, *Indigenous Peoples Preparatory Meeting: Comments on the First Revised Text of the Draft Declaration on Rights of Indigenous Peoples*, July 1989, UN Doc E/CN.4/Sub.2/AC.4/1990/3/Add.2.

United States–Chile Free Trade Agreement, United States–Chile, opened for signature 1 January 2004. Online. Available HTTP: <http://www.ustr.gov/trade-agreements/free-trade-agreements/chile-fta/final-text> (accessed 19 March 2012).

Universal Declaration of Human Rights (1948), UNGA Res 217 (AIII), UN GAOR, 3rd Sess, pt 1, at 71, UN Doc A/810.

Universal Declaration on the Rights of Mother Earth (1997), UN Doc FCCC/AWGLCA/2009/17. Online. Available HTTP: <http://motherearthrights.org/2010/04/27/world-peoples-conference-on-climate-change-and-the-rights-of-mother-earth/> (accessed 11 May 2012).

Vienna Convention for the Protection of the Ozone Layer, opened for signature 22 March 1985, TIAS No 11, 1513 UNTS 293 (entered into force 22 September 1988).

Vienna Convention on the Law of Treaties, 23 May 1969, 1155 UNTS 331 (entered into force 27 January 1980).

World Charter for Nature (1982) UNGA Res 37/7 (XXXVII), GAOR, 37th Sess, 22 ILM 455. Online. Available HTTP: <http://www.un.org/documents/ga/res/37/a37r007.htm> (accessed 23 July 2010).

World Commission on Environment and Development, *Our Common Future*, Oxford: Oxford University Press, 1987 (*Brundtland Report*).

WSSD, *Johannesburg Plan of Implementation* (2002), UN Doc A/CONF.199/20, Resolution 2.

WSSD, *Political Declaration* (2002), UN Doc A/CONF.199/20, 2002, Resolution 1.

Legislation

Australia

Aboriginal and Torres Strait Islanders Heritage Protection Act 1984 (Cth)

Acts Interpretation Act 1901 (Cth)

Carbon Credits (Carbon Farming Initiative) Act 2011 (Cth)

Clean Energy Act 2011 (Cth)

Clean Energy Regulator Act 2011 (Cth)

Climate Change Authority Act 2011 (Cth)

Coastal Waters (State Powers) Act 1980 (Cth)

Coastal Waters (State Title) Act 1980 (Cth)

Criminal Code Act 1983 (NT)

Electricity Supply Act 1995 (NSW).

Endangered Species Protection Act 1992 (Cth)

Environment Protection (Impact of Proposals) Act 1974 (Cth).

Environment Protection and Biodiversity Conservation Act 1999 (Cth)

Environment Protection and Biodiversity Conservation Regulations 2000 (Cth)

Fisheries Management Act 1991 (Cth)

Great Barrier Reef Marine Park Act 1975 (Cth)

Lemonthyme and Southern Forests (Commission of Inquiry) Act 1987 (Cth)

Mining Act 1992 (Cth)

National Greenhouse Energy Reporting Act 2007 (Cth)

Product Stewardship (Televisions and Computers) Regulations 2011 (Cth)

Quarantine Act 1908 (Cth)

Seas and Submerged Lands Act 1973 (Cth)

Water Act 2007 (Cth)

Environmental Planning and Assessment Act 1979 (NSW)

Fisheries Management Act 1994 (NSW)

Local Government Act 1993 (NSW)

Marine Parks Act 1997 (NSW)

National Parks and Wildlife Act 1974 (NSW)

Threatened Species Conservation Act 1995 (NSW)

Wilderness Act 1987 (NSW)

National Parks and Wildlife Act 1972 (SA)

Wildlife Act 1975 (Vic).

Nature Conservation Act 1992 (Qld)

Canada

Arctic Waters Pollution Prevention Act 1985 (Canada)

New Zealand

Climate Change Response (Emissions Trading) Amendment Act 2008 (NZ)

Climate Change Response Act 2002 (NZ)

Exclusive Economic Zone and Continental Shelf (Environmental Effects) Bill 2011 (NZ)

Local Government Act 2002 (NZ)

Resource Management (Energy and Climate Change) Amendment Act 2004 (NZ)

Resource Management (Marine Pollution) Regulations 1998 (NZ)

Resource Management (Simplifying and Streamlining) Amendment Act 2009 (NZ)
Resource Management Act 1991 (NZ)
Treaty of Waitangi Act 1975 (NZ)

United States

Alien Torts Claims Act 1789 (US)
Clean Air Act 1990 (US)
Endangered Species Act 1973 (US)
Federal Insecticide, Fungicide, and Rodenticide Act 1947 (US)
Magnuson-Stevens Fishery Conservation and Management Act 2006 (US)

Other countries

Endangered Species (Import and Export) Act 2006 (Singapore)

Various constitutions

Australian Constitution
Constitución Política de la República de Columbia
Constitución Política de la República del Ecuador
Constitución Política de la República Oriental del Uruguay
Constitution Act (NSW)
Constitution Act (NZ)
Constitution of Afghanistan
Constitution of Argentina
Constitution of the Republic of Rwanda
Constitution of the Republic of the Philippines
Kongeriket Norges Grunnlov (Constitution of the Kingdom of Norway)
Kosovo Constitution
Permanent Constitution of the State of Qatar
Philippines Constitution
Ra tta'tamma noon Ha'eng Raatcha anaaja'k Tai (Constitution of Thailand)
South African Constitution
Türkiye Cumhuriyeti Anayasasi (Constitution of the Turkish Republic)

Judicial decisions

Accord Asociación Para la Protección de Medio Ambiente y Educacion Ecologica '*18 de Octubre' v Aguas Argentinas S.A. & otros*, Fed. Appellate Tribunal of La Plata (2003).
Advisory Opinion of the Seabed Disputes Chamber of the International Tribunal for the Law of the Sea (1 February 2011) ('*Seabed Mining Advisory Opinion*'). Online. Available HTTP: <http://www.itlos. org/fileadmin/itlos/documents/cases/case_no_17/adv_op_010211.pdf> (accessed 11 May 2012).
Advisory opinion on Reparation for Injuries Suffered in the Service of the United Nations, Advisory Opinion (1949) ICJ Reports 174.
Advisory Opinion on the Legal Consequences for States of the Continued Presence of South Africa in Namibia (Southwest Africa) Notwithstanding Security Council Resolution 276 (1970), 21 June 1971, ICJ Rep 16, 31.
Advisory Opinion on the Legality of the Threat or Use of Nuclear Weapons (UNGA), opinion of 8 July 1996, 1996, ICJ Rep 95.
Advisory Opinion on the Legality of the Threat or Use of Nuclear Weapons, of 8 July 1996, [1996] ICJ Reports 226.
Advisory Opinion on the Use or Threat of Nuclear Weapons (1996), 35 ILM 809.
Advocate Kedar Bhakta Shrestha v HMG, Dep't of Transp. Mgmt., Writ No. 3109 of 1999 (Nepal), in UN Env't Programme [UNEP], *Compendium of Summaries of Judicial Decisions in Environment-Related Cases* 2005.

Aerial Herbicide Spraying (Ecuador v Colombia), Application of Ecuador, 31 March 2008.

AES Summit Generation Limited and AES-Tisza Erömü Kft. v Republic of Hungary (Award), ('2010') ICSID Case No. ARB/07/22.

Aguas Argentinas, SA, Suez, Sociedad General de Aguas de Barcelona, SA and Vivendi Universal, SA and the Argentine Republic, ICSID Case No. ARB/03/19, Order in response to a petition for transparency and participation as *amicus curiae*, 19 May 2005.

Aguas del Tunari S.A. v Republic of Bolivia (Petition of La Coordinadora para la defensa del Agua Y Vida and others,to the arbitral Tribunal), ICSID Case No. ARB/02/3. Online. Available HTTP: <http://ita.law.uvic.ca/documents/Aguaaboliviapetition.pdf> (accessed 19 December 2011).

Aguas Provinciales de Santa Fe SA and Others v Argentina (17 March 2006), Order in Response to a Petition for Participation as *Amicus Curiae*, ICSID Case No. ARB/03/17.

Air Transport Association of America and Others v Secretary of State for Energy and Climate Change, Case C-366/10, 21 December 2011.

Aldous v Greater Taree City Council [2009] NSWLEC 17.

Anvil Hill Project Watch Association Inc v Minister for the Environment and Water Resources [2007] FCA 1480.

Arco Iris v Instituto Ecuatoriano de Mineria, [Constitutional Court of Ecuador] Judgment No. 054-93-CP, Case No. 224/90.

Ashby v Minister of Immigration [1981] 1 NZLR 222.

Australian Conservation Foundation v La Trobe City Council (2004) 140 LGERA 100.

Banawasi Seva Ashram v State of Uttar Pradesh AIR 1987 SC 374.

Bandhua Mukti Morcha v Union of India, (1984) 3 SCC 161.

Bangladesh Environmental Lawyers Association v Bangladesh, represented by the Secretary, Ministry of Shipping Bangladesh Secretariat, Judgment 5 March 2009 and 17 March 2009.

BGP Properties Pty Limited v Lake Macquarie City Council [2004] NSWLEC 399.

Biwater Gauff (Tanzania) Ltd. v United Republic of Tanzania (Procedural Order No 5), ('2007') ICSID Case No ARB/05/22, International Centre for Settlement of Investment Disputes.

Brown v Forestry of Tasmania (No. 4) (2006) 157 FCR 1.

Case 240/83 *Procureur de la République v Association de Défense des Bruleurs d'huiles usagées* [1983] ECR 531.

Case 26/62 *Algemene Transport- en Expeditie Onderneming van Gend en Loos* v *Nederlandse Belastingsadministratie* [1963] ECR 1.

Case C-157/96 *National Farmers Union* [1998] ECR I-2211.

Case C-2/90 *Commission v Belgium* [1992] ECR I-4431.

Case C-209/98 *Sydhavnens Sten & Grus* [2000] ECR I-3743.

Case C-246/07 *Commission v Sweden (re POPs Convention)*, judgement 20 April 2010.

Case C-266/03 *Commission v Luxembourg (re Inland Waterways Agreement)* [2005] ECR I-4805, para. 60 and Case C-433/03 *Commission v Germany (re Inland Waterways Agreement)* [2005] ECR I-6985.

Case C-284/95 *Safety Hi-Tech Srl. v S. & T. Srl* [1998] ECR I-4301.

Case C-293/97 *Standley* [1999] ECR I-2603.

Case C-371/98 *R v Secretary of State for Environment, Transport and the Regions, ex parte First Corporate Shipping* [2000] ECR-I 9235.

Case Concerning Military and Paramilitary Activities in and against Nicaragua (Nicaragua v United States) [1986] ICJ Rep 14, 128.

Case Concerning Pulp Mills on the River Uruguay (Argentina v Uruguay) ('*Pulp Mills* case'). Online. Available HTTP: <http://www.icj-cij.org/docket/files/135/15877.pdf> (accessed 21 September 2011).

Case Concerning Pulp Mills on the River Uruguay (Argentina v Uruguay) ICJ Reports 2010.

Case concerning the Gabčíkovo-Nagymaros Project (Hungary v Slovakia). Online. Available HTTP: <http://www3.icj-cij.org/docket/files/92/7375.pdf?PHPSESSID=756c3208dcb4692850e8bbf72af34ed6> (accessed 21 September 2011).

Center for Minority Rights Development (Kenya) and Minority Rights Group International on behalf of the Endorois Welfare Council vs. Kenya, African Court for Human and Peoples' Rights, Case No. 276/2003.

Charan Lal Sahu v Union of India, AIR. 1990 S.C. 1480.

Chorzow Factory Case [1927] PCIJ Ser. A, No. 9, 21.

Clean Air Foundation Ltd. & Another v Gov't of H.K., 2007 WL 1824740.

Commonwealth v Tasmania [1983] HCA 21.

Connecticut v American Electric Power Company, Inc.

Corfu Channel (United Kingdom v Albania) (Merits), 1949 ICJ 4.

Corte Constitucional, Chamber of Civil and Agrarian Appeals, 19 November 1997, *Castrillon Vega v Federación Nacional de Algodoneros y Corporacion Autonoma Regional del Cesar (CORPOCESAR) /* Acción de Tutela Case No. 4577 (Colom.).

Costa v ENEL (case 6/64), 1964, ECR 585.

Decision regarding Communication 155/96 (*Social and Economic Rights Action Center/Center for Economic and Social Rights v Nigeria*), Case No. ACHPR/COMM/A044/1 (2002). Online. Available HTTP: <http://www.cesr.org/downloads/AfricanCommissionDecision.pdf> (accessed 30 November 2011).

Decision SC-1/3, adopted at the Conference of the Parties at its first meeting, Stockholm Convention, Rule 5.1(a).

Decision V/13 of COP 5 Convention on Biological Diversity, Doc UNEP/CBD/COP/5/23.

Defensoria de Menores Nro 3 v Poder Ejecutivo Municipal, Agreement 5, Superior Justice Court. Neuquen. March 2, 1999. (Arg.).

Dhungel v Godawari Marble Indus., WP 35/1992 (S.C. Nepal, 31 October 1995).

Dr. Mohiuddin Farooque v Bangladesh, 48 Dir 1996 (S.C. Bangl. App. Div., Civ.).

Environmental Defence Society (Inc) v Auckland Regional Council [2002] NZRMA 492.

Environmental Defence Society v South Pacific Aluminium (No 3) (1981) 1 NZLR 216.

Federal Republic of Germany/Netherlands) Judgment of 20 February 1969, [1969] *ICJ Reports* 3.

Federated Farmers of New Zealand (Inc) v New Zealand Post [1990–92] 3 NZBORR 339.

Flores v S. Peru Copper Corp., 343 F.3d 140, 160 (2d Cir. 2003).

FTR Holding SA, Philip Morris Products S.A. and Abal Hermanos S.A. v Oriental Republic of Uruguay, ICSID Case No. ARB/10/7.

Fundacion Natura v Petroecuador, [Tribunal of Constitutional Guarantees] Resolution No. 230-92-CP (15 October 1992).

Fundepublico v Mayor of Bugalagrande y otros, Interlocutorio #032, (Tulua, 19 December 1991) (Colom.).

Gabčíkovo-Nagymaros Project Case (Hungary/Slovakia) [1997] ICJ Rep 7.

Gabčíkovo-Nagymaros Project (Hungary v Slovakia) (separate opinion of Judge Weeramantry) [1997] ICJ Reports 7.

Georgia v Tennessee Copper Co., 206 US 230, 238 (1907).

Georgia v Tennessee Copper Co., 237 US 474 (1915).

Glamis Gold, Ltd. v The United States of America (Award), ('2009') UNCITRAL (NAFTA).

Gramin Sewa Sanstha v State of Uttar Pradesh, 1986(Supp) SCC 578.

Grand River Enterprises Six Nations, Ltd., et al. v United States of America (Award), ('2011') UNCITRAL (NAFTA).

Gray v Minister for Planning (2006) 152 LGERA 258.

Greenpeace Australia Limited v Redbank Power Company Pty Ltd and Singleton Council (1994) 84 LGERA 143.

Greenpeace New Zealand Inc v Genesis Power Ltd SC 94/2007 [2008] NZSC 112.

Greenpeace New Zealand v Northland Regional Council [2007] NZRMA 87.

Guerra and Others v Italy, 1998-I ECHR, Judgment of 19 February 1998.

Handelskwekerij GJ Bier v Mines de Potasses D'Alsace [1976] ECR 1735.

Hatton v The UK, judgment of 08 July 2003.

Horta v Commonwealth (1994) 181 CLR 183.

In re application of Chevron, 2010 WL 1801526 (SDNY, 20 May, 2010).

Indian Council for Enviro-Legal Action v Union of India, (1996) 3 SCC 212.

Irazu Margarita v Copetro S.A., Camara Civil y Comercial de la Plata, Ruling of 10 May 1993.

ITLOS, No. 11. (*Russian Federation v Australia*): The '*Volga*' Case (23 December 2002). Online. Available HTTP: <http://www.itlos.org/fileadmin/itlos/documents/cases/case_no_11/Judgment.Volga.E.pdf> (accessed 1 May 2012).

José Cuesta Novoa v the Sec'y of Pub. Health of Bogota (Const. Ct. Colom. 17 May, 1995).

Joseph Charles Lemire v Ukraine, (Decision on Jurisdiction and Liability) ('2010') ICSID Case No. ARB/06/18.

Karajan Jalasay Y.A.S.A.S. Samity v State of Gujarat, AIR 1987 SC 532.

Kattan, Alberto et al. v Nat'l Gov't, Juzgado Nacional de la Instancia en lo Contenciosoadministrativo Federal. No. 2, Ruling of 10 May 1983, La Ley, 1983-D, 576.

Khan v Branch Manager of NZ Immigration Services (High Court, Hamilton M 335/94, 11 August 1995).

Kyoto Protocol, *Decision 3/CMP.1, Modalities and Procedures for a Clean Development Mechanism as Defined in Article 12 of the Kyoto Protocol* (30 March 2006).

LG and E v Argentine Republic (Decision on Liability), ('2006') ICSID Case No. ARB/02/1.

Lopez-Ostra v Spain, ECHR (1994), Series A, No. 303C.

Lotus Case, PCIJ (1927) Ser. A. No. 10.

Lujan v Defenders of Wildlife 504 US 555 (1992); *Friends of the Earth v Laidlaw* 120 SCt 693 (2000).

M.C. Mehta v Union of India, A.I.R. (1987) 4 SCC 463 (India).

Mabo v Queensland (no 2) (1992) 175 CLR 1.

María Elena Burgos v Municipality of Campoalegre (Huila) (Const. Ct. Colom. 27 February 1997).

Metalclad Corporation v Mexico, ('2000') ICSID Case No. ARB(AF)97/1 (NAFTA).

Methanex v United States of America, Decision of the Tribunal on Petitions from Third Persons to Intervene as 'Amici Curiae', 15 January 2001.

Metro. Manila Dev. Auth. v Concerned Residents of Manila Bay, G.R. Nos. 171947–8 (SC, 18 December 2008).

Mighty River Power Ltd v Waikato Regional Council (23 and 24 October 2001) ECA 146/2001.

Minister for Arts, Heritage and Environment v Peko-Wallsend (1987) 75 ALR 218.

Minister for Environment and Heritage v Queensland Conservation Council Inc [2004] FCAFC 190.

Minister for Immigration and Ethnic Affairs v Teoh (1995) 183 CLR 273.

Minister for Planning v Walker [2008] NSWCA 224, (2008) 161 LGERA 423.

Ministry of Fisheries v Yoshimura and Urata (Unreported, District Court, Dunedin, O'Driscoll DCJ, 17 January 2005).

Minors Oposa v Factoran Jr., G.R. No. 10183, 224 SCRA 792 (30 July 1993). (Phil.), reprinted in 33 ILM 173, 175 (1994).

Murphyores Inc v Commonwealth (1976) 136 CLR 1.

Native Village of Kivalina v Exxon Mobil Corp., 663 F. Supp. 2d 863 (N.D. Cal. 2009).

New South Wales v Commonwealth (1975) 8 ALR 1.

New Zealand Air Line Pilots' Association v Attorney-General [1997] 3 NZLR 269, 289.

Newcrest Mining (WA) Ltd v Commonwealth (1997) 147 ALR 42.

Ng Ngau Chai v Town Planning Bd., [2007] HCAL 64/2007 (HK).

North Sea Continental Shelf Cases (Federal Republic of Germany v Denmark and Federal Republic of Germany v The Netherlands) (Judgment), Dissenting Opinion of Judge Lachs [1969] ICJ Rep 3, 230.

North Sea Continental Shelf cases (FRG v Denmark; FRG v The Netherlands) (1969) 41 ILR 29.

Nuclear Tests (Australia and New Zealand v France) (1974) ICJ Rep 253.

Olga Tellis v Bombay Municipal Corporation AIR 1986 SC 180.

Pacific Fur Seals Arbitration (Great Britain v United States) [1893] Moore's International Arbitration 755.

Pedro Flores v Codelco, División Salvador, Rol. 2.052 (Sup. Ct. Chile, June 23, 1988) ('*Pedro Flores*'), translated in *Georgetown International Environmental Law Review* 2, 251, p. 253 (1989) (Claudia C. Bohorquez trans.).

Philip Morris Asia Limited v Australia (Written Notification of Claim), UNCITRAL. Online. Available HTTP: <http://italaw.com/documents/PhilipMorrisAsiaLimited_v_Australia_NotificationOf Claim_22Jun2011.pdf> (accessed 19 December 2011).

Piero Foresti, Laura de Carli and others v Republic of South Africa (Letter from the Tribunal to the Parties, from 5 October 2009), ICSID Case No ARB/05/22, (International Centre for Settlement of Investment Disputes).

Prosecutor v Omar Al-Bashir, ICC-02/05-01/09-3. Decision on the Prosecution's Application for a Warrant of Arrest against Omar Hassan Ahmad Al-Bashir, 4 March 2009.

Prosecutor v Tadic, Case No. IT-94-1-I, Decision on Defense Motion for Interlocutory Appeal on Jurisdiction, 11 (2 October 1995), reprinted in 35 ILM *32*, 1996.

Proterra v Ferroaleaciones San Ramon S.A., Judgment No. 1156-90 (Sup. Ct. Peru, 19 November 1992).

Queensland v Commonwealth (1989) 167 CLR 232.

R v Secretary of State for Foreign and Commonwealth Affairs, ex parte World Development Movement [1995] 1 All ER 611.

Request for interpretation of the Judgment of 15 June 1962 in the case concerning the Temple of Preah Vihear (Cambodia v Thailand). Online. Available HTTP: <http://www.icj-cij.org/docket/index. php?p1=3&p2=3&k=46&case=151> (accessed 22 November 2011).

Re Minister for Immigration and Multicultural Affairs, ex parte Lam (2003) 214 CLR 1.

Re Xstrata Coal Queensland Pty Ltd and Ors [2007] QLRT 33.

Richardson v Forestry Commission [1988] HCA 10.

Salini Costruttori S.p.A. and Italstrade S.p.A. v Morocco, (Decision on Jurisdiction), ('2001') ICSID Case No. ARB/00/4.

Sierra Club v Morton 405 US 727 (1972).

Soc. and Econ. Rights Action Ctr. v Nigeria, Commc'n 155/96, African Commission on Human and Peoples' Rights (27 October 2001). Online. Available HTTP: <http://www.cesr.org/downloads/AfricanCommissionDecision.pdf> (accessed 11 May 2012).

Southern Bluefin Tuna Cases (*New Zealand v Japan; Australia v Japan*)(Cases Nos. 3 & 4), ITLOS, Order of 27 August 1999 (provisional measures), reprinted in 38 ILM 1634, 1999.

Southern Bluefin Tuna order (1999) 38 ILM 1624.

Subhash Kumar v State of Bihar, AIR 1991 S.C. 420.

Tavita v Minister of Immigration [1994] 2 NZLR 257.

Telstra Corporation Limited v Hornsby Shire Council [2006] NSWLEC 133.

Temple of Preah Vihear (Cambodia v Thailand) (Merits) [1962] ICJ Rep 6.

Thatcher G., Supreme Court Registrar, *Media Release, Greenpeace New Zealand Inc v Genesis Power Ltd SC 94/2007* [2008] NZSC 112, Supreme Court of NZ, 19 December 2008.

The Mayagna (Sumo) Awas Tingni Community v Nicaragua, Judgment of August 31, 2001, Inter-Am. Ct HR, (Ser. C) No. 79 (2001).

Total S.A. v Argentine Republic (Decision on Liability) ('2010'), ICSID Case No. ARB/04/01.

Trail Smelter Case (United States v Canada), Report of the International Arbitral Awards, the United Nations (2006), VOLUME III pp. 1905–82 at 1965. Online. Available HTTP: <http://untreaty.un.org/cod/riaa/cases/vol_III/1905-1982.pdf> (accessed 22 November 2011).

United Parcel Services of America Inc. v Canada (Decision of the Tribunal on Petitions for Intervention and Participation as Amici Curiae), ('2001') UNCITRAL.

United States – Import Prohibition of Certain Shrimp and Shrimp Products, WTO Doc WT/DS58/R (1998) (report of the Panel), WTO Doc WT/DS58/AB/R (1998) (report of the Appellate Body).

United States v Canada, Ad Hoc International Arbitral Tribunal, *1941 UN Reports of International Arbitral Awards 1911*, 1938.

US District Court for the Northern District of California Oakland Division, *Native Village of Kivalina and City of Kivalina v EXXONMOBIL Corp., et al.*, Case No: C08–1138 SBA.

Vattenfall AB, Vattenfall Europe AG, Vattenfall Europe Generation AG and Co. KG (Sweden and Europe) v The Federal Republic of Germany, (Award) ICSID Case No. ARB/09/6 (ECT).

Wilderness Society Inc v Turnbull, Minister for the Environment and Water Resources (2007) 158 LGERA 134.

Wildlife Preservation Society of Queensland Proserpine/Whitsunday Branch Inc v Minister for the Environment and Heritage (2006) 232 ALR 510.

Yogi Narahari Nath & Others v Honourable Prime Minister Girija Prasad Koirala & Others, 33 NLR 1955 (SC Nepal).

News articles

ABC, US second only to China in illegal wildlife trade: official. Online. Available HTTP: <http://www.abc.net.au/news/2008-06-10/us-second-only-to-china-in-illegal-wildlife-trade/2466308> (accessed 22 November 2011).

BBC News, 'Iran earthquake kills thousands', 26 December 2003. Online. Available HTTP: <http://news.bbc.co.uk/2/hi/3348613.stm> (accessed 3 November 2011).

BBC News, 'Plan for new Maldives homeland', 11 November 2008. Online. Available HTTP: <http://news.bbc.co.uk/go/pr/fr/-/2/hi/south_asia/7719501.stm> (accessed 19 March 2012).

BBC News, 'Russian and US Satellites Collide'. Online. Available HTTP: <http://news.bbc.co.uk/2/hi/science/nature/7885051.stm> (accessed 12 March 2012).

BBC News, 'Thai-Cambodia clashes "damage Preah Vihear temple"'. Online. Available HTTP: <http://www.bbc.co.uk/news/world-asia-pacific-12377626> (accessed 22 November 2011).

'Bering Sea Arbitration', *New York Times*, March 2, 1982. Online. Available HTTP: <http://query.nytimes.com/mem/archive-free/pdf?_r=1&res=9500E3D81631E033A25751C0A9659C94639ED7CF> (accessed 10 June 2010).

Bokhari, A., 'Setback in the water dispute', Dawn.com, 19 September 2011. Online. Available HTTP: <http://www.dawn.com/2011/09/19/comment-and-analysis-setback-in-the-water-dispute.html> (accessed 11 May 2012).

'CDM Registered Projects by Region', (2012). Online. Available HTTP: <http://cdm.unfccc.int/Statistics/Registration/RegisteredProjByRegionPieChart.html> (accessed 19 February 2012).

CITES Secretariat, 'African elephant fund launched at CITES meeting', 19 August 2011. Online. Available HTTP: <http://www.cites.org/eng/news/press/2011/20110819_SC61.php> (accessed 30 November 2011).

'Climate Change and Statelessness: An Overview', submitted by United Nations High Commissioner for Refugees (UNHCR) supported by IOM and NRC to the UNFCCC, 15 May 2009. Online. Available HTTP: <http://www.unhcr.org/refworld/docid/4a2d189d3.html> (accessed 19 March 2012).

'Deadly toxic waste dumping in Côte d'Ivoire clearly a crime – UN environmental agency', United Nations News Centre, 29 September 2006.

Dempsey, J. and Ewing, J., 'Germany, in Reversal, Will Close Nuclear Plants by 2022', New York Times, 30 May 2011.

Evans, G., 'Facing Up to Our Responsibilities.' The Guardian 12 May 2008. Online. Available HTTP: <http://www.guardian.co.uk/commentisfree/2008/may/12/facinguptoourresponsbilities> (accessed 3 November 2011).

'Focus Environment', IAEA Bulletin 49(2). Online. Available HTTP: <http://www.iaea.org/Publications/Magazines/Bulletin/Bull492/49205660610.html> (accessed 19 March 2012).

Fox, M., 'Finding No Fish, Ghanaians Turn to Bushmeat'. Planet Ark, 15 Nov 2004. Online. Available HTTP: <http://www.planetark.com/avantgo/dailynewsstory.cfm?newsid=28148> (accessed 30 September 2011).

Greenpeace International, 'Victory! New Greener Computer Released in India,' 4 February 2010. Online. Available HTTP: <http://www.greenpeace.org/international/en/news/features/victory-green-electronic-02032010/> (accessed 26 November 2011).

'Haiti Quake Aid Pledges Country Donations', Guardian. Online. Available HTTP: <http://www.guardian.co.uk/news/datablog/2010/jan/14/haiti-quake-aid-pledges-country-donations#data> (accessed 18 February 2012).

'Haze: Balls on UN table, Indonesia upset'. Online. Available HTTP: <http://www.jeffooi.com/2006/11/haze_balls_on_un_table_and_ind.php> (accessed 22 November 2011).

International Court of Justice Press Release, 'Costa Rica institutes proceedings against Nicaragua and requests the Court to indicate provisional measures', 19 November 2010. Online. Available HTTP: <http://www.icj-cij.org/docket/files/150/16239.pdf> (accessed 21 September 2011).

International Institute for Sustainable Development (IISD), 'AMCEN Special Session endorses African Common Climate Position', 19 September 2011.

Johnson, T., 'Law of Sea Implications for Gulf Spill', Interview with Caitlyn Antrim, Executive Director, Rule of Law Committee for the Oceans, Council on Foreign Relations, 2 July 2010. Online. Available HTTP: <http://www.cfr.org/publication/22585/law_of_sea_implications_for_gulf_spill.html> (accessed 30 July 2010).

Kahn, J. and Yardley, J., 'As China Roars, Pollution Reaches Deadly Extremes', New York Times, August 26, 2007. Online. Available HTTP: <http://www.nytimes.com/2007/08/26/world/asia/26china.html?pagewanted=print> (accessed 4 June 2010).

Kew, J., 'South Africa, Vietnam Agree to Work to Stem Rhino Poaching', Business Week, 28 September 2011. Online. Available HTTP: <http://www.businessweek.com/news/2011-09-28/south-africa-vietnam-agree-to-work-to-stem-rhino-poaching.html> (accessed 30 November 2011).

OECD, 'Debt Relief is Down: Other ODA Rises Slightly'. Online. Available HTTP: <http://www.oecd.org/document/8/0,3343,en_2649_201185_40381960_1_1_1_1,00.html> (accessed 18 February 2012).

'Pacific Has Some Wins in Tuna Treaty Talks with US', Radio Australia, 19 January 2012. Online transcript. Available HTTP: <http://www.radioaustralia.net.au/pacbeat/stories/201201/s3411645.htm> (accessed 19 January 2012).

Pacific News Center News Release, 'Pacific Regional Maritime Surveillance Effort Seeks to Stop Illegal Fishing', 22 November 2011. Online. Available HTTP: <http://www.pacificnewscenter.com/index.php?option=com_content&view=article&id=18840:pacific-regional-maritime-surveillance-effort-seeks-to-stop-illegal-fishing&catid=45:guam-news&Itemid=156> (accessed 18 January 2012).

'Palau seeks UN World Court opinion on damage caused by greenhouse gases', UN News Centre, 22 September 2011. Online. Available HTTP: <http://www.un.org/apps/news/story.asp?NewsID=39710&Cr=pacific+island&Cr1> (accessed 19 March 2012).

PRI's The World, Cautious Optimism in the Amazon, 28 July 2010. Online. Available HTTP: <http://www.theworld.org/2010/07/28/cautious-optimism-in-the-amazon/> (accessed 30 July 2010).

'PNG Returns to US Tuna Talks', ABC *Asia Pacific News*, 17 January 2012. Online. Available HTTP: <http://abcasiapacificnews.com/stories/201201/3410080.htm> (accessed 18 January 2012).

'Rhino poaching in South Africa reaches all-time high', *WWF*, 12 January 2011. Online. Available HTTP: <http://www.worldwildlife.org/who/media/press/2011/WWFPresitem19251.html> (accessed 30 November 2011).

Sacks, M., 'Supreme Court to Rule on Corporate Personhood for Crimes Against Humanity', *Huffington Post*, 17 October 2011. Online. Available HTTP: <http://www.huffingtonpost.com/2011/10/17/supreme-court_n_1015953.html> (accessed 26 November 2011).

'Seychelles Sink as Climate Change Advances', *National Public Radio*, 22 September 2010.

'Space Debris forces ISS astronauts to evacuate the station'. Online. Available HTTP: <http://thewatchers.adorraeli.com/2011/06/29/space-debris-forces-iss-astronauts-to-evacuate-the-station/> (accessed 26 July 2011).

'The Future We Want – Zero draft of the outcome document of the Rio+20 conference that is planned from 20–21 June 2012'. Online. Available HTTP: <http://www.uncsd2012.org/rio20/index.php?menu=140> (accessed 19 February 2012).

'The WEEE Directive and its Implementation in the EU', updated September 2009. Online. Available HTTP: <http://www.ecsn-uk.org/Legislation/WEEE/2WEEE%20directive%20&%20implementation%20in%20EU%20sept09v2.pdf> (accessed 2 December 2011).

'UN Watercourses Convention Global Initiative'. Online. Available HTTP: <http://www.dundee.ac.uk/water/projects/unwcglobalinitiative/> (accessed 21 September 2011).

Vidal, J. and Adam, D., 'China overtakes US as world's biggest CO2 emitter', *Guardian*, 19 June 2007. Online. Available HTTP: <http://www.guardian.co.uk/environment/2007/jun/19/china.usnews> (accessed 28 July 2010).

Vidal, J., 'China, India, Brazil and South Africa Prepare for Post-Copenhagen Meeting', *Guardian*, 13 January 2010. Online. Available HTTP: <http://www.guardian.co.uk/environment/2010/jan/13/developing-countries-basic-climate-change> (accessed 11 May 2012).

Websites and online documents

A Case Study on Indigenous People, Extractive Industries and the World Bank: Papua New Guinea, Presented at the workshop on 'Indigenous Peoples, the Extractive Industries and the World Bank', Exeter College in the University of Oxford, UK, 14–15 April 2003: <http://www.forestpeoples.org/sites/fpp/files/publication/2010/08/eirinternatwshoppngcaseapr03eng.pdf> (accessed 19 March 2012).

Adaptation Private Sector Initiative: <http://unfccc.int/adaptation/nairobi_work_programme/private_sector_initiative/items/4623.php> (accessed 23 February 2012).

Advancing Forestry Cooperation in International Year of Forest 2011: <http://www.aseansec.org/26733.htm> (accessed 13 January 2012).

Arctic Contaminants Action Program: <http://www.arctic-council.org/index.php/en/acap> (accessed 19 March 2012).

Arctic Council Nuuk developments: <http://www.arctic-council.org/article/2011/5/arctic_council_ministers_sign_agreement>.

Arctic Council, *Ilulissat Declaration* 2, Ilulissat, Greenland, 2008: <http://www.oceanlaw.org/downloads/arctic/Ilulissat_Declaration.pdf> (accessed 9 May 2012).

Arctic Council: <http://www.arctic-council.org/index.php/en/> (accessed 22 November 2011).

ASEAN Action Plan on Wildlife Trade: <http://www.indianjungles.com/280505.htm> (accessed 22 November 2011).

ASEAN Agreement on Transboundary Haze Pollution (Kuala Lumpur, 10 June 2002): < http://www.aseansec.org/pdf/agr_haze.pdf> (accessed 22 November 2011).

ASEAN and ADB, The Problem: Region-Wide Fires and Haze: <http://www.fire.uni-freiburg.de/se_asia/projects/asean.html> (accessed 22 November 2011).

ASEAN Cooperation on Environment: <http://www.aseansec.org/8914.htm> (accessed 22 November 2011).

ASEAN Declaration (Bangkok Declaration), Bangkok, 8 August 1967: <http://www.aseansec.org/1212.htm> (accessed 22 November 2011).

ASEAN Economic Community Blueprint: <http://www.asean.org/21083.pdf> (accessed 22 December 2011).

ASEAN Free Trade Area: <http://www.aseansec.org/12039.htm> (accessed 22 November 2011).

ASEAN Plus Three Cooperation Work Plan: <http://www.aseansec.org/21104.pdf> (accessed 22 November 2011).

ASEAN Political–Security Community Blueprint: <http://www.aseansec.org/5187-18.pdf> (accessed 22 December 2011).

ASEAN Regional Action Plan on Trade in Wild Fauna and Flora, 2005–2010: <http://www.asean.org/17753.pdf> (accessed 22 November 2011).

ASEAN Report of the Eminent Persons Group on the ASEAN Charter: <http://www.aseansec.org/19247.pdf> (accessed 22 November 2011).

ASEAN Report to the World Summit on Sustainable Development, 26 August–4 September 2002: Jakarta ASEAN Secretariat: <http://www.aseansec.org/pdf/WSSD.pdf> (accessed 22 November 2011).

ASEAN Roadmap for the Attainment of the Millennium Development Goals: <http://www.aseansec.org/documents/19th%20summit/MDG-Roadmap.pdf> (accessed 14 January 2012).

ASEAN Socio-Cultural Community Blueprint: <http://www.aseansec.org/5187-19.pdf> (accessed 22 December 2011).

ASEAN Statement on CITES: <http://www.aseansec.org/16470.htm> (accessed 22 November 2011).

ASEAN Vision 2020: <http://www.aseansec.org/1814.htm> (accessed 22 November 2011).

ASEAN, *Agreement on Conservation on Nature and Natural Resources* (1985), Art. 10(d): <http://sedac.ciesin.org/entri/texts/asean.natural.resources.1985.html> (accessed 17 February 2012).

ASEAN, ASEAN Sectoral Ministerial Bodies: <http://www.asean.org/21071.pdf> (accessed 2 February 2012).

ASEAN, Jakarta Resolution on Sustainable Development Jakarta, 30 October 1987: <http://www.aseansec.org/6081.htm> (accessed 2 February 2012).

ASEAN, Manila Declaration on the ASEAN Environment Manila, 30 April 1981: <http://www.aseansec.org/6077.htm> (accessed 2 February 2012).

ASEAN-WEN Support Program Assessment Report: <http://www.aseanwen.org/newscenter_typepopup.php?newsID=31> (accessed 1 September 2008).

Asian Development Banks, Safeguard Policy Statement (2009): <http://beta.adb.org/documents/safeguard-policy-statement> (accessed 18 February 2012).

Asian Nations Launch Regional Plan to Smash Wildlife Smuggling Rings: <http://www.aseansec.org/afp/75p.htm> (accessed 22 November 2011).

Atomic Energy and the Environment, IAEA Fact sheets and FAQs: <http://www.iaea.org/Publications/Factsheets/English/environment.html> (accessed 2 May 2012).

ATS pollution measures: <http://www.ats.aq/e/ep_marine.htm> (accessed 11 May 2012).

Australia's World Heritage: <http://www.environment.gov.au/heritage/about/world/index.html> (accessed 4 November 2011).

Australian Treaties Database: <http://www.dfat.gov.au/treaties/index.html> (accessed 4 November 2011).

Basel Action Network, 'The Basel Ban: A Triumph for Global Environmental Justice', October 2011: <http://www.ban.org/wp-content/uploads/2011/10/BP1_Oct_2011_Final_Letter.pdf> (accessed 23 November 2011).

Berlin Rules on Water Resources: <http://www.cawater-info.net/library/eng/l/berlin_rules.pdf> (accessed 21 September 2011).

Bernstein, S. and Brunnée, J., 'Options for Broader Reform of the Institutional Framework for Sustainable Development (IFSD): Structural, Legal, and Financial Aspects': <http://www.uncsd2012.org/rio20/content/documents/322IFSD%20FIVE%20OPTIONS%20REPORT%20-%20FINAL%20VERSION%201%20NOV%20for%20posting.pdf> (accessed 11 May 2012).

BioOne (2009), *CONDESAN: An Innovative and Multi-institutional Andean Platform in Continuing Evolution*: <http://www.bioone.org/doi/abs/10.1659/mrd.mp013> (accessed 11 May 2012).

Bonn Guidelines on Access to Genetic Resources and Fair and Equitable Sharing of the Benefits Arising out of Their Utilization (2002): <www.cbd.int/doc/publications/cbd-bonn-gdls-en.pdf> (accessed 8 March 2012).

CAFTA-DR Environmental Cooperation Program: <http://www.caftadr-environment.org/top_menu/countries/Regional/A_re_activiy_snapshot_polutant_release.html> (accessed 11 May 2012).

CAN (2007), *Andean Environmental Agenda 2006–2010*, 2nd edition: <http://www.comunidadandina.org/public/libro_54.htm> (accessed 11 May 2012).

Canada Model Foreign Investment Promotion and Protection Agreement (2004): <www.international. gc.ca/trade-agreements-accords-commerciaux/agr-acc/fipa-apie/index.aspx> (accessed 19 December 2011).

Carbon Pollution Reduction Scheme: <http://www.aph.gov.au/About_Parliament/Parliamentary_ Departments/Parliamentary_Library/Browse_by_Topic/ClimateChange/Governance/Domestic/ national/cprs> (accessed 24 April 2012).

CCAD (2009), *Central American Environmental Plan (PARCA 2010–2014)*, p. 16: <http://www.sica.int/ busqueda/busqueda_archivo.aspx?Archivo=pres_47436_1_12032010.pdf> (accessed 11 May 2012).

Charter of the Association of Southeast Asian Nations: <http://www.aseansec.org/21069.pdf> (accessed 22 November 2011).

Chemical Abstracts Service: <www.cas.org> (accessed 10 February 2012).

Clean Energy Legislative Package: <http://www.climatechange.gov.au/en/government/clean-energy-future/legislation.aspx> (accessed 24 April 2012).

Climate Analysis Indicators Tool (CAIT), Version 9.0, Washington, DC: World Resources Institute, 2011: <http://cait.wri.org> (accessed 28 December 2011).

Conference of Arctic Parliamentarians: <http://www.arcticparl.org/> (accessed 11 May 2012).

Congo Basin Forest Fund: <http://www.cbf-fund.org/> (accessed 22 February 2012).

Conservation International, 'Biodiversity Hotspots': <http://www.biodiversityhotspots.org/Pages/ default.aspx> (accessed 30 November 2011).

Convention on Biological Diversity, Thematic Programmes and Cross-Cutting Issues: <www.cbd.int/ programmes/> (accessed 1 July 2010).

Cooperation between the Asian Development Bank and the World Wide Fund for Nature: <http:// beta.adb.org/features/wwf-and-adb-two-heads-are-better-one> (accessed 20 February 2012).

Corpwatch, *Barrick's Dirty Secrets: An Alternative Annual Report* 14 (2007): <http://protestbarrick.net/ downloads/barrick_report.pdf> (accessed 29 December 2011).

Council of the European Union conclusions on Arctic issues, Brussels, 8 December 2009: <http://eur-lex. europa.eu/LexUriServ/LexUriServ.do?uri=COM:2008:0763:FIN:EN:pdf> (accessed 11 May 2012).

Council of the European Union, *Conclusion on a Comprehensive European International Investment Policy*, 3041st Foreign Affairs Council Meeting, Luxemburg, 25 October 2010: <www.consilium.europa. eu/uedocs/cms_data/docs/pressdata/EN/foraff/117328.pdf> (accessed 19 December 2011).

Customary International Humanitarian Law Database for rule 45: <http://www.icrc.org/customary-ihl/eng/docs/v2_rul_rule45> (accessed 23 August 2010).

Department for International Development (UKAID), 'Multilateral Aid Review: Ensuring maximum value for money for UK aid through multilateral organisations', (2011): <http://www.dfid.gov.uk/ Documents/publications1/mar/multilateral_aid_review.pdf> (accessed 22 February 2012).

EarthJustice, *Environmental Rights Report 2008*: <http://www.earthjustice.org/library/reports/2008-environmental-rights-report.pdf> (accessed 11 May 2012).

Environment Law Alliance Worldwide (E-Law), *Valuing Biodiversity in Costa Rica* (July 1999): <http:// www.elaw.org/node/866> (accessed 11 May 2012).

EU@UN website, 'Overview: European Union at the UN': <http://www.eu-un.europa.eu/articles/ articleslist_s88_en.htm> (accessed 11 May 2012).

European Bank for Reconstruction and Development, Environmental and Social Policy Guidelines: <http://www.ebrd.com/downloads/about/sustainability/2008policy.pdf> (accessed 18 February 2012).

European Commission Environment, 'Recast of the WEEE Directive': <http://ec.europa.eu/ environment/waste/weee/index_en.htm> (accessed 26 November 2011).

European Commission, 'Multilateral Environmental Agreements to which the EC is a Contracting Party or a Signatory': <http://ec.europa.eu/environment/international_issues/pdf/agreements_ en.pdf> (accessed 11 May 2012).

European Commission, *A Trade SIA Relating to the Negotiation of a Comprehensive Economic and Trade Agreement (CETA) Between the EU and Canada*, Final Report, June 2011: <http://www.eucanada-sia.org/docs/EU-Canada_SIA_Final_Report.pdf> (accessed 19 December 2011).

European Commission, External Trade, *Handbook for Sustainability Impact Assessment*, 2006: <http:// trade.ec.europa.eu/doclib/docs/2006/march/tradoc_127974.pdf> (accessed 19 December 2011).

European Commission, *Impact Assessment Guidelines*, 15 January 2009, SEC(2009)92: <http:// ec.europa.eu/governance/impact/commission_guidelines/docs/iag_2009_en.pdf> (accessed 19 December 2011).

European Union (2011), *EU External Action – Mid-Term Review and Regional Indicative Programme for 2011–2013*: <http://www.eeas.europa.eu/mercosur/rsp/11_13_mtr_en.pdf> (accessed 11 May 2012).

Executive Order 13141 of November 16, 1999 'Environmental Reviews of Trade Agreements': <http://ceq.hss.doe.gov/nepa/regs/eos/eo13141.html> (accessed 19 December 2011).

Expanding the Vision, 1998 Update, North American Waterfowl Management Plan: <http://www.fws.gov/birdhabitat/NAWMP/files/NAWMP1998.pdf> (accessed 11 May 2012).

Factsheet: ASEAN Heritage Parks: <http://www.news.gov.sg/public/sgpc/en/media_releases/agencies/nparks/press_release/P-20111019–1/AttachmentPar/00/file/Factsheet-%20Asean%20Heritage%20Parks.pdf> (accessed 22 December 2011).

FAO Code of Conduct for Responsible Fisheries, Adopted by the Twenty-eighth Session of the FAO Conference 31 October 1995: <http://www.fao.org/docrep/005/v9878e/v9878e00.htm> (accessed 18 January 2012).

FAO Code, (revised version) adopted by the 123 session of the FAO Council in November 2002, 'Preface': <http://www.fao.org/docrep/005/y4544e/y4544e01.htm#bm1> (accessed 15 November 2011).

FAO Conference Res 6/89 (1989) Appendix E: <http://ufdc.ufl.edu/UF00084642/00001/208j> (accessed 15 November 2011).

FAO legal office, *Sources of International Water Law*, Rome: FAO, 2001: <http://www.fao.org/DOCREP/005/W9549E/w9549e00.htm#Contents> (accessed 21 September 2011).

FAO, 'Guidance to Designated National Authorities on the Operation of the Rotterdam Convention: Introduction and Summary': <http://www.fao.org/docrep/007/y5423e/y5423e02.htm> (accessed 18 November 2011).

FAO, *Contemporary Thinking on Land Reforms* (1998): <http://www.fao.org/sd/ltdirect/ltan0037.htm> (accessed 11 May 2012).

FAO, *Control of Water Pollution from Agriculture*, Chapter 4, 'Pesticides as Water Pollutants': <http://www.fao.org/docrep/w2598e/w2598e07.htm> (accessed 15 November 2011).

FAO, *State of World Fisheries and Aquaculture 2010*: <http://www.fao.org/docrep/013/i1820e/i1820e.pdf> (accessed 18 January, 2012).

Fast Start Finance: <http://www.faststartfinance.org> (accessed 15 September 2011).

Financial Regulations for the World Heritage Fund, Art. IV: <http://whc.unesco.org/en/financialregulations/> (accessed 16 February 2012).

Food and Agriculture Organisation, *National Forest Programmes*: <http://www.fao.org/forestry/nfp/en/> (accessed 14 December 2011).

Food and Agriculture Organization (FAO), *International Code of Conduct on the Distribution and Use of Pesticides* (FAO Code), Art. 1(1): <http://www.fao.org/docrep/x5562E/X5562e0a.htm> (accessed 15 November 2011).

Food and Agriculture Organization of the United Nations (FAO), 'Famine spreads further in Somalia': <http://www.fao.org/news/story/en/item/89101/icode/> (accessed 30 November 2011).

Food and Agriculture Organization, (2011) 'Reforming Forest Tenure: Issues, Principles and Process', *FAO Forestry Paper* 165: <http://www.fao.org/docrep/014/i2185e/i2185e00.pdf> (accessed 14 December 2011).

Foreign Affairs and International Trade Canada, *Canada's Environmental Assessment Framework for Trade Negotiations*: <http://www.international.gc.ca/trade-agreements-accords-commerciaux/env/env-ea.aspx?lang=enandmenu_id=2andview=d> (accessed 8 March 2012).

Foreign Affairs and International Trade Canada, *Framework for Conducting Environmental Assessments of Trade Negotiations*, February 2001: <http://www.international.gc.ca/trade-agreements-accords-commerciaux/ds/Environment.aspx?lang=enandview=d> (accessed 19 December 2011).

Foreign Affairs and International Trade Canada, *Handbook for Conducting Environmental Assessments of Trade Negotiations*, March 2008: <http://www.international.gc.ca/enviro/assets/pdfs/EnvironA/overview/handbook-e.pdf> (accessed 19 December 2011).

Fourth Report on the Law of the Non-navigational Uses of International Watercourses (1998), S.C. McCaffrey, Special Rapporteur, UN Doc A/CN.4/412, p. 239: <http://untreaty.un.org/ilc/documentation/english/a_cn4_412.pdf> (accessed 21 September 2011).

French Embassy, *Burma – Cyclone Nargis*: <http://www.ambafrance-uk.org/Bernard-Kouchner-on-Burma-disaster.html> (accessed 3 November 2011).

Freshwater Reform: <http://www.mfe.govt.nz/issues/water/freshwater/fresh-start-for-fresh-water/index.html> (accessed 4 November 2011).

Global Biodiversity Outlook 3: <gbo3.cbd.int/> (accessed 8 March 2012).

Global Environment Facility, 'Evaluation of Incremental Costs Assessment', GEF/ME/C.30/2, 2 November 2006: <http://www.thegef.org/gef/sites/thegef.org/files/documents/GEFME-C30-2-IncrementalCostEvaluation110206.pdf> (accessed 13 February 2012).

Global Environment Facility, 'Operational Guidelines for the Application of the Incremental Cost Principle', 14 May 2007, GEF 31.1/12: <http://www.thegef.org/gef/policy/incremental_costs> (accessed 13 February 2012).

Global Environment Facility, 'Project Cycle: An Update', GEF/C.22/Inf.9 5 November 2003, para. 10: <http://www.thegef.org/gef/sites/thegef.org/files/documents/Loc...Update__FINAL__Nov_5_2003.pdf> (accessed 13 February 2012).

Global Environment Facility, 'Report on the Incremental Costs', GEF/C.14/5, 5 November 1999: <http://www.thegef.org/gef/sites/thegef.org/files/documents/gef_c14_5.pdf> (accessed 13 February 2012): <http://www.thegef.org/gef/policy/incremental_costs> (accessed 13 February 2012).

Global Environment Facility, Annual Report 2010: <http://www.thegef.org/gef/sites/thegef.org/files/publication/WBAnnualReportText.revised.pdf> (accessed 16 February 2012).

Global Environment Facility, *GEF Replenishments*: <www.thegef.org/gef/replenishment> (accessed 12 December 2011).

Global Environment Facility: 'Project Types and Programmatic Approach', <http://www.thegef.org/gef/project_types> (accessed 12 February 2012).

Global Environmental Facility, *What is the GEF?*: <www.thegef.org/gef/whatisgef> (accessed 12 December 2011).

GRAIN, 'Biodiversity Rights Legislation (BRL)': <www.grain.org/brl/> (accessed 8 March 2012).

Greenpeace International, 'Toxic Tech: Not in our Backyard': <http://www.greenpeace.org/international/Global/international/planet-2/report/2008/2/not-in-our-backyard.pdf> (accessed 15 November 2011).

Greenpeace International, 'Where Does E-waste Go?': <http://www.greenpeace.org/usa/en/campaigns/toxics/hi-tech-highly-toxic/e-waste-goes/> (accessed 15 November 2011).

High Seas Task Force, 'Closing the Net: Stopping Illegal Fishing on the High Seas', Final Report of the Ministerially-led Task Force on IUU Fishing on the High Seas, March 2006: <http://www.oecd.org/dataoecd/2/28/39375276.pdf> (accessed 25 January 2012).

Human Rights Committee, the Committee on the Elimination of Racial Discrimination, the Committee against Torture or the Committee on the Elimination of Discrimination against Women; Office of the United Nations High Commissioner for Human Rights, *Human Rights Treaty Bodies – Individual Communications*: <http://www2.ohchr.org/english/bodies/petitions/individual.htm> (accessed 5 September 2011).

Humanitarian Accountability Partnership – International, *The 2010 HAP Standard in Accountability and Quality Management*: <http://www.hapinternational.org/projects/standard/hap-2010-standard.aspx> (accessed 2 September 2011).

IAEA Bulletin (1973), *10: Test Ban Treaty*, 5 Aug. 1963 pp. 3, 8, 17 (series of articles commemorating the 10th anniversary of the signing of the Treaty and containing a list of ratifying states from 1963): <http://www.iaea.org/Publications/Magazines/Bulletin/Bull154/15403500322.pdf> (accessed 31 October 2011).

'Ibrahim Index 2010', *The Mo Ibrahim Foundation*: <http://www.moibrahimfoundation.org/en/section/the-ibrahim-index> (accessed 11 May 2012).

ICCAT, 'Supplemental Recommendations by ICCAT Concerning the Western Atlantic Bluefin Tuna Rebuilding Program, 10–03 [BFT], 2010: <http://www.iccat.int/Documents/Recs/compendiopdf-e/2010-03-e.pdf> (accessed 25 January 2012).

ICRC, *International Humanitarian Law – Treaties & Documents, 1949 Conventions & Additional Protocols*: <http://www.icrc.org/ihl.nsf/CONVPRES?OpenView> (accessed 29 February 2012).

ICTY, Office of the Prosecutor, *Final Report to the Prosecutor by the Committee Established to Review the NATO Bombing Campaign against the Federal Republic of Yugoslavia*, Prosecutor's Report: <http://www.icty.org/x/file/About/OTP/otp_report_nato_bombing_en.pdf> (accessed 4 August 2010).

IEA Database Search Results, 'Multilateral Environmental Agreements for the period from 2005 to 2011 (inclusive)': <http://iea.uoregon.edu/> (accessed 11 May 2012).

IFC, Performance Standards on Social and Environmental Sustainability, adopted by the IFC Board in 2011, with implementation starting on 1 January 2012: <http://www.ifc.org/ifcext/policyreview.nsf/Content/2012-Edition#PerformanceStandards> (accessed 11 May 2012).

ILA Berlin Conference 2004 – Water Resources Committee Report Dissenting Opinion, 9 August 2004: <http://www.internationalwaterlaw.org/documents/intldocs/ila_berlin_rules_dissent.html> (accessed 21 September 2011).

ILC, Analytical Guide: International Liability for Injurious Consequences arising out of Acts not Prohibited by International Law: <http://untreaty.un.org/ilc/guide/9.htm> (accessed 11 May 2012).

ILC, *Summary: International Liability for Injurious Consequences arising out of Acts not Prohibited by International Law*: <http://untreaty.un.org/ilc/summaries/9.htm> (accessed 11 May 2012).

ILC, *Summary: Prevention of transboundary damage from hazardous activities*: <http://untreaty.un.org/ilc/summaries/9_7.htm> (accessed 11 May 2012).

IMO Guidelines for Ships Operating in Arctic Ice-covered Waters: <http://www.fni.no/doc&pdf/FNI-R0207.pdf> (accessed 11 May 2012).

Indicative List of Incremental Costs in Annex VIII of the report of the Fourth Meeting of the Parties: <http://ozone.unep.org/Publications/MP_Handbook/Section_3.6_Annexes_The_Multilateral_Fund/Indicative_list.shtml> (accessed 16 February 2012).

Indigenous Portal, *Ilulissat Declaration from the Arctic Ocean Conference*, 24 June 2008: <http://www.indigenousportal.com/Politics/The-Ilulissat-declaration-from-the-Artic-Ocean-Conference.html> (accessed 11 May 2012).

Information on progress towards a mandatory polar code: <http://www.imo.org/mediacentre/meetingsummaries/de/pages/de-54th-session.aspx> (accessed 11 May 2012).

Initial Environmental Assessment Report of the Canada-Andean Community Free Trade Negotiations: <http://www.international.gc.ca/trade-agreements-accords-commerciaux/agr-acc/andean-andin/ea-toc.aspx?view=d> (accessed 16 May 2012).

Initial Environmental Assessment Report of the Canada-Panama Free Trade Negotiations: <http://www.international.gc.ca/trade-agreements-accords-commerciaux/agr-acc/ea-panama.aspx?lang=engandview=d> (accessed 19 December 2011).

Instrument for the Establishment of the Restructured Global Environment Facility, October 2011: <http://www.thegef.org/gef/sites/thegef.org/files/publication/GEF_Instrument_Oct2011_final_0.pdf> (accessed 22 February 2012).

Instrument with the Principles of Cooperation between Implementing Agencies, Global Environment Facility information report, 'About the Global Environment Facility 2009': <http://www.thegef.org/gef/> (accessed 10 September 2011).

Inter-American Forum on Environmental Law (FIDA), *Environmental Legislation*: <http://www.oas.org/dsd/FIDA/laws/database.htm> (accessed 11 May 2012).

Intergovernmental Panel on Climate Change, (2003) 'Good Practice Guidance for Land-Use, Land-Use Change and Forestry': <http://www.ipcc-nggip.iges.or.jp/public/gpglulucf/gpglulucf_contents.html> (accessed 14 December 2011).

International Centre for Integrated Mountain Development(ICIMOD), 'Toward an Access and Benefit Sharing Framework Agreement for the Genetic Resources and Traditional Knowledge of the Hindu Kush Himalayan Region', 2010: <www.icimod.org/abs> (accessed 8 March 2012).

International Law Commission (ILC), Introduction: Origin and background of the development and codification of international law: <http://untreaty.un.org/ilc/ilcintro.htm> (accessed 11 May 2012).

International Law Commission, *Summary: International Liability for Injurious Consequences arising out of Acts not Prohibited by International Law*: <http://untreaty.un.org/ilc/summaries/9.htm> (accessed 11 May 2012).

International Maritime Organization, *Background*. Online. HTTP: <http://www.imo.org/OurWork/Environment/PollutionPrevention/OilPollution/Pages/Background.aspx#2> (accessed 29 February 2012).

International Maritime Organization, *List of IMO Conventions*: <http://www.imo.org/About/Conventions/ListOfConventions/Pages/Default.aspx> (accessed 29 February 2012).

International Maritime Organization, *Statements by Delegations and Observers at the Closing Session of the Conference, Friday, 15 May 2009*: <http://www.sjofartsverket.se/pages/19514/sr-conf-inf8.pdf> (accessed 15 October 2011).

International Oil Pollution Compensation Funds: <http://www.iopcfund.org/> (accessed 29 February 2012).

International Polar Year 2007–2009: <http://www.ipy.org/> (accessed 11 May 2012).

IOTC, Resolution 10/01 – Timeclosure for Long-Liners in February 2011, IOTC Circular 2011/03, 12 January 2011: <http://www.iotc.org/files/circulars/2011/03-11%5BE%5D.pdf> (accessed 25 January 2012).

IUCN, Conservation and Sustainable Use of the Mesoamerican Barrier Reef System Project: <http://www.tbpa.net/page.php?ndx=66> (accessed 11 May 2012).

Johnston, E., 'Large-scale ADB projects draw criticism', *Japan Times*, 8 May 2007: <http://www.japantimes.co.jp/text/nn20070508a5.html> (accessed 20 February 2012).

Joint UNEP-OHCHR Expert Seminar on Human Rights and the Environment, Geneva, Switzerland, 14–16 January 2002, *Background Paper No. 1: Human Rights and Environment Issues in Multilateral Treaties Adopted Between 1991 and 2001* (prepared by D. Shelton): <http://www2.ohchr.org/english/issues/environment/environ/bp1.htm> (accessed 7 July 2011).

Lieber Code – Instructions for the Government of Armies of the United States in the Field, 1863: <http://www.icrc.org/ihl.nsf/FULL/110?OpenDocument> (accessed 29 February 2012).

London Guidelines (amended 1989): <http://www.chem.unep.ch/ethics/english/longuien.htm> (accessed 23 November 2011).

MEAs in Force: <http://www.mfe.govt.nz/laws/meas/meas-in-force.html> (accessed 4 November 2011).

Milan Declaration of the Sixth International Indigenous Peoples Forum on Climate Change 2003, UNSW Indigenous Law Centre (2011): <http://www.ilc.unsw.edu.au/sites/ilc.unsw.edu.au/files/mdocs/milan%20declaration.pdf> (accessed 29 December 2011).

Millennium Ecosystem Assessment, *Ecosystems and Human Well Being*, 2005: <www.millenniumassessment.org> (accessed 20 July 2010).

Nagoya Protocol on Access to Genetic Resources and the Fair and Equitable Sharing of Benefits Arising from Their Utilization: <www.cbd.int/abs/text/> (accessed 16 February 2012).

Nairobi–Helsinki Outcome, Second Meeting of the Consultative Group of Ministers or High Representatives on International Environmental Governance, Espoo, Finland, 21–23 November 2010: <http://www.unep.org/environmentalgovernance/Portals/8/documents/Events/Nairobi Helsinkifinaloutcomeedited.pdf> (accessed 11 May 2012).

NASA Policy Directive NPD 8020.7G, *Biological Contamination Control for Outbound and Inbound Planetary Spacecraft*, Revalidated 25 November 2008: <http://nodis3.gsfc.nasa.gov/npg_img/N_PD_8020_007G_/N_PD_8020_007G__main.pdf> (accessed 15 September 2011).

NASA Procedural Requirements for Limiting Orbital Debris, NPR 8715.6A. Effective Date 14 May 2009, Expiration Date 14 May 2014: <http://nodis3.gsfc.nasa.gov/npg_img/N_PR_8715_006A_/N_PR_8715_006A_.pdf> (accessed 15 September 2011).

National Forest Programme Facility (FAO), *Understanding National Forest Programmes: Guidance for Practitioners (2006)*: <http://www.fao.org/forestry/13533-0d0e0d879a9f3efc6ca9f847cd6ebb654.pdf> (accessed 14 December 2011).

National Policy Statement (NPS) for Freshwater Management 2011: <http://www.mfe.govt.nz/rma/central/nps/freshwater-management.html> (accessed 4 November 2011).

New England Governors' Conference, Inc., 'NEG/ECP Climate Change Program': <http://negc.org/main/?do=page&id=39> (accessed 11 May 2012).

NOAA/Hazardous Materials Response and Assessment Division, *Oil Spill Case Histories*, Seattle, 1992: <http://response.restoration.noaa.gov/sites/default/files/Oil_Spill_Case_Histories.pdf> (accessed 9 May 2012).

North American Waterfowl Management Plan: Strengthening the Biological Foundation, 2004 Implementation Framework: <http://www.fws.gov/birdhabitat/NAWMP/files/Implementation Framework.pdf> (accessed 11 May 2012).

North Atlantic Coast Guard Forum: <http://www.ccg-gcc.gc.ca/e0003559> (accessed 11 May 2012).

OAS Foreign Trade Information System (SICE) Canada: Trade Agreements: <http://www.sice.oas.org/ctyindex/CAN/CANagreements_e.asp> (accessed 11 May 2012).

OAS Foreign Trade Information System (SICE) United States of America: Trade Agreements: <http://www.sice.oas.org/ctyindex/USA/USAagreements_e.asp> (accessed 11 May 2012).

OCHA/IDMC, *Monitoring disaster displacement in the context of climate change – Findings of a study by the United Nations Office for the Coordination of Humanitarian Affairs and the Internal Displacement Monitoring Centre*, 2009: <http://www.internal-displacement.org/8025708F004CFA06/(httpPublications)/451D224B41C04246C12576390031FF63?OpenDocument> (accessed 11 May 2012).

OECD, 'Pollution Prevention and Control Extended Producer Responsibility in the OECD Area Phase 1 Report, Legal and Administrative Approaches in Member Countries and Policy Options for EPR Programs', OECD, 1996: <http://www.oecd.org/officialdocuments/publicdisplaydocument pdf/?cote=OCDE/GD(96)48&docLanguage=En> (accessed 28 November 2011).

OECD ODA report on 2010 results: <http://www.oecd.org/document/10/0,3746,en_2649_33721_ 44774218_1_1_1_1,00.html> (accessed 18 February 2012).

OECD Secretariat estimates on expected ODA: <http://www.oecd.org/dataoecd/17/12/44981982. pdf> (accessed 18 February 2012).

OECD, 'Environmental Outlook for the Chemicals Industry', OECD 2001, p. 19: <www.oecd.org/ dataoecd/7/45/2375538.pdf> (accessed 15 November 2011).

OECD, Committee on International Investment and Multinational Enterprises, *Foreign Direct Investment for Development: Maximising Benefits, Minimising Costs*, Paris: OECD, 2002: <http://www.oecd.org/ dataoecd/47/51/1959815.pdf> (accessed 19 December 2011).

OECD, *Council Recommendation Concerning the Application of the Polluter-Pays Principle to Accidental Pollution* (1989), C(89)88/Final: <http://acts.oecd.org/Instruments/ShowInstrumentView.aspx?In strumentID=38&InstrumentPID=35&Lang=en&Book=False> (accessed 17 February 2012).

OECD, *Council Recommendation on Guiding Principles Concerning the International Economic Aspects of Environmental Policies of the Organisation for Economic Co-operation and Development* (1972), C(72) 128: <http://acts.oecd.org/Instruments/ShowInstrumentView.aspx?InstrumentID=4&Lang=en&Boo k=False> (accessed 27 April 2012).

OECD, *Council Recommendation on the Implementation of the Polluter-Pays Principle* (1974), C(74) 223: <http://acts.oecd.org/Instruments/ShowInstrumentView.aspx?InstrumentID=11&InstrumentPI D=9&Lang=en&Book=False> (accessed 17 February 2012).

OECD, *OECD Guidelines for Multinational Enterprises*: <www.oecd.org/daf/investment/guidelines> (accessed 19 December 2011).

Oil Spill Solutions, *Tanker Spills Show Declining Trend*: <www.oilspillsolutions.org/majorspills.htm> (accessed 29 February 2012).

Organisation for Economic Co-operation and Development (OECD) report on 2010 development aid results: <http://www.oecd.org/document/10/0,3746,en_2649_33721_44774218_1_1_1_1,00. html> (accessed 18 February 2012).

Organization of American States: <http://www.oas.org/dil/indigenous_peoples.htm> (accessed 22 November 2011).

OSPAR Decision 9/3 on the Disposal of Disused Offshore Installations: <http://www.ospar.org/documents/ DBASE/DECRECS/Decisions/od98-03e.doc> (accessed 11 May 2012).

Petition to the Inter American Commission on Human Rights Seeking Relief from Violations Resulting from Global Warming Caused by Acts and Omissions of the U.S. 1 (7 December 2005): <http:// inuitcircumpolar.com/files/uploads/icc-files/FINALPetitionICC.pdf> (accessed 11 May 2012).

Pew Environmental Group, *Global Ocean Legacy*, 2011: <http://www.pewenvironment.org/campaigns/ global-ocean-legacy/id/8589941025/> (accessed 18 January 2012).

Planetary Protection Provisions for Robotic Extraterrestrial Missions, 20 April 2011: <http://nodis3.gsfc.nasa. gov/displayDir.cfm?t–PR&c=8020&s=12D> (accessed 15 September 2011).

Preparatory Committee for the United Nations Conference on Sustainable Development, First session, 17–19 May 2010, A/CONF.216/PC/2: <http://daccess-dds-ny.un.org/doc/UNDOC/GEN/ N10/302/56/PDF/N1030256.pdf?OpenElement> (accessed 30 July 2010).

Press Release, Inter-American Commission on Human Rights, IACHR Announces Webcast of Public Hearings of the 127th Regular Period of Sessions, No 8/07 (Feb. 26, 2007): <http://www.cidh. org/Comunicados/English/2007/8.07eng.htm> (accessed 21 January 2012).

Proposed National Policy Statement on Indigenous Biodiversity (2011): http://www.mfe.govt.nz/ publications/biodiversity/indigenous-biodiversity/index.html (accessed 4 November 2011).

Protecting New Zealand's Exclusive Economic Zone: <http://www.mfe.govt.nz/issues/oceans/ current-work/index.html> (accessed 4 November 2011).

Public Statement on the International Investment Regime, 31 August 2010: <http://www.osgoode. yorku.ca/public_statement> (accessed 19 December 2011).

Reducing Climate Change Impact: <http://www.iaea.org/newscenter/news/2009/climatechange. html> (accessed 11 May 2012).

Rights and Democracy, *Human Right Impact Assessments for Foreign Investment Projects: Learning from Community Experience in the Philippines, Tibet, the Democratic Republic of Congo, Argentina, and Peru*,

Montreal: Rights and Democracy, 2007: <www.dd-rd.ca/site/_PDF/publications/globalization/hria/full%20report_may_2007.pdf> (accessed 19 December 2011).

Rotterdam Convention Alliance (ROCA), ROCA Position Paper in Preparation of the Rotterdam Convention COP 5: <http://www.cela.ca/sites/cela.ca/files/Position%20paper%20ROCA9-2%20%28June%202011%29_0.pdf> (accessed 20 November 2011).

Secretariat of the UNCCD and the Common Fund for Commodities, (2009) *African Drylands Commodity Atlas*: <http://www.unccd.int/Lists/SiteDocumentLibrary/Publications/Atlas%20web.pdf> (accessed 15 May 2012).

Sharpiro, M., Report on the Amount of Funding that Flows to China under CDM: <http://e360.yale.edu/feature/perverse_co2_payments_send_flood_of_money_to_china/2350/> (accessed 19 February 2012).

Singapore Declaration on the ASEAN Charter: <http://www.aseansec.org/21233> (accessed 22 November 2011).

Singapore's Harsh Penalties Set Regional Precedent against Wildlife Smuggling: <http://www.asianturtlenetwork.org/library/news_articles/Singapore_Harsh_Penalties_Set_Regional_Precedent_Against_Wildlife_Smuggling.html> (accessed 22 November 2011).

Single European Act regarding the environment: <http://ec.europa.eu/economy_finance/emu_history/documents/treaties/singleuropeanact.pdf> (accessed 17 February 2012).

South African Report to CITES Secretariat (2011): <http://www.cites.org/common/com/SC/61/E61i-02.pdf> (accessed 30 November 2011).

Status of Agreement on Port State Measures to Prevent, Deter and Eliminate Illegal, Unreported and Unregulated Fishing: <http://www.fao.org/Legal/treaties/037s-e.htm> (accessed 19 January 2012).

Status of multilateral treaties deposited with the Secretary-General: <http://treaties.un.org/Pages/ViewDetails.aspx?src=UNTSONLINE&tabid=2&mtdsg_no=XXVII-12&chapter=27&lang=en#Participants> (accessed 21 September 2011).

Tamaqua Borough Corporate Waste and Local Control Ordinance of 1 May 2007 (Pennsylvania, USA): <http://www.celdf.org/article.php?id=439> (accessed 15 May 2012).

Tenth Meeting of the Conference of the Parties to the Basel Convention: <http://www.basel.int/COP10/tabid/1571/Default.aspx> (accessed 8 October 2011).

The Munden Project (2011), 'REDD and Forest Carbon: Market Based Critique and Recommendations': <http://www.rightsandresources.org/documents/files/doc_2215.pdf> (accessed 14 December 2011).

The Sphere Project: <http://www.sphereproject.org/> (accessed 2 September 2011).

UN Conference on Sustainable Development, *The Future We Want*, 2012: <http://www.uncsd2012.org/rio20/index.php?menu=17> (accessed 11 May 2012).

UN Division for Sustainable Development, *Partnerships for Sustainable Development*: <http://www.un.org/esa/dsd/dsd_aofw_par/par_index.shtml> (accessed 28 July 2010).

UN ECE, *Geneva Strategy and Framework for Monitoring Compliance with Agreements on Transboundary Waters* (2011), UN Doc MP.WAT/2000/5: <www.africanwater.org/Documents/compliance_strategy.doc> (accessed 21 September 2011).

UN Global Compact Office, 'A response from the Global Compact Office', 2: <http://www.unglobalcompact.org/docs/news_events/9.1_news_archives/2011_03_24/gco_jiu_response.pdf> (accessed 7 January 2012).

UN Global Compact Office, 'Frequently Asked Questions on the Integrity Measures': <http://www.unglobalcompact.org/docs/news_events/9.1_news_archives/2009_08_21/Integrity_Measures.FAQ.pdf> (accessed 7 January 2012).

UN Global Compact Office, *United Nations Guide to the Global Compact: A Practical Understanding of the Vision and the Nine Principles*, p. 4 ('United Nations Guide to the Global Compact'): <http://www.cosco.com/en/pic/research/7573381391844063.pdf> (accessed 9 May 2012).

UN Global Compact, *The Ten Principles*: <http://www.unglobalcompact.org/AboutTheGC/TheTenPrinciples/index.html> (accessed 7 January 2012).

UN Millennium Development Goals: <http://www.unicef.org/statistics/index_24304.html> (accessed 2 February 2012).

UN News Centre, 'Address as prepared for delivery to the Davos World Economic Forum', 2008: <www.un.org/apps/news/infocus/sgspeeches/search_full.asp?statID=177> (accessed 21 September 2011).

UN Permanent Forum on Indigenous Issues: <http://www.un.org/esa/socdev/unpfii/> (accessed 22 November 2011).

UNCCD, 'Action Programmes': <http://www.unccd.int/en/regional-access/Pages/regionalprofiles. aspx?region=Africa&ctx=pro> (accessed 15 May 2012).

UNCCD, 'UN Maps New Ways to Mainstream Desertification', 12 May, 2005: <http://archive. unccd.int/publicinfo/pressrel/showpressrel.php?pr=press12_05_05> (accessed 15 May 2011).

UNCCD, *Fact Sheet: Combating Desertification in Africa*: <http://www.unccd.int/Lists/SiteDocumentLibrary/ Publications/Fact_sheet_11eng.pdf> (accessed 15 May 2012).

UNCED, *Rio Declaration on Environment and Development* (1992), UN Doc A/CONF.151/26 (Vol. I) ('Rio Declaration'): <http://www.un.org/documents/ga/conf151/aconf15126-1annex1.htm> (accessed 18 January 2012).

UNEP (2007), *GEO Fact Sheet 3, The Air That We Breathe*: <http://www.unep.org/geo/GEO4/ media/fact_sheets/Fact_Sheet_3_Air.pdf> (accessed 11 May 2012).

UNEP (2010) *Latin America and the Caribbean Environmental Outlook (GEO-Latin America and the Caribbean 3)*: <http://www.unep.org/geo/pdfs/GEOLAC_3_ENGLISH.pdf> (accessed 11 May 2012).

UNEP (2010) *State of Biodiversity in Latin America and the Caribbean*, p. 1: <http://www.unep.org/DEC/ PDF/LatinAmerica_StateofBiodiv.pdf> (accessed 11 May 2012).

UNEP (2011) *UNEP Yearbook, Emerging Issues in Our Global Environment*, p. 70: <http://www.unep. org/yearbook/2011/> (accessed 11 May 2012).

UNEP (2011), *Keeping Track of Our Changing Environment, From Rio to Rio+20 (1992–2012)*, p. 24: <http://www.unep.org/geo/pdfs/Keeping_Track.pdf> (accessed 11 May 2012).

UNEP 'Stockholm Convention Centres': <http://chm.pops.int/Implementation/RegionalCentres/ TheCentres/tabid/583/Default.aspx> (accessed 23 November 2011).

UNEP Division of Environmental Conventions, *Development of a Framework for Harmonized Legislation to Implement Biodiversity-Related MEAs*: <http://www.unep.org/DEC/Support/Cross_Cutting/ Biodiv_Leg.asp> (accessed 11 May 2012).

UNEP, (2010) *State of Biodiversity in Africa*, p. 3: <http://www.unep.org/DEC/PDF/State%20of%20 biodiversity%20in%20Africa.pdf> (accessed 30 November 2011).

UNEP, 'Compliance Mechanisms Under Selected Multilateral Environmental Agreements': <http:// www.unep.org/DEC/docs/Compliance%20mechanisms%20under%20selected%20MEAs.pdf> (accessed 14 February 2012).

UNEP, 'Enhancing Synergies among the Basel Rotterdam and Stockholm Conventions': <http:// excops.unep.ch/documents/consproc/PPTEnhancingSynergies.pdf> (accessed 25 November 2011).

UNEP, 'Historic Agreement Ends 15 year Deadlock over Banning North–South Movements of Hazardous Waste', 25 October 2011: <http://www.basel.int/> (accessed 11 May 2012).

UNEP, 'Rotterdam Convention: How it was Developed': <http://www.pic.int/TheConvention/ Overview/Howitwasdeveloped/tabid/1045/language/en-US/Default.aspx> (accessed 18 November 2011).

UNEP, 'The Basel Convention Regional and Coordinating Centres at a Glance': <http://archive. basel.int/centers/description/BCRCataGlance.pdf> (accessed 9 May 2012).

UNEP, GEO-2000, 'Chapter Three: Policy Responses – Global and Regional Synthesis – MEAs and Non-binding Instruments': <http://www.grida.no/geo2000/english/0136.htm> (accessed 21 October 2011).

UNEP, *London Guidelines for the Exchange of Information on Chemicals in International Trade*: <http://www. chem.unep.ch/ethics/english/longuien.htm> (accessed 20 November 2011).

UNEP/CARICOM/UWI (2004) *Caribbean Environmental Outlook, Special Edition for the Mauritius International Meeting for the 10-year Review of the Barbados Programme of Action for the Sustainable Development of Small Island States*, p. 52: <http://www.unep.org/geo/pdfs/Caribbean_EO_final. pdf> (accessed 11 May 2012).

UNEP: Sustainable Innovation and Technology Transfer Industrial Sector Studies, 'Recycling – from E-Waste to Resources', Final Report July 2009: <http://ewasteguide.info/files/UNEP_2009_ eW2R.PDF> (accessed 25 November 2011).

UNESCO *Database of National Cultural Heritage Laws*: <http://www.unesco.org/culture/natlaws/ index.php?&lng=en> (accessed 29 February 2012).

UNESCO *Handbook of Legal and Practical Measures against Illicit Trafficking in Cultural Property*, Doc Ref CLT/CH/INS-06/22: <http://unesdoc.unesco.org/images/0014/001461/146118e.pdf> (accessed 29 February 2012).

UNESCO *Legal and Practical Measures Against Illicit Trafficking in Cultural Property: UNESCO Handbook*, International Standards Section, Division of Cultural Heritage, 2006: <http://unesdoc.unesco.org/images/0014/001461/146118e.pdf> (accessed 29 February 2012).

UNESCO Universal Declaration on Cultural Diversity, 2001: <unesdoc.unesco.org/images/0012/001271/127160m.pdf> (accessed 29 February 2012).

UNESCO World Heritage Centre, *The Operational Guidelines for the Implementation of the World Heritage Convention*: <http://whc.unesco.org/en/guidelines> (accessed 29 February 2012).

UNESCO, *1995 UNIDROIT Convention*: <http://www.unesco.org/new/en/culture/themes/movable-heritage-and-museums/illicit-traffic-of-cultural-property/1995-unidroit-convention/> (accessed 29 February 2012).

UNESCO, *Convention on the Means of Prohibiting and Preventing the Illicit Import, Export and Transfer of Ownership of Cultural Property – 1970*: <www.unesco.org/new/en/culture/themes/movable-heritage-and-museums/illicit-traffic-of-cultural-property/1970-convention/> (accessed 29 February 2012).

UNESCO, *Cultural Expression Technical Assistance: Strengthening the System of Governance for Culture in Developing Countries*: <http://www.unesco.org/new/en/culture/themes/cultural-diversity/diversity-of-cultural-expressions/programmes/technical-assistance/> (accessed 29 February 2012).

UNESCO, *Cultural Expressions: Parties to the Convention*: <http://www.unesco.org/new/en/culture/themes/cultural-diversity/diversity-of-cultural-expressions/the-convention/parties-to-the-convention/> (accessed 29 February 2012).

UNESCO, *Culture: The States Parties*: <http://www.unesco.org/new/en/culture/themes/movable-heritage-and-museums/armed-conflict-and-heritage/the-states-parties/> (accessed 29 February 2012).

UNESCO, *Databases*: <http://www.unesco.org/new/en/culture/themes/movable-heritage-and-museums/illicit-traffic-of-cultural-property/databases/> (accessed 29 February 2012).

UNESCO, *Encouraging Transmission of ICH: Living Human Treasures*: <http://www.unesco.org/culture/ich/index.php?lg=en&pg=00061> (accessed 29 February 2012).

UNESCO, *International Code of Ethics for Dealers in Cultural Property*: <http://portal.unesco.org/culture/en/ev.php-URL_ID=35190&URL_DO=DO_TOPIC&URL_SECTION=201.html) (accessed 29 February 2012).

UNESCO, *Text of the Convention for the Safeguarding of Intangible Cultural Heritage*. Online. HTTP: <http://www.unesco.org/culture/ich/index.php?lg=en&pg=00006> (accessed 29 February 2012).

UNFCCC Conference of the Parties Fifteenth Session (2009), Copenhagen, 7–18 December 2009, FCCC/CP/2009/L.7, ('Copenhagen Accord') para. 2: <http://unfccc.int/resource/docs/2009/cop15/eng/l07.pdf> (accessed 6 July 2011).

UNFCCC, *An Introduction to the Kyoto Protocol Compliance Mechanism*: <http://unfccc.int/kyoto_protocol/compliance/items/3024.php> (accessed 11 May 2012).

UNFCCC, *Investment and Financial Flows to Address Climate Change*, 2007: <unfccc.int/cooperation_and_support/financial_mechanism/items/4053.php> (accessed 19 December 2011).

UNFCCC, National Reports: <http://unfccc.int/national_reports/items/1408.php> (accessed 19 June 2010).

UNFCCC, *Share of Proceeds from the Clean Development Mechanism Project Activities for the Adaptation Fund*: <http://cdm.unfccc.int/Issuance/SOPByProjectsTable.html> (accessed 9 May 2012).

UNFCCC, *The CDM and Technology Transfer*: <http://cdm.unfccc.int/about/CDM_TT/index.html> (accessed 11 May 2012).

UNFCCC, *Thirteenth Conference of the Parties* (2008), Bali, Indonesia, Dec. 3–15, 2007, *Report of the Conference of the Parties*, UN Doc FCCC/CP/2007/6/Add.1: <http://unfccc.int/resource/docs/2007/cop13/eng/06a01.pdf> (accessed 5 July 2011).

United Nations Committee on the Peaceful Uses of Outer Space (1959), GA Res 1472(XIV), UN GAOR: <http://www.unoosa.org/oosa/en/COPUOS/members.html> (accessed 11 August 2011).

United Nations Deparatment for Information, 'Sustainable management of water resources rital to achieving anti-poverty goals delegatcs told, as Generally Assembly high-level dialogue marks World Water Day', 2010: <http://www.un.org/News/Press/docs/2010/ga10925.doc.htm> (accessed 21 September 2011).

United Nations Development Programme, (2011) *Human Development Index – 2011 Rankings*: <http://hdr.undp.org/en/statistics/> (accessed 30 November 2011).

United Nations Development Programme, *Protecting the Ozone Layer and Safeguarding the Global Climate*: <http://web.undp.org/ozone/> (accessed 9 May 2012).

United Nations Development Programme: China, *Poverty Reduction*: <http://www.undp.org.cn/modules.php?op=modload&name–ews&file=article&catid=10&sid=10> (accessed 28 July 2010).

United Nations Economic and Social Council, *Permanent Forum on Indigenous Issues: Report of the Seventh Session (21 April–2 May 2008) E/2008/43/E/C.19/2008/13* (2008) United Nations: <http://daccess-dds-ny.un.org/doc/UNDOC/GEN/N08/338/82/PDF/N0833882.pdf?OpenElement> (accessed 29 December 2011).

United Nations Economic Commission for Europe, 'Status of the Convention on Long-range Transboundary Air Pollution and its Related Protocols (as of March 1, 2011)': <http://www.unece.org/env/lrtap/status/lrtap_st.html> (accessed 31 October 2011).

United Nations Environment Programme (UNEP), (2003) *Action Plan of the Environment Initiative of the New Partnership for Africa's Development*: <http://www.uneca.org/unregionalconsultations/documents/NEPAD%20Action%20Plan%20–%20environment.pdf> (accessed 30 November 2011).

United Nations Environment Programme (UNEP), *Fourth ASEAN State of the Environment Report 2009*: <http://www.aseansec.org/publications/SoER4-Report.pdf> (accessed 22 November 2011).

United Nations Environment Programme Regional Seas Programmes: <www.unep.org/regionalseas> (accessed 11 May 2012).

United Nations Environment Programme, *Financing of the UNEP*: <www.unep.org/rms/en/Financing_of_UNEP/Environment_Fund/index.asp> (accessed 12 December 2011).

United Nations Environment Programme, *Financing of the UNEP*: <www.unep.org/rms/en/Financing_of_UNEP/Trustfunds/index.asp> (accessed 12 December 2011).

United Nations Forum on Forests, *IPF Proposal for Action*: <http://www.un.org/esa/forests/pdf/ipf-iff-proposalsforaction.pdf> (accessed 14 December 2011).

United Nations Forum on Forests, *Multi-Year Programme of Work 2007–2015*: <http://www.un.org/esa/forests/multi-year-work.html> (accessed 14 December 2011).

United Nations International Strategy for Disaster Reduction. *Hyogo Framework for Action*: <http://www.unisdr.org/we/coordinate/hfa> (accessed 3 November 2011).

United Nations Millennium Ecosystem Assessment (2005), *Synthesis Report: Ecosystems and Human Well-Being*: <http://www.maweb.org/documents/document.356.aspx.pdf> (accessed 28 December 2011).

United Nations Office for the Coordination of Humanitarian Affairs. *Guiding Principles on Internal Displacement*, 2nd edn, 2004: <http://www.brookings.edu/fp/projects/idp/resources/ GPEnglish.pdf> (accessed 5 September 2011).

United Nations Office of the High Representative for the Least Developed Countries, Landlocked Developing Countries and the Small Island Developing States (UN-OHRLLS), 'List of Least-Developed Countries': <http://www.unohrlls.org/en/ldc/25/> (accessed 30 November 2011).

United Nations, *Johannesburg Summit 2002, Basic Information*: <http://un.org/jsummit/html/basic_info/basicinfo.html> (accessed 26 July 2010).

United Nations, *Millennium Development Goals*: <http://www.un.org/millenniumgoals/poverty.shtml> (accessed 23 July 2010).

United Nations, *The Future We Want – zero-draft of the outcome document, January 10, 2012*: <www.uncsd2012.org/rio20/content/documents/370The%20Future%20We%20Want%2010Jan%20clean.pdf> (accessed 11 January 2012).

United Nations, *World Population Prospects: The 2010 Revision*. Online Database: <http://esa.un.org/unpd/wpp/index.htm> (accessed 9 May 2012).

United States and People's Republic of China Memorandum of Understanding for Fisheries Enforcement reported in UNGA (1993), Report of the Secretary-General, *Large-scale Pelagic Drift-net Fishing, Unauthorized Fishing in Zones of National Jurisdiction and on the High Seas, Fisheries By-catch and Discards, and other Developments*, UN Doc. A/55/386, 18 September 2000: <www.un.org/documents/ga/docs/55/a55386.pdf> (accessed 18 January 2012).

United States Trade Representative and Council on Environmental Quality, *Guidelines for Implementation of Executive Order 13141, Environmental Review of Trade Agreements*, December 2000: <http://www.ustr.gov/sites/default/files/guidelines%20for%2013141.pdf> (accessed 19 December 2011).

UN-Water, *Transboundary Waters: Sharing Benefits, Sharing Responsibilities*: <http://www.unwater.org/downloads/UNW_TRANSBOUNDARY.pdf> (accessed 21 September 2011).

US Climate Action Centre, *Copenhagen Climate Negotiations: The Briefing Book*, 2009: <http://www.usclimatenetwork.org/resource-database/biefingbook_basics.pdf> (accessed 2 December 2011).

US Energy Information Administration, 'International Energy Statistics': <http://www.eia.gov/cfapps/ipdbproject/IEDIndex3.cfm?tid=90&pid=44&aid=8> (accessed 30 November 2011).

US Environmental Protection Agency, 'Environmental Reviews of Trade and Investment Agreements': <http://www.epa.gov/international/trade/reviews.html> (accessed 19 December 2011).

US National Oceanic and Atmospheric Agency, *Marine Reserves in the United States*, 2011: <http://www.mpa.gov/pdf/helpful-resources/factsheets/us_marinereserves.pdf> (accessed 18 January 2012).

US Secretary of Commerce. *Report to the Congress of the United States Concerning US Actions Taken On Foreign Large-Scale High Seas Driftnet Fishing*, 2009, p. 7: <http://www.nmfs.noaa.gov/ia/intlbycatch/docs/congo_09rpt.pdf> (accessed 18 January 2012).

WIPO, *Intergovernmental Committee*: <www.wipo.int/tk/en/igc/> (accessed 8 March 2012).

World Bank and FAO, 'The Sunken Billions: the Economic Justification for Fisheries Reform', 2008: <http://go.worldbank.org/MGUTHSY7U0> (accessed 9 May 2012).

World Bank, *Introduction to the WBG's Environment Strategy*: <http://web.worldbank.org/WBSITE/EXTERNAL/TOPICS/ENVIRONMENT/0,,contentMDK:20268515~menuPK:242145~pagePK:148956~piPK:216618~theSitePK:244381,00.html> (accessed 12 December 2011).

World Health Organization, 'Toxic Hazards': <www.who.int/heli/risks/toxics/chemicals/en/index.html> (accessed 10 February 2012).

World Heritage Convention Secretariat, 'Rescuing the Congo's natural world heritage': <http://whc.unesco.org/en/news/700/> (accessed 30 November 2011).

World Resources Institute, *Bolivia's New Pro-Environment Constitution* (2009): <http://projects.wri.org/node/1206> (accessed 11 May 2012).

World Summit on Sustainable Development, 10 December 2002, A/C.2/57/L.83: <http://daccess-dds-ny.un.org/doc/UNDOC/LTD/N02/731/88/PDF/N0273188.pdf?OpenElement> (accessed 26 July 2010).

World Wildlife Fund, 'Underwriting Overfishing': <http://www.worldwildlife.org/what/globalmarkets/fishing/WWFBinaryitem8633.pdf> (accessed 23 January 2012).

WSSD, *Plan of Implementation*: <http://www.un.org/jsummit/html/documents/summit_docs/2309_planfinal.htm> (accessed 22 November 2011).

Index

Please note that IEL stands for international environmental law. References to Notes are followed by the letter 'n'.

An environmentally friendly book printed and bound in England by www.printondemand-worldwide.com

PEFC Certified

This product is
from sustainably
managed forests
and controlled
sources

www.pefc.org

PEFC/16-33-415

This book is made entirely of sustainable materials; FSC paper for the cover and PEFC paper for the text pages.

#0126 - 270114 - C0 - 246/174/45 [47] - CB